ROBERT BURNS
by Archibald Skirving

The Complete Letters of Robert Burns

The
Complete Letters
of
ROBERT
BURNS

Edited and Introduced by
JAMES A. MACKAY

Authorised by
THE BURNS FEDERATION

Alloway Publishing Ltd., Ayrshire.

First Published, 1987

© Introduction & Notes
James A. Mackay, 1987

ISBN 0-907526-31-4 Subscriber's Edition
ISBN 0-907526-32-2 Souvenir Edition

Alloway Publishing
AYR

Printed and bound in Scotland
Design and Printing
Walker & Connell Ltd., Darvel, Ayrshire.
Bell & Bain Ltd., Thornliebank, Glasgow.

Binding
Hunter & Foulis Ltd., Edinburgh.

Paper
Inveresk Paper Mills, Fife.

CONTENTS

Preface 7

Introduction 10

List of recipients of letters 24

Note on the text of the letters 29

List of verse epistles 32

Inscriptions in presentation copies of books 35

The Letters of Robert Burns 37

Appendix I
    Currie's list of letters to Burns
    Alphabetical 727
    Numerical 730

Appendix II
    The forgeries of Burns manuscripts by
    "Antique" Smith 762

    List of Subcribers 768

    Chronological list of Burns letters 792

    Index 810

The cover and title page reproduce the Silhouette of Burns by John Miers, 1787

To
Beth and Jimmy Anderson

PREFACE

This edition of the letters of Robert Burns is intended as a companion to the bicentenary edition of the *Complete Works*, which was published in July 1986 by the Burns Federation in association with Alloway Publishing Limited of Ayrshire. The runaway success of that volume inspired the Burns Federation, at its Conference held in Kilmarnock in September 1986, to vote unanimously that an edition of the poet's correspondence be prepared, uniform with the volume of poems.

This decision, resulting from a proposal by Donald Urquhart of the Southern Scottish Counties Burns Association, was not a new concept. Several years previously, when consideration was being given in the Executive Council of the Federation, to the publication of an authoritative edition of the poems, it was mooted by Samuel K. Gaw, a past-president of the Burns Federation, that devotees of the bard would be better served by the publication of a new edition of his letters. At that time the magnificent two-volume edition compiled by the late Professor J. De Lancey Ferguson, published by the Clarendon Press in 1931, had been out of print for many years. This matter was given serious consideration, but was shelved when it was discovered that a new edition was in course of preparation by the Clarendon Press, under the supervision of Professor G. Ross Roy.

The second Clarendon edition was published in 1985 in two volumes, and undoubtedly must be regarded as the definitive study of Burns's letters for many years to come. This splendid edition set the seal on the scientific scholarship which has steadily evolved over the past seventy years, following the sterling example set by Ferguson. Professor Roy re-collated every letter either from the original manuscript or from the earliest known printed source. Each letter was prefaced by the form of address used on the cover, and followed by details of its previous publishing history and its present whereabouts (if known). Moreover, Professor Roy was at great pains to reproduce the text of each letter exactly as Burns wrote it. Misspellings, deletions and grammatical mistakes were meticulously reproduced. The Roy text, in fact, represents the closest thing in print to the actual letters themselves, short of reproducing them photographically.

The major disadvantage of the Clarendon edition, however, was its exorbitant cost which has unfortunately priced it beyond the reach of many libraries and academics, far less the average Burns enthusiast. There are countless editions of the poems, but the only editions of the letters were either out of print (and very expensive in the antiquarian market) or outside the price range of all but the wealthiest. The appearance of the new edition was sufficient to whet the interest of the Burns movement, and thus it was that consideration of a new edition, at an affordable price, became imperative.

In producing this edition of the letters I realised from the outset that there was no point in trying to compete with the Roy edition. This towers head and shoulders over all previous compilations and will without any shadow of a doubt remain the standard work for many years to come. The first problem to be faced was how to reduce the text to a manageable form, so that it could be incorporated in a single volume. Forms of address and bibliographical end-notes have therefore been omitted. I have also aimed at a text which would be more easily readable; consequently, I have omitted Burns's crossings-out and presented a polished text as he would have intended it to be read by the recipients.

A much more fundamental change from the Ferguson and Roy editions, however, has been the arrangement of the letters according to their addressees. Previous editions have invariably printed the letters in strictly chronological order, beginning with those earliest compositions to William Niven and concluding with the poignant cries for help to Burness, Thomson and Armour, written from the Brow in July 1796. Admittedly, the chronological approach is not only the most direct but affords us a certain autobiographical insight. On the other hand, grouping the letters according to the recipient enables us to see with greater convenience and impact the relationship between Burns and each of his correspondents. This is particularly valuable in the case of the longer sequences of letters, such

8

as those addressed to Mrs Frances Dunlop of Dunlop, Agnes McLehose and George Thomson, but it is just as interesting and important to trace the development of Burns's relationships with Cunningham, Ballantine, Graham of Fintry, Peter Hill, Maria Riddell and many others. This approach has enabled me to preface each correspondence with biographical notes concerning each addressee and comments on the circumstances of and background to the letters.

In the course of preparing this edition of the poet's letters I have had a great deal of practical help and encouragement from John Inglis, past president of the Burns Federation (1984–5) who had previously been so instrumental in securing the success of the *Complete Works*. It would be invidious to single out the many librarians who have given me some assistance with this project, but I cannot refrain from expressing my great indebtedness to the staff of the British Library (London), the Mitchell Library (Glasgow) and, in particular, to William Anderson of the Dick Institute, Kilmarnock, and Alistair Cowper of the Ewart Library, Dumfries. Rita Turner of the Burns Federation has given me constant support at a practical level.

I must express my gratitude to Maurice Lindsay, whose *Burns Encyclopaedia* (3rd edition, 1980) has been my constant companion and *vade mecum* ever since it was published. I have had a great deal of support and encouragement from Donald Low and David Groves, but I am especially indebted to Professor Ross Roy, without whose assistance in ways too numerous to mention I doubt whether this daunting task could ever have been accomplished.

Last, but by no means least, I must express my heart-felt thanks to my wife Joyce, who not only has been of immeasurable help to me throughout this project, but also assisted with the proof-reading and compiled the alphabetical listing of Subscribers. On her capable shoulders has fallen all the work connected with the Subscription List, from keeping the accounts on behalf of the Burns Federation to the actual despatch of the Subscribers' copies.

JAMES A. MACKAY
Dumfries, 1987

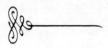

The poems and songs of Robert Burns are known and appreciated all over the world, but not one in a thousand that could sing *Auld Lang Syne* or quote *Tam o' Shanter* has so much as a nodding acquaintance with the letters written by Burns. His prose output, in the form of correspondence, was prodigious, especially in the last five years of his brief life. To those charges of dissipation which were often levelled by so-called biographers and detractors in the nineteenth century, it has long been customary to list, by way of rebuttal, the many poems composed and the many old ballads mended and revised at a time when the Poet was also carrying out the exceedingly onerous duties of an Excise Officer. A wider acquaintance with the letters of Burns from this period alone would surely give the lie to these old *canards*. Even if we were to assume that every letter written by Burns had survived in some shape or form, we would be astonished at this output, not only in sheer volume but in quality. These letters were the product of an alert and lively mind, the range of topics covered being matched by the wit and incisive phraseology of the writer.

It is obvious, however, that Burns's actual epistolary output was much greater than the surviving letters. For example, some 25 letters to Maria Riddell are extant, but from the numerical endorsements which she added to them on receipt it appears that she received at least 29 letters from Burns. The list compiled by Dr James Currie of the letters in the poet's possession at the time of his death (see Appendix I) reveals a great many names for whom no corresponding letters from Burns are known — yet it is safe to assume that in the majority of cases the letters from these people were either answered by Burns, or were received by him in response to a letter or letters from him.

Although we have to accept the fact that many of Burns's letters have been lost, we should be thankful that a sufficient number has survived to illumine the multi-faceted and multi-layered personality of Scotland's most complex genius. Contemporary eye-witness accounts suggest that Burns was highly articulate and nimble-tongued, a man who charmed and captivated individuals and audiences with the fire and passion of his speech. We have the evidence of his poetical works, ranging from epigrams produced extempore to major poems of immense power, testifying to his absolute mastery of the written word. And, in addition, we have evidence, time and time again, of his ability — without parallel among his compeers — to convert the dross of uncouth doggerel ballads into polished gems of song.

It used to be fashionable to contrast the genius of Burns, as evinced in the poems, with the mannered style of his prose. The perception of Burns as a writer of stiff and stilted letters — like so many of the distortions and untruths concerning his life and character — arose originally because of the incomplete and lopsided evidence presented to the public by the poet's early biographers. Francis Jeffrey succinctly expressed the viewpoint of the literary world of the early nineteenth century in his review of *Reliques of Robert Burns* by Cromek, which appeared in the *Edinburgh Review* of January 1809:

'[Burns's] letters seem to have been nearly all composed as exercises, and for display. There are few of them written with simplicity or plainness; and although natural enough as to the sentiment, they are generally very strained and elaborate in the expression. A very great proportion of them, too, relate neither to facts nor feelings peculiarly connected with the author or his correspondent — but are made up of general declamation, moral reflections and vague discussions — all evidently composed for the sake of effect and frequently introduced with long complaints of having nothing to say, and of the necessity and difficulty of letter-writing.'

Jeffrey's severe disparagement of Burns the letter-writer, however, was based entirely on the evidence as presented in Currie's *Works of Robert Burns, with an account of his life* (1800), together with Cromek's *Reliques* which, between them, reproduced no more than a third of the extant letters. Furthermore, a great many of them were presented in a heavily edited version. Passages which revealed the warmth and humanity of the writer, entire sections of a personal nature, were ruthlessly suppressed. Currie's selection of 180 letters were, for the most part, culled from the poet's correspondence with members of the aristocracy and the gentry, Burns's social superiors whose patronage he sought and assiduously cultivated. Taken in isolation, these letters tend to strike us nowadays as oddly at variance with the poet's fierce pride and independence of spirit; but they ought always to be regarded in the context of the times in which they were written, when making the right contacts, or obtaining preferment and advancement in one's chosen career, depended so largely on patronage.

Then again, the letters from Sylvander to Clarinda, that strange, almost ethereal correspondence between Burns and Agnes McLehose from December 1787 to March 1788, have provoked a great deal of comment by critics and biographers, most of whom have found it very difficult to be objective. As recently as 1928, for example, Dr. Robert Mackenna, in his introduction to *The Letters of the Poet* published by Collins, dismissed the Sylvander correspondence as 'a series of impassioned letters, in which he struts and swaggers, poses and makes fine gestures, pleads and reproaches, flatters and cajoles. This windy braggart, this loud-mouthed actor, this pietist frothing at the lips with airy bubbles of religiosity, this mean spurner of Jean Armour, is not the manly

Robert Burns we know and love.' And again, he contrasts rather harshly Burns the poetical genius with the pretentiousness of these particular letters: 'That perfect lyric *Ae fond kiss* is worth more than all the tumultuous words that were ever written by the delirious pen of Sylvander.' Quite so, but we ought never to lose sight of the fact that had there been no Clarinda there would never have been *Ae fond kiss.*

In fairness to Dr. Mackenna it should be pointed out that, over all, he was in no doubt as to the importance of Burns as a letter writer. Although his edition was selective, the vast majority of the letters now extant were available to him, as successive editors, especially between Robert Chambers (1851) and William Wallace (1896), had added more and more material to the canon. Certainly by the beginning of this century there was no doubt — among scholars at any rate — that Burns ranked high among the belletrists of all time. Any lingering doubts, in academic circles at least, were well and truly dispelled by the publication, in 1931, of Professor John De Lancey Ferguson's monumental, two-volume edition of the letters, published by the Oxford University Press. For the first time, the cumulative effect of the surviving letters, some 700 in all, could be felt; and Burns's merits as a letter-writer could at long last be properly recognised.

De Lancey Ferguson rightly surmised that some of the disappointment which the early critics experienced in reading Burns's letters was due to the contrast between what they expected and what they found. The image of the 'heav'n-taught ploughman' or the 'ploughing poet', which Burns himself shrewdly played for all it was worth during his sojourn in Edinburgh, gave the literary public of the late eighteenth century a perception of Burns as a rustic who produced poetic gems by pure inspiration. As late as 1805, for example, Sir Samuel Brydges could write of Burns: 'We can almost suppose in his athletic form and daring countenance, had he lived in times of barbarism, and been tempted by hard necessity to forego his principles such an one as we behold at the head of a banditti in the savage scenery of Salvator Rosa, gilding the crimes of violence and depredation by acts of valour and generosity'. Such preposterous notions of Burns as some kind of noble bandit were by no means untypical of that period. It must have jarred the sensibilities and the sentiment of Burns's early devotees when they first read the letters as edited by Currie and Cromek. They sought artlessness and found a highly polished artistry; they looked for rustic simplicity and found urbane sophistication.

Some critics in recent years, most notably Carol McGuirk, have emphasised even more starkly the contrast between Burns the talker and poet and Burns the letter-writer. In *Robert Burns and the Sentimental Era* she writes:

'It is surprising . . . to observe how indefatigably Burns himself indulges sentimental postures with his correspondents. Known for abrupt and somewhat explosive candor in discourse and for a self-sufficient and therefore successful adaptation of sentimental techniques in his early poetry, Burns is consistently, disappointingly, and derivatively sentimental in nearly all his letters."

Ms McGuirk then goes on to suggest that the conflict between creative impulse and the social requirements of the sentimental era in which Burns flourished provides 'an explanation for Burns's failure to emerge as himself in most of his letters. "Forced into periphrasis" might well be the epigraph to the two volumes of Burns's correspondence [the Oxford edition], so well does it describe the impression created by his defensive, over-written letters.'

This seems a very harsh and sweeping condemnation. To be sure, there is an overly emphatic self-consciousness in many of the letters to patrons and social superiors, the outcome of Burns's innate feelings of unease and inferiority. Burns was only too well aware of the social hurdles which he had to surmount. For a brief moment he was taken up and lionised by Scottish society in general and the Edinburgh *literati* in particular. The charm of his poetry and the brilliance of his conversation assured him his momentary place in the limelight. To sustain the interest and attention of those who mattered, Burns had to make his own terms; but the trouble was that he was not always sure what these terms should be.

One is left, inescapably, with the feeling that Burns was regarded as semi-literate by many of the people with whom he corresponded. Moreover, Burns himself was conscious of condescending and patronising attitudes in some of his correspondents, and countered this by demonstrating that when it came to letter-writing he could outshine them all. To this end he drafted his letters, polished and refined them and agonised over the appropriate turn of phrase, or the most apt quotation, before rendering them in their final form. The Sylvander letters are by no means the only ones in which the language is overheated and overblown. Letters to lawyers and professors and other professional men whose formal education was better than his own inspired Burns to heights of literary virtuosity. Reading between the lines we get the impression of Burns continually asserting that he is as good as, if not better than, his correspondents. To appreciate this, it is necessary to understand that, despite his peasant background, Burns was a highly educated man. What little formal schooling he had received, at the hands of John Murdoch and Hugh Rodger, was augmented considerably by his own reading which was astonishing in its variety and range.

To Burns, letter-writing was an art-form in its own right, and one that he strove consciously to master. His correspondence is

13

liberally sprinkled with the conscious efforts he was taking to perfect this art, and also revealing the masters on whom he modelled his prose. Thus, in a letter to Mrs Dunlop from Ellisland on 16th August 1788, he began 'I am in a fine disposition, my honored Friend, to send you an Elegiac Epistle; and want only genius to make it quite Shenstonian.' Or again, in a letter of 22nd January 1788, probably addressed to Henry Erskine, he writes: 'I have no great faith in the boasted pretensions to intuitive propriety and unlaboured elegance. – The rough material of Fine Writing is certainly the gift of Genius; but I as firmly believe that the workmanship is the united effort of Pains, Attention and Repeated – trial. – The Piece addressed to Mr. Graham is my first essay in that didactic, epistolary way; which circumstance I hope will bespeak your indulgence.' To James Candlish, then a student at Glasgow University, he wrote on 21st March 1787: '. . . I was determined to write a good letter, full of argument, amplification, erudition and, as Bayes says, *all that.*'

Only five days later, he wrote to Lady Henrietta Don at Coates: 'I have here sent you a parcel of my epistolary performances; happy at having it, in the smallest degree, in my power to show that gratitude, which, "while life's warm spirit beats within my breast" shall ever glow to the family of Glencairn. – I might have altered or omitted something in these letters; perhaps I ought to have done so; but I wished to show you the Bard and his style in their native colors.'

Throughout his life Burns made drafts of the more important letters before sending them, in their final, polished version, to the addressees. His motive for doing so may originally have been born of the anxiety of the semi-literate correspondent; but soon this was supplanted by the artist in him, intent on reworking and polishing a composition which, no matter how trivial the circumstances, might be a reflection on him as a writer. De Lancey Ferguson shrewdly pointed out that too often Burns's second thoughts failed to bring him to that last stage of artistry in which the art is hidden, but that this was not wholly his fault.

A legacy of this habit, however, was the accumulation of draft letters in which Burns seems to have taken inordinate pride. In April 1791 he prepared a collection of 'pieces local or unfinished, fragments the effusion of a poetical moment and bagatelles strung in rhyme' for his friend, Robert Riddell of Glenriddell, and subsequently prepared a companion volume containing copies of his prose. Writing to Mrs Dunlop on 15th December 1793, he mentioned:

'I have lately collected, for a Friend's perusal, all my letters; I mean those which I first sketched in a rough draft, and afterwards wrote out fair. – On looking over some old musty papers, which, from time to time, I had parcelled by, as trash that were scarce

14

worth preserving and which yet at the same time, I did not care to destroy I discovered many of these rude sketches, and have written and am writing them out, in a bound M.S.S., for my Friend's Library.'

Interestingly, he goes on, 'As I wrote always to you, the rhapsody of the moment, I cannot find a single scroll to you, except one, about the commencement of our acquaintance.' Certainly there is a freshness and originality about the Dunlop correspondence which is absent from many of his other formal letters to patrons.

Burns was not alone in regarding letter-writing as an art at which one should constantly strive. I have examined numerous other letters from the eighteenth and early nineteenth centuries and have found periphrasis and circumlocution, stilted expression and turgid thought to be all too common, even in letters between close members of a family. It must be remembered that in an age when the *cost* of sending letters through the post was exorbitant, the receipt of a letter was a great occasion (which usually burdened the recipient, rather than the sender, with the postage), and letter-writers perhaps conscious of the financial burden they were imposing upon their correspondents, strove to make their epistles worthwhile, in a quite literal sense.

Letter-writing was practised as an art among the wealthier and more leisured classes of society and anthologies of *belles lettres* were popular and required reading. Burns himself mentions a 'collection of letters by the Wits of Queen Anne's reign' which served as his model — possibly the collection edited by Alexander Pope containing the correspondence of Swift and Bolingbroke which, as De Lancey Ferguson puts it, 'are formal efforts to display to the best advantage wit, erudition, and skill in turning phrases.' Pompous effusions of this kind have no room for simple, straightforward language and the easy flow of colloquial narrative. 'It may be natural to wish always to put forward one's best foot', says Ferguson, 'but the gesture is bound to cramp the free rhythm of one's movements'.

In his long autobiographical letter to Dr. Moore, written at Mauchline in August 1787, Burns tells how

'The earliest thing of Composition that I recollect taking pleasure in was, The vision of Mirza and a hymn of Addison's beginning — "How are Thy servants blest O Lord!" I particularly remember one half-stanza which was music to my boyish ear . . . I met with these pieces in Masson's English Collection, one of my school-books.'

Burns probably studied the second edition of Arthur Masson's *Collection of Prose and Verse,* published in 1767, and there is ample evidence, from his letters, that he not only took its precepts to heart but committed whole passages to memory. In later life Burns was frequently to use literary allusions, biblical quotations and lines of verse to add seasoning to his letters. Writing to Clarinda, he confessed: 'I like to have quotations ready for every occasion — They give one's ideas so pat, and save one the trouble of finding expression adequate to one's feelings.'

The liberal sprinkling of one's letters with quotations may strike us nowadays as pretentious, but it was a fashion much admired in the eighteenth century, and Burns cannot be condemned for emulating his betters. In the letters to Clarinda, for example, Burns quotes Shakespeare (*Macbeth, Othello, Hamlet* and *Julius Caesar*), Pope (Essay *on Man, Prologue to the Satires* and, several times, *Eloisa* to *Abelard*), Addison (*Cato and The Spectator*), *Fingal* by 'Ossian', Thomas Southerne's *Fatal Marriage*, Gray's *Bard*, Milton's *Paradise Lost* and Edward Young's *Night Thoughts* and *First Epistle to Mr. Pope.* Goldsmith, Fielding, Locke, Bickerstaffe, Thomas D'Urfey and James Thomson supplied some of the more secular quotations. De Lancey Ferguson has demonstrated that a very high proportion of these authors appeared in Masson, Burns's school text-book. A significant number of quotations, however, came from the Bible. The Clarinda correspondence alone drew on Proverbs, Hebrews, the Song of Solomon, Joshua, Samuel, Numbers, Job and Genesis from the Old Testament, and Luke, John and Acts from the New Testament.

The quotations found in the letters to social equals and superiors alike are even more wide-ranging, from Homer and Virgil to Cervantes and Boileau-Despreaux. Nearer home, he drew heavily and frequently on those authors whom he admired the most, Henry Mackenzie (*Man of Feeling* and *Man of the World*), Tobias Smollett, Laurence Sterne, James Thomson, Edward Young and William Shenstone. Inevitably Shakespeare was a rich source, with quotations from no fewer than seventeen of the plays.

Oddly enough, those writers who had provided the models and inspiration for his poetry played only a minor role in the letters of Burns. Robert Fergusson, whose poems Burns freely acknowledged to mark the turning-point in his own career, yields but a single quotation, a couplet in a gloomy letter to George Thomson in April 1796. To be sure, Allan Ramsay was not only more liberally quoted — especially in those letters to Thomson anent the mending of old ballads — but also provided the poetic name for Nancy McLehose, Clarinda having been Ramsay's name for the Duchess of Queensberry.

Considering the old *canard* that Burns was irreligious, that notion is surely dispelled by Burns's familiarity with the King James Bible and the Metrical Psalms, both of which provided numerous quotations, actual, altered or paraphrased, as well as countless allusions. There are something like 130 biblical quotations and allusions, taken from 34 books of the Old and New Testaments, not to mention numerous phrases which, while they cannot be ascribed to any particular biblical source, probably came from the stock phraseology of contemporary sermons.

The lengthy autobiographical letter to Dr. Moore enumerates the relatively few books, diverse in subject matter, that were available to Burns in his formative years. These were read over and over again, until Burns must have had them almost off by heart. 'The Collection of Songs was my vade mecum.' he writes, 'I pored over them, driving my cart or walking to labor, song by song, verse by verse; carefully noting the true tender or sublime from affectation and fustian. − I am convinced I owe much to this for my critic-craft such as it is.' It is perhaps unfortunate that the same criteria were not applied to his more formal letters, but better models were not available to Burns at that time. When he abandoned these models, however, he wrote with a natural grace and a lively style.

Despite Burns's immense reputation as a poet in the vernacular of the Lowlands, only one prose letter is actually written in Lallans, the first of the series addressed to William Nicol (1st June 1787). Burns preferred to confine the vernacular to his poetry. Upwards of two dozen verse epistles in this vein are to be found in *The Complete Works*. Professor G. Ross Roy incorporated these into the second edition of the Letters (Oxford University Press, 1985) on the grounds that many, if not all of them, were actually transmitted through the post.

The chief value of the letters of Robert Burns is two-fold; they provide an immense amount of autobiographical detail which would otherwise be non-existent, and in a wider context they shed an interesting light on Scottish society in the Age of Enlightenment.

'No life of Burns,' wrote Professor Dewar in 1929, 'carries more conviction of truth, or frames a more speaking likeness, than the "honest narrative" of the poet's letter to Dr. Moore in August 1781'. And De Lancy Ferguson added two years later 'No autobiography has better withstood the probings − not infrequently hostile − of subsequent research.' There is a recurring motif in all of Burns's correspondence, one of absolute candour and a total lack of dissimulation or hypocrisy. Even in the Clarinda letters, which many biographers and critics have condemned for their highfalutin gush, the character of Burns the man shines through. All the romantic jargon of the time could not conceal the innate humour and personality of the writer.

The lengthy correspondence with Mrs Dunlop of Dunlop which endured for the last decade of the poet's life, started off in the rather stilted formal style which Burns adopted when writing to his patrons, but very quickly developed along more natural lines. Mrs Dunlop, the poet's senior by 29 years, became a kind of 'mother confessor' to him, and as a result many of the more self-revelatory passages are to be found among the 70-odd letters in this correspondence.

Of course it would be unwise to place too much reliance on the volume of letters which are presently known to have existed, but it is not without interest to analyse their composition. Of the extant letters no fewer than 217 — slightly less than a third — were written to women. With the exception of the 57 letters addressed to George Thomson, and which to a very large extent dealt with business matters, ladies head the list of the poet's chief correspondents: Mrs Dunlop received at least 77 letters, Agnes McLehose 52 and Maria Riddell 25. In descending order the other chief recipients of the poet's letters were James Johnson (21), Robert Ainslie (20), Alexander Cunningham and Peter Hill (both 19), Robert Graham of Fintry (15), John Ballantine (13) and Margaret Chalmers (12).

Until 1928 it was thought that the earliest extant letters written by Burns were the series of five addressed to that rather shadowy figure, Alison or Ellison Begbie who is said to have been the inspiration for 'Peggy Alison' and the 'lass of Cessnock banks'. Then a group of three letters addressed to Burns's friend from his Kirkoswald days, William Niven, came to light. Burns and Niven were pupils of Hugh Rodger and sharpened their wits in mutual debate and correspondence. At any rate the letter from Lochlee in July 1780, when Burns was 21 years old, is an extraordinary exercise in philosophical reflection. It is small wonder that Niven never got around to answering it, or a sequel penned a month or two later. In a third letter, dated 3rd November 1780 (actually the second letter now extant), Burns mildly reproaches his old school-friend for not replying. 'I am now beginning to think that, either they have not reached you, or else you are so wholly taken up in the pursuits of love, ambition, or some other of the cares and passions, that render human life one continued up-hill gallop from the cradle to the grave — that you have not time to remember an old acquaintance, who has nothing else to recommend him, but only he has an honest heart, and wishes you well.' Another letter, of 12th June, 1781, hints at a long gap in their correspondence and it would appear that Niven was not as avid a letter-writer as Burns.

Whether his correspondents were as enthusiastic, or as able, at the epistolary art as he was remains to be seen, but of one thing we may be certain. After Burns attained fame if not fortune his letters were treasured by their recipients and it is probably safe to assume that a fair proportion of them was preserved. Letters written by Burns before he became famous are few and far between — a mere score from the period between 1780 and the beginning of 1786. While we may lament the loss of letters from adolescence and young adulthood, we must be grateful for the fortuitous survival of any letters from this early period at all.

Through the letters of Burns we can study the expansion of his intellect, especially from the end of 1786 onwards. In the early period he measured himself against the best brains in Tarbolton, Mauchline and Ayr; from November 1786 onwards he matched his wits against the best minds in Scotland, holding his own among the professors and divines and *literati*. Equally at home in the salons of polite Edinburgh society and with his drinking companions of the Crochallan Fencibles, Burns could be all things to all men — and women — in his correspondence. Rarified passion might be the hallmark of the Clarinda correspondence and a certain genteel delicacy flavour the letters to Mrs Dunlop but Burns could at the same time be matter of fact with Cunningham, mildly bantering with James Smith or broadly candid with Robert Ainslie. The letters to his social equals are the more illuminating on account of their simple style and common sense permeated with a peasant realism.

Comparatively few letters were written to close relatives, but they form an interesting group. The first thing that strikes us is their formal tone. What young man nowadays would preface a letter to his father with 'Honored Sir' and conclude with 'I am, Honored Sir, your dutiful son'? The only extant letter which Burns wrote to his father (from Irvine in December 1781) is a curious piece of work, half of which is pre-occupied with melancholy musings on his poor state of health. Arising out of this gloomy introspection Burns confesses that his 'only pleasurable employment is looking backwards and forwards in moral and religious way. . .' and devotes the rest of the letter to religious metaphysical and moral speculation — though adding an oddly materialistic postscript 'my meal is nearly out but I am going to borrow till I get more.'

According to the list compiled by Dr. Currie, there were some fourteen letters from Gilbert Burns in the poet's possession at the time of his death, but only three letters from Robert to his brother have survived, and these are relatively formal pieces prefaced 'My dear Sir' or 'Dear Brother'. These epistles contrast with the ten letters Burns addressed to his younger brother William, between March 1789 and July 1790, shortly before the latter died. William was eight years his junior, and the impression formed by the letters is that the poet treated William like a son to whom he was, as Franklin B. Snyder has said, 'affectionate, loyal, serious, never over-bearing or dictatorial, and always frank with his counsel.' There is an interesting group of nine letters to his cousin James Burness, dealing mostly with family matters between 1783 and shortly before his death; and there is the quartet of letters addressed to his wife Jean Armour. The warmth and tenderness of the letters to 'My dearest Love' are worth more than all the euphuism in the Sylvander-Clarinda letters.

Turning to the business correspondence of Burns we find that the group of 57 letters to George Thomson, publisher of the *Select Collection*, not only provides us with invaluable insights into Burns's working methods in composition and in mending old ballads, but reveals a great deal about the character of Burns and 'the meddling amateur who did not hesitate to suggest "improvements", and to unauthorised alterations, in the poetry of Burns and the music of Beethoven'. That there were so many letters in the Thomson correspondence was solely due to Burns having to take the time and trouble to deal with such a conceited meddler. Moreover, we should never lose sight of the fact Burns undertook to collaborate with Thomson with no thought of recompense.

The correspondence with James Johnson, although very much smaller in volume, is also of immense interest. Burns was impressed by Johnson's 'honest Scotch enthusiasm' and gladly undertook to help him with his ambitious enterprise of collecting the words and music of the traditional songs for publication. Unlike Thomson, Johnson was only too well aware of his shortcomings and invariably bowed to Burns's superior knowledge and taste. The business relationship soon developed into something more intimate. In Johnson Burns found a kindred spirit, and his letters, ostensibly on business matters, often contain highly revealing passages. From Mauchline on 25th May 1788 Burns wrote: 'I am so enamoured with a certain girl's prolific twin-bearing merit, that I have given her a *legal* title to the best blood in my body; and so farewell Rakery!'

Burns's relationship with William Creech, publisher of the Edinburgh editions of his poems, was less happy. Creech has gone down in history as an incredibly vain and mean man who delayed paying Burns as long as he could. Of the five letters extant from Burns to Creech, however, only two touch upon money matters and then only elliptically. 'Why should I go into the country? till I clear with you, I don't know what to do, or what I have in my power to do.' complains Burns on 24th January 1788, after waiting for several months to get his account settled. The next letter on the subject, written at Mauchline on 31st March, begins by saying that Burns needs the 'sum procured me for my Copyright' (£100), but weakens the demand by adding 'but as I do not need the sum, at least I can make a shift without it till then, anytime between now and the first of May, as it may suit your convenience to pay it, will do for me'. This vexatious matter, however, was referred to in several letters to other people. On 22nd January he wrote to Margaret Chalmers: 'I have broke measures with Creech, and last week I wrote him a keen, frosty letter. He replied in a form of chastisement, and promised me upon his honor that I should have the account on Monday, but this is Tuesday, and yet I have heard not a word from him.' Later he wrote in similar vein to Dr. Moore, saying that Creech 'kept me hanging about Edinburgh from the 7th of August 1787, until the 13th April 1788, before he would condescend to give me a statement of affairs; nor had I got it even then but for an angry letter I wrote him, which irritated his pride.' Clearly other letters passed from Burns to his publisher than those which have been preserved, showing the poet taking a much tougher line.

No letters exist — if indeed they ever did — from Burns to John Wilson, his very first publisher, so we are denied information on the publication of the Kilmarnock Edition; but there are various letters to John Logan, John Ballantine, James Smith and Robert Aiken in the summer and autumn of 1786 which shed light on that transaction.

When Burns first met Peter Hill the latter was employed as a clerk at Creech's bookshop but in 1788 he broke away and established his own business. Hill acted on Burns's behalf in a number of financial and business matters, as well as supplying the poet with books either for himself or for the library of the Monkland Friendly Society which Burns and Robert Riddell organised. No fewer than nineteen letters to Peter Hill have survived; and although they mainly deal with business matters they are studded with personal observations.

More intriguing, perhaps, was Burns's dealings with newspaper editors, not only in Edinburgh but also in London. A surprising number of his poems and epigrams first saw the light of day in the pages of newspapers, notably *The Star,* edited by Peter Stuart who solicited contributions from Burns after reading the Kilmarnock Poems and even offered him a salary 'quite as large as his Excise office emoluments'. Burns, however, did not wish to tie himself down to one particular paper, although he agreed to submit occasional contributions. Significantly, he gently corrected Stuart regarding the signature R.B. Esq. appended to his contributions: 'No Poet, by statute of Parnassus, has a right, as an author, to assume Esquire . . . so I am, as yet, simply Mr. ROBERT BURNS, at your service. . . I must beg of you never to put my name to anything I send, except where I myself set it down at the head or foot of the piece.' Apart from occasional poems, Burns also wrote letters to the press on major topics of political importance. Needless to say, these polemical letters were published under pseudonyms.

Of Burns's later career, as an Excise officer, there is an abundance of material contained in the letters to Robert Graham of Fintry, whose influence secured him an appointment and subsequent transfer to Dumfries, to Alexander Findlater his immediate superior at Dumfries, to Mrs Dunlop who used her contacts to bring Burns before the attention of William Corbet, the General Supervisor, and of course, to John Mitchell, Collector at Dumfries. Correspondence with the last-named tended to be on the routine matters of the Dumfries port division, although Burns also deferred to Mitchell's opinions regarding many of his later poems and songs. Very few letters have survived relating to Burns's Excise dealings with the general public. There is a solitary letter to Robert Moore in 1789, intimating that he had been fined £1 for making bricks without a licence, and there is Burns's letter to Provost Staig in 1793 drawing attention to the unfair competition faced by Dumfries brewers who paid taxes from which their competitors in Bridgend (Maxwelltown) and Annan were exempt.

Other letters deal with the more trivial matters of every day life: Burns's dealings with local tradesmen such as Thomas Boyd, Alexander Crombie and David Newall; and, of course, the indirect references to that 'rascal of a Haberdasher' whose threats of legal proceedings certainly did nothing to prolong the poet's last days.

From correspondence we get tantalising glimpses of Burns the Freemason and Burns the patriot who played a leading role in the Dumfries Volunteers during the dark days of the French Revolutionary War when the threat of invasion was imminent. These aspects of the crowded life of the poet and Exciseman are far better known from his poems; and yet the letters give us another dimension.

The letters ought to dispel for once and for all any doubts, and certainly any lingering notion of Burns's last years being clouded by dissipation. To accomplish as much as Burns did in the last seven or eight years of his life, and maintain such wide-ranging interests as his letters illustrate, would have tried the stamina of any clean-living man in full health. Burns far too freely acknowledged the very occasional lapse, as when he wrote to Cunningham early in 1792, from the George Inn at 3 a.m., 'I am just now devilish drunk − if you doubt it, ask a Mr Campbell, whom I have just met with by lucky accident − He tells me he is connected with you by marriage'. Devilish drunk, perhaps, but not *too* drunk to pen a faultless letter. I suspect that this was nothing more than a jocular pose. One cannot deny the occasional references to drinking and drunkenness in Burns's letters, but when applied to himself they are usually in some jokey context. Contrast that, however, with his revulsion at the drunken scene following the roup of his crops. In a letter to Thomas Sloan, dated 1st September 1791, he writes: 'But such a scene of drunkenness was hardly ever seen in this country. − After the roup was over, about thirty people engaged in a battle, every man for his own hand and fought it out for three hours. − Nor was the scene much better in the house. − No fighting, indeed, but folks lieing drunk on the floor, and decanting, until both my dogs got so drunk by attending them, that they could not stand. − You will easily guess how I enjoyed the scene as I was no farther over than you used to see me.'

'For every apologetic or defiant reference in the letters to drunkenness', wrote De Lancey Ferguson, 'there are a dozen or a score to ill health'. And Professor Ferguson argues that a man as sensitive as Burns was to the impression he might make socially would be apt in the reaction following on excess to exaggerate the degree of his offence. Whatever the truth surrounding the so-called 'Rape of the Sabine Women' incident towards the end of

1793, there can be no doubt of the abject remorse expressed in the purple prose of the letter addressed to his outraged hostess: 'I daresay this is the first epistle you ever received from the nether world. I write to you from the regions of Hell, amid the horrors of the damned . . .' There follows what must surely be one of the most vivid descriptions of a hangover ever penned, but it is important to note that Burns tried to get the incident into perspective when he adds: 'To the men of the company I will make no apology. Your husband, who insisted on my drinking more than I chose, has no right to blame me; and the other gentlemen were partakers of my guilt.'

Regarding the generally poor state of his health throughout his adult life there can be no doubt. The letters bristle with references, direct and indirect, to the depression and nervous debilitation — 'the least anxiety, or perturbation in my breast, produces most unhappy effects on my whole frame' — oscillating with hyperactivity and burst of euphoria. Burns's cyclothymia is clearly evident in the sharply contrasting tones of letters written even on the same day, within hours of each other. One may detect elements of hysteria in some letters, notably those to Mrs Dunlop, but when Burns speaks of his hypochondria he is speaking not of any imagined illness but of the consequences of the chronic heart condition which he had endured since the overworked years of boyhood.

The physical illnesses and ailments which he suffered were likewise real enough. There are frequent references to headache, nausea, poor appetite, toothache and 'a malignant squinancy and low fever' as well as more immediate troubles such as a dislocated knee, a broken arm and influenza. Lest there be any doubt as to the reality of these illnesses we have the poignant record of his handwriting, usually bold and vigorous, reduced to a spidery scrawl during periods of illness and particularly over the last few weeks of his life.

Of Burns the poetic genius, his works are more than ample proof; but of Burns the man, as son, lover, husband, boon companion or true friend, as farmer, exciseman, collector and mender of old ballads, as polemicist or epigrammatist, as counsellor and literary collaborator, his letters are the surest record. Although only one letter was written as a form of autobiography in the strict sense, the remaining 700-odd letters reveal Burns as he really was, with all his faults and failings, his vices and his virtues, his strengths and his weaknesses, exhibited with a candour, honesty and integrity that can only enhance our love and understanding, our admiration and respect.

LIST OF THE RECIPIENTS
OF LETTERS WRITTEN BY BURNS

The following list is arranged in chronological order, according to the date of the first letter known to have been written by Burns.

William Niven, 29th July 1780 37
William Burnes, 27th December 1781 41
Alison Begbie, 1781 43
Thomas Orr, 7th September 1782 49
Sir John Whitefoord, November 1782 51
John Murdoch, 15th January 1783 54
James Burness, 21st June 1783 57
Gavin Hamilton, 18th October 1783 65
John Tennant of Glenconner, 13th September 1784 . . 72
Margaret Kennedy, October 1785 75
John Richmond, 17th February 1786 76
John Kennedy, 3rd March 1786 83
Robert Muir, 20th March 1786 86
Robert Aitken, 3rd April 1786 91
John Ballantine, April 1786 97
Mr McWhinnie, 17th April 1786 106
John Arnot, April 1786 107
David Brice, 12th June 1786 111
Dr John Mackenzie, 14th June 1786 113
Deed of Assignment, 22nd July 1786 115
James Smith about 1st August 1786 117
John Logan, 10th August 1786 123
Thomas Campbell, 19th August 1786 124
Mrs Stewart of Stair, September 1786 125
Archibald Lawrie, 13th November 1786 127
Mrs Frances Dunlop of Dunlop, 15th November 1786 . 130
Wilhelmina Alexander, 18th November 1786 216
William Chalmers & John McAdam, 20th Nov. 1786 . . . 218
George Reid, 29th November 1786 220
Rev. William Greenfield, December 1786 221
John Tennant 20th December 1786 222
Lord Monboddo, 30th December 1786 223
Henry Erskine December 1786 224
James, Earl of Glencairn, 13th January 1787 226
James Sibbald, January 1787 229
Margaret Chalmers, January 1787 230
Patrick Miller of Dalswinton, 15th January 1787 240
Dr John Moore, January 1787 246
Rev. George Lawrie, 5th February 1787 263
The Bailies of the Canongate, 6th February 1787 265
Earl of Buchan, 7th February 1787 266

James Dalrymple, February 1787 269
Earl of Eglinton, February 1787 271
James Candlish, 21st March 1787 272
Robert Cleghorn, March 1787 274
Lady Henrietta Don, 26th March 1787 280
Miss Farquhar, 20th April 1787 281
William Dunbar, 30th April 1787 282
Rev. Hugh Blair, 4th May 1787 288
Henry Mackenzie, 4th May 1787 289
William Tytler, 4th May 1787 291
James Johnson 4th May 1787 292
Dr M. Fyffe, 5th May 1787 304
William Creech, 13th May 1787 305
Alexander Pattison, 17th May 1787 308
Peter Hill, 17th May 1787 309
William Scott, 24th May 1787 326
Robert Ainslie, 29th May 1787 327
William Nicol, 1st June 1787 342
William — — —, 2nd July 1787 351
Lodge St. James, Tarbolton, 23rd August 1787 352
William Inglis, 4th September 1787 353
Josiah Walker, 5th September 1787 354
Gilbert Burns, 17th September 1787 357
William Cruikshank, 8th October 1787 359
James Hoy, 20th October 1787 361
Rev. John Skinner, 25th October 1787 363
Robert P-- — — — —n, 14th November 1787 365
Thomas Whyter, November 1787 366
Miss Isobel Mabane, 1st December 1787 367
John Beugo, December 1787 368
Mrs Agnes McLehose, 6th December 1787 370
William Hamilton, 12th December 1787 413
Charles Hay, 24th December 1787 414
Mr Thomson, 10th-24th December 1787 415
James Stewart, 26th December 1787 416
Francis Howden December 1787 417
Richard Brown 30th December 1787 418
Robert Graham of Fintry, January 1788 424
Mrs Elizabeth Rose, 17th February 1788 441
Anthony Dunlop, October 1787 - February 1788 . . . 443
William Stewart, 21st March 1788 444
Alexander Blair, 3rd April 1788 447
Dugald Stewart, 3rd May 1788 448
Samuel Brown, 4th May 1788 451
Andrew Dunlop, 31st May 1788 452
George Lockhart, 18th July 1788 453
John Smith, 18th July 1788 454
Alexander Cunningham, 27th July 1788 455
Miss Rachel Dunlop, 2nd August 1788 475

Robert McIndoe, 5th August 1788 476
Jean Armour Burns, 12th September 1788 477
Robert Riddell, 16th September 1788 480
Dr James Mundell, October 1788 485
Miss Agnes Dunlop, November 1788 486
The Edinburgh *Evening Courant*, 8th November 1788 . 487
Bruce Campbell, 13th November 1788 489
Dr Thomas Blacklock, 15th November 1788 490
John McMurdo, 26th November 1788 492
Lady Elizabeth Cunningham, 22nd January 1789 496
Peter Morison, 22nd January 1789 501
David Blair, 23rd January 1789 502
Alexander Dalziel, January 1789 505
Bishop John Geddes, 3rd February 1789 507
William Pitt, February 1789 509
Mrs Edward Whigham, 7th February 1789 512
Thomas Boyd, 8th February 1789 513
William Burns 2nd March 1789 514
Peter Stuart, April 1789 520
The Editor of the *Gazetteer*, 10th April 1789 525
James Hamilton, 27th April 1789 526
Rev. Patrick Carfrae, 27th April 1789 527
Jane Blair McMurdo, 2nd May 1789 529
The Editor of the Belfast *News-Letter* 18th May 1789 530
John McAuley, 4th June 1789 531
Miss Helen Maria Williams, July—August 1789 532
David Sillar, 5th August 1798 536
Alexander Fergusson, October 1789 538
Alexander Findlater, October 1789 539
Robert Moore, 26th October 1789 543
Mrs Patrick Miller, 2nd November 1789 245
David Newall, 7th November 1789 544
Lady Winifred Maxwell Constable, 16th Dec. 1789 . . . 546
Robert Maxwell, 20th December 1789 548
George S. Sutherland, 31st December 1789 549
David Staig, 1st March 1790 551
Mrs Elizabeth Graham, 10th June 1790 555
Captain Francis Grose, June 1790 557
Helen Craik of Arbigland, 9th August 1790 561
John Mitchell, August 1790 563
Answers to Petition of Thomas Johnston, Sep. 1790 . . 564
John Wilson, 11th September 566
John Somerville, 11th September 1790 567
Alexander Crombie & Co., 8th October 1790 568
Crauford Tait, 15th October 1790 569
Dr James Anderson, 1st November 1790 571
John Gillespie, January 1791 572
Rev. Archibald Alison, 14th February 1791 573
Rev. George H. Baird, 28th February 1791 574

Thomas Sloan, April 1791 576
Alexander Fraser Tytler, April 1791 578
Charles Sharpe, 22nd April 1791 580
James Gracie, April 1791 582
Alexander Coutts, 28th April 1791 583
Sir James Stirling, June 1791 584
Rev. Thomas Smith, 4th July 1791 585
Sir John Sinclair, August—September 1791 586
Alexander Williamson of Balgray, September 1791 . . . 588
Duke of Queensberry, 24th September 1791 589
Miss Deborah Duff Davies, October 1791 590
Colonel William Fullarton, 3rd October 1791 593
Rev. Joseph Kirkpatrick, 22nd Ocotber 1791 594
James Clarke, 10th January 1792 595
William Smellie, 22nd January 1792 597
William Corbet, February 1792 598
Maria Riddell, February 1792 600
Rev. William Moodie, February 1792 613
John Leven. March 1792 614
Stephen Clarke, 16th July 1792 615
George Thomson, 16th September 1792 616
William Johnston, 13th November 1792 680
Louisa Fontenelle, 22nd November 1792 681
Mary Peacock, 6th December 1792 684
Miss A.D. Benson, 21st March 1793 685
The Provost and Bailies of Dumfries, March 1793 553
John, Earl of Glencairn, March 1793 686
Thomas White, March 1793 687
Jessie Staig, Spring 1793 688
John Francis Erskine, 13th April 1793 689
Miss Lesley Baillie, May 1793 692
Miss Jean McMurdo, July 1793 693
Miss Janet Miller, 9th September 1793 245
Edward Whigham, November 1793 512
William Robertson, 3rd December 1793 695
Mrs Robert Riddell, December 1793 697
Patrick Miller, Jr., January 1794 699
Samuel Clark, February 1794 702
Captain John Hamilton, 24th March 1794 703
Lady Elizabeth Heron, 3rd April 1794 705
John Clark, 21st April 1794 706
Miss Eleanor Riddell, May 1794 707
John Syme, May 1794 708
John McLeod, 18th June 1794 710
David McCulloch, 21st June 1794 712
Robert Andrew Riddell, 22nd September 1794 713
The Editor of the *Morning Chronicle*, January 1795 . . 714
Patrick Heron of Heron, March 1795 715

Richard A. Oswald, 23rd April 1795 717
John Edgar, 25th April 1795 718
Lady Mary Douglas Hamilton, 2nd May 1795 719
Colonel A.S. de Peyster, 18th May 1795 720
William Lorimer, August 1795 721
James Armour, 10th July 1796 722
Miss Gordon (1791-6) 723
Sundry Unidentified Correspondents 724

NOTES ON THE TEXT OF THE LETTERS

The appearance of the Clarendon second edition of the letters (1985) has freed me from the constraints of producing a text which is exactly as Burns wrote it. It is of paramount importance to scholars to have a text which indicates the deletions. Sometimes this gives Burns's first thoughts, though more often than not it merely represents the poet's corrections of misspellings or ungrammatical expressions. The interpolation of square brackets and editorial notes in italics, however, is of much less interest to the ordinary reader and makes it difficult to follow the even flow of the prose. It has been my policy, therefore, to ignore such interpolations and deletions and present a text as Burns would have intended his recipients to read it.

In common with writers of his time, Burns had a somewhat unorthodox approach to spelling. This was largely due to the fact that orthography was not standardised in his day as it is in our time, though the purchase of a good English dictionary from Peter Hill (April 1789) must have been a great help. I have retained Burns's spelling without comment and have only exercised editorial licence in a very few instances where correction was necessary to make the sense clearer. Similarly I have retained his somewhat idiosyncratic punctuation. Burns, it must be admitted, was too free with his use of the comma which sometimes crops up in the unlikeliest of places. Here again, the insertion or deletion of a comma has only been resorted to in those cases where the sense of the text would otherwise have been difficult to follow.

The dating of letters was undergoing transition in the last decade of Burns's life. Previously the usual form was for writers to add the date at the *end* of the letter, in the left-hand corner below the conventional valediction and signature; but by the 1780s the practice of inserting the date and place of writing at the head of the letter, in the upper right-hand corner of the opening page, was gradually coming into fashion. Burns used both forms indiscriminately, and in the interests solely of uniformity I have inserted these details at the top of each letter, so that the reader may see at a glance when and from where each letter was written.

As the letters have been grouped according to each correspondent, I have considered it unnecessary to include the superscriptions which would have appeared on the outer cover of each letter. In the great majority of cases these forms of address vary little from letter to letter. The full text of these endorsements, of course, will be found in the Clarendon edition of 1985 if need be.

Burns was comparatively good about dating his letters, but there are many examples which were either undated, or merely endorsed 'Tuesday morning', 'Wednesday even' and so on. Where the date has been conjectured or deduced from external evidence, such as the postal markings or the docketing of the recipients, dates are shown in square brackets.

Much confusion has arisen in the past because successive editors were not fully conversant with the practice of the Post Office in postmarking letters. During the poet's lifetime, and for several years after his death, the only post office in the whole of Scotland which used datestamps was the General Post Office in Edinburgh. The datestamp took the form of an instrument not unlike a wooden clothes-peg, with two wooden segments bound together. On the ends of these pieces of wood, semi-circular in section, were engraved two letters (signifying the month) and one or two numerals (denoting the day of the month). England pioneered the postal datestamp in 1661 and from the fact that this device was introduced by Colonel Sir Henry Bishop during his tenure of office as Postmaster General following the Restoration, the resulting postmarks are known to postal historians as Bishop marks. The use of Bishop marks was extended to Edinburgh in 1693, but at first restricted to letters going furth of Scotland.

By the time of Burns, however, it was customary for the General Post Office to apply a Bishop mark not only to letters posted in Edinburgh, but also to letters passing through Edinburgh in transit, and to letters from other parts of the country arriving in the capital for delivery to addresses there. All other post offices in Scotland at that period used an undated stamp merely showing the name of the town. Thus a letter posted at Mauchline would bear in black ink a straight-line postmark MAUCHLINE, and if addressed to Edinburgh it would also bear a Bishop mark in red ink, appearing as a small circle with a horizontal line across the middle, and showing the abbreviated month and the day of its arrival. As letters from the southwest of Scotland took two or sometimes three days to reach Edinburgh, the Bishop mark is invariably later than the date written by the poet inside his letters. This apparent discrepancy has elicited comment from some previous editors, although it is exactly as one would expect.

Where the letters bear no internal date, however, the Bishop mark can only be regarded as giving an *approximate* date in the case of letters written to Edinburgh. In the case of letters written by Burns from Edinburgh, of course, the Bishop mark is an accurate guide to the date of actual composition. As a general rule, I have ignored the postmark, but where the Bishop mark is of use in dating letters this information is given in italics below the conjectural date in square brackets.

By courtesy of Professor Ross Roy the numbering of Burns's letters in the Clarendon edition (1985) is shown in parentheses, after the individual letter number, which I have given in roman numerals. The letters have been arranged in chronological order according to the date of the first known letter from Burns to the recipients. Within each group, naturally, all the letters to that particular correspondent are to be found in date sequence.

Where Burns quoted from his own works, or enclosed copies of his poems, I have given only their titles as rendered in that correspondence by Burns, together with the opening line, followed by a reference to the page in the companion volume on which the full text of the poem may be found, indicated in parenthesis by the abbreviation C.W. (*Complete Works*). Quotations from other sources, where they have been identified, are indicated by footnotes at the end of each letter for the sake of clarity and convenience.

In the Clarendon edition, Professor Roy interpolated the various verse epistles composed by Burns on the grounds that they were probably intended to be sent to the addressees in the form of letters and, indeed, many of them bear all the external indications of having been transmitted by post. Instead I have printed a separate list of them, with reference to their appearance in the companion volume. The numbers in brackets are those given in the 1985 edition by Professor Roy.

LIST OF VERSE EPISTLES, IN ALPHABETICAL ORDER OF RECIPIENT

Andrew Hunter Aiken, from Mossgiel 15th May 1786   (29C)
        I lang hae thought, my youthfu' friend   (C.W. p.221)

Rev. Dr Thomas Blacklock, from Ellisland 21st October 1789
(365B)
           Wow, but your letter made me vauntie!   (C.W. p.370)

Miss Jane Ferrier, enclosing a copy of *Elegy on the death of
Sir J. Hunter Blair* (C.W. p.281)
    from St James' Square, Edinburgh [July 1787?]   (168A)
    Madam
           Nae heathen Name shall I prefix   (C.W. p.283)

Alexander Findlater, from Ellisland 'Saturday morning' [1789?]   (380A)
           Dear Sir,
           our Lucky humbly begs   (C.W. p.378)

John Goldie, August 1785   (19F)
           O Gowdie, terror o' the whigs   (C.W. p.121)

Symon Gray, from Dunse 15th May 1787   (106A)
           Dear Cimon Gray,
           The other day,   (C.W. p.279)

Gavin Hamilton, from Mossgaville 3rd May 1786   (29B)
        I hold it, Sir, my bounden duty   (C.W. p.215)

Gavin Hamilton [April — May? 1786]   (30A)
        To you, Sir this summons I've sent   (C.W. p.210)

John Lapraik   1st April 1785   (19C)
        While briers an woodbines budding green   (C.W. p.101)

John Lapraik   21st April 1785   (19D)
        While new-ca'd kye rowte at the stake   (C.W. p.104)

John Lapraik   13th September 1785   (19G)
        Guid speed and Furder to you, Johnie   (C.W. p.127)

Jessie Lewars   26th June 1796   (698A)
        Thine be the volumes, Jessy fair   (C.W. p.567)

Captain William Logan   30th October 1786   (53B)
        Hail, thairm-inspirin, rattlin Willie!   (C.W. p.256)

John McAdam   [January — March? 1787]   (93A)
        Sir, o'er a gill I gat your card   (C.W. p.274)

Dr. John Mackenzie, from Mossgiel 14th June, A.M. [1786]   (31A)
        Friday first's the day appointed   (C.W. p.237)

Simon Mackenzie 1796?   (711)
        The friend who wild from Wisdom's way   (C.W. p.568)

Miss Isabella McLeod, from Edinburgh 16th March 1787   (88A)
        The crimson blossom charms the bee   (C.W. p.273)

BURNS AND HIGHLAND MARY
by W.H. Midwood

Ellisland near Dumfries 5th August, 1789

My dear Sir,

I was half in thoughts not to have written you at all, by way of revenge for the two *nimini* business letters you sent me. — I wanted to know all and about your Publication, what were your views, your hopes, fears, &c. &c. in commencing Poet in Print — in short, I wanted you to write to Robin like his old acquaintance, David; and not in the style of Mr o ffret, to Mr o ffret — Mr o ffret. —

Sir   this comes to advise you that your fifteen barrels of herrings were, by the blessing of God, shipped safe on board the Lovely Janet, Q. D. C. Duncan Mc Leerie Master, &c. &c. &c. —

I hear you have commenced Married Man; so much the better, though perhaps your Muse may not fare the better for it — I know not whether the Nine Gyp-Seys are jealous of my Lucky, but they are a good deal shyer since I could boast the important relation of Husband. —

I have got I think about eleven Subscribers for you — My acquaintance in this place is yet but very limited else I might have had more. — When you send Mr Aul in Dumfries his, you may with them pack me eleven; should I need more, I can write you, should there be too many, they can be returned. — My best compliments to Mrs Sillar; and believe me to be, Dear David ever yours R B Burns

Original Burns manuscript by courtesy of Irvine Burns Club
see page 536.

Rev. John McMath 17th September 1785 (19H)
    While at the stook the shearers cow'r   (C.W. p.129)

John Maxwell of Terraughty 7th February 1791 (435A)
    Health to the Maxwels' veteran Chief!   (C.W. p.417)

Dr. William Maxwell early September 1794 (635A)
    Maxwell, if merit here you crave   (C.W. p.519)

John Mitchell Hogmanai (sic) eve: 1795 (685C)
    Friend of the Poet, tried and leal   (C.W. p.561)

Hugh Parker [11th — 30th June? 1788] (248A)
    In this strange land, this uncouth clime   (C.W. p.322)

John Rankine December 1784 — March 1785 (19A)
    O rough, rude, ready-witted Rankine   (C.W. p.82)

John Renton about 18th May 1787 (108A)
    Your billet, Sir, I grant receipt;   (C.W. p.280)

Robert Riddell? [16th October 1789?] (365A)
    The King's most humble servant, I   (C.W. p.370)

Robert Riddell, From Ellisland June 1788 — October 1791 (481A)
Your News and Review, Sir, I've read through and through, Sir (C.W. p.427)

Robert Riddell, from Ellisland June 1788 — October 1791 (481B)
    Dear Sir, at ony time or tide   (C.W. p.428)

Mrs. Elizabeth Scott March 1787 (93B)
    Guidwife, I mind it weel in early date   (C.W. p.271)

David Sillar January 1785 (19B)
    While winds frae off Ben-Lomond blaw   (C.W. p.86)

David Sillar June — July 1786 (31B)
    Auld Neebor, I'm three times, doubly o'er your debtor   (C.W. p.213)

William Simpson May 1785 (19E)
    I gat your letter, winsome Willie   (C.W. p.107)

James Smith Winter 1785-6 (21A)
    Dear Smith, the sleest pawkie thief   (C.W. p.169)

Peter Stuart [June — July 1789?] (353A)
    Dear Peter, dear Peter   (C.W. p.359)

John Syme 17th December 1795 (685B)
    No more of your guests, be they titled or not   (C.W. p.560)

John Taylor [winter 1788-9] (292A)
    With Pegasus upon a day   (C.W. p.344)

James Tennant [January — April 1786?] (29A)
    Auld com'rade dear and brither sinner   (C.W. p.200)

Thomas Walker [August — September? 1786] (51A)
    What ails ye now, ye lousie bitch   (C.W. p.242)

Sir John Whitefoord   [about October 1793]   (475A)
       Thou, who thy honour as thy God rever'st   (C.W p.425)

Unidentified Correspondent   [1785-6?]   (59A)
       Yours this moment I unseal   (C.W. p.261)

Unidentified Correspondent, from Ellisland [summer 1789 — January 1790] (385A)
       Kind Sir, I've read your paper through   (C.W. p.379)

INSCRIPTIONS IN PRESENTATION COPIES OF BOOKS

On 28th February 1793 Burns, having learned that a new edition of his Poems had just been published, wrote to Creech asking for twenty copies. 'As I mean to present them among a few Great Folks whom I respect, & a few Little Folks whom I love, these twenty will not interfere with your sale . . .' Creech replied on 2nd March, sending the desired copies. Letters accompanying this two-volume edition were despatched to Thomas Sloan (18th March), and Agnes McLehose, Patrick Miller and the Earl of Glencairn, about the same time. In addition, lengthy inscriptions, which are nowadays classed as letters in their own right, were actually inscribed in the copies sent to Mrs. Graham of Fintry, Robert Riddell, John McMurdo, Lady Elizabeth Cunningham, David Blair and Thomas White, and these will be found in their respective places in the text.

In addition, however, there are several inscriptions of the utmost brevity, which do not warrant separate notice, but which are noted below.

To Elizabeth Burns ['Dear Bought Bess]:
    her Father's gift——
                    The Author

To Mrs. John Gillespie:
    A small but sincere mark of the most respectful esteem from —
                    The Author

To Mrs. Maria Riddell of Woodleypark:
    Un gage d'Amitie le plus sincére—
                    The Author

In addition to the letter sent to Patrick Miller of Dalswinton, the copy he received was inscribed:

    from his much indebted humble serv^t
                    The Author

It is assumed that the other presentation copies, accompanied by letters, were similarly endorsed. The known letters and inscriptions account for some thirteen of the presentation copies. A letter of June 1793 to Mrs. Dunlop mentions 'a parcel of books' sent 'a great while ago', so she may also have been the recipient of the 1793 edition, but of the remaining half dozen copies nothing is known.

One other book remains to be noted. In September 1793 Burns presented a copy of *The British Constitution* by Jean Louis De Lolme to the Dumfries public library. On the fly-leaf he penned an ambiguous inscription:

    Mr Burns presents this book to the Library & begs they will take it as a Creed of British Liberty — until they find a better.—

He subsequently thought better of such a rash act and took extraordinary steps to undo any damage to his Excise career, by glueing the fly-leaf and the adjoining page together in order to conceal the inscription. The pages have since been separated, and the volume with its radical sentiments is on display in the Burns House, Dumfries.

WILLIAM NIVEN

Born in Maybole in 1759, the second son of John Niven and Janet Spear, he became a prosperous merchant in his home town and eventually Deputy Lieutenant for Ayrshire (1810). He died in 1844. Niven was a fellow pupil of Burns under Hugh Rodger at Kirkoswald and after their schooldays they kept in touch by a correspondence that seems to have been largely one-sided. The three letters written by Burns to Niven between July 1780 and June 1781 are not only the earliest extant from the budding poet but among the most extraordinary literary exercises he ever produced. Niven obviously treasured these epistles and probably carried them around in his wallet, to judge by the fragmentary state of the first letter. The passages in italics are conjectural reconstructions in an attempt to restore the sense, if not the actual words, of the original.

Niven later claimed that Burns's *Epistle to a Young Friend*, dedicated to Andrew Hunter Aiken, had originally been intended for himself, although there is no documentary proof for this. The only other letter from Burns to Niven was written in August 1786 following a convivial meeting between Burns and some of his Maybole friends, including Niven and Thomas Piper, the 'spunkie, youthfu Tammie' referred to.

I (1)

Lochlee, 29th July 1786

I do not think I ever met with any *letter that was more* entertaining than the agreeable *one you wrote on* the 20th; the circumstances in it *are very cleverly* placed, and yet seem to rise natu*rally throughout* it, and tho' keenly satirical have *not a hint of the* indelicate. I shall not at present *attempt a defin*ite criticism on it as I am deter*mined to give you my* observations on the subject *at this very moment,* but I must first premise *these observations* are intirely my own, and consequently *may appear ill d*igested, nay perhaps to an unpre*judiced critic so*me of them may appear absurd: *but I am writing* to a Friend.—

There is some quality in the soul of man which *instills importan*t incentives in the human mind *which are the prin*cipal ingredients in every thing *that may be thought* manly, &c., this I call Pride and *regard it neither go*od nor bad in itself; but *when* joined *with other manly* dispositions it is part of the noblest virtues; or, when mixed with corrupted & disingenuous inclinations, it enters largely into the composition of many vices. I do not think I can convey my notion of it to you better, than by analizing some of the virtues in which it is most conspicuous. I look upon patience to be the possessing one's mind calmly in ruffling circumstances of life and is either a natural *born talent* or, an acquired command of *adulthood. If to* this you add a large portion of *Pride forement*ioned you have my idea of *manliness. Then* again, a generous, frank, open *mind promotes* an enlarged under-standing; *this is, in my* opinion, the genuine virtue of *magnanimity* or greatness of soul. Courage *I hold to be nothing* else than a large

37

portion of au*dacity combined* with a thoughtlessness of dan*ger which is check*ed & counterbalanced with *caution. When this* quality in its highest perfe*ction is manifest* it is called rashness: there is *also a kind of* ferocity which is sometimes ca*lled courage but which is* nothing akin to the former.—*It is bred from fear.* You see that according to my *opinion it is* absurd to say such a one *has courage. Each* person must have it in some *degree, but of all* pretensions to human nature . . . . . the ordinary acceptation of the . . . . . the forementioned principle . . . . . abilities such as render . . . . *There* are some characters that may be said to be without pride in a great measure: there is particularly one, may be said to be so which I have a great esteem for. The principal feature in this character is Indolence of temper: a man of this sort unless very much harrassed is always easy & calm: he is not soon offended & tho' ruffled . . . .

Three-quarters of a page is missing

. . . and fortitude of these *things* are natural evils, *but if* they *are* injuries from their fellow creatures they are impatient of abuse: they are particularly constant & kind in their friendships tho' indeed seldom with persons of their own character but if with those of the first kind I mention I know no friendly cement so strong. I shall only add that if to these you join a delicate taste & an uncommonly clear penetration you have the character of a friend of mind who shall here be nameless lest I should incur the imputation of being a flatterer which next to a backbiter is the most detestable character under the sun.—I am my dear friend yours since*rely.*

Robt Burns

As for my being in your country, I don't know when it will happen as I will have no business that I know of yet & such is our hurry that a pleasure jant is what I dare not ask. I have three acres of pretty good flax this season perhaps in the course of marketing it I may come your way.

R B

I have not reciev'd the letter you mention

II (2)

Lochlee, 3rd November 1780

Dear Sir,

I wrote you a letter in the latter end of Summer; I wrote you another as soon as the hurried season of Autumn was over, to neither of which, have I received any answer. I am now beginning to think that, either they have not reached you, or else you are so wholly taken up in the pursuits of love, ambition, or some other of the cares and passions, that render human life one continued up-hill gallop from the cradle to the grave—that you have not time to remember an old acquaintance, who has nothing else to recommend him, but only he has an honest heart, and wishes you well.—

I have nothing particular to tell you respecting myself. I am still so happy as to have a friend or two (tho' I am afraid I must no more have the honor of having you among that number) and I have now and then a sweetheart or two, but with as little view of matrimony as ever. I shall be happy to hear from you how you go on in the ways of life; I do not mean so much how trade prospers, or if you have the prospect of riches, or the dread of poverty; as how you go on in the cultivation of the finer feelings of the heart. For my own part, I now see it improbable that I shall ever acquire riches, and am therefore endeavouring to gather a philosophical contempt of enjoyments so hard to be gained & so easily lost.—

I hope to have the pleasure of a letter from you soon, and am,

Dear Sir, yours sincerely,

Robert Burns

III (3)

Lochlee, 12th June 1781

Dear Sir,

I shall not begin with considering whether you are to blame, or I am to blame, or who of us is most to blame for this long, long interval of our correspondence.

In my letter which I wrote you in February last, I touched a subject which, I thought, would have produced an immediate answer; but it seems I have been mistaken, tho' I suspect not altogether neither. Had not the hurried season of seed-time come on so soon as it did, I would have wrote you farther on the subject; but so fatigued was my body & so hebetated my mind, that I could neither think, nor write any thing to purpose.

I know you will hardly believe me when I tell you, that by a strange conjuncture of circumstances, I am intirely got rid of all connections with the tender sex, I mean in the way of courtship: it is, however absolutely certain that I am so; though how long I shall continue so, Heaven only knows; but be that as it may, I shall never be involved as I was again.—

Our communion was on Sunday se'en night, I mention this to tell you that I saw your cousin there, with some of Mr Hamilton's sons. You cannot imagine how pleased I was to steal a look at him, & trace the resemblance of my old friend—I was prepossessed in his favor on that account, but still more by that ingenuous modesty (a quality so rare amongst students, especialy in the divinity way) which is so apparent in his air & manner. I assure you my heart warmed to him: I was only sorry I could not tell him, how happy I would have been to have had it in my power to have obliged him. You know I am a Physiognomist, so will not be surprised at this. I shall expect to hear from you soon; & shall conclude with assuring you, that I am your sincere wellwisher & humble servant.

Robt Burns

IV (42)

Mossgiel, 30th August 1786

My Dear Friend,

I have been very throng ever since I saw you, and have not got the whole of my promise performed to you: but you know the old Proverb "The break o' a day's no the break o' a bargain"—Have patience and I will pay you all.—I thank you with the most heart-felt sincerity for the worthy knot of lads you introduced me to.—Never did I meet with so many congenial souls together, without one dissonant jar in the Concert. To all and each of them make my friendly Compliments particularly "spunkie, youthfu' Tammie." Remember me in the most respectful manner to the Baillie, and Mrs Niven, Mr Dun, and the two truly worthy old Gentlemen I had the honor of being introduced to on Friday; tho' I am afraid the conduct you forced me on may make them see me in a light I would fondly think I do not deserve.—

I will perform the rest of my promise soon.—In the mean time, remember this, never blow my Songs among the Million, as I would abhor to hear every Prentice mouthing my poor performances in the streets.—Every one of my Maybole friends are welcome to a Copy, if they chuse; but I wish them to go no farther.—I mean it as a small mark of my respect for them: a respect as sincere as the faith of dying SAINTS.—

I am ever, My Dear William Your oblidged,

Robt Burns

WILLIAM BURNES

The poet's father was born at Clochnahill near Dunnottar, Kincardine-shire in 1721, and trained as a gardener like his father before him; but the depression in the north-east in the aftermath of the Jacobite Rebellion forced him and his brother to move south in search of work. For two years William worked in Edinburgh before settling in Ayrshire, where he became head gardener at Doonholm, He leased seven and a half acres at Alloway for a market garden and built the 'auld clay biggin' to which he brought his bride, Agnes Broun, in December 1757. Their first child, Robert, was born in 1759, followed by three other sons and three daughters. In his auto-biographical letter to Dr. Moore (see page 246) Burns recounted the hard-ship and struggles endured by his father at Mount Oliphant (1766-77) and Lochlea from 1777 till his death of a 'phthisical consumption' on 13th February 1784, worn out by his labours and the stress brought on by his litigious landlord.

William Burnes gave his children a stern, Calvinistic upbringing, against which his eldest son occasionally rebelled, but there was genuine affection and respect in the letter from Irvine where Burns was learning the trade of flax-dressing, the only letter known from Burns to his father. William Burnes was the model for the toil-worn cotter, the priest-like father of *The Cotter's Saturday Night*. Burns was deeply indebted to his father, not only for his fierce pride and independent spirit, but also for the hard-won education which enabled Burns to develop his talents.

Irvin, December 27th 1781

Honored Sir,

I have purposely delayed writing in the hope that I would have the pleasure of seeing you on Newyearday but work comes so hard upon us that I do not chuse to come as well for that, as also for some other little reasons which I shall tell you at meeting.— My health is much about what it was when you were here only my sleep is rather sounder and on the whole I am rather better than otherwise tho it is but by very slow degrees.— The weakness of my nerves has so debilitated my mind that I dare not, either review past events, or look forward into futurity; for the least anxiety, or perturbation in my breast, produces most unhappy effects on my whole frame.—

Sometimes, indeed, when for an hour or two, as is sometimes the case, my spirits are a little lightened, I glimmer a little into futurity; but my principal, and indeed my only pleasurable employment is looking backwards & forwards in a moral & religious way — I am quite transported at the thought that ere long, perhaps very soon, I shall bid an eternal adieu to all the pains, & uneasiness & desquietudes of this weary life; for I assure you I am heartily tired of it, and, if I do not very much deceive myself I could contentedly & gladly resign it.—

> The Soul uneasy & confin'd from home,
> Rests & expatiates in a life to come.
>   Pope*

It is for this reason I am more pleased with the 15th, 16th & 17th verses of the 7th Chapter of Revelation than any ten times as many verses in the whole Bible, & would not exchange the noble enthusiasm with which they inspire me, for all that this world has to offer — As for this world I despair of ever making a figure in it — I am not formed for the bustle of the busy nor the flutter of the Gay I shall never again be capable of it.— Indeed, I am altogether unconcern'd at the thoughts of it. I foresee that very probably Poverty & Obscurity await me & I am, in some measure prepared & daily preparing to meet & welcome them.— I have but just time & paper to return you my grateful thanks for the many Lessons of Virtue & Piety you have given me — Lessons which were but too much neglected when they were given but which, I hope have been remembered ere it is yet too late — Present my dutiful respects to my Mother & my Compliments to Mr & Mrs Muir and with wishing you all a merry Newyearday I shall conclude—

I am, Honored Sir, your dutiful son

Robert Burns

my meal is nearly out but I am going to borrow till I get more—

Essay on Man, Epistle I, lines 97-8.

ALISON (or ELLISON) BEGBIE

A shadowy figure who was the recipient of five love letters from the poet in 1781, Alison Begbie was identified by Isabella Burns (Robert's sister). Both De Lancey Ferguson and Ross Roy remain sceptical on the grounds that (a) Burns often wrote letters for his shyer and less literate friends, and (b) four of the five letters are known only from drafts. The very formal, stilted language of these letters makes them suspect. Surely had Burns really been writing from the heart they would have been couched in more personal language. If, indeed they were from Burns to Alison Begbie, it is hardly surprising that she rejected him for someone else. Apart from the assertions of Isabella Burns, the story that Alison was courted by Burns is given credence by his statement to Dr. Moore: 'a Belle-fille whom I adored, and who had pledged her soul to me in the field of matrimony, jilted me, with peculiar circumstances of mortification.' The only evidence to suggest that the letters were sent is the fact that the final draft takes the form of a stoic acknowledgement of rejection.

Tradition states that Alison was the daughter of a farmer at Old Place in Galston parish. In 1781 she was working as a domestic servant at Carnell House on the bank of the River Cessnock and from this it is deduced that she was probably the inpiration for Burns's beautiful songs *The Lass Of Cessnock Banks* (C.W. p. 51) and *Bonie Peggy Alison* (C.W. p. 319).

I (5)

Lochlea, 1781?

What you may think of this letter when you see the name that subscribes it I cannot know; & perhaps I ought to make a long Preface of apologies for the freedom I am going to take, but as my heart means no offence but on the contrary is rather too warmly interested in your favor, for that reason I hope you will forgive me when I tell you that I most sincerely & affectionately love you.— I am a stranger in these matters Alison, as I assure that you are the first woman to whom I ever made such a declaration so I declare I am at a loss how to proceed.— I have more than once come into your company with a resolution to tell you what I have just now told you but my resolution always fail'd me, & even now my heart trembles for the consequence of what I have said — I hope my Dearest you will not despise me because I am ignorant of the flattering arts of courtship; I hope my inexperience of the world will plead for me — I can only say I sincerely love you & there is nothing on earth I so ardently wish for, or could possibly give me so much happiness as one day to see you mine — I think you cannot doubt my sincerity as I am sure that whenever I see you my very looks betray me, and when once you have too much goodness & humanity to allow an honest man to languish in suspense only because he loves you too well, but I am certain that in such a state of anxiety as I myself at present feel an absolute denial would be a more preferable state.—

43

Alison (or Ellison) Begbie

II(6)

I verily believe, my dear E., that the pure genuine feelings of love, are as rare in the world as the pure genuine principles of virtue and piety. This I hope will account for the uncommon style of all my letters to you. By uncommon, I mean, their being written in such a serious manner, which to tell you the truth, has made me often afraid lest you should take me for some zealous bigot, who conversed with his mistress as he would converse with his minister. I don't know how it is, my dear; for though, except your company, there is nothing on earth gives me so much pleasure as writing to you, yet it never gives me those giddy raptures so much talked of among lovers. I have often thought that if a well grounded affection be not really a part of virtue, 'tis something extremely akin to it. Whenever the thought of my E. warms my heart, every feeling of humanity, every principle of generosity, kindles in my breast. It extinguishes every dirty spark of malice and envy, which are but too apt to infest me. I grasp every creature in the arms of universal benevolence, and equally participate in the pleasures of the happy, and sympathise with the miseries of the unfortunate. I assure you, my dear, I often look up to the divine disposer of events, with an eye of gratitude for the blessing which I hope he intends to bestow on me, in bestowing you. I sincerely wish that he may bless my endeavours to make your life as comfortable and happy as possible, both in sweetening the rougher parts of my natural temper, and bettering the unkindly circumstances of my fortune. This, my dear, is a passion at least in my view, worthy of a man, and I will add worthy of a Christian. The sordid earth-worm may profess love to a woman's person, whilst in reality his affection is centered in her pocket: and the slavish drudge may go a wooing as he goes to the horse-market, to chuse one who is stout and firm, and as we may say of an old horse, one who will be a good drudge and draw kindly. I disdain their dirty, puny ideas. I would be heartily out of humour with myself, if I thought I were capable of having so poor a notion of the sex, which were designed to crown the pleasures of society. Poor devils! I don't envy them their happiness who have such notions. For my part I propose quite other pleasures with my dear partner.

III (7)

Lochlea, 1781?

My Dear E.

I do not remember in the course of your acquaintance and mine, ever to have heard your opinion on the ordinary way of falling in love, amongst people of our station in life: I do not mean the persons who proceed in the way of bargain, but those whose affection is really placed on the person.

Though I be, as you know very well, but a very aukward lover myself, yet as I have some opportunites of observing the conduct of others who are much better skilled in the affair of courtship than I am, I often think it is owing to lucky chance more than to good management, that there are not more unhappy marriages than usually are.

It is natural for a young fellow to like the acquaintance of the females, and customary for him to keep them company when occasion serves: some one of them is more agreeable to him than the rest; there is something he knows not what pleases him, he knows not how, in her company. This I take to be what is called love with the greatest part of us, and I must own, my dear E. it is a hard game such a one as you has to play when you meet with such a lover. You cannot refuse but he is sincere, and yet though you use him ever so favourably, perhaps in a few months, or at farthest in a year or two, the same unaccountable fancy may make him as distractedly fond of another, whilst you are quite forgot. I am aware that perhaps the next time I have the pleasure of seeing you, you may bid me take my own lesson home, as tell me that the passion I have professed for you is perhaps one of those transient flashes I have been describing; but I hope, my dear E., you will do me the justice to believe me, when I assure you, that the love I have for you is founded on the sacred principles of virtue and honour, and by consequence so long as you continue possessed of those amiable qualities which first inspired my passion for you, so long must I continue to love you. Believe me, my dear, it is love like this alone which can render the married state happy. People may talk of flames and raptures as long as they please; and a warm fancy, with a flow of youthful spirits, may make them feel something like what they describe; but sure I am, the nobler faculties of the mind with kindred feelings of the heart, can only be the foundation of friendship, and it has always been my opinion, that the married life was only friendship in a more exalted degree.

If you will be so good as to grant my wishes, and it should please providence to spare us to the latest period, of life, I can look forward and see, that even then, though bent down with wrinkled age; even then, when all other worldly circumstances will be indifferent to me, I will regard my E. with the tenderest affection, and for this plain reason, because she is still possessed of these noble qualities, improved to a much higher degree, which first inspired my affection for her.

> "O happy state! when souls each other draw,
> "When love is liberty, and nature law."*

Alison (or Ellison) Begbie

I know, were I to speak in such a style of many a girl, who thinks herself possessed of no small share of sense, she would think it ridiculous — but the language of the heart is, my dear E., the only courtship I shall ever use to you.

When I look over what I have written, I am sensible it is vastly different from the ordinary style of courtship — but I shall make no apology — I know your good nature will excuse what your good sense may see amiss.

*Pope: Eloisa to Abelard, lines 91-2

IV (8)

Lochlea, 1781?

My dear E.

I have often thought it a peculiarly unlucky circumstance in love, that though in every other situation in life, telling the truth is not only the safest, but actually by far the easiest way of proceeding. A lover is never under greater difficulty in acting, or more puzzled for expression, than when his passion is sincere, and his intentions are honorable. I do not think that it is very difficult for a person of ordinary capacity to talk of love and fondness, which are not felt, and to make vows of constancy and fidelity, which are never intended to be performed, if he be villain enough to practise such detestable conduct: but to a man whose heart glows with the principles of integrity and truth; and who sincerely loves a woman of amiable person, uncommon refinement of sentiment, and purity of manners — to such a one, in such circumstances, I can assure you, my dear, from my own feelings at this present moment, courtship is a task indeed. There is such a number of foreboding fears, and distrustful anxieties croud into my mind when I am in your company, or when I sit down and write to you, that what to speak or what to write I am altogether at a loss.

There is one rule which I have hitherto practised, and which I shall invariably keep with you, and that is, honestly to tell you the plain truth. There is something so mean and unmanly in the arts of dissimulation and falsehood, that I am surprised they can be acted by any one in so noble, so generous a passion as virtuous love. No, my dear E. I shall never endeavour to gain your favor by such detestable practices. If you will be so good and so generous as to admit me for your partner, your companion, your bosom friend through life; there is nothing on this side of eternity shall give me greater transport; but I shall never think of purchasing your hand by arts unworthy of a man, and I will add, of a Christian. There is one thing, my dear, which I earnestly request

46

of you, and it is this; that you would soon either put an end to my hopes by a peremptory refusal, or cure me of my fears by a generous consent.

It would oblige me much if you would send me a line or two when convenient. I shall only add further, that if a behaviour regulated (though perhaps but very imperfectly) by the rules of honor and virtue, if a heart devoted to love and esteem you, and an earnest endeavour to promote your happiness; if these are qualities you would wish in a friend, in a husband; I hope you shall ever find them in your real friend and sincere lover.

V (9)

Lochlea, June 1781?

I ought in good manners to have acknowledged the receipt of your letter before this time, but my heart was so shocked with the contents of it, that I can scarcely yet collect my thoughts so as to write you on the subject. I will not attempt to describe what I felt on receiving your letter. I read it over and over, again and again, and though it was in the politest language of refusal, still it was peremptory; "you were sorry you could not make me a return, but you wish me" what without you I never can obtain, "you wish me all kind of happiness." It would be weak and unmanly to say that without you I never can be happy; but sure I am, that sharing life with you, would have given it a relish, that, wanting you I can never taste.

Your uncommon personal advantages, and your superior good sense, do not so much strike me; these possibly in a few instances may be met with in others; but that amiable goodness, that tender feminine softness, that endearing sweetness of disposition, with all the charming offspring of a warm feeling heart — these I never again expect to meet with in such a degree in this world. All these charming qualities, heightened by an education much beyond any thing I have ever met in any woman I ever dared to approach, have made an impression on my heart that I do not think the world can ever efface. My imagination had fondly flattered itself with a wish, I dare not say it ever reached a hope, that possibly I might one day call you mine. I had formed the most delightful images, and my fancy fondly brooded over them but now I am wretched for the loss of what I really had no right to expect. I must now think no more of you as a mistress, still I presume to ask to be admitted as a friend. As such I wish to be allowed to wait on you, and as I expect to remove in a few days a little farther off, and you I suppose will perhaps soon leave this place, I wish to see you or hear from you soon; and if an ex-

pression should perhaps escape me rather too warm for friendship, I hope you will pardon it in, my dear Miss ———, (pardon
me the dear expression for once.) . . . . .

THOMAS ORR

A contemporary of Burns and Niven at Hugh Rodger's school in Kirkoswald, Orr had the dubious distinction of being the grandson of the notorious Julia Robinson, allegedly a witch and assuredly a receiver of stolen and smuggled goods. Orr helped out at the harvest in Lochlea in 1780-81, but went to sea in 1785 and was drowned on his first voyage. Of the three surviving letters from Burns to Orr, the first two (September and November 1782) are in the nature of literary exercises, but the third (1784) is of a personal nature and raises the intriguing speculation whether the 'Peggy' referred to therein was the same young lady as the recipient of the Alison Begbie letters.

I (10)

Lochlea, 7th September 1782

Dear Sir,

I have been designed to write to you of a long time but was at a loss for a direction as I am ignorant what place of the country you are in. I have nothing to tell you of news; for myself I am going on in my old way — taking as light a burden as I can, of the cares of the world; studying men, their manners, & their ways, as well as I can. Believe me Tom, it is the only study in this world will yield solid satisfaction. To be rich & to be great are the grand concerns of this world's men, & to be sure if moderately pursued it is laudable; but where is it moderately pursued? the greater part of men grasp at riches as eagerly as if Poverty were but another word for Damnation & misery whereas I affirm that the man whose only wish is to become great & rich; whatever he may appear to be, or whatever he may pretend to be; at the bottom he is but a miserable wretch. —Avoid this sordid turn of mind if you would be happy. Observe mankind around you; endeavour by studying the wisdom & Prudence of some and the folly & madness of others, to make yourself wiser & better.—I hope you will write me soon & tell me what your mind is employed in, what your studies principally are; & believe me, that you may be wise & virtuous, generous & humane is the sincere wish of your friend.

Robt Burns

II (11)

Lochlea, 17th November 1782

Dear Thomas,

I am to blame for not returning you an answer sooner to your kind letter. But such has been the backwardness of our harvest, and so seldom are we at Ayr that I have scarcely had one opportunity of sending a line to you.— I was extremely delighted with your letter. I love to see a man who has a mind superior to the world & the world's men — a man who, conscious of his own integrity, & at peace with himself, despises the censures &

opinions of the unthinking rabble of mankind. The distinction of a poor man & a rich man is something indeed, but it is nothing to the difference between either a wise man & a fool, or a man of honor & a knave.

> What is't to me, a Passenger God wot,
> Whether my Vessel be first rate or not;
> The Ship itself may make a better figure,
> But I who sail am neither less nor bigger.
>   Pope*

I have nothing farther to say to you but go on & prosper & if you miss happiness by enjoyment you will find it by contented resignation.—

Write me soon to let me know how you are to be disposed of during the winter & believe me to be ever

your sincere friend,

Robt Burns

*Satire VI, lines 291-4

III (19)

Mossgavil, 11th November 1784

Dear Thomas,

I am much oblidged to you for your last letter tho' I assure you the contents of it gave me no manner of concern.—I am at present so cursedly taken in with an affair of gallantry that I am very glad Peggy is off my hands as I am at present embarrassed enough without her.—I do'n't chuse to enter into particulars in writing but never was a poor rakish rascal in a more pitiful taking — I should be glad to see you to tell you the affair, meanwhile

I am your friend

Robt Burness

SIR JOHN WHITEFOORD

Third Baronet of Blairquhan (1734-1803), he was a notable agricultural reformer, a friend of the Earl of Glencairn and Master of St James's Masonic Lodge, Tarbolton. As a result of the losses he incurred through the collapse of the Douglas, Heron & Company Bank, Sir John was forced to sell his estate at Ballochmyle in 1785, living in Edinburgh thereafter. The first communication from Burns to Sir John takes the form of a draft petition of about November 1782, written on the back of the draft of the first letter to Alison Begbie. Four years later Burns composed quite a different letter soon after his arrival in Edinburgh, seeking advice and patronage. Sir John replied, advising Burns 'your character as a man as well as a poet entitles you, I think, to the assistance of every inhabitant of Ayrshire' and adding that if a sum could be raised by subscription for a second edition of the poems 'lay it out in the stocking of a small farm' — advice which Burns eventually took. Burns subsequently sent Sir John a manuscript copy of his *Lament for James, Earl of Glencairn* (C.W. p. 423).

I (12)

November, 1782

Sir

We who subscribe this are both members of St. James's Lodge Tarbolton & one of us in the office of Warden & as we have the honor of having you for Master of our Lodge, we hope you will excuse this freedom as you are the proper person to whom we ought to apply. We look on our Mason Lodge to be a serious matter both with respect to the character of Masonry itself, & likewise as it is a charitable society. This last indeed, does not interest you farther than a benevolent heart is interested in the welfare of its fellow-creatures; but to us Sir, who are of the lower orders of mankind, to have a fund in view on which we may with certainty depend to be kept from want should we be in circumstances of distress or old age, this is a matter of high importance. —We are sorry to observe that our lodge's affairs with respect to its finances have for a good while been in a wretched situation.— We have considerable sums in bills which lye by without being paid or put in execution; & many of our members never mind their yearly dues or anything else belonging to the lodge.—And since the separation from St. David's, we are not sure even of our existence as a Lodge.—Their has been a dispute before the Grand Lodge but how decided, or if decided at all we know not.—For these & other reasons we humbly beg the favor of you as soon as convenient to call a meeting & let us consider on some means to retrieve our wretched affairs.

We &

Sir John Whitefoord

II (61)

Sir,

Mr McKenzie, in Mauchline, my very warm and worthy friend, has informed me how much you are pleased to interest yourself in my fate as a man, and (what to me is incomparably dearer) my fame as a poet. I have, Sir, in one or two instances, been patronized by those of your character in life, when I was introduced to their notice by ***** friends to them, and honoured acquaintances to me; but you are the first gentleman in the country whose benevolence and goodness of heart has interested him for me, unsolicited and unknown. I am not master enough of the etiquette of these matters to know, nor did I stay to inquire, whether formal duty bade, or cold propriety disallowed, my thanking you in this manner, as I am convinced, from the light in which you kindly view me, that you will do me the justice to believe this letter is not the manoeuvre of the needy, sharping author, fastening on those in upper life who honour him with a little notice of him or his works. Indeed, the situation of poets is generally such, to a proverb, as may, in some measure, palliate that prostitution of heart and talents they have at times been guilty of. I do not think prodigality is, by any means, a necessary concomitant of a poetic turn; but I believe a careless, indolent attention to oeconomy, is almost inseparable from it; then there must be, in the heart of every bard of Nature's making, a certain modest sensibility, mixed with a kind of pride, that will ever keep him out of the way of those windfalls of fortune, which frequently light on hardy impudence and foot-licking servility. It is not easy to imagine a more helpless state than his, whose poetic fancy unfits him for the world, and whose character as a scholar gives him some pretensions to the *politesse* of life — yet is as poor as I am.

For my part, I thank Heaven, my star has been kinder; learning never elevated my ideas above the peasant's shed, and I have an independent fortune at the plough-tail.

I was surprised to hear that any one, who pretended in the least to the *manners of the gentleman,* should be so foolish , or worse, as to stoop to traduce the morals of such a one as I am, and so inhumanly cruel, too, as to meddle with that late most unfortunate, unhappy part of my story. With a tear of gratitude, I thank you, Sir, for the warmth with which you interposed in behalf of my conduct. I am, I acknowledge, too frequently the sport of whim, caprice, and passion — but reverence to God, and integrity to my fellow-creatures, I hope I shall ever preserve. I have no return, Sir, to make you for your goodness, but one — a return which, I am persuaded, will not be unacceptable — the honest, warm wishes of a grateful heart for your happiness, and

Sir John Whitefoord

every one of that lovely flock who stand to you in a filial relation. If ever calumny aim the poisoned shaft at *them*, may friendship be by to ward the blow!

JOHN MURDOCH

Born at Ayr in 1747, Murdoch as a young man of eighteen was employed by William Burnes and some neighbours at Alloway as a teacher. After they moved to Mount Oliphant Robert and Gilbert continued to attend Murdoch's school. Subsequently Murdoch left the district but returned to Ayr in 1772, where he taught English. During this period Robert took the opportunity to brush up his grammar with Murdoch who also took a keen interest in his most promising pupil and lent him many books. Curiously enough, Murdoch considered Gilbert to have more wit and imagination than Robert. Neither brother had much ear for music, Robert in particular being remarkably dull and 'untunable'! Alleged slanders against the Rev. Dr. Dalrymple led to his dismissal in February 1776. Murdoch went to London where he taught French, but was forced out by competition from the numerous French refugees who flocked to London at the outset of the Revolution. For some time he kept a shop, but died in extreme poverty in 1824. Burns contacted him again seven years later when his brother William went to London to work there as a saddler. Murdoch met William shortly before that young man died, and helped with the funeral arrangements.

I (13)

Lochlea, 15th January 1783

Dear Sir,

As I have an opportunity of sending you a letter without putting you to that experience which any production of mine would but ill repay; I embrace it with pleasure to tell you that I have not forgotten, nor never will forget, the many obligations I lie under to your kindness and friendship. I do not doubt, Sir, but you will wish to know what has been the result of all the pains of an indulgent father, and a masterly teacher; and I wish I could gratify your curiosity with such a recital as you would be pleased with; but that is what I am afraid will not be the case. I have, indeed, kept pretty clear of vicious habits; & in this respect, I hope, my conduct will not disgrace the education I have gotten; but as a man of the world, I am most miserably deficient.—One would have thought that, bred as I have been under a father who has figured pretty well as un hommes des affaires, I might have been, what the world calls, a pulsing, active fellow; but, to tell you the truth, Sir, there is hardly any thing more my reverse — I seem to be one sent into the world, to see, and observe; and I very easily compound with the knave who tricks me of my money, if there be any thing original about him which shews me human nature in a different light from any thing I have seen before. In short, the joy of my heart is to "Study men, their manners, and their ways:"[1] and for this darling subject, I chearfully sacrifice every other consideration: I am quite indolent about those great concerns that set the bustling, busy Sons of Care agog; and if I have to answer the present hour, I am very easy with regard to any thing further.—Even the last, worst shift of the unfortunate and the wretched, does not much terrify me: I know that even then, my talent for what country folks call "a sensible crack," when once it is sanctified by a hoary head, would procure me so much esteem, that even then — I would learn to be happy. However, I am under no apprehensions about that, for though indolent, yet so far as an extremely delicate constitution permits, I am not lazy; and in many things, especially in tavern matters, I am a strict eo-conomist; not, indeed, for the sake of the money, but one of the principal parts in my compostion is a kind of pride of stomach; and I scorn to fear the face of any man living: above every thing, I abhor as hell, the idea of sneaking in a corner to avoid a dun— possibly some pitiful, sordid wretch, who in my heart I despise and detest. 'Tis this, and this alone, that endears eo-conomy to me. In the matter of books, indeed, I am very profuse.—My favorite authors are of the sentimental kind, such as Shenstone, particularly his Elegies, Thomson, Man of feeling, a book I prize next to the Bible, Man of the World, Sterne, especially his Sentimental journey, McPherson's Ossian, & c. these are the glorious models after which I endeavour to form my conduct, and 'tis incongruous, 'tis absurd to suppose that the man whose mind glows with sentiments lighted up at their sacred flame — the man whose heart distends with benevolence to all the human race — he "who can soar above this little scene of things"[2] — can he descend to mind the paltry concerns about which the terrae-filial race fret, and fume, and vex themselves? O how the glorious triumph swells my heart! I forget that I am a poor, insignificant devil, unnoticed and unknown, stalking up and down fairs and markets when I happen to be in them, reading a page or two of mankind, and "catching the manners living as they rise,"[3] whilst the men of business jostle me on every side, as an idle encumbrance in their way.— But I dare say I have by this time tired your patience; so I shall conclude with begging you to give Mrs Murdoch — not my compliments — for that is a mere common place story; but my warmest, kindest wishes for her welfare; and accept of the same yourself from,

    Dear Sir, your sincere friend, and oblidged humble Servant

        Robert Burns

1 Pope: *January and May*, line 157
2 Thomson: *Autumn*, line 964
3 Pope: *Essay on Man*, Espistle I, line 14

II (405)

Ellisland near Dumfries. 16th July 1790

My dear Sir,

I received a letter from you a long time ago, but unfortunately as it was in the time of my peregrinations & journeyings through Scotland, I mislaid or lost the letter, & by consequence Your direction along with it.—Luckily my good Star brought me acquainted with Mr Kennedy, who, I understand, is an acquaintance of yours; & by his means & mediation I hope to replace that link which my unfortunate negligence has so unluckily broke in the chain of our correspondence. I was more vexed at the vile accident as my brother William, a journeyman Saddler, has been for some time in London; & wished above all things for your direction that he might have paid his respects to his father's friend.—His last address he sent me was, Wm. Burns, at Mr Barber's, Saddler, No. 181, Strand.—I write him by Mr Kennedy, but I neglected to ask him for your address; so if you find a spare half minute, please let my brother know by a card where & when he will find you, & the poor fellow will joyfully wait on you as one of the few surviving friends of the Man whose Name & Christian Name too, he has the honor to bear.—

Next letter I write you shall be a long one.—I have much to tell you of "hair-breadth 'scapes in th' iminent deadly breach"* with all the eventful history of a life the early years of which owed so much to your kind tutorage; but this at an hour of leisure.—My kindest compliments to Mrs Murdoch & family.—

I am ever,
My dear Sir,
your oblidged friend
Robt Burns

*Shakespeare: *Othello*, Act I, sc. 3.

JAMES BURNESS

The son of James Burnes (1717-61), elder brother of William Burnes, and therefore the first cousin of the poet, he was born in Montrose in 1750. His father was the first of the three brothers to realise the futility of farming at Clochnahill, for he went to Montrose in 1732 to be apprenticed to a merchant. In turn he too prospered as a merchant and played a prominent part in civic affairs. It is significant that the upward social mobility of the Burnes/Burness/Burns family only began when its members broke free of farming. James Jr. became a solicitor in Montrose; in turn his son James III became provost and his grandson, Sir Alexander Burns, was murdered at Kabul in 1841. That the families of James and William drifted apart is demonstrated by a letter from the latter (father of the poet) to James Jr. in April 1781 giving an account of himself and his family since his marriage in 1757. James Jr. has remained a shadowy figure, remembered solely on account of his correspondence with the poet, who wrote at least nine letters to him between June 1783 and July 1796. The first letter was written on William's behalf 'in his own opinion, & indeed in almost ev'ry body's else, in a dying condition', while the second deals briefly with the death of William Burnes. Thereafter a desultory exchange of letters took place. A letter of 4th September 1787 from Inverness arranged a meeting at 'Stonhive' (Stonehaven) which took place on 10th September. Subsequent letters show that James helped with the distribution of the first Edinburgh edition, and also offered financial assistance, which the poet was only too glad to accept. His last poignant letter, dated only days before his death, pleads 'Save me from the horrors of a jail! James sent £10 immediately, and after the poet's death sent another £5, with the offer to take Robert Jr. and educate him with his own children — a generous act which he could ill afford at the time. Jean did not wish to part with any of her children and politely declined the offer.

I (14)

Lochlee, 21st June 1783

Dear Sir,

My father received your favor of the 10th Current, and as he has been for some months very poorly in health, & is in his own opinion, & indeed in almost ev'ry body's else, in a dying condition; he has only, with great difficulty, wrote a few farewel lines to each of his brothers-in-law; for this melancholy reason I now hold the pen for him to thank you for your kind letter, & to assure you Sir, that it shall not be my fault if my father's correspondence in the North die with him.— My brother writes to John Caird, & to him I must refer you for the news of our family. I shall only trouble you with a few particulars relative to the present wretched state of this country. Our markets are exceedingly high; oatmeal 17 & 18d per peck, & not to be got even at that price. We have indeed been pretty well supplied with quantities of white pease from England & elsewhere, but that resource is likely to fail us; & what will become of us then, particularly the very poorest sort, Heaven only knows.—This country, till of late was flourishing incredibly in the Manufactures of Silk, Lawn & Carpet Weaving, and we are still carrying on a good deal in that way but much reduced from what it was; we had also a fine trade in the Shoe way, but now entirely ruined & hundreds driven to a starving condition on account of it.—Farming is also at a very low ebb with us. Our lands, generally speaking, are mountainous

& barren; and our Landholders, full of ideas of farming gathered from the English, and the Lothians and other rich soils in Scotland; make no allowance for the odds of the quality of land, and consequently stretch us much beyond what, in the event, we will be found able to pay. We are also much at a loss for want of proper methods in our improvements of farming: necessity compels us to leave our old schemes; & few of us have opportunities of being well informed in new ones. In short, my dear Sir, since the unfortunate beginning of this American war, & its as unfortunate conclusion, this country has been, & still is decaying very fast.

Even in higher life, a couple of our Ayrshire Noblemen, and the major part of our Knights & squires, are all insolvent. A miserable job of a Douglas, Heron, & Co.'s Bank, which no doubt you have heard of, has undone numbers of them; and imitating English, and French, and other foreign luxuries & fopperies, has ruined as many more.—There is great trade of smuggling carried on along our coasts, which, however destructive to the interests of the kingdom at large, certainly enriches this corner of it; but too often indeed at the expence of our Morals; however, it enables individuals to make, at least for a time, a splendid appearance; but Fortune, as is usual with her when she is uncommonly lavish of her favours, is generally even with them at the last; & happy were it for numbers of them if she would leave them no worse than when she found them—

My mother sends you a small present of a cheese, 'tis but a very little one as our last year's stock is sold off; but if you could fix on any correspondent in Edinburgh, or Glasgow, we would send you a proper one in the season. Mrs Black promises to take the cheese under his care so far, and then to send it to you by the Stirling carrier.

I shall conclude this long letter with assuring you that I shall be very happy to hear from you or any of our friends in your country when opportunity serves.—

My Father sends you, probably for the last time in this world, his warmest wishes for your welfare and happiness; and mother & the rest of the family desire to inclose their kind Compliments to you, Mrs Burness and the rest of your family along with

Dear Sir, Your affectionate Cousin,

Robt Burness

James Burness

II (16)

Lochlee, 17th February 1784

Dear Cousin,

I would have returned you my thanks for your kind favor of the 13th December sooner had it not been that I waited to give you an account of that melancholy event which for some time past we have from day to day expected.—On the 13th Current, I lost the best of fathers. Though to be sure we have had long warning of the impending stroke still the feelings of Nature claim their part and I cannot recollect the tender endearments and parental lessons of the best of friends and the ablest of instructors without feeling, what perhaps, the calmer dictates of reason would partly condemn.—

I hope my father's friends in your country will not let their connection in this place die with him. For my part I shall ever with pleasure — with pride acknowledge my connection with those who were allied by the ties of blood and friendship to a man whose memory I will ever honor and revere.—I expect therefore, My Dear Sir, you will not neglect any opportunity of letting me hear from you which will ever very much oblidge

My dear Cousin, yours sincerely,

Robert Burness

III (17)

Mossgiel 3rd August 1784

My dear Sir,

I ought in gratitude to have acknowledged the receipt of your last kind letter before this time, but without troubling you with any apology I shall proceed to inform you that our family are all in health at present and we were very happy with the unexpected favor of John Caird's company for near two weeks; & I must say it of him he is one the the most agreable, facetious, warm-hearted lads I was ever acquainted with.—

We have been surprized with one of the most extraordinary Phenomena in the moral world, which, I dare say, has happened in the course of this last Century.—We have had a party of the Presbytry Relief as they call themselves, for some time in this country. A pretty thriving society of them has been in the Burgh of Irvine for some years past, till about two years ago, a Mrs Buchan from Glasgow came among them, & began to spread some fanatical notions of religion among them, & in a short time made many converts among them & among others their Preacher, one Mr Whyte, who upon that account has continued however, to preach in private to this party, & was supported, both he, & their

59

spiritual Mother as they affect to call old Buchan, by the contributions of the rest, several of whom were in good circumstances; till in spring last the Populace rose & mobbed the old leader Buchan, & put her out of the town; on which, all her followers voluntarily quitted the place likewise, & with such precipitation, that many of them never shut their doors behind them; one left a washing on the green, another a cow bellowing at the crib without meat or any body to mind her, & after several stages, they are fixed at present in the neighbourhood of Dumfries.—Their tenets are a strange jumble of enthusiastic jargon, among others, she pretends to give them the Holy Ghost by breathing on them, which she does with postures & practices that are scandalously indecent; they have likewise disposed of all their effects & hold a community of goods, & live nearly an idle life, carrying on a great farce of pretended devotion in barns, & woods, where they lodge and lye all together, & hold likewise a community of women, as it is another of their tenets that they can commit no moral sin.—I am personally acquainted with most of them, & I can assure you the above mentioned are facts.—

This My Dear Sir, is one of the many instances of the folly in leaving the guidance of sound reason, & common sense in matters of Religion.—Whenever we neglect or despise these sacred Monitors, the whimsical notions of a perturbed brain are taken for the immediate influences of the Deity, & the wildest fanaticism, & the most inconsistant absurdities will meet with abettors & converts.—Nay I have often thought, that the more-out-of-the-way & ridiculous their fancies are, if once they are sanctified under the sacred name of RELIGION, the unhappy, mistaken votaries are the more firmly glued to them.—

I expect to hear from you soon, & I beg you will remember me to all friends, & believe me to be,

My Dear Sir your affectionate Cousin

Robert Burness

Direct to me at Mossgiel, Parish of Machline, near Kilmarnock.

IV (32)

Mossgiel, near Machlin, 5th July 1786

My Dear Sir,

I wrote to you about three half twelve months ago by post; I wrote you about a year ago, by a private hand; and I have not had the least return from you.—I have just half a minute to write you by an Aberdeen Gentleman of my acquaintance who promises to wait on you with this on his arrival, or soon after.—I intend to send you a letter accompanied with a singular curiosity, in about five or six weeks hence.—I shall then write you more at large; meanwhile you are just to look on this as a memento me;—-

I hope all friends are well.—

> I am ever, My Dear Sir, your affectionate Cousin,
>
> Robt Burness

V (134)

> Inverness, 4th September 1787

Dear Cousin,

I wrote to you from Edinburgh that I intended being north.—I shall be in Stonhive sometime on monday the 10th Instant, and I beg the favor of you to meet me there.—I understand there is but one Inn at Stonhive so you cannot miss me.—As I am in the country, I certainly shall see any of my father's relations that are any way near my road; but I do not even know their names, or where one of them lives, so I hope you will meet me and be my guide.—Farewell, till I have the pleasure of meeting you.—

> I am ever, Dear Sir, yours,
>
> Robt Burns

VI (136)

> Townfield six o'clock morning 13th September 1787

My dear Cousin,

Mr Nicol and Mr Carnegie have taken some freak in their head and have wakened me just now with the rattling of the chaise to carry me to meet them at Craigie to go on our journey some other road and breakfast by the way.—I must go, which makes me very sorry.—I beg my kindest best Compliments to your wife and all the good friends I saw yesternight.—

Write me to Edinburgh in this week, with a direction for your nephew in Glasgow.—Direct to me, Care of Mr Creech, Edinburgh.

> I am ever my dear Cousin Yours truly
>
> Robt Burns

James Burness

VII (138)

Edinburgh, 19th September 1787

My dear Cousin,

I send you along with this nine Copies which you will transmit as marked on the blank leaves.—The one to Lord Gardenstone you will transmit as soon as possible.—Your hints about young Hudson I shall carefully remember when I call for him.—

Anything you send me, direct to the care of Mr Andrew Bruce, Merchant, Bridge Street, Edinburgh — but I am afraid that your kind offer of the dry fish will cost more than they are worth, to Carriers.—My Compliments to your wife and all friends; and excuse this brevity in

Yours ever,
Robt Burns

VIII (314)

Ellisland, 9th February, 1789

My dear Sir,

Why I did not write you long ago is what, even on the rack I could not answer.—if you can in your mind form an idea of indolence, dissipation, hurry, cares, changes of country, entering on untried scenes of life — all combined; you will save me the trouble of a blushing apology.—It could not be want of regard for a ·man for whom I had a high esteem before I knew him — an esteem which has much increased since I did know him; and this caveat entered, I shall plead guilty to any other indictment with which you shall please to charge me.—

After I parted from you, for many months, my life was one continued scene of dissipation.—Here, at last, I am become stationary, and have taken a farm, and — a wife. The farm lies beautifully situated on the banks of the Nith, a large river that runs by Dumfries & falls into the Solway Firth.—I have gotten a lease of my farm as long as I pleased; but how it may turn out is just a guess, as it is yet to improve and inclose, & c.; however I have good hopes of my bargain on the whole.—

My Wife is my Jean, with whose story you are partly acquainted. —I found I had a much-loved fellow-creature's happiness or misery among my hands, and I durst not trifle with so sacred a deposite.—Indeed I have not any reason to repent the step I have taken, as I have attached myself to a very good wife, & have shaken myself loose of a very bad failing.—

I have found my book a very profitable business; and with the profits of it, have begun life pretty decently.—Should Fortune not favour me in farming, as I have no great faith in her fickly Ladyship, I have provided myself in another resource, which, however some folks may affect to despise it, is still a comfortable shift in the day of misfortune.—In the heyday of my fame, a gentleman whose name at least I dare say you know, as his estate lies somewhere near Dundee, Mr Graham of Fintry, one of the Commissioners of Excise, offered me the commission of an Excise-Officer.—I thought it prudent to accept the offer, and accordingly I took my Instructions, and have my Commission by me.—Whether I may ever do duty, or be a penny better for it, is what I do not know; but I have this comfortable assurance, that come whatever fate will, I can on my simple petition to the Excise board, get into employ.—

We have lost poor uncle Robert this winter.—He has long been weak and with very little alteration in him, he expired January 3rd.—His son William, has been with me this winter, & goes in May to bind himself to be a Mason with my fatherinlaw who is a pretty considerable architect in Ayrshire.— His other Son, the eldest, John, comes to me, I expect in summer.—They are both remarkable stout young fellows, & promise to do well.—His only daughter Fanny has been with me ever since her father's death and I purpose keeping her in my family till she be quite woman grown, & be fit for better service.—She is one of the cleverest girls, and has one of the most amiable dispositions that I have ever seen.—

All friends in this country and Ayrshire are well.—Remember me to all friends in the North.—My wife joins in Compliments to your bedfellow & family.—I would write your brother-in-law, but have lost his Address.—For goodness sake don't take example by me, but write me soon.—I am ever, My dear cousin,

yours most sincerely.—

Robt Burns

IX (705)

12th July 1796

My dearest cousin,

When you offered me money-assistance little did I think I should want it so soon.—A rascal of a Haberdasher to whom I owe a considerable bill taking it into his head that I am dying, has commenced a process against me & will infallibly put my emaciated body into jail.—Will you be so good as to accommodate me, & that by return of post, with ten pound.—O, James! did you know the pride of my heart, you would feel doubly for me! Alas! I am not used to beg! The worst of it is, my health was coming about finely; you know & my Physician assures me that melancholy & low spirits are half my disease, guess then my horrors since this business began.—If I had it settled, I would be quite well in a manner.—How shall I use the language to you, O do not disappoint me! but strong Necessity's curst command. –

I have been thinking over & over my brother's affairs & I fear I must cut him up; but on this I will correspond at another time, particularly as I shall want your advice.—

Forgive me for once more mentioning by return of Post.—Save me from the horrors of jail!

My compliments to my friend James, & to all the rest. I do not know what I have written,—The subject is so horrible, I dare not look it over again.—

Farewel

R Burns

GAVIN HAMILTON

The fifth son of a Mauchline lawyer, he was born in 1751 and followed in his father's footsteps. In 1775 he was appointed collector of stent, responsible for administering parish poor relief, but fell foul of Daddy Auld because of his liberal views. The resulting wrangle led to legal action which the Kirk Session lost. In revenge the Kirk Session attacked him on moral grounds, but the hearing in June 1785 before the Presbytery of Ayr ended in his favour. Hamilton became factor to the Earl of Loudoun, from whom he leased Mossgiel in 1784 as a summer retreat. His wife, Helen Kennedy of Daljarrock, did not favour this arrangement, so Hamilton sub-let Mossgiel to his friend Burns who later responded by dedicating the Kilmarnock Edition to him. In addition to the eight letters printed here, Burns addressed two verse epistles to Gavin Hamilton — 'I hold it, Sir, by bounden duty' (C.W. p. 215) and 'To you, Sir, this summons I've sent' (C.W. p. 210). Burns freely acknowledged the help Hamilton gave him in disposing of copies of his Poems (III). When Burns visited Harvieston in August 1787 he sent a detailed account of Hamilton's half-brothers and sisters whom 'I am told you have not seen these several years' (VI). The friendship cooled, however, when Hamilton suggested that Burns should stand guarantor for his brother Gilbert for a considerable sum. Burns replied as tactfully as possible (VIII): 'The language of refusal is to me the most difficult language on earth . . . ' As the closing lines feared, Burns seems to have incurred Hamilton's displeasure, and the correspondence appears to have ended in March 1788.

I (15)

Machline, 18th Ocotber 1783

Sir

As you were pleased to give us the otter of a private bargain of your cows you intend for sale, my brother & I this day took a look of them and a friend with us on whose judgement we could something depend to enable us to form an estimate— If you are still intending to let us have them in that way, please appoint a day that we may wait on you and either agree amongst ourselves cr else fix on men to whom we may refer it, tho' I hope we will not need any reference.—

I am Sir your humble servant

Robert Burness

P.S.
Whatever of your dairy utensils you intend to dispose of we will probably purchase.—

R.B.

II (25)

Mossgiel, Saturday morn: [15th April, 1786]

My proposals came to hand last night, and I know you would wish to have it in your power to do me a service as *early* as anybody, so I inclose you a sheet of them.—I must consult you, first opportunity, on the propriety of sending my *quondam* friend, Mr Aiken, a copy.—If he is now reconciled to my character as an honest man, I would do it with all my soul; but I would not be beholden to the noblest being ever God created, if he imagined me to be a rascal.—Apropos, old Mr Armour prevailed with him to mutilate that unlucky paper, yesterday.—Would you believe it? tho' I had not a hope, nor even a wish, to make her mine after her conduct; yet when he told me, the names were all cut out of the paper, my heart died within me, and he cut my very veins with the news.—Perdition seize her falsehood, and perjurious perfidy! but God bless her and forgive my poor, once-dear, misguided girl. —She is ill-advised.—Do not despise me, Sir: I am indeed a fool, but a *knave* is an infinitely worse character than any body, I hope, will dare to give

the unfortunate Robt Burns

III (62)

Edinburgh, 7th December 1786

Honored Sir,

I have paid every attention to your command, but can only say that, which perhaps you will have heard before this reach you, that Muirkirklands were bought by a John Gordon W.S. but for whom I know not; Mauchlands, Haugh Miln, & c. by a Frederick Fotheringham, supposed to be for Ballochmyle Laird; and Adamhill & Shawood were bought for Oswald's folks.— This is so imperfect an account, and will be so late ere it reach you, that were it not to discharge my Conscience I would not trouble you with this; but after all my diligence I could make it no sooner nor better.—

For my own affairs, I am in a fair way of becoming as eminent as Thomas a Kempis or John Bunyan; and you may expect henceforth to see my birthday inserted among the wonderful events, in the Poor Robin's and Aberdeen Almanacks, along with the black Monday, & the battle of Bothwell bridge.—My Lord Glencairn & the Dean of Faculty, Mr H. Erskine, have taken me under their wing; and by all probability I shall soon be the tenth Worthy, and the eighth Wise Man, of the world. Through my Lord's influence it is inserted in the records of the Caledonian Hunt, that they universally, one & all, subscribe for the 2d Edition.—My subscription bills come out tomorrow, and you shall get some of them next Post.—I have met in Mr Dalrymple of Orangefield what Solomon emphatically calls, "a Friend that sticketh close than a Brother."*—The warmth with which he interests himself in my affairs is of the same enthusiastic kind which you, Mr Aiken, and the few Patrons that took notice of my earlier poetic days, showed for the poor, unlucky devil of a Poet.—

I always remember Mrs Hamilton & Miss Kennedy in my poetic prayers, but you both in prose & verse.

> May Cauld ne'er catch you but a hap,
> Nor Hunger but in Plenty's lap!
>   Amen!

Robert Burns

*Proverbs 18:24

IV (72)

Edinburgh, 7th January 1787

. . . To tell the truth among friends, I feel a miserable blank in my heart, with want of her, and I don't think I shall ever meet with so delicious an armful again. She has her faults; and so have you and I; and so has every body.

> Their tricks and craft hae put me daft;
>   They've ta'en me in and a' that;
> But clear your decks, and here's the Sex,
>   I like the jads for a' that.
>   For a' that and a' that,
>   And twice as muckle's a' that. . .*

I have met with a very pretty girl, a Lothian farmer's daughter, whom I almost persuaded to accompany me to the west country, should I ever return to settle there. By the bye, a Lothian farmer is about an Ayrshire squire of the lower kind; and I had a most delicious ride from Leith to her house yesternight in a hackney-coach, with her brother and two sisters, and brother's wife. We had dined all together at a common friend's house in Leith, and danced, drank, and sang till late enough. The night was dark, the claret had been good, and I thirsty . . .

*The Jolly Beggars, lines 228-33

V (88)

Edinburgh, 8th March 1787

Dear Sir,

Yours came safe, and I am as usual much indebted to your goodness.—Poor Captain [James] Montgomerie is cast.—Yesterday it was tried whether the husband could proceed against the unfortunate Lover without first divorcing his wife, and their Gravities on the bench were unanimously of opinion that Maxwell may prosecute for damages directly, and need not divorce his wife at all if he pleases; and Maxwell is immediately, before the Lord ordinary to prove, what I dare say will never be

67

denied, the Crim-con then their Lordships will modify the damages, which I suppose will be pretty heavy, as their Wisdoms have expressed great abhorrence of my gallant Right Worshipfull Brother's conduct.—

O all ye Powers of love unfortunate and friendless woe, pour the balm of sympathising pity on the grief-torn, tender heart of the hapless Fair One!

My two Songs, on Miss W. Alexander and Miss P. Kennedy*were likewise tried yesterday by a jury of Literati, and found defamatory libels against the fastidious Powers of Poesy and Taste; and the Author forbid to print them under pain of forfeit-ure of character.—I cannot help almost shedding a tear to the memory of two Songs that cost me some pains, and that I valued a good deal, but I must submit.—

My most respectful Compliments to Mrs Hamilton and Miss Kennedy—

My poor unfortunate Songs come again across my memory — Damn the pedant, frigid soul of Critcism for ever and ever!

I am ever, Dear Sir, your oblidged,

Robt Burns

* *The Lass o Ballochmyle* (C.W. p. 199) and *Young Peggy* (C.W. p. 125)

VI (132)

Stirling, 28th August 1787

My dear Sir,

Here am I on my way to Inverness.—I have rambled over the rich, fertile carses of Falkirk and Stirling, and am delighted with their appearance: richly waving crops of wheat, barley, & c. but no harvest at all yet, except in one or two places an old wife's ridge.—Yesterday morning I rode from this town up the meandering Devan's banks to pay my last respects to some Ayrshire folks at Harvieston.—After breakfast, we made a party to go and see the famous Caudron-linn, a remarkable cascade in the Devan about five miles above Harvieston; and after spending one of the most pleasant days I ever had in my life. I returned to Stirling in the evening.—They are a family, Sir, though I had not had any prior tie, though they had not been the brother & sisters of a certain generous friend of mine, I would never forget them.— I am told you have not seen them in these several years, so you can have very little idea of what such young folks as they are now.—Your brother is as tall as you are, but slender rather than otherwise; and I have the satisfaction to inform you that he is getting the better of those consumptive symtoms which I suppose you know were threatening him.—His make & particularly his manner resemble you, but he will still have a finer face. (I put in the word, still, to please Mrs Hamilton).—Good-sense, modesty and at the same time a just idea of that respect that man owes to man and has a right in his turn to exact, are striking features in his character; and, what with me is the Alpha & the Omega, he has a heart might adorn the breast of a Poet.—Grace has a good figure and the look of health and chearfulness, but nothing else remarkable in her person.—I scarcely ever saw so striking a likeness between her & your little Beennie; the mouth and chin particularly.—She is reserved at first, but as we grew better acquainted; I was delighted with the native frankness of her manner, and the sterling sense of her observation. Of Charlotte I cannot speak in common terms of admiration: she is not only beautiful; but lovely.—Her form is elegant; her features not regular but they have the smile of Sweetness and the settled complacency of good nature in the highest degree; and her complexion, now that she has happily recovered her wonted health, is equal to Miss Burnet's.—After the exercise of our ride to the falls, Charlotte was exactly Dr Donne's Mistress:

> —"Her pure and eloquent blood
> "Flow'd in her cheeks and so distinctly wrought,
> "That one would almost say her body thought"*

Her eyes are fascinating; at once expressive of good-sense, tenderness, and a noble mind.—

I do not give you all this account, my good Sir, to flatter you; I mean it to reproach you.—Such relations, the first Peer in the realm might own with pride; then why but you keep up more correspondence with these so amiable young folks?—I had a thousand questions to answer about you all: I had to describe the little ones with the minuteness of Anatomy.—They were highly delighted when I told them that John was so good a boy and so fine a scholar, and that Willie was going on still very pretty; but I have it in commission to tell her from them that beauty is a poor silly bauble without she be good.—Miss Chalmers I had left in Edinburgh but I had the pleasure of meeting with Mrs Chalmers, only Lady Mckenzie being rather a little alarmingly ill of a sore throat somewhat marr'd our enjoyment.—

I shall not be in Ayrshire for four weeks.—My most respectful Compliments to Mrs Hamilton, Miss Kennedy and Doctor McKenzie.—I shall probably write him from some stage or other.—

I am ever, Sir, yours most gratefully

Robt Burns

---

*Donne: *The Second Anniversary*, lines 244-6, slightly misquoted.

Gavin Hamilton

VII (157)

My dear Sir,

It is indeed with the highest of pleasure that I congratulate you on the return of "Days of ease & nights of pleasure,"* after the horrid hours of misery, in which I saw you suffering existence when I was last in Ayr-shire.—I seldom pray for any body— "I'm baith dead sweer & wretched ill o't"—But most fervently do I beseech the Holy Trinity, or the holy Somebody that directs this world, that you may live long & be happy, but live no longer than you are happy.— It is needless for me to advise you to have a reverend care of your health.—I know you will make it a point never at one time to drink more than a pint of wine (I mean an English pint) & that you will never be witness to more than one bowl of punch at a time; & that cold drams you will never more taste: & above all things, I am convinced that after drinking perhaps boiling punch, you will never mount your horse & gallop home in a chill, late hour.—Above all things, as I understand you are now in habits of intimacy with that Boanerges of gospel powers, Father Auld, be earnest with him that he will wrestle in prayer for you, that you may see the vanity of vanities in trusting to, or even practising the carnal moral works of Charity, Humanity, Generosity & Forgiveness; things which you practised so flagrantly that it was evident you delighted in them; neglecting or perhaps prophanely despising the wholsome doctrine of, "Faith without Works, the only anchor of salvation." A hymn of thanksgiving would, in my opinion, be highly becoming from you at present; & in my zeal for your well-being, I earnestly press it on you to be diligent in chanting over the two inclosed pieces of sacred poesy. My best Compliments to Mrs Hamilton & Miss Kennedy.

Yours in the Lord

R.B.

* Pope: *Chorus of Youths and Virgins* from *Two Choruses to the Tragedy of Brutus*, line 154.

VIII (222)

Mossgiel, Friday Morn: [7th March? 1788]

Sir,

The language of refusal is to me the most difficult language on earth, and you are the man of the world, excepting One of Right Honourable designation, to whom it gives me the greatest pain to hold such language.—My brother has already got money, and shall want nothing in my power to enable him to fulfil his engagement with you; but to be security on so large a scale even for a brother, is what I dare not do, except I were in such circumstances of life

as that the worst that might happen could not greatly injure me.—
I never wrote a letter which gave me so much pain in my life, as I
know the unhappy consequences; I shall incur the displeasure of
a Gentleman for whom I have the highest respect, and to whom I
am deeply oblidged.—

I am ever, Sir,

your oblidged and very humble servant,

Robt Burns

JOHN TENNANT Jr.

The second son of John Tennant of Glenconner, in the parish of Ochiltree, he was born in 1760 and boarded with Burns at John Murdoch's home in the summer of 1773. Having failed in business, as a ship-builder and latterly as a distiller, Tennant took up farming at Auchenbay in his natal parish. Burns's three letters to John Tennant deal with local, domestic and business matters. It is particularly interesting to note the encouragement given by Burns in his letter of 22nd December 1788 to Tennant's liquor business, in view of the fact his younger brother Charles was to lay down the foundations of the dyeworks and breweries from which the present-day Glenconner family fortune sprang.

I (18)

Mossgiel, 13th September 1784

My dear Sir,

My unlucky illness of Friday last did not do me a greater disservice than in disappointing me of the pleasure I had promised myself in spending an hour with you.—I got so much better on Saturday as to be able to ride home, but I am still in a kind of slow fever, as I trouble you with this small letter rather to relieve a little the langor of my spirits than any thing particular I have to tell you.—I have been inform'd by Mr Robert Paterson how affairs went among you on Friday night, tho' by the bye I am apt to suspect his information in some particulars. He tells me you used all the powers of your eloquence, first on my friend Miss Ronald and next on Miss C ———, to have the liberty of escorting them home, but all to no purpose; and I assure you Mr Paterson plumes himself not a little that he has been able to foil so formidable an antagonist.—In short, as Mr Robert is very sanguine in all his projects, he seems fully assured of carrying his point; and I declare I never saw a man more intoxicated with success in my life.—However to do the gentleman justice his passion is but the raptures of a Lover in Romance, not the rant of a dramatic Hero.—Her sweet, sonsy face, which I have so often admir'd, he knows no more about it but only as it helps him to distinguish her from another person; and tho' he talks of her being "a grand cracker" to speak in Mr Paterson's own style, yet he seems to have little idea of her engaging frank, honest-hearted manner; and for good sense and education they are rather against him, as being so much superior to his own, they entangle him in a thousand difficulties; but, like a true Merchant he has stated it in the Ledgers of his fancy thus:

Stock, Dr to cash, by Mrs Paterson's portion} 300£.—

We talk of air & manner, of beauty & wit, and lord knows what unmeaning nonsense; but—there—is solid charms for you—Who would not be in raptures with a woman that will make him 300£ richer?—And then to have a woman to lye with when one pleases without running any risk of the cursed expence of bastards and all the other concomitants of that species of Smuggling—These are solid views of matrimony—

John Tennant Jr.

But I forget that tho' I am cheating my languid moments with this nonsensical letter I am putting your patience to penance, so I conclude with wishing to see you, tho' when or where I know not—

I am, My Dear Sir, yours Sincerely,

Robt Burns

II (291)

Ellisland, 22nd December 1788

My dear Sir,

I yesterday tried my cask of whisky for the first time, and I assure you it does you great credit.—It will bear five waters, strong; or six, ordinary Toddy.—The Whisky of this county is a most rascally liquor; and by consequence, only drunk by the most rascally part of the inhabitants.—I am persuaded, if you once got a footing here, you might do a great deal of business; both in the way of consumpt, and should you commence Distiller again, this is the native barley-country.—

I am ignorant if, in your present way of dealing, you would think it worth while to extend your business so far as this country-side —I write you this on the account of an accident which I must take the merit of having partly designed too.—A neighbour of mine, a John Currie, miller in Carse-mill, a man who is in a word, "a good man," a "very" good man, even for a 500£ bargain, he and his wife were in the country Publick-house & sell a great deal of foreign spirits but all along thought that Whisky would have degraded their house.—They were perfectly astonished at my whisky, both for its taste & strength, and by their desire I write you to know if you could supply them with liquor of an equal quality, and at what price.—Please write me by first Post, & direct to me, at Ellisland near Dumfries.—If you could take a jaunt this way yourself, I have a spare spoon, knife and fork, very much at your service.—My compliments to Mrs Tennant, and all the good folks in Glenconner & Barquharrie.—

I am most truly, My dear Sir, yours

Robt Burns

III (434)

My dear Sir,

I have from time to time called on the Maundersons for your money, but in vain. They must be prosecuted, but if you please, I wish you would do it in your own name, as it would raise an odium on me, who am living in the neighborhood.

Direct your mandate for prosecution to Edward Hyslop, Writer, Dumfries, & I shall give him the papers. Adieu!

Robt Burns

MISS MARGARET KENNEDY

Born in 1766, she was the daughter of Robert Kennedy of Daljarrock, factor to the Earl of Cassilis, and younger sister of Gavin Hamilton's wife Helen. Burns was introduced to Miss Kennedy at the Hamilton's house when she was only eighteen, and subsequently he wrote the song *Young Peggy* (C.W. p. 125) in her honour. The previous year, however, she had commenced an affair with Captain Andrew McDoual of Logan, Wigtownshire, the 'Sculdudd'ry' of the second Heron election ballad (C.W. p. 546). In 1794 she bore him a daughter, but the gallant Captain's disavowal of Miss Kennedy and the child led to an action in the Court of Session which was settled in 1798 in her favour. Miss Kennedy, however, never lived to see the successful outcome, as she died in 1795. In view of these tragic events, the final paragraph of Burns's letter has overtones of unconscious irony.

(20)

[early October 1785]

Madam,

Permit me to present you with the inclosed SONG, as a small, tho' grateful tribute for the honor of your acquaintance.—I have, in these verses, attempted some faint sketches of your Portrait in the unembellished simple manner of descriptive Truth.—Flattery, I leave to your Lovers; whose exaggerating Fancies may make them imagine you still nearer, if possible, to Perfection than you really are.—

Poets, Madam, of all Mankind, feel most forcibly the powers of Beauty; as, if they are really Poets of Nature's making, their feelings must be finer, and their taste more delicate than most of the world.—In The Chearful bloom of Spring, or the pensive mildness of Autumn; the Grandeur of Summer, or the hoary majesty of Winter; the Poet feels a charm unknown to the rest of his Species: even the sight of a fine flower, or the company of a fine Woman, (by far the finest part of God's works below) has sensations for the Poetic heart that the Herd of Man are strangers to.—On this last account, Madam, I am as in many other things, indebted to Mr Hamilton's kindness in introducing me to you.— Your Lovers may view you with a wish, I look on you with pleasure; their hearts, in your presence, may glow with desire, mine rises with Admiration.—

That the Arrows of Misfortune, however they should, as incident to Humanity, glance a slight wound, may never reach your Heart— that the snare of Villainy may never beset you in the road of Life—that Innocence may hand you, by the path of Honor, to the dwelling of Peace, is the sincere wish of him who has the honor to be,

Madam,
your most obedient
and very humble servant

JOHN RICHMOND

Born at Sorn in 1765, he became clerk in Gavin Hamilton's law office and it was through Richmond that Burns was introduced to James Smith. Until Richmond left the district in November 1785 to join a law firm in Edinburgh, he, Burns and Smith were bosom friends, forming the notorious 'Court of Equity' (C.W. p. 227). In January 1785 Richmond was forced to do public penance for fornicating with Jenny Surgeoner, who bore him a daughter. Burns (IV) upbraided his friend about his cavalier treatment of her: 'You are acting very wrong My friend; her happiness or misery is bound up in your affection or unkindness. . . ' — sentiments which later governed his own decision to settle down with Jean Armour. Richmond returned to Mauchline in 1789 and married Jenny two years later. Burns lodged with him in his room at Baxter's Close during his first sojourn in Edinburgh. De Lancey Ferguson avers that their friendship suffered under the strain of this prolonged intimacy, and that the perfunctory nature of later letters proves this; but there is no *prima facie* evidence to support this. The last three letters (VII-IX) of 1787-8 are as cordial as ever. In one (VIII) Burns writes: 'I long much to hear from you, how you are, what are your views, and how your little girl comes on' and adds with amazing casualness, 'By the way, I hear I am a girl out of pocket. . .'—a reference to the death of the girl twin of Jean's second set. What may be of greater significance, however, was the absence of any correspondence between Burns and Richmond after February 1788. Richmond died in 1846, having outlived his old friend by half a century, and in the moral climate of the early Victorian era was singularly reticent about youthful high-jinks with Burns and Smith. Nonetheless, he supplied Grierson of Dalgoner (c. 1805) with many anecdotes of Burns and his associates.

I (21)

Mossgiel, 17th February 1786

My Dear Sir,

I have not time at present to upbraid you for your silence and neglect, I shall only say I received yours with great pleasure.—I have inclosed you a piece of rhyming ware for your perusal.—I have been very busy with the muses since I saw you, and have composéd, among several others, The Ordination, a poem on Mr Mckinlay's being called to Kilmarnock, Scotch Drink a poem, the Cotter's Saturday Night, An Address to the Devil, &c. I have likewise compleated my Poem on the dogs, but have not shown it to the world.—My chief Patron now is Mr Aitken in Ayr who is pleased to express great approbation of my works.—Be so good as send me Ferguson by Connel and I will remit you the money.— I have no news to acquaint you with about Machlin, they are just going on in the old way.—I have some very important news with respect to myself, not the most agreable, news that I am sure you cannot guess, but I shall give you the particulars another time.—I am extremely happy with Smith; he is all the friend I have now in Machlin.—I can scarcely forgive your long neglect of me, and I beg you will let me hear from you regularly by Connel.—If you would act your part as a FRIEND, I am sure neither GOOD nor BAD fortune should estrange or alter me.—Excuse haste as I got yours but yesterday and am at present a little throng.—If you write me duely I shall afterwards give you letters as long as my arm. –

I am

My Dear Sir

yours

Robt Burness

II (33)

Mossgiel, 9th July 1786

My Dear Friend,

with the sincerest grief I read you letter.–You are truly a son of Misfortune.–I shall be extremely anxious to hear from you how your health goes on; if it is any way re-establishing; or if Lieth promises any thing: in short, how you feel in the inner man.–No news worth any thing; only godly Bryan was in the Inquisition yesterday, and half the countryside as witnesses against him.–He still stands out, a sturdy, denying Villain; but proof was led, yesternight, of circumstances highly suspicious; almost de facto: one of the Servant girls made faith that she, upon a time, rashly enter'd the house, to speak in your cant, "in the hour of Cause."–

I have waited on Armour since her return home, not by–from any the least view of reconciliation, but merely to ask for her health; and–to you I will confess it, from a foolish, hankering fondness–very ill-plac'd indeed.–The Mother forbade me the house; nor did Jean shew that penitence might have been expected.–However, the Priest, I am inform'd will give me a Certificate as a single man, if I comply with the rules of the Church, which for that very reason I intend to do.–

Sunday morn:} I am just going to put on Sackcloth & ashes this day.–I am indulged so far as to appear in my own seat.–Peccavi Pater, miserere mei–My book will be ready in a fortnight.–If you have any Subscribers return me them by Connell [the carrier].

The Lord stand wi' the Righteous–

Amen Amen

Robt Burns

III (36)

Old Rome Foord, 30th July 1786

My Dear Richmond,

My hour is now come.–You and I will never meet in Britain

77

John Richmond

more.—I have orders within three weeks at farthest to repair aboard the Nancy, Captain Smith, from Clyde, to Jamaica, and to call at Antigua.—This, except to our friend Smith, whom God long preserve, is a secret about Mauchlin.—Would you believe it? Armour has got a warrant to throw me in jail till I find security for an enormous sum.—This they keep an entire secret, but I got it by a channel they little dream of; and I am wandering from one friend's house to another, and like a true son of the Gospel "have no where to lay my head."*—I know you will pour an execration on her head, but spare the poor, ill-advised Girl for my sake: tho', may all the Furies that rend the injured, enraged Lover's bosom, await the old Harridan, her Mother, untill her latest hour! May Hell string the arm of Death to throw the fatal dart, and all the winds of warring elements rouse the infernal flames to welcome her approach! For Heaven's sake burn this letter, and never show it to a living creature.—I write it in a moment of rage, reflecting on my miserable situation,—exil'd, abandon'd, forlorn—

I can write no more—let me hear from you by the return of Connel.—I will write you ere I go.

I am, Dear Sir, yours here & hereafter

Robt Burns

*Matthew 8:20, paraphrased.

IV (43)

Mossgiel, 1st September 1786

My Dear Sir,

I am still here in statu quo, tho I well expected to have been on my way over the Atlantic by this time.—The Nancy, in which I was to have gone, did not give me warning enough.—Two days notice was too little for me to wind up my affairs and go for Greenock. I now am to be a passenger aboard the Bell, Captain Cathcart, who sails the end of this month.—I am under little apprehension now about Armour.—The warrant is still in existence, but some of the first Gentlemen in the county have offered to befriend me, and besides, Jean will not take any step against me, without letting me know, as nothing but the most violent menaces could have forced her to sign the Petition.—I have called on her once and again, of late; as she, at this moment is threatened with the pangs of approaching travail; and I assure you, my dear Friend, I cannot help being anxious, very anxious, for her situation.—She would gladly now embrace that offer she once rejected, but it shall never more be in her power.—

78

John Richmond

I saw Jenny Surgeoner of late, and she complains bitterly against you.—You are acting very wrong, My friend; her happiness or misery is bound up in your affection or unkindness.—Poor girl! she told me with tears in her eyes that she had been at great pains since she went to Paisley, learning to write better; just on purpose to be able to correspond with you; and had promised herself great pleasure in your letters.—Richmond, I know you to be a man of honour, but this conduct of yours to a poor girl who distractedly loves you, and whom you have ruined, forgive me, my friend, when I say it is highly inconsistent with that manly INTEGRITY that I know your bosom glows with.—Your little, sweet Innocent too—but I beg your pardon; 'tis taking an improper liberty.—

"He would not have done such a thing, but once,
"Tho' hid from all the world and none had known it—
"He could not have forgiven it to himself"—

Otway*.

I do not know if Smith wrote you along with my book; but I tell you now, I present you with that Copy, as a memento of an old friend, on these—conditions—you must bind it in the neatest manner and never lend it, but keep it for my sake.—I shall certainly expect to hear from you by the return of Connel and you shall hear from me yet before I go.—

I am, My Dear Sir, your ever faithful friend

Robt Burns

The Orphan, Act II, sc. 1.

V (45)

Mossgiel, 3rd September 1786

Wish me luck, dear Richmond! Armour has just now brought me a fine boy and girl at one throw. God bless them poor little dears!

"Green grow the rashes, O,
"Green grow the rashes, O,
"A feather bed is no sae saft,
"As the bosoms o' the lasses, O."

R.B.

VI (49)

27th September 1786

My Dear Sir,

I received yours of Connel's last return, and I have just a moment at present to tell you that I am in the land of the living, and in the place of hope.—I am going perhaps to try a second edition of my book—If I do, it will detain me a little longer in the country; if not, I shall be gone as soon as harvest is over.—

Bettsey Miller waits me—

God bless you

Robt Burns

VII (119)

Mossgiel, 7th July 1787

My dear Richmond,

I am all impatience to hear your fate since the old confounder of right & wrong has turned you out of place, by his journey to answer his indictment at the Bar of the other world. He will find the Practice of that court so different from the Practice in which he has for so many years been thoroughly hackneyed, that his friends, if he had any connection truly of that kind, which I rather doubt, may well tremble for his sake.

His Chicane, his Left-handed Wisdom, which stood so firmly by him, to such good purpose, *here,* like other accomplices in robbery and plunder, will, now the piratical business is blown, in all probability turn King's evidence, and then the Devil's bagpiper will touch him off, "Bundle and go."

If he has left you any legacy, I beg your pardon for all this; if not, I know you will swear to every word I have said about him.

I have lately been rambling over by Dumbarton & Inverary, and running a drunken race on the side of Loch Lomond with a wild Highlandman; his horse, which had never known the ornaments of iron or leather, zigzagged across before my old spavin'd hunter, whose name is Jenny Geddes, and down came the Highwayman, horse & all, and down came Jenny and my Bardship; so I have got such a skinful of bruises and wounds, that I shall at least be four weeks before I dare venture on my journey to Edinburgh.

Not one new thing under the sun has happened in Mauchline since you left it. I hope this will find you as comfortably situated as formerly, or, if heaven pleases, more so; but, at all events, I trust you will let me know by Connel how matters stand with you, well or ill.—'Tis but poor consolation to tell the world when matters go wrong; but, you know very well your connection & mine stands on a very different footing—

I am ever,

My dear friend,

yours

Robt Burns

John Richmond

Edinburgh, 25th October 1787

My dear Sir,

I have been rambling over the world ever since I saw you, through the heart of the Highlands as far as Inverness and back by the north coast the whole rout to Dundee.—I have done nothing else but visited cascades, prospects, ruins and Druidical temples, learned Highland tunes and pickt up Scotch songs, Jacobite anecdotes, &c. these two months.—It will be a fortnight before I leave Edinburgh, and if you come in for the winter session when it sits down, perhaps we shall have the mutual pleasure of meeting once more in auld Reekie.—I lodge at Mr Cruikshank's, No. 2d, St. James's square, Newtown.—

I hope you enjoy good health, good spirits and some hope, the great Beaume de vie in this world.—Give my Compliments to William Duncan first time you see him.—

I am busy at present assisting with a Collection of Scotch Songs set to Music by an Engraver in this town.—It is to contain all the Scotch Songs, those that have been already set to music and those that have not, that can be found.—

I long much to hear from you, how you are, what are your views, and how your little girl comes on.—By the way, I hear I am a girl out of pocket and by careless, murdering mischance too, which has provoked me and vexed me a good deal.—I beg you will write me by post immediately on receipt of this, and let me know the news of Armour's family, if the world begin to talk of Jean's appearance any way.—

Farewel, my dear Sir!

Robt Burns

IX (196)

Edinburgh, 7th February 1788

Dear Richmond,

As I hope to see you soon, I shall not trouble you with a long letter of Edinburgh news.—Indeed there is nothing worth mentioning to you; every thing going on as usual—houses building, bucks strutting, ladies flaring, blackguards sculking, whores leering,* &c. in the old way.—I have not got, nor will not for some time, get the better of my bruised knee; but I have laid

---

*These words have been cut out, but are Ferguson's conjectual reading.

John Richmond

aside my crutches.—A lame Poet is unlucky, lames verses is an every day circumstance.—I saw Smith lately; hale and hearty as formerly.—I have heard melancholly enough accounts of Jean: 'tis an unlucky affair.—

I am ever, My dear Sir, yours

Robt Burns

JOHN KENNEDY

Born in 1757, he was a cousin of Mrs Gavin Hamilton and her sister, Margaret Kennedy. He was factor to the Earl of Dumfries, at Dumfries House near Cumnock, when Burns first met him in 1786. Later he served the Earl of Breadalbane in a similar capacity for eighteen years before retiring to Edinburgh where he died in 1812. The correspondence between Burns and Kennedy was short-lived, being confined to the period from March till September 1786, but in that brief space Burns favoured Kennedy with copies of several poems, including a first sight of *To a Mountain Daisy* (C.W. p. 203). Kennedy helped Burns with the subscription to the Kilmarnock Poems.

I (22)

Mossgiel, 3rd March, 1786

Sir,

I have done myself the pleasure of complying with your request in sending you my Cottager.* If you have a leisure minute I should be glad if you would copy it, and return me either the original or the transcript, as I have not a copy of it by me, and I have a friend who wishes to see it.

Now Kennedy if foot or horse

R.B.

*The Cotter's Saturday Night, C.W. p. 147.

II (28)

Mossgiel, 20th April 1786

[Enclosing *To a Mountain-Daisy*, C.W. p. 203]

Sir,

by some neglect in Mr Hamilton, I did not hear of your kind request for a subscription paper till this day.—I will not attempt any acknowledgement for this, nor the manner in which I see your name in Mr Hamilton's subscription list.—Allow me only to say Sir, I feel the weight of the debt.—

I have here, likewise, inclosed a small piece, the very latest of my productions.—I am a good deal pleas'd with some sentiments in it myself; as they are just the native, querulous feelings of a heart, which, as the elegantly melting Gray says,

"Melancholy has marked for her own".—*

Our race comes on apace; that much expected scene of revelry and mirth; but to me it brings no joy equal to that meeting, with which your last flattered the expectation of,

Sir, your indebted humble servant

Robert Burns

*Gray: *Elegy in a Country Churchyard*, slightly misquoted.

John Kennedy

III (30)

Mossgiel, 16th May 1786

[Enclosing *Epistle to John Rankine*, C.W. p. 82]

Dear Sir,

I have sent you the above hasty copy as I promised. In about three of four weeks I shall probably set the Press agoing.—I am much hurried at present, otherwise your diligence so very friendly in my subscription, should have a more lengthen'd acknowledgement from.

Dear Sir, Your oblidged Servant,

R.B.

IV (38)

Kilmarnock, [10th] August 1786

My Dear Sir,

Your truly facetious epistle of the 3d Inst. gave me much entertainment.—I was sorry I had not the pleasure of seeing you as I passed your way, but we shall bring up all our lee-way on Wednesday the 16th Current when I hope to have it in my power to call on you and take a kind, very probably a last adieu, before I go for Jamaica; as I expect orders to repair to Greenock, every day.—I have at last made my public appearance, and am solemnly inaugurated into the numerous class of Authorship; but now you have them, let them speak for themselves.—

> Farewel Dear Friend! may Guid-luck hit you,
> And 'mang her favorites admit you!
> If e'er Detraction shore to smit you,
>   May nane believe him!
> And ony deil that thinks to get you,
>   Good Lord deceive him! ! !

Robt Burns

V (48)

Mossgiel, Tuesday noon, 26th September 1786

My Dear Sir

I this moment receive yours—receive it with the honest hospitable warmth of a friend's welcome.—Whatever comes from you, wakens always up the better blood about my heart; which your kind, little recollections of my Parental FRIEND carries as far as it will go.—'Tis there Sir, Man is blest! 'Tis there, my Friend, man feels a consciousness of something within him, above the trodden clod! The grateful reverence to the hoary, earthly Authors of his being—The burning glow when he clasps the Woman of his Soul to his bosom—the tender yearnings of heart for the little Angels to whom he has given existence—These, Nature has pour'd in milky streams about the human heart; and the Man who never rouses them into action by the inspiring influences of their proper objects, loses by far the most pleasureable part of his existence.

My departure is uncertain, but I do not think it will be till after harvest.—I will be on the very short allowance of time indeed, if I do not comply with your friendly invitiation.—When it will be, I do not know; but if I can make my wish good, I will endeavour to drop you a line some time before.—

My best Compliments to Mrs Kennedy.— I should be equally mortified should I drop in when she is abroad, but of that I suppose there is little chance.—

What I have wrote; Heaven knows: I have not time to review it; so accept of it in the beaten way of Friendship, with the ordinary phrase, perhaps, rather more than ordinary sincerity, of

I am   My Dear Sir, ever yours

Robt Burns

ROBERT MUIR

Born in Kilmarnock in 1758, he eventually joined his father in the family wine business. Burns took to him instantly when they first met in 1786 and the ensuing warm friendship was only terminated by Muir's early death on 22nd April 1788. Muir subscribed for 72 copies of the Kilmarnock Edition and 40 of the first Edinburgh Edition. The first two letters of the series were jocularly addressed 'Monsr Robert Muir' and by September 1786 (II) Burns was addressing him as 'My Friend my Brother'. Muir was one of the first to be apprised of the birth of Jean's first set of twins — 'poor Armour has repaid my amorous mortgages double'. Later Burns wrote to his friend during his first visit to Edinburgh (IV) and from Stirling (VI) during his Highland tour. In his last letter, on 7th March 1788, Burns hoped that 'the Spring will renew your shattered frame' — an allusion to the long bouts of illness which led to his death soon afterwards. Burns was greatly affected by this tragic event. In the curious self-pitying 'conscience' letter about Highland Mary, written to Mrs Dunlop (XLIV) in December 1789, Burns speculated about a hereafter — 'There should I meet the friend, the disinterested friend of my early life; the man who rejoiced to see me, because he loved me & could serve me — Muir, thy weaknesses were the aberration of Human-nature, but thy heart glowed with every thing generous, manly & noble. . .' Perhaps Burns had some premonition of his friend's impending death when he wrote his last letter, containing what must surely have been his frankest declaration of his religious beliefs.

I (23)

Mossgiel, 20th March 1786

Dear Sir,

I am heartily sorry I had not the pleasure of seeing you as you returned thro Machline; but as I was engaged, I could not be in town before the evening.—

I here inclose you my SCOTCH DRINK, and "may the ——— follow with a blessing for your edification."—I hope, sometimes before we hear the Gowk, to have the pleasure of seeing you, at Kilmarnock, when, I intend we shall have a gill between us, in a Mutchkin-stoup; which will be a great comfort and consolation to,

Dear Sir, your humble servant

Robt Burness

II (46)

Mossgiel, Friday morn
[8th September 1786]

[Enclosing a copy of *The Calf*. C.W. p. 252]

My Friend my Brother,

Warm recollection of an absent Friend presses so hard on my heart, that I send him the prefixed bagatelle pleased with the thought that it will greet the Man of my bosom, and be a kind of distant Language of Friendship.—

You will have heard that poor Armour has repaid my amorous mortgages double.—A very fine boy and girl have awakened a thousand feelings that thrill, some with tender pleasure and some with foreboding anguish, thro' my soul.—

This Poem was nearly an extemporaneous production, on a wager with Mr Hamilton that I would not produce a poem on the subject in a given time.—

If you think it worth while, read it to Charles* & Mr William Parker; and if they chuse, a copy of it is at their service, as they are men whose friendship I shall be proud to claim, both in this world and that which is to come.—

I believe all hopes of staying at home will be abortive, but more of this when, in the latter end of next week, you shall be troubled with a visit from

My Dear Sir,

your most devoted

Robt Burns

*Charles Samson

III (57)

Mossgiel, 18th November 1786

My dear Sir:

Inclosed you have "Tam Samson," as I intend to print him. I am thinking for my Edinburgh expedition on Monday or Tuesday, come se'ennight, for pos. I will see you on Tuesday first.

I am ever, Your much indebted,

R.B.

IV (64)

Edinburgh, 15th December 1786

My Dear Sir,

I delayed writing you till I was able to give you some rational account of myself and my affairs. I am got under the patronage of the Duchess of Gordon, Countess Dowager of Glencairn, Sir John Whitefoord, the Dean of Faculty, Professors Blair, Stewart, Gregory and several others of the noblesse and literati. I believe I shall begin at Mr Creech's as publisher. I am still undetermined as to the future; and, as usual, never think of it. I have now neither house nor home that I can call my own, and live on the world at large. I am just a poor wayfaring Pilgrim on the road to Parnassus; thoughtless wanderer and sojourner in a strange land. I received a very kind letter from Mr A. Dalziel, for which please return him my thanks; and tell him I will write him in a day or two. Mr Parker, Charles, Dr Corsan, and honest John [Wilson?] quondam printer, I remember in my prayers when I pray in rhyme. To all of whom, till I have an opportunity...

The rest is missing

I forgot to tell you how honest-hearted Andrew and his wife Matty... She is noblest of the Creator's...*

* Andrew and Martha Bruce

V (67)

20th December 1786

My Dear Friend,

I have just time for the Carrier, to tell you that I received your letter; of which I shall say no more but what a lass of my acquaintance said of her bastart wean; she said, she did na ken wha was the father exactly, but she suspected it was some o' that bony, blackguard Smugglers for it was LIKE THEM—so I only say, your oblidging epistle WAS LIKE YOU.—I inclose you a parcel of Subscription-bills.—Your affair of Sixty Copies is also LIKE YOU; but it would not be LIKE ME to comply.—

Your friend's notion of MY LIFE has put a crotchet in my head of sketching MY LIFE in some future epistle to you.—

My Compliments to Charles & Mr Parker.—

I am ever,
My Dear Sir,
yours
Robt Burns

VI (131)

Stirling, 26th August 1786

My dear Sir,

I intended to have written you from Edinburgh and now write you from Stirling to make an excuse.—Here am I on my way to Inverness, with a truly original, but very worthy man, a Mr Nicol; one of the Masters of the High-school in Edinburgh.—I left auld

Reekie yesterday morning, and have passt, besides by excursions, Linlithgow, Borrowstouness, Falkirk & here am I undoubtedly.— This morning I kneel'd at the tomb of Sir John the Graham, the gallant friend of the immortal WALLACE; and two hours ago, I said a fervent prayer for old Caledonia over the hole in a blue whin-stone where Robert de Bruce fixed his royal Standard on the banks of Bannockburn; and just now from Stirling castle I have seen by the setting-sun the glorious prospect of the windings of Forth through the rich carse of Stirling, and skirt the equally rich carse of Falkirk.—The crops are very strong but so very late that there is no harvest, except a ridge of two perhaps in ten miles, all the way I have travelled from Edinburgh.—

I left Andrew Bruce and family all well.—I will be at least three weeks in making my tour, as I shall return by the coast, and have many people to call for.—

My best Compliments to Charles, our dear kinsman and fellow-saint, and Messrs W. & H. Parkers.—I hope Hughoc is going on and prospering with God and Miss McCauslin.—

If I could think on any thing sprightly, I should let you hear every other post; but a dull, matter-of-fact business like this scrawl, the less & seldomer one writes, the better.—

Among other matters-of-fact I shall add this, that I am and ever shall be,

My dear Sir, your oblidged

Robt Burns

VII (221)

Mossgiel 7th March 1788

I have partly changed my ideas, my dear Friend, since I saw you.— I took old Glenconner with me to Mr Millar's farm, and he was so pleased with it, that I have wrote an offer to Mr Millar, which if he accepts, I shall sit down a plain farmer, the happiest of lives when a Man can live by it.—In this case I shall not stay in Edinburgh above a week.—I set out on Monday, and would have come by Kilmarnock but there are several small sums owing me for my first Edition, about Galston and Newmills; and I shall set off so early as to dispatch my business and reach Glasgow by night.—When I return, I shall devote a forenoon or two to make some kind of acknowledgement for all the kindness I owe your friendship.—Now that I hope to settle with some credit and comfort at home, there was not any friendship or friendly correspondence that promised me more pleasure than yours—I

Robert Muir

hope I will not be disappointed.—I trust the Spring will renew your shattered frame and make your friends happy.—You and I have often agreed that life is no great blessing on the whole.—The close of life indeed, to a reasoning eye, is "Dark as was chaos, ere the infant sun

> "Was roll'd together, or had try'd his beams
> Athwart the gloom profound"—*

But an honest man has nothing to fear.—If we lie down in the grave, the whole man a piece of broke machinery, to moulder with the clods of the valley,—be it so; at least there is an end of pain, care, woes and wants: if that part of us called Mind, does survive the apparent destruction of the man—away with old-wife prejudices and tales! Every age and every nation has had a different set of stories; and as the many are always weak, of consequence they have often, perhaps always been deceived: a man, conscious of having acted an honest part among his fellow creatures; even granting that he may have been the sport, at times, of passions and instincts; he goes to a great unknown Being who could have no other end in giving him existence but to make him happy; who gave him those passions and instincts, and well knows their force.—

These my worthy friend, are my ideas; and I know they are not far different from yours.—It becomes a man of sense to think of himself; particularly in a case where all men are equally interested, and where indeed all men are equally in the dark.—

These Copies of mine you have on hand; please send ten of them to M. John Ballantine of the bank in Ayr; for the remainder, I'll write you about them from Glasgow.—

Adieu, my dear Sir! God send us a chearful meeting!

Robt Burns

*Blair: The Grave, lines 15-16.

ROBERT AIKEN

Born in Ayr in 1739, the son of a sea-captain, he became one of the town's leading lawyers. He first met Burns in 1783 and was one of the first, outside the poet's immediate circle, to recognise the merit of his poetry. Indeed, Burns went so far as to declare that he never fully appreciated his own work until he heard Aiken read it aloud. Burns dedicated *The Cotter's Saturday Night* to him, and to his son Andrew, the *Epistle to a Young Friend* (C.W. p. 221). Aiken procured 145 subscriptions for the Kilmarnock Edition — almost a quarter of the entire printing. Burns freely acknowledged the help he had received, referring to Aiken in letters to other friends as his 'first poetic patron' (see Ballantine IV) or 'my first kind patron' (Ballantine V) and 'the few Patrons that took notice of my earlier poetic days' (Hamilton III). Undoubtedly the series of letters from Burns to Aiken was very much larger than the handful of surviving manuscripts suggests, and probably included some of the most revealing epistles he ever penned. Unfortunately most of them have disappeared. Aiken's daughter Grace declared that most of them were destroyed as the result of the dishonesty of a clerk in Aiken's office; but it is more likely that they were accidentally lost during a periodic weeding-out of legal papers. Letter III is important as containing the first mention of Burns's plans to enter the Excise service. Burns's admiration for 'Orator Bob' never wavered, despite an ephemeral coolness between them due to a misunderstanding of Aiken's role in the delicate negotiations with James Armour over Burns's original 'irregular' marriage to Jean.

I (24)

Mossgiel, 3rd April 1786

Dear Sir,

I received your kind letter with double pleasure in account of this second flattering instance of Mrs C———'s[1] notice and approbation.- I assure you I

"Turn out the brunt side o' my shin"[2]

as the famous Ramsay of jingling memory says, at such a Patroness.—Present her my most grateful acknowledgements, in your very best manner of telling Truth.—I have inscribed the following stanzas on the blank leaf of Miss More's works:—

Thou flattering mark of friendship kind

[See C.W. p. 202]

My Proposals for publishing I am just going to send to the Press.—

I expect to hear from you first opportunity.—

I am ever, Dear Sir, yours

Robt Burns

1 The identity of this lady has not been ascertained, but possibilities include Mrs William Campbell of Fairfield, Mrs Cunninghame of Lainshaw and Mrs Maxwell Campbell of Skerrington.
2 Allan Ramsay: *Answer to Hamilton of Gilbertfield's Second Epistle.*

Robert Aiken

II (51B)

[About 27th September 1786]

I never end a letter to you of late but I think of Mr Ballantine, tho' how to express that remembrance must be ever a dead point —to assume equality & talk of inclosing Compliments wou'd be a degree of presumption in the Bard that I hope the Man is incapable of, but will you tell him that my heart-warm pray'r for him is that he may never have a Draft on Expectation, Wishes on the House of enjoyment returned unaccepted, that as seldom as possible for humanity he may have occasion to discount, with the Agents of Remorse, that Happiness may give him a large Cash Account in this world, & an Eternal Cart Blanche in the world to come.

P.S. Forgive, My honor'd Sir, the impertinence of this Scrawl, it is written after a hard day's labour, if you think I have glanc'd at too much freedom with you in it, impute it to the Affectation of Wit, not to the want of feeling my proper distance.

III (53)

[About 8th October 1786]

Sir,

I was with Wilson, my printer, t'other day, and settled all our by-gone matters between us. After I had paid him all demands, I made him the offer of the second edition, on the hazard of being paid out of the *first and readiest,* which he declines. By his account, the paper of a thousand copies would cost about twenty-seven pounds, and the printing about fifteen or sixteen: he offers to agree to this for the printing, if I will advance for the paper; but this, you know, is out of my power; so farewell hopes of a second edition 'till I grow richer! an epocha, which, I think, will arrive at the payment of the British national debt.

There is scarcely any thing hurts me so much in being disappointed of my second edition, as not having it in my power to shew my gratitude to Mr Ballantine, by publishing my poem of *The Brigs of Ayr.* I would detest myself as a wretch, if I thought I were capable, in a very long life, of forgetting the honest, warm and tender delicacy with which he enters into my interests. I am sometimes pleased with myself in my grateful sensations; but, I believe, on the whole, I have very little merit in it, as my gratitude is not a virtue, the consequence of reflection, but sheerly the instinctive emotion of a heart too inattentive to allow worldy maxims and views to settle into selfish habits.

Robert Aiken

I have been feeling all the various rotations and movements within, respecting the excise. There are many things plead strongly against it; the uncertainty of getting soon into business, the consequences of my follies, which may perhaps make it impracticable for me to stay at home; and besides I have for some time been pining under secret wretchedness, from causes which you pretty well know—the pang of disappointment, the sting of pride, with some wandering stabs of remorse, which never fail to settle on my vitals like vultures, when attention is not called away by the calls of society or the vagaries of the muse. Even in the hour of social mirth, my gaiety is the madness of an intoxicated criminal under the hands of the executioner. All these reasons urge me to go abroad; and to all these reasons I have only one answer—the feelings of a father. This, in the present mood I am in, overbalances everything that can be laid in the scale against it.

* * * * *

You may, perhaps, think it an extravagant fancy, but it is a sentiment which strikes home to my very soul: though sceptical, in some points, of our current belief, yet, I think, I have every evidence for the reality of a life beyond the stinted bourne of our present existence: if so, then, how should I, in the presence of that tremendous Being, the Author of existence, how should I meet the reproaches of those who stand to me in the dear relation of children, whom I deserted in the smiling innocency of helpless infancy? O thou great, unknown Power! thou Almighty God! who hast lighted up reason in my breast, and blessed me with immortality! I have frequently wandered from that order and regularity necessary for the perfection of thy works, yet thou hast never left me nor forsaken me!

* * * * *

Since I wrote the foregoing sheet, I have seen something of the storm of mischief thickening over my folly-devoted head. Should you, my friends, my benefactors, be successful in your applications for me, perhaps it may not be in my power in that way to reap the fruit of your friendly efforts. What I have written in the preceding pages is the settled tenor of my present resolution; but should inimical circumstances forbid me closing with your kind offer, or, enjoying it only, threaten to entail farther misery—

* * * * *

To tell the truth, I have little reason for complaint, as the world, in general, has been kind to me, fully up to my deserts. I was, for some time past, fast getting into the pining distrustful snarl of the misanthrope. I saw myself alone, unfit for the struggle of life, shrinking at every rising cloud in the chance-directed atmosphere of fortune, while, all defenceless, I looked about in vain for a cover. It never occurred to me, at least never with the force it deserved, that this world is a busy scene, and man a creature destined for a progressive struggle; and that, however I might possess a warm heart and inoffensive manners, (which last, by the by, was rather more than I could well boast,) still, more than these passive qualities, there was something to be *done.* When all my school-fellows and youthful compeers, (those misguided few excepted who joined, to use a Gentoo phrase, the *hallachores* of the human race), were striking off wish eager hope and earnest intent on some one or other of the many paths of busy life, I was "standing idle in the market-place," or only left the chace of the butterfly from flower to flower, to hunt fancy from whim to whim.

* * * * *

You see, Sir, that if to *know* one's errors were a probability of *mending* them, I stand a fair chance; but, according to the reverend Westminster divines, though conviction must precede conversion, it is very far from always implying it.

* * * * *

IV (65)

Edinburgh, 16th December 1786

Dear Patron of my Virgin Muse,

I wrote Mr Ballantine at large all my operations and "eventful story," since I came to town.—I have found in Mr Creech, who is my agent forsooth, and Mr Smellie who is to be my printer, that honour and goodness of heart which I always expect in Mr Aiken's friends. Mr Dalrymple of Orangefield I shall ever remember: my Lord Glencairn I shall ever pray for. The Maker of man has great honor in the workmanship of his lordship's heart. May he find that patronage and protection in his guardian angel that I have found in him! His lordship has sent a parcel of subscription bills to the Marquiss of Graham, with downright orders to get them filled up with all the first Scottish names about Court.—He has likewise wrote to the Duke of Portland for their Graces' interest in behalf of the Scotch Bard's Subscription.

You will very probably think, my honoured friend, that a hint about the mischevous nature of intoxicated vanity may not be unseasonable, but, alas! you are wide of the mark.—Various concurring circumstances have raised my fame as a Poet to a height which I am absolutely certain I have not merits to support; and I look down on the future as I would into the bottomless pit.—

Robert Aiken

You shall have one or two more bills when I have an opportunity of a Carrier.—

> I am ever with the sincerest gratitude honored Sir
>
> Your most devoted humble servant
>
> Robert Burns

V (120)

> Mr Hamilton's Office, Saturday even:
> [14th July 1787]

[With a copy of the *Elegy for Sir James Hunter Blair.* C.W. p. 281]

My honored Friend,

The melancholly occasion of the foregoing Poem affects not only individuals but a Country.—That I have lost a Friend is but repeating after Caledonia.—This copy, rather an incorrect one, I beg you will accept, till I have an opportunity in person, which I expect to have on Tuesday first, assuring you how sincerely I ever am,

> honored & dear Sir,
>
> your oft oblidged
>
> Robt Burns

VI (354)

> [Ellisland, August 1789]

Dear Sir,

Whether in the way of my trade, I can be of any service to the Rev. Doctor William McGill, is I fear very doubtful. Ajax's shield consisted, I think, of seven bull hides and a plate of brass, which altogether set Hector's utmost force at defiance. Alas! I am not a Hector, and the worthy Doctor's foes are as securely armed as Ajax was. Ignorance, superstition, bigotry, stupidity, malevolence, self-conceit, envy—all strongly bound in a massy frame of brazen impudence. Good God, Sir! to such a shield, humor is the peck of a sparrow, and satire the pop-gun of a school-boy. Creation-disgracing *scelerats* such as they, God only can mend, and the Devil only can punish. In the comprehending way of Caligula, I wish they had all but one neck. I feel impotent as a child to the ardour of my wishes! O for a withering curse to blast the germins of their wicked machinations. O for a poisonous Tornado, winged from the Torrid Zone of Tartarus, to sweep the spreading crop of the villainous contrivances to the lowest hell!

Robert Aiken

VII (570)

Dumfries, 16th July 1793

My dear Sir,

I understand that our friend, Mrs Muir, of Tarbolton Mill, is likely to be involved in great difficulties as to the Settlement the late Miller made.—Will you be so obliging as to let me know the state of the case, &, if you think that it would answer any good purpose to advocate the business to Edinburgh at once? I can answer for an agent for her, a Writer to the Signet, an intimate friend of mine, Robert Ainslie, who will chearfully undertake the business without a single sixpence of fee; & our Countryman, David Cathcart, lies under promise to me, to be advocate at small expence wherever I represent Female poverty in distress.—I am much interested for her, & will, as far as I have interest in either, move Heaven and Earth in her behalf.—My interest in the first is vastly improved since you & I were first acquainted.—Ah! there is nothing like matrimony for setting a man's face Zion-ward! Whether it be that it sublimes a man above this visible, diurnal sphere—or whether it tires him of this Sublunary state—or whether the delicious morsel of happiness which he enjoys in the conjugal yoke gives him a longing for the feasts above — or whether a poor Husband thinks he has every chance in his favour, as should he go to Hell he can be no worse—I shall leave to a weel-waled Presbytery of Orthodox Ayrshire priests.

Yours most sincerely

Robt Burns

MRS. MARIA RIDDELL
by Sir Thomas Lawrence

Original Burns manuscript by courtesy of Irvine Burns Club — see page 536.

JOHN BALLANTINE

Born in Ayr in 1743, he became a merchant and banker and played a prominent part in civic affairs, becoming Dean of Guild, and then (in 1787) Provost of Ayr. In 1786 he was largely instrumental in the construction of the New Brig and he was the dedicatee of *The Brigs of Ayr* (C.W. p. 244). Ballantine (according to Gilbert Burns) offered to lend the poet the cash to pay for a second Kilmarnock edition but simultaneously advised him to try an Edinburgh publisher. Burns declined the loan but took the advice. Of the baker's dozen of surviving letters to Ballantine, the most interesting are those written by Burns during his Edinburgh days, discussing his activities and the people he met there. Ballantine was also kept informed of the progress of the first Edinburgh Edition, casting light on Burns's dealings with printer, publisher and booksellers alike. Only five letters were writen after April 1787, but Burns's friendship never diminished. Writing from Ellisland in September 1791 (XII) Burns warmly acknowledged the help of Ballantine in gaining him entree to the Ayrshire bourgeoisie — 'the Court of Gentiles in the temple of Fame. . .'

I (26)

Mr Hamilton's Office, Mon: night
[April ? 1786]

Sir,

I inclose you a parcel of pieces whose fate is undetermined; but if you can spare an hour to glance over them against I come down on Wednesday to meet Mr Aiken, I shall be in a good measure decided by your and his opinion.—I do not mean Dr Hornbook in this view; I send it merely to amuse you, as it is too trifling and prolix to publish.—To tell the truth I am almost decided against them all I here send, except The Fragments that begin, When Guilford good & c. and, Green grow the rashes.—It would be silly, after the repeated proofs I have received of your friendship, to make a fuss of apologising and excuses for troubling you & c.— I know you take a real and warm interest, both in the Bard and his works.—

I have the honor to be,
My much respected Friend,
your ever grateful humble servant
Robert Burns

II (51)

[Enclosing *The Brigs of Ayr*, C.W. p. 244]

Mossgiel, 27th September 1786

Sir,

I am no stranger to your friendly offices in my Publication; and had that been the only debt I owed you, I would long since have acknowledged it; as the next Merchant's phrase, dressed up a little would have served my purpose.

But there is a certain cordial, friendly welcome in my reception, when I meet with you; an apparent heart-warm, honest joy at having it in your power to befriend a man whose abilities you are pleased to honor with some degree of applause—befriending him in the very way too most flattering to his feelings, by handing him up to that dear lov'd NOTICE OF THE WORLD —— this, Sir, I assure you with brimful eyes this moment, I have often wished to thank you for, but was as often at a loss for expression suitable to the state of my heart.—God knows I know very little of GREAT FOLKS: and I hope He can be my witness, that for mere GREATNESS, I as little care.

Worth, in whatever circumstances I prize; but Worth conjoined with Greatness, has a certain irresistible power of attracting esteem.—

I have taken the liberty to inscribe the inclosed Poem to you.—I am the more at ease about this, as it is not the anxiously served up address of the Author wishing to conciliate a liberal Patron; but the honest Sincerity of heart-felt Gratitude.—Of its merits I shall say nothing; as I can truly say that whatever applauses it could receive would not give me so much pleasure as having it in my power, in the way I like best, to assure you how sincerely I am,

Sir,

your much indebted humble servant

Robert Burns

III (51C)

[With *The Brigs of Ayr* C.W. p. 244]

[late September or early October 1786]

Mr Ballantine will accept of the foregoing Ballad as all a Poet, who owes him much, can give.—I have seen a Print of the old Cross of Ayr—'tis not to be bought—could you send me one just now that I might take it with me.—I shall be here for about an hour yet.—

R.B.

IV (59)

[Enclosing *A Winter Night* C.W. p. 258]

Mossgiel, 20th November 1786

Sir,

Inclosed you have my first attempt in that irregular kind of measure in which many of our finest Odes are wrote.

How far I have succeeded I don't know, but I shall be happy to have your opinion on friday first, when I intend being in Ayr.—I hear of no returns from Edinburgh to Mr Aiken respecting my second Edition business; so I am thinking to set out beginning of next week, for the City myself.—

If my first poetic patron Mr Aiken is in town, I want to get his advice, both in my procedure, & some little Criticism affairs, much, if Business will permit you to honor me with a few minutes when I come down on Friday.—

I have the honor to be, Sir,
your much indebted humble servant
Robert Burns

V (63)

Edinburgh, 13th December 1786

My honored Friend,

I would not write you till I could have it in my power to give you some account of myself & my matters, which by the bye is often no easy task.—I arrived here on Tuesday was se'ennight, and have suffered ever since I came to town with a miserable head-ach & stomach complaint; but am now a good deal better.—I have found a worthy, warm friend in Mr Dalrymple of Orangefield who introduced me to lord Glencairn, a man whose worth and brotherly kindness to me I shall remember when time will be no more.— By this interest it is passed in the Caledonian Hunt, & entered in their books, that they are all to take each a Copy of the second Edition, for which they are to pay one guinea.—I have been introduced to a good many of the noblesse, but my avowed Patrons & Patronesses are, the Duchess of Gordon—the Countess of Glencairn, with my lord & lady Betty—the Dean of Faculty— Sir John Whiteford.—I have likewise warm friends among the Literati, Professors Stewart, Blair, Greenfield, and Mr McKenzie the Man of feeling.—An unknown hand left ten guineas for the Ayrshire Bard in Mr Sibbald's hand, which I got. I since have discovered my generous unknown friend to be Patrick Miller Esq. brother to the Justice Clerk; and drank a glass of claret with him by invitation at his own house yesternight.—I am nearly agreed with Creech to print my book; and, I suppose, I will begin on monday.—I will send a subscription bill or two next post; when I intend writing my first, kind Patron Mr Aiken. I saw his Son today, and he is very well.—

Dugald Stewart and some of my learned friends put me in the periodical paper called The Lounger, a copy of which I here inclose you.—I was, Sir, when I was first honored with your notice, too obscure, now I tremble lest I should be ruined by being dragged suddenly into the glare of polite & learned observation.—I shall certainly, my ever-honored Patron, write you an account of my every step; & better health and more spirits may enable me to make it something better than this stupid, matter-of-fact epistle.—

I have the honor to be, good Sir,
Your ever grateful humble servant
Robert Burns

If any of my friends write me, my direction is
Care of Mr Creech, Bookseller

VI (77)

Edinburgh, 14th January 1787

My honored Friend,

It gives me a secret comfort to observe in myself that I am not yet so far gone as Willie Gaw's Skate, "Past redemption;" for I have still this favorable symptom of grace, that when my Conscience, as in the case of this letter, tells me I am leaving something undone that I ought to do, it teases me eternally till I do it.—

I am still "dark as was Chaos"[1] in respect to Futurity.—My generous friend, Mr Peter Miller, brother to the Justice Clerk, has been talking with me about a lease of some farm or other in an estate called Dasswinton which he has lately bought near Dumfries.—Some life-rented, embittering Recollections whisper me that I will be happier any where than in my old neighborhood, but Mr Miller is no Judge of land; and though I dare say he means to favour me, yet he may give me, in his opinion, an advantageous bargain that may ruin me.—I am to take a tour by Dumfries as I return and have promised to meet Mr Miller on his lands some time in May.—

I went to a Mason-lodge yesternight where the Most Worshipful Grand Master Charters, and all the Grand lodge of Scotland visited.—The meeting was most numerous and elegant; all the different Lodges about town were present, in all their pomp.—The Grand Master who presided with great solemnity, and honor to himself as a Gentleman and Mason, among other general toasts gave, "Caledonia, & Caledonia's Bard, brother B———," which rung through the whole Assembly with multiplied honors and repeated acclamations.—As I had no idea such a thing would

100

happen, I was downright thunderstruck, and trembling in every nerve made the best return in my power.—Just as I finished, some of the Grand Officers said so loud as I could hear, with a most comforting accent, "Very well indeed!" which set me something to rights again.—

I have just now had a visit from my Landlady who, is a staid, sober, piously-disposed, sculdudery-abhoring Widow, coming on her grand climacterick.—She is at present in sore tribulation respecting some "Daughters of Belial" who are on the floor immediately above.—My Landlady who as I said is a flesh-disciplining, godly Matron, firmly believes her husband is in Heaven; and having been very happy with him on earth, she vigorously and perseveringly practices some of the most distinguishing Christian virtues, such as, attending Church, railing against vice, &c. that she may be qualified to meet her dear quon-dam Bedfellow in that happy place where the Unclean & the ungodly shall never enter.—This, no doubt, requires some strong exertions of Self-denial, in a hale, well-kept Widow of forty-five; and as our floors are low and ill-plaistered, we can easily distinguish our laughter-loving, night-rejoicing neighbors—when they are eating, when they are drinking, when they are singing, when they are &c., my worthy Landlady tosses sleepless & unquiet, "looking for rest but finding none,"[2] the whole night.—Just now she told me, though by the by she is sometimes dubious that I am, in her own phrase, "but a rough an' roun' Christian" that "We should not be uneasy and envious because the Wicked enjoy the good things of this life; for these base jades who, in her own words, lie up gandygoing with their filfthy fellows, drinking the best of wines, and singing abominable songs, they shall one day lie in hell, weeping and wailing and gnashing their teeth over a cup of God's wrath!"

I have today corrected my 152d page.—My best good wishes to Mr Aiken.—

I am ever
Dear Sir,
your much indebted humble servant
Robert Burns

1 Blair: *The Grave*, line 14.
2 Luke 11:24.

VII (86)

[Edinburgh, 24th February 1787]

My honored Friend,

I will soon be with you now *in guid black prent;* in a week or ten days at farthest—I am obliged, against my own wish, to print subscribers' names, so if any of my Ayr friends have subscription bills, they must be sent in to Creech directly.—

I am getting my Phiz done by an eminent Engraver; and if it can be ready in time, I will appear in my book looking, like other fools, to my title page.—

> I have the honor to be,
> Ever your grateful,
> Robt Burns

VIII (95)

Edinburgh, 18th April 1787

Sir,

I have taken the liberty to send a hundred copies of my book to your care.—I have no acquaintance with Forsyth; and besides I believe Booksellers take no less than the unconscionable Jewish tax of 25 per cent. by way of agency.—I trouble you then, Sir, to find a proper person, of the mercantile folks I suppose will be best, that for a moderate consideration will retail the books to subscribers as they are called for.—Several of the Subscription bills have been mislaid, so all who say they have subscribed must be served at subscription price; otherwise those who have not subscribed must pay six shillings.—Should more copies be needed, an order by post will be immediately answered.—

My respectful Compliments to Mr Aiken.—I wrote him by David Shaw which I hope he received.—

> I have the honor to be,
> with the most grateful sincerity,
> Sir, your oblidged & very humble servant
> Robert Burns

IX (173)

[undated]

Sir,

I have been wandering for some time past, like Satan in the first chapter of the book of Job, "Going to and fro in the earth, and walking up and down in it."[1]—Some weeks bypast indeed, I have been a cripple in one of my legs, owing to a fall by the drunken stupidity of a coachman.—I am got a good deal better, but can walk a little yet without my crutches.—"It is an ill-wind blows nobody good:"[2] the witlings of my acquaintance have made much of, "a Poet on stilts."—

My brother the bearer of this, has just now written me to assist him a little in money matters.—I cannot stir out, not even in a chair, to raise as much as he wants; and without my personal presence, I could not so well do it.—That account for my copies, in your or Mr Cowan's hands, you will please give it him.—Should he want half a dozen pounds or more, dare I ask you to accommodate him? I shall not on this side of eternity forget a pecuniary offer you once made me, when it was dangerous to accept it.—

So soon as I can walk, I return to Ayrshire; and I think I shall walk in ten days or a fortnight at farthest.—I beg you will take the trouble to present my most respectful compliment to the Patron of my virgin Muse, Mr Aiken.—I was with an old, worthy friend of his, or rather he was with me, last night, Mr Ainslie at Dunse; and on my telling him that Andrew Aiken was in Liverpool, he mentioned two gentlemen there, John Lawson Esqr of Carnatic; and Mr Clarke, an eminent merchant, who are Mr Ainslie's particular friends; and if introducing Andrew to them would do him any service, Mr Ainslie begs his old friend Mr Aiken will let him know.—Mr Ainslie's son is my most intimate friend here, so the channel is easy; or Mr Ainslie will be found

[rest of MS. missing]

1 Job 1:17
2 Shakespeare: *2 Henry IV*, Act IV, sc. 3.

X (259)

[With *The Fête Champêtre* C.W. p. 326]

Mauchline — Thursday-night

Sir,

"She never beuke a gude Cake that never beuke an ill ane": should the foregoing ballad, as I am afraid it may, be thought a dull one—it is not the *only* such I have composed.—

A bruised finger hindered me from transcribing my Poem myself; so I am oblidged to send you the inclosed, rather incorrect one.—

I have the honor to be, with the warmest sense of my many obligations to your goodness, Sir, your grateful humble servant.

Robt Burns

XI (442)

[March? 1791]

Sir,

While here I sit sad, & solitary, by the side of a fire in a little country inn, & drying my wet clothes, in pops a poor fellow of a

John Ballantine

sodger & tells me he is going to Ayr—By Heavens! say I to myself
with a tide of good spirits which the magic of that sound, Auld
toon o' Ayr conjured up, I will send my last song to Mr Ballantine
—Here it is.—

Ye flowery banks o' bonie Doon
[C.W. p. 419]

XII (468)

[Ellisland, September 1791]

Sir

Inclosed you will receive a draught on the Paisley-bank, for the
thirty two pounds I discounted in a bill at your Bank.—I did not
like to send money so far, else I would have sent you the cash,
but I suppose (for I am miserably ignorant in the business) that
the Draught will do quite as well.—Indeed I would have sent a
servant all the way with the money, but the Banker in Dumfries
who manages for the Paisley people assured me, that you
banking-folks hold Draughts on one another, as equal to cash.—

I am conscious that I must make so despicable a figure as a Man
of Business, that I am determined to appear before you in
another character, & one in which I shall stand more erect in your
presence: I beg leave to present you my last & not my worst
Ballad.—I have explained the occasion in an appendix to the Piece
—You will readily guess that the "Bard" mentioned in the Poem,
was a certain Poet whom a few years ago you handed up to the
"Court of the Gentiles" in the temple of Fame, where God grant
that he may make his footing good!

Lord Buchan lately sent me an invitation to make one at the
Coronation of a bust of Thomson, which is placed, or about to be
placed on Ednam-hill, the place where our Poet was born.—I
excused myself to his Lordship as they have fixed the middle of
harvest for the business, but I sent him the following stanzas, as
an Address to the Shade of the Bard, on crowning his Bust with
the Poetic Wreath.—I dare say you know the scenery alluded to in
the neighbouring country, else I fear the verses will lose any little
merit they may have.—

Address to the Shade of Thomson on
crowning his Bust with Bays—
While virgin Spring by Eden's flood
[C.W. p. 421]

I have not yet done any thing in the Excise matter you were so
good as interest yourself in, but I will in a few days.—

104

John Ballantine

Expressions of gratitude are now so prostituted by the Unmeaning & the Insincere, that a man, *in earnest*, does not know how to meddle with them, without contamination; but when I forget what I owe Mr Ballantine's goodness, may every Good Man forget me, & every Scoundrel tuck me under the arm & call me Brother ! ! !

I have the honor to be, Sir,
your obliged humble servant
Robert Burns

XIII (480)

Globe Inn, Dumfries
25th October [1791]

Sir,

The inclosed is my latest work.*—If the perusal of it gives you little pleasure, it at least gives me an opportunity of subscribing myself,

Sir, your obliged humble servant
R.B.—

*Probably *Tam o Shanter* (C.W. p. 410)

DAVID McWHINNIE

Little is known about this gentleman, whose tombstone can be seen in Ayr's Auld Kirk-yard off the High Street, beyond the fact that he was a lawyer in the town and died there in 1819. There is no record of him beyond Burns's letter from Mossgiel on 17th April 1786, regarding four copies of the Kilmarnock Edition. The poet added the hint — 'I have no less than eight dozen in whole, which is a great deal more that I shall ever need' — and McWhinnie responded nobly by securing 20 subscriptions in all.

(27)

Mossgiel, 17th April 1786

It is injuring some hearts, those that *elegantly* bear the impression of the good Creator, to say to them you give them the trouble of obliging a friend; for this reason, I only tell you that I gratify my *own* feelings in requesting your friendly offices with respect to the inclosed, because I know it will gratify *yours* to assist me in it to the utmost of your power.

I have sent you four copies, as I have no less than eight dozen in whole, which is a great deal more than I shall ever need.

Be sure to remember a poor Poet militant in your prayers. He looks forward with fear and trembling to that, to him, important moment which stamps the *die* with—with—with, perhaps the eternal disgrace of,

My dear Sir, Your humbled, afflicted, tormented
R. Burns

JOHN ARNOT

Born about 1738 at Dalquhatswood, north of Newmilns, the son of James Arnot, factor to the fourth Earl of Loudoun, he spent some years in Canton and Macao (1766-c.1770) before marrying and settling at Dalquhatswood. Arnot is the most enigmatic figure among Burns's contemporaries. Remarkably little record of him appears to have survived, leaving us immensely intrigued by Burns's reference to him, in the preamble to the copy of the letter made for the Glenriddell MS. What was that lack of prudence which earned for Arnot 'the world's contempt, & real misery, perhaps perdition'? The clue may lie in the fact that, in 1783, Arnot obtained an overdraft from the Ayrshire Bank of Hunter and Company, the year after he had borrowed £300, in conjunction with a partner, from Mrs Rachel Hamilton, the widow of an Edinburgh wine merchant. A letter from his father to Lord Loudoun (February 1760) had hinted at profligacy while his son was in London: 'Poor man he has lost some years of his youth. God grant he may see the folly of it.' From these admittedly scanty facts we may conjecture that John Arnot squandered his patrimony, got heavily into debt and died in disgrace, about 1789. The letter which Burns wrote 'about the latter end of 1785' — but patently about April 1786, from the reference to a subscription bill for the Kilmarnock Edition — describes in amusing but bawdy terms, full of sexual bragadoccio, how the poet had successfully besieged and captured Jean Armour, but was subsequently thwarted by James Armour in his bid to make her his wife.

(29)

The following was to one of the most accomplished of the sons of men that I ever met with—John Arnot of Dalquatswood in Ayrshire—alas! had he been equally prudent!—It is a damning circumstance in human-life, that Prudence, insular & alone, without another virtue, will conduct a man to the most envied eminences in life, while having every other good quality, & wanting that one, which at best is itself but a half virtue, will not save a man from the world's contempt, & real misery, perhaps perdition.—

The story of the letter was this—I had got deeply in love with a young Fair-One, of which proofs were every day *arising* more & more to view.—I would gladly have covered my Inamorato from the darts of Calumny with the conjugal Shield, nay, had actually made up some sort of Wedlock; but I was at that time deep in the guilt of being unfortunate, for which good & lawful objection, the Lady's friends broke all our measures, & drove me au desespoir.—

I think that the letter was written sometime about the latter end of 1785, as I was meditating to publish my Poems.—

> To John Arnot of Dalquhatswood Esquire, inclosing a Subscription-bill for my first edition, which was printed at Kilmarnock—

[April 1786]

Sir,

I have long wished for some kind of claim to the honor of your acquaintance, & since it is out of my power to make that claim by the least service of mine to you, I shall do it by asking a friendly office of you to me.—I should be much hurt, Sir, if any one should view my poor Parnassian Pegasus in the light of a spur-galled Hack, & think that I wish to make a shilling or two by him. —I spurn the thought.—

> It may-do—maun do, Sir, wi' them wha
> Maun please the great folk for a wame-fou;
> For me, sae laigh I need na bow,
> For, Lord be thankit. I can plough:
> And when I downa yoke a naig,
> Then, Lord be thankit! I can beg—[1]

You will then, I hope Sir, forgive my troubling you with the Inclosed; & spare a poor, heart-crushed devil, a world of apologies: a business he is very unfit for at any time, but at present, widowed as he is of every woman-giving comfort, he is utterly incapable of.—Sad & grievous, of late, Sir, has been my tribulation, & many & piercing, my sorrows; & had it not been for the loss the world would have sustained in losing so great a Poet, I had, ere now, done as a much wiser man, the famous Achitophel of long-headed memory, did before me, when "he went home & set his house in order."[2]—I have lost, Sir, that dearest earthly treasure, that greatest blessing here below, that last, best gift which compleated Adam's happiness in the garden of bliss, I have lost—I have lost—my trembling hand refuses its office, the frightened ink recoils up the quill—Tell it not in Gath—I have lost—a—a— A WIFE!

> Fairest of God's creation, last & best!
> *How art thou lost*[3]—

You have doubtless, Sir, heard my story, heard it all with all its exaggerations; but as my actions, & my motives for action, are peculiarly like myself, & that is peculiarly like nobody else, I shall just beg a leisure-moment & a spare-tear of you, untill I tell my own story my own way.—

I have been all my life, Sir, one of the rueful-looking, long-visaged sons of Disappointment.—A damned Star has always kept my zenith, & shed its baleful influence, in that emphatic curse of the Prophet—"And behold, whatsoever he doth, it shall not prosper!"[4]—I rarely hit where I aim; & if I want any thing, I am almost sure never to find it where I seek it. —For instance, if my pen-knife is needed, I pull out twenty things—a plough-wedge, a horse-nail, an old letter or a tattered rhyme, in short, every thing but my pen-knife; & that at last, after a painful fruitless search, will be found in the unsuspected corner of an unsuspected pocket, as if on purpose thrust out of the way.— Still, Sir, I had long had a wishing eye to that inestimable blessing, a wife.—My mouth watered deliciously, to see a young fellow, after a few idle, common-place stories from a gentleman in black, strip & go to bed with a young girl & no one durst say black was his eye; while I, for just doing the same thing, only wanting that ceremoney, am made a Sunday's laughing stock, & abused like a pick-pocket.—I was well aware though, that if my ill-starred fortune got the least hint of my connubial wish, my schemes would go to nothing.—To prevent this, I determined to take my measures with such thought & forethought, such caution & precaution, that all the malignant planets in the Hemisphere should be unable to blight by designs.—Not content with, to sue the words of the celebrated Westminster Divines, "The outward & ordinary means," I left no *stone* unturned; sounded every unfathomed *depth;* stopped up every *hole* & bore of an objection: but, how shall I tell it! notwithstanding all this turning of stones, stopping of bores, &c.—whilst I, with secret pleasure, marked my project *swelling* to the proper crisis, & was singing Te deum in my own fancy; or to change the metaphor, whilst I was vigorously pressing on the siege; had carried the counter-scarp, & made a practicable breach behind the curtin in the gorge of the very principal bastion; nay, having mastered the covered way, I had found means to slip a choice detachment into the very citadel; while I had nothing less in view than displaying my victorious banners on the top of the walls—"Heaven & Earth, must I remember"! my damned Star wheeled about to the zenith by whose baleful rays Fortune took the alarm, & pouring in her forces on all quarters, front, flank & rear, I was utterly routed, my baggage lost, my military chest in the hands of the enemy; & your poor devil of a humble servant, commander in chief forsooth, was obliged to scamper away, without wither arms or honors of war, except his bare bayonet & cartridge-pouch; nor in all probability had he escaped even with them, had he not made a shift to hide them under the lap of his military cloak.—

In short, Pharaoh at the Red Sea, Darius at Arbela, Pompey at Pharsalia, Edward at Bannockburn, Charles at Pultaway[5], Burgoyne at Saratoga — no Prince, Potentate or Commander, of ancient or modern unfortunate memory, ever got a more shameful or more total defeat.—

"O horrible! O horrible. Most horrible!"[6]

How I bore this, can only be conceived.—All powers of recital labor far, far behind.—There is a pretty large portion of bedlam in the composition of a Poet at any time; but on this occasion, I was nine parts & nine tenths, out of ten, stark staring mad.—At first, I was fixed in stuporific insensibility, silent, sullen, staring, like Lot's wife besaltified in the plains of Gomorrah.—But my second paroxysm chiefly beggars description.—The rifted northern ocean, when returning suns dissolve the chains of winter & loosening precipices of long accumulated ice tempest with hideous crash the foamy Deep—images like these may give some

John Arnot

faint shadow of what was the situation of my bosom.—My chained faculties broke loose; my maddening passions, roused to tenfold fury, bore over their banks with impetuous, resistless force, carrying every check & principle before them.—Counsel, was an unheeded call to the passing hurricane; Reason, a screaming elk in the vortex of Moskoe strom; & Religion, a feebly-struggling beaver down the roaring of Niagara.—I reprobated the first moment of my existence; execrated Adam's folly-infatuated wish for that goodly-looking but poison-breathing gift, which had ruined him, & undone me; & called on the womb of uncreated night to close over me & all my sorrows.—

A storm naturally overblows itself.—My spent passions gradually sank into a lurid calm; & by degrees, I have subsided into the time-settled sorrow of the sable widower, who, wiping away the decent tear, lifts up his grief-worn eye to look—for another wife.—

> "Such is the state of man; today he buds
> "His tender leaves of hope; tomorrow blossoms,
> "And bears his blushing honors thick upon him;
> "The third day comes a frost, a killing frost,
> "And nips his root, & then he falls as I do"—7

Such, Sir, has been this fatal era of my life.—"And it came to pass, that when I looked for sweet, behold bitter; & for light, behold darkness."—8

But this is not all.—Already the holy beagles, the houghma-gandie pack, begin to snuff the scent; & I expect every moment to see them cast off, & hear them after me in full cry: but as I am an old fox, I shall give them dodging & doubling for it; & by & bye, I intend to earth among the mountains of Jamaica.—

I am so struck, on a review, with the impertinent length of this letter, that I shall not increase it with one single word of an apology; but abruptly conclude with assuring you, that I am,

Sir, your, & Misery's most humble servant

1 A *Dedication to Gavin Hamilton*, lines 11-16. C.W. p. 216
2 Samuel 17:23
3 Milton: *Paradise Lost*, Bk. IX, lines 896 and 900.
4 Jeremiah 10:21, misquoted
5 Charles XII of Sweden, at Poltava, 1712. See *To A Gentleman*, lines 11-11-12 (C.W. p. 379)
6 Shakespeare: *Hamlet*, Act 1, sc. 5
7 Shakespeare: *Henry VIII*, Act III, sc. 2, altered
8 Job 30:26, altered

DAVID BRICE

A native of Mauchline who moved to Glasgow where he became a shoemaker. Nothing is known of him, although, from the intimate tone of the two letters from Burns in June and July 1786, it is evident that he and Burns were very close friends. These letters are invaluable for the light they shed on Burns's emotional turmoil, with those references to Jean as 'poor, ill-advised, ungrateful Armour' and later 'poor, foolish Armour'.

I (31)

Mossgiel, 12th June 1786

Dear Brice—

I received your message by G. Paterson, and as I am not very throng at present, I just write to let you know that there is such a worthless, rhyming reprobate, as your humble servant still in the land of the living, tho' I can scarcely say, in the place of hope.— I have no news to tell you that will give me any pleasure to mention, or you, to hear.—Poor, ill-advised, ungrateful Armour came home on Friday last.—You have heard all the particulars of that affair; and a black affair it is.—What she thinks of her conduct now, I don't know; one thing I know, she has made me compleatly miserable.—Never man lov'd, or rather ador'd, a woman more than I did her and, to confess a truth between you and me, I do still love her to destraction after all, tho' I won't tell her so, tho I see her which I don't want to do.—My poor dear, unfortunate Jean! how happy have I been in her arms!—It is not the losing her that makes me so unhappy; but for *her* sake I feel most severely.—I foresee she is on the road to, I am afraid, *eternal* ruin; and those who made so much noise, and showed so much grief, at the thought of her being *my wife,* may, some day, see her connected in such a manner as may give them more real cause of vexation.—I am sure I do not wish it: may Almighty God forgive her ingratitude and perjury to me, as I from my very soul forgive her! and may His grace be with her, to bless her in all her future life!—I can have no nearer idea of the place of eternal punishment than what I have felt in my own breast on her account.—I have tryed often to forget her: I have run into all kinds of dissipation and riot, Mason-meetings, drinking matches, and other mischief, to drive her out of my head, but all in vain: and now for a grand cure, the Ship is on her way home that is to take me out to Jamaica, and then, farewel, dear old Scotland, and farewel dear, ungrateful Jean, for never, never will I see you more!

You will have heard that I am going to commence Poet in print; and tomorrow, my works go to the press.—I expect it will be a Volume about two hundred pages.—It is just the last foolish action I intend to do; and then turn a wise man as fast as possible.—

I shall expect a letter from you first leisure moment; and believe me to be,

Dear Bryce, your friend & wellwisher

Robt Burns

II (34)

Mossgiel, 17th July 1786

. . . have been so throng printing my Poems, that I could scarcely find as much time.—Poor, foolish Armour is come back again to Mauchline, and I went to call for her, and her mother forbade me the house; nor did she herself express much sorrow for what she has done.—I have already appeared publickly in Church, and was indulged in the liberty of standing in my own seat.—I do this to get a certificate as a batchelor, which Mr Auld has promised me.—I am now fixed to go for the West Indies in October.—Jean and her friends insisted much that she should stand along with me in the kirk, but the minister would not allow it, which bred a great trouble I assure you; and I am blamed as the cause of it, tho I am sure I am innocent; but I am very well pleased, for all that, not to have her company.—I have no news to tell you that I remember.—I am really happy to hear of your welfare, and that you are so well in Glasgow tho I must certainly see you before I leave the country.—I shall expect to hear from you soon,

and am, Dear Bryce, yours

Robt Burns

Dr JOHN MACKENZIE

Born in Ayrshire about 1755, he studied medicine at Edinburgh University and at the behest of Sir John Whitefoord settled in Mauchline where he married Helen Miller, one of the 'Mauchline belles'. His house was purchased by the Burns Federation in 1917 and is now preserved as a museum largely on the strength of the fact that it was in a rented upstairs room that Burns and Jean Armour first set up home in February 1788. Dr Mackenzie's first impressions of the poet, whom he met in the spring of 1783 while attending William Burnes, are most revealing: 'The Poet seemed distant, suspicious, and without any wish to interest or please. He kept himself very silent in a dark corner of the room and before he took any part in the conversation, I frequently detected him scrutinising me during my conversation with his father and brother. But afterwards, when the conversation, which was on a medical subject, had taken the turn he wished, he began to engage in it, displaying a dexterity and a familiarity with topics apparently beyond his reach, by which his visitor was no less gratified than astonished.'

After Burns moved to Mossgiel he and Dr Mackenzie became good friends. The latter became Depute Master of St James Lodge, Tarbolton and it was in that capacity that he received the verse epistle 'Friday first's the day appointed' (C.W. p. 237), dated at Mossgiel 14th June A.M. 5790 — the 'year of the world' which translated into 1786. In *The Holy Fair* (C.W. p. 133) Mackenzie was personified as 'Commonsense' who left the assembly to keep a dinner engagement with Sir John Whitefoord at the home of the Earl of Dumfries, as soon as 'Peebles, frae the water-fit' began his sermon. Mackenzie also received a two-line note from Burns on 3rd September 1786, enclosing a copy of *The Calf* (C.W. p. 252): 'I am afraid the foregoing scrawl will be scarce intelligible.—The fourth, and the last Stanzas are added since I saw you today.—' Three other communications from Burns, dating between October 1786 and the following January, have survived. It was through Mackenzie that Burns was introduced to Professor Dugald Stewart, and Mackenzie also sent letters of introduction to Sir John Whitefoord and the Hon. Andrew Erskine, which helped Burns's *entree* to Edinburgh society. Mackenzie later moved to Irvine, where he died in 1837.

I (53A)

[Enclosing *Extempore Verses on Dining with Lord Daer.*
C.W. p. 254]

Wednesday morning
[25th October 1786]

Dear Sir,

I never spent an afternoon among great folks, with half that pleasure, as when in company with you I had the honour of paying my devoirs to that plain, honest, worthy man, the Professor [Dugald Stewart]. I would be delighted to see him perform acts of kindness and friendship, though I were not the object, he does it with such a grace.—I think his character, divided into ten parts, stands thus—four parts Socrates—four parts Nathaniel—and two parts Shakespeare's Brutus.

The foregoing verses were really extempore, but a little corrected since. They may entertain you a little, with the help of that partiality with which you are so good as favour the performances of,

Dear Sir, Your very humble servant,

Robert Burns

John Mackenzie

II (61A)

My dear Sir,

I have now been a week in Edinburgh and have been introduced to a great many of the Noblesse.—I have met very warm friends in the Literati, Professors Stewart, Blair, Greenfield, & your name-sake, the Author of The man of feeling. I am likewise kindly & generously Patronised by the Duchess of Gordon; Countess of Glencairn, with my lord & Lady Betty; Sir John Whiteford, and the Dean of Faculty, the honorable Mr H. Erskine, with several others.—Our worthy friend Mr Stewart, with that goodness truly like himself, got me in the periodical paper, The Lounger; a copy of which I here inclose you.—[1] You will[2]

1 Henry Mackenzie's review of Burns's poems in *The Lounger*, No. 97 December 1786
2 This letter, now in the Burns House Museum, Mauchline, was glued to a mount for framing, making it impossible to read the back of the sheet.

III (73)

Edinburgh, 11th January 1787

My Dear Sir,

Yours gave me something like the pleasure of an old friend's face, —I saw *your* friend and *my* honored Patron, Sir John Whitefoord just after I received your letter, and gave him your respectful Compliments.—He was pleased to say many handsome things of you which I heard with the more satisfaction as I knew them to be just.—

His son John, who calls very frequently on me, is in a fuss today like a coronation.—This is the great day—the Assembly & Ball of the Caledonian Hunt; and John has had the good luck to pre-engage the hand of the beauty-famed and wealth-celebrated Miss McAdam, our Country-woman.—Between friends, John is desperately in for it there; and I am afraid will be desperate indeed.—

I am sorry to send you the last Speech & dying words of the Lounger.—

A Gentleman waited on me Yesterday, and gave me, by Lord Eglintoun's order, ten guineas by way of subscription for a brace of Copies of my 2nd Edition.—

I met with Lord Maitland & a brother of his today, at breakfast.— They are exceedingly easy, accessible, agreable fellows; and seemingly pretty clever.—

I am ever, My Dear Sir, yours

Robt Burns

DEED OF ASSIGNMENT

This remarkable document was drawn up by Burns on 22nd July 1786, partly to avoid the consequences of any litigation brought by James Armour, and partly to wind up his business affairs before departing for Jamaica. In it he left the profit from the Kilmarnock Edition and the proceeds from the sale of his estate to his brother Gilbert, on condition that the latter brought up 'Dear Bought Bess'. Gilbert remained at Mossgiel till 1798. Subsequently, about May 1788, Burns lent Gilbert £180 to save him from ruin — a transaction to which Burns referred in his autobiographical letter to Dr Moore (see page 248). Gilbert was then supporting 'my aged mother, another still younger brother, and three sisters.' By surrendering himself almost half the profits from his first Edinburgh Edition, Burns gave his brother the money which enabled him to carry on farming and supporting the Burns family. The Deed of Assignment was lodged with the Sheriff-Clerk at Ayr, and is preserved in that office to this day, a facsimile being housed in the City Museum, Edinburgh.

35

Know all men by these presents that I Robert Burns in Mossgiel: whereas I intend to leave Scotland and go abroad, and having acknowledged myself the father of a child named Elizabeth, begot upon Elizabeth Paton in Largieside: and whereas Gilbert Burns in Mossgiel, my brother, has become bound, and hereby binds and oblidges himself to aliment clothe and educate my said natural child in a suitable manner as if she were his own, in case her Mother chuse to part with her, and that until she arrive at the age of fifteen years. Therefore, and to enable the said Gilbert Burns to make good his said engagement, Wit ye me to have assigned, disponed, conveyed and made over to, and in favors of, the said Gibert Burns his Heirs, Executors and Assignees, who are always to be bound in like manner with himself, all and Sundry Goods, Gear, Corns, Cattle, Horses, Nolt, Sheep, Household furniture, and all other moveable effects of whatever kind that I shall leave behind me on my departure from the kingdom, after allowing for my part of the conjunct debts due by the said Gilbert Burns and me as joint Tacksmen of the farm of Mossgiel. —And particularly, without prejudice of the aforesaid generality, the profits that may arise from the Publication of my Poems presently in the Press—And also, I hereby dispone and convey to him in trust for behoof of my said natural daughter, the Copyright of said Poems in so far as I can dispose of the same by law, after she arrives at the above age of fifteen years complete—Surrogating and Substituting the said Gilbert Burns, my brother and his foresaids in my full right, title, room and place of the whole Premises, with power to him to intromit with, and dispose upon the same at pleasure, and in general to do every other thing in the Premises that I could have done myself—before granting hereof, but always with and under the conditions before expressed.—And I oblidge myself to warrand this disposition and assignation from my own proper fact and deed allenarly—Consenting to the Registration hereof in the Books of Council and Session, or any other Judges Books competent, therein to remain for preservation, and constitute . . . whereof I have Procutars, &c.—In witness whereof I have wrote and signed these presents, consisting of this and the preceding page, on stamped paper, with my own hand, at Mossgiel the twenty second day of July, one thousand seven hundred and eighty-six years.

Robert Burns

JAMES SMITH

Born in 1765, the son of a Mauchline merchant who was accidentally killed when the lad was ten years old, he was the brother of Jean Smith, one of the 'Mauchline Belles'. He had an excessively strict and repressive upbringing from his step-father, James Lamie, and it is hardly surprising that he later kicked over the traces. With Burns and Richmond he formed the infamous Court of Equity, 'a happy triumvirate in village revelry'. Smith had a drapery business in Mauchline, opposite Nanse Tinnock's, but later he went to Linlithgow where he entered a partnership in a calico firm. When this failed, about 1788, he emigrated to St. Lucia in the West Indies. Though Cromek speaks of him being dead in 1808, it is probable that he survived till 1823. Burns addressed his verse epistle 'Dear Smith, the sleest, pawkie thief' (C.W. p. 169) to him over the winter of 1785-86, and followed this with a series of letters in 1786-8. The first two, when Smith was still resident in Mauchline, bore Burns's jocular 'Monsr' in the address, a conceit which he often adopted in writing to his more intimate friends. The four later letters, addressed to Smith at the Avon printfield in Linlithgow, were more formally endorsed. This small group of letters is of particular interest for details of Burns's turbulent courtship of Jean Armour, revealing his unguarded thoughts on sex and marriage.

I (37)

twelve o'clock
[about 1st August 1786]

My friend,

I need not tell you the receipt of yours gave me pleasure.—

> O Jeany, thou hast stolen away my soul!
> In vain I strive against the lov'd idea:
> Thy tender image sallies on my thoughts,
> My firm resolves become an easy prey!*

Against two things however, I am fix'd as Fate: staying at home, and owning her conjugally.—The first, by Heaven I will not do! the last, by Hell I will never do!

The inclosed may divert you.—

A good God bless you, and make you happy up to the warmest, weeping wish of parting Friendship!

For me, I am witless wild, and wicked; and have scarcely any vestige of the image of God left me, except a pretty large portion of honour and an enthusiastic, incoherent Benevolence.—

If you see Jean tell her, I will meet her, So help me Heaven in my hour of need!

Farewell till tomorrow morning!

Robt Burns

*First line paraphrased from Addison: Cato, Act I, sc. 6; the rest is apparently Burns's own.

117

James Smith

II (40)

Monday morn
[14th August 1786]

My Dear Sir,

I went to Dr Douglas yesterday fully resolved to take the opportunity of Captain Smith; but I found the Doctor with a Mr and Mrs White, both Jamaicans, and they have derang'd my plans altogether.—They assure him that to send me from Savannah la Mar to Port Antonio will cost my Master, Charles Douglas, upwards of fifty pounds; besides running the risk of throwing myself into a pleuratic fever in consequence of hard travelling in the sun.—On these accounts, he refuses sending me with Smith for pas; but a vessel sails from Greenock the first of Sept:, right for the place of my destination; the Captain of her is an intimate of Mr Gavin Hamilton's, and as good a fellow as heart could wish: with him I am destined to go.—Where I shall shelter, I know not, but I hope to weather the storm.—Perish the drop of blood of mine that fears them! I know their worst, and am prepared to meet it—

> I'll laugh, an' sing, an' shake my leg,
> As lang's I dow.[1]

Thursday morning, if you can muster as much self denial as be out of bed about seven o'clock, I shall see you as I ride thro' to Cumnock.—

I could not write to Richmònd by Connel,[2] but I will write by the Kilmarnock Carrier.—After all, Heaven bless the Sex. I feel there is still happiness for me among them.—

> O woman, lovely woman sure Heaven design'd you,
> To temper Man. we had been brutes without you.[3]

Robt Burns

1 Burns: *Second Epsitle to John Laplaik* (C.W. p. 104).
2 The Mauchline carrier.
3 Otway: *Venice Preserved*, Act I, sc. I, altered.

III (113)

Mauchline, 11th June 1787

My ever dear Sir,

I date this from Mauchline, where I arrived on Friday even last. I slept at John Dows, and called for my daughter; Mr. Hamilton and family; your mother, sister and brother; my quondam Eliza[1], &c. all, all well. If any thing had been wanting to disgust me compleatly at Armour's family, their mean servile compliance would have done it.

Give me a spirit like my favourite hero, Milton's Satan,

James Smith

"Hail, horrors! hail,
Infernal world! and thou, profoundest Hell,
Receive thy new possessor! one who brings
A mind not to be chang'd by *place* or *time!*"[2]

I cannot settle to my mind—Farming the only thing of which I know any thing, and Heaven above knows, but little do I understand even of that, I cannot, dare not risk on farms as they are. If I do not fix, I will go for Jamaica. Should I stay, in an unsettled state, at home, I would only dissipate my little fortune, and ruin what I intend shall compensate my little ones, for the stigma I have brought on their names.

I shall write you more at large soon; as this letter costs you no postage, if it be worth reading you cannot complain of your penny worth.

I am ever, my dear Sir, yours,

Robert Burns

P.S. The cloot[3] has unfortunately broke, but I have provided a fine buffaloe horn, on which I am going to affix the same cypher which you will remember was on the lid of the cloot.

1 Elizabeth Paton, mother of 'Dear Bought Bess'.
2 *Paradise Lost*, Bk I, lines 250-3.
3 A division of a cow's cloven hoof, hence a snuff-box made from the same material.

IV (117)

[30th June 1787]

On our return, at a Highland gentleman's hospitable mansion, we fell in with a merry party, and danced 'till the ladies left us, at three in the morning. Our dancing was none of the French or English insipid formal movements; the ladies sung Scotch songs like angels, at intervals; then we flew at *Bab at the Bowster, Tullochgorum, Loch Erroch side,* &c. like midges sporting in the mottie sun, or craws prognosticating a storm in a hairst day.— When the dear lasses left us, we ranged round the bowl till the good-fellow hour of six; except a few minutes that we went out to pay our devotions to the glorious lamp of day peering over the towering top of Benlomond. We all kneeled; our worthy landlord's son held the bowl; each man a full glass in his hand; and I, as priest, repeated some rhyming nonsense, like Thomas a Rhymer's prophecies I suppose.—After a small refreshment of the gifts of Somnus, we proceeded to spend the day on Lochlomond, and reached Dumbarton in the evening. We dined at another good fellow's house, and consequently push'd the bottle; when we went out to mount our horses, we found ourselves "No vera

119

fou but gaylie yet."[1] My Two friends and I rode soberly down the Loch side, till by came a Highlandman at the gallop, on a tolerably good horse, but which had never known the ornaments of iron or leather. We scorned to be out-galloped by a Highlandman, so off we started, whip and spur. My companions, though seemingly gayly mounted, fell sadly astern; but my old mare, Jenny Geddes, one of the Rosinante[2] family, she strained past the Highlandman in spite of all his efforts, with the hair-halter: just as I was passing him, Donald wheeled his horse, as if to cross before me to mar my progress, when down came his horse, and threw his rider's breekless arse in a clipt hedge; and down came Jenny Geddes over all, and my bardship between her and the Highlandman's horse. Jenny Geddes trode over me with such cautious reverence, that matters were not so bad as might well have been expected; so I came off with a few cuts and bruises, and a thorough resolution to be a pattern of sobriety for the future.

I have yet fixed on nothing with respect to the serious business of life. I am, just as usual, a rhyming, mason-making, raking, aimless, idle fellow. However, I shall somewhere have a farm soon. I was going to say, a wife too; but that must never be my blessed lot. I am but a younger son of the house of Parnassus, and, like other younger sons of great families, I may intrigue, if I choose to run all risks, but must not marry.

I am afraid I have almost ruined one source, the principal one indeed, of my former happiness; that eternal propensity I always had to fall in love. My heart no more glows with feverish rapture. I have no paradisical evening interviews stolen from the restless cares and prying inhabitants of this weary world. I have only ****. This last is one of your distant acquaintances, has a fine figure, and elegant manners; and in the train of some great folks whom you know, has seen the politest quarters in Europe. I do like her a good deal; but what piques me is her conduct at the commencement of our acquaintance. I frequently visited her when I was in ————, and after passing regularly the intermediate degrees between the distant formal bow and the familiar grasp round the waist, I ventured in my careless way to talk of friendship in rather ambiguous terms; and after her return to ————, I wrote to her in the same style. Miss, construing my words farther I suppose than even I intended, flew off in a tangent of female dignity and reserve, like a mounting lark in an April morning, and wrote me an answer which measured me out very completely what an immense way I had to travel before I could reach the climate of her favour. But I am an old hawk at the sport; and wrote her such a cool, deliberate, prudent reply as brought my bird from her aerial towerings, pop, down at my foot like corporal Trim's hat.

James Smith

As for the rest of my acts, and my wars, and all my wise sayings, and why my mare was called Jenny Geddes, they shall be recorded in a few weeks hence at Linlithgow, in the chronicles of your memory, by

Robert Burns

1 David Herd: *Ancient and Modern Scottish Songs*, II, 121, *We're gayly yet*.
2 Jenny Geddes, heroine of the Covenant, who threw her footstool at Bishop Lindsay in St Giles Cathedral (1637). Rosinante was Don Quixote's horse.

V (237)

Mauchline 28th April 1788

Beware of your Strasburg*, my good Sir! Look on this as the opening of a correspondence, like the opening of a twenty four gun battery! —

There is no understanding a man properly, without knowing something of his previous ideas (that is to say if the Man has any ideas for I know many who in the Animal-muster pass for Men that are the scanty Masters of only one idea on any given subject, and by far the greatest part of your acquaintances and mine can barely boast of Ideas 1.25, 1.5, 1.75, or some such fractional matter) so to let you a little into the secrets of my Pericranium, there is, you must know, a certain clean-limb'd, handsome be-witching young Hussy of your acquaintance to whom I have lately and privately given a matrimonial title to my Corpus. —

"Bode a robe, and wear it;
"Bode a pock, and bear it,"

says the wise old Scots Adage! I hate to presage ill-luck; and as my girl in some late random trials has been *doubly* kinder to me than even the best of women usually are to their Partners of our Sex, in similar circumstances; I reckon on twelve times a brace of children against I celebrate my twelfth wedding-day: these twenty four will give me twenty four Gossipings, twenty four christenings (I mean, one equal to two) and I hope by the blessing of the God of my fathers to make them twenty four dutiful children to their Parents, twenty four useful Members of Society, and twenty four approven servants of their God; not to mention twenty four times a hundred and eighty two Mason-meetings on the business that I hope to have with their Mother into the bargain. —

"Light's heartsome," quo' the wife when she was stealing sheep: you see what a lamp I have hung up to lighten your paths, when you are idle enough to explore the combinations and relations

121

of my ideas.—'Tis now as plain as a pike-staff why a twenty four gun battery was a Metaphor I would readily employ.—

Now for business.—I intend to present Mrs Burns with a printed shawl, an article of which I dare say you have variety, 'tis my first present to her since I have *irrevocably* called her mine, and I have a kind of whimsical wish to get her the said first present from an old and much valued friend of hers & mine, a trusty Trojan on whose friendship I count myself possessed of a life-rent lease; Connel goes to Edinburgh next week, it will oblidge me un-speakably if you will transmit by him the shawl, or you may send it by *[two or three words missing]* in Ronald's quarters which I believe will be best.—The quality, let it be of the best; the Pattern I leave to your taste.—The money I'll pay to your sister, or transmit to any Correspondent of yours in Edinburgh or Glasgow. Look on this letter as a "beginning of sorrows": I'll write you till your eyes ache with reading nonsense.—

Mrs Burns ('tis only her private designation) begs her best Compli-ments to you.—

I am, My dear Sir,
ever most truly
yours Robt Burns

*Its pentagonal citadel, built in 1682-84, was a byword for an impregnable fortress.

VI (251)

Mauchline, 26th June 1788

This, my dear Sir, is now the third letter I have written you since I have heard from you, or more properly speaking, since I, viva voce, heard of you. This is merely a business scrawl, consequently, "I expect your answer in course of Post."—I have waited on Mr Auld about my Marraige affair, & stated that I was legally fined for an irregular marriage by a Justice of the Peace.—He says, if I bring an attestation of this by the two witnesses, there shall be no more litigation about it.—As soon as this comes to hand, please write me in the way of familiar Epistle that, "Such things are."—Direct to me at Mauchline.—Mrs Burns joins in kindest Compliments to you along with, my dear friend,

yours most truly
Robt Burns

JOHN LOGAN

Proprietor of Knockshinnoch in the parish of New Cumnock, he married Martha MacAdam of Laight and was latterly styled 'of Afton and Laight'. He died in 1816. He was a friend of Gavin Hamilton who introduced him to Burns, and subsequently distributed 20 copies of the Kilmarnock Edition, referred to in the first letter in this group. In later years Burns visited Logan on several occasions at Laight, during his travels to and from Ayrshire, and during one of them is believed to have composed *Afton Water* (C.W. p. 351)

I (39)

Kilmarnock, 10th August 1786

Sir,

I gratefully thank you for your kind offices in promoting my subscription, and still more for your very friendly letter.— The first was doing me a Favour, but the last was doing me an Honour.—I am in such a bustle at present, preparing for my West-India voyage, as I expect a letter every day from the Master of the vessel, to repair directly to Greenock; that I am under a necessity to return you the subscription bills, and trouble you with the quantum of Copies till called for, or otherwise transmitted to the Gentlemen who have subscribed. Mr Bruce Campbell is already supplied with two copies, and I here send you 20 copies more.—If any of the Gentlemen are supplied from any other quarter, 'tis no matter; the copies can be returned.

If orders from Greenock do not hinder, I intend doing myself the honour of waiting on you, Wednesday the 16th Inst.

I am much hurt, Sir, that I must trouble you with the Copies; but circumstanced as I am, I know no other way your friends can be supplied.

I have the honour to be, SIR,
your much indebted humble Servant

Robert Burns

II (356)

[With *The Kirk's Alarm.* C.W. p. 359]

Ellisland near Dumfries, 7th August 1789

Dear Sir,

I intended to have written you long ere now, and as I told you, I had gotten three stanzas and a half on my way in a poetic epistle to you; but that old enemy of all *good works*, the Devil, threw me into a Prosaic mire, and for the soul of me, I cannot get out of it.—I dare not write you a long letter, as I am going to intrude on

123

your time with a long Ballad.—I have, as you will shortly see, finished, "The KIRK'S ALARM:" but now that it is done, and that I have laughed once or twice at the conceits in some of the Stanzas, I am determined not to let it get into the Publick; so I send you this copy, the first I have sent to Ayr-shire except some few of the Stanzas which I wrote off in embrio for Gavin Hamilton, under the express provision and request—that you will only read it to a few of us, and do not on any account, give, or permit to be taken, any copy of the Ballad.—If I could be of any service to Dr McGill, I would do it though it should be at a much greater expence than irritating a few bigotted Priests; but as I am afraid, serving him in his present embarras is a task too hard for me, I have enemies enow, God knows, tho' I do not wantonly add to the number.—Still, as I think that there is some merit in two or three of the thoughts, I send it you as a small but sincere testimony how much and with what respectful esteem

I am, Dear Sir, your oblidged humble servant

Robt Burns

THOMAS CAMPBELL

Several farmers by the name of Campbell lived in the Cumnock area, and Thomas owned his small estate of Pencloe, in Glen Afton, about a mile south of the town of New Cumnock. Most of Burns's friendships in this area were made in 1788 when he was commuting between Mauchline and Ellisland; but, as the date on this letter indicates, his acquaintance with Thomas Campbell belonged to a much earlier period. The letter, face-tiously addressed to 'Monsr. Thomas Campbell', was sent care of a Mr Good, whose identity is not known. Mr Logan referred to in the text was John Logan of Afton, himself the recipient of a letter from Burns dated 7th August 1789 (see page 123).

41

Mr J. Merry's, Saturday morn:
[New Cumnock, 19th August 1786]

My Dear Sir,

I have met with few men in my life whom I more wished to see again than you, and Chance seems industrious to disappoint me of that pleasure.—I came here yesterday fully resolved to see you, and Mr Logan, at New Cumnock, but a conjuncture of circum-stances conspired against me.—Having an opportunity of sending you a line, I joyfully embrace it.—It is perhaps the last mark of our friendship you can recieve from me on this side of the Atlantic.—Farewel! May you be happy up to the wishes of parting Friendship!

Robt Burns

MRS CATHERINE GORDON STEWART OF STAIR

Daughter of Thomas Gordon of Afton and Stair, she married in 1770 a grandson of the Earl of Galloway, Alexander Stewart of Stair. General Stewart was an improving landowner and MP for the Stewartry of Kirkcudbright. His death in 1795 caused the by-election in which Burns gave his poetic support to Patrick Heron (C.W. p. 543-9). After her husband's death Mrs Stewart sold Stair House and built a new house named Afton Lodge where she died in 1818. Mrs Stewart was one of Burns's earliest patrons and the first letter in this group was addressed to her in September 1786, on the eve of the poet's impending departure to Jamaica when he sent her 'a parcel of Songs', now known as the Stair MS. Five years later he compiled for her the collection now known as the Afton Lodge MS, preserved in the Birthplace Museum at Alloway, and included a prefatory note and dedication.

I (47)

[September, 1786]

Madam,

The hurry of my preparations for going abroad, has hindered me from performing my promise so soon as I intended.—I have here sent you a parcel of Songs, &c. which never made their appearance except to a friend or two at most.—Perhaps some of them may be no great entertainment to you; but of that I am far from being an adequate judge. The song* to the tune of Ettrick banks, you will easily see the impropriety of exposing much, even in manuscript.—I think, myself, it has some merit; both as a tolerable description of one of Nature's sweetest scenes, a July evening; & one of the finest pieces of Nature's workmanship, the finest indeed we know any thing of, an amiable, beautiful young woman: but I have no common friend to procure me that permission, without which I would not dare to spread the copy.—

I am quite aware, Madam, what task the world would assign me in this letter.—The obscure Bard, when any of the Great condescend to take notice of him, should heap the altar with the incense of flattery.—Their high Ancestry, their own great & godlike qualities & actions, should be recounted with the most exaggerated description.—This, Madam, is a task for which, I am altogether unfit.—Besides a certain disqualifying pride of heart; I know nothing of your connections in life, & have no access to where your real character is to be found—the company of your compeers; & more, I am afraid that even the most refined adulation, is by no means the road to your good opinion.—

One feature of your character I shall ever with grateful pleasure remember, the reception I got when I had the honor of waiting on you at Stair.—I am little acquainted with Politeness, but I know a good deal of benevolence of temper & goodness of heart. Surely, did those in exalted stations know how happy they could make some classes of the Inferiors by condescension & affability, they would never stand so high, measuring out with every look the height of their elevation, but condescend as sweetly as did Mrs Stewart of Stair.

*A song I had written on Miss Wilhelmina Alexander of Ballochmyle Vide, following letter [*Burns's note*].

II (477)

[Ellisland, October 1791]

Many Verses on which an Author would by no means rest his reputation, in print, may yet amuse an idle moment, in manuscript; and many Poems from the locality of the Subject, may be unentertaining or unintelligble to those who are strangers to that locality.—Most of, if not all the following Poems are in one or other of those predicaments; and the Author begs whoever into whose hands they may fall, that they will do him the justice not to publish what he himself thought proper to suppress.—

R.B.

To Mrs General Stewart of Afton—

The first person of her sex & rank that patronised his humble lays, this manuscript collection of Poems is presented, with the sincerest emotions of grateful respect, by—

The Author—

THE REV. ARCHIBALD LAWRIE

Born in 1768, the son of the Rev. George Lawrie of Loudoun, he was educated at Edinburgh University and became his father's assistant in 1793 succeeding him as minister in 1799. He continued to minister to Loudoun parish, at Newmilns, till his death in 1837. In 1794 he married Anne, sister of Dr. James McKittrick Adair whose wife, Charlotte Hamilton, was one of the poet's heroines and frequently mentioned in the letters to Margaret Chalmers. Lawrie was still at Newmilns when Burns first wrote to him, but some of the later letters were written to Lawrie at his lodgings in Edinburgh where he seems to have been a convivial companion. The last of them, incidentally, was addressed entirely in French — 'Monsr Archibd Lowrie, Colline de St Margaret' (St. Margaret's Hill was the name of the Loudoun Manse). The liberal use of French and Latin in these letters shows Burns's determination to be as 'lettered' as his university friend. The correspondence, however, does not seem to have continued beyond Lawrie's student days. On his return to Loudoun Lawrie doubtless developed into a serious divine.

I (54)

Mossgiel, 13th November 1786

Dear Sir,

I have along with this sent the two Volumes of Ossian, with the remaining Vol. of the Songs. Ossian I am not in such a hurry about; but I wish the Songs, with the Vol. of the Scotch Poets, returned as soon as they can conveniently be dispatched. If they are left at Mr. Wilson, the Bookseller's shop, Kilmarnock, they will easily reach me.

My most respectful compliments to Mr. and Mrs. Lowrie; and a poet's warmest wishes for their happiness to the young ladies; particularly the fair Musician, whom I think much better qualified than ever David was, or could be, to charms an evil spirit out of a Saul.*

Indeed, it needs not the feelings of a Poet to be interested in the welfare of one of the sweetest scenes of domestic Peace and kindred Love that ever I saw; as I think the peaceful unity of St. Margaret's hill can only be excelled'd by the harmonious concord of the Apocalyptic Zion.

I am, dear Sir, yours sincerely,

Robt Burns

*I Samuel 16:23.

II (83)

Lawn Market, Mond; noon [February? 1787]

Mon cher Monsieur

As tonight the Grand Master and Lodge of Masons appear at the Theatre in form, I am determined to go to the play.—I am afraid it will be impossible to form a Partie with our female

127

friends for this night, but I shall call on you a few minutes before the Theatre opens, when if Miss Lowrie can I shall be very happy; if not, I suppose you will have no objection to take a seat in the Pit with,

toujours le votre

R. Burns

III (92)

Sat. noon

Dear Sir,

I cannot be with you at tea tonight, as I have just now got a summons to wait on Lord Glencairn in the afternoon.—I expect to do myself the pleasure of calling on you between seven & eight.—I have wrote to Dr Blacklock, and sent him your direction and have promised to meet him at your house.—

Robt Burns

IV (127)

Edinburgh, 14th August 1787

My dear Sir,

Here am I—that is all I can tell you of that unaccountable BEING — Myself.—What I am doing, no mortal can tell; what I am thinking, I myself cannot tell; what I am usually saying, is not worth telling.—The clock is just strking, one, two, three, four, ——, ——, ——, ——, ——, ——, ——, twelve, forenoon; and here I sit, in the Attic story, alias, the garret, with a friend on the right hand of my standish—a friend whose kindness I shall largely experience at the close of this line—there—thank you—A Friend, my dear Mr Lowrie, whose kindness often makes me blush; A Friend who has more of the milk of human kindness than all the human race put together, and what is highly to his honor, peculiarly a friend to the friendless as often as they come in his way, in short, Sir, he is, without the least alloy, a universal Philanthropist; and his much beloved name is A BOTTLE OF GOOD OLD PORT! In a week, if whim and weather serve, I shall set out for the North, a tour to the Highlands.—

I ate some Newhaven broth, in other words, boiled mussles with Mr Farquhar's family t'other day—Now I see you prick up your ears—They are all well and Madamoiselle is particularly well.— She begs her respects to you all; along with which, please present those of your humble servant.—

BURNS AT THE HOUSE OF FRANCIS GROSE by R. Scott Lauder

Mauchline Octr 18th 1783

Sir

As you were pleased to give us the offer of a private bargain of your cows you intend
for sale, my brother & I this day took a look
of them and a friend with us on whose
judgement we could something depend to
enable us to form an estimate — If you are
still intending to let us have them in that
way, please appoint a day that we may wait
on you and either agree amongst ourselves
or else fix on men to whom we may refer
it, tho' I hope we will not need any reference.

I am
Sir
your humble servt
Robert Burness

P.S.
whatever of your dairy utensils you intend
to dispose of we will probably purchase

Original Burns manuscript by courtesy of
Kilmarnock & Loudoun District Council Museums Department
see page 65.

I can no more.—I have so high a veneration or rather idolatrization for the cleric character, that even a little futurum esse vel fuisse Priestling in his Penna, pennae, pennae, &c. throws an awe over my mind in his presence, and shortens my sentences into single ideas.—

Farewell, and believe me to be ever,

My dear Sir,

yours

Robt Burns

V (286)

Mauchline, 15th November 1788

Dear Sir,

If convenient, please return me by Connel the bearer, the 2 volumes of Songs I left, last time I was at St. Margaret's hill.—My best Compliments to all the good family.—

A Dieu je vous commende!

Robt Burns

MRS FRANCES ANNA DUNLOP OF DUNLOP

Eldest daughter of Sir Thomas Wallace of Craigie, who claimed descent from Sir Richard, cousin of Sir William Wallace of Elderslie, the great Scottish patriot, she was born in 1730. At the age of seventeen she eloped with John Dunlop of Dunlop, 27 years her senior. During the 37 years of her marriage she bore seven sons and six daughters. By the deaths of the mother (in 1761) and father (in 1774) she fell heir to the estates of Lochryan and Craigie respectively, but the latter passed to her eldest surviving son, Thomas Wallace who took his grandfather's surname on succeeding to the baronetcy. The young Sir Thomas married Eglintoune Maxwell (sister of the Duchess of Gordon) against his mother's wishes and by profligacy and mismanagement became so deeply in debt that the ancestral estate of Craigie had to be sold. As a result, Mrs Dunlop became estranged from her son when the estate was sold in 1783, and her distress was aggravated by the death of her husband two years later. In the autumn of 1786 her mind was, she says, 'in a state which, had it long continued, my only refuge would inevitably have been a madhouse or a grave; nothing interested or amused me; all around me served to probe a wound whose recent stab was mortal to my peace, and had already ruined my health and benumbed my senses.'

At this juncture she was given a copy of *The Cotter's Saturday Night* (C.W. p. 147) by Miss Betty McAdam, and was so moved by its noble sentiments that she wrote to Burns, ordering six copies of the Kilmarnock Edition. This was the beginning of a literary correspondence which gradually deepened into genuine friendship and endured until the end of 1794, when Burns gave grave offence by his outspoken condemnation of King Louis XVI and Queen Marie Antoinette of France (see letter LXXIV). Prior to that time, Burns had upset Mrs Dunlop by his outspoken support for the French Revolution. Four of her sons and a grandson were, or had been, Army officers and two of her daughters had married French royalist *emigres*, so it was singularly tactless of Burns to ignore the views which she expressed in many of her letters from 1792 onwards. Burns seems to have been oblivious of her outraged feelings, but his letter of 31st January 1796 hints at his unease: 'These many months you have been two packets in my debt.—What sin of ignorance I have committed against so highly a valued friend I am utterly at a loss to guess.' Even this appeal remained unanswered, adding a special poignancy to Burns's last letter to her, written barely ten days before his death. On 20th July 1796 Mrs Dunlop wrote to Gilbert seeking news of his brother, and, according to Currie, she did, in fact, reply to Burns shortly before he died. This appears to be confirmed by a letter by John Lewars to Mrs Dunlop soon afterwards.

Burns visited Mrs Dunlop on at least five occasions: in June 1787, February 1788 (when he stayed two days), May 1789 (two days), 21st June 1791 (at the time of Gilbert's wedding) and December 1792 (a four-day visit with Dr Adair). The contrast between the free-thinking young peasant poet and the rather conservative, middle-aged gentlewoman could hardly have been greater, yet a bond partly literary and partly of genuine affection was to develop between them, severed only by Burns's intemperate language.Mrs Dunlop saw her role as self-appointed critic. 'I have been told Voltaire read all his manuscripts to an old woman and printed nothing but what she would have approved. I wish you would name me to her office', she wrote to Burns who, though he never actually gave her this role, tolerated her patronising and criticism with a fair degree of good humour. Interestingly, Mrs Dunlop also gave Burns advice on possible choices of career, and weighed up the possibilities, which included an Army commission, the Salt Office and even professorship of Agriculture at Edinburgh University! After a time the correspondence settled down to a more desultory routine. Reading between the lines of Mrs Dunlop's letters, we get the feeling that the old lady was sometimes annoyed that Burns did not always reply as promptly as she would have wished, or pay close enough attention to the contents. For his part, however, Burns valued her frank and commonsense advice in general though he often discreetly overlooked her well-meant but frequently unsound literary counsel. Burns wrote more letters to her, and over a longer time-span, than to any other correspondent. The correspondence, however, began to deteriorate late in 1792, after Mrs Dunlop began expressing concern over the spread of the revolutionary spirit in Ayrshire. Subsequently she had to reprove him for writing 'improperly' to her. When he sent her his *Ode for General Washington's Birthday* (C.W. p. 515) in June 1794, she replied in September, observing that, while she too had once been fond of the theme of Liberty 'your Goddess has behaved in such a way as to injure her reputation, and acquire so very bad a name, that I find it no longer fit to acknowledge my favor for her. . . she is too much attached of late to the society of butchers . . .' a pointed reference to the Terror arising out of the French Revolution. Burns ignored this warning, and his violent remarks about the late King and Queen of France (12th January 1795) were the last straw. Nevertheless, possibly the last words Burns ever read were her message of reconciliation penned in July 1796.

She herself survived Burns by nineteen years, dying in the year of the Battle of Waterloo. Both sides of the correspondence were published in 1898 under the title of *Robert Burns and Mrs Dunlop* by her descendant, William Wallace.

1 (55)

Mossgiel, 15th November 1786

Madam,

I am truly sorry I was not at home yesterday when I was so much honored with your order for my Copies, and incomparably more so by the handsome compliments you are pleased to pay my poetic abilities.—I am fully persuaded that there is not any class of Mankind so feelingly alive to the titillations of applause as the Sons of Parnassus; nor is it easy to conceive how the heart of the poor Bard dances with rapture, when Judges honor him with their approbation.—

Had you been thoroughly acquainted with me, Madam, you could not have touched my darling heart-chord more sweetly, than by noticing my attempts to celebrate your illustrious Ancestor, the SAVIOUR OF HIS COUNTRY—

"Great Patriot hero! ill-requited Chief!"[1]

The first books I met with in my early years, which I perused with pleasure, were, the lives of Hannibal, and Sir William Wallace.—For several of my earlier years, I had few other Authors; and many a solitary hour have I stole out, after the laborious vocations of the day, to shed a tear over their glorious but unfortunate Story.—In those boyish days, I remember in particular, being much struck with that part of Wallace's history where these lines occur—

"Syne to the Leglen wood when it was late
"To make a silent and a safe retreat" —[2]

I chose a fine summer Sunday, the only day of the week in my power and walked half a dozen miles to pay my respects to the "Leglen wood," with as much devout enthusiasm as ever Pilgrim did to Lorreto; and as I explored every den and dell where I could suppose my heroic Countryman to have sheltered, I recollect (for even than I was a Rhymer) that my heart glowed with a wish to be able to make a Song on him equal to his merits.—

I have only been able to send you five Copies: they are all I can command.—I am thinking to go to Edinburgh in a week or two at farthest, to throw off a second Impression of my book: but on my return, I shall certainly do myself the honor to wait on you, and thank you in person for the obliding notice you have been pleased to take of.

Madam,
your much indebted
and very humble servant
Robert Burns

1   Thomson: *Autumn*, line 899.
2   William Hamilton of Gilbertfield's recension of Blind Harry's *History of Sir William Wallace*, Bk II, chap. I, lines 11-12, misquoted.

II (78)

Edinburgh, 15th January 1787

Madam,

Yours of the 9th current, which I am this moment honoured with, is a deep reproach to me for ungrateful neglect. I will tell you the real truth, for I am miserably awkward at a fib: I wished to have written Dr. Moore before I wrote to you; but though, every day since I received yours of Dec. 30, the idea, the wish to write to him, has constantly pressed on my thoughts, yet I could not for my soul set about it. I know his fame and character, and I am one of "the sons of little men." To write him a mere matter-of-fact affair, like a merchant's order, would be disgracing the little character I have; and to write the author of *The View of Society and Manners,* a letter of sentiment—I declare every artery runs cold at the thought. I shall try, however, to write to him to-morrow or next day.. His kind interposition in my behalf I have already experienced, as a gentleman waited on me the other day, on the part of Lord Eglinton, with ten guineas, by way of sub-scription for two copies of my next edition.

The word you object to in the mention I have made of my glorious countryman and your immortal ancestor, is indeed borrowed from Thomson; but it does not strike me as an improper epithet. I distrusted my own judgment on your finding fault with it, and applied for the opinion of some of the Literati here, who honour me with their critical strictures, and they all allow it to be proper. The song you ask, I cannot recollect, and I have not a copy of it. I have not composed any thing on the great Wallace, except what you have seen in print, and the inclosed, which I will print in this edition. You will see I have mentioned some others of the name. When I composed my *Vision* long ago, I had attempted a description of Koyle, of which the additional stanzas are a part, as it originally stood. My heart glows with a wish to be able to do justice to the merits of the *Saviour of his Country,* which, sooner or later, I shall at least attempt.

You are afraid I shall grow intoxicated with my prosperity as a poet. Alas! Madam, I know myself and the world too well. I do not mean any airs of affected modesty; I am willing to believe that my abilities deserved some notice; but in a most enlightened, informed age and nation, when poetry is and has been the study of men of the first natural genius, aided with all the powers of polite learning, polite books, and polite company- to be dragged forth to the full glare of learned and polite observation, with all my imperfections of awkward rusticity and crude unpolished ideas on my head—I assure you, Madam, I do not dissemble when I tell you I tremble for the consequences. The novelty of a poet in my obscure situation, without any of those advantages which are reckoned necessary for that character, at least at this time of day, has raised a partial tide of public notice, which has borne me to a height where I am absolutely feelingly certain my abilities are inadequate to support me; and too surely do I see that time when the same tide will leave me, and recede, perhaps, as far below the mark of truth. I do not say this in the ridiculous affectation of self-abasement and modesty. I have studied myself, and know what ground I occupy; and, however a friend or the world may differ from me in that particular, I stand for my own opinion, in silent resolve, with all the tenaciousness of property. I mention this to you, once for all, to disburthen my mind, and I do not wish to hear or say more about it—But

> "When proud fortune's ebbing tide recedes,"*

you will bear me witness, that, when my bubble of fame was at the highest, I stood, unintoxicated, with the inebriating cup in my hand, looking forward with rueful resolve to the hastening time when the blow of Calumny should dash it to the ground, with all the eagerness of vengeful triumph.

*   *   *   *   *

Your patronising me, and interesting yourself in my fame and character as a poet, I rejoice in; it exalts me in my own idea; and whether you can or cannot aid me in my subscription, is a trifle. Has a paltry subscription-bill any charms to the heart of a bard, compared with the patronage of the descendant of the immortal Wallace?

*Shenstone: *Elegy VII*, stanza 19.

Mrs Frances Anna Dunlop of Dunlop

III (90)

Edinburgh, 22nd March 1787

Madam,

When I was honoured with yours of the 26th February, I likewise received one from Dr Moore, where he informed me that he
had upon the way to Scotland his medical treatise, and his sketch
of Society and manners; the first he desired me to transmit to
you, the last he has done me the honor to present me with.– I
delayed writing you till the books should arrive, which they did
yesterday; and the first Carrier for your country-side I shall
send yours.–

I read your letter, Madam, with watery eyes.–A little, very little
while ago, I had scarce a friend but the stubborn pride of my own
bosom; now I am distinguished, patronised, befriended by
YOU.–Your friendly advices, I will not give them the cold name
of criticisms, I receive with reverence.–I have made some small
alterations in what I before had printed.–I have the advice of
some very judicious friends among the Literati here, but with
them I sometimes find it necessary to claim the priviledge of
thinking for myself.–The noble Earl of Glencairn, to whom I owe
more than to any man of earth, does me the honor of giving me
his strictures: his hints, with respect to impropriety or indelicacy,
I follow implicitly.–

You kindly interest yourself, my honored Patroness, in my future
views and prospects; then I can give you no light. It is all—

> "Dark as was Chaos ere the infant sun
> "Was roll'd together, or had try'd his beams
> "Athwart the gloom profound"—*

The appellation of a Scotch Bard is by far my highest pride; to
continue to deserve it is my most exalted ambition.—Scottish
scenes, and Scottish story are the themes I could wish my power,
unplagu'd with the routine of business, for which Heaven knows
I am unfit enough, to make leisurely pilgrimages through
Caledonia; to sit on the fields of her battles; to wander on the
romantic banks of her rivers; and to muse by the stately tower or
venerable ruins, once the honored abodes of her heroes.–

But these are all Utopian ideas: I have dallied long enough with
life; 'tis time to be in earnest.—I have a fond, aged Mother to care
for; and some other bosom-ties, perhaps equally tender.—Where
the Individual only suffers by the consequences of his own
thoughtlessness, indolence or folly, he may be excusable; nay
shining abilities, and some of the nobler virtues may half sanctify
the character; but where God and Nature have entrusted the welfare of others to his care, those whose weal or woe must depend
upon his, where the trust is sacred and the ties are dear, that man

must be far gone in unfeeling selfishness, or strangely lost to reflection and thought, whom these connections will not rouse to active attention and serious resolve.—

I guess that I shall clear between two and three hundred pounds by my Authorship; with that sum I intend, so far as I may be said to have any intention, to return to my old acquaintance, the plough, and, if I can meet with a lease by which I can live, to commence Farmer.—I do not intend to give up Poesy: being bred to labor secures me independance, and the Muses are my chief, sometimes have been my only enjoyment. — If my practice second my resolution, I shall have principally at heart the serious business of life; but while following my plough or building up my shocks, I shall cast a leisure glance to that dear, that only feature of my character which gave me the notice of Caledonia, and the patronage of a Wallace.—

Thus, honored Madam, I have given you the Bard, his situation and his views, native as they are in his own bosom.—An integritive character, honest pride, and my poetic fame, will, I hope, ever ensure my welcome with those whose esteem I value: the trappings and luxuries of upper stations, I have seen a little of them in Edinburgh—I can live without them.—I shall never blush for my own poverty, nor the poverty of my Country.—

> I am, with the sincerest throe of gratitude,
> Madam your much indebted, humble servant
> Robert Burns

P.S. I have today corrected the last proof sheet of my poems and have now only the Glossary and subscribers names to print. Printing this last is much against my will, but some of my friends whom I do not chuse to thwart will have it so.—I have both a second and a third Edition going on as the second was begun with too small a number of copies.—The whole I have printed is three thousand.—Would the profits of that afford it, with rapture I would take your hint of a military life, as the most congenial to my feelings and situation of any other, but, "What is wanting cannot be numbered."

> R.B.

* Blair: *The Grave*, lines 14-16.

IV (94)

Edinburgh, 15th April 1787

Madam,

There is an affectation of gratitude which I dislike.—The periods of Johnson and the pauses of Sterne may hide a selfish heart. For my part, Madam, I trust I have too much pride for servility, and too little prudence for selfishness.—I have this moment broke open your letter, but,

"Rude am I in Speech—
"And therefore little can I grace my cause
"In speaking for myself—"*

so shall not trouble you with any fine speeches and hunted figures.—I shall just lay my hand on my heart and say, I hope I will ever have the truest, the warmest sense of your goodness.

I come abroad in print, for certain, on Wednesday. Your orders I shall punctually attend to; only, by the way, I must tell you that I was paid before for Dr. Moore's & Miss Williams' copies through the medium of Commissioner Cochrane in this place, but that we can settle when I have the honor of waiting on you.—

Dr Smith was just gone to London the morning before I received your letter to him.—

I have the honor to be, Madam,
Your highly oblidged humble servant,
Robert Burns

* Based on *Othello*, Act I, sc. 3.

V (98)

Edinburgh, 30th April 1787

Madam,

I would not be capable of such an insult to you as to have sent the volumes in question to a woman who once bore the honored name of Lady Wallace.—There is a lady that I met with in town who I am told has a legal title to that designation, and I knew not of any other; but the lady discovered her and my mistake, and the other day returned the books, which you will receive by today's Carrier.—

Your criticism, Madam, I understand very well, and could have wished to have pleased you better.—You are right in your guesses that I am not very amenable to counsel.—Poets, much my superiors, have so flattered those who possessed the adventitious qualities of wealth and power that I am determined to flatter no created being, either in prose or verse, so help me God.—I set as little by kings, lords, clergy, critics, & c. as all these respectable Gentry do by my Bardship.—I know what I may expect from the world, by and by; illiberal abuse and perhaps contemptuous neglect: but I am resolved to study the sentiments of a very respectable Personage, Milton's Satan—"Hail horrors! hail, infernal world!*

I am happy, Madam, that some of my own favorite pieces are distinguished by your particular approbation.—For my DREAM which has unfortunately incurred your loyal displeasure, I hope in four weeks, or less, to have the honor of appearing, at Dunlop, in its defence in person.—

I have the honor to be, Madam,
your very highly indebted humble servant
Robt Burns

* *Paradise Lost*, Bk. I, lines 250-1.

VI (124)

Stewarton, 30th or 31st July 1787

I am sure, Madam, you have most effectually surprized me this morning.—Send your servant twenty miles to enquire for me! ! ! By all the towering flights of Pride; 'twas doing me an honor so far beyond my wildest expectation that for half a second the shadow of a Doubt eclipsed my belief, whether you might perhaps mean, to burlesque me.—I have indeed been ailing, but your verses have given my spirits a fillip for one day.—Without any Poetic licence, I assure you upon the honor of plain, unfettered, truth-delivering Prose, they are excellent.—I have a long letter to Dr Moore just ready to put into the Post Office, it is on a subject you have done me the honor to interest yourself in, so if you dare face twenty pages of an epistle, a reading of it is at your service.—I don't doubt but you will laugh at me; I know you will; and I insist on your taking that amusement at my expence, solely by yourself.—I am not bound to contribute at so dear a rate to the diversion of the rest of the family.—I have no copy of Dr Moore's letter, I mean the one I send him, so this you read must go to post.—If you can contrive a better way, I shall call for it myself tomorrow, as I am going for Edinburgh by way of Paisley & Glasgow, tomorrow morning.—

My most respectful Compliments to Lady Wallace, Miss Logan, who I heard at Ayr t'other day is at Dunlop, The Major & all your good family.—

I have the honor to be, with the highest respect and most sincere gratitude,

Madam, your much oblidged very humble servant
Robt Burns

VII (152A)

Edinburgh, 24th November 1787

Madam,

I will bear the reproaches of my conscience respecting this letter no longer.—I was indebted to you some time ago for a kind, long letter; (your letters, the longer the better) and again the other day I heard from you, enclosing a very friendly letter from Dr Moore. —I thought with myself in the height of my gratitude and pride of my remark that I would sit down some hour of inspiration, and write you a letter, at least worth twa groats; consequently you would have been a gainer, as you are so benevolent as bestow your epistolary correspondence on me, I am sure without the least idea of being paid *in kind*.—

When you talk of correspondence and friendship to me, Madam, you do me too much honor; but, as I shall soon be at my wonted leisure and rural occupation, if my remark on what I have read or seen, or any new rhyme I may twist, that is worth while, if such a letter, Madam, can give a person of your rank, information and abilities any entertainment, you shall have it with all my heart and soul.—

It requires no common exertion of good sense and Philosophy in persons of elevated rank, to keep a friendship properly alive with one much their inferior.—Externals, things totally extraneous of the man, steal upon the heart and judgments of almost, if not altogether, all mankind; nor do I know any more than one instance of a Man who fully and truly regards "all the world as a stage, and all the men and women merely Players",[1] and who, the dancing-school bow excepted only values these Players, the Dramatis Personae, who build Cities, or who rear hedges; who govern provinces, or superintend flocks, merely as they *act their parts*.—For the honor of Ayrshire, this Man is Professor Dugald Stewart of Catrine.—To him I might perhaps add another instance, a Popish Bishop [Geddes]; but I have outraged that gloomy Fury, Presbytereanism, enough already, though I don't spit in her lugubrious face by telling her that the first Cleric character I ever saw was a Roman Catholick.—

I ever could ill endure those surly cubs of "Chaos and old Night;"[2]—these ghostly beasts of prey, who foul the hallow'd ground of Religion with their nocturnal prowlings; but if the prosecution which I hear the Erebean Fanatics are projecting against my learned and truly worthy friend, Dr McGill, goes on, I shall keep no measure with the savages, but fly at them with the faulcons of Ridicule, or run them down with the bloodhounds of Satire, as lawful game, wherever I start them.—

I expect to leave Edinburgh in eight or ten days, and shall certainly do myself the honor of calling at Dunlop house as I return to Ayrshire.—

I have the honor to be, Madam,
your oblidged humble servant,
Robt Burns

1 Shakespeare: *As You Like It*, Act II, Sc. 7.
2 Milton: *Paradise Lost*, Bk I, line 543

Mrs Frances Anna Dunlop of Dunlop

VIII (184)

Edinburgh, 21st January 1788

After six weeks' confinement, I am beginning to walk across the room. They have been six horrible weeks, anguish and low spirits made me unfit to read, write, or think.

I have a hundred times wished that one could resign life as an officer resigns a commission: for I would not *take in* any poor, ignorant wretch, by *selling out*. Lately I was a sixpenny private; and, God knows, a miserable soldier enough: now I march to the campaign, a starving cadet; a little more conspicuously wretched.

I am ashamed of all this; for though I do want bravery for the warfare of life, I could wish, like some other soldiers, to have as much fortitude or cunning as to dissemble or conceal my cowardice.

As soon as I can bear the journey, which will be, I suppose about the middle of the next week, I leave Edinburgh, and soon after I shall pay my grateful duty at Dunlop house.

IX (198)

Edinburgh, 12th February 1788

The much respected Patroness of my early Muse certainly deserved a better return from me than to let her excellent, her kind letter remain so long unanswered.—Your elegant epistle, delivered, struck me so much, that I immediately made a private vow to give you a few verses on the subject; or at least, write you such a Post-sheet as would be a pennyworth at sixpence.—I have failed in both.—Some important business respecting my future days, and the miserable dunning and plaguing of Creech, has busied me till I am good for nothing.—Your criticisms and observations on the President's Elegy are just.—I am sick of writing where my bosom is not strongly interested.—Tell me what you think of the following? there, the *bosom* was perhaps a little *interested.*—

Clarinda, Mistress of my soul,
[C.W. p. 320]

Mr Schetky, the celebrated Musician, has done these lines the honor of setting them to music.—The following is a jeu d'esprit of t'other day, on a despairing Lover carrying me to see his Dulcinea—

Anna, thy charms my bosom fire,
[C.W. p. 306]

I don't know whether I have not, sometime or other, sent you my Epigram on Elphinstone's translation of, and commentaries on Martial, the famous Latin Poet—

> To Mr E—
> O thou, whom Poesy abhors;
> Whom Prose has turned out of doors!
> Heardst thou yon groan—proceed no further!
> 'Twas laurell'd Martial calling Murther!

I leave Edinburgh on saturday morning.—If my horse meet me at Glasgow, I will probably do myself the honor of calling at Dunlop-house.—

Some things, my revered Patroness, in your late letters hurt me: not that *you say them,* but that *you mistake me.*—Religion, my honored Madam, has not only been all my life my chief dependance, but my dearest enjoyment.—I have indeed been the luckless victim of wayward Follies; but, alas! I have ever been "more fool than knave."*—A Mathematician without Religion, is a probable character; an irreligious Poet, is a Monster.—I have been lately at Lady Wallace's and was delighted to find Miss Dunlop a daughter of the Mother: I shall call there again ere I leave town.—

I have the honor to be, Madam, your oblidged humble servant
Robt Burns

1 Shakespeare:*King Lear,* Act 1, sc. 4 (misquoted)

X (212)

Mossgiel, 29th February 1788

Madam,

I send you with this, Spencer, as I promised; and I already "rejoice with them that do rejoice"1 in anticipating the pleasure you will have in the fairy mazes of enchanted ground.—I return Belisarius2 to Miss Fanny, with my grateful thanks for one of the most glorious mental entertainments I ever enjoyed.—By the way, I suppose that hare-brain'd lady, Coila, is now about to move "in all the majesty of light."—

I think Miss Keith said she had never seen Gray's Poems: I send her a copy of them, which I beg she will do me the honor to accept of.—

The few days I have to spend at home are so hurried that I can only write a letter like a merchant's Order, and for some months to come yet, it must be so; but I look forward to the time when I shall have got into the routine of life, and then a correspondence with one or two friends will be, I hope, a great source of my happiness.—Allow me, Madam, to remind you of something like a promise of your continued favours in this way: this, I assure you, in the Presbyterean style, I ask of grace, not of debt.—

My most respectful compliments to your two young ladies.—

I have the honor to be, Madam,
your highly oblidged humble servant
Robt Burns

1 Romans 12:15.
2 Translated by Arthur Murphy, from the French of Jean-François Marmontel.

XI (219)

Mossgiel, 7th March 1788

Madam,

The last paragraph in yours of the 30th February affected me most, so I shall begin my answer where you ended your letter. That I am often a sinner with any little wit I have, I do confess; but I have taxed my recollection to no purpose to find out when it was employed against you. I hate an ungenerous sarcasm, a great deal worse than I do the devil; at least, as Milton describes him; and though I may be rascally enough to be sometimes guilty of it myself, I cannot endure it in others. You, my honoured friend, who cannot appear in any light but you are sure of being respectable—you can afford to pass by an occasion to display your wit, because you may depend for fame on your sense; or, if you choose to be silent, you know you can rely on the gratitude of many and the esteem of all; but God help us who are wits or witlings by profession, if we stand not for fame there, we sink unsupported!

I am highly flattered by the news you tell me of Coila. I may say to the fair painter who does me so much honour, as Dr. Beattie says to Ross the poet, of his muse Scota, from which, by the by, I took the idea of Coila: ('Tis a poem of Beattie's in the Scottish dialect, which perhaps you have never seen.)

> "Ye shak your head, but o' my fegs,
> Ye've set auld Scota on her legs:
> Lang had she lien wi' buffe [*for* beffs] and flegs,
>   Bombaz'd and dizzie,
> Her fiddle wanted strings and pegs,
>   Waes me, poor hizzie!"*

* Beattie: *To Mr. Alexander Ross at Lochlee, author of the Fortunate Shepherdess and other poems in the broad Scotch dialect*, Stanza 5.

Mrs Frances Anna Dunlop of Dunlop

XII (229)

Ayr, 26th March 1788

"Speak, Sister, is the deed done?"
"Long ago, long ago, long ago;
"Above twelve glasses since have run" 1

I have at last, my honored Friend, entered in the list of Country farmers.—I returned from Edinburgh on Saturday last, with my tack in my pocket; and since that time, I assure you, cares and business have occupied my every moment.—I have talked fondly of magnanimous resolution and persevering firmness, but every Declaimer talks of them: I wish to prove my claim to them by exertion.—I have given up all literary correspondence, all conversation, all reading (prose-reading) that is of the evapourating, dissipating kind.—My favorite quotation now, for I always have one, is from Young—

"On Reason build Resolve;
"That column of true majesty in Man"—2

I know you will be pleased with this; but were you as weak as most of the family of the Muses, you would be more pleased with what I am going to tell you.—I was one day, last time I was in Edinburgh, with Mr Mckenzie, the glorious Man of Feeling; and among other things, I read him such of your pieces as I thought proper, such of them as were quite general (they were the two I got from you when I last had the honor of being your guest) and he passed the highest enconiums on them.—He warmly begged leave to read them to Mrs Mckenzie, whose judgement he very deservedly highly values, and she admired them so much that she anxiously wished a copy; but this I positively declined.—If I had the pieces about me, I would mention to you the most admired lines.—

My letters, for some time to come, will be miserable scraps, and will not be worth half a glance except to such as you who honor me so much in interesting yourself in all that concerns me.—

My most respectful Compliments to all your family; the kind Tutoress of my friend Coila, deserves my particular acknowledgements.—The happiest night by much, of all I spent last in Edinburgh, was one at Lady Wallace's.—

I have the honor to be, Madam,
your ever grateful humble servant
Robt Burns

1 Not identified.
2 *Night Thoughts*, Night I, lines 30-1.

142

Mrs Frances Anna Dunlop of Dunlop

XIII (233)

Mauchline, 31st March 1788

I am truly sorry to tell you, Madam, that I fear it will not be in my power to meet you at the Mount on Sunday.—To come to Dunlop is impracticable; but I would earnestly wish, and will try to meet you at the old Major's.—

If you go on, Madam, in the same style of Complimenting me on the pleasure my correspondence gives you, you will bar my pen altogether.—Now that I am often—"Crazed with care,"[1] my letters will be

"like a twice-told tale,
"Vexing the dull ear of a drousy man"—[2]

I claim the kind promise of your correspondence as a priviledge, as an honor; and am never better pleased than when I see a letter from you, wrote out till there is hardly blank paper enough to close it.—

The Poems I promised you, I must confess debt and crave days.— Till Whitsunday I shall be immersed in business, partly my own, and partly on account of some near and dear friends, that I will not have a spare moment.—I will not speak a word about your present of the books.—Your kindness has already exhausted my every various expression of gratitude; and for this last instance, I am determined to be silent till I tax my invention for something new to say on the subject.—

I much fear I will not be able to meet you on Sunday, but I'll try.—

I have the honor to be, most gratefully,
Madam,
your obliged, humble servant

Robt Burns

1 Gray: *Elegy in a Country Churchyard*, line 108.
2 Shakespeare: *King John*, Act II, sc. 4

XIV (238)

Mauchline, 28th April 1788

Madam,

Your powers of Reprehension must be great indeed, as I assure you they made my heart ach with penitential pangs, even tho' I was really not guilty.—As I commence Farmer at Whitsunday,

143

you will easily guess I must be pretty throng; but that is not all. As I got the offer of the Excise business without solicitation; and as it costs me only six weeks attendance for instructions to entitle me to a Commission; which Commission lies by me, and at any future period on my simple petition can be resumed; I thought five & thirty pounds a years was no bad dernier resort for a poor Poet, if fortune in her jade tricks should kick him down from the little eminence to which she has lately helped him up.—For this reason, I am at present attending these instructions to have them completed before Whitsunday. Still, Madam, I prepared with the sincerest pleasure to meet you at the Mount, and came to my brother's on Saturday night to set out on Sunday: but for some nights preceding I had slept in an apartment where the force of the winds and rains was only mitigated by being sifted thro' numberless apertures in the windows, walls, &c. in consequence I was on Sunday, Monday, & part of Tuesday unable to stir out of bed with all the miserable effects of a violent cold.—

You see, Madam, the truth of the French maxim, "Le vrai n'est toujours le vraisemblable."*—Your last was so full of expostulation, and was something so like the language of an offended friend, that I began to tremble for a Correspondence which I had with grateful pleasure set down as one of the greatest enjoyments of my future life.—You see the consequence of all this.—I like to sit down, when I write to a *Friend indeed,* and give way to the unpremeditated miscellaneous effusions of my heart; instead of which, my unlucky Cold has forced me on a drawling epistle of dull apologies, that can serve no positive good end, but negatively I trust, will prevent that excomunication from the much esteemed privileges of your friendship, which, in appearance I so justly deserved; & which I dread infinitely more than all the Anathemas of the Vatican, or the equally infallible General Assembly.—

As I hold this no letter, but what the Quarrel-Brokers, alias, the Lawyers, call, A Reply I shall trouble you with a letter by our Edinburgh Carrier, who I believe sets out next week.—

I shall be going & coming frequently to Ayrshire thro' the Summer; and if I am not so happy as meet you at Dunlop, I shall be in Edinburgh some time before Midsummer, when if the irresistible hand of Predestination do not interpose, I shall see you at Haddington.—Your books have delighted me: Virgil, Dryden & Tasso were all equally strangers to me; but of this more in my next.—

I have the honor to be, Madam,
your much indebted humble servant
Robt Burns

---

1   Nicolas Boileau-Despreaux: *L'Art poetique,* Canto 3, line 48, misquoted

XV (241)

Mauchline, 4th May 1788

Madam,

I laid in a stock of apologies in my last which I intend shall serve me for the Season; so in this, and my future letters, I shall be brief or diffuse, witty or dull, as Time, genius, spirits, and the other auxiliaries of Composition, befriend me, without any kind of preface or preamble till the said stock of apologies are exhausted.—

Dryden's Virgil has delighted me.—I don't know whether the critics will agree with me, but the Georgics are to me by far the best of Virgil.—It is indeed a species of writing entirely new to me; and has filled my head with a thousand fancies of emulation: but alas! when I read the Georgics, and then survey my own powers, 'tis like the idea of a Shetland Pony drawn up by the side of a thorough bred Hunter, to start for the Plate.—

I own I am disappointed in the Eneid.—Faultless correctness may please, and does highly please the lettered Critic; but to that aweful character I have not the most distant pretentions.— I don't know whether I do not hazard my pretentions to be a Critic of any kind, when I say that I think Virgil, in many instances, a *servile* Copier of Homer.—If I had the Odyssey by me, I could parallel many passages where Virgil has evidently copied, but by no means improved Homer.—Nor can I think there is any thing of this owing to the Translators; for, from every thing I have seen of Dryden, I think him, in genius and fluency of language, Pope's master.—I have not perused Tasso enough, to form an opinion: in some future letter, you shall have my ideas of him; tho' I am conscious my criticisms must be very inaccurate and imperfect, as *there* I have ever felt & lamented my want of Learning most.—

I send you the inclosed Bagatelles by way of a sin-offering for past offences.—

My old Direction, at Mauchline, will find me for two or three weeks to come.—

> I have the honor to be,
> Madam, your oblidged humble servant,
> Robt Burns

XVI (244)

Mauchline, 27th May 1788

Madam,

I have been torturing my Philosophy to no purpose, to account for that kind Partiality of yours, which, unlike every other of my Patronesses & Patrons in upper life, has followed me in my return to my native shade of life, with assiduous benevolence.—Often did I regret in the fleeting hours of my late Will-o'-wisp appearance that, "Here I had no continuing city;"* and, but for the material consolation of a few solid guineas, could almost lament the time that a momentary acquaintance with Wealth & Splendour put me so much out of conceit with the sworn companions of my road through Life—Insignificance & Poverty.—

It is so common with Poets when their Patrons try their hand at a Rhyme, to cry up the Honorable or Right Honorable performance as Matchless; Divine, &c. that I am afraid to open my mouth respecting your Poetic Extempores that you occasionally favor me with: I will only say, you cannot oblidge me more than sending them me.—For my own part, I have extensive rhyming Projects in my head, but at present cannot for my soul tag a Stanza.—

29th—

There are few circumstances relating to the unequal distribution of the good things of this life that give me more vexation (I mean in what I see around me) than the Importance that the GREAT bestow on their trifles & small matters in family affairs, compared with the same, the very same things on the contracted Scale of a Cottage.—Last afternoon I had the honor to spend an hour or two at a good woman's fireside, where the homely planks that composed the floor were decorated with a splendid Carpet, and the gay table sparkled with Silver & China.—'Tis now about term day, and there has been a revolution among those creatures who, tho' in appearance, Partakers & equally noble Partakers of the same Nature with Madame; yet are from time to time, their nerves, their sinews, their health, strength, wisdom, experience, genius, time, nay a good part of their very thoughts, sold for months & years, anxious Drudges, sweating, weary slaves, not only to the necessities, the conveniences, but the Caprices of the IMPORTANT FEW.— We talk'd of the insignificant Creatures; nay, notwithstanding their general stupidity & Rascality, did some of the poor devils the honor to commend them—But, light be turf upon his breast who taught—"Reverence Thyself!" we looked down on the upolished Wretches, their impertinent wives and clouterly brats, as the lordly Bull does on the little, dirty Ant-hill, whose puny inhabitants he crushes in the carelessness of his ramble, or tosses in air in the wantonness of his pride.—

I return you the Poem with my thanks for the perusal.—Alas, Madam! the very ingenious Author deserves a better friend than the Press.—I feel most truly for him, but no writing in this our day will take, except very transcendant excellence indeed, or Novelty.—

Mrs Frances Anna Dunlop of Dunlop

I have often had it in my head to write to you in my miscellaneous way, a paragraph or sheet now & then as the spirit moves me; but with all my loyalty for his most sacred & most sapient Majesty, George 3d, By the grace of God, REX—I hate & abhor his exorbitant Postages.—

My old Direction—at Mauchline, will find me.—

I have the honor to be most gratefully
Madam, your humble servant
Robt Burns

Do, let me know when my brother Farmer's family increases.
R.B.

*From Hebrews 13:14.

XVII (247)

Ellesland, 13th June 1788

"Where'er I roam, whatever realms I see,
"My heart, untravell'd, fondly turns to thee;
"Still to my Friend it turns with ceaseless pain,
"And drags at each remove a lengthen'd chain"—[1]

This is the second day, my honored Friend, that I have been on my farm.—A solitary Inmate of an old, smoky 'SPENCE'; far from every Object I love or by whom I am belov'd, nor any acquaintance older than yesterday except Jenny Geddes the old mare I ride on; while uncouth Cares and novel Plans hourly insult my aukward Ignorance & bashful Inexperience.—There is a foggy Atmosphere native to my soul in the hour of care, consequently the dreary Objects seem larger than the life.— Extreme Sensibility, irritated and prejudiced on the gloomy side by a series of Misfortunes & Disappointments at that period of my existence when the soul is laying in her cargoe of ideas for the voyage of Life, is, I believe the principal cause of this unhappy frame of mind.—

"The valiant, in himself, what can he suffer?
"Or what need he regard his *single* woes?
"But when, alas, he multiplies himself
"To dearer Selves, to the lov'd, tender Fair,
"To those whose bliss whose beings hang upon him,
"To helpless children! then, O then! he feels
"The point of misery festering in his heart,
"And weekly weeps his fortune like a coward!"[2]

To excuse my long quotation, I must inform you, Madam, that your surname is just; I am indeed A HUSBAND. This information I from my inmost soul wished to give you but till you yourself should mention it, I did not know how to do it.—I found a once much-loved and still much lov'd Female, literally & truly cast out

147

to the mercy of the naked elements, but as I enabled her to *purchase* a shelter; and there is no sporting with a creature's happiness or misery.—The most placid good-nature & sweetness of disposition; a warm heart, gratefully devoted with its powers to love one; vigorous health & sprightly chearfulness, set off to the best advantage by a more than common handsome figure; these, I think, in a woman, may make a tolerable good wife, though she should never have read a page but The Scriptures of the Old & New Testament, nor have "danced in a brighter Assembly than a Penny-pay Wedding.—"

I have lately been at Dunlop, where, among other good company I met my old Acquaintance, Coila.—I am highly pleased with her.—The expression in the face; the adjustment of her head, particularly her own holly wreath; the tout ensemble of her attitude & air, especially her holding the wreath she is about to bestow are in my poor opinion admirably executed.—Some of your good family deserve to be lampoon'd for their prejudices against her.—A few things I ventur'd to hint at as rather imperfect, all which I saw, in a second call I made at Dunlop on tuesday last, are in a fair way of emulating the best finished parts of the work.—On the whole, it is such a high gratification to my vanity as none but an Author can have any idea of.—

Please keep my old Direction, "at Mauchline," as I will be there pretty often.—

I have the honor to be, Madam,
your ever grateful humble servant,
Robt Burns

1 Goldsmith: *The Traveller*, lines 6-10, slightly altered.
2 Thomson: *Edward and Eleanora*, Act IV, sc. 6.

XVIII (254)

Mauchline 10th August, 1788
[*Edinburgh Bishop mark* JY 17]
My much honored Friend,

Yours of the 24th June is before me.—I found it, as well as another valued friend—MY WIFE—waiting to welcome me to Ayrshire: I met both with the sincerest pleasure.—

When I write you, Madam, I do not sit down to answer every paragraph of yours, by echoing every sentiment—like, The faithful Commons of Great Britain, in parliament assembled, answering a speech from the best of Kings! I just write in the fulness of heart, and may perhaps be guilty of neglecting some of your kind enquiries—but not from your very odd reason that I do not read your letters.—All your epistles, for several months, have cost me nothing—except a deep-felt sentiment of respectful veneration, or a swelling throb of native Gratitude.—

Mrs Frances Anna Dunlop of Dunlop

Mrs Burns, Madam, is the identical woman who was the mother of twice twins to me in seventeen months.—When she first found herself—"As women wish to be who love their lords,"[1] as I lov'd her near to distraction, I took some previous steps to a private marriage.—Her Parents got the hint; and in detestation of my guilt of being a poor devil, not only forbade me her company & their house, but on my rumored West Indian voyage, got a warrant to incarcerate me in jail till I should find security in my about-to-be Paternal relation.—You know my lucky reverse of fortune.—On my eclatant return to Mauchline, I was made very welcome to visit my girl.—The usual consequences began to betray her; and as I was at that time laid up a cripple in Edinburgh, she was turned, literally turned out of doors, and I wrote to a friend to shelter her, till my return.—I was not under the least verbal obligation to her, but her happiness or misery were in my hands, and who could trifle with such a deposite?— To the least temptation to Jealousy or Infidelity, I am an equal stranger.—My preservative from the first, is the most thorough consciousness of her sentiments of honour, and her attachment to me; my antidote against the last, is my long & deep-rooted affection for her.—In housewife matters, of aptness to learn and activity to execute she is eminently mistress; and during my absence in Nithsdale, she is regularly & constantly apprentice to my Mother & Sisters in their dairy & other rural business.—In short, I can easily *fancy* a more agreable companion for my journey of Life, but, upon my honor, I have never *seen* the individual Instance!—You are right that a Bachelor state would have ensured me more friends; but, from a cause you will easily guess, conscious Peace in the enjoyment of my own mind, and unmistrusting Confidence in approaching my God, would seldom have been of the number. The Muses must not be offended when I tell them, the concerns of my wife & family will, in my mind, always take the Pas; but I assure them, their Ladyships shall ever come next in place.—Should my farm, which it possibly may, turn out a ruinous bargain, I have a certainty of an employment, poor as it may *comparatively* be, whose emoluments are luxury to any thing my first twenty five years of Life could promise.—I don't know if ever I mentioned to you my most favorite Quotation—

> "—On Reason build Resolve,
> "That column of true majesty in Man!"[2]

Circumstanced as I am, I could never have got a female partner for life who could have entered into my favorite studies, relished my favorite Authors, &c. without entailing on me at the same time, expensive living, fantastic caprice, apish affectation, with the other blessed, Boarding-school acquirements which (pardonnez moi, Madame!) are some times to be found among females of the upper ranks, but almost universally pervade the Misses of the Would-be-gentry.—In this kind of literary, sentimental correspondence, FRIENDSHIP must be my social channel; at the same time I declare to God, You are almost the [only] friend of this Kind I have.—So far from tiring of your correspondence, Madam, it would be one of the greatest misfortunes that could befall me, were I to lose it.—I really tremble at the idea that days & years are making you older, and that the all-conquering hand of Time may deprive me of a FRIEND whose WORTH I shall ever gratefully revere, and whose loss (should I be so unfortunate) I shall ever inconsolably deplore.—

I like your way in your Church-yard lucubrations.—Thoughts that are the spontaneous result of accidental situations, either respecting health, place, or company, have often a strength, and always an Originality, that would in vain be looked for in faded circumstances and studied paragraphs.—For me, I have often thought of keeping a letter, *in progression,* by me, to send you when the sheet was wrote out.—Now I talk of sheets, I must tell you, my reason for writing to you on paper of this kind is my pruriency of writing to you at LARGE.—A page of Post is on such a dissocial narrow-minded scale, that I cannot abide it; & double letters, at least in my miscellaneous, reverie manner, are a monstrous tax, in a close Correspondence.—

I have the honor to be, Madam,
your oblidged & most obedient humble servant,
Robt Burns

1 Home: *Douglas*, Act I, sc. 1.
2 Young: *Night Thoughts*, Night I, lines 30-1.

XIX (260)

Mauchline, 2nd August 1788

Honored Madam,

Your kind letter welcomed me, yesternight, to Ayr-shire.—I am indeed seriously angry with you at the Quantum of your "Luck-penny"; but vexed & hurt as I was, I could not help laughing very heartily at the noble Lord's apology for the miss'd Napkin.—[1]

I would write to you from Nithsdale, & give you my direction there, but I have scarce any opportunity of calling at a Post Office, once in a fortnight.—I am six miles from Dumfries; am scarcely ever in it myself; and as yet, have little acquaintance in the neighbourhood.—Besides, I am now very busy on my farm, building a dwelling-house; as at present I am almost an Evangelical man in Nithsdale, for I have scarce "Where to lay my head."—[2]

Mrs Frances Anna Dunlop of Dunlop

There are some passages in your last that brought tears in my eyes.—"The heart knoweth its own sorrows, and a Stranger intermeddleth not herewith."—[3] The repository of these "Sorrows of the heart" is a kind of Sanctum Sanctorum; & 'tis only a Chosen Friend, and that too at particular, sacred times, who dare enter into them.—

> "Heaven oft tears the bosom-chords
> "That nature finest strung"—[4]

You will excuse this quotation, for the sake of the Author.— Instead of entering on this subject farther, I shall transcribe you a few lines I wrote in a Hermitage belonging to a gentleman in my Nithsdale neighbourhood.—They are almost the only favours the Muses have conferred on me in that Country.—

> Thou whom Chance may hither lead
> [C.W. p. 324]

Since I am in the way of transcribing, the following were the production of yesterday, as I jogged through the wild hills of New Cumnock.—I intend inserting them, or something like them, in an epistle I am going to write the Gentleman on whose friendship my excise hopes depend—Mr Graham of Fintry, one of the worthiest and most accomplished Gentlemen, not only of this Country, but I will dare to say it, of this Age.—The following are just the first crude thoughts "unhousell'd, unannointed, unanneal'd."—[5]

> Pity the tuneful Muses' helpless train;
> Weak, timid Landsmen on Life's stormy main:
> The world were blest, did bliss on them depend;
> Ah! that "the Friendly e'er should want a Friend!"
> Their little Fate bestows they share as soon:
> Unlike sage, proverb'd Wisdom's hard-wrung boon.
> Let Prudence number o'er each sturdy son
> Who Life & Wisdom at one race begun;
> Who feel by Reason, & who give by Rule;
> Instinct's a brute and Sentiment a fool!
> Who make poor "will do" wait upon "I should;"
> We own they're Prudent—but who owns they're Good?
> Ye Wise Ones, hence! ye hurt the Social Eye;
> God's image rudely etch'd on base alloy!
> But come—[6]

Here the Muse left me.—I am astonished at what you tell me of Antony's writing me: I never received it.—Poor fellow! you vex me much by telling me that he is unfortunate.—I shall be in Ayrshire ten days from this date.—I have just room for an old Roman Farewell!

Robt Burns

1   An allusion to Mrs Dunlop's letter of 22nd July containing the lines:
    '. . . as Lord Bankton said when his fourth wife mist one napkin of a
    dozen fine ones in a parcel. "My dr., when my last wife was buried, I
    forgot to draw it out in putting her corpse into the coffin. I shall
    behave better next time." '
2   Matthew 8:20, paraphrased.
3   Proverbs 14:10.
4   Burns: *On Reading* . . *the Death of John McLeod*, lines 13-14. (C.W.
    p. 283)
5   Shakespeare: *Hamlet*, Act IV, sc. 5, misquoted.
6   Rough draft of *Epistle to Robert Graham Esq. of Fintry, requesting
    a Favour*. (C.W. p. 331, lines 49-65)

XX (264)

Ellisland, 16th August 1788

I am in a fine disposition, my honored Friend, to send you an
Elegiac Epistle; & want only genius to make it quite
Shenstonian.—

> "Why droops my heart with fancy'd woes forlorn?
> "Why sinks my soul beneath each wintry sky?"[1]

Or, in the more homely Poetry of "The Psalms of David in
metre"—

> "Why art thou then cast down, my Soul?
> "What should discourage thee?"[2]

A physical potion to expel a slight indispostion, with my
increasing Cares in this, as yet, Strange country—gloomy
conjecture in the dark vista of Futurity—consciousness of my
own inability for the struggle of the world—my broaden'd mark
to Misfortune in a Wife & children—I could indulge these, nay
they press for indulgence, till my humour would ferment into the
most acid vinegar of Chagrin, that would corrode the very thread
of Life.—

To counterwork these baneful feelings, I have sat down to write
to you; as I declare upon my soul, I always find *that* the most
sovereign balm under Heaven for my wounded Spirit.—

I was yesterday at Mr Miller's to dinner; the first time since I have
been his Tenant.—My reception was quite to my mind: from the
lady of the house, quite flattering.—I believe in my conscience that
she respects me more on account of my marrying a woman in
circumstances something similar to her own; when she
commenced Mrs Millar.—See what it is to be rich! I was going to
add, & to be great; but to be rich is to be great.— She sometimes
hits on a Couplet or two, impromptu.—She repeated one or two,
to the admiration of all present.—My suffrage as a professional
man, was expected: I for once went, agonizing, over the belly of
my conscience— Pardon me, ye, my adored Household gods, In-

dependance of Spirit, & Integrity of Soul! In the course of conversation, Johnson's musical Museum, A Collection of Scots
Songs with the music, was talked of.—We got a song on the Harpsichord, beginning—

> "Raving winds around her blowing"—
>
> [C.W. p. 314]

The Air was much admired: the Lady of the house ask'd me
whose were the words "Mine, Madam"—they are my very best
verses! sacre Dieu! she took not the smallest notice of them!—
The old Scots Proverb says well—"King's caff is better than ither
folks' corn."—I was going to make a New Testament quotation
about "casting Pearls,"[3] but that would be too virulent.—The
Lady is actually a woman of sense & taste: a proof, if the subject
needed one, that these said two qualities, so useful & ornamental
to Human Nature, are by no means inseparably of the family of
Gules, Purpure, Argent, Or, &c.—

After all that has been said on the other side of the question, Man
is by no means a happy creature.—I do not speak of the Selected
Few, favoured by partial Heaven; whose souls are tuned to Gladness amid Riches, & Honors, & Prudence, & Wisdom.—I speak of
the neglected Many, whose nerves, whose sinews, whose days,
whose thoughts, whose independance, whose peace, nay, whose
very gratifications & enjoyments, the instinctive gift of Nature,
are sacrificed & sold to these few bloated Minions of Heaven!—

If I thought you had never seen it, I would transcribe you a
stanza of an old Scots Ballad, called, "The life & age of Man;"
beginning thus—

> " 'Twas in the sixteenth hunder year
>   Of God & fifty three
> Frae Christ was born that bought us dear,
>   As Writings testifie"—[4]

I had an old Grand uncle with whom my Mother lived a while
in her girlish years; the good old man, for such he was, was long
blind ere he died, during which time, his most voluptuous enjoyment was to sit down & cry while my Mother would sing the
simple old song of The Life & Age of Man.—

It is this way of thinking, it is these melancholly truths, that
make Religion so precious to the poor, miserable Children of
men. If it is a mere phantasm, existing only in the heated
imagination of Enthusiasm—

> "What Truth on earth so precious as the Lie!"[5]

My idle reasonings sometimes make me a little sceptical, but the
Necessities of my heart always give the cold philosophisings the
lie.—Who looks for the heart weaned from earth; the Soul
affianced in her God; the Correspondence fixed with Heaven; the

pious supplication & devout thanksgiving, constant as the vicissitudes of even & morn; who thinks to meet with them in the Court, the palace, in the glare of public life? No: to find them in their precious importance & divine efficacy, we must search among the obscure recesses of Disappointment, Affliction, Poverty & Distress.—

I am sure, Dear Madam, you are now *more* than pleased with the *length* of my letters.—I return to Ayr-shire, middle of next week; and it quickens my pace to think that there will be a letter from you waiting me there.—I must be here again very soon for my Harvest.—I am really afraid you will wish me to return to my Post-sheet again.—

I have the honor to be, most sincerely & gratefully,

Madam, your humble servant
Robt Burns

1 Shenstone: *Elegy XX*, stanza 1.
2 Metrical Psalms 42:5; second line misquoted.
3 Matthew 7:6.
4 Unidentified
5 Young: *Night Thoughts*, Night VII, line 738.

XXI (265)

Mauchline, 21st August 1788

I came to Ayr-shire yesternight, my much-esteemed friend, and found your very alarming letter waiting me.—My father used to say, that in his whole life, whatever he was fondly set on, almost always failed him.—I am afraid it is all the heritage he has left me. —Since my Ambition dared to hope for your correspondence & friendship, the enthusiasm of Attachment has grown on me, till the enjoyment of your friendship is entwisted with my very enjoyment of Life; and your last letter has given me a thousand terrors.—I shall be here for ten days, & I conjure you to write me ever so short a scrap to inform me if you are getting rid of that ugly Distemper.To quit this disagreable subject; the following is the first Compliment I have paid the Nith, and was the work of an hour as I jogged up his banks yesterday morning.—The idea is a young Gentleman perhaps going abroad.—I do not affirm it has merit: the fact is, an Author is by no means a competent judge of his own composition; at least till the heyday of Novelty evaporate.—

The Thames flows proudly to the sea,
[C.W. p. 330]

You would know an Ayr-shire lad, Sandy Bell, who made a Jamaica fortune, & died some time ago.—A William Miller,

154

formerly a Mason, now a Merchant in this place, married a sister german of Bell's for the sake of a 500£ her brother had left her.— A Sister of Miller's who was then Tenant of my heart for the time being, huffed my Bardship in the pride of her new Connection; & I, in the heat of my resentment resolved to burlesque the whole business, & began as follows—

I

When Eighty-five was seven months auld,
[C.W. p. 157, lines 1-25]

—As I never wrote it down, my recollection does not entirely serve me.—

But now the gown, wi' rustling sound,
[C.W. p. 157, lines 26-43]

Against my Muse had come thus far, Miss Bess & I were once more in Unison, so I thought no more of the Piece.—Tho' the folks are rather uppish, they are such as I did not chuse to expose so I think this is about the second time I ever scrawled it.—

I wish these trifles may find you in a disposition to relish it.—

Adieu! Heaven send you more exhilerating moments than I fear you at present enjoy!

Robt Burns

XXII (267A)

Ellisland, 5th September, 1788

Here am I again, dear Madam, dating my letter from this haunt of the CUMMINS, this elbow of existence;—and here am I in the middle of my harvest, without good-weather when I may have Reapers, & without Reapers when I may have good weather.— The tremendous thunder-storm of yesternight & the lurid fogs of this morning have driven me, for refuge from the Hypocondria which I fear worse than the devil, to my Muse and my address to Mr Graham; so I have this last minute brought it to Finis, & this present minute sat down to give you a copy of it.—

To Robert Graham, Esq. of Fintry.—
When Nature her great Masterpiece designed,
[C.W. p. 330]

Will you give me your opinion of these verses? Direct to me, for three weeks yet to come at ELLISLAND, Care of Mr John Mcmurdo, Carse, Dunscore, by Dumfries.—You give so poor an account of your health still, that I shall not be easy till I hear of that circumstance, so essential to your own happiness and that of your friends.—Among which ELECT NUMBER you have done him the honor of giving a place to,

Madam, your ever grateful humble servant
Robt Burns

Mrs Frances Anna Dunlop of Dunlop

XXIII (275)

Mauchline, 27th September 1788

I have received twins, Dear Madam, more than once; but scarcely ever with more pleasure than when I recieved yours of the 12th Inst.—To make myself understood; I had wrote to Mr Graham, inclosing my Poem addressed to him, and the same post which favoured me with yours, brought me an answer from him.—It was dated the very day he had received mine; & I am quite at a loss to say whether it was most polite or kind.—

Your Criticisms, my honored Benefactress, are truly the work of a FRIEND.—They are not the blasting depredations of a canker-toothed caterpillar-Critic; nor are they the fair statement of cold Impartiality, balancing with unfeeling exactitude the pro & con of an Author's merits; they are the judicious observations of animated Friendship, selecting the beauties of the Piece.—

I have just arrived from Nithsdale, & will be here a fortnight.—I was on horseback this morning, for between my Wife & my farm is just 46 miles, by three o'clock.—As I jogged on in the dark, I was taken with a Poetic-fit, as follows—

Mrs Fergusson of Craigdarroch's lamentation for the death of her son; an uncommonly promising Youth of 18 or 19 years of age—

Fate gave the word, the arrow sped,

[C.W. p. 334]

You will not send me your Poetic-rambles, but, you see, I am no niggard of mine.—I am sure your Impromptus give me double pleasure: what falls from your Pen, can neither be unentertaining in itself, nor indifferent to me.—

The *one* fault you found, is just; but I cannot please myself in an emendation.—

What a life of solicitude is the life of a Parent! You interested me much in your young Couple.—I suppose it is not any of the ladies I have seen.—

I would not take my folio for this epistle, & now I repent it.—I am so jaded with my dirty long journey that I was afraid to drawl into the essence of Dulness with anything larger than a quarto, & so I must leave out another Rhyme of this morning's manufacture.

I will pay the sapientpotent George most chearfully, to hear from you ere I leave Ayrshire.—

I have the honor to be, Dear Madam, your much oblidged, and most respectful, humble servant.

Robt Burns

Mrs Frances Anna Dunlop of Dunlop

XXIV (280)

Sanquhar, 23rd October 1788

Dear Madam,

This is literally a letter en passant, for I write you while my horse baits, on my wonted journey.—Your two kind epistles came in course; but I shall much long for a third one, to inform me how you have recovered the horrid shock you must have felt in the dreadful catastrophe of Lady Wallace's house.—My blood runs cold when I think of it!

Apropos, I breakfasted this morning at Laicht, near New Cumnock, and Mrs Logan asked me, if I had heard that Miss Susan Dunlop was married to a Dane? I replied, the information was new to me.—As it is written, "that which is done in corners shall be proclaimed on the house-tops."[1]—Your last, Madam, is unanswerable.—The illustrious name of Wallace & the accomplishments of Mrs Dunlop have accustomed you so much to the superlatives of Commendation that I am afraid.

Ellisland, 26th Ocotber

My officious Landlady interrupted me, Madam, as I was going on to tell you that my Modesty called out, Murder! all the time I was reading your last.—Very unlike the fate of your other letters, I have never read it but once.—Though I never sit down to *answer* a letter, as our Pastoral Bards make their contending Swains answer one another, or as a be-periwigged Edinburgh Advocate answers his be-gowned brother, yet I cannot help thanking you particularly for the poetic compliment in your epistle the last I received but one.—Now I talk of Poetry, what think you of the following character: I mean the painting of it—

A little, upright, pert, tart tripping Wight—[2]
Another—

– Crochallan came,
The old cock'd hat, the brown surtout the same:
[C.W. p. 433 8 lines]

These are embryotic parts of what may, perhaps, one day, be A POEM.—

in Johnson's Scots Musical Museum, you will find my pieces, such as they are, for Heaven knows they are many of them dull enough! signed with one or other of the letters, R.B. or X.—The other marked pieces are by Poetic folks whom I dare say, except Dr Blacklock, you don't know.—

I may see you at Moreham mains, if you do not leave it for two or three months; as a little business of the devil's making will some time soon, drive me to Haddington.—Or if you return to Dunlop to keep your Halloween, I will meet you there also; as I must be at Dunlop & Kilmaurs' cow-fairs which happen on Halloween & Hallowday—old style.—I believe I shall move, bag

157

& baggage, to Nithsdale at Martinmass.—I am getting the loan of a neighbouring house till my own be ready.—

Before this can reach you, my direction will be again at Mauchline.—

> I have the honour to be, with the highest respect,
> Dear Madam, your oblidged & obedient humble servant
> Robt Burns

1   Luke 12:3, misquoted.
2   In the draft of a poem, much of which was later incorporated into *To Robert Graham of Fintry*. (C.W. p. 431).

XXV (281)

Mauchline, 29th October 1788

I give you joy, Dear Madam, of your new Grand-child.—I beg you will give my sincere Compliments to my brother farmer on the occasion.—

I wrote you the other day from Nithsdale, but I write you whenever I have leisure; and lest I should grow tiresome with my Egotisms & rhymes, just let the reading of them wait, till you too have leisure.—I began a Work lately, but what that work may be, I am totally ignorant.—As Young says, "'Tis nonsense destin'd to be future sense."*—I sent you a fragment of it by my last: take the following rough Sketch of the intended beginning, & let me know your opinion of the lines—

> The Poet's Progress. An embryotic Poem in the
> womb of Futurity.—
> Thou, Nature, partial Nature, I arraign,
> [C.W. p. 431]

Thus far only have I proceeded, & perhaps I may never again resume the subject.—I must mention one caution to you, Madam, with respect to these verses; I have a remote idea that I may one day use them as instruments of vengeance, & consequently I will hide them like a Conspirators dagger.—I mean this lest you might inadvertantly mention them, or acknowledge them as your old acquaintances, should you meet with them anonymously in a Newspaper.—I need not add that I allude to a certain Bookseller's connection & mine.—

How do you like the following Song, designed for an Air composed by a friend of mine, & which he had christened, The blue-eyed lassie.—

> I gade a waefu' gate yestreen,
> [C.W. p. 333]

I must have one line at least to make this new page appear with any grace, & now it is done, give me leave to subscribe myself, Dear Madam, your oblidged friend & grateful humble servant
> Robt Burns

* *Night Thoughts*, Night VII, line 597.

Mrs Frances Anna Dunlop of Dunlop

XXV. (285)

Mauchline, 13th November 1788

Madam

I had the very great pleasure of dining at Dunlop yesterday.—Men are said to flatter women because they are weak; if it is so, Poets must be weaker still; for Misses Rachel & Keith and Miss Georgina Mckay, with their flattering attentions & artful compliments, absolutely turned my head.—I own they did not lard me over as a Poet does his Patron or still more his Patroness, nor did they sugar me up as a Cameronian Preacher does Jesus Christ; but they so intoxicated me with their sly insinuations & delicate innuendoes of Compliment that if it had not been for a lucky recollection how much additional weight & lustre your good opinion & friendship must give me in that circle, I had certainly looked on myself as a person of no small consequence.—I dare not say one word how much I was charmed with the Major's friendly welcome, elegant manner & acute remark, lest I should be thought to balance my orientalisms of applause over against the finest Quey in Ayrshire which he made me a present of to help adorn my farm-stock.—As it was on Hallowday I am determined annually as that day returns to decorate her horns with an Ode of gratitude to the family of Dunlop.—

The Songs in the 2nd Vol. of the Museum, marked, D, are Dr Blacklock's; but as I am sorry to say they are far short of his other works, I, who only know the cyphers of them all, shall never let it be known. Those marked, T, are the work of an obscure, tippling, but extraordinary body of the name of Tytler: a mortal, who though he drudges about Edinburgh as a common Printer, with leaky shoes, a sky-lighted hat, & knee-buckles as unlike as George-by-the-grace-of-God, & Solomon-the-son-of-David, yet that same unknown drunken Mortal is Author & compiler of three fourths of Elliot's pompous Encyclopedia Brittanica.—Those marked, Z, I have given to the world as old verses to their respective tunes; but in fact, of a good many of them, little more than the Chorus is ancient; tho' there is no reason for telling every body this piece of intelligence.—Next letter I write you, I shall send one or two sets of verses I intend for Johnson's 3rd Volume.—

What you mention of the thanksgiving day is inspiration from above.—Is it not remarkable, odiously remarkable, that tho' manners are more civilized, & the rights of mankind better understood, by an Augustan Century's improvement, yet in this very reign of heavenly Hanoverianism, & almost in this very year, an empire beyond the Atlantic has had its REVOLUTION too, & for the very same maladministration & legislative misdemeanors in the illustrious & sapientipotent Family of Hanover as was complained of in the "tyranical & bloody house of STUART."—

So soon as I know of your arrival at Dunlop, I shall take the first conveniency to dedicate a day or perhaps two to You & Friendship, under the guarantee of the Major's hospitality.—There will soon be three score & ten miles of permanent distance between us; & now that your friendship & friendly correspondence is entwisted with the heart-strings of my enjoyment of life, I must indulge myself in a festive day of—

"The feast of reason & the flow of soul."*—

    I have the honor to be, Madam, your grateful humble servant
Robt Burns

*Pope: *First Satire of the Second Book of Horace*, line 128.

XXVII (290)

Ellisland, 7th December 1788

My dear honored Friend,

Yours, dated Edinburgh, which I have just read, makes me very unhappy.—"Almost blind and wholly deaf" are melancholy news of Human-nature; but when told of a much loved and honored friend, they carry misery in the sound.—Goodness on your part, and gratitude on mine, began a tie which has gradually & stongly entwisted itself among the dearest chords of my bosom; and I tremble at the omens of your late and present ailing habit, and shattered health.—You miscalculate matters widely, when you forbid my waiting on you lest it should hurt my worldyly concerns.—My small scale of farming is exceedingly more simple & easy than what you have lately seen at Moreham mains. —But be that as it may, the heart of the Man, and the fancy of the Poet are the two grand considerations for which I live: if miry ridges & dirty dunghills are to engross the best part of the functions of my soul immortal, I had better been a rook or a magpie all at once, & then I would not have been plagued with any ideas superior to breaking of clods & picking up grubs: not to mention Barn-door Cocks or Mallards, creatures with which I could almost exchange lives at any time.—If you contine so deaf, I am afraid a visit will be no great pleasure to either of us; but if I hear you are got so well as to be able to relish conversation, look you to it, Madam, for I will make my threatenings good, I am to be at the Newyearday fair of Ayr, by all that is Sacred in the word, Friend! I *will* come & see you!—As for G.R. whom you commiserate so much in your Moreham mains epistle (you see I have read both sheets, notwithstanding your wicked surmise) I am not sure whether he is not a gainer, by how much a Madman is a more respectable character than a Fool.—

If you have an opportunity of seeing the Edinburgh evening Courant of Saturday the 22nd of November, you will see a piece of my Politics, signed, A Briton.—Heaven forgive me for dissimulation in that Paragraph! I too, Madam, am just now Revolution-mad, but it is not the tarantula-frenzy of insulting Whiggism, like an ass's Colt capering over the generous hound breathing his last; mine is the madness of an enraged Scorpion shut up in a thumb-phial; the indignant groans and bloodshot glances of ruined Right, gagged on the pillory of Derision to gratify the idiot insolence of Usurpation.—

To show you that all your things don't lie by me unread, I have perused your inclosed verses more than half a dozen time, & as I am I believe the sole Depository of them as well as several other of your Parnassian flights, I treasure them by carefully with a felonious intention some day or other to give them here & there in my future Pieces as my own.- I tell you this in confidence, Madam, and I trust you will not betray me.--

My song, Clarinda, was a real affair.—It was un petit egaremen du coeur during my last stay in Edinburgh, but circumstances are too romantic to be credited even almost from the mouth of Truth* herself: I beg Truth's pardon if I have mistaken the Gender in the Pronoun foregoing marked with an Asterisk.—

Your meeting which you so well describe with your old School-fellow & friend was truly interesting.—Out upon the ways of the World! They spoil these "Social Offspring of the heart."—The old veterans of the "Men of the World" would have met with little more heart-workings than two old Hacks wore out on the road.—Apropos, is not the Scots phrase, "Auld lang syne," exceedingly expressive.—There is an old song & tune which has often thrilled thro' my soul.—You know I am an enthusiast in old Scots songs.—I shall give you the verses on the other sheet as I suppose Mr Ker will save you the Postage.—

My Address is now, at Ellisland near Dumfries.—I was favored with a most excellent & very kind letter accompanying a book, from Anthony.—It only reached me the other day, but is dated in April.—I received a heavy complaint, when I was at Dunlop, from Miss Keith, that you never shewed the family any of my things I sent you.—I must blame you, Madam, for this.—There are very few indeed whose applause would so much feast my vanity as one & all of the family of Dunlop; and where'er I deserve that applause, pray secure it for me.—I mean in things indifferent; for there are some things I have written to you that I would not have written, I believe, to any living individual else.—All I would say is; you are at perfect liberty to shew any of my fugitive things you may have, as Discretion et Bienseance direct you, to your amiable & worthy Family: a Family, where one may with propriety address you, my much honored Friend, "Hail, thou highly favoured among Women!"[1]

I see by your last that you will be at Dunlop by this time as this is the third day that this farrago of scraps has been by me; & I will e'en go on, till I have a private opportunity of transmitting the letter to Ayrshire, which will be by one of my own servants tomorrow night.—If you are very punctilious in the Christian Law —"Whatsoever ye would that others should do unto you, &c"[2] Heaven have mercy on your remnant of eyesight against you are got thus far! Page the twelfth! 'tis absolutely unconscionable! If Miss Georgina Mckay is still at Dunlop, I beg you will make her my Compliments, & request her in my name to sing you a song at the close of every page, by way of dissipating Ennui; as David (who, by the by, was, baiting the Sex, no bad Prototype of Miss Mc——, for he was not only fam'd for his musical talents, but was also "ruddy & well favor'd, & more comely than his breathren")[3] playing on his harp chased the Evil Spirit out of Saul.[4]—This Evil Spirit, I take it, was just, long-spun Sermons, &

many-pag'd Epistles, & Birthday Poetry, & patience-vexing Memorials, Remonstrances, Dedications, Revolution-Addresses, &c. &c. &c. while David's harp, I suppose was, mystically speaking, Tristram Shandy, Laugh & be fat, Cauld kail in Aberdeen, Green grows the rashes, & the rest of that inspired & inspiring family.—

> As life itself becomes disease,
> [C.W. p. 325]

I am sure it will by this time be no affectation to say that you must be tired with this Scots-mile-epistle.—Apropos to Scotsmile, I do not recollect having told you my Epitaph for J.H. Writer in Ayr—

> Here lies a Scots mile of a chiel,
> If he's in heaven, Lord, fill him weel!
> [C.W. p. 341]

To begin this sheet & conclude this letter, I shall give you a song I finished the other day, & sent it to Johnson for his Publication.— It sings to an excellent old lilt, known in Oswald's Collection of Scots Music by the name of, "The merry beggars."—I would give a bottle of wine to hear it sung, *en Mckai.*—

> My heart is a breaking, dear Titty,
> [C.W. p. 335]

I am not positively certain, after all, if I shall be at Ayr-fair; but I shall impatiently expect to hear a better account of your health.—

> A Dieu je vous commende!
>
> Robt Burns

Auld lang Syne—

Should auld acquaintance be forgot,
    And never thought upon?
Let's hae a waught o' Malaga,
    For auld lang syne.—

Chorus

For auld lang syne, my jo,
    For auld lang syne;
Let's hae a waught o' Malaga,
    For auld lang syne.—

And surely ye'll be your pint-stoup!
    And surely I'll be mine!
And we'll take a cup o' kindness yet,
    For auld lang syne.—
        For auld &c.

We twa hae run about the braes,
    And pou't the gowans fine;
But we've wander'd mony a weary foot
    Sin auld lang syne.—
        For auld &c.

We twa hae paidl't i' the burn
Frae morning sun till dine;
But seas between us braid hae roar'd
Sin auld lang syne.—
For auld &c.

And there's a han', my trusty fiere,
And gie's a han' o' thine!
And we'll tak a right gudewilly waught,
For auld lang syne!—

Light be the turf on the breast of the heaven-inspired Poet who composed this glorious Fragment! There is more of the fire of native genius in it, than in half a dozen of modern English Bacchanalians.—

Now I am on my Hobby-horse, I cannot help inserting two other old Stanzas which please me mightily.—

Go fetch to me a pint o' wine,

[C.W. p. 342]

I have made an alteration of the verses written in Glenriddel Hermitage: tell me which of them you like best—

Thou whom Chance may hither lead

[C.W. p. 325]

1 Luke 1:28, paraphrased
2 Matthew 7:12
3 See I Samuel 16:12, 18
4 I Samuel 26:23

XXVIII (293)

Ellisland Newyearday morning 1789

This, Dear Madam, is a morning of wishes; and would to God that I came under the Apostle James's description!—"The effectual, fervent PRAYER of a *righteous man* availeth much."[1] *In that case,* Madam, you should welcome in a Year full of blessings: every thing that obstructs or disturbs tranquility & self-enjoyment should be removed, and every Pleasure that frail Humanity can taste should be yours. I own myself so little a Presbyterean that I approve of set times & seasons of more than ordinary acts of Devotion; for breaking in on that habituated routine of life & thought which is so apt to reduce our existence to a kind of Instinct; or even sometimes & with some minds to a state very little superior to mere Machinery.—This Day; the first Sunday of May; a breezy, blue-skyed noon some time about the beginning, & a hoary morning & calm sunny day about the end, of Autumn; these, time out of mind, have been with me a kind of Holidays.—Not like the Sacramental, Executioner-face of a Kilmarnock Communion; but to laugh or cry, be chearful or pensive, moral or devout, according to the mood & tense of the Season & Myself.—

Mrs Frances Anna Dunlop of Dunlop

I believe I owe this to that glorious Paper in the Spectator, "The vision of Mirza"; a Piece that struck my young fancy, before I was capable of fixing an idea to a word of three syllables.—"on the fifth day of the moon which; according to the custom of my forefathers, I always *keep holy*; after having washed myself, and offered up my morning devotions, I Ascended the high hill of Bagdat, in order to pass the rest of the day in meditation & prayer."—&c.

We know nothing or next to nothing of the substance or structure of our Souls, so cannot account for those seeming caprices in them; that one should be particularly pleased with this thing, or struck with that, which on Minds of a different cast shall make no extraordinary impression.—I have some, favorite flowers in Spring, among which are the mountain-daisy, the hare-bell, the foxglove, the wild brier-rose, the budding birk & the hoary hawthorn, that I view and hang over with particular delight.—I never hear the loud, solitary whistle of the Curlew in a Summer noon, or the wild, mixing cadence of a troop of grey-plover in an Autumnal-morning, without feeling an elevation of soul like the enthusiasm of Devotion or Poesy.—Tell me, my dear Friend, to what can this be owing? Are we a piece of machinery that, like the Eolian harp, passive, takes the impression of the passing accident? Or do these workings argue something within us above the trodden clod? I own myself partial to these proofs of those aweful & important realities, a God that made all things, man's immaterial & immortal nature, & a World of weal or woe beyond death & the grave, these proofs that we diduct by dint of our own powers & observation.—However respectable, Individuals in all ages have been, I have ever looked on Mankind in the lump to be nothing better than a foolish, headstrong, credulous, unthinking Mob; and their universal belief has ever had extremely little weight with me.—Still I am a very sincere believer in the Bible but I am drawn by the conviction of a Man, not the halter of an Ass.—

Apropos to an Ass, how do you like the following Apostrophe to Dulness, which I intend to interweave in "The Poet's Progress."—

O Dulness, portion of the truly blest!
[C.W. p. 432, lines 56-75]

I have sketched two or three verses to you, but as a private opportunity offers immediately I must defer transcribing them.—[2] A servant of mine goes to Ayrshire with this, but I shall write you by Post. If I am to be so happy as have it in my power to see you when I go to Ayr-fair, which I very much doubt, I will try to dine at Dunlop on the wednesday of that week.—

If it is good weather on the fair-week, I shall try my utmost; for if I hit my aim aright, it will not be in my power in any given time again. Farewell!

Robt Burns

1 James 5:16.
2 *New Year's Day. To Mrs Dunlop* (C.W. p. 345)

164

XXIX (305)

Mossgiel, Wednesday morning,
[January 1789]

No ill-weather in Hay or Harvest ever gave me so chagrining a disappointment.—This morning I had set apart for a visit to my honored Friend—you cannot imagine, Madam, what happiness I had promised myself; when behold, "the snows descended, and the winds blew" and made my journey impracticable.—As it will be impossible for me to wait a journeyable day, I send you this to apologise for my seeming neglect, and to acknowledge the receipt of two kind Epistles from you, since I wrote you on Newyearsday.—I had got a hundred & fifty things to say to you, which a hundred & fifty sheets of Paper would not record; but I shall be in Ayrshire in the Spring, and you know with what rapture two Poetic folks will meet, amid opening daisies, budding hawthorns and fragrant birks.—Now I talk of Poetic, you must know, as I came to Sanquhar on Saturday evening—the landlord & landlady are my particular acquaintance—I had just dispatched my dinner, and was sitting in a family way over a friendly bowl, glad that my weary body & soul had found out so comfortable a place of rest—when lo, the quondam Mrs Oswald wheeled into the courtyard with an immense retinue, and the poor Bard is oblidged amid the shades of night, bitter frost, howling hills & icy cataracts to goad his jaded steed twelve miles farther on to another stage, I composed the following, and sent it off at the first Post-office for the Courant.—

Ode, sacred to the memory of Mrs Oswald of Auchencruive
Dweller in yon dungeon dark,
[C.W. p. 342]

To soften the matter a little, I altered the title to Mrs A—— of O——.—I was afraid they should suspect me for the Author.

I shall be impatient to hear from you.—
Adieu!

I am ever, Dear Madam,
your oblidged friend & humble servant
Robt Burns

XXX (310)

Ellisland, 5th February 1789

I have rummaged every Stationer's shop in Dumfries, for a long and broad, ample and capacious, sized sheet of writing paper, just to keep by me for epistles to you; and you see, dear Madam, by this honest-looking page, that I have succeeded to a miracle.—I own indeed you deserve a jolly letter.—In the first place, you are no niggard that way yourself, a quality absolutely necessary in a friendly correspondence; and in the next place, you seen determined not only to deserve my friendship such as it is, but to buy it.—There is a spirit in receiving as well as in giving presents; and I insist, Madam, that you shall give me credit for a very considerable portion of the former, as I have always accepted the

many kind instances of your beneficence, without expressing or
even feeling any of that pettishness of stricken pride which so
many people mistake for true spirit.—I am a miserable hand at
your fine speeches; and if my gratitude is to be reckoned by my
expression, I shall come poorly off in the account.—Your benevolent notices of my poor, little cousin, I cannot pass in silence:
for your goodness where your humble servant has been the object
a chearful honest, thank you, is all I can say about it.—In giving
me your friendship, Madam, you have given me a solid,
permanent addition to my happiness; and we shall not quarrel
about the ceremonials of it.—

I have received both your letters, and on the first, coming to
hand, I would have written you by post; but as it rejoices my
heart to send you a packet, I have waited for the return of one of
my Machline friends, who has been with me this week, to forward
it without that cursed postage.—

Your story of poor Mills[1] has much interested me.—If it is in my
power, Madam, to gratify your wishes by a little compliment, in
the way of my trade, to the memory of a friend of yours, you
know it will give me the highest pleasure to do it.—If the epistle
he has done me the honor to write me, come to your hand, open
it and welcome.—Still, you must make me this allowance in your
commands, that if the capricious baggage, my Muse, is not propitious, I will not attempt any thing on the subject.—I have had
themes on my hands for years, without being able to please
myself in my best efforts.—

There is a small river, Afton, that falls into Nith, near New-
Cumnock, which has some charming, wild, romantic scenery on
its banks.—I have a particular pleasure in those little pieces of
poetry such as our Scots songs, &c. where the names and
landskip-features of rivers, lakes, or woodlands, that one knows
are introduced.—I attempted a compliment of that kind, to
Afton, as follows: I mean in for Johnson's Musical Museum.—

Flow gently, clear Afton, among thy green braes,

[C.W. p. 351]

I believe I formerly mentioned some of the following verses to
you, but I have, since, altered them with a view to interweave
them in an epistle from an unfortunate lady whom you knew.—
Whether I may ever finish it, I do not know; but I have one or
two of the principal paragraphs already by me, of which the
following is one.—

Now, maddening, wild I curse that fatal night;
[discarded from Passion's Cry, C.W. p. 501]

I am very sorry that you should be informed of my supposed
guilt in composing, in some midnight frolic, a stanza or two perhaps not quite proper for a clergyman's reading to a company of
ladies.—That I am the author of the verses alluded to in your
letter, is what I much doubt.—You may guess that the convivial
hours of *men* have their mysteries of wit and mirth; and I hold it
a piece of comtemptible baseness, to detail the sallies of thought-

less merriment or the orgies of accidental intoxication, to the ear of cool Sobriety or female Delicacy.—

I intend setting out for Edinburgh on monday se'enight, & shall be there about a week.- I inclose you a piece of my prose,[2] which, for obvious reasons I send you for your *sole* amusement: it is dangerous ground to tread on.—

A lover of Scots Drink can never forgive the late usage of our distillers. If you honor me with a letter during my stay in town, please direct to the care of Peter Hill, Bookseller, Parliament square.—

I have the honor to be, Dear Madam,
your highly oblidged humble servant
Robt Burns

1   James Mylne, who died in 1788 leaving a MS. *To Mr. Burns, on his Poems* which appeared in his posthumous Poems, *Consisting of Miscellaneous Pieces, and Two Tragedies* (Edinburgh, 1790). Both Burns and Mrs Dunlop are included in the list of subscribers.
2   Letter to William Pitt (See page 509).

XXXI (316)

Edinburgh, Saturday morning,
21st February 1789

Your kind packet, my much esteemed friend, is just come to hand.—In my hurried hours in this place I have not yet had time to peruse Milne's verses, but I have three times o'er without interval perused your incomparable verses to your young lady.—It is evident, My dear Madam, that you were deeply interested in the Subject; as you have in these lines not only risen above yourself, but, upon the honor of a Man, and the skill of a Critic! you have risen above any thing of the kind done by any Author now living.—So soon as I return to Nithsdale, which will be in four or five days, I shall write a criticism on their merits.—

I am here more unhappy than I ever experienced before in Edinburgh.—I am a poor Man of business, and I have got some very serious business to do; I love the social pleasures in moderation, but here I am impressed into the service of Bacchus; and I am FROM HOME.—

But, truce, with peevish, poor complaining! I will not tax your friendship with my weakness.—Were it not for hurting your feelings, I would likewise add, that I will no more be thus indebted to your beneficence; but I checked a momentary pang of something like wounded pride and taxed my ingenuity to assist your wishes.—It oblidges me to let you into an intention of mine rather prematurely, but as it is the only way I can think of being oblidged by you, *in that manner,* I must tell it you.—I hope to be a father again in about two or three months, and I had resolved and indeed had told Mrs Burns, that the said child should be christened by the name of FRANCES DUNLOP, if a girl, or FRANCIS &c. if a boy; that while the child should exist it might be a witness of a Friendship to which I owe much of the pleasurable part of my life; a Friendship, which I wish to hand down to my Posterity as one of the honors of their Ancestor.—Let this said Miss Frances or Mr Francis be the object of your intended beneficence with all my soul.—Perhaps in the case of a boy, you would rather wish to wait for one of your own Sex, that might take the exact Name; and as I have not the smallest doubt of being very soon able to accommodate you in that way too, I shall expect your commands sometime before the important period.—I am here just in a vortex, so must conclude with a simple heart-felt

A Dieu je vous commende

Robt Burns

I'll write you on my return home—

XXXII (319)

Ellisland, 4th March 1789

Here am I, my honored Friend, returned safe from the Capital.—To a man who has a Home, however humble or remote; if that Home is like mine, the scene of Domestic comfort; the bustle of Edinburgh will soon be a business of sickening disgust.—

"Vain pomp and glory of this world, I hate you!"[1]

When I must sculk into a corner, lest the rattling equipage of some gaping blockhead, contemptible puppy, or detestable scoundrel should mangle me in the mire, I am tempted to exclaim—What merits have these Wretches had, or what demerit have I had, in some state of Pre-existence, that they are ushered into this scene of being with the sceptre of rule and the key of riches in their puny fists; and I am kicked into the world, the sport of their folly or the victim of their pride? I have read somewhere of a monarch, in Spain I think it was, who was so out of humour with the Ptolemean system of astronomy, that he said, had he been of the Creator's council he could have saved him a great deal of labor & absurdity.[2]—I will not defend this blasphemous speech; but often as I have glided with humble stealth through the pomp of Princes' street, it has suggested itself to me as an improvement on the present Human figure, that a man in proportion to his own conceit of his consequence in the world, could have pushed out the longitude of his common size, as a snail pushes out his horns, or as we draw out a perspective.—This trifling alteration; not to mention the prodigious saving it would be in the tear & wear of the neck and limb sinews of many of his Majesty's liege subjects in the way of tossing the head and tiptoe strutting, would evidently turn out a vast advantage in enabling us at once to adjust the ceremonials in making a bow or making way to a Great Man, and that too, within a second of the precise spherical angle of reverence, or an inch of the particular point of respectful distance, which the important creature itself requires; as a measuring glance at its towering altitude would determine the affair like instinct.—

You are right, Madam, in your idea of poor Mylne's poem[3] which he has addressed to me.—The piece has a good deal of merit, but it has one damning fault—it is by far too long.—Besides, my success has encouraged such a shoal of ill-spawned monsters to crawl into public notice under the title of Scots Poets, that the very term, Scots Poetry, borders on the burlesque.—When I write Mr Carfrae, I shall advise him rather to try one of his deceased friend's English Pieces.—I am prodigiously hurried with my own matters, else I would have requested a perusal of all Mylne's poetic performances; and would have offered his friends my assistance in either selecting or correcting what would be proper for the Press.—What it is that occupies me so much, and perhaps a little oppresses my present spirits, shall fill up a paragraph in some future letter.—In the mean time, allow me to close this epistle with a few lines done by a friend of mine; which for beauty I shall pit against any as many lines in our language.—I give you them, that, as you have seen the original, you may guess whether one or two alterations I have ventured to make in them, be any real improvement.—

> "Like the fair plant that from our touch withdraws,
> Shrink, mildly fearful, even from applause:
> Be all a Mother's fondest hope can dream,
> And all you are, my charming girl, seem.—
> Straight as the fox-glove e'er her bells disclose,
> Mild as the maiden blushing hawthorn blows,
> Fair as the fairest of each lovely kind,
> Your form shall be the image of your mind.—
> Your manners shall so true your soul express,
> That all shall long to know the worth they guess;
> Congenial hearts shall greet with kindred love,
> And even sickening Envy must approve."[4]

I have the honor to be, Madam, your obliged friend
& humble servant

Robert Burns

1 Shakespeare: *Henry VIII*, Act III, sc 2.
2 Alfonso X.
3 *To Mr Burns, on his Poems*, posthumously published in James Mylne's *Poems Consisting of Miscellaneous Pieces, and two tragedies* (Edinburgh 1790). The poem to Burns occupies thirteen pages.
4 Lines by Mrs Dunlop herself, revised by Burns.

XXXIII (324)

Ellisland, 25th March 1789

Dear Madam,

I have this moment your kind Packet of the 18th and tho' sore tired with the labours of the day
> "——Throwing the grain
> Into the faithful bosom of the ground"—*

yet, as I have a boy, my herd, going for Ayrshire tomorrow morning, & who will be at Kilmarnock, I shall make him go so much farther & leave this at Dunlop.—

You have a little miscalculated my feelings, my honored friend, respecting the naming of my child.—To name my child after any of the Great, with a view to their future beneficence, is quite foreign to my ideas: my motive is gratitude, not selfishness.— Though I may die a very Poor Man, yet I hope my children shall ever boast the character of their Father: and as that father has some few in the upper ranks of life to whom he is peculiarly indebted, or whom he holds peculiarly dear, he wishes his children likewise to indulge an honest pride on that account; and not only as a memento of these honors their father enjoyed, but as an incentive to noble action, he will call his children after the names of his illustrious friends & benefactors.—I intend, Madam, as first at my heart, to begin with your honored name; & my first child shall be Frances Wallace or F. Dunlop as you please, for really I dare not venture on the whole list of your appellations.—

As for Mr Graham's letter, Madam, it is of a piece with your usual goodness, and is what I highly approve of; only when I tell you the narrative of my situation, plans in life, &c. you will see the propriety of altering the scope of your epistle.—The latter part indeed of that epistle is what in no situation I could think on: I have marked in the epistle itself, where that part begins.—

You remember, Madam, I had two plans of life before me; the Excise & farming.—I thought, by the glimmering of my own prudence, the Excise was my most eligible scheme; but all my Great friends, and particularly You, were decidedly & therefore decided me, for farming.—My master, Mr Miller, out of real tho' mistaken benevolence, sought me industriously out, to set me this farm, as he said to give me a lease that would make me comfortable & easy.—I was a stranger to country, the farm and the soil, and· so ventured on a bargain, that instead of being comfortable, is & will be a very, very hard bargain, if at all practicable.—I am sorry to tell you this Madam, but it is a damning truth; though I beg, as the world think that I have got a pennyworth of a farm, you will not undeceive them.—To bring myself about, I thought of getting an Excise Division in the midst of which I live, and this was what took me last to Edinburgh; but there are in the Excise-Board certain regulations, which, notwithstanding Mr Graham's warmest exertions, baffled all my hopes.—By Mr Creech, who has at last settled amicably & fully as could have been expected, with me, I clear about 440 or 450£.— To keep my brother from ruin, and scattering my aged parent & three sisters comfortless in the world, I advanced him about 200£. of that money: this you know was an indispensible affair, as their wellbeing is certainly to me the same as my own.—What money rests for myself, you will guess is too little for my own stock; but my Master allows me some money to build & inclose, & with that, I could have done—if the farm would have done.—

But to close this tedious epistle, & to give you something more comfortable in my views: my brother's lease is near expiring, he may be able to live by my lease as he can with propriety do things that I *now* can not do; I will plant him in this farm & throw on the Excise at large, where I am sure of immediate & constant bread.—

Let these matters lie between you & I only.—

As for your writing Mr Graham, it is what pleases me above all things; but no plans in it if you please; I wish him to know how I labour under a sense of his goodness and, if you will, your thanks to him for his kindness to a man in whose welfare you have interested yourself: and if you give them a little different turn, now that you know my situation, send the verses above all things.—

Now I talk of verses, I own your criticism on my emendation of your line to be just; but one thing, Madam, has escaped your attention, "Envy", either a noun or verb, is accented on the first syllable, consequently the word cannot well close your line.

Forgive this miserable scrawl.—
I have the honor to be Madam.
your obliged friend & very humble servant
Robert Burns

If you write Mr Graham, his address is, George Street, Edinburgh—I must not seem to know any thing of the matter, so let it just go by the nearest Post Office.

R.B.

* Thomson: *Spring*, lines 45-6, misquoted.

XXXIV (326)

Ellisland, 3rd April 1789

Dear Madam

I have this moment finised the following political Squib, and I cannot resist the temptation of sending you a copy of it—the only copy indeed that I will send to any body except perhaps anonymously to some London Newspaper.—Politics is dangerous ground for me to tread on, and yet I cannot for the soul of me resist an impulse of any thing like Wit.—

Ode to the departed Regency Bill—

Daughter of Chaos' doting years!
[C.W. p. 352]

I have this moment an opportunity of sending this to Post, so can no more—not even review the past.—

R.B.

XXXV (330)

Ellisland, 21st April 1789

My honored friend,

If you knew my present hurry of building, planning, planting, sowing, &c. &c. you would give me great credit for this sheet-ful— If I live in leisure to fill it.—Every minute has five minutes' business to do, and every crown has a twenty-shilling errand to run.—I have just got a reading of some books I wanted much; and a parcel of Poems, now in the current of subscription, have given me, & daily give me, a world of trouble in revising them.—They are hopeless trash; but the Authoress is a poor young creature whose forefathers have seen better days; for which consideration I submit to the horrid drudgery.—I have over & above, the 3rd. vol. of the Scots Songs among my hands, among which will appear some delectable pieces of my Muse's dreams.—

Two mornings ago as I was, at a very early hour, sowing in the fields, I heard a shot, & presently a poor little hare limped by me, apparently very much hurt.—You will easily guess, this set my humanity in tears and my indignation in arms.—The following was the result, which please read to the young ladies—I believe you may include the Major, too; as whatever I have said of shooting hares, I have not spoken one irreverend word against coursing them.—This is, according to your just right, the very first copy I wrote.—

On seeing a fellow wound a hare with a shot—
Inhuman man! curse on thy barbarous art,

[C.W. p. 354]

It would truly oblige me, to have your opinion of the foregoing. —I must take some other opportunity to answer the particulars of your last.—I believe the Professorship you mention will be an idle project; but whatever it may be, I, or such as I, am quite out of the the question.—

You are rather premature on me, in expecting your Name-child so soon.—In about two months, I hope to tell you another story. By the way, should I have a boy, will you honor him with the Apellation, or will you wait a girl? you see, I am set in for trade. I wish I had lived in the days of Joktan, in whose days, says Moses, the earth was divided.* Then a patriarchal fellow like me might have been the father of a nation.—

Bur even in that case, I should have been a loser if I had then been denied the happiness & honor of subscribing myself, Dear Madam, your obliged friend & humble servant.

Robt Burns

* Genesis 10 : 25

XXXVI (335)

Ellisland, 4th April [May] 1789

You see, Madam, that I am returned to my folio epistles again. I no sooner hit on any Poetic plan or fancy but I wish to send it you; & if knowing & reading them gives half the pleasure to you, that communicating them to you gives to me, I am satisfied.—

As I am not devoutly attached to a certain monarch, I cannot say that my heart run any risk of bursting, on thursday was se'ennight, with the struggling emotions of gratitude.—God forgive me for speaking evil of dignities! but I must say, that I look on the whole business as a solemn farce of pageant mummery.—The following are a few Stanzas of new Psalmody for that "Joyful Solemnity" which I sent to a London Newspaper with the date & preface following—

Kilmarnock 25th April

Mr Printer

In a certain chapel, not fifty leagues from the market-cross of this good town, the following stanzas of Psalmody, it is said, were composed for, & devoutly sung on, the late joyful Solemnity of the 23rd.—

O sing a new song to the Lord,*

[C.W. p. 354]

So much for Psalmody.—You must know that the Publisher of one of the most blasphemous party London Newspapers is an acquaintance of mine, and as I am a little tinctured with Buff & Blue myself, I now & then help him to a Stanza.—

I have another Poetic whim in my head which I at present dedicate or rather inscribe to The Right Honourable Ch. J. Fox Esquire; but how long that fancy may hold, I can't say.—A few of the first lines I have just rough-sketched as follows—

Sketch—

How Wisdon & Folly meet, mix and unite;

[C.W. p. 356]

I beg your pardon for troubling you with the inclosed to the Major's tenant before the gate—it is to request him to look me out two milk cows; one for myself, & another for Captain Riddel of Glenriddel, a very oblidging neighbour of mine.—John very oblidgingly offered to do so for me; & I will either serve myself that way, or at Mauchline fair.—It happens on the 20th Current and the sunday preceding it I hope to have the honor of assuring you in person how sincerely I am, Madam, your highly oblidged

& most obedient humble servant

Robt Burns

*Published in the *Morning Star*, London, 14th May 1789, signed 'Duncan M'Leerie'.

XXXVII (350)

Ellisland, 21st June 1789

Dear Madam,

Will you take the effusions, the miserable effusion, of low spirits, just as they flow from their bitter spring? I know not of any particular cause for this worst of all my foes besetting me; but for some time my soul has been beclouded with a thickening atmosphere of evil imaginations and gloomy presages.

* * *

Monday evening [22nd June]

I have just heard the Rev. Joseph Kirkpatrick give a sermon. He is a man famous for his benevolence, and I revere him; but from such ideas of my Creator, good Lord deliver me! Religion, my honoured friend, is surely a simple business, as it equally concerns the ignorant and the learned, the poor and the rich. That there is an incomprehensibly Great Being, to whom I owe my existence, and that he must be intimately acquainted with the operations and progress of the internal machinery, and consequent outward deportment of this creature which he has made; these are, I think, self-evident propositions. That there is a real and eternal distinction between virtue and vice, and consequently that I am an accountable creature; that from the seeming nature of the human mind, as well as from the evident imperfection, nay, positive injustice, in the administration of affairs, both in the natural and moral worlds, there must be a retributive scene of existence beyond the grave—must, I think, be allowed by every one who will give himself a moment's reflection, I will go farther, and affirm, that from the sublimity, excellence, and purity of his doctrine and precepts un-paralleled by all the aggregated wisdom and learning of many preceding ages, though *to appearance,* he himself was the obscurest and most illiterate of our species; therefore Jesus Christ was from God.

*   *   *

Whatever mitigates the woes, or increases the happiness of others, this is my criterion of goodness; and whatever injures society at large, or an individual in it, this is my measure of iniquity.

What think you, Madam, of my creed! I trust that I have said nothing that will lessen me in the eye of one whose good opinion I value almost next to the approbation of my own mind.

Your little *dear* namesake has not yet made his appearance, but he is every day expected.—I promise myself great assistance in training up his young mind to dignity of sentiment and greatness of soul, from the honored name by which he is called.—I know many would despise & more would laught at, such a way of thinking; but with all reverence to the cold theorems of Reason, a few honest Prejudices & benevolent Prepossessions, are of the utmost consequence, and give the finishing polish to the illustrious characters of Patriot, Benefactor, Father & Friend; and all the tender relations included in the endearing word, What a poor, blighted, rickety breed are the Virtues & charities when they take their birth from geometrical hypothesis & mathematical demonstration? And what a vigorous Offspring are they when they owe their origin to, and are nursed with the vital blood of a heart glowing with the noble enthusiasm of Generosity, Benevolence and Greatness of Soul?—The first may do very well for those philosophers who look on the world of man as one vast ocean, and each individual as a little vortex in it whose sole business and merit is to absorb as much as it can in its own centre; but the last is absolutely & essentially necessary when you would make a Leonidas, a Hannibal, an Alfred, or a WALLACE.—

Whether this long letter may contribute to your entertainment is what I cannot tell; but one thing I know, my own spirits are a good the lighter for this opportunity of assuring you how sincerely I have the honor to be, Madam,

your obliged friend & humble servant
Robt Burns

Mrs Frances Anna Dunlop of Dunlop

Ellisland 7th July 1789

Yours of the 27th June, which came to hand yesternight, has given me more pain than any letter, one excepted, that I ever received.— How could you, my ever-honoured dear Madam, ask me, whether I had given up your correspondence and how you had offended me? Offended me! Your conduct to me, Madam, every since I was honoured with your notice, has been equally amiable as uncommon; and your Correspondence has been one of the most supreme of my sublunary enjoyments.—As I mentioned to you in a letter you will by this time have received, I have since I was at Dunlop been rather hurried and out of spirits; and some parts of your late conduct has laid me under peculiar embarrassments.—You had alarmed me lest that instead of the friend of your confidence, I was descending to be the creature of your bounty: for though you bestowed, not in the manner of serving me, but as if oblidging yourself; yet for the soul of me I could not help feeling something of the humiliating oppression of impotent gratitude.—

July 8th

I have been interrupted by the arrival of my aged Parent and my brother; and as he will convey this as far as Mauchline I shall finish my letter, though I cannot make it quite so long as I had otherwise intended.—As I have no romantic notions of independancy of spirit, I am truly obliged to you & Dr Moore for mentioning me to Mr Pulteney. From the manner in which God has divided the good things of this life, it is evident that He meant one part of Mankind to be the Benefactors & the other to be the Benefacted; and as he has thrown me among this latter Class, I would wish to acquiesce with chearfulness.—The Professorship is I know to me an unattainable object, but Mr Pulteney's character stands high as a Patron of merit, and of this, had I no other proof, you have made me believe that I have some share.—

I some time ago met with the following Elegy in M.S.S. for I suppose it was never printed, and as I think it has many touches of the true tender, I shall make no apology for sending it you: perhaps you have not seen it.—

Elegy.—
Straight is the spot & green the sod
From whence my sorrows flow,
And soundly sleeps the ever-dear
Inhabitant below.*

[20 stanzas in all]

I have marked the passages that strike me most.—I like to do so in every book that I read, & it will be a double pleasure in perusing the volumes you announce me, to see you favorite passages. Poor Mrs Henri! I shall be as impatient to hear news of her almost as I shall be of another woman whom I need not name.—I hope that you see her situation through the exaggerating medium of fearful apprehension.

Farewell, Madam! God send good news to us all! Do me the justice
to believe me when I assure you that there is scarcely any thing
which gives me so much pleasure as that

I have the honor to be,

Madam, your obliged friend & humble servant

Robt Burns

* By the Rev. John Mackenzie, of Portpatrick, *Scots Magazine*, March 1769.

XXXIX (352)

Ellisland, 17th July 1789

Dear Madam,

I assure you it is none of my least incentives to rhyme that it gives
me an opportunity not only of acknowledging, but you are good
enough to think, in some degree of repaying that hopeless debt of
kindness & friendship which I so largely owe you.—You know my
sentiments respecting the present two great Parties that divide our
Scots Ecclesiastics.—I do not care three farthings for Commentators
& authorities.—An honest candid enquirer after truth, I revere; but
illiberality & wrangling I equally detest.—You will be well
acquainted with the persecutions that my worthy friend, Dr Mcgill is
undergoing among your Divines.—Several of these reverend lads, his
opponents, have come thro' my hands before; but I have some
thoughts of serving them up again in a different dish.—I have just
sketched the following ballad, & as usual I send the first
rough-draught to you.—I do not wish to be known in it, tho' I know,
if ever it appear, I shall be suspected. If I finish it, I am thinking to
throw off two or three dozen copies at a Press in Dumfries, & send
them as from Edinburgh to some Ayr-shire folks on both sides of the
question.—If I should fail of rendering some of the Doctor's foes
ridiculous, I shall at least gratify my resentment in his behalf.—I long
to hear from you, not only for your criticism on this, but for a much
more important matter, to be informed of Mrs Henri's fate &
welfare.—Whatever interests you, can not be indifferent to me.—

The Kirk's Alarm—A Ballad—

Tune, Push about the brisk bowl—

Orthodox, Orthodox, who believe in John Knox,

[The first draft of 11 stanzas; C.W. p. 359]

This is all the length I have gone.—Whether I proceed any farther
is uncertain.—

Captain Grose, the well-known Author of the Antiquities of England
& Wales, has been through Annandale, Nithsdale & Galloway, in the
view of commencing another Publication, The Antiquities of
Scotland.—As he has made his headquarters with Captain Riddel, my
nearest neighbour, for these two months, I am intimately acquainted
with him; & I have never seen a man of more original observation,
anecdote & remark.—Thrown into the army from the Nursery, &
now that he is the father of a numerous family who are settled in
respectable situations in life, he has mingled in all societies, & knows
every body.—His delight is to steal thro' the country almost

unknown, both as favorable to his humour & his business.—I have to
the best of my recollection of the old buildings, &c. in the County,
given him an Itinerary thro' Ayr-shire.—I have directed him among
other places to Dunlop house, as an old building worthy of a place in
his Collection.—It would have been presumtion in such a man as I, to
offer an introductory letter between such folks as Captain Grose
& Major Dunlop, tho' for the honour of my native county, I could
have wished that Captain Grose had been introduced to the Dunlop
family, & the Major would have been of much use to him in
directing him thro' the farther corner of Cunningham, a place I little
know, however if you discover a chearful-looking grig of an old, fat
fellow, the precise figure of Slop, wheeling about your avenue in his
own carriage with a pencil & paper in his hand, you may conclude,
"Thou art the man!"*

Perhaps after all I may pluck up as much impudent importance as
write to the Major by him.—He will go for Ayr-shire in four or five
days, but I have directed him thro' Carrick & Kyle first.—

> I have the honor to be, Madam, your humble friend
> & most obedient servant
> Robt Burns

* 2 Samuel 12 : 7

XL (359)

Ellisland, 19th August 1789

Dear Madam

I had written you ere this time but for waiting the issue of two to
me important events which were hanging in the wind.—I mentioned
to you my Excise hopes and views.—I have been once more a lucky
fellow in that quarter.—The Excisemen's Salaries are now £50 per
Ann. and I believe the Board have been so obldging as fix me in the
Division in which I live; and I suppose I shall begin doing duty at the
commencement of next month.—I shall have a large portion of
country, but, what to me & my studies is no trifling matter, it is a
fine romantic Country.—

More luck still! About two hours ago I welcomed home your little
Godson.—He is a fine squalling fellow with a pipe that makes the
room ring.—His mother as usual.—Zelucco I have not thoroughly
read so as to give a critique on it.—To say it is an excellent
performance is but echoing the opinion of the world: I shall be more
particular in *my* remarks.—

You will easily guess that in the present situation of my family, and
in my preparations for the Excise, that I have indeed little spare
time.—To you, Madam, that little spare time is more chearfully
devoted than to any other person or purpose.—

Miss Charlottle Smith has delighted me.—Her Elegy in particular is
one of the first performances that I have ever seen.—Your Pencil has
in every mark prevented mine.—

> I have the honor to be, Dear Madam,
> Your obliged grateful humble servant
> Robt Burns

P.S.
The following lines I sent Mr Graham as my thanks for my appointment—
I call no goddess to inspire my strains,
[C.W. p. 362]

XLI (362)

Ellisland, 6th September 1789

Dear Madam,

I have mentioned, in my last, my appointment to the Excise, and the birth of little Frank, who, by the by, I trust, will be no discredit to the honourable name of Wallace, as he has a fine manly countenance, and a figure that might do credit to a little fellow two months older; and likewise an excellent good temper, though, when he pleases, he has a pipe, only not quite so loud as the horn that his immortal namesake blew as a signal to take out the pin of Stirling-bridge.

I had some time ago an epistle, part poetic, and part prosaic, from your poetess, Mrs Janet Little, a very ingenious but modest composition, I should have written her, as she requested, but for the hurry of this new business. I have heard of her and her compositions in this country; and, I am happy to add, always to the honour of her character. The fact is, I know not well how to write to her: I should sit down to a sheet of paper that I knew not how to stain. I am no dab at fine-drawn letter-writing; and except when prompted by friendship or gratitude, or which happens extremely rarely, inspired by the Muse (I know not her name) that presides over epistolary writing, I sit down, when necessitated to write, as I would sit down to beat hemp.

Some parts of your letter of the 20th August struck me with the most melancholy concern for the state of your mind at present.

*   *   *   *   *   *   *   *

Would I could write you a letter of comfort! I would sit down to it with as much pleasure as I would to write an epic poem of my own composition that should equal the *Iliad*. Religion, my dear friend, is the true comfort! A strong persuasion in a future state of existence; a proposition so obviously probable, that, setting revelation aside, every nation and people, so far as investigation has reached, for at least near four thousand years, have, in some mode or other, firmly believed it, In vain would we reason and pretend to doubt. I have myself done so to a very daring pitch; but when I reflected that I was opposing the most ardent wishes, and the most darling hopes of good men, and flying in the face of all human belief, in all ages, I was shocked at my own conduct.

I know not whether I have ever sent you the following lines, or if you have ever seen them; but it is one of my favourite quotations, which I keep constantly by me in my progress through life, in the language of the Book of Job,

"Against the day of battle and of war"[1]—
spoken of religion:

178

Mrs Frances Anna Dunlop of Dunlop

" 'Tis *this,* my friend, that streaks our morning bright,
'Tis *this* that gilds the horror of our night.
When wealth forsakes us, and when friends are few;
When friends are faithless, or when foes pursue;
'Tis this that wards the blow, or stills the smart,
Disarms affliction, or repels his dart;
Within the breast bids purest raptures rise,
 Bids smiling conscience spread her cloudless skies."[2]

I have been very busy with *Zeluco.* The Doctor [3] is so obliging as to request my opinion of it; and I have been revolving in my mind some kind of criticisms on novel-writing, but it is a depth beyond my research. I shall, however, digest my thoughts on the subject as well as I can. *Zeluco* is a most sterling performance.

Farewell! *A Dieu, le bon Dieu, je vous commende!*

1 Job 38 : 23
2 *Verses to Mr Hervey on his Meditations* (1748)
4 Dr John Moore

XLII (363)

Ellisland, 2nd October 1789

I beg your pardon, dear Madam, for this coarse paper, but I have no other large enough for a letter to you.—I have often said and thought that I had not time to write the letters I wished, when in fact, it was only the procrastinating, enfeebling tyranny of Indolence : now that excuse is literally true.- Five days in the week, or four at least, I must be on horseback, and very frequently ride thirty or forty miles ere I return; besides four different kinds of book-keeping to post every day.- Still, Madam, be not afraid, as you are pleased to express so much satisfaction in my correspondence, that this additional hurry will in the least detach my heart from that friendship with which you have honored me, or even abridge my letters; though it must at times prevent the regularity of my answers to yours.—I hold the epistles of a Friend to be the SACRAMENTS of Friendship.—To deface or destroy the shortest Billet of yours would shock my feelings as glaring Sacriledge.—

In this country we are just now Election-mad.—Sir James Johnston, the present Member for the Boroughs, has now opposite interest to the Great Man of this place, Queensberry.—His Grace is keenly attached to the Buff and blue Party : renegadoes and Apostates are, you know, always keen.—My Landlord's Son, a young Officer of twenty, is his Grace's creature, and is supported by the Foxites; Sir James, on the other hand, is backed by Ministerial influence.—The Boroughs are much divided, and veer about with much uncertainty: the *weight* of the arguments of the several Candidates will determine their success.—I tell you all this insignificant stuff to enable you to understand the following Ballad which I have just composed on the occasion.—The Boroughs are Dumfries; Lochmaben a small old town once the private residence of Robert Bruce and romantically situated among six or seven little lakes; Annan, Kircudbright and Sanquhar near which is the old castle of the Crightons.—

179

Mrs Frances Anna Dunlop of Dunlop

—The five Carlins o' the South—A Scotch Ballad—
Tune—Chevy chase.
There was five Carlins in the South,
[C.W. p. 364]

I dare say, Madam, you are by this, compleatly sick of Ballads; else I
might send you a new edition, much enlarged and improved, of
Doctor Mcgill's ballad.[1]—That, with some verses which I made on
Captain Grose, [2] may be the subject of such another Scots mile
Epistle.—

Your little squalling Godson, goes on, "improving in grace and in
favor with God and with man."[3]—Parental partiality apart he is in
fact and very deed almost the finest boy I ever saw; and seems to
say, by the vigorous tossings of his little limbs and the open
manliness of his infant brow, that he will one day stand on the legs
of INDEPENDANCE and hold up the face of AN HONEST MAN.—

I am happy to hear that your departed Bard is to get justice done
him in his Poetic remains.[4]—It was surely verging to borders of
Ceremony, your asking my permission to subscribe my Name.—Your
goodness, my honored friend, I can only acknowledge—I can never
repay it.—

Adieu! Le bon Dieu soulage et soutient ! ! !

Robt Burns

1 C.W. p. 359
2 C.W. p. 415
3 Luke 2 : 52 misquoted
4 James Mylne; see Letter, (pp. 166-7)

XLIII (371)

Ellisland, 8th November 1789

If I were to write you, my dear honored Friend, in order to sport
harmony of period or brilliancy of Point, I could not chuse a more
favourable moment than the present.—I have somehow got a most
violent cold; and in the stupid, disagreable predicament of a stuffed,
aching head and an unsound, sickly crasis, do I sit down to thank
you for yours of the nineteenth of October, Prose, Verse, &
whatever *else* was inclosed in it.—God help a poor man! for if ne
take a pecuniary favor from a friend with that acquiescence which is
natural to Poverty at finding so accommodating a thing, the poor
devil is in the greatest danger of falling into an abjectness of soul
equally incompatible with the independence of Man and the dignity
of Friendship: on the other hand, should he bristle up his feelings in
irritated Manhood, he runs every chance of degrading his magnanimity into an exceptious pride, as different from true spirit as the
vinegar acid of sour twopenny is from the racy smack of genuine
October.—

Your verses on Miss Gray are very pretty, but your motto on the
beechen bowl is inimitably fine.—You ask me to send you some
Poetry in return : I shall send you a Song I made the other day, of

which your opinion, as I am too interested in the subject of it, to be a Critic in the composition.—

Song—

Thou lingering star, with lessening ray,

[C.W. p. 372]

> I have the honor to be,
>> Madam,
>>> your obliged humble servant
>>>> Robt Burns

XLIV (374)

Ellisland, 13th December 1789

Many thanks, dear Madam, for your sheet-full of Rhymes.— Tho' at present I am below the veriest Prose, yet from you every thing pleases.— I am groaning under the miseries of a diseased nervous System; a System of all others the most essential to our happiness— our Misery.— For now near three weeks I have been so ill with a nervous head-ach, that I have been obliged to give up for a time my Excise-books, being scarce able to lift my head, much less to ride once a week over ten muir Parishes.— Lord, what is Man! Today, in the luxuriance of health, exulting in the enjoyment of existence; In a few days, perhaps in a few hours, loaded with conscious painful being, counting the tardy place of the lingering moments, by the repercussions of anguish, & refusing or denied a Comforter.—Day follows night, and night comes after day, only to curse him with life which gives him no pleasure; & yet the aweful, dark termination of that life, is a something— perhaps a Nothing—at which he recoils with still more horror.—

> "Tell us, ye Dead; will none of you in pity
> "Disclose the Secret—
> *"What 'tis you are, and we must shortly be!*
> "—'tis no matter:
> "A little time will make us learn'd as you are"[1]—

Can it be possible that when I resign this frail, feverish being, I shall still find myself in conscious existence! When the last gasp of agony has announced that I am no more to those that knew me & the few who loved me; when the cold, stiffened, unconscious ghastly corse is resigned into the earth, to be the prey of unsightly reptiles, & to become in time a trodden clod, shall I yet be warm in life, seeing & seen, enjoying & enjoyed? Ye venerable Sages & holy Flamens, is there any probability in your many conjectures any truth in your many stories, of another world beyond death; or are they all alike, baseless visions & fabricated fables? If there is another life, it must be only for the just, the benevolent, the amiable & the humane; what a flattering idea, then, is a World to come! Would to God I as firmly believed it as I ardently wish it! There I should meet an aged Parent, now at rest from the many buffetings of an evil world against which he so long & bravely struggled. There should I meet the friend, the disinterested friend of my early life; the man who rejoiced to see me, because he loved me & could serve me—Muir, thy

weaknesses were the aberrations of Human-nature, but thy heart
glowed with every think generous, manly & noble; and if ever
emanation from the All-Good Being animated a human form, it was
thine!—There should I, with speechless agony of rapture, again
recognise my lost, my ever dear MARY, whose bosom was fraught
with Truth, Honor, Constancy & LOVE.—

> My Mary, dear, departed Shade!
> Where is thy place of heavenly rest?
> Seest thou thy Lover lowly laid?
> Hear'st thou the groans that rend his breast![2]

Jesus Christ, thou amiablest of characters, I trust thou art no
Impostor, & that thy revelation of blissful scenes of existence
beyond death and the grave, is not one of the many impositions
which time after time have been palmed on credulous mankind.—I
trust that in Thee "shall all the Families of the earth be blessed"[3]
by being yet connected together in a better world, where every tie
that bound heart to heart in this state of existence shall be, far
beyond our present conceptions, more endearing.—

I am a good deal inclined to think with those who maintain that
what are called nervous affections are in fact diseases of the mind.—
I cannot reason, I cannot think; & but to You, I would not venture
to write any thing above an order to a Cobler.—You have felt too
much of the ills of life not to sympathise with a diseased wretch who
is impaired more than half of any faculties he possessed.—Your
goodness will excuse this distracted scrawl which the Writer dare
scarcely read, and which he would throw into the fire, were he able
to write any thing better, or indeed any thing at all.—

I am glad you have put me on transcribing my departed Friend's
epitaph.—Transcribing saves me the very great trouble of thinking.—

> Epitaph on R. Muir—
> What Man could esteem, or what Woman could love,
> Was He who lies under his sod:
> If Such Thou refusest admittance above,
> Then whom wilt thou favor, Good God!

[C.W. p. 322]

Rumour told me something of a Son of yours who was returned
from the East or West Indies.—If you have gotten news of James or
Anthony, it was cruel in you not to let me know; as I promise you
on the sincerity of a man who is weary of one world and anxious
about another, that scarce any thing could give so much pleasure as
to hear of any good thing befalling my honored Friend.—

If you have a minute's leisure, take up your pen in pity to le pauvre
Miserable—

Robt Burns

1 Blair: *The Grave*
2 *Thou Lingering Star* C.W. p. 372
3. Genesis 12 : 3, misquoted

Mrs Frances Anna Dunlop of Dunlop

Ellisland 25th January 1790

It has been owing to unremitting hurry of business that I have not written you, Madam, long ere now.—My health is greatly better, and I now begin once more to share in satisfaction and enjoyment with the rest of my fellow creatures.—

Many thanks, my much esteemed Friend, for your kind letters: only, why will you make me run the risk of being contemptible & mercenary in my own eyes? When I pique myself on my independant spirit, I hope it is neither Poetic licence nor Poetic rant; and I am so flattered with the honor you have done me in making me your Compeer in Friendship & Friendly Correspondence that I cannot without pain & a degree of mortification be reminded of the real inequality between our situations.

Most sincerely do I rejoice with you, dear Madam, in the good news of Anthony.—Not only your anxiety about his fate, but my own esteem for such a noble, warmhearted, manly young fellow, in the little snatch I had of his acquaintance, has interested me deeply in his fortunes.—

Falconer, the unfortunate Author of the Shipwreck, that glorious Poem which you so much admire, is no more.—After weathering that dreadful catastrophe he so feelingly describes in his Poem, and after weathering many hard gales of Fortune, he went to the bottom with the Aurora frigate! I forget what part of Scotland had the honor of giving him birth; but he was the son of obscurity & misfortune.—He was one of these daring adventurous spirits which old Caledonia beyond any other nation is remarkable for producing.—Little does the fond Mother think, as she hangs delighted over the sweet Little Leech at her bosom, where the poor fellow may hereafter wander and what may be his fate.—I remember a Stanza in an old Scots Ballad which notwithstanding its rude simplicity speaks feelingly to the heart—

"Little did my Mother think,
    "That day she cradled me,
"What Land I was to travel in,
    "Or what death I should die!"[1]

Old Scots Songs are, you know, a favorite study & pursuit of mine, and now I am on that subject allow me to give you two stanzas of another old simple Ballad which I am sure will please you.—The catastrophe of the Piece is, a poor ruined Female lamenting her fate.—She concludes with this pathetic wish—

"O that my father had ne'er on me smil'd;
    "O that my Mother had ne'er to me sung!
"O that my cradle it had never rock'd;
    "But that I had died when I was young!
"O that the Grave it were my bed;
    "My blankets were, my winding sheet;
"The clocks & the worms my bedfellows a';
    "And O, sae sound as I would sleep!"[2]

I do not remember in all my reading to have met with any thing more truly the language of Misery than the exclamation in the last line.—Misery is like Love; to speak its language truly, the Author must have felt it.—

I am every day expecting the doctor to give your little Godson the Smallpox.—They are *rife* in the country, & I tremble for his fate.—By the way, I cannot help congratulating you on his looks & spirit.—Every Person who sees him acknowledges him to be the finest. handsomest child they have ever seen.—I am myself delighted with the manly swell of his little chest, and a certain miniature dignity in the carriage of his head & the glance of his fine black .eye, which promises the undaunted gallantry of an Independant Mind.-

I thought to have sent you some rhymes, but time forbids.—I promise you Poetry untill you are tired of it, next time I have the honor of assuring you how truly I am,
Dear Madam, your oblidged humble servant
R.B.

1 Mary Hamilton (Child No. 173).

2 Not identified.

XLVI (396)

[Ellisland, about 6th March 1790]

Though I have just one hour & a half to do any thing for myself in, (I have laid down my watch by me, & shall scribble away, devil take the hindmost;) yet you see I have begun at the very top ot my fool's cap page; and how I shall fill the sheet, shall be, like many more important matters, left to time & chance.—I never perused a friendly letter, not even from yourself, Madam, that gave me more pleasure than yours of the 4th Inst. which I have just read.—You talk of sending me a Poem on the King by an English farmer, & an Ode to Hope by Janet Little, but I would rather have such another sheet of your Prose, than a second Poem on Achilles by Homer, or an Ode on Love by Sappho.—

You kindly lament the distance between us: that distance may soon be lessened.—My farm is a ruinous bargain & would ruin me to abide by it.—The Excise, notwithstanding all my objections to it, pleases me tolerably well: it is indeed my sole dependance.—At Martinmass 1791, my rent rises 20 £ per Annum, & *then,* I am, on the maturest deliberation, determined to give it up; & still, even *then,* I shall think myself well quit, if I am no more than a hundred pounds out of Pocket.—So much for Farming! Would to God I had never engaged in it!—I can have in the Excise-line what they call a foot-walk whenever I chuse; that is an appointment to a Division where I am under no necessity of keeping a horse.—There is in every Sea-port town, one or two Officers, called Port-Officers, whose income is at least seventy pounds per ann.—I will petition Mr. Graham & stretch all my interest, to get one of these; and if possible on Clyde.—Greenock & Port Glasgow are both lucrative places in that way, & to them my views are bent.—You formerly wrote me, if a Mr. Corbet in the Excise could be of use to me.—If it is a Corbet who is what we

Mrs Frances Anna Dunlop of Dunlop

Mrs Frances Anna Dunlop of Dunlop

call one of our General Supervisors, of which we have just two in
Scotland, he can do every thing for me.—Were he to interest himself
properly for me, he could easily by Martinmass 1791 transport me
to Port Glasgow port Division, which would be the ultimatum of my
present Excise hopes.—He is a William Corbet, & has his home, I
believe, somewhere about Stirling.—One word more, & then to have
done with this most ungracious subject; all this business of my farm,
&c. is for your most private ear: it would be of considerable
prejudice to me to have it known at present.—

Your little Godson is quite recovered, & is if possible, more thriving
than ever; but alas! one of the Servants has introduced the measles
into the house, & I shall be very uneasy untill we get them over.—

I have made a very considerable acquisition in the acquaintance of a
Mr. Sutherland, Manager of a company of Comedians at present in
Dumfries.—The following is a Prologue I made for his wife, Mrs.
Sutherland's benefit-night.—You are to understand that he is getting
a new Theatre built here, by subscription; & among his Subscribers
are all the first Names in the country.—

Prologue for Mrs. Sutherland's benefit night at Dumfries,
March 3rd 1790
What needs this din about the town o' Lon'on,
[C.W. p. 399]

I hope this will find you quite recovered from that alarming disorder
which, hostile to my happiness, threatened you so awefully.—You
will make me wish, as the Romans did of Augustus, that you had
never been born, or had never died; for should you leave this world
before me, it will give my heart-strings such a wrench that nothing in
my afterlife shall restore them to their proper tone.—I hope Madame
Henri is quite well again, & that the Goodwife of Morham-mains,
little ones, &c. are going on, encreasing in favor with God & with
Man.*   —I am still very hurried.—In May or June I shall be in
Ayr-shire, & may have an opportunity in propria-persona of assuring
you how much I have the honor to be

your devoted humble servant
Robt Burns

* Luke 2: 52

XLVII (397)

Ellisland 10th April 1790

I have just now, my ever honored Friend, enjoyed a very high luxury
in reading a paper of the Lounger.—You know my National
Prejudices.—I had often read & admired the Spectator, Adventurer,
Rambler, & World, but still with a certain regret that they were so
thoroughly & entirely English.—Alas! have I often said to myself,
what are all the boasted advantages which my Country reaps from a
certain Union, that can counterbalance the annihilation of her
Independance, & even her very Name! I often repeat that couplet of
my favorite poet, Goldsmith—

"—States of native liberty possest,
"Tho, very poor, may yet be very blest."—*

185

Mrs Frances Anna Dunlop of Dunlop

Nothing can reconcile me to the common terms, "English Embassador, English Court, &c." And I am out of all patience to see that equivocal Character, Hastings, empeached by "the Commons of England."—Tell me, my Friend, is this weak prejudice? I believe in my conscience such ideas as, "my Country; her independance; her honor; the illustrious Names that mark the history of my Native Land;" &c. I believe these, among your *Men of the world,* men who in fact guide for the most part & govern our world, *they* look on ways of thinking as just so many modifications of wrongheadedness.— They know the use of bawling out these terms to rouse or lead The Rabble; but for their own private use, with almost all the *able Statesmen* that ever existed or now exist, when they talk of Right & Wrong, they only mean Proper & Improper; & their measure of conduct is, not what they OUGHT but what they DARE.—For the truth of this I shall not ransack the history of Nations, but appeal to one of the ablest judges of men, & himself one of the ablest men that ever lived—the famous Earl of Chesterfield.—In fact, a Man who could thoroughly controul his vices whenever they interfered with his interest, & who could compleatly put on the appearance of every virtue so often as it suited his purposes, is, on the Stanhopian plan, the *perfect man;* a Man to lead Nations.—But are Great Abilities, compleat without a flaw, & polished without a blemish, the standard of Human Excellence? This is certainly the staunch opinion of *Men of the World;* but I call on Honor, Virtue & Worth to give the Stygian doctrine a loud Negative!—However, this must be allowed, that, if you abstract from Man the idea of an Existence beyond the Grave, *then,* the true measure of human conduct is, Proper & Improper: Virtue & Vice, as dispositions of the heart, are, in that case, of scarcely the same import & value to the world at large, as Harmony & Discord in the modifications of Sound; & a delicate sense of Honor, like a nice ear for Music, tho' it may sometimes give the Possessor an exta'sy unknown to the coarser organs of the HERD, yet, considering the harsh gratings & inharmonic jars in this ill-tuned state of Being, it is odds but the Individual would be as happy, & certainly would be as much respected by the true judges of Society as it would then stand, without either a good ear or a good heart.—

You must know, I have just met with the Mirror & Lounger for the first time, & I am quite in raptures with them.—I should be glad to have *your* opinion of some of the Papers.—The one I have just read, Lounger No.61 has cost me more honest tears than any thing I have read of a long time.—Mckenzie has been called the Addison of the Scots, & in my opinion, Addison would not be hurt at the comparison.—If he has not Addison's exquisite humour, he as certainly outdoes him in the tender & the Pathetic.—His Man of feeling (but I am not Counsel learned in the laws of Criticism) I estimate as the first Performance in its kind I ever saw.—From what book, moral or even Pious, will the susceptible young mind receive impressions more congenial to Humanity & Kindness, Generosity & Benevolence, in short, all that ennobles the Soul to herself, or endears her to others, than from the simple affecting tale of poor Harley? Still, with all my admiration of Mckenzie's writings I do not know if they are the fittest reading for a young Man who is about to

186

set out, as the phrase is, to make his way into life.—Do not you think, Madam that among the few favored of heaven in the structure of their minds (for such there certainly are) there may be a purity, a tenderness, a dignity, an elegance of Soul which are of no use, nay in some degree absolutely disqualifying for the truly important business of making man's way into life.—If I am not much mistaken, my gallant young friend, Anthony, is very much under these disqualifications; and for the young Females of a Family I could mention, well may they excite Parental Solicitude, for I, a common acquaintance, or as my vanity will have it, an humble friend, have often trembled for a turn of mind which will render them eminently happy—or peculiarly miserable!

I have been manufacturing some verses lately; but as I have got the most hurried season of Excise business over, I hope to have more leisure to transcribe any thing thay may show how much I have the honor to be, Madam, your oblidged humble servant.

Robt Burns

* *Deserted Village*, lines 425-6 misquoted.

XLVIII (399)

Ellisland, 6th June 1790

It is by no means impossible, my dear & much-honored Friend, but that you may see me, ere this reach you.—A particular & rather disagreable business calls me to Ayrshire—disagreable in every thing, but in that I hope it shall give me the pleasure of being at Dunlop & seeing you there.—Believe me, Madam, Heaven has few pleasures with which I am acquainted, equal to what I shall have on the seventeenth Current if not a day sooner, when I hope to assure you in person how much I have the honor to be,

Madam, your oblidged friend & humble servant
Robt Burns

P.S.

It is now near midnight, but I cannot resist the temptation my vanity, or, with respect to *you*, something perhaps more amiable than Vanity yet not quite so disinterested as Friendship, puts in my way to make me transcribe the following Ballad for you—it was finished only this day.—You know & with me, pity the amiable but unfortunate Mary Queen of Scots: To YOU, and your YOUNG LADIES, I particularly dedicate the following Scots Stanzas—

Queen Mary's Lament—

Now Nature hangs her mantle green

[C.W. p. 400]

P.S. the 2nd. The foregoing, tho' a shocking scrawl, is wonderfully well; considering that I have both dined & supped with the gentleman who does me the honor to frank this letter.—

XLIX (403)

Ellisland, 9th July 1790

I have this moment your two melancholy letters.—Owing to the carelessness of my servant in not calling at the Post-Office, I had not received your first untill now.—What answer shall I write you, Madam? What consolation shall I, or *can* I, offer to misfortunes so deep & heavy as yours! I am glad however to hear by your last, that Heaven seems inclined to spare you a daughter, though it has with such additional, heart-wringing circumstances deprived you of a Son.—Poor Mrs. Henri! May that BEING who supports all Nature support her under the very heavy weight of her sorrows; and endow her with extraordinary strength of mind, equal to her extraordinary trials!

> — "Of Heaven's protection who can be
> "So confident, as utter this,
> "Tomorrow I will spend in bliss!"[1]

What hidden trap-doors of disaster, what unseen arrows of misfortune, waylay, & beset our paths of life! And Heaven as if to shew its Omnipotence, often from the covert where Suspicion slept as having nothing to fear, looses the Shaft that wounds us to the very soul.—Thomson says finely—

> Attach thee firmly to the virtuous deeds
> And offices of life: to life itself,
> And all its transient joys, sit loose—[2]

and yet, like many other fine sayings, it has, I fear more of Philosophy than Human-nature in it.—Poor David's pathetic cry of grief is much more the language of Man; "O Absalom! My Son! My Son!!"[3] .A WORLD TO COME! is the only genuine balm for an agonising heart, torn to pieces in the wrench of parting forever (to mortal view) with Friends, inmates of the bosom and dear to the soul! The most cordial believers in a Future State have ever been the Unfortunate.—This of itself; if God is Good, which is I think the most intuitive truth in Nature; this very propensity to, and supreme happiness of, depending on a Life beyond Death & the Grave, is a very strong proof of the reality of its existence.—Though I have no objection to what the Christian system tells us of Another world; yet I own I am partial to those proofs & ideas of it which we have wrought out of our own heads & hearts.—The first has the demonstration of an authenticated story, the last has the conviction of an intuitive truth.—I have one favorite proof, because (though perhaps five thousand have done the same before me,) I have discovered it in its native rock, at least hewn it into shape myself.— There are not any first principles or component parts of the Human Mind, more truly radical than what is meant by, OUGHT, and OUGHT NOT; which all Mankind (a most respectable Suffrage!) have, for several thousand years, agreed are synonimous terms with Virtue Vice.—But, except our Existence *here,* have a reference to an Existence *hereafter,* Virtue & Vice are words without a meaning.—If *this scene* of Being is the whole of the *Drama,* then a man's individual Self, his own pleasures & enjoyments, are & should be the whole of his care; and the true standard, of his actions is, PROPER and IMPROPER.—There might be a few that would still be influenced by what are called, Feelings of the heart; but by this new System, these said Feelings are only no better nor more respectable than so many *Constitutional Weaknesses;* & the true MAN OF SENSE would be prudent in his Iniquity, & wisely wicked.—Should any object, the pleasure that would still be in the exercise of Generosity, &c. I answer, that farther than such Generosity was useful in promoting your own private purposes; that said pleasure was & ought to be of no higher estimation & value than what is called, An ear for Music: a little gratification of the organ of Sense, but of no *real* importance in life.—

There is sometimes a conjuncture of circumstances which looks like ominous.—When I received your letters, I was just finishing the following Stanza—

> Envy not the hidden treasure
> Finer Feelings can bestow;
> Chords that vibrate sweetest pleasure,
> Thrill the deepest notes of woe.—

I immediately & almost extempore added the following, too allusive to poor Mrs. Henri—

> Fairest Flower, behold the lily,
> Blooming in the sunny ray;
> Let the blast sweep o'er the valley,
> See it prostrate on the clay.—

[C.W. p. 402]

I have just got a summons to attend with my men-servants armed as well as we can, on Monday at one o'clock in the *morning* to escort Captain Miller from Dalswinton in to Dumfries to be a Candidate for our Boroughs which chuse their Member that day.—The Duke of Queensberry & the Nithsdale Gentlemen who are almost all friends to the Duke's Candidate, the said Captain, are to raise all Nithsdale on the same errand.—The Duke of Buccleugh's, Earl of Hopeton's people, in short, the Johnstons, Jardines, and all the Clans of Annandale, are to attend Sir James Johnston who is the other Candidate, on the same account.—This is no exaggeration.—On Thursday last, at chusing the Delegate for the boro' of Lochmaben, the Duke & Captain Miller's friends led a strong party, among others, upwards of two hundred Colliers from Sanquhar Coal-works & Mine Miners from Wanlock-head; but when they appeared over a hill-top within half a mile of Lochmaben, they found such a superiour host of Annandale warriors drawn out to dispute the Day, that without striking a stroke, they turned their backs & fled with all the precipitation the horrors of blood & murther could inspire.—What will be the event, I know not.—I shall go to please my Landlord, & to see the Combustion; but instead of trusting to the strength of Man, I shall trust to the heels of my horse, which are among the best in Nithsdale.—As our Royal Scottish Poet says—

> "He sud been swift that gat him
> Thro' speed that day."—[4]

The lad that takes my letter to town, is waiting with impatience.—
I beg, Madam, most fervently to hear by the first post of your
family, & particularly of your own health which I fear must have
suffered exceedingly.—

God send good news from Loudon-Castle!

Robt Burns

1 Not identified.
2 *Alfred: A Masque,* Act I, SC 5, misquoted.
3 2 Samuel 18:33.
4 *Christis Kirk on the Grene,* Canto 17, attributed to King James I.

L (411)

With *Elegy on Captain Matthew Henderson.*
[C.W. p. 337]

Ellisland, 30th July 1790

Ten minutes ago I had no idea, my dear honored Friend that your
distresses could be of comfort to me, which, odd as it may sound,
they have just now been. I had transcribed off for you the inclosed
Elegy on a much-valued acquaintance of mine, which I thought
might perhaps amuse you a little; and was just set down to write you
by this conveyance which is my wife & your little God-son going to
Ayr-shire to see their friends, when a servant of mine brought me
from town, your letter, & one from London acquainting me with the
death of a brother of mine who was there a journeyman Saddler.—
He was just twenty-three, a fine, worthy, young fellow; & while my
bosom laboured with the anguish consequent on the distressing
intelligence—Poor Mrs. Henri!—said I to myself; & lifted up my heart
in gratitude that I was not called to bear such a load of woe as hers.—

I am not collected enough to write to you a letter.—I am happy
however that Miss Dunlop is getting better, & particularly that YOU
are not likely to suffer so much as I dreaded in precious health.—
That was a shocking alarm respecting the Major.—It would indeed,
Madam, have been a load of sorrows more than you could have
borne.—

I have just finished the Stanzas I mentioned in my last.—Allow me,
my dear Friend, to dedicate them to you, as a Relique at the shrine
of friendship—a friendship that makes so large a share of the
enjoyment of my existence.—If ever I print it, permit me to prefix
your name; & if the period of publication should be at some (I hope
very) distant time, when you & I may perhaps be in worlds as
different as Heaven & Earth, & should I be the survivor, I shall
certainly mention it—

Sacred to the Memory of a much-valued & dearly respected Friend—

Do, let me hear from you! You cannot imagine what pleasure it will
give me!—

Adieu!

Robt Burns

Mrs. Dunlop of Dunlop

LI (412)

8th August 1790

Dear Madam,

After a long day's toil, plague, and care, I sit down to write to you. Ask me not why I have delayed it so long? It was owing to hurry, indolence, and fifty other things; in short, to any thing—but forgetfulness of *la plus aimable de son sexe*. By the by, you are indebted your best courtesy to me for this last compliment, as I pay it from my sincere conviction of its truth—a quality rather rare in compliments of these grinning, bowing, scraping times.

Well, I hope writing to *you* will ease a little my troubled soul. Sorely has it been bruised to-day! A ci-devant friend of mine, and an intimate acquaintance of yours has given my feelings a wound that I perceive will gangrene dangerously ere it cure. He has wounded my pride!

* * * * *

LII (423)

Ellisland 6th October 1790

Dear Madam

Your last letter came to me exceedingly opportune indeed.—I was just beginning to get the better of a malignant squinancy & slow fever which had tormented me for three weeks & had actually brought me to the brink of the grave.—

I inclose you Mr. Corbet's letter.—I have not seen him, but from the gentleman's known character for steady worth, there is every reason to depend on his promised friendship.—

I am glad to hear by my friend Mr. Archibald Lowrie that your good family are getting rather better in health & spirits.—Health! the greatest enjoyment on earth, & wanting which, all other enjoyments are of poor avail.—This Sentiment I have lately felt in all its force.—

I give you joy of the works of Mr. Bourne, which you tell me you are reading.*—I once had the first Volume, & was so delighted with it that I could have almost repeated it verbatim.—We can no more live without Religion, than we can live without air; but give me the Religion of Sentiment and Reason.—You know John Hildebroad's famous epitaph—

> "Here lies poor old John Hildebroad;
> "Have mercy on his soul, Lord God,
> "As he would do, were he Lord God,
> "And thou wert poor John Hildebroad."—

This speaks more to my heart, & has more of the genuine spirit of Religion in it, than is to be found in whole waggon-loads of Divinity.— I have not a moment more left.—

Adieu!

Robt Burns

---

* Revd. Samuel Bourn: *A Series of Discourses on the Principles and Evidences of Natural Religion and the Christian Revelation*, 4 vols. (London, 1760-64).

Mrs Frances Anna Dunlop of Dunlop

LIII (427)

[Ellisland, November 1790]

"As cold waters to a thirsty soul, so is good news from a far Country."[1]—

Fate, or Providence, or whatever is the true Apellation for the Power who presides over & directs the affairs of this our world, has long owed me a letter of good news from you, in return for the many tidings of sorrow & woe which I have received from you.—In this instance I most cordially obey the Apostle—"Rejoice with them that do rejoice."[2]—For me, *to sing* for joy, is no new thing; but *to preach* for joy, as I have done in the commencement of this Epistle, is a pitch of extravagant rapture to which I never rose before.—

I read your letter—I literally, *jumped for joy*—how such a mercurial creature as a Poet, lumpishly keep his seat on the receipt of the best news from his best Friend—I seized my gilt-headed Wangee rod, an instrument indispensably necessary in my left hand, in the moment of Inspiration & rapture—and stride—stride—quick & quicker—out skipt I among the broomy banks of Nith to muse over my joy by retail.—To keep within the bounds of Prose was impossible.—Mrs. Little's is a more elegant, but not a more sincere Compliment to the sweet little fellow, than I extempore almost poured out to him in the following verses—

A Monsr Monsr Henri—
Sweet Floweret, pledge o' meikle love,

[C.W. p. 406]

I am much flattered by your approbation of my, "Tam o' Shanter;" which you express in your former letter; tho' by the by, you load me in that said letter with accusations heavy & many; to all which I plead, Not Guilty!—Your book is, I hear, on the road to reach me.—As to printing of Poetry, when you prepare it for the Press, you have only to spell it right, & place the capital letters properly: as to the punctuation, the Printers do that themselves.—

I have a copy of my "Tam of Shanter" ready to send you by the first opportunity: it is too heavy to send by Post. I heard of Mr. Corbet lately.—He, in consequence of your recommendation, is most zealous to serve me.—Please favor me soon with an account of your good folks; if Mrs. Henri is recovering, & the young gentleman doing well.—

I am ever, my dear Friend & honored Patroness,

yours sincerely
Robt Burns

1 Proverbs 25:25
2 Romans 12:15

LIV (428)

Ellisland, 6th December 1790

Madam,
After tasking you with the perusal of so long a Poem,* it would be Egyptian to burthen you with an additional long letter.—

192

MRS. FRANCES DUNLOP OF DUNLOP

MISS ELIZABETH BURNETT OF MONBODDO

I wrote you two or three days ago, which I hope has come to hand.—
I hope you take care that the sweet little Floweret is properly
sheltered in this nipping Decemberly weather; for though Mrs. Little
& I have planted a Parnassian bower round him, yet I fear the laurel
will prove a very defenceless shade;—at least, it has ever turned out a
thin shelter for its Owners, & poorly qualified to fence off—

> "Poverty's cold wind & crushing rain!" [2]

I am half angry with you that you have not let me know ere now,
how poor Mrs. Henri recovers.—There is something so interesting in
her situation that I cannot get her out of my head, morning, noon or
night.—The first tragedy I ever saw performed, was Douglas; & Mrs.
Henri eternally puts me in mind of the horrors I felt for Lady
Randolph's distresses.—God forbid the sequel should be similar!—

There is a fine copy of Blind Harry's history of Wallace printed at
Perth, from a Manuscript of great antiquity in the Advocate's library;
with an Engraving of him from a genuine picture in the possession of
the Society of Antiquarians.—If I thought you had not seen it, I
would send it to you.—It is the most elegant piece of work that ever
came from any Printingpress in Great-britain.— [3]

There is likewise just published, Barbour's life of Robert Bruce, [4]
done from an old Manuscript in the Advocate's library.—If I could
get it safely sent, you might have it.—

Adieu!
Robt Burns

1 *Tam o' Shanter.*
2 Thomson: *Autumn*, line 276.
3. R. Morison, Perth.
4 *The Bruce*, ed. John Pinkerton, London, 1790.

LV (435)

Ellisland, 7th February 1791

When I tell you, Madam, that by a fall, not from my horse but with
my horse, I have been a cripple some time, & that this is the first day
my arm & hand have been able to serve me in writing, you will allow
that it is too good an apology for my seemingly ungrateful silence.—
I am now getting better, & am able to rhyme a little, which implies
some tolerable ease; as I cannot think that the most poetic genius is
able to compose on the rack.—

I do not remember if ever I mentioned to you my having an idea of
composing an Elegy on the late Miss Burnet of Monboddo.—I had
the honor of being pretty well acquainted with her, & have seldom
felt so much at the loss of an acquaintance as when I heard that so
amiable & accomplished a piece of God's works was no more.—I
have as yet gone no farther than the following fragment, of which
please let me have your opinion.—You know that Elegy is so
exhausted a subject that any new idea on the business is not to be
expected: 'tis well if we can place an old idea in a new light.—How
far I have succeeded as to this last, you will judge from what follows—

193

Mrs Frances Anna Dunlop of Dunlop

Elegy on the late Miss Burnet of Monboddo—
Life ne'er exulted in so rich a prize,

[C.W. p. 416]

I have proceeded no farther.*

Your kind letter, with your kind remembrance of your Godson came safe.—To this last, Madam, it is scarcely what my pride can bear.—As to the little fellow, he is, partiality apart, the finest boy I have of a long time seen.—He is now seventeen months old, has the small-pox & measles over, has cut several teeth, & yet never had a grain of Doctor's drugs in his bowels.—

I am truly happy to hear that the "little Floweret" is blooming so fresh & fair, & that "the Mother-Plant" is rather recovering her drooping head.—Soon & well may her "cruel wounds" be healed!— I have written thus far with a good deal of difficulty.—When I get a little abler you shall hear farther from,

Madam your oblidged & most devoted servant
Robt Burns

* Despite this, the entire poem was included.

LVI (443)

Ellisland, 11th April 1791

I am once more able, my honored friend, to return you with my own hand, thanks for the many instances of your friendship & particularly for your kind anxiety in this last disaster that my evil genius had in store for me.—However, life is chequered, joy & sorrow, for on Saturday morning last Mrs. Burns made me a present of a fine boy, rather stouter but not so handsome as your God-son at his time of life was.—Indeed I look on your little Namesake to be my chef d'oeuvre in that species of manufacture, as I look on "Tam o' Shanter" to be my standard performance in the Poetical line.—'Tis true, both the one & the other discover a spice of roguish waggery that might perhaps be as well spared; but then they also shew in my opinion a force of genius & a finishing polish that I despair of ever excelling.—Mrs. Burns is getting stout again, & laid as lustily about her today at breakfast as a Reaper from the cornridge.—That is the peculiar priviledge & blessing of our hale, sprightly damsels, that are bred among the hay & heather.—We cannot hope for that highly polished mind, that charming delicacy of soul, which is found among the Female world in the more elevated stations of life, which is certainly by far the most bewitching charm in that famous cestus of Venus.—It is indeed such an inestimable treasure, that where it can be had in its native heavenly purity, unstained by some or other of the many shades of affectation, & unallayed by some or other of the many species of caprice, I declare to Heaven I would think it cheaply purchased at the expence of every other earthly good!—But as this angelic creature is I am afraid extremely rare in any station & rank of life, & totally denied to such a humble one as mine; We meaner mortals must put up with the next rank of female excellence—as fine

194

a figure & face we can produce as any rank of life whatever; rustic, native grace; unaffected modesty, & unsullied purity; Nature's mother-wit, & the rudiments of Taste; a simplicity of soul, unsuspicious of, because unacquainted with; the crooked ways of a selfish, interested disingenuous world; & the dearest charm of all the rest, an yielding sweetness of disposition & a generous warmth of heart, grateful for love on our part, & ardently glowing with a more than equal return; these, with a healthy frame, a sound, vigorous constitution, which your higher ranks can scarcely ever hope to enjoy, are the charms of lovely woman in my humble walk of life.—

This is the greatest effort my broken arm has yet made.—Do, let me hear by first post, how cher, petit Monsieur, comes on with his pustules.—May Almighty Goodness preserve & restore him!!!

I have the honor to be, Madam
your obliged friend—
Robt Burns

In a letter I had lately from Doctor Moore he bids me to remember him to you, & beg of you not to think that his friendship flags when his pen lies still.—He says except on business, he now seldom lifts a pen at all.—But, this is from myself, the devil take such apathy of Friendship!!!

R.B.

LVII (481)

Dumfries, 26th October 1791

Forgive me, Madam for not writing you sooner.—I have been measuring my land that I had sold the crop of; taking a house here in town, & furnishing it; preparing my horses, cows, farming things, &c. for sale next week; &. in short, have not had a moment's rest to do any thing with a pen.—

I highly approve of Mrs. Henri's idea.—The lines she has written are at once, simple & energetic.—*As they are;* none of the amendments above the lines; is my judgement of the matter.—

Cursed business just now interferes—I can do nothing but seal this, & inclose some verses I mentioned to you.—

I am ever, Dear Madam,
your oblidged humble servant
R.B.

LVIII (485A)

Ellisland 17th [December] 1791

Dear Madam,
So it seems I have offended your feelings by the execration which closed my last letter; but here, at the beginning of this epistle, I insist that you shall stand by & give me leave to curse—"The devil take that cursed Rheumatism, which is wrecking the health, peace & self-enjoyment of my ever-dear & honored Friend! ! !—" And all the people shall say, Amen!—

195

Many thanks to you, Madam, for your good news respecting the little Floweret & the Mother-plant.—I hope my poetic prayers have been heard, & will be answered up to the warmest sincerity of their fullest extent; & then, Mrs. Henri will find her little darling the representative of his late Parent in every thing—but his abridged existence.—Apropos, is it not a kind of proof that I am "a righteous Man," since my "faithful, fervent prayer" avails so much?—

I have just finished the following Song, which to a lady the descendant of Wallace, & many heroes of his truly illustrious Line; & herself the mother of several Soldiers, needs neither preface nor apology.

The Song of Death—

Farewell, thou fair day, thou green earth, & ye skies
[C.W. p. 420]

The circumstance that gave rise to the foregoing verses was, looking over, with a musical friend Mcdonald's Collection of Highland airs was struck with one, an Isle of Skye tune, entitled, "Oran an aoig or The Song of Death," to the measure of which I have adapted my Stanzas.—

I have of late composed two or three pieces, which, ere yon full-orbed Moon, whose broad, impudent face now stares at old mother Earth all night, shall have shrunk into a modest crescent, just peeping forth at dewy dawn, I shall find an hour to transcribe for you.—

A Dieu je vous commende!   Robt Burns

* Patrick McDonald, *A Collection of Highland Vocal Airs*, Edinburgh, 1784.

LIX (491)

Dumfries, 14th January 1792

You will scarce think it credible when I tell you, dear Madam, that ever since I wrote you last, I have actually not had time to write you again.—Leaving my former habitation, settling here & getting deeply engaged in a line of our business to which I was an entire Stranger; not to mention hunting of Smugglers once or twice every week, & a ten days jaunt into Edinburgh; these have so entirely engrossed my time & attention, that, except letters of indispensible business, I have not put pen to paper on any given subject since you heard from me.—Now, that hurry is nearly over.—I have got into the routine of my occupation, & have far less occupation than in my former place; & upon the whole, I have every reason to believe that I shall be much more comfortable for my change.—Indeed, CHANGE, was, to me, become a matter of necessity.—Ruin awaited me as a Farmer; though by that peculiar Good Luck that for some years past, has attended all my motions, I have got rid of my farm with little, if any loss.—

Thus have I dedicated one page to my own concerns; & now I begin another with wishing, most sincerely wishing you the Compliments of the season.—Whatever number of years the Great Disposer of events may have allotted you, May the JOYS of those years very far overbalance the SORROWS!—Notwithstanding your many tender Relatives & near Connections, I do not think that there is an individual in the world who shall more desire or enjoy the prolongation of your existence than I; yet there is a period beyond which life is a burden too heavy to be borne, & it must be a very ungenerous, selfish attachment that would wish to have a Friend present with us at the expence of making that friend miserable.—As to your prediction of sixty three, I laugh at it.—You have a hale, antedeluvian constitution; & if you have any enemies in the world, wretches who are wicked enough to wish your departure from this state of Being, I have no doubt but you will hold out tough & hard, & live—& live, — & live, till these atrocious Scelerats gnash their teeth in the agonies of despair.—

I most cordially congratulate you on your good news from Anthony.— Pray, have you heard nothing lately of Mrs. Henri & her dear Babe?— Her worth & her misfortunes would interest the most hardened Bandit in her fate.—Oh, how often has my heart ached to agony, for the power, "To wipe away all tears from all eyes!"[1]

I am glad to hear so good an account of Jenny Little's affairs.—I have done next to nothing for her as yet, but I shall now set about & soon fill up my Subscription-bill.[2]

I feel much for your loss in the late excellent Lady Wallace.—Losing a Friend is a loss one can ill afford at any time, but taking an everlasting farewell of, the Friend of many years, is truly-distressing.— That it may be long ere any of your friends have occasion to feel for You, what you now feel for her, is the ardent wish & prayer of,

Dear Madam, your obliged & obedient humble servant
Robt Burns

1 Revelations 21:4
2 Janet Little, the 'Scotch Milkmaid,' published her *Poetical Works* at Ayr, 1792. Both Burns and Mrs. Dunlop were among the subscribers.

LX (493)

Dumfries, 3rd February 1792

Dear Madam

I have just five minutes less than no time at all to answer your kind letter.—Imprimis & in the first place, as to Mr. Corbet, I have some faint hopes of seeing him here this season: if he come, it will be of essential service to me.—Not that I have any immediate hopes of a Supervisorship; but there is what is called a Port Division, here, &, entre nous, the present incumbent is so obnoxious, that Mr. C———s presence will in all probability send him adrift into some other Division, & with equal probability will fix me in his stead.—A Port Division is twenty pounds a year more than any other Division, beside as much rum & brandy as will easily supply an ordinary family; which last consideration brings me to my second head of discourse, namely your unfortunate hunting of Smugglers for a little brandy; an article I believe indeed very scarce in your country.—I have however hunted these Gentry to better purpose than you, & as a servant of my brother's goes from here to Mauchline tomorrow morning, I beg leave to send you by him a very small jar, sealed full of as genuine Nantz as ever I tasted.—This freedom I hope you will forgive.—The jar will reach you, I trust, by some safe channel, though by what channel, I shall leave my brother to direct.—

Your little Godson sends his most grateful acknowledgements to you.—

Wilson's book I have not seen; but will be much obliged to you for a sight of it. [1] —My glass is run—A Dieu je vous commende!

Robt Burns

1 Alexander Wilson *Poems*, Paisley (1790)

LXI (505)

Annan Waterfoot, 22nd August 1792

Do not blame me for it, Madam—My own conscience, hacknied & weather-beaten as it is, in watching & reproving my vagaries, follies, Indolence, &c. has contrived to blame & punish me sufficiently.— These two or three months, besides my own business, I have been writing out for, & correcting the Press-work of two Publications.— One was for a friend; the other is, my own Poems, a new edition of which, in two volumes, will appear in a few weeks.—All this, you *must* allow, was enough & more than enough for such an idle, unthinking, musing rhyming, lazy wight as your humble servant.—Do not think it possible, my dear & honored friend, that I could be so lost to gratitude for many favours; to esteem for much worth & to the honest, kind, pleasurable tie of, *now* old acquaintance & I hope & am sure, of progressive, increasing friendship—as, for a single day, not to think of you—to ask the Fates what they are doing & about to do with my much-loved Friend & her many & wide-scattered Connections—& to beg of them to be as kind to you & yours as they possibly can?

Apropos (tho' how it is apropos I have not leisure to explain) do you know that I am almost in love with an acquaintance of yours. "Almost!" said I—I am in love, souse! over head & ears, deep as the most unfathomable abyss of the boundless ocean; but the word, "Love," owing to the intermingledoms of the good & the bad, the pure & impure, in this world, being rather an equivocal term for expressing one's sentiments & sensations, I must do justice to the sacred purity of my attachment.—Know, then, that the heart-struck awe, the distant humble approach; the delight we should have in gazing upon & listening to a Messenger of Heaven, appearing in all the unspotted purity of his Celestial Home, among the coarse, polluted, far inferiour sons of men, to deliver to them tidings that made their hearts swim in joy & their imaginations soar in transport— such, so delighting, & so pure, were the emotions of my soul on meeting the other day with Miss Lesley Bailie, your neighbout at Mayfield.—Mr. Bailie with his two daughters, accompanied by a Mr.

198

Mrs Frances Anna Dunlop of Dunlop

Hamilton of Grange, passing through Dumfries a few days ago, on their way to England, did me the honor of calling on me, on which I took my horse (tho' God knows I could ill spare the time) & convoyed them fourteen or fifteen miles & dined & spent the day with them.—'Twas about nine, I think, when I left them; & riding home I composed the following ballad, of which you will probably think you have a dear bargain, as it will cost you another groat of postage.—You must know that there is an old ballad, beginning with

My bonie Lizie Bailie,
I'll rowe thee in my plaidie & c[1]—

so I parodied it as follows, which is literally the first copy, "unanointed, unannealed,"[2] as Hamlet says—

The bonie Lesly Bailie,
To see her is to love her,
[C.W. p. 435]

So much for ballads.—I regret that you are gone to the East Country, as I am to be in Ayrshire in about a fortnight.—This world of ours, notwithstanding it has many good things in it yet it has ever had this curse, that two or three people who would be the happier, the oftener they met together are, almost without exception, always so placed as never to meet but once or twice a year, which considering the few years of a man's life, is a very great "evil under the sun,"[3] & which I do not recollect that Solomon has mentioned in his catalogue of the miseries of man.—I hope, & believe, that there is a state of existence beyond the grave where the worthy of this life will renew their former intimacies, with this endearing addition, that "we meet to part no more."[4]—Still the damned dogmas of reasoning Philosophy throw in their doubts; but upon the whole, I believe, or rather I have a kind of conviction, though not absolute certainty, of the world beyond the grave.—

"Tell us, ye Dead,
Will none of you, in pity, disclose the secret
What 'tis you are & *we* must shortly be!"   [5]

A thousand times have I made this apostrophe to the departed sons of men, but not one of them has ever thought fit to answer the question. "O that some courteous ghost would blab it out!"[6]—but it cannot be: you & I, my Friend, must make the experiment by ourselves.—However, I am so convinced that an unshaken faith in the doctrines of Christianity is not only necessary by making us better men, but also by making us happier men, that I shall take every care that your little godson, & every little creature that shall call me, Father, shall be firmly persuaded that "God was in Christ, reconciling the world unto himself, not imputing unto men their trespasses."[7]—

So ends this heterogeneous letter, written at this wild place of the world, in the intervals of my labor of discharging a vessel of rum from Antigua.—

Le bon Dieu vous benit! Amen!
Robt Burns

1 Child No. 227

2 Shakespeare: *Hamlet* Act I, sc. 5, misquoted.

199

3 Ecclesiastes 4:3:5:13:6:1: and 10:5.
4 Probably from Blair: *The Grave*, lines 760-1, altered.
5 Ibid., lines 431-2; 434, misquoted.
6 Ibid, line 433.
7 Corinthians 5: 19, slightly misquoted.

LXII (510)

24th September 1792

I have this moment, my dear Madam, yours of the twenty third.—All your other kind reproaches, your news, &c. are out of my head when I read, & think on poor Mrs. Henri's situation.—Good God! a heart-wounded, helpless young woman—in a strange, a foreign Land, & that Land convulsed with every horror that can harrow the human feelings—sick—looking, longing for a Comforter, but finding none—a Mother's feelings, too—but it is too much: He who wounded (He only can) may HE HEAL!—

As to your cold, you are so accustomed to, so hardened by our villianous climate, that I hope you will soon get the better of your complaint:—I wish the Farmer great joy of his new acquisition to his family.—I suppose he means to go on untill he shall count his children as one does wine—by the dozen.—He reminds me of a Scripture phrase, "And by these men was the earth *replenished* & divided."1 — I cannot say that I give him joy of his life as a Farmer.—'Tis, as a Farmer, paying dear, unconcionable rent, a *cursed life!*—As to a LAIRD farming his own property; sowing corn in hope, & reaping it, in spite of brittle weather, in gladness; knowing that none can say unto him, "What dost thou!"—fattening his herds; shearing his flocks; rejoicing at Christmas; & begetting sons & daughters, untill he be the venerated, grey-haired leader of a little Tribe—'tis a heavenly life!— but devil take the life of reaping the fruits that another must eat.—

Well, your kind wishes will be gratified, as to seeing me when I make my Ayrshire visit.—I cannot leave Mrs. B— untill her nine-month race is run, which may perhaps be in three or four weeks.—She, too, seems determined to make me the Patriarchal leader of a band.— However, if Heaven will be so obliging as let me have them in the proportion of three boys to one girl, I shall be so much the more pleased.—I hope, if I am spared with them, to shew a set of boys that will do honor to my cares & name; but I am not equal to the task of rearing girls.—Besides, I am too poor: a girl should always have a fortune.—Apropos, your little godson is thriving charmingly, but is a very devil.—He, though two years younger, has compleatly mastered his brother.—Robert is indeed the mildest, gentlest creature I ever saw.—He has a most surprising memory, & is quite the pride of his schoolmaster.—

You know how readily we get into battle upon a subject dear to our heart: you can excuse it.—God bless you & yours!

Robt Burns

* Probably derived from Genesis 9:1.

Mrs Frances Anna Dunlop of Dunlop

LXIII (512)

[October 1792]

I had been from home, and did not receive your letter until my return the other day. What shall I say to comfort you, my much-valued, much-afflicted friend! I can but grieve with you; consolation I have none to offer, except that which religion holds out to the children of affliction—*Children of affliction!*—how just the expression! and, like every other family, they have matters among them which they hear, see, and feel in a serious, all-important manner, of which the world has not, nor cares to have any idea. The world looks indifferently on, makes the passing remark, and proceeds to the next novel occurence.

Alas, Madam! who would wish for many years? What is it but to drag existence until our joys gradually expire, and leave us in a night of misery; like the gloom which blots out the stars one by one, from the face of night, and leaves us, without a ray of comfort, in the howling waste!

I am interrupted, and must leave off. You shall soon hear from me again.

LXIV (524)

Dumfries, 6th December 1792

I shall be in Ayrshire I think, next week; & if at all possible, I shall certainly, my much esteemed Friend, have the pleasure of visiting at Dunlop house.—Alas, Madam! how seldom do we meet in this world that we have reason to congratulate ourselves on accessions of happiness!—I have not passed half the ordinary term of an old man's life, & yet I do not see some names that I have known, & which I, & other acquaintances, little thought to meet with there so soon.—Every other instance of the mortality of our kind, makes us cast a horrid anxious look into the dreadful abyss of uncertainty, & shudder with apprehension for our own fate.—But of how different importance are the lives of different Individuals? Nay, of what importance is one period of the same life, more than another? A few years ago, I could have lain down in the dust, careless, as the book of Job elegantly says, "Careless of the voice of the morning",[1] & now, not a few, & these most helpless, individuals, would on losing me & my exertions, lose both their "Staff & Shield."—By the way, these helpless ones have lately got an addition; Mrs. B———having given me a fine girl since I wrote you.—There is a charming passage in Thomson's Edward & Eleonora—

> "The valiant, *in himself,* what can he suffer?
> Or what does he regard his single woes?
> But when, alas he multiplies himself
> To dearer selves, to the loved tender Fair,
> To those whose bliss, whose beings hang upon him,
> To helpless children! then, O then! he feels
> The point of misery festering in his heart,
> And weakly weeps his fortune like a coward"[2]—

As I am got in the way of quotations, I shall give you another from the same piece, peculiarly—Alas, too peculiarly apposite, my dear Madam, to your present frame of mind.—

> "Who so unworthy but may proudly deck him
> With his fair-weather virtue, that exults,
> Glad, o'er the summer main? the tempest comes,
> The rough winds rage aloud; when from the helm
> This virtue shrinks, & in a corner lies
> Lamenting—Heavens! if privileged from trial,
> How cheap a thing were virtue!"3—

I do not remember to have heard you mention Thomson's Dramas, as favorite walks of your reading.—Do you know, I pick up favorite quotations, & store them in my mind as ready armour, offensive, or defensive, amid the struggle of this turbulent existence.—Of these is one, a very favorite one, from Thomson's Alfred

> "Attach thee firmly to the virtuous deeds
> And offices of life: to life itself,
> With all its vain & transient joys, sit loose"4—

Probably I have quoted some of these to you formerly, as indeed when I write from the heart, I am apt to be guilty of these repetitions.—The compass of the heart, in the musical style of expression, is much more bounded, than the reach of invention; so the notes of the former are extremely apt to run into similar passages; but in return for the paucity of its compass, its few notes are much more sweet.—I must still give you another quotation, which I am almost sure I have given you before, but I cannot resist the temptation.—The subject is Religion.—Speaking of its importance to mankind, the Author says

> "'Tis this, my Friend, that streaks our morning bright;
> 'Tis this that gilds the horrors of our night.—
> When wealth forsakes us, & when friends are few:
> When friends are faithless, & when foes pursue;
> 'Tis this that wards the blow, or stills the smart,
> Disarms affliction, or repels its dart:
> Within the breast bids purest raptures rise,
> Bids smiling conscience spread her cloudless skies"5—

I see you are in for double Postage, so I shall e'en scribble out t'other sheet.—We, in this country, here have many alarms of the Reform, or rather the Republican spirit, of your part of the kingdom.—Indeed, we are a good deal in commotion ourselves, & in our Theatre here, "God save the king" has met with some groans & hisses, while Ça ira has been repeatedly called for.—For me, I am a *Placeman*, you know; a very humble one indeed, Heaven knows, but still so much so as to gag me from joining in the cry.—What my private sentiments are, you will find out without an Interpreter.—In the mean time, I have taken up the subject in another view, and the other day, for a pretty Actress's benefit-night, I wrote an Address, which I will give on the other page, called *The Rights of Woman.*

I shall have the honour of receiving your criticisms in person at Dunlop.

1 Quoted from another source; this phrase does not appear in the Book of Job or elsewhere in the Bible.
2 Act IV, sc. 6.
3 Act IV, sc. 7.
4 *Alfred: A Masque*, Act 1, sc. 5.
5 Previously quoted by Burns to Mrs. Dunlop, 6th September 1789.

LXV (529)

31st December 1792

Dear Madam,

A hurry of business, thrown in heaps by my absence, has untill now prevented my returning my grateful acknowledgements to the good Family of Dunlop, and you in particular, for that hospitable kindness which rendered the four days I spent under that genial roof, four of the pleasantest I ever enjoyed.—Alas, my dearest Friend! how few and fleeting are those things we call Pleasures! On my road to Ayr-shire, I spent a night with a friend whom I much valued; a man whose days promised to be many; & on Saturday last we laid him in the dust!

2nd January 1793

I have just received yours of the 30th & feel much for your situation.—However, I heartily rejoice in your prospect of recovery from that vile jaundice.—As to myself, I am better, though not quite free of my complaint.—You must not think, as you seem to insinuate, that in my way of life I want exercise.—Of that I have enough; but occasional hard drinking is the devil to me.—Against this I have again & again bent my resolution, & have greatly succeeded.— Taverns, I have totally abandoned: it is the private parties in the family way, among the hard drinking gentlemen of this country, that does me the mischief—but even this, I have more than half given over.—

Mr. Corbet can be of little service to me at present; at least I would be shy of applying.—I cannot possibly be settled as a Supervisor, for several years.—I must wait the rotation of the List, & there are twenty names before mine.—I might indeed get a job of officiating, where a settled Super was ill, or aged; but that hauls me from my family, as I could not remove them on such an uncertainty.—Besides, some envious, malicious devil has raised a little demur on my political principles, & I wish to let that matter settle before I offer myself too much in the eye of my Superiours.—I have set, henceforth a seal on my lips, as to these unlucky politics; but to you, I must breathe my sentiments.—In this, as in every thing else, I shall shew the undisguised emotions of my soul.—War I deprecate: misery & ruin to thousands, are in the blast that announces the destructive Demon.—But ...

[Three-quarters of a page cut away here]

. . . . the wisdom of their wickedness, & wither the strength of their iniquity! Set this seal upon their unrighteous resolves, "Behold, whatsoever you do, it shall not prosper".* That destruction THOU hast already begun to deal unto them, may it be the for...

Mrs Frances Anna Dunlop of Dunlop

[Three-quarters of a page missing]

5th January 1792 [for 1793]

You see my hurried life, Madam: I can only command starts of time.—However, I am glad of one thing; since I finished the other sheet, the political blast that threatened my welfare is overblown.—I have corresponded with Commissioner Graham, for the Board had made me the subject of their animadversions; & now I have the pleasure of informing that all is set to rights in that quarter.—Now, as to these inquisitorial Informers, Spies, Persecutors, &c. may the devil & his angels be let loose to—but hold! I was praying most fervently in my last sheet, & I must not so soon fall acursing in this.—

Alas! how little do the wickedly, or wantonly, or idly, officious, think what mischief they do by their malicious insinuations, indiscreet impertinence, or thoughtless blabbings.—What a difference there is, in intrinsic worth; Candour, Benevolence, Generosity, Kindness—in all the Charities & all the Virtues; between one class of human beings & another!—For instance, the amiable circle I so lately mixed with in the hospitable hall of Dunlop,—their gentle, generous hearts; their uncontaminated, dignified minds; their informed & polished understandings what a contrast, when compared—if such comparing were not downright sacrilege—with the prostituted soul of the miscreant wretch, who can deliberately & diabolically plot the destruction of an honest man who never offended him; & with a hellish grin of satisfaction can see the unfortunate man, his faithful wife, & prattling innocents, turned over to Beggary & Ruin.—Can such things be? Oui! telles choses se font! Je viens d'en faire une epreuve maudite.—(By the way, I don't know whether this is French; & much would it go against my soul, to mar anything belonging to that gallant people: though my real sentiments of them shall be confined alone to my correspondence with you.)

Your cup, my dear Madam, arrived safe.—I had two worthy fellows dining with me the other day, when I, with great formality, produced my whigmeleerie cup, & told them that it had been a family-piece among the descendants of Sir William Wallace.—This roused such an enthusiasm, that they insisted on bumpering the punch round in it; & by & by, never did your great Ancestor lay a *Suthron* more compleately to rest, than for a time did your cup my two friends.—

Your books I will send, but I wish to wait for a confirmed frost; as I know too well how much the carelessness of Carriers is apt to injure books in wet weather.—

Apropos, this is the season of wishing.—May God Almighty bless you, my dear Friend, & bless me the humblest & sincerest of your friends, by granting you yet many returns of the Season!—May all good things attend you, & yours, wherever they are scattered over the earth!—

Write me as soon as possible to let me know how your health recovers.—I tremble for you, when you meet the servants from France.—

Mrs Frances Anna Dunlop of Dunlop

> With the sincerest truth I ever am,
>> Dear Madam,
>>> your obliged Friend & humble servant
>>>> Robert Burns

*Psalms 1:3, altered

LXVI (563)

[June 1793]

I sent you a great while ago, a parcel of books, which I hope came safe to hand; & that they found my much respected friend in health & spirits & have afforded her some entertainment.—I have been doing little in my rhyming trade of a long while.—The following is an epigram which I made the other day on a stupid, money-loving dunderpate of a Galloway laird—Maxwell of Cardoness—

> Bless Jesus Christ, O Cardoness,
>> With grateful, lifted eyes;
> Who taught that not the soul alone,
>> But body too shall rise.—

> For had he said, the soul alone
> From death I will deliver:
> Alas, alas, O Cardoness!
>> Then hadst thou lain forever!

Here follows another.—

Extempore, on being asked why God had made Miss Davies so little, & Mrs S——[1] so big.—

Miss D—— you must know, is positively the least creature ever I saw, to be at the same time unexceptionably, & indeed uncommonly, handsome & beautiful; & besides has the felicity to be a peculiar favorite toast of mine.—On the contrary, Mrs S—— is a huge, bony, masculine, cowp-carl, horse-godmother, he-termagant of a six-feet figure, who might have been bride to Og, king of Bashan; or Goliath of Gath.—

Epigram
> Ask why God made the GEM so small,
>> And why so huge the Granite?
> Because, God meant mankind should set
>> That higher value on it.—

Though I think this last a pretty enough thought, yet I have been lately outdone by an humble acquaintance of mine, who is reckoned a very clever fellow among his fellow-tanners; for that is his trade.—I do not remember to have heard any thing of a good while that has pleased me so much.—

Epigram
> Silence in love shews deeper woe
>> Than words tho e're so witty:
> A beggar that is dumb, you know,
>> Deserves the greater pity.[2]—

205

I shall be too late for the post.—

Adieu!

R. B.

1 Not identified
2 Previously published in *Scots Magazine* (1740 and 1787), but probably originating with Sir Walter Raleigh.

LXVII (579)

25th August, [1793]

I have got a Frank for you*, my dear Madam, but I have unfortunately miscalculated the time.—The Post goes in ten minutes, so, to fill up my paper to the decent length of a letter, in such a moment of time, I shall write you a song which I composed the other day.—It is to an old Air called Allan water, a river in Perth-shire.—

Song
By Allan-side I chanc'd to rove,

[C.W. p. 498]

Are you, Madam, acquainted with any of the principal people, concerned in this new Royal Bank about to be established in Glasgow?—I am sure the Major will know them all.—Alas, too well do I know the up-hill business of asking a favor! But an uncommonly clever worthy young fellow, an intimate friend of mine, would wish a Clerk's place in it; & if you could any way serve him in that view, I would *indeed* esteem it as a high personal favour.—His name is, John Drummond: a native of Crieff: was bred four years a Clerk in a Banking-house (I forget its name) in Stirling; & has been now two years in the same capacity in a branch of the Paisley Bank here in Dumfries.—That branch is giving up, which is the reason of his being out of employ; & in these accursed times, employ is not easily found.—The Cashier of the Paisley Union bank can give his character.—Indeed, Recommendation in the strongest terms, he can have from all his former Employers; & *Pecuniary* Security he can furnish, to *any amount.*—Permit me to tax your most strenuous efforts.—

Adieu!
Robt Burns

* From Captain Patrick Miller, Jr. of Dalswinton, M.P.

LXVIII (603)

I mentioned to you a grand Publication of Scots songs, going on just now at London, where I have the honor (indeed it is all I have by it) of revising & composing the Scots Songs.*—The following are verses I intend for the sweet plaintive air, Logan-water—

A Song.—Tune Logan water

O Logan, sweetly didst thou glide,

[C.W. p. 490]

I have lately written two, or three ballads for the forementioned Collection which I will send you some other opportunity.—

Adieu!

* Thomson, *Select Collection.*   R. Burns

LXIX (605)

December 15th [1793]

My dear Friend,

As I am in a compleat Decembrish humour, gloomy, sullen, stupid, as even the deity of Dullness herself could wish, I will not drawl out a heavy letter with a number of heavier apologies for my late silence.—Only one I shall mention, because I know you will sympathise in it: these four months, a sweet little girl, my youngest child, has been so ill, that every day, a week or less threatened to terminate her existence.—I am sure that I have made my favorite quotation from Thomson's Edward & Eleanora, to you before; but it is so pat here, that I cannot resist it.—

> "The valiant, in himself, what can he suffer?
> "Or what does he regard his single woes?
> "But when, alas, he multiplies himself
> "To tender selves, to the lov'd tender Fair,
> "To those whose bliss, whose beings hang upon him,
> "To helpless children! then, O then! he feels
> "The point of misery fest'ring in his heart,
> "And weakly weeps his fortune like a coward"[1]—

There had much need be many pleasures annexed to the states of husband & father, for God knows, they have many peculiar cares.—I cannot describe to you, the anxious, sleepless hours these ties frequently give me. I see a train of helpless little folks; me, & my exertions, all their stay; & on what a brittle thread does the life of man hang! If I am nipt off, at the command of Fate; even in all the vigour of manhood as I am, such things happen every day—Gracious God! what would become of my little flock!—'Tis here that I envy your people of fortune.—A Father on his death-bed, taking an everlasting leave of his children, is indeed woe enough; but the man of competent fortune leaves his sons & daughters, independency & friends; while I—but, my God, I shall run distracted if I think any longer on the Subject!—

To leave talking of the matter so gravely, I shall sing with the old Scots ballad—

> "O that I had ne'er been married,
>   "I would never had nae care;
> "Now I've gotten wife & bairns,
>   "They cry, Crowdie!·ever mair.—
>
> "Crowdie! ance; Crowdie! twice;
>   "Crowdie! three times, in a day:
> "An ye, Crowdie! ony mair,
>   "Ye'll, Crowdie! a' my meal away."—

[C.W. p. 601]

I have often mentioned to you, a London Publication of Scots airs & songs, to which I have the honor to be Scots Composer.—The following I wrote the other day, for a beautiful Scots air; & I think it has some merit, so I send it you.—I have indeed, of late, written a good many things in that way; even though often far, far different from the complexion of my mind; but the Editor is a particular friend of mine, & I have pledged myself to assist him.—

Song—

Farewell, thou stream that winding, flows

[C.W. p. 486]

20th—

I have been, until this morning, unable to command half an hour, to finish this letter.- I am going to give you another little bagatelle of mine, of which I am really proud.—One favored hour of my Muse, I was reading the history of the battle of Bannockburn, & figuring to myself the looks & feelings of the Scots Patriot Heroes on that eventful day, as they saw their hated but powerful Tyrants advance. —The following, I have called, Bruce's Speech to his troops.—

Bannockburn—Tune, Lewis Gordon—

Scots wha hae with Wallace bled;
Scots whom Bruce has often led;
Welcome to your gory bed,
Or to glorious victorie.—

24th December

We have had a brilliant Theatre here, this season; only, as all other business has, it experiences a stagnation of trade from the epidemical complaint of the Country—"WANT OF CASH."—I mention our Theatre, merely to lug in an occasional Address which I wrote for the Benefit-Night of one of the Actresses, & which is as follows—

Address, spoken by Miss Fontenelle on her Benefit night December 4th at the Theatre, Dumfries,—Written by, Mr Burns

Still anxious to secure your partial favor,

[C.W. p. 508]

25th Christmas morning

This, my much lov'd Friend, is a morning of wishes: accept mine—so Heaven hear me, as they are sincere! that Blessings may attend your steps, & Affliction know you not!—In the charming words of my favorite Author, The Man of Feeling—"May the Great Spirit bear up the weight of thy grey hairs; & blunt the arrow that brings them rest"[2]

Now that I talk of Authors, how do you like Cowper? Is not the Task a glorious Poem? The Religion of The Task, bating a few scraps of Calvinistic Divinity, is the Religion of God & Nature; the Religion that exalts, that ennobles man.—Were not you to send me your Zeluco, in return for mine? Tell me, how you like my marks & notes through the Book. I would not give a farthing for a book, unless I were at liberty to blot it with my criticisms.—

Mrs Frances Anna Dunlop of Dunlop

I have lately collected, for a Friend's perusal, all my letters; I mean, those which I first sketched in a rough draught, & afterwards wrote out fair.—On looking over some old musty papers, which, from time to time, I had parcelled by, as trash that were scarce worth preserving & which yet at the same time, I did not care to destroy I discovered many of these rude sketches, & have written & am writing them out, in a bound M.S.S., for my Friend's Library.—As I wrote always to you, the rhapsody of the moment, I cannot find a single scroll to you, except one, about the commencement of our acquaintance.—If there were any possible conveyance, I would send you a perusal of it.—

Adieu! God bless you!
Robert Burns

1 Act IV
2 Henry Mackenzie, *The Man of Feeling*, XXXIV, 'He Meets an Old Acquaintance', slightly misquoted.

LXX (620A)

[13th March 1794]

I would have written you, my dear Friend, immediately on receipt of yours, but from day to day I had a prospect of going to Ayrshire when I would have had the very great pleasure of meeting you; but today I learn that all hopes of my west-country jaunt are cut off.—This has mortified me extremely, as now I shall not have it in my power to see you God knows when.—I shall indeed be in Ayrshire in summer, but then it is odds but you will be in the East-country.—

Pray, were not your son, James, & your grandson, Wallace, along with Cornwallis at Seringapatam?—I am just reading an exceedingly well written narrative of that campaign, done by a Major Dirom, who was Adjutant general there; & who has bought an estate & is now settling in this neighbourhood.—The Major frequently mentions Lieutenant Wallace, whom I take to be your grandchild; & lieutenant Agnew, who may possibly be a relation of yours.—They, two, were aidecamps to Colonel Maxwell.—I have often wished to have sat by you, & have read the narrative to you.—The circumstance of little Wallace being there, so near a relation of yours, & one in whom I know you are so much interested, made me all alive to the Story.—It was an admirable school for a young Soldier.—

How do you like the following verses, which I wrote the other day on a fantastical, fine-fashioned Dame of my acquaintance?

Monody on Maria————

How cold is that breast now which Folly once fired,

[C.W. p. 511]

Voílà un autre—In answer to one who affirmed of a well-known Character here, Dr Babbington, that there was Falsehood in his very looks—

That there is Falsehood in his looks,
I must & will deny;
They say, their Master is a KNAVE—
—And sure they do not lie.—

Yours ever
R. Burns

Mrs Frances Anna Dunlop of Dunlop

LXXI (628)

Castle Douglas, 25th June 1794

Here in a solitary inn, in a solitary village, am I set by myself, to amuse my brooding fancy as I may.—Solitary confinement, you know, is Howard's* favorite idea of reclaiming sinners; so let me consider by what fatality it happens that I have so long been exceeding sinful as to neglect the correspondence of the most valued Friend I have on earth.—To tell you that I have been in poor health, will not be excuse enough, though it is true.—I am afraid that I am about to suffer for the follies of my youth.—My Medical friends threaten me with a flying gout; but I trust they are mistaken.—

I am just going to trouble your critical patience with the first sketch of a stanza I have been framing as I passed along the road.—The Subject is, LIBERTY: you know, my honored Friend, how dear the theme is to me. I design it as an irregular Ode for General Washington's birth-day.—After having mentioned the degeneracy of other kingdoms I come to Scotland thus—

> Thee, Caledonia, thy wild heaths among,
> Thee, famed for martial deed & sacred Song,
> To thee I turn with swimming eyes;
> Where is that soul of Freedom fled?
> Immingled with the mighty Dead,
> Beneath the hallowed turf where WALLACE lies!
> Hear it not, WALLACE, in thy bed of death!
> Ye babbling winds, in silence sweep;
> Disturb ye not the hero's sleep,
> Nor give the coward secret breath
> Is this the Power in freedom's war
> That wont to bid the battle rage?
>
> Behold that eye which shot immortal hate,
> Crushing the despot's proudest bearing,
> That arm which, nerved with thundering fate,
> Braved Usurpation's boldest daring
> One quenched in darkness like the sinking star,
> And one the palsied arm of tottering, powerless Age.—

[C.W. p. 515]

You will probably have another scrawl from me in a stage or two.—

Yours ever most gratefully
Robt Burns

*John Howard, author of *The State of the Prisons in England and Wales* (1777).

LXXII (638)

[September, 1794]

Dear Madam,

I am so poorly today as to be scarce able to hold my pen, and so deplorably stupid as to be totally unable to hold it to any purpose; but as my good friend, The Member, franks it for me, it will only cost you the penance of reading.—I know you are pretty deep read in Medical matters, but I fear you have nothing in the Materia

Mrs Frances Anna Dunlop of Dunlop

Medica which can heal a diseased SPIRIT.—I think that the Poet's old companion, Poverty, is to be my attendant to my grave.—You know that my brother, poor fellow! was on the brink of ruin, when my good fortune threw a little money among my hands which saved him for a while.—Still his ruinous farm threatens to beggar him, & though, a bad debt of ten pounds excepted, he has every shilling I am worth in the world among his hands, I am nearly certain that I have done with it for ever.—This loss, as to my individual self, I could hold it very light; but my little flock would have been the better for a couple of hundred pounds: for *their* sakes, it wrings my heart!—

A propos, the other day, Mrs. Burns presented me with my fourth son, whom I have christened, James Glencairn; in grateful memory of my lamented Patron.—I shall make all my children's names, altars of gratitude.—Poor dear little souls, they are all the finest creatures in the world.—I gratefully thank my God for his goodness in that respect.—A fine constitution, & amiable dispositions, are of immense consequence to the happiness of the individual.—

When did you hear from the East?—Believe me, I am most anxiously interested in every thing dear to you.—Have you any correspondence with little Wallace; & does he promise well?—I know that he used to occupy a good deal of your thoughts.—Ah, my dear Madam, the feelings of a Parent are not to be described!—I sympathised much, the other day, with a father, a man whom I respect highly.—He is a Mr. Staig, the leading man in our Borough.—A girl of his, a lovely creature of sixteen, was given over by the Physician, who openly said that she had but few hours to live.—A gentleman who also lives in town, & who had studied medicine in the first schools—the Dr. Maxwell whom Burke mentioned in the House of Commons about the affair of the daggers—he was at last called in;—& his prescriptions, in a few hours altered her situation, & have now cured her.—Maxwell is my most intimate friend, & one of the first characters I ever met with; but on account of his Politics is rather shunned by some high Aristocrates, though his Family & Fortune entitle him to the first circles.—I addressed the following epigram to him on the occasion—

Maxwell, if merit here you crave,
[C.W. p. 519]

Here follows an Epigram of a different cast.—
On Walter Riddell Esq:
So vile was poor Wat, such a miscreant slave,
[C.W. p. 516]

I shall write you some ballads, in a day or two, the playthings of my fancy of late.—

Farewell!
Robt Burns

211

LXXIII (645)

29th October 1794

Dear Madam,

Your letter gives me great concern.—At this rigorous season, & at your time of life, a journey to London is no trifling matter.—Why did you not tell me which of the young Ladies was ill?—I regret extremely your journey, & I regret still more the occasion of it— One thing is in your favor; you will have the advice & friendly consolation of your & my very good Friend, Dr. Moore.—

Something else that was in your letter, I do not know how to mention.—You have effectively precluded my writing, you, at the time when sitting down to take up my pen to you was of most consequence to me: in the desponding hour of oppressing care.—My plaintive epistle, & the contents of your answer, give me, on my part, so much the air of mendicant insinuation, that I do not know how to lift up my head under it.—I know not how to be the object of Pity.—My Enemies may dislike (for they dare not despise me) & I can repay them in kind; but the Pity of a Friend is quite distressing.— But more than enough on the subject.—

I would without hesitation have crossed the country to wait on you, but for one circumstance—a week ago I gave my little James the small-pox, & he is just beginning to sicken.—In the mean time, I will comfort myself, that you will take Dumfries in your way: I shall be mortally disappointed if you do not.—Remember, it is by much your nearest route.—

At this time you will be all life & gayety, with your Ayr-races.—We have had the Caledonians here for this bypast fortnight; & of course, we have had a roar of Folly & Dissipation.—Most of our fashionable young men have all that Profligacy & Outrage which have sometimes accompanied Superior Understanding & brilliant Wit—but without those bright talents which might throw a kind of veil over mischievous Folly & unprincipled Wickedness.—One of the Corps provoked my ire the other day, which burst out as follows—

To the Honorable Mr. R. Maule of Panmure,
on his high Phaeton.
[C.W. p. 527]

Here is another on a more agreable subject—

On seeing Mrs. Kemble perform the part of Yarico,
on Dumfries theatre
[C.W. p. 526]

In the flattering hopes of seeing you, I remain your obliged friend—

Robt Burns

LXXIV (649)

Dumfries 20th December 1794

I have been prodigiously disappointed, in this London journey of yours.—In the first place, when your last to me reached Dumfries, I was in the country, & did not return untill too late to answer your

212

letter: in the next place, I thought you would certainly take this route; & now, I know not what is become of you, or whether this may reach you at all.—God grant that it may find you & yours in prospering health & good spirits!—Do, let me hear from you the soonest possible.—

As I hope to get a frank from my friend Miller, I shall, every leisure hour, take up the pen, & gossip away whatever comes first: Prose, or Poesy; Sermon, or Song.—In this last article, I have abounded, of late.—I have often mentioned to you, a superb Publication of Scotish Songs which is making its appearance in your Great Metropolis, & where I have the honor to preside over the Scotish verse, as no less a personage than Peter Pindar does over the English.—I wrote the following for a favorite air—

Song

My Chloris, mark how green the groves

[C.W. p.531]

29th December

Since I began this letter, I have been appointed to act in the capacity of Supervisor here, & I assure you, what with the load of business, & what with the business being new to me, I could scarcely have commanded ten minutes to have spoken to you, had you been in town, much less to have written you an epistle.—This appointment is only temporary, & during the illness of the present incumbent; but I look forward to an early period when I shall be appointed in full form: a consumation devoutly to be wished!—My Political sins seem to be forgiven me.—

[1st January 1795]

This is the season (Newyearsday is now my date) of wishing; & mine are most fervently offered up for you!—May life, to you, be a positive blessing while it lasts, for your own sake; & may it yet be greatly prolonged, is my wish for my own sake & for the sake of the rest of your friends!—What a transient business is life!—Very lately I was a boy; but t'other day I was a young man; & I already begin to feel the rigid fibre & stiffening joints of Old Age coming fast o'er my frame.—With all my follies of youth, & I fear, a few vices of manhood, still I congratulate myself on having had in early days religion strongly impressed on my mind.—I have nothing to say to any body, as, to which Sect they belong, or what Creed they believe; but I look on the Man who is firmly persuaded of Infinite Wisdom & Goodness superintending & directing every circumstance that can happen in his lot—I felicitate such a man as having a solid foundation for his mental enjoyment; a firm prop & sure stay, in the hour of difficulty, trouble & distress; & a never-failing anchor of hope, when he looks beyond the grave.—

12th January

You will have seen our worthy & ingenious friend, the Doctor, long ere this.—I hope he is well, & beg to be remembered to him.—I have just been reading over again, I dare say for the hundred & fiftieth time, his "View of Society & Manners;" & still I read it with unsated delight.—His humour is perfectly original.—It is neither the humour

of Addison, nor Swift, nor Sterne, nor any body, but Dr. Moore; &
is positively as rich a vein as any of them could boast.—By the bye,
you have deprived me of Zeluco: remember *that*, when you are
disposed to rake up the sins of my neglect from among the ashes of
my laziness.—

He has paid me a pretty compliment, by quoting me, in his last
Publication,[1] though I must beg leave to say, that he has not written
this last work in his usual happy manner.—Entre nous, you know my
Politics; & I cannot approve of the honest Doctor's whining over the
deserved fate of a certain pair of Personages.—What is there in the
delivering over a perjured Blockhead & an unprincipled Prostitute
into the hands of the hangman, that it should arrest for a moment,
attention, in an eventful hour, when, as my friend Roscoe in
Liverpool gloriously expresses it—

> "When the welfare of Millions is hung in the scale
> "And the balance yet trembles with fate!"[2]

But our friend is already indebted to People in power, & still looks
forward for his Family, so I can apologise for him; for at bottom I
am sure he is a staunch friend to liberty.—Thank God, these London
trials have given us a little more breath, & I imagine that the time is
not far distant when a man may freely blame Billy Pit, without being
called an enemy to his Country.—

Adieu!
Robt Burns

1 *Journal during a Residence in France* (London, 1793), II, 459.
2 William Roscoe: *Song: O'er the vine-covered hills and gay regions of France.*

LXXV (683)

[Enclosing *The Dumfries Volunteers.*]

[C.W. p. 537]

I am afraid, Dear Madam, that this parcel will be a bad bargain, at
the price it will cost you ere it reach you.—Miss Keith will see that I
have omitted the four lines on the ci-devant Commodore which gave
her so much offence.*—Had I known that he stood in no less
connection than the Godfather of my lovely young Friend, I would
have spared him for her sake.—

I expected to have heard from you, how you arrived home, & how
you found your friends; but in the hurry of momentous matters,
I suppose such a trifling circumstance had escaped your recollection.—

Adieu!
Robt Burns

* No lines of this description have survived.

LXXVI (688)

31st January 1796

These many months you have been two packets in my debt.—What
sin of ignorance I have committed against so highly a valued friend I
am utterly at a loss to guess.—Your son, John, whom I had the

pleasure of seeing here, told me that you had gotten an ugly accident of a fall, but told me also the comfortable news that you were gotten pretty well again.—Will you be so obliging, dear Madam, as to condescend on that my offence which you seem determined to punish with a deprivation of that friendship which once was the source of my highest enjoyments?—Alas! Madam, ill can I afford, at this time, to be deprived of any of the small remnant of my pleasures.—I have lately drank deep of the cup of affliction.—The Autumn robbed me of my only daughter & darling child, & that at a distance too & so rapidly as to put it out of my power to pay the last duties to her.—I had scarcely began to recover from that shock, when became myself the victim of a most severe Rheumatic fever, & long the die spun doubtful; until after many weeks of a sick-bed it seems to have turned up life, & I am beginning to crawl across my room, & once indeed have been before my own door in the street.—

> When Pleasure fascinates the mental sight,
> Affliction purifies the visual ray;
> Religion hails the drear, the untried night,
> That shuts, for ever shuts! Life's doubtful day.—[1]

As to other matters of my concern, my family, views, &c. they are all as successful as I could well wish.—

I know not how you are in Ayr-shire, but here, we have actual famine, & that too in the midst of plenty.—Many days my family & hundreds of other families, are absolutely without one grain of meal; as money cannot purchase it.—How long the *Swinish Multitude* will be quiet, I cannot tell : they threaten daily.[2]—

Farewel! May all good things attend you!

R. Burns

1 Paraphrased from Young: *Night Thoughts IX*
2 A reference to the Meal Riots in Dumfries, 12th-14th March 1796.

LXXVII (702)

10th July [1796]

Madam

I have written you so often without receiving any answer, that I would not trouble you again but for the circumstances in which I am.—An illness which has long hung about me in all probability will speedily send me beyond that bourne whence no traveller returns.*—Your friendship with which for many years you honored me was a friendship dearest to my soul.—Your conversation & especially your correspondence were at once highly entertaining & instructive.—With what pleasure did I use to break up the seal! The remembrance yet adds one pulse more to my poor palpitating heart!

Farewell!!!

Robert Burns

* Shakespeare: *Hamlet*, Act III, sc. 1.

MISS WILHELMINA ALEXANDER

Born at Paisley in 1756, she was the fourth daughter of Claud Alexander of Newtoun and sister of Claud Alexander, laird of Ballochmyle, an estate on the river Ayr near Mauchline. Burns encountered her while out walking, and composed *The Lass o Ballochmyle* (C.W. p. 199) as a result, sending a copy of the song with the following high-flown letter and requesting permission to publish it in 'a second edition of my poems'. She ignored the letter and Burns never forgave the snub — hence the note which he added to the copy made for the Glenriddell MS. The 'Lass o Ballochmyle' never married; in later life Burns's letter and the song were her most treasured possessions. She died an old maid, in Glasgow in 1843.

56

Mossgiel, 18th November 1786

Madam,

Poets are such outré Beings, so much the children of wayward Fancy and capricious Whim, that I believe the world generally allows them a larger latitude in the rules of Propriety, than the sober Sons of Judgement and Prudence.—I mention this as an apology all at once for the liberties which a nameless Stranger has taken with you in the inclosed; and which he begs leave to present you with.—

Whether it has poetical merit in any way worthy of the THEME, I am not the proper judge, but it is the best my abilites can produce; and, what to a good heart will perhaps be a superiour grace, it is equally sincere.—

The Scenery was nearly taken from real life; though I dare say, Madam, you don't recollect it: for I believe you scarcely noticed the poetic Reveur, as he wandered by you.—I had roved out as Chance directed, on the favorite haunts of my Muse, the banks of Ayr; to view Nature in all the gayety of the vernal year.—

The Sun was flaming o'er the distant, western hills; not a breath stirred the crimson opening blossom, or the verdant spreading leaf.

'Twas a golden moment for a poetic heart.—I listened the feathered Warblers, pouring their harmony on every hand, with a congenial, kindred regard; and frequently turned out of my path lest I should disturb their little songs, or frighten them to another station.—"Surely," said I to myself, "he must be a wretch indeed, who, regardless of your harmonious endeavours to please him, can eye your elusive flights, to discover your secret recesses, and rob you of all the property Nature gives you; your dearest comforts, your helpless, little Nestlings."

Even the hoary Hawthorn twig that shot across the way, what heart, at such a time, but must have been interested in its welfare, and wished it to be preserved from the rudely browsing Cattle, or the withering eastern Blast?

Miss Wilhemina Alexander

Such was the scene, and such the hour, when in a corner of my Prospect I spyed one of the finest pieces of Nature's workmanship that ever crowned a poetic Landskip; those visionary Bards excepted who hold commerce with aerial Beings.—

Had CALUMNY & VILLAINY taken my walk, they had, at that moment, sworn eternal peace with such an Object.—

What an hour of inspiration for a Poet! It would have raised plain, dull, historic Prose to Metaphor and Measure!

The inclosed Song was the work of my return home: and perhaps but poorly answers what might have been expected from such a scene.—I am going to print a second Edition of my Poems, but cannot insert these verses without your permission.—

I have the honor to be,
Madam,
Your most obedient & very humble servant,
Robert Burns

Well Mr Burns, & did the Lady give you the desired "Permission?"—No! She was too fine a Lady *to notice* so plain a compliment.—As to her great brothers, whom I have since met in life on more "equal" terms of respectability, why should I quarrel their want of attention to me?—When Fate swore that their purses should be full, Nature was equally positive that their heads should be empty.—"Men of their fashion were surely incapable of being unpolite?"—Ye canna mak a silk-purse o' a sow's lug.

WILLIAM CHALMERS

An Ayr lawyer and notary public, he was responsible for drawing up the Deed of Assignment (page 115) in July 1788, whereby Burns surrendered his property to his brother Gilbert when he was contemplating flight to Jamaica. At this time Chalmers asked Burns to write a poem for him to give to his sweetheart, and the result was the humorous piece of advice to the young lady beginning 'Wi braw new branks in mickle pride' (C.W. p. 231). With John McAdam of Craigengillan, William Chalmers was the recipient of the mock-mandate in the name of the nine Muses, a humorous send-up of legal phraseology which Chalmers no doubt could appreciate. The only other extant letter was written by Burns from Edinburgh in December 1786, enclosing copies of some of his poems including the *Address to Edinburgh* (C.W. p. 262). John McAdam, co-recipient of the letter of 20th November 1786, was a wealthy landowner and agricultural improver with estates at Barbeth, Straiton and Dunaskin. He himself was the recipient of the verse epistle beginning 'Sir, o'er a gill I gat your card' (C.W. p. 274) some time about January-March 1787.

I (58)

[Mauchline, 20th November 1786]

In the Name of the NINE. *Amen.*

We, ROBERT BURNS, by virtue of a Warrant from NATURE, bearing date the Twenty-fifth day of January, Anno Domini and BARD IN CHIEF in and over the Districts and Countries of KYLE, CUNNINGHAM, and CARRICK, of old extent, To our trusty and well-beloved WILLIAM CHALMERS and JOHN M'ADAM, Students and Practitioners in the ancient and mysterious Science of CONFOUNDING RIGHT and WRONG.

RIGHT TRUSTY,

Be it known unto you, That whereas, in the course of our care and watchings over the Order and Police of all and sundry the MANUFACTURERS, RETAINERS, and VENDERS of POESY; Bards, Poets, Poetasters, Rhymers, Songsters, Ballad-singers, &c. &c. &c. &c. &c. male and female—We have discovered a certain [bawdy], nefarious, abominable, and wicked SONG or BALLAD, a copy whereof We have here inclosed; Our WILL THEREFORE IS, that YE pitch upon and appoint the most execrable Individual of that most execrable Species, known by the appelation, phrase, and nickname of THE DEIL'S YELL NOWTE: and, after having caused him to kindle a fire at the CROSS of AYR, ye shall, at noontide of the day, put into the said wretch's merciless hands the said copy of the said nefarious and wicked Song, to be consumed by fire in the presence of all Beholders, in abhorrence of, and terrorem to, all such COMPOSITIONS and COMPOSERS. And this in nowise ye leave undone, but have it executed in every point as this OUR MANDATE bears, before the twenty-fourth current, when IN PERSON We hope to applaud your faithfulness and zeal.

GIVEN at MAUCHLINE, this twentieth day of November, Anno Domini one thousand seven hundred and eighty-six.

GOD SAVE THE BARD!

II (68)

Edinburgh, 27th December 1786

My dear friend,

I confess I have sinned the sin for which there is hardly any forgiveness, ingratitude to Friendship, in not writing you sooner; but

218

of all men living, I had intended to send you an entertaining letter, and by all the plodding, stupid Powers that in nodding, conceited majesty preside over the dull routine of Business—A heavily-solemn Oath this! I am, and have been, ever since I came to Edinburgh, as unfit to write a letter of humour, as to write a commentary on, The Revelation of Saint John the Divine, who was banished to the Isle of Patmos, by the cruel and bloody Domitian, son to Vespasian and brother to Titus both Emperors of Rome, and who was himself an Emperor, and raised the second or third Persecution, I forget which, against the Christians, and after throwing the said Apostle John, brother to the Apostle James commonly called James the greater to distinguish him from another James who was, on some account or other, known by the name of James the less, after throwing him into a caldron of boiling oil from which he was miraculously preserved, he banished the poor son of Zebedee to a desert island in the Archipelago, where he was gifted with the Second Sight, and saw as many wild beasts as I have seen since I came to Edinburgh; which, a circumstance not very uncommon in story-telling, brings me back to where I set out.—

To make some amends for what, against you reach this paragraph, you will have suffered; I inclose you two Poems I have carded and spun since I passed Glenbuck.—One blank in the Address to Edinburgh "Fair B——" is the heavenly Miss Burnet, daughter to lord Monbodo, at whose house I have had the honor to be more than once.—There has not been any thing nearly like her, in all the combinations of Beauty, Grace and Goodness the great Creator has formed, since Milton's Eve on the first day of her existence.—

I have sent you a parcel of subscription-bills, while I have wrote to Mr Ballantine & Mr Aiken to call on you for some of them if they want them.—

My direction is, Care of Andrew Bruce Merchant Bridge-street.
Adieu! Dear Chalmers—
Robt Burns

GEORGE REID

Farmer of Barquharie, near Ochiltree, he was born in 1762 and died in 1838.
In 1785 Reid married Agnes Tennant, eldest daughter by his second wife of
Burns's friend John Tennant of Glenconner. Burns borrowed from Reid the
pony on which he rode to Edinburgh in November 1786. In thanking him for
the loan of his 'pownie' Burns gave a brief account of his social activities up to
his arrival in the capital. The second letter, from Edinburgh the following
April, was addressed to Reid care of Mr. Ronald, the tobacconist in Mauchline,
and enclosed a couple of copies of the first Edinburgh Edition. Although he
promised to write again in about ten days time no further letter is extant.

I (60)

[Edinburgh, 29th November 1786]

My Dear Sir,

John Samson begged your pownie in such a manner, seconded by
Mr. Dalrymple of Orangefield, that I hope you will forgive my not
returning him by the Carrier.

I left Mr. Prentice's on Monday night. There was a most agreable
little party in the evening; a Mr. Lang, a dainty body of a clergyman;
a glorious good fellow, and with a still more glorious wife, Mr. and
Mrs. Stodart, with whom I breakfasted along with Mr. Prentice next
morning. For Mr. Prentice, no words can do him justice. Sound
sterling sense and plain warm hospitality are truly his.

R.B.

II (96)

Edinburgh, 19th April 1787

My dear Sir,

The fewer words I can tell my story in so much the better as I am in
an unco tirryfyke of a hurry.—I have sent two copies of my book to
you: one of them as a present to yourself, or rather your wife, the
other present in my name to Miss Jenny.—It goes to my heart that
time does not allow me to make some very fine turned periods on
the occasion, as I generally like pretty well to hear myself speak; at
least, fully as well as any body else.—

Tell Miss Jenny that I had wrote her a long letter wherein I had
taken to pieces right Honorables, Honorables, and Reverends not a
few but it, with many more of my written things were stolen from
my room, which terrified me from "scauding my lips in ither folks
kail" again.—By good luck the fellow is gone to Gibraltar, and I trust
in Heaven he will go to the bottom for his pains.—I will write you by
post when I leave auld Reekie, which will be in about ten days.—

Robt Burns

Rev. WILLIAM GREENFIELD

Professor of Rhetoric at Edinburgh University and minister of St. Andrew's, Edinburgh from 1784 to 1787, he later became Hugh Blair's associate at the High Church. In 1796 he became Moderator of the General Assembly and received his doctorate in divinity. Two years later, however, he was deposed and excommunicated by the Presbytery of Edinburgh, stripped of his University appointments and degrees and forced into exile. Presbytery records laconically mention 'certain flagrant reports concerning his conduct', from which Ferguson surmised that sexual misconduct lay at the heart of Greenfield's disgrace. Thenceforward he lived in northern England where he adopted the alias of Richardson and supported himself by writing. In 1809 he published his *Essays On The Sources Of The Pleasures* and was rehabilitated to the extent that he was permitted, through the intervention of Sir Walter Scott, to write for the *Quarterly Review* under his pseudonym. A very flattering description of him appears in Burns's Commonplace Book. Burns's sole letter to Greenfield enclosed 'two Songs, the composition of two Ayrshire Mechanics' and unburdened to him his doubts about his sudden fame, and his fears for the future.

(66)

December 1786

Reverend Sir

On raking the recesses of my memory the other day, I stumbled on two Songs which I here inclose you as a kind of curiosity to a Professor of the Belle lettres de la Nature; which, allow me to say, I look upon as an additional merit of yours; a kind of bye Professorship, not always to be found among the systematic Fathers and Brothers of scientific Criticism.—They were the works of Bards such as I lately was; and such as, I believe, I had better still have been.—

Never did Saul's armour sit so heavy on David when going to encounter Goliah,[1] as does the encumbering robe of public notice with which the friendship and patronage of some "names dear to fame" have invested me.—I do not say this in the ridiculous idea of seeming self-abasement, and affected modesty.—I have long studied myself, and I think I know pretty exactly what ground I occupy, both as a Man, & a Poet; and however the world, or a friend, may sometimes differ from me in that particular, I stand for it, in silent resolve, with all the tenaciousness of Property.—I am willing to believe that my abilities deserved a better fate than the veriest shades of life; but to be dragged forth, with all my imperfections on my head, to the full glare of learned and polite observation, is what, I am afraid, I shall have bitter reason to repent.—

I mention this to you, once for all, merely, in the Confessor style, to disburthen my conscience, and that—"When proud Fortune's ebbing tide recedes"[2]—you may bear me witness, when my buble of fame was at the highest, I stood, unintoxicated, with the inebriating cup in my hand, looking forward, with rueful resolve, to the hastening time when the stroke of envious Calumny, with all the eagerness of vengeful triumph, should dash it to the ground.—

I am ever, &c.

1 See 1 Samuel 17:38-9.
2 Shenstone: *Elegy VII*, stanza 19.

JOHN TENNANT OF GLENCONNER

In a letter to Clarinda on 2nd March 1788 (see page 400) Burns described John Tennant as 'A worthy, intelligent farmer, my father's friend and my own', and referred to him as 'guid auld Glen' in the verse-epistle to James Tennant of Glenconner (C.W. p. 200). Born in 1725, he was factor of the Ochiltree estate (1769-80) for the Dowager Countess of Glencairn and rented the farm of Glenconner. Previously he had been neighbour to William Burnes at Mount Oliphant, and accompanied the poet on his inspection of Ellisland, advising him somewhat injudiciously to undertake that losing bargain. He was one of the witnesses at the baptism of Robert Burns Junior. He had five sons and a daughter and died in 1810. His cousin, also called John Tennant, was blacksmith at Alloway and reputedly a witness at the poet's baptism.

I (67A)

20th December 1786

[In a copy of Marie Huber's *Letters Concerning the Religion Essential to Man. Translated from the French* (Glasgow, 1761).]

A paltry Present from Robt. Burns the Scotch Bard to his own friend & his Father's friend, John Tennant in Glenconner.—

II (197)

Edinburgh, 7th February 1788

My Dear Friend,

I shall see you in eight or ten days, so shall merely make this a business letter.—I go, on my return home to take the decisive look of a farm near Dumfries; where, if you will do me the favour to accompany me, your judgement shall determine me.—I met with an ugly accident about ten weeks ago, by the drunkeness of a Coachman; I fell and dislocated the cap of my knee, which laid me up a cripple, that I have but just lately laid aside my crutches.—I shall not have the use of my limb as formerly, for some months, perhaps years to come.—

My best Compliments to all your family, and Mr. Reid.—I am at present, crazed with thought and anxiety, but particulars I refer till meeting.—

I am ever, my dearest Sir, yours,
Robt Burns

JAMES BURNETT, LORD MONBODDO

Born in 1714, he was educated at Marischal College, Aberdeen and the universities of Edinburgh and Groningen. He studied Greek philosophy before turning to the law, and was called to the bar in 1737. His brilliant legal career was crowned in 1767 when he was made a Lord of Session, taking the title of Monboddo from his father's estate in Kincardineshire. A man of considerable scholastic attainments, though often eccentric opinions, he was also noted for his generosity and charm. A prolific writer, his best-known works include *Of the Origin and Progress of Language*, 6 vols. (1773-92) and *Antient Metaphysics*, 6 vols. (1778-99). His second daughter Eliza was 'the beautiful Miss Burnett' (C.W. p. 416) who died of tuberculosis in 1790 at the age of 25.

(69)

Saturday Eve
[30th? December 1786]

I shall do myself the honor, Sir, to dine with you tomorrow, as you obligingly request.—

My conscience twitting me with having neglected to send Miss Eliza a song which she once mentioned to me as a Song she wished to have —I inclose it for her; with one or two more, by way of a peace-offering.—

I have the honor to be, My Lord,
your very humble servant
Robt Burns

THE HON. HENRY ERSKINE

Born in 1746, the second son of the tenth Earl of Buchan, he was called to the bar in 1768 and became successively Dean of the Faculty (1786-96) and Lord Advocate (1783 and 1806-7). He was renowned for his forensic skill and his lively and witty courtroom manner. In his *Extempore in the Court of Session* (C.W. p. 273) Burns humorously contrasted Erskine with Sir Ilay Campbell the then Lord Advocate, who was his inferior as an orator. Burns first met Erskine at a meeting of the Canongate Kilwinning Lodge, through the mediation of Dalrymple of Orangefield. Latterly Erskine was MP for the Dumfries Burghs and died in 1817. Lord Cockburn alluded to his geniality: 'nothing was so sour as not to be sweetened by the glance, the voice, the gaiety, the beauty of Henry Erskine'. A plaque at his birthplace bears the words: 'No poor man wanted a friend while Harry Erskine lived'. The Captain Erskine referred to in Burns's letter of 22nd January 1789 was Captain Andrew Erskine, youngest son of the fifth Earl of Kellie, who drowned himself in the Forth in 1793 rather than face bankruptcy.

I (70)

[Enclosing *When Guilford Good.* C.W. p. 72]

Two o'clock—[End of December 1786]

Sir,

I showed the inclosed political ballad to my lord Glencairn, to have his opinion whether I should publish it; as I suspect my political tenets, such as they are, may be rather heretical in the opinion of some of my best Friends.—I have a few first principles in Religion and Politics which, I believe, I would not easily part with; but for all the etiquette of, by whom, in what manner, &c. I would not have a dissocial word about it with any one of God's creatures; particularly, an honored Patron, or a respected Friend.—His Lordship seems to think the piece may appear in print, but desired me to send you a copy for your suffrage.—I am, with the sincerest gratitude for the notice with which you have been pleas'd to honor the rustic Bard, Sir, your most devoted humble servant.

Robt Burns

II (299)

Ellisland near Dumfries, 22nd January 1788
[for 1789]

Sir

There are two things which, I believe, the blow that terminates my existence alone can destroy; my attachment and propensity to Poesy, and my sense of what I owe to your goodness.—There is nothing in the different situations of a Great and a Little man that vexes me more, than the ease with which one practises some virtues, that to the other are extremely difficult, or perhaps wholly impracticable.—A man of consequence and fashion shall richly repay a deed of kindness with a nod and a smile, or a hearty shake of the hand; while a poor fellow labors under a sense of gratitude, which like copper-coin, though it loads the bearer, is yet of small account in the currency and commerce of the World.—As I have the honor, Sir, to stand in the Poor fellow's predicament with respect to you, will you accept of a device I have thought on, to acknowledge these obligations I can never cancel?—Mankind in general agree in testifying their devotion, their gratitude, their friendship, or their love, by presenting whatever they hold dearest.—Every body who is in the least acquainted with the character of a Poet, knows that

JAMES 14th EARL OF GLENCAIRN

MARGARET CHALMERS (MRS LEWIS HAY)

there is nothing in the world on which he sets so much [value as his verses.—I desire, from time] to time as she may bestow her favors, to present you with the productions of my humble Muse.—The inclosed are the principal of her Works on the banks of Nith.—The Poem inscribed to R—— G—— Esq. is some verses, accompanying a request, which I sent to Mr Graham of Fintry; a gentleman who has given double value to some important favors he has bestowed on me, by his manner of doing them, and on whose future Patronage likewise I must depend for matters to me of the last consequence.—

I have no great faith in the boasted pretensions to intuitive propriety and unlaboured elegance.—The rough material of Fine Writing is certainly the gift of Genius; but I as firmly believe that the workmanship is the united effort of Pains, Attention & Repeated—trial.—The Piece addressed to Mr Graham is my first essay in that didactic, epistolary way; which circumstances I hope will bespeak your indulgence.—To your friend, Captain Erskine's strictures, I lay claim as a Relation; not, indeed, that I have the honor to be akin to the Peerage, but because he is a Son of Parnassus.—

I intend being in Edinburgh in four or five weeks when I shall certainly do myself the honor of waiting on you, to testify with what respect and gratitude I [*remainder missing*]

JAMES CUNNINGHAM, EARL OF GLENCAIRN

Born at Finlaystone in 1749, the younger son of the thirteenth Earl, he served as a captain in the West Fencible Regiment. His elder brother having predeceased him, he succeeded to the earldom when his father died in 1775. He was one of the representative Scottish peers in the House of Lords (1780-4) and was an ardent supporter of Fox's India Bill. As patron of Kilmarnock parish, he presented the Rev. William Mackinlay, a staunch 'Auld Licht', although he was himself more liberal in outlook. The appointment provoked Burns's satire *The Ordination* (C.W. p. 192). Glencairn's factor, Alexander Dalziel, brought the Kilmarnock Edition to the Earl's notice and when Burns arrived in Edinburgh with a letter of introduction from Dalrymple of Orangfield (whose wife was Glencairn's sister) the Earl received the poet warmly and introduced him to his friends. Glencairn's influence and contacts considerably facilitated Burns's success in Edinburgh — a fact freely acknowledged by the poet in a letter (III, see page 134) to Mrs Dunlop on 22nd March 1787: 'The noble Earl of Glencairn, to whom I owe more than any man of earth . . .' Glencairn gave Burns sound advice 'with respect to impropriety or indelicacy which I follow implicitly.' It was due to Glencairn that Burns secured the unanimous support of the Caledonian Hunt. Although the phraseology is stilted, one must be impressed by the obvious sincerity of Burns's letter to the Earl on 4th May 1787, written on the point of departure from Edinburgh.

When contemplating the Excise as a career, it was to Glencairn that Burns first turned for advice in January 1788.

Lord Glencairn never married and was latterly a semi-invalid. Late in 1790 he went to Portugal for his health's sake but returned to England and died at Falmouth soon after landing on 30th January 1791. Burns was deeply moved by the death of 'my best Friend, my first my dearest Patron and Benefactor; the man to whom I owe all that I am and have!' and composed his *Lament for James, Earl of Glencairn* (C.W. p. 423). Two of the three letters were addressed to Glencairn at Coates, the third being addressed to him at Barntown (Barnton).

I (75)

[Enclosing *Verses Intended to be Written Below a Noble Earl's Picture*]

[C.W. p. 265]

Lawnmarket, 13th January 1787

My Lord,

I wanted to purchase a Profile of your Lordship which I was told was to be got in town; but I am truly sorry to see that the Painter has spoiled a "Human face divine."*—The inclosed Stanzas I intended to have written below a Picture or Profile of your Lordship, could I have been so happy as to procure one with any thing of a likeness. — As I will soon return to my shades, I wanted to have something like a material object for my gratitude: I wanted to have it in my power to say to a Friend, there is my noble Patron, my generous Benefactor! —

Allow me, my Lord, to proffer my warm, my fond request, to be permitted to publish these verses.—I conjure your Lordship by the honest throe of Gratitude, by the generous wish of Benevolence, by all the Powers and Feelings which compose the magnanimous mind, do not deny me this my darling Petition.—I owe much, very much indeed, to your Lordship; and, what has not in some other instances been always the case with me, the weight of the obligation is a pleasing load.—I trust I have a heart as independent as your Lordship's, than which I can say nothing more; and I would not be beholden to favours that would crucify my feelings.—Your dignified character in life, and manner of supporting that character, are flattering to my Scottish pride; and I would be jealous of the purity of my grateful attachment, where I was under the Patronage of one of the much favored Sons of Fortune. —

Almost every Poet has celebrated his Patrons, particularly when they were Names dear to Fame, and illustrious in their Country; permit me then, my Lord, if you think the lines have intrinsic merit, to tell the World how much I have the honor to be

Your Lordship's highly indebted,
and ever grateful, humble servant
Robert Burns

* Milton: *Paradise Lost*, Bk, III, line 44.

II (103)

Edinburgh, Friday morn:
[4th May 1787]

My Lord,

I have followed your Lordship's orders, and have waited on Mr Elliot who will be supplied with the copies when he wants them.—

I go away tomorrow morning early; and allow me to vent the fullness of my heart in thanking your Lordship once more for all that patronage, that benevolence, that friendship with which you have honored me.—With brimful eyes I pray that you may find, in that Great Being whose image you so richly bear, that friend which I have found in you!

I came to this town without friend or acquaintance, but I met with your Lordship; and to YOU, Your good family I owe in a great measure all that at present I am and have.—My gratitude is not selfish design, that I disdain; it is not dodging after the heels of Greatness, that is an offering you disdain; it is a feeling of the same kind with my devotion.—

The only return I shall make your Lordship is, in all my future life and conduct to study never "To shame your favour".—

I have the honor to be, My noble Patron,
your gratefully indebted humble servant
Robt Burns

III (192)

[*Bishop mark* FE 1 (1788)]

My Lord

I know your Lordship will disapprove of my ideas in the request I am going to make to you, but I have weighed seriously my situation, my hopes and turn of mind, and am fully fixed to my scheme if I can possibly effectuate it.—I wish to get into the Excise; I am told that your Lordship's interest will easily procure me the grant from the Commissioners; and your Lordship's Patronage and Goodness which have already rescued me from obscurity, wretchedness and exile, embolden me to ask that interest.—You have put it in my power to save the little HOME that sheltered an aged mother, two brothers and three sisters, from destruction.—My brother's lease is but a wretched one, though I think he will probably weather out the remaining seven years of it.—After what I have given and will give him as a small farming capital to keep the family together, I guess my remaining all will be about two hundred pounds.—Instead of beggaring myself with a small dear farm, I will lodge my little stock, a sacred deposite, in a banking-house.—Extraordinary distress, or helpless old age have often harrowed my soul with fears; and I have one or two claims on me in the name of father: I will stoop to any thing that honesty warrants to have it in my power to leave them some better remembrance of me than the odium of illegitimacy.—

These my Lord, are my views: I have resolved on the maturest deliberation; and now I am fixed, I shall leave no stone unturned to carry my resolve into execution.—Your Lordship's Patronage is by far the strength of my hopes; nor have I yet applied to any body else.—Indeed I know not how to apply to any body else.—I am ill qualified to dog the heels of Greatness with the impertinence of Solicitation, and tremble nearly as much at the idea of the cold promise as the cold denial; but to your Lordship I have not only the honor, the happiness but the pleasure of being,

My Lord,
your Lordship's much oblidged and deeply indebted
Humble Servant
Robt Burns

P.S. I have inclosed your Lordship, Holy Willie; and will wait on you the beginning of next week, as against then I hope to have settled my business with Mr. Creech.—

JAMES SIBBALD

Born in Roxburghshire in 1745, he was the son of a farmer but himself worked as a farm labourer before going to Edinburgh where he worked for the bookseller Charles Elliot. Later he established his own business and, in 1783, founded the *Edinburgh Magazine*. In 1792 he became editor of the *Edinburgh Herald* and a decade later published his monumental literary history *Chronicle of the Poetry of Scotland*. The October 1786 issue of his magazine contained the very first review of the Kilmarnock Edition, saying of Burns that he was 'a striking example of native genius bursting through the obscurity of poverty and the obstructions of a laborious life'. Subsequent issues carried excerpts from the poems, moving Burns to write to Sibbald the following January to thank him. Sibbald was the person with whom Patrick Miller of Dalswinton left his anonymous ten guineas for Burns. Sibbald was a prolific writer on antiquarian subjects, and died at Edinburgh in 1803.

(71)

Lawn Market Friday morn:
[January 1787]

Sir,

so little am I acquainted with the Modes & Manners of the more publick and polished walks of life, that I often feel myself much embarrassed how to express the feelings of my heart, particularly Gratitude.—

"———Rude am I in speech,
"And little blest with the set, polish'd phrase;
"For since these arms of mine had seven years' pith,
"Till now, some nine moons wasted, they have us'd
"Their dearest effort in the rural field;
"And therefore, little can I grace my cause
"In speaking for myself———"*

The warmth with which you have befriended an obscure man and young Author, in your three last Magazines—I can only say, Sir, I feel the weight of the obligation, and wish I could express my sense of it.—In the mean time, accept of this conscious acknowledgement from,

Sir, your obliged, humble servant
Robt Burns

* Based on *Othello*, Act I, sc. 3.

229

MARGARET CHALMERS

Born at Fingland, Kirkcudbrightshire about 1763, her mother was a sister of Gavin Hamilton's stepmother. Her father James Chalmers was forced to dispose of his estate and subsequently leased a farm near Mauchline where Burns probably met her. She was a young lady of great culture and accomplishment, both literary and musical, and Burns appears to have been captivated by her. In December 1788 she married Lewis Hay, a partner in the banking house of Forbes, Hunter & Co. After her husband's death in 1800 she settled at Pau, where she died in 1843. Towards the end of her life she told Thomas Campbell, the poet, that Burns had proposed to her, but she tactfully declined him and they had remained good friends. From this it has been deduced that Margaret Chalmers was the recipient of the anonymous letter beginning 'My Dear Countrywoman', and may possibly have been the 'Miss [who] flew off in a tangent of female dignity and reserve' referred to in the letter to James Smith on 30th June 1787 (see page 122). Margaret often played the piano and sang for the blind Dr. Blacklock. In October 1787, at the end of the third Highland tour, Burns spent eight delightful days at Harvieston in her company. Burns recalled that happy occasion in his letter of 16th September 1788. In a letter which Burns dated December 1787, but which Ferguson has placed more precisely at 6th November, Burns sent her two love songs, *Where, braving angry winter's storms* (C.W. p. 298) and *My Peggy's Charms* (C.W. p. 297). Burns wished to publish them but she demurred on the grounds that she would easily be identified and thereby embarassed. Publication of *My Peggy's Charms* was, indeed, postponed till 1802. It is generally agreed that Margaret Chalmers was one of the only two intellectually able women with whom Burns enjoyed close friendship (the other being Maria Riddell). That his love for her was quite genuine was revealed in the letter (X) of 10th January 1788 to Mrs. McLehose (see page 381): 'Her I register in my heart's core - by Peggy Chalmers... She is worthy of a place in the same bosom with my Clarinda.'

Cromek states that Burns's letters to Margaret Chalmers were 'thrown into the fire by the late Mrs. Adair of Scarborough' (her cousin, Charlotte Hamilton) but omits to mention whether his text was taken from the charred fragments rescued from the fire, or from partial transcripts made before the originals were destroyed. Allan Cunningham states that 'nothing was saved except such fragments as were found among the Bard's memoranda', but this seems doubtful. Several of the fragmentary letters are dated, whereas Burns very seldom dated his drafts.

I (76)

[January? 1787]

My Dear Countrywoman,

I am so impatient to show you that I am once more at peace with you, that I send you the book I mentioned directly, rather than wait the uncertain time of my seeing you.—I am afraid I have mislaid or lost Collins' Poems which I promised to Miss Irvin.—If I can find them I will forward them by you; if not, you must apologize for me.—

I know you will laugh at it, when I tell you that your Piano and you together have play'd the deuce somehow, about my heart.—I was once a zealous Devotee to your Sex, but you know the black story at home. My breast has been widowed these many months, and I thought myself proof against the fascinating witchcraft; but I am afraid you will "feelingly convince me what I am."—I say, I am afraid, because I am not sure what is the matter with me.—I have one miserable bad symptom, when you whisper, or look kindly to another, it gives me a draught of damnation.—I have a kind of wayward wish to be with you ten minutes by yourself; though, what I would say, Heaven above knows, for I am sure, I know not.—I have no formed design in all this; but just in the nakedness of my heart write you down a mere matter-of-fact story.—You may perhaps give yourself airs of distance on this, and that will completely cure me; but I wish you would not: just let us meet if you please in the old, beaten way of friendship.—

I will not subscribe myself, your humble servant, for that is a phrase I think at least fifty miles off the heart; but I will conclude with sincerely wishing that the Great Protector of Innocence may shield you from the barbed dart of Calumny, and hand you by the covert snare of Deceit.—

II (145A)

[21st October 1787?]

I send Charlotte the first number of the songs; I would not wait for the second number; I hate delays in little marks of friendship, as I hate dissimulation in the language of the heart. I am determined to pay Charlotte a poetic compliment, if I could hit on some glorious old Scotch air, in number second. You will see a small attempt on a shred of paper in the book; but though Dr. Blacklock commended it very highly, I am not just satisfied with it myself. I intend to make it description of some kind: the whining cant of love, except in real passion, and by a masterly hand, is to me as insufferable as the preaching cant of old Father Smeaton, Whig-minister at Kilmaurs. Darts, flames, cupids, loves, graces, and all that farrago, are just a Mauchline sacrament, a senseless rabble.

I got an excellent poetic epistle yesternight from the old, venerable author of Tullochgorum, John of Badenyon, &c. I suppose you know he is a clergyman. It is by far the finest poetic compliment I ever got. I will send you a copy of it.[1]

I go on Thursday or Friday to Dumfries to wait on Mr. Miller about his farms.—Do tell that to Lady M'Kenzie, that she may give me credit for a little wisdom. "I Wisdom dwell with Prudence."[2] What a blessed fire-side! How happy should I be to pass a winter evening under their venerable roof! and smoke a pipe of tobacco, or drink water-gruel with them! What solemn, lengthened, laughter-quashing gravity of phiz! What sage remarks on the good-for-nothing sons and daughters of indiscretion and folly! And what frugal lessons, as we straitened the fire-side circle, on the uses of the poker and tongs!

Miss N.[3] is very well, and begs to be remembered in the old way to you. I used all my eloquence, all the persuasive flourishes of the hand, and heart-melting modulation of periods in my power, to urge her out to Herveiston, but all in vain. My rhetoric seems quite to have lost its effect on the lovely half of mankind. I have seen the day—but that is a "tale of other years."—In my conscience I believe that my heart has been so oft on fire that it is absolutely vitrified. I look on the sex with something like the admiration with which I regard the starry sky in a frosty December night. I admire the beauty of the Creator's workmanship; I am charmed with the wild but graceful eccentricity of their motions, and—wish them good night. I mean this with respect to a certain passion dont j'ai eu l'honneur d'etre un miserable esclave: as for friendship, you and Charlotte have given me pleasure, permanent pleasure, "which the world cannot give, nor take away" I hope; and which will outlast the heavens and the earth.

1 *Familiar Epistle to Robie Burns* by Rev. John Skinner.
2 Proverbs 8:12.
3 Miss Erskine Nimmo.

Margaret Chalmers

III (150)

Edinburgh, December 1787 [but probably 6th November]

My dear Madam,

I just now have read yours. The poetic compliments I pay cannot be misunderstood. They are neither of them so particular as to point *you* out to the world at large; and the circle of your acquaintances will allow all I have said. Besides I have complimented you chiefly, almost solely, on your mental charms. Shall I be plain with you? I will; so look to it. Personal attractions, madam, you have much above par; wit, understanding, and worth, you possess in the first class. This is a cursed flat way of telling you these truths, but let me hear no more of your sheepish timidity. I know the world a little I know what they will say of my poems; by second sight I suppose; for I am seldom out in my conjectures; and you may believe me, my dear madam, I would not run any risk of hurting you by an ill-judged compliment. I wish to show to the world the odds between a poet's friends and those of simple prosement. More for your information *both* the pieces go in. One of them "Where braving all the winter's harms," is already set—the tune is Neil Gow's lamentation for Abercairny; the other is to be set to an old Highland air in Daniel Dow's "collection of antient Scots music;"[1] the name is *Ha a Chaillich air mo Dheith*. My treacherous memory has forgot every circumstance about *Les Incas*, only I think you mentioned them as being in Creech's possession. I shall ask him about it. I am afraid the song of "Somebody" will come too late—as I shall, for certain, leave town in a week for Ayrshire, and from that to Dumfries, but there my hopes are slender. I leave my direction in town, so any thing, wherever I am, will reach me.

I saw your's to———it is not too severe, nor did he take it amiss. On the contrary, like a whipt spaniel, he talks of being with you in the Christmas days. Mr.———has given him the invitation, and he is determined to accept of it. O selfishness! he owns in his sober moments, that from his own volatility of inclination, the circumstances in which he is situated and his knowledge of his father's disposition, —the whole affair is chimerical—yet he *will* gratify an idle *penchant* at the enormous, cruel expense of perhaps ruining the peace of the very woman for whom he professes the generous passion of love! He is a gentleman in his mind and manners. *tant pis!*—He is a volatile school-boy: The heir of a man's fortune who well knows the value of two times two!

Perdition seize them and their fortunes, before they should make the amiable, the lovely———the derided object of their purse-proud contempt.

I am doubly happy to hear of Mrs. ———'s recovery, because I really thought all was over with her. There are days of pleasure yet awaiting her.

"As I cam in by Glenap
"I met with an aged woman;
"She bade me chear up my heart,
"For the best o' my days was comin."

232

This day will decide my affairs with Creech. Things are, like myself, not what they ought to be; yet better than what they appear to be.

"Heaven's sovereign saves all beings but himself—
That hideous sight—a naked human heart."[2]

Farewell! remember me to Charlotte.

R.B.

1 *A Collection of Ancient Scots Music* . . . Edinburgh, 1776
2 Young: *Night Thoughts*, Night III, line 226.

IV (152)

Edinburgh, 21st November 1787

I have one vexatious fault to the kindly-welcome, well-filled sheet which I owe to your and Charlotte's goodness—it contains too much sense, sentiment, and good-spelling. It is impossible that even you two, whom I declare to my God, I will give credit for any degree of excellence the sex are capable of attaining, it is impossible you can go on to correspond at that rate; so like those who, Shenstone says, retire because they have made a good speech,* I shall after a few letters hear no more of you. I insist that you shall write whatever comes first: what you see, what you read, what you hear, what you admire, what you dislike, trifles, bagatelles, nonsense; or to fill up a corner, e'en put down a laugh at full length. Now none of your polite hints about flattery: I leave that to your lovers, if you have or shall have any; though thank heaven I have found at last two girls who can be luxuriantly happy in their own minds and with one another, without that commonly necessary appendage to female bliss, A LOVER.

Charlotte and you are just two favorite resting places for my soul in her wanderings through the weary, thorny wilderness of this world—God knows I am ill-fitted for the struggle: I glory in being a Poet, and I want to be thought a wise man—I would fondly be generous, and I wish to be rich. After all, I am afraid I am a lost subject. "Some folk hae a hantle o' fauts, an' I'm but a ne'er-do-weel."

Afternoon.—To close the melancholy reflections at the end of last sheet, I shall just add a piece of devotion commonly known in Carrick, by the title of the "Wabster's grace."

> "Some say we're thieves, and e'en sae are we,
> "Some say we lie, and e'en sae do we!
> "Gude forgie us, and I hope sae will he!
> ——"Up and to your looms, lads."

* Shenstone: 'On Reserve', *Essays on Men, Manners, and Things.*

V (155)

[About 1st December 1787]

I have been at Dumfries, and at one visit more shall be decided about a farm in that country. I am rather hopeless in it; but as my brother is an excellent farmer, and is, besides, an exceedingly prudent, sober man, (qualities which are only a younger brother's fortune in our family,) I am determined, if my Dumfries business fail me, to return into partnership with him, and at our leisure take another farm in the neighbourhood. I assure you I look for high compliments from you and Charlotte on this very sage instance of my unfathomable, incomprehensible wisdom. Talking of Charlotte, I must tell her that I have to the best of my power, paid her a poetic compliment, now compleated. The air is admirable: true old Highland. It was the tune of a Gaelic song which an Inverness lady sung me when I was there; and I was so charmed with it that I begged her to write me a set of it from her singing; for it had never been set before. I am fixed that it shall go in Johnson's next number; so Charlotte and you need not spend your precious time in contradicting me. I won't say the poetry is first-rate; though I am convinced it is very well: and, what is not always the case with compliments to ladies, it is not only *sincere* but *just.*

(Here follows the song of "the Banks of the Devon.")*

[C.W. p. 298]

*Cromek who omitted the song from his edition.

VI (160)

Edinburgh 12th December 1787

I am here under the care of a surgeon, with a bruised limb extended on a cushion; and the tints of my mind vying with the livid horror preceding a midnight thunder-storm. A drunken coachman was the cause of the first, and incomparably the lightest evil; misfortune, bodily constitution, hell and myself, have formed a "Quadruple Alliance" to guarantee the other. I got my fall on Saturday, and am getting slowly better.

I have taken tooth and nail to the bible, and am got through the five books of Moses, and half way in Joshua. It is really a glorious book. I sent for my book-binder to-day, and ordered him to get me an octavo bible in sheets, the best paper and print in town; and bind it with all the elegance of his craft.

I would give my best song to my worst enemy, I mean the merit of making it, to have you and Charlotte by me. You are angelic creatures, and would pour oil and wine into my wounded spirit.

I inclose you a proof copy of the "Banks of the Devon," which present with my best wishes to Charlotte. The "Ochel-hills," you shall probably have next week for yourself. None of your fine speeches!

VII (162)

Edinburgh 19th December 1787

I begin this letter in answer to yours of the 17th current, which is not yet cold since I read it. The atmosphere of my soul is vastly clearer than when I wrote you last. For the first time, yesterday I crossed the room on crutches. It would do your heart good to see my bardship, not on my *poetic,* but on my *oaken* stilts; throwing my best leg with an air! and with as much hilarity in my gait and countenance, as a May frog leaping across the newly harrowed ridge, enjoying the fragrance of the refreshed earth after the long-expected shower!

*　　*　　*　　*

I can't say I am altogether at my ease when I see any where in my path, that meagre, squalid, famine-faced spectre, poverty; attended as he always is, by iron-fisted oppression, and leering contempt; but I have sturdily withstood his buffetings many a hard-labored day already, and still my motto is—I DARE! My worst enemy is *Moimême.* I lie so miserably open to the inroads and incursions of a mischievous, light-armed, well-mounted banditti, under the banners of imagination, whim, caprice, and passion; and the heavy armed veteran regulars of wisdom, prudence and fore-thought, move so very, very slow, that I am almost in a state of perpetual warfare, and alas! frequent defeat. There are just two creatures that I would envy, a horse in his wild state traversing the forests of Asia, or an oyster on some of the desert shores of Europe. The one has not a wish without enjoyment, the other has neither wish nor fear.

VIII (185)

[22nd January 1788?]

Now for that wayward, unfortunate thing, myself. I have broke measures with [Creech] and last week I wrote him a frosty, keen letter. He replied in terms of chastisement, and promised me upon his honor that I should have the account on Monday; but this is Tuesday, and yet I have not heard a word from him. God have mercy on me! a poor damned, incautious, duped, unfortunate fool! The sport, the miserable victim, of rebellious pride; hypochondriac imagination, agonizing sensibility, and bedlam passions!

"I wish that I were dead, but I'm no like to die!" I had lately "a hairbreadth 'scape in th' imminent deadly breach"* of love too. Thank my stars I got off heart-whole, "waur fleyd than hurt."— *Interruption.*

I have this moment got a hint. . . I fear I am something —but I hope for the best. Come, stubborn pride and unshrinking resolution! accompany me through this, to me, miserable world! You must not desert me! Your friendship I think I can count on, though I should date my letters from a marching regiment. Early in life, and all my life; I reckoned on a recruiting drum as my forlorn hope. Seriously though, life at present presents me with but a melancholy path: but—my limb will soon be sound, and I shall struggle on.

* Shakespeare: *Othello,* Act I, sc. 3, slightly altered.—

Margaret Chalmers

IX (207)

Edinburgh, Sunday [17th February 1788]

To-morrow, my dear madam, I leave Edinburgh . . . I have altered all
my plans of future life. A farm that I could live in, I could not find;
and indeed, after the necessary support my brother and the rest of
the family required, I could not venture on farming in that style
suitable to my feelings. You will condemn me for the next step I
have taken. I have entered into the excise. I stay in the west about
three weeks, and then return to Edinburgh for six weeks instructions;
afterwards, for I get employ instantly, I go *où il plait a Dieu,—et
mon Roi.* I have chosen this, my dear friend, after mature
deliberation. The question is not at what door of fortune's palace
shall we enter in; but what doors does she open to us? I was not likely
to get any thing to do, I wanted *un but,* which is a dangerous, an
unhappy situation. I got this without any hanging on, or mortifying
solicitation; it is immediate bread, and though poor in comparison of
the last eighteen months of my existence, 'tis luxury in comparison
of all my preceding life: besides, the commissioners are some of
them my acquaintances, and all of them my firm friends.

X (223)

Edinburgh 14th March 1788

I know, my ever dear friend, that you will be pleased with the news
when I tell you, I have at last taken a lease of a farm. Yesternight I
compleated a bargain with Mr. Miller, of Dalswinton, for the farm of
Ellisland, on the banks of the Nith, between five and six miles above
Dumfries. I begin at Whitsunday to build a house, drive lime, &c.
and heaven be my help! for it will take a strong effort to bring my
mind into the routine of business. I have discharged all the army of
my former pursuits, fancies and pleasures; a motley host! and have
literally and strictly retained only the ideas of a few friends, which I
have incorporated into a life-guard. I trust in Dr. Johnson's
observation, "Where much is attempted, something is done."
Firmness both in sufferance and exertion, is a character I would wish
to be thought to possess; and have always despised the whining yelp
of complaint, and the cowardly, feeble resolve.

*   *   *   *

Poor Miss Kennedy is ailing a good deal this winter, and begged me
to remember her to you the first time I wrote you. Surely woman,
amiable woman, is often made in vain! Too delicately formed for the
rougher pursuits of ambition; too noble for the dirt of avarice, and
even too gentle for the rage of pleasure: formed indeed for and
highly susceptible of enjoyment and rapture; but that enjoyment,
alas! almost wholly at the mercy of the caprice, malevolence,
stupidity, or wickedness of an animal at all times comparatively
unfeeling, and often brutal.

XI (235)

Mauchline April, 1788

I am indebted to you and Miss Nimmo for letting me know Miss
Kennedy. Strange! how apt we are to indulge prejudices in our

236

judgements of one another! Even I, who pique myself on my skill in marking characters; because I am too proud of my character as a man, to be dazzled in my judgement *for* glaring wealth; and too proud of my situation as a poor man to be biassed *against* squalid poverty; I was unacquainted with Miss K's very uncommon worth.

I am going on a good deal progressive in *mon grand bût,* the sober science of life. I have lately made some sacrifices for which, were I *viva voce* with you to paint the situation and recount the circumstances, you would applaud me.

XII (272)

Ellisland, near Dumfries, 16th September 1788

Where are you? and how are you? and is Lady M'Kenzie recovering her health? for I have had but one solitary letter from you. I will not think you have forgot me, Madam; and for my part—

> "When thee Jerusalem I forgot,
> "Skill part from my right hand!"[1]

"My heart is not of that rock, nor my soul careless at that sea." I do not make my progress among mankind as a bowl does among its fellows—rolling through the crowd without bearing away any mark or impression, except where they hit in hostile collision.

I am here, driven in with my harvest-folks by bad weather; and as you and your sister once did me the honor of interesting yourselves much *a l'egard de moi,* I sit down to beg the continuation of your goodness.—I can truly say that, all the exterior of life apart, I never saw two, whose esteem flattered the nobler feelings of my soul—I will not say, more, but, so much as Lady M'Kenzie and Miss Chalmers. When I think of you—hearts the best, minds the noblest, of human kind—unfortunate, even in the shades of life—when I think I have met with you, and have lived more of a real life with you in eight days, than I can do with almost any body I meet with in eight years—when I think on the improbability of meeting you in this world again—I could sit down and cry like a child!—If ever you honored me with a place in your esteem, I trust I can now plead more desert.—I am secure against that crushing grip of iron poverty, which, alas! is less or more fatal to the native worth and purity of, I fear, the noblest souls; and a late, important step in my life has kindly taken me out of the way of those ungrateful iniquities, which, however overlooked in fashionable license, or varnished in fashionable phrase, are indeed but lighter and deeper shades of VILLAINY.

Shortly after my last return to Ayrshire, I married "my Jean." This was not in consequence of the attachment of romance perhaps; but I had a long and much-loved fellow creature's happiness or misery in my determination, and I durst not trifle with so important a deposit. Nor have I any cause to repent it. If I have not got polite tattle, modish manners, and fashionable dress. I am not sickened and disgusted with the multiform curse of boarding-schoool affectation; and I have got the handsomest figure, the sweetest temper, the soundest constitution, and the kindest heart in the country. Mrs.

Burns believes, as firmly as her creed, that I am *le plus bel esprit, et le plus honnete homme* in the universe; although she scarcely ever in her life, except the Scriptures of the Old and New Testament, and the Psalms of David in metre, spent five minutes together on either prose or verse.—I must except also from this last, a certain late publication of Scots poems, which she has perused very devoutly; and all the ballads in the country, as she has (Oh the partial lover! you will cry) the finest "wood note wild" I ever heard.—I am the more particular in this lady's character, as I know she will henceforth have the honor of a share in your best wishes. She is still at Mauchline, as I am building my house; for this hovel that I shelter while occasionally here, is pervious to every blast that blows, and every shower that falls; and I am only preserved from being chilled to death, by being suffocated with smoke. I do not find my farm that pennyworth I was taught to expect, but I believe, in time, it may be a saving bargain. You will be pleased to hear that I have laid aside idle *eclat,* and bind every day after my reapers.

To save me from that horrid situation of at any time going down, in a losing bargain of a farm, to misery, I have taken my excise instructions, and have my commission in my pocket for any emergency of fortune. If I could set *all* before your view, whatever disrespect you in common with the world, have for this business, I know you would approve of my idea.

I will make no apology, dear Madam, for this egotistic detail: I know you and your sister will be interested in every circumstance of it. What signify the silly, idle gewgaws of wealth, or the ideal trumpery of greatness! When fellow partakers of the same nature fear the same God, have the same benevolence of heart, the same nobleness of soul, the same detestation at every thing dishonest, and the same scorn at every thing unworthy—if they are not in the dependance of absolute beggary, in the name of common sense are they not EQUALS? And if the bias, the instinctive bias of their souls run the same way, why may they not be FRIENDS?

When I may have an opportunity of sending you this, Heaven only knows. Shenstone says, "When one is confined idle within doors by bad weather, the best antidote against *ennui* is, to read the letters of, or write to one's friends;'[2] in that case then, if the weather continues thus, I may scrawl you half a quire.

I very lately, to wit, since harvest began, wrote a poem, not in imitation, but in the manner of Pope's Moral Epistles. It is only a short essay, just to try the strength of my Muse's pinion in that way. I will send you a copy of it, when once I have heard from you. I have like wise been laying the foundation of some pretty large works: how the superstructure will come on I leave to that great maker and marrer of projects—TIME. Johnson's collection of Scots songs is going on in the third volume; and of consequence finds me a consumpt for a great deal of idle metre.—One of the most tolerable things I have done in that way, is, two stanzas that I made to an air, a musical gentleman of my acquaintance composed for the anniversary of his wedding-day, which happens on the seventh of November. Take it as follows:

Margaret Chalmers

The day returns—my bosom burns,
[C.W. p. 333]

I shall give over this letter for shame. If I should be seized with a scribbling fit, before this goes away, I shall make it another letter; and then you may allow your patience a week's respite between the two. I have not room for more than the old, kind, hearty, FAREWEL!

To make some amends, *mes cheres Mesdames,* for dragging you on to this second sheet; and to relieve a little the tiresomeness of my unstudied and incorrectible prose, I shall transcribe you some of my later poetic bagatelles; though I have, these eight or ten months, done very little that way. One day, in an Hermitage on the Banks of Nith, belonging to a gentleman in my neighbourhood, who is so good as give me a key at pleasure, I wrote as follows; supposing myself the sequestered, venerable inhabitant of the lonely mansion.

Lines written in Friars' Carse Hermitage
[C.W. p. 324]

1 Metrical Psalms 137:5, slightly misquoted.
2 Shenstone: *Essays on Men, Manners and Things, XXIV,* misquoted.

PATRICK MILLER OF DALSWINTON

Born in 1731, he was a son of William Miller of Glenlee, Kirkcudbrightshire and brother of Sir Thomas Miller, President of the Court of Session. As a young man he had gone to sea, and this explains his later predeliction for nautical matters. Later he entered banking and became a director of the Bank of Scotland in 1767. In 1785 he purchased Dalswinton estate in the Nith valley north of Dumfries. Apparently he bought it 'blind' and was so disgusted at its run-down condition that he never meant to return. After he got over the initial shock, however, he settled down to a prolonged - and doubtless expensive - series of experiments in agricultural improvement. It has been said that Miller had sound ideas but tended to underestimate the time required to bring them to practical fruition. Burns himself suffered as a result of Miller's optimism, for although Ellisland eventually became a profitable farm it did not recover from its exhaustion till some years after Burns had given it up. Miller is probably best-remembered nowadays for his experiments with a catamaran driven by manually operated paddles and the more successful steamboat constructed by William Symington which made its maiden voyage on Dalswinton Loch in 1788. Tradition records that Burns was a passenger on that auspicious occasion, but if that is true it seems strange that he mentioned the fact in neither his poetry nor his correspondence. Patrick Miller left ten guineas for Burns with Sibbald. Later Burns discovered the identity of his benefactor and 'drank a glass of claret with him by invitation at his own house yesternight' (12th December 1786). Curiously enough, Burns got his new friend's name wrong at first, referring to him as Peter instead of Patrick, and the first three letters in this group are thus erroneously addressed.

In January 1787 Burns wrote to John Ballantine saying that Miller had discussed the possibility of a lease of a farm on his Dalswinton estate. Prophetically he wrote: 'Mr. Miller is no judge of land; and though I dare say he means to favour me, yet he may give me, in his opinion, an advantageous bargain that may ruin me.' Burns did not take him up on the offer till October 1787, and even then delayed a decision while he considered the Excise as a career. Eventually, in March 1788, he made up his mind, but soon regretted his part in the bargain and relations between him and his landlord were strained during the latter part of the tenancy. Once the business relationship was severed they became quite friendly again. Most of Burns's letters to Miller (I, III-V) deal mainly with the lease of Ellisland, but poetic matters were not overlooked. The last letter, written from Dumfries in the middle of March, 1793, accompanied a copy of the latest edition of the poems in which Burns placed the inscription from his much indebted humble servant THE AUTHOR.'

During his Ellisland period Burns also wrote a solitary letter to Mrs. Miller, on 2nd November 1789, enclosing *On the late Captain Grose's peregrinations Thro Scotland* (C.W. p. 373). The 'Political Ballad on a certain Borough Canvass' was the *Election Ballad for Westerha'* (C.W. p. 367) about Sir James Johnstone of Westerha' but really attacking the Duke of Queensberry. Despite (or because of) this poetic 'support' Johnstone lost the election to Patrick Miller Junior.

The letters of Burns to the latter gentleman are to be found on pp. 699-701. The only other letter to a member of the Miller family was written on 9th September 1793 to Janet Miller, eldest daughter and third child of Patrick Miller. Two years later she married John Thomas Erskine, later 28th Earl of Mar.

I (78A)

Lawn Market, Monday morn:

[15th January 1787]

Sir,

That I have not called on you, as you kindly gave me leave to do, is not owing to selfish or unfeeling Ingratitude, but a fear lest I should intrude on serious hours of Business.—Your kind beneficence to a man, at best obscure, and to you utterly unknown; I should detest myself as a wretch, if I could suspect myself capable of forgetting it.—

When you kindly offered to accommodate me with a Farm, I was afraid to think of it, as I knew my circumstances unequal to the proposal; but now, when by the appearances of my second edition of my book, I may reckon on a middling farming capital, there is not

nothing I wish for more than to resume the Plough.—Indolence and
Inattention to business I have been sometimes guilty of, but I thank
my God, Dissipation or Extravagance have never been a part of my
character.—If therefore, Sir, you could fix me in any sequester'd
romantic spot, and let me have such a Lease as by care and industry
I might live in humble decency, and have a spare hour now and then
to write out an idle rhyme, or wait on you, my honored Benefactor,
with my grateful respects, when you were in my neighborhood—I am
afraid, Sir, to dwell on the idea, lest Fortune have not such
happiness in store for me.—But however this may happen, I shall
ever be,

My honored, kind Patron,
your much indebted,
grateful,
humble servant
Robert Burns

II (139)

Edinburgh, 28th September 1787

Sir,

I have been on a tour through the Highlands and arrived in town but
the other day, so could not wait on you at Dalswinton about the
latter end of August as I had promised and intended.—Independant
of any views of future connections, what I owe you for the PAST, as
a FRIEND and BENEFACTOR when friends I had few and
benefactors I had none, strongly in my bosom prohibits the most
distant instance of ungrateful disrespect.—I am informed you do not
come to town for a month still, and within that time I shall certainly
wait on you, as by this time I suppose you will have settled your
scheme with respect to your farms.—

My journey through the Highlands was perfectly inspiring; and I
hope I have laid in a good stock of new poetical ideas from it.—I
shall make no apology for sending you the inclosed: it is a small but
grateful tribute to the memory of our common Countryman.—

I have the honor to be, with the most grateful sincerity,

Sir, your oblidged humble servant
Robt Burns

P.S.   I have added another Poem, partly as it alludes to some folks
nearly and dearly connected with Ayr-shire, and partly as rhymes are
the coin in which the poor Poet can only pay his debts of
Gratitude.—The Lady alluded to, is Miss Isabella M'Leod, Aunt to
the young Countess of Loudon.—

As I am determined not to leave Edinburgh till I wind up my matters
with Mr. Creech, which I am afraid will be a tedious business;
should I unfortunately miss you at Dalswinton, perhaps your Factor
will be able to inform me of your intentions with respect to the
Elesland farm, which will save me a jaunt to Edinburgh again.

There is something so suspicious in the professions of attachment
from a little man to a great man that I know not how to do justice
to the grateful warmth of my heart when I would say how truly I am
interested in the welfare of your little troop of angels, and how
much I have the honor to be, again,

Sir, your oblidged humble servant
Robt Burns

III (144)

Edinburgh, 20th October 1787

Sir,

I was spending a few days at Sir William Murray's, Oughtertyre and
did not get your oblidging letter till today I came to town.—I was
still more unlucky in catching a miserable cold for which the medical
gentlemen have ordered me into close confiement, "under pain of
Death!" the severest of penalties.—In two or three days, if I get
better, and if I hear at your lodgings that you are still at Dalswinton,
I will take a ride to Dumfries directly.—From something in your last,
I would wish to explain my idea of being your Tenant.—I want to be
a farmer in a small farm, about a plough-gang, in a pleasant country,
under the auspices of a good landlord.—I have no foolish notion of
being a Tenant on easier terms than another.—To find a farm where
one can live at all, is not easy.—I only mean living soberly, like an
old-style farmer, and joining personal industry.—The banks of Nith
are as sweet, poetic ground as any I ever saw; and besides, Sir, 'tis
but justice to the feelings of my own heart, and the opinion of my
best friends, to say that I would wish to call you landlord sooner
than any landed gentleman I know.—These are my views & wishes;
and in whatever way you think best to lay out your farms, I shall be
happy to rent one of them.—I shall certainly be able to ride to
Dalswinton about middle of next week, if I hear you are not gone.—

I have the honor to be, Sir,
your oblidged humble servant
Robt Burns

IV (214A)

Mauchline, 3rd March 1788

Sir,

I have been at Ellisland with Mr. Tennant, the gentleman on whose
judgement I told you I would so much depend.—I inclose you his
ideas on the subject, which are, I think, extremely just.—I am
fondest of a farming life; and that generosity and benevolence, so
very unlike the world but so very like yourself, make me ardently
wish to be your Tennant. I know a little of the world, Sir; the
sentiments of generosity and bowels of compassion they have
usually for one another from one in my situation of life to one in
yours, even the native grateful tribute of the heart is perhaps with
more propriety suppressed in silence.—

It is unusual, I understand, to make the entries to leases in your neighbourhood, at Whitsunday.—This will not do at Ellisland; the farm is so worn out, and every bit of it, good for any thing, is this year under tillage; at least the fields are so intersected with pieces under crop, that four horses which I will need this summer for driving lime and materials for building, with a cow for a married servant perhaps the first year, and one for myself as I must be on the spot, will eat up the whole pasture.—I'll pay for the grass & houses whatever they deserve for the summer, and if you please, make my entry to my lease at Martinmas.—I wish too, to have it at the present rent, 50£ for three years.—The lands are so exhausted, that to enter to the full rent would throw me under a disheartening load of debt.--Not, Sir, that I would mercenarily cheapen your goodness; if you do not chuse to drop the deficiency of 60£, I will try to pay it by small additions to my rent in subsequent years.—You offered me a long lease; I wish it, four nineteens.—I suppose you will have no objection to let me manage the farm as I think proper, till the last six years of the lease: these years I shall bind mysel not to crop above one third of the farm in one year, and what fields I lay down in grass to lay them down with manure.—I shall be in Edinburgh beginning of next week, when I shall wait on you.

I have the honor to be, Sir,
your highly oblidged humble servant
Robt Burns

V (224A)

St. James' Square, Sunday even:
[16th March 1788]

Sir,

I send you Mr. Gordon's scroll, and another which a professional man, a friend of mine, has done today.—This last is, I think, more distinctly what we have mutually agreed on; particularly the 300£.— According to your idea, I have mentioned the applying the surplus, if any be, to the improvement of the land; and as I told you, I wish to keep 50£ of the first received monies, to be the latest accounted for, in case my stock be rather scanty.—There is some fishing rights the present tenant possesses; if you intend that I should enjoy the same, it will be best, I suppose, to mention it in the tack; if you do not understand that I am to have that priviledge, 'tis but a trifling matter, and I don't much care.—If this scroll meets your approbation, I shall wait on Mr. Gordon to get the tack extended, so soon as you return me the papers.—

I have the honor to be ever,
Sir,
your highly oblidged and most respectful
humble servant
Robt Burns

VI (349)

Ellisland, 21st June 1789

Sometime ago I threatened you, my dear Sir, with a letter, and what was still worse, with a cargo of rhyme in it.—As I was in my fields early one morning in this last spring, I heard the report of a gun from a neighbouring wood, and presently a poor little hare, dragging its wounded limbs, limped piteously by me.—I have always had an abhorrence at this way of assasinating God's creatures without first allowing them those means of defence with which he has variously endowed them; but at this season when the object of our treacherous murder is most probably a Parent, perhaps the mother, and of consequence to leave two little helpless nurslings to perish with hunger amid the pitiless wilds, such an action is not only a sin against the letter of the law, but likewise a deep crime against the *morality of the heart.* We are all equally creatures of some Great Creator; and among the many enormous instances of capricious partiality in the Administration of this world which cry to Heaven for retribution & vengeance in some after state of existence. I think it is none of the least flagrant, that power which one creature of us has to amuse himself by and at the expence of another's misery, torture & death.—But to return to my Poem.—

On seeing a fellow wound a hare—,

Inhuman man! curse on thy barb'rous art

[C.W. p. 354]

VII (545)

[Dumfries, mid-March 1793]

Sir,

My Poems having just come out in another edition, will you do me the favour to accept of a copy—a mark of my gratitude to you, as a Gentleman to whose goodness I have been much indebted; of my respect for you, as a Patriot who, in a venal, sliding age, stands forth the champion of the liberties of my Country; & of my veneration for you, as a MAN whose benevolence of heart does honor to Human-nature.—There was a time, Sir, when I was your dependant: this language *then* would have been like the vile incense of flattery—I would not have used it.—Now that connection is at an end; do me the honor to accept of this honest tribute of respect from, Sir, your much indebted humble servant

Robt Burns

VIII (546A)

[In a copy of the 1793 Edition of the *Poems*, mid-March] from his much indebted humble servant

The Author

Mrs Patrick Miller   (368)

Ellisland, 2nd November 1789

Madam,

Inclosed I send you the verses on Captain Grose which you were pleased to honor so much with your approbation.—

I likewise take the liberty to present you with a copy of a song I composed two or three days ago: I hope it will shew you that my Muse takes an occasional excursion on the banks of Nith.—I intended to have troubled you with a Political Ballad on a certain Borough Canvass, but it is so foolish a production that even I its Author & Creator am out of humour with it.—I inclose the tune of the Song for Miss Miller, if she has not already seen it.—I believe both song & tune will appear in Johnson's Publication of Scots Songs.—

I have the honor to be, Madam,

Your much oblidged & ever grateful humble servant
Robt Burns

(585)

Miss Janet Miller *Dalswinton*
[With *Fair Jenny*; tune *Saw ye my Father?* C.W. p. 504]

Dumfries, 9th September 1793

Madam,

I have taken the liberty to make you the Heroine of the Song on the foregoing page.—Being little in the secret of young ladies' loves & lovers—how should I, you know? I have formed in my fancy a little love-story for you; & a lamentable ditty I have put in your Lover's mouth.—The air, you know, is excellent; & the verses, I hope, & think, are in my best manner.—It goes into Pleyel's songs: &, allow me to tell you a truth (what your Sex, Youth, & Charms, from *my* Sex, may not often hear) I am—Sincerely happy to have an opportunity of shewing, with what respect, I have the honor to be,

Madam,
your very humble servant
Robt Burns

DR. JOHN MOORE

Born at Stirling in 1729, he was the son of the Rev. Charles Moore. He was educated at Glasgow Grammar School and the University where he studied medicine. In 1747 he became surgeon's mate in the 54th (Duke of Argyll's) regiment and served in the Low Countries until peace was secured in 1748. He then went to Paris where he continued his medical studies. In 1770 he graduated M.D. at Glasgow University and from 1772 till 1778 was tutor and travelling companion to two successive young Dukes of Hamilton. In 1778 he settled in London where he continued to practise medicine till his death in 1802.

In 1779 he published his 2-volume *View of Society and Manners in France, Switzerland and Germany*, followed two years later by a further two volumes devoted to Italy. Among his other publications were *Medical Sketches* (1786) and a novel entitled *Zeluco*, a best-seller which Burns hailed enthusiastically as 'A glorious story'. In the autumn of 1786 Mrs. Dunlop sent him a copy of the Kilmarnock Edition. Moore was intrigued and interested, but rather than write to the poet direct he replied to Mrs. Dunlop, asking her to tell Burns to get in touch. Burns delayed writing to the great man, telling Mrs. Dunlop (on 15th January 1787): 'I wished to have written to Dr. Moore... yet I could not for my soul set about it. I know his fame and character, and I am one of "the sons of little men". Burns had an incredibly inflated notion of Moore's literary standing, but fortunately chose in the end to ignore the good doctor's advice, well-meaning but utterly mistaken as it was. Moore urged Burns to give up writing in the Scottish dialect and concentrate on standard English, producing something like Thomson's *Seasons*, only livelier. The one good and lasting thing to come out of this association, however, was Burns's long, autobiographical letter (IV) written on 2nd August 1787. The original of this remarkable document is now in the British Library and has served as the basis for all subsequent biographies of Burns. A subsequent letter (V), from Ellisland on 4th January 1789, brought the poet's story up to date.

In 1792 Dr. Moore was in Paris, an eye-witness to the bloody events of August and September following the dethronement of the king. These provided the raw material for *A Journal During a Residence in France* and *A View of the Causes and Progress of the French Revolution,* both of which won praise for their factual approach and balanced objectivity. Burns, however, struck a jarring note by criticising Moore, in his letter (LXXIV) to Mrs. Dunlop on 12th January 1795. Mrs. Dunlop took deep offence at Burns's justification of political murder. 'Since then', adds Maurice Lindsay, 'they have saddened those upholders of the liberal values who are admirers of Burns's work'.

I (79)

Edinburgh, January 1787

Sir,

my worthy honored Patroness Mrs. Dunlop has been so kind as send me extracts of letters she has had from you, where you do the rustic Bard the honor of noticing him and his works.—Those who have felt the anxieties of Authorship can only know what pleasure it gives to be noticed, in such a manner, by Judges of the first character.—

Your criticisms, Sir, I receive with reverence; only I am sorry they mostly came too late: a peccant passage or two that I would certainly have altered were gone to the Press.—

The hope to be admired for Ages is, in by far the greater part of what are even Authors of repute, an unsubstantial dream.—For my part, my first ambition was, and still my strongest wish is, to please my Compeers, the rustic Inmates of the Hamlet, while ever-changing language and manners will allow me to be relished and understood.—

I am very willing to admit that I have some poetical abilities; and as few, if any Writers, either moral or poetical, are intimately acquainted with the classes of Mankind among whom I have chiefly mingled, I may have seen men and manners in a different phasis, which may assist originality of thought.—Still I know very well, the novelty of my character has by far the greatest share in the learned and polite notice I have lately got; and in a language where Pope and Churchill have raised the laugh, and Shenstone and Gray drawn the

246

tear; where Thomson and Beattie have painted the landskip, and Littleton and Collins described the heart; I am not vain enough to hope for distinguished Poetic fame.—

I have the honor to be, &c.

II (85)

Edinburgh, 15th February 1787

Revered Sir,

Pardon my seeming neglect in delaying so long to acknowledge the honor, the very great honor you have done such a one as I, by your kind, your generous notice of me, Jan. 23.—It is not ingratitude; believe me, Sir, it is not.—A few months ago, I knew no other employment than the Plough-tail, nor could boast any thing higher than perhaps a distant acquaintance with a country Clergyman.—Mere Greatness never much embarrasses me; I have nothing to ask from their County, and I do not fear their judgement: but Genius, polished by Learning, and at its proper point of elevation in the eye of the World, this of late I frequently meet with, and tremble at the approach.—I scorn the affectation of seeming Modesty, to cover self-conceit.—I have very attentively studied myself; where I stand, both as a Man and a Poet.—That I have some merit, I do not deny, is my own opinion; but I see, with frequent wringings of heart, that the novelty of my character, and the honest, national prejudice of Scotchmen (a prejudice which do Thou, O God, ever kindle ardent in their breasts!) have borne me to a height altogether untenable to my abilities.—

For the honor Miss Williams has done me, please, Sir, return her my most grateful thanks.—I have more than once thought of paying her in kind, but have hitherto quitted the idea in hopeless despondency. —I had never before heard of her; but since, I have got her Poems, which for several reasons, some belonging to the head, and others the offspring of the heart, give me a great deal of pleasure.—I have little pretence to Critic Lore; I only know what pleases me, often without being able to tell why.—There are, I think, two particular, and to me, favorite characteristic features in Miss Williams' Muse—the wild, unfetter'd flight of native Poesy, and the querulous, sombre tenderness of "time-fettled Sorrow."—

My address is, Care of Mr. Creech, Bookseller, Edinburgh

I have the honor to be, my dearly much respected
Countryman, your ever gratefully indebted
humble servant
Robert Burns

III (97)

Edinburgh, 23rd April 1787

I received the books and sent the one you mentioned to Mrs. Dunlop. I am ill-skilled in beating the coverts of imagination for metaphors of gratitude. I thank you, Sir, for the honour you have done me; and to my latest hour will warmly remember it. To be highly pleased with your book, is what I have in common with the world; but to regard these volumes as a mark of the author's friendly esteem, is a still more supreme gratification.

Dr. John Moore

I leave Edinburgh in the course of ten days or a fortnight; and, after a few pilgrimages over some of the classic ground of Caledonia, *Cowden Knowes, Banks of Yarrow, Tweed,* &c. I shall return to my rural shades, in all likelihood never more to quit them. I have formed many intimacies and friendships here, but I am afraid they are all of too tender a construction to bear carriage a hundred and fifty miles. To the rich, the great, the fashionable, the polite, I have no equivalent to offer; and I am afraid my meteor appearance will by no means entitle me to a settled correspondence with any of you, who are the permanent lights of genius and literature.

My most respectful compliments to Miss Helen Maria Williams. If once this tangent flight of mine were over, and I were returned to my wonted leisurely motion in my old circle, I may probably endeavour to return her poetic compliment in kind.

IV (125)

Mauchline, 2nd August 1787

Sir

For some months past I have been rambling over the country, partly on account of some little business I have to settle in various places; but of late I have been confined with some lingering complaints originating as I take it in the stomach.—To divert my spirits a little this miserable fog of Ennui, I have taken a whim to give you a history of MYSELF.—My name has made a small noise in the country; you have done me the honor to interest yourself very warmly in my behalf; and I think a faithful account of, what character of a man I am, and how I came by that character, may perhaps amuse you in an idle moment.—I will give you an honest narrative, though I know it will be at the expence of frequently being laughted at; for I assure you, Sir, I have, like Solomon whose character, excepting the trifling affair of WISDOM, I sometimes think I resemble, I have, I say, like him "Turned my eyes to behold Madness and Folly;" [1] and like him too, frequently shaken hands with their intoxicating friendship.—In the very polite letter Miss Williams did me the honor to write me, she tells me you have got a complaint in your eyes.—I pray to God that it may be removed; for considering that lady and you are my common friends, you will probably employ her to read this letter; and then goodnight to that esteem with which she was pleased to honor the Scotch Bard.—After you have perused these pages, should you think them trifling and impertinent, I only beg leave to tell you that the poor Author wrote them under some very twitching qualms of conscience, that, perhaps he was doing what he ought not to do: a predicament he has more than once been in before.—

I have not the most distant pretensions to what the pyecoated guardians of escutcheons call, A Gentleman.—When at Edinburgh last winter, I got acquainted in the Herald's Office, and looking through that granary of Honors I there found almost every name in the kingdom; but for me,

"—My ancient but ignoble blood
Has crept thro' Scoundrels ever since the flood"—[2]

248

Gules, Purpure, Argent, &c. quite disowned me.—My Fathers rented land of the noble Keiths of Marshal, and had the honor to share their fate.—I do not use the word, Honor, with any reference to Political principles; loyal and disloyal I take to be merely relative terms in that ancient and formidable court known in this Country by the name of CLUB-LAW.—Those who dare welcome Ruin and shake hands with Infamy for what they sincerely believe to be the cause of their God or their King—"Brutus and Cassius are honorable men."—[3] I mention this circumstance because it threw my father on the world at large; where after many years' wanderings and sojournings, he pickt up a pretty large quantity of Observation and Experience, to which I am indebted for most of my little pretensions to wisdom.—I have met with few who understood "Men, their manners and their ways" [4] equal to him; but stubborn, ungainly Integrity, and headlong, ungovernable Irrascibility are disqualifying circumstances: consequently I was born a very poor man's son.—For the first six or seven years of my life, my father was gardiner to a worthy gentleman of small estate in the neighbourhood of Ayr.—Had my father continued in that situation, I must have marched off to be one of the little underlings about a farm-house; but it was his dearest wish and prayer to have it in his power to keep his children under his own eye till they could discern between good and evil; so with the assistance of his generous Master my father ventured on a small farm in his estate.—At these years I was by no means a favorite with any body.—I was a good deal noted for a retentive memory, a stubborn, sturdy something in my disposition, and an enthusiastic, idiot —I say idiot piety, because I was then but a child.—Though I cost the schoolmaster some thrashings, I made an excellent English scholar, and against the years of ten or eleven, I was absolutely a Critic in substantives, verbs and particles.—In my infant and boyish days too, I owed much to an old Maid of my Mother's, remarkable for her ignorance, credulity and superstition.—She had, I suppose, the largest collection in the county of tales and songs concerning devils, ghosts, fairies, brownies, witches, warlocks, spunkies, kelpies, elf candles, dead-lights, wraiths, apparitions, cantraips, giants, inchanted towers, dragons and other trumpery.—This cultivated the latent seeds of Poesy; but had so strong an effect on my imagination, that to this hour, in my nocturnal rambles, I sometimes keep a sharp look-out in suspicious places; and though nobody can be more sceptical in these matters than I, yet it often takes an effort of Philosophy to shake off these idle terrors.—The earliest thing of Composition that I recollect taking pleasure in was, The vision of Mirza and a hymn of Addison's beginning—"How are Thy servants blest, O Lord!" I particularly remember one half-stanza which was music to my boyish ear—

> "For though in dreadful whirls we hung,
> "High on the broken wave"—

I met with these pieces in Masson's English Collection, one of my school-books.—[5] The two first books I ever read in private, and which gave me more pleasure than any two books I ever read again, were, the life of Hannibal and the history of Sir William Wallace.— Hannibal gave my young ideas such a turn that I used to strut in raptures up and down after the recruiting drum and bagpipe, and wish myself tall enough to be a soldier; while the story of Wallace poured a Scotish prejudice in my veins which will boil along there till the flood-gates of life shut in eternal rest.—Polemical divinity about this time was putting the country half-mad; and I, ambitious of shining in conversation parties on sundays between sermons, funerals, &c. used in a few years more to puzzle Calvinism with so much heat and indiscretion that I raised a hue and cry of heresy against me which has not ceased to this hour.—

My vicinity to Ayr was of great advantage to me.—My social disposition, when not checked by some modification of spited pride, like our catechism definition of Infinitude, was "without bounds or limits."—I formed many connections with other Youngkers who possessed superiour advantages; the youngling Actors who were busy with the rehearsal of PARTS in which they were shortly to appear on that STAGE where, Alas! I was destined to druge behind the SCENES.—It is not commonly at these green years that the young Noblesse and Gentry have a just sense of the immense distance between them and their ragged Playfellows.—It takes a few dashes into the world to give the young Great man that proper, decent, unnoticing disregard for the poor, insignificant, stupid devils, the mechanics and peasantry around him; who perhaps were born in the same village.—My young Superiours never insulted the clouterly appearance of my ploughboy carcase, the two extremes of which were often exposed to all the inclemencies of all the seasons.—They would give me stray volumes of books; among them, even then, I could pick up some observations; and ONE, whose heart I am sure not even the MUNNY BEGUM'S scenes have tainted, helped me to a little French.—Parting with these, my young friends and benefactors, as they dropped off for the east or west Indies, was often to me a sore affliction; but I was soon called to more serious evils.—My father's generous Master died; the farm proved a ruinous bargain; and, to clench the curse, we fell into the hands of a Factor who sat for the picture I have drawn of one in my Tale of two dogs.—My father was advanced in life when he married; I was the eldest of seven children; and he, worn out by early hardship, was unfit for labour.—My father's spirit was soon irritated, but not easily broken. —There was a freedom in his lease in two years more, and to weather these two years we retrenched expences.—We lived very poorly; I was a dextrous Ploughman for my years; and the next eldest to me was a brother, who could drive the plough very well and help me to thrash.—A Novel-Writer might perhaps have viewed these scenes with some satisfaction, but so did not I: My indignation yet boils at the recollection of the scoundrel tyrant's insolent, threatening epistles, which used to set us all in tears.—

This kind of life, the chearless gloom of a hermit with the unceasing moil of a galley-slave, brought me to my sixteenth year; a little before which period I first committed the sin of RHYME.—You know our country custom of coupling a man and woman together as Partners in the labors of Harvest.—In my fifteenth autumn, my Partner was a bewitching creature who just counted an autumn less. —My scarcity of English denies me the power of doing her justice in that language; but you know the Scotch idiom, She was a bonie, sweet, sonsie lass.—In short, she altogether unwittingly to herself, initiated me in a certain delicious Passion, which in spite of acid Disappointment, gin-horse Prudence and bookworm Philosophy, I hold to be the first of human joys, our dearest pleasure here below.— How she caught the contagion I can't say; you medical folks talk much of infection by breathing the same air, the touch, &c. but I never expressly told her that I loved her.—Indeed I did not well know myself, why I liked so much to loiter behind with her, when returning in the evening from our labors; why the tones of her voice made my heartstrings thrill like an Eolian harp; and particularly, why my pulse beat such a furious ratann when I looked and fingered over her hand, to pick out the nettle-stings and thistles.—Among her other love-inspiring qualifications, she sung sweetly; and 'twas her favorite reel to which I attempted giving an embodied vehicle in rhyme.—I was not so presumtive as to imagine that I could make verses like printed ones, composed by men who had Greek and Latin; but my girl sung a song which was said to be composed by a small country laird's son, on one of his father's maids, with whom he was in love; and I saw no reason why I might not rhyme as well as he, for excepting smearing sheep and casting peats, his father living in the moors, he had no more Scholarcraft than I had.—

Thus with me began Love and Poesy; which at times have been my only, and till within this last twelvemonth have been my highest enjoyment.—My father struggled on till he reached the freedom in his lease, when he entered on a larger farm about ten miles farther in the country.—The nature of the bargain was such as to throw a little ready money in his hand at the commencement, otherwise the affair would have been impractible.—For four years we lived comfortably here; but a lawsuit between him and his Landlord commencing, after three years tossing and whirling in the vortex of Litigation, my father was just saved from absorption in a jail by phthisical consumption, which after two years promises, kindly stept in and snatch'd him away—"To where the wicked cease from troubling, and where the weary be at rest."—[6]

It is during this climacterick that my little story is most eventful.—I was, at the beginning of this period, perhaps the most ungainly, aukward being in the parish.—No Solitaire was less acquainted with the ways of the world.—My knowledge of ancient story was gathered from Salmon's and Guthrie's geographical grammars; my knowledge of modern manners, and of literature and criticism, I got from the Spectator.—These, with Pope's works, some plays of Shakespear, Tull and Dickson on Agriculture, The Pantheon, Locke's Essay on the human understanding, Stackhouse's history of the bible, Justice's British Gardiner's directory, Boyle's lectures, Allan Ramsay's works, Taylor's scripture doctrine of original sin, a select Collection of English songs, and Hervey's meditations had been the extent of my reading.[7] —The Collection of Songs was my vade mecum.—I pored over them, driving my cart or walking to labor, song by song, verse by verse; carefully noting the true tender or sublime from affectation and fustian.—I am convinced I owe much to this for my critic-craft such as it is.—

In my seventeenth year, to give my manners a brush, I went to a country dancing school.—My father had an unaccountable antipathy against these meetings; and my going was, what to this hour I repent, in absolute defiance of his commands.—My father, as I said before, was the sport of strong passions: from that instance of rebellion he took a kind of dislike to me, which, I believe was one cause of that dissipation which marked my future years.—I only say, Dissipation, comparative with the strictness and sobriety of Presbyterean country life; for through the will-o'-wisp meteors of thoughtless Whim were almost the sole lights of my path, yet early ingrained Piety and Virtue never failed to point me out the line of Innocence.—The great misfortune of my life was, never to have AN AIM.—I had felt early some stirrings of Ambition, but they were the blind gropings of Homer's Cyclops round the walls of his cave: I saw my father's situation entailed on me perpetual labor.—The only two doors by which I could enter the fields of fortune were, the most niggardly economy, or the little chicaning art of bargain-making: the first is so contracted an aperture, I never could squeeze myself into it; the last, I always hated the contamination of the threshold.—Thus, abandoned of aim or view in life; with a strong appetite for sociability, as well from native hilarity as from a pride of observation and remark; a constitutional hypochondriac taint which made me fly solitude; add to all these incentives to social life, my reputation for bookish knowledge, a certain wild, logical talent, and a strength of thought something like the rudiments of good sense, made me generally a welcome guest; so 'tis no great wonder that always "where two or three were met together, there was I in the midst of them."[8] —But far beyond all the other impulses of my heart was, un penchant à l'adorable moitiée du genre humain.—My heart was compleatly tinder, and was eternally lighted up by some Goddess or other; and like every warfare in this world, I was sometimes crowned with success, and sometimes mortified with defeat.—At the plough, scythe or reap-hook I feared no competitor, and set Want at defiance: and as I never cared farther for my labors than while I was in actual exercise, I spent the evening in the way after my own heart. —A country lad rarely carries on an amour without an assisting confident.—I possessed a curiosity, zeal and intrepid dexterity in these matters which recommended me a proper Second in duels of that kind; and I dare say, I felt as much pleasure at being in the secret of half the armours in the parish, as ever did Premier at knowing the intrigues of half the courts of Europe.—

The very goosefeather in my hand seems instinctively to know the well-worn path of my imagination, the favorite theme of my song; and is with difficulty restrained from giving you a couple of paragraphs on the amours of my Compeers, the humble Inmates of the farm-house and cottage; but the grave sons of Science, Ambition or Avarice baptize these things by the name of Follies.—To the sons and daughters of labor and poverty they are matters of the most serious nature: to them, the ardent hope, the stolen interview, the tender farewell, are the greatest and most delicious part of their enjoyments.—

Another circumstance in my life which made very considerable alterations in my mind and manners was, I spent my seventeenth[9] summer on a smuggling coast a good distance from home at a noted school, to learn Mensuration, Surveying, Dialling, &c. in which I made a pretty good progress.—But I made greater progress in the knowledge of mankind.—The contraband trade was at that time very successful; scenes of swaggering riot and roaring dissipation were as yet new to me; and I was no enemy to social life.—Here, though I learned to look unconcernedly on a large tavern-bill, and mix without fear in a drunken squabble, yet I went on with a high hand in my Geometry; till the sun entered Virgo, a month which is always a carnival in my bosom, a charming Fillette who lived next door to the school overset my Trigonometry and set me off in a tangent from the sphere of my studies.—I struggled on with my Sines and Co-sines for a few days more; but stepping out to the garden one charming noon, to take the sun's altitude, I met with my Angel,

> —"Like Proserpine gathering flowers,
> "Herself a fairer flower"— [10]

It was vain to think of doing any more good at school.—The remaining week I staid, I did nothing but craze the faculties of my soul about her, or steal out to meet with her; and the two last nights of my stay in the country, had sleep been a mortal sin, I was innocent.—

I returned home very considerably improved.—My reading was enlarged with the very important addition of Thomson's and Shenstone's works; I had seen mankind in a new phasis; and I engaged several of my schoolfellows to keep up a literary correspondence with me.—This last helped me much on in composition.—I had met with a collection of letters by the Wits of Queen Ann's reign, and I pored over them most devoutly.—I kept copies of any of my own letters that pleased me, and a comparison between them and the composition of most of my correspondents flattered my vanity.—I carried this whim so far that though I had not three farthings worth of business in the world, yet every post brought me as many letters as if I had been a broad, plodding son of Day-book & Ledger.—

My life flowed on much in the same tenor till my twenty third year. —Vive l'amour et vive la bagatelle, were my sole principles of action. —The addition of two more Authors to my library gave me great pleasure; Sterne and Mckenzie.—Tristram Shandy and the Man of Feeling were my bosom favorites.—Poesy was still a darling walk for my mind, but 'twas only the humour of the hour.—I had usually half a dozen or more pieces on hand; I took up one or other as it suited the momentary tone of this mind, and dismissed it as it bordered on fatigue.—My Passions when once they were lighted up, raged like so many devils, till they got vent in rhyme; and then conning over my verses, like a spell, soothed all into quiet.—None of the rhymes of those days are in print, except, Winter, a dirge, the eldest of my printed pieces; The death of Poor Mailie, John Barleycorn, And songs first, second and third: song second was the ebullition of that passion which ended the forementioned school-business.—

My twenty third year was to me an important era.—Partly thro' whim, and partly that I wished to set about doing something in life, I joined with a flax-dresser in a neighbouring town, to learn his trade and carry on the business of manufacturing and retailing flax.—This turned out a sadly unlucky affair.—My Partner was a scoundrel of the first water who made money by the mystery of thieving; and to finish the whole, while we were given a welcoming carousal to the New year, our shop, by the drunken carelessness of my Partner's wife, took fire and was burnt to ashes; and left me like a true Poet, not worth sixpence.—I was oblidged to give up business; the clouds of misfortune were gathering thick round my father's head, the darkest of which was, he was visibly far gone in a consumption; and to crown all, a belle-fille whom I adored and who had pledged her soul to meet me in the field of matrimony, jilted me with peculiar circumstances of mortification.—The finishing evil that brought up the rear of this infernal file was my hypochondriac complaint being irritated to such a degree, that for three months I was in diseased state of body and mind, scarcely to be envied by the hopeless wretches who have just got their mittimus, "Depart from me, ye Cursed." [11] —

From this adventure I learned something of a town-life.- But the principal thing which gave my mind a turn was, I formed a bosom-friendship with a young fellow, the first created being I had ever seen, but a hapless son of misfortune.—He was the son of a plain mechanic; but a great Man in the neighbourhood taking him under his patronage gave him a genteel education with a view to bettering his situation in life.—The Patron dieing just as he was ready to launch forth into the world, the poor fellow in despair went to sea; where after a variety of good and bad fortune, a little before I was acquainted with him, he had been set ashore by an American Privateer on the wild coast of Connaught, stript of every thing.—I cannot quit this poor fellow's story without adding that he is at this moment Captain of a large westindian man belonging to the Thames.—

This gentleman's mind was fraught with courage, independance, Magnanimity, and every noble, manly virtue.—I loved him, I admired him, to a degree of enthusiasm; and I strove to imitate him.—In some measure I succeeded: I had the pride before, but he taught it to flow in proper channels.—His knowledge of the world was vastly superiour to mine, and I was all attention to learn.—He was the only man I ever saw who was a greater fool than myself when WOMAN was the presiding star; but he spoke of a certain fashionable failing with levity, which hitherto I had regarded with horror.—Here his friendship did me a mischief; and the consequence was, that soon after I resumed the plough, I wrote the WELCOME inclosed. [12] —My reading was only encreased by two stray volumes of Pamela, and one of Ferdinand Count Fathom, which gave me some idea of Novels.- Rhyme, except some religious pieces which are in print, I had given up; but meeting with Fergusson's Scotch Poems, I strung anew my wildly-sounding, rustic lyre with emulating vigour.—When my father died, his all went among the rapacious hell-hounds that growl in the kennel of justice; but we made a shift to scrape a little money in the family amongst us, with which, to keep us together, my brother and I took a neighbouring farm.—My brother wanted my harebrained imagination as well as my social and amorous madness, but in good sense and every sober qualification he was far my superiour.—

I entered on this farm with a full resolution, "Come, go to, I will be wise!" [13] —I read farming books; I calculated crops; I attended markets; and in short, in spite of "The devil, the world and the flesh," I believe I would have been a wise man; but the first year from unfortunately buying in bad seed, the second from a late harvest, we lost half of both our crops: this overset all my wisdom, and I returned "Like the dog to his vomit, and the sow that was washed to her wallowing in the mire —". [14]

I now began to be known in the neighbourhood as a maker of rhymes.—The first of my poetic offspring that saw the light was a burlesque lamentation on a quarrel between two reverend Calvinists, both of them dramatis personae in my Holy Fair.—I had an idea myself that the piece had some merit; but to prevent the worst, I gave a copy of it to a friend who was very fond of these things, and told him I could not guess who was the Author of it, but that I thought it pretty clever.—With a certain side of both clergy and laity it met with a roar of applause.—Holy Willie's Prayer next made its appearance, and alarmed the kirk-Session so much that they held three several meetings to look over their holy artillery, if any of it was pointed against profane Rhymers.—Unluckily for me, my idle wanderings led me, on another side, point blank within the reach of their heaviest metal.—This is the unfortunate story alluded to in my printed poem, The Lament.—'Twas a shocking affair, which I cannot yet bear to recollect; and had very nearly given me one or two of the principal qualifications for the place among those who have lost the chart and mistake the reckoning of Rationality.—I gave up my part of the farm to my brother, as in truth it was only nominally mine; and made what little preparation was in my power for Jamaica. Before leaving my native country for ever, I resolved to publish my Poems.— I weighed my productions as impartially as in my power; I thought they had merit; and 'twas a delicious idea that I would be called a clever fellow, even though it should never reach my ears a poor Negro-driver, or perhaps a victim to that inhospitable clime gone to the world of Spirits.—I can truly say that pauvre Inconnu as I then was, I had pretty nearly as high an idea of myself and my works as I have at this moment.—It is ever my opinion that the great, unhappy mistakes and blunders, both in a rational and religious point of view, of which we see thousands daily guilty, are owing to their ignorance, or mistaken notions of themselves.—To know myself had been all along my constant study.—I weighed myself alone, I balanced myself with others; I watched every means of information how much ground I occupied both as a Man and as a Poet: I studied assiduously Nature's DESIGN where she seem'd to have intended the various LIGHTS and SHADES in my character.—I was pretty sure my Poems would meet with some applause; but at the worst, the roar of the Atlantic would deafen the voice of Censure, and the novelty of west-Indian scenes make me forget Neglect.—

I threw off six hundred copies, of which I had got subscriptions for about three hundred and fifty.—My vanity was highly gratified by the reception I met with from the Publick; besides pocketing, all expences deducted, near twenty pounds.—This last came very seasonable, as I was about to indent myself for want of money to pay my freight. So soon as I was master of nine guineas, the price of wafting me to the torrid zone, I bespoke a passage in the very first ship that was to sail, for

"Hungry ruin had me in the wind"- [15]

I had for some time been sculking from covert to covert under all the terrors of a Jail; as some ill-advised, ungrateful people had uncoupled the merciless legal Pack at my heels.—I had taken the last farewel of my few friends; my chest was on the road to Greenock; I had composed my last song I should ever measure in Caledonia. "The gloomy night is gathering fast,"[16] when a letter from Dr. Blacklock to a friend of mine overthrew all my schemes by rousing my poetic ambition.—The Doctor belonged to a set of Critics for whose applause I had not even dared to hope.—His idea that I would meet with every encouragement for a second edition fired me so much that away I posted to Edinburgh without a single acquaintance in town, or a single letter of introduction in my pocket.—The baneful Star that had so long shed its blasting influence in my Zenith, for once made a revolution to the Nadir; and the providential care of a good God placed me under the patronage of one of his noblest creatures, the Earl of Glencairn: "Oublie moi, Grand Dieu, si jamais je l'oublie!"—

I need relate no farther.—At Edinburgh I was in a new world: I mingled among many classes of men, but all of them new to me; and I was all attention "to catch the manners living as they rise."—[17]

You can now, Sir, form a pretty near guess what sort of a Wight he is whom for some time you have honored with your correspondence.— That Fancy & Whim, keen Sensibility and riotous Passions may still make him zig-zag in his future path of life, is far from being improbable; but come what will, I shall answer for him the most determinate integrity and honor; and though his evil star should again blaze in his meridian with tenfold more direful influence, he may reluctantly tax Friendship with Pity but no more.—

My most respectful Compliments to Miss Williams.—Her very elegant and friendly letter I cannot answer at present, as my presence is requisite in Edinburgh, and I set off tomorrow.—

If you will oblidge me so highly and do me so much honor as now and then to drop me a letter, Please direct to me at Mauchline, Ayrshire.—

> I have the honor to be, Sir
> your ever grateful humble servant
> Robt Burns

Edinburgh 23rd September

Sir

the foregoing letter was unluckily forgot among other papers at Glasgow on my way to Edinburgh.—Soon after I came to Edinburgh I went on a tour through the Highlands and did not recover this letter till my return to town which was the other day.—My ideas I picked up in my pilgrimage, and some rhymes of my earlier years, I

DR. JOHN MOORE

Engraved By W.&H. Hall

REV. DR. GEORGE LAWRIE

shall soon be at leisure to give you at large, so soon as I hear from you whether you are in London.—

I am again Sir, yours, most gratefully.—
R. Burns

1 Ecclesiastes 2 : 12.
2 Pope: *Essay on Man*, IV, 211.
3 Shakespeare: *Julius Caesar*, Act III, sc. 2.
4 Pope: *January and May*, line 157.
5 Arthur Masson, *A Collection of Prose and Verse, from the Best English Authors. For the Use of Schools.*
6 Job 3 : 17.
7 Thomas Salmon, *A New Geographical and Historical Grammar;* William Guthrie, *A New Geographical, Historical, and Commercial Grammar;* Jethro Tull, *The Horse-Hoing Husbandry: or, an Essay on Principles of Tillage and Vegetation;* Adam Dickson, *A Treatise on Agriculture;* John Taylor, *The Scripture Doctrine of Original Sin.*
8 Matthew 18 : 20, misquoted.
9 'Seventeenth' deleted and 'nineteenth or twentieth' substituted in another hand.
10 Milton: *Paradise Lost*, Bk, IV, line 269.
11 Matthew 25 : 41.
12 *A Poet's Welcome to his Lovebegotten Daughter.* (CW. p. 112).
13 Ecclesiastes 7 : 23.
14 2 Peter 2 : 22, misquoted.
15 Not identified.
16 C.W. p. 250.
17 Pope: *Essay on Man*, I, 14.

V (294)

Ellisland near Dumfries 4th January 1789

Sir,

As often as I think of writing to you, which has been three or four—times every week these six months, it gives me something so like the idea of an ordinary sized Statue offering at a conversation with the Rhodian Colossus that my mind misgives me; and the affair always miscarries somewhere between Purpose and Resolve.— I have at last got some business with you, and business-letters are written by the Style-book.—I say my business is with you, Sir; for you never had any with me, except the business that Benevolence has in the mansion of Poverty.—

The character and employment of a Poet were formerly my pleasure, but are now my pride.— I know that a very great deal of my late eclat was owing to the singularity of my situation, and the honest prejudice of Scotsmen; but still as I said in the preface to my first Edition, I do look upon myself as having some pretentions from Nature to the Poetic Character.—I have not a doubt but the knack, the aptitude to learn the Muses' trade, is a gift bestowed by Him "who forms the secret biass of the soul;"[1] but I as firmly believe that *excellence* in the Profession is the fruit of industry, labour, attention and pains.—At least I am resolved to try my doctrine by the test of Experience.—Another appearance from the Press, I put off to a very distant day; a day that may never arrive; but Poesy I am determined to prosecute with all my vigour.— Nature has given very few, if any, of the Profession, the talents of shining in every species of Composition: I shall try, for untill trial it is impossible to know, whether she has qualified me to shine in any one.— The worst of it is, against one has finished a Piece, it has been so often viewed and reviewed before the mental eye that one loses in a good measure the powers of critical discrimination.—Here the best criterion I know is A Friend; not only of abilities to judge, but with good nature enough, like a prudent teacher with a young learner, to give perhaps a little more than is exactly due, less the thin-skinned animal fall into that most deplorable of all Poetic diseases, heart-breaking despondency of himself.—Dare I, Sir, already immensely indebted to your goodness, ask the additional obligation of your being that Friend to me? I inclose you an Essay of mine in a walk of Poesy to me entirely new; I mean the Epistle addressed to R— G— Esq. or Robert Graham of Fintry Esquire; a gentleman of uncommon worth, to whom I lie under very great obligations.—The story of the Poem; like most of my poems, is connected with my own story; and to give you the one, I must give you something of the other.—

I cannot boast of Mr. Creech's ingenuous fair-dealing to me.—He kept me hanging on about Edinburgh from the 7th August 1787, untill the 13th April 1788, before he would condescend to give me a Statement of affairs; nor had I got it even then, but for an angry letter I wrote him which irritated his pride.—"I could" not a "tale" but a detail "unfold"[2] —but what am I that I should speak against the Lord's annointed Bailie of Edinburgh?—I believe I shall in whole, £100 Copy-right included, clear about £400, some little odds; and even part of this depends upon what the gentleman has yet to settle with me.—I give you this information because you did me the honor to interest yourself much in my welfare; but I give it to yourself only, for the world would accuse me of ingratitude, and I am still much in the gentleman's mercy.—Perhaps I injure the man in the idea I am sometimes tempted to have of him—God forbid I should! A little time will try, for in a month I shall go to town to wind up the business—if possible.—To give the rest of my story in brief, I have married "My Jean," and taken a farm: with the first step I have every day more & more reason to be satisfied; with the last it is rather the reverse.—I have a younger brother who supports my aged mother, another still younger brother & three sisters in a farm.—On my last return from Edinburgh it cost me about £180 to save them from ruin.—Not that I have lost so much; I only interposed between my brother and his impending fate by the loan of so much.—I give myself no airs on this, for it was mere selfishness on my part.—I was conscious that the opposite scale of the balance was pretty heavily charged, and I thought that throwing a little filial piety & fraternal affection into the scale in my favor, might help to smooth matters at the Grand Reckoning.—There is still one thing would make my circumstances quite easy.—I have an Excise-Officer's Commission, & I live in the midst of a country Division.—My request to Mr. Graham, who is one of the Commiss: of Excise, was, if in his power, to procure me that Division.—If I were very sanguine, I might hope that some of my Great Patrons might procure me a Treasury-warrant for Supervisor, Surveyor-general, &c. but thank Heaven I am in a good degree independant.—If farming will not do, a simple petition will get me into employ in the Excise somewhere; & poor as the salary comparatively is, it is luxury to what either my wife or I were in early life taught to expect.—Thus, secure of a livelyhood, "to thee sweet Poetry, delightful maid," I consecrate my future days.—

Dr. John Moore

With the highest esteem & warmest gratitude
I have the honor to be, Sir,
Your most humble servant

My address is, at Ellisland near Dumfries

Robt Burns

1 Akenside: *Pleasures of Imagination*, III, 522-3, slightly misquoted.
2 Shakespeare: *Hamlet*, Act I, sc. 5.

VI (322)

Ellisland, 23rd March 1789

Sir

The gentleman who will deliver you this, is a Mr. Nielson, a worthy clergyman in my neighbourhood, and a very particular acquaintance of mine.—As I have troubled him with this packet, I must turn him o'er to your goodness to recompense him for it in a way in which he much needs your assistance, and where you can effectually serve him.—Mr. Nielson is on his way for France to wait on his Grace of Queensberry on some little business of a good deal of importance to my friend, and he wishes for your instructions respecting the most eligible mode of travelling, &c., for him, when he has crossed the channel.—I would not have dared to take this liberty with you, but that I am told by those who have the honor of your personal acquaintance, that to be a poor honest Scotsman is such a letter of recommendation to you, and that to have it in your power to serve such a character gives you so much pleasure, that I am persuaded in soliciting your goodness in this business I am gratifying your feelings with a degree of enjoyment.—

The inclosed Ode is a compliment to the memory of the late Mrs. Oswald of Auchencruive.—You, probably, knew her personally, an honor of which I cannot boast; but I spent my early years in her neighbourhood, and among her servants and tenants I know that she was detested with the most heart-felt cordiality.—However, in the particular part of her conduct, which roused my Poetic wrath, she was much less blameable.—In January last, on my road to Ayrshire, I had put up at Bailie Whigham's in Sanqhuar, the only tolerable inn in the place.—The frost was keen, and the grim evening and howling wind were ushering in a night of snow and drift.—My horse & I were both much fatigued with the labors of the day, and just as my friend the Bailie and I, were bidding defiance to the storm over a smoking bowl, in wheels the funeral pageantry of the late great Mrs. Oswald, and poor I, am forced to brave all the horrors of the tempestuous night, and jade my horse, my young favorite horse whom I had just christened Pegasus, twelve miles farther on, through the wildest moors & hills of Ayrshire, to New Cumnock, the next Inn.—The powers of Poesy & Prose sink under me, when I would describe what I felt.—Suffice it to say, that when a good fire at New Cumnock had so far recovered my frozen sinews, I sat down and wrote the inclosed Ode.

I was at Edinburgh lately, and settled finally with Mr. Creech; and I must retract some illnatured surmises in my last letter, and own that at last, he has been amicable and fair with me.

I have the honor to be, with the sincerest gratitude,
Sir, your deeply indebted humble servant
Robt Burns

Dr. John Moore

Dumfries Excise Office, 14th July 1790

Sir

Coming into town this morning to attend my duty in this Office, it being Collection-Day, I met with a gentleman who tells me he is on his way to London; so I take the opportunity of writing you, as Franking is at present under a temporary death.—I shall have some snatches of leisure through the day, amid our horrid business & bustle, & I shall improve them as well as I can; but let my letter be as stupid as Boston's Four-fold State, as miscellaneous as a Newspaper, as short as a hungry Grace-before-meat, or as long as a Lawpaper in the Douglas-cause, [1] as ill-spelt as Country John's Billet-doux; or as unsightly a scrawl as Betty Byre-mucker's answer to it; I hope, considering circumstances, you will forgive it; and as it will put you to no expence of Postage, I shall have the less reflection about it.—

I am sadly ungrateful in not returning you my thanks for your most valuable present—Zelucco.—In fact, you are in some degree blameable for my neglect.—You were pleased to express a wish for my opinion of the Work, which so flattered me that nothing less would serve my over-weening fancy than a formal criticism on the Book. In fact, I have gravely planned a Comparative view of You, Fielding, Richardson & Smollet, in your different qualities & merits as Novel-Writers.—This, I own, betrays my ridiculous vanity, and I may probably never bring the business to bear; but I am fond of the spirit young Elihu shews in the book of Job—"And I said I will also declare my Opinion"—[2].—I have quite disfigured my copy of the Book with my annotations.—I never take it up without at the same time taking my pencil, & marking with asterisms, parenthesis, & c. wherever I meet with an original thought, a nervous remark on life & manners, a remarkably well-turned period, or a character sketched with uncommon precision.—

Though I shall hardly think of fairly writing out my "comparative view," I shall certainly trouble you with my remarks such as they are.—

I have just received from my Gentleman that horrid Summons in the Book of the Revelations—"That, time shall be no more!"[3]

The little Collection of Sonnets have some charming Poetry in them. —If *indeed* I am indebted to the fair Author for the book, & not as I rather suspect to a celebrated Author of the other Sex, I should certainly have written the Lady with my grateful acknowledgements & my own ideas of the comparative excellence of her Pieces.—I would do this last, not from any vanity of thinking that my remarks could be of much consequence to Miss Smith, but merely, from my own feelings as an Author, Doing as I would be done by.—

[*About five lines of the letter missing*]
"—the demons of despair & death,
Ride on the blast, & urge the howling storm."—

I inclose you three late Pieces of my own.—If you would at a leisure-hour cast a critic-eye over them & let me know any weak lines, &c. you may remark in them, it would indeed by very oblidging.—

Dr. John Moore

I hope Miss Williams is well & going in favor with Apollo & the Nine.—

I have the honor to be, Sir,
your highly oblidged & ever grateful humble servant
Robt Burns

1 The popular name for the long drawn-out legal action, Duke of Hamilton v. Archibald Douglas of Douglas over the right to the title and inheritance. James Boswell was retained as Douglas's counsel, 1778.
2 Job 32:10 or 17.
3 Revelation 10:6.

VIII (437)

Ellisland near Dumfries, 28th February 1791

I do not know, Sir, whether you are a Subscriber to Grose's Antiquities of Scotland.—If you are, the inclosed poem will not be altogether new to you.—Captain Grose did me the favor to send me a dozen copies of the Proof-sheet, of which this is one.—Should you have read the piece before, still this will answer the principal end I have in view: it will give me another opportunity of thanking you for all your goodness to the rustic Bard; & also of shewing you, that the abilities you have been pleased to commend & patronise, are still employed in the way you wish.—

The Elegy on Captain Henderson, is a tribute to the memory of a Man I loved much.—Poets have in this the same advantages as Roman Catholics; they can be of service to their Friends after they have past that bourne where all other kindness ceases to be of any avail. Whether after all, either the one or the other be of any real service to the Dead, is, I fear, very problematical; but I am sure they are highly gratifying to the Living: and as a very orthodox text, I forget where, in Scripture says, "Whatsoever is not of faith, is sin;"[1] —so, say I, Whatsoever is not detrimental to Society, & is of positive Enjoyment, is of God the Giver of all good things, & ought be received & enjoyed by His creatures with thankful delight.—As almost all my Religious tenets originate from my heart, I am wonderfully pleased with the idea that I can still keep us a tender intercourse with the dearly beloved Friend, or still more dearly beloved Mistress, who is gone to the world of Spirits.—

The Ballad on Queen Mary, was begun while I was busy with Percy's Reliques of English Poetry.—By the way, how much is every honest heart which has a tincture of *genuine* Caledonian Prejudice, oblidged to you for your glorious story of Buchanan & Targe.—'Twas an unequivocal proof of your loyal gallantry of Soul, giving Targe the victory.[2] —I should have been mortified to the ground, if you had not.—What a rocky-hearted, perfidious Succubus was that Queen Elizabeth!—Judas Iscariot was a sad dog to be sure, but still his demerits shrink to insignificance, compared with the doings of the infernal Bess Tudor.—Judas did not know, at least was by no means sure, what or who that Master was; his turpitude was simply betraying a worthy man who had ever been a good Master to him: a degree of turpitude which has even been outdone by many of his kind since.—Iscariot, poor wretch, was a man of nothing at all per Annum, & by consequence, thirty pieces of silver was a very serious

261

Dr. John Moore

temptation to *him*; but, to give but one instance, the Duke of Queensberry, the other day, just played the same trick to *his* kind Master, tho' His Grace is a man of thirty thousand a year, & come to that imbecille period of life when no temptation but Avarice can be supposed to affect him.—

I have just read over, once more of many times, your Zelucco.—I marked with my pencil, as I went along every passage that pleased me particularly above the rest, & one, or two I think, which with humble deference I am disposed to think unequal to the merit of the Book.—I have sometimes thought to transcribe these marked passages, or at least so much of them as to point out where they are & send them to you.—Original strokes, that strongly depict the human heart, is your & Fielding's province, beyond any other Novellist, I have ever perused.—Richardson indeed might perhaps be excepted; but unhappily. his Dramatis personae are beings of some other world; & however they may captivate the unexperienced, romantic fancy of a boy or a girl, they will ever, in proportion as we have made human nature our study, disgust our riper minds.—

As to my private concerns, I am going on, a mighty Taxgatherer before the lord, & have lately had the interest to get myself ranked on the list of Excise as a Supervisor.—I am not yet employed as such, but in a few years I will fall into the file of Supervisorship by seniority.—I have had an immense loss in the death of the Earl of Glencairn; the Patron from whom all my fame & good fortune took its rise.—Independant of my grateful attachment to him, which was indeed so strong that it pervaded my very soul, & was entwined with the thread of my existence; so soon as the Prince's friends had got in, (& every dog you know has his day) my getting forward in the Excise would have been an easier business than otherwise it will be.— Though this was a consummation devoutly to be wished, yet, thank Heaven, I can live & rhyme, as I am; & as to my boys, poor, little fellows! if I cannot place them on as high an elevation in life, as I could wish; I shall, if I am favored so much of the Disposer of events as to see that period, take care to fix them on as broad and independant basis as possible.—Among the many wise adages which have been treasured up by our Scotish Ancestors, this is one of the best—"Better be the head o' the Commonality, as the tail o' the Gentry."—

But I am got on a subject, which however interesting to me, is of no manner of consequence to you; so I shall give you a short poem on the other page, & close this with assuring you how sincerely I have the honor to be

Sir, your obliged & ever grateful humble servant
Robt Burns

Written on the blank leaf of a book which I presented to a very young lady,[3] whom I had formerly characterised under the denomination of, The Rose-bud.—

Beauteous Rose-bud, young & gay,
[C.W. p. 367]

1 Romans 14:23.
2 George Buchanan and Duncan Targe, characters in Dr. Moore's *Zeluco*.
3 Miss Janet Cruikshank.

REV. GEORGE LAWRIE

The father of the Rev. Archibald Lawrie, previously noted (see page 127), and himself the son of a Kirkmichael minister, he was born in 1727 and educated at Edinburgh University. In 1763 he was ordained minister of Loudoun Parish, at Newmilns and remained there till his death in 1799. In 1764 he married Mary, daughter of Archibald Campbell, Professor of Divinity at St. Andrews University. Their daughter Christina, who is mentioned in this letter, was born in 1766 and married Alexander Wilson, a Glasgow bookseller, in April 1787. 'Miss Lowrie (*sic*) and her Piano forte' greatly impressed Burns, and according to Gilbert, the first time that Robert ever heard the piano (or rather a spinet) played was at the Lawrie manse in Newmilns, and this gave him a taste for concert recitals. Miss Lawrie herself was in Edinburgh at the same time as Burns who evidently had great pleasure in passing on to her parents the complimentary remarks of Henry Mackenzie, author of *The Man of Feeling*.

(80)

Edinburgh, 5th February 1787

Reverend and Dear Sir

When I look at the date of your kind letter my heart reproaches me severely with ingratitude in neglecting so long to answer it.—I will not trouble you with any account, by way of apology, of my hurried life & distracted attention: do me the justice to beleive that my delay by no means proceeded from want of respect.—I feel, and ever shall feel for you the mingled sentiments of esteem for a friend & reverence for a father.—

I thank you Sir, with all my soul for your friendly hints; though I do not need them so much as my friends are apt to imagine.—You are dazzled with news-paper accounts & distant reports, but in reality I have no great temptation to be intoxicated with the cup of Prosperity.—Novelty may attract the attention of mankind a while; to it I owe my present eclat: but I see the time not distant far when the popular tide which has borne me to a height of which I am perhaps unworthy shall recede with silent celerity and leave me a barren waste of sand, to descend at my leisure to my former station. I do not say this in the affectation of modesty; I see the consequence is unavoidable and am prepared for it.—I had been at a good deal of pains to form a just, impartial estimate of my intellectual Powers before I came here; I have not added, since I came to Edinburgh, any thing to the account; and I trust, I shall take every atom of it back to my shades, the coverts of my unnoticed, early years.—

In Dr. Blacklock, whom I see very often, I have found what I would have expected in our friend, a clear head and an excellent heart.—

By far the most agreable hours I spend in Edinburgh must be placed to the account of Miss Lowrie and her Piano forte.—I cannot help repeating to you & Mrs. Lowrie a compliment that Mr. Mckenzie the celebrated "Man of feeling" paid to Miss Christie the other night at the Concert.—I had come in at an interlude and sat down by him, till I saw Miss Lowrie in a seat not very distant, and went up to pay my respects to her.—On my return to Mr. Mckenzie, he asked me who she was; I told him 'twas the daughter of a reverend friend of mine in the West country.—He returned there was something very striking to his idea in her appearance. On my desiring to know what it was, he was pleased to say, "She has a great deal of the elegance of a well-bred Lady about her, with all the sweet simplicity of a Country girl."—

Rev. George Lawrie

My Compliments to all the happy Inmates of Saint Margaret's.—
                    I am, Dear Sir, Yours most gratefully,
                                        Robt Burns

FERGUSSON'S TOMBSTONE

Burns was thoroughly versed in the poetry of Robert Fergusson (1750-74) whose works were published barely a year before he died in an Edinburgh mad-house. Fergusson's mastery of the vernacular inspired Burns to even greater heights, but both in the structure and the subject-matter of his poems Burns was considerably influenced by the man whom he regarded as:

'O Thou, my elder brother in misfortune,
By far my elder brother in the muse,'

Burns was not slow to acknowledge his debt to Fergusson, notably in the *Epistle to William Simpson* (C.W. p. 107) and *Apostrophe to Fergusson* (C.W. p. 269), but his gratitude took a more practical form when he wrote the following letter to the Bailies of the Canongate, Edinburgh, seeking permission to erect a headstone over Fergusson's unmarked grave. The bailies forwarded Burns's request to the authorities in charge of the cemetery. Burns commissioned the architect Robert Burn to erect the stone, for which the four lines beginning 'No sculptured Marble here, nor pompous lay' (C.W. p. 269) were composed. Burns did not settle the bill till 1792. Commenting on the delay in a letter to Peter Hill (see page 321), he wrote of Mr. Burn: 'He was two years in erecting it, after I commissioned him for it; and I have been two years paying him, after he sent me his account; so he and I quits. He had the hardiesse to ask me interest on the sum; but considering that the money was due by one Poet, for putting a tombstone over another, he may, with grateful surprise, thank Heaven that he ever saw a farthing of it.'

(81)

To the Honorable the BAILIES OF THE CANONGATE, *Edinburgh.*

Edinburgh, 6th February 1787

Gentlemen,

I am sorry to be told that the remains of Robert Ferguson the so justly celebrated Poet, a man whose talents for ages to come will do honor, to our Caledonian name, lie in your church yard among the ignoble Dead unnoticed and unknown.—Some memorial to direct the steps of the Lovers of Scottish Song, when they wish to shed a tear over the "Narrow house" of the Bard who is now no more, is surely a tribute due to Ferguson's memory: a tribute I wish to have the honor of paying.—I petition you then, Gentlemen, for your permission to lay a simple stone over his revered ashes, to remain an unalienable property to his deathless fame.—

I have the honor to be Gentlemen,
your very humble servant
Robert Burns

DAVID ERSKINE, EARL OF BUCHAN

Born in 1742, he succeeded his father as eleventh earl in 1767. The Hon. Henry Erskine (see page 224) was his younger brother. A literary dilettante, he was a founder of the Society of Antiquaries of Scotland in 1780. He fancied himself as a patron of the arts, although his very canny approach to spending money invariably limited his patronage to what he regarded as good advice. On 1st February 1787 he wrote to Burns an exceedingly patronising and pompous letter: 'I have redd (*sic*) with great pleasure several of your poems... These little doric pieces of yours in our provincial dialect are very beautiful...' but he then went on to advise Burns to keep his 'Eye upon Parnassus and drink deep of the fountains of Helicon, but beware of the Joys that is (*sic*) dedicated to the Jolly God of wine.' Burns replied six days later in appropriately high-flown fashion, though noting in his Edinburgh Commonplace Book that he was writing 'in answer to a bombast epistle'. The copy of this letter which appears in the Don MS is headed 'in answer to an epistle of critisms (*sic*) and advices from his Lordship'.

In August 1791 Lord Buchan invited Burns to one of those self-advertising literary 'festivals' which he was fond of promoting, suggesting that Burns might compose a poem suitable for the occasion, the crowning of a bust of the poet Thomson. Burns replied that he could not attend because of the harvest, though he sent his *Address to the Shade of Thomson* (C.W. p. 421). The event was a farce: the bust itself was broken in a drunken frolic before its erection, and the earl had to be content with laying a wreath on a book of Thomson's poems. Burns's letter (II) and the poem were published by the earl in 1792 as part of his *Essays on the Lives and Writings of Fletcher of Saltoun and the Poet Thomson*. Burns himself was to be the subject of a similar celebration, which the earl staged on the banks of the Tweed in 1814, but his most preposterous act was to intrude on the family of Sir Walter Scott when he was ill in 1819. Lord Buchan had elaborate plans for the funeral ceremony! Sir Walter, in fact, outlived the earl (who died in 1829) by some three years. Scott later described Buchan as 'a person whose immense vanity, bordering on insanity, obscured, or rather eclipsed, very considerable talents...'

I (82)

Lawnmarket, 7th February 1787

My Lord,

the honor your Lordship has done me by your notice and advice in yours of the 1st Inst I shall ever gratefully remember.—

"Praise from thy lips 'tis mine with joy to boast,
"They best can give it who deserve it most"—[1]

Your Lordship touches the darling chord of my heart when you advise me to fire my Muse at Scottish story and Scottish scenes.—I wish for nothing more than to make a leisurely Pilgrimage through my native country; to sit and muse on those once hard-contended fields where Caledonia, rejoicing, saw her bloody lion borne through broken ranks to victory and fame; and catching the inspiration, to pour the deathless Names in Song.—But, my Lord, in the midst of these delighting, enthusiastic Reveries, a long-visaged, dry, moral-looking Phantom strides across my imagination, and with the frigid air of a declaiming Preacher sets off with a text of Scripture—"I, Wisdom, dwell with Prudence"—[2]

"Friend, I do not come to open the ill-closed wounds of your "Follies and Misfortunes, merely to give you pain; I wish through "these wounds to imprint a lasting impression on your heart!— I will "not mention how many of my salutary advices you have despised.— "I have given you line upon line, precept upon precept; and while I "was chalking you out the straight way to Wealth and Character, "with audacious effrontery you have zigzagged across the path, "contemning me to my face.—You know the consequences.—It is "not yet three months since Home was so hot for you, that you "were on the wing for the western shore of the Atlantic; not to "make a fortune, but to hide your disgrace.—

266

"Now that your dear-lov'd Scotia, about whom you make such a
"racket, puts it in your power to return to the situation of your
"forefathers, will you follow these, will-o'whisp meteors of Fancy
"and Whim till they bring you once more to the brink of ruin? I
"grant the utmost ground you can occupy is but half a step from the
"veriest Poverty, but still it is half a step from it.—If all that I urge is
"ineffectual, let HER who seldom calls to you in vain, let the call of
"Pride prevail with you.—You know how you feel at the iron grip of
"ruthless Oppression: you know how you bear the galling sneer of
"contumelious Greatness.—I hold you out, the conveniences the
"comforts of life, independence and character, in the one hand; I
"tender you, servility, dependance and wretchedness, in the other: I
"will not insult your Common sense by bidding you make a
"choice."—

This, my Lord, is an unanswerable harangue.—I must return to my
rustic station, and, in my wonted way, woo my rustic Muse at the
Ploughtail.—Still, my Lord, while the drops of life, while the sound
of Caledonia, warm my heart; gratitude to that dear-priz'd Country
in which I boast my birth, and gratitude to those her distinguished
Names who have honored me so much with their Approbation and
Patronage, shall while stealing through my humble Shades, ever
distend my bosom, and at times as now draw forth the swelling
tear.—

> I have the honor to be, with the highest respect,
> My Lord, your much indebted, humble servant
> Robert Burns

1 Unidentified. G. Ross Roy suggests that these lines may have been
paraphrased from the closing couplet of Addison: *The Campaign.*
2 Proverbs 8:12.

II (465)

[With *Address to the Shade of Thomson*, C.W. p. 421]

> Ellisland near Dumfries
> 29th August 1791

My Lord,

Language sinks under the ardour of my feelings, when I would thank
your Lordship for the honour, the very great honour, you have done
me, in inviting me to the coronation of the bust of Thomson.—In my
first enthusiasm, on reading the card you did me the honour to write
to me, I overlooked every obstacle, and determined to go; but I fear
it will not be in my power.—A week or two in the very middle of my
harvest, is what I much doubt I dare not venture on.—I once already
made a pilgrimage *up* the whole course of the Tweed, and fondly
would I take the same delightful journey *down* the windings of that
charming stream.

Your Lordship hints at an ode for the occasion: but who would
write after Collins? I read over his verses to the memory of
Thomson, and despaired. I attempted three or four stanzas in the
way of address to the shade of the bard, on crowning his bust.—I

trouble your Lordship with the inclosed copy of them, which I am afraid will be but too convincing a proof how unequal I am to the task you would obligingly assign me.—However, it affords me an opportunity of approaching your Lordship, and declaring how sincerely I have the honour to be,

My Lord, Your Lordship's highly obliged,
And most devoted humble servant
Robert Burns

III (612)

Dumfries, 12th January 1794

My Lord

will your Lordship allow me to present you with the inclosed little composition of mine,* as a small tribute of gratitude for that acquaintance with which you have been pleased to honor me. Independant of my enthusiasm as a Scotchman, I have rarely met with any thing in History which interests my feelings as a Man, equally with the story of Bannockburn.—

On the one hand, a cruel but able Usurrper, leading on the finest army in Europe, to extinguish the last spark of Freedom among a greatly-daring and greatly injured People; on the other hand, the desperate relics of a gallant Nation, devoting themselves to rescue their bleeding Country, or perish with her.—

Liberty! Thou art a prize truly & indeed invaluable!—for never canst thou be too dearly bought!

If my little Ode has the honor of your Lordship's approbation it will gratify my highest ambition.—

I have the honor to be, MY LORD,
your Lordship's deeply indebted
& most devoted humble servant
Robt Burns

* *Scots Wha Hae*, C.W. p. 500.

JAMES DALRYMPLE OF ORANGEFIELD

Born about 1752, the son of Charles Dalrymple of Ayr, who had married Miss Macrae McGuire, the heiress of Orangefield in 1750. James Dalrymple succeeded to the estate in 1785. When Burns went to Edinburgh the following year Dalrymple, with John Samson of Kilmarnock, appears to have guaranteed George Reid of Barquharie the safe return of the 'pownie' lent to the poet for the journey. Dalrymple also favoured Burns with a letter of introduction to his cousin, the Earl of Glencairn, circumstances which Burns described in a letter to John Ballantine on 13th December 1786 (see page 99), On 7th December 1786 Dalrymple introduced Burns at a meeting of Canongate Kilwinning Lodge. Only one letter from Burns to Dalrymple is extant, written in February 1787 on receipt of a rhyming epistle from Dalrymple. Thereafter he disappears from the correspondence. He squandered his fortune and was declared bankrupt in 1791, dying four years later. Orangefield House for several years formed part of the terminal complex at Prestwick Airport, but has since been demolished.

(84)

To JAMES DALRYMPLE, Esq. *of Orangefield, on receiving a rhyming epistle from him—*

Edinburgh, February 1787

Dear Sir,

I suppose the devil is so elated at his success with you that he is determined by a coup de main to effect his purposes on you all at once in making you a Poet.—

I broke open the letter; hummed over the rhymes; and as I saw they were extempore, said to myself they were very well: but when I saw at the bottom, a name that I shall ever value with grateful respect—

"I gapit wide but naething spak"—[1]

I was nearly as much struck as the three friends of Job, of affliction-bearing memory, when "they sat down with him seven days and seven nights and spake not a word;"[2] or, to go farther back, as the brave but unfortunate Jacobite Clans who, as John Milton tells us, after their unhappy Culloden lay "nine times the space that measures day & night," [3] in oblivious astonishment, prone-weltering on the fiery Surge.—I am naturally of a superstitious cast, and so soon as my wonder-scared imagination regained its consciousness and resumed its functions, I cast about in my pericranium what this might portend.—

My foreboding ideas had the wide stretch of Possibility; and several events, great in their magnitude and important in their consequences, recurred to my fancy.—The downfall of the Conclave, or the crushing of the Cork-rumps; a ducal coronet to Lord George Gordon and the Protestant interest, or St. Peter's keys to the hell-mouthing John Russell; Family-prayers in the house of Orangefield, or another brace of bantlings to a certain bard already over-charged with a numerous issue.—

You want to know how I come on.—I am just in statu quo, or, not to insult a gentleman with my latin, in auld use and wont.—The noble Earl of Glencairn took me by the hand today, and interested himself in my concerns, with a goodness like that benevolent B E I N G whose image he so richly bears.—"Oubliez moi, grand Dieu, si jamais je l'oublie!" He is a stronger proof of the immortality of the Soul than any that Philosophy has ever produced.—A Mind like his can never die.—Let the Worshipfull Squire Hugh Logan, or Mass James

269

James Dalrymple of Orangefield

Mckindlay, go into their primitive nothing.—At best they are but ill-digested lumps of Chaos, only one of them strongly tinged with bituminous particles, and sulphureous effluvia.—But my noble Patron, eternal as the heroic swell of Magnanimity and the generous throb of Benevolence, shall look on with princely eye—

"Unhurt amid the war of elements,
The wrecks of Matter, and the crush of Worlds"—[4]

For the blind, mischief-making little urchin of a Deity, you mention, he and I have been sadly at odds ever since some dog tricks he play'd me not half a century ago.—I have compromised matters with his godship of late by uncoupling my heart and fancy, for a slight chase, after a certain Edinburgh Belle.—My devotions proceed no farther than a forenoon's walk, a sentimental conversation, now and then a squeeze of the hand or interchanging an oeillade, and when peculiar good humor and sequestered propriety allow—

—"Brethren, salute one another with a holy kiss,"—
Paul [5]

"Kissin in the key o' love,
"An' clappin is the lock,
"An' making o's the best thing
"That ere a young thing got"—

An auld Sang o' my Mither's.
I have the honor to be, &c.

---

1 *The Death and Dying Words of Poor Mailie,* line 11.(C.W. p. 62)
2. Job 2:13, misquoted.
3 *Paradise Lost,* Bk I, line 50.
4 Addison: *Cato,* Act V, sc. I.
5 1Corinthians 16:20, misquoted.

ARCHIBALD MONTGOMERIE, EARL OF EGLINTON

Born in 1726, he had a distinguished military career. In 1757 he raised the 77th Regiment of Foot and was appointed its lieutenant colonel, and later rose to the rank of general. He succeeded to the earldom in 1769, after having been MP for Ayrshire, and was chosen in 1776 as one of the Scottish Representative Peers in the House of Lords. In 1782 he was appointed Governor of Edinburgh Castle, in which position he was succeeded by his cousin, Colonel Hugh Montgomerie, the 'sodger Hugh' of *The Author's Earnest Cry and Prayer* (C.W. p. 176). Lord Eglinton sent ten guineas per a Mr. Wauchope, to Burns when he arrived in Edinburgh, as a subscription for two copies of the Edinburgh Poems. This following letter was sent by Burns in reply.

(86A)

Edinburgh, February 1787

My Lord

As I have but slender pretentions to philosophy, I cannot rise to the exalted ideas of a Citizen of the world at large; but have all those national prejudices, which, I believe, glow peculiarly strong in the breast of a Scotchman.—There is scarcely any thing to which I am so feelingly alive as the honor and welfare of old Scotia; and, as a Poet, I have no higher enjoyment than singing her Sons and Daughters.—Fate had cast my station in the veriest shades of Life, but never did a heart pant more ardently than mine to be distinguished; though, till very lately, I looked round for a ray of light in vain.—It is easy then to guess how supremely I was gratified, in being honored with the countenance and approbation of one of my dear lov'd Country's most illustrious Sons, when Mr. Wauchope called on me yesterday on the part of your Lordship.—Your munificence, my Lord, certainly deserves my very grateful acknowledgements; but your patronage is a bounty peculiarly suited to my feelings.—I am not master enough of the etiquette of life to know, whether there be not some impropriety in troubling your Lordship with my thanks, in this manner; but my heart whispered me to do it.—From the emotions of my inmost Soul I do it.

Selfish ingratitude, I hope I am incapable of; and mercenary servility, I trust I shall ever have so much honest pride as to detest.—

I have the honor to be,
with the most grateful sincerity
My Lord
your much indebted & very humble servant

JAMES CANDLISH

Born McCandlish in 1759, he was a boyhood neighbour and schoolmate of Burns. He studied medicine at Glasgow University and in 1794 married one of the 'Mauchline Belles', Jean Smith, sister of James Smith (see page 119). He settled in Edinburgh about 1788 where he lectured in medicine at the University. In a letter to Peter Hill (X) dated March 1791 Burns mentions Candlish as 'the earliest friend except my only brother that I have on earth, and one of the worthiest fellows that ever any man called by the name of Friend.'

I (89)

Edinburgh, 21st March 1787

My ever dear old acquaintance,

I was equally surprised and pleased at your letter, tho' I dare say you will think by my delaying so long to write you, that I am so drowned in the intoxication of good fortune as to be indifferent to old and once dear connections.—The truth is, I was determined to write a good letter, full of argument, amplification, erudition and, as Bayes says,[1] *all that.*—I thought of it, and thought of it, but for my soul I cannot; and lest you should mistake the cause of my silence, I just sit down to tell you so.—Don't give yourself credit though, that the strength of your logic scares me: the truth is, I never mean to meet you on that ground at all.—You have shown me one thing, which was to be demonstrated, that strong pride of reasoning, with a little affectation of singularity, may mislead the best of hearts.—I likewise, since you and I were first acquainted, in the pride of despising old women's stories, ventured in "the daring path Spinosa trod;"[2] but experience of the weakness, not the strength, of human powers made me glad to grasp at revealed Religion.

I must stop, but don't impute my brevity to a wrong cause.—I am still, in the apostle Paul's phrase, "The old man with his deeds"[3] as when we were sporting about the Lady thorn.—I shall be four weeks here yet, at least; and so I shall expect to hear from you—welcome sense, welcome Nonsense.—

I am with the warmest sincerity,
My Dear old Friend, yours
Robt Burns

1 A catch-phrase of Bayes, a character in *The Rehearsal* by George Villiers, 2nd Duke of Buckingham (1671).
2 John Brown, *Essay on Satire* (1748)
3 Colossians 3:9

II (153A)

[Edinburgh, late November 1787]

My dear friend,

If once I were gone from this scene of hurry and dissipation, I promise myself the pleasure of that correspondence being renewed which has been so long broken. At present I have time for nothing.—Dissipation and business engross every moment.—I am engaged in assisting an honest Scots Enthusiast, a friend of mine, who is an Engraver, and has taken it into his head to published a collection of all our songs set to music, of which the words and music are done by Scotsmen.—This, you will easily guess, is an undertaking exactly to

James Candlish

my taste.—I have collected, begg'd, borrow'd and stolen all the songs I could meet with.—Pompey's Ghost, words and music, I beg from you immediately, to go into his second number: the first is already published.—I shall show you the first Number when I see you in Glasgow, which will be in a fortnight or less.—Do be so kind as send me the song in a day or two; you cannot imagine how much it will oblidge me.—

I am ever, My Dear Sir, Yours
Robt Burns

Direct to me at Mr. William Cruikshank's, St. James's square, Newtown, Edinburgh

ROBERT CLEGHORN

Born at Corstorphine, then on the outskirts of Edinburgh, his date of birth is unknown as he belonged to an Episcopalian family which did not register his birth in the parish register of the Established Church. He farmed at Saughton Mills and married a widow named Allen whose son John later showed Burns's letters to his step-father to Lord Byron, apparently upsetting the puritanical streak in that strange personality! Burns was a frequent visitor at Saughton Mills during his Edinburgh sojourns and joined Cleghorn in the Crochallan Fencibles. It was through Cleghorn that Burns conveyed a great deal of bawdy verse, some traditional, some original, which later provided the basis for *The Merry Muses of Caledonia* (published 1799). Cleghorn had a good voice and an ear for music and apart from that 'violent propensity to Bawdy' shared Burns's interests in collecting old Scots ballads.

I (91)

[Enclosing *Bonie Dundee*]

[C.W. p. 280]

[Edinburgh, 1787?]

Dr. Cleghorn,

You will see by the above that I have added a Stanza to bony Dundee.—If you think it will do, you may set it a going

"Upon a ten-string Instrument
"And on the Psaltery"—*

R.B.

To Mr. Cleghorn, farmer. God bless the trade.

* Metrical Psalms 92:3, misquoted.

II (230)

Mauchline, 31st March 1788

Yesterday, my dear Sir, as I was riding thro' a parcel of melancholy, joyless muirs, between Galloway and Ayrshire; it being Sunday, I turned my thoughts to "Psalms, and hymns and spiritual Songs;" and your favourite air, Captain Okean, coming in my head, I tryed these words to it.—You will see that the first part of the tune must be repeated—

Song—tune—Captain Okean—
The small birds rejoice in the green leaves returning,

[C.W. p. 322 (1 stanza only).]

I am tolerably pleased with these verses, but as I have only a sketch of a tune, I leave it with you to try if they suit the measure of the music.—

I am so harrassed with Care and Anxiety about this farming project of mine, that my Muse has degenerated into the veriest prose-wench that ever picked cinders, or followed a Tinker.—When I am fairly got into the routine of business, I shall trouble you with a longer epistle; perhaps with some queries respecting farming: at present, the world sits such a load on my mind that it has effaced almost every trace of the image of God in me.—

My very best Compliments and good wishes to Mrs. Cleghorn.—

I am ever, My dear Sir,
your oblidged humble servant
Robt Burns

Robert Cleghorn

III (302)

Ellisland near Dumfries, 23rd January 1789

I must take shame and confusion of face to myself, my dear friend and brother farmer, that I have not written you much sooner.—The truth is, I have been so tossed about between Ayrshire and Nithsdale that, till now I have got my family here, I have had time to think of nothing—except now and then a distich or Stanza as I rode along.—Were it not for our gracious monarch's cursed tax of postage, I had sent you one or two Pieces of some length that I have lately done.—I have no idea of the Press.—I am now able to support myself & family, though in a humble, yet an independant way; and I mean, just at my leisure, to pay my court to the tuneful Sisters, in hopes that they may one day enable me to carry on a Work of some importance. The following are a few verses I wrote in a neighbouring Gentleman's Hermitage, to which he is so good as let me have a key.—

Written in Friars' Carse Hermitage

[C.W. p. 324]

I shall be in Edinburgh for a few days, sometime about the latter end of February or beginning of March, when I shall shew you other Pieces.—My farming scheme too, particularly one, the management of one inclosure of Holming land, is to be decided by your superior judgement.—I find, if my farm does well with me, I shall certainly be an Enthusiast in the business.—

[*Remainder missing*]

IV (407)

Ellisland, 23rd July 1790

Do not ask me, my dear Sir, why I have neglected so long to write you.—Accuse me of indolence, my line of life of hurry, my stars of perverseness—in short, accuse anything, but me of forgetfulness.— You knew Matthew Henderson. At the time of his death I composed an elegiac Stanza or two, as he was a man I much regarded; but something came in my way so that the design of an Elegy to his memory gave up.—Meeting with the fragment the other day among some old waste papers, I tried to finish the Piece, & have this moment put the last hand to it.—This I am going to write you is the first fair Copy of it.—

Elegy on Captain Matthew Henderson—
O Death, thou tyrant fell & bloody!

[C.W. p. 337]

Let me know how you like the foregoing.—
My best Compliments to Mrs. Cleghorn & family.—

I am ever most truly, My dear Sir, Yours
Robt Burns

V (416)

Ellisland, 29th August 1790

My Dear Sir,

Give me leave to introduce the Bearer, Mr. Tennant, to your acquaintance.—He is not only one of the most respectable farmers, but also one of the most respectable men, both as to his character & connections, in Ayr-shire.—He is on a tour of pleasure thro' the East part of Scotland, or rather on a tour of information; for he is a keen Farmer, & as such, I have taken the liberty to put him under your instruction for an afternoon when he comes to your Country.—

I am in a hurry, a damn'd hurry; so take this scrawl.—Why don't you return me my Collection of [*word missing*] Songs? The inclosed is quite new.—

My Compliments to Mrs. Cleghorn, the Miss Cleghorns, & Miss Cleghorn of Saughton Mills.—I should like much to see the little Angel.—

Adieu!
Robt Burns

VI (473)

[Ellisland, October? 1791]

My dear Friend,

I inclose you a proof-sheet, one out of a dozen I got from the Publisher, to give among my friends.—It is a Poem of mine which perhaps you have seen from our friends Dunbar or Cunningham, who got M.S.S. copies of it.—

I have not time to write you at large, but wish much to hear from you, & to know whether I could venture to write you by post without any risk of the letter being read by any body but yourself.— In so many words, I may perhaps have occasion to tell you somewhat & ask a little advice too, which I would not wish even Mrs. Cleghorn to see, & I believe the Good Women in general take a freedom to break up or peep into their husband's letters.—

This is indeed all a perhaps; but let me hear from you.—

I am giving up my farm: it is a bad bargain; & as my Landlord is offering the lands to sale, I took the hint, & have got some little consideration for my lease.—The Excise, after all has been said against it, is the business for me.—I find no difficulty in being an honest man in it; the work of itself, is easy; & it is a devilish different affair, managing money matters where I care not a damn whether the money is paid or not; from the long faces made to a haughty Laird or still more haughty Factor, when rents are demanded, & money, Alas! not to be had!—Besides, I am now ranked on the Supervisor list, which will in a little time, place me in a respectable situation, even as an Excise-Man.—

My best Compliments to Mrs. Cleghorn & your little ones; & believe me to be ever, most sincerely, My dear Sir,

Your oblidged Friend & humble servant
Robt Burns

VII (488)

My best Compliments to Mrs. Cleghorn and all your friends of my acquaintance.—Many happy returns of the season to you, my worthy Sir, and (pardon me) your fully as worthy Bedfellow.—The foregoing poem is for her: for you, I make you a present of the following new Edition of an old Cloaciniad song, a species of composition which I have heard you admire, and a kind of song which I know you wanted much.—It is sung to an old tune, something like Take your auld cloak about you—

There was twa wives, and twa witty wives,

[C.W. p. 435]

God speed the plough, & send a good seed time! Amen!

Farewell!
Robt Burns

VIII (527)

[Enclosing *Why Should na Poor Folk Mowe.*]

[C.W. p. 476]

Sanquhar, 12th December 1792

My dear Cleghorn,

By our friend Crosbie I send you a song, just finished this moment.—May the ——— follow with a blessing!

Amen!

Robt Burns

IX (592)

25th October [1793?]

I have just bought a quire of Post, & I am determined, my Dear Cleghorn, to give you the maidenhead of it.—Indeed, that is all my reason for, & all that I can propose to give you by, this present scrawl.—From my late hours last night, & the dripping fogs & damn'd east-wind of this stupid day, I have left me as little soul as an oyster.—"Sir John, you are so fretful, you cannot live long."—"Why, there is it! Come, sing me a BAUDY-SONG to make me merry!!!"[1]

ACT SEDERUNT OF THE SESSION—A Scots Ballad—
Tune, O'er the muir amang the heather—
In Edinburgh town they've made a law,

[C.W. p. 506]

Well! the Law is good for something, since we can make a Bawdy-song out of it.—(N.B. I never made anything of it any other way—) There is, there must be, some truth in original sin.—My violent propensity to Bawdy convinces me of it.—Lack a day if that species of Composition be the Sin against "the Haly Ghaist," "I am the most offending soul alive."[2]—Mair for taiken, A fine chiel, a hand-wail'd friend & crony o' my ain, gat o'er the lugs in loove wi' a braw, bonie, fodgel hizzie frae the English-side, weel-ken'd i' the brugh of

277

Annan by the name o' Bonie Mary; & I tauld the tale as follows.—
N.B. The chorus is auld—

    Chorus—Tune, *Minnie's aye glowrin o'er me*—
  Come cowe me, minnie, come cowe me;

           [C.W. p. 506]

Forgive this *wicked* scrawl.—Thine, in all the sincerity of a brace of
honest Port.—

                      R.B.

1 Shakespeare: *I Henry IV*, Act, III, sc. 3.
2 Shakespeare: *Henry V*, Act IV, sc. 3.

X (680)

               [Dumfries, 21st August 1795]

My dear Cleghorn,

Inclosed you have Clarke's Gaffer Gray.—I have not time [to make
a] copy of it, so, when you have taken a copy for yourself, please
return me the Original.—I need not caution you against giving copies
to any other person.—"Peggy Ramsay," * I shall expect to find in
Gaffer Gray's company, when he returns to Dumfries.—

I intended to have taken the advantage of the Frank, & given you a
long letter; but cross accident has detained me untill the Post is just
going.—Pray, has Mr. Wight got the better of his fright, & how is Mr.
Allan? I hope you got all safe home.—Dr. Maxwell & honest John
Syme beg leave to be remembered to you all.—They both speak in
high terms of the acquisition they have made to their acquaintance.
—Did Thomson meet you on Sunday? If so, you would have a world
of conversation. Mrs. Burns joins in thanks for your obliging, *very
obliging* visit.—

                  Yours ever
                  R Burns
P.S.
Did you ever meet with the following, Todlin hame—By the late Mr.
McCulloch, of Ardwell—Galloway—

When wise Solomon was a young man o' might,
He was canty, & liked a lass ilka night;
But when he grew auld that he was na in trim,
He cried out, "In faith, Sirs! I doubt it's a sin!"
Todlen hame, todlen hame,
Sae round as a neep we gang todlen hame.—

But we're no come to that time o' life yet, ye ken;
The bottle's half-out—but we'll fill it again:
As for Solomon's doubts, wha the deevil cares for't!
He's a damn'd churlish fallow that likes to spill sport.—
Todlen &c.

A bicker that's gizzen'd, it's nae worth a doit;
Keep it wat, it will haud in—it winna let out:
A chiel that's ay sober, is damn'd ill to ken;
Keep him wat wi' gude drink—& ye'll find him out then.—
  Todlen &c.

May our house be weel theekit, our pantry ay fu',
Wi' rowth in our cellar for weetin our mou';
Wi' a tight, caller hizzie, as keen as oursels,
Ay ready to souple *the whistle & bells*!!
    Todlen hame &c.

---

* An ancient bawdy ballad, mentioned by Shakespeare in *Twelfth Night*, Act II, sc. 3.

XI (687)

[Enclosing *O, That's the Lassie o' my Heart*]

[C.W. p. 559]

[Dumfries, January 1796]

My ever dear Cleghorn,

The foregoing had been sent you long ago but for reasons which you may have heard.—Since I saw you, I have indeed been much the child of disaster.—Scarcely began to recover the loss of an only daughter & darling child, I became my self the victim of a rheumatic fever, which brought me to the borders of the grave.—After many weeks of a sick-bed, I am just beginning to crawl about.—

Thanks, many thanks, for my Gawin Douglas.—This will probably be delivered to you by a friend of mine, Mr. Mundell, surgeon whom you may remember to have seen at my house.—He wants to enquire after Mr. Allan.—Best Compliments to the amiablest of my friends, Mrs. Cleghorn, to little Miss, though she will scarcely remember me, & to my thunder-scared friend, Mr. Wight.—

Yours
R. Burns

LADY HENRIETTA DON

Born in 1752, she was the elder daughter of the thirteenth Earl of Glencairn and sister of Burns's patron, Earl James. In 1778 she married Sir Alexander Don, Bart. of Newton-Don in Berwickshire. Her daughters, Elizabeth and Mary, were accidentally drowned in 1793; Burns referred to one of them as 'Lady Harriet's little angel whose epithalamium I am pledged to write'. Her only son (born 1779), succeeded to the baronetcy in 1815, Lady Don herself having died in 1801. The 'parcel of epistolary performances' referred to in the first letter below now constitutes the Don MS in Edinburgh University Library.

I (93)

Edinburgh, 26th March 1787

Madam,

I have here sent you a parcel of my epistolary performances; happy at having it, in the smallest degree, in my power to show that gratitude, which, "while life's warm spirit beats within my breast" shall ever glow to the family of Glencairn.—I might have altered or omitted somethings in these letters; perhaps I ought to have done so; but I wished to show you the Bard and his style in their native colors.—

I have the honor to be
with the most heart-warm, grateful sincerity,
Madam, your much indebted & very humble servant
Robt Burns

II (479)

Ellisland near Dumfries, 23rd October 1791

My Lady

The inclosed is a tribute to the memory of a MAN, the memory of whom shall mix with my latest recollection.—As all the world knows my obligations to the late noble Earl of Glencairn, I wish to make my gratitude equally conspicuous, by publishing this Poem.—But in what way shall I publish it?—It is too small a piece to publish —The way which suggests itself to me is, to send it to the Publisher of one of the most reputable periodical works; The Bee, for instance. —Lady Betty has referred me to you.—The Post is just going, else I would have taken the opportunity of the frank, & sent your Ladyship some of my late pieces.—

I have the honor to be, My Lady
Your Ladyship's grateful humble servant
Robt Burns

Lament for James, Earl of Glencairn
The wind blew hollow frae the hills
[C.W. p. 423]

To Lady Hariot Don, this Poem, not the fictitious creation of poetic fancy, but the breathings of real woe from a bleeding heart, is respectfully & gratefully presented by

THE AUTHOR

MISS FARQUHAR

Possibly the daughter of James Farquhar, one of the subscribers to the first edition of the Edinburgh Poems, with whom Burns dined at Newhaven in August 1787. In a letter (IV) to the Rev. Archibald Lawrie (see page 128) Burns mentions this occasion and adds: 'They are all well and Madamoiselle is particularly well. - She begs her respects to you all...' From this it has been deduced that Lawrie had a particular interest in Miss Farquhar, although he subsequently married Anne McKittrick Adair in 1794. Miss Farquhar was the recipient of a copy of the first Edinburgh Edition, which Burns inscribed for her about 20th April 1787, as follows:

(96A)

To Miss Farquhar as a mark of the most respectful PERSONAL esteem, and sincere gratitude for many kindnesses he owes to her nearest Relations and dearest Friends, from,

THE AUTHOR

WILLIAM DUNBAR

Born in Nairnshire, the third son of Alexander Dunbar of Boath who claimed kinship with the tenth Earl of Buchan through his wife, Lady Agnes Randolph. He became a Writer to the Signet in 1769 and in the years before his death in 1807 was also Inspector General of Stamp Duties in Scotland. A convivial bachelor, he was Depute Master of the Canongate Kilwinning Lodge and 'colonel' of the Crochallan Fencibles. As such, he was the 'Rattlin, roarin Willie' of Burns's poem (C.W. p. 320). At least seven letters passed between Burns and Dunbar from 1787 to 1791, and one may deduce from this correspondence that Dunbar wrote less often than Burns would have wished. Of particular interest is the letter (VI) written between 14th January and 2nd February 1790 giving details of Burns's arduous workload as farmer, exciseman and poet.

I (99)

Lawnmarket, Monday morn.
[30th April 1787]

Dear Sir,

In justice to Spencer I must acknowledge that there is scarcely a Poet in the language could have been a more agreable present to me, and in justice to you, allow me to say, Sir, that I have not met with a man in Edinburgh to whom I would so willingly have been indebted for the gift.—The tatter'd Rhymes I herewith present you, and the handsome volumes of Spencer for which I am indebted to your goodness, may perhaps seem as out of proportion to one another as to their late owners but be that as it may, my gift, though far less valuable, is as sincere a mark of esteem as yours.—

The time is approaching when I shall return to my shades; and I am afraid my numerous Edinburgh friendships are of so tender a construction that they will not bear carriage with me.—Yours is one of the few that I could wish of a more robust constitution. It is indeed very probable that when I leave this City, we part never more to meet in this sublunary Sphere; but I have a strong fancy that in some future excentric Planet, the Comet of a happier System than any with which Astronomy is yet acquainted, you and I, among the harum-scarum Sons of Imagination and Whim, with a hearty shake of a hand, a Metaphor and a Laugh, shall recognise OLD ACQUAINTANCE—

Where Wit may sparkle all its rays,
Uncurst with Caution's fears;
And Pleasure, basking in the blaze,
Rejoice for endless years!

I have the honor to be, with the warmest Sincerity,
Dear Sir, your oblidged & very humble servant
Robert Burns

II (199A)

Weden: morn:
[13th February 1788]

I have put off my thanks for your book and kind letter, my dear Sir, thinking I would find time to express what I felt on the occasion; but I am so hurried, on the wing for Ayrshire, that I can only say with Don John in Shakespeare, "I thank you; I am not a man of many words, but I thank you."—*

William Dunbar

Your correspondence I have often wished to ask: I will do myself the honor to say that I think there is something strongly congenial in our minds.—

My direction is, at Mauchline.—I'll write you from Glasgow or Mauchline.—

I am most sincerely and gratefully yours—

Robt Burns

* *Much Ado About Nothing*, Act I, sc. 1.

III (236)

Mauchline, 7th April 1788

I have not delayed so long to write you, my much respected Friend, because I thought no farther of my promise.—I have long since given up that kind of formal correspondence, where one sits down irksomely to write a letter, because we think we are in duty bound so to do.—

I have been roving over the Country, as my farm I have taken is forty miles from this place, hiring servants and preparing matters: but most of all, I am earnestly busy to bring about a revolution in my own mind.—As, till within these eighteen months, I never was the wealthy master of ten guineas, my knowledge of business is to learn add to this, my late scenes of idlesness and dissipation have enervated my mind to an alarming degree.—Skill in the sober Science of Life is my most serious and hourly study.—I have dropt all conversation and all reading (prose reading) but what tends in some way or other to my serious aim. Except one worthy young fellow, I have not one single Correspondent in Edinburgh.—You have indeed kindly made me an offer of that kind, an offer which gives me the highest pleasure.—The world of Wits, and Gens comme il faut which I lately left, and with whom I never again will intimately mix, from that Port, Sir, I expect your Gazette: what les beaux Esprits are saying, what they are doing, and what they are singing.—Any sober intelligence from my sequestered walks of life; any droll Original; any passing remark, important forsooth because it is mine; any little Poetic effort, however embryotic; these, my dear Sir, are all you have to expect from me. When I talk of Poetic efforts, I must have it always understood, that I appeal from your wit and taste to your friendship and good nature.—The first would be my favorite tribunal where I defied Censure; but the last, where I declined Justice.—

I have scarcely made a single Distic since I saw you.—When I meet with an old Scots Air that has any facetious idea in its Name, I have a peculiar pleasure in following out that idea for a verse or two.—

I trust that this will find you in better health than I did, last time I called for you.—A few lines from you, directed to me, at Mauchline, were it but to let me know how you are, will set my mind a good deal.—Now, never shun the idea of writing me because perhaps you may be out of humour or spirits; I could give you a hundred good consequences attending a dull letter; one for example, and the remaining ninety nine some other time; it will always serve to keep in countenance, my much respected Sir, your oblidged friend, and humble servant

Robt Burns

William Dunbar

IV (274)

Ellisland near Dumfries, September 25th 1788

My ever dear Friend,

You, yourself, are to blame for my long, ungrateful silence.—You wrote me such an excellent letter, at once so marked with Friendship & Genius, that I resolved not to answer it, in the usual way, "at my first leisure hour," but to watch some favored moment of inspiration & call up my little scattered Powers, to give you as well as I could, an adequate return.—I waited a moment that never came; so in my plain, dull ordinary way, accept of my thanks for your letter; your Cowper's Poems, the best Poet out of sight since Thomson; & accept of my best wishes for your welfare, & the welfare of Mrs. Fordyce & your two little Neices.—I was going to call them, two little Angels; but when I consider, though their looks have all that celestial Sweetness, guileless Sprightliness & ingenuous Modesty that one would expect in a young Inhabitant of Heaven, a Seraph newly entered on existence, nay, their air, their manner, their figure (for whatever Milton had, I have no idea of a Cherub six feet high) are quite Angelic; yet there is a Something, and not a little Something neither, about their eyes, as well as in the *enchanting* shape & colors of the organs themselves, as in their *fascinating* way of using them—in short, for I hate to dwell on so disagreeable a subject as accusing a fellow-creature, I am positively of opinion that there is more bewitching destructive mischief in one of their GLANCES, than in the worst half of "Satan's invisible world discovered."[1] now witchcraft can never make a part in the character, at least of a GOOD Angel.—I am sorry for the young ladies' sakes that I am forced to bear this witness against them; but however I may deal in fiction, under my Poetic Licence, I sacredly stick to truth in Prose.—To say no more on this unlucky business I give the young Ladies notice, that, married man as I am, & consequently out of the field of Danger, still I have so much regard for the welfare of the world I lately left, that I have half a thought of advertising them in RHYME, to put mankind on their guard against such a dangerous & still *growing* Mischief.—

I inclose you a Poem I have just finished.— It is my first Essay in that kind of Poetry, & I ask your Criticisms on it, both how far you think that such a species of poetic composition seems to suit my Muse, & what faults you find, or emmendations you would propose, in it.—I am determined, from this time forth, whatever I may write, to do it leisurely & to the utmost of my power, correctly.—I must caution you, should you think the Poem[2] worth mentioning to mention it but sparingly; & the gentleman's name to whom it is addressed, not at all.—My connection with him is at present very delicate, & highly important to myself.

I am ever most truely, My dear Sir, yours—
Robt Burns

1 A popular treatise on witchcraft, by George Sinclair (1685).
2 Probably *To Robert Graham, Esq., of Fintry*, C.W. p. 431.

William Dunbar

V (309)

[With both versions of *verses in Friars' Carse Hermitage*.]
[C.W. pp. 324-5.]

[Early February 1789]

In vain do we talk of reason, my dear Sir; we are the offspring of
Caprice, and the nurslings of Habitude.--The most pleasurable part
of our existence, the strings that tie heart to heart, are the
manufacture of some hitherto undescribed and unknown Power
within us.--The circle of our acquaintance, like a wide horizon, is
too large for us to make any thing of it.- We are amused for a little
with the ill-defined, distant objects; but our tired eye soon fixes with
delighted discrimination on the towering cliffs, or the winding river,
a hoary ruin, or a woody vale, just as that namelcss Something
within us directs.—

I returned from my late hare-brained ramble into life, with two or
three attachments of that kind in my bosom; but from my
uncouthness when out of my native sphere, and my obscurity in that
sphere, I am oblidged to give most of them up in despair of a mutual
return.—I often say to myself why may not a son of Poverty with an
intelligent mind and an independant spirit, make an agreable
Intimate or an entertaining Correspondent? What are all, even the
most exalted advantages to which we can be born, compared with
good Sense, native taste and amiable dispositions; and what are the
richest attainments of Fortune, to Intelligence and Worth?—

You made me happy once in the idea that I should enjoy your
correspondence in my rustic obscurity, but must I think of you what
I never thought of you before, that you are one of the herd of
mankind?—I had set so much store by your friendship, that I shall
not very easily part with the hope I had fondly induldged of its
being one of the permanent enjoyments of my life.—In my
Professional line, too, I want you much.--Before an Author gets his
Piece finished, he has viewed and reviewed it so often—he has
brought it so near the mental eye, that it is within the sphere of
vision, and he is no longer a judge of its merits.—A judicious candid
friend is then all he has to trust to; and I had set you down as that
friend for me.—

The foregoing Poems are of my late productions, and if they will
bear your criticism, I should be glad that you would honor them
with your strictures.—I shall be in Edinburgh for two or three days,
very soon, and I hope then to have the pleasure of assuring you in
person, how sincerely I am,

Dear Sir, your most obedient humble servant
Robt Burns

VI (382)

Ellisland 14th January 1790

Since we are here creatures of a day, since a "few summer days, and
a few winter nights, and the life of man is at an end," why, my dear
much-esteemed Sir, should You and I let negligent indolence, for I

285

know it is nothing worse, step in between us, and bar the enjoyment of a mutual correspondence?–We are not shapen out of the common, heavy, methodical Clod, the elemental Stuff of the plodding, selfish Race, the Sons of Arithmetick and Prudence; our feelings & hearts are not benumbed & poisoned by the cursed influence of riches, which, whatever blessing they may be in other respects, are no friends to the nobler qualities of the heart; in the name of random Sensibility then, let never the moon change on our silence any more.–I have had a tract of bad health most part of this winter, else you had heard from me long ere now.–Thank Heaven, I am now got so much better as to be able to partake a little in the enjoyments of life.–

Our friend, Cunningham, will perhaps have told you of my going into the excise.–The truth is, I found it a very convenient business to have 50£ Per Ann., nor have I yet felt any of these mortifying circumstances in it that I was led to fear.–

February 2nd
I have not for sheer hurry of business been able to spare five minutes to finish my letter.–Besides my farm business, I ride on my Excise matters at least 200 miles every week.–I have not by any means given up the Muses.–You will see in the 3rd Vol. of Johnson's Scots Songs that I have contributed my mite there.–

But, my dear Sir, little ones that look up to you for parental Protection, are an important charge · I have already two fine healthy stout little fellows, & I wish to throw some light upon them.–I have a thousand reveries & schemes about them, & their future destiny.–Not that I am a Utopian Projector in these things.–I am resolved never to breed up a Son of mine to any of the learned Professions.–I know the value of independance; and since I cannot give my Sons an independant fortune I shall give them an independant line of life.–What a chaos of hurry, chance & change is this world, when one sits soberly down to reflect on it!–To a Father who himself knows the world, the thought that he shall have Sons to usher into it, must fill him with dread; but if he have Daughters, the prospect in a thoughtful moment is apt to shock him.–

I hope Mrs. Fordyce & the two young ladies are well.–Do, let me forget that they are nieces of yours, & let me say that I never saw a more interesting, sweeter pair of Sisters in my life.–I am the fool of my feelings & attachments.–I often take up a Volume of my Spenser to realize you to my imagination, and think over the social scenes we have had together.–God grant that there may be another world more congenial to honest fellows, beyond this.–A world where these rubs & plagues of absence, distance, misfortunes, ill health, &c. shall no more damp hilarity and divide friendship.–

This I know is your throng season, but half a page will much oblige, my dear Sir,

yours sincerely,
Robt Burns

William Dunbar

VII (431)

Ellisland, 17th January 1791

I am not gone to Elysium, most noble Colonel, but am still here in this sublunary world, serving my God by propagating his image, and honoring my king by begetting him loyal subjects.

Many happy returns of the season await my friend. May the thorns of care never beset his path! May peace be an inmate of his bosom, and rapture a frequent visitor of his soul! May the blood-hounds of misfortune never track his steps, nor the screech-owl of sorrow alarm his dwelling! May enjoyment tell thy hours, and pleasure number thy days, thou friend of the Bard! "Blessed be he that blesseth thee, and cursed be he that curseth thee!!!"*

As a farther proof that I am still in the land of existence, I send you a poem, the latest I have composed. I have a particular reason for wishing you only to show it to select friends, should you think it worthy a friend's perusal: but if at your first leisure hour you will favour me with your opinion of, and strictures on the performance, it will be an additonal obligation on,

Dear Sir,

Your deeply indebted humble servant,

R.B.

1 Numbers 24:9, misquoted.

REV. DR. HUGH BLAIR

Born in 1718, the only son of John Blair, a businessman who lost his fortune in the ill-fated Darien Scheme, Hugh was educated at the High School and University of Edinburgh, from which he graduated MA in 1739. He was licensed to preach in 1741 and subsequently became tutor in the family of Simon, son of Lord Lovat. The patronage of the Earl of Leven secured for him the parish of Collessie in Fife, whence he went as junior minister to the Canongate Church, Edinburgh. In 1754 he was called to Lady Yester's and in 1760 obtained the High Kirk, St Giles. From 1762 onwards he also held the chair of Rhetoric at Edinburgh University and earned wide renown for his lectures on taste. He played a prominent role in the Age of Enlightment among those who constantly tried to 'un-Scotch' themselves. His sermons were extremely popular, and reveal a degree of liberal humanism conspicuously absent in the writings of his narrower contemporaries.

When Burns first came to Edinburgh, Dr. Blair was at the pinnacle of his career and more than forty years the poet's senior. Yet, despite the wide gulf in age, temperament and social position. Blair became one of Burns's warmest supporters. Like other members of the Edinburgh *literati*, Blair's well-intentioned advice sometimes had unfortunate results. It was at least partly due to him that Burns omitted *The Jolly Beggars* from the Edinburgh Edition, as well as a poem entitled *The Prophet and God's Complaint*, now lost. Blair outlived the poet by four years and advised Dr Currie not to publish too much about Burns's character and to make the selection of his poems 'with much delicacy and caution'. Burns has left a shrewd portrait of Dr. Blair in his *Second Commonplace Book:* 'his vanity is proverbially known among his acquaintances; but he is justly at the head of what may be called fine writing.'

(101)

Lawnmarket, Friday morn.
[4th May 1787]

Reverend & much respected Sir,

I leave Edinburgh tomorrow morning, but could not go without troubling you with half a line, sincerely to thank you for that kindness, that patronage, that friendship you have shown me.—

I often felt the embarrasment of my very singular situation; drawn forth from the veriest shades of life to the glare of remark; and honored by the notice of those illustrious Names of my country, whose Works, while they are applauded to the end of time, will ever instruct and mend the heart. However the meteor-like novelty of my appearance in the world might attract notice, and honor me with the acquaintance of the permanent lights of genius and literature, those who are truly Benefactors of the immortal nature of Man, I knew very well that my utmost merit was far unequal to the task of preserving that character, when once that novelty was over; and have made up my mind that abuse or almost even neglect will not surprize me in my quarters.—

I have sent you a proof impression of Beugo's work for me, done on Indian paper, as a trifling but sincere testimony with what heart-warm gratitude

I have the honor to be,
Revered Sir,
your much indebted humble servant
Robt Burns

REV. DR. HUGH BLAIR

WILLIAM CREECH

HENRY MACKENZIE

Born in 1745, the son of Joshua Mackenzie an Edinburgh physician and his wife Margaret, daughter of Hugh Rose of Kilravock, he was educated at the High School and University of Edinburgh. He read law in Edinburgh and London and began practising in 1768 in the Scottish Court of Exchequer. He was a prominent Freemason and founder-member of the Royal Society of Edinburgh in 1783 and the Highland and Agricultural Society in 1784. His paper on the German theatre to the Royal Society in 1788 triggered off an interest in drama which later had a profound influence on Sir Walter Scott. He became Comptroller of Taxes for Scotland in 1799 and held that office until his death in 1831. For half a century he was a pillar of the Scottish Establishment and was on intimate terms with all the important personalities of the kingdom from David Hume to Sir Walter Scott. In 1776 he married Penuel, daughter of Sir Ludovic Grant of Grant, by whom he had fourteen children. It was through Mackenzie that Burns secured introductions to Sir James Grant of Castle Grant and Mrs Rose of Kilravock, during the Highland tour of 1787.

Mackenzie had a long and illustrious literary career, beginning in 1771 when his great novel *The Man of Feeling* was published anonymously. This was followed in 1773 by *The Man of the World* under his own name, and *Julia de Roubigne* in 1777. Several of his plays were staged in Edinburgh and London. He was successively editor of *The Mirror* and then *The Lounger*. In the issue of the latter dated 9th December 1786 he wrote the laudatory piece on the Kilmarnock Poems which materially assisted Burns in gaining entree to Edinburgh's literary circles. It was Mackenzie who coined the phrase 'this Heaven-taught ploughman' which Burns played up for all it was worth, although he was not a ploughman and was considerably more 'lettered' than the patronising Mackenzie. For his part, Burns had an exaggerated admiration of Mackenzie whose *Man of Feeling* he confessed to John Murdoch was 'a book I prize next to the Bible'. Mackenzie advised Burns regarding the disposal of his copyright to Creech, and it was in Mackenzie's house, on 17th April 1787, that the deal was worked out. For this, Mackenzie has often been accused of selling Burns short, but the 100 guineas paid to the poet was a handsome sum by the standards of the time, and perfectly reasonable given the comparatively limited nature of Burns's fame. A more disinterested party, however, might have safeguarded the copyright. 'Mr. Harley', referred to in Burns's letter of thanks, was the hero of *The Man of Feeling*. Mackenzie later endorsed this letter 'Remarkable Anecdote to shew the good Effects of *Moral Reading*.

(101A)

Revered Sir,   Lawn Market Friday morn: [4th May 1787]

I leave Edinburgh tomorrow morning, and send you this to assure you that no little petulant self-conceit, no distance or absence shall ever make me forget how much I owe YOU.—

Allow me, Sir, to thank you most sincerely on another account; whatever is good about my heart is much indebted to Mr. Harley.— It is said often that the world reads and is never mended: I shall tell you a real matter of fact which happened in my own observation, and I tell it you because you are a little interested in it.—A dear friend of mine, and the truly cleverest fellow I ever saw, was very fond of a girl in the neighbourhood who doated on him distractedly. —He was bred to the sea, a lad of much better than ordinary education, and glowed with unbounded ambition; she too was very pretty, and knew a little more of the politesse of life than most of her compeers.—He was going abroad not to return for some time, and stung with passion, knowing she had many admirers, he formed a common but very wicked resolution respecting her, and hinted to me his plan.— I had just then got the Man of the World and lent it him, not indeed with a moral design but as something that pleased me.—This was two evenings before the fatal interview was to have happened; and calling on him, as usual, next evening to ask his opinion of the book, I shall never forget the horror with which he mentioned his tomorrow night's enterprise; and this moment she makes him one of the best of wives.

289

Henry Mackenzie

I give you this seemingly romantic but real story, because as an Author and as a Man it must highly gratify your feelings.—

I have sent you by the bearer of this a trifling but a very sincere testimony of that gratitude with which I have the honor to be,

Sir, your much indebted humble servant
Robt Burns

WILLIAM TYTLER OF WOODHOUSELEE

Born in 1711, the son of a Writer to the Signet in whose legal footsteps he himself followed, he is best remembered for his collaboration with James Johnson in the early volumes of the *Scots Musical Museum*, later helping Burns to collect material for subsequent volumes. A historian and antiquarian, he was a regular contributor to the *Transactions* of the Society of Antiquaries. He edited *The Poetical Remains of James I of Scotland*, but his most famous work was his spirited defence of Mary Queen of Scots (1760) against the attacks of his contemporaries Robertson and Hume which inspired Burns to write 'Revered Defender of beauteous Stuart' (C.W. p. 276). Like Burns, he had a sentimental attachment to the deposed House of Stuart and encouraged George Thomson to embark on *Select Scottish Airs*. His son Alexander, later Lord Woodhouselee, was also a fervent admirer of Burns (see page 578).

I (102)

[With the poet's portrait, and *Epistle to Mr. Tytler of Woodhouselee, Author of a Defence of Mary Queen of Scots.*

[C.W. p. 276]

Lawnmarket, Friday noon [4th May 1787]

My muse jilted me here, and turned a corner on me, and I have not got again into her good graces. I have two requests to make. Burn the above verses when you have read them, as any little sense that is in them is rather heretical, and do me the justice to believe me sincere in my grateful remembrance of the many civilities you have honoured me with since I came to Edinburgh, and in assuring you that I have the honour to be,

Revered Sir, your oblidged and very humble servant
R. Burns

II (126)

Lawnmarket, Monday noon
[August 1787]

Sir,

Inclosed I have sent you a sample of the old pieces that are still to be found among our Peasantry in the West. I once had a great many of these fragments and some of these here entire; but as I had no idea then that any body cared for them, I have forgot them.—I invariably hold it sacriledge to add any thing of my own to help out with the shatter'd wrecks of these venerable old compositions; but they have many various readings.—If you have not seen these before, I know they will flatter your true old-style Caledonian feelings; at any rate I am truly happy to have an opportunity of assuring you how sincerely I am,

Revered Sir,
your gratefully indebted, humble servant
Robert Burns

JAMES JOHNSON

Born about 1750 in the Ettrick area of Roxburghshire, he served his apprenticeship as an engraver under James Reed before setting up in Bell's Wynd, Edinburgh as an engraver and music-seller. He devised a process for reproducing sheet-music by means of pewter plates, but earned little from his invention. Some time before Burns first came to Edinburgh Johnson had the notion of collecting the words and music of all the old Scots ballads. When he first met Burns the first volume of the *Scots Musical Museum*, containing 100 airs, was already in the press. Burns needed little encouragement to become involved in this project and soon became even more enthusiastic than Johnson himself. From 1787 until his death, Burns was to all intents and purposes the editor of the *Museum*, contributing at least 177 songs of his own, and mending and restoring many others which had been reduced to mere fragments. Three further volumes, each containing 100 airs, were published in Burns's life time and a fifth was in production at the time of his death. It is significant that, without Burns's aid, it took Johnson till 1803 to publish the sixth volume. Johnson's lack of formal education is evident in his letters, atrociously spelled even by the low standards of the period. Unlike Thomson, however, Johnson knew his limitations and always deferred to Burns in matters of taste and knowledge. Never far from penury himself, Johnson nevertheless managed to contribute £4 to the fund raised on behalf of Burns's widow and family. When he died in poverty in 1811 his widow was less fortunate than Jean Armour and died destitute in a workhouse in 1819. Johnson's work was neglected and under-rated by his contemporaries, but posterity recognises that the *Scots Musical Museum* was, and still is, the most important repository of Scottish song ever compiled. The 21 extant letters from Burns to Johnson, penned between May 1787 and June 1796, reveal something of Burns's working methods, as well as the harmony that existed between him and his publisher, without that element of exasperation which we may detect in the correspondence with Thomson.

I (104)

Lawnmarket, Friday noon
[4th May 1787]

Dear Sir,

I have sent you a Song never before known, for your collection; the air by McGibbon, but I know not the Author of the words, as I got it from Dr. Blacklock. Farewell, my dear Sir! I wished to have seen you, but I have been dreadfully throng as I march tomorrow.—Had my acquaintance with you been a little older, I would have asked the favor of your correspondence; as I have met with few people whose company & conversation gave me so much pleasure, because I have met with few whose sentiments are so congenial to my own.—When Dunbar & you meet, tell him that I left Edinburgh with the idea of him hanging somewhere about my heart.—

Keep the original of this Song till we meet again, whenever that may be.—

Robt Burns

II (147A)

[October or November 1787]

. . .These lines will set [to the tune better thus] than as they are printed.—

To the song in the first Volume, "Here awa there awa," must be added this verse, the best in the song—

"Gin ye meet my love, kiss her & clap her,
"An gin ye meet my love, dinna think shame:
"Gin ye meet my love, kiss her and clap her,
"And shew her the way to had awa hame."

There is room enough on the plate for it.—

292

James Johnson

For the tune of the Scotch queen, in Oswald; take the two first, and the two last stanzas of the Poem entitled, The Lament, in Burns' Poems; which . . .
To daunton me —

> "The blude red rose at yule may blaw,
> "The simmer lilies bloom in snaw,
> "The frost may freeze the deepest sea
> "But an auld man shall never daunton me,

> Chorus —

> "To daunton me, to daunton me,
> "An auld man shall never daunton me."—

The chorus is set to the first part of the tune, which just suits it, when *once* play'd or sung over.—

III (151)

[With *My Peggy's Charms*]
[C.W. p. 297]
[Edinburgh? mid-November 1787?]

Dear Mr. Publisher,

I hope against I return, you will be able to tell me from Mr. CLARKE if these words will suit the tune.—If they don't suit, I must think on some other Air; as I have a very strong private reason for wishing them in the 2nd Volume.—Don't forget to transcribe me the list of the Antiquarian Music. Farewel!

R. Burns

IV (242)

Mauchline, 25th [May] 17 [88]

My dear Sir,

I am really uneasy about that money which Mr. Creech owes me per Note in your hand, and I want it much at present as I am engaging in business pretty deeply both for myself & my brother. A hundred guineas can be but a trifling affair to him, and 'tis a matter of most serious importance to me.—Tomorrow I begin my operations as a farmer, and God speed the Plough!—

I am so enamoured with a certain girl's prolific twin-bearing merit, that I have given her a *legal* title to the best blood in my body; and so farewell Rakery! To be serious, my worthy friend; I found I had a long and much loved fellow-creature's happiness or misery among my hands; and tho' Pride & seeming Justice were murderous King's Advocates on the one side, yet Humanity, Generosity & Forgiveness were such powerful such irresistible Counsel on the other side, that a Jury of old Endearments & new attachments brought in a unanimous verdict—*NOT GUILTY*! And the Panel, Be it known unto all whom it concerns, is installed & instated into all the Rights, Priviledges, Immunities, Franchises, Services & Paraphernalia that at present do, or in any time coming may belong to the Name, Title & Designation [*four or five words missing*]

293

Present my best Compliments [*three or four words missing*] and please let me hear from you by return of Carrier.—

I am, my dear sir, yours sincerely,
Robt Burns

V (258)

Ellisland, 28th [July? 1788]

My dear Sir,

I send you here another cargo of Songs.—I long to know whether you are begun yet, & how you come on.—Pray, did that cheese I sent to Mr. Clarke & by your care, come to hand?—

I have still a good number of Dr Blacklock's Songs among my hands, but they take sad hacking & hewing.—I sent you some weeks ago, another parcel of Songs, but I have not heard if you have recieved them.—I am in hopes that I shall pick some fine tunes from among the Collection of Highland airs which I got from you at Edinburgh—I have had an able Fiddler two days already on it, & I expect him every day for another review of it.—I have got one most beautiful air out of it, that sings to the measure of Lochaber.—I shall try to give it my very best words.

How does your Father do; & my worthy brother Bard, Mr Barclay? Give them my very best Compliments.—

I have troubled you with some letters which you will please put into the Penny-post Office.—

Have you never a fair goddess that leads you a wild-goose chace of amorous devotion? Let me know a few of her qualities, such as, whether she be rather, black, or fair; plump, or thin; short, or tall; &c. & chuse your air, & I shall task my Muse to celebrate her.—

Adieu!
Robt Burns

VI (267)

Mauchline August 1788
[*Edinburgh Bishopmark* SE 2]

My dear Sir,

I this moment have your last. The Caledonian Hunt's delight is a most glorious tune but, Alas! I am told it is Irish. I once made a verse to it a while ago.—I see, Young Philander woo'd me lang, in your list in hand.—If you have not done much, pray alter it: the tune is, The Pier of Leith, & I have two verses of the original song which are excellent.—I am on the way to my farm again where I will be busy for about a month; after that, have at you.—Putting in, "Fanny fair," to the Mill Mill O is loss of time; I doubt it is an English thing. —The post goes, & I inclose you a few more.—You are mistaken in "Killiecrankie"; it is a different air totally.—Look in Aird's Selection for the original tune . . .

* James Aird, ed., *A Selection of Scotch, English Irish and Foreign Airs.* ·6 vols. (1782-99).

James Johnson

VII (288)

[With *Whistle o'er the lave o't* and *Tam Glen.*]
[C.W. pp. 335-6]

Mauchline 15th November 1788

My dear Sir,

I have sent you two more Songs.—If you have got any tunes or any thing to correct, please send them by return of the Carrier.—his name is Connel; he puts up at Campbell's, Grass market.—Please, send the inclosed to Mr Clarke.—

I can easily see, my dear Friend, that you will very probably have four Volumes.—Perhaps you may not find your account, *lucratively*, in this business; but you are a Patriot for the Music of your Country; and I am certain, Posterity will look on themselves as highly indebted to your Publick spirit.—Be not in a hurry; let us go on correctly; and your name shall be immortal.—

My Compliments to your father & Mr Barclay.—I am preparing a flaming Preface for your third Volume.—I see every day, new Musical Publications, advertised; but what are they? Gaudy, hunted butterflies of a day, & then vanish for ever: but your Work will outlive the momentary neglects of idle Fashion, & defy the teeth of Time.—Adieu!

Robt Burns

VIII (303)

Ellisland, 23rd January [1789]

Tune Caledonian Hunt's delight—Mr Gow's

There was on a time, but old Time was then young,
[C.W. p. 349]

I shall be in Edinburgh my dear Sir, in about a month, when we shall overhaul the whole Collection and report progress.—The foregoing, I hope, will suit the excellent air it is designed for.—

Adieu, till we meet.—

Robt Burns

IX (331)

Ellisland, 24th April 1789

Dear Sir,

My trunk was unaccountably delayed in Edinburgh & did not reach me till about ten days ago, so I had not much time of your music.— I have sent you a list that I approve of, but I beg & insist that you will never allow my opinion to overrule yours.—I will write you more at large next Post, as I, at present, have scarce time to subscribe myself, Dear Sir, yours sincerely.—

Robt Burns

X (348)

Ellisland, 19th June 1789
My dear friend,

What are you doing, and what is the reason that you have sent me no
proof sheet to correct? Though I have been rather remiss in writing
you, as I have been hurried, puzzled, plagued & confounded with
some disagreable matters, yet believe me, it is not owing to the
smallest neglect or forget of you, my good Sir, or your patriotic
work.—Mr Clarke & I have frequent meetings & consultations on
your work.—I have given him three or four songs which he is
preparing for you.—One is, the Caledonian Hunt, as it seems the
verses I sent you don't suit it; another is, The Braes o' Ballochmyle,
to which I have likewise given him new words, & a third is, The poor
Thresher.—Let me hear from you first post, and forgive this seeming
neglect in a careless fellow of an indolent Poet, who is as lazy as the
Packman that laid down his pack until he would f—t.

My best compliments to your father & Mr Barclay.

I am ever, dear Sir, yours sincerely,
Robt Burns

P.S. If you send a parcel, direct to the care of Walter Auld, Saddler,
Dumfries; & write me at the same time by post to let me know what
Carrier you have employ'd, as they are careless rascals.

R.B.

XI (452)

[Ellisland, 1791?]
Dear Sir,

I received your letter with the Proofs of two songs, but Mr Clarke
has mistaken one of them, the Song, Craigieburnwood, sadly, having
put the Chorus to the wrong part of the tune—so I have given it him
to correct.—I send you thirteen songs, with two Numbers of a
Publication called, the Bee, in which are two Scots songs with the
music which are well worthy your insertion.—Please take care of the
two Numbers, as the loss of them would break my Set.—On second
thoughts, I send you also two other songs with directions where to
find the tunes.—I have besides many other Songs on the stocks, so
you need not fear a want of materials—I was so lucky lately as to
pick an entire copy of Oswald's Scots Music & I think I shall make
glorious work out of it.—I want much Anderson's Collection of
strathspeys [1] &c. & then I think I will [have] all the Music of th[e
cou]ntry.—Send me your Proofs as soon as ready.

Send two copies of Captain Riddel's Strathspeys,[2] by the Dumfries
Carrier, directed to Captain Craik of Arbigland, care of Captain
Hamilton, Dumfries; & your price shall be sent you by any channel
you appoint.—

Yours—
R. Burns

1 John Anderson, *A Collection of New Highland Strathspey Reels for the
Violin or German Flute with a Harpsichord & Violoncello Bass, etc.*
Edinburgh, c. 1790.

James Johnson

2 Robert Riddell: *New Music for the Piano Forte or Harpsichord Composed by a Gentleman Consisting of a Collection of Reels, Minuets, Hornpipes, Marches and two Songs in the Old Scotch Taste, with Variations to Five Favourite Tunes* Edinburgh: James Johnson c. 1785.

XII (503)

[Dumfries, May 1792?]

Dear Sir,

this will be presented to you by one of your Subscribers, & a gentleman to whose musical talents you are much indebted for getting you Scotch tunes.—Let him know your progress, & how you come on with the work.—Inclosed is one Song out of many I have yet to send you; & likewise I inclose you another & I think a better set of Craigieburnwood, which you will give to Mr Clarke to compare with the former set, as I am extremely anxious to have that song right.—

I am, Dear Sir, yours
Robt Burns

XIII (513)

[Dumfries, October 1792?]

My dear Friend,

I would have returned you your Songs much sooner but for unavoidable hurry.—I am now at work correcting a new edition of my Poems & this, with my ordinary business keeps me in full employment.—
[*Half a page of MS. missing*]
. . . chuse.—Get some body to class the first lines of the Songs alphabetically, & I will draw out an Index of Authors' names, &c. as soon as you send me the list, & return
[*two or three words missing*]
A much-valued musical acquaintance of [mine, *one or two words missing*] . . . g of Ayr, is thinking of publishing a Collection of Strathspeys & Reels.—
[*Several lines missing*]
. . . terms as you would another; but as you will be well paid, let him have your lowest terms.—Write to me as to this matter, in a post or two at farthest.—

As to our Musical Museum, I have better than a dozen songs by me for the fifth volume.—Send with Mr Clarke when he comes to
[*several lines missing*]
If we cannot finish the fifth volume any other way—what would you think of Scots words to some beautiful Irish airs? In the mean time, at your leisure, give a copy of the Museum to my worthy friend Mr Peter Hill, Bookseller, to bind for me interleaved with blank leaves, exactly as he did the laird of Glenriddell's, that I may insert every anecdote I can learn, together with my own criticisms and remarks on the songs. A copy of this kind I shall leave with you, the Editor, to publish at some after period, by way of making the Museum a book famous to the end of time, and you renowned for ever.

In haste, yours
R.B.

James Johnson

XIV (591)

[Dumfries, October 1793?]

I was much obliged to you, my dear Friend, for making me acquainted with Gow.—He is a modest, intelligent, worthy fellow; besides his being a man of great genius in his way.—I have spent many happy hours with him in the short while he has been here.—

Why did you not send me those tunes & verses that Clarke & you cannot make out? — Let me have them as soon as possible, that, while he is at hand, I may settle the matter with him.—He & I have been very busy providing & laying out materials for your fifth volume.—I have got about a dozen by me.—If you can conveniently, let me have half a dozen copies of your fourth volume; I want no more.—As soon as the Bound copy of all the volumes is ready, take the trouble of forwarding it.—In haste—

Yours ever—
R.B.

XV (616)

[Dumfries, February 1794]

My dear Sir,

I send by my friend, Mr Wallace, forty-one songs for your fifth volume.—Mr Clarke has also a good many, if he have not, with his usual indolence, *cast them at the cocks.*—I have still, a good parcel among my hands, in scraps & fragments; so that I hope we will make a shift for our last volume.—

You should have heard from me long ago; but, over & above some vexatious share in the pecuniary losses of these accursed times, I have, all this winter, been plagued with low spirits & blue devils, so that I have almost hung my harp on the willow-trees.—

I have got an old Highland durk, for which I have a great veneration; as it once was the durk of Lord Balmerino.—It fell into bad hands who stripped it of the silver mounting, as well as the knife and fork. I have some thoughts of sending it to your care, to get it mounted anew.—Our friend, Clarke, owes me an account somewhere about one pound, which would go a good way in paying the expence.—I remember you once settled an account in this way before; & as you will still have money-matters to settle with him, you might accommodate us both.—I do not, my dear Sir, wish you to do this; & I beg you will not hint it to Mr Clarke.—If we do it at all, I will break it to him myself.—

My best Compliments to your worthy old Father, & your better half.—

Yours
Robt Burns

XVI (630)

June 29th [1794]

My dear Friend,

I thank you for your kind present of poor Riddell's Book.—Depend upon it that your 5th Volume shall not be forgotten.—In the mean time, I have gotten you two new Subscribers—Peter Heron Esquire of Kirochtree, & Major Heron at Kirochtree.—Please put up two sets of your four volumes, & direct them as above, and leave them at Mr Heron's, George's Square.—Please do it on receipt of this, as there will be a Carrier from Kirochtree in Edinburgh this week.

I have just been getting three or four songs for your book.—Pray, will you let me know, how many, & what are the songs Urbani has borrowed from your Museum?—

Yours
RB

XVII (667)

Weden:eve:
[1795]

My dear Friend

now to the subject of your songs.—The song to Ginglan Geordie if my memory serves me right, is one of Dr Blacklock's.—We all knew the Doctor's merit; but his songs, in general, were very silly.—I inclose you one to the tune which has much more merit, & I beg you will insert it.[1]—

"Ken ye what Meg o' the mill has gotten," I send you the old words. —Any fiddler will give you the tune, if you ask for it by the name of, "Jacky Hume's lament."—

"Gude ale comes & gude ale goes"—I send you all that I recollect of the words, as you say you have the tune.—

"Lay thy loof in mine Lassie"—you say you have the words.—The tune you will find in Aird's Selection[2] under the name of "The Cordwainer's march."—

"My Lady's gown & gairs upon't"—I think I can yet procure.—"The Lochmaben harper" I fear I shall never recover; & it is a famous old song.—The rest are I doubt irrecoverable.—I think it hard that after so much trouble in gathering these tunes they should be lost in this trifling way.—Clarke has been shamefully careless.—If I had Oswald's old Collection, I could yet recover some, besides picking out some beautiful airs yet unappropriated to words. My Oswald I lent to a friend who is at a distance at present; so I beg you will favor me with a glance of yours for a week or two.—Please send it the first convenience.—

Pray, is not the song mentioned in the list, No 55th, under the title of "Gloomy December" the same with—"Ance mair I hail thee thou gloomy December" which you say is among the lost?—

"Peggy in devotion"—is surely English.—Tell Clarke from me, on no account to insert an English song in this volume.—The last parcel I sent you, I do not see at all in your list.—

"The rock & the wee pickle tow"[3] put in only the two first stanzas. —It would be idle folly to trouble yourself with any more.—

"O bonie Jean, where hast thou been
"Father & mother seeking thee—&c."

is a fine song which we have all along overlooked.—The song is in
Witherspoon, [4] & the tune is the air of one Gay's songs in the
Beggar's Opera, where it is mentioned by name.[5]—This music you
can easily procure.—

Did I not send you song to "Lumps o' puddings," & what has
become of it?—"Go from my window" is a song so old as to be
mentioned as a popular song in the days of our James the 4th, & I
wish Mr Clarke would try to make it do.—

Queen Mary's lament, you will find in the two volume edition of my
Poems.—Call it "Queen Mary's lament on the return of Spring."

In a day or two, I will write you more at large.—

Yours
R Burns

1 Johnson published the song in Vol. V of the *Scots Musical Museum* with
Blacklock's words.
2 See footnote to Letter VI (267).
3 Not published by Johnson.
4 David Herd, *The Ancient and Modern Scottish Songs* (published by Martin &
Wotherspoon 1769).
5 The song, entitled *Jeany, where hast Thou been*, is in David Herd's *Ancient
and Modern Scottish Songs*, Vol. II, p. 57. The air is entitled *O Jenny, where
hast Thou been*, No. 9 in John Gay's *The Beggar's Opera*.

XVIII (684)

[August? 1795]

My dear Friend

without any apology for my laziness which indeed will admit of no
apology, I proceed to business.—I inclose you four new songs,
together with a Stanza of another song which you had some time
ago.—

"The Bob o' Dumblane," remains to be added in your fifth volume.
—Take it from the "Orpheus Caledonius": if you have not this Book,
I will send you a reading of it.—At the end of this set, (the same with
that in the Tea-table Miscellany) let the old words follow.—

Old words

Lassie, lend me your braw hemp-heckle,
  And I'll lend you my thripplin kame:
My heckle is broken, it canna be gotten,
  And we'll gae dance the Bob o' Dumblane.—
Twa gaed to the wood, to the wood, to the wood,
  Twa gaed to the wood, three cam hame:
An't be na weel bobbit, weel bobbit, weel bobbit,
  An't be na weel bobbit, we'll bob it again. [1]

Another song—"A health to Betty"—See the Orpheus Caledonius,
vol. 1st.—
Another Song—"The carl he cam o'er the craft"—for by far the best
set of this, See also the Orpheus, vol. 1st.—
Another Song—"For o'er lang biding here"—For this, See the
Orpheus, vol. 2d.—

Another song—"Ewe bughts Marion"- a quite different set from the one you have already published—See, for this, the Orpheus, vol. 2d.—

Another song—"My Jockey blithe for what thou's done" for this, see also the Orpheus, vol. 2d.—Though, by the by,this is nearly the same air with, "Had I the wyte she bade me"; a song you already have.—

Another song—"The glancing o' her apron"—see in the Orpheus—vol. 2d.—

Another song—"John Ochiltree" see in the Orpheus, vol. 2d.—

Another song—"Willy's rare & Willie's fair"- I do not remember if you have it already in any of your four volumes; if you have not yet inserted it, you will find it in the Orpheus, vol. 2d.—

Another Song—"Here's a health to them that's awa"—was published sometime ago by Corri—in a single sheet.—

Another song—"The auld man's mare's dead"—see the air in Aird's Selection,[2] & the words in the "Scots nightingale."—

"Fairly shote of her"- get the old words ⎫ But let me have
"When I was a young thing"⎱ get the old ⎬ the verses
"I chappit at the study" ⎰ words ⎭ to correct.—

"Hazel green" send me the tune, & I will furnish words.

"Jenny's bawbee"—take the old verses you mention—

"Gude night & joy be wi' you a'."—let this be your last song of all the Collection; & set it to the old words; & after them, insert my "Gude night & joy be wi' you a'" which you will find in my Poems.[3]—

The old words are—

> The night is my departing night,
>   The morn's the day I maun awa:
> There's no a friend or fae o' mine
>   But wishes that I were awa.—
> What I hae done, for lake o' wit,
>   I never, never can raca':
> I trust ye're a' my friends as yet,
>   Gude night & joy be wi' you a'.—

I will overhaul Ritson, in my next; & I have besides, ten or a dozen songs to send you.—

Two new Subscribers to your Museum, please insert in your list; & forward the volumes, four each, by the *very first* Carrier to their respective places of abode.—Let them know how to remit you the cash & it is on demand. They are—

James Gracie, Bank of Scotland's Office, Dumfries.—
Archibald Richardson, Brewer, Newton Douglas [4]—

Your book is here coming in to be a great favorite.—A Singing Master in this place has borrowed my copy, & has learned ten or a dozen of them which he sings on all occasions.—As he is very popular here, & has much in his power, I do not know but it would be sound policy in you to present him with a copy.—

Inclosed is a job which I beg you will finish pretty soon.—It is a Bill, as you will see, for a tavern.—The Tavern-keeper, Hyslop, is a good honest fellow; & as I lie under particular obligations to him, I

James Johnson

request that you may do it for him on the most reasonable terms.—
If there is any fancy that you would wish to introduce, by way of
additional ornament, let me know; but I think, the simpler it is, the
better.—The tavern is at the sign of "the Globe"- for which reason it
must have a Globe at the top.—I think the model of the Bill which is
inclosed, is a good size; but you are a better judge.—Let me have a
proof sheet, ere you finish it.—I write you in a day or two.-

Yours ever
R Burns

1 C.W. p. 561.
2 See footnote to Letter VI (267).
3 See *The Farewell* (C.W. p. 237).
4 Now Newton Stewart.

XIX (690)

Weden: Noon
[23rd September 1795] *

My dear Friend,

Mr Clarke will have acquainted you with the unfortunate reasons of
my long silence.—When I get a little more health, you shall hear from
me at large on the subject of the songs.—

I am highly pleased with Hyslop's bill, only you have, in your usual
luck, mispelt two words.—The article—*"Postages* & porter"—you
have made, *"Porterages* & porter"—pray, alter that.—In the article—
"Pipes & Tobacco"- you have spelt Tobacco thus—To*bb*acco—
whereas it is spelt with a single b, thus—"Tobacco".—When you have
amended these two faults, which please do directly, throw off five
hundred copies, & send them by the very first coach or fly.—

Farewel! my ever valued Friend!
R Burns.

* This letter is undated, but its cover bears a poorly struck Bishop mark —
E 24, denoting *arrival* in Edinburgh on the 24th of a month, either September
(1795) or February (1796). This implies posting at noon of the previous day
in Dumfries and the only month in which the 23rd fell on a Wednesday was
September 1795. This ties in with the reference to the printing of Hyslop's bill
ordered in the previous letter.
Previous editors have misunderstood the significance of the postmark and
dated this letter to February 1796, doubtless also misled by the reference to a
'long silence' in line 1. But this could also have alluded to a gap of several
weeks in the correspondence.

XX (692)

[Dumfries, March 1796]

My dear Friend,

For Hyslop's plate, many thanks for your goodness: I have made
him a present of it; a present he well deserved at my hand.—Thank
you likewise for the copies of my Volunteer Ballad.—Our friend has
done *indeed* well! 'Tis chaste & beautiful.—I have not met with any
thing has pleased me so much.—You know, I am no Connoisseur; but
that I am an Amateur will be allowed me.—I return you your packet
of songs; & in a day or two, by post, expect to hear *at large* from—

Yours affectionately
R Burns

James Johnson

XXI (696)

[About 1st June 1796]

How are you, my dear Friend? & how comes on your fifth volume? —You may probably think that for some time past I have neglected you & your work; but, Alas, the hand of pain, & sorrow, & care has these many months lain heavy on me!—Personal & domestic affliction have almost entirely banished that alacrity & life with which I used to woo the rural Muse of Scotia.—In the mean time, let us finish what we have so well begun.—The gentleman Mr Lewars, a particular friend of mine, will bring out any proofs (if they are ready) or any message you may have.—

Farewel!
R Burns

turn over

You should have had this when Mr Lewars called on you, but his saddle-bags miscarried.—I am extremely anxious for your work, as indeed I am for every thing concerning you & your welfare.—You are a good, worthy, honest fellow, & have a good right to live in this world—because you deserve it.—Many a merry meeting this Publication has given us, & possibly it may give us more, though, alas! I fear it.—This protracting, slow, consuming illness which hangs over me, will, I doubt much, my ever dear friend, arrest my sun before he has well reached his middle career, & will turn over the Poet to far other & more important concerns than studying the brilliancy of Wit or the pathos of Sentiment.—However, Hope is the cordial of the human heart, & I endeavour to cherish it as well as I can.—Let me hear from you as soon as convenient.—Your Work is a great one; & though, now that it is near finished, I see if we were to begin again, two or three things that might be mended, yet I will venture to prophesy, that to future ages your Publication will be the text book & standard of Scotish Song & Music.[1]—

I am ashamed to ask another favor of you because you have been so very good already, but my wife has a very particular friend of hers, a young lady[2] who sings well, to whom she wishes to present the Scots Musical Museum, if you have a spare copy, will you be obliging as to send it by the very first Fly, as I am anxious to have it soon.

Yours ever
R. Burns

1 cf. letter to George Thomson XI (554) in April 1793, expressing the same sentiment.
2 Jessie Lewars (see p. 32).

FYFE or FYFFE

The following letter was addressed by Burns to 'Mr Fyfe, Surgeon Colege (*sic*)'. Inexplicably, this has become expanded to 'Dr. M. Fyffe' in the Appendix to Ferguson's 1931 edition of the Letters, copied by Maurice Lindsay in his *Encyclopaedia* and by Ross Roy in his edition of the Letters (1985). The Royal College of Surgeons, however, has no record of him, and no graduate of Edinburgh University answers this description. Likewise, the identity of the Mr McCartney who received a print of the Beugo engraving is unknown.

(105)

Saturday morn: six o'clock [5th May 1787]

My dear Sir,

my loins are girded, my sandals on my feet, and my staff is in my hand; * and in half an hour I shall set off from this venerable, respectable, hospitable, social, convivial, imperial Queen of cities, AULD REEKIE.—My compliments to Mr McCartney, and I have sent him that engraving.—Farewell!

> Now, God in heaven bless REEKIE'S town
> With plenty, joy and peace!
> And may her wealth and fair renown
> To latest times encrease!!!—Amen

Robt Burns

* Exodus 12:11, paraphrased.

WILLIAM CREECH

Born at Newbattle in 1745, the son of the Rev. William Creech who died soon afterwards, he was raised by his mother at Dalkeith and later Perth. He finished his schooling in Edinburgh where he began medical studies at the University. His mother, however, secured for him a position in the printing and publishing business of Kincaid and Bell, Alexander Kincaid being a close friend of the widow Creech. After a Continental interlude, travelling with his boyhood friend Lord Kilmaurs (later fourteenth Earl of Glencairn, Burns's patron), Creech entered into a partnership with Kincaid in a new venture in 1771, the latter retiring two years later. Creech ran his printing, publishing and bookselling business for 44 years, right down to his death in 1815. In 1788 he became a magistrate and was Lord Provost of Edinburgh in 1811-13. His High Street premises became a centre for the *literati* and he was on close terms with Hugh Blair, James Beattie, Henry Mackenzie, Dugald Stewart and the Earl of Glencairn. It was the last named who introduced Burns to Creech soon after his arrival in the capital. Lord Glencairn asked Creech if he would undertake a second and expanded edition of Burns's poems. Creech, however, recommended a subscription edition, for which he promised to subscribe 500 copies. Later, Burns and Creech drew up a memorandum of agreement, on the advice of Henry Mackenzie, whereby Burns sold his copyright for 100 guineas. Although this is not as mean as it seems to posterity, Creech compounded it by delaying payment not only of this sum but also the money due to Burns from the subscriptions. It was mainly for the purpose of settling with Creech that Burns returned to Edinburgh late in 1787, and one may appreciate the poet's mounting exasperation with his publisher in the letter (III) of 24th January 1788, and the 'chaser' (IV) nine weeks later. Creech's pathological fear of parting with money provoked scathing comment from Burns in both verse and prose, notably the sketch of him in the Second Commonplace Book. After Creech settled his debts, however, Burns moderated his views and even collaborated with him in the two-volume edition of November 1793 (see letters VI and VII); though when Burns delayed correcting the proofs Creech blithely went ahead with publication regardless.

I (106)

[Enclosing the *Lament* (Auld chuckie Reekie's sair distrest).

[C.W. p. 277]

Selkirk 13th May 1787

My honored Friend,

The inclosed I have just wrote, nearly extempore, in a solitary Inn in Selkirk, after a miserable wet day's riding.—I have been over most of East Lothian, Berwick, Roxburgh & Selkirk Shires; and next week I begin a tour through the north of England.—Yesterday I dined with Lady Hariot, sister to my noble Patron, Quem Deus conservit! I would write till I would tire you as much with dull Prose as I dare say by this time you are with wretched Verse, but I am jaded to death; so, with a grateful farewel, I have the honor to be,

good Sir, yours sincerely
Robt Burns

II (115)

Glasgow, 24th June 1787

Dear Sir

If you have any Copies of mine on hand, please send fifty to Mr Smith Bookseller here for supply of Subscribers.—If you cannot, write me to Mauchline.—

I am, Dear Sir, yours
Robt Burns

III (185 A)

24th January 1788

Sir,

when a business, which could at any time be done in a few hours, has kept me four months without even a shadow of any thing else to do but wait on it, 'tis no very favourable symptom that it will be soon done, when I am a hundred miles absent.—At any rate, I have no mind to make the experiment, but am determined to have it done before I leave Edinburgh.—But why should I go into the country? till I clear with you, I don't know what to do, or what I have in my power to do.—You have declared yourself to the Publick at large, my friend, my Patron; at all times I gratefully own it: I beg you will continue to be so; and rather make a little exertion amid your hurried time, than trifle with a poor man in his very existence; I shall expect to hear from you tomorrow, or next day; and have the honor to be,

Sir,

your very humble servant

IV (231)

Mauchline 31st March 1788

Sir

As I am seriously set in for my farming operations, I shall need that sum your kindness procured me for my Copyright.—I have sent the line to Mr John Sommerville, a particular friend of mine, who will call on you; but as I do not need the sum, at least I can make a shift without it till then, any time between now and the first of May, as it may suit your convenience to pay it, will do for me.—

I have the honor to be,
Sir, your oblidged, humble servant
Robt Burns

V (502)

Dumfries, 16th April 1792

Sir

I this moment have yours, & were it not that habit, as usual, has deafened conscience, my criminal indolence should lead me an uneasy life of Reproach.—I ought long ago to have written you on this very business.—

Now, to try a language of which I am not half master, I shall assume as well as I can, the man of business.—I suppose, at a gross guess, that I could add of new materials to your two volumes, about fifty pages.—I would also correct & retrench a good deal.—These said fifty pages you know are as much mine as the thumb-stall I have just now drawn on my finger which I unfortunately gashed in mending my pen. A few Books which I very much want, are all the recompence I crave, together with as many copies of this new edition of my own works as Friendship or Gratitude shall prompt me to *present*.—There are three Men whom you know, & whose friendly Patronage I think I can trouble so far, Messrs Mckenzie, D. Stuart, & F. Tytler; to any of these I shall submit my M.S.S. for their strictures, & also let them say on my informing them, I mean any of them, what Authors I want, to what value of them I am entitled.—If he adjudge me only a Thom-thumb, I am content.—The Man of Feeling & Professor Stuart, are, I hear, busy with Works of their own, for which reason I shall prefer Mr Tytler.—So soon as I hear from you, I shall write Mr Tytler; & in a fortnight more I shall put my M.S.S. in his hands.—

If the thing were possible that I could receive the Proof-Sheets by our Dumfries Fly, which runs three times a week, I would earnestly wish to correct them myself.—

> I have the honor to be, sir,
> your very humble servant
> Robt Burns

VI (——)

[late 1792?]

Sir,

I have been from home, and very throng for some time, else I would have sent you the remaining MSS. I suppose that there will be fifteen or eighteen pages yet, at least. Please send me, by first carrier, Darwin's Botanic Garden, and his Loves of the Plants, as also Professor D. Stewart's Elements of the Philosophy of the Human Mind. If I exceed in this commission I will pay the balance. Adieu! They gallop fast whom the Devil drives, and I am just going to mount on an excise ride.

"There's threesome reels, there's foursome reels,
There's hornpipes and strathspeys, man;
But the ae best dance e'er came to the land,
Was the deil's awa wi the Exciseman!!!"

Ca ira!

> I am ever, sir
> Your very humble servant,
> R Burns

[Not in Ferguson (1931) or Ross Roy (1985).
Printed in the Appendix of *The Edinburgh Literary Journal* Vol. V. (1831) with a comment by Henry Glassford Bell. The original MS has been lost.]

VII (538)

Dumfries, 28th February 1793

Sir,

I understand that my Book is published.—I beg that you will, *as soon as possible*, send me twenty copies of it.—As I mean to present them among a few Great Folks whom I respect, & a few Little Folks whom I love, these twenty will not interfere with your sale.—If you have not twenty copies ready, send me any number you can.—It will confer a particular obligation to let me have them by first Carrier.—

> I have the honor to be, Sir,
> your obedient humble servant
> Robt Burns

ALEXANDER PATTISON

Despite Burns's rather facetious epithet of 'bookseller' in the address of this letter, Pattison was actually a textile manufacturer in Paisley. He earned the nickname because of his success in gathering subscriptions for the first Edinburgh Edition. Mr Cowan was apparently his partner. Burns visited Pattison on his return from Edinburgh in February 1788 and graphically described the occasion in a long letter to Clarinda from Kilmarnock (XXXIII). Pattison's wife died in April 1784 at the early age of 34, leaving a son and a daughter. He subsequently emigrated to the United States, but nothing is known of his later career.

(107)

Berrywell near Dunse
17th May 1787

Dear Sir,

I am sorry I was out of Edinburgh making a slight pilgrimage to the classic scenes of this country when I was favored with yours of the 11th inst inclosing an order of the Paisley banking company on the Royal Bank for twenty two pounds seven shillings Sterling, payment in full, after carriage deducted, for ninety copies of my book I sent you.—According to your motions I see you will have left Scotland before this reaches you otherwise I would send you Holy Willie with all my heart.—I was so hurried that I absolutely forgot several things I ought to have minded, among the rest sending books to Mr Cowan, but any order of yours will be answered at Creech's shop.—You will please remember that non-subscribers pay six shillings, this is Creech's profit; but those who have subscribed, though their names may have been neglected in the printed list which is very incorrect, they are supplied at the subscription price.—I was not at Glasgow, nor do I intend for London; and I think Mrs Fame is very idle to tell so many lies on a poor Poet.—

When you or Mr Cowan write for Copies, if you should want any, direct to Mr Hill at Mr Creech's shop, and I write to Mr Hill by this post to answer either of your orders. Hill is Mr Creech's first Clerk, and Creech himself is presently in London. I suppose I shall have the pleasure, against your return to Paisley, of assuring you how much I am,

Dear Sir, your oblidged humble servant
Robt Burns

PETER HILL

Born at Dysart, Fife in 1754, the son of James Hill and Mary Russell, he moved to Edinburgh and was 'first clerk' in Creech's bookshop in the High Street when Burns first met him in 1787. The following year, however, Hill left Creech and established his own business. His wife Elizabeth Lindsay, whom he married in 1780, was his social superior and is reputed to have disapproved of her husband's friendship with Burns. Hill later became City Treasurer and treasurer of Heriot's Hospital, and was appointed Collector of Cess in 1814.

Some nineteen letters of Burns to Hill have been recorded, dating between May 1787 and the end of January 1796. In the earlier letters it is obvious that Hill acted as Burns's man of business in Edinburgh, carrying out financial transactions. Later on, he helped Burns with the procurement of books for the Monkland Friendly Society library which Burns and Robert Riddell organised. Gradually, however, the tone of the correspondence became more personal and intimate, revealing the humour and humanity of Burns in many ways. Several letters including the very last, refer to, or were accompanied by, an 'annual kipper' (a smoked salmon), a delicacy much esteemed by the Edinburgh bookseller. It was Hill who actually carried out the payment of the money owed by Burns to Robert Burn in respect of Fergusson's tombstone (see page 265). Hill, together with Cameron the papermaker and Ramsay, printer of the *Edinburgh Evening Courant*, paid a visit to Burns at Dumfries in 1794, subsequently alluded to by Burns (XVII) when sending some of his latest compositions along with the customary 'kippered salmon'. Letter XVIII does not bear the recipient's name and was at one time attributed to Creech, but Ferguson demonstrated conclusively that Peter Hill must have been the addressee.

I (108)

17th May 1787

Dear Sir,

If Mr Alexr Pattison, or Mr Cowan from Paisley, or in general any other of those to whom I have sent copies on credit before, apply to you, you will give them what number they demand when they require it; provided always that those who are non-subscribers shall pay one shilling more than subscribers.—This I write to you when I am miserably fou, consequently it must be the sentiments of my heart.—

Robert Burns

II (109)

Berrywell, 24th May 1787

Dear Sir,

Any more letters for me that may come to your care, send them to Dumfries, directed to be detained till called for.—I mean this direction only for a week; afterwards direct to me at Mossgiel near Mauchline.—Today I set out for a ride thro' Northumberlandshire.—I beg you or Mr Creech will acquaint me, whenever he returns.—

I am, Dear Sir, yours,
Robt Burns

P.S. I received a bill from Mr Pattison which he has wrote to you about.—My letter granting receipt has miscarried, but I have wrote him again today—

R.B.

III (121)

Mauchline, 19th July 1787

Dear Sir,

I have just got a letter from Scot the Bookbinder, where he tells me he needs a little money at present.—I have written him to call on you; & I beg you will pay him his account or give him part payment as you see proper.—

When Mr Creech returns, I beg you will let me know by first convenient Post.—I am,

Dear Sir, your very humble servant
Robt Burns

IV (255)

Mauchline, 18th July 1788

You injured me, my dear Sir, in your construction of the cause of my Silence.—From Ellisland in Nithsdale to Mauchline in Kyle, is forty & five miles; there, a house a building, & farm inclosures & improvements to tend; here, A new—not so much indeed a *new* as a *young* wife—Good God, Sir, could my dearest BROTHER expect a regular correspondence from me!—I who am busied with the sacred Pen of Nature, in the mystic Volume of Creation, can I dishonor my hand with a dirty goose feather, on a parcel of mash'd old rags? I who am "Called as was Aaron" to offer in the Sanctum Sanctorum, not indeed the mysterious bloody types of future MURDER, but the thrice hallowed quintessences of future EXISTENCE; can I—but I have apologised enough: I am certain that You, my liberal-minded & much-respected Friend, would have acquitted me, tho' I had obeyed to the very letter that famous Statute among the irrevocable Decrees of the Medes and Persians; "Not to ask Petition, for forty days, of either god or man, save *THEE, O Queen*, only—[1]

I am highly oblidged to you, my dearest Sir, for your kind, your elegant compliments, on my becoming one of that most respectable, that truly venerable Corps; they who are, without a metaphor, the Fathers of Posterity, the Benefactors of all coming Generations; the Editors of Spiritual Nature, & the Authors of Immortal Being.—Now that I am "one of you," I shall humbly but fervently endeavour to be a conspicuous Member.—Now it is "called Today," with my powers & me; but the time fast approacheth, when, beholding the debilitated victim of all-subduing Time, they shall exclaim, "How are the Mighty fallen, & the weapons of war perished!!"[2]

Your book came safe, and I am going to trouble you with farther Commissions.—I call it troubling you, because I want only, Books; the cheapest way, the best; so you may have to hunt for them in the evening Auctions.—I want Smollet's works, for the sake of his incomparable humor.—I have already Roderick Random & Humphrey Clinker.—Peregrine Pickle, Lancelot Greaves & Ferdinand Count Fathom, I still want; but as I said, the veriest ordinary Copies will serve me.—I am nice only in the appearance of my Poets.—I forget the price of Cowper's Poems, but I believe I must have them. —I saw the other day, proposals for a Publication entitled, "Bankes's new & complete Christian's family bible;" Printed for C. Cooke, Paternoster row, London.—He promises at least to give in the Work, I think it is, three hundred & odd Engravings, to which he has put the Names of the first Artists in London.—You will know the character of the Performance, as some Numbers of it are published;

and if it is really what it pretends to be, set me down as a Subscriber, & send me the Published Numbers.—

Let me hear from you, your first leisure minute, & trust me, you shall, in future, have no reason to complain of my Silence.—The dazzling perplexity of Novelty will dissipate, & leave me to pursue my course in the quiet Path of methodical Routine.—

I might go on to fill up the Page, but I dare say you are already sufficiently tired of,

My dear Sir, yours sincerely,
Robt Burns

1 Esther, paraphrased.
2 2: Samuel 1:27.

V (276)

Mauchline, 1st October 1788

My dear Friend,

I have been here in this Country, about three days, and all that time, my chief reading has been, the Address to Lochlomond[1] you were so oblidging as send me.—Were I impannelled, one of the Author's Jury to determine his criminality respecting the Sin of Poesy, my verdict should be "Guilty! A Poet of Nature's making!"—It is an excellent method for improvement, and what I beleive every Poet does; to place some favorite classic Author, in our own walks of study & composition, before us a Model. Tho' your Author has not mentioned the name, I could have, at half a glance, guessed his Model to be Thomson.—Will my brother Author forgive me, if I venture to hint, that his imitation of that Immortal Bard is in two or three places rather more servile than such a genius as his required.

E.G. They soothe the madding passions all to peace—
Address.
To soothe the throbbing passions into peace—
Thomson [2]

I have read Thomson at the same time, & I think the verification of the Address, in simplicity, harmony, & elegance, fully equal to the Seasons. Like Thomson too, he has looked into Nature for himself: you meet with no copied description.—One particular Criticism I made, at first reading; in no one instance has he said too much.—He never flags in his progress, but like a true Poet of Nature's making, kindles in his course.

His beginning is simple, and modest, as if distrustful of the strength of his pinion; only, I do not altogether like—

—"Truth,
"The soul of every song that's nobly great"—

Fiction is the soul of many a Song that's nobly great.—Perhaps I am wrong: this may be but a Prose Criticism. Is not the phrase, in line 7th page 6th, "Great lake," too much vulgarised by every-day language, for so sublime a Poem?

"Great mass of waters, theme for nobler Song"–is perhaps no emendation.–His enumeration of, & comparison with other lakes, is at once harmonious & poetic. Every Reader's ideas must sweep the

"——winding margin of an hundred miles"–

The following perspective of a mountains blue–the imprisoned billows beating in vain–the wooded isles–the digression on the yew-tree–Benlomond's lofty, cloud-enveloped head, &c. are beautiful–A thunder-storm is a subject which has been often tried, yet our Poet in his grand picture has interjected a circumstance, so far as I know, entirely original–

"——the gloom
"Deep seamed with frequent streaks of moving fire——"

In his preface to the storm, "The glens how dark between," is noble Highland landscape! The "rain plowing the red mould," too, is beautifully fancied.–Benlomond's "Lofty, pathless top" is a good expression; & the surrounding view from it is truly great: the–"Silver mist"–

"Beneath the beaming sun"——is well described; & here, he has contrived to enliven his Poem with a little of that passion which bids fair, I think, to usurp the modern muses altogether. I know not how far this episode is a beauty upon the whole, but the Swain's wish to carry–"Some faint idea of the vision bright," to entertain her "partial listening ear," is a pretty thought.–But in my opinion the most beautiful passages in the whole Poem, are the fowls crouding, in wintry frosts, to Loch-lomond's "hospitable flood"–Their wheeling round, their lighting, mixing, diving, &c.–and the glorious description of the Sportsman.–This last is equal to any thing in The Seasons: the idea of "the floating tribes, distant seen, far glistening to the moon," provoking his eye as he is oblidged to leave them, is a noble ray of poetic genius.–"The howling winds"–The "hideous roar" of "the white cascades"–are all in the same style.–

I forget that while I am thus holding forth with the heedless warmth of an Enthusiast, I am perhaps tiring you with nonsense.–I must however mention that the last verse of the 16th page is one of the most elegant Compliments I have ever seen.–I must likewise notice that beautiful paragraph, beginning,–"The gleaming lak;" &c. I dare not go into the particular beauties of the two last paragraphs, but they are admirably fine, & truly Ossianic.–

I must beg your pardon for this lengthened scrawl–I had no idea of it when I began. I should like to know who the Author is; but whoever he be, please, present him with my grateful thanks for the entertainment he has afforded me.–

A friend of mine desired me to commission for him, two books–"Letters on the Religion essential to man," a book you sent me before; and, "The world unmasked, or the Philosopher the greatest cheat." [3]–Send me them by the first opportunity.–The Bible you sent me is truly elegant, only I wish it had been in two volumes.–

I wrote you about a week ago, by Mr Clarke the Organist.–

I am most sincerely, my dear Sir, yours
Robt Burns

Peter Hill

1 James Cririe: *Address to Loch Lomond*, (1788).
2 *Autumn*, line 966.
3 Both by Marie Huber.

VI (325)

Ellisland 2d April 1789

I will make no excuses, my dear Bibliopolus, (God forgive me for murdering language) that I have sat down to write you on this vile paper, stained with the sanguinary scores of "thae curst horse leeches o' th' Excise."—It is economy, Sir; it is that, cardinal virtue, Prudence; so I beg you will sit down & either compose or borrow a panegyric (if you are going to borrow, apply to our friend, Ramsay,* for the assistance of the author of those pretty little buttering paragraphs of eulogiums on your thrice-honored & never-enough-to-be-praised MAGISTRACY—how they hunt down a housebreaker with the sanguinary perseverance of a bloodhound—how they outdo a terrier in a badger-hole, in unearthing a Resettor of stolen goods—how they steal on a thoughtless troop of Night-nymphs as a spaniel winds the unsuspecting Covey—or how they riot o'er a ravaged Bawdy-house as a cat does o'er a plundered Mouse-nest—how they new-vamp old Churches, aiming at appearances of Piety—plan Squares & Colledges, to pass for men of taste & learning, &c. &c. &c. —while old Edinburgh, like the doting Mother of a parcel of rakehelly Prodigals, may sing "Hooly & fairly," or cry, "Waes me that e'er I saw ye," but still must put her hand in her pocket & pay whatever scores the young dogs think proper to contract)—

I was going to say, but this damn'd Parenthesis has put me out of breath, that you should get that manufacturer of the tinselled crockery of magistratial reputations, who makes so distinguished & distinguishing a figure in the Evening Courant, to compose or rather to compound something very clever on my remarkable frugality; that I write to one of my most esteemed friends on this wretched paper, which was originally intended for the venal fist of some drunken Exciseman, to take dirty notes in a miserable vault of an Ale-cellar.—

O Frugality! thou mother of ten thousand blessings! Thou Cook of fat beef & dainty greens! Thou Manufacturer of warm Shetland hose & comfortable surtouts! Thou old Housewife, darning thy decayed stockings, with thy ancient spectacles on thy aged nose!!! Lead me, hand me in thy clutching, palsied fist, up those heights & through those thickets hitherto inaccessible & impervious to my anxious, weary feet—not those damned Parnassian Crags, bleak & barren, where the hungry worshippers of Fame are, breathless, clambering, hanging between heaven & hell; but these glittering cliffs of Potosi where the all-sufficient, all-powerful deity, WEALTH, holds his immediate court of joys & pleasures; where the sunny exposure of Plenty & the hot-walls of profusion produce those blissful fruits of LUXURY, exotics in this world and natives of Paradise!!! Thou withered Sybill, my sage Conductress, usher me into the refulgent, adored Presence! The Power, splended & potent as he now is, was once the puling nursling of thy faithful care & tender arms! Call me thy son, thy cousin, thy kinsman, or favorite; and adjure the god by

313

the scenes of his infant years, no longer to repulse me as a Stranger or an alien, but to favor me with his peculiar countenance & protection! He daily bestows his greatest kindnesses on the undeserving & the worthless, assure him that I bring ample documents of meritorious demerits! Pledge yourself for me, that for the glorious cause of LUCRE I will do any thing, be any thing—but the horse-leech of private Oppression, or the vulture of public Robbery!!!!!!—

But to descend from heroics—what, in the name of all the devils at once, have you done with my trunk? Please let me have it by first Carrier, except his name be, Niven; he is a rascal who imposed or would have imposed on me the other day most infamously.—I want a Shakespear—let me know what plays your used Copy of Bell's Shakespear wants: I want likewise an English dictionary, Johnson's I suppose is best.—These & all my *Prose* commissions, the cheapest is always the best for me.—There is a small debt of honor that I owe Mr Robt Cleghorn in Saughton mills, my worthy friend, & your wellwisher; please give him, & urge him to take it, the first time you see him, ten shillings' worth of any thing you have to sell, & place it to my account.—

The Library scheme that I mentioned to you is already begun, under the direction of Captain Riddel, & ME!—There is another in emulation of it, going on at Closeburn, under the auspices of Mr Mentieth of Closeburn, which will be on a greater scale than ours; I have likewise secured it for you.—Captain R— gave his infant society a great many of his old books, else I had written you on that subject; but one of these days I shall trouble you with a Commission for "the Monkland friendly Society."—A copy of the Spectator, Mirror & Lounger, Man of feeling, Man of the world, Guthrie's Geographical grammar, with some religious pieces, will likely be our first order.—

Write me first post, & send me the Address to Stuart, Publisher of the Star newspaper: this I beg particularly but do not speak of it.— I'll expect along with the trunk, my Ainslie's map of Scotland; & if you could send your boy to Mr Beugo, Engraver, he has a picture of mine a framing which will be ready by this time.—You see the freedom I take with you.—Please direct any parcels to me, to the care of Walter Auld, Saddler, Dumfries.—

When I grow richer, I will write you on gilt Post, to make amends for this sheet.—

At present every guinea has a five-guinea errand with,

My dear Sir,
Your faithful, poor but honest, friend
R.B.

* David Ramsay, proprietor of the Edinburgh *Courant*.

Peter Hill

VII (387)

Ellisland 2nd February 1790

No! I will not say one word about apologies or excuses for not writing you.—I am a poor, damn'd, rascally Gager, condemned to gallop at least 200 miles every week to inspect dirty Ponds & yeasty barrels, and where can I find time to write to, or importance to interest, any body? The upbraidings of my conscience, nay the upbraidings of my Wife, have persecuted me on your account these two or three months past.—I wish to God I was a Great Man that my correspondence might throw light upon you, to let the world see what you really are; and then I would make your fortune, without putting my hand in my pocket for you, which, like all other Great Men, I suppose I would avoid as much as possible.—What are you doing, and how are you doing? Have you lately seen any of my few friends? What is become of the Borough Reform, or how is the fate of my poor Namesake, Mademoiselle Burns, decided? Which of their grave Lordships can lay his hand on his heart and say that he has not taken the advantage of such frailty; nay, if we may judge by near six thousand years experience, can the World do without such frailty? O Man! but for thee & thy selfish appetites & dishonest artifices, that beauteous form, & that once innocent & still ingenuous mind might have shone conspicuous & lovely in the faithful wife and the affectionate mother; and shall the unfortunate sacrifice to thy pleasures have no claim on thy humanity! As for those flinty-bosomed, puritannic Prosecutors of Female Frailty & Persecutors of Female Charms—I am quite sober—I am dispassionate—to shew you that I am so I shall mend my Pen ere I proceed—It is written, "Thou shalt not take the name of the Lord thy God in vain," so I shall neither say, G— curse them! nor G— blast them! nor G— damn them! but may Woman curse them! May Woman blast them! May Woman damn them! May her lovely hand inexorably shut the Portal of Rapture to their most earnest Prayers & fondest essays for entrance! And when many years, and much port and great business have delivered them over to Vulture Gouts and Aspen Palsies, *then* may the dear, bewitching Charmer in derision throw open the blissful Gate to tantalize their impotent desires which like ghosts haunt their bosoms when all their powers to give or receive enjoyment, are for ever asleep in the sepulchre of their fathers!!!

Now for business.—Our book Society owe you still £1—4—A friend of mine will I suppose have given you some money for me.—It is about £3—10sh. or so, from which pay yourself the Monkland Friendly Society's account, & likewise Mr Neilson's account, and send me a copy of it.—The gentleman that will have given you the money will be Mr Allan Masterton, Writing Master in Carruber's Close.—I saw lately in a review, some extracts from a new Poem called, "The Village Curate," [1] I think; send it me.—I want likewise a cheap Copy of THE WORLD.—Mr Armstrong, the young Poet who does me the honor to mention me so kindly in his Works, please give him my best thanks for the copy of his book.[2]—I shall write him, my first leisure hour.—I like his Poetry much, but I think his style in Prose quite astonishing.—What is become of that old Veteran in Genius, Wit and B—dry, Smellie, & his book? Give him my

315

compliments.—Does Mr Graham of Gartmore ever enter your Shop now? He is the noblest instance of great talents, great fortune & great Worth that ever I saw in conjunction. Remember me to Mrs Hill, & believe me to be

My dear Sir, ever Yours
Robt Burns

1 Rev. James Hurdis.
2 John Armstrong: *Juvenile Poems*, Edinburgh (1789).

VIII (395)

Ellisland 2nd March 1790

My dear Sir,

At a late meeting of the Monkland friendly Society it was resolved to augment their Library by the following books which you are to send us as soon as possible.—The Mirror—The Lounger—Man of feeling—Man of the world (these for my own sake I wish to have by the first Carrier) Knox's history of the Reformation—Rae's history of the Rebellion 1715 [1]—Any good history of the Rebellion 1745 —A display of the Secession Act & Testimony by Mr Gib—Hervey's Meditations—Beveridge's thoughts—& another copy of Watson's body of Divinity—This last heavy Performance is so much admired by many of our Members, that they will not be content with one Copy, so Captain Riddel our President & Patron agreed with me to give you private instructions not to send Watson, but to say that you could not procure a Copy of the book so cheap as the one you sent formerly & therefore you wait farther Orders.—I wrote Mr A. Masterton three or four months ago to pay some money he owed me into your hands, & lately I wrote you to the same purpose, but I have heard from neither one nor other of you.—

In addition to the books I commissioned in my last, I want very much—An Index to the Excise laws, or An Abridgement of all the Statutes now in force relative to the Excise, by Jellinger Symons I want three Copies of this book.—If this book is now to be had, cheap or dear, get it for me.—An honest Country neighbor of mine wants too, a family bible, the larger the better, but second-handed, for he does not chuse to give above ten shillings for the book.—I want likewise for myself, as you can pick them up, second-handed, or any way cheap copies of Otway's dramatic works, Ben Johnson's Ditto Dryden's Congreve's, Wycherly's, Vanburgh's, Cibber's, or any Dramatic works of the more Moderns, Mackline Garrick, Foote, Colman, or Sheridan's.—A good Copy too of Moliere in French I much want.—Any other good Dramatic Authors, in their native language I want them; I mean Comic Authors chiefly, tho' I should wish Racine, Corneille & Voltaire too.—I am in no hurry for all or any of these, but if you accidentally meet with them very cheap, get them for me.—

And now, to quit the dry walk of business, how do you do, my dear Friend? & how is Mrs Hill? I trust, if now and then, not so *elegantly* handsome; at least as amiable, & sings as divinely as ever.—My Goodwife too, has a charming "woodnote wild;" now could we four get any way snugly together in a corner in the New Jerusalem (remember I bespeak your company there) you & I tho' Heaven knows we are no Singers, yet, as we are all to have harps you know, we shall contrive to support the ladies' pipes, as we have oft done before, with all the powers of our *instruments*!

I am out of all patience with this vile world for one thing.—Mankind are by nature benevolent creatures; except in a few scoundrelly instances, I do not think that avarice of the good things we chance to have is born with us; but we are placed here amid so much Nakedness, & Hunger, & Poverty, & want, that we are under a damning necessity of studying Selfishness in order that we may Exist! Still there are, in every age, a few souls that all the Wants & Woes of life cannot debase to Selfishness, or even give the necessary alloy of Caution & Prudence.—If ever I am in danger of vanity, it is when I contemplate myself on this side of my disposition & character.—God knows I am no Saint; I have a whole host of Follies & Sins to answer for; but if I could, & I believe I do it as far as I can, I would "wipe away all tears from all eyes."[2]—Even the knaves who have injured me, I would oblidge them; tho' to tell the truth, it would be more out of vengeance to shew them that I was independant of, & above them, than out of the overflowings of my benevolence.—
Adieu!

Robt Burns

1 Peter Rae: *History of the Late Rebellion*, Dumfries (1718).
2 Revelation 7:17.

IX (430)

Ellisland, 17th January 1791

Take these three guineas & place them overgainst that damned account of yours, which has gagged my mouth these five or six months!—I can as little write Good Things as write Apologies to the man I owe money to.—O the supreme curse of making three guineas do the business of five!—Not all the twelve labors of Hercules, not all the Hebrews' three centuries of Egyptian bondage, were such an insuperable business, such an infernal task.—

Poverty! Thou half-sister of Death, thou cousin-german of Hell, where shall I find force of execration equal to thy demerits!—By thee, the venerable Ancient, though in thy invidious obscurity, grown hoary in the practice of every virtue under Heaven, now laden with years & wretchedness, implores from a stony-hearted son of Mammon whose sun of prosperity never knew a cloud, a little, little aid to support his very existence, and is by him denied & insulted.—By thee, the Man of Sentiment whose heart glows with Independance & melts with sensibility, inly pines under the neglect or writhes in bitterness of soul under the contumely, of arrogant, unfeeling Wealth.—By thee the Man of Genius whose ill-starred ambition plants him at the tables of the Fashionable & Polite, must see in suffering silence his remark neglected & his person despised, while shallow Greatness in his idiot attempts at wit shall meet with countenance & applause.—

Nor is it only the family of Worth that have reason to complain of thee: the children of Folly & Vice, tho' in common with thee the offspring of Evil, smart equally under thy rod.—Owing to thee, the Man of unfortunate dispositions & neglected education, is condemned as a fool for his dissipation; despised & shunned as a needy wretch, when his follies as usual have brought him to want; & when his unprincipled necessities drive him to dishonest practices, he is abhorred as a miscreant, & perishes by the justice of his country.— But far otherwise is the lot of the Man of Family & Fortune.—His early extravagance & folly, are fire & spirit; his consequent wants, are the embarrassments of an Honest Fellow; & when, to remedy the matter, he sets out with a legal commission to plunder distant provinces & massacre peaceful nations, he returns laden with the spoils of rapine & murder, lives wicked & respected, & dies a Villain & a Lord.—Nay, worst of all—Alas for hapless Woman!—the needy creature who was shivering at the corner of the street, waiting to earn the wages of casual prostitution, is ridden down by the chariot wheels of the CORONETED REP, hurrying on to the adulterous assignation; she, who without the same necessities to plead, riots nightly in the same guilty trade!!!

Well, Divines may say what they please, but I maintain that a hearty blast of execration is to the mind, what breathing a vein is to the body: the overloaded sluices of both are wonderfully relieved by their respective evacuations.—I feel myself vastly easier than when I began my letter, & can now go on to business.—You will be so good then as send by the first Dumfries Carrier, all, or as many as you have by you, of the following books.—

The Adventurer—Joseph Andrews—Don Quixote—The Idler— Arabian nights entertainment—Dr Price's dissertations on Providence, prayer, Death & Miracles—Roderick Random—&—the 5th Volume of the Observer—for these books take your fair price, as our Society are no judges of the matter, & will insist on having the following damned trash, which you must also send us, as cheap as possible—Scots Worthies—Boston's 4 fold State—Marrow of Modern divinity—Cole on God's Sovereignty—Newton's letters—Doddridge's thoughts* — Gib's Act & Testimony—Confession of faith—& Captain Robert Boyle.—I forgot to mention among the valuable books, Blair's Sermons & the latest edition of Guthrie's Geographical grammar, which two books be sure to send us.

* Philip Doddridge, *Free Thoughts on the Most Probable Means of Reviving the Dissenting Interest* London, (1730).

X (440)

[Ellisland, March 1791]

My dear Hill

I shall say nothing at all to your mad present.—You have long & often been of important service to me, & I suppose you mean to go on confering obligations untill I shall not be able to lift up my face before you.—In the mean time, as Sir Roger de Coverley, because it happened to be a cold day in which he made his will, ordered his servants, Great Coats, for mourning, so, because I have been this week plagued with an indigestion, I have sent you by the Carrier a fine old ewe-milk Cheese.—

Indigestion is the devil: nay, 'tis the devil & all.—It besets a man in every one of his senses.—I lose my appetite at the sight of successful Knavery; sicken to loathing at the noise & nonsense of self-important Folly.—When the hollow-hearted wretch takes me by the hand, the feeling spoils my dinner; the proud man's wine so offends my palate that it choaks me in the gullet; & the *pulvilis'd*, feathered, pert coxcomb is so horrible in my nostril that my stomach turns.—

If ever you have any of these disagreable sensations, let me prescribe for you, Patience & a bit of my Cheese.—I know that you are no niggard of your good things among your friends, & some of them are in much need of a slice.—There in my eye is our friend, Smellie; a man positively of the first abilities & greatest strength of mind, as well as one of the best hearts & keenest wits that I have ever met with; when you see him, as, Alas! he too often is, smarting at the pinch of distressful circumstance aggravated by the sneer of contumelious greatness—a bit of my cheese alone will not cure him; but if you add a tankard of Brown Stout & superadd a magnum of right Oporto, you will see his sorrows vanish like the morning mist before the summer sun.—

Candlish, the earliest friend except my only brother that I have on earth, & one of the worthiest fellows that ever any man called by the name of Friend, if a luncheon of my Cheese would help to rid him of some of his superabundant Modesty, you would do well to give it him.—

David with his Courant* comes, too, across my recollection, & I beg you will help him largely from the said ewe-milk cheese, to enable him to digest those damn'd, bedaubing paragraphs with which he is eternally larding the lean characters of certain Great Men in a certain Great Town.—I grant you the periods are very well turned; so, a fresh egg is a very good thing, but when thrown at a man in a Pillory it does not at all improve his figure, not to mention the irreparable loss of the egg.—

My facetious little friend, Colonel Dunbar, I would wish also to be a Partaker; not to digest his spleen for that he laughs off, but to digest his last night's wine at the last field-day of the Crochallan corps.—

Among our common friends, I must not forget one of the dearest of them, Cunningham.—The brutality, insolence & selfishness of a world unworthy of having such a fellow as he in it, I know sticks in his stomach, & if you can help him to any thing that will make a little easier on that score, it will be very obliging.—

As to honest John Sommerville, he is such a contented happy man that I know not what can annoy him, except perhaps he may not have got the better of a parcel of modest anecdotes which a certain Poet gave him one night at supper, the last time the said Poet was in town.-

Though I have mentioned so many men of Law, I shall have nothing to do with them professedly—the Faculty are beyond my prescription—As to their *CLIENTS*, that is another thing; GOD KNOWS THEY HAVE MUCH TO DIGEST!!!—

The Clergy, I pass by—their profundity of erudition, & their liberality of sentiment; their total want of Pride, & their detestation of Hypocrisy, are so proverbially notorious, as to place them far, far above either my Praise or Censure.—

I was going to mention a man of worth whom I have the honor to call Friend, the Laird of Craigdarroch; but I have spoken to the landlord of the Kings-Arms Inn here, to have at the next County Meeting, a large ewe-milk cheese on the table, for the benefit of the Dumfries-shire Whigs, to enable them to digest the Duke of Queensberry's late political conduct.—

I have just this moment an opportunity of a private hand to Edinburgh, as perhaps you would not Digest double Postage—So God bless you—

Robt Burns

* David Ramsay, proprietor of the *Edinburgh Courant*.

XI (475)

[Ellisland, October? 1791]

My dear Friend,

I was never more unfit for writing.—A poor devil nailed to an elbow chair, writhing in anguish with a bruised leg, laid on a stool before him, is in a fine situation truly for saying bright things.

I may perhaps see you about Martinmass.—I have sold to My Landlord the lease of my farm, & as I roup off every thing then, I have a mind to take a week's excursion to see old acquaintances.—At all events you may reckon on your account about that time.—So much for business.—I do not know if I ever informed you that I am now got ranked on the list as a Supervisor; & I have pretty good reason to believe that I shall soon be called out to employ.—The appointment is worth from one to two hundred a year, according to the place of the country in which one is settled.—I have not been so lucky in my farming.—Mr Miller's kindness has been just such another as Creech's was; but this for your private ear.—

His meddling vanity, a busy fiend,
Still making work his selfish craft must mend. *—

By the way, I have taken a damned vengeance of Creech.—He wrote me a fine, fair letter, telling me that he was going to print a third Edition; & as he had a brother's care of my fame, he wished to add every new thing I have written since, & I should be amply rewarded with—a copy or two to present to my friends!—He has sent me a copy of the last Edition to correct, &c.—but I have as yet taken no notice of it; & I hear he has published without me.—You know & all my friends know, that I do not value money; but I owed the gentleman a debt, which I am happy to have it in my power to repay.—

Farewel! & Prosperity attend all your undertakings!—I shall try, if my unlucky limb would give me a little ease, to write you a letter a little better worth reading.—Put the inclosed to post.—

R. Burns

* Rejected lines from *Epistle to Robert Graham, Esq., of Fintry* C.W. p. 330.

Peter Hill

XII (495)

My dear Friend,

I send you by the bearer, Mr Clarke, a particular friend of mine, six pounds & a shilling, which you will dispose of as follows.—£5-10, per account I owe to Mr Robt Burn, Architect, for erecting the stone over poor Ferguson.—He was two years in erecting it, after I commissioned him for it; & I have been two years paying him, after he sent me his account; so he & I are quits.—He had the hardiesse to ask me interest on the sum; but considering that the money was due by one Poet, for putting a tomb-stone over another, he may, with grateful surprise, thank Heaven that ever he saw a farthing of it.

With the remainder of the money, pay yourself the "Office of a Messenger"* that I bought of you, & send me by Mr Clarke a note of its price.—Send me likewise the fifth volume of the Observer by Mr Clarke; & if any money remain, let it stand to account.

My best Compliments to Mrs Hill.—I sent you a Maukin by last week's Fly, which I hope you received.—

Yours most sincerely,
Robt Burns

* Robert Thomson: *The Duty and Office of a Messenger at Arms*, Edinburgh (1790).

XIII (553)

[Dumfries, April 1793]

I would have written you sooner, my dear Friend, but as our Treasurer was out of town untill today, I did not wish to write except I could write to the purpose.—Today, I believe, our T——remits you the cash.—On Monday next our Committee meets, when you shall have a new order.—

I hope & trust that this unlucky blast which has overturned so many, & many worthy characters who four months ago little dreaded any such thing—will spare my Friend.—

O! may the wrath & curse of all mankind, haunt & harrass these turbulent, unprincipled misc[reants] who have involved a People in this ruinous business!!!

I have not a moment more.—Blessed be he that blesseth thee, & CURSED be he that curseth thee![1] & wretch whose envious malice would injure thee, may the Giver of every good & perfect gift say unto him "Thou shalt not prosper!"[2]—

R.B.

1 Numbers 24:9.
2 Deuteronomy 28:29.

XIV (565)

Dumfries, 13th June 1793

My dear Friend,

I take Glenriddel's kind offer of a corner for a Postscript to you,

though I have got nothing particular to tell you.—It is with the
greatest pleasure I learn from all hands, & particularly from your
warm friend & Patron, the Laird here, that you are going on,
spreading & thriving like the Palm-tree that shades the fragrant vale
in the Holy Land of the Prophet.—May the richest juices from
beneath, & the dews of Heaven from above, foster your root &
refresh your branches, untill you be as conspicuous among your
fellows, as the stately Goliah towering over the little Pigmy
Philistines around him!
Amen! So be it!!!

Robt Burns

XV (614)

February 1794

My Dear Sir,

I am half angry with you, that you are not any pains to keep squares
with our Library here. They complain much of your not attending
properly to their orders; &, but for the exertions of Mr Lewars a
young man whom I once introduced to you, they had applied
elsewhere.—Apropos, the first volume of Dalrymple's Memoirs,[1] Mr
Lewars had the ill-luck to get spoilt in his possession; which unless
he can replace, will bring him in for the whole book.—It was
published, I think, in separate volumes, so that with a little industry
you may possibly be able to supply him.—Mr Wallace, the gentleman
who will deliver you this, can inform you of the Edition &c.—

Now that business is over, how are you? & how do you weather this
accursed time?—God only knows what will be the consequence; but
in the mean time, the country, at least in our part of it, is still
progressive to the devil.—For my part, "I jouk & let the jaw flee
o'er."—As my hopes in this world are but slender, I am turning very
rapidly, Devotee, in the prospect of sharing larger in the world to
come.—

How is old sinfull Smellie coming on with this world? for as to the
other, I suppose he has given that up.—Is there any talk of his second
volume?[2]—If you meet with my much-valued old friend, Colonel
Dunbar of the Crachallan Fencibles, remember me most
affectionately to him.—Alas! not infrequently, when my heart
is in a wandring humor, I live past scenes over again—to my mind's
eye, you, Dunbar, Cleghorn, Cunningham, &c—present their friendly
phiz; my bosom aches with tender recollections!

Adieu!
Robt Burns

1 Sir John Dalrymple: *Memoirs of Great Britain and Ireland* 1790
2 *The Philosophy of Natural History*, vol. II not published till 1799.

XVI (623)

[May 1794]

My dear Friend,

Allow me to introduce Mr Findlater to you, our Supervisor of
Excise; & a gentleman of great information & the first worth.—I lie

& have long lain under great obligations to him, & by way of recompense (& what I assure you I think no small one) I wish to make him acquainted with a man of worth equal to his own, & of respectability, I am happy to hear, great & daily increasing.—He is just going; so I have not a moment to tell you of my Poetic business. —Of that soon.—

I have been making a Collection of all the blotted scrolls of any letters I have written, & which I had scrolled, which I intended to have given to poor Glenriddell.—Alas! he is gone, & in him a worthy Friend, both of yours & mine.—Many of my letters to you, you were pleased to think well of, but writing to you was always the ready business of my heart, & I scarcely ever scrolled a line.—Perhaps a perusal of my Manuscript would please you—you shall have it—

Findlater can wait no longer—Let me recommend him to your civilities—

Adieu!
Robt Burns

XVII (643)

[October 1794]

My dear Hill,

By a Carrier of yesterday, Henry Osburn by name, I sent you a Kipperred Salmon, which I trust you will duly receive, & which I also trust will give you many a toothful of satisfaction.—If you have the confidence to say that there is any thing of the kind in all your great City, superior to this in true Kipper relish & flavour, I will be avenged of your slander by—not sending you another next season.— In return, the first party of Friends that dine with you (provided that your fellow-travellers, & my trusty & well-beloved veterans in intimacy, Messrs Ramsay & Cameron, be of the party) about that time in the afternoon when a relish, or devil, becomes grateful; give them two or three slices of the Kipper, & drink a bumper to your friends in Dumfries.—

Moreover, by last Saturday's Fly, I sent you a hare; which I hope came & carriage free, safe to your hospitable mansion—& social table.—So much for business.—

How do you like the following Pastoral, which I wrote the other day for a tune that I dare say you well know.

Ca' the yowes to the knowes [*second version*]

Chorus (old)
[C.W. p. 519]

And how do you like the following—

On seeing Mrs Kemble in Yarico.—

Or This.— [C.W. p. 526]

On W—— R—— Esquire
[C.W. p. 516]

My best good wishes to Mrs Hill; & believe me to be

ever yours
R. Burns

Peter Hill

XVIII (671)

Dumfries, 30th May [1795]

[With the following epigrams and song]

On being asked why God had made Miss Deborah Davies so little &
Mrs A [Honorable Mrs Stewart?] so big—
[C.W. p. 491]

On hearing it asserted that there was falsehood in the Revd Dr
Babington's very looks—
[C.W. p. 514]

On Captain Lascelles—
[C.W. p. 521]

On Captain William Roddick, Esq: of Corbieton —
[C.W. p. 505]

Epitaph on John Bushby Writer, of Tinwald Downs—
[C.W. p. 521]

Pinned to Mrs Walter Riddell's carriage.—
[C.W. p. 514]

On William Graham Esq: of Moss knowe—
[C.W. p. 522]

On James Morine, Esq: of Laggan—
[C.W. p. 495]

On the laird of Cardonness [David Maxwell] —
[C.W. p. 491]

Extempore—On being shewn a beautiful Country seat belonging to
the same—
[C.W. p. 492]

On seeing the beautiful country-seat of lord Galloway, John Stewart—
On the same nobleman —
On the same ——
To the same, on the Author being threatened with his resentment—
[C.W. p. 494]

On seeing Mrs Kemble in Yarico—
[C.W. p. 526]

On a lady [Jean Lorimer] requesting me to give her a sprig of
blossomed thorn—
[C.W. p. 534]

To the beautiful Miss Eliza J——n, on her principles of Liberty &
Equality—
[C.W. p. 336]

A Song.—Tune, My lodging is on the cold ground
My Chloris mark how green the groves,
[C.W. p. 531]

Peter Hill

Sir

I had intended to have troubled you with a long letter; but at present the delightful sensations of an omnipotent TOOTHACH so engross all my inner man, as to put it out of my power even to write Nonsense.—However, as in duty bound, I approach my BOOKSELLER with an offering in my hand—a few poetic Clinches & a song: to expect any other kind of offering from the Rhyming Tribe, would be to know them much less than you do.—I do not pretend that there is much merit in these Morceaux, but I have two reasons for sending them; primo, they are mostly ill-natured, so are in unison with my present feelings while fifty troops of infernal Spirits are riding post from ear to ear along my jaw-bones; & secondly, they are so short, that you cannot leave off in the middle, & so hurt my pride in the idea that you found any Work of mine too heavy to get through.—

I have a request to beg of you, & I not only beg of you, but conjure you—By all your Wishes & by all your HOPES, that the MUSE will spare the Satyric wink, in the moment of your foibles; that she will warble the song of rapture round your Hymeneal couch; & that she will shed on your turf the honest tear of Elegiac gratitude!—grant my request as speedily as possible.—Send me, by the very first Fly or Coach for this Place, three copies of the last edition of my Poems; which place to my account.—

Now, may the good things of Prose, & the good things of Verse, come among thy hands, untill they be filled with the good things of Life! prayeth.

R. Burns

XIX (686)

Dumfries, 29th January 1796

My dear Hill,

By the chaise, the driver of which brings you this, I send your *annual* KIPPER:—but on the express condition that you do not, like a fool as you were last year, put yourself to five-times the value in expence of a return.—

I have just time to beg that you will make my best Compliments to my fair friend, Mrs Hill; CAMERON, my kinsman; & RAMSAY, my yoke-fellow in the Lord! God be with you all!—In a week, or ten days, thou shalt hear *at large* from—

Thine—
R Burns

WILLIAM SCOTT

Partner in the firm of James and William Scott, bookbinders in Forrester's Wynd, Edinburgh who produced some of the finest bindings in late-eighteenth century Scotland. William Scott's name appears in the list of subscribers to the first Edinburgh Edition. The 1787 edition of the Poems was published by Creech in blue paper wrappers, and it was then left to individual purchasers to have their copies put into more permanent bindings of their own choice. Clearly Scott was entrusted with the binding of the copies which Burns had despatched to his own friends. Note also the use made of carriers, a system which, of course, survives to this day but, before the advent of the parcel post in 1883, afforded the only means for the transmission of books and other bulky packets.

I (109A)

Dunse, 24th May 1787

(Mr Scot,

As you have still some of the ordinary bound copies which I suppose are all ready, parcel up two of them each by itself, and seal them up. One of them direct to Miss Ainslie at Berrywell near Dunse, & send it by Dunse carrier, if possible this week as the Dunse carrier does not leave Edinburgh till Saturday morning early.—The other direct to Mr Gilbert Ker Farmer in Stodrigg near Kelso & send it by the Kelso carrier.—Paste the inclosed labels on the blank leaves or inside of the cover.—

I am your friend
Robt Burns

From what I have just now learnt you cannot get the parcels sent by this week's carrier, but do not fail the next opportunity.

R.B.

II (128)

Saturday morn [1787?]

Mr Scott,

Give the gentleman who delivers you this, Mr Richmond, my Small "on Ploughs."*

Robt Burns

* James Small: *A Treatise on Ploughs and Wheel Carriages*, (1794).

ROBERT AINSLIE

Born at Berrywell, near Duns, Berwickshire in 1766, the son of the steward of Lord Douglas's estates in that county, he was a pupil in Samuel Mitchelson's law office in Edinburgh when Burns first met him early in 1787. His happy-go-lucky outlook and his devotion to wine, woman and song rapidly endeared him to Burns, whom he accompanied on the first part of the Border tour in May of that year. At Eyemouth they were both made 'Royal Arch Masons' of the local masonic lodge, Ainslie being charged a guinea, although Burns was admitted gratis — this explains the term 'brother Arch' with which Burns opened his letter (II) of 25th June 1787. Ainslie had to get back to work in Edinburgh, so Burns had to continue his journey, over the Border and into northern England, alone. In a racy account of his travels (I) Burns conveys something of the contrast between the carefree company of Ainslie and the more sober-sided atmosphere he found in Northumberland. In a later letter (III) he clearly expresses how much he values Ainslie's friendship : 'I have not a friend upon earth besides yourself, to whom I can talk nonsense without forfeiting some degree of his esteem'. Ainslie seems to have had an uncanny knack of matching Burns's moods in all their ups and downs. Ainslie was one of the very few people with whom Burns never felt constrained to strike some kind of a pose, and consequently the letters are extremely candid and self-revealing. Ainslie was privy to the poet's affair with Mrs McLehose and was also the recipient of the notorious 'horse-litter' letter (VII). It was to Ainslie that Burns turned in July 1788 when he learned that May Cameron was pregnant and had lost her job. Burns asked Ainslie (IX) to sort out this mess for him, adding 'But don't for Heaven's sake meddle with her as a *Piece.*' Ainslie became a reformed character later in life, a Writer to the Signet, an elder of the Kirk and the author of pious homilies and religious works. Ferguson pithily comments 'His piety did not prevent his preserving, and allowing to be published, the most damaging of his former friend's letters.' Ainslie died in 1838.

I (110)

Newcastle, 29th May 1787

Mon cher Compagnon de voyage,

Here am I, a woeful wight on the banks of Tyne.—Old Mr Thomas Hood has been persuaded to join our Partie, and Mr Kerr & he do very well, but alas! I dare not talk nonsense lest I lose all the little dignity I have among the sober sons of wisdom & discretion, and I have not had one hearty mouthful of laughter since that merry-melancholy moment we parted.—

Mr Sherriff tired me to death; but as my good star directed Sir James Hall detained him on some business as he is Sir James's tenant, till near eleven at night, which time I spent with Miss —— till I was, in the language of the royal Voluptuary, Solomon, "Sick of Love!"*

Next morning, Sir James who had been informed by the Sherriffs of my Bardship's arrival, came to breakfast with us and carried me with him, and his charming Lady & he did me the honor to accompany me the whole forenoon through the glorious, romantic Deane of Dunglass.—I would not stay dinner; and when I returned to my horse, I found Miss —— ready equipp'd to escort me to Dunbar with the view of making a parade of me as a Sweetheart among her relations by the way & at Dunbar.—She was "bien poudré, bien frisé" in her fine cream-colored riding clothes, mounted on an old, dun carthorse that had once been fat; a broken, old side saddle, without crupper, stirrup or girth; a bridle that in former times had had buckles, and a crooked meandring hazle stick which might have borne a place with credit in a scrubbed besom.—In the words of the Highlandman when he saw the Deil on Shanter-hill in the shape of five swine—"My hair stood and my p— stood, and I swat & trembled."—Nothing could prevail with her, no distant insinuation,

327

no broad hint would make her give over her purpose; at last vexed, disgusted, enraged, to a high degree, I pretended a fire-haste and rode so hard that she was almost shaken to pieces on old Jolly, and, to my great joy found it convenient to stop at an uncle's house by the way: I refused to call with her, and so we quarreled & parted.—

You shall hear from me at Dumfries.—Farewell!

* Song of Solomon 2:5.

Robt Burns

II (116)

Arrochar, near Crocharibas, by Loch Loang
June 25th 1787

My dear Friend & brother Arch,

I write you this on my tour through a country where savage streams tumble over savage mountains, thinly overspread with savage flocks, which starvingly support as savage inhabitants. My last stage was Inverary—tomorrow night's stage, Dumbarton. I ought sooner to have answered your kind letter, but you know I am a man of many sins.

. . . the Devil's Day-book only April 14 or fifteen so cannot yet have increased her growth much. I begin, from that, and some other circumstances to suspect foul play; and to tell the truth I w . . .

III (122)

Mauchline, 23rd July 1787

My Dear Ainslie,

There is one thing for which I set great store by you as a friend, and it is this, that I have not a friend upon earth, besides yourself, to whom I can talk nonsense without forfeiting some degree of his esteem. Now, to one like me, who never cares for speaking any thing else but nonsense, such a friend as you is an invaluable treasure: I was never a rogue, but have been a fool all my life; and, in spite of all my endeavours, I see now plainly that I shall never be wise. Now it rejoices my heart to have met with such a fellow as you, who, though you are not just such a hopeless fool as I, yet I trust you will never listen so much to the temptations of the devil as to grow so very wise that you will in the least disrespect an honest fellow because he is a fool. In short, I have set you down as the staff of my old age, when the whole list of my friends will, after a decent share of pity, have forgot me.

> "Though in the morn comes sturt and strife,
> Yet joy may come at noon;
> And I hope to live a merry merry life,
> When a' thir days are gone."

Write me soon, were it but a few lines just to tell me how that good sagacious man your father is,—that kind dainty body your mother,— that strapping chield your brother Douglas—and my friend Rachel, who is as far before Rachel of old, as she was before her blear-eyed sister Leah.

R.B.

IV (122A)

Mauchline, 29th July 1787

Give you joy, give you joy, My dear brother! may your child be as strong a man as Samson, as wise a man as Solomon, & as honest a man as his father.– I have double health & spirits at the news.– Welcome, Sir, to the society, the venerable Society, of FATHERS!!!

> "L——s children are God's heritage;
>   The womb's fruit his reward;
> The sons of youth as arrows are
>   In strong men's hands prepar'd.–
>
> O, happy is the man that hath
>   His quiver fill'd with those!
> He unashamed in the gate
>   Shall speak unto his foes!'*

But truce, with the Psalmist! I shall certainly give you a congratulatory Poem on the birth day myself.–My ailing child is got better– and the Mother is certainly in for it again– and Peggy will bring a gallant half-Highlander– and I shall get a farm, and keep them all about my hand, and breed them in the fear of the Lord and an oakstick, and I shall be the happiest man upon earth–

> "Sing up wi't, Aily, Aily;
>   Down wi' kimmerland Jock:
> Deil ram their lugs quo' Willie,
>   But I hae scour'd her dock!"   Encore!

Take the following random verses to the tune of Black Joke–

> My girl she's airy, she's buxom and gay

[C.W. p. 82]

A letter I just now got from Creech's oblidges me to be in Edinburgh against this day, or tomorrow se'ennight, and then what a shaking of hands, and what coveys of *good things*, between you & I, I will call for you at Mitchelson's the moment I arrive–

> Then hey for a merry, good fellow;
>   And hey, for a glass of good strunt:
> May never WE SONS OF APOLLO
>   E'er want a good friend and a —

[C.W. p. 376]

Writing Sense is so damn'd, dry, hide-bound a business, I am determined never more to have any thing to do with it.–I have such an aversion to right line and method, that when I can't get over the hedges which bound the highway, I zig-zag across the road just to keep my hand in.–I am going to church, and will remember you in my prayers.–Farewel!

Robt Burns

---

* Metrical Psalms 127:3-5, slightly misquoted.

Robert Ainslie

V (130)

Edinburgh, 23rd August 1787

"As I gaed up to Dunse
"To warp a pickle yarn,
"Robin, silly body,
"He gat me wi' bairn."—

From henceforth, my dear Sir, I am determined to set off with my letters like the periodical Writers, viz. prefix a kind of text quoted from some Classic of undoubted authority, such as the Author of the immortal piece of which my text is a part.—What I have to say on my text is exhausted in a letter I wrote you the other day, before I had the pleasure of receiving yours from Inverleithing; and sure never was any thing more lucky; as I have but the time to write this, that Mr Nicol on the opposite side of the table takes to correct a proof-sheet of a thesis.—They are gabbling latin so loud that I cannot hear what my own soul is saying in my own scull, so must just give you a matter-of-fact sentence or two, and end if time permit with a verse de rei generatione.—

Tomorrow I leave Edinburgh in a chaise: Nicol thinks it more comfortable than horse-back, to which I say, Amen; so Jenny Geddes goes home to Ayr-shire, to use a phrase of my Mother's, "wi' her finger in her mouth."—

Now for a modest verse of classical authority:

"The cats like kitchen;
    The dogs like broo;
The lasses like the lads weel,
    And th' auld wives too.—

Chorus

An' we're a' noddin
    Nid, nid, noddin,
We're a' noddin fou at e'en.—"

If this does not please you, let me hear from you: if you write any time before the first of September direct to Inverness, to be left at the post Office till call'd for; the next week at Aberdeen; the next at Edinburgh.—The sheet is done, and I shall just conclude with assuring you that I am, and ever with pride shall be

My dear Sir,
Robt Burns

Call your boy what you think proper, only interject Burns.—What do you to a scripture name; for instance—

Zimri Burns Ainslie

or

Achithophel, &c., &c.—

look your bible for these two heroes.—If you do this, I will repay the Compliment.—

Robert Ainslie

VI (153)

Sunday morn
[25th November 1787]

I beg, my dear Sir, you would not make any appointment to take us to Mr Ainslie's tonight.—On looking over my engagements. constitution, present state of health, some little vexatious soul concerns, &c. I find I can't sup abroad tonight.—

I shall be in today till one o'clock.—If you have a leisure-hour, &c.—

You will think it romantic when I tell you that I find the idea of your friendship almost necessary to my existence.—You assume a proper length of face in my bitter hours of blue-devilism, and you laugh fully up to my highest wishes at my *good things*.—I don't know upon the whole if you are one of the first fellows in God's world, but you are so to me.—I tell you this just now in the conviction that some inequalities in my temper and manner may perhaps sometimes make you suspect that I am not so warmly as I ought to be

your friend
Robt Burns

VII (215)

Mauchline, 3rd March, 1788

My dear Friend,

I am just returned from Mr. Miller's farm. My old friend whom I took with me was highly pleased with the bargain, and advised me to accept of it. He is the most intelligent sensible farmer in the county, and his advice has staggered me a good deal. I have the two plans before me: I shall endeavour to balance them to the best of my judgment, and fix on the most eligible. On the whole, if I find Mr. Miller in the same favourable disposition as when I saw him last, I shall in all probability turn farmer.

I have been through sore tribulation and under much buffeting of the Wicked One since I came to this country. Jean I found banished, like a martyr—forlorn destitute and friendless: All for the good old cause. I have reconciled her to her fate, and I have reconciled her to her mother. I have reconciled her to her mother. I have taken her a room. I have taken her to my arms. I have given her a mahogany bed. I have given her a guinea, and I have f——d till she rejoiced with joy unspeakable and full of glory. But, as I always am on every occasion, I have been prudent and cautious to an astonishing degree. I swore her privately and solemnly never to attempt any claim on me as a husband, even though anybody should persuade her she had such a claim (which she had not), neither during my life nor after my death. She did all this like a good girl, and I took the opportunity of some dry horse litter, and gave her such a thundering scalade that electrified the very marrow of her bones. Oh, what a peacemaker is a guid weel-willy pintle! It is the mediator, the guarantee, the umpire, the bond of union, the solemn league and covenant, the plenipotentiary, the Aaron's rod, the Jacob's staff, the prophet Elisha's pot of oil, the Ahasuerus' Sceptre, the sword of

331

mercy, the philosopher's stone, the Horn of Plenty, and Tree of Life between Man and Woman.

I shall be in Edinburgh the middle of next week. My farming ideas I shall keep private till I see. I got a letter from Clarinda yesterday, and she tells me she has got no letter of mine but one. Tell her that I wrote to her from Glasgow, from Kilmarnock, from Mauchline, and yesterday from Cumnock, as I returned from Dumfries. Indeed she is the only person in Edinburgh I have written to till this day today. How are your soul and body putting up?—A little like man and wife, I suppose.

Your faithful friend,
R.B.

VIII (243)

Mauchline, 26th May 1788

My dear Friend,

I am two kind letters in your debt, but I have been from home & horridly busy, buying & preparing for that farming business; over & above the plague of my Excise Instructions which this week will finish.—

As I flatter my wishes that I foresee many future years' Correspondence between us, 'tis foolish to talk of excusing dull epistles: a dull letter may be a very kind one.—

I have the pleasure to tell you that I have been extremely fortunate in all my buyings and bargainings hitherto; Mrs Burns not excepted, which title I now avow to the World.—I am truly pleased with this last affair: it has indeed added to my anxieties for Futurity but it has given a stability to my mind & resolutions, unknown before; and the poor girl has the most sacred enthusiasm of attachment to me, and has not a wish but to gratify my every idea of her deportment.—

I am interrupted

Farewel My dear Sir!—
Robt Burns

Direct to me at Mauchline.

IX (246)

[Dumfries, about 1st June 1788]

My Dear friend,

My first welcome to this place was the inclosed letter.—I am very sorry for it, but what is done is done.—I pay you no compliment when I say that except my old friend Smith there is not any person in the world I would trust so far.—Please call at the James Hog mentioned, and send for the wench* and give her ten or twelve shillings, but don't for Heaven's sake meddle with her as a *Piece*.—I insist on this, on your honor; and advise her out to some country friends.—You may perhaps not like the business, but I just tax your friendship thus far.—Call for God sake, lest the poor soul be starving. —Ask her for a letter I wrote her just now, by way of token.—it is unsigned.—Write me after the meeting.—

Robt Burns

* May Cameron, who had written the 'inclosed letter' begging for help as she was jobless, destitute and 'in trouble'.

Robert Ainslie

X (248)

Ellisland, 14th June 1788

This is now the third day, My dearest Sir, that I have sojourned in these regions; and during these three days you have occupied more of my thoughts than in three weeks preceeding: in Ayr-shire I have several Variations of Friendship's Compass, here it points invariably to the Pole.—My Farm gives me a good many uncouth Cares & Anxieties, but I hate the language of Complaint.—Job, or some one of his friends, says well—"Why should a living man complain?"—*

What books are you reading, or what is the subject of your thoughts, besides the great studies of your Profession? You said something about Religion in your last, I don't exactly remember what it was, as the letter is in Ayrshire, but I thought it not only prettily said but nobly thought.—

Keep my old Direction "at Mauchline," till I inform myself of another.—Adieu¹

Robt Burns

* Lamentations 3 :39, slightly altered.

XI (249)

[June? 1788]

. . . I have lately been much mortified with contemplating an unlucky imperfection in the very framing and construction of my soul; namely, a blundering inaccuracy of her olfactory organs in hitting the scent of craft or design in my fellow creatures. I do not mean any compliment to my ingenuousness, or to hint that the defect is in consequence of the unsuspicious simplicity of conscious truth and honor: I take it to be, in some way or other an imperfection in the mental sight; or, metaphor apart, some modification of dulness. In two or three small instances lately, I have been most shamefully out.

I have all along, hitherto, in the warfare of life, been bred to arms among the light-horse—the piquet-guards of fancy; a kind of Hussars and Highlanders of the *Brain*; but I am firmly resolved to *sell out* of these giddy battalions, who have no ideas of a battle but fighting the foe, or of a siege but storming the town. Cost what it will, I am determined to buy in among the grave squadrons of heavy-armed thought, or the artillery corps of plodding contrivance.

You will make a noble fellow if once you were married. I make no reservation of your being *well*-married: You have so much sense, and knowledge of human nature, that though you may not realize perhaps the ideas of romance, yet you will never be *ill-married*.

Were it not for the terrors of my ticklish situation respecting provision for a family of children. I am decidedly of opinion that the step I have taken is vastly for my happiness. As it is, I look to the excise scheme as a certainty of maintenance; a maintenance, luxury to what either Mrs. Burns or I were born to.

Adieu.

Robert Ainslie

XII (250)

Mauchline, 23rd June 1788

This letter, my dear Sir, is only a business scrap.—Mr Miers, Profile painter in your own town, has executed a profile of Dr Blacklock for me; do me the favor to call for it, and sit to him yourself for me which put in the same size as the Doctor's: the amount of both profiles will be fifteen shillings which I have given to James Connel, our Mauchline Carrier, to pay you when you give him the parcel.— You must not, my friend, refuse to sit.—The time is short: when I sat to Mr Miers, I am sure he did not exceed two minutes.—I propose hanging Lord Glencairn, the Doctor & you, in trio, over my new chimney-piece that is to be.—Adieu!

Robt Burns

XIII (252)

Ellisland, 30th June 1788

My Dear Sir,

I just now received your brief Epistle; and to take vengeance on your laziness, I have you see taken a long sheet of writing paper, & begun at the top of the page, intending to scribble on to the very last corner.—I am vexed at that affair of the girl, but dare not enlarge on the subject until you send me your direction, as I suppose that will be altered on your late Master and Friend's death.—I am concerned for the old fellow's exit, only as I fear it may be to your disadvantage in any respect: for an old man's dying; except he have been a very benevolent character, or in some particular situation of life that the welfare of the Poor or the Helpless depended on him, I think it an event of the most trifling moment to the world.—Man is naturally a kind, benevolent animal, but he is dropt into such a damn'd needy situation here in this vexatious world, and has such a whoreson, hungry, growling, multiplying Pack of Necessities, Appetites, Passions & Desires about him, ready to devour him for want of other food; that in fact he must lay aside his cares for others that he may look properly to himself.—Every One, more or less, in the words of the old Scots Proverb, "Has his cods in a cloven stick, and maun wyse them out the best way he can."—

You have been imposed on in paying [*word missing*] Mr Miers for the profile of a Mr Hamilton.—I did not mention it in my letter to you, nor did I ever give Mr Miers any such order.—I went once indeed with young Hamilton of Bangour, to shew him some Profiles I was getting done for Mrs Blacklock, and he sat to Miers of his own accord to send it as he said to a sweetheart; but for my own part, I would as soon think of ordering a Profile of Tibby Nairn or Julie Rutherford as of such a contemptible puppy as H— I beg you will take the trouble to return the Profile to Mr Miers: I have no objection to lose the money, but I won't have any such Profile in my possession.—I desired the Carrier to pay you, but as I mentioned only 15sh. to him, I will rather inclose you a guinea note.—I have it not indeed to spare here, as I am only a sojourner in a strange land in this place; but in a day or two I return to Mauchline, and there I have the Bank-notes through the house like salt-Permits.—

There is a great degree of folly in talking unnecessarily of one's private affairs.—I have just now been interrupted by one of my new Neighbours, who has made himself absolutely contemptible in my eyes by his silly, garrulous pruriency.—I know it has been a fault of my own too; but from this moment I abjure it as I would the service of Hell! Your Poets, Spendthrifts, and other fools of that kidney, pretend forsooth to crack their jokes on Prudence; but 'tis a squalid Vagabond glorying in his rags.—Still, Imprudence respecting money-matters is much more pardonable than imprudence respecting character. I have no objection to prefer Prodigality to Avarice in some few instances; but I appeal to your observation if you have not met, & often met with the same little disengenuousness, the same hollow-hearted insincerity and disintegritive depravity of principle, in the hackneyed victims of Profusion as in the unfeeling children of Parsimony.—I have every possible reverence for the much-talk'd-of World beyond the Grave, and I wish that which Piety believes and Virtue deserves may be all matter of fact; but in things belonging to and terminating in this present Scene of Existence, man has serious and interesting business on hand.—Whether a man shall shake hands with Welcome in the distinguished elevation of Respect, or shrink from Contempt in the abject corner of Insignificance; Whether he shall wanton under the Tropic of Plenty, at least, enjoy himself in the comfortable latitudes of easy Convenience, or starve in the Artic circle of dreary Poverty; Whether he shall rise in the manly consciousness of a self-approving mind, or sink beneath a galling load of Regret & Remorse—these are alternatives of the last moment.—

You see how I preach.—You used occasionally to sermonize too; I wish you would in charity favor me with a little in your own way.—At any rate, write me with your convenience, to let me know your direction. I admire the close of a letter Lord Bolingbroke writes to Dean Swift, "Adieu, dear Swift! with all thy faults well I love thee; make an effort and love me with all mine."—Humble servant, & all that trumpetry, is now such a perversion, such a Sodomy of Language, that Honest friendship in her sincere way, must have recourse, to simple, Farewell!

P.S. I am a subscriber to Ainslie's large map of Scotland; if you are in the shop, please ask after the progress; and when published, secure me one of the earliest Impressions of the Plate.—Forgive me for all this trouble.—I seldom see a Newspaper, so do not know the state of Publications, the Stage, &c.

R.B.

XIV (266)

Mauchline, 23rd August 1788

I received your last, my dear friend, but I write you just now on a vexatious business.—

I don't know if ever I told you some very bad reports that Mrs McLehose once told me of Mr Nicol. I had mentioned the affair to Mr Cruikshank, in the course of conversation about our common friend, that a lady had said so & so, which I suspected had originated from some malevolence of Dr Adams.—* He had mentioned this story to Mr Nicol cursorily, & there it rested; till now, a prosecution has commenced between Dr A— & Mr N—, & Mr N— has press'd me over & over to give up the lady's name.—I have refused this; & last post Mr N— acquaints me, but in very good natured terms, that if I persist in my refusal, I am to be served with a summonds [*sic*] to compear & declare the fact.—

Heaven knows how I should proceed! I have this moment wrote Mrs Mc—se, telling her that I have informed you of the affair; & I shall write Mr Nicol by Tuesday's post that I will not give up my female friend till farther consideration; but that I have acquainted you with the business & the name; & that I have desired you to wait on him, which I intreat, my dear Sir, you will do; & give up the name or not, as Your & Mrs Mc—se's prudence shall suggest.—

I am vexed to the heart that Mr Ainslie has disappointed my brother: I grasp at your kind offer, & wish you to enquire for a place among the Saddler's shops. If I get him into a first rate shop, I will bind him a year or two, I almost do not care on what terms.—He is about eighteen; really very clever; & in what work he has seen, not a despicable tradesman; but I will have him a first rate hand if possible.—

Why trouble yourself about Hamilton? let me pay the expence, for I don't know where he is now to be found.—Dr Blacklock where he lodged, which caused me to meet with him; & Signior Dasti, Junr one of his greatest cronies, are the only intelligencers to whom I can refer you.—

Adieu! I am ever most cordially yours
Robt Burns

* Dr Alexander Adam, Rector of the High School, Edinburgh.

XV (279)

Dumfries, [16th October 1788]
[*Bishop mark* OC 18]

I am not entirely sure of my farm's doing well.—I hope for the best: but I have my Excise Commission in my pocket; I don't care three skips of a Cur-dog for the up-and-down gambols of Fortune.—

I am vexed at your seeming dispiritedness.—I am afraid somewhat is going cross with you.—The devil sometimes half whispers me, that you are wearying of an idle barren Correspondence.—

XVI (295)

Ellisland, 6th January 1789

Many happy returns of the season to you, my dear Sir! May you be comparatively happy up to your comparative Worth, among the sons of men; which wish would, I am sure, make you one of the most blest of the Human-race.—

I do not know if passing "a Writer to the Signet" be a trial of scientific merit, or a mere business of friends & interest.—However it be, let me quote you my two favorite passages, which, tho' I have repeated them ten thousand times, still they rouse my manhood &

steel my resolution like Inspiration—

> —On Reason build Resolve,
> That column of true majesty in man!

Young. [1]

> Hear, Alfred, hero of the State,
> Thy Genius Heaven's high will declare;
> The triumph of the truly great
> Is never, never to despair!
> Is never to despair!

Masque of Alfred. [2]

I grant you enter the lists of life, to struggle for bread, business, notice and distinction in common with hundreds.—But who are they? Men, like yourself: and of that aggregate body, your compeers, seven tenths of them come short of your advantages, natural & accidental; while two of those that remain either neglect their parts, as flowers blooming in a desert or mispend their strength, like a bull goring a bramble-bush.—

But to change the theme, I am still catering for Johnson's publication; and among others, I have brushed up the following old favorite Song a little, with a view to your worship.—I have only altered a word here & there; but if you like the humour of it, we shall think of a Stanza or two to add to it.—

O Robin sure in hairst,

[C.W. p. 348]

I shall be in town in about four or five weeks, & I must again trouble you to find & secure for me a direction where to find Jenny Clow, for a main part of my business in Edinburgh is to settle that matter with her, & free her hand of the process.—

I shall not be above two or three nights in town; but one of them I shall certainly devote to witness with how much esteem & affection I am,

My dear Friend, yours—
Robt Burns

1 *Night Thoughts*, Night I, lines 30-31.
2 Thomson: *Alfred: A Masque*, Act I, sc. 3.

XVII (347)

Ellisland, 8th June 1789

My dear Friend,

I am perfectly ashamed of myself when I look at the date of your last. It is not that I forget the friend of my heart and the companion of my peregrinations; but I have been condemned to drudgery beyond sufferance, though not, thank God, beyond redemption. I have had a collection of poems by a lady put into my hands to prepare them for the press; which horrid task, with sowing my corn with my own hand, a parcel of masons, wrights, plaisterers, &c. to attend to, roaming on business through Ayrshire—all this was against me, and the very first dreadful article was of itself too much for me.

13th. I have not had a moment to spare from incessant toil since the 8th. Life, my dear Sir, is a serious matter. You know by experience that a man's individual self is a good deal, but believe me, a wife and family of children, whenever you have the honor to be a husband and a father, will shew you that your present most anxious hours of solicitude are spent on trifles. The welfare of those who are very dear to us, whose only support, hope and stay we are—this, to a generous mind, is another sort of more important object of care than any concerns whatever which center merely in the individual. On the other hand, let no young, unmarried, rakehelly dog among you, make a song of his pretended liberty and freedom from care. If the relations we stand in to king, country, kindred, and friends, be any thing but the visionary fancies of dreaming metaphysicians; if religion, virtue, magnanimity, generosity, humanity and justice be aught but empty sounds; then the man who may be said to live only for others, for the beloved, honorable female whose tender faithful embrace endears life, and for the helpless little innocents who are to be the men and women, the worshippers of his God, the subjects of his king, and the support, nay the very vital existence of his COUNTRY, in the ensuing age;—compare such a man with any fellow whatever, who, whether he bustle and push in business among laborers, clerks, statesmen; or whether he roar and rant, and drink and sing in taverns—a fellow over whose grave no one will breathe a single heigh-ho, except from the cobweb-tie of what is called good fellowship—who has no view nor aim but what terminates in himself —if there be any grovelling earthborn wretch of our species, a renegado to common sense, who would fain believe that the noble creature, man, is no better than a sort of fungus, generated out of nothing, nobody knows how, and soon dissipating in nothing, nobody knows where; such a stupid beast, such a crawling reptile might balance the foregoing unexaggerated comparison, but no one else would have the patience.

Forgive me, my dear Sir, for this long silence. *To make you amends*, I shall send you soon, and more encouraging still, without any postage, one or two rhymes of my later manufacture.

XVIII (367)

Ellisland, 1st November 1789

My dear Friend

I had written you long ere now, could I have guessed where to find you; for I am sure you have more good sense than to waste the precious days of vacation time in the dirt of Business & Edinburgh.— Wherever you are, God bless you, & lead you not into temptation but deliver you from evil!

I do not know if I have informed you that I am now appointed to an Excise Division, in the middle of which my house & farm lie.—In this I was extremely lucky.—Without ever having been an Expectant, as they call their Journeymen Excisemen, I was directly planted down to all intents & purposes an officer of Excise, there to flourish & bring forth fruits—worthy of repentance.—I know how the word, Exciseman, or still more opprobrious, Gauger, will sound in your

ears.—I too have seen the day when my auditory nerves would have
felt very delicately on this subject, but a wife & children are things
which have a wonderful power in blunting these kind of sensations.—
Fifty pounds a year for life, & a provision for widows & orphans,
you will allow, is no bad settlement for a Poet.—For the ignominy of
the Profession, I have the encouragement which I once heard a
recruiting Sergeant give to a numerous if not a respectable audience
in the Streets of Kilmarnock—"Gentlemen, for your farther &
"better encouragement, I can assure you that our regiment is
"the most blackguard corps under the crown, and consequently
"with us an honest fellow has the surest chance for preferment."—

You need not doubt that I find several very unpleasant and
disagreable circumstances in my business; but I am tired with and
disgusted at the language of complaint against the evils of life.—
Human existence in the most favourable situations does not abound
with pleasures, and has its inconveniences and ills; capricious, foolish
Man mistakes these inconveniences & ills as if they were the peculiar
property of his particular situation; and hence that eternal fickleness
that love of change which has ruined & daily does ruin many a fine
fellow as well as many a Blockhead; and is almost without exception
a constant source of disappointment & misery.—

So far from being with my present lot, I earnestly pray the Great
Disposer of Events that it may never be worse, & I think I can lay
my hand on my heart and say, "I shall be content."

I long to hear from you how you go on—not so much in business as
in life. Are you pretty well satisfied with your own exertions, and
tolerably at ease in your internal reflections? 'Tis much to be a great
character as a lawyer, but beyond comparison more to be a great
character as a man. That you may be both the one and the other is
the earnest wish, and that you *will* be both is the firm persuasion of,

My dear Sir, &c.

XIX (482)

[Dumfries, November? 1791?]

My dear Ainslie,

Can you minister to a mind diseased?* Can you, amid the horrors of
penitence, regret, remorse, head-ache, nausea, and all the rest of the
d——d hounds of hell, that beset a poor wretch, who has been guilty
of the sin of drunkenness—can you speak peace to a troubled soul?

Miserable perdu that I am! I have tried every thing that used to
amuse me, but in vain: here must I sit, a monument of the vengeance
laid up in store for the wicked, slowly counting every chick of the
clock as it slowly—slowly, numbers over these lazy scoundrels of
hours, who, d——n them, are ranked up before me, every one at his
neighbour's backside, and every one with a burden of anguish on his
back, to pour on my devoted head—and there is none to pity me. My
wife scolds me! my business torments me, and my sins come staring
me in the face, every one telling a more bitter tale than his fellow.—
When I tell you even *** [bawdry?] has lost its power to please,
you will guess something of my hell within, and all around me.—I

Robert Ainslie

began *Elibanks and Elibraes,* but the stanzas fell unenjoyed and
unfinished from my listless tongue: at last I luckily thought of
reading over an old letter of yours that lay by me in my book-case,
and I felt something, for the first time since I opened my eyes, of
pleasurable existence.—Well—I begin to breathe a little, since I began
to write you. How are you, and what are you doing? How goes Law?
Apropos, for connexion's sake, do not address to me supervisor, for
that is an honour I cannot pretend to—I am on the list, as we call it,
for a supervisor, and will be called out by and by to act as one; but at
present I am a simple gauger, tho' t' other day I got an appointment
to an excise division of 25£ *per ann.* better than the rest. My present
income, down money, is 70£ *per ann.*

* * * * *

I have one or two good fellows here whom you would be glad to
know . . .

* Shakespeare: *Macbeth*, Act V, sc. 3, altered.

XX (561)

[26th April 1793]

I am damnably out of humour, my dear Ainslie, & that is the reason
why I take up the pen to *you*: 'tis the nearest way, (probatum est)
to recover my spirits again.—

I received your last, & was much entertained with it; but I will not at
this time, nor at any other time, answer it.—Answer a letter? I never
could answer a letter in my life!—I have written many a letter in
return for letters I have received; but then—they were original matter
—spurt—away! zig, here; zag, there; as if the Devil that, my grannie
(an old woman *indeed!*) often told me, rode on Will-o'-wisp, or, in
her more classic phrase, SPUNKIE, were looking over my elbow.—
A happy thought that idea has ingendered in my head! SPUNKIE—
thou shalt henceforth be my Symbol, Signature, & Tutelary Genius!
Like thee, hap-step-&-lowp, here-awa-there-awa, higglety-pigglety,
pell-mell, hither-&-yon, ram-stam, happy-go-lucky, up-tails-a'-by-the-
light-o'-the-moon, has been, is, & shall be, my progress through the
mosses & moors of this vile, bleak, barren wilderness of a life of
ours.—

Come, then, my guardian Spirit! like thee, may I skip away, amusing
myself by & at my own light: and if any opaque-souled lubber of
mankind complain that my elfine, lambent, glimmerous wanderings
have misled his stupid steps over precipices, or into bogs; let the
thick-headed blunderbuss recollect, that he is not SPUNKIE—that

> "SPUNKIE'S wanderings could not copied be;
> Amid these perils none durst walk but he"*

I feel myself vastly better.—I give you friendly joy of Robie Waters'
brother.—'Twas a happy thought, his begetting him against a *Book
press.*—No doubt, as you with equal sagacity & science remark, it
will have an astonishing effect on the young BOOK-WORM'S head-
piece. I have no doubt but your Scholarcraft may be caught, as a
Scotsman catches the itch, by friction.—How else can you account

340

for it, that born blockheads, by mere dint of *handling* books, grow so wise that even they themselves are equally convinced of & surprised at their own parts?—I once carried this Philosophy to that degree that in a knot of Country folks who had a library amongst them, and who, to the honor of their good sense, made me Factotum in the business, one of our members, a little, wise-looking, squat, upright, jabbering body of a Taylor, I advised him, instead of turning over the leaves, *to bind the book on his back.*—Johnie took the hint; and as our meetings were every fourth saturday, & Prick-Louse having a good Scots mile to walk in coming, &, of course, another in returning, BODKIN was sure to lay his hand on some heavy Quarto, or ponderous Folio, with & under which, wrapt up in his grey plaid, he grew wise as he grew weary all the way home.—He carried this so far, that an old, musty Hebrew Concordance, which we had in a present from a neighbouring Priest, by mere dint of applying it as doctors do a blistering plaister, between his shoulders, STITCH, in a dozen pilgrimages, acquired as much *rational* Theology as the said priest had done by forty years perusal of the pages.—

Tell me and tell me truly what you think of this theory.—

yours—
SPUNKIE

* Dryden: *Prologue to The Tempest* (paraphrased).

WILLIAM NICOL

Son of a tailor in Ecclefechan, he was born in 1744 at Dumbretton in the parish of Annan. His father died when he was very young, and he received his early education from an itinerant teacher, John Orr. While still a teenager he established an elementary school in his mother's house, but later he managed to attend classes at Annan Academy before going to Edinburgh University. At first he studied for the ministry but then switched to medicine. In 1774 he took part in an open competition for the position of classics master at the High School of Edinburgh and having won he remained in that post till 1795. After a violent quarrel with the rector, Dr Alexander Adam, he founded a school of his own and ran it successfully until his death two years later. Nicol was a man of undoubted ability, energy and drive, but these admirable qualities were balanced by vanity and irascibility. Lord Cockburn, in *Memorial of his Times*, describes his schooldays, when he was a pupil of Nicol's: 'Unacquainted with the nature of youth. . . he had nothing for it but to drive them: and this he did by constant and indiscriminate harshness. The efforts of this were very hurtful to all his pupils. Out of the whole four years of my attendance there were probably not ten days in which I was not flogged, at least once. . .'

Despite his uncertain temper, Nicol enjoyed convivial company and it was this that probably brought him and Burns together. It is not known how or when they first met, some time early in 1787, but the friendship was sufficiently well advanced for Nicol to be the recipient of a letter (I) from Carlisle during the Border tour, addressed to 'Kind, honest-hearted Willie' - the only extant letter written by Burns in the vernacular. Nicol accompanied Burns on the Highland tour which began on 25th August 1787, but their friendship was sorely tried by Nicol's tiresome and unreasonable behaviour. Burns bore Nicol's tantrums with considerable equanimity, even though he was greatly embarrassed at times. Some laconic entries in the journal of the Highland tour, and the apologetic letter to James Hoy (see page 361) give some inkling of the strain on the relationship. Nevertheless, Burns and Nicol remained on good terms and a desultory correspondence continued till 1793 at least. The last extant letter which can be accurately dated (IX) shows Burns in brilliantly flippant mood, in response to Nicol's advice to temper his views to the political climate then prevailing.

Burns named his second surviving son William Nicol in 1791, telling George Thomson in May 1795 (see page 674) of 'that propensity to witty wickedness and manfu' mischief, which even at twa days auld I foresaw would form the striking features of his disposition'.

I (112)

Carlisle 1st June 1787—or
I believe the 39th o' May rather

Kind, honest-hearted Willie,

I'm sitten down here, after seven and forty miles ridin, e'en as forjesket and forniaw'd as a forfoughten cock, to gie	exhausted, worn out
you some notion o' my landlowper-like stravaguin sin the sorrowfu' hour that I	vagrant roaming
sheuk hands and parted wi' auld Reekie.—	
My auld, ga'd Gleyde o' a meere has huchyall'd up hill and down brae, in Scotland	galled, hawk, mare, tottered
and England, as teugh and birnie as a	rough-tempered
vera devil wi' me.—It's true, she's as poor's a Sang-maker and as hard's a kirk, and	
tipper-taipers when she taks the gate first	teeters
like a Lady's gentlewoman in a minuet or a hen on a het girdle, but she's a yauld,	griddle, alert, dusty.
poutherie Girran for a' that; and has a	pony.
stomach like Willie Stalker's meere that wad hae digeested tumbler-wheels, for	cartwheels
she'll whip me aff her five stimparts o'	quarts
the best aits at a down-sittin and ne'er	oats,
fash her thumb.—When ance her ring-	trouble
banes and spavies, her crucks and cramps,	spavins, limps

342

William Nicol

are fairly soupl'd, she beets to, beets to, and ay the hindmost hour the tightest.— *submissive, accelerates*

I could wager her price to a thretty pennies that, for twa or three wooks ridin at fifty mile a day, the deil-sticket a five gallopers acqueesh Clyde and Whithorn could cast saut in her tail.— *thirty* / *devil-botched* / *between* / *salt*

I hae daunder'd owre a' the kintra frae Dumbar to Selcraig, and hae forgather'd wi' monie a guid fallow and monie a weel-far'd hizzie.—I met wi' twa dink quines in particular, ane o' them a sonsie, fine, fodgel lass, baith braw and bonie; the tither was a clean-shankit, straught, tight, weel-far'd winch, as blythe's a lintwhite on a flowrie thorn, and as sweet and modest's a new blawn plumrose in a hazle shaw.—They were baith bred to mainers by the beuk, and onie ane o them has as muckle smeddum and rumble-gumtion as the half o' some Presbytries that you and I baith ken.—They play'd sik a deevil o' a shavie that I daur say if my harigals were turn'd out, ye wad see twa nicks i' the heart o' me like the mark o' a kail-whittle in a castock.— *saundered, country* / *handsome hussy, trim girls* / *buxom* / *plump, fine* / *clean-limbed, straight* / *linnet* / *primrose* / *much spirit, commonsense* / *trick* / *entrails* / *knife cabbage-stem*

I was gaun to write you a lang pystle, but, Gude forgie me, I gat myself sae notouriously bitchify'd the day after kail-time that I can hardly stoiter but and ben.— *epistle* / *God* / *drunk* / *stagger out and in*

My best respecks to the guidwife and a' our common friens, especiall Mr & Mrs Cruikshank* and the honest Guidman o' Jock's Lodge.—

I'll be in Dumfries the morn gif the beast be to the fore and the branks bide hale.— *if* / *intact harness remains*

Gude be wi' you, Willie! Amen——
Robt Burns

* William Cruikshank (see page 359).

II (114)

Mauchline, 18th June 1787

My dear friend,

I am now arrived safe in my native country after a very agreable jaunt; and have the pleasure to find all my friends well.—I breakfasted with your gray-headed, reverend friend Mr Smith; and was highly pleased both with the cordial welcome he gave me, and his most respectable appearance & sterling good sense.—

William Nicol

I have been with Mr Miller at Dalswinton, and am to meet him again in August.—From my view of the lands and his reception of my Bardship, my hopes in that business are rather mended; but still they are but slender.—

I am quite charmed with Dumfries folks.—Mr Burnside the Clergyman, in particular, is a man whom I shall ever gratefully remember; and his wife, Gude forgie me, I had almost broke the tenth commandment on her account.—Simplicity, elegance, good sense, sweetness of disposition, good humour, kind hospitality, are the constituents of her manner and heart; in short—but if I say one word more about her, I shall be directly in love with her.—

I never, My friend, thought mankind very capable of any thing generous; but the stateliness of the Patricians in Edinburgh, and the damn'd servility of my plebeian brethren, who perhaps formerly eyed me askance, since I returned home, have nearly put me out of conceit altogether with my species.—I have bought a pocket Milton which I carry perpetually about with me, in order to study the sentiments—the dauntless magnanimity; the intrepid, unyielding independance; the desperate daring, and noble defiance of hardship, in that great Personage, Satan.—'Tis true, I have just now a little cash; but I am afraid the damn'd star that hitherto has shed its malignant, purposeblasting rays full in my zenith; that noxious Planet so baneful in its influences to the rhyming tribe, I much dread it is not yet beneath my horizon. Misfortune dodges the path of human life; the poetic mind finds itself miserably deranged in, and unfit for the walks of business; add to all, that, thoughtless follies and hare-brained whims, like so many Ignes fatui, eternally diverging from the right line of sober discretion, sparkle with step-bewitching blaze in the idlygazing eyes of the poor heedless Bard, till, pop, "he falls like Lucifer, never to hope again." [1]—God grant this may be an unreal picture with respect to me! but should it not, I have very little dependance on mandkind.—I will close my letter with this tribute my heart bids me pay you—the many ties of acquaintance & friendship which I have, or think I have in life, I have felt along the lines and, damn them! they are almost all of them of such frail contexture, that I am sure they would not stand the breath of the least adverse breeze of Fortune; but from you, My ever dear Sir, I look with confidence for the Apostolic love that shall wait on me "Through good report & bad report" [2] —the love which Solomon emphatically says "Is strong as Death." [3] —My Compliments to Mrs Nicol, & all the circle of our common friends.—

Robt Burns

P.S. I shall be in Edinburgh about the latter end of July.—

R.B.

1 Shakespeare: *Henry VIII*, Act III, sc. 2.
2 2 Corinthians 6 :8, misquoted.
3 Song of Solomon 8 :6.

William Nicol

III (123)

Mauchline, 29th July 1787
[*Bishop mark AU 1*]

My dear Friend,

how oft I have written you since I left Edinburgh I know not, but I know I have never once heard from you.—A lingering indisposition has hung about me for some time and has beaten me out of the use of pen and ink, otherwise you should have had letters from me as long as my arm.—A letter from Creech's I just now received oblidges me to be in Edinburgh against this day or tomorrow se'ennight, though my stay will be but a few days.—If you do not leave the town immediately at the commencement of the vacation, I hope to have the heart-felt pleasure of once more meeting a friend to whom I owe so much, and for whom I have so high an esteem.—I had promised to lodge with our common friend Mr Cruikshank, but I know it will be quite inconvenient as he will be leaving town in this your precious hour of rest.—My Compliments to Mrs Nicol, Mr & Mrs Cruikshank, the worthy Farmer at Jock's Lodge, and all our common friends.—

I am ever My dear Sir, yours most sincerely
Robt Burns

IV (141)

Auchtertyre, Monday. [8th October 1787]

My dear Sir,

I find myself very comfortable here, neither oppressed by ceremony nor mortified by neglect.—Lady Augusta is a most engaging woman, and very happy in her family, which makes one's outgoings and incomings very agreable.—I called at Mr Ramsay's of Ochtertyre as I came up the country, and am so delighted with him that I shall certainly accept of his invitation to spend a day or two with him as I return.—I leave this place on wednesday or thursday.—

Make my kindest compliments to Mr & Mrs Cruikshank and Mrs Nicol is she is returned.—

I am ever, Dear Sir, your deeply indebted
Robert Burns

V (222A)

Mauchline, 8th March 1788

My dear Sir,

My life, since I saw you last has been one continued hurry.—That savage hospitality which knocks a man down with strong liquors, is the devil and all.—I have a sore warfare in this world! The Devil, the World and the Flesh, are three formidable foes. The first, I generally try to fly from; the second, Alas! generally flies from me; but the third is my plague, worse than the ten plagues of Egypt.—

I have been looking over several farms in the Country: one in particular in Nithsdale pleased me so well, that if my offer to the Proprietor is accepted, I shall commence Farmer at Whitsunday, if farming do not appear eligible, I shall have recourse to my other shift—but this to a friend.—

I set out for Edinburgh, Monday morning.—How long I stay there, is uncertain; but you will know so soon as I can inform you myself However I determine, Poesy must be laid aside for some time: my mind has been vitiated with Idleness, and it will take a good deal of effort to habituate it to the routine of business.—

I am ever, My dear Sir, yours sincerely,
Robt Burns

VI (375)

Ellisland, Sunday morning
[13th December? 1789]

I have been so ill, my ever dear Friend, that I have not been able to go over the threshold of my door since I saw you.—As I could not see & inspect Laggan farm personally, I have sent for two friends of mine that know it well, and on whose judgement of land I could depend very far, & from what they inform me, I think you have every reason to proceed in your purchase.—One of my friends says it will without a doubt bring Seventy guineas of rent; and as he is a plain intelligent country farmer, I like *his* decision on the business.—The other says that if it is bought under seventeen hundred pounds it is by no means too dear.—

Now for your unfortunate old mare.—Ihave tried many dealers for her, & I am ashamed to say that the highest offer I have got for her, is fifty shillings.—However, I tried her yesterday in the Plough, & I find the poor creature is extremely willing to do what she can, so I hope to make her worth her meat to me, untill I can try her, at some fair.—

I can no more.—I hope this will find your remaining family in health & better spirits than,

My dear Sir,
your miserable humble oblidged friend
Robt Burns

My warmest most respectful Compliments to Mrs Nicol.—

R.B.

VII (390)

Ellisland, 9th February 1790

My dear Sir,

That damned mare of yours is dead. I would freely have given her price to have saved her: she has vexed me beyond description. Indebted as I was to your goodness beyond what I can ever repay, I eagerly grasped at your offer to have the mare with me. That I might at least shew my readiness in wishing to be grateful, I took every care of her in my power. She was never crossed for riding above half a score of times by me or in my keeping. I drew her in the plough, one of three, for one poor week. I refused fifty-five shillings for her, which was the highest bode I could squeeze for her. I fed her up and had her in fine order for Dumfries fair; when four or five days before the fair, she was seized with an unaccountable disorder in the sinews, or somewhere in the bones of the neck; with a weakness or total want of power in her fillets, and in short the whole vertebrae of her spine seemed to be diseased and unhinged, and in eight and forty hours, in spite of the two best farriers in the country, she died and be d-mned to her! The farriers said that she had been quite strained in the fillets beyond cure before you had bought her, and that the poor devil, though she might keep a little flesh, had been jaded and quite worn out with fatigue and oppression. While she was with me, she was under my own eye, and I assure you, my much valued friend, every thing was done for her that could be done; and the accident has vexed me to the heart. In fact I could not pluck up spirits to write you, on account of the unfortunate business.

There is little new in this country. Our theatrical company, of which you must have heard, leave us in a week. Their merit and character are indeed very great, both on the stage and in private life; not a worthless creature among them; and their encouragement has been accordingly. Their usual run is from eighteen to twenty-five pounds a night; seldom less than the one, and the house will hold no more than the other. There have been repeated instances of sending away six, and eight, and ten pounds in a night for want of room. A new theatre is to be built by subscription; the first stone is to be laid on Friday first to come. Three hundred guineas have been raised by thirty subscribers, and thirty more might have been got if wanted. The manager, Mr Sutherland, was introduced to me by a friend from Ayr; and a worthier or cleverer fellow I have rarely met with. Some of our clergy have slipt in by stealth now and then; but they have got up a farce of their own. You must have heard how the Rev. Mr. Lawson of Kirkmahoe, seconded by the Rev. Mr. Kirkpatrick of Dunscore, and the rest of that faction, have accused in formal process, the unfortunate and Rev. Mr. Heron of Kirkgunzeon, that in ordaining Mr. Nelson to the cure of souls in Kirkbean, he, the said Heron, feloniously and treasonably bound the said Nelson to the confession of faith, *so far as it was agreeable to reason and the word of God!*

Mrs. B. begs to be remembered most gratefully to you. Little Bobby and Frank are charmingly well and healthy. I am jaded to death with fatigue. For these two or three months, on an average, I have not ridden less than two hundred miles per week. I have done little in the poetic way. I have given Mr. Sutherland two Prologues; one of which was delivered last week. I have likewise strung four or five barbarous stanzas, to the tune of Chevy Chase, by way of Elegy on your poor unfortunate mare, beginning the name she got here was Peg Nicholson)

> Peg Nicholson was a good bay mare,
> As ever trod on airn;
> Bur now she's floating down the Nith,
> And past the Mouth o' Cairn.

[C.W. p. 380]

William Nicol

My best compliments to Mrs. Nicol, and little Neddy, and all the family. I hope Ned is a good scholar, and will come out to gather nuts and apples with me next harvest.

> I am ever, my dearest Friend, yours,
> Robt Burns

VIII (398A)

28th May 1790

My ever dear Sir

I was on Laggan yesterday.—I had provided myself with a phial of Spirit of Salt, & a man who is the best judge of limestone in the Country.—A gentleman, brotherinlaw to the present Tenant was also with me.—The herd shewed me where he suspected the limestone, which is by the side of, & along the burn that runs down through the farm.—The man whom I had hired along with me was puzzled what to think.—He could not imagine that limestone could be found among whinstone rocks, but we certainly found a species of stone all along the burn, sometimes in thick Strata & sometimes in loose pieces, which effervesced, & in several instances pretty strongly with the acid.—It is very unlike most of the limestone in this Country, but I have seen much limestone in Ayr-shire of the same color.—I send in a servant this evening to Dumfries with a bundle containing seven different samples of the stone, to get it transmitted to you by the first Edinburgh Fly.—You will forgive this additional expence for I was afraid to trust the drunken uncertainty of a Stupid Carrier.—I do not pretend to say that the samples will burn to lime.—They are only the shattered, weather-beaten, outside chips of rocks, which, as they evidently betray some thing calcareous in their composition, may in all probability lie over limestone.—One thing is certain; the next adjoining farm, which has a name beginning with, "Brecken"-side—I think it is, & which is just a continuation of your field, does, as I am positively assured, contain lime.—

As to the farm itself, it is a most beautiful one, & in my opinion, as well the whole neighbourhood's opinion, is an exceeding cheap purchase.—

The servant will be late & I can no more.—My best Compliments, in which MY RIB desires to join me, to Mrs Nicol & family.—I expect little Neddy is a good boy, & that I shall have him here to gather apples & nuts against harvest.—

The Parcel is directed to the care of Peter Hill, as I don't know your street.—

Adieu!

> yours ever gratefully
> Robt Burns

I have just burnt a bit of the stone & though it does not offer to crumble like lime, its effervescence is vastly increased.—

R.B.

William Nicol

IX (460A)

[Mauchline, 21st June? 1791]

. . . I propose it as an annual tribute which, my dearest Sir, you must allow me to tax myself with, while I am a Farmer.—My best Compliments to Mrs Nicol, little Ned and all the family.—Would to God, Sir, that instead of this lame dull epistle, I could send you a transcript of my glowing heart . . . I think of you, Louis Cauvin* [*one or two words missing*] ble. Except [*word missing*] the general doctrine of Original Sin, remember me to him.—Mr Vair, too, please give him my Compliments.

* Burns's French tutor.

X (537)

[20th February 1793]

As my friend Nicol, though one of the worthiest, & positively the cleverest fellow I ever knew, yet no man, in his humours, having gone greater lengths in imprudence, unholiness, &c. than he; I wrote him as follows.—(*Burns's headnote in Glenriddell MS.*)

O thou, wisest among the Wise, meridian blaze of Prudence, full-moon of Discretion, & Chief of man Counsellors!—How, infinitely is thy puddle-headed, rattle-headed, wrong-headed, round-headed slave indebted to thy supereminent goodness, that from the luminous path of thy own right-lined rectitude, thou lookest benignly down on an erring Wretch, of whom the zig-zag wanderings defy all the powers of Calculation, from the simple copulation of Units up to the hidden mystery of Fluxions! May one feeble ray of that light of wisdom which darts from thy sensorium, straight as the arrow of Heaven against the head of the Unrighteous, & bright as the meteor of inspiration descending on the holy & undefiled Priesthood —may it be my portion; so that I may be less unworthy of the face & favour of that father of Proverbs & master of Maxims, that antipode of Folly & magnet among the Sages, the wise & witty Willie Nicol! Amen! Amen! Yea, so be it! ! !

For me, I am a beast, a reptile, & know nothing.—From the cave of my ignorance, amid the fogs of my dulness & pestilential fumes of my Political heresies, I look up to thee, as doth a toad through the iron-barred lucarne of a pestiferous dungeon to the cloudless glory of a summer sun!—Sorely sighing in bitterness of soul, I say, when shall my name be the quotation of the Wise, & my countenance be the delight of the Godly, like the illustrious lord of Laggan's* many hills?—As for him, his works are perfect: never did the pen of Calumny blur the fair page of his reputation, nor the bolt of Hatred fly at his dwelling.—At his approach is the standing up of men, even the Chief & the Ruler; & before his presence the frail form of lovely Woman, humbly awaiting his pleasure, is extended on the dust.— Thou mirror of purity, when shall the elfine lamp of my glimmerous understanding, purged from sensual appetites & gross desires, shine like the constellation of thy intellectual powers? As for thee, thy thoughts are pure, & thy lips are holy.—Never did the unhallowed breath of the Powers of darkness & the pleasures of darkness, pollute

William Nicol

the sacred flame of the sky-descended, & heavenward-bound desires:
never did the vapours of impurity stain the unclouded serene of thy
cerulean imagination.—O, that like thine were the tenor of my life,
like thine the tenor of my conversation! Then should no friend fear
for my strength, no enemy rejoice in my weakness!Then should I lie
down, & rise up, & none to make me afraid!—

May thy pity & thy prayer be exercised for,—
O thou lamp of Wisdom & mirror of Morality!
Thy devoted slave—
RB

* A small estate of his—[*Burns's note*].

XI (712)

[1787-96]

[conclusion]

O Mr Nicol, can Time ever extinguish the glowing remembrance of
you in my bosom! The idea of your uncommon abilities may
dissipate a little in comparison, but where, except surrounding the
Fountain of Goodness, shall I find a heart to equal yours!

Adieu!
Robt Burns

MR WILL . . .

The following fragment was written by Burns from Mossgiel on 2nd July 1787. The manuscript, which was in the Gribbel Collection, was badly mutilated and only the opening sentence is more or less intact. It was addressed to a gentleman whose first name was William, but so many correspondents of this period exist with that Christian name - Nicol, Niven, Creech, Cruikshank, Parker, Dunbar, Craik, Reid, Tennant, Stewart and Smellie - that it is quite impossible to hazard a guess as to the identity of the addressee. The letter was sent with a copy of *A Poet's Welcome to his Love-Begotten Daughter* (C.W. p. 112). The present location of the manuscript is unknown.

(118)

Mossgiel, 2nd July 1787

My dear Sir,

the above is the Poem I promised you, and much good may it do you! I owe it to my much esteemed friend to send him a copy of it.—

My brother, Rog[   ] sometime in Nov[ember   ]
minate himself [   ]-stance cannot aid [   ]
best advice will ever be at the command of

My dear Sir, yours sincerely
Robt Burns

LODGE ST JAMES KILWINNING NO. 135 TARBOLTON

Formerly amalgamated with Lodge St David on 25th June 1781, this lodge broke away on 8th July 1782 and was reconstituted as a separate masonic lodge, number 135. Burns was initiated into the masonic movement on 4th July 1781, at the age of 22, and passed and raised on 1st October 1781. Although he was the first freemason inducted into the joint lodge, he left St David for St James at the time of the secession the following year. On 27th July 1784 he was elected Depute Master, a position which he held until 1788. In this capacity Burns presided over many meetings of the lodge, and several of the minutes are preserved in his handwriting. The lodge met in the inn kept by James Manson, to whose care the following letter was addressed. Manson's inn, on the east side of Burns Street at the junction with Garden Street, was demolished some years ago, but its site is indicated by a plaque mounted, on a pillar in the garden of the house now erected on that spot. Manson himself was referred to in Burns's poem *To Dr Mackenzie, Mauchline* (C.W. p. 237). Lodge St James itself was the subject of *The Farewell* (C.W. p. 237-8), thought to have been composed for the meeting on 24th June 1786, well before the publication of the Kilmarnock Edition, when Burns was still set on emigrating to Jamaica.

(129)

Edinburgh, 23rd August 1787

MEN & BRETHREN,

I am truly sorry it is not in my power to be at your quarterly meeting.—If I must be absent in body, beleive me I shall be present in spirit. I suppose those who owe us monies by bill or otherwise will appear; I mean those we summoned.—If you please, I wish you would delay prosecuting defaulters till I come home.—The Court is up, and I will be home before it sits down. In the mean time, to take a note of who appear and who do not of our faulty debtors will be right in my humble opinion; and those who confess debt and crave days, I think we should spare them.—Farewell!

Within your dear Mansion may wayward Contention
    Or withered Envy ne'er enter!
May Secrecy round be the mystical bound,
    And brotherly Love be the Center!!!

Robt Burns

ROBERT AINSLIE

REV. JOHN SKINNER

WILLIAM INGLIS

Born in 1747 in Inverness, he became a merchant and banker as well as the foremost and best-remembered of that burgh's civic heads. He became Burgh Treasurer in 1775, a bailie in 1780 and provost in 1797. He retired from office in 1800 and died in February 1801. His most lasting achievement was the foundation of the Northern Infirmary which he laboured for many years to initiate. Many of the fine public buildings in Inverness dating from the late-eighteenth century were established by him and for upwards of 30 years he was the chief promoter of all the improvements in the town. He is chiefly remembered, however, for having extended hospitality to Burns at his home, Kingsmills House, during the Highland tour. Burns dined with the Inglis family on Wednesday 5th September, as an inscription in the lobby of Kingsmills House (now an hotel) testifies to this day.

Ettles Hotel where Burns lodged, may have been the hotel erected in 1776 by the two Masonic Lodges, John Ettles being the resident manager. It was renamed the Caledonian Hotel in 1825.

(133)

Ettles Hotel, Tuesday Evening [4th September 1787]

Mr. Burns presents his most respectful compliments to Mr. Inglis—would have waited on him with the inclosed, but is jaded to death with the fatigue of to-day's journey—won't leave Inverness till Thursday morning.

JOSIAH WALKER

Born in 1761, the youngest son of the Rev. Thomas Walker of Dundonald, Ayrshire by his third wife, Anne Shaw, he graduated from Edinburgh University in 1780. He taught privately in Edinburgh till 1787 when he became tutor to the Marquis of Tullibardine, nine year-old son of the fifth Duke of Atholl. Later he accompanied the boy to Eton and lived with him there until the young Marquis died in 1796. An Edinburgh friend wrote to Walker in 1787 at Blair Atholl, Perthshire, telling him of the latest literary sensation and promising to bring him a copy of the Poems on his next visit. Walker records that his expectations were 'very moderately excited' at this and goes on; 'I instantly classed the poetical ploughman with the poetical milkmaids and thrashers of England, of whose productions I was no violent admirer. . .' When he actually read the Poems, however, Walker 'experienced emotions of surprise and delight of which I had never been so conscious before. . . On every page the stamp of genius was impressed.'
Walker subsequently met Burns in Edinburgh, and later at Blair Atholl during the Highland tour. The latter occasion resulted in the two letters now extant. Walker admits that 'The language that I had begun to despise, as fit for nothing but colloquial vulgarity, seemed to be transfigured by the sorcery of genius', but this did not deter him from offering his criticism of Burns's use of the vernacular, criticism which Burns (II) patiently refuted. Walker visited Burns at Dumfries in November 1795, shortly before the poet was assailed by that period of prolonged illness that culminated in his death. On the basis of these three brief meetings Walker compiled a critical memoir as a preface to the 1811 edition of the Poems. Though not without some shrewd observations, the general tone of this memoir is one of condescension. Walker's anecdote of Burns in the Globe Inn rattling off epigrams and dogmatising on this and that between calling for more drinks may be explained by the poet's deteriorating health at the time, but Ferguson trenchantly hypothesises 'that Burns's abrupt and decisive manner was due to irritation at being patronised by an ass.' The full text of Walker's memoir may be found in Maurice Lindsay's Encyclopaedia (1980 edition), pp.368-70. Walker later became Collector of Customs at Perth and edited the Perth Courier for a time. In 1815 he was appointed Professor of Humanity at Glasgow University and died in 1831.

I (135)

Inverness, 5th September 1787

[With *The humble petition of Bruar Water.*]

[C.W. p. 290]

My dear Sir,

I have just time to write the foregoing, and to tell you that it was, at least most part of it, the effusion of the half hour that I spent at Bruar.—I don't mean it was extempore, for I have endeavoured to brush it up as well as Mr Nicol's chat and the jogging of the chaise would allow.—It eases my heart a good deal, as Rhyme is the coin with which a Poet pays his debts of honor or gratitude: what I owe to the noble Family of Athole of the first kind, I shall ever proudly boast; what I owe of the last, so help me God in my hour of need! I shall never forget!—

The little angel band, I declare I prayed for them very sincerely today at the falls of Fyars: you know from experience the bedlam warmth of a Poet's heart.—I shall never forget the fine family piece I saw at Blair; the amiable, the truly noble Dutchess with her smiling little seraph in her lap, at the head of her table; the lovely "olive plants," as the Hebrew Bard finely says, * round the happy mother; the beautiful Mrs Graham: the lovely, sweet Miss Cathcart, &c. I wish I had the powers of Guido [Reni?] to do them justice! My lord Duke's kind hospitality, markedly kind indeed; Mr Graham of Fintrie's charms of conversation; Sir William Murray's friendship; in short the recollection of all that polite agreable company raises on honest glow in my bosom.—

354

If you write to me, to be left at the post office, Dundee, any time before the 12th Inst I will find it, as by my calculation I shall pass that night in Dundee.—

Farewell!

Robt Burns

* Psalms 128 :3.

II (140)

Edinburgh, 29th September 1787

My dear friend & Countryman,

Why I have not answered your most welcome letter sooner is partly owing to yourself.—I was conscious I was deeply in your debt, and was resolved to pay you *in kind* by writing you a most devlish good letter; but among a Poet's Creditors usually, "The spirit is willing, but the flesh is weak;" * so I send you this in the interim merely "to confess debt and crave days."—I assure you I have "turn'd out the brunt side o' my shin" at the idea of my Petition for the poor naked Falls of Bruar being so well received at Blair.—I wrote it with all the pith and marrow of Gratitude.—I was so flattered by the cordial welcome I got from the truly noble Family, and so delighted with the little Seraphs, the future hope of Caledonia, that I swore in my own mind by the Great Fountain of Generosity and Hospitality, if my Muse did not, within twenty four hours from the date of my leaving Blair, pay her illustrious friends at Athole some poetic compliment, the very best the time and circumstances could produce —I would with unrelenting vengeance throw her into the House of Correction and finally banish her to Botany bay.—

Your Criticism I do not just approve of: To say that a thing is "Worth gaun a mile to see," is indefinitely saying worth going a great way to see, which in my opinion is better than marking any particular length of way.—Pardonnez moi; you may perhaps be right for all that.—I would not like it published in any other newspaper than a magazine, nor there, but as if by chance, and "said" to be done by such a Man: but it is to me a matter totally indifferent: you are at perfect liberty to do as you please.—

I should go on to tell you the particulars of my pilgrimage after you saw me: what pleasure I had in your account of the adventure at Bruar, and the story of Miss Cathcart,—by the way, I am convinced fully now, that those who tell me I have no second-sighted skill in human-nature are mistaken; I had not been fifteen minutes in Miss Cathcart's company till I set her down in the dearest records of my observation as one of those "Ministring Spirits" who delight in doing kind offices to "The Heirs of Salvation"—I was going to say that if, on consulting your feelings you can promise that a letter from Poet Burns, in whatever mood, tense, time, number or case his Bardship may be, and that whether it be the consequence of unforeseen misfortune or thoughtless folly; shall be welcome: if you can to this, with all your heart, and with all your soul, and with all your strength, and with all your mind, & say, YEA, and AMEN—then, Sir; so aid me, My Muse, in my hour of Song, as I now speak the truth and nothing but the truth! I ever shall be happy to send you the cogitations of my mind; the occurrencies of my life, or the productions of my Muse; on condition that you just pay me, as I said before, *in kind.*—I have no idea of corresponding as a clock strikes; I only write when the spirit moves me.—Direct to me at Mauchline, as it is now a post-town.—On Thursday I shall be at Auchtertyre, where I shall remain for five or six days, and then a day or two at Edinburgh sends me for the west Country.—

Adieu!
Robt Burns

you may direct to me

* Matthew 26 :41.

GILBERT BURNS

Born on 28th September 1760, the second son of William Burnes and Agnes Broun, he was the brother and partner of the poet in his early farming ventures, renting Mossgiel from Martinmass 1783 but not actually moving thence from Lochlea till March 1784. It was to Gilbert that Burns made his Deed of Assignation in 1786 (see page 115), while contemplating flight to Jamaica. Gilbert continued to work Mossgiel until 1798, supporting his widowed mother and the poet's younger brother and sisters. In 1798 Gilbert moved to Dinning in Nithsdale where he spent two years before becoming manager of Captain John Dunlop's farm of Morham West Mains, East Lothian. In 1804 he became factor to Lady Katherine Blantyre's East Lothian estates, making his home at Grant's Braes, near Haddington, where he died in 1827. In 1791 Gilbert married Jean Breckenridge of Kilmarnock, by whom he had eleven children, including the Rev. Dr Thomas Burns, founder of Otago province, New Zealand. About May 1788 Burns lent his brother £180 - about half the profits from the Edinburgh Edition - to save Gilbert and his dependants from ruin. It was not until 1820 that Gilbert was able to pay off the loan, mainly by editing an edition of his brother's poems for Cadell and Davies. Gilbert set out with the laudable intention of vindicating Robert's character and correcting 'the too strong statement Dr Currie has given of the irregularities of the latter part of his life', but in the end he acquiesced in his publisher's demands that he say nothing that might give offence to Dr Currie's family and friends. Gilbert Burns has come down to posterity as a rather colourless, timid soul, in complete contrast to the fiercely independent spirit of his famous brother. John Murdoch, however, wrote of his former pupils: 'Gilbert always appeared to me to possess a more lively imagination, and to be more of a wit, than Robert. . . Robert's countenance was generally grave and expressive of a serious, contemplative and thoughtful mind. Gilbert's face said, "Mirth with thee I mean to live", and certainly if any person who knew the two boys had been asked which of them was most likely to court the Muses, he would surely never have guessed that Robert had a propensity of that kind.' Gilbert's notes and reminiscences of his brother have yielded much of interest and value to biographers of the poet, notably the lengthy biographical letter to Mrs Dunlop of Dunlop.

I (137)

Edinburgh, 17th September 1787

My dear Sir,

I arrived here safe yesterday evening after a tour of 22 days, and travelling near 600 miles; windings included.—My farthest stretch was, about 10 miles beyond Inverness.—I went through the heart of the Highlands by Crieff, Taymouth the famous seat of Lord Breadalbine, down the Tay, among cascades & Druidical circles of stones, to Dunkel a seat of the Duke of Athole, thence cross Tay and up one of his tributary streams to Blair of Athole another of the Duke's seats, where I had the honor of spending nearly two days with his Grace and Family, thence many miles through a wild country among cliffs grey with eternal snows and gloomy, savage glens till I crossed Spey and went down the stream through Strathspey so famous in Scotish Music, Badenoch, &c. till I reached Grant Castle, where I spent half a day with Sir James Grant and Family, then cross the country for Fort George—call by the way at Cawdor the ancient seat of Mcbeth you know in Shakespear, there I saw the identical bed in which Tradition says king Duncan was murdered, lastly from Fort George to Inverness.—

I returned by the coast; Nairn, Forres, and so on to Aberdeen, thence to Stonhive where James Burness from Montrose met me by appointment.—I spent two days among our relations, and found our aunts, Jean and Isbal still alive and hale old women, John Caird, though born the same year with our father, walks as vigourously as I can; they have had several letters from his son in New York.— William Brand is likewise a stout old fellow; but farther particulars I delay till I see you, which will be in two or three weeks. The rest of

357

my stages are not worth rehearsing—warm as I was from Ossian's country where I had seen his very grave, what cared I for fisher-towns and fertile Carses?—I slept at the famous Brodie of Brodie's one night and dined at Gordon castle next day with the Duke, Dutchess and family.—I am thinking to cause my old mare meet me by means of John Ronald at Glasgow, but you shall hear farther from me before I leave Edinburgh.—My duty and many Compliments from the North to my Mother; and my brotherly Compliments to the rest.—I have been trying for a berth for William, but am not likely to be successful.—Farewel!

Robt Burns

II (381)

11th January 1790

Dear Brother

I mean to take advantage of the Frank though I have not in my present frame of mind much appetite for exertion in writing.—My nerves are in a damnable State.—I feel that horrid hypochondria pervading every atom of both body & Soul.—This Farm has undone my enjoyment of myself.—It is a ruinous affair on all hands.—But let it go to hell! I'll fight it out and be off with it.—

We have gotten a set of very decent Players here just now. I have seen them an evening or two.—David Campbell in Ayr wrote me by the Manager of the Company, a Mr Sutherland, who is indeed a man of genius and apparent worth.—On Newyearday evening I gave him the following Prologue which he spouted to his Audience with great applause.—

No Song nor dance I bring from yon great City
That queens it o'er our taste—the more's the Pity:
[C.W. p. 376]

I can no more.—If once I were clear of this accursed farm, I shall respire more at ease.—

I am yours
Robt Burns

III (703)

10th July [1796]

Dear Brother

It will be no very pleasing news to you to be told that I am dangerously ill, & not likely to get better.—An inveterate rheumatism has reduced me to such a state of debility, & my appetite is gone, so that I can scarce stand on my legs.—I have been a week at sea-bathing, & I will continue there or in a friend's house in the country all the summer.—God help my wife & children, if I am taken from their head!—They will be poor indeed.—I have contracted one or two serious debts, partly from my illness these many months & partly from too much thoughtlessness as to expense when I came to town that will cut in too much on the little I leave them in your hands.—Remember me to my Mother.—

Yours
R Burns

WILLIAM CRUIKSHANK

A native of Berwickshire, he trained as a schoolmaster under his uncle and namesake at Duns, before going on to Edinburgh University where he graduated M.A. In 1770 he was appointed rector of the Canongate High School and in 1772 became classics master at the High School of Edinburgh, and thus a colleague of William Nicol. Burns lodged with the Cruikshank family in St James's Square from September/October 1787 till he left Edinburgh in February 1788. *The Rosebud* (C.W. p. 318) was inspired by Cruikshank's 12 year-old daughter Janet (Jeany).

I (142)

Auchtertyre, Monday morn:
8th October 1787

I have nothing, my dear Sir, to write you, but that I feel myself exceedingly comfortably situated in this good family; just notice enough to make me easy but not to embarrass me.—I was storm-steaded two days at the foot of the Ochel hills with Mr Tait at Herveyston & Mr Johnston at Alva, but was so well pleased that I shall certainly spend a day on the banks of Devon as I return.—I leave this place, I suppose, on Wednesday, and shall devote a day to Mr Ramsay at Ochtertyre near Stirling; a man to whose worth I cannot do justice.—My most respectful, kind Compliments to Mrs Cruikshank and my dear little Jeany; and if you see Mr Masterton please remember me to him.—

I am ever, My dear Sir,
yours most gratefully
Robt Burns

II (214)

Mauchline, 3rd March 1788

My dear Sir,

Apologies for not writing are frequently like apologies for not singing—the apology better than the—song.—I have fought my way severely through the savage hospitality of this Country—to send every guest drunk to bed if they can.—

I executed your commission in Glasgow, and I hope the Cocoa came safe.—'Twas the same price and the very same kind as your former parcel; for the gentleman recollected your buying there before perfectly well—

I should return my thanks for your   hospitality (I leave a blank for the epithet, as I know none can do it justice;) to a poor, wayfaring Bard who was spent and almost overpowered fighting with Prosaic wickednesses in high places; but I am afraid lest you burn the letter whenever you come to the passage, so I pass over it in silence.—

I am just returned from visiting Mr Miller's farm.—The friend whom I told you I would take with me, was highly pleased with the farm; and as he is without exception the most intelligent farmer in the Country, he has staggered me a good deal.—I have the two plans of life before me; I shall balance them to the best of my judgement; and fix on the most eligible.—I have written Mr Miller, and shall wait on him when I come to town which will be the beginning or middle of next week: I would be in sooner, but my unlucky knee is rather

William Cruikshank

worse, and I fear for some time will scarcely stand the fatigue of my Excise instructions.—I only mention these ideas to you, and indeed except Mr Ainslie whom I intend writing to tomorrow, I will not write at all to Edinburgh till I return to it.—I would send my compliments to Mr Nicol, but he would be hurt if he knew that I wrote to any body and not to him: so I shall only beg my best, kindest Compliments to my worthy Hostess and the sweet little Rose-bud.—So soon as I am settled in the routine of life, either as an Excise Officer or as a farmer, I propose myself great pleasure from a regular correspondence with the only Man almost I ever saw who joined the most attentive prudence with the warmest generosity.—

I am much interested for that best of men, Mr Wood; I hope he is in better health and spirits than when I saw last.—

> I am ever, My dearest friend,
> your oblidged humble servant
> Robt Burns

III (292)

[Ellisland, August 1788 (*Cunningham*)]
[Mid-December 1788-January 1789] [1]

I have not room, my ever dear friend, to answer all the particulars of your last kind letter. I shall be in Edinburgh on some business very soon, and as I shall be two days, or perhaps three, we shall discuss matters viva voce. My knee, I believe, never will be entirely well; and an unlucky fall this winter, has made it still worse. I well remember the circumstance you allude to respecting Mr Creech's opinion of Mr Nicol, but as the first gentleman owes me still about 50*l.* I dare not meddle in the affair.

It gave me a very heavy heart to read such accounts of the consequence of your quarrel with that puritanic, rottenhearted, hell-commissioned scoundrel A——.[2] If, notwithstanding your unprecedented industry in public, and your irreproachable conduct in private life, he still has you so much in his power, what ruin may he not bring on some others I could name?

Many and happy returns of the seasons to you, with your dearest and worthiest friend, and the lovely little pledge of your happy union. May the Great Author of life, and of every enjoyment that can render life delightful, make her that comfort and blessing to you both which you so ardently wish for, and which, allow me to say, you so well deserve. Glance over the foregoing verses, and let me have your blots. Adieu!

> Robt Burns

1 Ross Roy suggests this date on the grounds that Burns received a letter from Cruikshank dated 13th December 1788.
2 Dr. Alexander Adam (1741-1809), Rector of the High School, Edinburgh.

JAMES HOY

Born in 1747, he was for almost half a century librarian and companion to the Duke of Gordon at Castle Gordon. William Wallace (1896) described him as 'a well-read man. . . . [who never lost] the Dominie-Sampson-like purity of heart and simplicity of manners by which he was distinguished. Burns met him at Castle Gordon during his Highland tour, on that memorable occasion when, to humour the irascible Nicol, Burns had to forego the pleasure of dining with the Duke and Duchess. It was this 'unlucky predicament' which moved Burns to write his first letter to Hoy—Nicol being 'that obstinate Son of Latin Prose' whom he curses in the opening paragraph. The main reason for writing, however, was to bring to Hoy's attention Johnson's *Scots Musical Museum* and request a copy of the Duke's words for 'Cauld Kail in Aberdeen'. Burns wrote again to thank Hoy for complying with this request.

I (145)

[Enclosing *Castle Gordon* C.W. p. 293]

Edinburgh, 20th October 1787

Sir,

I will defend my conduct, in giving you this trouble, on the best of Christian principles—"Whatsoever ye would that men should do unto you, do ye even so unto them."—[1] I shall certainly, among my legacies, leave my latest curse to that unlucky predicament which hurried me, tore me away from Castle Gordon.—May that obstinate Son of Latin Prose be curst to Scotch-mile periods, and damn'd to seven-league paragraphs; while Declension & Conjugation, Gender, Number and Time, under the ragged banners of Dissonance and Disarrangement eternally rank against him in hostile array!!!!!!

Allow me, Sir to strengthen the small claim I have to your acquaintance by the following request. An Engraver, James Johnson, in Edinburgh has, not from mercenary views but from an honest Scotch enthusiasm, set about collecting all our native Songs and setting them to music; particularly those that have never been set before.—Clarke, the well known Musician, presides over the musical arrangement; and Drs Beattie & Blacklock, Mr Tytler, Woodhouslee, and your humble servant to the utmost of his small power, assist in collecting the old poetry, or sometimes for a fine air to make a stanza, when it has no words.—The inclosed is one which, like some other misbegotten brats, "too tedious to mention,"[2] claims a parental pang from my Bardship.—I suppose it will appear in Johnson's second Number; the first was published before my acquaintance with him.—My request is; "Cauld kail in Aberdeen" is one intended for this number; and I beg a copy of his Grace of Gordon's words to it, which you were so kind as repeat to me.—You may be sure we won't prefix the Author's name, except you like; tho' I look on it as no small merit to this work that the names of many of the Authors of our old Scotch Songs, names almost forgotten, will be inserted.—I do not well know where to write to you, I rather write at you; but if you will be so obliging, immediately on receipt of this, as to write me a few lines; I shall perhaps pay you in kind, tho' not in quality.—Johnson's terms are: each Number, a handsome pocket volume, to consist at least of a hundred Scotch Songs, with basses for the Harpsichord, &c.; the price to Subscribers, 5, to non sub: 6sh—He will have three Numbers I conjecture.—

My direction for two or three weeks will be, at Mr William Cruikshank's, St James's Square, Newton, Edinburgh.—

I am, Sir, yours to command—
Robt Burns

1 Matthew 7:12.
2 Shakespeare: *Pericles*, Act V, sc. I, misquoted.

II (149)

Edinburgh, 6th November 1787

Dear Sir,

I would have wrote you immediately on receipt of your kind letter, but a mixed impulse of gratitude and esteem whispered to me that I ought to send you *Something* by way of return.—When a Poet owes any thing, particularly when he is indebted for good offices; the payment that usually recurs to him, the only coin indeed in which he probably is conversant, is Rhyme. Johnson sends the books by the fly as directed, and begs me to inclose his most grateful thanks: *my* return, I intended should have been one or two poetic bagatelles which the world have not seen, or perhaps for obvious reasons, cannot see.—These I shall send you before I leave Edinburgh.—They may make you laugh a little, which on the whole is no bad way of spending one's precious hours and still more precious breath: at any rate they will be, tho' a small, yet a very sincere mark of my respectful esteem for a gentleman whose farther acquaintance I should look upon as a peculiar obligation.—

The Duke's song, independent totally of his *dukeship*, charms me.— There is I know not what of wild happiness of thought and expression peculiarly beautiful in the old Scottish song style, of which his Grace, old venerable Skinner, the Author of Tullochgorum &c.; and the late Ross at Lochlee of true Scottish poetic memory, are the only *modern* instances that I recollect, since Ramsay with his contemporaries, and poor Bob Fergusson went to the World of deathless existence and truly immortal song.—The Mob of mankind, that "many-headed beast,"[1] would laugh at so serious a speech about "an old Song;" but, as Job says, "O that mine adversary had written a book!"[2] Those who think that composing a Scotch song is a trifling business—let them try.—

I wish my Lord Duke would pay a proper attention to the Christian admonition—"Hide not your candle under a bushel,"[3] but "Let your light shine before men."[4]—I could name half a dozen Dukes that I guess are a devilish deal worse employed; nay I question if there are half a dozen better: perhaps there are not half that scanty number whom Heaven has favored with the tuneful, happy, and, I will say, glorious gift.—

I am, Dear Sir, Your obliged humble Servant
Robt Burns

1 Pope: *Epistle* I, Bk. II, line 30 misquoted.
2 Job 31:35.
3 Matthew 5:15, Mark 4:21, Luke 11:33, from one of which Burns has misquoted.
4 Matthew 5:16.

REV. JOHN SKINNER

Born at Balfour, Aberdeenshire in 1721, he was educated at Marischal College and ordained in the Episcopal Church in 1742. He was the incumbent of Langside, Aberdeenshire from then until his death in 1807, apart from an initial two years spent in Shetland as preceptor to the Sinclairs of Scalloway. Among his numerous theological works, the best-known was his monumental *Ecclesiastical History of Scotland.* Although he subscribed to the oath of allegiance after the Jacobite Rebellion, Skinner was imprisoned for six months in Aberdeen for preaching to an assembly of more than four persons, and his church was wrecked by the troops of the 'Butcher' Duke of Cumberland. Skinner was a pioneer song-collector and composed several well-known ballads, including *Tullochgorum, John o' Badenyon* and *Ewie wi the Crookit Horn.* Inspired by the Edinburgh Edition of 1787, the Rev. John Skinner wrote to Burns in October that year, enclosing his rhyming *Familiar Epistle to Robie Burns the Ploughman Poet, In his own style.* This verse epistle, together with two prose letters from Skinner and the following two letters by Burns were subsequently published in volume III of Skinner's *Posthumous Works* (1809).

I (147)

[Edinburgh, 25th October 1787.]

Reverend and Venerable Sir,

Accept, in plain dull prose, my most sincere thanks for the best poetical compliment I ever received. I assure you, Sir, as a poet, you have conjured up an airy demon of vanity in my fancy, which the best abilities in your *other* capacity would be ill able to lay. I regret, and while I live shall regret, that when I was in the north, I had not the pleasure of paying a younger brother's dutiful respect to the Author of the best Scotch song ever Scotland saw,—"Tullochgorum's my delight!" The world may think slightingly of the craft of song-making, if they please; but, as Job says, "O! that mine adversary had written a book!"[1] let them try. There is a certain something in the old Scotch songs, a wild happiness of thought and expression, which peculiarly marks them, not only from English songs, but also from the modern efforts of song-wrights, in our native manner and language. The only remains of this enchantment, these spells of the imagination, rests with you. Our true brother, Ross of Lochlee, was likewise "owre cannie,"—a "wild warlock"—but now he sings among the "sons of the morning."[2] I have often wished, and will certainly endeavour, to form a kind of common acquaintance among all the genuine sons of Caledonian song. The world, busy in low prosaic pursuits, may overlook most of us;—but "reverence thyself." The World is not our *peers,*—so we challenge the jury. We can lash that world,—and find ourselves a very great source of amusement and happiness independent of that world. There is a work going on in Edinburgh, just now, which claims your best assistance. An Engraver in this town has set about collecting and publishing all the Scotch Songs, with the Music, that can found. Songs in the English language, if by Scotchmen, are admitted; but the Music must all be Scotch. Drs Beattie and Blacklock are lending a hand, and the first musician in town presides over that department. I have been absolutely crazed about it, collecting old stanzas, and every information remaining, respecting their origin, authors, &c. This last is but a very fragment business; but at the end of his second number, —the first is already published,—a small account will be given of the Authors, particularly to preserve those of latter times. Your three songs, *"Tullochgorum" "John of Badenyon,"* and *"Ewie wi' the crookit Horn,"* go in this second number. I was determined, before I got your letter, to write you, begging that you would let me know where the editions of these pieces may be found, as you would wish them to continue in future times; and if you would be so kind to this undertaking, as send any Songs, of your own or others, that you would think proper to publish. Your name will be inserted among the other authors, *"Nill ye, will ye."* One half of Scotland already give your songs to other authors. Paper is done. I beg to hear from you,—the sooner the better, as I leave Edinburgh in a fortnight or three weeks.

I am, with the warmest sincerity, Sir,
your obliged humble servant,
Robert Burns

My direction—*At Mr William Cruiksbanks, St James's Square, New Town, Edinburgh.*

1 Job 31:35.
2 Isaiah 14:12.

II (203)

[Edinburgh, 14th February 1788.]

Reverend and dear Sir,

I have been a cripple now near three months, though I am getting vastly better, and have been very much hurried beside, or else I would have wrote you sooner. I must beg your pardon for the epistle you sent me appearing in the Magazine. I had given a copy or two to some of my intimate friends, but did not know of the printing of it till the publication of the magazine. However, as it does great honour to us both, I hope you will forgive it. The second volume of the songs I mentioned to you in my last, is published to-day. I send you a copy, which I beg you will accept as a mark of the veneration I have long had, and shall ever have, for your character, and of the claim I make to your continued acquaintance. Your songs appear in the third volume, with your name in the index, as I assure you, Sir, I have heard your *Tullochgorum*, particularly among our west country folks, given to many different names, and most commonly to the immortal Author of the *Minstrel*,[1] who, indeed, never wrote any thing superior to *"Gie's a Sang, Montgomery cried."*[2] Your brother has promised me your verses to the Marquis of Huntly's reel, which certainly deserves a place in the Collection. My kind host, Mr Cruikshank, of the High School here, and said to be one of the best Latins in this age, begs me to make you his grateful acknowledgements for the entertainment he has got in a Latin publication of yours that I borrowed for him from your acquaintance, and my much respected friend, in this place, the reverend Dr Webster. Mr Cruikshank maintains that you write the best Latin since Buchanan. I leave Edinburgh to-morrow, but shall return in three weeks. Your song you mentioned in your last, to the tune of *"Dumbarton Drums,"* and the other, which you say was done by a brother by trade of mine, a ploughman, I shall thank you much for a copy of each.

I am ever, reverend Sir,
with the most respectful esteem,
and sincere veneration, yours,
Robert Burns

1 James Beattie.
2 The opening line of *Tullochgorum.*

ROBERT P------------N

The *Literary Magnet*, Vol.2 (1824) which published the following letter states that it was written 'to the late Mr. Robert P-----n, of Alnwick. Mr P. was eminently distinguished as a pious and philanthropic character; and he was also capable of appreciating highly the beauty of Burns's poems; but he felt the deepest regret tht many of them were of an immoral and dangerous tendency to the minds of his readers, as well as injurious to the best interest of the bard himself.'

(150A)

Edinburgh, 14th November 1787

Sir,—I have always held it a maxim in life, that in this bad world, those who truly wish us well, are entitled to a pretty large share at least of our gratitude; that you are so obliging as to interest yourself in my most important concerns, I can easily see by your rather extraordinary letter.

When good will to a fellow creature leads us a little out of the ordinary line, it is not only excusable, but highly laudable. Accept my thanks Sir, as sincere as your advice, and believe me to be,

Your obliged humble servant,
R. Burns

THOMAS WHITER

A Nottingham hosier who happened to be in Edinburgh in 1787, probably on business, when Burns made his acquaintance. Whiter became a burgess of Nottingham in 1800, his address being then given as Short Hill in that city. He died in Edinburgh of typhus fever on 9th November 1803. His obituary in the *Nottingham Journal* called him 'a man of uncommon strength of mind, great warmth of heart, and most active benevolence.'

(153B)

Sunday 8 o'clock P.M.
[End of November? 1787]

My Friend,

I hate to delay any thing in the little commerce of kindness, so I send you the book and scroll.—My direction is, at Mr Cruikshank's, Saint James's square, Newtown, Edinburgh.—

Adieu!
Robt Burns

You will return me the things, if I should not see you, against this day se ennight.—

MISS ISOBEL or ISABELLA MABANE

Nothing is known about this lady beyond the tantalising scraps furnished by Chambers (1851): 'Died in Edinburgh many years ago' and Douglas (1877): 'She became Mrs Col. Wright, but there is no tradition of any connecting link between her and Burns except this short letter'. Burns had evidently visited Miss Mabane and promised to try and get some small object of *vertu*, possibly a patch-box, repaired. The following letter, accompanying the trinket, provides an excellent example of the verbiage Burns could produce on occasion when he had nothing to say: the first paragraph of this letter says absolutely nothing at all.

(154)

Satur: noon newtown [1st December 1787]
No 2d St James' sqr

Here have I sat, my dear Madam, in the stony attitude of perplexed study, for fifteen vexatious minutes; my head askew, bending over the intended card; my fixed eye insensible to the very light of day poured around; my pendulous goose-feather loaded with ink, hanging over the future letter;—all for the important purpose of writing a complimentary Card to accompany your trinket.— Compliments, is such a miserable Greenland expression, lies at such a chilly, Polar distance from the torrid zone of my constitution, that I cannot for the very soul of me use it to any person for whom I have the twentieth part of the esteem every one must have for you who knows you.—

As I leave town in three or four days, I can give myself the pleasure of calling for you only for a minute.—Tuesday evening, sometime about seven, or after, I shall wait on you for your farewel commands.—

The hinge of your box I put into the hands of the proper connoisseur; but, it is, like Molly Gaw's skate, "Past redemption." The broken glass likewise went under review, but deliberative Wisdom thought it would too much endanger the whole fabric.—

I am, Dear Madam,
with all the sincerity of Enthusiasm,
your very humble servant
Robt Burns

JOHN BEUGO

Born at Edinburgh in 1759, he served his apprenticeship as an engraver and eventually set up in business on his own account. He was commissioned by Creech to engrave Burns's portrait for the frontispiece of the first Edinburgh Edition, after the painting by Alexander Nasmyth. Beugo waived his fee, emulating the generous example of Nasmyth himself. Writing to John Ballantine on 24th November 1787 (see page 102) Burns mentions: 'I am getting my phiz done, by an eminent engraver, and if it can be ready in time, I will appear in my book, looking like all other *fools*, to my title-page.' Burns subsequently favoured several of his correspondents with proofs of the engraving. It seems probable that Beugo required further sittings from Burns. At any rate, the two men became friends and later studied French together under the tuition of Louis Cauvin who, incidentally, commented that Burns made as much progress in three months as any of his ordinary pupils did in three years. Beugo was widely read and himself dabbled in poetry. In 1797 he published anonymously *Poetry, Miscellaneous and Dramatic, by an Artist*. Subsequently he organised the first exhibition of paintings held in Sir Henry Raeburn's rooms in York Place, and was a pillar of the Scottish artistic Establishment. He was the foremost Scottish engraver of his day, producing book illustrations, reproductions of several of Raeburn's best-known paintings and also vignettes for Lizars who produced cheques and banknotes for the Commercial and British Linen Company banks. Beugo married Elizabeth McDowall, by whom he had a daughter. He died at Edinburgh in 1841.

I (156)

St James's Square, Tuesday even. [Dec. 1787?]

My dear Sir,

a certain sour faced old acquaintance called Glauber's salts hinders me from my lesson tonight.—Tomorrow night I will not fail.—

Robt Burns

II (268)

Ellisland near Dumfries, 9th September 1788

My dear Sir,

There is not, in Edinburgh, above the number of the Graces whose letters would have given me so much pleasure as yours of the 3d Inst, which only reached me yesternight.—I am here on my farm, busy with my harvest; but for all that most pleasurable part of Life called, Social Communication, I am here at the very elbow of Existence.— The only things that are to be found in this country, in any degree of perfection, are Stupidity & Canting.—Prose, they only know in Graces, Prayers, &c. and the value of these they estimate as they do their plaiding webs—by the Ell; as for the Muses, they have as much idea of a Rhinoceros as of a Poet. For my old, capricious but good-natured hussy of a Muse—

By banks of Nith I sat and wept,
When Coila I thought on;
In midst thereof I hung my harp
The willow trees upon.—[1]

I am generally about half my time in Ayrshire, with my "Darling Jean," and then I, at *lucid intervals*, throw my horny fist across my be-cobwebbed Lyre, much in the same manner as an old wife throws her hand across the spokes of her Spinning wheel.—

I will send you the Fortunate Shepherdess [2] as soon as I return to Ayrshire; for there I keep it with other precious treasure.—I shall send it by a careful hand, as I would not for any thing it should be mislaid or lost.—I do not wish to serve you, from any benevolence,

John Beugo

or other grave Christian virtue; 'tis purely a selfish gratification of my own feelings, whenever I think of you.—

You do not tell me if you are going to be married.—Depend upon it, if you do not make some damned foolish choice it will be a very great improvement on the Dish of Life.—I can speak from Experience; tho' God knows, my choice was as random as Blindman's-buff.—I like the idea of an honest country Rake of my acquaintance, who, like myself, married lately.—Speaking to me of his late Step, "L——d, man," says he, "a body's baith cheaper and better sair't!"—

If your better functions would give you leisure to write me, I should be extremely happy at it: that is to say, if you neither keep nor look for a regular correspondence.—I hate the idea of being *oblidged* to write a letter! I sometimes write a friend twice a week, at other times, once a Quarter.—

I am exceedingly pleased with your fancy in making the Author you mention, place a map of Iceland instead of his Portrait before his Works.—'Twas a glorious idea.—

Could you conveniently do one thing.—Whenever you finish any head, I should like to have a proof Copy of it.—I might tell you a long story about your fine genius; but as what every body knows cannot have escaped you, I shall not say one syllable about it.—

If you see Mr Naesmith,[3] remember me to him most respectfully, as he both loves & deserves respect; tho', if he would pay less respect to the mere Carcase of Greatness, I should think him much nearer perfection.—

My best direction, for four or five months to come, is "at Mauchline."—

I am most truly, my dear Sir, yours to command,
Robt Burns

1 Metrical Psalms 137:1-2, parodied.
2 By Alexander Ross.
3 Alexander Nasmyth, the portrait painter.

AGNES McLEHOSE

Born in 1759, the daughter of Andrew Craig, a Glasgow surgeon, Agnes - or as she was known to her family and friends, Nancy - was barely three months younger than Burns. Her charms, more physical than intellectual, first attracted James McLehose, a rakish young Glasgow solicitor, when she was still a teenager. Nancy's father disapproved of McLehose and forbade him from calling at the house, but 'love will find a way'. When Nancy had occasion to board the coach bound for Edinburgh she found herself alone with James who had guaranteed privacy by purchasing all the other seats! Nancy was literally swept off her feet, and at the age of seventeen became Mrs McLehose. In four years Nancy bore him as many children, though one died in infancy. She was expecting her fourth child when her husband's brutality towards her became intolerable and she returned with her young family to the care of her father. Andrew Craig died two years later, so Nancy moved to Edinburgh and took an apartment in Potter Row. She lived on a small annuity, supplemented by assistance from her cousin.William Craig, Sheriff-Depute of Ayrshire. In 1784 James McLehose went to Jamaica, determined to turn over a new leaf. Doubtless in a more liberal and enlightened age, Nancy would have divorced her dissolute husband; but in the 1780s the machinery for even a legal separation does not seem to have existed.

When Burns was lionised by Edinburgh society, Nancy was keen to meet him and her wish was fulfilled on 4th December 1787. Burns had been kept hanging around Edinburgh that winter trying to get Creech to pay up, and had whiled away his enforced idleness in an endless round of parties and other social gatherings. It was at a tea party given by Miss Nimmo, an elderly friend of Margaret Chalmers, that Burns was introduced to Mrs McLehose. Mutual attraction appears to have been instantaneous. As soon as she got home that evening Nancy sent Burns a note inviting him to tea with her the following Thursday. In his reply (I) Burns had to decline the invitation due to a prior engagement but suggested the following Saturday instead. He expected to leave Edinburgh very shortly and did not anticipate returning for two years, and regretted that he had only just got to know her. Had everything gone according to plan, it is probable that Mrs McLehose would have taken her place among those ladies with whom the poet conducted a sporadic correspondence. But chance intervened. The carelessness of a drunken coachman caused a carriage accident in which Burns was injured and confined to bed, so that the Saturday tea party had to be postponed (II). Nancy's sympathetic response provoked an even more cordial note (III) from Burns on 12th December. Within a fortnight the correspondence had taken a more intense, passionate turn and before the year was out that sentimental but somewhat artificial flirtation had commenced between 'Sylvander' and 'Clarinda'. There can be no doubt that Burns embarked on amatory conquest. Previous affairs of the heart had involved girls who were his social equal or inferior.Jean Armour, May Cameron, Jenny Clow and Elizabeth Paton), and intellectually on a much lower plane altogether. That Burns had occasional yearnings for ladies on a higher social or intellectual level is seen in his tentative approaches to Margaret Chalmers; perhaps even Wilhelmina Alexander comes into this category. But until December 1787 he had been singularly unsuccessful. Now the Junoesque Mrs McLehose, the grass-widow with a measure of refinement and culture, appeared to offer distinct possibilities. Burns set out to woo her with words. Nancy, for her part, was flattered by his attentions but while she was quite prepared to go so far in a platonic entanglement, her side of the correspondence makes it clear that Burns would be permitted to go so far and no further. While Sylvander's letters became bolder and more passionate, Clarinda began retreating behind 'reason' and 'religion' and duty to her children. When Burns mentioned love (III) - even though in a fairly innocent context - Nancy was swift to reprove him : 'Do you remember that she whom you address is a married woman?' Burns expanded on this theme (V), which led to a further reproof which, in turn, he countered with a compromise (IX). Thereafter, the poet who had counselled his younger brother to 'try at once for intimacy' (see page 516) retreated, baffled, in the face of Nancy's intransigence. One may imagine the turmoil in Clarinda's breast, anxious on the one hand to prolong the correspondence with this fascinating man, but fearful lest news of her amorous dalliance should come to the attention of her dour, Calvinistic cousin, William Craig, on whom she depended so much financially, or her equally uncompromising minister, Mr Kemp. On 30th December Burns confided in Richard Brown (see page 419): 'I am at this moment ready to hang myself for a young Edinburgh widow.' The platonic friendship entered a new phase on 12th January, when Burns was sufficiently recovered to pay her a visit. When she wrote the following day she expressed her mixed feelings: 'But though our enjoyment did not lead beyond the limits of virtue, yet today's reflections have not been altogether unmixed with regret'. Burns tried to reassure her (XIII) but when they met on 23rd January he seems to have tried for a more physical, less platonic relationship which inevitably provoked a reproach: 'If you wish Clarinda to regain her peace, determine against everything but what the strictest delicacy warrants'. To this, Sylvander replied 'Clarinda, my life, you have wounded my soul' (XX).

By now even Burns must have begun to realise that he was not getting anywhere with Mrs McLehose. One may detect some flagging in his ardour by the end of January; and by this time Burns was slaking his amorous thirst with Jenny Clow, a servant girl who later bore his son. Nevertheless the literary love affair with Clarinda continued to ebb and flow a little longer. Nancy tried to terminate the affair, and this precipated the extraordinary outburst of 13th February (XXVII) which begins in italics *My ever dearest Clarinda*. This letter was written in immediate reply, as Burns was about to join a social gathering for dinner. Later the same evening he wrote again to Clarinda at greater length and two further letters followed the very next day, expressing something of the misery and anguish he was going through. There was a further hectic exchange of letters on 18th February, triggered off by a warning which Nancy had received - a 'haughty dictatorial letter', probably from Lord Criag. Burns left Edinburgh about this time, with the promise to marry Clarinda as soon as her husband's death should release her — an event which did not occur till Burns himself had been in his grave for several years.

On 23rd February 1788 Burns wrote from Mossgiel (XXXIV) telling Nancy of his reunion with Jean Armour which he summarily dismissed in language wholly unworthy of him: 'I have done with her, and she with me . . .' Notwithstanding the disgraceful language of this notorious 'farthing taper' letter, Burns and Jean were formally married six weeks later, a matter which he left to Robert Ainslie to impart to Nancy. Mercifully, the letter which she wrote to Burns on that occasion has not survived, but we may guess at its tone and content from his dignified answer on 9th March 1789 (XLII) where he pointedly reminded her that, even if he might have been imprudent and foolish, he had not actually done anything to deserve the epithets she now hurled at him, and he added, pretty sharply, that the credit for not having taken final advantage of her was his. 'When you call over the scenes that have passed between us, you will survey the conduct of an honest man, struggling successfully with temptations the most powerful that ever beset humanity . . .'

By February 1790, however, Clarinda's anger at Sylvander's 'perfidious treachery' had so abated that she reopened the correspondence. Burns spent some time in Edinburgh in December 1791 and saw Nancy several times but by now she was attempting a reconciliation with her husband and planned to sail for Jamaica the following February. On his return to Dumfries, Burns wrote (L) enclosing *Ae fond Kiss* (C.W. p. 434), inspired by their last meeting on 6th December. When Nancy got to Jamaica she discovered that James had taken a Negro mistress in the interim, by whom he had had a daughter. Within three months, Nancy was on her way back to Scotland, claiming the excessive heat and the mosquitoes as her reason for not remaining in the West Indies. Only two further letters appear to have been written after Nancy's return; indeed, the first of these (LI) reproached her for not having let Burns know of her arrival in Scotland. Although the passion of the earlier correspondence had long since evaporated there is a note of poignancy in the very last letter, written from Castle Douglas about 25th June 1794: 'Ah! my ever dearest Clarinda! - Clarinda? - What a host of Memory's tenderest offspring crowd on my fancy at that sound! - But I must not indulge that subject: - you have forbid it.'

In her diary, under the date of 6th December 1831, Nancy wrote: 'This day I can never forget. Parted with Burns, in the year 1791, never more to meet in this world. Oh, may we meet in Heaven!' Mrs McLehose never remarried after her husband's death. Many years later Sir Walter Scott mentioned having seen her at the home of his friend Lord Craig when she was 'old, charmless and devout'. When she died in 1841 the Sylvander letters in her possession were valued at a mere £25.

A problem which has faced biographers and students of this remarkable correspondence was Nancy's habit of mutilating letters. Sometimes names, words or phrases were cut out, pasted over, or so heavily scored through as to become illegible, and dates altered for some inexplicable reason.

I (158)

Thursday even:
[6th December 1787]

Madam,

I had set no small store by my tea-drinking tonight, and have not often been so disappointed.—Saturday evening I shall embrace the opportunity with the greatest pleasure.—I leave this town this day se'ennight, and probably for a couple of twelvemonth but must ever regret that I so lately gott an acquaintance I shall ever highly esteem, and in whose welfare I shall ever be warmly interested.—

Our worthy common friend, [Miss Nimmo], in her usual pleasant way, rallied me a good deal on my new acquaintance, and in the humor of her ideas I wrote some lines which I inclose you, as I think they have a good deal of poetic merit; and Miss N—— tells me, you are not only a Critic but a Poetess.—Fiction, you know, is the native region of Poetry; and I hope you will pardon my vanity in sending you the bagatelle as a tolerable off-hand jeux d'esprit.—I have several poetic trifles which I shall gladly leave with Miss N—— or you, if they were worth houseroom; as there are scarcely two people on earth by whom it would mortify me more to be forgotten, tho, at the distance of nine-score miles.—

> I am, Madam, with the highest respect,
> your very humble servant
> Robt Burns

II (159)

Saturday even:
St James Square No 2 [8th December 1787]

I can say with truth, Madam, that I never met with a person in my life whom I more anxiously wished to meet again than yourself.— Tonight I was to have had that very great pleasure—I was intoxicated with the idea—but an unlucky fall from a coach has so bruised one of my knees that I can't stir my leg off the cushion. So, if I don't see you again, I shall not rest in my grave for chagrin.—I was vexed to the soul I had not seen you sooner; I determined to cultivate your friendship with the enthusiasm of Religion; but thus has Fortune ever served me.—I cannot bear the idea of leaving Edinburgh without seeing you—I know not how to account for it—I am strangely taken with some people; nor am I often mistaken. You are a stranger to me; but I am an odd being: some yet unnamed feelings; things not principles, but better than whims, carry me farther than boasted reason ever did a Philosopher.—

Farewel! every happiness be yours!

> Robt Burns

III (161)

[12th December 1787]

I stretch a point indeed, my dearest Madam, when I answer your card on the rack of my present agony.—Your friendship, Madam! by Heavens, I was never proud before.—Your lines, I maintain it, are Poetry; and good Poetry; mine, were indeed partly fiction, and partly a friendship which had I been so blest as to have met with you *in time*, might have led me—God of love only knows where.—Time is too short for ceremonies—I swear solemnly (in all the tenor of my former oath) to remember you in all the pride and warmth of friendship until—I cease to be!—

Tomorrow, and every day till I see you, you shall hear from me.—

Farewell! May you enjoy a better night's repose than I am likely to have.

> Robt Burns

IV (163)

[20th December? 1787]

Your last, my dear Madam, had the effect on me that Job's situation had on his friends, when "they sat down seven days and seven nights astonied, and spake not a word."[1]—"Pay my addresses to a married woman!" I started, as if I had seen the ghost of him I had injur'd: I recollected my expressions; some of them indeed were, in the law phrase, "habit and repute," which is being half guilty.—I cannot positively say, Madam, whether my heart might not have gone astray a little; but I can declare upon the honor of a Poet that the vagrant has wandered unknown to me.—I have a pretty handsome troop of Follies of my own; and, like some other people's retinue, they are but undisciplined blackguards: but the luckless rascals have something of honor in them; they would not do a dishonest thing.—

To meet with an unfortunate woman, amiable and young; deserted and widowed by those who were bound by every tie of Duty, Nature and Gratitude, to protect, comfort and cherish her; add to all, when she is perhaps one of the first of Lovely Forms and Noble Minds, the Mind too that hits one's taste as the joys of Heaven do a Saint— should a vague infant-idea, the natural child of Imagination, thoughtlessly peep over the fence—were you, My Friend, to sit in judgement, and the poor, airy Straggler brought before you, trembling self-condemned; with artless eyes, brimful of contrition, looking wistfully on its Judge—you could not, My dear Madam, condemn the hapless wretch to "death without benefit of Clergy?"

I won't tell you what reply my heart made to your raillery of "Seven Years;" but I will give you what a brother of my trade says on the same allusion—

> The Patriarch to gain a wife
> Chaste, beautiful and young,
> Serv'd fourteen years a painful life
> And never thought it long:
> O were you to reward such cares,
> And life so long would stay,
> Not fourteen but four hundred years
> Would seem but as one day![2]

I have written you this scrawl because I have nothing else to do, and you may sit down and find fault with it if you have no better way of consuming your time; but finding fault with the vaguings of a Poet's fancy is much such another business as Xerxes chastising the waves of Hellespont.—

My limb now allows me to sit in some peace; to walk I have yet no prospect of, as I can't mark it to the ground.—

I have just now looked over what I have written, and it is such a chaos of nonsense that I daresay you will throw it into the fire, and call me an idle, stupid fellow; but whatever you think of my brains, believe me to be, with the most sacred respect, and heart-felt esteem,

My Dear Madam, your humble servant
Robt Burns

1 Job 2:13, misquoted.
2 *Tea-Table Miscellany*, III, song cix.

V (166)

Friday eve
[28th December 1787]

I beg your pardon, my dear "Clarinda," for the fragment scrawl I sent you yesterday.—I really don't know what I wrote. A gentleman for whose character, abilities and critical knowledge I have the highest veneration, called in, just as I had begun the second sentence, and I would not make the Porter wait.—I read to my much-respected friend several of my own bagatelles and among others your lines which I had copied out.—He began some criticisms on them as on the other pieces, when I informed him they were the work of a young lady in this town; which I assure you made him stare.—My learned friend seriously protested that he did not believe any young woman in Edinburgh was capable of such lines; and if you know any thing of Professor Gregory you will neither doubt of his abilities nor his sincerity.—I do love you if possible still better for having so fine a taste and turn for Poesy.—I have again gone wrong in my usual unguarded way, but you may erase the word, and put esteem, respect, or any other tame Dutch expression you please in its place. —I believe there is no holding converse or carrying on correspondence, with an amiable woman, much less a *gloriously amiable, fine woman,* without some mixture of that delicious Passion, whose most devoted Slave I have more than once had the honor of being: but why be hurt or offended on that account? Can no honest man have a prepossession for a fine woman, but he must run his head against an intrigue? Take a little of the tender witchcraft of Love, and add it to the generous, the honorable sentiments of manly Friendship; and I know but *one* more delightful morsel, which few, few in any rank ever taste.—Such a composition is like adding cream to strawberries— it not only gives the fruit a more elegant richness, but has a peculiar deliciousness of its own.—

I inclose you a few lines I composed on a late melancholy occasion. —I will not give above five or six copies of it at all, and I would be hurt if any friend should give any copies without my consent.—*

You cannot imagine, Clarinda, (I like the idea of Arcadian names in a commerce of this kind) how much store I have set by the hopes of your future friendship.—I don't know if you have a just idea of my character, but I wish you to see me *as I am.*—I am, as most people of my trade are, a strange will o' wisp being; the victim too frequently of much imprudence and many follies.—My great constituent elements are Pride and Passion: the first I have endeavoured to humanize into integrity and honour; the last makes me a Devotee to the warmest degree of enthusiasm, in Love, Religion, or Friendship; either of them or all together as I happen to be inspired.—'Tis true, I never saw you but once; but how much acquaintance did I form with you in that once! Don't think I flatter you, or have a design upon you, Clarinda; I have too much pride for the one, and too little cold contrivance for the other; but of all God's creatures I ever could approach in the beaten way of acquaintance, you struck me with the deepest, the strongest, the most permanent impression.—I say the most permanent, because I know myself well, and how far I can promise either on my prepossessions or powers.—Why are you unhappy? and why are so many of our fellow creatures, unworthy to belong to the same species with you, blest with all they can wish? You have a hand all benevolent to give, why were you denied the pleasure? You have a heart form'd, gloriously form'd, for all the most refined luxuries of love; why was that heart ever wrung? O Clarinda! shall we not meet in a state, some yet unknown state of Being, where the lavish hand of Plenty shall minister to the highest wish of Benevolence; and where the chill north-wind of Prudence shall never blow over the flowery fields of Enjoyment? if we do not, Man was made in vain! I deserv'd most of the unhappy hours that have linger'd over my head; they were the wages of my labour; but what unprovoked Demon, malignant as Hell, stole upon the confidence of unmistrusting busy Fate, and dash'd your cup of life with undeserved sorrow?—

Let me know how long your stay will be out of town: I shall count the hours till you inform me of your return.—Cursed etiquette forbids your seeing me just now; and so soon as I can walk, I must bid Edinburgh adieu.—Lord, why was I born to see misery which I cannot relieve, and to meet with friends whom I can't enjoy! I look back with the pang of unvailing avarice on my loss in now knowing you sooner: all last winter; these three months past; what luxury of intercourse have I not lost! Perhaps tho' 'twas better for my peace.— You see I am either above, or incapable of Dissimulation.—I believe it is want of that particular genius.—I despise Design because I want either coolness or wisdom to be capable of it.—I may take a fort by storm, but never by Siege.—

I am interrupted—Adieu! my dear Clarinda!

Sylvander

* Probably *On the Death of Lord President Dundas* (C.W. p. 300).

VI (169)

[3rd January 1788?]

My dear Clarinda,

Your verses, my dearest Madam, have so delighted me that I have copied them in among some of my own most valued pieces, which I keep sacred for my own use.—Do, let me have a few now and then.—

Did you, Madam, know what I feel when you talk of your sorrows! Good God! that one who has so much worth in the sight of Heaven, and is so amiable to her fellow-creatures should be so unhappy! I can't venture out for cold.—My limb is vastly better, but I have not any use of it without my crutches.—Monday, for the first time, I dine at a neighbour's next door: as soon as I can go so far, *even in a coach*, my first visit shall be to you.—Write me when you leave town and immediately when you return, and I earnestly pray your stay may be short.—You can't imagine how miserable you made me when you hinted to me not to write. Farewell.

Sylvander

VII (170)

[4th January 1788]

You are right, my dear Clarinda: a friendly correspondence goes for nothing, except one write their undisguised sentiments.—Yours please me for their intrinsic merit, as well as because they are *yours;* which, I assure, is to me a high recommendation.—Your religious sentiments, Madam, I revere.—If you have, on some suspicious evidence, from some lying oracle, learnt that I despise or ridicule so sacredly important a matter as real Religion, you have, my Clarinda, much misconstrued your friend.—"I am not mad, most noble Festus!"* 'Have you ever met a perfect character? Do we not sometimes rather exchange faults than get rid of them? For instance; I am perhaps tired with and shocked at a life, too much the prey of giddy inconsistencies and thoughtless follies; by degrees I grow sober, prudent and statedly pious—I say statedly, because the most unaffected devotion is not at all inconsistent with my first character —I join the world in congratulating myself on the happy change.— But let me pry more narrowly into this affair; have I, at bottom, any thing of a secret pride in these endowments and emmendations? have I nothing of a Presbyterean sourness, a hypercritical severity when I survey my less regular neighbours? in a word, have I miss'd all those nameless and numberless modifications of indistinct selfishness, which are so near our own eyes we can scarcely bring them within our sphere of vision, and which the known spotless cambric of our character hides from the ordinary Observer?—

My definition of Worth is short: Truth and Humanity respecting our fellow-creatures; Reverence and Humility in the presence of that Being, my Creator and Preserver, and who, I have every reason to believe, will one day be my Judge.—The first part of my definition is the creature of unbiassed Instinct; the last is the child of after Reflection.—Where I found these two essentials; I would gently note, and slightly mention, any attendant flaws—flaws, the marks, the consequences of Human nature.—

I can easily enter into the sublime pleasures that your strong imagination and keen sensibility must derive from Religion, particularly if a little in the shade of misfortune; but I own I cannot without a marked grudge, see Heaven totally engross so amiable so charming a woman as my friend Clarinda; and should be very well pleased at *a circumstance* that would put it in the power of Somebody, happy Somebody! to divide her attention, with all the delicacy and tenderness of an earthly attachment.—

You will not easily persuade me that you have not gotten a grammatical knowledge of the English language.—So far from being inaccurate, you are elegant beyond any woman of my acquaintance, except one whom I wish I knew.—

Your last verses to me have so delighted me, that I have got an excellent old Scots air that suits the measure, and you shall see them in print in the "Scots musical Museum," a work publishing by a friend of mine in this town.—I want four stanzas; you gave me but three, and one of them alluded to an expression in my former letter; so I have taken your two first verses with a slight alteration in the

second, and have added a third, but you must help me to a fourth.—
Here they are: the latter half of the first stanza would have been
worthy of Sappho; I am in raptures with it—

> Talk not of Love, it gives me pain,
>   For love has been my foe:
> He bound me with an iron chain,
>   And sunk me deep in woe.—

> But Friendship's pure and lasting joys
>   My heart was form'd to prove:
> There, welcome win and wear the prize,
>   But never talk of Love!—

> Your Friendship much can make me blest,
>   O, why that bliss destroy!
>   only
> Why urge the odious, one request
>   will
> You know I must deny!

The alteration in the second stanza is no improvement, but there was
a slight inaccuracy in your rhyme.—The third, I only offer to your
choice, and have left two words for your determination.—The air is
"The banks of Spey," and is most beautiful.—

Tomorrow evening, I intend taking a chair and paying a visit at
Park-place to a much valued old friend.—If I could be sure of finding
you at home, and I will send one of the chairmen to call, I would
spend from five to six o'clock with you, as I go passt, I cannot do
more at this time, as I have something on my hand that hurries me
much.—I propose giving you the first call, my old friend the second,
and Miss Nimmo as I return home.—Do not break any engagement
for me, as I will spend another evening with you at any rate before I
leave town.—

Do not tell me that you are pleased when your friends inform you of
your faults.—I am ignorant what they are; but I am sure they must
be such evanescent trifles, compared with your personal and mental
accomplishments, that I would despise the ungenerous, narrow soul
who would notice any shadow of imperfections you may seem to
have, any other way than in the most delicate, agreeable rallery.—
Coarse minds are not aware how much they injure the keenly feeling
tie of bosom-friendship, when in their foolish officiousness they
mention what nobody cares for recollecting.—People of nice
sensibility and generous minds have a certain intrinsic dignity, that
fires at being trifled with, or towered, or even too nearly
approached.—

You need make no apology for long letters: I am even with you.—
Many happy New-years to you, charming Clarinda! I can't dissemble
were it to shun perdition.—He who sees you as I have done and does
not love you, deserves to be damn'd for his stupidity! He who loves
you and would injure you, deserves to be doubly damn'd for his
villainy! Adieu!

Sylvander

Agnes McLehose

P.S.—What would you think of this for a fourth stanza

> Your thought, if love must harbour there,
> Conceal it in that thought,
> Nor cause me from my bosom tear
> The very friend I sought.

* Acts 26:25.

VIII (171)

Saturday noon [5th January 1788]

Some days, some nights, nay some *hours*, like the "ten righteous persons in Sodom,"[1] save the rest of the vapid, tiresome, miserable months and years of life.—One of these *hours*, my dear Clarinda blesst me with yesternight—

> ——"One well spent hour,
> "In such a tender circumstance for Friends,
> "Is better than an age of common time!"
> Thomson[2]

My favorite feature in Milton's Satan is, his manly fortitude in supporting what cannot be remedied—in short, the wild broken fragments of a noble, exalted mind in ruins.—I meant no more by saying he was a favorite hero of mine.—

I mention'd to you my letter to Dr Moore, giving an account of my life: it is truth, every word of it; and will give you the just idea of a man whom you have honor'd with your friendship.—I am afraid you will hardly be able to make sense of so torn a piece.—Your verses I shall muse on—deliciously—as I gaze on your image in my mind's eye, in my heart's core: they will be in time enough for a week to come.—I am truly happy your head-ach is better—O, how can Pain or Evil be so daringly, unfeelingly, cruelly savage as to wound so noble a mind, so lovely a form!—

My little fellow is all my Namesake.—Write me soon.—My every, strongest good wishes attend you, Clarinda

Sylvander

I know not what I have wrote—I am pestered with people around me—

1 Genesis 18:32, paraphrased.
2 *Alfred: A Masque*, Act I, sc. 6, altered.

IX (174)

Tuesday night
[8th January 1788]

I am delighted, charming Clarinda, with your honest enthusiasm for Religion. Those of either sex, but particularly the female, who are lukewarm in that most important of all things, "O my soul, come not thou into their secrets!"[1]—I feel myself deeply interested in your good opinion, and will lay before you the outlines of my belief. He, who is our Author and Preserver, and will one day be our Judge, must be, (not for his sake in the way of duty, but from the native

378

impulse of our hearts,) the object of our reverential awe and grateful adoration: He is almighty and all-bounteous, we are weak and dependent; hence, prayer and every other sort of devotion.—"He is not willing that any should perish, but that all should come to everlasting life;"[2] consequently, it must be in every one's power to embrace His offer of "everlasting life;" otherwise He could not, in justice, condemn those who did not. A mind pervaded, actuated and governed by purity, truth and charity, though it does not *merit* heaven, yet is an absolutely necessary pre-requisite, without which heaven can neither be obtained nor enjoyed; and, by Divine promise, such a mind shall never fail of attaining "everlasting life:" hence, the impure, the deceiving, and the uncharitable, extrude themselves from eternal bliss, by their unfitness for enjoying it. The Supreme Being has put the immediate administration of all this, for wise and good ends known to himself, into the hands of Jesus Christ, a great Personage, whose relation to Him we cannot comprehend, but whose relation to us is a Guide and Saviour; and who, except for our own obstinacy and misconduct, will bring us all, through various ways and by various means, to bliss at last.

These are my tenets, my lovely friend; and which, I think, cannot be well disputed. My creed is pretty nearly expressed in the last clause of Jamie Dean's grace, an honest weaver in Ayrshire; "Lord grant that we may lead a gude life! for a gude life maks a gude end, at least it helps weel!"

I am flattered by the entertainment you tell me you have found in my packet. You see me as I have been, you know me as I am, and may guess at what I am likely to be. I too may say, "Talk not of Love, &c." for indeed he has "plung'd me deep in woe!"[3] Not that I ever saw a woman who pleased unexceptionably, as my Clarinda elegantly says, "In the companion, the friend, and the mistress."[4] *One* indeed I could except—*One*, before passion threw its mists over my discernment I knew it, *the* first of women! Her name is indelibly written in my heart's core—but I dare not look in on it—a degree of agony would be the consequence.—Oh, thou perfidious, cruel, mischief-making demon, who president o'er that frantic passion—thou mayst, thou dost poison my peace, but shall not taint my honour—I would not for a single moment give an asylum to the most distant imagination, that would shadow the faintest outline of a selfish gratification, at the expence of *her* whose happiness is twisted with the threads of my existence—May she be happy as she deserves! And if my tenderest, faithfulest friendship can add to her bliss—I shall at least have one solid mine of enjoyment in my bosom! *Don't guess at these ravings!*

I watched at our front window to-day, but was disappointed. It has been a day of disappointments. I am just risen from a two-hours bout after supper, with silly or sordid souls, who could relish nothing in common with me—but the Port. "One"—'Tis now "witching time of night;"[5] and whatever is out of joint[6] in the foregoing scrawl, impute it to enchantments and spells; for I can't look over it, but will seal it up directly, as I don't care for tomorrow's criticisms on it.

Your are by this time fast asleep, Clarinda; may good angels attend and guard you as constantly and faithfully as my good wishes do!

"Beauty, which whether waking or asleep,
"Shot forth peculiar graces—"[7]

John Milton, I wish thy soul better rest than I expect on my pillow to-night! O for a little of the cart-horse part of human nature! Good night, my dearest Clarinda!

Sylvander

1 Genesis 49:6.
2 John 3:16, misquoted.
3 From Clarinda's own verses, reproduced in letter I (168) to Captain Richard Brown.
4 From Mrs. McLehose's letter to Burns of the previous night.
5 Shakespeare: *Hamlet*, Act III, sc. 2.
6 See Shakespeare: *Hamlet*, Act I, sc. 5.
7 Milton: *Paradise Lost*, Bk. V, lines 14-15.

X (175)

Thursday noon
[10th January 1788]

I am certain I saw you, Clarinda; but you don't look to the proper story for a Poet's lodging—

"Where Speculation roosted near the sky"—[1]

I could almost have thrown myself over, for very vexation.—Why didn't you look higher? It has spoilt my peace for this day.—To be so near my charming Clarinda; to miss her look when it was searching for me—I am sure the soul is capable of disease, for mine has convulsed itself into an inflamatory fever.—

I am sorry for your little *boy*: *do, let me* know tomorrow how he is.—You have converted me, Clarinda.—(I shall love that name while I live: there is heavenly music in it.—) Booth and Amelia I know well.—[2] Your sentiments on that subject, as they are on every subject, are just and noble.—"To be feelingly alive to kindness—and to unkindness,"[3] is a charming female character.—

What I said in my last letter, the Powers of fuddling sociality only know for me.—By yours, I understand my good Star has been partly in my horizon, when I got wild in my reveries.—Had that evil Planet which has almost all my life shed its baleful rays on my devoted head, been, as usual, in my zenith [*sic*], I had certainly blab'd something that would have pointed out to you the dear Object of my tenderest friendship, and, in spite of me—something more.—Had that fatal information escaped me, and it was merely chance or kind stars that it did not; I had been undone! you would never have wrote me, except perhaps *once*, more!—O, I could curse circumstances! and the coarse tie of human laws which keep fast what Common Sense would loose; and which bars that happiness itself cannot give—Happiness which otherwise Love and Honor would warrant! But hold—I shall make no more "hairbreadth 'scapes"—[4]

My friendship, Clarinda, is a life-rent business.—My Likings are both strong, and eternal.—I told you I had but one Male friend: I have but two female.—I should have a third, but she is surrounded by the blandishments of Flattery and Courtship.—Her I register in my heart's core—by Peggy Chalmers.—Miss Nimmo can tell you how divine she is.—She is worthy of a place in the same bosom with my Clarinda.—That is the highest compliment I can pay her.—

Farewel, Clarinda! Remember

Sylvander!

1 Young: *First Epistle to Mr. Pope*, line 10.
2 Henry Fielding: *Amelia*.
3 From Clarinda's letter dated Wednesday [9th January].
4 Shakespeare: *Othello*, Act I, sc. 3.

XI (176)

Saturday Morn:
[12th January 1788]

Your thoughts on Religion, Clarinda, shall be welcome.—You may perhaps distrust me when I say 'tis also *my* favorite topic; but mine is the Religion of the bosom.—I hate the very idea of controversial divinity; as I firmly believe, that every honest, upright man, of whatever sect, will be accepted of the Deity.—If your verses, as you seem to hint, contain censure, except you want an occasion to break with me, don't send them.—I have a little infirmity in my disposition, that where I fondly love or highly esteem, I cannot bear reproach.—

"Reverence thyself" is a sacred maxim, and I wish to cherish it.—I think I told you Lord Bolingbroke's saying to Swift—"Adieu, dear Swift! with all thy faults I love thee entirely; make an effort to love me with all mine."—A glorious sentiment, and without which there can be no friendship! I do highly, very highly esteem you indeed, Clarinda; you merit it all! Perhaps, too, I scorn dissimulation! I could fondly love you: judge, then, what a maddening sting your reproach would be.—"Oh, I have sins to *Heaven*, but none to *you*!"[1] With what pleasure would I meet you today, but I cannot walk to meet the fly.—I hope to be able to see you, *on foot*, about the middle of next week.—

I am interrupted—Perhaps you are not sorry for it—You will tell me —but I won't anticipate blame.—O Clarinda! did you know how dear to me is your look of kindness, your smile of approbation! you would not, either in prose or verse, risque a censorious remark.—

"Curst be the verse, how well soe'er it flow,
That tends to make one worthy man my foe!"[2]

Sylvander

1 Thomas Southerne: *The Fatal Marriage*, Act I. altered slightly.
2 Pope: *Prologue to the Satires*, lines 283-4.

Agnes McLehose

XII (177)

[12th January 1788]

You talk of weeping Clarinda; some involuntary drops wet your lines as I read them.—Offend me, my dearest Angel! you cannot offend me: you never offended me! If you had ever given me the least shadow of offence; so pardon me, my God, as I forgive Clarinda—I have read yours again: it has blotted my paper.—Tho' I find your letter has agitated me into a violent headache, I shall take a chair and be with you about eight.—A friend is to be with us at tea on my account, which hinders me from coming sooner.—Forgive, my dearest Clarinda, my unguarded expressions.—For Heaven's sake forgive me, or I shall never be able to bear my own mind!—

Your unhappy
Sylvander

XIII (178)

Monday Even, 11 o'clock
[14th January 1788]

Why have I not heard from you, Clarinda!—Today I well expected it; and before supper, when a letter to me was announced, my heart danced with rapture: but behold, 'twas some fool who had taken it into his head to turn Poet, and made me an offering of the first-fruits of his nonsense. "It is not poetry, but prose run mad."[1] Did I ever repeat to you an epigram I made on a Mr Elphinstone, who has given a translation of Martial, a famous Latin poet? The poetry of Elphinstone can only equal his prose-notes. I was sitting in a merchant's shop of my acquaintance, waiting somebody; he put Elphinstone into my hand, and asked my opinion of it; I begged leave to write it on a blank leaf, which I did—

To Mr Elphinstone, &c.—

O thou, whom Poesy abhors!
Whom Prose has turned out of doors!
Heard'st thou yon groan? proceed no further!
'Twas laurel'd Martial calling murther!
[C.W. p. 270]

I am determined to see you, if at all possible, on Saturday evening. Next week I must sing—

The night is my departing night,
    The morn's the day I maun awa';
There's neither friend nor foe o' mine
    But wishes that I were awa'!

What I hae done for lack o' wit,
    I never, never can reca';
I hope ye're a' my friends as yet—
    Gude night, and joy be wi' you a'![2]

If I could see you sooner, I would be so much the happier; but I would not purchase the *dearest gratification* on earth, if it must be at your expence in wordly censure; far less, inward peace!—

I shall certainly be ashamed of thus scrawling whole sheets of incoherence.—The only *unity*, (a sad word with Poets & Critics!) in my ideas, is Clarinda.—There my heart "reigns and revels."—

> "What art thou Love! whence are those charms,
> "That thus thou bear'st an universal rule!
> "For thee the soldier quits his arms,
> "The king turns slave, the wise man fool.—
>
> "In vain we chase thee from the field,
> "And with cool thoughts resist thy yoke:
> "Next tide of blood, Alas! we yield;
> "And all those high resolves are broke!"—[3]

I like to have quotations ready for every occasion.—They give one's ideas so pat, and save one the trouble of finding expression adequate to one's feelings.—I think it is one of the greatest pleasures attending a Poetic genius, that we can give our woes, cares, joys, loves, &c. an embodied form in verse, which, to me, is ever immediate ease.—Goldsmith says finely of his Muse—

> "Thou source of all my bliss and all my woe,
> "Who found'st me poor at first, and keep'st me so"—[4]

My limb has been so well today that I have gone up and down stairs often without my staff.—Tomorrow, I hope to walk once again on my own legs to dinner.—It is only next street.—Adieu!

Sylvander

1 Pope: *Prologue to the Satires*, line 188.
2 Traditional song of parting to the air *Goodnight and joy by wi' you a'*.
3 Anonymous song in *The Hive*, 1724, p. 33.
4 *The Deserted Village*, lines 413-14.

XIV (179)

Tuesday Evening [15th January 1788]

That you have faults, my Clarinda, I never doubted; but I knew not where they existed, and Saturday night made me more in the dark than ever. O, Clarinda, why will you wound my soul by hinting that last night must have lessened my opinion of you! True; I was "behind the scenes with you," but what did I see? A bosom glowing with honour and benevolence; a mind ennobled by genius, informed and refined by education and reflection, and exalted by native religion, genuine as in the climes of heaven; a heart formed for all the glorious meltings of friendship, love and pity. These I saw.—I saw the noblest immortal soul, creation ever shewed me.

I looked long, my dear Clarinda, for your letter; and am vexed that you are complaining. I have not caught you so far wrong as in your idea, that the commerce you have with *one* friend hurts you, if you cannot tell every tittle of it to *another*. Why have so injurious a suspicion of a good God, Clarinda, as to think that Friendship and Love, on the sacred, inviolate principles of Truth, Honour and Religion, can be any thing else than an object of His divine approbation?

I have mentioned, in some of my former scrawls, Saturday evening next. Do, allow me to wait on you that evening. Oh, my angel! how soon must we part! and when can we meet again! I look forward on the horrid interval with tearful eyes! What have I lost by not knowing you sooner. I fear, I fear my acquaintance with you is too short, to make that *lasting* impression on your heart I could wish.

Sylvander

XV (180)

Weden noon:
[16th January 1788]

Clarinda,

Your letter found me writing to you.—I read yours two or three times by way of welcome: by and by, I shall do it more justice.—Friday evening, about eight, expect me.—If I can't walk all the way, I'll take a chair to Nicolson's square, or so; and walk the rest.—You talk of vanity; in mercy remember me, when you praise my letter-writing talents so extravagantly.—Inured to flattery as I have been for some time past, I am not proof against the applauses of one whom I love dearer, and whose judgement I esteem more, than I do all the world beside.—I forget the chairman waits—God bless you! Remember

Sylvander

XVI (181)

Saturday Morning—
[19th January 1788]

There is no time, my Clarinda, when the conscious thrilling chords of Love and Friendship give such delight, as in the pensive hours of what our favourite Thomson calls, "Philosophic Melancholy."[1] The sportive insects who bask in the sunshine of Prosperity, or the worms that luxuriant crawl amid their ample wealth of earth, they need no Clarinda; they would despise Sylvander- if they durst.—The family of Misfortune, a numerous group of brothers and sisters! they need a resting-place to their souls: unnoticed, often condemned by the world; in some degree perhaps condemned by themselves, they feel the full enjoyment of ardent love, delicate tender endearments, mutual esteem and mutual reliance.—

In this light I have often admired Religion.—In proportion as we are wrung with grief, or distracted with anxiety, the ideas of a compassionate Deity, an Almighty Protector, are doubly dear.—

" 'Tis this, my friend, that streaks our morning bright;
" 'Tis this that gilds the horrors of our night"—[2]

I have been this morning taking a peep thro', as Young finely says, "the dark postern of time long elaps'd;"[3] and you will easily guess, 'twas a rueful prospect.—What a tissue of thoughtlessness, weakness and folly! My life reminded me of a ruin'd temple: what strength, what proportion in some parts! what unsightly gaps, what prostrate ruins in others! I kneeled down before the Father of mercies and said, "Father, I have sinned against Heaven and in thy sight, and am

MRS. AGNES McLEHOSE (CLARINDA)

ROBERT GRAHAM OF FINTRY

no more worthy to be called thy son!"[4] I rose, eased and strengthened.—I despise the superstition of a Fanatic, but I love the Religion
of a Man.—"The future," said I to myself, "is still before me: there
let me—

> On Reason build Resolve,
> "That column of true majesty in Man!"—[5]

"I have   difficulties many to encounter," said I; "but they are not
"absolutely insuperable: and where is firmness of mind shewn, but
"in exertion? mere declamation, is bombast rant.—Besides, wherever
I am, or in whatever situation I may be—

> —" 'Tis nought to me:
> "Since God is ever present, ever felt,
> "In the void waste as in the city full;
> "And where He vital breathes, there must be joy!"[6]

Saturday Night—half after ten—

What luxury of bliss I was enjoying this time yesternight! My ever-
dearest Clarinda, you have stolen away my soul but you have
refined, you have exalted it; you have given it a stronger sense of
Virtue, and a stronger relish for Piety.—Clarinda, first of your Sex, if
ever I am the veriest wretch on earth to forget you; if ever your
lovely image is effaced from my soul,

> "May I be lost, no eye to weep my end;
> "And find no earth that's base enough to bury me!"[7]

What trifling silliness is the childish fondness of the every day
children of the world! 'tis the unmeaning toying of the younglings of
the fields and forests: but where Sentiment and Fancy unite their
sweets; where Taste and Delicacy refine; where Wit adds the flavour,
and Good-sense gives strength and spirit to all, what a delicious
draught is the hour of tender endearment! Beauty and Grace in the
arms of Truth and Honor, in all the luxury of mutual love!

Clarinda, have you ever seen the picture realized? not in all its very
richest colouring: but

> "Hope thou Nurse of young Desire;
> "Fairy promiser of joy"—[8]

Last night, Clarinda, but for one slight shade, was the glorious
Picture—

> Innocence
> Look'd, gayly smiling on; while rosy Pleasure
> Hid young Desire amid her flowery wreath,
> And pour'd her cup luxuriant; mantling high,
> The sparkling heavenly vintage, Love and Bliss![9]

Clarinda, when a Poet and Poetess of Nature's making, two of
Nature's noblest productions! when they drink together of the same
"cup of Love and Bliss"—Attempt not, ye coarser stuff of Human-
nature, profanely to measure enjoyment ye never can know!

Goodnight, my dear Clarinda!

Sylvander

1 *Autumn*, line 1003.
2 One of several "Verses to Mr. Hervey on his Meditations" reproduced in
James Hervey's *Meditations and Contemplations*, 2 vols. (Glasgow, 1768).
3 *Night Thoughts*, Night I, line 224.
4 Luke 15:18-19.
5 *Night Thoughts*, Night I, lines 30-1.
6 Thomson: *A Hymn on the Seasons*, lines 104-7.
7 Not identified.
8 Bickerstaffe: *Love in a Village*, Act I, sc. 1.
9 In J .B. Reid: *Concordance to the Poems and Songs of Robert Burns*
(Glasgow, 1889), these lines are attributed to Burns himself.

XVII (182)

Sunday night—[20th January 1788]

The impertinence of fools has joined with a return of an old
indisposition, to make me good for nothing today.—The paper has
lain before me all this evening, to write to my dear Clarinda, but—

Fools rush'd on fools, as waves succeed to waves"—[1]

I cursed them in my soul: they sacreligiously disturbed my
meditations on her who holds my heart.—What a creature is man! A
little alarm last night and today that I am mortal, has made such a
revolution on my spirits! There is no Philosophy, no Divinity, comes
half so home to the mind.—I have no idea of courage that braves
Heaven.—'Tis the wild ravings of an imaginary hero in Bedlam.—

I can no more, Clarinda; I can scarce hold up my head: but I am
happy you don't know it, you would be so uneasy.—

Sylvander

Monday morning—

I am, my lovely friend, much better this morning, on the whole; but
I have a horrid languor on my spirits.—

"Sick of the world, and all its joy,
"My soul in pining sadness mourns:
"Dark scenes of woe my mind employ,
"The past and present in their turns"—[2]

Have you ever met with a saying of the Great and likewise Good Mr
Locke, Author of the famous essay on the human understanding.—
He wrote a letter to a friend, directing it, "not to be delivered till
after my decease;" it ended thus—"I know you loved me when
"living, and will preserve my memory now I am dead.—All the use to
"be made of it is; that this life affords no solid satisfaction, but in
"the consciousness of having done well, and the hopes of another
"life.—Adieu! I leave my best wishes with you—J. Locke—"[3]

Clarinda, may I reckon on your friendship for life? I think I may.—
Thou Almighty Preserver of Men! Thy friendship, which hitherto I
have too much neglected, to secure it shall, all the future days and
nights of my life, be my steady care!—The idea of my Clarinda
follows—

"Hide it my heart, within that close disguise,
"Where mix'd with God's her lov'd idea lies"—[4]

But I fear that inconstancy, the consequent imperfection of human weakness.—Shall I meet with a friendship that defies years of Absence and the chances and changes of Fortune? Perhaps "such things are"; *One* honest man I have great hopes from, that way: but who, except a Romance-writer, would think on a *love* that could promise for life, in spite of distance, absence, chance and change; and that too, with slender hopes of Fruition?—For my own part, I can say to myself in both requisitions, "Thou art the man!"[5] I dare, in cool resolve I dare, declare myself that Friend, and that Lover.—If Womankind is capable of such things, Clarinda is.—I trust that she is; and feel I shall be miserable, if she is not.—There is not one Virtue which gives worth, or one Sentiment which does honor to the Sex, that she does not possess superiour to any woman I ever saw: her exalted mind, aided a little perhaps by her situation, is, I think, capable of that nobly-romantic Love-enthusiasm.—

May I see you on Wednesday evening, my dear angel? The next wedensday again will, I conjecture, be a hated day to us both.—I tremble for censorious remark, for your sake; but in extraordinary cases, may not usual and useful Precaution be a little dispensed with? Three evenings, three swift-winged evenings, with pinions of down, are all the past—I dare not calculate the future.—I shall call at Miss Nimmo's tomorrow-evening; 'twill be a farewell call.—

I have wrote out my last sheet of paper, so I am reduc'd to my last half-sheet—What a strange, mysterious faculty is that thing called Imagination? We have no ideas almost at all, of another world; but I have often amused myself with visionary schemes of what happiness might be enjoyed by small alterations, alterations that we can fully enter to, in this present state of existence—For instance; suppose you and I just as we are at present; the same reasoning Powers, sentiments and even desires; the same fond curiosity for knowledge and remarking observation in our minds; & imagine our bodies free from pain and the necessary supplies for the wants of nature, at all times and easily within our reach: imagine farther that we were set free from the laws of gravitation which binds us to this globe, and could at pleasure fly, without inconvenience, through all the yet unconjecture'd bounds of Creation—what a life of bliss would we lead, in our mutual pursuit of virtue and knowledge, and our mutual enjoyment of friendship and love!—

I see you laughing at my fairy fancies, and calling me a voluptuous Mahometan; but I am certain I would be a happy creature, beyond any thing we call bliss here below: nay, it would be a paradise congenial to you too.—Don't you see us hand in hand, or rather my arm about your lovely waist, making our remarks on Sirius, the nearest of the fixed stars; or surveying a Comet flaming inoxious by us, as we just now would mark the passing pomp of a travelling Monarch: or, in a shady bower of Mercury or Venus, dedicating the hour to love; in mutual converse, relying honor and revelling endearment—while the most exalted strains of Poesy and Harmony would be the ready, spontaneous language of our souls! Devotion is the favorite employment of your heart; so is it of mine: what incentives then to, and powers for, Reverence, Gratitude, Faith and Hope in all the fervours of Adoration and Praise to that Being whose unsearchable Wisdom, Power and Goodness so pervaded, so inspired every Sense and Feeling!—By this time, I dare say, you will be blessing the neglect of the maid that leaves me destitute of Paper.—

Sylvander

1 Not identified.
2 Not identified.
3 Letter to Anthony Collins of 23rd August 1704.
4 Pope: *Eloisa to Abelard*, lines 11-12, altered to fit the opposite sex.
5 2 Samuel 12:7.

XVIII (183)

[21st January 1788]

*   *   * I am a discontented ghost a perturbed spirit. Clarinda, if ever you forget Sylvander, may you be happy, but he will be miserable.

O, what a fool I am in love!—what an extravagant prodigal of affection! Why are your sex called the tender sex, when I never have met with one who can repay me in passion? They are either not so rich in love as I am, or they are niggards where I am lavish.

O Thou, whose I am, and whose are all my ways! Thou see'st me here, the hapless wreck of tides and tempests in my own bosom: do Thou direct to thyself that ardent love, for which I have so often sought a return, in vain, from my fellow-creatures! If Thy goodness has yet such a gift in store for me, as an equal return of affection from her who, Thou knowest, is dearer to me than life, do Thou bless and hallow our band of love and friendship; watch over us, in all our outgoings and incomings, for good; and may the tie that unites our hearts be strong and indissoluble as the thread of man's immortal life!

I am just going to take your Blackbird,* the sweetest, I am sure, that ever sung, and prune its wings a little.

Sylvander

* Clarinda's *To a Blackbird Singing on a Tree* which Burns revised

(C.W. p. 319)

XIX (186)

Thursday morning
[24th January 1788]

"Unlavish Wisdom never works in vain"—*

I have been tasking my reason, Clarinda, why a woman, who for native genius, poignant wit, strength of mind, generous sincerity of soul, and the sweetest female tenderness, is without a peer; and whose personal charms have few, very, very few parallels, among her sex; why, or how she should fall to the blessed lot of a poor hairum-scairum Poet, whom Fortune has kept for her particular use to wreak her temper on, whenever she was in ill-humour. One time I conjectured that as Fortune is the most capricious jade ever known; she may have taken, not a fit of remorse, but a paroxysm of whim, to raise the poor devil out of the mire, where he had so often and so conveniently served her as a stepping-stone, and give him the most glorious boon she ever had in her gift, merely for the maggot's sake, to see how his fool head and his fool heart will bear it. At other times I was vain enough to think that Nature, who has a great deal to say with Fortune, had given the coquettish goddess some such hint as, "Here is a paragon of Female Excellence, whose equal, in all my former conpositions, I never was lucky enough to hit on, and despair of ever doing so again; you have cast her rather in the shades of life; there is a certain Poet, of my making; among your frolicks, it would not be amiss to attach him to this master-piece of my hand, to give her that immortality among mankind which no woman of any age ever more deserv'd, and which few Rhymesters of this age are better able to confer."

Evening, 9 o'clock
I am here, absolutely unfit to finish my letter—pretty hearty after a bowl, which has been constantly plied since dinner, till this moment. I have been with Mr. Schetki, the musician, and he has set it finely. —I have no distinct ideas of any thing, but that I have drunk your health twice tonight, and that you are all my soul holds dear in this world.—

Sylvander

Clarinda, Mistress of My Soul
[C.W. p. 320]

* Thomson: *Spring*, line 731.

XX (187)

[25th January 1788]

Clarinda, my life, you have wounded my soul.—Can I think of your being unhappy, even tho' it be not described in your pathetic elegance of language, without being miserable? Clarinda, can I bear to be told from you, that "you will not see me tomorrow night—that you wish the hour of parting were come"! Do not let us impose on ourselves by sounds: if in the moment of fond endearment and tender dalliance, I perhaps trespassed against the *letter* of Decorum's law; I appeal, even to you, whether I ever sinned in the very least degree against the *spirit* of her strictest statute.—But why, My Love, talk to me in such strong terms; every word of which cuts me to the very soul? You know, a hint, the slightest signification of your wish, is to me a sacred command.—Be reconciled, My Angel, to your God, your self and me; and I pledge you *Sylvander's honor,* an oath I dare say you will trust without reserve, that you shall never more have reason to complain of his conduct.—Now, my Love, do not wound our next meeting with any averted looks or restrained caresses: I have marked the line of conduct, a line I know exactly to your taste, and which I will inviolably keep; but do not *you* show the least inclination to make boundaries: seeming distrust, where you know you may confide, is a cruel sin against Sensibility.—

"Delicacy, you know it, was which won me to you at once—"*take care* you do not loosen the dearest most sacred tie that unites us"—"Clarinda, I would not have stung *your* soul, I would not have bruised *your* spirit, as that harsh crucifying, "Take care," did *mine*; no, not to have gained heaven! Let me again appeal to your dear Self, if Sylvander, even when he seemingly half-transgressed the laws of Decorum, if he did not shew more chastised, trembling, faultering delicacy, than the MANY of the world do in keeping these laws.—

O Love and Sensibility, ye have conspired against My Peace! I love to madness, and I feel to torture! Clarinda, how can I forgive myself, that I ever have touched a single chord in your bosom with pain! would I do it willingly? Would any consideration, any gratification make me do so? O, did you love like me, you would not, you could not deny or put off a meeting with the Man who adores you; who would die a thousands deaths before he would injure you; and who must soon bid you a long farewell!—

I had proposed bringing my bosom friend, Mr Ainslie, tomorrow evening, at his strong request, to see you; as he only has time to stay with us about ten minutes, for an engagement; but—I shall hear from you: this afternoon, for mercy's sake! for till I hear from you I am wretched.—O Clarinda, the tie that binds me to thee, is entwisted, incorporated with my dearest threads of life!

Sylvander

XXI (188)

[26th January 1788]

I was on the way, *my Love,* to meet you (I never do things by halves) when I got your card.—Mr [Ainslie] goes out of town tomorrow morning, to see a brother of his who is newly arrived from France.—I am determined that he and I shall call on you together; so look you, lest I should never see tomorrow, we will call on you.— Tonight.—Mary and you may put off tea till about seven; at which time, in the Galloway phrase, "an the beast be to the fore, and the branks bide hale," expect the humblest of your humble servants, and his dearest friend.—We only propose staying half an hour,—"for ought we ken."—I could suffer the lash of Misery eleven months in the year, were the twelfth to be composed of hours like yesternight. —You are the soul of my enjoyment: all else is of the stuff of stocks & stones.—

Sylvander

XXII (189)

Sunday noon [27th January 1788]

I have almost given up the excise idea.—I have been just now to wait on a great person, Miss Nimmo's friends, Mrs Stewart.—Why will Great people not only deafen us with the din of their equipage, and dazzle us with their fastidious pomp, but they must also be so very dictatorially wise? I have been question'd like a child about my matters, and blamed and schooled for my Inscription on Stirling window.[1]—Come, Clarinda—"Come, curse me Jacob; come, defy me Israel!"[2]

Sunday Night
I have been with Miss Nimmo. She is indeed, "a good soul," as my
Clarinda finely says.—She has reconciled me, in a good measure, to
the world, with her friendly prattle.—

Schetki has sent me the song, set to a fine air of his composing.—I
have called the song, Clarinda: I have carried it about in my pocket,
and thumbed it over all day.—

I trust you have spent a pleasant day: and that no idea or
recollection of me gives you pain.—

Monday morning—
If my prayers have any weight in Heaven, this morning looks in on
you and finds you in the arms of peace; except where it is
charmingly interrupted by the ardours of Devotion.—

I find so much serenity of mind, so much positive pleasure, so much
fearless daring toward the world, when I warm in devotion, or feel
the glorious sensation, a consciousness of Almighty Friendship, that
I am sure I shall soon be a honest Enthusiast—

> "How are Thy servants blest, O Lord,
> How sure is their defence!
> Eternal wisdom is their guide,
> Their help Omnipotence!"[3]

I am, my dear Madam,
yours,
Sylvander

1 See *Poems*, 166.
2 Numbers 23 :7, misquoted.
3 Addison: *Spectator*, 20th September 1712.

XXIII (190)

Tuesday morn
[29th January 1788]

I cannot go out today, my dearest *Love*, without sending you half a
line by way of a sin offering; but believe me, 'twas the sin of
Ignorance.—Could you think that I *intended* to hurt you by
anything I said yesternight? Nature has been too kind to you for
your happiness.—Your Delicacy, your Sensibility—O why should
such glorious qualifications be the fruitful source of woe!—You have
"murder'd sleep"[1] to me last night.—I went to bed, impress'd with
an idea that you were unhappy; and every start I closed my eyes,
busy Fancy painted you in such scenes of romantic misery that I
would almost be persuaded you are not well this morning.—

> —"If I unweeting have offended,
> "Impute it not"—[2]
> —"But while we live,
> "But one short hour perhaps, between us two
> "Let there be peace".—[3]

If Mary is not gone by this reaches you, give her my best
Compliments.—She is a charming girl, and highly worthy of the
noblest love.—

I send you a Poem to read, till I call on you this night, which will be about nine.—I wish I could procure some potent spell, some fairy charm, that would protect from injury, or restore to rest, that bosom-chord, "tremblingly alive all o'er,"[4] on which hangs your peace of mind.—I thought, vainly, I fear, thought, that the devotion of Love, Love strong as even you can feel; Love guarded, invulnerably guarded, by all the purity of Virtue, and all the pride of Honor; I thought such a love might make you happy—will I be mistaken? I can no more, for hurry.—

Thine,
Sylvander

1 Shakespeare: *Macbeth*, Act II, sc. 2.
2 Addison: *Cato*, Act V, sc. 4, altered.
3 Not identified.
4 Pope: *Essay on Man*, I, 297.

XXIV (191)

Friday Morning 7 o'clock, [1st February 1788]

Your fears for Mary are truly laughable. I suppose, my love, you and I showed her a scene which, perhaps, made her wish that she had a swain, and one who could love like me; and 'tis a thousand pities that so good a heart as hers should want an aim, an object. I am miserably stupid this morning. Yesterday I dined with a Baronet, and sat pretty late over the bottle. And "who hath woe—who hath sorrow? they that tarry long at the wine; they that go to seek mixed wine."* Forgive me, likewise, a quotation from my favourite author. Solomon's knowledge of the world is very great. He may be looked on as the "Spectator" or "Adventurer" of his day: and it is, indeed surprising what a sameness has ever been in human nature. The broken, but strongly characterizing hints, that the royal author gives us of the manners of the court of Jerusalem and country of Israel are, in their great outlines, the same pictures that London and England, Versailles and France exhibit some three thousand years later. The loves in the "Song of songs" are all in the spirit of Lady M.W. Montague, or Madame Ninon de l'Enclos; though, for my part, I dislike both the ancient and modern voluptuaries; and will dare to affirm, that such an attachment as mine to Clarinda, and such evenings as she and I have spent, are what these greatly respectable and deeply experienced Judges of Life and Love never dreamed of.

I shall be with you this evening between eight and nine, and shall keep as sober hours as you could wish.

I am ever, my dear Madam, yours,
Sylvander

1 Proverbs 23:29-30.

XXV (194)

Sunday morning—[3rd February 1788]

I have just been before the throne of my God, Clarinda; according to my association of ideas, my sentiments of love and friendship, I next devote myself to you.—Yesternight I was happy: happiness "that the world cannot give."—I kindle at the recollection; but it is a flame where Innocence looks smiling on, and Honor stands by, a sacred guard.—Your heart, your fondest wishes, your dearest thoughts, these are yours to bestow: your Person is unapproachable, by the laws of your country; and he loves not as I do, who would make you miserable.—

You are an Angel, Clarinda; you are surely no mortal that "the earth owns."—To kiss your hand, to live on your smile, is to me far more exquisite bliss than the dearest favours that the fairest of the Sex, yourself excepted, can bestow,—

Sunday even:
You are the constant companion of my thoughts.—How wretched is the condition of one who is haunted with conscious guilt, and trembling under the idea of dreaded Vengeance! And what a placid calm what a charming secret enjoyment it gives to bosom—the kind feelings of friendship, and the fond throes of love! Out upon the tempest of Anger, the acrimonious gall of fretful Impatience, the sullen frost of lowring Resentment, or the corroding poison of withered Envy! They eat up the immortal part of Man! If they spent their fury only on the unfortunate objects of them, it would be something in their favor; but these miserable passions, like traitor Iscariot, betray their lord and master.—

Thou Almighty Author of peace and goodness and love! Do thou give me the social heart that kindly tastes of every man's cup! It is a draught of joy—warm and open my heart to share it with cordial, unenvying rejoicing! Is it the bitter potion of sorrow—melt my heart with sincerely sympathetic woe!—Above all, do Thou give me the manly mind that resolutely exemplifies in life and manners those sentiments which I would wish to be thought to possess! The friend of my soul—there may I never deviate from the firmest fidelity, and most active kindness! Clarinda, the dear object of my fondest love; there, may the most sacred, inviolate Honor, the most faithful, kindling Constancy ever watch and animate my every thought and imagination!—

Did you ever meet with the following lines—spoken of Religion, your darling topic—

> " 'Tis *this*, my friend, that streaks our morning bright:
> " 'Tis *this* that gilds the horror of our night!
> "When wealth forsakes us, and when friends are few;
> "When friends are faithless, or when foes pursue;
> " 'Tis this that wards the blow or stills the smart,
> "Disarms affliction, or repels its dart:
> "Within the breast bids purest rapture rise,
> "Bids smiling Conscience spread her cloudless skies."—*

I met with these verses very early in life, and was so delighted with them that I have them by me, copied at school.—

Good night, and sound rest, my dearest Clarinda!

Sylvander

* Another verse from the preface of Hervey's *Meditations*.

Agnes McLehose

XXVI (195)

Thursday night
[7th February 1788]

I cannot be easy, my Clarinda, while any sentiment respecting me in your bosom gives you pain.—If there is no man on earth to whom your heart and affections are justly due, it may savour of imprudence but never of *criminality* to bestow that heart and those affections where you please.—The God of love meant and made those delicious attachments to be bestowed on somebody; and even all the imprudence lies in bestowing them on an unworthy Object.— If this reasoning is conclusive, as it certainly is, I must be allowed to "talk of Love."—

It is perhaps rather wrong to speak highly to a friend of his letter; it is apt to lay one under a little restraint in their future letters, and restraint is the death of a friendly epistle; but there is one passage in your last charming letter, Thomson or Shenstone never exceeded it, nor often came up to it.—I shall certainly steal it, and set in some future poetic production, and get immortal fame by it.—'Tis when you bid the scenes of Nature remind me of Clarinda.—Can I forget you, Clarinda? I would detest myself as a tasteless, unfeeling, insipid, infamous Blockhead! I have lov'd women of ordinary merit, whom I could have loved for ever. You are the first, the only unexceptionable individual of the beauteous Sex that I ever met with; and never woman more intirely possessed my soul.—I know myself, and how far I can depend on passions, well.—It has been my peculiar study.—

I thank you for going to Miers.—Urge him, for necessity calls, to have it done by the middle of next week: wednesday the latest day. —I want it for a breast-pin, to wear next my heart.—I propose to keep sacred set times to wander in the woods and wilds for meditation on you.—Then, and only then, your lovely image shall be produced to the day, with a reverence akin to Devotion.—

You must not . . .

[*More than half a page of MS. missing*]

. . . Man I trust."—Tomorrow night shall not be the last.—Goodnight! I am perfectly stupid, as I supped late yesternight.—

Sylvander

XXVII (199)

[13th February 1788]

My ever dearest Clarinda,

I make a numerous dinner party wait me while I read yours and write this—Do not require that I should cease to love you, to adore you in my soul—'tis to me impossible—your peace and happiness are to me dearer than my soul—name the terms on which you wish to see me, to correspond with me, and you have them—I must love, pine, mourn and adore in secret—this you *must* not deny me—you will ever be to me—

"Dear as the light that visits these sad eyes,
"Dear as the ruddy drops that warm my heart;"*

394

Agnes McLehose

I have not patience to read the puritanic scrawl.—Vile sophistry!—
Ye heavens! thou God of nature! thou Redeemer of mankind! ye
look down with approving eyes on a passion inspired by the purest
flame, and guarded by truth, delicacy and honour: but the half-inch
soul of an unfeeling, cold-blooded, pitiful presbyterian bigot, cannot
forgive any thing above his dungeon bosom and foggy head.

Farewell! I'll be with you to-morrow evening—and be at rest in your
mind—I will be yours in the way you think most to your happiness!
I dare not proceed—I love, and will love you, and will with joyous
confidence approach the throne of the Almighty Judge of men, with
your dear idea, and will despise the scum of sentiment and the mist
of sophistry.

Sylvander

* Gray: *The Bard*, lines 40-1, slightly altered.

XXVIII (200)

Weden:—midnight—
[13th February 1788]

Madam

After a wretched day, I am preparing for a sleepless night.—I am
going to address myself to the Almighty Witness of my actions—
some time, perhaps *very* soon, my Almighty Judge.—I am not going
to be the advocate of Passion—be Thou my Inspirer and testimony,
O God, as I plead the cause of truth!—

I have read over your friend's haughty, dictatorial letter: you are
only answerable to your God, in such a manner.—Who gave any
fellow-creature of yours (a fellow-creature incapable of being your
judge because not your Peer) a right to catechize, scold, undervalue,
abuse and insult, wantonly and inhumanly to insult you thus?—I
don't wish, not even *wish* to deceive you, Madam. The Searcher of
hearts is my witness how dear you are to me; but tho' it were
possible you could be still dearer to me—I would not even kiss your
hand, at the expence of your conscience.—Away with declamation!
let us appeal to the bar of Common Sense.—It is not mouthing every
thing sacred; it is not vague, ranting assertions; it is not assuming,
haughtily and insultingly assuming, the dictatorial language of a
Roman Pontiff, that must dissolve a union like ours.—Tell me,
Madam, are you under the least shadow of an obligation to bestow
your love, tenderness, caresses, affections, heart and soul, on Mr
Mcilhose—the man who has repeatedly, habitually and barbarously
broke thro' every tie, of Duty, Nature, or Gratitude to you? The
laws of your Country indeed, for the most useful reasons of Policy
and sound government, have made your person inviolate; but are
your heart and affections bound to one who gives not the least
return of either to you? You cannot do it; it is not in the nature of
things that you are bound to do it; the common feelings of
humanity forbid it.—Have you then a heart and affections which are
no man's right? you have: it would be highly, ridiculously absurd to
suppose the contrary.—Tell me then in the name of Common Sense
can it be wrong, is such a supposition compatible with the plainest
ideas of Right and Wrong, that it is improper to bestow that heart
and those affections to another; while that bestowing is not in the

395

smallest degree hurtful to your duty to God, to your children, to yourself, or to Society at large?—

This is the great test; the consequences: let us see them. In a widowed, forlorn, lonely situation, with a bosom glowing with love and tenderness, yet so delicately situated that you cannot indulge these noble feelings except you meet with a man who has a soul capable

XXIX (201)

[14th February 1788]

"I am distressed for thee, my brother Jonathan!"[1] I have suffered, Clarinda, from your letter.—My Soul was in arms at the sad perusal: I dreaded that I had acted wrong.—If I have robbed you of (*two words illegible*) friend God forgive me! But, Clarinda, be comforted: let us raise the tone of our feelings a little higher and bolder.—A fellow-creature who leaves us, who spurns us without just cause, tho' once our bosom friend—up with a little honest pride—let them go! How shall I comfort you who am the cause of the injury? Can I wish that I had never seen you? that we had never met? No: I never will! But have I thrown you friendless? there is almost distraction in that thought.—

Father of mercies! against thee often have I sinned; through thy grace I will endeavor to do so no more! She who, Thou knowest, is dearer to me than myself; Pour Thou the balm of peace into her past wounds, and hedge her about with Thy peculiar care, all her future days and nights! Strengthen her tender, noble mind firmly; to suffer, and magnamimously to bear! Make me worthy of that friendship, [that love] she honors me with! May my attachment to her be pure as Devotion and lasting as immortal life! O Almighty Goodness, hear me! Be to her at all times, particularly in the hour of distress or trial, a Friend and Comforter; a Guide and Guard!

"How are Thy servants blest, O Lord,
"How sure is their defence!
"Eternal Wisdom is their guide,
Their help, Omnipotence!"[2]

Forgive me, Clarinda, the injury I have done you!—Tonight I shall be with you; as indeed I shall be ill at ease till I see you.—

1 2 Samuel 1:26.
2 Addison: *Spectator*, 20th September 1712.

XXX (202)

2, o'clock [14th February, 1788]

I just now received your first letter of yesterday, by the careless negligence of the Penny post.—Clarinda, matters are grown very serious with us: then seriously hear me, and hear me Heaven—I met you, my dear Clarinda, by far the first of womankind, at least to me; I esteemed, I lov'd you at first sight, both of which attachments you have done me the honor to return; the longer I am acquainted with you, the more innate, amiableness and worth I discover in you—You have suffered a loss I confess for my sake; but if the firmest, steaddiest, warmest Friendship; if every endeavor to be worthy of *your* friendship; if a love, strong as the ties of Nature, and holy as the duties of Religion—if all these can make any thing like a compensation for the evil I have occasioned you, if they be worth your-acceptance, or can in the least add to your enjoyments—So help Sylvander, ye Powers above, in his hour of need, as he freely gives these all to Clarinda!

I esteem you, I love you, as a friend; I admire you, I love you, as a Woman, beyond any one in all the circle of Creation: I know I shall continue to esteem you, to love you; to pray for you—nay to pray for *myself* for *your* sake.—[*one line missing*]

Expect me at eight—and believe me to be ever, My dearest Madam, yours most entirely—

Sylvander

XXXI (204)

[15th February 1788]

When matters, My Love, are desperate, we must put on a desperate face—

"On Reason build Resolve,
"That column of true majesty in man"—[1]

Or as the same Author finely says in another place—

——"Let thy Soul spring up
"And lay strong hold for help on him that made thee"—[2]

I am yours, Clarinda, for life.—Never be discouraged at all this.—Look forward; in a few weeks I shall be some where or other out of the possibility of seeing you: till then, I shall write you often, but visit you seldom. Your fame, your welfare, your happiness, are dearer to me than any gratification whatever.—Be comforted, my Love! the present moment is the worst; the lenient hand of Time is daily and hourly either lightening the burden, or making us insensible to the weight.—None of these friends, I mean Mr K[emp?] and the other gentleman can hurt your worldly support; and for friendship, in a little time you will learn to be easy, and by and by, to be happy without it.—A decent means of livelyhood in the world, an approving God, a peaceful conscience and one firm trusty friend—can any body that has these, be said to be unhappy? These are yours.—

Tomorrow evening I shall be with you about eight: probably for the last time, till I return to Edinburgh—In the mean time, should any of these two *unlucky* friends question you respecting me, whether I am *the Man;* I do not think they are entitled to any information.—As to their jealousy and spying, I despise them.—Adieu! my dearest Madam!

Sylvander

1 Young: *Night Thoughts*, Night I, lines 30-1.
2 Ibid., Night VI, lines 90-1, paraphrased.

Agnes McLehose

XXXII (208)

Glasgow Monday even: 9 o'clock
[18th February 1788]

The attraction of love, I find, is in an inverse proportion to the attraction of the Newtonian Philosophy: in the system of Sir Isaac, the nearer objects were to one another, the stronger was the attractive force; in my system, every milestone that marked my progress from Clarinda, awaked a keener pang of attachment to her. —How do you feel, my Love? is your heart ill at ease? I fear it.—God forbid that these Persecutors should harass that Peace which is more precious to me than my own.—Be assured I shall ever think of you, muse on you, and in my moments of devotion, pray for you.—The hour that you are not in all my thoughts—"be that hour darkness! let the shadows of Death cover it! let it not be numbered in the hours of the day!"[1]

  ——"When I forget the darling theme—
  "Be my tongue mute! may fancy paint no more!
  "And dead to joy, forget my heart to beat!"[2]

I have just met with my old friend, the ship Captain; guess my pleasure: to meet you could alone have given me more.—My brother William too, the young Saddler, has come to Glasgow to meet me; and here are we three spending the evening.–

I arrived here too late to write by post; but I'll wrap half a dozen sheets of blank paper together, and send it by the Fly under the name of a—parcel.–You shall hear from me, next post town.—I would write you a longer letter but for the present circumstance of my friend.—Adieu, My Clarinda! I am just going to propose your health by way of grace-drink.–

                                                            Sylvander

1 Job 3:5.
2 Thomson: *A Hymn on the Seasons*, lines 94, 98-9.

XXXIII (209)

Kilmarnock, Friday [22nd February 1788]

I wrote you, my dear Madam, the moment I lighted in Glasgow; since then, I have not had opportunity; for in Paisley, where I arrived next day, My worthy, wise, friend, Mr Pattison, did not allow me a moment's respite.—I was there ten hours; during which time I was introduced to nine men worth six thousands; five men worth ten thousand; his brother, richly worth twenty thousands; and a young Weaver who will have thirty thousands good, when his father, who has no more children than the said Weaver and a Whigkirk, dies.—Mr P——was bred a zealous Antiburgher; but, during his widowerhood, he has found their strictness incompatible with certain compromises he is often obliged to make with those Powers of darkness, the devil, the world and the flesh; so he, good, merciful man! talked privately to me, of the absurdity of eternal torments, the liberality of sentiment in indulging the honest instincts of Nature, the mysteries of Concubinage, &c. He has a son however, that at sixteen has repeatedly minted at certain priviledges,—only proper for sober, staid men, who can use the *good things* of this life without *abusing*

398

them; but the father's parental vigilance has hitherto hedged him in, amid a corrupt and evil world.—His only daughter, who, "if the beast be to the fore, and the branks bide hale," will have seven thousand pound, when her old father steps into the dark Factory-Office of Eternity with his well-thrumm'd web of life; has put him again and again in a commendable fit of indignation by requesting a harpsichord—"O, these damn'd Boarding-schools" exclaims my prudent friend; "she was a good spinner and sower, till I was advised by her foes and mine to give her a year of Edinburgh!"

After two bottles more, my much-respected friend opened up to me a project, a legitimate child of Wisdom and Goodsense—'twas no less than a long-thought-on and deeply-matur'd design to marry a girl, fully as elegant in her form as the famous Priestess whom Saul consulted in his last hours;* and who had been second maid of honor to his deceased wife.—This, you may be sure I highly applauded; so I hope for a pair of gloves by and by.—

I spent the two bypast days at Dunlop-house with that worthy family to whom I was deeply indebted early in my poetic career; and in about two hours I shall present your "twa wee sarkies" to the little fellow.—

My dearest Clarinda, you are ever present with me; and these hours that drawl by among the fools and rascals of this world, are only supportable in the idea that they are the forerunners of that happy hour that ushers me to "The Mistress of my soul."—Next week I shall visit Dumfries, and next again, return to Edinburgh.— My letters, in these hurrying dissipated hours, will be heavy trash— but you know the Writer.—

God bless you!
Sylvander

* See I Samuel 28.

XXXIV (210)

[Mossgiel, 23rd February 1788]

I have just now, My ever dearest Madam, delivered your kind present to my sweet, little Bobbie; who I find a very fine fellow.—Your letter was waiting me.—Your interview with Mr K——[1] opens a wound, ill-closed, in my breast: not that I think his friendship of so much consequence to you, but because you set such a value on it.— Now for a little news that will please you.—I, this morning as I came home, called for a certain woman.—I am disgusted with her; I cannot endure her! I, while my heart smote me for the prophanity, tried to compare her with my Clarinda: 'twas setting the expiring glimmer of a farthing taper beside the cloudless glory of the meridian sun.—Here was tasteless insipidity, vulgarity of soul, and mercenary fawning; there, polished good sense, heaven-born genius, and the most generous, the most delicate, the most tender Passion.—I have done with her, and she with me.—

[*One line of MS. cut away here*] I set off tomorrow for Dumfries-shire.—'Tis merely out of Compliment to Mr Miller, for I know the Excise[2] must be my lot.- I will write you from Dumfries, if these horrid postages don't frighten me.—

Agnes McLehose

"Whatever place, whatever land I see,
"My heart, untravell'd, fondly turns to thee:
"Still to "Clarinda" turns with ceaseless pain:
"And drags, at each remove, a lengthen'd chain!"[3]

I just stay to write you a few lines before I go to call on my friend, Mr Gavin Hamilton.—I hate myself as an unworthy sinner, because these interviews of old, dear friends make me for half a moment almost forget Clarinda.—

Remember tomorrow evening at eight o'clock: I shall be with the Father of mercies, at that hour, on your account.—Farewell! if the post goes not tonight, I'll finish the other page tomorrow morning.—

Sylvander

1 Kemp.
2 Heavily scored through. Douglas misread this as 'the Indies.'
3 Goldsmith: *The Traveller*, lines 7ff., paraphrased.

XXXV (213)

Cumnock, 2nd March 1788

I hope and am certain that my generous Clarinda will not think my silence for now a long week has been in any degree owing to my forgetfulness.—I have been tosst about thro' the Country ever since I wrote you; and am here, returning from Dumfries-shire, at an Inn, the Post-Office of the place, with just so long time as my horse eats his corn to write you.—I have been hurried with business and dissipation almost equal to the insidious degree of the Persian Monarch's mandate, when he forbade asking petition of god or man for forty days: had the venerable Prophet been as throng as I, he had not broke the decree; at least, not thrice a day.—

I am thinking my farming scheme will yet hold.—A worthy, intelligent farmer, my father's friend and my own, has been with me on the spot: he thinks the bargain practicable.—I am myself, on a more serious review of the lands, much better pleased with them.—I won't mention this in writing to any body but you and Mr Ainslie.—Don't accuse me of being fickle: I have the two plans of life before me, and I wish to adopt the one most likely to procure me independance. I shall be in Edinburgh next week.—I long to see you: your image is omnipresent to me: nay, I am convinced I would soon idolatrize it most seriously; so much do absence and memory improve the medium thro' which one sees the much loved Object.—Tonight, at the sacred hour of eight, I expect to meet you—at the Throne of Grace.- I hope as I go home tonight, to find a letter from you at the Post-Office in Mauchline.—I have just once seen that dear hand since I left Edinburgh; a letter indeed which much affected me. —Tell me, first of womankind, will my warmest attachment, my sincerest friendship, my correspondence, will they be any compensation for the sacrifices you make for my sake? If they will, they are yours. If I settle on the farm I propose, I am just a day and a half's ride from Edinburgh—we will meet—don't you say, "perhaps too often!"—

Farewel, my fair my charming Poetess! May all good things ever attend you!

I am ever, My dearest Madam,
yours—
Sylvander

400

Agnes McLehose

XXXVI (217)

[6th March 1788]

I own myself guilty, Clarinda; I should have wrote you last week: but when you recollect, my dearest Madam, that yours of this night's Post is only the third I have got from you, and that this is the fifth or sixth I have sent to you, you will not reproach me with a good grace for unkindness.—I have always some kind of idea, not to sit down to write a letter except I have time and possession of my faculties so as to do some justice to my letter; which at present is rarely my situation.—For instance, yesterday I dined at a friend's at some distance; the savage hospitality of this Country spent me the most part of the night over the nauseous potion in the bowl; this day —sick—head-ache—low-spirits—miserable—fasting, except for a draught of water or small-beer now eight o'clock at night—only able to crawl ten minutes' walk into Mauchline, to wait the Post in the pleasurable hope of hearing from the Mistress of my soul.—

But, truce with all this! When I sit down to write to you all is harmony and peace.—A hundred times a day do I figure you, before your taper, your book or work laid aside as I get within the room.— How happy have I been! and how little of that scantling portion of time, called the life of man, is sacred to happiness; much less transport!

I could moralize tonight, like a Death's head.—

> "O what is life, that thoughtless wish of all!
> "A drop of honey in a draught of gall"—[1]

Nothing astonishes me more, when a little sickness clogs the wheels of life, than the thoughtless career we run, in the hour of health.— "None saith, where is God, my Maker, that giveth songs in the night: who teacheth us more knowledge than the beasts of the field, and more understanding than the fowls of the air"—[2]

Give me, my Maker, to remember thee! Give me to act up to the dignity of my nature! Give me to feel "another's woe"; and continue with me that dear-lov'd Friend that feels with mine!—

The dignified and dignifying consciousness of an honest man, and the well-grounded trust in approving Heaven, are two most substantial foundations of happiness.—[*Four or five words missing*] the soul, and give [*four or five words missing*] his native worth. [*Four or five words missing*] I shall set out soon [*four or five words missing*] which are very [*four or five words missing*] me, on mond[ay] [*four or five words missing*] Clarinda.—[*Four or five words missing*] pleasure.—I have just [had Bobbie inoculated][3] in the small-pox, as they are in the neighborhood: he is as yet, doing very well.—

I could not have wrote a page to any mortal, except yourself.—I'll write you by Sunday's post.—

Adieu! Good-night!
Sylvander

1 Not identified.
2 Job 36:10-11, misquoted.
3 Conjectural reading by Ferguson (1931) rejected by Ross Roy (1985).

Agnes McLehose

XXXVII (218)

Mossgiel 7th March 1788

Clarinda, I have been so stung with your reproach for unkindness, a sin so unlike me, a sin I detest more than a breach of the whole Decalogue, fifth, sixth, seventh and ninth articles excepted; that I believe I shall not rest in my grave about it, if I die before I see you. —You have often allowed me the head to judge, and the heart to feel the influence of female excellence: was it not blasphemy then, against your own charms, and against my feelings to suppose that a short fortnight could abate my Passion? You, my Love, may have your cares and anxieties to disturb you, but they are the usual recurrencies of life; your future views are fix'd, and your mind in a settled routine.—Could not you, my ever dearest Madam, make a little allowance for a man, after long absence, paying a short visit to a Country full of friends, relations, and early intimates? Cannot you guess, my Clarinda, what thoughts, what cares, what anxious forebodings, hopes and fears, must crowd the breast of the man of keen sensibility, when no less is on the tapis than his aim, his employment, his very existence thro' future life? To be overtopped in anything else, I can bear; but in the lists of generous love, I defy all mankind!—Not even to the tender, the fond, the loving Clarinda; she whose strength of attachment, whose melting soul, may vie with Eloisa and Sappho; not even She can overpay the Affection She owes me!

Now that, not my apology, but my defence is made; I feel my soul respire more easily.—I know you will go along with me in my justification—would to Heaven you could in my Adoption too! I mean an Adoption beneath the stars: an Adoption where I might revel in the immediate beams of

"She, the bright sun of all her Sex"—[1]

I would not have you, my dear Madam, so much hurt at Miss Nimmo's coldness.—'Tis placing yourself below her, an honor she by no means deserves.—We ought, when we wish to be economists in happiness; we ought in the first place to fix the standard of our own character; and when, on full examination, we know where we stand, and how much ground we occupy, let us contend for it as property; and those who seem to doubt, or deny us what is justly ours, let us either pity their prejudices or despise their judgement.—I know, my Dear, you will say this is self-conceit; but I call it self-knowledge: the one is the overweening opinion of a fool, who fancies himself to be, what we would wish himself to be thought; the other is the honest justice that a man of sense, who has thoroughly examined the subject, owes to himself.—Without this standard, this column in our own mind; we are perpetually at the mercy of the petulance, the mistakes, the prejudices, nay, the very weakness and wickedness of our fellow-creatures.—

I urge this, my Dear, both to confirm myself in the doctrine which I assure you, I sometimes need; and because I know that this, causes you often much disquiet.—To return to Miss Nimmo: she is most certainly a worthy soul; and equalled by very, very few in goodness of the heart.—But, can she boast more goodness of heart than

402

Clarinda? not even prejudice will dare to say so: for penetration and discernment, Clarinda sees far beyond her: to wit, Miss Nimmo dare make no pretence; to Clarinda's wit, scarce any of her sex dare make pretence. Personal charms, it would be ridiculous to run the parallel: and for conduct in life, Miss Nimmo was never called out, either much to do, or to suffer; Clarinda has been both; and has performed her Part, where Miss Nimmo would have sunk at the bare idea.—

Away, then, with these disquietudes! Let us pray with the honest weaver of Kilbarchan, "Lord, send us a gude conceit o' oursel'!" Or in the words of the auld sang,

"Who does me disdain, I can scorn them again,
"And I'll never mind any such foes"

There is an error in the commerce of intimacy which has led me far astray . . . .

[Several lines of MS erased]

. . . way of exchange, have not an equivalent to give; and what is still worse, have no idea of the value of our goods.—Happy is our lot, indeed, when we meet with an honest Merchant, who is qualified to deal with us on our own terms; but that is a rarity: with almost every body we must pocket our pearls, less or more; and learn, in the old Scots phrase—"To gie sic-like as we get."—For this reason one should try to erect a kind of bank or store-house in one's own mind; or as the Psalmist says, "We should commune with our own hearts and be still."[2] This is exactly . . .

[Several lines of MS. erased]

. . . friend be so peculiarly favored of heaven as to have a soul as noble and exalted as yours, sooner or later your bosom will ach with disappointment. I wrote you yesternight which will reach you long before this can.—I may write Mr Ainslie before I see him, but I am not sure.—

Farewel! ! ! and remember

Sylvander

1 Burns: *Clarinda, Mistress of my Soul,* line 13, altered.
2 Psalms 4:4, misquoted.

XXXVIII (222B)

Wednesday Morning, [12th March 1788]

Clarinda, will that envious night-cap hinder you from appearing at the window as I pass? "Who is she that looketh forth as the morning; fair as the sun, clear as the moon, terrible as an army with banners?"[1]

Do not accuse me of fond folly for this line; you know I am a cool lover. I mean by these presents greeting, to let you to wit, that arch-rascal, Creech, has not done my business yesternight, which has put off my leaving town till Monday morning. Tomorrow at eleven, I meet with him for the last time; just the hour I should have met far more agreable company.

You will tell me this evening, whether you cannot make our hour of meeting to-morrow one o'clock. I have just now written Creech such a letter, that the very goose-feather in my hand shrunk back from the line, and seemed to say, "I exceedingly fear and quake!"[2] I am forming ideal schemes of vengeance. O for a little of my will on him! I just wished he loved as I do—as glorious an object as Clarinda—and that he were doomed. Adieu, and think on

Sylvander

1 Song of Solomon 6:10.
2 Hebrews 12:21.

XXXIX (224)

Friday, Nine o'clock Night.
[14th March 1788]

I am just now come in, and have read your letter. The first thing I did, was to thank the Divine Disposer of events, that he has had such happiness in store for me as the connexion I have with you. Life, my Clarinda, is a weary, barren path; and woe be to him or her that ventures on it alone! For me, I have my dearest partner of my soul: Clarinda and I will make out our pilgrimage together. Wherever I am, I shall constantly let her know how I go on, what I observe in the world around me, and what adventures I meet with. Will it please you, my love, to get, every week, or, at least, every fortnight, a packet, two or three sheets, full of remarks, nonsense, news, rhymes, and old songs?

Will you open, with satisfaction and delight, a letter from a man who loves you, who has loved you, and who will love you to death, through death, and for ever? Oh Clarinda! what do I owe to Heaven for blessing me with such a piece of exalted excellence as you! I call over your idea, as a miser counts over his treasure! Tell me, were you studious to please me last night? I am sure you did it to transport. How rich am I who have such a treasure as you! You know me; you know how to make me happy, and you do it most effectually. God bless you with

"Long life, long youth, long pleasure, and a friend!"[1]

Tomorrow night, according to your own direction, I shall watch the window: 'tis the star that guides me to paradise. The great relish to all is, that Honour, that Innocence, that Religion, are the witnesses and guarantees of our happiness. "The Lord God knoweth," and, perhaps, "Israel he shall know,"[2] my love and your merit. Adieu, Clarinda! I am going to remember you in my prayers.

Sylvander

1 Pope: *To Mrs. M.B.*, line 2.
2 Joshua 22:22, altered slightly.

XL (225)

Monday, Noon
[17th March 1788]

I will meet you to-morrow, Clarinda, as you appoint. My Excise affair is just concluded, and I have got my order for instructions: so far good. Wednesday night I am engaged to sup among some of the principals of the Excise: so can only make a call for you that evening; but next day, I stay to dine with one of the Commissioners, so cannot go till Friday morning.

Your hopes, your fears, your cares, my love, are mine; so don't mind them. I will take you in my hand through the dreary wilds of this world, and scare away the ravening bird or beast that would annoy you. I saw Mary in town today, and asked her if she had seen you. I shall certainly bespeak Mr Ainslie as you desire.

Excuse me, my dearest angel, this hurried scrawl and miserable paper; circumstances make both. Farewell till to-morrow.

Sylvander

XLI (225A)

Edinburgh March 17th 1788

Fair Empress of the Poet's soul,
[C.W. p. 321]

Sylvander

XLII (226)

Tuesday morn:
[18th March 1788]

I am just hurrying away to wait on the Great Man, Clarinda, but I have more respect to my own peace and happiness than to set out without waiting on you; for my imagination, like a child's favorite bird, will fondly flutter along with this scrawl till it perch on your bosom.—I thank you for all the happiness you bestowed on me yesterday.—The walk—delightful; the evening-rapture.—Do not be uneasy today, Clarinda; forgive me.—I am in rather better spirits today, though I had but an indifferent night: care, anxiety, sat on my spirits; and all the chearfulness of this morning is the fruit of some serious, important ideas that lie in their realities beyond "the dark and the narrow house,"* as Ossian, prince of Poets, says. The Father of Mercies be with you, Clarinda! and every good thing attend you!

Sylvander

* *Fingal*, Bk. I, section 15.

XLIII (320)

9th March 1789

Madam

The letter you wrote me to Heron's carried its own answer in its bosom: you forbade me to write you, unless I was willing to plead, Guilty, to a certain Indictment that you were pleased to bring against me.- As I am convinced of my own innocence, and though conscious of high imprudence & egregious folly, can lay my hand on my breast and attest the rectitude of my heart; you will pardon me, Madam, if I do not carry my complaisance so far, as humbly to acquiesce in the name of, Villain, merely out of compliment even to YOUR opinion; much as I esteem your judgement, and warmly as I regard your worth.—I have already told you, and I again aver it, that

at the Period of time alluded to, I was not under the smallest moral
tie to Mrs B——; nor did I, nor could I then know, all the powerful
circumstances that omnipotent Necessity was busy laying in wait for
me.—When you call over the scenes that have passed between us, you
will survey the conduct of an honest man, struggling successfully
with temptations the most powerful that ever beset humanity, and
preserving untainted honor in situations where the austerest Virtue
would have forgiven a fall—Situations that I will dare to say, not a
single individual of all his kind, even with half his sensibility and
passion, could have encountered without ruin; and I leave you to
guess, Madam, how such a man is likely to digest an accusation of
perfidious treachery!

Was I to blame, Madam, in being the distracted victim of Charms
which, I affirm it, no man ever approached with impunity?—Had I
seen the least glimmering of hope that these Charms could ever have
been mine—or even had not iron Necessity—but these are unavailing
words.—

I would have called on you when I was in town, indeed I could not
have resisted it, but that Mr A[inslie] told me that you were
determined to avoid your windows while I was in town, lest even a
glance of me should occur in the Street.—

When I have regained your good opinion, perhaps I may venture to
solicit your friendship: but be that as it may, the first of her Sex I
ever knew, shall always be the object of my warmest good wishes.—

XLIV (388)

[February 1790]

I have, indeed, been ill, Madam, this whole winter. An incessant
headache, depression of spirits, and all the truly miserable
consequences of a deranged nervous system, have made dreadful
havoc of my health and peace. Add to all this, a line of life, into
which I have lately entered, obliges me to ride, upon an average, at
least 200 miles every week. However, thank heaven I am now greatly
better in my health. . . . I cannot, will not, enter into extenuatory
circumstances; else I could show you how my precipitate, headlong,
unthinking conduct leagued, with a conjuncture of unlucky events,
to thrust me out of a possibility of keeping the path of rectitude; to
curse me, by an irreconcileable war between my duty and my
nearest wishes, and to damn me with a choice only of different
species of error and misconduct.

I dare not trust myself further with this subject. The following song
is one of my latest productions; and I send it you as I would do
anything else, because it pleases myself.

> Thine am I, my faithful fair,
> Thine, my lovely Nancy;
> Ev'ry pulse along my veins,
> Ev'ry roving fancy.*

[3 additional stanzas; C.W. p. 505]

* In September 1794 Burns instructed Thomson to delete 'Nancy' and
substitute 'Chloris'.

Agnes McLehose

XLV (389)

[Ellisland, February 1790]

. . . in health. I do not rate the fatigue a farthing.—This labourious life secures me independance, a blessing which you know few people prize higher than I.

I could not answer your last letter but one when you in so many words tell a man that "you look on his letters with a smile of contempt", in what language Madam, can he answer you? Though I were conscious that I had acted wrong—and I am conscious that I have acted wrong—yet I would not be bullied into repentance but your last letter quite disarmed me.—Determined as you . . .

XLVI (462)

[Ellisland, July 1791?]

I have received both your last letters, Madam, & ought & would have answered the first long ago.—But on what subject shall I write you? How can you expect a Correspondent should write you, when you declare that you mean to preserve his letters with a view, sooner or later, to expose them on the pillory of derision & the rack of criticism? This is gagging me compleatly as to speaking the sentiments of my bosom; else, Madam, I could perhaps too truly

"Join grief with grief & echo sighs to thine!"[1]

I have perused your most beautiful but most pathetic Poem—do not ask me how often, or with what emotions.—

You know that, "I dare to *sin*, but not to *lie*."[2]—Your Verses wring the confession from my inmost soul that—I will say it—expose it if you please—that—I have more than once in my life been the victim of a damning conjuncture of circumstances; & that to me you must be ever

"Dear as the light that visits those sad eyes"[3]—

*   *   *

Sweet Sensibility how charming,
[C.W. p. 402]

I have just, *since I had yours,* composed the inclosed Stanzas.—Let me know your opinion of them.—I have one other Piece in your taste, but I have just a snatch of time.—

1 Pope: *Eloisa to Abelard,* line 42, misquoted.
2 Not identified.
3 Gray: *The Bard,* strophe 3, line 12.

XLVII (483)

Dumfries, 23rd November 1791

It is extremely difficult, my dear Madam, for me to deny a lady anything; but to a lady whom I regard with all the endearing epithets of respectful esteem and old friendship, how shall I find the language of refusal? I have, indeed, a shade of the lady, which I keep, and shall ever keep in the *sanctum sanctorum* of my most anxious care.

407

That lady, though an unfortunate and irresistible conjuncture of circumstances has lost me her esteem, yet she shall be ever, to me

"Dear as the ruddy drops that warm my heart."*

I am rather anxious for her sake, as to her voyage. I pray God my fears may be groundless. By the way, I have this moment a letter from her, with a paragraph or two conceived in so stately a style, that I would not pardon it in any created being except herself; but, as the subject interests me much, I shall answer it to you, as I do not know her present address. I am sure she must have told you of a girl, a Jenny Clow, who had the misfortune to make me a father, with contrition I own it, contrary to the laws of our most excellent constitution, in our holy Presbyterian hierarchy.

Mrs M— tells me a tale of the poor girl's distress that makes my very heart weep blood. I will trust that your goodness will apologise to your delicacy for me, when I beg of you, for Heaven's sake, to send a porter to the poor woman—Mrs M., it seems, knows where she is to be found—with five shillings in my name; and, as I shall be in Edinburgh on Tuesday first, for certain, make the poor wench leave a line for me, before Tuesday, at Mr Mackay's, White Hart Inn, Grassmarket, where I shall put up; and, before I am two hours in town, I shall see the poor girl, and try what is to be done for her relief. I would have taken my boy from her long ago, but she would never consent.

I shall do myself the very great pleasure to call for you when I come to town, and repay you the sum your goodness shall have advanced . . . .

and most obedient,
Robert Burns

* Shakespeare: *Julius Caesar*, Act II, sc. 1.

XLVIII (484)

Leadhills, Thursday noon
[8th December 1791]
[*Bishop mark* DE 11]

[With the *Lament of Mary Queen of Scots*]
[C.W. p. 400]

Such, My dearest Nancy, were the words of the amiable but unfortunate Mary.—Misfortune seems to take a peculiar pleasure in darting her arrows against "Honest Men & bony Lasses."[1]—Of this You are too, too just a proof; but may your future fate be a bright exception to the remark.—In the words of Hamlet—

"Adieu, adieu, adieu! Remember me!"[2]

Robt Burns

1 *Tam o Shanter*, line 16. C.W. p. 410.
2 Shakespeare: *Hamlet*, Act I, sc. 5, altered.

XLIX (485)

Dumfries, 15th December 1791

I have some merit, my ever dearest of women, in attracting & securing the heart of Clarinda.—In her I met with the most accomplished of all women-kind, the first of all God's works, & yet I, even I, had the good fortune to appear amiable in her sight.—

By the bye, this is the sixth letter that I have written you, since I left you; & if you were an ordinary being, as you are a creature very extraordinary, an instance of what God Almighty in the plentitude of his power & the fullness of his goodness, can make!! I would never forgive you for not answering my letters.—

I have sent in your hair, a part of the parcel you gave me, with a measure, to Mr Bruce the Jeweller in Prince's Street, to get a ring done for me.—I have likewise sent in the verses on Sensibility, altered to—

Sensibility how charming
Dearest, Nancy, thou canst tell—&c,
[C.W. p. 402]

in to the Editor of the Scots Songs, of which you have three volumes, to set to a most beautiful air; out of compliment to the first of women, my ever beloved, my ever sacred Clarinda.—

I shall probably write you tomorrow.—In the mean time, from a man who is literally drunk, accept & forgive! ! !

R.B—

L (486)

Dumfries, 27th December 1791

I have yours, my ever dearest Nancy, this moment.—I have just ten minutes before the Post goes, & these I shall employ in sending you some Songs I have just been composing to different tunes for the Collection of Songs, of which you have three volumes—& of which you *shall* have the fourth.—

Song—Tune, Rory Dall's port—

Ae fond kiss, & then we sever;
[C.W. p. 434]

Song—To an old Scots tune—

Behold the hour, the boat arrive!
[C.W. p. 503]

Song, To a charming plaintive Scots air—

Ance mair I hail thee, thou gloomy December!
[C.W. p. 433, lines 1-8]

The rest of this song is on the wheels.—

Adieu! Adieu! ! !

Agnes McLehose

LI (544)

The following was never scrolled, but is copied from the original letter.—

[March? 1793]

I suppose, my dear Madam, that by your neglecting to inform me of your arrival in Europe, a circumstance which could not be indifferent to me, as indeed no occurrence relating to you can—you meant to leave me to guess & gather that a correspondence I once had the honor & *felicity* to enjoy, is to be no more.—Alas, what heavy laden sounds are these—"no more!"—The wretch who has never tasted pleasure, has never known woe; but what drives the soul to madness, is the recollection of joys that are—"no more!"—But this is not language to the world.—They do not understand it.—But, come, ye children of Feeling & Sentiment; ye whose trembling bosom chords ach, to unutterable anguish, as recollection gushed on the heart! Ye who are capable of an attachment, keen as the arrow of Death, and strong as the vigour of Immortal Being— Come! & your ears shall drink a tale—but hush!—I must not, can not tell it! Agony is in the recollection, & frenzy is in the recital!—

But to leave these paths that lead to madness, I congratulate your friends, Madam, on your return; and I hope that the precious health which Miss Peacock tells me is so much injured, is restored, or restoring.—There is a fatality attends Miss Peacock's correspondence & mine.—Two of my letters, it seems she never received; and her last, which came when I was in Ayrshire, was unfortunately mislaid, and only found about ten days or a fortnight ago, on removing a desk of drawers.

I present you a book: may I hope you will accept of it.—I dare say you have brought your books with you.—The fourth volume of the Scots Songs is published: I will also send it you.—

Shall I hear from you?—But first, hear me!—No cold language—no prudential documents—I despise Advice, & scorn Controul—If you are not to write such language, such sentiments, as you know I shall wish, shall delight to receive; I conjure you, By wounded Pride! By ruined Peace! By frantic disappointed Passion! By all the many ills that constitute that sum of human woes—A BROKEN HEART!—To me be silent for ever! ! !—If you insult me with the unfeeling apothegms of cold-blooded Caution, May all the—but hold—a Fiend could not breathe a malevolent wish on the head of *MY* Angel!—

Mind my request!—If you send me a page baptised in the font of sanctimonious Prudence—By Heaven, Earth & Hell, I will tear it into atoms!—

Adieu! May all good things attend you!

R.B.

I need scarcely remark that the foregoing was the fustian rant of enthusiastic youth.*—

* Burns's comment in the Glenriddell MS.

Agnes McLehose

LII (629)

[Castle Douglas 25th June? 1794]

Before you ask me why I have not written you; first let me be informed of you, *how* I shall write you? "In Friendship," you say; & I have many a time taken up my pen to try an epistle of "Friendship" to you; but it will not do: 'tis like Jove grasping a pop-gun, after having wielded his thunder.—When I take up the pen, Recollection ruins me.—Ah! my ever dearest Clarinda!—Clarinda?— What a host of Memory's tenderest offspring crowd on my fancy at that sound!—But I must not indulge that subject:—you have forbid it.—

I am extremely happy to learn that your precious health is re-established, & that you are once more fit to enjoy that satisfaction in existence, which health alone can give us.—My old Friend, Ainslie, has indeed been kind to you.—Tell him that I envy him the power of serving you.—I had a letter from him a while ago, but it was so dry, so distant, so like a card to one of his Clients, that I could scarce bear to read it, & have not yet answered it.—He is a good, honest fellow; & *can* write a friendly letter, which would do equal honor to his head & his heart, as a whole sheaf of his letters I have by me will witness; & though Fame does not blow her trumpet at my approach *now,* as she did *then,* when he first honored me with his friendship, yet I am as proud as ever; & when I am laid in my grave, I wish to be stretched at my full length, that I may occupy every inch of ground which I have a right to.—

You would laugh, were you to see me, where I am just now:—would to Heaven you were here to laugh with me, though I am afraid that crying would be our first employment.—Here am I set, a solitary hermit, in the solitary room, of a solitary inn, with a solitary bottle of wine by me—as grave & as stupid as an owl—but like that owl, still faithfull to my own song; in confirmation of which, my dear Mrs Mack, here is your good health! May the hand-wal'd bennisons o' Heaven bless your bonie face; & the wretch wha skellies at your weelfare, may the auld tinkler deil get him to clout his rotten heart! Amen!

You must know, my dearest Madam, that these now many years, whereever I am, in whatever company, when a married lady is called as a toast, I constantly give you; but as your name has never passed my lips, even to my most intimate friend, I give you by the name of Mrs Mack.—This is so well known among my acquaintances, that when my married lady is called for, the toast-master will say—"O, we need not ask him who it is—here's Mrs Mac!" I have also among my convivial friends, set on foot a round of toasts, which I call, a round of Arcadian Shepherdesses; that is, a round of favourite Ladies, under female names celebrated in ancient song; & then, you are my Clarinda:—so my lovely Clarinda, I devote this glass of wine to a most ardent wish for your happiness!—

> In vain would Prudence, with decorous sneer,
> Point out a cens'ring world, & bid me fear:
> Above that world on wings of love I rise,
> I know its worst—& can that worst despise.—

411

Agnes McLehose

"Wronged, injured, shunned; unpitied, unredrest;
The mocked quotation of the scorner's jest"–
Let Prudence direst bodements on me fall,
Clarinda, rich reward! o'erpays them all!

I have been rhyming a little of late, but I do not know if they are worth Postage.–

* * *

Tell me what you think of the following–

Monody–

How cold is that bosom which folly once fired,
[C.W. p. 511]

The subject of the foregoing is a woman of fashion in this country, with whom, at one period, I was well acquainted.–By some scandalous conduct to me, & two or three other gentlemen here as well as me, she steered so far to the north of my good opinion, that I have made her the theme of several illnatured things.–The following Epigram struck me the other day, as I passed her carriage.–

Pinned to Mrs R——'s coach–

If you rattle along like your Mistress's tongue,
[C.W. p. 514]

WILLIAM HAMILTON

The recipient of the following letter has not been identified, although it is evident that he was on good terms with John Tait, at whose Edinburgh residence of Park Place he was residing when Burns sent him a package containing this letter. Possibly he had connexions with Clackmannanshire.

(159A)

Weden even:
[12th December 1787]

My dear Sir,

I send you two copies of a song, one for Mr Adair[1] and another for yourself.—The letter to Miss Chalmers,[2] I beg you will take the trouble to send to the Clackmannan Carrier tonight.—I have got an ill bruised limb, but am growing better.—Cannot you call in? T'would oblidge your friend

R. Burns

My Compliments to Crawford[3]

1 James Adair, who accompanied Burns to Harviestoun, October 1787.
2 Margaret Chalmers.
3 Crawford Tait, son of John Tait of Harviestoun.

413

CHARLES HAY

Born in 1747, he was the son of James Hay of Cocklaw. He studied law in Edinburgh and was called to the bar in 1768. In 1806 he was raised to the Bench and then took the title of Lord Newton. He enjoyed the honorific title of 'muster-master-general' in the Crochallan Fencibles, his duties apparently consisting of 'drilling' the recruits! Lord Cockburn says that Hay was noted for 'law, punch, whist, claret, and worth', and Forbes Gray added that 'his bibulous performances were really remarkable at a time when drinking records were not easily established.' He had no taste for literature, so it must be assumed that his friendship with Burns was purely convivial, although Burns's comments in the following letter seem to give the lie to that suggestion. Lord Newton died in 1811.

(164)

[Enclosing the lines *On the death of Lord President Dundas*]
[C.W. p. 300]

Monday morn:
[24th December? 1787]

Sir

the inclosed Poem was in consequence of your suggestion, last time I had the pleasure of seeing you.—It cost me an hour or two of next morning's sleep, but did not please me; so it lay by, an ill-digested effort, till the other day that I gave it a Critic brush.—These kind of subjects are much hackneyed; and besides, the wailings of the rhyming tribe over the ashes of the Great, are damnably suspicious, and out of all character for sincerity.—These ideas damp'd my Muse's fire; however, I have done the best I could; and at all events, it gives me an opportunity of declaring that I have the honor to be, Sir,

your oblidged humble servant
Robt Burns

MR THOMSON

The recipient of the following brief note has not been identified. The note was addressed to him at Mr——s, St James square, but the surname has been heavily scored through. Ross Roy thinks that it may have begun with 'St' or 'Sh'. It is chiefly of interest as mentioning the injury sustained by Burns in a carriage accident on 8th December 1787. From this it has been deduced that the undated note was written some time between 10th and 24th December.

(164A)

Monday morn:
[10th-24th December 1787]

Dear Sir

I am laid up with a bruised limb, and shall be glad to see you if you can call in for half a minute any time today or tomorrow.

I am
yours sincerely
Robt Burns

JAMES STEWART

The recipient of the following letter was the keeper of Cleland's Gardens, a public house in North St James Street, Edinburgh where a Jacobite dinner was held on 31st December 1787 to celebrate the birthday of the Young Pretender, Prince Charles Edward Stuart. Burns was replying to an invitation to this event. The stanzas quoted in the letter are taken from his *Address to Wm. Tytler, Esq., of Woodhouselee* (C.W. p. 276).

(165)

St James square, Weden: even
[26th December 1787]

Sir

Monday next is a day of the year with me hallowed as the ceremonies of Religion, and sacred to the memory of the sufferings of my King and my Forefathers.—The honour you do me by your invitation, I most cordially and gratefully accept.—

> Tho' something like moisture conglobes in my eye,
>   Let no one misdeem me disloyal;
> A poor friendless Wanderer may well claim a sigh,
>   Still more if that Wanderer were royal.—
>
> My fathers that Name have rever'd on a throne;
>   My fathers have died to right it;
> Those fathers would spurn their degenerate Son,
>   That Name should he scoffingly slight it!

I am, Sir, your oblidged humble servant
Robt Burns

FRANCIS HOWDEN

An Edinburgh jeweller in Parliament Square who, in 1792, obtained the royal warrant as medallist and goldsmith to HRH the Prince of Wales. The following letter was accompanied by a small silhouette by Miers which Burns wished to have mounted in a locket as a wedding present, but for whom is not known. Burns presented these 'shades' to several of his friends - invariably the paper cuts which Miers supplied at sixpence each. It is evident, from this letter, that Howden had had several previous commissions of this sort from Burns.

(167)

St. James's Square No. 2d Attic story.

The bearer of this will deliver you a small shade to set; which, my dear Sir, if you would highly oblidge a poor cripple devil as I am at present, you will finish at farthest against tomorrow evening.—It goes a hundred miles into the country; and if it is at me by five o'clock tomorrow evening, I have an opportunity of a private hand to convey it; if not, I don't know how to get it sent.—Set it just as you did the others you did for me, "in the neatest and cheapest manner;" both to answer as a breastpin and with a ring to answer as a locket.—Do, despatch it; as it is, I believe, the pledge of Love, and perhaps the prelude to ma-tri-mo-ny.—Everybody knows the auld wife's observation when she saw a poor dog going to be hang'd—"God help us! it's the gate we hae a' to gang!"—

The Parties, one of them at least, is a very particular acquaintance of mine; the honest lover.—He only needs a little of an advice which my grandmother, rest her soul! often gave me, and I as often neglected—"Leuk twice or ye loup ance!"—

Let me conjure you, my friend, by the bended bow of Cupid; by the unloosed cestus of Venus; by the lighted torch of Hymen, that you will have the locket finished by the time mentioned! And if your Worship would have as much Christian charity as call with it yourself, and comfort a poor wretch, not wounded indeed by Cupid's arrow, but bruised by a good, serious agonizing, damn'd, hard knock on the knee—you will gain the earnest prayers, when he does pray, of,

Dear Sir, your humble servant
Robt Burns

CAPTAIN RICHARD BROWN

Born in Irvine in 1753, where Burns met him in the autumn of 1781 while
learning the trade of flax dressing. Brown, six years the poet's senior and
already quite the man of the world as befitted a sea-farer, exerted a
tremendous influence on Burns, then at an impressionable age and away from
home for the first time. Burns describes his friendship with Brown in the
Autobiographical letter to Dr Moore (see page 254) which, incidentally, sheds
some light on Brown's colourful background. The son of 'a plain mechanic', he
had become the protegé of a great man of the neighbourhood, who had given
him a genteel education. The death of his benefactor, however, had robbed
him of advancement, so he had gone to sea. Shortly before Burns first met him
he had been captured by an American privateer and cast ashore on the
Connaught coast. By the time Burns wrote to Moore, however, Brown was
captain of a large west indiaman, the *Mary and Jean*. To Moore Burns also
confided that 'He was the only man I ever saw who was a greater fool than
myself when WOMAN was the presiding star. . .' Brown married late in 1787
and settled in Port Glasgow which remained his home until his death in 1833.
After his marriage Brown acquired a veneer of respectability and became
estranged from his erstwhile friend when it came to his attention that Burns
had been telling people that Brown had initiated him into the arts of
seduction. Consequently the correspondence ends with Burns's letter (VII) of
November 1789. Virtually the only copy of the Kilmarnock Edition
personally inscribed for presentation by Burns was that sent to Brown. It only
came to light after Brown's death and was discovered hidden at the back of a
sideboard!

Of the seven extant letters, perhaps the most interesting is that written from
Mauchline on 7th March 1788 (III) in which Burns adopts some amusing
nautical metaphors to describe Jean Armour's predicament on his return from
Edinburgh, when he found her pregnant for the second time, and cast out by
her family. The phrase 'have taken command myself - not ostensibly, but for a
time, in secret' has been taken to refer to the timing of Burns's regular
marriage to Jean.

I (168)

Edinburgh, 30th December 1787

My dear Sir,

I have met with few things in my life which has given me more
pleasure than Fortune's kindness to you, since those days in which
we met in the vale of misery, as I can honestly say that I never met
with a man who more truly deserved it, or to whom my heart more
truly wish'd it.—I have been much indebted, since that time, to your
story and sentiments, for steeling my mind against evils of which I
have had a pretty decent share.—My will o' wisp fate, you know: do
you recollect a sunday we spent in Eglinton woods? you told me, on
my repeating some verses to you that you wondered I could resist
the temptation of sending verses of such merit to a magazine: 'twas
actually this that gave me an idea of my own pieces which
encouraged me to endeavour at the character of a Poet.—I am happy
to hear that you will be two or three months at home: as soon as a
bruised limb will permit me, I shall return to Ayrshire—and we *shall*
meet!

"And faith, I hope we'll no sit dumb,
    Nor yet cast out!" [1]

I have much to tell you, of "Men, their manners & their ways," [2]
perhpas a little of t'other Sex.—Apropos, I beg to be remembered to
Mrs Brown; there, I doubt not, my dear friend, but you have found
substantial happiness.—I am impatient to see her, as well as you.—I
expect to find you something of an altered, but not, a different
man: the wild, bold, generous young fellow, composed into the
steady affectionate husband, and the fondly careful Parent.—For me,
I am just the same will-o'-wisp being I used to be.—About the first,
and fourth quarters of the moon, I generally set in for the trade-

winds of wisdom; but about the full, and change, I am the luckless victim of mad tornadoes, which blow me into chaos.—Almighty Love still "reigns and revels" in my bosom; and I am at this moment ready to hang myself for a young Edinburgh widow, who has wit and beauty more murderously fatal than the assassinating stiletto of the Sicilian Banditti, or the poisoned arrow of the savage African. My Highland durk, that used to hang beside my crutches, I have gravely removed into a neighbouring closet, the key of which I cannot command; in case of spring-tide paroxysms.—You may guess of her wit by the following verses which she sent me the other day—

> "Talk not of Love, it gives me pain,
>   "For Love has been my foe;
> "He bound me with an iron chain,
>   "And plung'd me deep in woe!
>
> "But Friendship's pure and lasting joys
>   "My heart was form'd to prove:
> "There welcome win and wear the prize,
>   "But never talk of Love.
>
> "Your Friendship much can make me blest,
>   "O, why that bliss destroy!
> "Why urge the odious, one request
>   "You know I must deny!"

My best compliments to our friend, Allan.—Adieu!   Robt Burns

1 Ramsay: *Answer to Hamilton of Gilbertfield's First Epistle*, closing lines.
2 Pope: *January and May*, line 157.

II (205)

Edinburgh, 15th February 1788

My Dear Sir,

I received yours with the greatest pleasure—I shall arrive at Glasgow on Monday evening, and beg if possible, you will meet me on Tuesday: I shall wait you tuesday all day.—I shall be found at Durie's, Blackbull Inn.—I am hurried as if hunted by fifty devils, else I would come to Greenock: but if you cannot possibly come, write me, if possible, to Glasgow on Monday; or direct to me at Mossgiel, by Mauchline, and name a day and place in Ayrshire, within a fortnight in Ayrshire, & return to Edinburgh.—

I am ever, My dearest friend, yours
Robt Burns

III (211)

Mossgiel, 24th February 1788

My dear Friend,

I cannot get the properest direction for my friend in Jamaica, but the following will do—To Mr John Hutchison, at John Brownrigs Esqr—Care of Mr Benjamin Henriques, Merchant, Orange Street, Kingston.—

I arrived here, at my brother's, only yesterday; after fighting my way thro' Paisley and Kilmarnock against those old powerful foes of mine, the Devil, the World, and the Flesh; so terrible in the fields of Dissipation.—

I have met with few incidents in my life which gave me so much pleasure as meeting you in Glasgow.—There is a time of life beyond which, we cannot form a tie worth the name of Friendship.—

"Oh youth, enchanting stage, profusely blest!"—[1]

Life is a fairy scene; almost all that deserves the name of enjoyment, or pleasure, is only charming delusion; and in comes ripening Age, in all the gravity of hoary wisdom, and wickedly chases away the dear, bewitching Phantoms.—

When I think of life, I resolve to keep a strict look out in the course of Economy, for the sake of wordly convenience and independance of mind; to cultivate intimacy with a few of the companions of youth, that they may be the friends of Age; never to refuse my liquorish humour a handful of the Sweetmeats of life, where they come not too dear; and for Futurity,

"The present moment is our ain,
"The neist we never saw!"[2]

How do you like my Philosophy?—Give my best Compliments to Mrs Brown; and believe me to be ever,

My dear Sir, your most truly
Robt Burns

1 Shenstone: *Elegy XI*, stanza 10.
2 Jean Adams: *There's nae luck about the house*, lines 51-2.

IV (220)

Mauchline, 7th March 1788

I have been out of the country, my dear friend; and have not had an opportunity of writing till now, when I am afraid you will be gone out of the country too.—I have been looking at farms; and after all, perhaps I may settle in that character.—I have got such a vicious bent to idleness, and have ever been so little a man of business, that it will take no ordinary effort to bring my mind properly in to the routine of business; but you will say—"A great effort is worthy you;" I say so to myself, and butter up my vanity with all the stimulating compliments I can think of.—Men of grave, geometrical minds, the sons of, "Which was to be demonstrated," may cry up reason as much as they please; but I have always found an honest passion, or native instinct, the trustiest auxiliary in the warfare of this world.— Reason almost always comes to me, like an unlucky wife to a poor devil of a husband—just in time enough to add her reproaches to his other grievances.—

I found Jean—with her cargo very well laid in; but unfortunately moor'd, almost at the mercy of wind and tide: I have towed her into convenient harbour where she may lie snug till she unload; and have taken the command myself—not ostensibly, but for a time, in secret. —I am gratified by your kind enquiries after her; as after all, I may say with Othello—

420

Captain Richard Brown

"Excellent wretch!
"Perdition catch my soul but I do love thee!"*

I go for Edinburgh on monday, but will return in a week.—I'll send you the Directory on Weden: next, which I suppose will find you time enough.—I got a letter from my Edinburgh correspondent, who tells me he has not sent it you; for which I am very angry with him.—

Prosperity and safe return attend you!

I am ever, my dear Sir, yours most sincerely,
Robt Burns

* Act III, sc. 2.

V (228)

Glasgow, 20th March 1788

I am monstrously to blame, my dear Sir, in not writing you, and sending you the Directory.*—I have been getting my tack extended, as I have taken a farm; and I have been racking shop accounts with Mr Creech; which, both together, with watching, fatigue, and a load of Care almost too heavy for my shoulders, have in some degree actually fever'd me.—I really forgot the directory yesterday, which vexes me: but I was convuls'd with rage a good part of the day.—

I am to thank you much for the ingenious friendly, indeed elegant epistle from your friend Mr Crawford.—I will certainly write him, but not now: this is only a card to you, as I am posting to my farm in Dumfries shire, where many perplexing arrangements await me.—

I am vexed about the Directory; but, my·dear Sir, forgive me: these eight days, I have been positively crazed.—

My Compliments to Mrs Brown.—I'll write to you to Grenada.—

I am ever, my dearest Friend, yours—
Robt Burns

* Probably *Jones's Directory of the City of Glasgow* (1787).

VI (344)

Mauchline, 21st May 1789

My dear Friend,

I was just in this country by accident and hearing of your safe arrival, I could not resist the temptation of wishing you joy on your return—wishing you would write me before you sail again—wishing you would always set me down as your bosom-friend—wishing you long life & prosperity & that every good thing may attend you—wishing Mrs Brown and your little ones as few of the evils of this world as is consistent with humanity—wishing you & she were to make two at the ensuing lying-in with which Mrs Burns threatens very soon to favor me; that I had longer time to write you at present—& finally, wishing that if there is to be another state of existence, Mrs Brown, Mrs Burns, our little ones in both families, & you and I in some snug paradisical retreat, may make a jovial Party to all eternity! Amen ! ! !—

421

There is a lad, a James Miller, a surgeon from this place that I hear is to sail your Passenger.—He is a good, honest blunt lad, by no means destitute of abilities; and the son of a most respectable man, a particular friend of mine. Should it be in your power to oblige him in any little civility, it would oblidge me likewise.—Farewell! God bless you! my long-loved, dearest friend ! ! !—I have time for no more than that I am ever,

Most sincerely yours,
Robert Burns
turn over

My direction is, at Ellisland near Dumfries.—

VII (369)

Ellisland, 4th November 1789

I have been so hurried my ever dear Friend, that tho' I got both your letters I have not been able to command an hour to answer them *as I wished*; and even now, you are to look upon this merely as confessing debt and craving days.—Few things could have given me so much pleasure as the news that you were once more safe & sound on Terra Firma, & happy in that place where happiness is alone to be found—in the fire-side circle.—May the BENEVOLENT DIRECTOR OF ALL THINGS peculiarly bless you in all those endearing connections consequent on the tender and venerable names—Husband & Father!—

I have indeed been lucky, extremely lucky, in getting an additional income of 50£ a year, while at the same time the appointment will not cost me above 10, or 12£ per Ann. of expences, more than I must inevitably have been [*four or five letters missing*]

The worst of it is, the excise Division which I have got is so extensive, no less than ten parishes to ride over, & besides abounds with so much business, that I can scarce steal a spare moment.—However, Labour endears Rest, and both are absolutely necessary for the proper enjoyment of Human Existence.—

I cannot meet you any where; no less than an order from the Board of Excise at Edinburgh is necessary before I can have so much time as meet you in Ayr-Shire.—But, do you come and see me! We must have a Social Day & perhaps lengthen it out with half the night, before you go again to Sea.—You are the earliest Friend I now have on earth, my brother excepted, & is not that an endearing circumstance? When you & I first met, we were at a green period of human life when the twig would easily take a bent—but would as easily return to its former state.—You & I not only took a mutual bent; but by the melancholy tho' strong influence of being both of the family of the Unfortunate, we were intertwined with one another in our growth towards advanced Age; and blasted be the sacreligious hand that shall attempt to undo the UNION!—You & I must have one bumper to my favorite toast—May the Companions of our Youth be the Friends of our Old Age!—Come and see me, one year; I shall see you at P. Glasgow the next; & if we can contrive to have a gossiping between our two bedfellows, it will be much additional pleasure.—Mrs Burns joins me in kindest Compliments to you & Mrs Brown.—

Adieu! I am ever, My dear Sir,
Yours
Robt Burns

ROBERT GRAHAM OF FINTRY

Born in 1749 into an ancient noble family connected with the Grahams of Strathcarron and Claverhouse, he became the twelfth laird of Fintry, a designation which he retained although he disposed of the estate in 1780. He married Elizabeth Mylne of Mylnefield, by whom he had four sons and ten daughters. In 1787 he was appointed a Commissioner of the Scottish Board of Excise and in this capacity exerted considerable influence on Burns's behalf. Burns met him at Athole House on 31st August 1787 during his Highland tour, but it was not until the following January that Burns put their acquaintance to the test and solicited his patronage. Some fifteen letters from the poet are extant from then until 1794, from which it is appraent that Graham became not only a staunch friend but an invaluable supporter, especially in bending the Excise regulations to accommodate Burns - employed first in the district in which he resided, and then in the rather curious matter of his transfer to the more lucrative Port Division of Dumfries. In particular, Graham played an important part in the ticklish affair of Burns's political sympathies (XI-XII). Other letters (XIII-XV) show Burns manoeuvring for promotion and also outlining his plans for the re-organisation of the Dumfries divisions (7th January 1794). To the charges, made in recent years, that Burns was unscrupulous in pulling strings on his behalf it is only fair to point out that he lived in an age when men depended heavily on their connexions for preferment and patronage, and even in a later generation William Wordsworth was rewarded with the virtual sinecure of Distributor of Stamps for Westmorland, at a salary far in excess of that for which Burns had to work very hard.

I (172)

St James' Square, Monday morn:
[7th January 1788]

Sir,

When I had the honor of being introduced to you at Atholehouse, I did not think of putting that acquaintance so soon to the test.— When Lear, in Shakespeare, asks old Kent why he wished to be in his service, he answers, "Because you have that in your face I could like to call Master:"* for some such similar reason, Sir, do I now solicit your Patronage.—You know, I dare say, of an application I lately made to your Board, to be admitted an Officer of Excise.—I have, according to form, been examined by a Supervisor, and today I give in his Certificate with a request for an Order for instructions.—In this affair, if I succeed, I am afraid I shall but too much need a patronising Friend.—Propriety of conduct as a Man, and fidelity and attention as an Officer, I dare engage for; but with any thing like business, I am totally unacquainted.—The man who till within these eighteen months was never the wealthy master of ten guineas, can be but ill-acquainted with the busy routine.—I had intended to have closed my late meteorous appearance on the stage of Life, in the country Farmer; but after discharging some filial and fraternal claims, I find I could only fight for existence in that miserable manner, which I have lived to see repeatedly throw a venerable Parent in the jaws of a Jail; where, but for the Poor Man's last and often best friend, Death, he might have ended his days.—

I know, Sir, that to need your goodness is to have a claim on it: may I therefore beg your Patronage to forward me in this affair till I be appointed to a Division; where, by the help of rigid Economy, I shall try to support that Independance so dear to my soul, but which has too often been so distant from my situation.—

I have the honor to be, Sir,
your most humble servant
Robert Burns

* *King Lear*, Act I, sc. 4, slightly misquoted.

Robert Graham of Fintry

II (228B)

Mauchline, 25th March 1788

Sir

I have been lucky enough to find an Excise Officer here who is exceedingly clever, and who enters with the warmth of a friend in my ideas of being instructed.—I got Mr Dickson, the Officer whom formerly I chose for my Instructor, to assign over his Order to this gentleman; but it seems the Supervisor in Ayr, who must examine me, is superstitiously strict, and to make all things fast I must trouble you, as you were so very good as to give me permission, to order the Secretary to make out a new Order for my instruction, and direct it to Mr James Findlay, Excise Officer at Tarbolton, Ayr District.—

I find every thing suit well with that kind Patronage you are pleased to honor me with.—My brother, who is an excellent farmer, has six years of a poor lease to run, but he can at any time be rid of it into his master's hands; so I can at any warning place him in my farm.—Not, Sir, that I would approach the character of Rapacity dunning Benevolence: you have generously offered me the shelter of your Patronage in such a manner as even the caprice of Delicacy might be gratified in accepting.—

With the warmest sincerity of native gratitude, I have the honor to be, Sir,

your highly oblidged humble servant
Robt Burns

P.S.
The Secretary may direct to me, if he chuses rather than Mr Findlay, at MAUCHLINE.—

R.B.

III (269)

[Enclosing *Epistle To Robert Graham Esqr. of Fintry requesting a Favour*. The Poem is headed - *Ellisland—September* 8th 1788.]

[C.W. p. 330]

Ellisland near Dumfries—September 10th—1788

Sir—

The scrapes and premunires into which our indiscretions and follies, in the ordinary constitution of things, often bring us, are bad enough; but it is peculiarly hard that a man's virtues should involve him in disquiet, and the very goodness of his heart cause the persecution of his peace.—You, Sir, have patronized and befriended me, not by barren compliments which meerly fed my vanity, or little marks of notice which perhaps only encumbered me more in the awkwardness of my native rusticity, but by being my persevering Friend in real life; and now, as if your continued Benevolence had given me a prescriptive right, I am going again to trouble you with my importunities.—

Your Honorable Board, sometime ago, gave me my Excise Commission; which I regard as my sheet anchor in life.—My farm, now that I have tried it a little, tho' I think it will in time be a saving bargain, yet does by no means promise to be such a Pennyworth as I was taught to expect.—It is in the last stage of worn-out poverty, and will take some time before it pay the rent.—I might have had Cash to supply the deficiencies of these hungry years, but I have a young brother who is supporting my aged mother, another still much younger brother and three sisters, on a farm in Ayr-shire; and it took all my surplus, over what I thought necessary for my farming capital, to save not only the comfort but the very existence of that fireside family-circle from impending destruction.—This was done before I took the farm; and rather than abstract my money from my brother, a circumstance which would ruin him, I will resign the farm and enter immediately into the service of your HONOURS.—But I am embarked now in the farm; I have commenced married man; and I am determined to stand by my Lease, till resistless Necessity compel me to quit my ground.—

There is one way by which I might be enabled to extricate myself from this embarrassment, a scheme which I hope and am certain is in your power to effectuate.—I live here, Sir, in the very centre of a country Excise-Division; the present Officer lately lived on a farm which he rented in my nearest neighbourhood; and as the gentleman, owing to some legacies, is quite opulent, a removal could do him no manner of injury; and on a month's warning, to give me a little time to look again over my Instructions, I would not be afraid to enter on business.—I do not know the name of his Division, as I have not yet got acquainted with any of Dumfries Excise People; but his own name is, Leonard Smith.—It would suit me to enter on it, beginning of next Summer; but I shall be in Edinburgh to wait upon you about the affair, sometime in the ensuing winter.—

When I think how and on what I have written to you, Sir, I shudder at my own Hardiesse.—Forgive me, Sir! I have told you my situation. —If asking anything less could possibly have done, I would not have asked so much.—

If I were in the Service, it would likewise favor my Poetical schemes. —I am thinking of something, in the rural way, of the Drama-kind.— Originality of character is, I think, the most striking beauty in that Species of Composition, and my wanderings in the way of my business would be vastly favorable to my picking up original traits of Human nature.—

I again, Sir, earnestly beg your forgiveness for this letter.—I have done violence to my own feelings in writing it.—

> ——"If I in aught have done amiss,
> "Impute it not!"[1]

My thoughts on this business, as usual with me when my mind is burdened, vented themselves, in the inclosed verses, which I have taken the liberty to inscribe to you.—

You, Sir, have the power to bless: but the only claim I have to your friendly Offices, is my having already been the Object of your goodness, which indeed looks like producing my debt instead of my discharge.—

I am sure I go on Scripture-grounds in this affair; for, I "ask in faith, nothing doubting;"[2] and for the true Scripture-reason too—Because I have the fullest conviction that, "my Benefactor is good."—

I have the honor to be, Sir,
your deeply indebted humble servant
Robt Burns

1 Addison: *Cato*, Act V, sc. 4, misquoted.
2 James I: 6, misquoted.

IV (273)

Ellisland, 23rd September 1788

Sir,

Though I am scarce able to hold up my head with this fashionable Influenza, which is just now the rage hereabouts, yet, with half a spark of Life I would try to thank you for your most generous favour of the 14th; which, owing to my infrequent calls at the Post-Office in the hurry of harvest, came only to hand yesternight.—I assure you, my ever-honored Sir, I read it with eyes brimful of other drops than those of anguish.—Oh, what means of happiness the Author of Goodness has put in their hands to whom he has given the power to bless; & what real happiness has he given to those on whom he has likewise bestowed, kind, generous, benevolent Dispositions!—Did you know, Sir, from how many fears & forebodings the friendly assurances of your patronage & protection has freed me, it would be some reward for your goodness.—

I am curst with a melancholy Prescience, which makes me the veriest coward, in Life.—There is not any exertion which I would not attempt rather than be in that horrid situation—to be ready to call on the mountains to fall on me, & the hills to cover me from the presence of a haughty Landlord, or his still more haughty Underling, to whom I owed—what I could not pay.—My Muse, too, the circumstance that after my Domestic Comfort is by far the dearest to my soul, to have it in my power to cultivate her acquaintance to advantage—in short, Sir, you have, like the G R E A T B E I N G whose image you so richly bear, made a Creature happy who had no other claim to your goodness than his necessity, & who can make you no other return than his grateful Acknowledgement.—

My farm I think I am certain will, in the long run, be an Object for me; & as I rent it in the first three years something under, I will be able to weather by a twelvemonth or perhaps more; tho' it would make me set Fortune more at defiance, if it can be in your power to grant my request as I mentioned, in the beginning of next Summer.— I was thinking that as I am only a little more than five miles from Dumfries, I might perhaps officiate there, if any of these Officers could be removed with more propriety than Mr Smith; but besides the monstrous inconvenience of it to me, I could not bear to injure a poor fellow by outing him to make way for myself: to a wealthy Son of good-fortune like Smith, the injury is imaginary, where the propriety of your rules admit.—

Had I been well, I intended to have troubled you farther with a description of my Soil, & Plan of farming; but business will call me

to town about February next, I hope then to have the honor of
assuring you in propria persona how much & how truly

> I am, Sir, your deeply indebted
> & ever grateful humble servant
> Robt.Burns

V (341)

Ellisland, 13th May 1789

Sir,

though I intend making a little manuscript book of my unpublished
Poems for Mrs Graham, yet I cannot forbear in the mean time
sending her the inclosed, which was the production of the other day.
—In the plea of Humanity, the ladies, to their honour be it spoken,
are ever warmly interested.—That is *one* reason of my troubling you
with this—another motive I have is a hackneyed subject in my letters
to you.—God help a poor devil, who carries about with him a load of
gratitude, of which he can never hope to ease his shoulders but at
the expence of his heart!—I waited on Collector Mitchell with your
letter.—It happened to be Collection-day, so he was very throng, but
he received me with the utmost politeness and made me promise to
call on him soon.—As I don't wish to degrade myself to a hungry
rook gaping for a morsel, I shall just give him a hint of my wishes.—I
am going on with a bold hand in my farm, and am certain of holding
it with safety for three or four years; and I think if some cursed
malevolent star have not taken irremoveable possession of my
zenith, that your Patronage & my own priority then as an
Expectant should run a fair chance for the Division I want.—By the
by the Excise-instructions you mentioned were not in the bundle.—
But 'tis no matter; Marshal in his Yorkshire,* & particularly that
extraordinary man, Smith, in his Wealth of Nations, find my leisure
employment enough.—I could not have given any mere *man*, credit
for half the intelligence Mr Smith discovers in his book. I would
covet much to have his ideas respecting the present state of some
quarters of the world that are or have been the scenes of
considerable revolutions since his book was written.—

Though I take the advantage of your goodness, & presume to send
you any new Poetic thing of mine, I must not tax you with answers
to each of my idle letters.—I remember you talked of being this way
with my honored friend, Sir William Murray, in the course of this
summer.—You cannot imagine, Sir, how happy it would make me,
should you, two illuminate my humble domicile.—You will certainly
do me the honor to partake of a Farmer's dinner with me.—I shall
promise you a good piece of good old beef, a chicken, or perhaps a
Nith salmon fresh from the ware, & a glass of good punch, on the
shortest notice; and allow me to say, that Cincinnatus, or Fabricius,
who presided in the august Roman Senate, & led their invincible
armies, would have jumped at such a dinner.—I expect your Honors
with a kind enthusiasm.—I shall mark the year & mark the day, &
hand it down to my children as one of the most distinguished honors
of their Ancestor.—

Robert Graham of Fintry

I have the honor to be, with the sincerest gratitude,
sir, your oblidged & very humble servant
Robt Burns

* William Marshall: *The Rural Economy of Yorkshire* (London 1788).

VI (353)

Ellisland, 31st July 1789

Sir

The language of Gratitude has been so prostituted by servile adulation and designing flattery, that I know not how to express myself when I would acknowledge the receipt of your last letter.—I beg and hope, ever-honored

"Friend of my life! *true Patron of my rhymes*"—[1]

that you will always give me credit for the sincerest, chastest gratitude!

The callous Hypocrite may be louder than I, in his grateful professions, professions which he never felt; or the selfish heart of the Covetous may pocket the bounties of Beneficence with more rejoicing exultation; but for the brimful eye, springing from the ardent throbbings of an honest bosom, at the goodness of a kindly active Benefactor and politely generous Friend, I dare call the SEARCHER OF HEARTS & AUTHOR OF ALL GOODNESS to witness, how truly these are mine to you.—

Mr Mitchel did not wait my calling on him, but sent me a kind letter giving me a hint of the business, and on my waiting on him yesterday, he entered with the most friendly ardour into my views and interests.—He seems to think, and from my own private knowledge I am certain he is right, that removing the Officer who now does, and for these many years has done duty in the Division in the middle of which I live, will be productive of at least no disadvantage to the Revenue, and may likewise be done without any detriment to him.—Should the Honorable Board think so, and should they deem it eligible to appoint me to officiate in his present place, I am then at the top of my wishes.—The emoluments of my Office will enable me to carry on and enjoy those improvements in my farm, which, but for this additional assistance, I must in a year or two have abandoned.—Should it be judged improper to place me in this Division, I am deliberating whether I had not better give up farming altogether, and go into the Excise wherever I can find employment.—Now that the Salary is £50 per ann. the Excise is surely a much superior object to a farm which, without some foreign assistance, must for half a lease be a losing bargain.—The worst of it is, I know that there are some respectable Characters who do me the honor to interest themselves in my welfare & behaviour, and as leaving the farm so soon may have an unsteady, giddy-headed appearance, I had perhaps better lose a little money than hazard such people's esteem.—

You see Sir, with what freedom I lay before you all my little matters —little indeed to the World, but of the most important magnitude to me.—You are so good, that I trust I am not troublesome.—I have heard and read a good deal of Philanthropy, Generosity and Greatness of soul, and when rounded with the flourish of declamatory periods, or poured in the mellifluence of Parnassian measure, they have a tolerable effect on a musical ear; but when these high sounding professions are compared with the very act and deed as they are usually performed, I do not think there is any thing in or belonging to Human Nature, so baldly disproportionate.—In fact, were it not for a very few of our Kind, among whom an honored Friend of mine that to you Sir I will not name is a distinguished individual, the very existence of Magnanimity, Generosity, and all their kindred Virtues, would be as much a question among Metaphysicians, as the existence of Witchcraft.— Perhaps the nature of man is not so much to blame for all this, as the situation in which, by some miscarriage or other, he is placed in this world.—The poor, naked, helpless wretch, with such voracious appetites and such a famine of provision for them, is under a kind of cursed necessity of turning selfish in his own defence.—Except here & there a Scelerate who seems to be a Scoundrel from the womb by Original Sin, thorough-paced Selfishness is always a work of time.— Indeed in a little time we generally grow so attentive to ourselves, and so regardless of others, that I have often in Poetic frenzy looked on this world as one vast ocean, occupied and commoved by innumerable vortices, each whirling round its centre, which vortices are the children of men; and that the great design, & merit if I may say so, of every particular vortex consists, in how wide it can extend the influence of its circle, and how much floating trash it can suck and absorb.—

I know not why I have got into this preaching vein, except it be to shew you, Sir, that it is not my ignorance but my knowledge of mankind which makes me so much admire your goodness to your humble servant.—

I hope this will find my amiable young acquaintance, John, recovered from his indisposition, and all the members of your charming fire-side circle well and happy.—I am sure I am anxiously interested in all their welfares; I wish it with all my soul; nay I believe I sometimes catch myself praying for it.—I am not impatient of my own impotence under that immense debt which I owe to your goodness, but I wish and beseech that BEING who has all good things in his hands to bless and reward you with all those comforts and pleasures which HE knows I would bestow on you were they mine to give.—

I shall return your books very soon: I only wish to give Dr Smith one other perusal, which I will do in two or three days.—I do not think that I must trouble you for another cargo, at least for some time, as I am going to apply to Leadbetter & Symons on Gaging,[2] and to study my Sliding rule, Branan's rule, &c. with all possible attention.—

An apology for the impertinent length of this epistle, would only add to the evil.—

> I have the honor to be, Sir,
> your deeply indebted humble servant
> Robt Burns

Robert Graham of Fintry

1 Burns: *To Robt Graham of Fintry*, line 69. C.W. pp. 330-2.
2 Charles Leadbetter: *The Royal Gauger; or, Gauging Made Easy.* Jelinger Symons: *The Excise Laws Abridged and Digested.*

VII (373)

Ellisland, 9th December 1789

Sir

I have of a good while had a wish to trouble you with a letter, and had certainly done it long ere now but for a humilating something that throws cold water on the resolution; as who should say, "You have found Mr Graham a very powerful & kind friend indeed, and "that interest he is so kindly taking in your concerns you ought by "every thing in your power to keep alive and cherish."—Now, though since God has thought proper to make one Powerful & another Helpless, the connection of Oblidger and Oblidgee is all fair; & though the situation of my being Client under your Patronage is to me highly honorable, yet, Sir, allow me to flatter myself that as a Poet & an Honest Man you first interested yourself in my welfare, and principally as such still you permit me to approach you.—

I have found the Excise business go on a great deal smoother with me than I apprehended; owing a good deal to the generous friendship of Mr Mitchel my Collector, and the kind assistance and instruction of Mr Findlater my Supervisor.—I dare to be honest, and I fear no labor.—Nor do I find my hurried life greatly inimical to my correspondence with the Muses.—Their visits to me indeed, and I believe to most of their acquaintances, like the visits of good angels are short, & far between, but still I meet them now and then as I jog through the wild hills of Nithsdale.—I take the liberty to inclose you a few bagatelles, all of them the vagaries of my leisure thoughts in my Excise-rides.—

If you know, or have ever seen, Captain Grose the Antiquarian, you will enter into any humor that is in the verses on him.[1]—Perhaps you have seen them already, as they found their way into a London newspaper.—

Though I dare say you have none of the Solemn-league-&-covenant fire which shone so conspicuous in Lord George Gordon and the Kilmarnock weavers, yet I think you must have heard of Dr Mcgill, one of the clergymen of Ayr, and his heretical book.[2]—God help him, poor man! though he is one of the worthiest as well as one of the ablest, in the whole priesthood of the Kirk of Scotland, in every sense of that ambiguous term, yet, for the blasphemous heresies of squaring Religion by the rules of Common Sense, and attempting to give a decent character to Almighty God and a rational account of his proceedings with the Sons of Men, the poor Doctor and his numerous family are in imminent danger of being thrown out to the mercy of the winter winds.—The inclosed Ballad[3] on that business is I confess too local, but I laughed at some conceits in it myself, though I am convinced in my conscience that there are several heavy stanzas in it too.—

The Election-ballad[4] alludes, as you will see, to the present canvass in our string of Boroughs.—I do not believe there will be a harder run

431

match in the whole General Election.—The Great Man here, like all
Renegadoes, is a flaming Zealot.—Kick'd out before the astonished
indignation of his deserted Master, and despised I suppose by the
Party who took him in to be a mustering faggot at the mysterious
orgies of their midnight iniquities, and a useful drudge in the dirty
work of their Country Elections, he would fain persuade this part of
the world that he is turned Patriot; and, where he knows his men,
has the impudence to aim away at the unmistrusting manner of a
Man of Conscience and Principle.—Nay to such an intemperate
height has his zeal carried him, that, in convulsive violence to every
feeling in his bosom, he has made some desperate attempts at the
hopeless business of getting himself a character for benevolence and
in one or two late terrible strides in pursuit of Party-interest, has
actually stumbled on something like meaning the welfare of his
fellow-creatures.—I beg your pardon, Sir, if I differ from you in my
idea of this Great Man; but were you to know his sins as well of
Omission as Commission to this outraged Land, you would club
your curse with the execrating voice of the Country.—I am too little
a man to have any political attachments; I am deeply indebted to
and have the warmest veneration for, Individuals of both Parties; but
a man who has it in his power to be the Father of a Country, and
who is only known to that Country by the mischiefs he does in it, is
a character of which one cannot speak with patience.—

Sir James Johnston does "what man can do," but yet I doubt his
fate.—Of the Borough of Annan, he is secure.—Kirkcudbright is
dubious.—He has the Provost; but lord Daer, who does the honors of
Great Man to the place, makes every effort in his power for the
opposite interest.—Luckily for Sir James, his lordship though a very
good lord, is a very poor politician.—Dumfries & Sanquhar are
decidedly the Duke's "to let or sell;" so Lochmaben, a city
containing upwards of fourscore living souls that cannot discern
between their right hand or left—for drunkenness, has at present the
balance of power in her hands.—The Honorable Council of that
ancient borough are fifteen in number; but alas! their fifteen names
indorsing a bill of fifteen pounds, would not discount the said bill in
any banking-office.—My lord Provost who is one of the soundest
headed, best hearted, whisky-drinking fellows in the south of
Scotland, is devoted to Sir James, but His Grace thinks he has a
majority of the Council; tho' I who have the honor to be a Burgess
of the town & know somewhat behind the curtain, could tell him a
different story.—

The worst of it for the Buff & blue folks is, that their Candidate,
Captain M——,[5] my landlord's son, is, entre nous, a youth by no
means above mediocrity in his abilities; and is said to have a
huckster-lust for shillings, pence & farthings.—This is the more
remarkable as his father's abilities & benevolence are so justly
celebrated.—

The Song beginning, "Thou lingering Star" &c. is the last, & in my
opinion by much the best of the inclosed Compositions.—I beg leave
to present it with my most respectful Compliments to Mrs
Graham.—

I return you by the Carrier, the bearer of this, Smith's Wealth of Nations, Marshal's Yorkshire & Angola.[6]–Les Contes de Fontaine is in the way of my trade & I must give it another reading or two; Chansons joyeuses, & another little French book, I keep for the same reason.– I think you will not be reading them, & I will not keep them long.–

Forgive me, Sir, for the stupid length of this epistle.–I pray Heaven it may find you in a humour to read "The Belfast new Almanack," or, "The Bachelor's garland, containing five excellent new Songs;" or the Paisley Poet's version of the Psalms of David,[7] and then my impertinence may disgust the less.–

> I have the honor to be, Sir,
> your ever grateful humble servant
> Robt Burns

1 *On the Late Captain Grose's Peregrinations thro' Scotland, collecting the Antiquities of that Kingdom* C.W. p. 373.
2 *A Practical Essay on the Death of Jesus Christ*, Edinburgh (1786).
3 *The Kirk's Alarm*; C.W. p. 359.
4 *The Five Carlins* C.W. p. 364.
5 Miller.
6 Probably *Angola, histoire indienne*, attributed to C.J.L.A. Rochette de la Morlière.
7 James Maxwell: *A New Version of the Whole Book of Psalms in Metre . . . Adapted to the Present State of the Christian Church*, Glasgow (1773).

VIII (402A)

Ellisland, 10th June 1790

"Epistle to Robert Graham Esq: of Fintry on the Election for the Dumfries string of Boroughs, Anno 1790–"

[C.W. p. 402]

I have the honor to be, & the happiness to be, Sir, your oblidged & ever grateful humble servant

> Robt Burns

IX (419)

Dumfries, Globe Inn, 4th September 1790

Sir

The very kind letter you did me the honor to write me, reached me just as I was setting in to the whirlpool of an Excise-fraud-Court, from the vortex of which I am just emerged—Heaven knows, in a very unfit situation to do justice to the workings of my bosom when I sit down to write to the

"Friend of my life—true Patron of my rhymes!"[1]

As my Division consists of ten large parishes, & I am sorry to say, hitherto very carelessly surveyed, I had a good deal of business for the Justices; & I believe my Decreet will amount to between fifty & sixty pounds.—I took, I fancy, rather a new way with my Frauds.—I recorded every Defaulter; but at the Court, I myself begged off every poor body that was unable to pay, which seeming candour gave me so much implicit credit with the Hon. Bench that with high Compliments they gave me such ample vengeance on the rest, that my Decreet is double the amount of any Division in the District.–

I am going either to give up, or subset my farm directly.—I have not liberty to subset, but if my Master will grant it me, I propose giving it just as I have it to myself, to an industrious fellow of a near relation of mine.—Farming this place in which I live, would just be a livelyhood to a man who would be the greatest drudge in his own family, so is no object; & living here hinders me from that knowledge in the business of Excise which it is absolutely necessary for me to attain.—

I did not like to be an incessant beggar from you.—A Port Division I wish if possible to get; my kind funny friend Captain Grose, offered to interest Mr Brown, & perhaps Mr Wharton for me, a very handsome opportunity offered of getting Mr Corbet superior general, to pledge every service in his power; then I was just going to acquaint you with what I had done, or rather what was done for me, that as every body have their particular friends to serve, you might find the less obstacle in what, I assure you, Sir, I constantly count on—your wishes & endeavors to be of service to me.—

As I had an eye to getting on the Examiners list, if attainable by me, I was going to ask you if it would be of any service to try the interest of some Great, & some *very* Great folks to whom I have the honor to be known; I mean in the way of a Treasury Warrant.—But much as early impressions have given me of the horror of Spectres, &c. still, I would face the Arch-fiend, in Miltonic pomp, at the head of all his legions; and hear that infernal shout which blind John says: "Tore hell's concave;"[2] rather than crawl in, a dust-licking Petitioner, before the lofty presence of a Mighty Man, & bear, amid all the mortifying pangs of Self-annihilation, the swelling consequence of his damn'd State, & the cold monosyllables of his hollow heart!—

It was in the view of trying for a Port, that I asked Collector Mitchel to get me appointed, which he has done, to a vacant foot-walk in Dumfries.—If ever I am so fortunate as to be called out to do business as a Supervisor, I would then chuse the North of Scotland; but untill that Utopian period, I own I have some wayward feelings at appearing as a simple Gauger in a Country where I am only known by fame.—Portglasgow, Greenock, or Dumfries, Ports, would be in the mean time my ultimatum.—

I inclose you a tribute I have just been paying to the memory of my friend, Matthew Henderson, whom I dare say you must have known. —I had acknowledged your goodness sooner, but for want of time to transcribe the Poem.—Poor Matthew!—I can forgive Poverty for hiding Virtue & Piety.—They are not only plants that flourish best in the shade, but they also produce their sacred fruits more especially for another world.—But when the haggard Beldam throws her invidious veil over Wit, Spirit, &c. but I trust another world will cast light on the subject.—

I have the honor to be, Sir,
your deeply oblidged
And very humble servant
Robt Burns

1 Epistle *to Robert Graham, Esq., of Fintry.* C.W. p. 332, line 69.
2 Milton: *Paradise Lost*, Book I, line 502.

Robert Graham of Fintry

X (476)

[With *To Robert Graham Esq., of Fintry* which is dated Ellisland 5th October 1791.]

[C.W. p. 431]

Bishop mark OC 6 [1791]

Postscript—

Sir,

I ought to have written you long ago, but a mere letter of thanks must to you be an insipid business: I wish to give you something that will give you at least as much amusement as "The Aberdeen new Prognostication;" or, "Six excellent new Songs."- Along with two other Pieces, I inclose you a sheetful of groans, wrung from me in my elbow chair, with one unlucky leg on a stool before me.—I make no apology for addressing it to *you*: I have no longer a *choice* of Patrons: the truly noble Glencairn is no more!—I intend soon to do myself the honor of writing Mrs Graham & sending her some other lesser Pieces of late date.—My Muse will sooner be in mischief than be idle; so I keep her at work.—

I thought to have mentioned some Excise ideas that your late goodness has put in my head, but 'tis so like the sorning impudence of a sturdy beggar, that I cannot do it.—It was something in the way of an Officiating job.—With the most ardent wish that you may wish that you may be rewarded by HIM who can do it, for your generous patronage to a man, who, tho' feelingly sensible of it, is quite unable to repay it,

I have the honor to be, Sir,
your most devoted humble servant
R. Burns

XI (528)

Dumfries December 31st [1792]

Sir,

I have been surprised, confounded & distracted by Mr Mitchel, the Collector, telling me just now, that he has received an order from your Honorable Board to enquire into my political conduct, & blaming me as a person disaffected to Government.—Sir, you are a Husband—& a father—you know what you would feel, to see the much-loved wife of your bosom, & your helpless, prattling little ones, turned adrift into the world, degraded & disgraced from a situation in which they had been respectable & respected & left almost without the necessary support of a miserable existence.—Alas, Sir! must I think that such, soon, will be my lot! And from the damned, dark insinuations of hellish, groundless Envy too!—I believe, Sir, I may aver it, & in the sight of Omnipotence, that I would not tell a deliberate Falsehood, no, not though even worse horrors, if worse can be, than those I have mentioned, hung over my head; & I say, that the allegation, whatever villain has made it, is a LIE! To the British Constitution, on Revolution principles, next after my God, I am most devoutly attached!—

You Sir, have been much & generously my Friend—Heaven knows how warmly I have felt the obligation, how gratefully I have thanked you.—Fortune, Sir, has made you powerful & me impotent; has given you patronage, & me dependance.—I would not for my *single Self* call on your Humanity; were such my insular, unconnected situation, I would despise the tear that now swells in my eye—I could brave Misfortune, I could face Ruin: for at the worst, "Death's thousand doors stand open;"* but, Good God! the tender concerns that I have mentioned, the claims & ties that I, at this moment, see & feel around me, how they ennerve Courage, & wither Resolution! To your patronage, as a man of some genius, you have allowed me a claim; & your esteem, as an honest Man, I know is my due: to these, Sir, permit me to appeal; & by these may I adjure you to save me from that misery which threatens to overwhelm me, & which, with my latest breath I will say it, I have not deserved.—

Pardon this confused scrawl.—Indeed I know not well what I have written.--

I have the honor to be Sir,
your deeply indebted
& ever grateful humble servant
Robt Burns

* Blair: *The Grave*, line 394.

XII (530)

Dumfries 5th January 1793

Sir,

I am this moment honored with your letter: with what feelings I received this other instance of your goodness, I shall not pretend to describe.—

Now, to the charges which Malice & Misrepresentation have brought against me.—

It has been said, it seems, that I not only belong to, but head a disaffected party in this place.—I know of no party in this place, either Republican or Reform, except an old party of Borough-Reform, with which I never had any thing to do.—Individuals, both Republican & Reform, we have, though not many of either; but if they have associated, it is more than I have the least knowledge of: & if there exists such an association, it must consist of such obscure nameless beings, as precludes any possibility of my being known to them, or they to me.—

I was in the playhouse one night, when Ça ira was called for.—I was in the middle of the pit, & from the Pit the clamour arose.—One or two individuals with whom I occasionally associate were of the party, but I neither knew of the Plot, nor joined in the Plot; nor ever opened my lips to hiss, or huzza, that, or any other Political tune whatever.—I looked on myself as far too obscure a man to have any weight in quelling a Riot; at the same time, as a character of higher respectability, than to yell in the howlings of a rabble.—This was the conduct of all the first Characters in this place, & these Characters know, & will avow, that such was my conduct.—

I never uttered any invectives against the king.—His private worth, it is altogether impossible that such a man as I, can appreciate; and in his Public capacity, I always revered, & ever will, with the soundest loyalty, revere, the Monarch of Great-britain, as, to speak in Masonic, the sacred KEYSTONE OF OUR ROYAL ARCH CONSTITUTION.—

As to REFORM PRINCIPLES, I look upon the British Constitution, as settled at the Revolution, to be the most glorious Constitution on earth, or that perhaps the wit of man can frame; at the same time, I think, & you know what High and distinguished Characters have for some time thought so, that we have a good deal deviated from the original principles of that Constitution; particularly, that an alarming System of Corruption has pervaded the connection between the Executive Power and the House of Commons.—This is the Truth, the Whole truth, of my Reform opinions; opinions which, before I was aware of the complection of these innovating times, I too unguardedly (now I see it) sported with: but henceforth, I seal up my lips.—However, I never dictated to, corresponded with, or had the least connection with, any political association except, that when the Magistrates & principal inhabitants of this town, met to declare their attachment to the Constitution, & their abhorrence of Riot, which declaration you would see in the Papers, I, as I thought my duty as a Subject at large, & a Citizen in particular, called upon me, subscribed the same declaratory Creed.—

Of Johnston, the publisher of the Edinburgh Gazetteer, I know nothing.—One evening in company with four or five friends, we met with his prospectus which we thought manly & independant; & I wrote to him, ordering his paper for us.—If you think that I act improperly in allowing his Paper to come addressed to me, I shall immediately countermand it.—I never, so judge me, God! wrote a line of prose for the Gazetteer in my life.—An occasional address, spoken by Miss Fontenelle on her benefit night here, which I called, the Rights of Woman, I sent to the Gazetteer; as also, some extempore stanzas on the Commemoration of Thomson: both these I will subjoin for your perusal.—You will see that they have nothing whatever to do with Politics.—At the time when I sent Johnston one of these poems, but which one, I do not remember, I inclosed at the request of my warm & worthy friend, Robert Riddel Esq: of Glenriddel, a prose Essay, signed Cato, written by him, & addressed to the delegates for the County Reform, of which he was one for this County.—With the merits, or demerits, of that Essay I have nothing to do, farther than transmitting it in the same Frank, which Frank he had procured me.—

As to France, I was her enthusiastic votary in the beginning of the business.—When she came to shew her old avidity for conquest, in annexing Savoy, &c. to her dominions, & invading the rights of Holland, I altered my sentiments.—A tippling Ballad* which I made on the Prince of Brunswick's breaking up his camp, & sung one convivial evening, I shall likewise send you, sealed up, as it is not every body's reading.—This last is not worth your perusal; but lest Mrs FAME should, as she has already done, use, & even abuse, her old priviledge of lying, you shall be the master of every thing, le pour et le contre, of my political writings & conduct.—

437

This, my honored Patron, is all.—To this statement I challenge disquisition.—Mistaken Prejudice, or unguarded Passion, may mislead, & often have misled me; but when called on to answer for my mistakes, though, I will say it, no man can feel keener compunction for his errors, yet, I trust, no man can be more superiour to evasion or disguise.—

I shall do myself the honor to thank Mrs Graham for her goodness, in a separate letter.—

If, Sir, I have been so fortunate as to do away these misapprehensions of my conduct & character, I shall with the confidence which you were wont to allow me, apply to your goodness on every opening in the way of business, where I think I with propriety may offer myself.—An instance that occurs just now; Mr Mcfarlane, Supervisor of the Galloway District is & has been for some time, very ill.—I spoke to Mr Mitchel as to his wishes to forward my application for the job, but though he expressed & ever does express every kindness for me, he hesitates, in hopes that the disease may be of short continuance.—However, as it seems to be a paralytic affection, I fear that it may be some time ere he can take charge of so extended a District.—There is a great deal of fatigue, & very little business in the District; two things suitable enough to my hardy constitution, & inexperience in that line of life.—

I have the honor to be, Sir,
your ever grateful, as highly obliged humble servant
Robt Burns

* *Why should na Poor Folk Mowe* C.W. p. 476.

XIII (533)

Dumfries, 7th January [1793]
Sir,

Collector Mitchel has acquainted me that today he applies to your Honorable Board for somebody to officiate in the District of Galloway, untill Mr McFarlane recovers.—I mentioned this business in the last letter I troubled you with.— You, Sir, are the best judge whether I can with propriety be appointed to the job, or whether you can, as matters at present stand, befriend my wishes.—

I have the honor to be,

Good Sir, (an epithet from me, you most truly deserve)

your ever grateful humble servant
Robt Burns

XIV (610)

[7th January 1794]
Sir,

I am going to venture on a subject which I am afraid may appear, *from me,* improper; but as I do it from the best of motives, if you should not approve of my ideas, you will forgive them.—

Economy of the Public Monies is, I know, highly the wish of your Honorable Board; & any hint conducive thereto which may occur to any, though the meanest, individual in your service, it is surely his duty to communicate it.—

I have been myself accustommed to labour, & have no notion that a servant of the Public should eat the bread of idleness; so, what I have long digested, & am going to propose, is the reduction of one of our Dumfries Divisions.—Not only in these unlucky times, but even in the highest flush of business, my Division, though by far the heaviest, was mere trifling.—The others were likely still less.—I would plan the reduction as thus.—Let the second Division be annihilated; & be divided among the others.—The Duties in it, are, two chandlers, a Common Brewer, & some Victuallers; these, with some Tea & Spirit Stocks, are the whole Division.—The two Chandlers, I would give to the 3d, or Tobacco Division; it is the idlest of us all.—That I may seem impartial, I shall willingly take under my charge, the Common Brewer & the Victuallers.—The Tea & Spirit Stocks, divide between the Bidgend, & Dumfries 2d Itinerant Divisions: they have at present but very little, *comparatively,* to do, & are quite adequate to the task.—

I assure you, Sir, that, by my plan, the Duties will be equally well charged, & thus an Officer's appointment saved to the Public.—You must remark one thing; that our Common Brewers are, every man of them in Dumfries, completely & unexceptionably, Fair Traders.—One, or two, rascally creatures are in the Bridgend Division, but besides being nearly ruined, as all Smugglers deserve, by fines & forfeitures, their business is on the most trifling scale you can fancy.—

I must beg of you, Sir, should my plan please you, that you will conceal my hand in it, & give it as your own thought.—My warm & worthy friend, Mr Corbet, may think me an impertinent inter-meddler in his department; & Mr Findlater, my Supervisor, who is not only one of the first, if not the very first of Excisemen in your Service, but is also one of the worthiest fellows in the universe; he, I know, would feel hurt at it; & as he is one of my most intimate friends, you can easily figure how it would place me, to have my plan known to be mine.—

For farther information on the Subject, permit me to refer you to a young beginner whom you lately sent among us, Mr Andrew Pearson; a gentleman that I am happy to say, from manner, abilities & attention, promises to be indeed a great acquisition to the service of your Honorable Board.—

This is a letter of business: in a future opportunity I may & most certainly will trouble you with one in my own way a la Parnasse.—

I have the honor to be,
Sir, you much indebted,
& ever grateful humble servant
Robt Burns

P.S. I forgot to mention, that if my plan takes, let me recommend to your humanity & justice, the present Officer of the 2nd Division.—

He is a very good Officer, & is burdened with a family of small children, which, with some debts of early days, crush him much to the ground.—

RB

XV (615A)

[Dumfries, February 1794]

Sir,

The language of supplication is almost the only language in which I have it in my power to approach you; & I have your generous commands for coming to you with it, on every opportunity.—I hope, & know then, that you will forgive me, for mentioning to you a circumstance which has come to my knowledge, & which it is possible, though, I am afraid, by no means probable, may be of some service to me.—

Mr Corbet is I know, at the top of the Collectors' List; & as they are most of them old men, it is extremely probably that the place he holds may be soon vacant.—That place—Supervisor-General—is, I understand, nearly secured for Mr Findlater, my Supervisor here.— Could it be possible then, Sir, that an old Supervisor who may still be continued, as I know is sometimes the case, after they are rather too infirm for much DUTY, could not such an Officer be appointed to Dumfries, & so let the OFFICIATING JOB fall to my share?— This is a bare possibility, if it be one; so I again beg your pardon for mentioning it, & I have done with the subject.—

You will have seen, or heard of a Publication of Scots Songs, under the hand of Pleyel; & where I appear in some of the Scots Poesy of the Work.—Miss GRAHAM will do me the honor to accept of a Copy —a trifling, but most fervent tribute of Gratitude, to the best Friend & truest, almost only, Patron, I have in the world: a GENTLEMAN, whose MANNER of bestowing, would give a pleasure to the feelings of unfortunate Royalty.—

Should the Chapter of Chances & Changes, which God forbid! ever place a Child of yours in the situation to need a Friend, as I have done; may they likewise find that Generous Friend, that I have found in YOU!

I shall order a Copy of the Sonatas, as I have none by me, to be sent from the Publisher.—

I have the honor to be,

Sir, your ever grateful humble
Robt Burns

MRS ELIZABETH ROSE OF KILRAVOCK

Born Elizabeth Rose in 1747, she married her cousin Dr Hugh Rose, 19th laird of Kilravock, in 1778. He died two years later and was succeeded by his baby son Hugh. Mrs Rose never remarried and died in 1815. She was a cousin of Henry Mackenzie, who gave Burns a letter of introduction to her on his Highland tour of 1787. Burns called at Kilravock near Inverness and later jotted down in his *Journal*: 'Old Mrs Rose, sterling sense, warm heart, strong passions, honest pride, all in an uncommon degree - Mrs Rose jnr. a little milder than the Mother, this perhaps owing to her being younger.' His hostess, of course, was the younger of the two ladies. Also present on that occasion was her niece, Miss Rose of Kildrummie, who sang two Highland airs. Burns requested copies of them for inclusion in Johnson's *Museum*, and in thanking Mrs Rose he sent this letter with the second volume, which was published three days earlier. Mrs Rose's musical accomplishments were renowned. Cosmo Innes, in his history of the Rose family, described her as 'the choice companion, the leader of all cheerful amusements, the humorous story-teller, the clever mimic, the very soul of society . . . she sung the airs of her own country, and she had learned to take a part in catches and glees, to make up the party with her father and brother. The same motive led her to study the violin . . .'

(206)

Edinburgh, February 17th, 1788

Madam:

You are much indebted to some indispensable business I have had on my hands, otherwise my gratitude threatened such a return for your obliging favour as would have tired your patience. It but poorly expresses my feelings to say, that I am sensible of your kindness: it may be said of hearts such as yours is, and such, I hope, mine is, much more justly than Addison applies it,—

"Some souls by instinct to each other turn."[1]

There was something in my reception at Kilravock so different from the cold, obsequious, dancing-school bow of politeness, that it almost got into my head that friendship had occupied her ground without the intermediate march of acquaintance. I wish I could transcribe, or rather transfuse into language, the glow of my heart when I read your letter. My ready fancy, with colours more mellow than life itself, painted the beautiful wild scenery of Kilravock—the venerable grandeur of the castle—the spreading woods—the winding river, gladly leaving his unsightly, heathy source, and lingering with apparent delight as he passes the fairy walk at the bottom of the garden;—your late distressful anxieties—your present enjoyments—your dear little angel, the pride of your hopes;—my aged friend, venerable in worth and years, whose loyalty and other virtues will strongly entitle her to the support of the Almighty Spirit here, and his peculiar favour in a happier state of existence. You cannot imagine, Madam, how much such feelings delight me; they are my dearest proofs of my own immortality. Should I never revisit the north, as probably I never will, nor again see your hospitable mansion, were I, some twenty years hence, to see your little fellow's name making a proper figure in a newspaper paragraph, my heart would bound with pleasure.

I am assisting a friend in a collection of Scottish songs, set to their proper tunes; every air worth preserving is to be included: among others I have given "Morag," and some few Highland airs which pleased me most, a dress which will be more generally known, though far, far inferior in real merit. As a small mark of my grateful esteem, I beg leave to present you with a copy of the work, as far as it is printed; the Man of Feeling,[2] that first of men, has promised to transmit it by the first opportunity.

I beg to be remembered most respectfully to my venerable friend, and to your little Highland chieftain. When you see the "two fair spirits of the hill," at Kildrummie,[3] tell them that I have done myself the honour of setting myself down as one of their admirers for at least twenty years to come, consequently they must look upon me as an acquaintance for the same period; but, as the Apostle Paul says, "this I ask of grace, not of debt."[4]

I have the honour to be, Madam, &c.
R.B.

1 Addison: *The Campaign*, line 101. Said of Marlborough and Prince Eugene. misquoted.
2 Henry Mackenzie
3 Miss Sophia Brodie and Miss Rose of Kildrummie, (niece of Mrs Rose).
4 Romans 4:4.

ANTHONY DUNLOP

Born in 1775, the seventh son of Mrs Dunlop of Dunlop, he entered the merchant navy at the age of twelve. In 1803 he married Ann Cunningham, daughter of the Collector of Customs at Irvine and subsequently purchased a small estate in the Isle of Man, which he named Ellerslie in allusion to his illustrious ancestor, Sir William Wallace. Later he became involved in an expensive lawsuit and, greatly impoverished, he committed suicide in June 1828 in an Edinburgh hotel.

(207)

St James' Square, Wed. Morn.
[October 1787 - February 1788]

[With *Holy Willie's Prayer.*]

[C.W. p. 93]

Sir,

Inclosed you have Holy Willie, and much good may he do you. I have prefixed a small preface, like a lamp stuck before a Presbyterian Pulpit to throw light not on the subject, that is commonly *light-proof*, but on the speaker:

I wish you a happy voyage, and all the success an honest man can enjoy.

> Get wealth and power, if possible with grace
> If not; I wish you neither wealth nor place.*

These, Sir, are my *wishes*; from my inmost soul I would *pray* for you too; but I like to oblige every man his own way.

I am Sir,
Your very Humble Servant,
Robert Burns

* Pope: *The First Epistle of the First Book of Horace Imitated*, lines 103-4, misquoted.

WILLIAM STEWART

Born about 1749, the son of a publican at Closeburn, Dumfriesshire. He became factor of the Closeburn estate of the Rev. James Stuart Menteith of Barrowby, Lincolnshire. His daughter was the Lovely Polly Stewart of Burns's song (C.W. p. 523). Burns was a frequent visitor at Closeburn while on Excise business, and engraved the song *You're Welcome Willie Stewart* (C.W. p. 522) on a crystal glass at Closeburn Inn. The landlady (Stewart's mother) being angry at what she considered the disfigurement of her glass, a gentleman present appeased her by paying a shilling and carried off the relic, which eventually came into the hands of Sir Walter Scott. Stewart's sister Catherine was the wife of Mr Bacon, publican of Brownhill and subject of the poem (III). The first letter in the following series does not bear the name of the recipient, but from the reference to Brownhill it has been assumed that Stewart was the addressee. The last letter (IV) gives some idea of the dire financial straits in which Burns found himself in his last eighteen months. As the endorsement in Stewart's handwriting shows, he sent Burns three guineas. Like Cleghorn and McMurdo, Stewart shared Burns's predelection for bawdy verse (II).

I (228A)

Mauchline, 21st March 1788

Sir,

I have at last fairly signed my tack with Mr Miller, and must commence operations at Whitsunday.—I am an entire Stranger in your Country; and Heaven knows shall need advice enough: will you be so very good as take a poor devil of a sojourning Rhymster under your care? I assure you I keep the scripture in my eye, for I "ask in faith, nothing wavering."[1]—Old Kent, in Shakespeare, says to poor king Lear, that he wished to be in his service "Because he had that in his face he could like to call Master":[2] forgive me, Sir, when I say, you have something in like manner I could wish to call friend.—

I shall be at Brownhill for any thing I know on thursday night; will you be able to spare me an hour or two on friday? I want two men servants for the summer; if you know of any, please bespeak me them, or direct me to them.—I could like one of them a married man, as I can give him a house, and perhaps for this summer, a cow's grass; but I won't make a custom of that any more than this season.—

If you did not know me for a Scots Poet, I dare say you would suspect me for a Hibernian—

> "Hibernia fam'd, 'bove every other grace,
> "For matchless intrepidity of face"—[3]

> Forgive my freedom; and believe me to be sincerely,
> Sir, your very humble Servant
> Robt Burns

1 James 1:6.
2 *King Lear*, Act I, sc. 4.
3 Churchill: *The Rosciad*, lines 339-40.

II (253)

Ellisland wedensday even:
[9th July? 1788]

My dear Sir,

I go for Ayrshire tomorrow, so cannot have the pleasure of meeting you for some time; but anxious for your "Spiritual welfare & growth in grace," I inclose you the Plenipo.[1]—You will see another, "The Bower of bliss;" 'tis the work of a Reverend Doctor of the Church of

William Stewart

Scotland—Would to Heaven a few more of them would turn their fiery Zeal *that way*! There, they might *spend* their Holy fury, and shew the *tree* by its *fruits*!!!² There, the *in-bearing workings* might give hopeful presages of a *New-birth*!!!!!

The other two are by the author of the Plenipo, but "The Doctor" is not half there, as I have mislaid it.— I have no copies left of either, so must have the precious pieces again:—

I am ever your oblidged humble servant
Robt Burns

I understand old David's Daughter, your tenant's sister means to treat a few friends with A Wedding: Her Mother tells me just now, "Mr Stewart is sick a hamely, kind gentleman that he shall be at it, were it but one of half a dozen"—"I'll meet thee at Philippi!"³

1 *The Plenipotentiary*. In *The Merry Muses of Caledonia*.
2 Matthew 12:33, paraphrased.
3 Shakespeare: *Julius Caesar*, Act IV, sc. 3.

III (306)

Brownhill Monday even:
[early 1789?]

Dear Sir,

In honest Bacon's ingle-neuk,
[C.W. p. 350]

Robt Burns

P.S.
In a week I shall be ready with two horses to drive lime; but I hope to see you on Wednesday

R.B.

IV (606)

Glencairn kirk Thursday even:

My dear Sir,

Smellie's Philosophy of Natural History I had lent to Mr Findlater, & he is in Edinburgh at present.—I tell you this because I hate breaking a promise, were it even to the most [*three or four words erased*] that ever [*four or five words erased*] much less to a Man whose head is a credit & whose heart is an honor to the works of God.—

That Misconduct or Mischance may never put a weapon in the hands of Ill-luck to wound your Peace, is the prayer of

Robt Burns

V (652)

Dumfries, 15th January 1795

This is a painful, disagreable letter; & the first of the kind I ever wrote.—I am truly in serious distress for three or four guineas: can you, my dear Sir, accommodate me?—It will indeed truly oblige me. —These accursed times, by stopping up Importation, have for this year at least lopt off a full third part of my income: &, with my large Family, this is to me a distressing matter.—

Farewell! & God bless you!
R Burns

William Stewart

[Closeburn Castle 16th January 1795
This day forwarded and inclosed in a letter to Mr Burns £3:3s
sterling and for which I hold no security in writing.

William Stewart]

ALEXANDER BLAIR

Nothing is known of the recipient of the following letter, addressed to him at 'Catrine House Catrine', and Ferguson inferred that he was somehow connected with Professor Dugald Stewart, perhaps as pupil or employee - but, of course, he may merely have been a house-guest at the professor's country residence. Ferguson has cast doubt on the authenticity of this letter on grounds of 'a certain vagueness and awkardness in the expression' and adds that from 1787 onwards Burns very rarely signed his name 'Robert', whereas 'Antique' Smith and other forgers frequently tried to make their work more attractive by so doing. It should also be noted that the address 'Catrine House Catrine' is rather suspect. Writing from Mauchline, Burns would have been content to address such a letter to Catrine House. It was not, in fact, until 1788 that Claud Alexander of Ballochmyle and David Dale erected a cotton mill on the River Ayr, and developed the model village of Catrine to accommodate the millworkers. This enterprise was hardly under way at the time this letter was allegedly written.

(234)

Mauchline, 3rd April 1788.

Sir,

I returned here yesterday, and received your letter, for which I return you my heartiest and warmest thanks. I am afraid I cannot at this moment accede to your request, as I am much harrassed with the care and anxiety of farming business, which at present is not propitious to poetry; but if I have an opportunity you shall learn of my progress in a few weeks.

I cannot but feel gratitude to you for the kindly manner by which you have shewn your interest in my endeavours; and I remain,

your obedient servant,
Robert Burns

DUGALD STEWART

Born at Edinburgh in 1753, the son of Dr. Matthew Stewart, professor of mathematics at the University. In 1775 Dugald succeeded his father in this chair, exchanging it in 1785 for the chair of moral philosophy. He enjoyed a high reputation as a lecturer, although his standing as a metaphysician has been subject to re-assessment by posterity. In August 1786 Dr. Mackenzie of Mauchline sent a copy of the Kilmarnock Edition to Stewart, then vacationing at his country seat, Catrine House. Professor Stewart was greatly impressed by the poems and invited Burns to dinner with him on 23rd October. On that occasion the guests included Lord Daer, the first member of the aristocracy that Burns actually encoutered in the flesh. Over the winter of 1786-7 Burns enjoyed a great deal of attention and hospitality from Stewart in Edinburgh. In turn, Burns was the means of introducing Captain Grose to Stewart (III-IV). Stewart died at Edinburgh in 1828 and was commemorated by a statue by W.H. Playfair, erected on Calton Hill in 1832.

I (239)

Mauchline, 3rd May 1788

Sir,

I inclose you one or two more of my bagatelles, If the fervent wishes of honest gratitude have any influence with that great unknown Being, who frames the chain of causes and events, prosperity and happiness will attend your visit to the Continent, and return you safe to your native shore.

Wherever I am, allow me, Sir, to claim it as my privilege, to acquaint you with my progress in my trade of rhymes; as I am sure I could say it with truth, that, next to my little fame, and the having it in my power to make life more comfortable to those whom nature has made dear to me, I shall ever regard your countenance, your patronage, your friendly good offices, as the most valued consequence of my late success in life.

I have the honour to be most truly,
Sir, your much indebted humble servant
Robt Burns

II (297)

Ellisland near Dumfries 20th January 1789.

Sir,

the inclosed sealed packet I sent to Edinburgh a few days after I had the happiness of meeting you in Ayrshire, but you were gone for the Continent.—I have now added a few more of my productions, those for which I am indebted to the Nithsdale Muses.—The Piece inscribed to R—— G—— Esq. is a copy of verses I sent Mr Graham of Fintry accompanying a request for his assistance in a matter, to me, of very great moment.—To that gentleman I am already doubly indebted: for deeds of kindness of serious import to my dearest interests, done in a manner grateful to the delicate feelings of Sensibility.—This Poem is a species of Composition new to me, but I do not intend it shall be my last essay of the kind, as you will see by the "Poet's Progress."—These fragemnts, if my design succeed, are but small part of the intended Whole.—I propose it shall be the work of my utmost exertions ripened by years; of course I do not wish it much known.—The fragment, beginning—"A little, upright, pert, tart," &c. I have not shown to man living till I now send it you.—It is the postulata, the axioms, the definition, of a CHARACTER, which, if it appear at all, shall be placed in a variety of lights.—This particular part, I send you merely as a sample of my hand at Portrait sketching; but lest idle Conjecture should pretend to point out the Original, please to let it be for your single, sole inspection.—

Need I make any apology for this trouble to a gentleman who has treated me with such marked benevolence and peculiar kindness, who has entered into my interests with so much zeal, and on whose critical decisions I can so fully depend?—A Poet as I am by trade, these decisions to me are of the last consequence.—My late transient acquaintance among some of the mere rank and file of Greatness, I resign with ease; but to the distinguished Champions of Genius and Learning, I shall be ever ambitious of being known.—The native genius and accurate discernment, in Mr Stewart's critical strictures; the justness (Iron justice, for he has no bowels of compassion for a poor poetic sinner) of Dr Gregory's remarks, and the delicacy of Professor Dalziel's taste, I shall ever revere.—I shall be in Edinburgh some time next month.

I have the honor to be, Sir,
Your highly oblidged and very humble servant
Robt Burns

III (409)

[Ellisland, July 1790]

Sir,—

I will be extremely happy if this letter shall have the honor of introducing you to Captain Grose, a gentleman whose acquaintance you told me you so much coveted. I inclose this to him, and should his pursuits lead him again to Ayrshire, and should his time, and (what I am sorry to say is more precarious) his health permit, I have no doubt but you will have the mutual pleasure of being acquainted.

I am, &c.
R.B.

IV (410)

Ellisland, 30th July 1790

Sir,

It would be a reason sufficiently just, if I were to tell you that I have not sent you my Poetic Epistle to Fintry, because I actually could not find time to transcribe it; but a better reason is, I am out of conceit with it myself, & transcribing a thing of my own I do not like, is a drudgery I know not how to bear.—I dare say if you have not met with Captain Matthew Henderson about Edinburgh, you must have heard of him.—He was an intimate acquaintance of mine, & of all Mankind I ever knew, he was one of the first, for a nice sense of honour, a generous contempt of the adventitious distinctions of Men, and sterling tho' sometimes outré Wit.—The inclosed Elegy has pleased me beyond any of my late poetic efforts.—Perhaps 'tis "the memory of joys that are past," and a friend who is no more, that biasses my criticism.—It is likewise, ever since I read your, Aiken on the poetical use of Natural history,* a favorite study of mine, the characters of the Vegetable & the manners of the Animal kingdoms.—I regret much that I cannot have an opportunity of

Dugald Stewart

waiting on you to have your strictures on this Poem—How I have succeeded on the whole—if there is any incongruity in the imagery— or whether I have not omitted some apt rural paintings altogether.— I will not pretend to say, whether it is owing to my prejudice in favor of a gentleman to whom I am so much indebted, or to your critical abilities; but in the way of my trade, as a Poet, I will subscribe more implicitly to *your* strictures, than to any Individual on earth.—

I have written Captain Grose, & inclosed him a billet to you.—If he comes to your neighborhood, you will probably see him.—

I shall have leisure soon, to write off for you, several of my pieces.—

I have the honor to be, Sir,
your oblidged humble servant
Robt Burns

* John Aikin, *Essays on Song-Writing* (1772).

SAMUEL BROWN

Born at Craigenton in 1739, the third son of Gilbert Brown and Agnes Rennie, he was the brother of Agnes Brown and thus uncle of the poet. Burns lodged with him at Kirkoswald in 1775 while studying mathematics under Hugh Ródger. Brown married Margaret Nevin in April 1765, after they had done penance before the Kirk Session on a charge of antenuptial fornication. Their only child Jenny (mentioned by Burns in *Hallowe'en*) was baptised on 12th July 1765. These facts, together with allegations that Brown was connected in some way with smuggling, explain the rather broad humour of the following letter.

(240)

Masgiel, 4th May 1789 [for 1788]

Dear Uncle,

These I hope will find you and your Conjugal yoke-fellow in your good old Ordinary.—I am impatient to hear if the Ailsa fowling be Comenced for this Season yet, as I want three or four stones of feathers, and hope you will bespeak them for me.—it would be a vain attempt for me to enumerate the various transactions I have been engaged in since I saw you Last.—But this know.—I engaged in the smuggling Trade and God knows if ever any poor man experienced better returns—two for one.—But as freight and Delivery has turned out so D—md Dear I am thinking about takeing out a Licence and beginning in a Fair trade.—I have taken a Farm on the Banks of Nith and in imitation of the old Patriarchs get Men servants and Maid Servants—Flocks and herds and beget sons and Daughters.

Your Obedient Nephew,
Robert Burns

ANDREW DUNLOP OF DUNLOP

The fourth son of Mrs Dunlop, he attained the rank of major in the Army during the American War of Independence and then retired to manage the family estate near Stewarton, following his father's death in 1785. During the French Revolutionary War he raised and commanded the Ayrshire Fencible Cavalry. He died unmarried in 1804. Burns's only known letter to him commented philosophically on the decline of his fame, but dealt mainly with his recent marriage and his motive for settling down at last: 'I saw, Sir, that I had a once, & still much lov'd fellow-creature's happiness or misery among my hands; and I could not dally with such a matter.'

(245)

Mauchline, Saturday morn:
[31st May 1788]

Sir,

I mentioned to your Mother in a letter I wrote her yesterday, which is the third of fourth I have wrote to her to Haddington, that my Philosophy was gravelled to account for that Partiality from the house of Dunlop of which I have the honor to be so much the Object.—Do you know that except from your Mother and the good family, my existence or non-existence is now of as little importance to that Great World I lately left, as the satellites of the Georgium Sidus is to a parcel of your Ditchers.—I foresaw this from the beginning.—Ambition could not form a higher wish than to be wedded to Novelty; but I retired to my shades with a little comfortable pride and a few comfortable pounds; and even there I enjoy the peculiar happiness of Mrs Dunlop's friendship & Correspondence, a Happiness I shall ever gratefully prize next to the dearest ties that wind about my heart, so in my Ploughman Compliment I bid the World—GUDE SPEED.—

Your Mother never hinted at the report of my late change in life, and I did not know how to tell her.—I am afraid that perhaps she will not entirely enter into the motives of my conduct, so I have kept aloof from the affair altogether.—I saw, Sir, that I had a once, & still much-lov'd fellow-creature's happiness or misery among my hands; and I could not dally with such a matter.—Pride & seeming Justice like true murderous King's Advocates talked much of injuries & wrongs; but Generosity, Humanity & Forgiveness were such irresistible Counsel for the poor Pannel, that a Jury of old Attachments & new Endearments brought in a verdict—NOT GUILTY!—

I shall be at Glasgow in the middle of next week, and if I find you at home, I shall certainly take the opportunity of assuring you in propria persona how much I have the honor to be,

Sir,
your ever grateful humble servant
Robert Burns

452

GEORGE LOCKHART

Nothing is known of George Lockhart, apart from what one may glean from the address on this letter: 'Merchant at Miss Gray's, Glasgow'. The name of George Lockhart, merchant and manufacturer,appears in the first *Directory of Glasgow* (1787). A later edition noted that Miss Hanna Gray let lodgings above the post office in Princes Street, and from this it may be inferred that Lockhart lodged there. This is confirmed by Burns's reference to 'Mr Purden' (*sic*): the Glasgow directories show John Purdon, merchant and linen-printer as a fellow-lodger at Miss Gray's in 1787-9. By 1790 Purdon had moved with Miss Gray to 110 Trongate, but there is no further mention of Lockhart.

(256)

Mauchline, 18th July 1788

My Dear Sir,

I am just going for Nithsdale, else I would certainly have transcribed some of my rhyming things for you.—The Miss Bailies I have seen in Edinburgh.—"Fair & lovely are Thy Works, Lord God Almighty! who would not praise Thee for these Thy Gifts in Thy goodness to the sons of men! ! !"[1]—It needed not your fine taste to admire them.—I declare, one day I had the honor of dining at Mr Bailie's, I was almost in the predicament of the Children of Israel, when they could not look on Moses' face for the glory that shone in it when he descended from mount Horeb.—[2]

I did once write a poetic Address from the falls of Bruar to his Grace of Athole, when I was in the Highlands. When you return to Scotland let me know, & I will send such of my pieces as please myself best.—

I return to Mauchline in about ten days.—

My Compliments to Mr Purden.—
I am in truth, but, at present, in haste
Yours sincerely
Robt Burns

1 Not identified, but probably common formulae in contemporary sermons.
2 See Exodus 34:29-35.

JOHN SMITH

Born in 1753, the eldest son of John Smith who founded the well-known firm of Glasgow stationers and booksellers in 1751. The company name was changed to John Smith & Son some time between 1774 and 1777, when John Smith Jr. was taken into partnership. John Smith Sr. retired in 1781, but in 1803 John Smith Jr. took his son, also named John, into partnership and the company has retained the name John Smith & Son to this day, the oldest Scottish bookselling firm in existence at the present time. The company subscribed for a dozen copies of the first Edinburgh Edition, but it is apparent from (I) that it subsequently ordered a further nine. It is obvious (II) that the company also acted as agents on behalf of individual subscribers. Ross Roy quotes an anecdote from the firm's history (1921) about this operation. Smith charged only 5 per cent for this service, and when Burns learned of such a modest charge he is said to have exclaimed 'You seem a very decent sort of folk, you Glasgow booksellers; but, eh! they're sair birkies in Edinburgh.'

I (256A)

Mauchline, 18th July 1788

Sir

I received per the Mauchline Carrier £11.19s 1d. as mentioned in yours of the 16th Current.—I can-not lay my hand on the Account but I suppose the nine Copies sent from Kilmarnock are not included in this payment.—I only mention this, en passant; but I will probably be in Glasgow in a month or two myself.—

I am, Sir, your humble servant
Robt Burns

To Mr Jno Smith Junr
Bookseller—Glasgow—

II (296A)

Mauchline, 17th January 1789

Dear Sir,

Please send me if convenient the value of the nine copies of my book which I sent you last from Kilmarnock and are yet unaccounted for, by John Glover, Carrier to Dumfries.—My address is, at Ellisland near Dumfries.—

I am, Dear Sir, your very humble servant
Robt Burns

ALEXANDER CUNNINGHAM

The eldest son of James Cunningham of Hyndhope and nephew of the historian, Principal William Robertson, he was born about 1763 and practised law in Edinburgh. When Burns first met him he was engaged to Anne Stewart of East Craigs but in 1788 she 'prostituted her character' as Burns puts it by jilting Cunningham in favour of Forest Dewar, an Edinburgh surgeon. Cunningham eventually got over this and married Agnes Moir in 1792. In 1797 he purchased the business of the jeweller William Robertson, probably as the result of wealth brought to the marriage by his wife who was heiress to an estate in South Carolina. It seems likely that Robertson the jeweller was a close relative; Maurice Lindsay records that by 1806 he was in partnership with his uncle Patrick Robertson in this venture. In 1798 he became a Writer to the Signet. He was one of the poet's closest friends; apart from Cleghorn and Peter Hill, he was the only one of the Edinburgh group who had not drifted away before Burns died, as shown by the fact that no fewer than nineteen letters from the poet are known, including one of the very last he ever wrote. Cunningham played the principal role in promoting the subscription for Burns's widow and orphans.

I (257)

Ellisland in Nithsdale, 27th July 1788

My godlike Friend—nay do not stare,

[C.W. p. 328]

My spur-galled, spavin'd Pegasus makes so hobbling a progress over the Course of Extempore, that I must here alight & try the foot-path of plain prose.—I have not met with any thing this long while, my dear Sir, that has given my inward man such a fillip as your kind Epistle.—

For my own Biographical story, I can only say with the venerable Hebrew Patriarch; "Here am I, with the Children God has given me!"[1] I have been a Farmer since Whitsunday, & am just now building a house—not a Palace to attract the train-attended steps of pride-swoln Greatness; but a plain, simple Domicile for Humility & Contentment.—I am, too, a married man.—This was a step of which I had no idea, when you & I were together.—On my return to Ayr-shire, I found a much-lov'd Female's positive happiness, or absolute Misery among my hands; and I could not trifle with such a sacred Deposite.—I am, since, doubly pleased with my conduct.—I have the consciousness of acting up to that generosity of principle I would be thought to possess; & I am really more & more pleased with my Choice.—When I tell you that Mrs Burns was once, *my Jean*, you will know the rest.—Of four children she bore me, in seventeen months, my eldest boy is only living.—By the bye, I intend breeding him up for the Church; and from an innate dexterity in secret Mischief which he possesses & a certain hypocritical gravity as he looks on the consequences, I have no small hopes of him in the sacerdotal line.—

Mrs Burns does not come from Ayr-shire, till my said new house be ready, so I am eight or ten days at Mauchline & this place alternately.—Hitherto my direction was only, "at Mauchline;" but, "at Ellisland near Dumfries;" will now likewise find me; tho' I prefer the former.—I need not tell you, that I shall expect to hear from you soon.—Adieu!

Robt Burns

Lowe's Poem[2] I shall transcribe in my first leisure-hour.

R.B.

1 Genesis 33:5, paraphrased.
2 Rev. John Lowe: *Mary's Dream.*

Alexander Cunningham

II (307)

Ellisland, 24th January 1789

My dear Cunningham

When I saw in my last Newspaper that a Surgeon in Edinburgh was married to a certain amiable and accomplished young lady whose name begins with, Ann; a lady with whom I fancy I have the honor of being a little acquainted, I sincerely felt for a worthy much-esteemed friend of mine.—As you are the single only instance that ever came within the sphere of my observation of her human nature, of a young fellow, dissipated but not debauched, a circumstance that has ever given me the highest idea of the native qualities of your heart, I am certain that a disappointment in the tender passion must, to you, be a very serious matter.—To the hopeful youth, keen on the badger-foot of Mammon, or listed under the gaudy banners of Ambition, a love-disappointment, as such, is an easy business; nay, perhaps he hugs himself on his escape; but to your scanty tribe of mankind, whose souls bear, on the richest materials, the most elegant impress of the Great Creator, Love enters deeply into their existence, it is entwisted with their very thread of life.—I myself can affirm, both from bachelor and wedlock experience, that Love is the Alpha and the Omega ·of human enjoyment.—All the pleasures, all the happiness of my humble Compeers, flow immediately and directly from this delicious source.—It is that spark of celestial fire which lights up the wintry hut of Poverty, and makes the chearless mansion, warm, comfortable and gay.—It is the emanation of Divinity that preserves the Sons and Daughters of rustic labour from degenerating into the brutes with which they daily hold converse.—Without it, life to the poor inmates of the Cottage would be a damning gift.—

I intended to go on with some kind of consolatory epistle, when, unawares I flew off in this rhapsodical tangent.—Instead of attempting to resume a subject for which I am so ill qualified, I shall ask your opinion of some verses I have lately begun, on a theme of which you are the best judge I ever saw.—It is Love too; tho' not just warranted by the law of nations.—A married lady of my acquaintance, whose crim. con. amour with a certain Captain, has made some noise in the world writes to him, now in the West Indies as follows—

> By all I lov'd neglected and forgot,
> [12 lines] *
>
> Now, raving wild, I curse that fatal night
> [C.W. p. 501, two variant lines and lines 11-26.]

I intend being in Edinburgh about the end of February—

Adieu!
Robt Burns

* Captain James Montgomerie and Mrs Maxwell Campbell of Skerrington. See letter to Gavin Hamilton of 8th March 1787, (p. 67-8).

456

Alexander Cunningham

III (336)

Ellisland, 4th May 1789

My dear Sir,

Your *duty-free* Favor of the 26th April I received two days ago.—I will not say, I received it with pleasure; that is the cold compliment of ceremony; I perused it, Sir, with delicious satisfaction.—In short it is such a letter that not you, nor your friend, but the Legislature, by express Proviso in their Postage laws should frank.—A letter informed with all the glowing soul of friendship is such an honor to Human nature, that they should order it, free ingress & egress to & from their bags & mails, as an encouragement and mark of distinction to supereminent Virtue.—

I have just put the last hand to a little Poem, which I think will be something to your taste.—One morning lately as I was out pretty early in the fields sowing some grass-seeds, I heard the burst of a shot from a neighbouring Plantation, & presently a poor little wounded hare came crippling by me.—You will guess my indignation at the inhuman fellow, who could shoot a hare at this season when they all of them have young ones; & it gave me no little gloomy satisfaction to see the poor injured creature escape him.—Indeed there is something in all that multiform business of destroying for our sport individuals in the animal creation that do not injure us materially, that I could never reconcile to my ideas of native Virtue & eternal Right.—

On Seeing a Fellow Wound a Hare with a Shot—

April—1789

Inhuman man! curse on thy barb'rous art,

[C.W. p. 354]

Thank you, my dearest Sir, for your concern for me in my contest with the London News-men.—Depend on it that I will never deign to reply to *their* Petulance.—The Publisher of the Star has been polite.— He may find his account in it; though I would scorn to put my name to a Newspaper Poem.—One instance, indeed, excepted; I mean, your two Stanzas.—Had the Lady kept her character, she should have kept my verses but as she prostituted the one, I no longer made anything of the other; so sent them to Stuart as a bribe, in my earnestness to be cleared from the foul aspersions respecting the Duchess of Gordon.—

Let me know how you like my Poem.—I am doubtful whether it would not be an improvement to keep out the last Stanza but one, altogether.

Cleghorn is a glorious production of the Author of Man.—You, He, & the noble Colonel of the Crochallan Fencibles are to me

Dear as the ruddy drops that warm my heart—*

I have a good mind to make verses on you all, to the tune of, Three guid fellows ayont yon glen.—By the way, do, look in on poor Johnson how he comes on.—I sent him a list of what *I would chuse* for his third Volume.—

Adieu! God bless you!

Robt Burns

* Shakespeare: *Julius Caesar*, Act II, sc.1, misquoted.

IV (392)

Ellisland 13th February 1790.

I beg your Pardon my dear & much valued Friend, for writing you on this very unfashionable unsightly Sheet—

"My Poverty but not my Will consents"—[1]

but to make amends, since modish Post I have none, except one poor widowed half-sheet of Gilt, which lies in my drawer among my plebeian foolscap pages, like the widow of a Man of fashion whom that unpolite Scoundrel, Necessity, has driven from Burgundy and Pine-apple, to a dish of bohea with the scandal-bearing Help-mate of a village Priest, or a glass of whisky-toddy with the ruby-nosed Yoke-fellow of a foot-padding Exciseman—I make a vow to inclose this sheet-full of epistolary fragments in that, my only scrap of Gilt paper.—

I am indeed your unworthy debtor for three friendly letters.—I ought to have written to you, long ere now, but it is a literal fact, I have not almost a spare-moment.—It is not that I *will* not write you: MISS BURNET is not more dear to her Guardian Angel, nor his Grace of Queensberry to the Powers of Darkness, than my friend Cunningham to me.—It is not that I *can* not write you: should you doubt it, take the following fragment which was intended for you some time ago, and be convinced that I can *antithesize* Sentiment & *circumvolute* Periods, as well as any Coiner of phrases in the regions of Philology.—

December 1789
My dear Cunningham
Where are you? And what are you doing? Can you be that son of Levity who takes up a friendship as he takes up a fashion; or are you, like some other of the worthiest fellows in the world, the victim of Indolence, laden with fetters of ever-increasing weight?

What strange things we are! Since we have a portion of conscious existence, equally capable of enjoying Pleasure, Happiness & Rapture, or of sufferieng Pain, Wretchedness & Misery, it is surely worthy of enquiry whether there be not such a thing as A SCIENCE OF LIFE; whether Method, Economy and Fertility of expedients, be not applicable to Enjoyment; and whether there be not a want of dexterity in Pleasure which renders our little scantling of happiness still less, and a profuseness, an intoxication in bliss which leads to Satiety, Disgust and Self-abhorrence.—There is not a doubt but that health, talents, character, decent competency, respectable friends, are real and substantial blessings, and yet do we not daily see those who enjoy many or all of these good things, and notwithstanding, contrive to be as unhappy as others to whose lot few of them have fallen.—I believe one great source of this mistake or misconduct is owing to a certain stimulus within us called Ambition, which goads us up the hill of life, not as we ascend other eminences for the laudable curiosity of viewing an extended landscape, but rather for the dishonest pride of looking down on others of our fellow-creatures seemingly diminutive in humbler stations.—&c. &c. &c. &c. &c.

Sunday—14th February 1790
God help me! I am now oblidged to join

"—Night to day, & Sunday to the week—"[2]

If there be any truth in the Orthodox faith of these Churches, I am
damned past redemption, and what is worse, damned to all eternity.
—I am deeply read in Boston's fourfold State, Marshal on Sanctification, Guthrie's trial of a Saving Interest, &c. &c. but "There is no
balm in Gilead, there is no physician there,"[3] for me; so I shall e'en
turn Ariminian, & trust to, "Sincere though imperfect obedience."—

Tuesday 16th
Luckily for me I was prevented from the discussion of the knotty
point at which I had just made a full stop.—All my fears & cares are
of this world: if there is Another, an honest man has nothing to fear
from it.—I hate a Man that wishes to be a Deist, but I fear, every fair,
unprejudiced Enquirer must in some degree be a Sceptic.—It is not
that there are any very staggering arguments against the Immortality
of Man; but like Electricity, Phlogiston, &c. the subject is so
involved in darkness that we want Data to go upon.—One thing
frightens me much: that we are to live for ever, seems too good news
to be true.—That we are to enter into a new scene of existence,
where exempt from want & pain we shall enjoy ourselves & our
friends without satiety or separation—how much would I be
indebted to any one who could fully assure me that this were
certain fact!

"Tell us, ye Dead! will none of you, in pity
"To those you left behind, disclose the secret,
"What 'tis you are, and we must shortly be!"[4]

My time is once more expired.—I will write Mr Cleghorn soon.—God
bless him & all his concerns! And may all the Powers that preside
over conviviality & friendship be present with all their kindest
influence when the bearer of this, Mr Syme, & you meet! I wish I
could also make one.—I think we should be trinity in unity.—

Finally, Brethren, farewell! Whatsoever things are lovely, whatsoever
things are gentle, whatsoever things are charitable, whatsoever things
are kind, think on these things, and think on[5]

Robt Burns

1 Shakespeare: *Romeo and Juliet*, Act V, sc. 1.
2 Young: *Love of Fame*, Satire V, line 102.
3 Jeremiah 8:22.
4 Blair: *The Grave* lines 431-2, 434.
5 Based on Philippians 4:8.

V (411B)

Ellisland, 8th August 1790

Forgive me, my once dear & ever dear Friend, my seeming
negligence.—You cannot sit down and fancy the busy life I lead.—I
laid down my Goose-feather to beat my brains for a pat Simile, &
had some thoughts of a country Grannum at a family-christening; a
Bride on the market-day before her marriage; an Orthodox Clergyman at a Paisley Sacrament; an Edinburgh Bawd on a Sunday

evening; a tavern-keeper at an Election-dinner; &c. &c. &c.—but the resemblance that hits my fancy best is, that poor, blackguard Miscreant, Satan, who, as Holy Writ tells us, roams about like a roaring lion, seeking, *searching*, whom he may devour.[1]—However, tossed about as I am, if I chuse (& who would not chuse) to bind down with the crampets of Attention the brazen foundation of Integrity, I may rear up the Superstructure of Independance, & from its daring turrets bid defiance to the storms of Fate.—And is not this a "consummation devoutly to be wished?"[2]

> "Thy spirit, Independance, let me share;
> "Lord of the lion-heart, & eagle-eye!
> "Thy steps I follow with my bosom bare,
> "And brave each blast that sails along the sky!"

Are not these glorious verses? They are the introduction of Smollet's Ode to Independance: if you have not seen the Poem I will send it to you.—How wretched is the man that hangs on & by the favors of the Great! To shrink from every dignity of Man at the approach of a lordly piece of Self-consequence, who, amid all his tinsel glitter & stately hauteur, is but a creature formed as thou art—& perhaps not so well formed as thou art—came into the world a puling infant as thou didst, & must go out of it as all men must, a stinking corpse—& should the important piece of clay-dough deign to cast his supercilious eye over you, & make a motion as if to signify his tremendous fiat—then—in all the quaking pangs & staring terrors of self-annihil- ation, to stutter in crouching syllables—"Speak! Lord!! for thy servant heareth!!!"[3]—If such is the damned state of the poor devil, from my soul I pity him!...

1 Peter 5:8.
2 Shakespeare: *Hamlet*, Act III, sc. 1.
3 I Samuel 3:9.

VI (433)

Ellisland, 23rd January 1791.

Many happy returns of the season to you, my dear friend! As many of the good things of this life as is consistent with the usual mixture of good and evil in the cup of Being!

I have just finished a poem, which you will receive enclosed. It is my first essay in the way of tales.

I have these several months been hammering at an elegy on the amiable and accomplished Miss Burnet. I have got, and can get, no farther than the following fragment, on which please give me your strictures. In all kinds of poetic composition, I set great store by your opinion; but in sentimental verses, in the poetry of the heart, no Roman Catholic ever set more value on the infallibility of the Holy Father than I do on yours.

I mean the introductory couplets as text verses.

ELEGY

On the late Miss Burnet *of* Monboddo
[C.W. p. 416 lines 1-24.]

Let me hear from you soon. Adieu!

Alexander Cunningham

VII (441)

Ellisland, 11th March 1791

My dear Cunningham

I recieved your first letter two days ago: the last came to hand this moment.—I was highly delighted with the well-carried on Allegory in your friend's letter.—I read it to two or three acquaintances who had souls to enjoy a good thing, & we had a very hearty laugh at it.—I have felt along the line of my Muse's inclination, & I fear your Archery-subject would be uphill work with her.—I have two or three times in my life composed from the wish, rather than from the impulse, but I never succeeded to any purpose.—One of these times I shall ever remember with gnashing of teeth.—'Twas on the death of the late Lord President Dundas.—My very worthy & most respected Friend, Mr Alexander Wood, Surgeon, urged me to pay a compliment in the way of my trade to his Lordship's memory.—Well, to work I went, & produced a copy of Elegiac verses, some of them I own rather common place, & others rather hide-bound, but on the whole though they were far from being in my best manner, they were tolerable; & had they been the production of a Lord or a Baronet, they would have been thought very clever.—I wrote a letter, which however was in my very best manner, & inclosing my Poem, Mr Wood carried altogether to Mr Solicitor Dundas that then was, & not finding him at home, left the parcel for him.—His Solicitorship never took the smallest notice of the Letter, the Poem, or the Poet.—From that time, highly as I respect the talents of their Family, I never see the name, Dundas, in the column of a newspaper, but my heart seems straitened for room in my bosom; & if I am obliged to read aloud a paragraph relating to one of them, I feel my forehead flush, & my nether lip quivers.—Had I been an obscure Scribbler, as I was then in the heyday of my fame; or had I been a dependant Hangeron for favor or pay; or had the bearer of the letter been any other than a gentleman who does honor to the city in which he lives, to the Country that produced him, & to the God that created him, Mr Solicitor might have had some apology.—

But enough of this ungracious subject.—A friend of mine who transcribed the last parcel I sent you, is to be with me in a day or two, & I shall get him to copy out the two Poems you mention.—I have this evening sketched out a Song, which I have a good mind to send you, though I foresee that it will cost you another groat of postage.—By the way, you once mentioned to me a method of franking letters to you, but I have forgot the direction.—My song is intended to sing to a Strathspey reel of which I am very fond, called in Cummin's Collection of Strathspeys, "Ballendalloch's reel;" & in other Collections that I have met with, it is known by the name of, "Camdelmore".—It takes three Stanzas of four lines each, to go through the whole tune.—I shall give the song to Johnson for the fourth vol. of his Publication of Scots Songs, which he has just now in hand.—

Song—

Sweet are the banks, the banks o' Doon,

[C.W. p. 612]

461

Alexander Cunningham

If the foregoing Piece be worth your strictures, let me have them.—
For my own part, a thing that I have just composed, always appears
through a double portion of that partial medium in which an Author
will ever view his own works.—I believe in general, Novelty has
something in it that inebriates the fancy; & not unfrequently,
dissipates & fumes away like other intoxication, & leaves the poor
Patient as usual with an aching heart.—A striking instance of this
might be adduced in the revolution of many a Hymeneal
honeymoon.—But lesst I sink into stupid Prose, so sacreligiously
intrude on the office of my Parish-priest, who is in himself one vast
constellation of dullness, & from his weekly zenith rays out his
contradictory stupidity to the no small edification & enlightening of
the heavy & opaque pericraniums of his gaping Admirers; I shall fill
up the page in my own way, & give you another Song of my late
composition, which will appear perhaps in Johnson's work as well as
the former.—You must know a beautiful Jacobite Air, There'll never
be peace till Jamie comes hame.—When Political combustion ceases
to be the object of Princes & Patriots, it then, you know, becomes
the lawful prey of Historians & Poets.—

Song—

By yon castle wa', at the close of the day,

[C.W. p. 418]

If you like the air, & if the stanzas hit your fancy, you cannot
imagine, my dear Friend, how much you would oblige me if by the
charms of your delightful voice you would give my honest effusion
to "The memory of joys that are past," to the few friends whom
you indulge in that pleasure.—But I have scribbled on till I hear the
clock has intimated the near approach of—

"That hour, o' night's black arch the key-stane"*—So Goodnight to
you! And sound be your sleep, & delectable your dreams! Apropos,
how do you like this thought in a ballad I have just now on the
tapis?

I look to the west, when I gae to rest—
That happy my dreams & my slumbers may be:
[For] far in the west lives he I lo'e best—
The man that is dear to my babie & me!

[C.W. p. 419]

[Good] night, once more; & God bless you!

Robt Burns

* *Tam o' Shanter*, line 69.

VIII (456)

11th June 1791

Let me interest you, my dear Cunningham, in behalf of the
gentleman who gives you this—He is a Mr Clarke of Moffat, principal
schoolmaster there, & is at present suffering severely under the
persecution of one or two malicious but powerful individuals of his
employers.—He is accused of harshness to some perverse dunces that
were placed under his care.—God help the Teacher, a man of genius

462

& sensibility, for such is my friend Clarke, when the blockhead Father presents him his booby son, & insists on having the rays of science lighted up in a fellow's head whose scull is impervious & inaccessible by any other way than a positive fracture with a cudgel! —A fellow, whom in fact it savours of Impiety to attempt making a scholar of, as he has been marked, "A Blockhead," in the book of fate at the Almighty fiat of his Creator.—

The Patrons of Moffat-school are, the Ministers, Magistrates & Town Council of Edinburgh, & as the business comes now before them, let me beg my dearest Friend to do every thing in his power to serve the interests of a man of genius, a man of worth, & a man whom I particularly respect & esteem—You know some good fellows among the Magistrates & Council, though, God knows, 'tis generally a very unfit soil for good fellows to flourish in, but particularly you have much to say with a Reverend Gentleman to whom you have the honor of being very nearly related, & whom this Country & Age have had the honor to produce—I need not name the Historian of Charles the fifth.*—I tell him through the medium of his nephew's influence, that Mr Clarke is a gentleman who will not disgrace even his Patronization.—

I know the merits of the cause thoroughly; & I say it, that my friend is falling a sacrifice to prejudiced Ignorance, & envious, *causeless* Malice.—God help the children of Dependance! Hated & persecuted by their enemies, & too often—Alas, almost unexceptionably, *always* —received by their friends with insulting disrespect, & heart-stinging reproach, under the thin disguises of cold civility, & humiliating advice.—O, to be a sturdy Savage, stalking in the pride of his indepandance amid the solitary wilds of his desarts! Rather than in civilized life helplessly to tremble for a subsistence, precarious as the caprice of a fellow-creature! Every man has his virtues, & no man is without his failings; & curse on that privileged plaindealing of friendship, which, in the hour of my calamity, cannot reach forth the helping hand, without at the same time pointing out those failings, & assigning their share in my present distress.—My friends, for such the world calls you, & such ye think yourselves to be, pass by my Virtues if you please; but do, also, spare my follies: the first will witness in my breast for themselves, & the last will give pain enough to the ingenuous mind without you.—And, since deviating, more, or less, from the paths of Propriety & Rectitude must be incident to Human-nature, do thou, Fortune, put it in my power, always from my own pocket to pay the penalties of those errors.—I do not want to be independant, that I may sin; but I want to be independant in my sinning.—

To return in this rambling letter to the Subject I set out with; let me recommend my friend, Clarke, to your acquaintance & good offices: his Worth entitles him to the first, & his Gratitude will merit the last.—

I long much to hear from you, Adieu!

* William Robertson.

IX (463)

[summer/early autumn 1791]

It gave me the highest the sincerest pleasure, your account of your noble [*two or three words obliterated*].—As to [wisdom?] 'worshipping the rising sun,' I know no reason why we should not; but it is his merit not his *place*, that you or I are capable of paying adoration to My late noble Patron *shall* be the theme of my Muse; but it shall not be a hasty abortive sally.—I shall to the last throb of parting life remember & revere him.—My miniature of him is only a profile shade, not a painting; but it is the most striking likeness of him, Lady H—— Don said, that ever had been done.- It is literally true, that my wife knew him perfectly, tho' she had not the least idea of his being in the country.—Miers, . . .

[*Half a page of MS. is missing here*]

going to publish another Edition of my book; one copy of which, with the best address my abilities can produce, either Prose or Verse, shall be forwarded to the Earl of Glencairn.—From what you have said, I venerate his character.—

I am so completely nettled with the fumes of wine, that I cannot write any thing like a letter.—

I shall give you a new Song—

Tune, the Quaker's wife—
Come cowe me, Davie . . .

[*Three more lines obliterated in the MS., but see* C.W. *p. 506 of which this may be a variant.*]

X (496)

Dumfries, 5th February 1792

My ever dear Cunningham,

Tomorrow, or some day soon, I will write you as entertaining a letter as I can; in the mean time, take a scrawl of very serious business.—You remember Mr Clarke Master of the grammar School at Moffat, whom I formerly recommended to your good offices: the crisis of his fate is just at hand.—Mr Mcmurdo of Drumlanrig, Ferguson of Craigdarroch & Riddel of Glenriddel, gentlemen who know Clarke personally & intimately, have strained & are straining every nerve to serve him, but, alas! poor Clarke's foes are mighty! Lord Hoptoun, spurred on by those infernal creatures that always go between a Great Man & his inferiours, has sworn his destruction; irritated as he justly is, that any Plebeian & the Son of a Plebeian, should dare to oppose his—*existence*—a trifling affair! against his Lordship s high & mighty will.- What I know & *You* know that I would for a friend of Yours, I ask of you for a friend, a much-esteemed friend, of mine.—Get the Principal's interest in his favor.— Be not denied!—To interpose between lordly Cruelty & helpless merit, is a task worthy of you to ask & him to execute! In the mean time, if you meet with Craigdarroch or chance to wait on him (by the bye, I wish you w[ould on this] very business) he will inform you of the merits of one party & the demerits of the other.—

You shall hear from me again soon.

God bless you!
Robt Burns

464

Alexander Cunningham

XI (502A)

George Inn, 3 o'clock morn:
[Apr or May 1792]

My dear Cunningham

I am just now devilish drunk—if you doubt it, ask a Mr Campbell, whom I have just met with by lucky accident—He tells me he is connected with you by marriage—You will allow me I know, to be a judge of mankind—he may have his faults—but I wish to see him again.—You were more than generous to poor Clarke! Most—cordially do I thank you for it.—In your present situation you will probably meet with many congratulatory compliments—but none more sincere than mine, when I wish you all the happiness—'tis more than human nature is entitled to—the happiness, that I wish you; & that you deserve!—

Adieu!
Robt Burns

XII (506)

Dumfries, 10th September 1792

No! I will not attempt an apology.—Amid all my hurry of business, grinding the faces of the Publican & the Sinner on the merciless wheels of the Excise; making ballads, & then drinking, & singing them; & over & above all, the correcting the Presswork of two different Publications; still, still I might have stolen five minutes to dedicate to one of the first of my Friends & Fellow-creatures.—I might have done, as I do at present, snatched an hour near "witching time of night"[1]—& scrawled a page or two.—I might have congratulated my Friend on his marriage; or, I might have thanked the Caledonian Archers for the honor they have done me: (though, to do myself justice, I intended to have done both in RHYME, else I had done both long ere now.—) Well then, here is to your good health! for you must know, I have set a nipperkin of TODDY by me, just by way of SPELL to keep away the meikle horned Deil, or any of his subaltern Imps who may be on their nightly rounds.—

But what shall I write to you?—"The Voice said, Cry! and I said, What shall I cry?"[2]—O, thou Spirit! whatever thou art, or wherever thou makest thyself visible! Be thou a Bogle by the eerie side of an auld thorn, in the dreary glen through which the herd-callan maun bicker in his gloamin route frae the fauld!—Be thou a BROWNIE, set, at dead of night, to thy task by the blazing ingle, or in the solitary barn where the repercussions of thy iron flail half affright thyself, as thou performest the work of twenty of the sons of men, ere the cock-crowing summon thee to thy ample cog of substantial BROSE!—Be thou a KELPIE, haunting the ford, or ferry, in the starless night, mixing thy laughing yell with the howling of the storm & the roaring of the flood, as thou viewest the perils & miseries of Man on the foundering horse, or in the tumbling boat!—Or, lastly, be thou a GHOST, paying thy nocturnal visits to the hoary ruins of decayed Grandeur; or performing thy mystic rites in the shadow of the time-worn Church while the Moon looks, without a cloud, on the silent, ghastly dwellings of the dead around thee; or taking thy

465

stand by the bed-side of the Villain, or the Murderer, pourtraying on his dreaming fancy, pictures, dreadful as the horrors of unveiled Hell, & terrible as the wrath of incensed Deity! ! !—Come, thou Spirit, but not in these horrid forms; come with the milder, gentle, easy inspirations which thou breathest round the wig of a prating ADVOCATE, or the tête of a tea-bibbing Gossip, while their tongues run at the light-horse gallop of clishmaclaiver for ever & ever—come, & assist a poor devil who is quite jaded in the attempt to share half an idea among half a hundred words; to fill up four quarto pages, while he has not got one single sentence of recollection, information, or remark, worth putting pen to paper for!—

I feel, I feel the presence of Supernatural assistance! Circled in the embrace of my elbow-chair, my breast labors, like the bloated Sybil on her three-footed stool, & like her too, labors with Nonsense.—Nonsense, auspicious name!—Tutor, Friend & Finger-post in the mystic mazes of Law; the cadaverous paths of Physic; & particularly in the sightless soarings of SCHOOL DIVINITY, who, leaving Common Sense confounded at his strength of pinion, Reason delirious with eyeing his giddy flight, & Truth creeping back into the bottom of her well, cursing the hour that ever she offered her scorned alliance to the wizard Power of Theologic Vision—raves abroad on all the winds, "On Earth, Discord! A gloomy Heaven above "opening her jealous gates to the nineteen thousandth part of "the tithe of mankind! And below, an inescapable & inexorable "Hell, expanding its leviathan jaws for the vast residue of "Mortals! ! !" O, doctrine! comfortable & healing to the weary, wounded soul of man!—Ye sons & daughters of affliction, ye pauvres Miserables, to whom day brings no pleasure, & night yields no rest, be comforted! " 'Tis but *one* to "nineteen hundred thousand, that "your situation will mend in this world;" so, alas, the Experience of the Poor & the Needy too truly affirms; & 'tis nineteen hundred thousand to *one,* by the dogmas of Theology, that you will be damned eternally in the World to come!

But of all Nonsense, Religious Nonsense is the most nonsensical; so enough, & more than enough of it—Only, by the bye, will you, or can you tell me, my dear Cunningham, why a religioso turn of mind has always a tendency to narrow & illiberalize the heart? They are orderly; they may be just; nay, I have known them merciful: but still your children of Sanctity move among their fellow-creatures with a nostril snuffing putrescence, & a foot spurning filth, in short, with that conceited dignity which your titled Douglases, Hamiltons, Gordons, or any other of your Scots Lordlings of seven centuries standing, display when they accidentally mix among the many-aproned Sons of Mechanical life.—I remember, in my Plough-boy days, I could not conceive it possible that a noble Lord could be a Fool, or that a godly Man could be a Knave.—How ignorant are Plough-boys!—Nay, I have since discovered that a *godly woman* may be a——!—But hold—Here's t'ye again—This Rum is damn'd generous Antigua, so a very unfit menstruum for scandal.—

Apropos, how do you like, I mean *really* like, the Married Life?—Ah, my Friend! Matrimony is quite a different thing from what your love-sick youths & sighing girls take it to be!—But Marriage, we are told, is appointed by God & I shall never quarrel with any of HIS Institutions.—I am a Husband of older standing than you, & I shall give you *my* ideas of the Conjugal State.—(En passant, you know I am no Latin, is not "Conjugal" derived from "Jugum" a yoke?) Well then, the scale of Good-wife ship I divide into ten parts.—Good Nature, four; Good-Sense, two; Wit, one; Personal Charms, viz. a sweet face, eloquent eyes, fine limbs, graceful carriage, (I would add a fine waist too, but that is so soon spoilt you know) all these, one: as for the other qualities belonging to, or attending on, a Wife, such as, fortune, connections education, (I mean, education extraordinary) family-blood, &c. divide the two remaining degrees among them as you please; only, remember that all these minor properties must be expressed by *fractions;* for there is not any one of them, in the aforesaid scale, entitled to the dignity of an *integer.*—

As for the rest of my fancies & reveries—How I lately met with Miss Lesley Bailie, the most beautiful, elegant woman in the world—How I accompanied her & her Father's Family fifteen miles on their journey, out of pure devotion to admire the loveliness of the works of God in such an unequalled display of them—How, in galloping home at night, I made a ballad on her of which these two Stanzas make a part—

> Thou, bonie Lesley, art a queen,
> Thy subjects we before thee;
> Thou, bonie Lesley, art divine,
> The hearts o' men adore thee.—
>
> The very Deil, he could na scathe
> Whatever wad belang thee!
> He'd look into thy bonie face,
> And say, "I canna wrang thee—"[3]

Behold all these things are written in the Chronicles of my imaginations, & shall be read by thee, my dear Friend, & by thy beloved Spouse, my other dear Friend, at a more convenient season.—

Now, to thee, & to thy before-designed *bosom*-companion, be given the precious things brought forth by the Sun, & the precious things brought forth by the Moon, & the benignest influences of the Stars, & the living streams which flow from the fountains of Life & by the tree of Life, for ever & ever! AMEN! ! !

Robt Burns

1 Shakespeare: *Hamlet*, Act III, sc. 2.
2 Isaiah 30:6.
3 Original version, extensively revised in the published form. C.W. p. 435.

XIII (536)

20th February 1793

What are you doing, what hurry have you got on your hands, my dear Cunningham, that I have not heard from you? Are you deeply engaged in the mazes of Law, the mysteries of Love, or in the profound wisdom of modern politics?—Curse on the word which ended the period!

Alexander Cunningham

Quere, What is Politics?
Answer, Politics is a science wherewith, by means of nefarious
cunning, & hypocritical pretence, we govern civil Polities for the
emolument of ourselves & our adherents.—
Quere, What is a Minister?
Answer, A Minister is an unprincipled fellow, who by the influence
of hereditary, or acquired wealth; by superiour abilities; or by a
lucky conjuncture of circumstances, obtains a principal place in the
administration of the affairs of government.—
Q. What is a Patriot?
A. An individual exactly of the same description as a Minister, only,
out of place.—

I have been interrupted in my Catechism, & am returned at a late
hour, just to subscribe my name; to put you in mind that there is a
forgotten friend of yours of that name, still in the land of the living,
though I can hardly say, in the place of hope.—

I made the following Sonnet the other day, which has been so lucky
as to obtain the approbation of no ordinary judge—our friend
Syme.—

Sonnet

—on hearing a thrush in a morning walk in January—

[C.W. p. 483]

Adieu!—
Robt Burns

XIV (593A)

[Dumfries, November 1793]

Urbani has told a damned falsehood—I made no engagements or
connections with him whatever.—After he & I had met at Lord
Selkirk's we lived together three or four days in this town, & had a
great deal of converse about our Scots Songs.—I translated a verse of
an *Italian* song for him, or rather made an English verse to suit his
rythm & added two verses which had been already published in
Johnson's Museum.—I likewise gave him a simple old Scots song
which I had pickt up in this country, which he promised to set in a
suitable manner.—I would not even have given him this, had there
been any of Mr Thomson's airs, *suitable to it,* unoccupied.—I shall
give you the Song on the other page.—Urbani requested me to lend
him a hand now & then in his work.—I told him, & told him truly,
that such was my enthusiasm for the subject, had I met with him
previous to my acquaintance with Mr Thomson, I would most gladly
have lent him any assistance in my power, but that now, untill Mr
T—'s publication was finished, I could not promise any thing:
however, that at a future period, when the humour was on me, I
would chearfully write a song for him.—He hinted, I remember,
something about mentioning my name in an advertisement, which I
expressly forbade.—One thing he may mean; Johnson, I know, has
given him full permission to any thing I have written in the Museum.
—Beyond that, he had no right to expect, &, for his impudence, shall
never receive, any assistance from me.—

468

Alexander Cunningham

So much, my dear Cunningham, as you say, as to business: now for the Song.—I would, to tell the fact, most gladly have seen it in our Friend's publication; but, though I am charmed with it, it is a kind of Song on which I know we would think very differently.—It is the only species of Song about which our ideas disagree.—What to me, appears the simple & the wild, to him, & I suspect to you likewise, will be looked on as the ludicrous & the absurd.—

Song—

O my Love's like the red, red rose,
  That's newly sprung in June:
My Love's like the melodie
  That's sweetly play'd in tune.—

As fair art thou, my bonie lass,
  So deep in love am I;
And I can love thee still, my Dear,
  Till a' the seas gang dry.—

Till a' the seas gang dry, my Dear,
  And the rocks melt wi' the sun:
I will love thee still, my Dear,
  While the sands o' life shall run.—

And fare thee weel, my only Love,
  O fare thee weel a while!
And I will come again, my Love,
  Tho' 'twere ten thousand mile.—

Yours most sincerely
RB

N.B. As to retorting on the Signior, I scorn it.—Let him, his lies & his works, go to hell in their own way—

RB

XV (619)

25th February 1794.

Canst thou minister to a mind diseased?[1] Canst thou speak peace and rest to a soul tost on a sea of troubles without one friendly star to guide her course, and dreading that the next surge may overwhelm her? Canst thou give to a frame, tremblingly alive as the tortures of suspense, the stability and hardihood of the rock that braves the blast? If thou canst not do the least of these, why wouldst thou disturb me in my miseries with thy inquiries after me?

*   *   *   *   *

For these two months I have not been able to lift a pen. My constitution and frame were, *ab origine*, blasted with a deep incurable taint of hypochondria, which poisons my existence. Of late a number of domestic vexations, and some pecuniary share in the ruin of these ***** times; losses which, though trifling, were yet what I could ill bear, have so irritated me, that my feelings at time could only be envied by a reprobate spirit listening to the sentence that dooms it to perdition.

469

Are you deep in the language of consolation? I have exhausted in reflection every topic of comfort. *A heart at ease* would have been charmed with my sentiments and reasonings; but as to myself, I was like Judas Iscariot preaching the gospel; he might melt and mould the hearts of those around him, but his own kept its native incorrigibility.

Still there are two great pillars that bear us up, amid the wreck of misfortune and misery. The ONE is composed of the different modifications of a certain noble, stubborn something in man, known by the names of courage, fortitude, magnanimity. The OTHER is made up of those feelings and sentiments, which, however the sceptic may deny them, or the enthusiastic disfigure them, are yet, I am convinced, original and component parts of the human soul; those *senses of the mind,* if I may be allowed the expression, which connect us with and link us to, those awful obscure realities—an all-powerful and equally beneficent God; and a world to come, beyond death and the grave. The first gives the nerve of combat, while a ray of hope beams on the fireld:—the last pours the balm of comfort into the wounds which time can never cure.

I do not remember, my dear Cunningham, that you and I ever talked on the subject of religion at all. I know some who laugh at it, as the trick of the crafty FEW, to lead the undiscerning MANY; or at most as an uncertain obscurity, which mankind can never know any thing of, and with which they are fools if they give themselves much to do. Nor would I quarrel with a man for his irreligion, any more than I would for his want of a musical ear. I would regret that he was shut out from what, to me and to others, were such superlative sources of enjoyment. It is in this point of view, and for this reason, that I will deeply imbue the mind of every child of mine with religion. If my son should happen to be a man of feeling, sentiment, and taste, I shall thus add largely to his enjoyments. Let me flatter myself that this sweet little fellow, who is just now running about my desk, will be a man of a melting, ardent, glowing heart; and an imagination, delighted with the painter, and rapt with the poet. Let me figure him wandering out in a sweet evening to inhale the balmy gales, and enjoy the growing luxuriance of the spring, himself the while in the blooming youth of life. He looks abroad on all nature, and through nature up to nature's God. His soul, by swift delighting degrees, is rapt above this sublunary sphere, until he can be silent no longer, and bursts out into the glorious enthusiasm of Thomson,

"These, as they change, Almighty Father, these
"Are but the varied God.—The rolling year is full of thee."2

And so on in all the spirit and ardour of that charming hymn.

These are no ideal pleasures; they are real delights; and I ask what of the delights among the sons of men are superior, not to say equal, to them? And they have this precious, vast addition, that conscious Virtue stamps them for her own, and lays hold on them to bring herself into the presence of a witnessing, judging, and approving God.

1 Shakespeare: *Macbeth*, Act V, sc. 3, altered.
2 Thomson: *A Hymn on the Seasons*, lines 1-3.

Alexander Cunningham

XVI (620)

Since I wrote you the last lugubrious sheet, I have not had time to write you farther.—When I say, that I had not time; that, as usual, means that the three Demons, Indolence, Business & Ennui, have so completely shared my hours among them, as not to leave me a five-minutes fragment to take up a pen in.—

Thank Heaven, I feel my spirits buoying upwards with the renovating year.—Now I shall in good earnest take up Thomson's songs.—I dare say, he thinks I have used him unkindly, & I must own with too much appearance of truth; though if offences come only from the heart, I assure him that I am innocent.—Apropos, do you know the much admired old Highland air called, "The Sutor's dochter?" It is a first-rate favorite of mine, & I have written what I reckon one of my best songs to it.—I will send it you, set as I think it should be, & as it was sung with great applause in many fashionable groups by Major Robertson of Lude, who was here with his Corps.—By the bye, if you do not know him, let me beg of you, as you would relish a high acquisition to your social happiness, to get acquainted with him.—He always, every time I had the very great pleasure of being in his company, reminded me of a forcible saying of Charlie Caldwell, a drunken Carrier in Ayr:—Charles had a Cara Sposa after his own heart, who used to take "caup-out" with him till neither could see the other.—When those honest Genii of old Scotch Social Life—"REAMING SWATS"—used to transport the tender Pair beyond bounds of sober joy, to the region of rapture, the ardent Lover would grapple the yielding Fair to his bosom—"MARGET! YE'RE A GLORY TO GOD, & THE DELIGHT O' MY SOUL!!"

As I cannot in conscience tax you with the postage of a packet, I must keep this bizarre melange of an epistle untill I find the chance of a private conveyance.—Here follows the song I have mentioned—

Song—Tune, Sutor's dochter—

Wilt thou be my Dearie?

[C.W. p. 512]

There is one commission that I must trouble you with.—I lately lost a valuable Seal, a present from a departed friend, which vexes me much.—I have gotten one of your Highland pebbles, which I fancy would make a very decent one; & I want to cut my armorial bearings on it: will you be so obliging as enquire what will be the expence of such a business?—I do not know that my name is matriculated, as the Heralds call it, at all; but I have invented one for myself; so, you know, I will be chief of the Name; & by courtesy of Scotland, will likewise be entitled to Supporters.—These, however, I do not intend haveing on my Seal.—I am a bit of a Herald; & shall give you, Secundum artem, my ARMS.—On a field, azure, a holly-bush, seeded, proper, in base; a Shepherd's pipe & crook, Saltier-wise, also proper, in chief.—On a wreath of the colors, a woodlark perching on a sprig of bay-tree, proper, for Crest.—Two Mottoes: Round the top of the Crest—"Wood-notes wild"—At the bottom of the Shield, in the usual place—

"Better a wee bush than nae bield."—

By the Shepherd's pipe & crook, I do not mean the nonsense of Painters of Arcadia; but a Stock-&-horn, & a Club; such as you see at the head of Allan Ramsay, in David Allan's quarto Edition of the Gentle Shepherd.—By the bye, do you know Allan?—He must be a man of very great genius.—Why is he not more known? Has he no Patrons; or do "Poverty's cold wind & crushing rain beat keen & heavy" on him?—I once, & but once, got a glance of that noble edition of the noblest Pastoral in the world, & dear as it was; I mean, dear as to my pocket, I would have bought it; but I was told that it was printed & engraved for Subscribers only.—He is the *only* Artist who has hit *genuine* Pastoral costume.—What, my dear Cunningham, is there in riches, that they narrow & encallous the heart so? I think, that were I as rich as the sun, I would be as generous as day; but as I have no reason to imagine my soul a nobler one than every other man's I must conclude that wealth imparts a bird-lime quality to the Possessor, at which the man, in native poverty, would have revolted.—What has led me to this, is the idea of such merit as Mr Allan possesses, & such riches as a Nabob, or Government Contractor possesses, & why do not they form a mutual league?—Let Wealth shelter & cherish unprotected Merit, and the gratitude & celebrity of that Merit will richly repay.—

March 22

In fact, I am writing you a Journal, & not a letter.—A bustle of business has laid my epistolary pen aside in silence, since I took it up last to you.—

I have just received a letter from Thomson, which has filled me with self-reproaches.—I will, directly, & in good earnest, set about his Work.—I am sorry I did not know him, when I was in Edinburgh; but I will tell you a plot which I have been contriving: you & he shall, in the course of this Summer, meet me half-way; that is, at the Bield Inn; & there we will pour out a Drink Offering before the Lord, & enter into a solemn League & Covenant, never to be broken nor forgotten.—

> Wha first shall rise to gang awa,
> A cuckold coward loun is he;
> Wha first beside his chair shall fa',
> He is the king amang us THREE!*

Burns

* *Willie brew'd a peck o' maut*, lines 17-20. See *Poems.* 268.

XVII (677)

[Enclosed in the letter to George Thomson, 3rd August 1795]

Scotch Song—

> Now Spring has clad the grove in green,
> [C.W. p. 528]

Scottish Song—

> O bonie was yon rosy brier,
> [C.W. p. 558]

Alexander Cunningham

Written on the blank leaf of a copy of the last edition of my Poems, presented to the lady whom in so many fictitious reveries of Passion but with the most ardent sentiments of *real* friendship, I have so often sung under the name of—CHLORIS*—

'Tis Friendship's pledge, my young, fair FRIEND;

[C.W. p. 557]

To Mr Cunningham—

—Une bagatelle de l'Amitié.—

Coila.—

* Jean Lorimer.

XVIII (700)

Brow-Sea-bathing quarters—
7th July [1796]

My dear Cunningham

I received yours here this moment and am indeed highly flattered with the approbation of the literary circle you mention; a literary circle inferiour to none in the two kingdoms.—Alas! my friend, I fear the voice of the Bard will soon be heard among you no more! For these eight or ten months I have been ailing, sometimes bedfast & sometimes not; but these last three months I have been tortured with an excruciating rheumatism, which has reduced me to nearly the last stage.— You actually would not know me if you saw me.—Pale emaciated, & so feeble as occasionally to need help from my chair—my spirits fled! fled!—but I can no more on the subject—only the Medical folks tell me that my last & only chance is bathing & country quarters & riding.—The deuce of the matter is this; when an Excise-man is off duty, his salary is reduced to 35£ instead of 50£.— What way, in the name of thrift, shall I maintain myself & keep a horse in Country-quarters—with a wife & five children at home, on 35£? I mention this, because I had intended to beg your utmost interest & all friends you can muster to move our Commissioners of Excise to grant me the full salary.—I dare say you know them all personally.—If they do not grant it me, I must lay my account with an exit truly en poete, if I die not of disease I must perish with hunger.—

I have sent you one of the songs: the other, my memory does not serve me with, & I have no copy here; but I shall be at home soon, when I will, send it you.—Apropos to being at home, Mrs Burns threatens in a week or two, to add one more to my Paternal charge, which, if of the right gender, I intend shall be introduced to the world by the respectable designation of Alexander Cunningham Burns. My last was James Glencairn, so you can have no objection to the company of Nobility.—

Farewel
RB

[The last page of the letter is filled with a transcript of *Lord Gregory* C.W. p. 482]

473

Alexander Cunningham

XIX (704)

Bishop mark JY 12* [1796]

Did Thomson shew the following song, the last I made or probably will make for some time.—The air is my favorite.—

Here's a health to ane I lo'e dear.

Tune, Here's a health to them that's awa

[C.W. p. 565]

I shall be impatient to hear from you.—As to me, my plan is to address the Board by petition & then if any friend has thrown in a word 'tis a great deal in my favor.—

Adieu!
RBurns

* Actually two different postmarks: the undated name-stamp of Dumfries, where this letter was put into the post, and the Bishop datestamp applied on arrival at Edinburgh. The actual date of composition, at the Brown, was probably no later than Sunday 10th July; the tone of this letter seems to imply that it was written *before* the last letters to Mrs Dunlop (p. 215) and Gilbert Burns (p. 358).

RACHEL DUNLOP

The fifth daughter of Mrs Dunlop, she was unmarried and still living with her mother at Dunlop House, near Stewarton, when Burns wrote to her. Subsequently she married Robert Glasgow of Montgreenan, who died without issue in 1827.

(261)

Mauchline, 2nd August 1788—

Madam,

I was in Nithsdale when your kind present and kinder letter came to Mauchline, so did not see it until yesternight that I came here.—

I am in perpetual warfare with that doctrine of our Reverend Priesthood, that "we are born into this world bond slaves of iniquity & heirs of perdition, wholly inclined" to that which is evil and wholly disinclined to that which is good until by a kind of Spiritual Filtration or rectifying process Called effectual Calling &c.—The whole business is reversed, and our connections above & below completely change place.—I believe in my conscience that the case is just quite contrary—We come into this world with a heart & disposition to do good for it, untill by dashing a large mixture of base alloy called Prudence alias Selfishness, the too precious Metal of the Soul is brought down to the blackguard Sterling of ordinary currency, this I take it is the reason why we of the Barbarian Sex who are so much Called out to act on that profligate Stage—the World—come so far short of your Gentler Kind who bear on much richer materials an equally more elegant impression & image of infinite purity goodness & truth. As I am a married man neither my knowledge of facts or impartial testimony can be doubted; & while I can produce your kind correspondence with the poet, or in general while I can name Mrs Dunlop with all her daughters I can be at no loss for corroborative evidence.

Mrs B begs me to return to you her most grateful thanks for your elegant little work on the Cap—she says she will be hard pushed indeed for family linens if she do not make your cap grace the head of her hindmost child, tho' she should have a score.—I rejoice in Coila's progress to perfection, tho' you have awakened my curiosity much to pay her my grateful respects again; but when that curiosity will be gratified heaven knows.—

I have the honor to be Madam
your obedient Humble Servant
Robt Burns

475

ROBERT McINDOE

A silk merchant with premises at Horn's Land, off Virginia Street, Glasgow.
Nothing is apparently known of Andrew McCulloch, mentioned in this letter.

(262)

Mauchline, 5th August 1788

My Dear Sir,

I am vexed for nothing more that I have not been at Glasgow, than
not meeting with you.—I have seldom found my friend Andrew
McCulloch wrong in his ideas of Mankind; but respecting your
Worship, he was true as Holy Writ.—This is the night of our Fair, and
I, as you see, cannot keep well *in a line*; but if you will send me by
the bearer, John Ronald Carrier, between Glasgow and Mauchline,
fifteen yards of black silk, the same kind as that of which I bought a
gown & petticoat from you formerly, Lutestring I think is its name,
I shall send you the money & a more coherent letter, when he goes
again to your good town.—To be brief, send me fifteen yards black
lutestring silk, such as they use to make gowns & petticoats of, & I
shall chuse some sober morning before breakfast, & write you a
sober answer, with the sober sum which will then be due you from,

Dear Sir, fu' or fasting, yours sincerely
Robt Burns

JEAN ARMOUR BURNS

Born in 1767, the daughter of James Armour, master mason in Mauchline. Burns appears to have made her acquaintance soon after moving to Mossgiel in 1784 and she ranked among the 'Mauchline Belles'. Tradition has it that Burns and Jean met at a dance during Race Week in April that year, but it was not until after the interlude with Elizabeth Paton that Burns began to pay serious court to Jean in 1785. Before the end of that year intimacy had taken place and Jean became pregnant. In March or April 1786 Burns gave her a paper which constituted a marriage contract under Scots law at the time, but James Armour took the document to his lawyer, Robert Aiken, who cut out the names of the contracting parties. This act had absolutely no legal significance and it can only be supposed that it was merely done on the spur of the moment to mollify the irate father. Until 1940, marriage by declaration alone, with or without documentary back-up, was perfectly valid in Scotland. Burns regarded this, and Jean's flight to Paisley, as 'desertion'. Consequently he now sought a certificate from Mauchline Kirk Session that he was a bachelor. On 25th June 1786 he appeared before the Session and acknowledged his share in fornication, as a result of which he made the three obligatory appearances before the congregation and eventually got his certificate from 'Daddy Auld'.

Letters to Arnot and Brice give graphic details of this episode, soon followed by the affair with Mary Campbell and then, when he was being hounded by the vindictive James Armour, the decision to emigrate to Jamaica and, arising out of that, the publication of the Kilmarnock Edition. Old Armour modified his view of Burns after he became famous and, more significantly, had secured the patronage of some very powerful and influential gentlemen. Jean gave birth to twins at the beginning of September, but at that time Burns was still set on emigrating with Mary Campbell. Even after 'Highland Mary' died the following month, Burns does not appear to have considered settling down with Jean. During his first winter in Edinburgh he formed an association 'with a very pretty girl, a Lothian farmer's daughter. . .' and there was also the affair with May Cameron who gave birth to Burns's child in May 1787. In June, however, he was back in Mauchline and was sufficiently reconciled to Jean that she became pregnant again. Another prolonged sojourn in Edinburgh resulted in the affair with Jenny Clow and the platonic relationship with Mrs McLehose. In February 1788 Burns returned to Mauchline. Despite the 'farthing taper' letter to Clarinda (see page 399) Burns set up house with Jean at Mauchline. Jean's second set of twins was born early in March, only to die soon afterwards. Burns and Jean were privately remarried about 25th May, but it was not until June that Burns settled at Ellisland and prepared to send for Jean, and not until 5th August 1788 that the marriage of Burns and Jean was recognised by the Mauchline Kirk Session. In December 1788 Jean moved from Mauchline to Ellisland, and the first two letters below date from the period when they were still living apart. The only other letters were written while Burns was in Edinburgh in February 1789 and from the Brow shortly before he died.

Jean bore Burns nine children, the last on the very day of her husband's funeral. Though intellectually far below Burns, she seems to have been a remarkably generous and compliant woman, remaining loyal to him 'not weighing his merits, but pardoning his offences'. Few women would have been so big-hearted as Jean in bringing up his bastard daughter by Anna Park, shrugging off the affair with the remark 'Our Robbie should have had twa wives'. Ferguson points out that the fact that Burns managed to raise a large family on a limited income says a lot for Jean's careful management. She outlived her husband by 38 years, continuing to reside in the same house in Dumfries. She gave her children a good up-bringing and saw them launched in middle-class careers. With commonsense and good humour she patiently dealt with the tourists, biographers, hagiologists, pilgrims and curiosity-seekers whom Burns's fame impelled to visit her. The only portraits of her were painted relatively late in life. Mrs Grant of Laggan described Jean, aged 55, as 'a very comely woman with plain sound sense and very good manners.' Burns composed fourteen songs associated with Jean, the most noteworthy being *Of a' the Airts the Wind can Blaw* (C.W. p. 329) which he stated 'I composed out of compliment to Mrs Burns. N.B. It was during the honeymoon.' Burns's attitude to Jean and the reason which impelled him to settle down in the end are summed up in his letter to Margaret Chalmers on 16th September 1788 (see page 237): 'not in consequence of the attachment of romance perhaps; but I had a long and much-loved fellow creature's happiness or misery in my determination, and I durst not trifle with so important a deposit.'

I (270)

Ellisland, Friday 12th September 1788

My dear Love,

I received your kind letter with a pleasure which no letter but one from you could have given me.—I dreamed of you the whole night

477

last; but alas! I fear it will be three weeks yet, ere I can hope for the happiness of seeing you.—My harvest is going on.—I have some to cut down still, but I put in two stacks today, so I am as tired as a dog.—

You might get one of Gilbert's sweet milk cheeses, [*two or three words torn away*] & send it to [*MS. torn*]

On second thoughts, I believe you had best get the half of Gilbert's web of Table-linen, and make it up; tho' I think it damnable dear, but it is no out-laid money to us you know.—I have just now consulted my old Landlady about table-linen, & she thinks I may have the best for two shillings per yard; so after all, let it alone untill I return; and some day soon I will be in Dumfries, and will ask the prices there.—I expect your new gowns will be very forward, or ready to make, against I be home to get the Baiveridge.—I have written my long-thought-on letter to Mr Graham, the Commissioner of Excise; & have sent him a sheetful of Poetry besides.—Now I talk of Poetry, I had a fine Strathspey among my hands to make verses to, for Johnson's Collection which I . . . [*remainder of MS. missing*]

II (278)

Ellisland Tuesday 14th October 1788

My dearest Love,

You need not come on Sunday to meet me on the road, for I am engaged that day to dine with Mr Logan at Laycht, so it will be in the evening before I arrive at Mauchline.—

You must get ready for Nithsdale as fast as possible, for I have an offer of a house in the very neibourhood with some furniture in it, all which I shall have the use of for nothing till my own house be got ready; and I am determined to remove you from Ayrshire immediately, as I am a sufferer by not being on the farm myself.—We will want a Maid servant, of consequence: if you can hear of any to hire, ask after them.—The apples are all sold & gone.—I am extremely happy at the idea of your coming to Nithsdale, as it will save us from these cruel separations.—The house is one in which a Mr Newal* lived during the summer, who is gone to Dumfries in Winter. —It is a large house, but we will only occupy a room or two of it.—

I am ever, my dearest Madam,
your faithful husband & humble servant
Robt Burns

* David Newall (see page 544).

III (315)

Edinburgh Friday morning [20th February 1789]
[*Bishop mark* FE 20]

I cannot precisely say when I will leave this town, my dearest friend, but at farthest I think I will be with you on sunday come eight days, perhaps sooner.—I had a horrid journey . . .

[*About three lines of MS. missing here*]

I have settled matters greatly to my satisfaction with Mr Creech.—He is certainly not what he should be, nor has he given me what I should have, but I am better than I expected.—Farewel! I long much to see you—God bless you!

> yours most sincerely
> Robt Burns

IV (708)

> Brow, Thursday.
> [14th July 1796]

My dearest Love,

I delayed writing until I could tell you what effect sea-bathing was likely to produce. It would be injustice to deny that is has eased my pains, and, I think, has strengthened me, but my appetite is still extremely bad. No flesh nor fish can I swallow; porridge and milk are the only thing I can taste. I am very happy to hear, by Miss Jess Lewars, that you are all well. My very best and kindest compliments to her, and to all the children. I will see you on Sunday.

> Your affectionate husband,
> R. B.

ROBERT RIDDELL OF GLENRIDDELL

Born in 1755, the eldest son of Walter Riddell of Glenriddell in Glencairn parish, Dumfriesshire, he was educated at Dumfries (where a fellow-pupil was James Currie, Burns's biographer). Later he studied at the universities of St. Andrews and Edinburgh, obtained an ensign's commission in the Royal Scots and was eventually promoted to captain in the 83rd Regiment in 1781 in the closing phase of the American War. He retired on half-pay the following year and in 1784 married Elizabeth Kennedy of Manchester. He purchased the estate of Friars' Carse six miles north of Dumfries and continued to live there after he inherited Glenriddell in 1788, selling the latter about that time. Riddell was an antiquarian and numismatist, a man not without some musical talent who shared Burns's enthusiasm for collecting old ballads. About 1785 he published a collection of reels, minuets, hornpipes and marches, set for the piano or harpsichord, and in 1794 published a collection of Scotch, Galwegian and Border Tunes for violin and piano.

It is not known precisely how or where Burns first met Robert Riddell, but it seems likely that they were introduced by Patrick Miller of Dalswinton soon after Burns took up the lease of Ellisland. Within two weeks of the move Burns was composing his *Lines written in Friars' Carse Hermitage* (C.W. p. 325), having been given a key by Riddell. The friendship developed rapidly and Riddell was the subject of several poems and verse-epistles. Burns and Riddell organised the Monkland Friendly Society Library, many of whose books were procured by Burns from Peter Hill in Edinburgh. Burns later compiled two volumes of poetic and prose manuscripts for his friend, and this collection became known as the Glenriddell MS. Only the volume of poems, however, was actually handed over to Riddell. Riddell also had a copy of the *Scots Musical Museum* interleaved with annotations, although it transpires that most of the latter were by Burns himself.

Riddell's conviviality found expression in such spectacles as the drinking contest over the Whistle and the so-called 'Rape of the Sabine Women' incident. It has been hinted that his early death at the age of 39 was precipitated by alcoholic excess. Burns was deeply distressed at his death, especially as he had not had the opportunity to become reconciled to his erstwhile friend, although he was at pains to recover the Glenriddell MS from the widow. Posterity has dealt rather harshly with Riddell, largely on account of the estrangement which arose from an incident in which he was by no means blameless. Burns himself kept things in perspective when he wrote of the Riddells: 'At their fire-side I have enjoyed more pleasant evenings than at all the houses of fashionable people in this country put together . . .'

I (271)

[Enclosing *The Day Returns*]

[C.W. p. 333]

Ellisland—Tuesday even.
[16th September 1788]

Sir,

as I was busy behind my harvest-folks this forenoon, and musing on a proper theme for your, "Seventh of November," some of the conversation before me accidently suggested a suspicion that this said Seventh of Nov. is a Matrimonial Anniversary with a certain very worthy Neighbour of mine.—I have seen very few who owe so much to a Wedding-day as Mrs Riddel & you; and my imagination took the hint accordingly, as you will see in the next page.—A little gratitude too, had a pretty large share in firing my Muse; as amidst all the enjoyment I have in your hospitable Mansion, there is nothing gives me more pleasure than to see the minute, cordial attentions and the sparkling glances of the Lover, while in so many Conjugal scenes in the World, a third person is hourly hurt with the insipid yawn of Satiety or the malignant squint of Disgust.—

I return you my most grateful thanks for your lad today.—Dare I ask him for tomorrow? I dare not ask more: I would not ask even that one, did not staring Necessity compel me. I have not a person I can command but three; your servant makes a fourth which is all my forces.—

I have the honor to be, equally in prose & verse,
Sir, your grateful humble servant
Robt Burns

ALEXANDER CUNNINGHAM

JEAN ARMOUR BURNS

Robert Riddell of Glenriddell

II (340)

[Ellisland, 1789?]

Sir,

I wish from my inmost soul it were in my power to give you a more substantial gratification & return for all your goodness to the Poet, than transcribing a few of his idle rhymes.—However, "an old Song," tho' to a proverb an instance of insignificance, is generally the only coin a Poet has to pay with.—If my Poems which I have transcribed & mean still to transcribe into your Book were equal to the grateful respect & high esteem I bear for the Gentleman to whom I present them, they would be the finest Poems in the language.—As they are, they will at least be a testimony with what sincerity I have the honor to be,

Sir, your devoted humble servant
Robt Burns

P.S. I send you the books.—Mr Sloan & I will do ourselves the honor to wait on you tomorrow at your hour—

R.B.

III (365)

Ellisland, October 16th 1789.

Sir,

Big with the idea of this important day[1] at Friars Carse, I have watched the elements and skies in the full persuasion that they would announce it to the astonished world by some phenomena of terrific portent.—Yesternight until a very late hour did I wait with anxious horror, for the appearance of some Comet firing half the sky; or aerial armies of sanguinary Scandinavians, darting athwart the startled heavens rapid as the ragged lightning, and horrid as those convulsions of nature that bury nations.

The elements, however, seem to take the matter very quietly: they did not even usher in this morning with triple suns and a shower of blood, symbolical of the three potent heroes, and the mighty claret-shed of the day.—For me, as Thomson in his Winter says of the storm—I shall

"Hear astonished, and astonished sing"[2]

The whistle and the man; I sing
The man that won the whistle, &c.[3]

"Here are we met, three merry boys,
"Three merry boys I trow are we;
"And mony a night we've merry been,
"And mony mae we hope to be.

"Wha first shall rise to gang awa,
"A cuckold coward loun is he:
"Wha *last* beside his chair shall fa'
"He is the king amang us three."[4]

To leave the heights of Parnassus and come to the humble vale of prose.—I have some misgiving that I take too much upon me, when I request you to get your guest, Sir Robert Lowrie [Laurie], to frank

the two inclosed covers for me, the one of them, to Sir William
Cunningham, of Robertland, Bart. at Auchenskeith, Kilmarnock—
the other, to Mr. Allan Masterton, Writing-Master, Edinburgh.[4] The
first has a kindred claim on Sir Robert, as being a brother Baronet,
and likewise a keen Foxite; the other is one of the worthiest men in
the world, and a man of real genius; so, allow me to say, he has a
fraternal claim on you. I want them franked for to-morrow as I
cannot get them to the post to-night.—I shall send a servant again for
them in the evening. Wishing that your head may be crowned with
laurels to-night, and free from aches tomorrow,

> I have the honor to be, Sir,
> Your deeply indebted humble Servant
> Robt Burns

1 The day of the contest for 'The Whistle', C.W. p. 368.
2 Line 110.
3 These lines do not appear in *The Whistle* but obviously they were inspired
by the poem.
4 Neither of these franked letters has survived.

IV (449)

27th April 1791

[POEMS WRITTEN BY Mr ROBt BURNS *and selected by him from
his unprinted Collection, for Robert Riddell of Glenriddell Esqr.*] *

As this Collection almost wholly consists of pieces local or unfinished,
fragments the effusion of a poetical moment & bagatelles strung in
rhyme simply pour passer le temps, the Author trusts that nobody
into whose hands it may come will without his permission give or
allow to be taken, copies of any thing here contained; much less to
give to the world at large, what he never meant should see the light.
—At the Gentleman's request, whose from this time it shall be, the
Collection was made; and to him, & I will add, to his amiable Lady,
it is presented, as a sincere though small tribute of gratitude for the
many many happy hours the Author has spent under their roof.—
There, what Poverty even though accompanied with Genius must
seldom expect to meet with at the tables in the circles of Fashionable
Life, his welcome has ever been, The cordiality of Kindness, & the
warmth of Friendship. As, from the situation in which it is now
placed, this M.S.S. may be preserved, & this Preface read, when the
hand that now writes & the heart that now dictates it may be mouldering in the dust; let these be regarded as the geniune sentiments of a
man who seldom flattered any, & never those he loved.—

> Robt Burns

* Taken from the holograph title-page of the first volume of the 'Glenriddell
Manuscripts'.

V (472)

Tuesday noon
[27th September 1791]

Sir,

I will be writing Peter Hill next week, when I will remember M'nish's
book.—You know I don't like asking favors of the gentleman—dare I

trouble you, if you meet with the Member, to get me a Frank,
"October the second, 1791

"Colonel Fullarton of Fullarton
"Fullarton-house,
"Irvine"—

I am to send the Colonel some things, beside the Whistle; & do not
wish to put him to expense.—

I inclose you the letter to the Duke that you were pleased to think
so well of.—I also send you the first, the very first sketch of a few
stanzas, almost extempore, on a very amiable Subject.—I am pleased
with some of the lines; perhaps because they are new; but they shall
see a few chosen friends, or be entirely supprest, as it shall be their
fate to meet with your & Mrs Riddel's applause or disapprobation.—

I shall not be able to go to town tomorrow.—

I have the honor to be, Sir,
your deeply indebted humble servant
Robt Burns

VI (473A)

Thursday noon
[September 1788-October 1791?]

Sir,

I send you some Magazines which I met with yesternight.—You may
perhaps see something in them to cheat the tedious hour.—I would
have brought you them in person, but the unrelenting demon,
Necessity, nails me to the oar of business for the day.—

I have the honor to be, Sir,
your deeply indebted humble servant
Robt Burns

VII (473B)

[September 1788-October 1791?]

Sir,

I have just received a newspaper & a letter from Mr Sloan both of
which I send you, as the former contains some foreign & the latter
some Manchester* news which you may not have seen.—But for the
hurry of Excise scribbling I would have done myself the honor of
waiting on you with them.—

* Elizabeth Riddell was a Mancunian.

VIII (487)

[*Prefatory Note to the Abridgement of the First Common-place
Book*]

On rummaging over some old papers, I lighted on a M.S.S. of my
early years, in which I had determined to write myself out; as I was
placed by Fortune among a class of men to whom my ideas would
have been nonsense—I had meant that the book would have lain by

me, in the fond hope that, some time or other, even after I was no more, my thoughts would fall into the hands of somebody capable of appreciating their value.—It sets off thus—

Observations, hints, Songs, scraps of Poetry &c. by R.B. . . .

[Here follows the *Abridgement*]

IX (548)

[In a copy of the 1793 Edition of the *Poems*, mid-March]

When you & I, my dear Sir, have passed that bourne whence no traveller returns, should these volumes survive us, I wish the future Reader of this Page to be informed, that they were the pledge of Friendship, ardent & grateful on my part, as it was kind & generous on yours.—

That Enjoyment may mark your days, & Pleasure number your years, is the earnest prayer of, my dear Sir,

your much indebted friend—
The Author

DR. JAMES MUNDELL

Born in Dumfries of an old Nithsdale family, he served in the Navy as a surgeon but returned to his home town after the American War and practised medicine, being appointed surgeon at the Infirmary in 1794. His widowed mother lived at Rosebank, and his sister married Provost Gabriel Richardson. As a general practitioner, he attended Burns and his family at Ellisland and during their early years in Dumfries itself, although he was superseded as physician to Burns by Dr William Maxwell in 1794. Mundell was part-owner of a cotton mill in Dumfries, powered by a treadmill driven by an ox, referred to in a letter from Burns to Maria Riddell in December 1793 (see page 606). Burns lists Mundell as one of the subscribers for *The Bee* when he wrote to its editor, Dr. James Anderson on 1st November 1790 (see page 571). 'Mundell the quack' was among those friends of Burns lampooned by the right-wing Loyal Natives in January 1793, which inspired Burns's epigram (C.W. p. 515). With Burns, Mundell was a founder-member of the Dumfries Volunteers in January 1795. The only extant letters from Burns to Mundell deal with purely domestic matters. The little boy whose 'sore mouth has again inflamed Mrs B——'s Nipples' was Francis Wallace Burns, born on 18th August 1789, which probably places this undated letter in the following January. Dr. Mundell's nephew Peter was chairman of the Birth Centenary celebrations at Dumfries in 1859.

I (277)

Isle, Sunday morn [1788]

Dear Sir,

As my symptoms are continuing milder, I have not waited on you; but my liquid drug has failed.—You will please send me by my servant the bearer, a recruit of the G——d L——n.—I am still using the unction, tho' thank Heaven, not extreme unction.—I shall be in town on wedensday.—

I am, Dear Sir, your humble servant
Robt Burns

II (383)

[January 1790]

Dear Doctor

The bearer, Janet Nievison, is a neighbour, and occasionally a laborer of mine.—She has got some complaint in her shoulder, and wants me to find her out a Doctor that will cure her, so I have sent her to you. —You will remember that she is just in the jaws of MATRIMONY, so for heaven's sake, get her "hale & sound" as soon as possible.—We are all pretty well; only the little boy's sore mouth has again inflamed Mrs B——'s Nipples.—

I am yours
Robt Burns

AGNES ELEANOR DUNLOP

The eldest daughter of Mrs Dunlop, she married Joseph Elias Perochon, a French Royalist *emigre*, with whom she moved to London. When he retired from business, the couple retired to Castlebank, Dumfries where she died in 1825. After the poet's death, Mrs Perochon showed considerable kindness to his widow, and in gratitude Jean gave her the burial plot in St. Michael's Churchyard where Burns had originally been interred, before his remains were transferred to the Mausoleum. Mrs Perochon's grave can be seen there to this day. At the time of Burns's letter, she was still unmarried and living at Dunlop House.

(282)

Monday morn:
[November? 1788]

Madam,

Tho' I am not always what Glenalvon calls, "The shallow fool of coward Conscience,"* yet I have a Something in my bosom, a kind of feeling of Propriety or Impropriety where I am the veriest Coward on earth.—My horrid sin of this kind against you has compleatly gagged me, that I can't write to, or approach you, were it to redeem me from perdition.—If I can pluck up so much courage. I'll call at Dunlop-house on wednesday or thursday, perhaps at wednesday's breakfast hour.—

I have the honor to be, Madam
your most penitent humble servant
Robt Burns

* Home: *Douglas,* Act II, sc. 2.

LETTER TO THE EDINBURGH EVENING COURANT

The following letter, signed 'A Briton' was Burns's first polemical contribution to any newspaper. It was inspired by the celebrations that marked the centenary of the outbreak of the 'Glorious Revolution' of 1688 which led to the flight of James VII and II, and the accession of William and Mary. Burns, a secret Jacobite in sentiment if not in politics, was revolted by the 'harsh political prejudice' in the diatribe by the Rev. Joseph Kirkpatrick from the pulpit at his local centenary celebration on 5th November, and in this essay called for moderation and a proper perspective on the House of Stuart, concluding by drawing a parallel between the rebels of 1688 and the Americans of 1776. The fourth of July, as it has turned out, is celebrated just as fervently today, whereas the fifth of November is nowadays remembered only in the context of an earlier *coup d'etat*, the attempt by Guy Fawkes to blow up the Houses of Parliament in 1605. This letter was published in the *Courant* of 22nd November 1788.

(283)

8th November [1788]

Sir,

Notwithstanding the opprobrious epithets with which some sour philosophers and gloomy sectaries have branded our nature—the principle of universal selfishness, or the proneness to all evil, which they have given us—still the detestation in which inhumanity to the distressed, or insolence to the fallen, are held by all mankind, shews that they are not natives of the human heart. Even those unhappy partners of our kind that are undone, the bitter consequences of their follies or their crimes—who but sympathizes with the miseries of a ruined profligate brother?—We forget the injuries, and feel for the man.

I went last Wednesday to my parish church, most cordially to join in grateful acknowledgements to the Author of all Good, for the consequent blessings of the Glorious Revolution. To that auspicious event we owe no less than our liberties religious and civil—to it we are likewise indebted for the present Royal Family, the ruling features of whose administration have ever been, mildness to the subject, and tenderness of his rights. Bred and educated in revolution principles, the principles of reason and common sense, it could not be any silly political prejudice that made my heart revolt at the harsh abusive manner in which the Reverend Gentleman mentioned the House of Stuart, and which, I am afraid, was too much the language of that day. We may rejoice sufficiently in our deliverance from past evils, without cruelly raking up the ashes of those whose misfortune it was, perhaps, as much as their crimes, to be the authors of those evils; and may bless God for all his goodness to us as a nation, without, at the same time, cursing a few ruined powerless exiles, who only harboured ideas, and made attempts, that most of us would have done, had we been in their situation.

"The bloody and tyrannical house of Stuart" may be said with propriety and justice, when compared with the present Royal Family, and the liberal sentiments of our days. But is there no allowance to be made for the manners of the times? Were the royal contemporaries of the Stuarts more mildly attentive to the rights of man? Might not the epithets of "bloody and tyrannical" be with at least equal justice applied to the house of Tudor, of York, or any other of their predecessors?

487

Letter to the Edinburgh Evening Courant

The simple state of the case, Mr Printer, seems to me to be this—At that period, the science of government—the true relation between King and subject, like other sciences, was but just in its infancy, emerging from the dark ages of ignorance and barbarism. The Stuarts only contended for prerogatives which they knew their predecessors enjoyed, and which they saw their contemporaries enjoying; but these prerogatives were inimical to the happiness of a nation and the rights of subjects. In this contest between Prince and People, the consequence of that light of science which had lately dawned over Europe, the Monarch of France, for example, was victorious over the struggling liberties of the subject: With us, luckily, the Monarch failed, and his unwarrantable pretensions fell a sacrifice to our rights and happiness. Whether it was owing to the wisdom of leading individuals, or to the justlings of party, I cannot pretend to determine; but, likewise happily for us, the kingly power was shifted into another branch of the family, who, as they owed the throne solely to the call of a free people, could claim nothing inconsistent with the covenanted terms which placed them there.

The Stuarts have been condemned and laughed at for the folly and impracticability of their attempts, in 1715 and 1745. That they failed, I bless my God most fervently; but cannot join in the ridicule against them.—Who does not know that the abilities or defects of leaders and commanders are often hidden until put to the touchstone of exigence; and that there is a caprice of fortune, an omnipotence in particular accidents, and conjunctures of circumstances, which exalt us as heroes, or brand us as madmen, just as they are for or against us?

Man, Mr. Printer, is a strange, weak, inconsistent being—Who would believe, Sir, that in this our Augustan age of liberality and refinement, while we seem so justly sensible and jealous of our rights and liberties, and animated with such indignation against the very memory of those who would have subverted them, who would suppose that a certain people, under our national protection, should complain, not against a Monarch and a few favourite advisers, but against our whole legislative body, of the very same imposition and oppression, the Romish religion not excepted, and almost in the very same terms as our forefathers did against the family of Stuart! I will not, I cannot, enter into the merits of the cause; but I dare say, the American Congress, in 1776, will be allowed to have been as able and as enlightened, and, a whole empire will say, as honest, as the English Convention in 1688; and that the fourth of July will be as sacred to their posterity as the fifth of November is to us.

To conclude, Sir, let every man, who has a tear for the many miseries incident to humanity, feel for a family, illustrious as any in Europe, and unfortunate beyond historic precedent; and let every Briton, and particularly every Scotsman, who ever looked with reverential pity on the dotage of a parent, cast a veil over the fatal mistakes of the Kings of his forefathers.

A Briton

BRUCE CAMPBELL

Born in 1734, he was the laird of Mayfield and Milrig in Galston parish, Ayrshire. His wife Annabella was daughter of James Wilson of Kilmarnock who may, or may not, have been a relative of John Wilson, Burns's printer. Campbell was James Boswell's cousin and agent. In writing to Campbell, Burns hoped to secure an introduction to Boswell but so far as is known they never met. This letter was subsequently annotated by Boswell 'Mr Robert Burns the Poet expressing very high sentiments of me.'

(284)

Mauchline, 13th November 1788

Sir

I inclose you, for Mr Boswell, the Ballad* you mentioned; and as I hate sending waste paper or mutilating a sheet, I have filled it up with one or two of my fugitive Pieces that occurred.—Should they procure me the honor of being introduced to Mr Boswell, I shall think they have great merit.—There are few pleasures my late will-o'-wisp character has given me, equal to that of having seen many of the extraordinary men, the Heroes of Wit & Literature in my Country; & as I had the honor of drawing my first breath almost in the same Parish with Mr Boswell, my Pride plumes itself on the connection.—To crouch in the train of mere, stupid Wealth & Greatness, except where the commercial interests of wordly Prudence find their account in it, I hold to be Prostitution in any one that is not born a Slave, but to have been acquainted with such a man as Mr Boswell, I would hand down to my Posterity as one of the honors of their Ancestor.—

I am, Sir, your most obedient
& very humble servant
Robt Burns

* The Fête Champêtre (C.W. p. 326).

DR. THOMAS BLACKLOCK

Born at Annan, Dumfriesshire in 1721, the son of a bricklayer, he was blinded by smallpox in infancy, but managed to overcome his disability. Largely self-educated, he studied divinity at Edinburgh University and was ordained minister of Kirkcudbright in 1762. His parishioners, however, complained that his blindness rendered him unfit for his parochial duties, so in 1765 he retired to Edinburgh on a small annuity which he eked out by running a boarding-house for scholars and students. A man of keen intellect and broak outlook, he was the friend of Samuel Johnson and Benjamin Franklin, as well as writers, philosophers and savants of the period, and a pillar of the Age of Enlightenment. Johnson regarded him with reverence, while David Hume pronounced him 'a very elegant genius . . . with that delicate pride which so naturally attends virtue in distress.' The Rev. George Lawrie sent him a copy of the Kilmarnock Edition and he replied on 4th September 1786, full of praise. Lawrie communicated this to Burns. Blacklock was then at the pinnacle of his career and enjoyed an immense reputation as a poet and scholar. Black-lock's advice and encouragement decided Burns against emigration. Instead he went to Edinburgh and the entire course of his life was dramatically altered. Blacklock's letter has sometimes been regarded with the same impact as Paul's conversion on the road to Damascus, but. despite Burns's colourful description in the Autobiographical Letter to Dr Moore, it was only one of several factors that combined to make him change his mind. It is significant that Burns allowed several weeks to pass, after his arrival in Edinburgh, before he called on Blacklock. In the interim, Blacklock wrote to Lawrie regretting that Burns had not contacted him, and this impelled Lawrie to write to Burns. It was not until 5th February 1787 that Burns was able to write to Lawrie (see page 263) to say that he had, indeed, called on Blacklock. From then onwards, however, a genuine friendship developed between the two men who exchanged rhyming epistles in 1789. Burns's only recorded prose letter to Dr Blacklock deals with his move to Ellisland.

I (287)

Mauchline, 15th November 1788

Reverend & dear Sir,

As I hear nothing of your motions but that you are, or were, out of town, I do not know where this may find you, or whether it will find you at all.—I wrote you a long letter, dated from the land of matrimony, in June; but either it had not found you at all; or, what I dread more, it found you or Mrs Blacklock in too precarious a state of health & spirits, to take notice of an idle Packet.—

I have done many little things for Johnson, since I had the pleasure of seeing you; & I have finished one Piece, in the way of Pope's moral epistles; but from your silence, I have everything to fear so I have only sent you two melancholy things, which I tremble lest they should too well suit the tone of your present feelings.—

In a fortnight, I move, bag & baggage to Nithsdale; Till then, my direction is, at this place; after that period, it will be, at Ellisland near Dumfries.—It would extremely oblidge me, were it but half a line, to let me know how you are, & where you are.—Can I be indifferent to the fate of a Man, to whom I owe so much? a Man whom I not only esteem but venerate?

My warmest good wishes & most respectful Compliments to Mrs Blacklock, & Miss Johnston, if she is with you.—

I cannot conclude without telling you that I am more & more pleased with the step I took respecting "my Jean". Two things, from my happy experience, I set down as Apothegms in Life:—A wife's head is immaterial, compared with her heart—&—Virtue's (for Wisdom, what Poet pretends to it)—"ways are ways of pleasantness, & all her paths are peace."*—

Adieu!
Robt Burns

Dr. Thomas Blacklock

A Mother's lament for the loss of her Son.
Fate gave the word, the arrow sped
[C.W. p. 334]
The lazy Mist.—A tune in Oswald—
The lazy mist hangs from the brow of the hill,
[C.W. p. 334]

* Proverbs 3:17.

JOHN McMURDO

Born in 1743 at Drumlanrig, the son of the chamberlain to the Duke of Queensberry, he in turn became chamberlain in 1780 and continued in that position till he retired to Hardriggs, Dumfries in 1797. He died in 1803. After Burns's death he became a trustee of the funds being raised for the poet's family and in this capacity he was named in the agreement for the publication of the Currie edition of 1800. It is not known how or when Burns and McMurdo first met but presumably this happened in the summer of 1788 when Burns was settling in at Ellisland. McMurdo shared Burns's interest in bawdy verse and was lent the poet's collection (IV). Burns became a frequent visitor at Drumlanrig and wrote a number of songs for McMurdo's family, as well as persuading Stephen Clarke, musical editor of the *Scots Musical Museum*, to come to Drumlanrig to give some of McMurdo's children music lessons. In March 1793, however, Burns had too much to drink during one of his visits and became 'a little turbulent'. This necessitated a remorseful apology the following day (V), accompanied by a song 'hammered out' that morning. In the same month McMurdo was the recipient of a copy of the 1793 edition of the Poems with a somewhat self-deprecatory inscription (VI). Something of a more accurate self-assessment is to be found in a later letter (VII). Kings might bestow coronets, while he could only give a ballad; but his presents were superior to those of monarchs, being the presents of genius.

I (289)

[Perhaps enclosing *To Mr McMurdo, with a pound of Lundiefoot snuff* C.W. 356].

Sanquhar, 26th November 1788

Sir,

I write to you this & the inclosed literally en passant, for I am just baiting on my way to Ayr-shire.—I have Philosophy or Pride enough, to support me with unwounded indiference against the neglect of my mere dull Superiors, the nameless rank & file of Noblesse & Gentry, nay even to keep my vanity quite sober under the larding of their Compliments; but from those who are equally distinguished by their Rank & Character, those who bear the more elegant impressions of the Great Creator, on the richest materials, their little notices & attentions are to me among the first of earthly enjoyments.—The honor you did my fugitive Pieces in requesting copies of them, is so highly flattering to my feelings & Poetic Ambition that I could not resist even this half-opportunity of scrawling off for you the inclosed as a small but honest testimony how truly & gratefully I have the honor to be,

Sir, you deeply indebted humble servant
Robert Burns

II (296)

Ellisland 9th January 1789

Sir,

A Poet and a Beggar are in so many points of view alike, that one might take them for the same individual character under different designations; were it not that though, with a trifling Poetic license, most Poets may be styled Beggars, yet the converse of the proposition does not hold, that every Beggar is a Poet.—In one particular however they remarkably agree; if you help either the one or the other to a mug of ale or the picking of a bone, they will very willingly repay you with a Song.—This occurs to me at present, as I have just dispatched a well-lined rib of J. Kilpatrick's Highlander; a bargain for which I am indebted to you, in the style of our Ballad-printers, "Five excellent new Songs."—The inclosed is nearly my newest Song, and one that has cost me some pains, though that is

492

but an equivocal mark of its excellence.—Two or three others which I have by me shall do themselves the honor to wait on your after-leisure: petitioners for admittance into favour must not harass the condescension of their Benefactor.—

You see Sir, what it is to patronise a Poet.—'Tis like being a magistrate in a petty Borough; you do them the favour to preside in their Council for one year, and your name bears the prefatory stigma of Bailie, for life.—

With, not the Compliments, but the best wishes the sincerest prayers of the Season for you, that you may see many and happy years with Mrs McMurdo and your family—two blessings, by the by, to which your rank does not by any means entitle you; a loving wife and fine family being almost the only good things of this life to which the Farm-house and Cottage have an exclusive right—

I have the honor to be

Sir, your much indebted And very humble servant
Robt Burns

III (411A)

[With *Elegy on Captain Matthew Henderson.*]
[C.W. p. 337.]

Ellisland, 2nd August 1790

Sir,

Now that you are over with the sirens of Flattery, the harpies of Corruption, & the furies of Ambition, these infernal deities that on all sides and in all parties preside over the villainous business of Politics, permit a rustic Muse of your acquaintance to do her best to sooth you with a song.—

You knew Henderson—I have not flattered his memory.—

I have the honor to be, Sir,
Your oblidged humble servant
R. Burns

IV (499A)

Monday six o'clock
Dumfries, [February? 1792]

Sir,

'tis said that we take the greatest liberties with our greatest friends, & I pay myself a very high compliment by the manner in which I am going to apply the remark.—I have owed you money longer than ever I owed it to any man.—Here is Kerr's account, & here is the six guineas; & now, I don't owe a shilling to man or WOMAN either.—But for these damned, dirty, dogs-ear'd, little pages, I had done myself the honor to have waited on you long ago.—Independant of the obligations your hospitable kindness has laid me under, the consciousness of your superiority in the ranks of MAN & GENTLE-MAN, of itself, was fully as much as I could ever make head to; but to owe you money, too, was more than I could face.—

John McMurdo

I think I once mentioned something to you of a Collection of Scots Songs I have for some years been making: I send you a perusal of what I have gathered.—I could not conveniently spare them above five or six days, & five or six glances of them will probably more than suffice you.—When you are tired of them, please leave them with Mr Clint of the King's Arms.—There is not another copy of the Collection in the world, & I should be sorry that any unfortunate negligence should deprive me of what has cost me a good deal of pains.—

I have the honor to be,
Sir,
Your deeply indebted & ever grateful humble servant
Robt Burns

V (542A)

[March 1793?]

Sir,

I believe last night that my old enemy, the Devil, taking the advantage of my being in drink (he well knows he has no chance with me in my sober hours) tempted me to be a little turbulent.— You have too much humanity to heed the maniac ravings of a poor wretch whom the powers of Hell, & the potency of Port, beset at the same time.—

In the mean time, allow me to present you with the following Song which I have hammered out this morning.—

I am ever
Your poetical humble servant
R.B.

Song
Lang here awa, there awa wandering Willie,
[C.W. p. 480]

VI (549)

(In a copy of the 1793 Edition of the *Poems*, mid-March)

Will Mr McMurdo do me a favor to accept of these Volumes; a trifling, but sincere mark of the very high respect I bear for his worth as a Man, his manners as a Gentleman, & his kindness as a Friend.—However inferiour, now, or afterwards, I may rank as a Poet; one honest virtue, to which few Poets can pretend, I trust I shall ever claim as mine:—to no man, whatever his station in life, or his power to serve me, have I ever paid a compliment at the expence of TRUTH.

The Author

VII (571)

[July 1793]

Sir,

There is a beautiful, simple little Scots air which Mr Clarke tells me has the good fortune to meet your approbation, & which he says he has taught your young ladies, together with the rudiments of a Song which I intended to suit the tune.— That Ballad I inclose, finished; & in my own opinion, in my best style: & I now beg leave to present to Miss Mcmurdo the Composition when I think I have made it worthy in some degree of the Subject.—She, I from the beginning, meant for the Heroine of it.—*

Sincere respect, Sir, even from those who can bestow nothing else, or who are themselves of no consequence as folks of the world, still that tribute of the heart is an offering grateful to every worthy mind.—You know, that is a tribute I never pay, but in the willing ardour of my soul.—Kings give Coronets; Alas, I can only bestow a Ballad.—Still however I proudly claim one superiority even over Monarchs: My presents, so far as I am a Poet, are the presents of Genius; & as the gifts of R. BURNS, they are the gifts of respectful gratitude to the WORTHY.—I assure you, I am not a little flattered with the idea, when I anticipate children pointing out in future Publications the tribute of respect I have bestowed on their Mothers.—The merit of the Scots airs, to which many of my Songs are, & more will be, set, give me this pleasing hope.—

You, I believe, are a Subscriber to that Splendid Edition of Scots Music in which Pleyel presides over the musical department.—In a future Number of that Work, the first Number is already published, this Ballad will probably appear.—

I have the honor to be,

Sir, your obliged humble servant

Robt. Burns

* There was a lass & she was fair (C.W. p. 493)

VIII (607)

[Dumfries, Dec 1793]

Sir,

I just finished the inclosed, and I do my Ballad the honour to sent you it.—I shall be through your country-side in about the middle of next week; if you have an hour to spare for so trifling a purpose....

LADY ELIZABETH CUNNINGHAM

Born about 1750 at Finlaystone, she was the daughter of the thirteenth Earl of Glencairn and sister of Earl James, Burns's patron. She lived with her mother, the Dowager Countess, at Coates House near Edinburgh, and died unmarried in 1804. She was the recipient of four extant letters from Burns, as well as a lengthy dedication in a copy of the 1793 edition of the Poems. She was the first person to receive a copy of his *Lament for James Earl of Glencairn* (C.W. p. 423).

I (298)

Ellisland near Dumfries, 22nd January 1789

My Lady

As the officious gratitude of a poor creature, however it may be a little troublesome, can never be disagreeable to a good heart, I have ventured to send your Ladyship this packet.—That from a dabble in rhymes I am become a professed Poet; that my attachment to the Muses is heated into enthusiasm; that my squalid Poverty is changed for comfortable Independance, is the work of your Ladyship's noble Family.—Whether I may ever make my footing good, on any considerable height of Parnassus, is what I do not know; but I am determined to strain every nerve in the trial.—Though the rough material of fine writing is undoubtedly the gift of Genius, the workmanship is as certainly the united effort of labor, attention and pains.—Nature has qualified few, if any, to shine in every walk of the Muses: I shall put it to the test of repeated trial, whether she has formed me capable of distinguishing myself in any one.—

In the first great concern of life, the means of supporting that life, I think myself tolerably secure.—If my farm should not turn out well, which after all it may not, I have my Excise-Commission in reserve.—This last is comparatively a poor resource, but it is luxury to any thing the first five & twenty years of my life taught me to expect; and I would despise myself if I though I were not capable of sacrificing any one little liquorish gratification on the altar of Independance.—A little spice of indolence excepted. I thank Heaven there is not any species of dissipation that I cannot set at defiance.—The indolent reveries of a bemused mind, are indeed the sins that easily beset me; but, like the noxious vapours that annoy Miners, I am afraid they are evils that necessarily rise from my very Profession.—

The inclosed Poems are the favors of the Nithsdale muses.—The piece inscribed to R—— G—— Esq. is a copy of verses which I sent to Mr Graham of Fintry, with a request for his assistance to procure me an Excise Division in the middle of which I live.—On my return from Edinburgh last, I found my aged mother, my brothers & sisters on the brink of ruin with their farm; and as I am certain the remainder of their lease will be worth holding, I advanced them nearly one half of my capital to keep their little Commonwealth together, and place them in comfort.—My own farm here, I am pretty sure will in time do well; but for several years it will require assistance more than my pocket can affod.—The Excise-salary would pay half my rent, and I could manage the whole business of the Division without five guineas of additional expence.—

I shall be in Edinburgh in about a month when I shall do myself the honour to inform your Ladyship farther of these to me important matters, as I know your Goodness will be interested in them.—

In all my other domestic concerns, I find myself extremely comfortable.—I muse & rhyme, morning, noon & night; & have a hundred different Poetic plans, pastoral, georgic, dramatic, &c. floating in the regions of fancy, somewhere between Purpose and resolve.—To secure myself from ever descending to any thing unworthy of the independant spirit of Man, or the honest pride of Genius, I have adopted Lord Glencairn as my titular Protector, what your scholars call by the Heathen name of Dii penates, I think it is.— I have a large shade of him, with the verses I intended for his picture, wrote out by Butterworth, pasted on the back; and a small shade of him both by Miers, set in a gold breast-pin, with the words, "Mon Dieu et toi," engraved on the shell.—The first, I have hung over my Parlour chimney-piece; the last I keep for gala days.—I have often, during this hard winter, wished myself a Great-man, that I might, with propriety in the etiquette of the world, have enquired after Lady Glencairn's health.—One of the sons of little men as I am, I can only wish fervently for her welfare; or in my devouter moods, pray for her, in the charming language of Mckenzie, that "the Great Spirit may bear up the weight of her grey hairs and blunt the arrow that brings them rest."—*

I shall not add to this unconscionable letter by a tedious apology, or any thing more than assuring your Ladyship, that with the warmest sincerity of heart-felt, though powerless gratitude,

I have the honor to be, My Lady,
your Ladyship's deeply indebted
and ever grateful humble servant
Robt. Burns

* *The Man of Feeling*, chapter XXXIV

II (342)

Ellisland near Dumfries 15th May 1789
[*Bishop mark* MY 19]

My Lady

Though I claim the priviledge your Ladyship's goodness allows me of sending you copies of any thing I compose in the way of my Poetic Trade, I must not tax you with noticing each of my idle epistles.— The inclosed piece pleading the cause of Humanity, is for your Ladyship; the other, a specimen of the Author's Political Piety, I present with my humble respects to the noble Earl to whom I owe my All.—

Though I had no other motive, I would continue to cultivate the acquaintance of the Muses for the sake of having an opportunity of assuring the Noble Family of Glencairn with what enthusiasm I have the honor to be,

The grateful creature of their bounty,
and their very humble Servant
Robert Burns

Lady Elizabeth Cunningham

III (379)

Ellisland 23rd December 1789

My Lady,

The honor you have done your poor Poet in writing him so very obliding a letter, and the pleasure the inclosed beautiful verses have given him, came very seasonable to his aid amid the chearless gloom and sinking despondency of December weather and diseased nerves.—As to forgeting the Family of Glencairn, with which you tax me, Heaven is my witness with what sincerity I could use those simple, rude, but I think strongly expressive old verses—

> If thee, Jerus'lem I forget,
> Skill part from my right hand.—
> My tongue to my mouth's roof let cleave,
> If I do thee forget
> Jerusalem, and thee above
> My chief joy do not set!—*

When I am tempted to do any thing improper, I dare not because I look on myself as accountable to your Ladyship and Family; when now and then I have the honor to be called to the tables of the Great, if I happen to meet with any thing mortifying from the stately stupidity of self-sufficient Squires, or the luxuriant insolence of upstart Nabobs, I get above the creatures by calling to remembrance that I am patronised by the noble House of Glencairn; and at gala times such as Newyearsday, a Christening, or the Kirn-night, when my punch-bowl is brought from its dusty corner and filled up in honor of the occasion, I begin with, The Countess of Glencairn! My Good Woman with the enthusiasm of a grateful heart next cries, My Lord! And so that toast goes on untill I end with Lady Hariet's little Angel whose Epithalamium I have pledged myself to write.—

When I received your Ladyship's letter, I was in the act of transcribing the inclosed Poems such as they are for you; and meant to have sent them my first leisure hour and acquainted you with a late change in my way of life.—By the generous friendship of one of the first of men, Mr Graham of Fintry, I have got the Excise Division in the midst of which I live; and considering my unlucky bargain of a farm, I find £50 per An. which is now our Salary, an exceeding good thing.—

People may talk as they please of the ignominy of the Excise, but what will support my family and keep me independant of the world is to me a very important matter, and I had much rather that my Profession borrowed credit from me, than that I borrowed credit from my Profession.—Another advantage I have in this business is, the knowledge it gives me of the various shades of Human Character; and consequently assisting me in my trade as a Poet.—Not that I am in haste for the Press, as my Lord has been told: had it been so, I would have been highly wanting to myself, not to have consulted my noble, generous Patron; but still, to be Poet, is my highest ambition, my dearest wish, and my unwearied study.—I am aware that though I were to give to the world Performances superiour to my former works, if they were productions of the same kind, the comparative reception they would meet with would mortify me.—For this reason I wish still to secure my old friend, Novelty, on my side, by the *kind* of my performances: I have some thoughts of the Drama.— Considering the favorite things of the day, the two and three act pieces of Okeefe, Mrs Inchbald, &c. does not your Ladyship think that a Scotish Audience would be better pleased with the Affectation, Whim & Folly of their own native growth, than with manners which to by far the greatest of them can be only second hand?—No man knows what Nature has fitted him for untill he try; and if after a preparatory course of some years' study of Men and Books, I should find myself unequal to the task, there is no great harm done— Virtue and Study are their own reward.—I have got Shakespeare, and begun with him; and I shall stretch a point & make myself master of all the Dramatic Authors of any repute, in both English and French, the only languages which I know.—

I ought to apologise to your Ladyship for sending you some of the inclosed rhymes, they are so silly.—Every body knows now of poor Dr Mcgill.—He is my particular friend, & my Ballad on his persecution has virulence enough if it has not wit.—You must not read Lady Glencairn the stanza about the Priest of Ochiltree.— Though I know him to be a designing, rotten-hearted Puritan, yet perhaps her Ladyship has a different idea of him.—The Ode to the Regency bill was mangled in a Newspaper last winter.—The Election ballad alludes to our present canvass in this string of Boroughs.—I do not suppose there will be a harder run match in the whole General Election.—I have avoided taking a Side in Politics.—The Song is the only one of the inclosed Pieces that I think worthy of being sent to so good a judge as your Ladyship.—

I will not add to this tedious epistle more than to assure your Ladyship with what grateful sincerity I have the honor to be,

your Ladyship's highly oblidged
and most obedient humble servant
Robt Burns

* Metrical Psalms 137:5-6

IV (467)

[Enclosing *Lament for James, Earl of Glencairn.*]
[C.W. p. 423]

[late September? 1791]

My Lady,

I would, as usual, have availed myself of the privilege your goodness has allowed me, of sending you any thing I compose in my poetical way; but as I had resolved, so soon as the shock of my irreparable loss would allow me, to pay a tribute to my late benefactor, I determined to make that the first piece I should do myself the honour of sending you. Had the wing of my fancy been equal to the ardour of my heart, the inclosed had been much more worthy your perusal: as it is, I beg leave to lay it at your ladyship's feet. As all the world knows my obligations to the late Earl of Glencairn, I would wish to shew as openly that my heart glows, and shall ever glow, with the most grateful sense and remembrance of his lordship's goodness. The sables I did myself the honour to wear to his lordship's memory, were not the "mockery of woe." Nor shall my gratitude perish with me!—If, among my children, I shall have a son that has a heart, he shall hand it down to his child as a family honour, and a family debt, that my dearest existence I owe to the noble house of Glencairn!

I was about to say, my lady, that if you think the poem may venture to see the light, I would, in some way or other, give it to the world. . . .

V (550)

[In a copy of the 1793 Edition of the *Poems*, mid-March]

But for the generous patronage of the late James Earl of Glencairn to the Author, these volumes had never been.—In memory of the obligations he conferred on me, & in gratitude to your Ladyship for your goodness, do me the honor to accept of these volumes.—

Robt Burns

PETER MORISON

A carpenter and cabinetmaker of Mauchline, he lived in Beechgrove Cottage on the west side of the Cowgate at its junction with the road to Catrine. Morison made the furniture for Ellisland, and from the following letter it can be seen that he kept his famous customer waiting. According to Andrew Boyle, there is a local tradition that while Burns was at Mossgiel he was in the habit of joining the Morison family for lunch after Sunday morning services and that on one such occasion he composed the *Address to a Haggis* (C.W. p. 264), although it must be pointed out that it has also been claimed that this poem was written at Edinburgh or Craigie.

(300)

Isle 22nd January 1789

My dear Sir,

Necessity oblidges me to go into my new house, even before it be plaistered.—I will inhabit the one end untill the other is finished.—About three weeks more, I think, will at farthest be my time beyond which I cannot stay in this present house.—If ever you wished to deserve the blessing of him that was ready to perish; if ever you were in a situation that a little kindness would have rescued you from many evils; if ever you hope to find rest in future states of untryed being; get these matters of mind ready.—My servant will be out in the beginning of next week for the Clock.—My Compliments to Mrs Morison.—

I am, after all my tribulation, Dear Sir, yours,
Robt Burns

DAVID BLAIR

Born in Birmingham about 1755, he is listed in Pye's *Directory of Birmingham* as a gunmaker from 1787 onwards, and may have had a connection with Blair and Lea, gunmakers of Navigation Street, who were established in 1783. Blair's name appears in several subscription lists for the relief of the poor in 1812-13, indicating that he was a person of substance. In 1813 he was a founder member of the Birmingham Chamber of Manufacturers and Commerce. Two of his sons died in May 1812 and he himself died in May 1814. Blair supplied Burns with the brace of pistols which the poet subsequently gave to Dr William Maxwell, and which are now preserved in the Royal Museum of Scotland, Edinburgh.

I (301)

Ellisland, 23rd January 1789.

My dear Sir,

My honor has lien bleeding these two months almost, as 'tis near that time since I received your kind tho' short epistle of the 29th Oct. The defensive tools do more than half mankind do, they do honor to their maker; but I trust that with me they shall have the fate of a miser's gold—to be often admired, but never used.

Long before your letter came to hand, I sent you, by way of Mr. Nicol, a copy of the book, and a proof-copy of the print, loose, among the leaves of the book. These, I hope, are safe in your possession some time ago. If I could think of any other channel of communication with you than the villainous expensive one of the Post, I could send you a parcel of my Rhymes; partly as a small return for your kind, handsome compliment, but much more as a mark of my sincere esteem and respect for Mr. Blair. A piece I did lately I shall try to cram into this letter, as I think the turn of thought may perhaps please you.

Written in Friars-Carse Hermitage, on the Banks

of the Nith. Oct. 1788

[C.W. p. 325]

I remember with pleasure, my dear Sir, a visit you talked of paying to Dumfries, in Spring or Summer.—I shall only say, I have never parted with a man, after so little acquaintance, whom I more ardently wished to see again. At your first convenience, a line to inform me of an affair in which I am much interested—just an answer to the question, How you do, will highly oblige, my dear Sir,

Yours very sincerely,
Robt Burns

II (360)

Ellisland, 27th August 1789

I have been sadly to blame, my Dear Sir, but, do forgive me! If, as is said, Offences proceed only from the heart, mine is guiltless.—Know you any thing of a worse than Galley-bondage, a slavery where the soul with all her powers is laden with weary fetters of ever-increasing weight; a Slavery which involves the mind in dreary darkness and almost a total eclipse of every ray of God's image; and all this the work the baneful doings of that arch-fiend known among mortals by the name of Indolence? But this is not all my apology.—I have for

502

some time had in view to commence acting Excise Officer.—I say, acting, for I have had an Excise Commission by me nearly these two years; and now that the Salary is augmented to £50 per Ann. I thought it an object worth my notice.—I believe I am now appointed to a Division in the middle of which I live, and may perhaps enter on business in a week or ten days; and as several months ago I foresaw this event peering above the horizon of Probability, I was accordingly very busy with the theory of my future occupation, which, to those who wish to be masters of their business, is a theory not a little intricate and perplexed.—Add to all, that in a day or two after I received your last oblidging packet, Mrs Burns presented me with a fine chopping boy, which, with improving a farm, building a steading of farm-houses, &c., has kept me I assure you, very busy.

I am the more earnest to excuse myself, as I scarce ever met with a man whose good opinion on so little acquaintance, I would so fondly covet as Mr Blair's.—

I am much oblidged to you for the Magazine you sent me; of which, though the most elegant of that species of Publications that I have ever seen, I had never so much as heard the Name.—Never mind the bagatelle of a Poem.—I know nothing how the Publishers could get it, but as I had given several copies to my friends, it has found its way I suppose thro' the well-meant though blameable officiousness of some of them.—I have a little altered, and I think improved that Poem, and would just now transcribe it to you, but for that cursed tax of Postage.—That, and another Poem I have written since, I shall make the contents of another epistle which expect to be troubled with soon.—
I am, ever,

My dear Sir, yours most sincerely
Robt Burns

III (376)

[With a copy of *The Five Carlins.*]
[C.W. p. 364]

My dear Sir, [December 1789]

I meant to have sent you a larger packet, but Mr Chalmers our friend tells me that he is sending you some things, so I send you this foolish Ballad.—I have not yet forgiven Fortune for her mischievous game of Cross Purposes that deprived me of the pleasure of seeing you again when you were here.—

Adieu!
R. Burns

IV (551)

[In a copy of the 1793 Edition of the *Poems*, mid-March]
Dear Sir,

Accept of these volumes, as a mark of the most sincere esteem & regard—and when, perhaps, he is but a memory, let these call to your tender friendly recollection—

The Author

David Blair

V (682)

Dumfries, 25th August 1795

The following, my dear Sir, is the history of Lord Balmerino's durk which you now have.—In the year 1745, a Bailie in Glasgow (I once knew his name, but have forgotten it) who was a secret abettor of the Jacobite interest, sent some hundred pairs of shoes to the Prince's army, through the medium of Lord Balmerino; & that with many compliments to my Lord's personal character.—His Lordship, who was truly a brave, generous, worthy character, wrote back a grateful letter of thanks to the Bailie, & accompanied the letter with a present of his own durk.—This durk & letter came into the possession of a son of the Bailie, a dissipated worthless fellow, who sold the durk to a particular friend of mine* for an anker of Ferintosh whisky. —My friend, who is a gentleman of the most undoubted probity, has often perused the letter; & well had it been for the interests of the durk, had my friend's chastity been equal to his Integrity! For one evening the devil & the flesh tempted him, in the moment of intoxication, to a house of a certain description, where he was despoined of his durk, & that durk despoiled of its knife & fork, & silver mounting which had been indeed very rich; His Lordship's arms, cypher, Crest, &c. being elegantly engraved on several places of it.— My friend, after a diligent search, at last recovered his durk in this mutilated situation; from him it came to me.—

This history, I pledge myself to you, if authentic.—

Yours ever
Robt Burns

* Dr William Maxwell, himself the scion of an old Jacobite family. It is interesting to note that, by giving to Blair the dirk which came from Maxwell, it was fitting that in due course Burns should present Blair's pistols to Maxwell as a dying gift. The dirk is now on display in the Tower at Mauchline.

ALEXANDER DALZIEL

Born at Noblehouse, Peebles-shire where his father was the innkeeper, Dalziel had the distinction of being a personal friend of Robert Fergusson, and later became one of Burns's most accomplished correspondents. He was factor to the Earl of Glencairn's estate of Finlaystone, Renfrewshire. According to Cromek it was Dalziel who brought the Kilmarnock Edition to the Earl's attention (a claim which has also been made on behalf of Dalrymple of Orangefield, though Ferguson points out that one claim does not necessarily invalidate the other). Dalziel played a prominent role in the foundation of the Greenock Burns Club in 1801. He himself died in 1819.

I (304)

Ellisland, Friday night—

I sit down to write my friend in not the best plight— . . .

> The carlin clew her wanton tail
> Her wanton tail sae ready
> "I learnt a sang in Annandale. . . .*

Miers, lately in Edinburgh, now in Leeds, has the original Shade, from which he did mine.—However, if his Lordship wishes it, he shall have it to get copied. . . .

Do, write me soon.—

Adieu!
Robt Burns

* *Come Rede Me Dame* (C.W. p. 348).

II (422)

Ellisland, 5th October 1790

Dear Sir,

I suppose that by this time & long before this time, your Indignation has given me over to as many devils as chuse to accept of me.—A few days after I received yours I was seized with a slow, illformed Fever, from which I am just risen out of the weary bed of Sickness; & if this is not apology enough, I must inform you farther that I have likewise had a most malignant Squinancy which had me very near the precincts of the Grave.—I am now got greatly better, though by no means in a confirmed state of health.—Yesterday, for the first time, I rode as far as Dumfries.—So much for myself & my seeming neglect of your commands.—

As to Miss G——, I have very little acquaintance with her character, but a most intimate friend of mine, a Mr Frederick Maxwell, is married to a Sister of Mr Glendinning of Parton, who, as you know is married to a sister of Miss G——'s.—Thro' this channel I can know every thing that is proper to ask.—

Miss G—— has of late years been a good deal on the reserve in her temper.—There was a match much talked of between her & a Mr David Blair, a gentleman of a tolerable decent estate in this neighbourhood.—Blair has very little on the positive side of his character. —When I have said that he is a good, honest, harmless fellow, you will have a pretty just idea of him.—Miss G——, after trying a gentle tour in vain for her health, came to the George Inn, in Dumfries, where, in the very room in which her father died, she took her last residence, & there payed the great debt of Nature.—Her Sister, Mrs Glendinning, has been ever since so inconsolable that she has seen

nobody, has scarcely spoken to an individual in her own family, &
was with difficulty diverted from a resolution to hang the room, in
which her father & sister died, with mourning, & there spend her
future days.—

If there were any particular circumstances with which you would
wish to be acquainted, or, if I can pick up any farther anecdotes
respecting the lady, you shall have them.—

I am most sincerely sorry to hear from several quarters of my Noble
Patron's bad health.—God send him that best & dearest of blessings,
Health: of late I have been taught its value.—

I am ever, Dear Sir, yours
Robt Burns

III (439)

Ellisland near Dumfries
10th March 1791

Mr dear Sir

I have taken the liberty to frank this letter to you, as it incloses an
idle Poem of mine, which I send you; & God knows you may
perhaps pay dear enough for it, if you read it through.—not that this
is my own opinion; but an Author by the time he has composed &
corrected his work, has quite pored away all his powers of critical
discrimination.—

I can easily guess from my own heart what you have felt on a late
most melancholy event.—God knows what I have suffered, at the
loss of my best Friend, my first my dearest Patron & Benefactor; the
man to whom I owe all that I am & have! I have gone into mourning
for him, & with more sincerity of grief than I fear some will, who by
Nature's ties ought to feel on the occasion.—

I will be exceedingly oblidged to you indeed, to let me know the
news of the Noble Family, how the poor Mother & the two sisters
support their loss.—I had a packet of Poetic bagatelles ready to send
to Lady Betty, when I saw the fatal tidings in the Newspaper.—I see
by the same channel that the honored REMAINS of my noble
Patron are designed to be brought to the Family Burial place.—Dare
I trouble you to let me know privately before the day of interment,
that I may cross the country & steal among the croud, to pay a tear
to the last sight of my ever revered Benefactor?—It will oblige me
beyond expression.—

I am, My dear Sir, yours sincerely,
Robt Burns

THE RIGHT REV. JOHN GEDDES,
BISHOP OF DUNKELD

Born in 1735, of an old Catholic family, both he and his brother Alexander (the noted biblical critic and theologian) became bishops. Burns first met him at Lord Monboddo's early in 1787 and subsequently described him as 'the first (i.e. the foremost) Cleric character I ever saw'. Prior to his appointment to the diocese of Dunkeld, Geddes had been rector of the Royal Scots College at Valladolid, Spain and was responsible for getting it, and four other Catholic seminaries, to subscribe to the Edinburgh Edition of 1787. Geddes himself does not appear among the list of subscribers, although he later obtained a copy which he had rebound with blank end-papers. Burns borrowed this copy during his Highland tour and was extremely tardy about returning it, as the following letter, written a year and a half later, testifies. On Geddes's death this volume passed to his sister Mrs Hyslop and eventually came into the hands of the well-known Burnsian, W.K. Bixby of St Louis who had it reprinted in 1908, in an edition of 473 copies, this facsimile being known as *The Geddes Burns*. The chief interest of this facsimilie lies in the fourteen poems in Burns's handwriting which he inserted on the end-papers before returning it. The original is now in the Huntington Library, San Marino, California. Bishop Geddes died at Aberdeen in February 1799. The following letter was sent to Bishop Geddes, care of Dr James Gregory, inventor of Gregory's powder, the famous laxative.

Ellisland near Dumfries 3rd February —1789—

Venerable Father

As I am conscious that wherever I am, you do me the honour to interest yourself much in my welfare, it gives me pleasure to inform you that I am here, at last, stationary in the serious business of life; and have now, not only the retired leisure, but the hearty inclination, to attend to those great and important questions, what I am, where I am, and for what I am destined.—In that first concern, the conduct of the Man, there was ever but one side on which I was habitually blameable; and there I have secured myself in the way pointed out by Nature and Nature's God.—I was sensible that to so helpless a creature as a poor Poet, a wife and family were incumbrances which a species of prudence would bid him shun; but when the alternative was, being at eternal warfare with myself, on account of habitual follies, to give them no worse name, which no general example, no licentious wit, no sophistical infidelity could me ever justify, I must have been a fool to have hesitated, and a madman to have made another choice.—   Besides, I had, in "My Jean," a long and much-loved fellow-creature's happiness or misery among my hands, and who could trifle with such a deposite?—

In the affair of a Livelyhood, I think myself tolerably secure: I have good hopes of my farm, but should they fail, I have an Excise commission which, on my simple petition will at any time procure me bread.—There is a certain stigma affixed to the character of an Excise-Officer, but I do not intend to borrow honour from any profession; and though the Salary be comparatively small, it is luxury to any thing that the first twenty five years of my life taught me to expect.—

Thus, with a rational aim and method in life, you may easily guess, my Reverend and much-honored Friend, that my characteristical trade is not forgotten.—I am, if possible, more than ever an enthusiast to the Muses.—I am determined to study man and Nature, in that view, incessantly; and to try if the ripening and corrections of years can enable me to produce something worth preserving.—

The Right Rev. John Geddes, Bishop of Dunkeld

You will see in your book, which I beg your pardon for detaining so long, that I have been tuning my lyre on the banks of Nith.—Some larger Poetic plans that are floating in my imagination, or partly put in execution, I shall impart to you when I have the pleasure of meeting with you; which, if you are then in Edinburgh, I shall have about the beginning of March.—That acquaintance, worthy Sir, with which you were pleased to honour me, you must still allow me to challenge: for, with whatever unconcern I give up my transient connexion with the merely Great, those self-important beings whose intrinsic worthlessness is concealed under the accidental advantages of their rank, I cannot lose the patronising notice of the Learned and the Good without the bitterest regret.—

> I have the honor to be, Venerable Sir, your most respectful
> and very humble servant—
> Robt Burns

WILLIAM PITT, THE YOUNGER

Born in the same year as Burns, he was the younger son of William Pitt the Elder, Earl of Chatham. Pitt was something of an infant prodigy - a brilliant scholar by the age of ten and author of a political tragedy at the age of thirteen. After Cambridge, he entered Parliament as M.P. for Appleby at the age of 21, and took the House by storm with his maiden speech which brought him to the attention of Shelburne, in whose administration he became Chancellor of the Exchequer. In December 1783, at the age of 24, he became Prime Minister.

Early in his career as Prime Minister Pitt had tried to abolish 36 pocket boroughs and transfer their seats to towns and cities which were either under-represented or unrepresented altogether, but was defeated. He never again attempted parliamentary reform, and after 1792, when fear of contagion from the French Revolution induced paranoia in the Government, he suspended the Habeas Corpus Act and condoned the notorious sedition trials of the Friends of the People, sentenced to transportation for nothing more heinous than advocating constitutional reform and universal suffrage. To Burns, therefore, 'Billy Pit' epitomised tyranny and repression - a viewpoint which is not shared by posterity. Although an inspired leader, Pitt lacked the common touch. As one biographer put it, 'he was revered, but not loved'. Pitt's administration came very close to defeat in 1789 over the question of the Regency Bill, precipitated by the crisis over the King's temporary insanity. This was a matter to which Burns referred in his lengthy *Ode on the Departed Regency Bill* (C.W. p. 352), but the matter which inspired him to write the following open letter, published in the *Edinburgh Evening Courant* of 9th February 1789, was the Government's unfair treatment of the Scottish distillers. Burns subsequently made a copy of this letter for the Glenriddell MS, differing from the printed version in a number of minor textual points.

At the juncture of the king's illness, while the Regency Bill was pending, & when every body expected the Premier's downfall, Addresses crouded in to him from all quarters; &, among the rest, the following appeared in a Newspaper.—The Addressers, the late Distillers of Scotland, had just been ruined by a positive breach of the Public faith, in a most partial tax laid on by the House of Commons, to favour a few opulent English Distillers, who, it seems, were of vast Electioneering consequence.—

[About 1st February 1789]

Sir,

While pursy Burgesses croud your gates, sweating under the weight of heavy addresses, permit us, the late Distillers in that part of Great Britain called Scotland, to approach you, not with venal approbation but with fraternal condolence; not as what you just now are, or for some time have been, but as what in all probability you will shortly be.—We will have the merit of countenancing not deserting our friends in the day of their calamity, and you will have the satisfaction of perusing at least one honest Address.—

You are well acquainted, Sir, with the dissection of Human Nature; nor do you need the assistance of a fellow-creature's bosom to inform you, that Man is always a selfish, often a perfidious being.—This assertion, however the hasty conclusions of superficial observation may doubt of it, or the raw inexperience of youth may deny it, those who make the fatal experiment that we have done, will feel it.—You are a Statesman, and consequently are not ignorant of the traffic of these Corporation-compliments.—The little Great-man who drives the Borough to market, and the very Great-man who buys the Borough in that market, they, two, do the whole business, and you well know, that they, likewise, have their price.—With that sullen disdain which you can so well assume, rise, illustrious Sir, and spurn these hireling efforts of venal

Stupidity!—At best, they are the compliments of a wretch's friends on the morning of his execution: they take a decent farewil; resign him to his fate; and hurry away from his approaching hour.—

If fame say true, and omens be not very much mistaken, you are about to make your exit from that world where the sun of gladness guilds the paths of properous men: permit us, great Sir, with the sympathy of fellow-feeling, to hail your passage to the realms of ruin.—Whether the sentiment proceed from the selfishness or cowardice of mankind, is immaterial; but to a child of misfortune, pointing him out those who are still more unhappy, is giving him some degree of positive enjoyment.—

In this light, Sir, our downfal may be again useful to you: though not exactly in the same way, it is not perhaps the first time that it has gratified your feelings.—

It is true, the triumph of your evil star has been exceedingly despiteful.—At an age when other men are the votaries of pleasure, or underlings in business, you had attained a British Statesman's highest wish; and with the ordinary date of human life, what a prospect was before you!—Deeply rooted in Royal Favor, you overshadowed the land: the birds of passage; which follow ministerial sunshine through every clime of political faith and manners, flocked to your branches; and the beast of the field, the lordly Possessors of hills and vallies, [sic] crowded under your shade.—"But behold a watcher, a holy one came down from Heaven, and cried aloud, and said this; hew down the tree and, cut off his branches, shake off his leaves, and scatter his fruit: let the beasts get away from under it and the fowls from his branches!"*—A blow from an unthought of quarter, one of those terrible accidents which peculiarly mark the hand of Omnipotence, overset your career, and laid all you fancied honours in the dust.—

But turn your eyes, Sir, to the tragic scenes of our fate.—An ancient nation that for many ages had gallantly maintained the unequal struggle for independence with her much more powerful neighbour, at last agrees to a union which should ever after make them one people.—In consideration of certain circumstances, it was solemnly convenanted, that the Former should always enjoy a stipulated alleviation in her share of the public burdens, particularly in that branch of the revenue known by the name of, the Excise.—

This just priviledge had of late given great umbrage to some invidious powerful individuals of the more potent half of the Empire, and they have spared no wicked pains, under insidious pretexts to subvert, what they yet too much dreaded the spirit of their ancient enemies, openly to attack.—

By this conspiracy we fell; nor did we alone suffer, our Country was deeply wounded.—A number of, we will say it, respectable characters, largely engaged in trade where we were not only useful but absolutely necessary to our Country, in her dearest interest; we, with all that was near and dear to us, were sacrificed, without remorse, to the infernal deity of Political Expediency!-Not that sound policy, the good of the whole; we fell victims to the wishes of dark Envy and unprincipled Ambition.—Your foes, Sir, were avowed; they were too brave to take an ungenerous advantage; your defeat was in the face of day.—

Our enemies, to compleat our overthrow, contrived to make their private treachery the villainy of a Nation: not content with their own guilt they made the Public infamous! Your downfal only drags with you, your friends and partisans; in our misery are more or less involved the most numerous and most useful part of the Community, all those who immediately depend on the cultivation of the soil, from the landlord of a Province down to his lowest hind.—

Allow us, Sir, yet farther, just to hint at another rich vein of comfort in the dreary regions of Adversity;—the gratulations of an approving conscience.—In a certain great Assembly of which you are a distinguished member, panegyrics on your private virtues have so often wounded your delicacy, that we shall not distress you with any thing on the subject.—There is, however, one part of your public conduct which our feelings will not permit us to pass in silence—our gratitude must trespass on your modesty—we mean, worthy Sir, the whole of your behaviour to the Scots Distillers.—In evil hours, when obtrusive memory presses bitterly on the sense, let that recollection come, Sir, like a healing angel, and speak the peace to your soul which the world can neither give nor take away.—

We have the honour to be, Sir

Your grateful, sympathising, humble servants

John Barleycorn—Preses—

* Part of the dream of Nebuchadnezzar. Daniel 4:13-14.

MR AND MRS EDWARD WHIGHAM

The following letter was addressed to the wife of Edward Whigham (1750-1823), keeper of the Queensberry Arms at Sanquhar, and Provost of that burgh from 1793 till 1800. It seems likely that it was due to Whigham that Burns was made an honorary burgess and freeman of Sanquhar on 23rd December 1794. Burns met the Whighams on his first jaunt into Nithsdale in 1788 and thereafter was a frequent guest at their inn. He described the Whighams as 'my particular acquaintances'. It was with the Whighams that Burns was taking a drink on that Saturday night in January 1789 when the arrival of Mrs Oswald's funeral party forced him to ride a further twelve miles to the next inn, and therefore inspired his savage satire, the *Ode Sacred to the Memory of Mrs Oswald* (C.W. p. 342). It is not known which poems he refers to in this letter. The 'Bailie' is, of course, Edward Whigham. An undated memorandum is also included at this juncture. As it was addressed by Burns to Provost E—— W—— it must belong to the period 1793-6.

(312)

Ellisland 7th February 1789

Dear Madam,

I received the books safe and sound; and in return, I inclose you the Poem you wanted.—You will. likewise see the first sketch of the Poem, on a something different plan.—

My best Compliments to the Bailie: I am much indebted to your kindness and his to the two boys, my brothers in law.—

I am, Dear Madam, your oblidged & most humble servant
Robt Burns

(598)

Memorandum for Provost E[dward] W[higham]

To get from John French his sets of the following old Scots airs—

1st. The auld yowe jumpt o'er the tether—
2d. Nine nights awa, welcome hame my dearie—
3d. A' the nights o' the year, the chapman drinks nae water.

If Mr Whigham will either of himself, or through the medium of that hardy Veteran of original wit, and social procure these airs, it will be extremely obliging to

R.B.

DR. THOMAS BLACKLOCK

CAPTAIN FRANCIS GROSE

THOMAS BOYD

Born in 1753, he was a stonemason, building contractor and architect in Dumfries, responsible for the erection of Burns's farmhouse at Ellisland. Apart from Ellisland, he is best-remembered for his work on the new bridge over the Nith at Dumfries, built in 1791-4, and the Theatre Royal. The three brief letters from Burns indicate the poet's exasperation at the inordinate time taken by Boyd to complete the house while Burns was in temporary accommodation at Isle. The third letter, however, shows that Burns got his own back by delaying the settlement of his bill! Boyd married Jane Waddell, and died in September 1822.

I (313)

Isle, Sunday morn:
[8th February 1789]

I see at last, dear Sir, some signs of your executing my house within the current year.—I am oblidged to set out for Edinburgh tomorrow se'ennight so I beg you will set as many hands to work as possible during this week.—I am distressed with the want of my house in a most provoking manner.—It loses me two hours work of my servants every day, besides other inconveniences. For God's sake let me but within the shell of it!

I am, Dear Sir, yours,
Robt Burns

II (317)

Isle Sunday morn: [1st March 1789]

I arrived from Edinburgh yesternight and was a good deal surprised at finding my house still lying like Babylon in the prophecies of Isiah.*—I beg, dear Sir, for humanity's sake, that you will send me out your hands tomorrow, and oblidge

Dear Sir, yours sincerely,
Robt Burns

* See Isaiah 13:19-20.

III (458)

Ellisland, 16th June 1791

Dear Sir,

As it is high time that the account between you & me were settled, if you will take a bill of Mr Alexander Crombie's to me for twenty pounds in part, I will settle with you immediately; at least, against Wednesday se'ennight, as I am to be out of the country for a week.— Mr Crombie cannot take it amiss that I endeavour to get myself clear of his bill in this manner, as you owe him and I owe you.—

I am, Dear Sir, yours,
Robt Burns

WILLIAM BURNS

Born in 1767, the third son of William Burnes and Agnes Brown, he still was a
teenager when his father died and it was then left to his eldest brother Robert
to take care of him. By all accounts, William was a gentle, rather diffident
youth, lacking the restless ambition of Robert or the steadiness of Gilbert.
Clearly William had no vocation for farming, and Robert cast around for some
suitable form of employment for him. At first he tried Robert Ainslie, with a
view to getting William a saddler's apprenticeship in Edinburgh. When that
came to nothing, William moved in with Robert and Jean at Ellisland and
lodged there for several months until he obtained saddlery work at Longtown
near Carlisle. From there he moved to Newcastle upon Tyne, where he worked
for Messrs Walker and Robson. On completing his apprenticeship he became a
journeyman saddler with William Barber in the Strand, London. Poor William
had only been in the metropolis a few months when he succumbed to 'a putrid
fever' and died on 24th July 1790. The ten letters extant from Burns to his
younger brother reveal an endearing side to his nature. Although only eight
years older than William, the poet was something of a father figure to him; but
it is only fair to point out that he imparted his more elaborately sententious
advice (VIII) because William had specifically sought it. Burns's advice to
William concerning falling in love (V), however, is ruefully self-revealing.

I (318)

Isle, 2nd March 1789

My dear William,

I arrived from Edinburgh only the night before last, so could not
answer your epistle sooner.—I congratulate you on the prospect of
employ, and I am indebted to you for one of the best letters that has
been written by any Mechanic-lad in Nithsdale or Annandale or any
Dale on either side of the Border this twelvemonth.—Not that I
would have you always affect the stately stilts of studied composition,
but surely writing a handsome letter is an accomplishment worth
courting; and with attention & practice, I can promise you that it
will soon be an accomplishment of yours.—

If my advices can serve you, that is to say, if you can resolve
yourself, not only in reviewing your own deportment, manners, &c.
but also in carrying your consequent resolutions of amending the
faulty parts into practice, my small knowledge & experience of the
world is heartily at your service.—

I intended to have given you a sheetful of counsels, but some business
has prevented me.—In a word, Learn Taciturnity: let that be your
motto.—Through you had the wisdom of Newton, or the wit of
Swift, garrulousness would lower you in the eyes of your fellow-
creatures.—

You will receive by the carrier 2 coarse & one fine shirt, a neckcloth
and your velveret waistcoat.—I'll probably write you next week.—

I am
your brother
Robt Burns

II (321)

Isle—Tuesday even: [10th March 1789]

Dear William,

In my last I recommended that invaluable apothegm, Learn
taciturnity.—It is absolutely certain that nobody can know our
thoughts; and yet, from a slight observation of mankind, one would
not think so.—What mischiefs daily arise from silly garrulity or

foolish confidence! There is an excellent Scots Saying, that "A man's mind is his kingdom."—It is certainly so; but how few can govern that kingdom with propriety.—

The serious mischiefs in Business which this Flux of language occasion, do not come immediately to your situation; but in another point of view, the dignity of the man, now is the time that will either make or mar you.—Yours is the time of life for laying in habits; you cannot avoid it, though you would chuse; and these habits will stick to your last sand.—At after periods, even at so little advance as my years, 'tis true, one may still be very sharp-sighted to one's habituall failings and weaknesses, but to eradicate or even amend them is a quite different matter.—Acquired at first, by accident, they, by and by, begin to be as it were convenient; and in time are in a manner a necessary part of our existence.—

I have not time for more.—Whatever you read, whatever you hear, concerning the ways and works of that strange creature, MAN, look into the living world about you, look into Yourself, for the evidence of the fact, or the application of the doctrine.—

I am ever, yours
Robt Burns

III (323)

Isle—March 25th—1789

I have stolen from my corn-sowing, this minute, to write a line to accompany your shirt & hat, for I can no more.—Your sister Nannie arrived here yesternight, & begs to be remembered to you.—Write me every opportunity: never mind Postage.—My head, too, is as addle as an egg this morning, with dining abroad yesterday.—I received yours by the Mason.—Forgive me this foolish-looking scrap of an epistle.—

I am ever, My dear William,
yours
Robt Burns

P.S. If you are not then gone from Longtown, I'll write you a long letter by this day se'ennight. If you should not succeed in your tramps, don't be dejected or take any rash step.—Return to us; in that case, and we will court Fortune's better humour.—Remember this I charge you

R B

IV (329)

Isle 15th April 1789

My dear William

I am extremely sorry at the misfortune of your legs; I beg you will never let any worldly concern interfere with the more serious matter, the safety of your life & limbs.—I have not time in these hurried days to write you any thing other than a mere howd'ye letter.—I will only repeat my favorite quotation—

> "What proves the Hero truly great,
> "Is never, never to despair—*

515

My house shall ever be your welcome home; & as I know your prudence (would to God you had *resolution* equal to your *prudence*!) if any where at a distance from friends, you should need money, you know my direction by post.—

The inclosed is from Gilbert brought by your sister Nanny.—It was unluckily forgot.—Yours to Gilbert goes by post.—I heard from them yesterday, they are all well.—

Adieu!
Robt Burns

* Thomson: *Alfred*, Act I, sc. 3.

V (337)

Ellisland, 5th May, 1789

My dear William,

I am happy to hear by yours from Newcastle, that you are getting some employ. Remember

> "On reason build Resolve,
> "That column of true majesty in man."—[1]

I had a visit of your old landlord. In the midst of a drunken frolic in Dumfries, he took it into his head to come and see me; and I took all the pains in my power to please and entertain the old veteran. He is high in your praises, and I would advise you to cultivate his friendship, as he is, in his way, a worthy, and to you may be a useful man.

Anderson I hope will have your shoes ready to send by the waggon tomorrow. I forgot to mention the circumstance of making them pumps; but I suppose good calf shoes will be no great mistake. Wattie[2] has paid me for the thongs.

What would you think of making a little inquiry how husbandry matters go, as you travel, and if one thing fail, you might perhaps try another?

Your falling in love is indeed a phenomenon. To a fellow of your turn it cannot be hurtful. I am, you know, a veteran in these campaigns, so let me advise you always to pay your particular assiduities and try for intimacy as soon as you feel the first symptoms of the passion: this is not only best, as making the most of the little entertainment which the sport-abilities of distant addresses always gives, but is the best preservative for one's peace. I need not caution you against guilty amours—they are bad and ruinous everywhere, but in England they are the very devil. I shall be in Ayrshire about a fortnight. Your sister send their compliments. God bless you.

Robert Burns

1 Young: *Night Thoughts*, Night I, lines 30-1.
2 Walter Auld

VI (357)

Ellisland, 14th August 1789

My Dear William

I received your letter, and am very happy to hear that you have got settled for the winter.—I inclose you the two guinea notes of the

Bank of Scotland, which I hope will serve your need; It is, indeed, not quite so convenient for me to spare money as it once was, but I know your situation, and I will say it, in some respect, your worth.— I have no time to write at present, but I beg you will endeavour to pluck up a little more of THE MAN, than you used to have. Remember my favorite quotations

—on Reason build Resolve,
That column of true majesty in Man;"[1]

"What proves the hero truly great
Is never, never to despair."[2]

Your Mother & Sisters beg their Compliments

A Dieu je vous commende

Robt Burns

1 Young: *Night Thoughts*, Night I, lines 30-1.
2 Thomson: *Alfred: A Masque*, Act I, sc. 3.

VII (372)

Ellisland 10th November 1789

Dear William

I would have written you sooner but I am so hurried and fatigued with my Excise-business, that I can scarcely pluck up resolution to go through the effort of a letter to any body.—Indeed you hardly deserve a letter from me, considering that you have spare hours in which you have nothing to do at all, and yet it was near three months between your two last letters.—

I know not if you heard lately from Gilbert.—I expect him here with me on the latter end of this week.—They are all well, as I heard very lately.—My Mother is returned, now that she has seen my little boy, Francis, fairly set to the world.—I suppose Gilbert has informed you that you have gotten a new Nephew.—He is a fine thriving fellow, & promises to do honor to the Name he bears.—I have named him, Francis Wallace, after my worthy friend Mrs Dunlop of Dunlop.—

The only Ayr-shire news that I remember, in which I think you will be interested is, that Mr Ronald* is bankrupt.—You will easily guess that from his insolent vanity in his sunshine of life, he will now feel a little retaliation from those who thought themselves eclipsed by him, for, poor fellow! I do not think he ever intentionally injured any one.—I might indeed perhaps except his wife, whom he certainly has used very ill; but she is still fond of him to distraction, and bears up wonderfully, much superiour to him, under this most severe shock of Fortune.—Women have a kind of sturdy sufferance which qualifies them to endure beyond, much beyond the common run of Men; but perhaps part of that fortitude is owing to their short-sightedness, as they are by no means famous for seeing remote consequences in all their real importance.—

I am very glad at your resolution of living within your income be that what it will.—Had poor Ronald done so, he had not this day been a prey to the dreadful miseries of Insolvency.—You are at the time of life when those habitudes are begun which are to mark the character of the future Man.—Go on, and persevere; & depend on less or more success.—

All the family have their Compliments to you.—

I am, dear William, your brother
Robt Burns

* Not Ronald of the Bennals as previous editors supposed, but a tobacconist in Mauchline of the same name.

VIII (391)

Ellisland, 10th February 1790

My dear William

I would have written you sooner but I have mislaid Mr Murdoch's* letter, and cannot for my life lay my hand on it; so I cannot write him for want of a Direction.—If I find it afterwards, I will write him & inclose it to you in London.—Now that you are setting out for that place, put on manly resolve, & determine to persevere; & in that case you will less or more be sure of success.—One ot two things allow me to particularize to you.—London swarms with worthless wretches who prey on their fellow-creatures' thoughtlessness or inexperience.—Be cautious in forming connections with comrades and companions.—You can be pretty good company to yourself, & you cannot be too shy of letting any body know you farther than to know you as a Sadler.—Another caution; I give you great credit for your sobriety with respect to that universal vice, Bad Women.—It is an impulse the hardest to be restrained, but if once a man accustoms himself to gratifications of that impulse, it is then nearly or altogether impossible to restrain it.—Whoring is a most ruinous expensive species of dissipation; is spending a poor fellow's money with which he ought clothe & support himself nothing? Whoring has ninety nice chances in a hundred to bring on a man the most nauseous & excrutiating diseases to which Human nature is liable; are disease & an impaired constitution trifling considerations? All this is independant of the criminality of it.—

I have gotten the Excise Division in the middle of which I live.—Poor little Frank is this morning at the height in the Small-pox.—I got him inoculated, & I hope he is in a good way.—

Write me before you leave Newcastle, & as soon as you reach London.—In a word, if ever you be, as perhaps you may be, in a strait for a little ready cash, you know my direction.—I shall not see you beat, while you fight like a Man.—

Farewell! God bless you!
Robt Burns

* John Murdoch, Robert's former teacher, then giving French lessons in London.

IX (400)

Dumfries June Seventh 1790
[*London Bishop mark* JU 10 90]

My dear William

I have scare time to write a line, but as I have an opportunity of a Frank, I shall just write you that line.—I duely received your two letters, but indeed I have been very throng.—I am exeedingly happy to hear of your welfare, & that you are getting rather forward as otherwise.—Let me quote a Couplet of my own to you

"That whether, doing, suffering, or forbearing,
You may do miracles by persevering"*

I shall write you soon, & shall get your shirts forwarded to you.—All your friends in Nithsdale are well, & beg to be remembered to you.—

I am ever, yours
E. Burns

* *Prologue Spoken at the Theatre of Dumfries*, lines 23-4

X (406)

Ellisland, 16th July 1790

My dear William,

I have leisure only for a very short letter, but it will cost you nothing, as I write by a friend going to London.—I have not been able to find Mr Murdoch's address as I have mislaid or lost his letter, but I have found means to write him & to send him your direction, & have desired to send you a card intimating when & where to call for him.—I heard lately from the West, & all friends are well.—I wish much to hear from you.—

I am ever yours
Robt Burns

PETER STUART

Second of three brothers who went to London and made a career in journalism. The eldest, Charles, later turned to playwriting, while Daniel, the youngest, took over the *Morning Post* in 1788 and developed it into the leading centre-Tory paper. Peter was about the same age as Burns, founded the *Oracle* in the mid-1780s and on 3rd May 1788, with partners in the book trade, founded the *Star and Evening Advertiser*, the first regular London evening paper. Peter quarrelled with his partners over the Regency controversy - he championed the Prince of Wales against the Prime Minister - and on 13th February 1789 he and his brother Charles, with James Mackintosh (brother of his fiancee), founded a rival *Star*, later renamed Stuart's *Star and Evening Advertiser*, and later still, the *Morning Star* which ceased publication in the middle of June 1789. Stuart subsequently returned to the *Oracle*, and his defence of Henry Dundas, Lord Melville in that periodical led to a reprimand before the bar of the House of Commons in 1805. Stuart became an ardent admirer of Burns after reading the Kilmarnock Edition and offered Burns a salary as large as his Excise emoluments if he would agree to become a regular contributor. Burns declined, though he agreed to send in occasional pieces, for which Stuart put him on the complimentary list.

I (326A)

[April? 1789?]

My dear Sir,

You may think, and too justly, that I am a selfish ungrateful fellow, having received so many repeated instances of kindness from you, and yet never putting pen to paper to say—thank you; but if you knew what a devil of a lie my conscience has led me on that account, your good heart would think yourself too much avenged. By the by, there is nothing in the whole frame of man which seems to me so unaccountable as that thing called conscience. Had the troublesome yelping cur powers efficient to prevent a mischief, he might be of use; but, at the beginning of the business, his feeble efforts are to the workings of passion as the infant frosts of an autumnal morning to the unclouded fervour of the rising sun: and no sooner are the tumultuous doings of the wicked deed over, than, amidst the bitter native consequences of folly, in the very vortex of our horrors, up starts conscience, and harrows us with the feelings of the d*****.

I have inclosed you, by way of expiation, some verse and prose, that, if they merit a place in your truly entertaining miscellany, you are welcome to. The prose extract is literally as Mr. Sprott sent it me.

The Inscription on the Stone is as follows:

HERE LIES ROBERT FERGUSSON, POET.

Born September 5th, 1751—Died, 16th October 1774.[1]

No sculptur'd marble here, nor pompous lay,
"No storied urn nor animated bust,"[2]
This simple stone directs pale Scotias' way
To pour her sorrows o'er her poet's dust.[3]

On the other side of the Stone is as follows:

"By special grant of the Managers to Robert Burns, who erected this stone, this burial-place is to remain for ever sacred to the memory of Robert Fergusson."

1 Burns misdated the year of Fergusson's birth, (1750).
2 Gray: *Elegy in a Country Churchyard*, line 41, altered.
3 C.W. p. 269.

Peter Stuart

II (328)

Ellisland, near Dumfries
13th April [1789]

[The Printer feels himself exceedingly proud of the receipt of the following Letter; and as it comes from the pen of a *very ingenious Poet,* whose productions are now the delight and admiration of every Reader of Taste, the Printer believes, that the best mode of answering the Author's intentions is by a publication of his sentiments on a subject which appears interesting to his literary reputation.]

Mr. Printer,

I was much surprised last night on being told that some silly verses on the Duchess of Gordon, which had appeared in a late paper of yours, were said to be my composition.—As I am not a Reader of any *London Newspaper,* I have not yet been able to procure a sight of that paper. I know no more of the matter than what a friend of mine, from having slightly glanced over the paragraph, could recollect; but this I know, I am not the author of the verses in question. My friend told me that the Printer himself expressed a doubt whether the poem was mine: I thank you, Sir, for that doubt. A Conductor of another London paper* was not so candid when he lately inserted a disrespectful stanza on the same highly respectable personage, which he, with unqualified assurance, asserted to be mine; though in fact, I never composed a line on the Duchess of Gordon in my life. I have such a sense of what I personally owe to her Grace's benevolent patronage, and such a respect for her exalted character, that I have never yet dared to mention her name in any composition of mine, from a despair of doing justice to my own feelings.

I have been recollecting over the sins and trespasses, peccadilloes and backslidings of myself and my forefathers, to see if I can guess why I am thus visited and punished with this vile calamity [calumny?], to be, at one time, falsely accused of the two most damning crimes, of which, as a man and as a poet, I could have been guilty— INGRATITUDE and STUPIDITY.

I beg of you, Sir, that in your very first paper, you will do justice to my injured character with respect to those verses, falsely said to be mine; and please mention farther that in the Gazeteer and New Daily Advertiser, of March 28, another forgery of the like nature was committed on me, in publishing a disrespectful stanza on the Duchess of Gordon. I have written to the Conductor of that Paper, remonstrating on the injury he has done me; but lest from some motive or other, he should decline giving me that redress I crave, if you will undeceive the Public, by letting them know through the channel of your universally known paper, that I am guiltless of either the one or the other miserable pieces of rhyme, you will much oblige,

Sir, Your very humble servant,
Robert Burns

[The Printer has the happiness of flattering himself with an

assurance of the future correspondence of Mr. Burns, the sublime
flights and inspirations of whose Muse, must raise the reputation of
the first print.]

* *The Gazetteer*, see p. 525.

III (331)

Kilmarnock 25th April

[For a transcription of part of this letter, see Letter XXXVI (335) to
Mrs Dunlop].

IV (338)

Mr. Printer,

I know not who is the author of the following poem, but I think it
contains some equally well-told and just compliments to the
memory of a Matron, who, a few months ago, much against her
private inclinations, left this good world, and twice five good
thousands *per annum* behind her.

We are told, by very respectable authority, that "the *righteous* die,
and none regardeth;"* but as this was by no means the case in point
with the departed beldam, for whose memory I have the honour to
interest myself, it is not easy guessing why prose and verse have both
said so little on the death of the owner of ten thousand a year.

I disike partial respect of persons, and am hurt to see the public
make a fuss when a poor pennyless gipsey is consigned over to Jack
Ketch, and yet scarce take any notice when a purse-proud Priestess
of Mammon is, by the inexorable hand of death, pinioned in everlasting fetters of ill-gotten gold, and delivered up to that arch-brother
among the finishers of the law, emphatically called, by our Bard, the
Hangman of Creation.

Tim Nettle

[Here follows the *Ode Sacred to the Memory of the late Mrs. Oswald
of Auchencruive*]

Dweller in yon dungeon dark,
[C.W. p. 342]

* Not identified, but possibly suggested by Isaiah 57:1.

V (339)

Mr. Printer,

Your goodness oppresses me—

"Talbot's death
"Was woe enough though it had ended there."[1]

Your polite exculpation of me in your paper was enough—the paper
itself is more than I can in decency accept of, as I can do little or
nothing on my part to requite the obligation. For this reason, I am
to be at liberty to resign your favour at pleasure, without any
imputation of little pride or pettish humour.

I have had my usual luck in receiving your paper.—They have all
come to hand except the two which I most wanted, the 17th and

18th, in which I understand my verses are.—So it has been with me always.—A damned Star has almost all my life usurped my zenith, and squinted out the cursed rays of its malign influences, in the strong language of the old Hebrew Seer—"And behold, whatsoever he purposeth, it shall not come to pass; and whatsoever he doth, it shall not prosper."[2]

Any alterations you think necessary in my trifles, make them and welcome. In political principles, I promise you I shall be seldom out of the way; as I could lay down my life for that amiable, gallant, generous fellow, our heir apparent. Allow me to correct the addresses you give me.—I am not R.B. Esq.—No Poet, by statute of Parnassus, has a right, as an author, to assume Esquire, except he has had the honour to dedicate, "by permission," to a Prince, if not to a King; so I am as yet simply, Mr. ROBERT BURNS, at your service.—The preceding are yours, "as you like it."—The Ode is a compliment I paid to that veneralbe votary of iron avarice and sordid pride—the late Mrs. Os[wal]d of Ach[encruive] N[orth] A[yr]shire. The Epitaph is not mine. I must beg of you never to put my name to any thing I send, except where I myself set it down at the head or foot of the piece. I am charmed with your paper. I wish it were more in my power to contribute to it; but over and above a comfortable stock of laziness, of which, or rather *by* which I am possessed, the regions of my fancy are dreadfully subject to baleful east-winds, which, at times, for months together, wither every bud and blossom, and turn the whole into an arid waste. From which evil, good Lord deliver us! Amen!

R.B.

1 Shakespeare: *Romeo and Juliet*, Act III, sc. 2, misquoted.
2 Probably inspired by Isaiah 46:11.

VI (343)

Ellisland, near Dumfries
18th May 1789

[With *Delia*]
[C.W. p. 358]

Mr. Printer,

If the productions of a simple ploughman can merit a place in the same paper with Sylvester Otway, and the other favorites of the Muses who illuminate *The Star* with the lustre of genius, your insertion of the inclosed trifle will be succeeded by future communications from

Yours, &c.,
R. Burns

VII (361)

[late August or early September 1789]

My dear Sir,

The hurry of a farmer in this particular season, and the indolence of a poet at all times and seasons, will, I hope, plead my excuse for neglecting so long to answer your obliging letter of the 5th of August.

Peter Stuart

That you have done well in quitting your laborious concern in ***
[the *Morning Star*] I do not doubt; the weighty reasons you
mention, were, I hope, very, and deservedly indeed, weighty ones,
and your health is a matter of the last importance; but whether the
remaining proprietors of the paper have also done well, is what I
much doubt. The *** [*Morning Star*], so far as I was a reader,
exhibited such a brilliancy of point, such an elegance of paragraph,
and such a variety of intelligence, that I can hardly conceive it
possible to continue a daily paper in the same degree of excellence;
but if there was a man who had abilities equal to the task, that man's
assistance the proprietors have lost.

*　　　*　　　*

When I received your letter, I was transcribing for *** [the *Morning
Star*]. my letter to the magistrates of the Canongate, Edinburgh,
begging their permission to place a tomb-stone over poor Fergusson,
and their edict in consequence of my petition, but now I shall send
them to *** [the *Oracle*?]. Poor Fergusson! If there be a life
beyond the grave, which I trust there is; and if there be a good God
presiding over all nature, which I am sure there is; thou art now
enjoying existence in a glorious world, where worth of the heart
alone is distinction in the man; where riches, deprived of all their
pleasure-purchasing powers, return to their native sordid matter;
where titles and honours are the disregarded reveries of an idle
dream; and where the heavy virtue, which is the negative
consequences of steady dulness, and those thoughtless, though often
destructive follies, which are the unavoidable aberrations of frail
human nature, will be thrown into equal oblivion as if they had
never been!

Adieu, my dear Sir! So soon as your present views and schemes are
concentred in an aim, I shall be glad to hear from you; as your
welfare and happiness is by no means a subject indifferent to

Yours, &c.

THE LONDON GAZETTEER
AND NEW DAILY ADVERTISER

The 28th March 1789 issue of this newspaper contained the following quatrain attributed to Burns:

> Her Grace was mucklest of them aw,
> Like Saul, she tower the tribes aboon;
> Her gawn was whiter than the snaw,
> Her face was redder than the moon.

The following letter remonstrated with the editor who admitted to having lifted these lines from the *Star*. Burns subsequently complained to Peter Stuart in similar vein (see page 521). This episode is of particular interest as showing Burns's attitude towards his reputation as well as his loyalty to his patrons.

(327)

Ellisland near Dumfries
10th April 1789

Sir,

By accident I met with your Paper of March the 28th, in which there are four disrespectful lines on the Duchess of Gordon, that you tell us are the composition of "Mr. Burns, the ploughing poet;" who, as you at the same time remind the world, "owes much of his good fortune to her Grace's patronage." I am that Burns, Sir; and I affirm that the wretched Stanza in question is not mine, nor do I know any thing of the Author.—It is indeed true, that I have the honour to be deeply indebted to the Duchess of Gordon's goodness, and for that reason I now write to you: had you only forged dullness on me, I should not have thought it worth while to reply: but to add ingratitude too, is what I cannot in silence bear. In justice to the private character of a man, which must suffer much by your injurious imputation, allow me, Sir, to insist on your retracting your assertion, of my being the Author of those verses.

I am, Sir, Your injured humble servant,
Robert Burns

[Note by the Editor of *The Gazetteer:*

'Mr. Burns will do right in directing his petulance to the proper delinquent, the Printer of *The Star*, from which Paper the Stanza was literally copied into the Gazetteer. We can assure him, however, for his comfort, that the Duchess of Gordon acquits him both of the ingratitude and the dullness. She has, with much difficulty, discovered that the *Jeu d' Esprit* was written by the Right honourable the Treasurer of the Navy*, on her Grace's dancing at a ball given by the Earl of Findlater; this has been found out by the industry and penetration of Lord Fife. The lines are certainly not so dull as Mr. Burns insinuates, and we fear he is jealous of the poetical talents of his rival, Mr. Dundas.']

* Henry Dundas, later Viscount Melville.

JAMES HAMILTON

A grocer with premises at 86 Trongate Glasgow, he communicated with Burns over the purchase of copies of the poems of Gavin Turnbull, the Kilmarnock poet and actor. The second letter, dated 26th May 1789, hints at misfortunes which had befallen Hamilton, and from the fact that his name disappeared from the Glasgow directory about this time it is inferred that they were of a business nature.

I (332)

Ellisland near Dumfries, 27th April 1789

My dear Sir,

I have written twice to my brother Poet, Mr Turnbull, but as I have not had a word in return from him, I suspect that he has left Glasgow.—I owe him some money for copies of his poems.—He sent me 6; one of them I had paid before, and one of them is still on hand; so the price of four is ready for him, if he will authorise any body in Dumfries to recieve it; or, as I shall be in Mauchline at Whitsunday or thereabouts, I shall then send it to you by John Ronald, for I am not acquainted with any of the Carriers in this country.—

This country has nothing new.—Mankind are the same every where.— In this place, as in Glasgow I suppose too, of the men called honest, and the women called chaste, a number supposed to be near the full half of them are not what they pretend to be; and of the remaining half, many of them are thought to have still worse faults.—My Rib begs her compliments to you.—I am, Dear Sir, yours sincerely

Robt Burns

II (345)

Ellisland, 26th May 1789

R. Burns Dr to G. Turnbull for 5 copies of his Poems @ 2/6 pr. o : 12 : 6

Dear Sir,

I send you by John Glover Carrier the above account for Mr Turnbull, as I suppose you know his address.—

I would fain offer, my dear Sir, a word of sympathy with your misfortunes; but it is a tender string, & I know not how to touch it. —It is easy to flourish a set of high flown sentiments on the subject that would give great satisfaction to—a breast quite at ease; but as ONE observes, who was very seldom mistaken in the theory of life, "The heart knoweth its own sorrows, & a stranger intermeddleth not therewith."*—

Among some distressful emergencies that I have experienced in life, I ever laid this down as my foundation of comfort—"THAT HE WHO HAS LIVED THE LIFE OF AN HONEST MAN, HAS BY NO MEANS LIVED IN VAIN!"

With every wish for your welfare & future success,

I am, My dear Sir, sincerely yours
Robt Burns

* Proverbs 14:10, altered.

526

REV. PATRICK CARFRAE

Born in 1742, he was educated at Edinburgh University and ordained minister of Morham, near Haddington in 1766, moving to Dunbar in 1795 and receiving a doctorate of divinity in the latter year. He remained at Dunbar till he retired in 1820 and died two years later. His account of Morham parish appears in the first *Statistical Account of Scotland*, and he was involved in the preparation for publication of James Mylne's poems, referred to in the following letter. Mrs Dunlop (who was one of Carfrae's parishioners at Morham) and Burns were both subscribers to Mylne's poems. Unlike many of his contemporaries, who preached extempore, Carfrae preferred to read from prepared scripts, a habit which earned him the nickname of Paper Pate.

(333)

Ellisland, 27th April—1789

Reverend Sir,

I do not recollect that I have ever felt a severer pang of conscious shame, than when I just now looked at the date of your oblidging letter which accompanied Mr Mylne's excellent Poem*.—I could make a great many apologies, Sir; & some of them, very plausible ones; but none of them would exculpate me to *myself*, so I do not wish they should satisfy *you*.—I am much to blame: the honor Mr Mylne did me, greatly enhanced in value by the endearing though melancholly circumstance of its being the last production of his truly amiable Muse, deserved a better return.—

I have, as you hint, thought of sending a copy of the Poem to some Periodical Publication; but on farther reflection, I am afraid, in the present case, that it would be an improper step.—My success, perhaps as much accidental as merited, has brought an innundation of nonsense over the Land.—Subscription bills for Scots Poems have so dunned and do daily so dun the Public, that the very term, Scots Poetry, totters on the brink of contempt.—For these reasons, if publishing in magazines, &c. any of Mr Mylne's Poems, be at all prudent, in my opinion it should certainly not be a Scots Poem.— The profits of the labours of a Man of genius are, I hope, at least as honorable as nay other profits whatever; and Mr Mylne's relations are most justly entitled to that honest harvest which Fate has denied himself to reap.—But let the friends of Mr Mylne's fame, among whom I crave the honor of ranking myself, always keep in eye his respectability as a Man, and as a Poet; and take no measure that, before the World knows any thing of his character, would risk his name & Productions being classed with the fools & nonsense of the times.—

I have, Sir, some experience of publishing; and the way in which I would proceed with Mr Mylne's Poems is this.—I would publish in two or three English & Scots Public Papers, any one of his English Poems which should, by private judges, be thought the most excellent, and mention it, at the same time, as one of many poetical productions which a Lothian Farmer of respectable character left behind him at his death.—That his friends had it in idea to publish soon, by subscription, a Collection of his Poems, for the sake of his numerous family (I think Mrs Dunlop informed me that he had a numerous family)—not in pity to that Family, but in justice to what his friends think the Poetic Merits of the deceased; and to secure in the most effectual manner, to those tender connections whose right it is, the pecuniary reward of those merits.—After thus advertising the Public of the design, I would proceed to disperse Subscription bills.—Suppose the book to be 200, a few odd pages, and that there are printed, 600 copies.—This, on elegant paper, & stitched, or in boards, will be done for less than forty pounds.—Though not above 300 Subscribers are got, that at 4sh. or even at 3sh. per Copy price to Subscribers, will more than pay costs; and thus, without risking any thing and with a probability of considerable profits as the work should succeed in the world, I would bring Mr Mylne's poetic Merits to that Bar which is alone competent to decide on them, the VOICE OF THE PUBLIC.—

From what I have seen of his works, & from what an abler Judge, my honored friend Mrs Dunlop, has often mentioned to me of those works of his which I have not seen, I have the Most sanguine hopes that Mr Mylne's Poems will be a very respectable & much esteemed addition to that species of Polite Literature.—

I expect to be in Haddingtonshire sometime in the coming summer, & if then, or at any time prior or subsequent to then, my information or assistance can be of help in the business, employing me in it will be giving a real pleasure to, Reverend Sir,

your oblidged humble servant
Robt Burns

My direction is—Mr R.B.
Ellisland near Dumfries

* John Mylne: *To Mr Burns, on his Poems.*

JANE BLAIR McMURDO

Born in 1749, the daughter of Provost Blair of Dumfries, she was the sister of Mrs de Peyster and wife of John McMurdo, chamberlain at Drumlanrig. She was alluded to in the *Election Ballad* of 1790 (C.W. p. 402). She died in 1836.

(334)

[Ellisland, 2nd May 1789]

Madam

I have finished the [*word illegible*] Piece which had the happy fortune to be honored with your approbation; & never did little Miss shew her applauded Sampler with more [*word illegible*] sparkling pleasure to partial Maman, than I now send my Poem* to you & Mr Mcmurdo, if he is returned to Drumlanrig.—You cannot easily imagine what thin-skinned animals, what sensitive plants, poor Poets are.—How do we shrink into the embittered corner of self-abasement, when neglected or condemned by those to whom we look up! and how do we, in erect importance, add another cubit to our stature, on being noticed & applauded by those whom we honor & respect! My late visit to Drumlanrig has, I can tell you, Madam, given me a balloon waft up Parnassus, where on my fancied elevation I regard my Poetic self with no small degree of complacency.—Surely, with all their sins, the rhyming tribe are not ungrateful creatures. I recollect your goodness to your humble guest—I see Mr Mcmurdo adding to the politeness of the Gentleman the kindness of a Friend, and my heart swells as it would burst, with warm emotions and ardent wishes! It may be it is not gratitude; it may be a mixed sensation. That strange, shifting, doubling animal MAN is so generally, at best, but a negative, often a worthless, creature, that we cannot see real goodness and native worth without feeling the bosom glow with sympathetic approbation.

With every sentiment of grateful respect,
I have the honor to be, Madam,
Your obliged and grateful humble Servant
Robt Burns

* Probably *To John McMurdo, Esq., of Drumlanrig* (C.W. p. 356).

THE BELFAST NEWS-LETTER

The following note accompanied a copy of *Delia* (C.W. p. 358) which allegedly Burns sent for publication. The poem was published in the issue of 3rd June 1789, and was reprinted by James Dewar in his *Tribute to the Memory of Robert Burns*, published at Belfast in 1893. From the close similarity of the wording in the note accompanying the same poem to Peter Stuart on the same date, it has been surmised that the Belfast paper lifted this material from Stuart's *Morning Star* (see page 523). No manuscript to confirm or rebut this theory, however, exists.

Ellisland, near Dumfries,
18th May 1789.

To the Printer,

Sir,—If the production of a simple plough-boy can merit a corner in your paper, your insertion of the enclosed trifle will be succeeded by future communications from

Yours, &c.,
R. Burns

JOHN McAULEY

Town clerk of Dumbarton at the time of Burns's west Highland tour in 1787.
It is thought that Burns stayed with McAuley at his home, Levengrove House
(now demolished but sited in what is now Levengrove Park). McAuley
obtained a number of subscriptions for the first Edinburgh Edition. Nothing
else is known about him, except that he died in 1799.

(346)

[Ellisland] 4th June 1789

Dear Sir,

Though I am not without my fears respecting my fate, at that grand, universal inquest of right and wrong, commonly called *The Last Day*, yet I trust there is one sin, which that arch vagabond, Satan, who I understand is to be king's evidence, cannot throw in my teeth, I mean ingratitude. There is a certain pretty large quantum of kindness for which I remain, and, from inability, I fear must still remain, your debtor; but, though unable to repay the debt, I assure you, Sir, I shall ever warmly remember the obligation. It gives me the sincerest pleasure to hear, by my old acquaintance, Mr Kennedy, that you are, in immortal Allan's language, "Hale and weel, and living;" and that your charming family are well, and promising to be an amiable and respectable addition to the company of performers, whom the Great Manager of the Drama of Man is bringing into action for the succeeding age.

With respect to my welfare, a subject in which you once warmly and effectively interested yourself, I am here in my old way, holding my plough, marking the growth of my corn, or the health of my dairy; and at times sauntering by the delightful windings of the Nith, on the margin of which I have built my humble domicile, praying for seasonable weather, or holding an intrigue with the muses, the only gipseys with whom I have now any intercourse. As I am entered into the holy state of matrimony, I trust my face is turned completely Zion-ward; and as it is a rule with all honest fellows to repeat no grievances, I hope that the little poetic licences of former days will of course fall under the oblivious influence of some good-natured statute of celestial proscription. In my family devotion; which, like a good presbyterian, I occasionally give to my household folks, I am extremely fond of the psalm, "Let not the errors of my youth,"[1] &c. and that other, "Lo, children are God's heritage,"[2] &c. in which last Mrs. Burns, who, by the by, has a glorious "wood-note wild" at either old song or psalmody, joins me with the pathos of Handel's Messiah . . .

1 Metrical Psalms 25:7.
2 Ibid. 127:3.

531

HELEN MARIA WILLIAMS

Born in 1762 in London, she spent her formative years in Berwick-upon-Tweed before settling in the metropolis where she worked for Dr Moore as his amanuensis while dabbling in poetry herself. In 1790 she moved to Paris where she supported the Girondist faction. For this partisanship she was imprisoned until the downfall and death of Robespierre. Later she condemned the Revolution and espoused the Bourbon cause. Her novel *Julia* was published in 1790 and later she translated Bernardin de St. Pierre's romantic tragedy *Paul et Virginie* into English. She also wrote several volumes on France, and died at Paris in 1827. The following letter thanked Miss Williams for the sonnet which she had composed in his honour, after reading *To a Mountain Daisy* (C.W. p. 203). This had been sent to Burns by Dr Moore and on hearing of Burns's approval of it, she had replied that 'a much less portion of applause' from him would have been gratifying. With her letter she enclosed a much more ambitious poem entitled *The Slave Trade*, which had been published in 1788. In writing to her, Burns went to extraordinary lengths to give her 'a few strictures' on her poem, ending that 'my conscience tells me that for once in my life I have acted up to the duties of a Christian in doing as I would be done by.'

(353B)

[Ellisland, late July or early August] 1789

Madam,

Of the many problems in the nature of that wonderful creature, Man, this is one of the most extraordinary, that he shall go on from day to day, from week to week, from month to month, or perhaps from year to year, suffering a hundred times more in an hour from the impotent consciousness of neglecting what he ought to do, than the very doing of it would cost him. I am deeply indebted to you, first for a most elegant poetic compliment; then for a polite, obliging letter; and, lastly, for your excellent poem on the Slave-Trade;* and yet, wretch that I am! though the debts were debts of honour, and the creditor a lady, I have put off and put off even the very acknowledgment of the obligation, until you must indeed be the very angel I take you for, if you can forgive me.

Your poem I have read with the highest pleasure. I have a way, whenever I read a book, I mean a book in our own trade, Madam, a poetic one, and when it is my own property, that I take a pencil and mark at the ends of verses, or note on margins and odd paper, little criticisms of approbation or disapprobation as I peruse along. I will make no apology for presenting you with a few unconnected thoughts that occurred to me in my repeated perusals of your poem. I want to shew you that I have honesty enough to tell you what I take to be truths, even when they are not quite on the side of approbation; and I do it in the firm faith that you have equal greatness of mind to hear them with pleasure.

I had lately the honour of a letter from Dr. Moore, where he tells me that he has sent me some books. They are not yet come to hand, but I hear they are on the way.

Wishing you all success in your progress in the path of fame; and that you may equally escape the danger of stumbling through incautious speed, or losing ground through loitering neglect.

I have the honour to be, &c.

* *A Poem on the Bill Lately Passed for Regulating the Slave Trade*, (London 1788).

Helen Maria Williams

[Enclosed with the foregoing letter]

A few strictures on Miss Williams Poem on the Slave trade—I know very little of scientific criticism, so all I can pretend to in that intricate art is merely to note as I read along, what passages strike me as being uncommonly beautiful, & where the expression seems to me perplexed or faulty.—

The Poem opens finely.—There are none of these idle prefatory lines which one may skip over before one comes to the subject.—Verses ninth & tenth in particular

> Where Ocean's unseen bound
> Leaves a drear world of waters round—

are truly beautiful.—The simile of the hurricane is likewise fine; & indeed, beautiful as the Poem is, almost all the similes rise decidedly above it.—From verse 31st to verse 50th is a pretty eulogy on Britain.—Verse 36th—that foul drama deep with wrong, is nobly expressive.—Verse 46th I am afraid is rather unworthy of the rest: "to dare to feel," is an idea that I do not altogether like. The contrast of valour & mercy, from the 46th verse to the 50th is admirable.—

Either my apprehension is dull, or there is something a little confused in the apostrophe to Mr Pit.—Verse 55th is the antecedent to verses 57th & 58th but in verse 58th the connection seems ungrammatical.—

> —Powers. . . . .
> . . . .
> With no gradations mark'd their flight,
> But *rose* at once to glory's height—

ris'n should surely be the word instead of *rose*. Try it in Prose:—Powers,—their flight marked by no gradations, but these same powers $^{risen}_{rose}$ at once to the height of glory.—Likewise, verse 53rd "For this!" is evidently meant to lead on the sense of verses 59th, 60th, 61st, & 62nd, but let us try how the thread of connection runs.

> For this! . . . .
> . . . .
> The deeds of Mercy, that embrace
> A distant sphere, an alien race,
> Shall Virtue's lips record, and claim
> The fairest honors of thy name!

I beg pardon if I misapprehend the matter, but this appears to me the most if not the only imperfect passage in the Poem.—The comparison of the sunbeam is fine.—

The compliment to the Duke of Richmond is, I hope, as just as it is certainly elegant. The thought—

Helen Maria Williams

"Virtue . . .
. . . .
—lends, from her unsullied source,
The gems of thought their purest force"

—is exceedingly beautiful.—The idea, from verse 81st, to the 85th, that the "blest decree" is like the beams of morning ushering in the glorious day of liberty, ought not to pass unnoticed nor unapplauded. —From verse 85th to verse 108th is an animated contrast between the unfeeling selfishness of the Oppressor, on the one hand, & the misery of the captive on the other.—Verse 88th might perhaps be amended, thus—"Nor ever *quit* her narrow maze"—we are said to *pass* a bound, but we *quit* a maze. Verse 100th is exquisitely beautiful

—They, whom wasted blessings tire—

Verse 110th is, I doubt, a clashing of metaphors: to load a span, is, I am afraid, an unwarrantable expression. ["Cast the universe in (*deleted*)] In verse 114th "Cast the universe in shade, " is a fine idea. —From the 115th verse to the 142nd is a striking description of the wrongs of the poor African.—Verse 120th "The load of unremitted pain," is a remarkable strong expression.

The address to the advocates for abolishing the slave-trade, from verse 143d to verse 208th is animated with the true life of Genius.— The picture of Oppression—

"While she links her impious chain,
And calculates the price of pain,
Weighs Agony in sordid scales,
And marks if Death or Life prevails"—

is nobly executed.

What a tender idea is in verse 180th! indeed that whole description of Home may vie with Thomson's description of Home, somewhere in the beginning of his Autumn.—I do not remember to have seen a stronger expression of misery than is contained in these verses

"Condemn'd, severe extreme, to live
When all is fled that life can give!"—

the comparison of our distant joys to distant objects is equally original & striking.

The character & manners of the dealer in this infernal traffic is a well done though a horrid picture.—I am not sure how far introducing the Sailor, was right; for though the Sailor's common characteristic is generosity, yet in this case his is certainly not only an unconcerned witness but in some degree an efficient agent in the business.—Verse 224 is a nervous [*words torn out*] expressive—"The heart convulsive anguish breaks."

The description of the captive wretch when he arrives in the West Indies is carried on with equal spirit.—The thought that the Oppressor's sorrow on seeing his slave pine, is like the butcher's regret when his destined lamb dies a natural death, is exceedingly fine.—

I am got so much into the cant of criticism, that I begin to be afraid lest I have nothing except the cant of it; and instead of elucidating my Author, am only benighting myself.—For this reason, I will not pretend to go through the whole Poem. Some few remaining beautiful lines, however, I cannot pass over.—Verse 280, is the strongest description of selfishness I ever saw; the comparison in verses 285 & 286, is new & fine; and the line, "Your alms to Penury ye lend," is excellent.—

In verse 317, Like, should surely be As, or, So: for instance—

> "His sway the harden'd bosom leads
> To Cruelty's remorseless deeds;
> As (or So) the blue lightning when it springs
> With fury on its livid wings,
> Darts to the goal with rapid force,
> Nor heeds that ruin marks its course."—

If you insert the word, Like, where I have placed, As, you must alter, Darts, to, Darting, &, Heeds, to, Heeding, in order to make it grammar. A Tempest, is a favorite subject with the Poets, but I do not remember any thing, even in Thomson's Winter, superiour to your verses from the 344th to the 351st.—Indeed that last Simile, beginning with, Fancy may dress &c. & ending with the 350th verse, is, in my opinion, the most beautiful passage in the whole Poem.—it would do honor to the greatest names that ever graced our Profession.—

I will not beg your pardon, Madam, for these strictures, as my conscience tells me that for once in my life I have acted up to the duties of a Christian in doing as I would be done by.—

DAVID SILLAR

Born in 1760, the third son of Patrick Sillar of Spittalside near Lochlea, he was largely self-educated. He was appointed interim teacher at Tarbolton parish school, but failed to get the permanent post, awarded to John 'Dr Hornbook' Wilson instead. He then founded a school of his own, but this proved unsuccessful. Even in affairs of the heart he was something of a failure, for his engagement to Peggy Orr was broken off and she later married an Edinburgh shoemaker. In 1783 he moved to Irvine where he had a go at the grocery business but this led to bankruptcy. Nothing daunted, he then founded a school for navigation and later inherited a fortune from the death of an uncle, a partner in the Liverpool mercantile house of Sillar and Henderson. Prosperous at last, he served for some years on Irvine burgh council. Sillar was a versifier himself, although not in the same class as Burns, and he tried to emulate Burns's success in 1789 when his own volume of poems was published at Kilmarnock by the self-same John Wilson. It has been alleged that Sillar resented Burns's success where he himself failed, but it should be noted that he was one of the first subscribers to the Burns monument at Alloway and was a founder-member of Irvine Burns Club in 1826, three years before his death. Sillar was the recipient of two verse epistles from Burns (C.W. pp. 86 and 213), composed in January 1785 and June-July 1796 respectively. Burns took a lively interest in the publication of his brother poet (I-II) but when Sillar went bankrupt in 1791, all Burns could offer was sympathy (III).

I (355)

Ellisland near Dumfries, 5th August 1789

My dear Sir,

I was half in thoughts not to have written you at all, by way of revenge for the two d-mn'd business letters you sent me.—I wanted to know all and about your Publication, what were your views, your hopes, fears, &c. &c. in commencing Poet in Print—in short, I wanted you to write to Robin like his old acquaintance, Davie; and not in the style of Mr Tare, to Mr Tret—

Mr. Tret,
Sir,
this comes to advise you that your fifteen barrels of herrings were, by the blessing of God, shipped safe on board the Lovely Janet, Q.D.C. Duncan Mcleerie Master, &c. &c. &c.—

I hear you have commenced, Married Man; so much the better, though perhaps your Muse may not fare the better for it.—I know not whether the NINE GIPSEYS are jealous of my Lucky, but they are a good deal shyer since I could boast the important relation of Husband.—

I have got I think about eleven Subscribers for you.—My acquaintance in this place is yet but very limited else I might have had more. —When you send Mr Auld in Dumfries his, you may with them pack me eleven; should I need more, I can write you, should these be too many, they can be returned.—My best Compliments to Mrs Sillar; and believe me to be, Dear David,

Ever yours
Robt Burns

II (384)

Ellisland, 22nd January 1790

My dear Friend

Inclosed I send you £2-4s the price of eleven copies of your Poems which I got.—I have been much pleased with them, & I hope you will find your account in the business.—I would write you a long letter, but the bearer is in a devil of a hurry, & I am in another.—I beg you

536

David Sillar

will let me know how the work has turned out.—

With my best Compliments to Mrs Sillar

I am, my dear Davie yours sincerely
Robt Burns

III (461)

[Early summer 1791]

My dear Sir,

I am extremely sorry to hear of your misfortune, & the more so, as it is not in my power to give you any assistance.—I am just five shillings rich at present; tho' I was considerably richer three days ago, when I was obliged to pay twenty pounds for a man* who took me in, to save a rotten credit.—I heedlessly gave him my name on the back of a bill wherein I had no concern, & he gave me the bill to pay.—To write you a long letter, of news, &c. would but insult your present unfortunate feelings: I trust your many rich & powerful friends will enable you to get clear of that flinty-hearted scoundrel, whose name I detest.—

Yours
Robt Burns

---

* Alexander Crombie of Dumfries. See letters of Burns to James Gracie (p. 582) and Thomas Boyd (p. 513) concerning this matter.

ALEXANDER FERGUSSON OF CRAIGDARROCH

Born about 1746, a descendant of Annie Laurie, he was Laird of Craigdarroch, a lawyer by profession and a Justice of the Peace for Dumfriesshire. He married Deborah, daughter of Robert Cutlar of Arroland, Kirkcudbrightshire. Fergusson was a prominent Freemason, and was present on that memorable occasion in Edinburgh when Burns was hailed as Caledonia's Bard. Fergusson was noted for his prowess as a hard drinker, winning the drinking contest immortalised by Burns in *The Whistle* (C.W. p. 368). On that occasion Fergusson downed 'upwards of five bottles of claret'. William Hunter, one of the servants at Friars' Carse, later testified that 'When the gentlemen were put to bed, Burns walked home, without any assistance, not being the worse for drink' — yet another piece of evidence refuting the *canard* about Burns being a heavy drinker, in an age when excessive alcoholic consumption was widespread. Fergusson died in 1796, in his fiftieth year. Burns wrote the following, however, strictly on a legal matter but showed characteristic compassion.

(364)

Globe Inn, Noon, Wednesday
[October? 1789]

Blessed be he that kindly doth
The poor man's case consider.*

I have sought you all over the town, good Sir, to learn what you have done, or what can be done, for poor Robie Gordon. The hour is at hand when I must assume the execrable office of whipper-in to the bloodhounds of justice, and must, must let loose the ravenous rage of the carrion sons of bitches on poor Robie. I think you can do something to save the unfortunate man, and I am sure, if you can, you will. I know that Benevolence is supreme in your bosom, and has the first voice in, and the last check on, all you do; but that insidious whore Politics may seduce the honest cully Attention until the practicable moment of doing good is no more.

I have the honor to be, Sir,
your obliged, humble servant,
Robt Burns

* Metrical Psalms 41:1, misquoted.

538

ALEXANDER FINDLATER

Born at Burntisland in 1754, the son of the Rev. Thomas Findlater, minister of Linton, Peeblesshire, he entered the Excise in 1774 and was appointed Examiner in June 1790. In April 1791 he became Supervisor at Dumfries, and six years later was promoted to General Supervisor at Edinburgh. In 1811 he succeeded William Corbet as Collector at Glasgow and remained there until he retired in 1825. He died in 1839, having lived long enough to be able to rebut some of the *canards* about Burns published by 'Honest Allan' Cunningham in 1834. At an earlier date (1815) he had also refuted the calumnies of Heron, Currie and other early biographers, in a long letter to Alexander Peterkin who reprinted it in his edition of Currie's *Life and Works of Burns* published that year. Findlater was in an excellent position to know Burns well. He had been Supervisor at Dumfries for about six months when the poet moved into the town, but it seems that he had known him in an official capacity prior to that time. This is borne out by the following correspondence, which begins with a letter from Ellisland about October 1789, and it is obvious from (II) that Findlater had given a good account of the poet to Corbet. A close friendship developed between the two men and Burns was in the habit of sending parcels of new-laid eggs to his superior - a custom alluded to in the verse-epistle commencing 'Dear Sir, our Lucky humbly begs . . .' (C.W. p. 378) and a brief note (III) about February 1790. Subsequent notes and letters often accompanied poems and songs, but friendship did not blunt Findlater's scrutiny of Burns's work (V). When Findlater was ill for some months in 1794-5 Burns was appointed Acting Supervisor in his place. Findlater also defended Burns at the enquiry of December 1792 into his loyalty and efficiency.

I (364A)

Ellisland, Thursday morning—
[October? 1789]

I do not recollect, Sir, whether 'twas you who promised me, or I who requested you, to take the trouble of a letter to a friend of mine in Glasgow; but I remember it *was* mentioned, and you obligingly said you would do it.—Any Porter knows where to find Mr George Lockhart.—I have farther presumed on your goodness, & have written my friend that if he has leisure to send me an epistle & will wait on you with it, that you will take charge of it.

That you may have a safe journey, & a happy meeting with that dearest of all connections, your fireside circle, is the sincere wish of,

Sir,
your obliged humble servant
Robt Burns

II (366A)

Ellisland, 28th October 1789

Sir

I believe I mentioned something to you yesternight of the character that Mr Corbet told me you had given of me to our Edinburgh Excise folks, but my conscience accuses me that I did not make the proper acknowledgements to you for your Goodness.—Most sincerely & gratefully do I thank you, Sir, for this uncommon instance of kindness & friendship.—

I mean not by this as if I would propitiate your future inspection of my conduct.—No, Sir; I trust to act, and I *shall* act, so as to defy Scrutiny; but I send this as a sheer tribute of Gratitude to a Gentleman whose goodness has laid me under very great obligations, and for whose character *as* a GENTLEMAN I have the highest esteem.—It may very probably never be in my power to repay, but it is equally out of my power to forget, the obligations you have laid on,

Sir, your deeply indebted & very humble servant
Robt Burns

Alexander Findlater

III (393)

[Ellisland] Saturday Morn:

Dear Sir,

Mrs B——, like a true good wife, looking on my taste as a Standard, &
knowing that she cannot give me any thing— *eatable*—more agreable
than a new-laid egg, she begs your acceptance of a few.—

They are all of them *Couch*; not thirty hours out.—

I am, Dear Sir, your oblidged humble servant
Robt Burns

IV (414)

Sending a letter to Captain Grose, & being at a loss for his direction,
I inclosed it to Mr Cardonnel* of the customs in Edinburgh who is
acquainted with the Captain's motions & is like himself a profound
Antiquarian. On the inside of the cover I wrote to Cardonnel
extempore & anonymous the following lines, alluding to an old Song
"Heard ye e'er of Sir John Malcolm,

"Igo & ago"
Ken ye ought o' Captain Grose?
[C.W. p. 415]

* Adam de Cardonnel Lawson, author of works on Scottish antiquities.

V (460)

Sunday even:
[June, 1791]

Dear Sir,

I am both much surprised & vexed at that accident of Lorimer's
Stock.—The last survey I made prior to Mr Lorimer's going to
Edinburgh I was very particular in my inspection & the quantity was
certainly in his possession as I stated it.—The surveys I have made
during his absence might as well have been marked *"key absent"* as I
never found any body but the lady, who I know is not mistress of
keys, &c. to know any thing of it, and one of the times it would
have rejoiced all Hell to have seen her so drunk.—I have not surveyed
there since his return.—I know the gentleman's ways are, like the
grace of God, past all comprehension; but I shall give the house a
severe scrutiny tomorrow morning, & send you in the naked facts.—I
know, Sir, & regret deeply, that this business glances with a malign
aspect on my character as an Officer; but as I am really innocent in
the affair, & as the gentleman is known to be an illicit Dealer, &
particularly as this is the *single* instance of the least shadow of
carelessness or impropriety in my conduct as an Officer, I shall be
peculiarly unfortunate if my character shall fall a sacrifice to the
dark maneouvres of a Smuggler.*—

I am, Sir, your oblidged & obedient humble servant
Robt Burns

I send you some rhymes I have just finished which tickle my fancy a
little.—

* William Lorimer, father of Chloris.

Alexander Findlater

VI (561A)

[In a copy of Thomson's *A Select Collection of Original Scotish Airs*, early May 1793]

A pledge of rooted Friendship, well watered with many a bottle of good WINE—

Robt Burns

VII (601)

Nanie Welsh's Ep 4*

Dear Findlater,

Will you give & receive happiness—both very pleasant business—some bets of wine are to use up—you will find Messrs Simm, Hyslop, & a stranger to whom you will like to be known—COME!!!

R.B.

* Previous editors have been mystified by this endorsement. My reading of it is Evg 4, i.e. 4 p.m..

VIII (615)

[Dumfries, February 1794]

Sir,

Inclosed are the two schemes. I would not have troubled you with the collector's one, but for suspicion lest it be not right. Mr Erskine promised me to make it right, if you will have the goodness to shew him how. As I have no copy of the scheme for myself, and the alterations being very considerable from what it was formerly, I hope that I shall have access to this scheme I send you, when I come to face up to my new books. *So much for schemes.*—And that no scheme to betray a FRIEND, or mislead a STRANGER; to seduce a YOUNG GIRL, or rob a HEN-ROOST; to subvert LIBERTY, or bribe an EXCISEMAN; to disturb the GENERAL ASSEMBLY, or annoy a GOSSIPPING; to overthrow the credit of ORTHODOXY, or the authority of OLD SONGS; to oppose *your wishes*, or frustrate *my hopes*—MAY PROSPER—is the sincere wish and prayer of

Robt Burns

IX (639)

[September 1794]

My dear Sir,

This is the second letter of at least *my directing* which you will receive by this day's post.—I have been among the Angelic World, this forenoon.—Ah!

"had ye but been whare I hae been,
"Ye wad hae been sae canty, O!"[1]

But don't be afraid: I did not dare to touch the ark of the Covenant; nor even to cast a prophane eye to the mercy-seat, where it is hid among the feathered Cherubim.—I am in the clouds elsewhere—

Alexander Findlater

"Ah, Chloris, could I now but sit
"As unconcerned as when
"Your infant beauty could beget
"Nor happiness nor pain"[2] —

Let Yesternight—Oh yesternight!

"Kist yestreen—kist yestreen—
"O as she was kist yestreen—
"I'll never forget while the hollin grows green,
"The bonie sweet Lassie I kist yestreen."[3] —

I am truly sorry that God has not given you taste enough to relish Rothemurche's Strathspey, else I would tell you over some verses I have begun to it.

Chorus—(to the first part of the air)

Lassie wi' the lint-white locks,

[C.W. p. 528]

By the bye, I have not been able to please myself with verses to—"We'll gang nae mair to yon town"—but I have pledged myself to give to the fair Aracdian, the original verses on her—

Sylvia
"Thine am I, my Celia fair"[4] —
Cloe
Lesbia

1 *Killiecrankie.*
2 From Sir Charles Sedley's *The Mulberry Garden* in Ramsay's *Tea-Table Miscellany*, Vol. I.
3 Altered from Herd's *Ancient and Modern Scottish Songs*, 226 (Edinburgh 1776).
4 *Thine am I, my Chloris fair*, C.W. p. 505.

ROBERT MOORE

The following note is the sole surviving example of Burns's dealings with the general public in his capacity as an Excise officer. It is interesting to note that Moore's transgression arose over the manufacture of bricks - a craft which was relatively new to Scotland. In fact it was James Maxwell of Kirkconnell, father of Dr William Maxwell, who imported this technology to Scotland in the 1750's following his return from Jacobite exile in France. Kirkconnell House near Dumfries in now the oldest brick-built house in Scotland, having been built by James Maxwell of bricks manufactured on the spot, from local clay deposits.

(366)

26th October 1789

Robert Moore in Dumfries I hereby intimate to you that by decreet of the Justices of the Peace for the County of Dumfries you are fined in the sum of 1£ Ster. for making bricks without entry—and if the said sum be not paid within 14 days from this date you will incur an additional expence of 2d on each 1 sh. Sterling.

Robt Burns

DAVID NEWALL

A Dumfries lawyer in whose house at the Isle Burns and Jean lodged while Ellisland was being built. He came from a very old Dumfries family whose name frequently occurs in the burgh records. He practised law in the town and became Procurator Fiscal, but also speculated in property and developed parts of Dumfries at the end of the eighteenth century. He served as first lieutenant in the Dumfries Volunteers. Burns is said to have been a frequent visitor at his home, Bushy Bank, where his daughter would play on the piano old Scottish airs which Burns collected and to which he composed lyrics. The only extant letters from Burns to Newall deal mainly with business matters, but Newall was also the recipient of at least one of Burns's poems.

I (370)

Ellisland, 7th November 1789

Dear Sir,

The bearer, James Halliday is the lad who executed the drain between Isle & Ellisland.—It is now finished, at least four or five days work more will conclude it; and these few days work must I doubt stand over untill next Spring, as the business is impracticable in wintry weather.—I have not called any body to inspect it, as I have expected your Worship out to pass your judgement on it in the first place; but I am of opinion that with the said four or five days work more, it will do.—I have not taken an accurate measure of the drain, but by a pretty near guess, I take it to be about 80 Roods in length.—Seventeen pence per rood was the bargain, which, taking 85 roods as the just length, makes the whole amount £6. 0s. 5d.—but at this rate the poor fellows will scarce have 1/- per day, as I know tolerably exactly how many days they were altogether; & between you and me, they very well deserve 14 or 15d per day, as they wrought both hard & dirty & kept no stated hours, but from sun to sun almost.—However you & I will settle that at meeting.—In the mean time they want some money; I have fully paid them one half viz. £3. 0s. 2½d. & if you please, you may I think, give them a couple of guineas, or so, untill you see the Work yourself.—Inclosed you have the Ballad I formerly mentioned.—*

My Landlord, &c. I understand are rather cool at the Production.— They think the butter not thick enough on the bread, for one party; while I, for my part, scorn to belong to either party—except I were devilishly well paid.—For this reason, whether the thing entertain or tire you, keep it to yourself.—I have just given one or two copies of it in all; but this I send *you* has several alterations, which in fact do not mend the formentioned fault, but rather unfortunately perhaps the contrary.—However, I will not offend folks with whom, & under whom, & under whom I am connected, and shall give no more copies of it—unless you make my vanity boil it over by your being pleased with it.—

I am, dear Sir,
Your oblidged & obedient humble servant
Robt Burns

* *The Five Carlins*, C.W. p. 364.

544

David Newall

[Spring? 1790]

Dear Sir—

Enclosed is a state of the account between you and me and James Halliday respecting the drain. I have stated it at 20d. per rood, as, in fact, even at that, they have not the wages they ought to have had, and I cannot for the soul of me see a poor devil a loser at my hand.

Humanity, I hope, as well as Charity, will cover a multitude of sins; a mantle of which—between you and me—I have some little need.

I am, sir, yours,
R.B.

LADY WINIFRED MAXWELL CONSTABLE

Born in 1736, the only surviving child of the sixth and last Earl of Nithsdale who forfeited his lands for his part in the Jacobite Rebellion of 1715, she was herself a staunch Jacobite. In 1758 she married William Haggerston Constable of Everingham, Yorkshire, who assumed the name and arms of Maxwell. In the 1780s she returned to Scotland and set about rebuilding her ancestral home, Terregles, two miles west of Dumfries. Burns was an occasional visitor there and *Nithsdale's Welcome Hame* (C.W. p. 377) was composed to mark Lady Winifred's return. Burns's first letter to Lady Winifred dwelt on the fact that he shared her espousal of the lost cause, repeating the family myth of having been 'out' in the 1715 Rebellion. The verses enclosed with this letter were the *Address to Wm. Tyler* (C.W. p. 276). In the spring of 1791 Lady Winifred sent Burns a snuff-box with a miniature portrait of Mary Queen of Scots set into the lid. Burns was then laid up with a broken arm, but in his reply (II) he enclosed his *Lament of Mary Queen of Scots* (C.W. p. 400). The snuff-box eventually passed into the hands of William Nicol Burns who took it to India and damaged the portrait irreparably while leaping aboard a ship.

I (377)

Ellisland, 16th December 1789

My Lady

In vain have I from day to day expected to hear from Mrs Young, as she promised me at Dalswinton, that she would do me the honor to introduce me at Tinwald; and it was impossible, not from your Ladyship's accessibility but from my own feelings, that I could go alone.—Lately indeed Mr Maxwell of Carruchen, in his usual goodness, offered to accompany me, when an unlucky indisposition on my part hindered my embracing the opportunity.—

To court the notice or the tables of the Great, except where I sometimes have had a little matter to ask of them or more often the pleasanter task of witnessing my gratitude to them, is what I never have done, and I trust never shall do.—But with your Ladyship I have the honor to be connected by one of the strongest & most endearing ties in the whole Moral World—Common Sufferers in a Cause where even to be unfortunate is glorious, the Cause of Heroic Loyalty!—Though my Fathers had not illustrious Honors and vast properties to hazard in the contest; though they left their humble cottages only to add so many units more to the unnoted croud that followed their Leaders; yet, what they could they did, and what they had they lost: with unshaken firmness and unconcealed Political Attachments, they shook hands with Ruin for what they esteemed the cause of their King and their Country.—

This language, and the inclosed verses, are for your Ladyship's eyes alone.—Poets are not very famous for their prudence; but as I can do nothing for a Cause which is now nearly no more, I do not wish to hurt myself.—

I have the honour to be, My Lady,
Your Ladyship's oblidged & obedient humble servant—
Robt Burns

II (448)

Ellisland near Dumfries
25th April 1791

My Lady

nothing less than the unlucky accident of having lately broken my right arm, could have prevented me, the moment I received your Ladyship's elegant present by Mr Miller, from returning you my

546

warmest & most grateful acknowledgements.—I assure your Ladyship, I shall set it apart: the symbols of Religion shall only be more
sacred.—In the moment of Poetic composition, the Box shall be my
inspiring Genius.—When I would breathe the comprehensive wish of
Benevolence for the happiness of others, I shall recollect Your Ladyship; when I would interest my fancy in the distresses incident to
Humanity, I shall remember the unfortunate MARY.—I inclose your
Ladyship a poetic compliment I lately paid to the memory of our
greatly injured, lovely Scotish Queen.—

I have the honor to be, My Lady,
Your Ladyship's highly oblidged
& ever devoted humble servant
Robt Burns

PROVOST ROBERT MAXWELL

Provost of Lochmaben from September 1782 till September 1790, he then retired from civic affairs and died in October 1792. In a letter to Robert Graham of Fintry (see page 432) Burns described him as 'one of the soundest headed, best hearted, whisky-drinking fellows in the south of Scotland. From the following letter it appears that Provost Maxwell shared the poet's penchant for bawdy verse. 'Mr Jeffry' was the Rev. Andrew Jaffray, at whose Lochmaben manse Burns sometimes stayed while on Excise business in that neighbourhood.

(378)

Ellisland, 20th December 1789

Dear Provost,

As my friend Mr Graham goes for your good old town tomorrow, I cannot resist the temptation to send you a few lines; and as I have nothing to say, I have chosen this sheet of foolscap, and begun, as you see, at the top of the first page, because I have ever observed that when once people who have nothing to say have fairly set out, they know not when to stop.—Now that my first sentence is concluded, I have nothing to do but to pray Heaven to help me to another.—Shall I write you on Politics, or Religion, two master-subjects for your Sayers of nothing? Of the first, by this time you are, I dare say, nearly surfeited; & for the last, whatever they may talk of it who make it a kind of Company concern, I never could endure it beyond a Soliloquy.—I might write you on farming, on building, on marketing, on planning, &c. but my poor distracted mind is so torn, so jaded, so racked & bedevil'd with the task of the superlatively Damn'd—MAKING ONE GUINEA DO THE BUSINESS OF THREE—that I detest, abhor and swoon at the very word, Business, though no less than four letters of my very short Sirname are in it.—

Well, to make the matter short, I shall betake myself to a subject ever fertile of themes, a Subject, the turtle-feast of the Sons of Satan, and the delicious, secret Sugar-plumb of the Babes of Grace; a Subject, sparkling with all the jewels that Wit can find in the mines of Genius, and pregnant with all the stores of Learning, from Moses & Confucius to Franklin & Priestly—in short, may it please Your Lordship, I intend to write BAUDY!

Song—Tune—Auld Sir Symon

I'll tell you a tale of a Wife,

[C.W. p. 375]

You see, Sir, I have fulfilled my promise: I wish you would think of fulfilling yours, and come & see the rest of my Collection.—

If at any time you expect a Field-day in your town, a Day when Dukes, Earls and Knights pay their court to Weavers, Taylors, and Coblers, I should like to know of it two or three days beforehand.— It is not that I care three skips of a cur-dog for the Politics, but I should like to see such an exhibition of Human Nature.—

If you meet with that worthy old Veteran in Religion and Good-fellowship, Mr Jeffry, or any of his amiable Family, I beg you will give them my best Compliments.—

I am, Dear Sir, yours sincerely,
Robt Burns

GEORGE STEPHENS SUTHERLAND

Little is known of this actor-manager who played a prominent part in the foundation of the Theatre Royal, Dumfries. He had been a member of John Jackson's company in the winter season of 1781-2 at the Theatre Royal in Edinburgh. He played Don Garcia in Mrs Cowley's *A Bold Stroke for a Husband* in 1784. He was also the author of the song *The Bowmen of the Border* published in 1790. He formed his own theatrical company and came to Dumfries in 1789, playing at the Old Assembly Room in the George Hotel. Burns's first letter to Sutherland was sent with the *Prologue* (C.W. p. 376) which Sutherland declaimed on New Year's Evening. Burns wrote to his brother Gilbert on 11th January 1790 reporting that Sutherland had 'spouted to his Audience with great applause'.

Early in the New Year Sutherland began canvassing influential people in Dumfries for the establishment of a permanent theatre, made possible under the more liberal Licensing Act of 1788. Burns described the background to this project in a letter to William Nicol on 2nd February 1790 (see page 347): 'The manager, Mr Sutherland, was introduced to me by a friend from Ayr; and a worthier or cleverer fellow I have rarely met with.' A meeting of the subscribers was held on 18th February 1790, at which Sutherland announced that he had feued from Thomas Bushby a part of the gardens at East Barnraws (later Queen Street). Plans were drawn up by the architect Thomas Boyd and approved by the meeting. The foundation stone was laid later that year. The founding deed for the Theatre was drawn up in favour of Robert Riddell of Glenriddell and the Theatre staged its first production on 29th September 1792, the scenery being painted by Alexander Nasmyth, then down on his luck because of his radical politics. From a preliminary sketch for one of the Dumfries sets, now preserved in the National Gallery of Scotland, it seems that Nasmyth secured the work at the behest of Robert Burns. Burns himself played an active part in the Theatre's early years. In a letter to Mrs Dunlop in March 1790 (see page 000) Burns enclosed the *Scots Prologue* (C.W. p. 399) which he wrote for Mrs Sutherland's benefit night.

I (380)

[With *Prologue Spoken at the Theatre of Dumfries*]

[C.W. p. 376]

Ellisland Thursday morn:
[31st December 1789]

Sir,

Jogging home yesternight it occurred to me that as your next night is the first night of the New Year, a few lines allusive to the Season, by way of Prologue, Interlude, or what you please, might take pretty well.—The inclosed verses are very incorrect because they are almost the first crude suggestions of my Muse, by way of bearing me company in my darkling journey.—I am sensible it is too late to send you them; but if they can any way serve you, use, alter, or if you please neglect them.—I shall not be in the least mortified though they are never heard of; but if they can be of any service to Mr Sutherland and his friends, I shall kiss my hand to my lady Muse, and own myself much her debtor.—

I am Sir, your very humble Servant
Robt Burns

II (394A)

Monday morning
[1st March? 1790]

Sir,

I was much disappointed, my dear Sir, in wanting your most agreeable company yesterday. However, I heartily pray for good weather next Sunday; and whatever aerial Being has the guidance of the elements, may take any other half dozen of Sundays he pleases, and clothe them with

"Vapours, and clouds, and storms,"*

until he terrify himself at combustion of his own raising—

I shall see you on Wednesday forenoon.

In the greatest hurry, &c.
R.B.

* Thomson: *Winter*, line 3.

DAVID STAIG

Born in 1740 of an old Dumfries family, he was for upwards of forty years agent of the Bank of Scotland in the burgh and probably the best provost the town has ever had in its long history. He first became provost at Michaelmas 1783 and from then until 1817 he held the chief office no fewer than nine times, covering a total of twenty years in office. Under his vigorous and enterprising administration Dumfries got its first paving, cleansing, lighting and police, followed by a massive reform of the civic revenues (1788). The new Academy, the shipping quay, the new bridge over the Nith and the first regular mail-coach service were all due to his energy and drive. Burns's suggestions for improvements in the local beer tax (III) were subsequently adopted. As Staig was provost in 1792-4, Burns's letter (IV) addressed to the 'Lord Provost, Bailies & Town Council of Dumfries' is included in this group. In it Burns reminded the council that he had been made an honorary burgess (in 1787) and, as such, entitled to be relieved of the higher scale of school fees charged on 'Strangers'. Provost Staig played a prominent part in the Mausoleum fund, and was a founder member, in 1820, of Dumfries Burns Club. He died in 1824.

I (394)

Ellisland Monday morn:
[1st March 1790]

Sir

My friend and fellow-laborer in scaling the barren heights of Parnassus, Mr Sutherland, having asked me for a Prologue, or something like it, for Mrs Sutherland's benefit-night, I have composed a Prologue, "or something like it," for him, as you will see by the Inclosed.—It is not for its *merit* that I trouble you with a copy of it: if it escape damnation, it will be "of *Grace*, not of *Works*;"* but there is a dark stroke of Politics in the belly of the Piece, and like a faithful loyal Subject, I lay it before You, as the chief Magistrate of the Country, at least the only Magistrate whom I have met with in the Country who had the honor to be very conspicuous as a Gentleman; that if the said Poem be found to contain any Treason, or words of treasonable construction, or any *Fama clamosa* or *Scandalum magnatum*, against our Sovereign lord the King, or any of his liege Subjects, the said Prologue may not see the light.—Mr Sutherland may probably mention the circumstance, for your strictures, or I may possibly meet with you on wednesday in your market-day perambulations.—

To tell you the truth, the whole truth, (in the language of that elegant Science, the Law,) the real reason why I trouble you with this, is, that I had a woman's longing for an opportunity of this kind to assure You, how gratefully & truly,

I have the honor to be, Sir,
your oblidged & obedient humble servant
Robt Burns

* Romans 11:6, paraphrased.

II (533B)

Thursday Noon
[Dumfries, 10th January 1793]

Sir,

There are such things as people writing what they ought not to have written, & writing what they wish they had never written—possibly, nay very probably, this epistle with which I am going to trouble you, is in one or both of these predicaments.

David Staig

I come to beg of you Sir, not for myself, that indeed I do as seldom as possible, though were I under the necessity of taxing the fraternal feelings of my Bretheren of Mankind, Mr Staig is one of the few characters whom I would with chearfulness and confidence approach.—

Among the Company of Players here there is one to whose merits, as an Actor, you must be no stranger; his name is Guion.—Strolling Comedians are a class of folks with whom you will readily believe I wish to have very little communication.—

When Mr Guion came here, he was introduced to my acquaintance by a friend of mine in Edinburgh, a Gentleman of distinguished character there who begged me to serve Guion in anything I could with propriety do.—I have found Mr Guion to be truly what my friend represented him, a man of more than common information & worth—his Benefit comes on tomorrow night—Now Sir—is there any periphrasis of Language, any circumlocution of phrase, in which I could convey a request without at the same time seeming to convey it, that your amiable Lady & lovely daughters would grace my friend Mr Guion's Boxes.—Such a petition I have no right to make—Nay, it is downright impertinence in me to make it, but if I were in your rank of life & you in mine I would forgive you such a fault.—

If your good family will be so very obliging as to accord with the prayer of my petition I hereby promise & engage that when you are made a Commissioner of the Customs I will write a congratulatory Ode on the subject, that every one of your charming Girls as she is married shall have an Epithalamium & your Lady shall command my Muse on any theme she pleases.

Pray do Sir forgive this impertinence in a man for the sake of his friend, what he would have been three fourths starved before he would have been guilty of for himself.—

> I have the Honor to be
> Sir
> Your Obliged & Obedient Servant
> Robt Burns

III (534)

> Friday Noon
> [January 1793?]

I know, Sir, that any thing which relates to the Burgh of Dumfries's interest will engage your readiest attention, so shall make no apology for this letter.—I have been for some time turning my attention to a branch of your good town's revenue, where I think there is much to amend; I mean the "Twa pennies" on Ale.—The Brewers & Victuallers within the jurisdiction pay accurately; but three Common Brewers in the Bridgend[1] whose consumpt is almost entirely in Dumfries, pay nothing; Annan Brewer, who daily sends in great quantities of ale, pays nothing; because in both cases, Ale Certificates are never asked for: & of all the English Ale, Porter, &c. scarcely any of it pays.—For my part, I never recorded an Ale Certificate in Dumfries, & I know most of the other Officers are in the same predicament.—It makes no

David Staig

part of our official duty, & besides, untill it is universally assessed, on all Dealers, it strikes me as injustice to assess one.—I know that our Collector has a per centage on the Collection; but as it is no great object to him, he gives himself no concern about what is *brought in* to the town.—The Supervisor would suit you better.—He is an abler & a keener man, &, what is all-important in the business, such is his official influence over, & power among, his Officers, that were he to signify that such was his wish, not a "pennie" would be left uncollected.—It is by no means the case with the Collector.—The Officers are not so immediately among his hands, & they would not pay the same attention to his mandates. Your Brewers here, the Richardsons, one of whom, Gabriel,[2] I survey, pay annually in "twa pennies," about thirty pounds; & they complain, with great justice, of the unfair balance against them, in their competition with the Bridgened, Annan, & English Traders.—As they are respectable characters, both as Citizens and Men of Business, I am sure they will meet with every encouragement from the Magistracy of Dumfries.— For their sakes partly I have interested my self in this business, but still much more on account of many obligations which I feel myself to lie under to Mr Staig's civility & goodness.—Could I be of the smallest service in any thing which he has at heart, it would give me great pleasure.—I have been at some pains to ascertain what your annual loss on this business may be, & I have reason to think that it may amount fully to one third of what you at present receive.—

These crude hints, Sir, are entirely for your private use.—I have by no means any wish to take a sixpence from Mr Mitchel's income: nor do I wish to serve Mr Findlater: I wish to shew any attempt I can, to do any thing that might declare with what sincerity I have the honor to be

Sir, your obliged humble servant
Robt Burns

P.S. A variety of other methods might be pointed out, & will easily occur to your reflection on the subject.—

RB

1 The settlement on the West bank of the Nith (later the burgh of Maxwell-town), in Kirkcudbrightshire and therefore beyond the jurisdiction of Dumfries.
2 Gabriel Richardson (1759-1820), Provost in 1801 and brother-in-law of Dr Mundell.

IV (542)

[March 1793]

My Lord & Gentlemen,

The literary taste & liberal spirit of your good town has so ably filled the various departments of your schools, as to make it a very great object for a Parent to have his children educated in them.—Still, to me, a Stranger, with my large family & very stinted income, to give my young ones that education I wish, at the high School-fees which a Stranger pays, will bear hard upon me.—

Some years ago your good Town did me the honor of making me an Honorary Burgess*.—Will your Honors allow me to request that this mark of distinction may extend so far, as to put me on the footing of a real Freeman of the Town, in the Schools?—

553

David Staig

That I may not appear altogether unworthy of this favor, allow me to state to you some little services I have lately done a branch of your Revenue: the twopennies exigible on foreign Ale vended within your limits.—In this rather neglected article of your income, I am ready to shew that, within these few weeks, my exertions have secured for you of these duties nearly the sum of ten pounds: & in this too, I was the only one of the gentlemen of the Excise (except Mr Mitchell, whom *you pay* for his trouble,) who took the least concern in the business.

If you are so very kind as to grant my request, it will certainly be constant incentive to me to strain every nerve, where in that, or any other way, I can officially serve you & will, if possible, increase that grateful respect with which I have the honor to be,

My Lord & Gentlemen,
Your devoted humble servant

* On 4th June 1787.

MRS ELIZABETH GRAHAM OF FINTRY

Three letters from Burns to the wife of his patron, Robert Graham of Fintry, exist. The first was written to accompany letter (VIII) addressed to her husband, but included a ballad, possibly *Lament of Mary Queen of Scots* (C.W. p. 400). The remaining letters consisted of mere notes, one accompanying *The Rights of Woman* (C.W. p. 471) and the other being a lengthy and rather high-flown inscription in a copy of the 1793 edition of the Poems.

I (402)

[Enclosing Letter VIII (402A) to Robert Graham.]

Ellisland, 10th June 1790

Madam

Whether it is that the story of our Mary Queen of Scots has a peculiar effect on the feelings of a Poet, or whether in the inclosed ballad I have succeeded beyond my usual poetic success, I know not; but it has pleased me beyond any late effort of my Muse: on that account I beg leave to inclose it particularly to You.—It is true, the purity of my motives may be suspected—I am already deeply indebted to your & Mr Graham's goodness; and, what *in the usual ways of men* is of infinitely greater importance, Your & His Patronage can be of the utmost service to me in time to come.—I was born a poor dog; and however I may occasionally pick a better bone than I used to do, I know that a poor dog I must live & die.—But I will indulge the flattering faith that my Poetry will considerably outlive my Poverty; and without any fustian affection of spirit I can promise & affirm that it must be no ordinary demand of the latter shall ever make me do any thing injurious to the honest fame of the former.—Whatever shall be my failings, for failings are a part of Human-nature, may they ever be those of a generous heart & an independant mind!—It is not my *fault* that I was born to dependance; nor is it Mr Graham's chiefest praise *that he can command influence*; but it is *his* merit to bestow with the politeness of a Gentleman and the kindness of a Brother; and I trust it is *mine* to receive with ingenuous thankfulness, and to remember with undiminished gratitude.—

I have the honor to be, Madam,
your highly oblidged & most obedient humble servant
Robert Burns

II (531)

[With *The Rights of Woman.*]
[C.W. p. 471]

[Dumfries, 5th January 1793]

To Mrs Graham of Fintry, this little poem, written in haste on the spur of the occasion, & therefore inaccurate; but a sincere Compliment to that Sex, the most amiable of the works of God—is most respectfully presented by—

The Author

Mrs Elizabeth Graham of Fintry

III (547)

[In a copy of the 1793 Edition of the *Poems,* mid-March]

It is probable, Madam, that this page may be read when the hand that now writes it, is mouldering in the dust.– May it then bear witness, that I present you these volumes, as a tribute of gratitude, on my part, ardent and sincere; as your & Mr Graham's goodness to me has been generous & noble!–May every child of yours, in the hour of need, find such a FRIEND, as I shall teach every child of mine that their father found in YOU!

Robt Burns

CAPTAIN FRANCIS GROSE

Born in London in 1731, the son of a Swiss jeweller who worked on the crown for the coronation of King George II in 1728. Grose entered the Army, attaining the rank of captain, but resigned his commission to devote his life to art and antiquity. He was at one time Richmond Herald in the College of Arms, but sold his appointment to Henry Pugolas for 600 guineas. Subsequently he became Paymaster and Adjutant of the Surrey Militia, a role in which he seems to have been singularly inept, squandering the huge fortune inherited from his father in making good the deficiencies in his regimental accounts. He had much more success in the antiquarian field, publishing his six volumes of *Antiquities of England and Wales* between 1773 and 1787. Two companion volumes dealing with Scotland followed in 1789 and 1791. It was while in Scotland gathering material for the latter project that Grose met Burns. Burns recounted the circumstances of their meeting in a letter to Mrs Dunlop on 17th July 1789 (see page 176). Grose stayed with the Riddells at Friars' Carse while gathering material in Nithsdale and Annandale. Burns found a kindred spirit in this fat, jovial man with an inexhaustible fund of anecdotes and jokes. Grose agreed to include Alloway Kirk in his forthcoming volume, provided that Burns furnished a tale of witchcraft to accompany his drawing. In June 1790 Burns sent the following prose narrative, a prelude to that superb mock-epic *Tam o Shanter* (C.W. p. 410) which was despatched with (III) in December of that year. Grose also inspired those witty lines *On the late Captain Grose's Peregrinations through Scotland* (C.W. p. 373), as well as the parody of an oyster-dredging song and *Epigram on Francis Grose the Antiquary* (C.W. p. 415). Grose died at Dublin in 1791.

I (401)

[June? 1790]

Among the many Witch Stories I have heard relating to Aloway Kirk, I distinctly remember only two or three.

Upon a stormy night, amid whirling squalls of wind and bitter blasts of hail, in short, on such a night as the devil would chuse to take the air in, a farmer or farmer's servant was plodding and plashing homeward with his plough-irons on his shoulder, having been getting some repairs on them at a neighbouring smithy. His way lay by the Kirk of Aloway, and being rather on the anxious look-out in approaching a place so well known to be a favourite haunt of the devil and the devil's friends and emissaries, he was struck aghast by discovering through the horrors of the storm and stormy night, a light, which on his nearer approach, plainly shewed itself to proceed from the haunted edifice. Whether he had been fortified from above on his devout supplication, as is customary with people when they suspect the immediate presence of Satan; or whether, according to another custom, he had got courageously drunk at the smithy, I will not pretend to determine; but so it was that he ventured to go up to, nay into the very kirk. As good luck would have it, his temerity came off unpunished. The members of the infernal junto were all out on some midnight business or other, and he saw nothing but a kind of kettle or caldron, depending from the roof, over the fire, simmering some heads of unchristened children, limbs of executed malefactors, &c. for the business of the night. It was, in for a penny, in for a pound, with the honest ploughman: so without ceremony he unhooked the caldron from off the fire, and pouring out the damnable ingredients, inverted it on his head, and carried it fairly home, where it remained long in the family a living evidence of the truth of the story.

Another story which I can prove to be equally authentic was as follows.

557

On a market day in the town of Ayr, a farmer from Carrick, and consequently whose way lay by the very gate of Aloway kirk-yard, in order to cross the river Doon at the old bridge, which is about two or three hundred yards further on than the said gate, had been detained by his business, 'till by the time he reached Aloway, it was the wizard hour, between night and morning. Though he was terrified, with a blaze streaming from the kirk, yet as it is a well-known fact that to turn back on these occasions is running by far the greatest risk of mischief, he prudently advanced on his road. When he had reached the gate of the kirk-yard, he was surprised and entertained, through the ribs and arches of an old gothic window which still faces the highway, to see a dance of witches merrily footing it round their old sooty blackguard master, who was keeping them alive with the powers of his bag-pipe. The farmer stopping his horse to observe them a little, could plainly descry the faces of many old women of his acquaintance and neighbourhood. How the gentleman was dressed, tradition does not say; but the ladies were all in their smocks: and one of them happening unluckily to have a smock which was considerably too short to answer all the purpose of that piece of dress, our farmer was so tickled that he involuntarily burst out, with a loud laugh,"Well luppen Maggy wi' the short sark!" and recollecting himself, instantly spurred his horse to the top of his speed. I need not mention the universally known fact, that no diabolical power can pursue you beyond the middle of a running stream. Lucky it was for the poor farmer that the river Doon was so near, for notwithstanding the speed of his horse, which was a good one, against he reached the middle of the arch of the bridge, and consequently the middle of the stream, the pursuing, vengeful, hags, were so close at his heels, that one of them actually sprung to seize him; but it was too late, nothing was on her side of the stream but the horse's tail, which immediately gave way to her infernal grip, as if blasted by a stroke of lightning; but the farmer was beyond her reach. However, the unsightly, tailless condition of the vigorous steed was to the last hour of the noble creature's life, an awful warning to the Carrick farmers, not to stay too late in Ayr markets.

The last relation I shall give, though equally true, is not so well identified as the two former, with regard to the scene: but as the best authorities give it for Aloway, I shall relate it.

On a summer's evening, about the time that Nature puts on her sables to mourn the expiry of the chearful day, a shepherd boy belonging to a farmer in the immediate neighbourhood of Aloway Kirk, had just folded his charge, and was returning home. As he passed the kirk, in the adjoining field, he fell in with a crew of men and women, who were busy pulling stems of the plant ragwort. He observed that as each person pulled a ragwort, he or she got astride of it and called out, "Up horsie!" on which the ragwort flew off, like Pegasus, through the air with its rider. The foolish boy likewise pulled his ragwort, and cried with the rest "Up horsie!" and, strange to tell, away he flew with the company. The first stage at which the cavalcade stopt, was a merchant's wine cellar in Bourdeaux, where, without saying by your leave, they quaffed away at the best the cellar could afford, until the morning, foe to the imps and works of darkness, threatened to throw light on the matter, and frightened them from their carousals.

The poor shepherd lad, being equally a stranger to the scene and the liquor, heedlessly got himself drunk, and when the rest took horse, he fell asleep, and was found so next day by some of the people belonging to the merchant. Somebody that understood Scotch, asking him what he was, he said he was such-a-one's herd in Aloway; and by some means or other getting home again, he lived long to tell the world the wondrous tale.

I am, &c. &c.
Rob Burns

II (408)

[Enclosing Letter to Professor Dugald Stewart III (409) see page 450]

[Ellisland, July 1790]

Sir,

I believe among all our Scots literati you have not met with professor Dugald Stewart, who fills the moral philosophy chair in the University of Edinburgh. To say that he is a man of the first parts, and what is more, a man of the first worth, to a gentleman of your general acquaintance, and who so much enjoys the luxury of unincumbered freedom and undisturbed privacy, is not perhaps recommendation enough:—but when I inform you that Mr. Stewart's principal characteristic is your favorite feature; *that* sterling independence of mind, which, though every man's right, so few men have the courage to claim, and fewer still the magnanimity to support:—When I tell you, that unseduced by splendor, and undisgusted by wretchedness, he appreciates the merits of the various actors in the great drama of life, merely as they perform their parts—in short, he is a man after your own heart, and I comply with his earnest request in letting you know that he wishes above all things to meet with you. His house, Catrine, is within less than a mile of Sorn Castle, which you proposed visiting; or if you could transmit him the inclosed, he would with the greatest pleasure, meet you any where in the neighbourhood. I write to Ayrshire to inform Mr. Stewart that I have acquitted myself of my promise. Should your time and spirits permit your meeting with Mr. Stewart, 'tis well; if not, I hope you will forgive this liberty, and I have at least an opportunity of assuring you with what truth and respect,

I am, Sir, Your great admirer,
And very humble servant.

III (427A)

[With *Tam o Shanter*.]

[C.W. p. 410]

Ellisland 1st December 1790.

Sir,

The Post is just going, but 'tis no matter.—I am not, God knows, vain of my Composition, & you like intellectual food more substantial, than the whipt syllabub of epistolary Compliment.—

Inclosed is one of the Aloway-kirk Stories, done in Scots verse.—Should you think it worthy a place in your Scots Antiquities, it will lengthen not a little the altitude of my Muse's pride.—If you do me the honor to print it, I am afraid it will be impossible to transmit me the Proof-Sheets, otherwise I should like to see them.—After all, Sir, do by me as I would do by you, or any body; print my piece or not as you think proper.—Authors have too often very little to say in the disposal of this world's affairs, but it would be very hard if they should not be absolute in their own Works.—

Your draught of Kilwinning is finished, but not come to hand.—I shall send it you the minute it reaches me.—I hope it will answer your wishes, but at all events it has one merit, it will cost you nothing but the Postage.—I wish I could give you a more substantial proof, with how much respectful regard & sincere esteem I have the honor to be,

Sir,
your oblidged humble servant
Robt Burns

HELEN CRAIK

Born about 1750, she was the unmarried daughter of the family which owned
Arbigland, Kirkbean parish, on the Solway coast where John Paul Jones had
been the gardener's son. She was a friend of Robert Riddell, and it may have
been through him that Burns was introduced to her. They shared a passion for
Goethe's *Werther* and other sentimental favourites of the period. She
composed the lines, in a hand other than Burns's, inscribed on the title page of
the Glenriddell MS. She died at Flimby Lodge, Cumbria in 1825.

I (413)

Ellisland, 9th August 1790

Madam

Some unlooked for accidents have prevented my doing myself the
honor of a second visit to Arbigland, as I was so hospitably invited,
and so positively meant, to have done.—However, I still hope to have
that pleasure before the commencement of the busy days of
harvest.—

I inclose you two of my late Pieces, as some kind of return for the
pleasure I have received in perusing a certain manuscript volume of
Poems, in the possession of Captain Riddel.—To repay one with "an
old Song," is a proverb, whose force, you, Madam, I know will not
allow.—What is said of Illustrious Descent, is, I believe, equally true
of a Talent for Poesy; none ever despised it who had the least
pretensions to it.—

It is often a reverie of mine, when I am disposed to be melancholy,
the characters & fates of the Rhyming tribe.—There is not among all
the Martyrologies that ever were penned, so rueful a narrative as
Johnson's Lives of the Poets.—In the comparative view of Wretches,
the criterion is not, what they are doomed to suffer, but how they
are formed to bear.—Take a being of our kind; give him a stronger
imagination and more delicate sensibility, which will ever between
them engender a more ungovernable set of Passions, than the usual
lot of man; implant in him an irresistible impulse to some idle
vagary, such as, arranging wild-flowers in fantastical nosegays,
tracing the grasshopper to his haunt by his chirping song, watching
the frisks of the little minnows in the sunny pool, or hunting after
the intrigues of wanton butterflies—in short, send him adrift after
some wayward pursuit which shall eternally mislead him from the
paths of Lucre; yet, curse him with a keener relish than any man
living for the pleasures that only Lucre can bestow; lastly, fill up the
measure of his woes, by bestowing on him a spurning sense of his
own dignity; and you have created a weight nearly as miserable as a
Poet.—

To you, Madam, I need not recount the fairy pleasures the Muse to
counterbalance this catalogue of evils, bestows on her Votaries.—
Bewitching Poesy is like bewitching WOMAN: she has in all ages
been accused of misleading Mankind from the counsels of Wisdom
and the paths of Prudence; involving them in difficulties, baiting
them with Poverty, branding them with Infamy, and plunging them
in the vortex of Ruin; yet, where is the Man but must own, that all
our happiness on earth is not worthy the Name! that even the holy
hermit's solitary prospect of paradisical bliss, is but the glitter of a
northern sun rising over a frozen region! Compared with the many
pleasures, the nameless raptures, we owe to the lovely QUEEN OF
THE HEARTS OF MEN!!!

Please present my most respectful Compliments to Mr Craik, & the Captain.—

I have the honor to be, Madam,
Your very humble servant
Robt Burns

II (490)

Dumfries, 12th January 1792

I have just a snatch of time at present to put pen to paper in, but in that moment, allow me, Dear Madam, to grant your obliging, flattering request; as unceremoniously as a how-d'ye, to a friend, & as sincerely as a burst of indignation to the person we hate.—Setting my obligations to & respect for the Arbigland Family out of the question, any friend of a gentleman whom I value & respect as I do Mr Maxwell of Carruchen, may command me, nay would honor me with his or her commands, in a much more important matter than a copy of a Poetic bagatelle.—

As to HELEN, I shall certainly bestow my utmost attention on it, if possible that I can start a hint that may not have occurred to you, in smoothing a line or improving a thought.—Now that I have, by my removal to town, got time & opportunity, I shall often intrude on you with my assurance, how sincerely & respectfully I am, Dear Madam, your obliged & obedient humble servant

Robt Burns

JOHN MITCHELL

Born in Aberdeenshire in 1731, he studied for the ministry but later turned to the Excise instead and served successively at Fraserburgh and Kilmarnock before being appointed Collector at Dumfries in 1788. He was transferred to Haddington in 1802, but from the omission of his name from the list of Excise officers after 1804 it has been surmised that he either retired, or died in that year. During his Dumfries period he was Burns's immediate superior. Burns called upon him in May 1789, armed with a letter of introduction from Graham of Fintry. Later he was able to report to his patron that Mitchell 'sent me a kind letter giving me a hint of the business, and on my waiting on him yesterday, he entered with the most friendly ardour into my views and interests.' About two weeks later Burns got his Excise appointment, although he did not commence work till the beginning of September. Burns later acknowledged the help given by Mitchell and Findlater in breaking him in.

Burns's first extant letter to Mitchell was written from Ellisland in September 1790 and illustrates the problems that faced an Exciseman in doing his duty without fear or favour. Burns had reported a farmer, Thomas Johnston of Mirecleugh, for illicit maltings. As a result, Johnston had been tried and convicted, and fined £5, but appealed against the fine. Fergusson of Craigdarroch and Riddell of Glenriddell, in their capacity as magistrates, ordered Collector Mitchell to suspend proceedings till Johnston's appeal could be investigated. Burns, who had been exceedingly busy at this time, was clearly annoyed at the intervention of Fergusson and Riddell on Johnston's behalf, and there was more than a hint of exasperation in the final sentence of this letter. Burns's answer to Johnston's petition is appended, The only other letters to Mitchell are brief notes, seeking permission for leave of absence to attend Gilbert's wedding (II) and dealing with his accounts (III).

I (417)

[Ellisland, 1790]

Sir,

I shall not fail to wait on Captain Riddel tonight.—I wish & pray that the goddess of Justice herself would appear tomorrow among our Honorable Gentleman, merely to give them a word in their ear, that, "Mercy to the Thief, is Injustice to the Honest Man"—For my part, I have galloped over my ten parishes these four days, untill this moment that I am just alighted, or rather, that my poor jackass skeleton of a horse has let me down; for the miserable devil has been on his knees half a score of times, within the last twenty miles, telling me in his own way—"Behold, am not I thy faithful jade" of a horse, on which thou hast ridden these many years!!!"* In short, Sir, I have broke my horse's wind, & almost broke my own neck, besides some injuries in a part that shall be nameless, owing to a hard-hearted stone of a saddle, & I find that every Offender has so many Great Men to espouse his cause, that I shall not be surprised if I am committed to the strong Hold of the Law tomorrow for insolence to the dear friends of the Gentlemen of the Country.—

I have the honor to be, Sir,
Your oblidged & obedient humble servant
Robt Burns

* Numbers 22:30, paraphrased.

II (457)

[Ellisland, 16th June 1791]

Sir,

A very pressing occasion, no less than witnessing the wedding of an only brother, calls me to Ayr-shire for which I shall take your permission as granted, except I be countermanded before Sunday, the day I set out.—I shall remember that three days are all that I can expect.—The inclosed *official* paper came to my hand, & I take the liberty to lay it before you.—

> I have the honor to be, sir,
> your obliged, humble servant
> Robt Burns

III (521)

30th November 1792

Sir,

On looking over my accounts I find that I have received £8–3s to account of 2d & 3. Rounds' Salary.—

> I have the honor to be most sincerely,
> Sir, Your much obliged humble servant
> Robt Burns

(418)

Answers to the Petition of THOMAS JOHNSTON—

[September 1790]

1^{rmo} Whether the Petitioner has been in use formerly to malt all his grain at one operation, is foreign to the purpose: this last season he certainly malted his crop at four or five operations; but be that as it may, Mr Johnston ought to have known, that by express Act of Parliament, no Malt however small the quantity can be legally manufactured *until* previous Entry be made, in writing, of all the ponds, barns, floors, &c. so to be used before the grain be put to steep.—In The Excise Entry books for the Division, there is not a syllable of Thomas Johnston's name for a number of years bygone.—

2d True it is, that Mr Burns on his first ride, in answer to Mr Johnston's question anent the conveyance of the Notices, among other ways, pointed out the sending it by post as the most eligible method; but at the same time added this express Cluase, & to which Mr Burns is willing to make faith,—"At the same time, remember, Mr Johnston, that that Notice is at your risk, untill it reach me!"— Farther, when Mr Burns came to the Petitioner's kiln, there was a servant belonging to Mr Johnston ploughing at a very considerable distance from the kiln, who left his plough & three horses without a driver, & came into the kill, which Mr B—— thought was rather suspicious circumstance; as there was nothing extraordinary in an Excise Officer going into a legal Maltfloor, so as to leave three horses yoked to a plough in the distant middle of a moor.—

This Servant on being repeatedly questioned by Mr Burns could not tell when the malt was put to steep, when it was taken out; in short was determined to be entirely ignorant in the affair.—Bye & bye, Mr Johnston's Son came in, & on being questioned as to the steeping, taking out of the grain, &c. Mr Johnston Junior referred me to this said servant, this ploughman, who, he said must remember it best as having been the principal actor in the business. The lad *then*, having gotten his cue, circumstantially recollected all about it.—

All this time though I was telling the Son & Servant the nature of the premunire they had incurred, though they pleaded for mercy keenly, the affair of the Notice having been sent never once occurred to them, not even the son who is said to have been the Bearer.—This was a stroke reserved for & worthy of the gentleman himself.—As to Mrs Kellock's oath, it proves nothing.—She did indeed depone to a line being left for me at her house, which said line miscarried.—It was a sealed letter; she could not tell whether it was a Malt Notice or not.—She could not even condescend on the Month, nor so much as the season of the year.—The truth is, Thomas Johnston & his family being Seceders, & consequently coming every Sunday to Thornhill Meeting-house, they were a good conveyance for the several Maltsters & Traders in their neighborhood to transmit to Post their Notices, Permits, &c.—

But why all this tergiversation? It was put to the Petitioner in open Court, after a full investigation of the Cause, "Was he willing to swear that he meant no fraud in the matter?" And the Justices told him that if he swore to that, he would be assoilzied, otherwise he should be fined; still, the Petitioner, after ten minutes' consideration, found his Conscience unequal to the task & declined the Oath.—

Now indeed he says he is willing to swear; he has been excercising his Conscience in private & will perhaps stretch a point.—But the fact to which he is to swear was equally & in all its parts known to him on that day when he refused to swear, as today: nothing can give him farther light as to the intention of his mind, respecting his meaning or not meaning a fraud in the affair.—No time can cast light farther on the present resolves of the mind; but Time will reconcile, & has reconciled many a Man to that Iniquity which at first he abhorred.—

JOHN WILSON

Born about 1751, the son of a Glasgow weaver, he studied at Glasgow University, then taught at Craigie near Kilmarnock and was appointed schoolmaster at Tarbolton in 1781. A horn book was a children's primer, hence the nickname 'Dr Hornbook' which Burns bestowed on Wilson. To augment his low salary, Wilson also ran a grocer's shop where he sold a few medicines and advertised that 'advice would be given in common disorders at the shop gratis'. He was the secretary of Tarbolton's masonic lodge (1782-7) and it was after hearing him discourse on his medical knowledge at a masonic meeting that Burns was inspired to write *Death and Doctor Hornbook* (C.W. p. 96). It is utterly untrue that this satire ruined him. He continued as schoolmaster and session clerk at Tarbolton till 1793. Oddly enough when Wilson contemplated moving from Tarbolton to take up a clerical post in Edinburgh, it was to his satirist that he turned for help and advice. The following letter was full of commonsense and sound practical advice which Wilson heeded. Instead, he eventually went to Glasgow where he taught in the High Street, subsequently establishing a commercial academy in Buchanan Street. He became Session Clerk of Gorbals parish, an appointment which he held for thirty years till his death in 1839.

(420)

Ellisland, 11th September 1790

I am truly sorry, my dear Sir, that you find yourself so uncomfortably situated in Tarbolton; the more so, as I fear you will find on trial that the remedy you propose, is worse than the disease.—The life of an Edinburgh Quill-driver at twopence a page, is a life I know so well —that I should be very sorry any friend of mine should ever try it.— To young lads, bred to the law, & meaning to push their way in that department & line of life, practising as a copying Clerk is to them a necessary step; but to a gentleman who is unacquainted with the science of law, & who proposes to live merely by the drudgery of quill, he has before him a life o many sorrows.—Pardon me, my dear Sir, this freedom: I wish only to keep you, as far as my knowledge of life can, from being misled by that seducing Slut, Fancy, under the mask of Hope.—The Excise is impracticable to you.—No man above thirty, or who has more than two children, is admissible.— However, you are the best judge of your present situation & future hopes; & as I wish to be of all the service to you that is in my scanty power, I inclose you a card to a friend of mine*, the only one I have in Edinburgh, to whom I could with any hope of success make such a request.—

Allow me to mention one suggestion to you.—Your present appointment may be held by deputy, at least untill you go to Edinburgh & see what you have to expect there: let me beg of you for Mrs Wilson's sake & your sweet little flock, not to quit the Present, poor as it is, untill you be pretty sure of your hold of the Future.—

I am afraid, too, that at this season, in vacation, you will find few of the Gentlemen of the law in town.—Had you not better defer your journey untill the Court sit down?

Mrs Burns joins me in best Compliments to Mrs Wilson.—

> Farewell! & believe me to be, my dear Sir,
> Yours sincerely
> Robt Burns

* See next page.

JOHN SOMERVILLE

Very little is known of this Edinburgh lawyer who lived at 67 Princes Street and had his office at the head of the Cowgate. He may have been the 'J. Sommervill' whose name appears in almanac lists of Advocate First Clerks (solicitors) in 1805 and 1809. Clearly he was a friend of Burns, as he subscribed for four copies of the Edinburgh edition of 1787. It was to Somerville that Burns wrote a letter of introduction on behalf of John Wilson, when the latter was contemplating a legal career. The second letter to Somerville, written in May 1791, introduced William Lorimer of Kemmishall who was seeking a lawyer in Edinburgh. Lorimer was, of course, the father of Jean Lorimer, the 'Chloris' of the poems.

(421)

[Enclosed with the foregoing]

Ellisland 11th September 1790

My dear Sir,

the Bearer, Mr Wilson, from Ayrshire is a particular friend of mine.— He comes to your good City I believe to see for a job as a Clerk, Copyist, or so, for which whoever employes him will find him eminently qualified.—If you can be of any service to him, it will truly oblidge me.—

My best Compliments to Mrs Sommerville, little Harry, & all the little Cherubs.—

I am ever, My dear Sir,
your oblidged & obedient humble servant
Robt Burns

II (451)

Ellisland, near Dumfries, 11th May 1791.

Allow me, my dear Sir, to introduce a Mr Lorimer a particular friend of mine, to your acquaintance, as a gentleman worth your knowing, both as a man and (what is case in point), as a man of property and consequence, who goes to town just now, to advise with and employ an Agent in some law-business. By way of serving him, I put him in the best hands when I introduce him to Mr Somerville. My kindest compliments to Mrs Somerville, little Harry, and all your little folks. By the way, about ten months ago, I collected . . . a little fellow,* whom, for strength, size, figure, and pitch of note, I will match against, any boy in Nithsdale, Annandale, or any dale whatever. So, in a mug of porter, here goes the Gudewife o' Diltammies' toast— "The Gudeman an' the bill! for they keep a' the roun in milk,"

Yours
Robt Burns

* William Nicol Burns, born 9th April 1791; 'months' must have been a slip of the pen for 'days'.

ALEXANDER CROMBIE

Born in Dumfries in 1757, the son of Alexander Crombie Sr. who had moved from Haddington about 1750 and married Elizabeth Murray. Alexander junior married Charlotte, sister of a fellow stone-mason, Thomas Watson, and established a flourishing business. He was tacksman of the Castledykes Quarry and built a number of country houses, notably the Miller residence at Dalswinton. He also had a business in Dumfries as sculptor, monumental mason and manufacturer of ornamental ironwork. Many of the tombstones in St. Michael's churchyard were produced by Crombie & Co. His son Andrew diversified into sanitary engineering, and the firm supplied Dumfries with its first public water supply. Alexander junior died in 1828. The following note was annotated 2/9 (two shillings and ninepence).

(424)

Ellisland, 8th October 1790

Please send me by the Bearer, my servant, a bar of shoeing iron, which place to account of

Gentlemen, your very humble servant
Robt Burns

CRAUFORD TAIT

Born about 1765, the son of John Tait of Harviestoun by whom Burns was entertained in October 1787, he was educated in Edinburgh, became a Writer to the Signet, and succeeded to the Harviestoun estate on his father's death in 1800. His wife was a daughter of Sir Ilay Campbell, the Lord President, and his son Archibald Campbell Tait was Archbishop of Canterbury (1869-82). The following letter introducing William Duncan exists as a copy in the Glenriddell MS and a draft in the Rosebery Collection, but the original has apparently not survived.

(425)

Ellisland, 15th October 1790

Dear Sir

Allow me to introduce to your acquaintance the bearer, Mr William Duncan, a friend of mine whom I have long known & long loved.—His father, whose only son he is, has a decent little Property in Ayrshire, & has bred the young man to the Law; in which department he comes up an adventurer to your Good Town.—I shall give you my friend's character in two words: as to his head, he has talents enough & more enough for common life; as to his heart, when Nature had kneaded the kindly clay that composes it, she said, "I can no more."—

You, my good Sir, were born under kinder stars; but your fraternal sympathy, I well know, can enter fully into the feelings of the young man who enters life with the laudable ambition to do something & to be something among his fellow creatures; but whom the consciousness of friendless obscurity presses to the earth & wounds the soul!—Even the fairest of his virtues are against him.—That independant spirit & that ingenuous modesty, qualities inseparable from a noble mind, are, with the Million, circumstances not a little disqualifying.—What pleasure is in the power of the Fortunate & the Happy, to glad the heart of such depressed Youth, by their notice and patronage!—I am not angry with mankind at their deaf economy of the purse.—The goods of this world cannot be divided without being lessened.—But why be a niggard of that which bestows bliss on a fellow-creature, yet takes nothing from their own means of enjoyment?—We wrap ourselves up in the cloak of our own better fortune, & turn away our eyes, lest the wants & woes of our brother-mortals should disturb the selfish apathy of our souls.—

I am the worst hand in the world at asking a favor.—That indirect address, that insinuating implication, which without any positive request, plainly expresses your wish, is not a talent to be acquired at a plough-tail.—Tell me, for you can, in what periphrasis of language, in what circumvolution of phrase, I shall envelope yet not conceal this plain story—"My dear Mr Tait, my friend Mr Duncan whom I have the pleasure of introducing to you, is a young lad of your own profession, & a gentleman of much modesty & great worth.—Perhaps it may be in your power to assist him in the, to him, important consideration of getting a Place; but at all events, your notice & acquaintance will be to him a very great acquisition; & I dare pledge myself that he will never disgrace your favor."—

You may probably be surprised, Sir, at such a letter from me: 'tis, I own, in the usual way of calculating these matters, more than our acquaintance entitles me to.—But my answer is short; of all the men at your time of life whom I knew in Edinburgh you are the most accessible on the side on which I have assailed you.—You are very much altered indeed from what you were when I knew you, if Generosity point the path you will not tread, or Humanity call to you in vain.—

As to myself, a being to whose interest I believe you are still a well-wisher; I am here, breathing at all times, thinking sometimes, and rhyming now and then. Every situation has its share of the cares and pains of life, and my situation I am persuaded has a full ordinary allowance of its pleasures and enjoyments.

My best compliments to your father and Miss Tait. If you have an opportunity, please remember me in the solemn league and covenant of friendship to Mrs. Lewis Hay. I am a wretch for not writing her; but I am so hackneyed with self-accusation in that way, that my conscience lies in my bosom with scarce the sensibility of an oyster in its shell. Where is Lady M'Kenzie? wherever she is, God bless her! I likewise beg leave to trouble you with compliments to Mr. Wm. Hamilton; Mrs. Hamilton and family; and Mrs. Chalmers, when you are in that country. Should you meet with Miss Nimmo, please remember me kindly to her.

I am &c. &c—

DR. JAMES ANDERSON

Born in 1739 at Hermiston, west of Edinburgh, he was a pioneer of agricultural improvement and a journalist who wrote on a wide range of topics. He was given a doctorate of law by Aberdeen University in 1780. Between December 1790 and January 1794 he edited *The Bee or Literary Intelligencer*, a literary and scientific periodical. Burns and his friends were subscribers, as the following letter shows. Although Anderson asked Burns to contribute to his magazine, the only thing from his pen was a letter to the Earl of Buchan, which it is thought the Earl sent in himself (see page 267).

(426)

Ellisland near Dumfries
1st November 1790

Sir,

I am much indebted to Dr Blacklock for introducing me to a Gentleman of Dr Anderson's celebrity, & to you, Sir, for your flattering opinion of my abilities.—Your elegant Prospectus gave me much pleasure; & in your hands I have no doubt but your work will form an addition to Scottish literature worthy of a place with any thing it yet can boast.—I hope the Honey that your BEE will gather on the banks of Forth shall be found equal, either for delicacy of flavor, or virtues nutritive & medical, to any that ever was amassed amid all the blossoming fragrance of the Vale of Glocester, or the flowery luxuriance of the plains of Kent.—

As to any assistance that I can give you, I am afraid it will all evaporate in good wishes.—My fingers are so wore to the bone in holding the noses of his Majesty's liege subjects to the grindstone of Excise that I am totally unfitted for wielding a pen in any generous subject.—In the mean time, set me down as a Subscriber, bona fide for I will not, nor can not accept of your kind offer.—Set down likewise, for your first volume at least, in terms of your Proposals:

Alexr Findlater Supervisor of Excise, Dumfries—
John Lewars ⎫
Archibd Thomson ⎬ Officers of Excise, Dumfries—
Willm Pen ⎪
Hugh Marques ⎭
Thomas Sloan—Dumfries (to my care)
Willm Lorimer in Kemyshall near Dumfries—
Willm Hyslop, Innkeeper, Dumfries—
James Mundell, Surgeon, Dumfries—
Frederick Maxwell, Terreagles, near Dumfries
Willm Stewart, Factor, Closeburn, via Dumfries

I would wish, if convenient, to have one or two copies more of your Prospectus.—Perhaps I may add still farther to your Subscription list. —I always did, & now more than ever shall like an honest fellow the better, for "having a Bee in his bonnet-lug"—

I am, Sir, your great Admirer
& most obedient humble servant
Robt Burns

JOHN GILLESPIE

An Excise colleague of Burns at Dumfries, later transferred to Portpatrick, Wigtownshire. While stationed in Dumfriesshire, Gillespie had got to know Jean Lorimer, but his attempts to woo 'Chloris' got nowhere. As late as 1791, however, as this letter indicates, Burns was still trying to convince Gillespie that he had a hope. Jean, however, confounded the poet's prognostications by eloping to Gretna Green with a young rake named Whelpdale who, after three weeks of marriage, left his wife to escape his creditors. Of the two dozen songs which Burns composed about or to Chloris, it has been said that at least three of them were written on behalf of Gillespie. Recent research by Dr David Groves, however, suggests that Burns had a more personal motive. Messrs Lewars and Thomson were John Lewars Jr. and James Thomson, the latter eventually marrying the former's sister Jessy.

(432)

[Ellisland, 1791?]

[With *Craigieburn Wood.*]
[C.W. p. 436]

The inclosed Song, my dear Sir, is the work of t' other day, based on a bonie Lass, once near & dear to your heart, the charming Miss Lorimer.—She was born near Craigieburn-wood, a beautiful place still in her father's possession.—There is a sweet old tune, called Craigieburn wood, which, if you were a musical Man would delight you.—I drank tea with the young lady at her home yesternight; & on my whispering her that I was to write you, she begged me to inclose you her Compliments.—In fact, the lady, to my certain knowledge, is down on her marrow bones of repentance, respecting her usage of a certain gentleman.—I never meet with her, but you are, sooner or later, introduced on the carpet.—Last night when she & I were a few minutes by ourselves after tea, she says to me—"I wonder, Mr Burns what pet Mr Gillespie has taken at this country, that he does not come & see his friends again?"—

Pray, why did you go away, my good Sir, & never take leave of your friends at Ellisland?—I assure you Mrs Burns is very much in dudgeon, & says that she won't send you her Compliments untill you make an apology for your abrupt departure. The great rivals now with Miss Jenny, are our brethren Officers Messrs Lewars & Thomson.—They are both deeply in love, but the Lady does not favor the one or the other.—

Let me hear from you soon.

I am ever, my dear Sir, Yours,
Robt Burns

REV. ARCHIBALD ALISON

Born in 1757 at Edinburgh, he was educated at Glasgow University and Balliol College, Oxford and entered holy orders in 1784. In the same year he married a daughter of Dr John Gregory. After holding a number of Anglican pluralities in England, he returned to Scotland in 1800 and was appointed senior minister of the Edinburgh Episcopal Chapel, a position which he held till his retirement in 1831. He died eight years later. He met Burns when the latter visited Edinburgh in February 1789. The following year he published *Essays on the Nature and Principles of Taste*, a copy of which he sent to Burns who made up for the tardiness of his thanks by writing the following excessively fulsome letter.

(436)

Ellisland, near Dumfries, 14th February 1791

Sir,

You must by this time have set me down as one of the most ungrateful of men.—You did me the honor to present me with a Book which does honor to Science & the intellectual powers of man, & I have not even so much as acknowledged the receipt of it.*—The fact is, you yourself are to blame for it.—Flattered as I was by your telling me that you wished to have my opinion of the Work, the old spiritual enemy of mankind, who knows well that vanity is one of the sins that most easily beset me, put it into my head to ponder over the performance, with the look-out of a Critic, & to draw up forsooth a deep, learned digest of strictures on a Composition, of which in fact, untill I read the book, I did not even know the first principles.—

I own, Sir, that at first glance, several of your propositions startled me as paradoxical.—That the martial clangor of a trumpet had something in it vastly more grand, heroic & sublime, than the twingle-twangle of a jews-harp; that the delicate flexure of a rose-twig, when the half-blown flower is heavy with the tears of the dawn, was infinitely more beautiful & elegant than the upright stub of a burdock; & that from something innate, & independant of all association of ideas; these I had set down as irrefragable, orthodox truths, untill perusing your book shook my faith.—In short, Sir, except Euclid's elements of Geometry, which I made a shift to unravel by my father's fire-side, in the winter-evenings of the first season I held the plough, I never read a book which gave me such a quantum of information & added so much to my stock of ideas, as your "Essay on the principles of taste."—One thing, Sir, you must forgive my mentioning as an uncommon merit in the work, I mean the language.—To clothe abstract Philosophy in elegance of Style, sounds something like a contradiction in terms; but you have convinced me that they are quite compatible.—

I inclose you some poetic bagatelles of my late composition.—The one in print is my first essay in the way of telling a Tale.—

I am, Sir, your great admirer
& obliged humble servant
Robt Burns

* *Essays on the Nature and Principles of Taste* (1790).

REV. GEORGE HUSBAND BAIRD

Born in 1761, he was ordained minister of Dunkeld in 1787 and translated to Greyfriars in Edinburgh five years later. In 1792 he was also appointed joint professor of Oriental languages at Edinburgh University. The following year he became Principal and in 1800 was chosen as Moderator of the General Assembly of the Church of Scotland. Early in 1791 he wrote to Burns, informing him of his plans to publish an edition of the poems of Michael Bruce, the proceeds to be employed in helping Bruce's elderly mother. Baird also wished Burns to look over the late poet's manuscripts and supply some memorial verses for his headstone. Burns declined to add his criticisms to Bruce's manuscripts but enclosed a proof-sheet of *Tam o Shanter* (C.W. p. 410), to be forwarded with a letter (VIII) to Dr Moore (see page 261), saying that Baird could have this for inclusion in the Bruce volume. For his part, Baird rejected Burns's masterpiece as hardly appropriate to a volume of predominantly religious and spiritual peotry.

(438)

Ellisland near Dumfries
28th February 1791

Why did you, my dear Sir, write to me in such a hesitating style on the business of poor Bruce? Don't I know, & have I not felt, the many ills, the peculiar ills, that Poetic Flesh is heir to?—You shall have your choice of all the unpublished poems I have; & had your letter had my address, so as to have reached me in course of post (it but came to hand this morning) I should have directly put you out of suspense about it.—I suppose I need not premise, that I still reserve these my works so much in my power, as to publish them on my own account, if so the spirit move me, at any *after* period.—I only ask that some prefatory advertisement in the Book, as well as the Subscription bills, may bear, that the Publication is solely for the behoof of Bruce's Mother; I would not leave Ignorance the least room to surmise, or Malice to insinuate, that I clubbed a share in the work from mercenary motives.—

Nor need you give me credit for any remarkable generosity in my part of the business.—I have such a host of Peccadillos, Failings, Follies, & Backslidings (anybody but myself might perhaps give some of them a worse appellation) that by way of some balance, however trifling, in the account, I am fain, so far as my very limited power reaches, to do any good I can to my fellow-creatures, merely for the selfish purpose of clearing a little the vista of Retrospection. —You who are a Divine, & accustomed to soar the wild-goose heights of Calvinistic Theology, may no doubt look down with contempt on my creeping notions; but I, who was forced to pick up my fragments of knowledge as the hog picks up his husks, at the plough-tail, can understand nothing sublimer than this debtor & creditor system.—

I sincerely feel for the lamentable, incurable breach, in the family of your truly illustrious Patron.—I ever remember with grateful pride, my reception at Athole-house, & when I saw in the Newspapers the accounts of his Grace's conjugal Piety, my heart ached again, to have it in my power to take him by the hand & say, "Sir, you are an honor to Human-nature; & I not only esteem, but revere you!" I intended to have strung my rustic Lyre to her Grace's ever-dear & sacred memory; but soon, all my ideas were absorbed in the agonies of a violent wrench Fate gave the dearest chords of my bosom, the death of the Earl of Glencairn.—He also was a Being who did honor to that Omnipotence which called him into existence.—From him all my fame & fortune took its rise: to him I owe every thing that I am or have, & for his Sake I wear these Sables with as much devout sincerity as ever bleeding Gratitude did for departed Benevolence.—

My kindest Compliments to Mr Walker.—Do you know an acquaintance of Mr Walker's, & a Countryman of mine, a Mr Wyat? If you have an opportunity, please remember me kindly to him.—

You need not send me Bruce's M.S.S. for my criticisms.—It is among very good hands, indeed among hands superior to mine, already.—*

I have taxed your friendship with the trouble of transmitting the inclosed letter to Dr Moore, the celebrated Author of Zelucco.—I leave it open for your perusal, I mean the printed sheet.—It is one of my latest productions; & I dare say you may have it, if you will, to accompany Bruce's works.—Please inclose it with the card, & seal it with black, & send it to the Doctor.—I do not know his particular address, but it will not be difficult to find, in a Man of his celebrity & rank.—

I am most sincerely, Yours
Robt Burns

* Michael Bruce's *Poems on Several Occasions* was not actually published till 1796, with a lengthy preface, unsigned but believed to have been by Baird.

THOMAS SLOAN

A native of Wanlockhead whom Burns is believed to have first encountered in 1788 when travelling from Ayrshire to Ellisland. Sloan and Burns were to have paid a joint visit to Robert Riddell, but a lame horse and a broken arm prevented Burns from keeping the appointment, as indicated by the first letter, which Ferguson conjecturally dated in April 1791. Sloan was a subscriber to *The Bee* and Ferguson considers that he may have been the recipient of the invitation to spend New Year's Day 1791 with Burns (see page 724). Nothing else is known about Sloan, except that he appears to have got into some kind of business difficulties. Burns was unsuccessful in soliciting John Ballantine's help in the matter (II). From 1791 onwards Sloan resided in Manchester, and it is not known whether he actually received the 1793 edition of the Poems that Burns promised (III).

I (444)

[April 1791]

I am truly sorry, my dear Sir, that my black mare has hurt one of her hind legs so ill that she cannot travel, else she should have been at your service.—

Many thanks for your attention.—I much wish to see you. I called on Captain Riddel today, who enquired kindly for you: he is getting better.—

Excuse this brief epistle from a broken arm.—

Yours,
R.B.

P.S. I have recruited my purse since I saw you, & you may have a guinea or two if you chuse.

II (466)

Ellisland, 1st September 1791

My dear Sloan,

Suspence is worse than disappointment, for that reason I hurry to tell you that I just now learn that Mr Ballantine does not chuse to interfere more in the business.—I am truly sorry for it, but cannot help it.—

You blame me for not writing you sooner, but you will please to recollect that you omitted one little necessary piece of information—your Address.—However, you know equally well, my hurried life, indolent temper, & strength of attachment.—It must be a longer period than the longest life "in the world's hale & undegenerate days" that will make me forget so dear a friend as Mr Sloan.—I am prodigal enough at times, but I will not part with such a treasure as that.—

I can easily enter into the *embaras* of your present situation.—You know my favorite quotation from Young—

"On Reason build RESOLVE!
"That column of true majesty in Man"[1]—

And that other favorite one from Thomson's Alfred—

"What proves the heroe truly Great,
"Is, never, never to despair"——[2]

Or shall I quote you an Author of your acquaintance?

MRS. CATHERINE BRUCE

MRS. JAMES THOMSON (JESSIE LEWARS)

Thomas Sloan

"—Whether DOING, SUFFERING, or FORBEARING,
"You may do miracles by—PERSEVERING"[3]—

I have nothing new to tell you.—The few friends we have are going on in the old way.—I sold my crop on this day se'ennight past, & sold it very well: a guinea an acre, on an average, above value.—But such a scene of drunkenness was hardly ever seen in this country.— After the roup was over, about thirty people engaged in a battle, every man for his own hand, & fought it out for three hours.—Nor was the scene much better in the house.—No fighting, indeed, but folks lieing drunk on the floor, & decanting , untill both my dogs got so drunk by attending them, that they could not stand.—You will easily guess how I enjoyed the scene as I was no farther over than you used to see me.—

Mrs B—— & family have been in Ayr-shire these many weeks.—

Farewel & God bless You! My dear Friend.—
Robt Burns

1 *Night Thoughts*, Night I, lines 30-1.
2 *Alfred: A Masque*, Act I, sc. 3.
3 *Prologue* (C.W. p. 377)

III (539)

Friars Carse, 18th March 1793

My dear Sloan,

Do not ask me why I have never written you.—Blame any thing, but forgetfulness.—I often remember you over my cups, & to my cups.— My present incentive, which has roused me from my lethargy, is a complaint from Mr Riddell, that you have not taken notice of a late letter & business of his.—I have insisted that you are incapable of ingratitude; & I beg that next post you will vindicate & excuse yourself.—

I have just made my appearance, in two volumes.—A Copy waits you.—

Yours
Robt Burns

ALEXANDER FRASER TYTLER

Born in 1747, the son of William Tytler of Woodhouselee, he was educated at the High School and University of Edinburgh and called to the bar in 1770. With John Pringle he was, in 1780, appointed joint professor of Universal History, becoming sole professor in 1786. Four years later he was appointed Judge-Advocate General of Scotland and in 1802 became a Lord of Session, with the title of Lord Woodhouselee. He published several books, including *Decisions of the Court of Session*, *Elements of German History* and a biography of Lord Kames. He was also something of a poetaster and, like his father William Tytler, took a keen interest in Burns and his work. When *Tam o Shanter* was first published by Francis Grose, it was Tytler who persuaded Burns to drop the lines beginning 'Three lawyers' tongues turn'd inside out', suppressed in the 1793 *Poems* and most editions thereafter. Tytler also appears to have corrected the proofs of the 1793 edition of the *Poems*, a matter for which Burns thanked Tytler in his second letter, below. Tytler encouraged Burns to develop the narrative skills which were latent in his composition of *Tam o Shanter*, saying 'you will eclipse Prior and La Fontaine; for with equal wit, equal power of numbers and equal naivete of expression, you have a bolder and more vigorous imagination.' Burns alluded to this in his reply (I) but, as Maurice Lindsay says, 'an apparent decline in Burns's capacity for sustained creative effort, prevented these dreams from being realised.'

I (445)

[Ellisland, April 1791]

Sir,

Nothing less than the unfortunate accident I have met with could have prevented my grateful acknowledgements for your letter. His own favourite poem, and that an essay in a walk of the muses entirely new to him, where consequently his hopes and fears were on the most anxious alarm for his success in the attempt; to have that poem so much applauded by one of the first judges, was the most delicious vibration that ever thrilled along the heart-strings of a poor poet. However, Providence, to keep up the proper proportion of evil with the good, which it seems is necessary in this sublunary state, thought proper to check my exultation by a very serious misfortune. A day or two after I received your letter, my horse came down with me and broke my right arm. As this is the first service my arm has done me since its disaster, I find myself unable to do more than just in general terms to thank you for this additional instance of your patronage and friendship. As to the faults you detected in the piece, they are truly there: one of them, the hit at the lawyer and priest*, I shall cut out: as to the falling off in the catastrophe, for the reason you justly adduce, it cannot easily be remedied. Your approbation, Sir, has given me such additional spirits to persevere in this species of poetic composition, that I am already revolving two or three stories in my fancy. If I can bring these floating ideas to bear any kind of embodied form, it will give me an additional opportunity of assuring you how much I have the honour to be, &c.

* Four lines omitted from most published versions of *Tam o Shanter*, C.W. p. 413:

> Three lawyers' tongues, turn'd inside out,
> Wi lies seam'd like a beggar's clout;
> Three priests' hearts, rotten, black as muck,
> Lay stinking, vile, in every neuk.

These lines appeared in Grose's *Antiquities of Scotland* but Burns omitted them from the 1793 edition of the Poems.

Alexander Fraser Tytler

II (526)

6th December [1792]

Sir,

A poor caitiff, driving, as I am at this moment, with an Excise-quill, at the rate of Devil take the hindmost, is ill-qualified to round the period of Gratitude, or swell the pathos of Sensibility.—Gratitude, like some other amiable qualities of the mind, is nowadays so abused by Imposters, that I have sometimes wished that the project of that sly dog, Momus I think it is, had gone into effect—planting a window in the breast of Man.—In that case, when a poor fellow comes, as I do at this moment, before his Benefactor, tongue-tied with the sense of these very obligations, he would have had nothing to do but place himself in front of his Friend, & lay bare the workings of his bosom.—

I again trouble you with another, & my last, parcel of Manuscript.—I am not interested in any of these; blot them at your pleasure.—I am much indebted to you for taking the trouble of correcting the Press-work. One instance indeed may be rather unlucky: if the lines to Sir John Whiteford are printed, they ought to end,

"And tread the *shadowy* path to that dark world unknown"*— "Shadowy," instead of, "dreary," as I believe it stands at present.—I wish this could be noticed in the Errata.—This comes of writing, as I generally do, from the memory.—

I have the honor to be, Sir, your deeply indebted humble servant Robt Burns

* *Lines to Sir John Whitefoord, Bart.* C.W. p. 425.

CHARLES SHARPE

Born in 1750, the grandson of Sir Thomas Kirkpatrick of Closeburn, he changed his surname to Sharpe on succeeding to the Hoddam estate of his kinsman, Matthew Sharpe, in 1769. In the following year he married Eleanora, daughter of John Renton of Lamerton to whom Burns addressed a short verse-epistle in 1787. Sharpe trained as a lawyer, but never practised. He was a talented amateur musician and also a minor poet, hence Burns's reference to 'our common Family . . . of the Muses'. Burns's *nom de plume*, Johnie Faa, was derived from a celebrated Irish tinker.

(446)

Dumfries, 22nd April 1791

It is true, Sir, you are a gentleman of rank & fortune & I am a poor devil; you are a feather in the cap of Society, & I am a very hobnail in his shoes; yet I have the honor to belong to the same Family with you, & on that score I now address you.—You will perhaps suspect that I am going to claim affinity with the equally ancient & honorable House of Kilpatrick?—No, no, Sir: I cannot indeed be properly said to belong to any House, or even any Province or Kingdom, as my mother, who for many years was spouse to a marching regiment, gave me into this bad world, aboard the packet-boat, somewhere between Donaghadee & Portpatrick.—By our common Family, I mean, Sir, the Family of the Muses.—I am a Fiddler & a Poet; & you, I am told, play an exquisite Violin, & have a standard taste in the belles lettres.—The other day, a brother Cat-gut gave me a charming Scots air of your composition.—If I was delighted with the tune, I was in raptures with the name you have given it; & taking up the idea, I have spun it into the three stanzas inclosed.—Will you allow me, Sir, to present you them, as the dearest offering that a misbegotten son of Poverty & Rhyme has to bestow? —I have a woman's longing to take you by the hand & unburthen my heart by saying, "Sir, I honor you as a Man who supports the "dignity of human-nature in an age when Frivolity & Avarice "have between them debased us below the brutes that "perish!"—But, Alas, Sir! to me you are unapproachable.—It is true, the Muses baptized me in Castalian streams, but the thoughtless gipseys forgot to give me A NAME.—As some others of the Sex have served many a poor fellow, they have given me a great deal of pleasure, but the bewitching jades have beggared me.—

Would they but spare me a little of their cast-linen!—Were it only to put it in my power to say, that I have a shirt on my back!—But the idle wenches, like Solomon's lilies, "toil not, neither do they spin;"* so I must e'en continue to tie my remnant of a cravat, like the hangman's rope, round my naked throat; & coax my galligaskins to keep together their many colored fragments, & conceal with all their remaining strength (a strength, alas! seldom equal to the task!) the indecent efforts & obscene exhibitions of their unruly INMATE.—As to the affair of Shoes, I have given that up.—My pilgrimages in my ballad-trade from town to town, & on your stony-hearted turnpikes too, are what not even the hide of Job's behemoth could bear.—The coat on my back is no more: I shall not speak evil of the Dead.—It would be equally unhandsome & ungrateful to find fault with my old Surtout, which so kindly supplies & conceals the loss of my departed coat.—My hat indeed is a great favorite; & though I got it literally for "an old song," I would not exchange it for the best

Charles Sharpe

beaver in Britain.—I was for several of my earlier years, a kind of factotum servant to a country Clergyman, where I pickt up, among other scraps of learning, a smattering in some branches of the mathematicks.—Whenever I feel inclined to rest myself on my way, I take my seat under a hedge, & laying my wallet of ballads on the one side, & my fiddle-case on the other, I place my hat between my legs, & can by means of its brim, or rather brims, go through the whole doctrine of the Conic Sections.—

However, Sir, don't let me mislead you, as if I meant to interest your pity.—Fortune has so much forsaken me, that she has taught me to live without her; & amid my ragged poverty, I am as independant, & much more happy, than a monarch of the world.—According to the hackneyed metaphor, I value the several Actors in the great Drama of Life, simply as they perform their Parts.—I can look on a worthless fellow of a Duke with unqualified contempt, & can regard an honest scavenger with sincere respect.—As you, Sir, go thro' your Role with such distinguished merit, permit me to make one in the chorus of universal applause, & have the honor of subscribing myself, with the highest respect for your character, & the warmest wish for your welfare,

Sir, your most devoted humble servant
Johnie Faa—

* Matthew 6:28-9.

JAMES GRACIE

Born at New Abbey, Kirkcudbrightshire about 1756, he became manager of the Dumfries Commercial Bank, Dean of Guild and captain in the Dumfries Volunteers. He was the subject of the epigram 'Gracie, thou art a man of worth' (C.W. p. 420). When the Commercial Bank failed Gracie turned to accountancy as a career, but died bankrupt in 1814. The first letter below sheds light on the hazards of discounting bills, a form of financial transaction common in an era before cheques and money orders became fashionable. Burns had taken Alexander Crombie's bill for £20, but about two months later was using it in partial settlement of his own debt to Thomas Boyd who, in turn was indebted to Crombie (see page 000). The second letter was in reply to Gracie's offer of a convalescent outing in his carriage, but Burns was dying by that date.

I (447)

Globe Inn, 8 *o'clock* p.m.
[April? 1791]

Sir—

I have your letter anent Crombie's bill. Your forbearance has been very great. I did it to accommodate the thoughtless fellow. He asks till Wednesday week. If he fail, I pay it myself. In the meantime, if horning and caption be absolutely necessary, *grip him by the neck, and welcome.*

Yours,
Robert Burns

II (707)

Weden: morn:
[Brow, 13th July 1796]

My dear Sir,

It would be doing high injustice to this place not to acknowledge that my rheumatisms have derived great benefit from it already; but alas, my loss of appetite still continues. I shall not need your kind offer, *this week*, & I return to town the beginning of next week it not being a tide-week.—I am detaining a man in a burning hurry—So God bless you!

R Burns

ALEXANDER COUTTS

A minor poet, resident in Whitehaven, Cumbria who wrote to Burns on 21st April 1791 enclosing a verse-epistle. So far as can be ascertained, however, Burns never got around to sending a rhyming reply.

(450)

Ellisland, near Dumfries,
28th April 1791.

Dear Sir,

I am much your debtor for your two elegant epistles. I had written you long ago but I still hoped my Muse would enable me to answer you *in kind*; but the Muses are capricious gipseys, at least I have ever found them so. In the meantime I send you this verse, like other poor devils who are in debt, to beg a little time—"have patience, and I will pay thee all."* I shall reprobate my Muse to all eternity, if she do not very soon inspire me to tell you in Verse how sincerely I am,

Dear Sir, Yours,
Robt Burns

* Matthew 18:26.

SIR JAMES STIRLING

Born in 1740-1, the son of Alexander Stirling and Jane Muir of Edinburgh, he went to the West Indies where he amassed a large fortune. On his return to Edinburgh he became a partner in a bank and married Alison Mansfield, daughter of his senior partner. He was Lord Provost of Edinburgh in 1790, 1794, and 1798 and was created a baronet in 1792 for his 'firm yet prudent conduct in connection with the reform riots' in that year. He died in 1805. As one of the trustees of Moffat Grammar School he was in receipt of the following letter which Burns drafted on behalf of James Clarke. Burns later transcribed a copy of it for the Glenriddell MS.

(459)

[June 1791]

My Lord

It may be deemed presumption in a man, obscure & unknown as I am, & an entire stranger to your Lordship, to trouble you in this manner, but when I inform you that the subject on which I address you is of the last importance to me, & is so far connected with you, that on your determination, in a great measure, my fate must depend, I rely on your Lordship's goodness that you will think any farther apology unnecessary.—I have been for nearly five years Schoolmaster in Moffat; an appointment of which, your Lordship will know, you, with the rest of the Magistracy & Town Council, together with the Clergy of Edinburgh, have the Patronage.—The trust with which these my highly respectable Patrons had honored me, I have endeavoured to discharge with the utmost fidelity, & I hope, with a good degree of success; but of late, one or two powerful individuals of my employers have been pleased to attack my reputation as a Teacher; have threatened no less than to expell me the school; & are taking every method, some of them, I will say it, insidious & unfair to the last degree, to put their threats in execution. —The fault of which I am accused is, some instances of severity to the children under my care.—Were I to tell your Lordship, that I am innocent of the charge; that any shade of cruelty, particularly that very black one of cruelty to tender infancy, will be allowed by every unbiassed person who knows any thing of me, to be tints unknown in my disposition; you would certainly & justly look on all this *from me*, as words of course; so I shall trouble you with nothing on the merits of my cause, untill I have a fair hearing before my Right Honorable Patrons.—

A fair hearing, my Lord, is what above all things I want; & what I greatly fear, will be attempted to be denied me.—It is to be insinuated, that I have vacated my place; that I never was legally appointed; with I know not how many pretences more, to hinder the business from coming properly before your Lordship & the other Patrons of the School: all which I deny; & will insist on holding my appointment untill the dignified Characters who gave it me, shall find me unworthy of it.—In your Lordship's great acquaintance with Human-life, you must have known of, & seen, many instances of Innocence, nay, of Merit, disguised & obscured, & sometimes for ever buried, by the dark machinations of unprincipled Malevolence, & envious Craft; & till the contrary be made appear, 'tis at least equally probable that my case is in that unfortunate & undeserved predicament.—

I have the honor to be, &c.

REV. THOMAS SMITH

Born in 1764 at Dumfries, he was educated at Edinburgh University and after graduating in 1785 went to Alloa Seminary. In 1789 he was licensed to preach by the Presbytery of Dumfries and ordained the following year. Later in 1790 he received a call from the congregation of Mecklenburgh County, North Carolina, but declined it and worked for ten years as a home missionary. In 1800, however, he emigrated to the United States where he did missionary and supply work for eleven years. He was then appointed minister of a United Presbyterian congregation in Huntingdon, Pennsylvania where he remained till his death in August 1825. In 1814 he was appointed Moderator of the Synod of the American Church. Smith was doing missionary work at Auchinleck when Burns wrote the following letter, enclosing copies of *Wilt thou be my Dearie* (C.W. p. 512) and *O wat ye wha's in yon town* (C.W. p. 541).

(462A)

[With *Wilt thou be my Dearie* and *O wat ye wha's in yon town.*]
[C.W. pp. 512, 541]

Bailie Kellock's
4th July 1791

My dear Sir—

I know you will be setting me down in the book of your remembrance as an ungrateful fellow for not answering your kind obliging letter.—People will pretend business, and make fifty apologies, all of them frivolous and untrue.—Five minutes you will say would do the business, and what man so hurried that he cannot spare five minutes? So 'tis impossible to exculpate the Poet from the vile charge, of unkindly neglecting his Friend:—But, if you know the French proverb, "Le vrai n'est toujours le vraisemble,"* It was never more applicable than in the present case.—A few days after I got your valued letter, I fell or rather my horse fell with me, and I broke my right arm.—

This, you will allow, was too good an apology.—I would gladly, since my recovery, have written you, but you are such a bird of passage there is no guessing where to find you; but by the same good luck that I met with you and at the same fireside too, I fell in just now with a pleasant, jolly fellow, a gentleman of your cloth, a Mr Ferrier, from Paisley, a man who may be stiled, a Body, or rather, *Corporation* of Divinity; and he has obligingly promised to convey you this dry scrawl.—

I expect a printed copy of "Logie o' Buchan," by the first post.—I will take care to forward a Copy of it for you, if I should advertise for your address in the newspapers.—It is a sweet little air, and the stanza equally beautiful.—

I must break off here; for I find this dull rainy day and consequently, low spirits, have sunk me to such a miserable, matter-of-fact, drawling style that I am unequal to a higher task than a hand-bill Advertisement.—

Adieu my dear Sir! and believe me to be yours, sincerely.—
Robt Burns

* Nicolas Boileau-Despreaux: *L'Art poetique*, Canto 3, line 48, misquoted.

SIR JOHN SINCLAIR OF ULBSTER, BART.

Born in 1754 at Thurso Castle, he was successively MP for Caithness (1780), Lostwithiel (1784) and Petersfield (1796-1811). He was the first President of the Board of Agriculture and died at Edinburgh in 1835. In 1793 he published his monumental *History of the Revenue of the British Empire*, but this was eclipsed by the work for which he has become immortal, his *Statistical Account of Scotland*, published in 21 volumes between 1791 and 1799. This was the first systematic attempt to compile socio-economic statistics for the whole country and was prepared largely as a result of the co-operation of the parish ministers. Robert Riddell was very disappointed with the account of Dunscore produced by the minister of that parish, so he prevailed on Burns to send Sir John a supplementary article, dealing with the Monkland Friendly Society Library which he and the poet had founded. The following letter included Burns's account which shows that Burns rather than Riddell had been the chief instigator of this pioneering attempt at a community library. This is confirmed by Riddell's own admission to Sir John which accompanied Burns's letter: 'Mr Burns was so good as to take the whole charge of this small concern. He was treasurer, librarian, and censor to this little society, who will long have a grateful sense of his public spirit and exertions for their improvement and information.' Burns's contribution was published as an appendix to volume III (pp. 598-600).

(469)

[Ellisland, August or September 1791]

Sir,

The following circumstance has, I believe, been omitted in the Statistical Account, transmitted to you, of the parish of Dunscore, in Nithsdale. I beg leave to send it you, because it is new, and may be useful. How far it is deserving of a place in your patriotic publication, you are the best judge.

To store the minds of the lower classes with useful knowledge, is certainly of very great consequence, both to them as individuals, and to society at large. Giving them a turn for reading and reflection, is giving them a source of innocent and laudable amusement; and besides, raises them to a more dignified degree in the scale of rationality. Impressed with this idea, a gentleman in this parish, ROBERT RIDDELL, Esq.; of Glenriddel, set on foot a species of circulating library, on a plan so simple, as to be practicable in any corner of the country; and so useful, as to deserve the notice of every country gentleman, who thinks the improvement of that part of his own species, whom chance has thrown into the humble walks of the peasant and the artisan, a matter worthy of his attention.

Mr. Riddell got a number of his own tenants, and farming neighbours, to form themselves into a society, for the purpose of having a library among themselves. They entered into a legal engagement, to abide by it for 3 years; with a saving clause or two, in cases of removal to a distance, or of death. Each member, at his entry, paid 5s.; and at each of their meetings, which were held every fourth Saturday, 6d. more. With their entry money, and the credit which they took on the faith of their future funds, they laid in a tolerable stock of books at the commencement. What authors they were to purchase, was always to be decided by the majority. At every meeting, all the books, under certain fines and forfeitures, by way of penalty, were to be produced; and the members had their choice of the volumes in rotation. He whose name stood, for that night, first on the list, had his choice of what volume he pleased in the whole collection; the second had his choice after the first; the third after the second, and so on to the last. At the next meeting, he who had been first on the list at the preceding meeting, was last at this; he

586

who had been second, was first; and so on, through the whole 3 years. At the expiration of the engagement, the books were sold by auction, but only among the members themselves; and each man had his share of the common stock, in money or in books, as he chose to be a purchaser or not.

At the breaking up of this little society, which was formed under Mr. Riddell's patronage, what with benefactions of books from him, and what with their own purchases, they had collected together upwards of 150 volumes. It will easily be guessed, that a good deal of trash would be bought. Among the books, however, of this little library, were, Blair's Sermons, Robertson's History of Scotland, Hume's History of the Stewarts, the Spectator, Idler, Adventurer, Mirror, Lounger, Observer, Man of Feeling, Man of the World, Chrysal, Don Quixotte, Joseph Andrews, &c. A peasant who can read, and enjoy such books, is certainly a much superior being to his neighbour, who, perhaps, stalks beside his team, very little removed, except in shape, from the brutes he drives.

Wishing your patriotic exertions their so much merited success,

I am, SIR, Your humble servant,
A Peasant

ALEXANDER WILLIAMSON OF BALGRAY

For many years factor to the Earl of Hopetoun, nothing is known of him other than that he died at Edinburgh on 12th July 1805. He was the recipient of yet another letter drafted by Burns on behalf of James Clarke during the Moffat dispute of 1791. The text of this letter was later copied by Burns for the Glenriddell Ms, hence the comment at the foot. The Glenriddell version is headed '. . . to Mr Williamson, Factotum & Favorite to the Earl of Hopeton'.

(470)

[September 1791]

Sir

most sincerely do I regret that concurrence of accident, prejudice & mistake, which, most unfortunately for me, has subjected me, as master of Moffat Grammar-School, to the displeasure of the Earl of Hopeton & those in whom he places confidence.—Protestations of my innocence will, from me, be thought words of course.—But I hope, & I think I have some well-grounded reasons for that hope, that the gentlemen in whose hands I immediately am, the Right Honorable Patrons of the School, will find the charges against me groundless, & my claims just; & will not allow me to fall a sacrifice to the insidious designs of some, & the well-meant, though misinformed, zeal of others.—However, as disputes & litigations must be of great hurt both to the School & Me, I most ardently wish that it would suggest itself to Mr Williamson's good sense & wish for the welfare of the country, the propriety of dropping all disputes, & allowing me peaceable admission to my School & the exercise of my function.—This, Sir, I am persuaded, will be serving all parties; & will lay *me* under particular & lasting obligations to your goodness.—I propose opening school tomorrow; & the quiet possession of my schoolhouse is what I have to request of you: a request which if refused, I must be under the very disagreable necessity of asking in the way pointed out by the laws of my Country.—Whatever you, Sir, may think of other parts of my conduct, you will at least grant the propriety of a man's straining every nerve in a contest, where not only RUIN but INFAMY must attend his defeat.—

Bravo! Clarke.—In spite of Hopeton & his myrmidons thou camest off victorious!—

WILLIAM DOUGLAS, 4th DUKE OF QUEENSBERRY

Born in 1724, the only son of William, second Earl of March, and Lady Anne Hamilton, he succeeded to the earldom in 1731. On the death of a cousin in 1786 he succeeded to the dukedom of Queensberry. A notorious hell-rake, gambler and patron of the turf, he was familiarly though unfavourably known in contemporary memoirs and gossip columns as 'Old Q'. He has been blamed for the corruption of Charles James Fox, the politician, who became a compulsive gambler and almost ruined his career. Queensberry was Lord of the Bedchamber to King George III from 1760 till 1789, but was dismissed for backing the Prince of Wales in the Regency controversy. He died unmarried in 1810, despite a numerous illegitimate progeny, and his titles were then dispersed. The dukedom, together with Drumlanrig Castle, then passed to the third Duke of Buccleuch. Despite the following fulsome letter, which accompanied a copy of *The Whistle* (C.W. p. 368), Burns had little time for 'Drumlanrig's haughty Grace' whom he lampooned in his election ballads.

(471)

Ellisland, 24th September 1791

My Lord Duke

Will your Grace pardon this approach in a poor Poet, who perhaps intrudes on your converse with Princes to present you—all he has to offer—his best Ballad; & to beg—all he has to ask of you—your gracious acceptance of it.—Whatever might be my opinion of the poem, I would not have dared to take the liberty of presenting it thus, but for your Grace's acquaintance with the dramatis personae of the piece.—

When I first thought of sending my poem to your Grace, I had some misgivings of heart about it.—Something within me seemed to say— "A Nobleman of the first rank & the first taste, & who has lived in "the first Court of Europe, what will he care for you or your ballad? "Depend upon it that he will look on this business as some one or "other of the many modifications of that servility of soul, with "which Authors, & particularly you, Poets, have ever approached the "Great."—No! said I to myself: I am conscious of the purity of my motives.—And as I never crouch to any man, but the man I have wronged; nor even him, except he forgives me; I will approach his Grace with tolerable upright confidence, that even were I & my ballad poorer stuff than we are, the Duke of Queensberry's polite affability would make me welcome; as my sole motive is to shew how sincerely I have the honor to be,

My Lord Duke,
Your Grace's most devoted humble servant
Robt Burns

[This was written shortly after I had the honor of being introduced to the Duke, at which introduction I spent the evening with him, when he treated me with the most distinguished politeness, & marked attention.—Though I am afraid his Grace's character as a Man of worth is very equivocal, yet he certainly is a Nobleman of the first taste, & a Gentleman of the first manners—]*

* The comment in parenthesis appears with the transcription of the letter in the Glenriddell MS.

DEBORAH DUFF DAVIES

Daughter of Dr Daniel Davies of Tenby, Pembrokeshire and a relative of the Riddell family whom Burns probably met at Woodley Park, she was noted for her petite beauty which inspired several songs and epigrams by the poet. She went to France for the sake of her health, but apparently died young of consumption. Cunningham adds, without any substantiation, that she was jilted by a Captain Delaney and went into a decline as a consequence. Miss Davies was staying at Drungans Lodge near Beeswing on the western side of the Nith estuary in October 1791 when she received Burns's first letter. Miss Davies, by virtue of her social position, was in an untouchable and unattainable category so far as Burns was concerned, and although a chatty and amiable letter from her, written at Fontainebleu in March 1793, is extant, Burns's letters to her were all couched in his most turgid and high-flown style, clearly intent on impressing this girl who was his social superior.

I (472A)

Inclosing a ballad[1]

[early October? 1791] [2]

Madam,

I understand that my very worthy neighbour, Mr Riddell, has informed you that I have made you the subject of some verses.— There is something in the idea of being the burdeñ of a ballad, that I do not think Job or Moses, though such patterns of patience & meekness, could have resisted the curiosity to know what that ballad was: so my worthy friend, what I dare say he never intended, has done me a mischief; & reduced me to the unfortunate alternative of leaving your curiousity ungratified, or else disgusting you with foolish verses, the unfinished production of a random moment, & never meant to have met your ear.—I have heard or read somewhere, of a gentleman, who had some genius, much eccentricity, & very considerable dexterity with his pencil.—In the accidental groupes of social life into which one is thrown, whenever this gentleman met with a Character in a more than ordinary degree congenial to his soul, he used to steal a sketch of the face, merely, he said, as a nota bene to point out the agreeable recollection to his memory.—What this Gentleman's pencil was to him, is my Muse to me; & the inclosed verses I do myself the honor to send you, are a memento exactly of the same kind.—It may be more owing to the fastidious-ness of my caprice than the delicacy of my taste, but I am so often tired, disgusted & hurt with the insipidity; affectation & pride of mankind, that when I meet with a person "after my own heart," I positively feel what an orthodox Protestant would call a species of idolatry, & which acts on my mind like inspiration, & I can no more resist rhyming on the impulse, than an Eolian harp can refuse its tones to the streaming air.—A distich or two would be the consequence, though the object of my fancy were grey-bearded, wrinkled age; but where my theme is Youth & Beauty, a young Lady whose personal charms, wit & sentiment are equally striking & unaffected—by Heavens! though I had lived threescore years a married man, & threescore years before I was a married man, my imagination would hallow the very idea; & I am truly sorry that the inclosed stanzas have done such poor justice to such a Subject—

I have the honor &c.—

1 Miss Davies replied that she was 'vain of the poem addressed' to her, but goes on to speak of its 'Jacobite sentiments'. This would suggest that either *Lovely Davies* (C.W. p. 422) was not the poem enclosed, or that her comment dealt with another poem.
2 Miss Davies thanked Burns in a letter of 10th October 1791.

Deborah Duff Davies

II (556A)

[Enclosing *Wee Thing*.]

[C.W. p. 446]

6th April 1793

It is impossible, Madam, that the generous warmth & angelic purity of your youthful mind can have any idea of that moral disease under which I, unhappily, must rank as the chief of sinners; I mean, a torpitude of the Moral Powers that may be called, A Lethargy of Conscience.—In vain the provoked Fury rears her horrent crest, & rouses all her snakes: beneath the deadly-fixed eye & leaden hand of INDOLENCE, their wildest ire is charmed into the torpor of the bat, slumbering out the rigours of winter in the chink of a ruined wall.— Nothing less, Madam, than this vile depravity of soul could have made me so long neglect your obliging commands.—Indeed I had one apology: the bagatelle was not worth presenting.—Besides, so strongly as I am interested in Miss DAVIES'S fate & welfare, in the serious business of life, amid its chances & changes; that to make her the subject of a silly BALLAD, is downright mockery of these ardent feelings.—'Tis like an impertinent jest to a dying friend.—

Good God, why this disparity between our wishes & our powers!— Why is the most generous wish to make others blest, impotent & ineffectual as the idle breeze that crosses the pathless desart!—In my walks of life, I have met with a few people to whom how gladly would I have said—"Go, be happy!—I know that your hearts have been wounded by the scorn of the Proud whom accident has placed above you, or worse still, in whose hands, perhaps, are placed many of the comforts of your life: but, there! ascend that rock of Independance, & look, justly, down on their littleness of soul.—Make the Worthless tremble under your indignation, & the Foolish sink before your contempt; & largely impart that happiness to others which I am certain will give yourselves so much pleasure to bestow!"

Why, dear Madam, must I awake from this delightful reverie, & find it all a dream?—Why, amid my generous enthusiasm, must I find myself a poor, powerless devil, incapable of wiping one tear from the eye of Misery, or of adding one comfort to the Friend I love!—Out upon the world! say I; that its affairs are administered so ill!—They talk of REFORM—My God! what a reform would *I* make among the Sons, & even the Daughters of men!

DOWN, immediately, should go FOOLS from the high places where misbegotten CHANCE has perked them up, & through life should they sculk, ever haunted by their native insignificance, as the body marches accompanied by its shadow.—As for a much more formidable class, the knaves, I am at a loss what to do with them.—Had *I* a world, there should not be a knave in it: & on the other hand, Hell as our Theologians paint it, particularly an eternal Hell, is a deeper damnation than I could bear to see the veriest scoundrel in earth plunged into.—But the hand that could give, I would liberally fill: & I would pour delight on the heart that could kindly forgive, & generously love.—

591

Still, the inequalities of life are, among MEN, comparatively tolerable: but there is a DELICACY, a TENDERNESS, accompanying every view in which one can place lovely WOMAN, that are grated & shocked at the rude, capricious distinctions of Fortune.—Woman is the BLOOD-ROYAL of life: let there be slight degrees of precedency among them, but let them be all sacred.—

Whether this last sentiment be right, or wrong, I am not accountable: it is an original, component feature of my mind.—I remember, & 'tis almost the earliest thing I do remember, when I was quite a boy, one day at church, being enraged at seeing a young creature, one of the maids of his house, rise from the mouth of the pew to give way to a bloated son of Wealth & Dullness, who waddled surlily past her.— Indeed the girl was very pretty; & he was an ugly, stupid, purse-proud, money-loving, old monster, as you can imagine.

I will make no apology for this rhapsodical sheet.—If you are provoked to take your revenge in kind, it will highly honor & oblige,

Madam, Your most obedient humble servant
Robt Burns

III (564)

Tuesday Evening
[June? 1793]

Happy is the man, Madam, that ever has it in his power to contribute to your enjoyments. *Ah, quelle enviable sorte!* (N.B. If this is not French, it ought to be so.) If the following Song gives you any entertainment, it more than repays me for composing it. (The singularity of this compliment is, that it is true.) It is written on the only toast I have in the world besides yourself—a lovely woman, a Miss Lesley Baillie, of Mayfield, in Ayrshire. Why you and she have appeared so lovely in my eyes, is the Creator's business to answer for: so I am glad the burden is off my shoulders.

Song.

Blythe hae I been on yon hill,
[C.W. p. 490]

By the bye, I am a great deal luckier than most poets. When I sing Miss Davies or Miss Lesley Baillie, I have only to feign the passion— the charms are real.

That never in your presence may the son of man speak to deceive, or hear to betray, is the devout prayer of,

Madam, Your devoted bard, and humble servant
Robert Burns

COLONEL WILLIAM FULLARTON

Born in 1754, the son of the botanist William Fullarton of Fullarton, near Dundonald, Ayrshire, he was educated at Edinburgh University and undertook the Grand Tour in the care of Patrick Brydone. Later he entered the Army and served with distinction, eventually commanding the 98th Regiment. Following the outbreak of the French Revolutionary War in 1793 he raised the 23rd Light Dragoons, also known as Fullarton's Light Horse, and saw service at the Cape and in India. He represented Ayrshire in Parliament from 1796 till 1803, becoming Governor of Trinidad in the latter year. He died in 1808. His publications include an *Account of Agriculture in Ayrshire* (1793) and a *View of English Interests in India.* He was referred to in *The Vision* (C.W. p. 114). Fullarton and a friend visited Burns at Ellisland in 1791, and as a result Burns wrote the following letter, enclosing some poems.

(474)

Ellisland, 3rd October 1791

Sir,

I have just this minute got the frank*; & next minute must send it to Post, else I purposed to have sent you two or three other bagatelles, that might have amused a vacant hour about as well as, "Six excellent new Songs," or, "The Aberdeen Prognostication for the year to come."—I shall probably trouble you soon with another packet.— About the "gloomy month of November, when the people of England hang & drown themselves," any thing generally is better than one's own thought.—

Fond as I may be of my own productions, it is not for their sake that I am so anxious to send you them.—I am ambitious, covetously ambitious of being known to a gentleman whom I am proud to call my Countryman: a gentleman who was a Foreign Embassador as soon as he was a Man; & a Leader of Armies as soon as he was a Soldier; & that with an eclat unknown to the usual minions of a Court, men who with all the adventitious advantages of Princely Connections and Princely Fortune, must yet, like the Caterpillar, labor a whole lifetime before they reach the wished height, there to roost a stupid Chrysalis, & doze out the remaining glimmering existence of old age.—

If the gentleman who accompanied you when you did me the honor of calling on me is with you, I beg to be respectfully remembered to him.—

I have the honor to be Sir,
your highly obliged & most devoted humble servant
Robt Burns

* Referred to in Letter V (472) to Robert Riddell of Glenriddell (see page 483).

REV. JOSEPH KIRKPATRICK

Born in 1750, he was ordained minister of Dunscore in 1777 and moved to Wamphray in 1806 where he remained till his death in 1824. He married Anne McMillan, daughter of the minister of Torthorwald, Dumfriesshire. While he resided at Ellisland, Burns attended services at Dunscore parish church, and it was Kirkpatrick's ill-advised attack on the House of Stuart, on the centenary of the Glorious Revolution of 1688, which inspired Burns to write to the Edinburgh *Evening Courant* in November 1788 (see page 487). Apart from this political disagreement, Burns found his minister a dreadful bore, 'one vast constellation of dullness, and from his weekly zenith rays out his contradictory stupidity to the no small edification and enlightenment of the heavy and opaque pericraniums of his gaping Admirers', as he described him to Alexander Cunningham in March 1791 (see page 462). Robert Riddell, however, put it more tersely when he expressed his extreme dissatisfaction of the Dunscore parish account, to Sir John Sinclair when sending in addenda to Kirkpatrick's contribution: '. . .the worst account yet printed, except the account of the parish of Terregles. Much more may be said of Dunscore, but the ignorance and stupidity of the minister is such, and so great a Mule is he, that no good can be done with him.' Nevertheless, Burns observed the social niceties when he informed Kirkpatrick of his impending move to Dumfries.

(478)

Ellisland, Saturday Noon
[22nd? October 1791]

Reverend & Dear Sir,

On Thursday first I intend doing myself the pleasure of waiting on you, as I am thinking to flit the Monday or Tuesday following.—If the weather is such that she can accompany me, Mrs Burns will also do herself the pleasure of waiting on Mrs Kirkpatrick before we leave Dunscore.—If I do not hear from you I shall conclude that our waiting on you will not be inconvenient for you.—

I am, with sincere respect, Dear Sir,
Your very humble servant
Robt Burns

JAMES CLARKE

Born at Closeburn about 1761, he was educated at Wallacehall Academy in that parish and became a teacher at Moffat Grammar School in 1786. He organised the subscription library in that town and about 1790 married Jane Simpson from Cumbria. In 1791 Clarke fell foul of some parents of his pupils and they conspired with the Earl of Hopetoun, the local landowner, to have him dismissed. Burns exerted himself on Clarke's behalf and, as he mentions in a letter (X) to Alexander Cunningham (see page 464), secured the help of Robert Riddell, Fergusson of Craigdarroch and John McMurdo of Drumlanrig. The first two letters in this series allude to this unpleasant incident. Clarke went to Edinburgh in February 1792 to seek redress and, incidentally, carried a letter (XII) from Burns to Peter Hill. Burns also drafted a letter for Clarke to send to the Lord Provost of Edinburgh, one of the school's patrons, to seek a fair hearing. Clarke was vindicated and continued at Moffat until 1794 when he was promoted to Forfar. He became rector of Cupar Grammar School in 1802. In retirement he kept a boarding-house at Dollar, where he died in 1825. Though hard-pressed himself, Burns lent his friend a considerable sum of money which Clarke was still paying off at the time of the poet's death. Burns's last letter, less than a month before he died, acknowledged one of these repayments and appealed for another by return of post.

I (489)

Dumfries, 10th January 1792

I received your letters this moment, my dear Sir.—I sup with Captain Riddel in town tonight, else I had gone to Carse directly.—Courage, mon ami! The day may, after all, be yours: but at any rate, there is other air to breathe than that of Moffat, pestiferously tainted as it is with the breath of that Arch Scoundrel, Johnston.—There are two quotations from two of our Poets which, in situations such as yours, were congenial to my soul.—

Thomson says—

"What proves the hero truly great,
"Is never, never to despair."[1]—

And Dr Young

—"On REASON build RESOLVE,
"That column of true majesty in Man!"[2]

Tomorrow you shall know the result of my consultation with Captain Riddel.—

Yours
Robt Burns

1 *Alfred: A Masque*, Act I, sc. 3.
2 *Night Thoughts*, Night I, lines 30-1.

II (499)

Dumfries 17th February 1792

My dear Sir,

If this finds you at Moffat, or so soon as it finds you at Moffat, you must without delay wait on Mr Riddel, as he has been very kindly thinking of you in an affair that has occurred of a Clerk's place in Manchester, which, if your hopes are desperate in your present business, he proposes procuring it for you.—I know your gratitude for past, as well as hopes of future favors, will induce you to pay every attention to Glenriddel's wishes; as he is almost the only, & undoubtedly the *best* friend that your unlucky fate has left you.—

Apropos, I just now hear that you have beat your foes, *every tail hollow*. Huzza! Io! triomphe! Mr Riddel, who is at my elbow, says

595

that if it is so, he begs that you will wait on him directly—& I know you are too good a man not to pay your respects to your Saviour.—

Yours
Robt Burns
turn over

Mr Riddel will be in Dumfries untill Sunday midday, so you will find him here.—If you don't come & wait on him directly—You will never be forgiven.—

R.B.—

III (698)

Dumfries, 26th June 1796

My dear Clarke,

Still, still the victim of affliction, were you to see the emaciated figure who now holds the pen to you, you would not know your old frined.—Whether I shall ever get about again, is only known to HIM, the Great Unknown, whose creature I am.—Alas, Clarke, I begin to fear the worst!—As to my individual Self, I am tranquil;—I would despise myself if I were not: but Burns's poor widow! & half a dozen of his dear little ones, helpless orphans, there I am weak as a woman's tear.*—Enough of this! 'tis half my disease!—

I duly received your last, inclosing the note.—It came extremely in time, & I was much obliged to your punctuality.—Again I must request you to do me the same kindness.—Be so very good as *by return of post* to inclose me another note.—I trust you can do it without much inconvenience, & it will seriously oblige me.—If I must go, I leave a few friends behind me, whom I shall regret while consciousness remains—I know I shall live in their remembrance.—

Adieu dear Clarke! That I shall ever see you again, is, I am afraid, highly improbable.—

R. Burns

* Shakespeare: *Troilus and Cressida*, Act I, sc. 1, altered.

WILLIAM SMELLIE

Born in 1740 at Edinburgh, the son of a prosperous stonemason, he was educated at Duddingston parish school and Edinburgh High School. He became apprenticed to a printer in 1752, but also attended classes at the University and studied at home. He acquired a wide knowledge of science and literature and a reputation as the printer of many learned works. In 1771 he became the first editor of the *Encyclopaedia Britannica*, writing many of the entire works himself. With Gilbert Stuart he founded the *Edinburgh Magazine*, translated the works of Buffon, and compiled a *Philosophy of Natural History* which was widely acclaimed at the time. He wore his erudition lightly and had a name for conviviality, being the founder of the Crochallan Fencibles to which he introduced Burns. Undoubtedly many letters must have passed between Burns and Smellie, but the only one that has survived is the following, intended to introduce Maria Riddell who was seeking a publisher for her book entitled *Voyages to the Madeira and Leeward Caribbee Islands*. Unfortunately, as Robert Kerr (Smellie's biographer) writes: 'Many letters of Burns. . . being totally unfit for publication, and several of them containing severe reflections on many respectable people still in life, have been burnt.' Smellie visited Burns and Maria Riddell in the summer of 1792; there is a local tradition that Burns and Smellie were then accorded some kind of civic reception in Dumfries. Smellie died in 1795.

(492)

[Dumfries, 22nd January] 1792

I sit down, my dear Sir, to introduce a young lady to you, & a lady in the first ranks of fashion too.—What a task! You, who care no more for the herd of animals called, "Young Ladies," than for the herd of animals called—"Young Gentlemen"; You, who despise & detest the groupings & combinations of Fashion—an idiot Painter! who seems industrious to place staring Fools, and unprincipled Knaves in the fore-ground of his Picture, while Men of Sense & Honesty are too often thrown into the dimmest shades.—Mrs Riddel who takes this letter to town with her, is a Character that even in your own way, as a Naturalist & a Philosopher, would be an acquisition to your acquaintance.—The Lady too, is a votary of the Muses; and as I think I am somewhat of a judge in my own trade, I assure you that her verses, always correct, & often elegant, are very much beyond the common run of the Lady Poetesses of the day.—She is a great admirer of your Book;* & hearing me say that I was acquainted with you, she begged to be known to you, as she is just going to pay her first visit to our Caledonian Capital.—I told her that her best way was, to desire your intimate friend & her near relation, Craigdarroch, to have you at his house while she was there; & lest you should think of a lively West-Indian girl of eighteen, as girls of eighteen too often deserve to be thought of, I should take care to remove that prejudice—To be impartial, however, the Lady has one unlucky failing; a failing which you will easily discover, as she seems rather pleased with indulging it; & a failing which you will as easily pardon, as it is a sin that very much besets yourself;—where she dislikes, or despises, she is apt to make no more a secret of it—than where she esteems & probably respects.—

I will not send you the unmeaning "Compliments of the season," but I will send you, my warmest wishes, & most ardent prayers, that Fortune may never throw your subsistence to the mercy of a Knave, nor set your character on the judgement of a Fool! But that, upright & erect, you may walk to an honest grave, where men of letters shall say, here lies a man who did honor to Science, & men of worth shall say, here lies a man who did honor to Human Nature.—I am ever, with the most grateful sincerity,

* *The Philosophy of Natural History* (1790).

my dear Sir, yours,
Robt Burns

WILLIAM CORBET

Born in 1755, he served in the Army with great distinction, and took command of the British forces in Jersey after the death of Major Peirson when the French invaded that island in 1781. At the end of the American War of Independence he retired with the rank of colonel and entered the Excise service where his promotion seems to have been just as meteoric. By 1784 he was a Supervisor at Linlithgow and two years later was Supervisor-General at Stirling, then Acting Supervisor-General at Edinburgh (1789) and promoted to that position on a permanent basis two years later. In 1797 he was translated to Glasgow, as Collector. During his Glasgow period he belonged to a convivial club known as the Board of Green Cloth. In 1811 he died at Meadowside, then on the western outskirts of Glasgow. Three of his sons attended Glasgow University.

In February 1790 Mrs Dunlop wrote to Burns asking if a Mr Corbet in the Excise 'could be of any use' in advancing his career. If this were the case, she would renew an old friendship with Mrs Corbet on Burns's behalf. After some delay and confusion, the connexion was re-established and by the end of 1790 Corbet was in touch with Findlater, seeking an assessment of the poet's character and ability. On 23rd December Findlater replied, saying that Burns was 'an active, faithful and zealous officer. . . capable of achieving (sic) a much more arduous task than any difficulty that the theory or practice of our business can exhibit'. It now seems probable that Corbet secured Burns a transfer to the less-demanding Dumfries third division, rather than the 'first itinerary' which would have involved a great deal of hard riding. When doubts were cast on Burns's loyalty in December 1792, Corbet came to Dumfries to conduct an enquiry. Findlater testified that Burns was 'exact, vigilant, and sober, that in fact he was one of the best officers in the district'. The two extant letters from Burns both deal with the poet's transfer to the more lucrative port division, which he achieved in February 1792.

I (494)

[February?] 1792

Sir,

I have in my time taken up the pen on several ticklish subjects, but none that ever cost me half so much as the language of supplication. —To lay open one's wants & woes to the mercy of another's benevolence, is a business so prostituted by the worthless & unfeeling, that a man of Principle & Delicacy shrinks from it as from Contamination.—

Mr F[indlater] tells me that you wish to know from myself, what are my views in desiring to change my Excise Division.—With the wish natural to man, of bettering his present situation, I have turned my thoughts towards the practicality of getting into a Port Division. —As I know that the General Supervisors are omnipotent in these matters, my honored friend, Mrs Dunlop of Dunlop, offered me to interest you in my behalf.—She told me that she was well acquainted with Mrs Corbet's goodness, & that on the score of former intimacy, she thought she could promise some influence with her: and added, with her usual sagacity & knowledge of human nature, that the surest road to the good offices of a man was through the meditation of the woman he loved.—On this footing, Sir, I venture my application; else, not even the known generosity of your character would have emboldened me to address you thus.—

I have the honor &c.

II (508)

[Dumfries, September 1792]

Sir

When I was honored with your most obliging letter, I said to myself, —"A simple letter of thanks will be a very poor return for so much kindness; I shall likewise send the gentleman a cargo of my best & newest rhymes."—However, my new Division holds me so very busy, & several things in it being rather new to me, my time has hitherto been totally engrossed.—When a man is strongly impressed with a sense of something he ought to do; at the same time, that want of leisure, or want of opportunity, or want of assistance, or want of information, or want of paper, pen & ink, or any other of the many wants which FLESH is heir to—when Sense of Duty pulls one way, & Necessity (or, Alas! too often INDOLENCE under Necessity's garb) pulls another; you are too well acquainted with poor Human Nature, to be told what a devil of a life that arch-vixen, Conscience leads us.—Old as I am in acquaintance, & growing grey in connection, with Slips, Frips, Failings, Frailties, Back-slidings in the paths of grace, & Forward fa's upon a naked wame, and all the other light-horse militia of Iniquity, never did my poor back suffer such scarification from the scourge of Conscience, as during these three weeks that your kind epistle has lain by me unanswered.—A negro wench under the rod of a West-Indian Mistress; a nurse under the caprice of a spoilt child, the only son & heir of a booby Squire; nay, a hen-peckt Husband under the displeasure of his virago Wife—were enviable predicaments to mine.—At last, by way of compromise, I return you by this my most grateful thanks for all the generous friendship & disinterested patronage, for which, now & formerly, I have the honor to be indebted to you; and as to the Rhymes, another edition, in two volumes, of my Poems being in the Press, I shall beg leave to present a copy to Mrs Corbet, as my first, & I will venture to add, most effectual mediator with you on my behalf.—

I have the honor to be, &c.

MARIA BANKS WOODLEY RIDDELL

Born in 1772 in London or Dorset, she was the third and youngest daughter of William Woodley, Governor of the Leeward Islands, and his wife Frances Payne of St Christopher. Maria was brought up in England, but in 1788 accompanied her father on a visit to the West Indies that was to form the basis for her book entitled *Voyages to the Madeira and Leeward and Caribbee Islands,* published in November 1792. In the Indies she met Walter Riddell (1764-1802), younger brother of Robert Riddell of Glenriddell. Walter was then a young widower with an estate in Antigua. They were married in St Christopher on 16th September 1790 and returned to England soon afterwards. Her first daughter Anna Maria, was born in London in August 1791. Early in 1792 Walter Riddell purchased the estate of Goldielea near Dumfries, and renamed it Woodley Park in honour of his wife. Burns was already on close terms with Maria's brother-in-law at Friars' Carse, where he met her prior to her moving into Woodley Park. Clearly their friendship had matured sufficiently by January 1792 for Burns to write to Smellie introducing Maria. The following month, after she had returned from London, he was writing to her as 'My Dearest Friend' (I). Over the ensuing five and a half years some 25 extant letters passed from Burns to Maria, but according to her docketing at least another four letters have not survived. Maria has been described as 'the only really first-class woman with whom Burns ever went any distance', although it must be added that theirs was a purely platonic relationship. She was a poetess (on a par with Clarinda), possessed of immense charm, vivacity and wit and, as Sir Thomas Lawrence's portrait shows, great beauty. Burns was captivated by 'this lively West-Indian girl of eighteen'. Her only failing was her forthrightness. From (II) it is clear that there was little love lost between the Riddells of Friars' Carse and Woodley Park. By April Burns was hinting 'It will be absolutely necessary for me to get in love, else I shall never be able to make a line worth reading on the subject.' (VI). The correspondence continued warmly, after Walter Riddell went off to the West Indies in June 1793, leaving his young wife at Woodley Park. There are references to Burns joining Maria in her box at the theatre (IX). Reading between the lines, one can sense the friendship gathering momentum. Then, however, came the lapse generally known as the 'Rape of the Sabine Women' incident at Friars' Carse in December 1793. Robert and Elizabeth Riddell were outraged by the poet's behaviour and Maria felt bound by family loyalty to support them and snub Burns. There is an uneasy, jokey element in his letter (XIII) ending 'Farewell, thou first of Friends, & most accomplished of Women; even with all they little caprices!!!. The following letter, however, was an attempt to retrieve the situation, accompanying a copy of Goethe's *Werther*, but admitting 'Tis true, Madam, I saw you once since I was at Woodley park; & that once froze the very life-blood of my heart. . .' In vain he tried a peace offering, sending her the epigram *On Maria Riddell* (C.W. p. 501) which had probably been composed in August 1793. When she spurned this, Burns retaliated (XVI) by returning her Commonplace Book: 'I have perused it with much pleasure, & would have continued my criticisms; but as it seems the Critic has forfeited your esteem, his strictures must lose their value.' Thereafter he took a particularly mean revenge, prostituting his Muse in the composition of unpleasant and spiteful epigrams (C.W. pp. 511, 514). If Maria's 21 year-old heart was really as rotten as he alleged, her later conduct would have been very different. There is no evidence that Burns ever sent her these dreadful verses, but he circulated them widely and doubtless they got back to her. Yet she had forgiven him by the end of 1794 when she sent him a book, which he duly acknowledged, in a very stiff letter (XVII) written in the third person. Within two months the friendship had been resumed, Maria lending him *Anacharsis* and Burns lending her Reid's portrait miniature of him. By now Maria was living more humbly at Tinwald House, Colonel Goldie having repossessed Woodley Park as Walter Riddell had not managed to raise the balance of the purchase price. Later she and Walter moved to Halleaths, west of Dumfries, to judge by the address on the letters from the summer of 1795 onwards. These last letters mention illness (XXI) and domestic misfortune (XXII) - the death of the poet's daughter - and culminate in that last pathetic note in June 1796, declining Maria's invitation to the King's Birthday ball. Maria subsequently arranged for a carriage to bring Burns to her lodgings when he was at the Brow; her description of their last meeting on 5th July 1796 is particularly poignant.

Maria Riddell was the most constant of all his friends. She composed the obituary published in the Dumfries *Weekly Journal*, a generous sketch which she later revised for inclusion in Currie's 1800 edition. Maria also busied herself concerning the welfare of Jean and the bairns, but she did not long outlive the poet. Her worthless husband died at Antigua in 1802, leaving Maria and one surviving daughter as state pensioners at Hampton Court. In 1807 she married Phillips Lloyd Fletcher, an officer in the Dragoons, but died at Chester on 15th December 1808.

Maria Banks Woodley Riddell

I (497)

[February 1792]

My Dearest Friend,—

Yours by Mr Stoddart was the welcomest letter I ever received. God grant that now when your health is re-established, you may take a little, little more care of a life so truly valuable to Society and so truly invaluable to your friends! As to your very excellent epistle from a certain Capital of a certain Empire, I shall answer it in its own way sometime next week; as also settle all matters as to little Miss. Your goodness there is just like your kindness in everything else. I am happy to inform you I have just got an appointment to the first or Port Division as it is called, which adds twenty pounds per annum more to my Salary. My Excise Income is now Cash paid, Seventy pounds a year: and this I hold untill I am appointed Supervisor. So much for my usual good luck. My Perquisites I hope to make worth 15 or 20£ more. So Rejoice with them that do Rejoice.*

Apropos has little Mademoiselle been inoculated with the Small-pox yet? If not let it be done as soon as it is proper for her habit of body, teeth, &c.

Once more let me congratulate you on your returning health. God grant that you may live at least while I live, for were I to lose you it would leave a Vacuum in my enjoyments that nothing could fill up. Farewell . . .

Robt Burns

* Romans 12:15.

II (509)

[Early autumn 1792]

Fate seems determined, Madam, to set you & I at cross purposes.— On Sunday I am engaged to go to Drumlanrig with my friend Clarke, the Organist from Edinburgh, who goes to give the young ladies the instruction of his profession.—I was the Agent between Mr Mcmurdo & him, & by express appointment I must go to Drumlanrig on that day.—However, it is not likely that I shall see Glenriddel at that time; but if I should, I shall say nothing at all, & listen to nothing at all, in which you are, mediately, or immediately, concerned.—So, Vive l'amour, & vive la bagatelle! For I dare say that one, or both of these Mighty Deities are at the bottom of this most extraordinary, inexpressible, & inexplicable mystery.—

Robt B——

III (517)

[November 1792]

Madam,

I return you my most sincere thanks for the honor you have done me in presenting me a copy of your Book.*—Be assured I shall ever keep it sacred, as a boasted testimony how much I have the honor to be,

Madam,
your highly obliged humble servant
Robt Burns

* *Voyages to the Madeira and Leeward and Caribee Islands*

Maria Banks Woodley Riddell

IV (533A)

Madam,

You were so very good as to promise me to honour my friend with your presence on his benefit-night. That night is fixed for Friday first: the play a most interesting one! *The Way to keep Him.*[1] I have the pleasure to know Mr. G.[2] well. His merit as an actor is generally acknowledged. He has genius and worth which would do honour to patronage: he is a poor and modest man; claims which, from their very *silence*, have the more forcible power on the generous heart. Alas, for pity! that from the indolence of those who have the good things of this life in their gift, too often does brazen-fronted importunity snatch that boon, the rightful due of retiring, humble want! Of all the qualities we assign to the author and director of Nature, by far the most enviable is—to be able "To wipe away all tears from all eyes."[3] O what insignificant, sordid wretches are they, however chance may have loaded them with wealth, who go to their graves, to their magnificent *mausoleums*, with hardly the consciousness of having made one poor honest heart happy!

But I crave your pardon, Madam; I came to beg, not to preach.

1 Arthur Murphy.
2 F.J. Guion.
3 Revelation 7:17.

V (550A)

[In a copy of the 1793 Edition of the *Poems*, mid-March]

Un gage d'Amitie le plus sincere—

The Author

VI (554A)

Friday noon
[April 1793]

I remember, Madam, to have heard you lately inveigh against this unfortunate Country, that it was so barren of comforts, the very necessaries of life were not to be found in it.—In particular, you told me, you could not *exist* without FRENCH GLOVES.—Had Fate put it in my power any way to have added one comfort to your existence, it could not perhaps have done any thing which would have gratified me more; yet, poor as I am in every thing, except Inclination, I have been fortunate enough to obviate the business of FRENCH GLOVES.—In order that you may have the higher idea of my merits in this MOMENTOUS affair, I must tell you, that all the Haberdashers here are on the alarm, as to the necessary article of French Gloves.—You must know that FRENCH GLOVES are contraband goods, & expressly prohibited by the laws of this wise-governed Realm of ours.—A Satirist would say, that this is one reason why the ladies are so fond of them; but I, who have not one grain of GALL in my composition, shall alledge, that it is the PATRIOTISM of the dear Goddesses of man's idolatry, that makes them so fond of dress from the LAND OF LIBERTY & EQUALITY.

Maria Banks Woodley Riddell

—There was a search very lately through this town, for the express purpose of discovering French Gloves, at which search I assisted in the very respectable character of a Revenue Officer; & three of our principal Merchants are at this moment, subpona'd before the Court of Exchequer (a crabbed law expression, for being ruined in a revenue court) for that day's work.—Still, I have discovered one Haberdasher, who, at my particular request, will clothe your fair hands as they ought to be, to keep them from being profaned by the rude gaze of the gloting eye, or—Horrid!—from perhaps A RAPE by the unhallowed lips, of the Satyr Man.—You will remember though, that you are to tell no body, but the ladies of your acquaintance, & that only on the same condition so that the secret may be sure to be kept, & the poor Haberdasher not ruined by his kindness.—

So much for this very important matter.—

I had a long letter the other day from Mr Thomson, the gentleman who presides over the Publication of Scots Music to which Mr R—— is a Subscriber; & he tells me we may expect twenty five of the Songs by the end of next month.—There are several airs that have verses far unworthy of their merit, to which Mr T. wishes me to give him new ones.—Would you honor the publication with a Song from you?—For instance, the fine pathetic air, "My lodging on the cold ground;"—The present song is an improper measure: the Stanza ought to run as thus—

"O'er moorlands & mountains, rough, barren & bare,
"Bewilder'd & wearied I roam"—

I have just sent him a new song to "the last time I came o'er the moor;" but I do not know if I have succeeded.—I inclose it for your strictures.—Mary was the name I intended my Heroine to bear, but I altered it into your Ladyship's, as being infinitely more musical.—I am afraid that my song will turn out a very cold performance, as I never can do any good with a love theme, except when I am really & devoutely in love.—

I have the honor to be, Madam,
the most devoted & humblest of your
devoted & humble servants
The Bard

The last time I came o'er the moor

"The last time I came o'er the moor,
And left Maria's dwelling,*

On reading over this song, I see it is but a cold, inanimate composition. —It will be absolutely necessary for me to get in love, else I shall never be able to make a line worth reading on the subject.—

* Alternative opening lines of *Farewell, Thou Stream*, C.W. p. 486.

603

VII (590)

Friday morn:
[October 1793]

I am extremely sorry, Dear Madam, that an equally unexpected & indispensible bustle of business, will deprive me of the very great pleasure of waiting on you to-day.

What think you of the following Clinch on W—— R——*

> Light lay the earth on Billy's breast,
>   His chicken heart so tender;
> But build a Castle on his head—
>   His scull will prop it under.—

I have just put the last hand to the following song: how does it please you?—

> Thine am I, my faithful Fair,
>   Thine, my lovely Nancy;
>   [C.W. p. 505]

Le bon Dieu vous bénisse!

RB

*William Roddick of Corbieton, C.W. p. 505.

VIII (594)

[November? 1793]

Dear Madam

I meant to have called on you yesternight, but as I edged up to your Box-door, the first object which greeted my view was one of these lobster-coated PUPPIES, sitting, like another dragon, guarding the Hesperian fruit.—On Sunday I shall have the pleasure & honor of assuring you, in propria persona, how sincerely

I am yours
RB

IX (595)

[November? 1793]

On the conditions & capitulations you so obligingly make, I shall certainly make my plain, weather-beaten, rustic phiz a part of your box furniture on Tuesday; when we may arrange the business of the visit.—

My friend Clarke, has taken an enthusiasm for an old Scots air, hitherto little noticed, & makes it truly delightful.—As soon as he goes to Edinburgh, he is to give it to the world, with accompany-ments, in his best manner.—My song,

> "For pity's sake, forgive me"—

suits the air exactly, & I give it to him to set to it.—I alter the first four lines thus—

"Farewell, thou stream, that winding flows
"Around Maria's dwelling!
"O cruel Mem'ry, spare the throes,
"Within my bosom swelling!
"Condemn'd to drag &c."—

Tell me, thou first & fairest of Critics, is it mended?—

Among the profusion of hollow compliments which insidious Craft, or unmeaning folly, incessantly offer at your Shrine—A Shrine, my God! how far exalted above such adoration—permit me, were it but for Rarity's sake, to pay you the honest tribute of a warm heart & an independant mind; & assure you, that I am,

Thou most amiable & most accomplished of Thy Sex,
with the most respectful esteem & fervent regard—
Thine—
RB

X (595A)

[November 1793]

On Monday, my dear Madam, I shall most certainly do myself the honor of waiting on you: whether the Muses, ere then, will wait on me, is, I fear, dubious.—

Please accept a new Song, which I have this moment received from Urbani.—It is a trifling present, but—"Give all thou canst"—

Were my esteem for a certain Lady to be measured by a musical offering, that could not be less than the music of the Spheres in Score, or the Haleluias of the Hierarchies with all their accompaniments.—

Yours—
R. B.

XI (599A)

[late November or December 1793]

I have at last, my Fair friend, determined to write you out these lines which you were pleased to commend so much.—To tell you the truth, I would long ago have written them, but for a certain expence of recollection which bankrupts my peace—

"I cannot but remember such things were,
"And were most dear to me"*—

In vain would Prudence, with decorous sneer,

[C.W. p. 501]

Now for another piece of Poetry of mine, that is also from the heart.—

[*Scots Wha Hae*]

[C.W. p. 500]

So much for my two favorite topics, Love & Liberty.—

A Dieu je vous commende;
RB

* Shakespeare: *Macbeth*, Act IV, sc. 3, altered.

Maria Banks Woodley Riddell

XII (600A)

[December? 1793]

I will wait on you, my ever-valued Friend; but whether in the morning, I am not sure.—Sunday closes a period of our cursed revenue business, & may probably keep me employed with my pen until Noon.—Fine employment for a Poet's pen! There is a species of the Human genus that I call, the Gin-horse Class: what enviable dogs they are!—Round, & round, & round they go—Mundell's ox that drives his cotton-mill, their exact prototype—without an idea or wish beyond their circle; fat sleek, stupid, patient, quiet & contented:—while here I sit, altogether Novemberish, a damn'd melange of Fretfulness & melancholy; not enough of the one to rouse me to passion; nor of the other to repose me in torpor; my soul flouncing & fluttering round her tenement, like a wild Finch caught amid the horrors of winter & newly thrust into a cage.—

Well, I am persuaded that it was of me that the Hebrew Sage prophesied, when he foretold—"And behold, on whatsoever this man doth set his heart, it shall not prosper!*—If my resentment is awaked, it is sure to be where it dare not squeak; & if in LOVE, as, God forgive me! I sometimes am; Impossibility presents an impervious barrier to the proudest daring of Presumption, & poor I, dare much sooner peep into the focus of Hell, than meet the eye of the goddess of my soul!

Pray that Wisdom & Bliss may [*word missing*?] be more frequent visitors of

RB

* Not Biblical, but perhaps a sermon cliché.

XIII (603A)

[December 1793]

I have often told you, my Dear Friend, that you had a spice of Caprice in your composition, & you have as often disavowed it; even perhaps while your opinions were, at the moment, irrefragably proving it.—Could *any thing* estrange me from a Friend such as you?—No!—Tomorrow, I shall have the honor of waiting on you.—

Farewell, thou first of Friends, & most accomplished of Women; even with all thy little caprices! ! !

RB

XIV (609)

[January 1794]

I have this very moment got the song from Sim*, & I am sorry to see that he has spoilt it a good deal.—It shall be a lesson to me how I lend him any thing again.—

I have sent you Werter: truly happy to have any, the smallest, opportunity of obliging you.—

'Tis true, Madam, I saw you once since I was at Woodley park; & that once froze the very life-blood of my heart.—Your reception of me was such, that a wretch, meeting the eye of his Judge, about to pronounce sentence of death on him, could only have envied my feelings & situation.—

But I hate the theme; & never more shall write or speak of it.—

One thing I shall proudly say; that I can pay Mrs R— a higher tribute of esteem, & appreciate her amiable worth more truly, than any man whom I have seen approach her—nor will I yield the pas to any man living, in subscribing myself with the sincerest truth

Her devoted humble servant
RB

* David Sime, the music editor.

XV (610A)

[early January 1794]

To Maria—

Epigram—on Lord Buchan's assertion, that "Women ought always to be flattered grossly, or not spoken to at all"—

'Praise woman still!' his Lordship says,
'Deserved, or not, no matter,'
But thee, Maria, while I praise,
There Flattery cannot flatter.—

Maria, all my thought and dream,
Inspires my vocal shell:
The more I praise my lovely Theme
The more the truth I tell.—

[C.W. p. 501]

R.B.

XVI (611)

Dumfries, 12th January 1794

Madam

I return your Common Place Book.—I have perused it with much pleasure, & would have continued my criticisms; but as it seems the Critic has forfeited your esteem, his strictures must lost their value.—

If it is true, that "Offences come only from the heart;"*—before you, I am guiltless:—To admire, esteem, prize and adore you, as the most accomplished of Woman, & the first of Friends—if these are crimes, I am the most offending thing alive.—

In a face where I used to meet the kind complacency of friendly confidence, *now* to find cold neglect & contemptuous scorn—is a wrench that my heart can ill bear.—It is however some kind of miserable good luck; that while De-haut-en-bas rigour may depress an unoffending wretch to the ground, it has a tendency to rouse a stubborn something in his bosom, which, though it cannot heal the wounds of his soul, is at least an opiate to blunt their poignancy—

With the profoundest respect for your exalted abilities; the most sincere esteem & ardent regard & for your gentle heart & amiable manners; & the most fervent wish & prayer for your welfare, peace & bliss—

I have the honor to be,
MADAM,
your most devoted humble servant
Robt Burns

* Pope: *The Rape of the Lock*, Canto I, line 1, misquoted.

XVII (650)

Friday eve [January? 1795]

Mr Burns's Compliments to Mrs Riddell—is much obliged to her for her polite attention in sending him the book.—Owing to Mr B——s's being at present acting as Supervisor of Excise, a department that occupies his every hour of the day, he has not that time to spare which is necessary for any Belle Lettre pursuit; but, as he will, in a week or two, again return to his wonted leisure, he will then pay that attention to Mrs R——'s beautiful Song "To thee, loved Nith," which it so well deserves.

When "Anacharsis Travels" come to hand, which Mrs Riddell mentioned as her gift to the Public Library, Mr B—— will thank her for a reading of it, previous to her sending it to the Library, as it is a book Mr B—— has never seen, & wishes to have a longer perusal of than the regulations of the Library allow.

P.S. Mr Burns will be much obliged to Mrs. Riddell if she will favor him with a perusal of any of her poetical pieces which he may not have seen.

XVIII (658)

[Dumfries, March? 1795]

I cannot express my gratitude to you for allowing me a longer perusal of Anacharsis.—In fact, I have never met with a book that bewitched me so much; & I as a member of the Library, must warmly feel the obligation you have laid us under. Indeed to me, the obligation is stronger than to any other individual of our Society; as Anacharsis is an indispensable desideratum to a Son of the Muses.—

Pleyel is still in statu quo.—In a little time, however, we will have all the work.—He is still in Strasbourg; but the Messrs Coutts, the London bankers, have been so obliging as to allow my friend Thomson, the Editor, the channel of their correspondence in Switzerland, through which medium the business is going forward.—Thomson has enlarged his plan.—The hundred pathetic airs are to be as proposed, only he means to have four plates, instead of two.—He likewise has increased his number of facetious songs & lively airs & proposes adorning them here & there with vignettes. Among others in the lively way, he has taken one or two Irish tunes; chiefly, I believe, from the partiality which his friendship to me makes him feel for the verses I have written for them.—The following I wrote the other day for an Irish air which I highly admire; & for the sake of my verses he has obligingly adopted the air into his Selection.—

WILLIAM SMELLIE

GEORGE THOMSON

Maria Banks Woodley Riddell

Song—

Their groves o' sweet myrtle

[C.W. p. 550]

Song—

My Chloris, mark how green the groves

[C.W. p. 531]

Song—

Long, long the night

[C.W. p. 542]

I cannot help laughing at your friend's conceit of my picture; & I
suspect you are playing off on me some of that fashionable wit,
called HUMBUG.—Apropos to pictures, I am just sitting to Reid in
this town for a miniature; & I think he has hit by far the best
likeness of me ever was taken.—When you are at any time so idle, in
town, as to call at Reid's painting-room, & mention to him that I
spoke of such a thing to you, he will shew it you; else, he will not;
for both the Miniature's existence & its destiny, are an inviolable
secret, & therefore very properly trusted in part *to you.*—

Song—

Canst thou leave me thus, my Katie

[C.W. p. 530]

I am sure you are now most heartily inclined to drowsy rest, so Bon
repos.

RB

XIX (668)

Saturday, six P.M.
[Spring, 1795]

Par accident, meeting with Mrs Scot on the street, & having the
miniature in a Book in my pocket, I send you it; as I understand that
a servant of yours is in town.—The painter, in my opinion, has spoilt
the likeness.—Return me the bagatelle per first opportunity.—I am so
ill as to be scarce able to hold this miserable pen to this miserable
paper.—

RB

XX (673A)

[Summer 1795]

I think there is little doubt but that your interest, if judiciously
directed, may procure a Tide-waiter's place for your protege, Shaw;
but, alas, that is doing little for him!—Fifteen pounds per ann. is the
Salary; & the perquisites, in some lucky stations, such as Leith,
Glasgow, Greenock, may be ten more; but in such a place as this,
for instance, they will hardly amount to five.—The appointment is
not in the EXCISE, but in the CUSTOMS.—The way of getting
appointed, is just the application of GREAT FOLKS to the
Commissioners of the CUSTOMS: the Almanack will give you their

Maria Banks Woodley Riddell

names.—The EXCISE is a superior object, as the salary is fifty Per annum.—You mention that he has a family: if he has more than three children, he cannot be admitted as an Excise Officer.—To apply there, is the same business as at the Customs.—Garthland, if you can commit his sincere zeal in the cause, is, I think, able to do either the one or the other.—Find out, among your acquaintances, who are the private friends of the Commissioners of the particular BOARD at which you wish to apply, & interest them—the more, the better.—The Commissioners of both Boards are people quite in the fashionable circle, & must be known to many of your friends.—I was going to mention some of your Female acquaintance who might give you a lift, but, on recollection, your interest with the WOMEN is, I believe, but a sorry business.—So much the better! 'tis God's judgement upon you for making such a despotic use of your sway over the MEN.—*You* a Republican!—You have an Empire over us; & you know it too: but the Lord's holy name be praised, you have something of the same propensity to get giddy—(intoxicated is not a lady's word) with power; & a devilish deal of aptitude to the same blind, undistinguishing FAVORITISM, which makes other Despots less dangerous to the welfare & repose of mankind than they otherwise might be.—

So much for scolding you.—

I have perused your M.S.S. with a great deal of pleasure.—I have taken the liberty to make a few marks with my pencil which I trust you will pardon.—

Farewel!

R. Burns

XXI (674)

[June or July 1795]

The health you wished me in your Morning's Card is I think flown from me for ever.—I have not been able to leave my bed today, till about an hour ago.—These wickedly unlucky advertisements I lent (I did wrong) to a friend, & I am ill able to go in quest of him.—

The Muses have not quite forsaken me.—The following detached Stanzas I intend to interweave in some disastrous tale of a Shepherd

"Despairing beside a clear stream"[1] —

L'amour, toujours l'amour!

Volte Subito.

The trout in yonder wimpling burn

[C.W. p. 555]

Have you seen Clarke's Sonatas, the subjects from Scots Airs?[2] If not, send for my Copy—

RB

1 Nicholas Rowe: *Colin's Complaint*, line 1.
2 Stephen Clarke: *Six Sonatas for the Harpsichord*, Edinburgh (c.1790).

Maria Banks Woodley Riddell

XXII (685)

[Dumfries, October or November 1795]

A severe domestic misfortune has put all literary business out of my head for some time past.—Now I begin to resume my wonted studies.—I am much correspondence in your debt: I shall pay it soon.—Clarke's Sonatas are of no use to me, & I beg you will keep them.—

That you, my friend, may never experience such a loss as mine, sincerely prays*—

RB

* The poet's daughter, Elizabeth Riddell Burns, died in September 1795.

XXIII (685A)

[November 1795]

I have been a grievous sinner against all etiquette of correspondence, in not writing you long ere now.—'Tis now ten o'clock: too late to detain your poor fellow of a servant untill I hawk up an apology.— The following is new.—

Scotch Song.—

O bonie was yon rosy brier,

[C.W. p. 558]

Bon repos!

RB

XXIV (685D)

[December 1795 or January 1796]

I have perused with great pleasure your elegiac verses.—In two or three instances I mark inequalities, rather than faults.—A line that in an ordinary mediocre production might pass, not only without censure, but with applause, in a brilliant composition glares in all its native halting inferiority.—The last line of the second stanza I dislike most.—If you cannot mend it (I cannot, after beating my brains to pap) I would almost leave out the whole stanza.—

A Dieu je vous recommende!

RB

XXV (697)

[Dumfries, 1st June 1796]

I am in such miserable health as to be utterly incapable of shewing my loyalty in any way.—Rackt as I am with rheumatisms, I meet every face with a greeting like that of Balak to Balaam—"Come, curse me Jacob; & come, defy me Israel!"[1]—So, say I, Come, curse me that East-wind; & come, defy me the North!!! Would you have me in such circumstances copy you out a Love-song? No! if I must write, let it be Sedition, or Blasphemy, or something else that begins with a B, so that I may grin with the grin of iniquity, & rejoice with the rejoicing of an apostate Angel.[2]

611

Maria Banks Woodley Riddell

–"All good to me is lost;
"Evil, be thou my good!"[3]–

I may perhaps see you on Saturday, but I will not be at the Ball.–
Why should I?–"Man delights not me, nor woman either!"[4] Can
you supply me with the Song, "Let us all be unhappy together."–

Do, if you can, & oblige

le pauvre miserable
RB

1 Numbers 23:7.
2 Romans 12:15, paraphrased.
3 Milton: *Paradise Lost*, Bk. IV, lines 109-10.
4 Shakespeare: *Hamlet*, Act II, sc. 2.

WILLIAM MOODIE

Born in 1760 he was appointed minister of St Andrew's, Edinburgh in 1787 and became professor of Hebrew at the University in 1793. A noted theologian of the period down to his death in 1812, he was a prolific publisher of religious tracts and sermons. His sole relevance to Burns correspondence was as the recipient of the following letter, believed to be one of several addressed to ministers in Edinburgh at this time, on behalf of the poet's friend James Clarke of Moffat. The text is taken from the transcript in the Glenriddell MS.

(498)

[early February] 1792

Reverend & Dear Sir,

this will be presented you by a particular Friend of mine, a Mr Clarke, Schoolmaster in Moffat, who has lately become the unfortunate & undeserved subject of persecution from some of his Employers.—The ostensible & assigned reason on their part is, some instances of severity to the boys under his care; but I have had the best opportunities of knowing the merits of the cause, & I assure you, Sir, that he is falling a sacrifice to the weakness of the MANY following in the cry of the villainy of the FEW.—The business will now come before the Patrons of the School, who are, the Ministers, Magistrates & Town-council of Edinburgh, & in that view I would interest your goodness in his behalf.—'Tis true, Sir, & I feel the full force of the observation, that a man in my powerless, humble station very much mistakes himself, & very much mistakes the way of the world, when he dares presume to offer influence among so highly respectable a Body as the Patronage I have mentioned; but what could I do? A man of Abilities, a man of Genius, a man of Worth, and my Friend, before I would stand quietly & silent by, & see him perish thus, I would down on my knees to the rocks & the mountains, & implore them to fall on his Persecutors & crush their malice & them in deserved destruction!—Believe me, Sir, he is greatly injured man.—The humblest individual, though, Alas! he cannot so redress the wrong, may yet as ably attest the fact, as a Lord.—Mr Moodie's goodness I well know; & that acquiantance with him I have the honor to boast of, will forgive my addressing him thus in favour of a Gentleman, whom, if he knew as well, he would esteem as I do.—

613

JOHN LEVEN

General Supervisor of Excise at Edinburgh from 1801 till his retirement or death two years later, he was thus erroneously addressed by Burns in the following letter sent about March 1792. At that time, however, Leven was only a Supervisor, although he may have been acting temporarily in the higher grade. Lawson was a Dumfries grocer and wine-merchant. This letter is a good example of Burns writing to a superior in his official capacity, but not neglecting to take the opportunity to enclose his latest ballad.

(500)

[March? 1792]

Sir,

I have sealed & secured Lawson's Tea, but no permit has yet appeared, nor can it appear before Tuesday at the nearest; so there is the greater chance of a condemnation.—I shrewdly suspect the Newcastle House, Rankine & Sons is the Firm, will think that the goods being regularly delivered to a Carrier, with proper permit, will exonerate them as to any farther responsibility; & Lawson, on his part, is determined not to have any thing to do with it; so our process may be the easier managed.—

The moment that the Permits arrive, if they do arrive, as I am pretty certain they will, I shall inform you; but, in the mean time, when the three remaining boxes arrive, as they cannot, in *quantity*, correspond with Permit, & besides, will be at least beyond the limited time a full week; are not they also seizable?—

Mr Mitchell mentioned to you a ballad which I composed & sung at one of his Excise-court dinners: here it is.—

The deil's awa wi' th' Exciseman—Tune, madam Cassey*
[C.W. p. 467]

If you honor my ballad by making it one of your charming, bon vivant effusions, it will secure it undoubted celebrity.—

I have the honor to be, Sir
Your obliged & devoted humble servant
Robt Burns

* Madam Cossy, the Quaker's Wife and the Hemp-dresser are all believed to be the same tune.

614

STEPHEN CLARKE

Organist of the Episcopal Chapel in Edinburgh when Burns first met him, in 1787, a position which passed to his son when he died ten years later. Clarke was employed by James Johnson to harmonise the melodies for the *Scots Musical Museum*. In this respect he seems to have been rather lazy, and sometimes careless, and one will find numerous references to Burns's exasperation, in letters to both Johnson and George Thomson. Posterity has not dealt too kindly with Clarke whose harmonisations are regarded as pretty rudimentary, although they are more acceptable than the florid accompaniments composed by Beethoven, Haydn and Pleyel. Clarke also compiled *Sonatas based on Scots Airs* which Burns forwarded to Maria Riddell with the comment that they were of no use to him. In July 1792 he promised the McMurdo family that he would get Clarke to come to Drumlanrig to give two of the daughters music lessons. Clarke appears to have ignored Burns's original request, but the following mock-formal letter evidently did the trick. Clarke's visit to Drumlanrig was subsequently mentioned by Burns to Thomson (XVI) when he sent the latter Clarke's transcription of the air 'There was a lass and she was fair' which he had taught to the McMurdo girls. Thomson, however, disliked this melody and promptly lost it. In a subsequent letter to Thomson (XVII) Burns mentioned, in a postscript, that Clarke was also teaching music to the family of Patrick Miller of Dalswinton.

(504)

16th July 1792

Mr Burns begs leave to present his most respectful Compliments to Mr Clarke—Mr B—— some time ago did himself the honor of writing Mr C—— respecting coming out to the country to give a little Musical instruction in a highly respectable family where Mr C—— may have his own terms, & may be as happy as Indolence, the Devil, & the Gout will permit him.—Mr B—— knows well that Mr C—— is engaged so long with another family; but cannot Mr C—— find two or three weeks to spare to each of them? Mr B—— is deeply impressed with, & awefully conscious of, the high importance of Mr C——'s time, whether in the winged moments of symphonious exhibition at the keys of Harmony, while listening Seraphs cease their own less delightful strains;—or in the drowsy, hours of slumbrous repose, in the arms of his dearly beloved elbow-chair, where the frowsy but potent Power of Indolence, circumfuses her vapours round, & sheds her dews on, the beard of her Darling Son—but half a line conveying half a meaning from Mr C—— would make Mr B the very happiest of mortals.—

GEORGE THOMSON

Born in 1757, the son of Robert Thomson, schoolmaster at Limekilns, Dunfermline, he was taught by his father, first at Limekilns and later at Banff. In 1774 Thomson obtained employment as a clerk in the office of a Writer to the Signet, but in 1780, on the recommendation of John Home (author of *Douglas*), he was appointed junior clerk to the Board of Trustees. Shortly afterwards, on the death of the principal clerk, Thomson was promoted to fill that position, which he held for upwards of half a century. In 1781 he married Katherine Miller of Kelso, daughter of a lieutenant in the 50th Regiment, by whom he had six daughters and two sons. One of his grand-daughters, Catherine Thomson Hogarth, was the unhappy wife of Charles Dickens. Thomson retired from the Board in 1839 and then moved to London to be near his sons (a colonel of Engineers and an assistant-commissary-general respectively) and their families. Mrs Thomson died in 1841 while visiting her daughter, Mrs Hogarth. Thomson subsequently returned to Edinburgh for a public dinner, held on 3rd March 1847 to mark his ninetieth birthday. Lord Cockburn took the chair, and presented Thomson with an inscribed vase. He finally settled at Vanbrugh Place, Leith where he died in February 1851. He was buried in Kensal Green cemetery alongside his wife. Dickens composed the epitaph on his headstone.

The abiding passion of Thomson's long and otherwise uneventful life was music. An accomplished violinist, he played in the orchestra at the St Cecilia concerts and enjoyed playing the violin quartets of Pleyel and Haydn. Apart from the florid compositions of Pleyel he had a predilection for Italianate renderings of Scottish songs by the eminent *castrato* Tenducci and the arias performed by Domencia Corri. As a result of hearing Tenducci and Corri Thomson 'conceived the idea of collecting all our best melodies and songs, and of obtaining accompaniments to them worthy of their merit.' At first he turned for help to the Hon. Andrew Erskine (see page 224), younger brother of the amateur musician and composer Earl of Kellie, but Erskine's suicide left Thomson to carry on his grand designs alone. Thomson found that 'the melodies in general were without any symphonies to introduce and conclude them, and the accompaniment (for the piano only) meagre and commonplace; while the verses united with the melodies were in a great many instances coarse and vulgar, the productions of a rude age, and such as could not be tolerated or sung in good society'. The musical problems were solved by securing the services of Pleyel in the first instance, and latterly also of Haydn, Beethoven, Weber, Hummell and the other great musicians and composers at the end of the eighteenth century.

The problems with the lyrics were solved by approaching Burns, whose *Cotter's Saturday Night* particularly impressed him. It was ironic, therefore, that Thomson, like the *literati* of 1786-7 should have admired the poet for what was, in truth, one of his weakest compositions. Thomson wrote to Burns in September 1792 setting out his ideas: 'To render this work perfect, we are desirous to have the poetry improved wherever it seems unworthy of the music . . . Some charming melodies are united to mere nonsense and doggerel, while others are accommodated with rhymes so loose and indelicate as cannot be sung in decent company.' Thomson then asked Burns to write 20 to 25 songs suitable to the melodies he proposed sending him, along with a few songs 'exceptionable only in some of their verses . . . leaving it to you either to mend these or make new songs in their stead.'

Burns replied enthusiastically on 16th December 1792, and this was the beginning of a prolific correspondence which endured right to the end of the poet's life. Burns was doubtless attracted by the idea of working on a project that promised to be better printed and more lavishly produced than Johnson's *Scots Musical Museum*. Unfortunately Burns made it plain to Thomson that he would always abide by the editor's decision. This had worked perfectly well with Johnson, but it created numerous problems with Thomson who had neither Johnson's commonsense nor his humility. Consequently, the following correspondence was much fuller and more frequent than it ought otherwise to have been, as Burns was forced to justify his viewpoint. Indirectly, it has provided an invaluable insight into Burns's working methods, with particular reference to the collecting and mending of traditional ballads and fragments. With characteristic forthrightness Burns had, at the outset, made it clear to Thomson that he would not take any payment for this work. This quixotic gesture is understandable, but hardly business-like. When Thomson sent Burns £5 on the publication of the first part of his *Select Collection of Scotish Airs* the poet responded indignantly (XVII). Although Burns himself was noticing a drop in his emoluments as a result of the French war, the last thing he wanted, or would take, was payment for work which he regarded as a sacred duty. Thomson never attempted to repeat the gesture until the very last days of the poet's life when he responded to the pathetic plea (LVII) 'After all my boasted independance, curst necessity compels me to implore you for five pounds', to stave off the haberdasher (David Williamson) who was dunning him. Although Thomson thought Burns was exaggerating he sent him a draft for the sum by return.

During the period when Burns was working for Thomson he continued to work for Johnson, a situation that caused the former a great deal of professional jealousy. Burns asked Thomson to return any songs which he considered unsuitable, so that Johnson might have them. Thomson, however, was inclined to be a dog in the manger in this respect. Burns attempted to clarify the vexed question of the ownership of his songs (XII): 'Though I give Johnson one edition of my songs, that does not give away the copy-right. . .' Nevertheless, Thomson subsequently tried - fortunately without success - to secure the copyright of Burns's contribution to his *Select Collection*. Some time later, Burns put the record straight in a Deed of Assignment of Copyright (XIX). Generous though the terms in this document were, Thomson did not publish it in any of the volumes produced in Burns's lifetime, but waited till 1798, and then printed it in a carefully edited version which appeared to give him sole rights.

Not content with falsifying the Deed of Assignment, Thomson played an ignoble part in the biographical distortions initiated by Heron and Currie. He frequently and flagrantly altered or suppressed passages in Burns's letters prior to sending them to Currie for inclusion in the 1800 edition. Ferguson, in a devastating exposé (*Burns Chronicle*, 1929), showed Thomson for the mean, vain and arrogant person he was. Thomson was not without detractors during his lifetime. When 'Christopher North' (Professor John Wilson) delivered a blistering attack on Thomson in his *Land of Burns* (1838), Thomson replied with a vigorous rebuttal, dated 29th March 1838, which the publisher, Robert Chambers, subsequently printed in later editions of that book in a well-meaning attempt to correct the balance. In this long, rambling, autobiographical letter Thomson cited Burns's letter (XVII) and asked rhetorically: 'Who that reads the letter. . . can think I have deserved the abuse which anonymous scribblers have poured upon me for not endeavouring to remunerate the poet? If I had dared to go further than I did, in sending him money, is it not perfectly clear that he would have deemed it an insult, and ceased to write another song for me?' He then went on, sanctimoniously: 'Had I been a selfish or avaricious man, I had a fair opportunity, upon the death of the poet, to put money in my pocket; for I might then have published, for my own behoof, all the beautiful lyrics he had written for me, the original manuscripts of which were in my possession. . .' Instead, the old humbug tells us how he made all these manuscripts, both songs and letters, freely availabe to Dr Currie. 'For thus surrendering the manuscripts, I received both verbally and in writing, the warm thanks of the trustees for the family Mr John Syme and Mr Gilbert Burns; who considered what I had done as a fair return for the poet's generosity of conduct to me.' And he ended with a fulsome testimonial written on his behalf by Josiah Walker in April 1811. In 1843 and 1845 Thomson again refuted the charges of meanness, in letters to the publisher Blackie and *Tait's Magazine*. All that can be said in his favour is that he played a considerable part in fund-raising for the Burns memorial on Calton Hill, Edinburgh.

I (507)

Dumfries 16th September 1792

Sir

I have just this moment got your letter.—As the request you make to me will positively add to my enjoyments in complying with it, I shall enter into your undertaking with all the small portion of abilities I have, strained to their utmost exertion by the impulse of Enthusiasm. —Only, don't hurry me: "Deil tak the hindmost" is by no means the Crie de guerre of my Muse.—Will you, as I am inferiour to none of you in enthusiastic attachment to the Poetry & Music of old Caledonia, &, since you request it, have chearfully promised my mite of assistance, will you let me have a list of your airs with the first line of the verses you intend for them, that I may have an opportunity of suggesting any alteration that may occur to me—you know 'tis in the way of my trade—still leaving you, Gentlemen, the undoubted right of Publishers, to approve, or reject, at your pleasure in your own Publication?—I say, the first line of the verses, because if they are verses that have appeared in any of our Collections of songs, I know them & can have recourse to them. Apropos, if you are for *English* verses, there is, on my part, an end of the matter.— Whether in the simplicity of *the Ballad*, or the pathos of *the Song*, I can only hope to please myself in being allowed at least a sprinkling of our native tongue.—English verses, particularly the works of Scotsmen, that have merit, are certainly very eligible.—Tweedside; Galashiels, viz. Ah! the poor shepherd's mournful fate &c. Gilderoy, viz. Ah, Chloris, could I now but sit, except, excuse my vanity, you should for Gilderoy prefer my own song, "From thee, Eliza, I must go" &c. all these you cannot mend; but such insipid stuff, as, "To Fanny fair could I impart" &c. usually set to The Mill Mill O, 'tis a disgrace to the Collections in which it has already appeared, & would doubly disgrace a Collection that will have the very superiour merit of yours.—But more of this in the farther prosecution of the Business, if I am to be called on for my strictures & amendments—I say, amendments; for I will not *alter* except where I myself at least think that I *amend*.—

As to any remuneration, you may think my Songs either *above*, or *below* price; for they shall absolutely be the one or the other.—In the honest enthusiasm with which I embark in your undertaking, to talk of money, wages, fee, hire, &c. would be downright Sodomy of Soul!—A proof of each of the Songs that I compose or amend, I shall receive as a favor.—In the rustic phrase of the Season, "Gude speed the wark!"

I am, Sir, your very humble servant
Robt Burns

P.S. I have some particular reasons for wishing my interferance to be known as little as possible.—

R. B.

II (511)

Friday night [26th October 1792]

My dear Sir,

Let me tell you, that you are too fastidious in your ideas of Songs & ballads.—I own that your criticisms are just—the Songs you specify in your list have, *all but one*, the faults you remark in them—but who shall mend the matter?—Who shall rise up & say, "Go to, I will make a better!"—For instance; on reading over, The lea-rig, I immediately set about trying my hand on it; & after all, I could make nothing more of it than the following, which Heaven knows is poor enough.—

When o'er the hill the Eastern star,
[C.W. p. 474]

Your observation as to the aptitude of Dr Percy's ballad to the air, Nanie O, is just.—It is, besides, perhaps, the most beautiful Ballad in the English language.—But let me remark to you, in the sentiment & style of our Scotish airs, there is a pastoral simplicity, a something that one may call, the Doric style & dialect of vocal music, to which a dash of our native tongue & manners is particularly, nay peculiarly apposite.—For this reason, & upon my honor, for this reason alone, I am of opinion, (but, as I told you before, my opinion is yours, freely yours, to approve, or reject as you please) that my ballad of Nanie O might perhaps do for one set of verses to the tune.—Now, don't let it enter into your head, that you are under any necessity of taking my verses.—I have long ago made up my mind as to my own reputation in the business of Authorship; & have nothing to be pleased, or offended at, in your adoption or rejection of my verses.—

618

Tho' you should reject one half of what I give you, I shall be pleased with your adopting t'other half; & shall continue to serve you with the same assiduity.—

In the printed copy of my, Nanie O, the name of the river is horridly prosaic—I will alter it,

Behind yon hills where $\left\{\begin{array}{l} \text{Girvan} \\ \text{Lugar flows''} \end{array}\right.$ —

"Girvan" is the river that suits the idea of the stanza best, but "Lugar" is the most agreable modulation of syllables.—

I intended to have given you, & will soon give you, a great many more remarks on this business; but I have just now an opportunity of conveying you this scrawl, postage-free, an expence that it is ill able to pay: so, with my best Compliments to honest Allan,[1] Good b'w'ye, to you!—

R. B.—

Remember me to the first & dearest of my friends, Alexander Cunningham, who, I understand, is a coadjutor with you in this business.—

R. B.

Saturday morning—

I find that I have still an hour to spare this morning before my conveyance goes away.—I shall give you Nanie O, at length.—

[C.W. p. 45]

Your remarks on, Ewe bughts Marion, are just; Still, it has obtained a place among our more classical Scots songs; & what with many beauties in its·composition, & more prejudices in its favor, you will not find it easy to supplant it.—In my very early years, when I was thinking of going to the West Indies, I took the following farewell of a dear girl.—It is quite trifling, & has nothing of the merit of "Ewebughts;" but it will fill up this page.—You must know, that all my earlier love-songs were the breathings of ardent Passion; & tho' it might have been easy in aftertimes to have given them a polish, yet that polish, to me, whose they were, & who perhaps alone cared for them, would have defaced the legend of my heart which was so faithfully inscribed on them.—Their uncouth simplicity was, as they say of wines, their RACE.—

Will ye go to the Indies, my Mary[2]

[C.W. p. 468]

Galla water & auld Rob Morris, I think will most probably be the next subjects of my musings.—However, even on *my verses*, speak out of your criticisms with equal frankness.—My wish is, not to stand aloof, the uncomplying bigot of opiniatretê; but cordially to join issue with you in the furtherance of the work.—

GUDE SPEED THE WARK! AMEN ! ! !

R. B.

1 David Allan.
2 'This is a very poor Song—which I do not mean to include in my Collection. I think it were a pity to publish any thing of the Poet's which he did not himself consider to be worth publication. G.T.'

George Thomson

III (514)

8th November 1792

If you mean, my dear Sir, that all the Songs in your Collection shall be Poetry of the first merit, I am afraid you will find difficulty in the undertaking more than you are aware of.—There is a peculiar rhythmus in many of our airs, a necessity of adapting syllables to the emphasis, or what I would call, the *feature notes*, of the tune, that cramps the Poet, & lays him under almost insuperable difficulties.— For instance, in the air, My wife's a wanton wee thing, if a few lines, *smooth & pretty*, can be adapted to it, it is all that you can expect.— The following I made extempore to it; & though, on farther study I might give you something more profound, yet it might not suit the light-horse gallop of the air so well as this *random clink*.—

My wife's a winsome wee thing—
[C.W. p. 469]

I have just been looking over "the Collier's bony dochter," & if the following rhapsody which I composed the other day on a charming Ayr-shire girl, Miss Lesley Bailie of Mayfield, as she passed thro' this place to England, if it will suit your taste better than the Collier lassie, fall on & welcome.—

O saw ye bonie Lesley,
[C.W. p. 435]

Every seventh line ends with three syllables, in place of the two in the other lines, but you will see in the sixth bar of the second part, the place where these three syllables will always recur, that the four semiquavers usually sung as one syllable will with the greatest propriety divide into two—thus

For Na - ture made her   what she   is,   And &c., &c., &c.,

I have hitherto deferred the sublimer, more pathetic airs, untill more leisure, as they will take, & deserve, a greater effort.—However, they are all put into thy hands, as clay into the hands of the Potter; to make one vessel to honor, & another to dishonor.*—Farewel!

Robt Burns

* Romans 9:21, paraphrased.

IV (518)

[With *Highland Mary*, to the tune, *Katherine Ogie*.]
[C.W. p. 470]

14th November 1792

My dear Sir,

I agree with you that the song, K. Ogie, is very poor stuff, & unworthy, altogether unworthy, of so beautiful an air.—I tried to mend it; but the awkward sound, "Ogie", recurring so often in the rhyme, spoils every attempt at introducing *Sentiment* into the Piece.

George Thomson

The foregoing Song pleases myself; I think it is in my happiest manner: you will see at first glance that it suits the air.—The Subject of the Song is one of the most interesting passages of my youthful days; & I own that I would be much flattered to see the verses set to an Air which would insure celebrity.—Perhaps, after all, 'tis the still glowing prejudice of my heart, that throws a borrowed lustre over the merits of the Composition.—

I have partly taken your idea of "Auld Rob Morris."—I have adopted the two first verses, & am going on with the Song on a new plan, which promises pretty well.—I take up one or another, just as the Bee of the moment buzzes in my bonnet-lug; & do you, sans ceremonie, make what use you chuse of the productions.—

Adieu!
Robt Burns

V (522)

Dumfries 1st December 1792

Your alterations of my "Nanie O", are perfectly right.—So are those of, "My wife's a wanton wee thing."—Your alteration of the 2d Stanza is a positive improvement.—Now, my dear Sir, with the freedom which characterizes our correspondence, I must not, cannot alter, "Bonie Lesley."—You are right; the word "Alexander," makes the line a little uncouth, but I think the thought is pretty.—Of Alexander beyond all other heroes it may be said in the sublime language of Scripture, that "he went forth, conquering, & to conquer."*—

"For Nature made her *what she is,*
 And never made anither.—(Such a person as she is)
this is my opinion more poetical than

"Ne'er made sic anither."—

However, it is immaterial: make it either way.—"Caledonie," I agree with you, is not so good a word as could be wished, tho' it is sanctioned in three or four instances by Allan Ramsay; but I cannot help it.—In short, that species of Stanza is the most difficult that I have ever tried.—The lea-rig, is as follows—

When o'er the hill the E'enin star ⎫
            parting sun   ⎭

[C.W. p. 474]

I am interrupted.—Please transmit the inclosed by a careful hand.—

Yours
Robt Burns

* Revelation 6:2.

George Thomson

VI (523)

4th December [1792]

[With *Auld Rob Morris* and *Duncan Gray*.]

[C.W. pp. 474-5.]

The foregoing I submit, my dear Sir, to your better judgement. Acquit them, or condemn them, & as seemeth good in thy sight.— Duncan Gray is that kind of light-horse gallop of an air, which precludes sentiment.—The ludicrous is its ruling feature.—

Yours
Robt Burns

VII (532)

[With *Poortith Cauld* and *Braw Lads o Galla Water*.]

[C.W. p. 481]

[Received 7th January 1793]

Many returns of the season to you! my dear Sir.—How comes on your publication? will these two foregoing, be of any service to you? Dispose of them as seemeth good in thy sight. If you are begun with the Work, I could like to see one of your proofs, merely from curiosity; & perhaps to try to get you a subscriber, or two.—I should like also to know what other songs you print to each tune, besides the verses to which it is set.—In short, I would wish to give you my opinion on all the poetry you publish.—You know, it is my trade; & a man in the way of his trade may suggest useful hints that escape men of much superiour parts & endowments in other things.

If you meet with my dear & much-valued Cunningham, greet him, in my name, with the Compliments of the season.—

Yours
Robt Burns

Regarding these songs Thomson wrote: 'These verses I humbly think have too much of *uneasy* & cold reflection, for this Air, which is pleasing, & rather gay than otherwise'.—Burns replied: 'The objections are just, but I cannot make it better.—The stuff won't bear mending; yet for *private* reasons I should like to see it in print'—

VIII (535)

26th January, 1793

I approve greatly, my dear Sir, on your plans.—Dr Beattie's essay will of itself be a treasure.—On my part, I mean to draw up an appendix to the Dr's essay, containing my stock of anecdotes, &c. of our Scots Airs & Songs.—All the later Mr Tytler's anecdotes, I have by me, taken down in the course of my acquaintance with him from his own mouth.—I am such an enthusiast, that in the course of my several peregrinations through Scotland, I made a pilgrimage to the individual spot from which the song took its rise.—Lochaber, & The braes of Ballenden, excepted, so far as the locality, either from the title of the air, or the tenor of the Song, could be ascertained, I have paid my devotions at the particular shrine of every Scots Muse.—

I do not doubt but you might make a very valuable Collection of Jacobite songs, but would it give no offence? In the mean time, do n't you think but some of them, particularly "The Sow's tail to Geordie," as an *Air*, with other words, might be well worth its place in your Collection of lively Songs?

If it were possible to procure songs of merit, I think it would be proper to have one set of Scots words to every air,—& that the set of words to which the notes ought to be pricked.—There is a naivete, a pastoral simplicity, in a slight intermixture of Scots words & phraseology, which is more in unison (at least to my taste, & I will add, to every genuine Caledonian taste, with the simple pathos, or rustic sprightliness, of our native music, than any English verses whatever. —For instance, in my, Auld Rob Morris, you propose instead of the word, "descriving," to substitute the phrase, "all telling," which would spoil the rusticity, the pastoral, of the Stanza.—

The very name of Peter Pindar is an acquisition to your work.—His "Gregory" is beautiful.—I have tried to give you a set of Stanzas in Scots, on the same subject, which are at your service.—Not that I intend to enter the lists with Peter: that would be presumption indeed.—My Song, though much inferior in poetic merit, has I think more of the ballad simplicity in it.—

Lord Gregory—

O mirk, mirk is this midnight hour

[C.W. p. 482]

Your remark on the first Stanza of my, "Highland Mary," is just; but I cannot alter it without injuring the poetry in proportion as I mended the perspicuity; so, if you please, we will let it stand as it is. —My other songs, you will see what alterations I have made in them. If you think that my name can be of any service to your advertisement, you are welcome.—

My most respectful Compliments to the Honorable Gentleman who favored me with a postscript in your last.—He shall hear from me & receive his M.S.S. soon.—

Yours
Robt Burns

IX (540)

20th March [1793]

[With *Mary Morison.*]
[C.W. p. 69]

My dear Sir,

the Song prefixed is one of my juvenile works.—I leave it among your hands.—I do not think it very remarkable, either for its merits, or demerits.—It is impossible, at least I feel it in my stinted powers, to be always original, entertaining & witty.—

What is become of the list, &c. of your songs?—I shall be out of all temper with you by & by.—I have always looked on myself as the Prince of indolent correspondents, & valued myself accordingly; & I will not, cannot, bear rivalship from you, nor any body else.—

I wish much to have the list, & to hear how you come on.—

Yours
Robt Burns

George Thomson

X (552A)

Bishop mark MR 27 [1793]

Song

Lang here awa, there awa wandering, Willie,
[C.W. p. 480]

I leave it to you, my dear Sir, to determine whether the above, or
the old, "Thro' the lang muir," be the best.—

Yours
Robt Burns

XI (554)

[April 1793]

Open the door to me Oh

Oh, open the door, some pity to shew,
[C.W. p. 485]

I do not know whether this song be really mended.—

Song—Tune, Bonie Dundee—

True-hearted was he, the sad swain o' the Yarrow,
[C.W. p. 486]

These verses suit the tune exactly, as it is in the Museum. There is a
syllable wanting at the beginning of the first line of the second
Stanza, but I suppose it will make little odds.—There is so little of
the Scots language in the composition that the mere English Singer
will find no difficulty in the Song.—

I have yours, my dear Sir, this moment.—I shall answer it, & your
former letter, in my desultory way of saying whatever comes
uppermost.—

I am decidedly against setting, "The gloomy night &c." to the air,
"my Nanie O."—Musical expression is, as you said in one of your
late letters, very ambiguous; but whatever a few Cognoscenti may
think, you would find that eight out of ten of your Scots Subscribers,
would prefer for that air my, "Nanie O," though an inferiour song,
to "The Banks of Ayr."—Besides, the Banks of Ayr has been set by a
Mr Dasti to an original air; & being a favorite song with Sutherland's
Company of strolling Comedians, it is now a well-known & popular
air, over the West & South of Scotland.—

That business of many of our tunes wanting at the beginning what
Fiddlers call, a starting-note, is often a rub to us poor Rhymers.—

"There's braw, braw lads in Yarrow braes"—

You may alter to,

"Braw, braw lads on Yarrow braes,
"Rove among the blooming heather"—

My Song, Here awa there awa, as amended by Mr Erskine, I entirely
approve of, & return you.—The Yellow hair'd laddie, I would dispose
of thus.—I would set the air to the oldest of the Songs to that tune,

624

George Thomson

"The yellow-hair'd laddie sat on yon burn brae"—& place in letter-press after it, as an English Set,—"In April when primroses paint the sweet plain."—

Give me leave to criticise your taste in the only thing in which it is in my opinion reprehensible: (you know I ought to know something of my own trade) of pathos, Sentiment & Point, you are a compleat judge; but there is a quality more necessary than either, in a Song, & which is the very essence of a Ballad, I mean Simplicity—now, if I mistake not, this last feature you are a little apt to sacrifice to the foregoing.—

Ramsay, as every other Poet, has not been always equally happy in his pieces: still I cannot approve of taking such liberties with an Author, as Mr Walker has done with "The last time I cam o'er the moor."—Let a Poet, if he chuses, take up the idea of another, & work it in to a piece of his own; but to mangle the works of the poor Bard whose tuneful tongue is now mute for ever in the dark & narrow house, by Heaven 'twould be Sacriledge! I grant that Mr Walker's version is an improvement; but, I know Mr Walker well, & esteem him much; let him mend the Song, as the Highlander mended his gun: he gave it a new Stock, a new lock, & a new barrel.—

I do not by this, object to leaving out improper Stanzas, where that can be done without spoiling the whole.—One Stanza in, "The lass o' Patie's mill" must be left out: the Song will be nothing worse for it. —I am not sure if we can take the same liberty with, "Corn-riggs are bonie.— "Perhaps it might want the last Stanza, & be the better for it.—

I shall be extremely sorry, if you set any other song to the air, "She rose & loot me in," except the Song of that title.—It is cruel to spoil the allusion in poor unfortunate McDonald's pretty ode.—

Could you spare me for a while, "My lodging is on the cold ground" —I mean, could you defer it untill the latest period of your Publication, and I will try to make a new Song to it?—

I would be happy to be favored with a list of the twenty five you mean to publish first.—Remember that on them will in a great measure depend the fate of your Work with the Public; for that reason, it will be necessary to select & arrange them with double circumspection.—

Cauld kail in Aberdeen, you must leave with me yet a while.—I have vowed to have a song to that air, on the lady whom I attempted to celebrate in the verses, "Poortith cauld & restless love."—At any rate, my other Song, "Green grow the rashes" will never suit.—That Song is current in Scotland under the old title, & sung to the merry old tune of that name; which of course would mar the progress of your Song to celebrity.—*Your Book will be the Standard of Scots Songs for the future:* [1] let this idea ever keep your judgement on the alarm.—

I send you a song, on a celebrated fashionable Toast in this Country, to suit Bonie Dundee.—I send you also a Ballad to the Mill mill O.—

"The last time I came o'er the moor" I would fain attempt to make a Scots Song for, & let Ramsay's be the English Set.—

625

You shall hear from me soon.—When you go to London on this business, can you come by Dumfries? I have still several M.S.S. Scots airs by me, which I have pickt up, mostly from the singing of country lasses.—They please me vastly; but your learned lugs would perhaps be displeased with the very feature for which I like them.—I call them Simple; you would pronounce them Silly.—Do you know a fine air, called Jackie Hume's lament?—There I have a Song of considerable merit, to that air, beginning—

> O ken ye what Meg o' the mill has gotten,
> An ken ye what Meg o' the mill has gotten:
> She's gotten a Coof wi' a claut o' siller,
> And broken the heart o' the barley Miller.[2]—

I'll inclose you both the Song & tune, as I had them ready to send to Johnson's Museum.—I send you likewise, to me a beautiful little air, which I had taken down from viva voce.—On the other page, I will give you a Stanza or two of the Ballad to it.—

> There was a lass and she was fair,

[C.W. p. 493]

I know these Songs are not to have the luck to please you, else you might be welcome to them.—Preserve them carefully, & return them to me, as I have no other copy.-

Adieu!
RB

1 Cf. Burns's letter to Johnson, XXI (696), saying the same of the *Scots Musical Museum* (p. 303).
2 Plus four other stanzas on a separate sheet.

XII (557)

7th April 1793

Thank you, my dear Sir, for your packet.—You cannot imagine how much this business of composing for your publication has added to my enjoyments.—What with my early attachment to ballads, Johnson's Museum, your book; &c. Ballad-making is now as compleatly my hobby-horse, as ever Fortification was Uncle Toby's; so I'll e'en canter it away till I come to the limit of my race, (God grant that I may take the right side of the winning-post!) & then chearfully looking back on the honest folks with whom I have been happy, I shall say, or sing, "Sae merry as we a' hae been"—& then, raising my last looks to the whole Human-race, the last voice of Coila shall be—"Good night & joy be wi' you a'!"*—

So much for my last words: now for a few present remarks, as they have occurred at random, on looking over your List.—

The two first lines of "The last time I came o'er the moor" & several other lines in it, are beautiful; but in my opinion,—pardon me, revered Shade of Ramsay!—the song is unworthy of the divine air.—I shall try to *make,* or *mend.*—"For ever Fortune wilt thou &c." is a charming Song; but "Logan burn & Logan braes," are sweetly susceptible of rural imagery: I'll try that likewise, & if I succeed, the other Song may class among the English ones.—I remember two ending lines of a verse in some of the old Songs of "Logan water"

626

George Thomson

(for I know a good many different ones) which I think pretty—

"Now my dear lad maun face his faes,
"Far, far frae me & Logan braes!"

"My Patie is a lover gay," is also unequal.—"His mind is never muddy," is a muddy expression indeed.—

"Then I'll resign & marry Pate,
"And syne my cockernony"

This is surely far unworthy of Ramsay, or your book.—My Song, Rigs of barley" to the same air, does not altogether please me; but if I can mend it, & thresh a few loose sentiments out of it, I shall submit it to your consideration.—I need not here repeat that I leave you, without the smllest partiality, or constraint, to reject, or approve any thing of mine.—

"The lass o' Patie's mill," is one of Ramsay's best songs; but there is one loose sentiment in it, which my much-valued friend Mr Erskine, who has so well improved "Down the burn Davie lad," will take into his critical care & keeping.—In Sir J. Sinclair's Statistical volumes, are two claims, one I think from Aberdeen-shire, & the other from Ayr-shire, for the honor of this Song.—The following anecdote which I had from the present Sir William Cunningham of Robertland, who had it of the late John, Earl of Lowdon, I can, on such authorities, believe.—Allan Ramsay was residing at Lowdon castle with the then Earl, father to Earl John; & one forenoon, riding, or walking out together, his Lordship & Allan passed a sweet, romantic spot on Irvine water, still called, "Patie's mill," where a bonie lass was "tedding hay, bareheaded on the green."—My Lord observed to Allan that it would be a fine theme for a song.—Ramsay took the hint; &, lingering behind, he composed the first sketch of it, which he produced at dinner.—

"The yellow-hair'd laddie" deserves the best verses that ever were composed; but I dare not venture on it. The verses you intend, though good, are not quite worthy of it.—

"I wish I were where Helen lies"—The only tolerable set of this song, that I know, is in Pinkerton's collection.—

"One day I heard Mary say"—is a fine Song; but, for consistency's sake, alter the name, "Adonis."—Was there ever such bans published, as a purpose of marriage between *Adonis* & *Mary*?—These Greek & Roman pastoral appellations have a flat, insipid effect in a Scots song.—

I agree with you, that my song, "There's nought but care on every hand," is much superiour to "Poortith cauld &c."—

The original song, "The Mill, mill O" though excellent, is on account of decency, inadmissible; still I like the title; & I think a Scots song would suit the notes best, & let your chosen song, which is very pretty, follow as an English set.—

Though I give Johnson one edition of my songs, that does not give away the copy-right; so you may take—"Thou lingering star with lessening ray," to the tune of Hughie Graham, or other songs of mine; & likewise the song, "Ye gallants bright, I rede you right" &c., for it also is my composition.—

627

Banks of the Dee, is, you know, literally, Langolee, to slow time.—
The song is well enough, but has some false imagery in it, for
instance—

>   "And sweetly the *nightingale* sung from the *tree*"—

In the first place, the nightingale sings in a low bush, but never from
a tree; & in the second place, there never was a nightingale seen, or
heard, on the banks of the Dee, or on the banks of any other river in
Scotland.—*Exotic* rural imagery is always comparatively flat.—If I
could hit on another Stanza, equal to, "The small birds rejoice"
&c., I do myself honestly avow that I think it a superiour song.—

"John Anderson my jo"—the song to this tune in Johnson's Museum,
is my composition, & I think it not my worst: if it suit you, take it
& welcome.—

Your Collection of Sentimental & pathetic songs, is, in my opinion,
very compleat; but not so your Comic ones.—Where is Tullochgorum,
Lumps o' puddins, Tibbie Fowler, Rattlin roarin Willie, & several
others, which in my humble opinion, are well worthy of preservation.
There is also one sentimental song, of mine, the first in the 4th Vol.
of the Museum, which never was known out of the immediate
neighbourhood, untill I got it taken down from a country girl's
singing.—It is called, Craigieburnwood; & in the opinion of Mr Clarke,
is one of the sweetest Scots Songs.—He is quite an enthusiast about
it; & I would take his taste in Scots music against the taste of most
connoisseurs.—

You are quite right in inserting the last five, though they certainly
are Irish.—"Shepherds, I have lost my love," is, to me, a Heavenly
air.—What would you think of a set of Scots verses to it?—I have
made one, a good while ago, which I think, is the best love-song I
ever composed in my life; but in its *original* state, is not quite a
lady's song.—I inclose the Original, which please present, with my
best Compliments to Mr Erskine; & I also inclose an *altered*, not
amended, copy for you, if you chuse to set the tune to it, & let the
Irish verses follow.—

You shall hear from me again, & have your Songs.—Mr Erskine's are
all pretty, but his, "Lone vale," is divine.—I have one criticism to
make on a line in his fine song to, "I wish my Love were in a mire"—
but more of this, when I return your parcel.—

Yours
RB

Let me know just how you like these random hints.

RB

* The traditional farewell song before *Auld Lang Syne*.

XIII (559)

Bishop mark AP 26 [1793]

>   The last time I came o'er the moor,
>   And left Maria's dwelling,
>   What throes, what tortures, passing cure,
>   Were in my bosom swelling.[1]

George Thomson

My dear Sir,

I had scarcely put my last letter into the Post-Office, when I took up the subject of, "The last time I came o'er the moor," & e'er I slept, drew the outlines of the foregoing.—How far I have succeeded, I leave, as I do every other I send you, to you to decide.—I own my vanity is flattered, when you give my works a place in your elegant & superb Work; but to be of service to that Work, is my first wish.— As I have often told you, I do not in a single instance wish you, out of compliment to me, to insert any thing of mine.—

If you can send me, as I said in my last hotch-potch epistle, a list of your first twenty-five songs, I will add the Author's names, & return you the list.—One hint let me give you: where you have, as in Katharine Ogie, set another song to the air, it will be proper always to prefix the old name of the tune—thus—

Highland Mary.—Tune, Katharine Ogie.—

Another hint you will forgive. Whatever Mr Pleyel does, let him not alter one iota of the original Scots Air; I mean, in the Song department.—Our friend, Clarke, than whom, you know, there is not a better judge of the subject, complains that in the air, "Lee-rigg," the accent is to be altered.—But, let our National Music preserve its native features.—They are, I own, frequently wild, & unreduceable to the more modern rules; but on that very eccentricity, perhaps, depends a great part of their effect.[2]—Farewel!

R. Burns

1 With a further 20 lines, the first of several variants of what eventually became *Farewell, Thou Stream* (C.W. p. 486).
2 Thomson annotated this: 'The Poet must have misunderstood the matter. As a Song the Lee-rigg will not be altered in any respect whatever - in the Sonatas Mr Pleyel is permitted to vary the Airs as he pleases.'

XIV (566)

25th June 1793

Have you ever, my dear Sir, felt your bosom ready to burst with indignation, on reading of, or seeing, how these mighty villains who divide kingdom against kingdom, desolate provinces & lay Nations waste out of the wantonness of Ambition, or often from still more ignoble passions?—In a mood of this kind today, I recollected the air of Logan water, & it occurred to me that its querulous melody probably had its origin from the plaintive indignation of some swelling, suffering heart, fired at the tyrannic strides of some Public Destroyer; & overwhelmed with private distresses, the consequence of a Country's ruin.—If I have done any thing at all like justice to my feelings, the following song, composed in three-quarters of an hour's lucubrations in my elbow-chair, ought to have some merit.—

Song—Tune Logan Water

O, Logan, sweetly didst thou glide,

[C.W. p. 490]

Do you know the beautiful little fragment, in Witherspoon's Collection* of Scots Songs?

"O gin my love were yon red rose,
"That grows upon the castle wa'!
"And I mysel' a drap o' dew,
"Into her bonie breast to fa'!

"Oh, there beyond expression blest
"I'd feast on beauty a' the night;
"Seal'd on her silk-saft faulds to rest,
"Till fley'd awa by Phebus' light!"

This thought is inexpressibly beautiful; & quite, so far as I know, original.—It is too short for a song, else I would forswear you altogether, except you gave it a place.—I have often tried to eke a stanza to it, but in vain.—

After balancing myself for a musing five minutes, on the hind-legs of my elbow-chair, I produced the following.—The verses are far inferiour to the foregoing, I frankly confess; but if worthy of insertion at all, they might be first in place; as every Poet knows any thing of his trade, will husband his best thoughts for a concluding stroke.—

O were my Love yon Lilack fair,
[C.W. p. 492]

Yours ever—
Robt Burns

* David Herd: *The Ancient and Modern Scots Songs*, published by Martin & Wotherspoon (1769).

XV (567)

Bishop mark JU 30 [1793]

When I tell you, my dear Sir, that a friend of mine in whom I am much interested has fallen a sacrifice to these accursed times, you will easily allow that it might unhinge me for doing any good among ballads.—My own loss, as to pecuniary matters, is trifling; but the total ruin of a much lov'd Friend, is a loss indeed.—Pardon my seeming inattention to your last commands.—

I cannot alter the disputed line, in the Mill Mill O.—What you think a defect, I esteem as a positive beauty: so you see how Doctors differ.—

I shall now, with as much alacrity as I can muster, go on with your commands.—

You know Fraser, the Hautboy player in Edinburgh. He is here, instructing a band of Music for a Fencible Corps quartered in this country.—Among many of his airs that please me, there is one, well known as a Reel by the name of, "The quaker's wife;" & which I remember a grand Aunt of mine used to sing, by the name of "Liggeram cosh, my bonie wee lass."—Mr Fraser plays it slow, & with an expression that quite charms me.—I got such an enthusiast in it, that I made a Song for it, which I here subjoin, & inclose Fraser's set of the tune.—If they hit your fancy, they are at your service; if not, return me the tune, & I will put it in Johnson's Museum. I think the song is not in my worst manner.—

George Thomson

Song—Tune, Liggeram cosh—
Blythe hae I been on yon hill,
[C.W. p. 490]

I should wish to hear how this pleases you.—

Yours—
R B

XVI (568)

[2nd July? 1793]

My dear Sir,

I have just finished the following ballad, & as I do think it in my best style, I send it you.—You had the tune, with a verse or two of the song, from me, a while ago.—Mr Clarke, who wrote down the air from Mrs Burns's wood-note wild, is very fond of it; & has given it celebrity, by teaching it to some young ladies of the first fashion here.—If you do not like the air enough to give it a place in your Collection, please return me the air.—The song you may keep, as I remember it.—

There was a lass & she was fair,
[C.W. p. 493]

I have some thoughts of inserting in your index or in my notes, the names of the fair-ones, the themes of my Songs.—I do not mean the name at full; but dashes or asterisms, so as ingenuity may find them out.—

Yours—
RB

The heroine of the foregoing is, Miss M^cmurdo, daughter to Mr ——of Drumlanrig—one of your Subscribers.—

XVII (569)

[July 1793]

I assure you, my dear Sir, that you truly hurt me with your pecuniary parcel.—It degrades me in my own eyes.—However, to return it would savour of bombast affectation; But as to any more traffic of that Debtor & Creditor kind, I swear by that HONOUR which crowns the upright Statue of ROB^t BURNS'S INTEGRITY!—On the least motion of it, I will indignantly spurn the bypast transaction, & from that moment commence entire Stranger to you!—BURNS'S character for Generosity of Sentiment, & Independance of Mind, will, I trust, long outlive any of his wants which the cold, unfeeling, dirty Ore can supply: at least, I shall take care that such a Character he shall deserve.—

Thank you for my Copy.—Never did my eyes behold, in any Musical work, such elegance & correctness.—Your Preface, too, is admirably written; only your partiality to me has made you say too much: however, it will bind me down to double every effort in the future progress of the Work.—

Now for business.—Must I return you the List? The following are a

631

few remarks on it.—I never copy what I write you, so I may be often tautological, or perhaps contradictory.—

The flowers of the forest, is charming as a poem; & should be & must be, set to the notes; but, though out of your rule, the three Stanzas, beginning,

"I hae seen the smiling o' Fortune beguiling"—

are worthy of a place, were it but to immortalize the Author of them, who is an old Lady of my acquaintance, & at this moment living in Edinburgh.—She is a Mrs Cockburn[1]; I forget of what place; but from Roxburgh-shire.—What a charming apostrophe is—

"O fickle Fortune, why this cruel sporting,
Why, why torment us—*poor sons of a day*!"

The old Ballad, "I wish I were where Helen lies"—is silly, to contemptibility.—My alteration of it in Johnson, is not much better. —Mr Pinkerton, in his, what he calls ancient ballads (many of them notorious, tho' beautiful enough forgeries) has the best set.—It is full of his own interpolations, but no matter.[2]—

In the lea-rig, I have altered my mind as to the first line, & will, if you please, have it as at first—

"When o'er the hill the eastern star"—

It is much more poetical.—

The verses of "the bony Brucket lassie," are poor.—They, I believe, are the production of that odd being, Balloon Tytler[3].—The air deserves fine verses.—

The Measure of "Hughie Graham" will answer exactly to my favorite fragment—"O if my love were yon red rose"—Will the expression suit?

The Jacobite verses, "Ther'll never be peace till Jamie comes hame" are mine, made on the idea suggested by the title of the air.—If you object to their sentiment, there is another song of mine, Museum, vol: 4th, Page 340, which will suit the measure.—It is a little irregular in the flow of the lines; but where two short syllables, that is to say, one syllable more than regular feet, if these two syllables fall to the space of one, crochet-time, composed of two different quavers under a slur, it has, I think, no bad effect, to divide them.—Thus it may flow—

Yon wild mossy mountains &c.
That nurse &c.
Where the grous thro' the heath lead their coveys to feed,
And the shepherd &c.

After all, perhaps the expression of the air requires something more solemn.—

If you look into the Museum, vol: 4th P. 320, you will see an altered set of the Ballad, "O let me in this ae night."—Apropos, in Oswald, under the name of

"Will ye lend me your loom lass"—

you will meet with a different set, & perhaps a better one, than in Johnson's Museum.—

In my next, I will suggest to your consideration, a few songs which may have escaped your hurried notice.—In the mean time, allow me to congratulate you, now, as a brother of the quill.—You have *committed* your character & fame; which will now be tried, for ages to come, by the illustrious Jury of the SONS & DAUGHTERS of Taste—all whom Poesy can please, or Music charm.—Being a Bard of Nature, I have some pretensions to Second Sight; & I am warranted by the Spirit to fortell & affirm, that your great great grandchild will hold up your volumes, & say with honest pride, "This so much admired Selection was the work of my Ancestor."—

Yours
RB

P.S. Robert Riddell Esqr of Glenriddell, subscribed to me for the Songs.—Send him a copy, to my care, the first opportunity.—Walter Riddell of Woodley-park, is a Subscriber for the whole Work; but he is at present out of the Country.—John Mcmurdo Esq: Drumlanrig, is, I believe, another Subscriber for the whole work, & also, I think, Patrick Miller of Dalswinton but Mr Clarke our friend who is at present teaching in both families, I will write or speak to him about it.—However, all your Subscribers here are determined to transmit you, the *full* price, without the intervention of these Harpies the Booksellers.

Do not forget Glenriddell's Copy of the Songs—

RB

1 Mrs Alison Cockburn (1712-94) from Fairnilee, Selkirkshire.
2 John Pinkerton: *Scottish Tragic Ballads*, London (1781).
3 James Tytler (1747-1805), thus nicknamed for having made the first manned flights in the British Isles, 1784.

XVIII (574)

[August 1793]

My dear Thomson,

I hold the pen for our Friend, Clarke, who at present is studying the Music of the Spheres at my elbow.—The Georgium Sidus he thinks is rather out of tune; so, untill he rectify that matter, he cannot stoop to terrestrial affairs.—

He sends you six of the Songs, & if more are wanted, he says you shall have them.—

RB

Damn your long stairs!

XIX (574A)

[Deed of Assignment of Copyright to GEORGE THOMSON]

I do hereby certify to all those whom it may concern, that *all* the Songs of my composition, published & to be published along with Scotish airs by Mr George Thomson of Edinburgh, are so published by my authority & consent: & in particular, that I never authorised any other person to publish *any* of those songs which were written by me for his work.—

AND, only reserving to myself the power of publishing these songs, at any future period, & in any manner I may think proper, I DO HEREBY, *as far as I legally can*, prohibit any other person than the said George Thomson from publishing the before mentioned Songs; & do also empower him to prosecute in terms of law any person or persons pirating, publishing, or vending the said Songs, or any of them, without his consent; & that at his own expence & for his own behoof.—

In witness whereof, I have written & subscribed these Presents, at Dumfries, the second day of August, one thousand, seven hundred & ninety three years.—

Robt Burns

XX (575)

Bishop mark AU 13 [1793]

Your objection, my dear Sir, to the passages in my song of Logan-water,[1] is right in one instance: the phrase "cruel joys" is, there, improper; but it is difficult to mend it: if I can, I will.—The other passage you object to, does not appear in the same light to me.—

The phrase, "Mammie's wark," universally among the peasantry signifies, "Mother's wark," if you think this last better, you may adopt it.—Your other objections to this song will vanish, when you consider that I have not painted Miss McMurdo in the rank which she holds in life, but in the dress & character of a Cottager; consequently the utmost simplicity of thought & expression was necessary.—

Had you not better send me a list of the next parcel of songs which you intend to publish? As to your large list you sent me, it is so blurred & blotted, that nobody besides myself could make me any thing of it.—

I have looked over, "There'll never be peace till Jamie" &c. but I cannot make any better of it.[2]—

I was yesternight in a composing humour, & behold the fruits of it.—

Let me in this ae night—

O lassie art thou sleepin yet,

[C.W. p. 538]

I need not hint to you, that the chorus goes to the high part of the tune.—

I likewise tried my hand on, "Robin Adair," & you will probably think, with little success; but it is such a d-mned, cramp, out-of-the way measure, that I despair of doing any thing better to it.—

Phillis the fair.—Tune Robin Adair—

While larks with little wing,

[C.W. p. 495]

So much for Namby Pamby.—I may after all, try my hand on it in Scots verse.—There I always find myself most at home.—

I have just put the last hand to the song I meant for "Cauld kail in Aberdeen."—If it suits you, to insert it, I shall be pleased; as the heroine is a favorite of mine: if not, I shall also be pleased, because I wish, & will be glad, to see you act decidedly in the business.—'Tis a tribute as a Man of taste, & as an Editor, which you owe yourself.—

Song—Tune, Cauld kail in Aberdeen—

O poortith cauld, & restless love,

[C.W. p. 481]

Among your Subscribers, is, for the Songs, The Honorable John Gordon Esquire of Kenmore: send his to my care.—For the Songs & Sonatas both, Walter Riddell Esq: of Woodleypark: send to the care of Mrs Riddell, Dumfries.—

Yours
Robt Burns

1 C.W. p. 490.
2 C.W. p. 418.

XXI (576)

[mid-August 1793]

That crinkum crankum tune, Robin Adair, has run so in my head, & I succeeded so ill in my last attempt, that I have ventured in this morning's walk, one essay more.—You, my dear Sir, will remember an unfortunate part of our worthy friend, Cunningham's story, which happened about three years ago.—That struck my fancy, & I endeavoured to do the idea justice as follows—

Song

Had I a cave on some wild, distant shore;

[C.W. p. 496]

By the way, I have met with a musical Highlander in Breadalbane's Fencibles which are quartered here, who assures me that he well remembers his mother's singing Gaelic Songs to both, Robin Adair, & Gramachree. They certainly have more of the Scotch than Irish taste in them.—This man comes from the vicinity of Inverness; so it could not be any intercourse with Ireland that could bring them— except, what I shrewdly suspect to be the case, the wandering Minstrels, Harpers, or Pipers, used to go frequently errant through the wilds both of Scotland & Ireland, & so some favorite airs might be common to both;—Case in point.—They have lately in Ireland, with great pomp, published an Irish air, as they say, called, Caun de deish: the fact is, in a publication of Corri's, a great while ago, you find the same air, called a Highland one, with a Gaelic song *set* to it.—Its name there, I think is, "Oran Gaoil" —& a fine air it is.— Do, ask honest Allan, or the Reverend Gaelic Parson, about these matters.—

Robt Burns

XXII (577)

Bishop mark AU 19 [1793]

My dear Sir,

That unlucky song, "O poortith cauld,"[1] &c. must stand as it stands —I won't put my hand to it again.—"Let me in this ae night"[2]—I shall overlook.—I am glad that you are pleased with my song, "Had I a cave,"[3] &c.—as I liked it myself.—

I walked out yesterday evening, with a volume of the Museum in my hand, when turning up "Allan water," "What numbers shall the muse repeat," &c. it appeared to me rather unworthy of so fine an air; & recollecting that it is on your list, I sat, & raved, under the shade of an old thorn, till I wrote one to suit the measure.—I may be wrong; but I think it not in my worst style.—You must know, that in Ramsay's tea-table, where the modern Song first appeared, the ancient name of the tune, Allan says, is "Allan water," or, "My love, Annie's very bonie."—This last has certainly been a line of the original song; so I took up the idea, &, as you will see, have introduced the line in its place which I presume it formerly occupied; though I likewise give you a chusing line, if it should not hit the cut of your fancy—

Allan water

By Allan- stream / side I chanc'd to rove,

[C.W. p. 498]

Bravo! say I: it is a good song.—Should you think so too, (not else) you can set the music to it, & let the other follow as English verses.—

I cannot touch, "Down the burn Davie." "The last time I came o'er the muir," I shall have in my eye.[4]—

Autumn is my propitious season.—I make more verses in it, than in all the year else.—

God bless you!
RB

1 C.W. p. 481. 2 Ibid. p. 538. 3 Ibid. p. 496. 4 Ibid. p. 501.

XXIII (578)

[about 25th August 1793]

You may readily trust, my dear Sir, that any exertion in my power, is heartily at your service.—But one thing I must hint to you, the very name of Peter Pindar is of great Service to your Publication; so, get a verse from him now & then, though I have no objection, as well as I can, to bear the burden of the business.—

Is, Whistle & I'll come to you, my lad—one of your airs?—I admire it much; & yesterday I set the following verses to it.—Urbani, whom I have met with here, begged them of me, as he admires the air much; but as I understand that he looks with rather an evil eye on your WORK, I did not chuse to comply.—However, if the song does not suit your taste, I may possibly send it him.—He is, entre nous, a narrow, contracted creature; but he sings so delightfully, that whatever he introduces at your concert, must have immediate celebrity.—

The set of the air which I had in my eye, is in Johnson's Museum.—

Song—

O whistle, & I'll come to you, my jo / lad,

[C.W. p. 496]

636

George Thomson

Another favorite air of mine, is, The muckin' o' Geordie's byre.—
When sung slow with expression, I have wished that it had had better
poetry: that, I have endeavored to supply, as follows—

Song—

Adown winding Nith I did wander,

[C.W. p. 497]

Mr Clarke begs you to give Miss Phillis a corner in your Book, as she
is a particular Flame of his, & out of compliment to him, I have
made the Song.—She is a Miss Phillis Mcmurdo, sister to the "Bonie
Jean" which I sent you sometime ago.—They are both pupils of his.—

Clarke begs his Compliments to you, & will send you some more airs
in a few days.—

You shall hear from me, the very first grist I get from my Rhyming
Mill.—

Yours
RB

XXIV (580)

[28th August 1793]

That tune, Cauld kail in Aberdeen, is such a favorite of yours, that I
once more roved out yesterevening for a gloaming-shot at the Muses;
when the Muse that presides o'er the shores of Nith, or rather my
old Inspiring dearest Nymph, Coila, whispered me the following.—I
have two reasons for thinking that it was my early, sweet, simple
Inspirer, that was by my elbow, "smooth gliding without step," &
pouring the Song on my glowing fancy: in the first place, since I left
Coila's native haunts, not a fragment of a Poet has arisen to chear
her solitary musings by catching inspiration from her; so I more than
suspect that she has followed me hither, or at least makes me
occasional visits: secondly, the last stanza of this song I send you, is
the very words that Coila taught me many years ago, & which I set
to an old Scots reel in Johnson's Museum.—

Song, Tune, Cauld kail—

Come let me take thee to my breast,

[C.W. p. 498]

If you think the above will suit your idea of your favorite air, I shall
be highly pleased.—

"The last time I came o'er the moor,"[1] I cannot meddle with, as to
mending it;—& the musical world have been so long accustomed to
Ramsay's words, that a different song, though positively superior
would not be so well received.—

I am not fond of choruses to songs, so I have not made one for the
foregoing.—

Apropos, there is a song of mine in the 3d vol: of the Museum,
which would suit Dainty Davie, tell me how it will suit.—It begins

O were I on Parnassus Hill[2]—

Let me have the list of your 1st hundred songs as soon as possible.—

I am ever, my dear Sir, yours Sincerely
Robt Burns

1 C.W. p. 486
2 Ibid. p. 329

XXV (581)

Bishop mark AU 28 [1793]

My dear Sir,

I have written you already by today's post, where I hinted at a song of mine which might suit Dainty Davie.—I have been looking over another & a better song of mine in the Museum, which I have altered as follows, & which I am persuaded will please you.—The words, "Dainty Davie," glide so sweetly in the air, that to a Scots ear, any song to it, without "Davie" being the hero, would have a lame effect.—

Dainty Davie—

Now rosy May comes in wi' flowers,
[C.W. p. 499]

So much for Davie—The chorus, you know, to the low part of the tune.—See Clarke's set of it in the Museum—

Yours
RB

N.B. In the Museum they have drawled out the tune to twelve lines of poetry which is damn'd nonsense—Four lines of Song, & four of Chorus, is the way—

XXVI (582)

[about 30th August 1793]

My dear Sir,

You know that my pretensions to musical taste, are merely a few of Nature's instincts, untaught & untutored by Art.—For this reason, many musical compositions, particularly where much of the merit lies in Counterpoint, however they may transport & ravish the ears of you, Connoisseurs, affect my simple lug no otherwise than merely as medodious Din.—On the other hand, by way of amends, I am delighted with many little melodies, which the learned Musician despises as silly & insipid.—I do not know whether the old Air, "Hey tutti taitie," may rank among this number; but well I know that, with Fraser's Hautboy, it has often filled my eyes with tears.—There is a tradition, which I have met with in many places of Scotland, that it was Robert Bruce's March at the battle of Bannock-burn.—This thought, in my yestenight's evening walk, warmed me to a pitch of enthusiasm on the theme of Liberty & Independance, which I threw into a kind of Scots Ode, fitted to the Air, that one might suppose to be the gallant ROYAL SCOT'S address to his heroic followers on that eventful morning.—

Robert Bruce's march to BANNOCKBURN—

To its ain tune—

638

SCOTS, wha hae wi' WALLACE bled,
SCOTS, wham BRUCE has aften led,
Welcome to your gory bed,—
    Or to victorie.—

Now's the day, & now's the hour;
See the front o' battle lower,
See approach proud EDWARD'S power,
    Chains & Slaverie.—

Wha will be a traitor-knave?
Wha can fill a coward's grave?
Wha sae base as be a Slave?
    —Let him turn & flie.—

Wha for SCOTLAND'S king & law,
Freedom's sword will strongly draw,
FREE-MAN stand, or FREE-MAN fa',
    Let him follow me.—

By Oppression's woes & pains!
By your Sons in servile chains!
We will drain our dearest veins,
    But they *shall* be free!

Lay the proud Usurpers low!
Tyrants fall in every foe!
LIBERTY'S in every blow!
    Let US DO—or DIE!!!

So may God ever defend the cause of TRUTH and Liberty, as he did
that day!—Amen!

                              RB

P.S. I shewed the air to Urbani, who was highly pleased with it, &
begged me to make soft verses for it; but I had no idea of giving
myself any trouble on the Subject, till the accidental recollection of
that glorious struggle for Freedom, associated with the glowing ideas
of some other struggles of the same nature, *not quite so ancient,**
roused my rhyming Mania.—Clarke's set of the tune, with his bass,
you will find in the Museum; though I am afraid that the air is not
what will entitle it to a place in your elegant selection.—However, I
am so pleased with my verses, or more properly, the Subject of my
verses, that although Johnson has already given the tune a place, yet
it shall appear again, set to this Song, in his next & last Volume.—

                              RB

* A reference to the trial of Muir and Palmer for sedition, then taking place at
Edinburgh.

XXVII (583)

                         [September 1793]

I dare say, my dear Sir, that you will begin to think my correspondence is persecution.—No matter—I can't help it—a Ballad is my
hobby-horse; which, though otherwise a simple sort of harmless,
idiotical beast enough has yet this blessed headstrong property, that
when once it has fairly made off with a hapless wight, it gets so
enamoured with the tinkle-gingle, tinkle-gingle of its own bells, that
it is sure to run poor Pilgarlick, the bedlam Jockey, quite beyond
any useful point or post in the common race of MAN.—

George Thomson

The following song I have composed for, "oran-gaoil," the Highland air that you tell me in your last, you have resolved to give a place to in your Book.—I have this moment finished the song; so you have it glowing from the Mint.—If it suits you—Well!—If not—'tis also—Well!—

Song—Tune, Oran gaoil—

Behold the hour, the boat arrive;

[C.W. p. 503]

RB

XXVIII (584)

Bishop mark SE 8 [1793]

I am happy, my dear Sir, that my Ode pleases you so much.—Your idea, "honour's bed," is, though a beautiful, a hacknied idea; so, if you please, we will let the line stand as it is.—I have altered the Song as follows.—

BANNOCKBURN—A Song—

Robert Bruce's Address to his Army.—

Scots wha hae wi' Wallace bled,
Scots wham Bruce has aften led;
Welcome to your gory bed,
 Or to glorious victorie.—

Now's the day, & now's the hour;
See the front o' battle lour;
See approach proud Edward's power—
 Edward! Chains & Slaverie!

Wha will be a traitor knave?
Wha can fill a coward's grave?
Wha sae base as be a slave?
 Traitor! Coward! turn & flie!

Wha for Scotland's King & Law
Freedom's sword will strongly draw,
Free-man stand, or Free-man fa',
 { Soger! Hero! on wi' me!
 { Caledonian! on wi' me!

By Oppression's woes & pains!
By your sons in servile chains!
We will drain our dearest veins,
 But they shall be—shall be free!

Lay the proud usurpers low!
Tyrants fall in every foe!
Liberty's in every blow!
 Forward! Let us Do, or Die!!!

N.B. I have borrowed the last stanza from the common Stall edition of Wallace—

"A false usurper sinks in every foe,
 And liberty returns with every blow"*—

A couplet worthy of Homer.—Yesterday you had enough of my correspondence—the post goes—& my head achs miserably.—One comfort: I suffer so much, just now, in this world, for last night's debauch, that I shall escape scot-free for it in the world to come.— Amen!

RB

---

* William Hamilton of Gilbertfield: *The Life and Heroic Actions of Sir William Wallace* Bk VI, chap, 2, lines 92-3.

XXIX (586)

[early September 1793]

I have received your list, my dear Sir, & here go my observations on it.—

No 1. "An thou wert my ain"—I have not Pinkerton; but before me, in Witherspoon's first vol: (Entitled, Ancient & modern Scotish Songs & heroic ballads) I have three songs to this air, & with the same chorus—

> 1st Of race divine thou needs must be—
> 2d   Like bees that suck the morning dew—
> 3d   As round the elm th' enamour'd vine—

Of these, all of them good, the first, in my opinion, is the best.—The English Song, "Ah dear Marcella" &c. is not in my copy of the Charmer.—

No 2d Down the burn Davie—I have, this moment, tried an alteration; leaving out the last half of the 3d stanza, & the first half of the last Stanza—thus—

> As down the burn they took their way,

[C.W. p. 501]

No 3d Nothing to remark—

No 4th Katharine Ogie—I should like to see this in your next number.—

No 5th Low down in the broom—In my opinion, deserves more properly, a place among your lively & humorous Songs.—I shall, by & by, point out some in this last list, which rather belong to the first.—

No 6th Lewie Gordon—Jamie Dawson is a beautiful ballad, but it is a great length: cannot you, for sake of economy in the Press-work, substitute a shorter one?—

No 7th—Nothing—

No 8th Cowdenknowes—Remember, in your index, that the English Song—"When Summer comes the Swains on Tweed"—is the production of CRAWFORD.—Robert, was his Christian name.—

No 9th & 10th—Nothing—

No 11th Bonie Dundee—Your objection of the stiff line, is just; but mending my colouring would spoil my likeness; so the Picture must stand as it is.[1]—

No 12th The last time I came o'er the moor—why encumber yourself with another English Song to this tune?—Ramsay's is English already, to your hand.—

No 13th Flowers o' the forest—The verses, I have seen the smiling &c. —with a few trifling alterations; putting no more, for, nae mair; & the word, "turbid," in a note at the bottom of your page, to shew the meaning of the word, "drumlie," the song will serve you for an English set.—

A small sprinkling of Scoticisms, is no objection to an English reader.—

No 14th Nothing—Except, Despairing beside a clear stream, is a very popular song, to its own tune: would it not be better to have another in the same measure, (there are plenty of them) which has never been set to music?—

No 15th Nothing—

No 16th Thro' the wood laddie—I am decidedly of opinion, that both in this, & There'll never be peace till Jamie come hame, the second, or high part of the tune is only for instrumental music, & would be much better ommitted in singing.—

No 17th Lord Gregory—please insert in your next Number.—Two or three copies of the song have got into the world, & I am afraid lest they find their way to some pilfering Magazine, or Newspaper.—

No 18 Thou art gane awa frae me, Mary—See the best set of this Song in the Museum.—

Nos 19. 20. 21.—Nothing—

No 22. Peggy I must love thee.—Please, let me take this into consideration: it will do for your 3d Number.—

No 23d Nothing—

No 24. Logan water—shall wait my revisal.—Only one passage I think faulty: "Cruel joys," is a damned stupid expression.—

No 25th Nothing.—

Nos 26. & 27. Nothing

No 28. My lodging is on the cold ground—please, let it wait your 3d Number, to gain time.—

Nos 29. & 30. Nothing—

No 31. Fair Helen—is not an air that charms me.—

No 32. Bonie Jean—Nothing—

No 33. Bonie Jean the 2d—Change the name to "There was a lass & she was fair"—which, by the by, is the old name of the air.—Do, make a point of publishing this Song to its own tune, & in your next Number, you will highly oblige me by it.—Please, likewise insert, Bonie Dundee, in your next number.—

No 34. Gill Morice—I am unalterably, for leaving out altogether.—It is a plaguey length, which will put you to great Press-expence; the air itself, is never sung; & its place can be well supplied with one of two fine Songs which are not at all in your list—Craigieburn wood, & Roy's wife.—The first, beside its intrinsic merit, has Novelty; & the last has high merit, as well as great celebrity.—Of the last, I have the original Set, as written by the Lady who composed it; & is superiour to any edition of the Song which the Public has yet seen.—

No 35. Nothing—

No 36. Is the real tune of "Hughie Graham," as sung in some places; in others, it is sung to a different, & very pleasing little air, yet unknown to the world.—I neglected to take down the notes, when I met with it; & now, it is out of my power.—This air, you will find in Oswald's Collection, Book, 8th, under the title of, Drimen Duff.—

George Thomson

No 37. Laddie lie near me—must *lie by me*, for some time.—I do not know the air; & untill I am compleat master of a tune, in my own singing, (such as it is) I never can compose for it.—My way is: I consider the poetic Sentiment, correspondent to my idea of the musical expression; then chuse my theme; begin one Stanza; when that is composed, which is generally the most difficult part of the business, I walk out, sit down now & then, look out for objects in Nature around me that are in unison or harmony with the cogitations of my fancy & workings of my bosom; humming every now & then the air with the verses I have framed: when I feel my Muse beginning to jade, I retire to the solitary fireside of my study, & there commit my effusions to paper; swinging, at intervals, on the hind-legs of my elbow-chair, by way of calling forth my own critical strictures, as my pen goes on.—

Seriously, this, at home, is almost invariably my way.—What damn'd Egotism!

No 38. Nothing—
No 39. Highland laddie—The old set will please a mere Scotch ear best; & the new, an Italianised one.—There is a third, & what Oswald calls, the old Highland laddie, which pleases me more than either of them.—It is sometimes called, Ginglan Johnie; it being the air of an old humorous bawdy song of that name.—You will find it in the Museum, vol: 4th P. 342—"I hae been at Crookieden" &c.—only, instead of the time being, "lively," it ought to be, andante.—I would advise you, in this musical quandary, to offer up your prayers to the Muses for Inspiring direction; & in the mean time, waiting for this direction, bestow a libation to Bacchus; & there is not a doubt but you will hit on a judicious choice.—PROBATUM EST—
No 40. Nothing—
No 41. O bonie lass will ye lie in a barrack—must infallibly have Scots verses.—
No 42. Unknown—
No 43. 1st Woes my heart that we should sunder—Do you know a song in the Museum,

> Go fetch to me a pint o' wine,
> And fill it in a silver tassie," &c.[2]

It is a song of mine, & I think not a bad one.—It precisely suits the measure of this air.—You might set it to this; & for an English song, take, either—

> With broken words &c.—

or Speak on, speak thus &c.—this last is the best—Remember I am no Dictator.—Ad libitum is the word.—
No 43d. 2d John Anderson my jo—I have already told you, is my composition.—
No 44. Nothing—
No 45. Nothing—
No 46. 47. 48. 49. & 50. Nothing—
No 51. The bonie brucket lassie—I inclose you a song to it, as I think it should be set; & with a better effect than the modulation in the Museum, where it first appeared, & whence every body else has borrowed it.—The tune is a very early acquaintance of mine. The

643

George Thomson

verses, if they deserve the name, in the Museum, are the work of a gentleman known by the appellation of, Balloon Tytler[3].—

No 52. le roi s'advisera—

No 53. Banks of the Dee—Leave it out entirely—'tis rank Irish—every other Irish air you have adopted, is in the Scotch taste: but Langolee! why 'tis no more like a Scots air, than Lunardi's balloon[4] is like Diogenes' tub.—I grant you that it is pretty; but why don't you take also, The humours of glen, Captain O'kean, Coolen, & many other Irish airs much more beautiful than it.—In place of this blackguard Irish jig, let me recommend to you, our beautiful Scots air, Saw nae ye my Peggy—a tune worth ten thousand of it; or, Fy—let us a' to the bridal, worth twenty thousand of it.—

No 54. Nothing—

No 55. White Cockade—I have forgot the Cantata you allude to, as I kept no copy, & indeed did not know that it was in existence; however, I remember that none of the songs pleased myself, except the last—something about,

"Courts for cowards were erected,
"Churches built to please the priest"[5]—

But there is another song of mine, a composition of early life, in the Museum, beginning—

Nae gentle dames, tho' e'er sae fair[6]—

which suits the measure, & has tolerable merit.—

No 56. It suits best to make it, Whistle & I'll come t'ye my lad—

No 57. Auld Sir Symon—I must beg you to leave out, & put in its place, The quaker's wife—"Blythe hae I been o'er the hill"—which is one of the finest Songs ever I made in my life; & besides is composed on a young lady, positively the most beautiful, lovely woman in the world.—As I purpose giving you the names & designations of all my heroines, to appear in some future edition of your work, perhaps half a century hence, you must certainly include "the boniest lass in a' the warld" in your Collection.—

No 58. Nothing.—

59. Dainty Davie,—I have heard sung, nineteen thousand, nine hundred & ninety nine times, & always with the chorus to the low part of the tune; & nothing, since a Highland wench in the Cowgate once bore me three bastards at a birth, has surprised me so much, as your opinion on this Subject.—If it will not suit, as I proposed, we will lay two of the stanzas together, & make the chorus follow that, exactly as "Luckie Nansie" in the Museum.—

No 60. Fee him, father—I inclose you, Fraser's set of this tune when he plays it slow; in fact, he makes it the language of Despair.—I shall here give you two stanzas, in that style; merely to try, if it will be any improvement.—Were it possible, in singing, to give it half the pathos which Fraser gives it in playing, it would make an admirably pathetic song.—I do not give these verses for any merit they have.—I composed them at the time in which Patie Allan's mither die'd—that was, "About the back o' midnight"—& by the lea-side of a bowl of punch which had overset every mortal in company, except the Hautbois & the Muse.—

Thou hast left me ever, Jamie, Thou hast left me ever

[C.W. p. 503]

644

No 61. Jockie & Jenny—I would discard; & in its place would put—
"There's nae luck about the house,"—which is a very pleasant air, &
positively the finest love-ballad, in that style, in the Scots, or
perhaps any other language.—Or, "When she came ben she bobbit,"
is a more beautiful air by much, than either of them; & in the
andante way, would make a charming sentimental Ballad.—
No 62. Nothing—
No 63. Maggie Lauder,—is a good tune, but there is, I don't know
what, of vulgarism about it; at least to me it has always that effect.—
There is an English Song to which it is set in the Museum.—
Nos 64. 65. & 66. Nothing—
No 67. Saw ye my father—is one of my greatest favorites.—The
evening before last, I wandered out, & began a tender song, in what I
think is its native style.—I must premise, that the old way, & the way
to give most effect, is to have no starting note, as the Fiddlers call it,
but to burst at once into the pathos.—Every country girl sings—

Saw ye my *fa*ther &c.
I saw not &c.—

this last, to be sure hurts the poetry, "*I* saw," instead of, "I *saw*" but
I am speaking of the air.—My song is but just begun; & I should like,
before I proceed, to know your opinion of it.—I have sprinkled it
with the Scotch dialect, but it may be easily turned into correct
English.—

Fragment—tune, Saw ye my father—

Where are the joys I hae met in the morning,
[C.W. p. 504]

No 68. Nothing—
No 69. Todlin hame—Urbani mentioned an idea of his, which has
long mine; that this air is highly susceptible of pathos: accordingly,
you will soon hear him, at your concert, try it to a song of mine in
the Museum—"Ye banks & braes o' bonie Doon"—I mention this as a
hint worth your attending to.—Johnson has made him free of the
Museum, from which he will [*one or two words illegible*] several
new things—I pointed out some verses that were yet unknown to
him, to give them a trial for celebrity.—Clarke has told me what a
creature he is, but if he will bring any more of our tunes from
darkness into light, I would be pleased.—
No 70. Nothing—
No 71. Geordie's byre—call the tune so, for decency's sake) I agree
with you that the song will be the better to want the Stanza—

The primrose is o'er for the Season—

I'll rather write a new song altogether, than make this, English.—The
sprinkling of Scotch in it, while it is but a sprinkling, gives it an air
of rustic naivete, which time will rather increase than diminish.—
Nos 72. & 73. Nothing.—
No 74. & last—Tranent Muir—I am altogether averse to.—The song is
fine, & eke the tune, but it is not a piece with the rest of your
pieces.—Instead of it, allow me mention a particular favorite of
mine, which you will find, in the Museum—"I had a horse, & I had
nae mair"—It is a charming song, & I know the story of the Ballad.—

George Thomson

One Song more, & I have done.—Auld lang syne—The air is but mediocre; but the following song, the old Song of the olden times, & which has never been in print, nor even in manuscript, untill I took it down from an old man's singing; is enough to recomment any air—

Auld lang syne—

Should auld acquaintance be forgot,
And never brought to mind?
Should auld acquaintance be forgot,
And days o' lang syne?

Chorus

For auld lang syne, my Dear,
For auld lang syne,
We'll tak a cup o' kindness yet,
For auld lang syne—

We twa hae run about the braes,
And pu't the gowans fine;
But we've wander'd mony a weary foot,
Sin auld lang syne.—
For auld lang &c.—[7]

Now, I suppose, I have tired your patience fairly.—

You must, after all is over, have a Number of Ballads, properly so called—Gill morice—Tranent Muir—Mcpherson's Fareweel—Battle of Sheriff muir, or, We ran & they ran (I know the author of this charming ballad, & his history) Hardiknute—Barbara Allan (I can furnish a finer set of this tune than any that has yet appeared) & besides, do you know that I really have the old tune to which The Cherry & the Slae was sung, & which is mentioned as a well known air in Scotland's complaint, a book published before poor Mary's days.—It was then called, The banks o' Helicon; an old poem which Pinkerton has brought to light.—You will see all this is Tytler's Hist: of Scots Music.—The tune, to a learned ear, may have no great merit; but it is a great curiosity.—I have a good many original things of this kind.—

Good b'ye to ye—
R. B.

1 C.W. p. 280. 2 Ibid. p. 342.
3 See footnote to XVII (569).
4 Vincenzo Lunardi (1759-1806) made numerous balloon flights in England and Scotland, upstaging his predecessor 'Balloon Tytler'. See *To a Mouse* C.W. p. 131.
5 *The Jolly Beggars*, lines 256-7. (C.W. p. 191).
6 *My Highland Lassie, O.* (C.W. p. 224).
7 Followed by stanzas 4, 5 and 2 of *Auld Lang Syne* in that order. C.W. p. 341.

XXX (587)

Bishop mark SE 15 [1793]

"Who shall decide, when Doctors disagree?"*—My Ode pleases me so much that I cannot alter it.—Your proposed alterations would, in my opinion, make it tame.—I am exceedingly obliged to you for putting me on reconsidering it; as I think I have much improved it.—Instead of "Soger! Hero!" I will have it to be, "Caledonian! on wi' me!"—I have scrutinized it over & over; & to the world some way or other, it

646

shall go as it is.—At the same time, it will not in the least hurt me, tho' you leave the song out altogether, & adhere to your first idea of adopting Logan's verses.—

I have finished my song to "The grey cock," & in English, as you will see.—Your objection of a syllable too much for the *expression* of the air, is just; but, allow me to say, that the mere dividing of a dotted crotchet into a crotchet & quaver, is not a great matter: however, in that I have no pretensions to cope in judgement with you.—Of the Poetry, I speak with confidence; but the Music is a business where I hint my ideas with the utmost diffidence.—The old verses have merit, though unequal; & are popular: my advice is, to set the air to the old words, & let mine follow as English verses.— Here they are.—

Fair Jenny—Tune, The grey cock—

Where are the joys I have met in the morning,

[C.W. p. 504]

Adieu, My dear Sir!
The post goes; so I shall defer some other remarks untill more leisure.—

RB

* Pope: *Moral Essays, Epistle III*, line 1.

XXXI (588)

[September 1793] [1]

I have been turning over some volumes of English songs to find verses whose measures would suit the airs for which you have allotted me to find English songs.—The following I pickt up in an old Collection, which will suit very well for, "Nansie's to the green-wood gane." You must not, my dear Sir, expect all your English songs to have superlative merit: 'tis enough if they are passable.—

The other night, with all her charms,
My ardent passion crowning,
Fair Celia sank within my arms
An equal transport owning.—

[With five additional stanzas] [2]

As for the air, "Whistle & I'll come to ye my lad," there is a fine English song for it in Ramsay's Tea-table Miscellany, beginning—

"Ah Chloe! thou treasure, thou joy of my breast"[3]—

For, "John Anderson my jo," you have also in Ramsay's Miscellany, an excellent song, beginning—

"What means this niceness now of late"[4]—

George Thomson

In the same Miscellany is not a bad song, by Crawford,[5] to, "Peggy I must love thee"—beginning—

> "Beneath a beech's grateful shade"[6] —

As for English verses to, "Geordie's Byre," take the following, altered a trifle from Ramsay—

> O Mary, thy graces & glances,
>   Thy smiles so enchantingly gay,
> And converse bewitchingly charming,
>   Bright wit & good humour display.—
>
> [With four stanzas] [7]

Since I am in the way of amending & abridging, let me recomment the following abridgement from a beautiful poem of Hamilton's to suit, "Take your auld cloak about ye."—

> Alas! the sunny hours are past;
> The cheating scene, it will not last:
> Let not the flatt'rer, Hope, persuade;
> Ah, must I say, that it will fade!
>
> [With 40 additional lines] [8]

For, "Willie was a wanton wag"—you have a song made on purpose, also by Hamilton, which you will find in Ramsay's Miscellany—beginning—

> "Willy, ne'er enquire what end"[9] —

English verses for, "The tither morn as I forlorn,"—you have, in my song—

> The last time I came o'er the moor,
>   And left Maria's dwelling"[10] —

For, "Todlin hame," take the following old English song, which I daresay is but little known—

> The Primrose—Tune, Todlin hame—
>
> Dost ask me, why I send thee here,[11]
>
> [C.W. p. 502]

N.B.—I have altered it a little.

For "Muirland Willie," you have, in Ramsay's Tea-table, an excellent song, beginning—

> "Ah, why those tears in Nelly's eyes"[12] —

As for "The Collier's Dochter," take the following old Bacchanal—

> Deluded swain, the pleasure
>   The fickle Fair can give thee,
> Is but a fairy treasure,
>   Thy hopes will soon deceive thee.—
>
> The billows on the ocean,
>   The breezes idly roaming,
> The clouds' uncertain motion,
>   They are but types of Woman.—

> O! art thou not ashamed
> To doat upon a feature?
> If Man thou wouldst be named,
> Despise the silly creature.—
>
> Go find an honest fellow;
> Good claret set before thee:
> Hold on; till thou art mellow,
> And then to bed in glory.[13]—

The faulty line in Logan water, I mend thus—

> How can your flinty hearts enjoy,
> The widow's tears, the orphan's cry[14]—

The song, otherwise, will pass.—

I am extremely sorry that the "Quaker's wife" is not a wife to your taste.—I am pleased with my song; & very proud of my acquaintance with the lovely Heroine.—

As to McGregoir a Rua-Ruth, you will see a song of mine to it, with a set of the air superiour to yours, in the Museum, vol: 2d P. 181.— the song begins—

> Raving winds around her blowing[15]—

Your Irish airs are pretty, but they are rank Irish.—If they were, like the Banks of Banna for instance, though really Irish, yet in the Scotish taste, you might adopt them.—Since you are so fond of Irish music, what say you to twenty five of them in an additional Number?—We could easily find the quantity of charming airs; I will take care that you shall not want songs; & I assure you that you would find it the most saleable of the whole.—If you do not approve of "Roy's wife" for the music's sake, we shall not insert it.—

"Deil tak the wars," is a charming song; so is, Saw ye my Peggy.— "There's nae luck about the house," well deserves a place.—I cannot say that "O'er the Hills & far awa" strikes me, as equal to your Selection.—"This is no my ain house," is a great favorite air of mine; & if you will send me your set of it, I shall task my Muse to her highest effort.—What is your opinion of, "I hae laid a herrin in sawt" —I like it much.—Your Jacobite airs are pretty; & there are many others of the same kind pretty; but you have not room for them.— You cannot, I think, insert, Fye let us a' to "the bridal," to any other words than its own:

Now let me declare off from your taste.—Toddlin hame is a song that to my taste is an exquisite production of genius.—That very Stanza you dislike

> "My kimmer & I lay down to sleep"

is to me a piece of charming native humour.—What pleases me, as simple & naive, disgusts you as ludicrous & low.—For this reason, "Fee him, father," "Fye gie me my coggie Sirs," "Fye let us a' to the bridal," with several others of that cast, are, to me, highly pleasing; while, "Saw ye my father or saw ye my mother" delights me with its descriptive, simple pathos.—Thus my song, "Ken ye what Meg o' the mill has gotten"[16] pleases myself so much, that I cannot

George Thomson

without disgust try my hand at another song to the air; so I shall not attempt it.—I know you will laugh at all this; but, "Ilka man wears his belt his ain gate."—

Yours
R. Burns

1 Thomson's note to Currie: '*Nothing* in this letter for the general eye, nor are any of the Songs Mr. Burns's own, except the first which is too warmly coloured. G.T.'
2 Altered from Tom Brown's *Celia's Rundlet of Brandy* from Thomas D'Urfey's *Wit and mirth: or Pills to Purge Melancholy,* London (1719), IV, 185-6. Thomson's note: 'Unpublishable surely!' Burns apparently altered the opening stanza and added a stanza to the song.
3 Allan Ramsay: *The Tea-Table Miscellany,* Vol. I, under the title *Song Complaining of Absence.*
4 Ibid. under the title *Song.*
5 Robert Crawford.
6 *Tea-Table Miscellany,* Vol. I, under the title *Song.*
7 Ibid. under the title *To L.M.M.*
8 *Tea-Table Miscellany,* Vol. II, under the title *Ode. To Mrs. A.R.* ('Now spring begins her smiling round.')
9 Ibid. under the title *Horace, book I. Ode II* [for XI] *to W.D.* [William Dalrymple of Cranstoun?]
10 C.W. p. 486
11 Robert Herrick: *Hesperides.*
12 *Tea-Table Miscellany,* Vol. I, under the title *Where Helen lies.*
13 Burns altered the first four lines of an anonymous eight-line song in John Watts's *Musical Miscellany* (London, 1730), IV, 98-9. The remaining four lines in Watts bear no resemblance to the song Burns sent to Thomson and we must therefore accept as Burns's the last three stanzas.
14 C.W. p. 491, See lines 29-30.
15 C.W. p. 314.   16 C.W. p. 489.

XXXII (593)

Bishop mark OC 29 [1793]

Your last letter, my dear Thomson, was indeed laden with heavy news.—Alas, poor Erskine!—The recollection that he was a coadjutor in your Publication has till now scared me from writing you, or turning my thoughts on composing for you.—

I am pleased that you are reconciled to the air of the Quaker's wife; though by the by, an old Highland gentleman & a deep Antiquarian, tells me that it is a Gaelic air, & known by the name of "Leiger m' choss," which name you may if you think fit, prefix as the name of the tune.—It bears that name in the West country, where there is still half a stanza of the song preserved, which I take to have been the chorus—The Gaelic phrase they have corrupted into Liggeram coss

> "Leiger m' choss, my bonie wee lass,
> "Leiger m' choss, my Dearie:
> "A' the lee-lang winter night,
> "Leiger m' choss, my Dearie."—

The following verses, I hope will please you, as an English Song to the air.—

Thine am I, my faithful Fair,

[C.W. p. 505]

Your objection to the English song I proposed for "John Anderson my jo" is certainly just.—The following is by an old acquaintance of mine, & I think has merit.—You will see that each fifth line is made to suit the peculiar note you mention.—The song was never in print,

650

which I think is so much in your favor.—The more original, *good* Poetry your Collection contains, it certainly has so much the more merit.—

Song—By Gavin Turnbull—

O condescend, dear, charming maid,
  My wretched state to view;
A tender swain to love betray'd,
  And sad despair by you:—

While here, all melancholy,
  My passion I deplore;
Yet urged by some resistless fate,
  I love thee more & more.—

[With two more stanzas.] *

The following address of Turnbull's to the Nightingale, will suit as an English Song to the air "There was a lass & she was fair"—By the by, Turnbull has a great many songs in M.S.S. which I can command, if you like his manner.—Possibly, as he is an old friend of mine, I may be prejudiced in his favor: but I like some of his pieces very much.—

The Nightingale—By G. Turnbull

Thou sweetest minstrel of the grove,
  That ever tried the plaintive strain,
Awake thy tender tale of love,
  And sooth a poor forsaken swain.—

Who, though the muses deign to aid,
  And teach him smoothly to complain;
Yet Delia, charming, cruel maid,
  Is deaf to her forsaken swain.—

[With two more stanzas.]

I shall just transcribe another of Turnbull's which would go charmingly to Lewis Gordon.—

Laura—By G. Turnbull

Let me wander where I will,—
Shady wood, or winding rill,—
Where the sweetest may-born flowers
Paint the meadows, deck the bowers,
Where the linnet's early song
Echoes sweet the woods among;
Let me wander where I will,
Laura haunts my fancy still.—

[With two more stanzas.]

The rest of your letter I shall answer at some other opportunity.—

Yours
R. B.

---

* Thomson did not publish these three songs by Turnbull which, however, appear in *The Contemporaries of Burns* by James Paterson, Edinburgh (1840).

George Thomson

XXXIII (602)

[December 1793]

Tell me, my dear Sir, you like the following verses to "Jo Janet."—

Husband, husband, cease your Strife,

[C.W. p. 510]

Yours
R B

XXXIV (625)

[May 1794]

My dear Sir,

I return you the plates, with which I am highly pleased; only your criticism on the grouping of the young lad being introduced to the mother, excepted.—There I entirely agree with you.—I would humbly propose that in No 1st instead of the Younker knitting stockings, I would, in preference to your "Trump", to put a Stock & horn among his hands, as if he were screwing & adjusting it.—I would have returned them sooner; but I waited the opinion of a friend of mine who is positively the ablest judge on the subject I have ever met with, & though an unknown, is yet a superior Artist with the *Burin*, & he is quite charmed with Allen's manner.[1]—I got him a peep of the Gentle Shepherd; & he pronounces Allen a most Original Artist of great excellence.—

For my part, I look on Mr Allen's chusing my favorite Poem for his Subject, to be one of the highest compliments I have ever received.[2]—

I am quite vexed at Pleyel's being cooped up in France,[3] as it will put an entire stop to our work.—Now, & for six or seven months, *I shall be quite in song*, as you shall see by & by.—I know you value a Composition, because it is made by one of the Great Ones, as little as I do.—However, I got an air, pretty enough, composed by Lady Elizabeth Heron of Heron, which she calls "The bank of Cree."— Cree is a beautiful romantic stream; & as her Ladyship is a particular friend of mine, I have written the following song to it.[4]

Banks of Cree

Here is the glen, & here the bower,

[C.W. p. 513]

The air I fear is not worth your while, else I would send it you.—

I am hurried; so, farewel untill next post.—My "seal" is all well, except that my "Holly" must be a *bush*, not a *tree*, as in the present shield.—I also inclose it; & will send the pebble by the first opportunity.—

Yours
R B

1 David Allan (1744-96).
2 *The Cotter's Saturday Night.* In the work Burns's likeness (taken from Alexander Nasmyth's portrait which was engraved by John Beugo for the frontispiece of the 1787 edition of Burns's poems) was used by Allan as a model for the head of the eldest son.

3 Ignaz Joseph Pleyel (1757-1831), born in Vienna but from 1793 domiciled in Paris where he founded the Pleyel piano factory, still in existence.
4 Daughter of Thomas Cochrane, 8th Earl of Dundonald. Thomson did not like *Banks of Cree* and published *Here is the Glen* in 1798, after Burns's death, to the tune *Flowers of Edinburgh*.

XXXV (632)

[July 1794]

Is there no news yet, my dear Sir, of Pleyel?—Or is your work to be at a dead stop untill these glorious Crusaders, the Allies, set our modern Orpheus at liberty from the savage thraldom of Democratic Discords?[1]—Alas the day! And woe is me! That auspicious period, pregnant with the happiness of Millions—that golden age, spotless with Monarchical innocence & Despotic purity—That Millenium, of which the earliest dawn will enlighten even Republican turbulence, & shew the swinish multitude that they are but beasts & like beasts must be led by the nose & goaded in the backside—these days of sweet chords & concords seem by no means near!—Oh, that my eyes were fountains of waters,[2] for thy rueful sake, poor Prussia! that, as thy ire has deluged the plains of Flanders, so might my grief innundate the regions of Gallovidia!—Ye children of Success, ye sons of prosperity—ye who never shed the tear of sorrow, or felt a wish unsatisfied; spare your reproaches on the left-handed shifts & shuffling of unhappy Brandenburg! Once was his Rectitude straight as the shaft of the Archers of Edina, & stubborn as the granite on the Gallovidian hills—the Batavian witnessed his bowels of compassion,[3] & Sarmatia rejoiced in his truth—But Alas—

"The needy man who has known better times" &c.[4]

While Princes & Prelates & het-headed zealots

[C.W. p. 476][5]

So much for nonsense.—I have sent you by my much-valued Friend, Mr Syme of this place, the pebble for my seal.—You will please remember that my holly is a bush, not a tree.—

I have three or four songs on the way for you, but I have not yet put the last hand to them.—Pray are you going to insert, "Bannockburn"; or, "Wilt thou be my Dearie," in your Collection? If you are not, let me know; as in that case I will give them to Johnson's Museum. I told you that our friend, Clarke, is quite an enthusiast in the idea that the Air, "Nansy's to the green-wood gane" is capable of sentiment & pathos in a high degree.—In this, if I remember right, you did not agree with him.—I intend setting my verses, which I wrote & sent you, for the "Last time I came o'er the moor"—to this air; [& Clarke is to take it in hand as an adagio air.] I have made an alteration in the beginning of the song, which you will find on the new page.—

Song—

Farewell, thou stream that winding flows
Around Eliza's dwelling:

[C.W. p. 486]

George Thomson

I have presented a copy of your songs to the daughter of a much-valued & much-honored friend of mine, Mr Graham of Fintry.—I wrote, on the blank side of the titlepage, the following address to the young lady—

Here, where the Scotish Muse immortal lives,

[C.W. p. 511]

I have also promised the young Lady a copy of your Sonatas: will you have the goodness to send a copy, directed to Miss Graham of Fintry.—

Another friend of mine goes to town in a week or so, when you shall again have another packet of nonsense from—

Yours
RB

1 Pleyel went to France early in 1794, but was subsequently unable to return to Britain due to the escalation of the French Revolutionary War.
2 Jeremiah 9:1, paraphrased.
3 John 3:17. This passage is peppered with quasi-biblical phraseology.
4 Home: *Douglas*, Act III, sc. 1.
5 Annotated: 'What a pity this is not publishable. G.T.'

XXXVI (635)

30th August [1794]

The last evening as I was straying out & thinking of your favorite air, O'er the hills & far away—I spun the following stanzas for it; but whether my spinning will deserve to be laid up in store like the precious thread of the Silk-worm, or brushed to the devil like the vile manufacture of the Spider, I leave my dear Sir, to your usual candid criticism.—I was pleased with several lines in it at first; but I own that now, it appears rather a flimsy business.—This is just a hasty sketch, untill I see whether it be worth a critique.—We have many Sailor Songs, but as far as I at present recollect, they are mostly the effusions of the jovial Sailor, not the wailings of his love-lorn Mistress [*sic*].—I must here make one sweet exception—Sweet Annie frae the Seabeach came.—Now for the song—

On the seas & far away—Tune, O'er the hills &c.

How can my poor heart be glad,

[C.W. p. 517]

I give you leave to abuse this song, but do it in the spirit of Christian Meekness.—

Yours ever
RB

XXXVII (637)

[September 1794]

Little do the Trustees for our Manufacturers, when they frank my letters to you, little do they consider what kind of manufacture they are encouraging.—The manufacture of NONSENSE was certainly not in idea when the Act of Parliament was framed; & yet, under my hands & your *cover*, it thrives amazingly.—Well, there are more pernicious manufactures, that is certain.—[1]

654

I shall withdraw my, "O'er the seas & far away," altogether: it is unequal, & unworthy the Work.—Making a poem is like begetting a son: you cannot know whether you have a wise man or a fool, untill you produce him to the world & try him.—For that reason I send you the offspring of my brain, *abortions* & all; & as such, pray look over them, & forgive them, & burn them.—

I am flattered at your adopting, "Ca' the yowes to the knowes," as it was owing to me that ever it saw the light.—About seven years ago, I was well acquainted with a worthy little fellow of a Clergyman, a Mr Clunzie[2], who sung it charmingly; & at my request, Mr Clarke[3] took it down from his singing.—When I gave it to Johnson, I added some Stanzas to the song & mended others, but still it will not do for *you*. —In a solitary stroll which I took today, I tried my hand on a few pastoral lines, following up the idea of the chorus, which I would preserve.—Here it is, with all its crudities & imperfections on its head.—

Chorus

Ca' the yowes to the knowes, [*second version*]

[C.W. p. 519]

I shall give you my opinion of your other newly adopted songs, my first scribbling fit.—

Adieu!
RB

1 A cynical admission of a blatant abuse of the franking privilege,
2 Rev. John Clunie (1757-1819).
3 Stephen Clarke (d. 1797). See p. 615 for Burns's letter to him.

XXXVIII (637)

[September 1794]

Do you know, my dear Sir, a blackguard Irish song called "OOnagh's waterfall, or The lock that scattered OOnagh's p-ss?" Our friend Cunningham sings it delightfully.—The air is charming, & I have often regretted the want of decent verses to it.—It is too much, at least for *my* humble rustic Muse to expect that every effort of hers must have merit: still I think that it is better to have mediocre verses to a favorite air than none at all.—On this principle I have all along proceeded in the Scots Musical Museum; & as that publication is at its last volume, I intend the following song to the air I mentioned, for that work.—If it does not suit you as an Editor, but if you know the air, you may be pleased to have verses to it that you may sing it before Ladies.—

She says she lo'es me best of a'.—

Tune, Onagh's waterfall—

Sae flaxen were her ringlets,

[C.W. p. 520]

Not to compare small things with great, my taste in music is like the mighty Frederic of Prussia's taste in painting: we are told that he frequently admired what the Connoisseurs decried, & always without any hypocrisy confest his admiration.—I am sensible that my taste in Music must be inelegant & vulgar, because people of undisputed & cultivated taste can find no merit in many of my favorite tunes.—Still, because I am cheaply pleased, is that any reason why I should deny myself that pleasure?[1]—Many of our Strathspeys, ancient & modern, give me most exquisite enjoyment, where you & other judges would probably be shewing signs of disgust.—For instance, I am just now making verses for Rother-murche's Rant, an air which puts me in raptures: & in fact, unless I be pleased with the tune I never can make verses to it.—Here I have Clarke on my side, who is a judge that I will pit against any of you.—Rothemurche, he says, is an air both original & beautiful; & on his recommendation I have taken the first part of the tune for a chorus, & the fourth or last part for the song.—I am but two stanzas deep in the work, & possibly you may think, & justly, that the poetry is as little worth your attention as the music.—

Chorus

Lassie wi' the lintwhite locks,

[C.W. p. 528]

I have begun anew, Let me in this ae night.—Do you think that we ought to retain the old Chorus? I think we must retain both the old chorus & the first Stanza of the old Song.—I do not altogether like the third line of the first Stanza, but cannot alter it to please myself. —I am just three stanzas deep in it.

O lassie are ye sleeping yet,

[C.W. p. 538]

How do you like this? and would you have the denouement to be successful or otherwise? Should she "let him in," or not?—

Did you not once propose the Sow's tail to Geordie, as an air for your work?—I am quite delighted with it; but I acknowledge that is no mark of its *real* excellence.—I once set about verses for it, which I meant to be in the alternate way of a lover & his Misstress chanting together.—I have not the pleasure of knowing Mrs Thomson's christian name, & yours I am afraid is rather burlesque for sentiment, else I had meant to have made you the hero & heroine of the little piece.—I had just written four stanzas at random, which I intend to have woven somewhere into, probably at the conclusion of the Song.—

He

The bee that thro' the sunny hour

[C.W. p. 529, lines 25 ff.]

So much for an idle farago of a gossiping letter.—You once asked my air for "Brunswic's great Prince"[2]—It is, The Campbells are comin.—

Do you know a droll Scots song, more famous for its humour than delicacy, called, The grey goose & the gled?—Mr Clarke took down the notes, such as they are, at my request, which I shall give with some decenter verses to Johnson.—Mr Clarke says that the tune is positively an old Chant of the ROMISH CHURCH; which corrobor-ates the old tradition, that at the Reformation, the Reformers burlesqued much of the old Church Music with setting them to bawdy verses.—As a farther proof; the common name for this song is, Cumnock Psalms.—As there can be no harm in transcribing a stanza of a Psalm, I shall give you two or three: possibly the song is new to you.—

Cumnock Psalms—

As I looked o'er yon castle wa'
I spied a grey goose & a gled;
They had a fecht between them twa,
And O, as their twa hurdies gade.

Chorus

With a hey ding it in, & a how ding it in,
And a hey ding it in, it's lang to day:
Tal larietal, tal larietal
Tal larietal, tal larie tay.

2.

She strack up & he strack down,
Between them twa they made a mowe,
And ilka fart that the carlin gae,
It's four o' them wad fill a bowe.
With a hey ding it in &c.

3.

Temper your tail, Carlin, he cried,
Temper your tail by Venus' law;
Double your dunts, the dame replied,
Wha the deil can hinder the wind to blaw!
With a hey &c.

4.

For were ye in my saddle set,
And were ye weel girt in my gear,
If the wind o' my arse blaw you out o' my cunt,
Ye'll never be reckoned a man o' weir.—
With a hey &c.

5.

He placed his Jacob whare she did piss,
And his ballocks whare the wind did blaw,
And he grippet her fast by the goosset o' the arse
And he gae her cunt the common law.
With a hey &c.[3]

So much for the Psalmody of Cumnock.—

How do you like the following Epigram, which I wrote the other day a lovely young girl's recovery from a fever.—A Doctor Maxwell,[4] the identical Maxwell whom Burke mentioned in the House of COMMONS, was the Physician who seemingly saved her from the grave; & to him I address the following—

George Thomson

To Dr Maxwell, on Miss Jessy Staig's recovery.

> Maxwell, if merit here you crave,
>   That merit I deny:
> *You* save fair Jessy from the grave!
>   An ANGEL could not die.—

[C.W. p. 519.]

God grant you patience with this stupid epistle. Amen!
RB

1 See John Moore: *View of Society and Manners in France, Switzerland and Germany*, 6th edn. (1786).
2 *Why Should na Poor Folk Mowe*, line 9.
3 Annotated: 'Delicate psalmody indeed. G.T.'
4 Dr. William Maxwell (1760-1834). The girl was Jessie Staig (C.W. p. 519).

XXXIX (644)

19th October [1794]

My dear Friend,

By this morning's post I have your list, & in general, I highly approve of it.—I shall, at more leisure, give you a critique on the whole: in the meantime, let me offer at a new improvement, or rather, restoring old simplicity, one of your newly adopted songs.—

> O When she cam ben she bobbit,
>   (a crochet stop here)
> O when she cam ben she bobbit; (a crochet stop)
> And when she cam ben, she kist Cockpen,
> And syne denied that she did it.— (a crochet stop)

This is the old rhythm, & by far the most original & beautiful.—Let the harmony of the bass, at the stops, be full; & thin & dropping through the rest of the air; & you will give the tune a noble & striking effect.—Perhaps I am betraying my ignorance; but Mr Clarke is decidedly of my opinion.—He goes to your town by today's Fly, & I wish you would call on him & take his opinion in general: you know his taste is a standard.—He will return here again in a week or two; so, please do not miss asking for him. One thing I hope he will do, which would give me high satisfaction, persuade you to adopt my favorite, Craigieburnwood, in your Selection: it is as great a favorite of his as of mine.—The Lady on whom it was made, is one of the finest women in Scotland; & in fact (entre nous) is in a manner to me what Sterne's Eliza was to him—a Mistress, or Friend, or what you will, in the guileless simplicity of Platonic love.—(Now don't put any of your squinting construction on this, or have any clishmaclaiver about it amòng our acquaintances)—I assure you that to my lovely Friend you are indebted for many of your best songs of mine.[1]—Do you think that the sober, gin-horse routine of existence could inspire a man with life, & love, & joy—could fire him with enthusiasm, or melt him with pathos, equal to the genius of your Book?—No! No ! ! !—Whenever I want to be more than ordinary in *song*; to be in some degree equal to your diviner airs; do you imagine I fast & pray for the celestial emanation?—Tout au contraire! I have a glorious recipe, the very one that for his own use was invented by the Divinity of Healing & Poesy when erst he piped to the flocks of

658

Admetus.—I put myself in a regimen of admiring a fine woman; & in proportion to the adorability of her charms, in proportion you are delighted with my verses.—

The lightning of her eye is the godhead of Parnassus, & the witchery of her smile the divinity of Helicon!—

To descend to the business with which I began; if you like my idea of—"when she cam ben she bobbit"—the following stanzas of mine, altered a little from what they were formerly when set to another air, may perhaps do instead of worse stanzas.—

Saw ye my Phely (quasi dicat, Phillis)

Tune, When she cam ben she bobbit—

O saw ye my dearie, my Phely?

[C.W. p. 523]

Now for a few miscellaneous remarks.—

"The Posie," is my composition; the air was taken down from Mrs Burns's voice.—It is well known in the West Country, but the old words are trash.—By the by—take a look at the tune again, & tell me if you do not think it is the original from which Roslin Castle is composed.—The second part, in particular, for the first two or three bars, is exactly the old air.—"Strathallan's lament," is mine:[2] the music is by our right trusty & deservedly well-beloved, Allan Masterton.—The "Young Highland rover," Morag, is also mine;[3] but is not worthy of the fine air.—

"Donochthead," is not mine: I would give ten pounds it were.—It appeared first in the Edinburgh Herald; & came to the Editor of that Paper with the Newcastle Post-mark on it.—

"Whistle o'er the lave o't," is mine: the music said to be by a John Bruce, a celebrated violin-player, in Dumfries about the beginning of this century.—This I know, Bruce, who was an honest man, though a red-wud Highlandman, constantly claimed it; & by all the old musical people here, is believed to be the Author of it.—

"O how can I be blythe & glad,"[4] is mine; but as it is already appropriated to an air by itself, both in the Museum & from thence into Ritson—(I have got that book) I think it would be as well to leave it out.—However, do as you please.—

"Mcpherson's Farewel,"[5] is mine, excepting the chorus & one stanza.—

"Andrew & his cutty gun"—the song to which it is set, in the Museum, is mine; & was composed on Miss Euphemia Murray of Lintrose, commonly & deservedly called, the Flower of Strathmore.—

"The Quakers wife"—do not give the tune that name, but the old Highland one, Leiger m' chose—the only fragment remaining of the old words, is the chorus, still a favorite lullaby of my old mother, from whom I learned it—

Leiger m' chose, my bonie wee lass,

An leiger m' chose, my dearie;

A' the lee-lang winter night,

Leiger m' chose, my dearie.—

The current name for the reel, to this day, at country weddings is, Liggeram cosh, a Lowland corruption of the original Gaelic.—I have altered the first stanza, which I would have to stand thus—

> Thine am I, my faithful Fair,
> Well thou may'st discover;
> Every pulse along my veins
> Tells the ardent Lover.--

"Saw ye my father"—I am still decidedly of opinion that you should set the tune to the old song, & let mine follow for English verses; but as you please.—Clarke laughed at your objection to my airs & songs; 'tis mere whim & caprice of taste—

"In summer when the hay was mawn," "An O for ane & twenty Tam," are both mine.—The set of the last in the Museum, does not please me; but if you will get any of our ancienter Scots Fiddlers to play you, in Strathspey time, "The Moudiewort," (that is the name of the air) I think it will delight you.—

"How long & dreary is the night,"—I met with some such words in a Collection of songs somewhere, which I altered & enlarged; & to please you, & to suit your favorite air of "cauld kail" I have taken a stride or two across my room, & have arranged it anew, as you will find on the other page.—

Tune, Cauld Kail in Aberdeen

How long & dreary is the night,

[C.W. p. 524]

Tell me how you like this.—I differ from your idea of the expression of the tune.—There is, to me, a great deal of quereluous tenderness in it.—You cannot, in my opinion, dispense with a bass to your addenda airs.—A lady of my acquaintance, a noted performer, plays, "Nae luck about the house," & sings it the same time so charmingly, that I shall never bear to see it sent into the world as naked as Mr What-d-ye-call-um has done in his London Collection.—[By the by, I am much obliged to him for his interesting Essay, as it has nearly preoccupied the ground, & to much better purpose, on which I was to have built my system.—All that is now left for me is, a few anecdotes & miscellaneous remarks.—] [6]

These English Songs gravel me to death.—I have not that command of the language that I have of my native tongue.—In fact, I think that my ideas are more barren in English than in Scotish.—I have been at "Duncan Gray," to dress it in English, but all I can do is deplorably stupid.—For instance—

Song—Tune, Duncan Gray—

Let not Woman e'er complain

[C.W. p. 525]

If you insert both Peter's song & mine, to "The bonie brucket lassie," it will cost you engraving the first verse of both songs, as the rhythm of the two is considerably different. As, "Fair Eliza" is already published, I am totally indifferent whether you give it a place or not; but to my taste, the rhythm of my song, to that air, would have a much more original effect.—

660

George Thomson

"Love never more shall give me pain," has long been appropriated to
a popular air of the same title, for which reason, in my opinion, it
would be improper to set it to, "My lodging is on the cold ground."
—There is a song in the Museum, by a ci-devant Goddess of mine,[7]
which I think not unworthy of the air, & suits the rhythm equally
with "Love never more" &c.—It begins—

Talk not of love, it gives me pain[8]—

Since the above, I have been out in the country taking a dinner with
a friend, where I met with the lady whom I mentioned in the second
page of this odds-&-ends of a letter.—As usual I got *into song*; &
returning home, I composed the following—

The Lovers morning salute to his Mistress—

Tune, Deil tak the wars

Sleep'st thou, or wauk'st thou, fairest creature;

[C.W. p. 526]

I allow the first four lines of each Stanza to be repeated; but if you
inspect the air, in that part, you will find that it, also, without a
quaver of difference, is the same passages repeated: which will
exactly put it on the footing of our other slow Scotish airs, as they,
you know, are twice sung over.—If you honor my verses by setting
the air to it, I will vamp up the old Song & make it English enough
to be understood.—I have sent you my song noted down to the air,
in the way I think that it should go: I believe you will find my set of
the air to be one of the best.—

I inclose you a Musical curiousity, an East Indian air, which you
would swear was a Scotish one.—I know the authenticity of it, as the
gentleman who brough it over is a particular acquaintance of mine.—
Do, preserve me the copy I send you, as it is the only one I have.—
Clarke has set a Bass to it, & I intend putting it into The Musical
Museum.—Here follow the verses I intend for it.—

The auld man's winter thought—

But lately seen in gladsome green

[C.W. p. 525]

I would be obliged to you if you could procure me a sight of Ritson's
Collection of English Songs, which you mention in your letter.—I
can return them three times a week by the Fly.—The Scotish
Collection, as I told you, I have gotten.—

I will thank you for another information, & that as speedily as you
please—whether this miserable, drawling, hotch-potch wounded
[*word illegible*] Epistle has not compleatly tired you of the
correspondence of,

Yours
R. Burns

1 C.W. p. 458. 2 Ibid. p. 458. 3 Ibid. p. 293. 4 Ibid. p. 442 5 Ibid. p. 308
6 Cancelled by Thomson: reconstruction conjectural.
7 Agnes McLehose.
8 *To a Blackbird* (SMM, 1788) or *Revision for Clarinda* (C.W. p. 319).

George Thomson

XL (646)

Many thanks to you, My dear Sir, for your present: it is a book of the utmost importance to me.[1]—I have, yesterday, begun my anecdotes, &c. for your work.—I intend drawing it up in the form of a letter to you, which will save me from the tedious, dull business of Systematic arrangement.—Indeed, as all I have to say is, unconnected remarks, anecdotes, scraps of old songs, &c. it would be impossible to give the work a beginning, a middle & an end; which the Critics insist to be absolutely necessary in a Work.—As soon as I have a few pages in order, I will send you them as a Specimen.—I only fear that the matter will grow so large among my hands as to be more expence than you can allot for it.—Now for my desultory way of writing you.—

I am happy that I have at last pleased you with verses to your right-hand tune, "Cauld kail:" I see a little unpliancy in the line you object to, but cannot alter it for a better.—It is one thing to know one's error, & another & much more difficult affair to amend that error.—

In my last, I told you my objections to the song you had selected for, "My lodging is on the cold ground." On my visit the other day to my fair Chloris (that is the poetic name of the lovely goddess of my inspiration)[2] she suggested an idea, which I, in my return from the visit, wrought into the following Song.—It is exactly in the measure of, "My dearie an thou die," which you say is the precise rhythm of the air—

Song

My Chloris, mark how green the groves,

[C.W. p. 531]

How do you like the simplicity & tenderness of this Pastoral?—I think it pretty well.—

I like you for entering so candidly & so kindly into the story of Ma chere Amie.—I assure you, I was never more in earnest in my life, than in the account of that affair which I sent you in my last.—Conjugal-love is a Passion which I deeply feel, & highly venerate; but somehow it does not make such a figure in Poesy as that other species of the Passion—

"Where Love is liberty & Nature law[3].—"

Musically speaking, the first is an instrument of which the gamut is scanty & confined, but the tones inexpressibly sweet; while the last, has powers equal to all the intellectual Modulation of the Human Soul.—Still, I am a very Poet in my enthusiasm of the Passion.—The welfare & happiness of the beloved Object, is the *first* & *inviolate* sentiment that pervades my soul; & whatever pleasures I might wish for, or whatever might be the raptures they would give me, yet, if they interfere & clash with that *first* principle, it is having these pleasures at a dishonest price; & Justice forbids, & Generosity disdains the purchase!—As to the herd of the Sex, who are good for little or nothing else, I have made no such agreement with myself; but where the Parties are capable of, & the Passion is, the true Divinity of love—the man who can act otherwise than I have laid down, is a Villain!—It was impossible, you know, to take up the subject of your songs in the last sheet: that would have been a falling off indeed.—

Despairing of my own powers to give you variety enough in English Songs, I have been turning over old Collections to pick out songs of which the measure is something similar to what I want, & with a little alteration so as to suit the rhythm of the air exactly, to give you them for your Work.—Where the Songs have hitherto been but little noticed, nor have ever been set to music, I think the shift a fair one.—A Song, which, under the same first verse of the first stanza, you will find in Ramsay's Tea-table Miscellany, & elsewhere, I have cut down for an English dress to your "Daintie Davie," as follows—

Song, altered from an old English one—

It was the charming month of May,

[C.W. p.527]

You may think meanly of this; but take a look at the bombast original, & you will be surprised that I have made so much of it.—

I have finished my song to Rothemurche's rant; & you have Clarke to consult, as to the set of the air for singing.—

Lassie wi' the lintwhite locks—

Tune, Rothemurche

[C.W. p. 528]

This piece has at least the merit of being a regular Pastoral: the vernal morn, the summer noon, the Autumnal evening & the Winter night, are regularly rounded. If you like it, well: if not, I will insert it in the Museum.—

I am out of temper that you should set so sweet, so tender an air, as "Deil tak the war," to the foolish old verses.—You talk of the silliness of, "Saw ye my father:" by Heavens, the odds is, Gold to Brass!—Besides, the old song, though now pretty well modernised into the Scotish language, is originally, & in the early editions, a bungling, low imitation of the Scotish manner, by that genius, Tom D'urfey; so has no pretensions to be a Scotish production.—There is a pretty English song, by Sheridan, in the Duenna, to the air which is out of sight superiour to D'urfey.—It begins—

When sable night, each drooping plant restoring.[4]

The air, if I understand the expression of it properly, is the very native language of Simplicity, Tenderrness & Love.—I have again gone over my song to the tune, as follows—

Sleep'st thou, or wauk'st thou, fairest creature;

[C.W. p. 526]

I could easily throw this into an English mould; but to my taste, in the simple & tender of the Pastoral song, a sprinkling of the old

Scotish, has an imitable effect.—You know, I never encroach on
your priviledge as an Editor.—You may reject my Song altogether, &
keep by the old one; or you may give mine, as a second Scotish one;
or, lastly, you may set the air to my verses, still giving the old song,
as a second one, & as being well known; in which last case, I would
find you, in English verses of my own, a song, the exact rhythm of
my Scotish one.—If you keep by the old words, Sheridan's song will
do for an English one.—I once more conjure you, to have no manner
of false delicacy in accepting, or refusing my compositions, either in
this, or any other of your songs.—

Now for my English Song to "Nansie's to the greenwood"—

Farewell, thou stream that winding flows
[C.W. p. 486]

"Young Jockey was the blythest lad"—my English song—"Here is
the glen & here the bower," cannot go to this air it was written on
purpose for an original air composed by Miss Heron of Heron.
However, the measure is so common, that you may take your choice
of five hundred English Songs.—Do you know the air, "Lumps o'
puddings"? It is a favorite of mine, & I think would be worth a place
among your additional Songs, as soon as several in your list.—It is in
a measure, in which you will find songs enow to chuse on; but if you
were to adopt it, I would take it in my own hand.—

There is another air, "The Caledonian hunt's delight," to which I
wrote a song that you will find in Johnson—"Ye banks & braes o'
bonie Doon"—; this air, I think, might find a place among your
hundred—as Lear says of his Knights.—To make room for it, you
may take out (to my taste) either, "Young Jockey was the blythest
lad," or "There's nae luck about the house," or, "The collier's bonie
lassie," or, "The tither morn," or, "The sow's tail"—& put into your
additional list.—Not but that these songs have great merit; but still
they have not the pathos of "The banks o' Doon."—Do you know
the history of the air?—It is curious enough.—A good many years
ago, a Mr Jas Miller, Writer in your good town, a gentleman whom
possibly you know, was in company with our friend, Clarke; &
talking of Scots music, Miller expressed an ardent ambition to be
able to compose a Scots air.—Mr Clarke, partly by way of joke, told
him, to keep to the black keys of the harpsichord, & preserve some
kind of rhythm; & he would infallibly compose a Scots air.—Certain
it is, that in a few days, Mr Miller produced the rudiments of an air,
which Mr Clarke, with some touches & corrections, fashioned into
the tune in question.—Ritson, you know, has the same story of the
"Black keys;" but this account which I have just given you, Mr
Clarke informed me of, several years ago.—Now, to shew you how
difficult it is to trace the origin of our airs, I have heard it repeatedly
asserted that it was an Irish air; nay I met with an Irish gentleman
who affirmed he had heard it in Ireland among the old women;
while, on the other hand, a Lady of fashion, no less than a Countess,
informed me, that the first person who introduced the air into this
country was a Baronet's Lady of her acquaintance, who took down
the notes from an itinerant Piper in the Isle of Man.—How difficult
then to ascertain the truth respecting our Poesy & Music! I myself,
have lately seen a couple of Ballads sung through the streets of

Dumfries, with my name at the head of them as the Author, though it was the first time ever I had seen them.—

I thank you for admitting Craigieburnwood; & I shall take care to furnish you with a new Chorus.—In fact, the Chorus was not my work, but a part of some old verses to the air.—If I can catch myself in a more than ordinary propitious moment, I shall write a new Craigieburnwood altogether.—My hear is much in the theme.—

I am ashamed, my dear Fellow, to make the request—'tis dunning your generosity—but in a moment, when I had forgot whether I was rich or poor, I promised Chloris a copy of your songs. It wrings my honest pride to write you this; but an ungracious request is doubly so, by a tedious apology.—To make you amends, as soon as I have extracted the necessary information out of them, I will return you Ritson's volumes.—

The Lady is not a little proud that she is to make so distinguished a figure in your Collection, & I am not a little proud that I have it in my power to please her so much.—

On second thoughts, I send you Clarke's singing set of Rothemurche, which please return me in your first letter.—I know it will not suit you.—

I have no more post-paper, & it is too late to go to the Shop; so you must e'en take an envelope of Excise-paper.—Lucky it is for your patience that my paper is done, for when I am in a scribbling humor, I don't know when to give over.—

Adieu!
R. Burns

1 Joseph Ritson (ed.), *A Select Collection of English Songs*, 3 vols., London (1783).
2 Jean Lorimer.
3 Pope: *Eloisa to Abelard*, line 92.
4 Sheridan: *La Duenna*, Act I, sc. 5.
5 The first version of Craigieburn Wood (C.W. p. 436) appeared in SMM vol. IV. The second version (C.W. p. 536) was sent to Thomson in January 1795.

XLI (647)

19th November [1794]

You see, my dear Sir, what a punctual correspondent I am; though indeed you may thank yourself for the tedium of my letters, as you have so flattered me on my horsemanship with my favorite Hobby & have praised the grace of his ambling so much, that I am scarcely off his back.—For instance, this morning, though a keen blowing frost, in my walk before breakfast, I finished my Duet which you were pleased to praise so much.—Whether I have uniformly succeeded, I will not say; but here it is to you, though it is not an hour old.—

Song—Tune—The Sow's tail.—

He.
O Philly, happy be that day
[C.W. p. 529]

Tell me honestly how you like it; & point out whatever you think faulty.—

I am much pleased with your idea of singing our songs in alternate stanzas, & regret that you did not hint it to me sooner.—In those that remain, I shall have it in my eye.—I remember your objections to the name Philly; but it is the common abbreviation of Phillis, which is now a common Christian name.—Nelly, & Sally, the only name that suits, has, to my ear, a vulgarity about them, which unfits them for any thing except burlesque.—The legion of Scotish Poetasters of the day, whom your brother Editor, Mr Ritson, ranks with me as my coevals, have always mistaken vulgarity for simplicity; whereas Simplicity is as much eloignee from vulgarity, on the one hand, as from affected point & puerile conceit, on the other.—

I agree with you, as to the air, Craigieburnwood, that a chorus would in some degree spoil the effect; & shall certainly have none in my projected song to it.—It is not, however, a case in point with Rothemurche: there, as in "Roy's wife of Aldivaloch," a chorus, to my taste, goes well enough.—As to the chorus going first, you know it is so with "Roy's wife" also.—In fact, in the first part of both tunes, the rhythm is so peculiar & irregular, & on that irregularity depends so much of their beauty, that we must e'en take them with all their wildness, & humour the verse accordingly.—Leaving out the starting-note, in both tunes, has I think an effect that no regularity could counterbalance the want of.—Try

> O Roy's wife &c.
> O Lassie wi' the lintwhite locks—

and compare with

> Roy's Wife of Aldivaloch—
> Lassie wi' the lintwhite locks—

does not the tameness of the prefixed syllable strike you?—In the last case, with the true furor of genius, you strike at once into the wild originality of the air; whereas in the first insipid business, it is like the grating screw of the pins before the fiddle is brought in tune. —This is my taste: if I am wrong, I beg pardon of the Cognoscenti.—

I am also of your mind, as to the "Caledonian hunt;" but to fit it with verses to suit these dotted crotchets will be a task indeed.—I differ from you, as to the expression of the air.—It is so charming, that it would make any Subject in a song go down; but pathos is certainly its native tongue.—Scots Bacchanalians we certainly want, though the few that we have are excellent.—For instance, Todlin hame, is, for Wit & Humour, an unparalleled composition; &, Andrew & his cutty gun, is the work of a Master:—By the way, are you not quite vexed to think that these men of genius, for such they certainly were, who composed our fine Scotish lyrics, should be unknown?—It has given me many a heart-ach.—A propos to Bacchan- alian songs in Scotish, I composed one yesterday, for an air I like much—"Lumps o' puddings."—

Song—

Contented wi' little, & cantie wi' mair,
[C.W. p. 531]

If you do not relish the air, I will send it to Johnson.—

The two songs you saw in Clarke's, are, neither of them, worth your attention.—The words of, Auld lang syne, are good; but the music is an old air, the rudiments of the modern tune of that name.—The other tune, you may hear as a common Scotish country dance.

20th Since yesterday's penmanship, I have framed a couple of English Stanzas, by way of an English song to "Roy's wife."—You will allow me that in this instance, my English corresponds in sentiment with the Scotish.—

> Can you leave me thus, my Katy, Tune, Roy's wife
>
> [C.W. p. 530]

Well! I think this to be done in two or three turns across my room, & with two or three pinches of Irish blackguard, is not so far amiss. —You see, I am determined to have my quantum of applause from Somebody.—Now for, "when she cam ben she bobbit"—

> Song—
>
> O saw ye my Dear, my Mary,
>
> [C.W. p. 523]

I think these names will answer better than the former; & the rhythm of the song is as you desired.—

I dislike your proposed alterations in two instances.—Logie o' Buchan, & There's my thumb I'll ne'er beguile thee, are certainly fittest for your additional songs; & in their place, as two of the hundred, I would put the most beautiful of airs, "Whistle & I'll come to ye, my lad"—at all rates, as one.—It is surely, highly capable of feeling & sentiment & the song is one of my best.—For the other, Keep your favorite; Muirland Willie; & with it, close your hundred.— As to the first being Irish, all that you can say is, that it has a twang of the Irish manner; but to infer from that, that *of course* it must be an Irish production, is unfair.—In the neighbourhood & intercourse of the Scots & Irish, & both musical nations too, it is highly probably that composers of one nation would sometimes imitate, or emulate, the manner of the other.—I never met with an Irishman who claimed this air: a pretty strong proof that it is Scotish.—Just the same is the case with Gramachree; if it be really Irish, it is decidedly in the Scotish taste.—That other air in your Collection, Oran Gaoil; which you think is Irish, that nation claim as theirs, by the name of Caun du delish; but, look into Gow's Publication of Scotish Songs, & you will find it as a Gaelic song, with the words in that language; a wretched translation of which original words is set to the tune in the Museum.—Your worthy Gaelic priest, gave me that translation; and at his table I heard both the original & the translation sung by a large party of Highland gentlemen, all of whom had no other idea of the air than that it was a native of their own country.—

I am obliged to you for your goodness in your three copies, but will certainly return you two of them.—Why should I take money out of your pocket?—

Tell my friend, Allen (for I am sure that we only want the trifling circumstance of being known to one another, to be the best friends on earth) that I much suspect he has, in his plates, mistaken the figure of the stock & horn,—I have, *at last*, gotten one; but it is a very rude instrument.—It is composed of three parts; the stock, which is the hinder thigh-bone of a sheep, such as you see in a mutton-ham: the horn, which is a common Highland cow's horn, cut off at the smaller end, untill the aperture be large enough to admit the "Stock" to be pushed up through the horn, untill it be held by the thicker or hip-end of the thigh-bone: & lastly, an oaten reed exactly cut & notched like that which you see every shepherd-boy have, when the corn-stems are green & full-grown.—The reed is not made fast in the bone, but is held by the lips, & plays loose in the smaller end of the "stock;" while the "Stock," & horn hanging on its larger end, is held by the hands in playing.—The "Stock" has six, or seven, ventiges on the upper side, & one back-ventige, like the common flute.—This of mine was made by a man from the braes of Athole, & is exactly what the shepherds wont to use in that country. —However, either it is not quite properly bored in the holes, or else we have not the art of blowing it rightly; for we can make little of it. —If Mr Allen chuses, I will send him a sight of mine; as I look on myself to be a kind of brother-brush with him.—"Pride in Poets is nae sin," & I will say it, that I look on Mr Allen & Mr Burns to be the only genuine & real Painters of Scotish Costume in the world.—

Farewel!

R. Burns

* David Allan.

XLII (648)

Bishop mark DE 9 [1794]

My dear Sir,

It is, I assure you, the pride of my heart to do any thing to forward, or add to the value of your book; & as I agree with you that the Jacobite song, in the Museum, to "There'll never be peace till Jamie comes hame," would not so well consort with Peter Pindar's excellent love-song to that air, I have just framed for you the following.—

My Nanie's awa— Tune, There'll never be peace—

Now in her green mantle blythe Nature arrays

[C.W. p. 532]

How does this please you?—

I have thought that a song, in Ramsay's Colln beginning, "Come fill me a bumper my jolly brave boys"—might do, as an English song for "Todlen hame."—It might do thus—

Come fill me a bumper, my jolly, brave boys,
Let's have no more female impert'nence & noise:
I've tried the endearments & witchcraft of love,
And found them but nonsense & whimsies, by Jove.

Chorus
Truce with your love, no more of your love;
The bottle henceforth is my Mistress, by Jove.*

&c.—&c.—&c.—

As to the point of time, for the Expression, in your proposed Print from my "Soger's return:" It must certainly be at—

"She gaz'd"—

The interesting dubiety & suspense, taking possession of her countenance; & the gushing fondness, with a mixture of roguish playfulness, in his; strike me, as a subject of which a Master will make a great deal.—

In great haste, but in great truth—
Yours—
RB

* Ramsay: *Tea-Table Miscellany*, vol. I. Burns added the chorus when emending the song to the air *Todlin Hame*.

XLIII (651)

[January 1795]

My dear Sir,

I fear that my songs, however a few, one, or two, or three, or even four, may please; yet, originality is a coy feature, in Composition, & in a multiplicity of efforts in the same style, disappears altogether.— For these three thousand years, we, poetic folks, have been describing the Spring, for instance; & as the Spring continues the same, there must soon be a sameness in the imagery, &c. of these said rhyming folks.—To wander, a little from my first design, which was to give you a new song, just hot from the mint, give me leave to squeeze in a clever anecdote of my *Spring originality*.—

Some years ago, when I was young, & by no means the saint I am now, I was looking over, in company with a belle lettre friend, a Magazine Ode to Spring, when my friend fell foul of the recurrence of the same thoughts, & offered me a bet that it was impossible to produce an Ode to Spring on an original plan.—I accepted it; & pledged myself to bring in the verdant fields,—the budding flowers,— the chrystal streams,—the melody of the groves—& a love-story into the bargain, & yet be original.—Here follows the piece, & wrote for music too!—

Ode to Spring— Tune, The tither morn.—

When maukin bucks, at early f——s,
[C.W. p. 535]

Now for decency.—A great critic, Aikin on songs,[1] says, that love & wine are the exclusive themes for song-writing.—The following is on neither subject, & consequently is no Song; but will be allowed, I think, to be two or three pretty good *prose* thoughts, inverted into rhyme.—

Song—For a' that & a' that.—

Is there, for honest Poverty
[C.W. p. 535][2]

January 15th The foregoing has lain by me this fortnight, for want of a spare-moment.—The Supervisor of Excise here being ill, I have been acting for him, & I assure you, I have hardly five minutes to

myself to thank you for your elegant present of Pindar.—The
typography is admirable, & worthy of the truly original Bard.—

I do not give you the foregoing song for your book, but merely by
way of vive la bagatelle; for the piece is not really Poetry.—How will
the following do for Craigieburnwood.—

Sweet fa's the eve on Craigieburn,
[C.W. p. 536]

Farewell! God bless you!

RB

1 John Aikin, *Essays on Song-Writing* 1772.
2 First published in *The Glasgow Magazine* (August 1795) and several times
thereafter before Thomson published it in the *Select Collection* 1805 with the
title *The Honest Man the Best of Men* to the tune *Up and War them a', Willie.*

XLIV (656)

[Dumfries, 6th February 1795]

I am afraid, my dear Sir, that printing your Songs in the manner   of
Ritson's would counteract the sale of your Greater Work; but,
secluded as I am from the World, its humours & caprices, I cannot
pretend to judge in the matter.—If you are ultimately frustrated of
Playel's assistance, what think you of applying to Clarke?—This, you
will say, would be breaking faith with your Subscribers; but, bating
that circumstance, I am confident that Clarke is equal, *in Scotish
Song*; to take up the pen, even after Pleyel.—[1]

I shall, at a future period, write you my sentiments as to sending my
bagatelles to a newspaper.—

Here is another trial at your favorite air.—

Song.

O lassie, art thou sleeping yet,
[C.W. p. 538]

I do not know whether it will do.—

Yours ever.—
RB
See the wrapper

The bird that charm'd his summer day,
Is now the cruel Fowler's prey;
Let witless, trusting Woman say,
How aft her fate's the same, jo.
I tell you now &c.—

By G—— I have thought better!

The bird that charm'd his summer day,
And now the cruel Fowler's prey,
Let that to witless woman say
The gratefu' heart o' Man jo.[2]—

1 See footnote p. 653. Thomson ignored this suggestion and instead contracted
with Kozeluch, Mozart's successor as Court Composer to the Emperor
Leopold II.

2 The first version of the above stanza is scored through. Thomson has written in the margin, 'I would omit both this Verse & the one which the Poet has scored out, on the preceding page, or retain the scored one as being the best. G.T.'

XLV (657)

Ecclefechan 7th February 1795

My dear Thomson,

you cannot have any idea of the predicament in which I write you.— In the course of my duty as Supervisor (in which capacity I have acted of late) I came yesternight to this unfortunate, wicked, little village.—I have gone forward—but snows of ten feet deep have impeded my progress: I have tried to "gae back the gate I cam again," but the same obstacle has shut me up within insuperable bars.—To add to my misfortune; since dinner, a Scraper has been torturing Catgut, in sounds that would have insulted the dying agonies of a Sow under the hands of a Butcher—and thinks himself, *on that very account,* exceeding good company.—In fact, I have been in a dilemma, either to get drunk, to forget these miseries; or to hang myself, to get rid of these miseries:—like a prudent man (a character congenial to my every thought, word & deed) I, of two evils have chosen the least, & am very drunk—at your service!—

I wrote you yesterday from Dumfries.—I had not time *then* to tell you all I wanted to say; &, Heaven knows, at present I have not capacity.—

Do you know an air—I am sure you must know it—"We'll gang nae mair to yon town"?—I think, in slowish time, it would make an excellent song.—I am highly delighted with it; & if you should think it worthy of your attention, I have a fair Dame in my eye to whom I would consecrate it.—You will find a good set of it in Bowie's Collection; & try it with this doggerel—untill I give you a better—

Chorus

O wat ye wha's in yon town,
Ye see the e'enin sun upon;
The dearest maid's in yon town
The e'enin sun is shynin on.—

O sweet to me yon spreading tree,
Where Jeanie wanders aft her lane;
The hawthorn flower that shades her bower,
Oh, when shall I behold again!—*

As I am just going to bed, I shall wish you a good night.—

RB

P.S. As I am likely to be stormstead here tomorrow, if I am in the humor, you shall have a long letter from me.—

RB

* C.W. p. 541. 'Jeanie' could be Jean Armour, Jean Lorimer or Jean Scott (daughter of the Postmaster of Ecclefechan).

George Thomson

XLVI (661)

[April 1795]

Song— Tune, We'll gang nae mair to yon town.—

O wat ye wha's in yon town,
[C.W. p. 541]

Your objection to the last two stanzas of my Song, "Let me in this ae night,"[1] does not strike me as just.—You will take notice that my heroine is replying quite at her ease; & when she talks of "faithless man," she gives not the least reason to believe that she speaks from her own experience, but merely from observation of what she has seen around her.—but of all boring matters in this boring world, criticising my own works is the greatest bore.—

Song—Tune, Where'll bonie Ann lie.—
(or a still better tune, the rhythm of which it suits
better than the drawling stuff in the Museum).
Locheroch-side.—
Address to the woodlark.—

O stay, sweet warbling woodlark stay,
[C.W. p. 550]

Song—Tune, Ay wakin O—
(On Chloris being ill)

Chorus—
Long, long the night,
[C.W. p. 542]

How do you like the foregoing?—As to my address to the woodlark, Johnie Cope is an air will do it very well.—Still, whether it be the association of ideas, I cannot say, but there is a squalidity, an absence of elegance, in the sentiment & expression of that air, that does not altogether suit the spirit & delicacy I have endeavoured to transfuse into the song.—

As to English verses for Craigieburn, you have them in Ritson's English Selection,[1] vol. 1st Song 22d.—By Sir Walter Raleigh, beginning—

"Wrong not, sweet Mistress of my heart."—

"The lammy" is an air that I do not much like.—"Laddie lie near me," I am busy with—And in general have them all in the eye.—

The Irish air, "Humours of glen" is a great favorite of mine, & as, except the silly verses in "The poor Soldier," there are not any decent verses for it, I have written for it, as follows—

Song—

Their groves o' sweet myrtle let Foreign Lands reckon,
[C.W. p. 550]

Yours
R.B.
Stop!
turn over

EUPHEMIA MURRAY OF LINTROSE

JOHN SYME

George Thomson

Song—Tune, Laddie lie near me

'Twas na her bonie blue e'e was my ruin;

[C.W. p. 551]

Let me hear from you—

RB

1 C.W. p. 538.
2 Joseph Ritson (ed.) : *A Select Collection of English Songs*, 3 vols., London (1783).

XLVII (665)

Altered from an old English song.—

Tune, John Anderson my jo.—

How cruel are the Parents

[C.W. p. 551]

Song. Tune, Deil tak the wars—

Mark yonder pomp of costly fashion,

[C.W. p. 552]

[3rd? May 1795]

Well! this is not amiss.—You see how I answer your orders: your taylor could not be more punctual.—I am just now in a high fit of Poetizing, provided that the strait-jacket of Criticism don't cure me. —If you can in a post or two administer a little of the intoxicating potion of your applause, it will raise your humble servant's phrenzy to any height you want.—I am at this moment "holding high converse" with the Muses, & have not a word to throw away on such a Prosaic dog as you are.—

RB

XLVIII (670)

[May 1795]

Ten thousand thanks, my dear Sir, for your elegant present; though I am ashamed of the value of it, being bestowed on a man who has not by any means merited such an instance of kindness.—I have shewn it to two or three judges of the first abilities here, & they all agree with me in classing it as a first rate production.—My phiz is *sae kenspeckle*, that the very joiner's apprentice whom Mrs Burns employed to break up the parcel (I was out of town that day) knew it at once.—You may depend upon my care that no person shall have it in their power to take the least sketch from it.—My most grateful compliments to Allan, that he has honored my rustic Muse so much with his masterly pencil.—One strange coincidence is, that the little one who is making the felonious attempt on the cat's tail, is the most striking likeness of an ill-deedie, damn'd, wee, rumble-gairie hurchin of mine, whom, from that propensity to witty wickedness & manfu' mischief, which, even at twa days auld I foresaw would form the striking features of his disposition, I named Willie Nicol; after a certain Friend of mine, who is one of the Masters of a Grammar-school in a city which shall be nameless.—Several people think that Allan's likeness of me is more striking than Nasemith's for which I sat to

673

him half a dozen times.—However there is an artist* of very
considerable merit, just now in this town, who has hit the most
remarkable likeness of what I am at this moment, that I think ever
was taken of any body.—It is a small miniature; & as it will be in
your town getting itself be-crystallized, &c. I have some thoughts of
suggesting to you, to prefix a vignette taken from it to my song,
"Contented wi' little & cantie wi' mair," in order that the portrait of
my face & the picture of my mind may go down the stream of Time
together.—

Now to business.—I inclose you a Song of merit, to a wellknown air,
which is to be one of yours.—It was written by a lady, & has never
yet seen the Press.—If you like it better than the ordinary "Woo'd
& married," or if you chuse to insert this also, you are welcome;
only, return me this copy.—"The Lothian Lassie," I also inclose: the
song is well known, but was never in notes before.—The first part is
the old tune.—It is a great favorite of mine, & here I have the honor
of being of the same opinion with STANDARD CLARKE.—I think
it would make a fine Andante ballad.—

Give the inclosed Epigram to my much-valued friend, Mr Cunningham;
& tell him that on wednesday I go to visit a friend of his to whom
his friendly partiality in speaking of the Bard in a manner introduced
me—I mean a well-known Military & Literary character, Colonel
Dirom.—

As to what you hint of my coming to Edinburgh, I know of no such
arrangement.—You do not tell me how you liked my two last songs?
Are they condemned?—

Yours
RB

* Alexander Reid (1747-1823) of Kirkennan. See also letters to Maria Riddell
XVIII and XIX (p. 609) for conflicting opinions.

XLIX (672)

[June 1795]

English Song—Tune, Let me in this ae night—

Forlorn, my Love, no comfort near,
[C.W. p. 554]

How do you like the foregoing? I have written it within this hour:
so much for the *speed* of my Pegasus; but what say you to his
bottom?—

R B

L (673)

[3rd July 1795]

Scotish Ballad.—Tune the Lothian lassie—

Clarke has this air

Last May a braw wooer cam down the lang glen,
[C.W. p. 555]

George Thomson

Fragment, Tune, The Caledonian Hunt's delight.–
Why, why tell thy lover,
[C.W. p. 556]

Such is the damned peculiarity of the rhythm of this air, that I find it impossible to make another stanza to suit it.–

"This is no my ain house," puzzles me a good deal.–In fact, I think to change the old rhythm of the first, or chorus part of tune will have a good effect.–I would have it something in the gallop of the following–

Chorus

O this is nae my ain BODY,
[C.W. p. 558]

I am at present quite occupied with the charming sensations of the TOOTH-ACH; so have not a word to spare. I know your letters come post-free to you, so I trouble you with the inclosed, which as it is a business letter, please cause to be delivered at first convenience.

Yours
R. Burns

LI (676)

Bishop mark AU 3 [1795]

Your objection is just, as to the verse of my song.–I hope the following alteration will please you–

Cold, alter'd friends with cruel art
Poisoning fell Misfortune's dart;–
Let me break thy faithful heart,
And say that fate is mine, love.[1]–

Did I mention to you, that I wish to alter the first line of the English song to Leiger m' choss, alias, The Quaker's wife–from, "Thine am I, my faithful Fair"–to "Thine am I, my Chloris fair."[2]–If you neglect this alteration, I call on all the NINE, conjunctly & severally, to anathematise you![3]–

In "Whistle & I'll to ye, my lad"– the iteration of that line is tiresome to my ear.–Here goes the old first four lines of every Stanza, & here follows what I think is an improvement–

"O whistle, & I'll come to ye, my lad,
"O whistle, & I'll come to ye, my lad;
"Tho' father, & mother, & a' should gae mad,
"O whistle, & I'll come to ye, my lad."

Or

"O whistle, & I'll come to ye, my lad,
"O whistle, & I'll come to ye, my lad;
"Tho father, & mother, & a' should gae mad,
"Thy JEANY will venture wi' ye, my lad."–

In fact, a fair Dame at whose Shrine I, the priest of the NINE, offer up the incense of Parnassus; a Dame, whom–the GRACES have attired in witchcraft, & whom the LOVES have armed with lightening—a Fair One, *herself the heroine of the song,* insists on the amendment; & dispute her commands, if you dare!—

"Gateslack"—the word you object to, in my last ballad, is positively the name of a particular place, a kind of passage up among the Lawther hills, on the confines of this Country.—"Dalgarnock" is also the name of a romantic spot, near the Nith, where are still a ruined Church, & a burial-place. However, let the line run, "He up the lang loan" &c.[4]—

"This is no my ain body" alter into, This is no my ain lassie.

Song—Tune, This is no my ain house.—

O This is no my ain lassie,

[C.W. p. 558]

Do you know that you have roused the torpidity of CLARKE at last? He has requested me to write three or four songs for him, which he is to set to music himself.—The inclosed sheet contains two songs for him: the sheet please present to my very much valued friend whose name is at the bottom of the sheet.—I will write him a long letter one of these days.—I inclose the sheet open, both for your inspection, & that you may copy off the song, "O bonie was yon rosy brier."[5]—I do not know whether I am right; but that song pleases me;—& as it is extremely probably that Clarke's newly-roused CELESTIAL SPARK will be soon smothered in the fogs of indolence, if you like the song, it will go, *as Scotish verses,* to the air, "I wish my love was in a mire" & poor Mr Erskine's English lines may follow.—

I inclose you a "For a' that & a' that" which was never in print: it is a much superiour song to mine.—I have been told that it was composed by a lady.—[6]

1 *English Song*, lines 13-16 ('Forlorn, my Love, no comfort near', C.W. p. 554).
2 C.W. p. 505.
3 Annotated by Thomson: 'N.B. The Poet afterwards disapproves of the name Chloris altogether—& restores the word here proposed to be altered'.
4 *The Braw Wooer*, C.W. pp. 555-6.
5 C.W. p. 558.
6 Not identified. The lady's verses were rejected by Thomson.

LII (689)

[February 1796]

Many thanks, my dear Sir, for your handsome, elegant present to Mrs B—— & for my remaining vol. of P. Pindar. Peter is a delightful fellow, & a first favorite of mine.—Now to business. How are you paid by your Subscribers here?—I gave you in the names of Robert Riddell of Glenriddel, & his brother, Walter Riddell of Woodleypark. —Glenriddell subscribed only for the songs; Walter Riddell for both the Songs & Sonatas.—Glenriddell's widow, to whom he left all his fortune, lives now in your town, & Walter is also at present in it: call on them for their cash.—I mention these matters because probably you may have a delicacy on my account, as if I had presented them with their copies; a kindness neither of them deserve at my hands.— They are bona fide Subscribers, & as such treat them.—I also

George Thomson

supplied another Subscriber, Mr Sharpe of Hoddam, with the second
set of Sonatas (my own copy) so charge him accordingly.—Mr
Gordon of Kenmure, who subscribes for the songs only, unknown to
me at the time in a money transaction where I was concerned, paid
the 10/6 to my account; so there I am your debitor.—

I am much pleased with your ideas of publishing a Collection of our
songs in Octavo with etchings.—I am extremely willing to lend every
assistance in my power.—The twenty-five Irish Songs, in one
number, is a business that you will find your account in more than
anything.—I shall chearfully undertake the task of finding verses for
them.—I have already, you know, equipt three Irish airs with words,
and the other day I strung up a kind of rhapsody to another
Hibernian melody which I admire much.—

Hey for a lass wi' a tocher Tune, Balinamona & ora

Awa wi' your witchcraft o' beauty's alarms,

[C.W. p. 563]

If this will do, you have now four of my Irish engagement—Humours
of glen, Captain Okean, Oonagh's Waterfall, & Balinamona. In my
bypast songs, I dislike one thing; the name, Chloris.[1] I meant it as
the fictitious name of a certain lady; but, on second thoughts, it is a
high incongruity to have a Greek appellation to a Scotch Pastoral
ballad.—Of this, & something else in my next: I have more amendments to propose. What you once mentioned of "flaxen locks"[2] is
just: they cannot enter into an *elegant* description of beauty.—Of
this again.—

God bless you!
RB—

1 Annotated by Thomson: 'N.B. The Bard never explained what name he
wanted for Chloris.—Mr. Syme knows the Lady I believe. I think if her name
has two syllables, we should use it whatever it may be.—Or, shall it remain
Chloris, as the Poet left it?'
2 She Says she lo'es Me best of a', line 1. C.W. p. 520.

LIII (693)

[April 1796]

Alas, my dear Thomson, I fear it will be sometime ere I tune my lyre
again! "By Babel streams" &c.[1]—Almost ever since I wrote you last,
I have only known Existence by the pressure of the heavy hand of
SICKNESS; & have counted Time by the repercussions of PAIN!
Rheumatism, Cold & Fever, have formed, to me, a terrible Trinity in
Unity, which makes me close my eyes in misery, & open them
without hope.—I look on the vernal day, & say with poor Ferguson—

"Say wherefore has an all indulgent Heaven
Light to the comfortless & wretched given?"[2]—

This will be delivered to you by a Mrs Hyslop[3], Landlady of the
Globe Tavern here, which for these many years has been my
HOWFF, & where our friend Clarke & I have had many a merry
squeeze.—I mention this, because she will be a very proper hand to
bring that Seal you talk of.—

677

George Thomson

I am highly delighted with Mr Allan's etchings. "Woo'd & married & a' "—is admirable! The *grouping* is beyond all praise.—The *expression* of the figures, conformable to the story in the ballad, is absolutely faultless perfection.—I next admire, "Turnimspyke."—What I like least is, "Jenny said to Jocky."—Besides the female being in her appearance *quite a virago*, if you take her stooping into account, she is at least two inches taller than her lover.—

I will thank you much for a number or two of that magazine you mention.—Poor Cleghorn! I sincerely sympathise with him! Happy I am to think that he yet has a wellgrounded hope of health & enjoyment in this world.—

As for me—but that is a *damning* subject!

FAREWEL ! ! !
RB

1 Psalms 137:1, misquoted.
2 Robert Fergusson: *Job, Chap. III, Paraphrased*, lines 39-40.
3 Margaret 'Meg' Hyslop. See C.W. p. 409.

LIV (604)

[May 1796]

My dear Sir,

I once mentioned to you an air which I have long admired—"Here's a health to them that's awa, hiney"—but I forget if you took any notice of it.—I have just been trying to suit it with verses; & I beg leave to recommend the air to your attention once more.—I have only begun with it.—

Chorus

Here's a health to ane I lo'e dear,

[C.W. p. 565]

This will be delivered by a Mr Lewars, a young fellow of uncommon merit—indeed, by far the cleverest fellow I have met with in this part of the world.—His only fault is—Democratic heresy. As he will be a day or two in town, you will have leisure, if you chuse, to write me by him; & if you have a spare half-hour to spend with him, I shall place your kindness to my account.—

I have no copies of the songs I have sent you, & I have taken a fancy to review them all, & possibly may mend some of them; so, when you have compleat leisure, I will thank you for either the Originals, or copies.—I had rather be the author of five well-written songs than of ten otherwise.—My verses to "Cauld kail" I will suppress; as also those to "Laddie lie near me."—They are neither worthy of my name, nor of your book.—

I have great hopes that the genial influence of the approaching summer will set me to rights, but as yet I cannot boast of returning health.—I have now reason to believe that my complaint is a flying gout:—a damnable business!

Do, let me know how Cleghorn is, & remember me to him.—

Yours ever—
R. Burns
turn over

678

This should have been delivered to you a month ago, but my friend's trunk miscarried, & was not recovered until he came home again.—I am still very poorly, but should like much to hear from you.—

RB

LV (695)

[About 18th May 1796]

My dear Sir,

Inclosed is a Certificate, which, though a little different from Mr Mcknight's model, I suppose will amply answer the purpose: & I beg you will prosecute the miscreants without mercy.—When your Publication is finished, I intend publishing a Collection, on a cheap plan, of all the songs I have written for you, the Museum, &c.—at least of all the songs of which I wish to be called the Author.—I do not propose this so much in the way of emolument, as to do justice to my Muse, lest I should be blamed for trash I never saw, or be defrauded by other claimants of what is justly my own.—The post is going: I will write you again tomorrow.—Many, many thanks for the beautiful seal!—

RB

LVI (699)

Brow 4th July [1796]

My dear Sir,

I received your songs, but my health being so precarious nay dangerously situated, that as a last effort I am here at a seabathing quarters. —Besides my inveterate rheumatism, my appetite is quite gone; & I am so emaciated as to be scarce able to support myself on my own legs.—Alas! is this a time for me to woo the Muses! However, I am still anxiously willing to serve your work; & if possible shall try:—I would not like to see another employed, unless you could lay your hand upon a poet whose productions would be equal to the rest.— You will see my alterations & remarks on the margin of each song.— You may perhaps think me hard as to "Cauld kail in Aberdeen," but I cannot help it.—My address is still Dumfries.—

Farewel! & God bless you!
R Burns

LVII (706)

12th July [1796]

After all my boasted independance, curst necessity compels me to implore you for five pounds.—A cruel scoundrel of a Haberdasher to whom I owe an account, taking it into his head that I am dying, has commenced a process & will infallibly put me into jail.[1]—Do, for God's sake, send me that sum, & that by return of post.—Forgive me this earnestness, but the horrors of a jail have made me half distracted.—I do not ask all this gratuitously; for upon returning health, I hereby promise & engage to furnish you with five pounds' worth of the neatest song genius you have seen.—I tryed my hand on Rothiemurchie this morning.—The measure is so difficult that it is

679

impossible to infuse much genius into the lines—they are on the other side.—Forgive, forgive me!

Yours
RBurns
Turn

Song, tune, Rothiemurchie

Chorus
Fairest maid on Devon banks,[2]

[C.W. p. 568]

1 Annotated by Thomson: 'This idea is exaggerated—he could not have been in any such danger at Dumfries nor could he be in such necessity to implore aid from *Edinr*.' Nevertheless Thomson wrote to Burns on 14th July enclosing a draft for the sum requested.
2 Annotated: 'These I presume are the last verses which came from the great Bard's pen, as he died very soon after. G.T.'

CAPTAIN WILLIAM JOHNSTON

Founder of the Edinburgh *Gazetteer* in November 1792, he was a radical politician who advocated parliamentary reform and earned a prison sentence a few months later for his trouble. Burns responded to the prospectus for the new periodical by writing (I) and asking to be enrolled as a subscriber. Burns's lines *On Some Commemorations of Thomson* (C.W. p. 421) first appeared in the *Gazetteer*. The only other letter from Burns was a brief note a fortnight after the initial contact, enclosing *The Rights of Woman*. A few weeks later, when someone denounced Burns to the Board of Excise, his sympathy with Johnston was one of the charges laid. This provoked Burns to write to Graham of Fintry (see page 437): 'Of Johnston. . . I know nothing. One evening in company with four or five friends, we met with his prospectus which we thought manly and independent. . . If you think that I act improperly in allowing his paper to come addressed to me, I shall immediately countermand it. I never, so judge me, God! wrote a line of prose for the Gazetteer in my life.' He did admit that he had sent Johnston an essay on the extension of the franchise, penned by Robert Riddell of Glenriddell, under the *nom de plume* of Cato. That essay, perfectly reasonable and moderate by present-day standards, would probably have been regarded as treasonable in the paranoid climate of the 1790s.

I (515)

Dumfries, 13th November 1792

Sir,

I have just read your Prospectus of the Edinburgh Gazetteer.—If you go on in your Paper with the same spirit, it will, beyond all comparison, be the first Composition of the kind in Europe.—I beg leave to insert my name as a Subscriber; & if you have already published any papers, please send me them from the beginning.— Point out your own way of settling payments in this place, or I shall settle with you through the medium of my friend, Peter Hill, Bookseller in Edinburgh.—

Go on, Sir! Lay bare, with undaunted heart & steady hand, that horrid mass of corruption called Politics & State-Craft! Dare to draw in their native colors these

"Calm, thinking VILLAINS whom no faith can fix"*—

whatever be the shiboleth of their pretended Party.—

The address, to me at Dumfries, will find,

Sir, your very humble Servant
Robt Burns

* Pope: *The Temple of Fame*, line 410.

II (520A)

Dumfries, 27th November 1792

Sir,

Send your paper from the first to Robert Riddel Esquire of Glenriddel by Dumfries.—The inclosed is (entre nous) by him; & if you chuse, it is at the service of your Publication.—

I am, Sir,
your fervent wellwisher,
& very humble servant
Robt Burns

For the Edinburgh Gazetteer—

The Rights of Woman—An occasional Address spoken, on her Benefit Night, November 26th, at Dumfries, by Miss Fontenelle.—

[C.W. p. 508]

LOUISA FONTENELLE

Born in London in 1773, she made her debut at Covent Garden on 6th November 1788 in *The Highland Reel* by O'Keefe, playing the role of Moggy. She repeated her success in this role at Edinburgh in October 1789, with John Jackson's company at the Theatre Royal. She played in Edinburgh during the winter season of 1789-90, then acted at the Theatre Royal, Haymarket, London in the summer seasons of 1790 to 1792. By January 1793 she was back in Edinburgh, playing Lucy in *The Beggars' Opera*. She also acted at the Glasgow theatre in Dunlop Street and, with Sutherland's company, performed at the Theatre Royal, Dumfries in the winter of 1792. She married John Brown Williamson, actor-manager at Dumfries in succession to Sutherland, and a friend of Burns who composed *The Rights of Woman* (C.W. p. 471) and a prologue for her benefit night in December 1793 (C.W. p. 508). In 1796 Mr and Mrs Williamson emigrated to the United States, where they played in Boston and New York, before joining the South Carolina Company of Comedians, at Charleston where she died of yellow fever on 31st October 1799. Jackson's memoir of the Edinburgh stage ranked her with Mesdames Yates, Esten, Jordan and Siddons as 'the most capital performers that could be had.'

I (519)

[Enclosing *The Rights of Woman*—C.W. p. 471]

[22nd November 1792]

Madam,

In such a bad world as ours, those who add to the scanty sum of our pleasures, are positively our Benefactors.—To you, Madam, on our humble Dumfries boards, I have been more indebted for entertainment, than ever I was in prouder Theatres.—Your charms as a woman would insure applause to the most indifferent Actress, & your theatrical talents would secure admiration to the plainest figure.—This Madam, is not the unmeaning, or insidious compliment of the Frivolous or Interested, I pay it from the same honest impulse that the Sublime of Nature excites my admiration, or her beauties give me delight.—

Will the foregoing lines be of any service to you on your approaching benefit night? If they will, I shall be prouder of my Muse than ever. —They are nearly extempore: I know they have no great merit; but though they shall add but little to entertainment of the evening, they give me the happiness of an opportunity to declare how much I have the honor to be

Madam, your very humble servant

II (520)

[November 1792]

I am thinking to send my *Address* to some periodical publication, but it has not got your sanction, so pray look over it.

As to the Tuesday's play, let me beg of you, my dear Madam, to give us, *The Wonder, a Woman keeps a Secret!*[1] to which please add, *The Spoilt Child*[2]—you will highly oblige me by so doing.

Ah, what an enviable creature you are! There now, this cursed gloomy blue-devil day, you are going to a party of choice spirits—

> ... "To play the shapes
> Of frolic fancy, and incessant form
> Those rapid pictures, that assembled train
> Of fleet ideas, never join'd before,
> Where lively *wit* excites to gay surprise;

Louisa Fontenelle

Or folly-painting *humour*, grave himself,
Calls laughter forth, deep-shaking every nerve.'³

But as you rejoice with them that do rejoice, do also remember to
weep with them that weep,⁴ and pity your melancholy friend.

1 Susan Centlivre (née Carroll).
2 Attributed to Isaac Bickerstaffe.
3 Thomson: *Winter*, lines 610-16.
4 Romans 12:15.

III (599)

[With the Prologue beginning
Still Anxious to Secure your partial Favor C.W. p. 508.]

[about 1st December 1793]

Inclosed is the "Address," such as it is; & may it be a prologue to an
overflowing House!— If all the Town put together, have half the
ardour, for your success & welfare, of my individual wishes, my
prayer will most certainly be granted.—Were I a man of gallantry &
fashion, strutting & fluttering in the fore-ground of the picture of
Life, making the speech to a lovely young girl might be construed to
be one of the doings of All-powerful Love; but you will be surprised,
my dear Madam, when I tell you, that it is not Love, nor even
Friendship, but sheer Avarice.—In all my justlings & jumblings,
windings & turnings, in life, disgusted at every corner, as a man of
the least taste & sense must be, with vice, folly, arrogance, impertinence, nonsense & stupidity, my soul has ever, involuntarily &
instinctively, selected as it were for herself, a few whose regard,
whose esteem, with a *Miser's Avarice* she wished to appropriate &
preserve.—It is truly from this cause, ma chere Madmoiselle, that
any, the least, service I can be of to you, gives me most real pleasure.
—God knows I am a powerless individual. And when I thought on
my Friends, many a heart-ach it has given me! But if Miss Fontenelle
will accept this honest compliment to her personal charms, amiable
manner & gentle heart, from a man, too proud to flatter, though too
poor to have his compliments of any consequence; it will sincerely
oblige her *anxious* Friend, & most devoted humble servant

MARY PEACOCK

Little is known of this lady who was a friend of Mrs McLehose, other than that she married (as his second wife) James Gray, a master in the High School, Edinburgh. According to Chambers, she died in India. Burns apparently wrote to Miss Peacock on three occasions, but only the following letter survived. Writing to Mrs McLehose in March 1793, Burns mentioned his abortive correspondence with Mary Peacock: 'Two of my letters, it seems, she never received; and her last, which came when I was in Ayrshire, was unfortunately mislaid, and only found about ten days or a fortnight ago, on removing a desk of drawers.'

(525)

[Dumfries] 6th December 1792

Dear Madam,—

I have written so often to you and have got no answer, that I had resolved never to lift up a pen to you again, but this eventful day, *the sixth of December*, recalls to my memory such a scene! Heaven and earth! when I remember a far distant person!—but no more of this, until I learn from you a proper address, and why my letters have lain by you unanswered, as this is the third I have sent you. The opportunities will be all gone now, I fear, of sending over the book I mentioned in my last. Do not write me for a week, as I shall not be at home; but as soon after that as possible.

> Ance mair I hail thee, thou gloomy December!
> Ance mair I hail thee wi' sorrow and care;
> Dire was the parting thou bidst me remember,
> Parting wi' Nancy, oh! ne'er to meet mair.

[C.W. p. 433]

Yours,—
B—.

ANNA DOROTHEA BENSON

Born about 1773, the daughter of James Benson, a wine merchant in York and a friend of the Craiks of Arbigland, in whose house Burns met her. Her first husband was Thomas Skepper, a barrister at York. After his death she became the third wife of Basil Montague of London in 1808, and spent the rest of her long life in the metropolis where she died in 1856. She is chiefly remembered for her friendship with Jane Welsh and Thomas Carlyle, from whose extensive correspondence we learn that she was meddling, mawkish and self-opinionated. The following letter mentions a sonnet which Burns enclosed with it, but unless this was a misdescription, nothing is known of this lost work.

When Allan Cunningham ascribed to her a statement that Burns drank 'as other men drank', she wrote to Jane Welsh on 25th February 1834: 'Burns was incapable of rudeness or vulgarity. . . well bred and gentlemanly in all the courtesies of life', adding that even during the meeting of the Caledonian Hunt she 'never saw Burns once intoxicated, though the worthy Member for Dumfries, and the good Laird of Arbigland, and twenty more. . . were brought home in a state of glorious insensibility.'

(541)

21st March 1793

Madam,

Among many things for which I envy those hale, long-lived old fellows before the flood, is this in particular, that when they met with any body after their own heart, they had a charming long prospect of many, many happy meetings with them in after-life.

Now, in this short, stormy, winter day of our fleeting existence, when you now and then, in the Chapter of Accidents, meet an individual whose acquaintance is a real acquisition, there are all the probabilities against you that you shall never meet with that valued character more. On the other hand, brief as this miserable being is, it is none of the least of the miseries belonging to it, that if there is any miscreant whom you hate, or creature whom you despise, the ill-run of the chances shall be so against you, that in the overtakings, turnings, and jostlings of life, pop, at some unlucky corner, eternally comes the wretch upon you, and will not allow your indignation or contempt a moment's repose. As I am a sturdy believer in the powers of darkness, I take these to be the doings of that old author of mischief, the devil. It is well known that he has some kind of shorthand way of taking down our thoughts, and I make no doubt that he is perfectly acquainted with my sentiments respecting Miss B——; how much I admired her abilities and valued her worth, and how very fortunate I thought myself in her acquaintance. For this last reason, my dear Madam, I must entertain no hopes of the very great pleasure of meeting with you again.

Miss Hamilton tells me that she is sending a packet to you, and I beg leave to send you the inclosed sonnet, though, to tell you the real truth, the sonnet is a mere pretence, that I may have the opportunity of declaring with how much respectful esteem I have the honour to be, &c.

JOHN CUNNINGHAM, 15th EARL OF GLENCAIRN

Born in 1750, he was the younger brother of Burns's patron, Earl James. After military service as an officer in the 14th Dragoons, he took holy orders in the Church of England. He married Lady Isabella Erskine, daughter of the Earl of Buchan, but died in 1796 without issue, and the earldom of Glencairn became extinct. Burns sent the following letter to him with a copy of the 1793 edition of the Poems.

(546)

Dumfries Monday even:
[mid-March 1793]

My Lord,

when you cast your eye on the name at the bottom of this letter, & on the title -page of the book I do myself the honor to send your Lordship, a more pleasurable feeling than my vanity tells me, that it must be a name not entirely unknown to you.—The generous patronage of your late illustrious BROTHER, found me in the *lowest obscurity*: he introduced my rustic Muse to the partiality of my Country; & to him I owe all.—My sense of his goodness; & the anguish of my soul at losing my truly noble Protector & Friend; I have endeavored to express in a Poem to his memory, wich I have now published.—This Edition is just from the press; & in my gratitude to the DEAD, & my respect for the LIVING (Fame belies you, my Lord, if you possess not the same Dignity of Man, which was your noble brother's characteristic feature) I had destined a copy for the Earl of Glencairn.—I learnt just now that you are in town: allow me to present it you.—

I know, my Lord, such is the vile, venal contagion which pervades the world of Letters, that professions of respect from an Author, particularly from a Poet, to a LORD, are more than suspicious.—I claim my bypast conduct, & my feelings at this moment, as exceptions to the too just conclusion.—Exalted as are the honors of your Lordship's name, and unnoted as is the obscurity of mine, with the uprightness of an honest man, I come before your Lordship, with an offering, however humble, 'tis all I have to give, of my grateful respect; & to beg of you, my Lord, 'tis all I have to ask of you, that you will do me the honor to accept of it.—

I have the honor to be, My Lord,
your Lordship's most devoted humble servant
Robt Burns

THOMAS WHITE

Born in 1758 in Hexham, Northumberland, he taught mathematics at Dumfries Academy for forty years, latterly becoming rector. He served in the Dumfries Volunteers as a second lieutenant. As a mathematician he was very highly regarded, and one contemporary in Dumfries, at the time of his death in 1825, said '... as a man, he has not left an honester behind him'. A tradition in the White family speaks of Burns being a regular Saturday guest in their home. The circular ends of the dining-table from White's home where Burns is said to have regularly taken breakfast are now preserved in Burns House, Dumfries. White did much to promote interest in Burns's works, and remained a friend even in the last months when the poet's revolutionary opinions alienated many of his other friends. White composed a verse tribute to the memory of Burns in 1796. Apart from a copy of the 1793 edition of the Poems, Burns presented White with Voltaire's *La Pucelle*.

(552)

[In a copy of the 1793 Edition of the *Poems*, mid-March]

Mr White will accept of this Book as a mark of the most sincere Friendship, from a man who has ever had too much respect for his Friends, & too much contempt for his enemies, to flatter either the one or the other—

The Author

JANET or JESSIE STAIG

Born in 1775, the daughter of David Staig of Dumfries. She married Major William Miller, second son of Burns's landlord at Ellisland, Patrick Miller of Dalswinton. Apart from *Young Jessie* (C.W. p. 486) which Burns enclosed with the following letter, he composed the lines to Dr Maxwell, when he brought her back from the brink of death in September 1794. Sad to say, the 'Angel' of those lines died in 1801, in her 26th year.

(554B)

[Enclosing *Young Jessie* C.W. p. 486]

[Spring 1793]

Mr Burns presents his most respectful compliments to Miss Staig, & has sent her the song.—MrB— begs to be forgiven his delaying so long to send it; & allows Miss S— to impute the neglect to any cause under Heaven, except want of respect for her commands.—Mr B— would just give the hint to Miss S—, that should the respectful timidity of any of her lovers deny him his powers of speech, that then she will teach him Mr B—'s song; so that the poor fellow may not lie under the double imputation of being neither able TO SING NOR SAY.—Monday even:

JOHN FRANCIS ERSKINE, 27TH EARL OF MAR

Born in 1741, the son of Lady Frances Erskine and grandson of the 26th Earl
of Mar who suffered attainder for his part in the Rebellion of 1715. It was not
until 1824 that, by Act of Parliament, John Francis Erskine, as 'grandson and
lineal heir' of the attainted Earl, had his lands and titles restored to him. He
and Burns never met, but when he got to hear a rumour that the poet had
been dismissed from his Excise post because of his radicalism, Erskine wrote
to Robert Riddell offering to head a subscription on Burns's behalf. The
details of this generous act are set out below, in the preamble to the copy of
the letter which Burns made for the Glenriddell MS.

(558)

In the year of 1792/93, when Royalist & Jacobin had set all Britain
by the ears, because I unguardedly, rather under the temptation of
being witty than disaffected, had declared my sentiments in favor of
Parliamentary Reform, in the manner of that time, I was accused to
the Board of Excise of being a Republican; & was very near being
turned adrift in the wide world on that account.—Mr Erskine of Mar,
a gentleman indeed, wrote to my friend Glenriddell to know if I was
really out of place on account of my Political principles; & if so, he
proposed a Subscription among the friends of Liberty for me, which
he offered to head, that I might be no pecuniary loser by my
political Integrity.—This was the more generous, as I had not the
honor of being known to Mr Erskine. I wrote him as follows.—

[Dumfries, 13th April 1793]

Sir,
degenerate as Human Nature is said to be, & in many instances,
worthless & unprincipled it certainly is; still there are bright
examples to the contrary; examples, that even in the eye of Superiour
Beings must shed a lustre on the name of Man.—Such an example
have I now before me, when you, Sir, came forward to patronise &
befriend a distant, obscure stranger; merely because Poverty had
made him helpless, & his British hardihood of mind had provoked
the arbitrary wantonness of Power.—My much esteemed friend, Mr
Riddell of Glenriddell, has just read me a paragraph of a letter he
had from you.—Accept, Sir, of the silent throb of gratitude; for
words would but mock the emotions of my soul.—

You have been misinformed, as to my final dismission from the
Excise: I still am in the service.—Indeed, but for the exertions of a
gentleman who must be known to you, Mr Graham of Fintry, a
gentleman who has ever been my warm & generous friend, I had,
without so much as a hearing, or the smallest previous intimation,
been turned adrift, with my helpless family, to all the horrors of
Want.—Had I had any other resource, probably I might have saved
them the trouble of a dismissal; but the little money I gained by my
Publication, is almost every guinea embarked, to save from ruin an
only brother; who, though one of the worthiest, is by no means one
of the most fortunate of men.—

In my defence to their accusations, I said, that whatever might be
my sentiments of Republics, ancient or modern as to Britain, I
abjured the idea.—That a Constitution which, in its original principles,
experience had proved to be every way fitted for our happiness in
society, it would be insanity to sacrifice to an untried, visionary
theory.—That, in consideration of my being situated in a department,

689

however humble, immediately in the hands of the people in power, I
had forborne taking any active part, either personally, or as an
author, in the present business of Reform.—But that, where I must
declare my sentiments, I would say that there existed a system of
corruption between the Executive Power & the Representative part
of the Legislature, which boded no good to our glorious Constitution;
& which every patriotic Briton must wish to see amended.—Some
such Sentiments as these I stated in a letter to my generous Patron,
Mr Graham, which he laid before the Board at large, where it seems
my last remark gave great offence; & one of our Supervisors general,
a Mr Corbet, was instructed to enquire, on the spot, into my
conduct, & to document me—"that *my* business was to *act*, not to
think; & that whatever might be Men or Measures, it was my
business to be silent & obedient"—Mr Corbet was likewise my steady
friend; so, between Mr Graham & him, I have been partly forgiven:
only, I understand that all hopes of my getting officially forward are
blasted.—

Now, Sir, to the business in which I would more immediately
interest you.—The partiality of my Countrymen has brought me
forward as a man of genius, & has given me a Character to support.—
In the Poet, I have avowed manly & independant sentiments, which I
trust will be found in the Man.—Reasons of no less weight than the
support of a wife & children have pointed out as the eligible, &
indeed the only eligible line of life for me, my present occupation.—
Still, my honest fame is my dearest concern, & a thousand times
have I trembled at the idea of the degrading epithets that Malice, or
Misrepresentation may affix to my name.—I have often, in blasting
anticipation, listened to some future hackney Magazine Scribbler,
with the heavy malice of savage stupidity, exulting in his hireling
paragraphs that "Burns, notwithstanding the fanfaronade of
independance to be found in his works, & after having been held
forth to Public View & Public Estimation as a man of some genius,
yet, quite destitute of resources within himself to support this
borrowed dignity, he dwindled into a paltry Exciseman; & slunk out
the rest of his insignificant existence in the meanest of pursuits &
among the vilest of mankind."—

In your illustrious hands, Sir, permit me to lodge my strong
disavowal & defiance of these slanderous falsehoods.—BURNS was a
poor man, from birth; & an Exciseman, by necessity: but—I will say
it!—the sterling of his honest worth, no poverty could debase; & his
independant British mind, Oppression might bend, but could not
subdue!—Have not I, to me, a more precious stake in my Country's
welfare, than the richest Dukedom in it?—I have a large family of
children, & the probability of more.—I have three sons, whom, I see
already, have brought with them into the world souls ill qualified to
inhabit the bodies of Slaves.—Can I look tamely on, & see any
machination to wrest from them, the birthright of my boys, the
little independant Britons in whose veins runs my own blood?—No! I
will not!—should my heart stream around my attempt to defend it!—

Does any man tell me, that my feeble efforts can be of no service; &
that it does not belong to my humble station to meddle with the
concerns of a People?—I tell him, that it is on such individuals as I,

that for the hand of support and the eye of intelligence, a Nation has to rest.—The uninformed mob may swell a Nation's bulk, & the titled, tinsel Courtly throng may be its feathered ornament, but the number of those who are elevated enough in life, to reason & reflect; & yet low enough to keep clear of the venal contagion of a Court; these are a Nation's strength.—

One small request more: when you have honored this letter with a perusal, please commit it to the flames.—BURNS, in whose behalf you have so generously interested yourself, I have here, in his native colours, drawn *as he is*; but should any of the people in whose hands is the very bread he eats, get the least knowledge of the picture, it would ruin the poor Bard for ever.—

My Poems having just come out in another edition, I beg leave to present you with a copy; as a small mark of that high esteem & ardent gratitude with which I have the honor to be—

Sir,
Your deeply indebted,
And ever devoted humble servant

LESLEY BAILLIE

Born at Mayville, Stevenston on 6th March 1768, the daughter of Robert Baillie. She married Robert Cumming of Logie in 1799 and died at Edinburgh in July 1843. Local legend maintains that Burns visited the Baillie family in Stevenston, but there is no evidence to suggest that he visited them either there or at their town house in Edinburgh. The circumstances of their first authenticated meeting are to be found in Burns's letter (LXI) to Mrs Dunlop (see page 198), when the Baillie family called on Burns at Dumfries on their way to England. Later she was the heroine of *Saw Ye Bonie Lesley* (C.W. p. 435) and *Blythe Hae I Been on yon Hill* (C.W. p. 490), the latter being enclosed with the following letter.

(562)

[Enclosing *Blythe hae I been on yon Hill*, C.W. p. 490.]

[Dumfries, May 1793]

Madam,

I have just put the last hand to the inclosed song; & I think that I may say of it, as Nature can of you—"There is a work of mine, finished in my very finest style!"—

Among your sighing swains, if there should be one whose ardent sentiment & ingenuous modesty fetter his powers of speech in your presence; with that look & attitude so native to your manner, & of all others the most bewitching—Beauty listening to Compassion—put my Ballad in the poor fellow's hand, just to give a little breathing to the fervour of his soul.—

I have some pretence, Madam, to make you the theme of my song, as you & I are two downright singularities in human nature.—You will probably start at this assertion; but I believe it will be allowed that a woman exquisitely charming, without the least seeming consciousness of it; & a Poet who never paid a compliment but where it was justly due; are two of the greatest rarities on earth.—

I have the honor to be—&c.—

JEAN McMURDO

Born in 1777, the eldest daughter of John McMurdo and Jane Blair of
Drumlanrig. About this time Stephen Clarke was at Drumlanrig, teaching Jean
and her sister Philadelphia to play the piano. Jean Armour sang an old song
which Clarke transcribed and taught to the McMurdo girls, and as a compliment
to Miss McMurdo - and possibly also his own wife - Burns composed the lyrics
of *Bonie Jean* (C.W. p. 493). Part of the song, together with Clarke's manuscript of the music, went to Thomson in April 1793, and Burns described the
circumstances of both words and music in a letter (XVI) to Thomson on 2nd
July (see page 631), asking Thomson to send back the melody if he did not
like it. Thomson rejected Burns's 'beautiful little air', which has been lost to
posterity, publishing the lyrics to the tune of 'Willie was a wanton wag' instead
- a typical example of Thomson's cavalier attitude to Burns's suggestions.

(572)

To Miss [JEAN] McMURDO *Drumlanrig;*
inclosing a song composed on her, by RB

daughter to John McMurdo factor to the Duke of Queensberry;
inclosing a ballad I had composed on her.—The ballad will appear in
Pleyel's Publication of Scots Songs; & begins—

There was a lass & she was fair—

[C.W. p. 493]

Copy

[Dumfries, July 1793]

Madam,

Amid the profusion of complimentary address which your age, sex,
& accomplishments will now bring you, permit me to approach you
with my devoirs, which, however deficient may be their consequence
in other respects, have the double novelty & merit, in these frivolous,
hollow times of being poetic & sincere.—In the inclosed ballad I
have, I think, hit off a few outlines of your portrait.—The personal
charms, the purity of mind, the ingenuous naivete of heart &
manners, in my heroine, are, I flatter myself, a pretty just likeness of
Miss Mcmurdo in a Cottager.—

Every composition of this kind must have a series of dramatic
incident in it; so I have had recourse to my invention to finish the
rest of my ballad.—

So much for the Poet: now let me add a few wishes which every man
who has himself the honor of being a father, must breathe, when he
sees female Youth, Beauty & Innocence about to enter into this
much chequered & very precarious world.—May you, my young
Madam, escape that FRIVOLITY which threatens universally to
pervade the minds & manners of Fashionable life.—

To pass by the rougher, & still more degenerate Sex; the mob of
fashionable Female Youth, what are they? Are they any thing? They
prattle, laugh, sing, dance, finger a lesson, or perhaps turn over the
leaves of a fashionable Novel; but are their minds stored with any
information, worthy of the noble powers of reason & judgement; or
do their hearts glow with Sentiment, ardent, generous & humane?—
Were I to poetise on the Subject, I would call them the butterflies of
the human kind: remarkable only for & distinguished only by, the
idle variety of their gaudy glare; sillily straying from one blossoming
weed to another, without a meaning & without an aim; the idiot
prey of every pirate of the skies, who thinks them worth his while as

693

he wings his way by them; & speedily, by wintry Time, swept to that oblivion whence they might as well never have appeared.—

Amid this crowd of Nothings, may you, Madam, be Something! May you be a Character, dignified as Rational & Immortal being.—

A still more formidable plague in life, unfeeling interested Selfishness; is a contagion too impure to touch you.—The selfish drift to bless yourself alone; to build your fame on another's ruin; to look on the child of Misfortune without commiseration, or even the victim of Folly without pity—these, & every other feature of a heart rotten at the core, are what you are totally incapable of.—

These wishes, Madam, are of no consequence to you, but to me they are of the utmost; as they give me an opportunity of declaring with what respect I have the honor to be,

&c.

MAJOR WILLIAM ROBERTSON OF LUDE

Born about 1762, the son of James Robertson of Lude, Perthshire, he succeeded to the family estate in 1802. He obtained an ensign's commission at the age of fifteen and served in the American War of Independence and the French Revolutionary War, in the Walcheren expedition and the seizure of St Lucia. In 1794 he raised the Perthshire Fencibles and, in 1804, a Volunteer corps. The following year he accompanied Pulteney's expedition to Spain, and later served on the general staff in Scotland, England and the Channel Islands. He retired from the Army in 1813 with the rank of lieutenant-general and died in 1820. Major Robertson's regiment was stationed at Dumfries in 1793 when Burns made his acquaintance in company with Robert Riddell, and sent him the following letter, together with a copy of *Scots Wha Hae* (C.W. p. 500). Burns also gave Robertson two copies of *Wilt Thou Be My Dearie* (C.W. p. 512), about the second of which there is an amusing note (II) written in February or March 1794.

I (600)

Tuesday morn:
[3rd December 1793]

[Enclosing *Scots Wha Hae*, C.W. p. 500.]

Sir,—

heated as I was with wine yesternight, I was perhaps rather seemingly impertinent in my anxious wish to be honored with your acquaintance.—You will forgive it: 'twas the impulse of heart-felt respect.—"He is the father of Scotch County Reform; and is a man who does honor to the Business, at the same time that the Business does honor to him!" Said my worthy friend Glenriddel, to somebody by me, who was talking of your coming to this country with your Corps.—Then, I replied, I have a woman's longing to take him by the hand, and to say to him—Sir, I honor you, as a man to whom the interèsts of Humanity are dear; and as a Patriot to whom the Rights of your Country are sacred.

In times such as these, Sir, when our Commoners are barely able, by the glimmer of their own twilight understandings, to scrawl a frank; and when Lords are—what Gentlemen would be ashamed to be—to whom shall a sinking Country call for help?—to the *independant Country Gentleman!*—To Him, who has too deep a stake in his Country not to be in earnest for her welfare; and who, in the honest pride of Man, can view with equal contempt, the insolence of Office, and the allurements of Corruption.

I mentioned to you, a Scots Ode, or Song, I had lately composed, and which, I think, has some merit: allow me to inclose it.—When I fall in with you at the Theatre, I shall be glad to have your opinion of it.—Accept of it, Sir, as a very humble, but most sincere tribute of respect from a man, who, dear as he prizes Poetic Fame, yet dearer holds an Independant Mind.

I have the honor to be,
Sir,
Your very humble servant,
Robert Burns

II (617)

[Enclosing *Wilt Thou be my Dearie*. C.W. p. 512]

[February or March 1794]

Mr Burns presents his most respectful Compliments to Major Robertson—begs leave to present him with another copy of the Song

695

—as Mr B— understands that in a "Treaty of Commerce" with a fair Lady, the little song was among the articles ceded by Major R—.—

Apropos, Mr B—'s most devout wish, & earnest prayer for Major Robertson's welfare, is,—"That in his commerce with the FAIR, the Balance of Trade may never be against him! Amen!"

As the charms of Major R—'s voice gave the first celebrity to the Song, Mr B— begs that he will continue his kindness to his Protegée.—

MRS RIDDELL

Controversy continues to rage over the correct identity of the 'Mrs R*****' to whom Burns addressed the following letter. When it was published by Dr. Currie in 1800 Maria Riddell wrote to him: (I am puzzled to guess how you came by it. I had somehow mislaid it, and it was certainly not among those I delivered for your perusal. Some other person must have pirated a copy. It is a pity you inserted it, at any rate; the stile is not fanciful enough for the intention of the composition, and it is not altogether a creditable one to Burns.' Currie had, in fact, consulted Glenriddell's sister-in-law, Miss Kennedy, about this letter and she had replied: 'I think that the letter ought not to appear as it refers to some circumstances of improper Conduct of Burns to Mrs Walter Riddell, which she represented to Mr Riddell and which he thought (in his Brother's absence) he ought to resent and therefore declin'd taking any further notice of Burns.'

This implies that Maria Riddell was the recipient of the letter; but if this were the case it makes a nonsense of Burns expressly stating that it was the husband of the offended lady who had made him drink too much. Maria's involvement in the episode misled some biographers into thinking that the drunken lapse, traditionally known as the 'Rape of the Sabine Women' incident, must have taken place at Woodley Park; but at that time Walter Riddell was in the West Indies and could not have been the husband referred to in this letter. Consequently - unless we accept the ingenious theory of Maria's descendant, Angus Macnaghten, that some other lady of Nithsdale fitted the description 'Mrs R' - only Mrs Robert Riddell of Glenriddell could have been meant. This is confirmed by Burns's own letters (XIV-XVI) to Maria in January 1794 (see pages 606-7) which do not sound like sequels to the 'letter from hell'. One can only assume, therefore, that Maria Riddell was drawn into the dispute at a later stage. After all, there is nothing in her letter to Currie which actually says that the letter was addressed to her - merely that she had had it in her possession.

This also ties in with the fact that after Robert Riddell's death his widow sold Friars' Carse and retired to Bath where she died in 1801. It seems likely that she surrendered papers of Burnsian interest to Maria about the time of her departure from Scotland. She has been described as a lady of uncertain temper and a narrow, unbending outlook. Francis Grose wrote to Burns on 3rd January 1791 that 'after the scene between Mrs Riddel Junr. and your humble servant, to which you was witness, it is impossible I can ever come under her Roof again.' She sold Friars' Carse to spite her brother-in-law, Walter Riddell whom she 'most cordially hated' - further evidence of her unforgiving nature.

(608)

[January 1794?]

Madam,

I daresay this is the first epistle you ever received from this nether world. I write you from the regions of Hell, amid the horrors of the damned. The time and manner of my leaving your earth I do not exactly know, as I took my departure in the heat of a fever of intoxication, contracted at your too hospitable mansion; but, on my arrival here, I was fairly tried, and sentenced to endure the purgatorial tortures of this infernal confine for the space of ninety-nine years, eleven months, and twenty-nine days, and all on account of the impropriety of my conduct yesternight under your roof. Here am I, laid on a bed of pityless furze, with my aching head reclined on a pillow of everpiercing thorn, while an infernal tormentor, wrinkled and old, and cruel, his name I think is *Recollection*, with a whip of scorpions, forbids peace or rest to approach me, and keeps anguish eternally awake. Still, Madam, if I could in any measure be reinstated in the good opinion of the fair circle whom my conduct last night so much injured, I think it would be an alleviation to my torments. For this reason I trouble you with this letter. To the men of the company I will make no apology.—Your husband, who insisted on my drinking more than I chose, has no right to blame me, and the other gentlemen were partakers of my guilt. But to you, Madam, I have much to apologize. Your good opinion I valued as one of the greatest acquisitions I had made on earth, and I was truly a beast to forfeit it. There was a Miss I——, too, a woman of fine sense, gentle and unassuming manners—do make, on my part, a miserable damned

697

wretch's best apology to her. A Mrs. G——, a charming woman, did me the honour to be prejudiced in my favour; this makes me hope that I have not outraged her beyond all forgiveness.—To all the other ladies please present my humblest contrition for my conduct, and my petition for their gracious pardon. O, all ye powers of decency and decorum! whisper to them that my errors, though great, were involuntary—that an intoxicated man is the vilest of beasts—that it was not in my nature to be brutal to any one—that to be rude to a woman, when in my senses, was impossible with me—but—

*   *   *   *   *

Regret! Remorse! Shame!* ye three hell-hounds that ever dog my steps and bay at my heels, spare me! spare me!

Forgive the offences, and pity the perdition of, Madam,

Your humble slave,

* *Man was Made to Mourn*, line 52. C.W. p. 123.

CAPTAIN PATRICK MILLER

Born in 1769, he was the son of Patrick Miller of Dalswinton, Burns's landlord at Ellisland. He entered the Army at a very early age and had purchased a captaincy by the time he was twenty. At that tender age he stood as Whig candidate for the Dumfries Burghs in the election of 1790 and, with the backing of the Duke of Queensberry, won the contest. Burns composed *The Five Carlins* (C.W. p. 364) to mark the occasion. Although Burns described Captain Miller, in a letter of 9th December 1789 to Graham of Fintry (see page 432) as 'a youth by no means above mediocrity in his abilities'. Miller was a friend of Perry, the proprietor of the *Morning Chronicle*, who offered Burns a position on the paper's literary staff. Burns declined, but sent Miller a copy of *Scots Wha Hae* for anonymous publication.

I (613)

[Enclosing *Bannockburn*, second version. -
See also letter XXVIII to George Thomson (584).]

[Dumfries, January 1794]

Dear Sir,

The following Ode is on a subject which I know you by no means regard with indifference

> "O, Liberty—
> "Thou mak'st the gloomy face of Nature gay,
> "Giv'st beauty to the sun, & pleasure to the day!"*

It does me so much good to meet with a Man whose honest bosom glows with the generous enthusiasm, the heroic daring, of Liberty, that I could not forbear sending you a composition of my own on the subject, which I really think is in my best manner.—

I have the honor to be, Dear Sir,
your very humble servant
Robt Burns

* Addison: *Letter from Italy to Lord Halifax*.

II (620B)

[Dumfries, mid-March 1794]

Dear Sir,

Your offer is indeed truly generous, & most sincerely do I thank you for it; but in my present situation, I find that I dare not accept it.— You well know my Political sentiments; & were I an insular individual, unconnected with a wife & a family of children, with the most fervid enthusiasm I would have volunteered my services: I then could & would have despised all consequences that might have ensued.—

My prospect in the Excise is something; at least, it is, encumbered as I am with the welfare, the very existence of near half-a-score of helpless individuals, what I dare not sport with.—

In the mean time, they are most welcome to my Ode; only, let them insert it as a thing they have met with by accident, & unknown to me.—Nay, if Mr Perry, whose honor, after your character of him I cannot doubt, if he will give me an Address & channel by which any thing will come safe from these spies with which he may be certain that his correspondence is beset, I will now & then send him any bagatelle that I may write.—In the present hurry of Europe, nothing but news & politics will be regarded; but against the days of Peace, which Heaven send soon, my little assistance may perhaps fill up an idle column of a Newspaper.—I have long had it in my head to try my hand in the way of little Prose Essays, which I propose sending into the world through the medium of some Newspaper; & should these be worth his while, to these Mr Perry shall be welcome; & all my reward shall be, his treating me with his Paper, which, by the bye, to any body who has the least relish for Wit, is a high treat indeed.—

How do you like the following clinch?

> Extempore, Pinned to a Lady's coach—

> If you rattle along like your Mistress's tongue,
>   Your speed will out-rival the dart:
> But, a fly for your load, you'll break down on the road,
>   If your stuff be as rotten's her heart.—
>   —Nith.—
>   [C.W. p. 514]

If your friends think this worth insertion, they are welcome.—

Almost every day, I am manufacturing these little trifles, &, in a dearth of News, they may have a corner.—

Voila un autre—

> Epigram—On a noted coxcomb—

> "Light lay the earth on Billy's breast,"
>   His chicken heart so tender;
> But build a castle on his head,
>   His scull will prop it under.—
>   —Clincher.—

>   [C.W. p. 505]

This is also theirs, if they please.—

> With the most grateful esteem, I am ever,
> Dear Sir, Your most obedient.—
> Robt Burns

P.S. A new Scots Song. Tune, The Sutors dochter

> Wilt thou be my Dearie;
>   [C.W. p. 512]

III (659)

8th March [1795]

My anxiety to answer, your kind epistle has delayed my writing you so long.—This, you will say, is an Irishcism; but it is even so.—The task you obligingly assigned me of writing out some of my rhyming bagatelles for your fair English friend, I was determined to execute on a large scale; & thus waiting for leisure to make up a Packet for you, I could not write you a line.—In despair of that leisure, I now take up the pen to tell you so, by way of apology for my seeming inattention to a Gentleman whom I so highly esteem, quo ad, a *Man*! independantly of his being a man of rank of fortune: circumstances which I trust will ever be a very trifle indeed, in my appreciation of mankind —

Captain Patrick Miller

Inclosed, is a Song, I wrote the other day.—The lady I mean to compliment in it, is, Mrs Oswald; a woman with whom every body here is quite enchanted.—I throw the little drama of my Song—Mr Oswald, seeing the evening sun shine on the habitation of his Lucy.— Oswald, I am sure you must know; else I would draw you his portrait—the portrait of an independant-minded Country Gentleman, who dares to think & act for himself: a Character, my dear Sir, which I know you must highly value; as it is a Character in which I prophesy that you will one day make a determined, steady, respectable figure yourself.—

Talking of Oswald, the Galloway interest will infallibly be overthrown at the approaching Election: this you may depend on.—

When you return to the country, you will find us all *Sogers*.—(This, a propos, brings to my mind an old Scotish Stanza.—

> There cam a soger here to stay,
>   He swore he wadna steer me;
> But, lang before the break o' day,
>   He cuddl'd, muddl'd near me:
>
> He set a stiff thing to my wame,
>   I docht na bide the bends o't;
> But lang before the grey morn cam,
>   I soupl'd baith the ends o't.—)

I have not a moment more than just to say—

God bless You!
Robt Burns

SAMUEL CLARK, JR.

Born in Dumfries in 1769, he was, like his father before him, a solicitor in the town, and latterly Conjunct Commissary Clerk and Clerk of the Peace for the County. He married Mary Wight in 1798 and had fourteen children before his death in August 1814. He was a friend of Burns who seems, if the following letters are anything to go by, to have been more than usually convivial in his company. Clark was with Burns on that memorable occasion in January 1794, when the poet's ambivalent toast 'May our success in our present war be equal to the justice of our cause' roused the ire of a certain Captain Dods, so graphically recalled the next day (II). Burns was afraid that word of his conduct might get back to the Commissioners of Excise, hence these two undated letters appealing for Clark's help in ensuring that the matter was not misrepresented to William Corbet. Fortunately the incident seems to have been no more than a storm in a teacup.

I (618)

My dear Sir,

I recollect something of a drunken promise yesternight to breakfast with you this morning.—I am very sorry that it is impossible.—I remember too, your very oblidgingly mentioning something of your intimacy with Mr Corbet our Supervisor General.—Some of our folks about the Excise Office, Edinburgh, had & perhaps still have conceived a prejudice against me as being a drunken dissipated character.—I might be all this, you know, & yet be an honest fellow, but you know that I am an honest fellow and am nothing of this.— You may in your own way let him know that I am not unworthy of subscribing myself

My dear Clarke, YOUR FRIEND
R. Burns

II (631)

Sunday morning—

Dear Sir

I was, I know, drunk last night, but I am sober this morning.—From the expressions Captain Dods made use of to me, had I had nobody's welfare to care for but my own, we should certainly have come, according to the manners of the world, to the necessity of murdering one another about the business.—The words were such as generally, I believe, end in a brace of pistols; but I am still pleased to think that I did not ruin the peace welfare of a wife & a family of children in a drunken squabble.—Farther, you know that the report of certain Political opinions being mine, has already once before brought me to the brink of destruction.—I dread lest last night's business may be misrepresented in the same way —YOU, I beg, will take care to prevent it.—I tax your wish for Mr Burns's welfare with the task of waiting as soon as possible, on every gentleman who was present, & state this to him, & as you please shew him this letter.—What after all was the obnoxious toast?—"May our success in the present war be equal to the "justice of our cause"—A toast that the most outrageous frenzy of loyalty cannot object to.—I request & beg that this morning you will wait on the parties present at the foolish dispute.— The least delay may be of unlucky consequence to me.—I shall only add, that I am truly sorry that a man who stood so high in my estimation as Mr Dods, should use me in the manner in which I conceive he has done.—

I am, Dear Sir, yours sincerely
Robt Burns

CAPTAIN JOHN HAMILTON OF ALLERSHAW

Captain in the Dumfries Volunteers and Burns's landlord in Dumfries, both in the Wee Vennel (now Bank Street) where he rented a three-room apartment in 1791-3, and in Mill Street (now Burns Street) where Burns rented a much larger, detached house from May 1793 till his death. Unfortunately Burns soon found himself in arrears of rent, due mainly to the unexpected drop in his emoluments as a result of the war with France which had brought imports to a virtual standstill. The following series of four letters deals entirely with this matter. When Burns managed to pay three guineas towards his arrears (III), Hamilton wrote back, asking if he had in any way offended the poet. Burns replied by return (IV) and we may read between the lines the bitter memories of the humiliation which debt had brought upon his father.

I (620C)

24th March 1794

Sir,

It gives me most sincere pleasure to have it in my power to fulfill part of my pecuniary engagements to you.—Inclosed I send you a five pound bank-note.—The following is the statement on my side—

	L — s — d
To a bed & press, per account of Thomas Blan, joiner	1 — 13 — 0
To a quey Calf	0 — 10 — 0
To Cash	5 — 0 — 0
	7 — 3 — 0

With the sincerest gratitude for your kind forbearance & kindness on all occasions,

I am, Sir, your obliged humble servant
Robt Burns

II (633)

[July 1794]

Sir,

It is even so.—You are the only person in Dumfries or in the world, to whom I have *run in debt*; & I took the freedom with you, because I believed, & do still believe that I may do it with more impunity as to my feelings than any other person almost that I ever met with.—I will settle with you soon; & I assure you, Sir, it is with infinite pain that I have transgressed on your goodness.—The unlucky fact for me is, that about the beginning of these disastrous times, in a moment of imprudence I lent my name to a friend who has since been unfortunate; & of course, I had a sum to pay which my very limited income & large family could ill afford.—God forbid, Sir, that any thing should ever distress you as much as writing this card has done me.—

With the sincerest gratitude & most respectful esteem—

I have the honor to be,
Sir,
your very humble servant
Robt Burns

Captain John Hamilton of Allershaw

III (653)

D.fries, 29th January 1795

Sir,

it is needless to attempt an apology for my remissness to you in money-matters: my conduct is beyond all excuse.—Literally, Sir, I had it not.—The distressful state of Commerce at this town, has this year taken from my otherwise scanty income no less than 20£.— That part of my Salary depended upon the Imports, & they are no more, for one year.—I inclose you three guineas: & shall soon settle all with you.—

I shall not mention your goodness to me: it is beyond my power to describe either the feelings of my wounded soul at not being able to pay you as I ought; or the grateful respect with which I have the honor to be,

Sir, your deeply obliged humble servant
Robt Burns

IV (655)

Saturday morn:
[31st January 1795]

Sir,

I was from home, & had not the opportunity of seeing your more than polite, your most friendly Card.—It is not possible, most worthy Sir, that you can do any thing to offend any body: my backwardness proceeds alone from the abashing consciousness of my obscure situation in the ranks of life.—Many an evening have I sighed to call in & spend it at your social fireside; but a shyness of appearing obtrusive amid the fashionable visitants occasionally there kept me at a distance.—It shall do so no more.—On Monday, I must be in the country; & most part of the week: but the first leisure evening I shall avail myself of your hospitable goodness.—

With the most ardent sentiments of Gratitude & Respect,

I have the honor to be,
Sir, your highly obliged, humble servant
Robt Burns

LUCY JOHNSTONE (MRS. RICHARD OSWALD)

JEAN LORIMER (CHLORIS)

LADY ELIZABETH HERON

Born in 1745, the daughter of Thomas Cochrane, eighth Earl of Dundonald, she married Patrick Heron of Heron in 1775 and bore him two daughters. A talented amateur musician, she composed 'The Banks o Cree' for which Burns wrote *Here is the Glen* (C.W. p. 513), a copy of which he sent Lady Heron with the following letter. Burns sent this song to Thomson, who disliked the air Lady Heron had composed and published the song to the tune 'Flowers of Edinburgh' - though he waited till Burns was dead before going against his express wishes in this matter.

(620D)

Dumfries, 3rd April 1794

My Lady,

By my much valued Friend, Mr Syme, I some time ago received a beautiful air which your Ladyship did me the honor to send me, with your obliging commands to suit it with verses.—The inclosed, I am afraid, will not be found in any degree worthy of the charming melody.—The post just going denies me the opportunity at present of pointing out to your Ladyship several different Publications just now going on, in some one of which, if you have no objection, the song may appear.—In a day or two, I shall do myself the honor to write your Ladyship again, & probably trouble you with a longer epistle on the subject.—

My song has at least done me one service, as it has given me an opportunity of declaring how much I have the honor to be,

My Lady, your Ladyship's most devoted servant
Robt Burns

JOHN CLARK

Born in 1750, the son of John Clark of Nunland, he was provost of Dumfries (1777-9) and died in 1813. He lived at Locharwoods, an estate on the north bank of the Lochar Water some six miles south-east of Dumfries and two miles west of the Brow. Clark was a close friend of Robert Riddell, and in that capacity was the recipient of a copy of Burns's *Sonnet on the Death of Robert Riddell* (C.W. p. 513), enclosed with the first letter. Burns prevailed on Clark to lend him the means of transport after his ineffectual sojourn at the Brow.

I (621)

Monday noon
[21st April 1794]

[Enclosing *Sonnet on the Death of Robert Riddell.* C.W. p. 513.]

Dear Sir,

This morning's loss I have severely felt.—Inclosed is a small heart-felt tribute to the memory of the *man I loved.*—I shall send it to some Newspaper with my name.—

Mr Clarke will accept of this M.S.S. copy, as a testimony how sincerely I am,

his devoted humble servant
Robt Burns

II (709)

Saturday noon
[Brow, 16th July 1796]

My dear Sir,

my hours of bathing have interfered so unluckily as to have put it out of my power to wait on you.—In the mean time, as the tides are over I anxiously wish to return to town, as I have not heard any news of Mrs Burns these two days.—Dare I be so bold as to borrow your Gig? I have a horse at command, but it threatens to rain, & getting wet is perdition.—Any time about three in the afternoon, will suit me exactly.—

Yours most gratefully & sincerely
R Burns

ELEANOR OR SOPHY RIDDELL

The identity of the lady to whom the following letter was written has never been satisfactorily established. Currie, who first printed the letter in 1800, merely gave it as addressed to 'Miss ——'. Wallace (1896) suggested 'Miss Woodley', but that was impossible, as both of Maria Riddell's sisters were married. Ferguson (1931) suggested that the recipient may have been a Miss Kennedy, sister of Mrs Elizabeth Riddell, in whose album Burns is known to have written three of his epigrams. The names 'Elinor or Sophy' were thus given by Hugh Gladstone in his paper 'Maria Riddell, the Friend of Burns' (*Transactions of the Dumfries and Galloway Natural History and Antiquarian Society*, Third Series, vol. 3, 1914-15) and followed by W.M. Wood in his *Robert Burns and the Riddell Family* (Dumfries, 1922). The impression was given that both names pertained to the same lady. Robert Riddell, however, had two sisters - Eleanor, who died unmarried in 1797, and Sophia, who died young. Maria Riddell named her younger daughter Sophia after the latter aunt. Miss Eleanor Riddell left a small legacy to Maria Riddell's surviving daughter, Anna Maria. On balance, it seems likely that Eleanor Riddell was the addressee in this instance.

(624)

[Dumfries, May? 1794]

Madam,

Nothing short of a kind of absolute necessity could have made me trouble you with this letter. Except my ardent and just esteem for your sense, taste, and worth, every sentiment arising in my breast, as I put pen to paper to you, is painful. The scenes I have past with the friend of my soul, and his amiable connections! the wrench at my heart to think that he is gone, for ever gone from me, never more to meet in the wanderings of a weary world! and the cutting reflection of all, that I had most unfortunately, though most undeservedly, lost the confidence of that soul of worth, ere it took its flight!

These, Madam, are sensations of no ordinary anguish.—However you, also, may be offended with some *imputed* improprieties of mine; sensibility you know I possess, and sincerity none will deny me.

To oppose those prejudices which have been raised against me, is not the business of this letter. Indeed it is a warfare I know not how to wage. The powers of positive vice I can in some degree calculate, and against direct malevolence I can be on my guard; but who can estimate the fatuity of giddy caprice, or ward off the unthinking mischief of precipitate folly?

I have a favour to request of you, Madam; and of your sister Mrs.——,[1] through your means. You know that, at the wish of my late friend, I made a collection of all my trifles in verse which I had ever written. They are many of them local, some of them puerile and silly, and all of them unfit for the public eye. As I have some little fame at stake, a fame that I trust may live, when the hate of those who "watch for my halting,"[2] and the contumelious sneer of those whom accident has made my superiors, will, with themselves, be gone to the regions of oblivion I am uneasy now for the fate of those manuscripts—Will Mrs. —— have the goodness to destroy them, or return them to me? As a pledge of friendship they were bestowed; and that circumstance, indeed, was all their merit. Most unhappily for me, that merit they no longer possess; and I hope that Mrs. ——'s goodness, which I well know, and ever will revere, will not refuse this favour to a man whom she once held in some degree of estimation.

With the sincerest esteem I have the honour to be, Madam, &c.

1 Robert Riddell's widow, Elizabeth.
2 Jeremiah 20:10.

JOHN SYME

Born in 1755, the son of the Laird of Barncailzie, Kirkcudbrightshire, he followed in his father's footsteps as a Writer to the Signet in Edinburgh. In his early years, however, he served as an ensign in the 72nd Regiment, but then retired to manage the family estate. His father lost heavily as a result of the failure of the Douglas, Heron & Co. Bank at Ayr and the estate had to be sold. In 1791 he obtained the sinecure of Distributor of Stamps in Dumfries and had his office on the ground floor of the house in the Wee Vennel (now Bank Street) where Burns resided. Syme's villa, Ryedale, was in Maxwelltown, on the west bank of the Nith, and Burns was a frequent guest there. Syme accompanied Burns on tours of Kirkcudbright and Galloway in the summers of 1793 and 1794. Syme visited Burns at the Brow on 15th July 1796, and at his home in Dumfries a few days later, and was appalled at the rapid deterioration in the poet's condition. After Burns's death Syme, with Dr Maxwell, organised the funeral and, with Alexander Cunningham, laboured unceasingly on behalf of Jean and her family. He left some vivid reminiscences of Burns, while his correspondence with Cunningham was serialised in the *Burns Chronicle* (1934-42).

I (624A)

Jerusalem Tavern Monday even:
[Dumfries, May 1794]

To Mr Syme—with a present of a dozen of Porter—

O had the Malt thy strength of mind,
Or Hops the flavour of thy wit;
'Twere Drink for first of Humankind,
A Gift that e'en for SYME were fit.—

II (669)

Monday eve [May? 1795]

You know, that among other high dignities, you are my Supreme Court of Critical Judicature, from which there is no appeal.—I inclose you a Song which I composed since I saw you; & am going to give you the history of it.[1]—

Do you know that among much that I admire in the characters & manners of those Great Folks whom I have now the honor to call my acquaintances, the OSWALD FAMILY[2], there is nothing charms me more, than his unconcealable, enthusiastic attachment to that incomparable woman.—By the way, did you ever, my dear SYME, meet with a man who owed more to the Divine Giver of all good things than Mr Oswald? A fine fortune; a pleasing, engaging exterior, self-evident amiable dispositions, with an ingenuous, upright mind, & that too informed much beyond the usual run of young fellows of his rank & fortune: &, add to all this, such a Woman!—but of her I shall say nothing, in despair of saying any thing adequate—only, I have done some justice to *his* feelings, according to the scene I have drawn.—

As I am a good deal pleased with my performance, I, in my first fervour, thought of sending it to Mrs O——; but on reflection, perhaps, from the well-known character of Poverty & Poetry, what I would offer as the honest incense of genuine esteem & grateful respect, might be construed into some modification of that servility which my soul abhors.—

Do, let me know some convenient moment, ere the WORTHY FAMILY leave the town, that I, *with propriety*, may wait on them.— In the circle of the fashionable herd, those who come either to shew

708

their own consequence, or to borrow consequence from the visit—in such a MOB I will not appear:—mine is different errand.—

Yours

Robt Burns

1 *'O wat ye wha's in yon town'*—C.W. p. 541.
2 Richard and Lucy Oswald of Auchencruive. Burns had clearly modified his opinions since 1789 (see page 259).

JOHN McLEOD OF COLBECKS

The recipient of this letter has not been identified, and the suggestion that he may have been one of the McLeods of Raasay is extremely doubtful, as Burns's acquaintance with that family dated back to 1787, whereas this gentleman was referred to as a 'lately-acquired friend'. Even the name of his estate has not been identified, although it was probably somewhere in the north of England. McLeod had, in fact, written to Burns about the sale of Friars' Carse on 16th May 1794.

(626)

Dumfries, 18th June 1794

Sir,

the fate of Carse is determined.—A majority of the trustees have fixed its *sale*.—Our friend, John Clarke, whom you remember to have met with here, opposed the measure with all his might; but he was over-ruled.—He, wishing to serve Walter Riddell, the surviving brother, wanted the widow to take a given annuity, & make over to him the survivancy of the paternal estate; but luckily, the widow most cordially hates her brotherinlaw, &, to my knowledge, would rather you had the estate, though five hundred cheaper, than that Wattie should.—In the mean time, Wattie has sold his Woodleypark to Colonel Goldie, the last Proprietor.—Wattie gave 16000£ for it; laid out better than 2000£ more on it; & has sold it for 15000£.—So much for Master Wattie's sense & management which, entre nous, are about the same pitch as his worth.—

The Trustees have appointed a gentleman to make out an estimate of the value of the terra firma in the estate, which you know is by far the principal article in the purchase: the house & woods will be valued by some professional man.—The gentleman they have pitched on, is a Mr William Stewart, factor & manager for Mr Menteath of Closeburn.—Stewart is my most intimate friend; & has promised me a copy of his estimate—but please let this be a dead secret.—Stewart was the intimate & confidential friend of poor Riddell that is gone, & will be trusted & consulted in all the business; & from him I am to know every view & transaction.—I assure you it has cost me some manoeuvring to bring this to bear; but as this kind of underhand intelligence may & will be of very considerable service to you, if you are still thinking of the purchase, I have in a manner beset & waylaid my friend Stewart, untill I have prevailed on him.—By this day se'ennight Stewart will have made out his estimate, & against that day, you shall hear from me.—As soon as the advertisement appears in the papers, which will be, Stewart tells me, in a fortnight or so, I will go over the woods with an acquaintance of mine, who is a twenty years experienced judge in the way of buying woods; & you shall have the exact value of every stick on the property.—I could not go over the estate in that way, you know, untill the sale be formally announced.—The idea of the Trustees is, to bring on the sale in October; so that the Purchaser may enter at Martinmass.—

Now, my lately-acquired, but much-valued & highly honored Friend, let me urge you to be in earnest with this business.—Here is positively the most beautiful spot in the lowlands of Scotland; absolutely the masterpiece of Nature in that part of the kingdom; & would you not wish to call it yours?—This country is charmingly romantic & picturesque, in the whole; 'tis besides highly improving & improveable, & a cheap Country to live in—you will be within six

John McLeod of Colbecks

miles of the third town for importance & elegance in Scotland—your neighbourhood will abound in "Honest men & bonie lasses"*—do, come & be happy, & make me in particular, & the whole country happy by adding Mr McLeod's worth & Mrs McLeod's amiableness—not to speak of their splendid fortune & distinguished rank—to this already deserving & enchanting part of the kingdom.—

You see with what selfishness I have the honor to be,

Dear Sir, your obliged & devoted humble servant
Robt Burns

* *Tam o Shanter*, line 16. C.W. p. 410.

DAVID McCULLOCH OF ARDWALL

Born in 1769, the fourth son of David McCulloch of Ardwall and Jane Corsane, he travelled extensively, and was in France when the Revolution broke out. He returned to Scotland in 1793 when his father was dying of cancer and managed the estate in the absence of his elder brothers then abroad. A high-flown testimonial to his filial piety was published at this time, somewhat negated by the minutes of Anwoth Kirk Session which record a charge of fornication made against him and Peggy Bailey, a serving maid at Ardwall. Lockhart tells a story, in his biography of Sir Walter Scott, about Burns being ostracised by polite society early in 1794 (possibly arising out of the 'Rape of the Sabines' incident), and being snubbed by the ladies and gentlemen coming into Dumfries for a county ball. McCulloch immediately dismounted and crossed the street to join Burns who greeted him warmly, took him home and entertained him very agreeably until the hour of the ball arrived. McCulloch was an exceptionally fine singer, on whom Burns tested many of his songs before sending them to Thomson. Encouraged by his elder brother, David went to India in 1796 and thence to Malaya where he had a thriving export business at Prince of Wales Island. He returned to England in 1820 and settled at Cheltenham where he died in 1825.

(627)

Dumfries, 21st June 1794

My dear Sir,

My long projected journey through your country is at last fixed; & on Wedensday next, if you have nothing of more importance than take a saunter down to Gatehouse, about two or three o'clock, I shall be happy to take a draught of Mckune's best with you.— Collector Syme will be at Glens about that time, & will meet us about dish-of-tea-hour.—Syme goes also to Kiroughtree; & let me remind you of your kind promise to accompany me there.—I will need all the friends I can muster, for I am indeed ill at ease whenever I approach your Honorables & Right Honorables.—

Yours sincerely
Robt Burns

ROBERT ANDREW RIDDELL

A minor landscape painter who only exhibited at the Royal Academy on one
occasion (1793), and then only contributed a single painting. He resided at 13
Hart Street, Bloomsbury, in London and was therefore a near neighbour of
John Murdoch at that period, which may explain the connexion with Burns.
Riddell wrote to Burns on 2nd July 1794, sending him a set of twelve
topographical prints. The following letter was a rather belated response from
the poet. It is probable that the prints were those engraved by A. Robertson,
from paintings by Riddell, one of which was subsequently inscribed by Jean
Burns to J. Logie in 1826 and featured in a sale catalogue of September 1879
(see the *Burns Chronicle* of 1902 for further details). Riddell appears to have
done an extensive series of Scottish views, the last to be published (in 1812)
being a view of Glencoe. Judging by extant reproductions, the paintings of
Robert Riddell seem to have possessed little artistic merit.

(640)

Dumfries, 22nd September 1794

My dear Sir,

You must by this time have set me down as one of the most unkind
& ungrateful of the sons of men, not untill now to have answered
your extremely obliging letter.—The fact is, I was determined to
answer you in the way *of my trade*; in a poetic Epistle in one of our
Newspapers.—I have not yet been able to arrange my NUMBERS, to
please myself; but if the Muse is not extremely restive, you shall
hear, *in my own way*, from,

My dear Sir,
Your obliged friend & humble servant
Robt Burns

THE EDITORS OF THE *MORNING CHRONICLE*

The following letter was first published by Cromek in his *Reliques* (1808), stating that it was written by Burns on behalf of a neighbour in Dumfries. Burns is said to have had second thoughts about it, as it was never forwarded to the newspaper, and asked his neighbour to return it to him. The text is from Burns's draft in the Rosenbach Museum and Library, Philadelphia, and collated in that form by Ross Roy.

(654)

[January 1795]

Gentlemen:

You will see by your subscribers' list, that I have now been about nine months one of that number.—I am sorry to inform you, that in that time, seven or eight of your Papers either have never been sent me, or else have never reached me.—To be deprived of any one Number of the first Newspaper in Britain, for information, ability & independance, is what I can ill brook & bear; but to be deprived of that most admirable Oration of the Marquis of Lansdowne, when he made the great though ineffectual attempt, (in the language of the Poet, I fear too true,) "to save a Rotten State"*—this was a loss which I neither can, nor will forgive you.—That Paper, Gentlemen, never reached me; but I demand it of you.—I am a Briton; & must be interested in the cause of Liberty: I am a man; & the rights of Human Nature cannot be indifferent to me.—However, do not let me mislead you: I am not a man in that situation of life, which, as your Subscriber, can be of any consequence to you, in the eyes of those, to whom *Situation of Life alone* is the criterion of Man—I am but a plain Tradesman, in this distant, obscure country town: but that humble domicile in which I shelter my wife & children, is the Castellum of a Briton; & that scanty, hard-earned Income which supports them, is as truly my Property, as the most magnificent fortune, of the most puissant member of your House of Nobles.

These, Gentlemen, are my sentiments; & to them I subscribe my Name: & were I a man of ability & consequence enough to address the Public, with that Name should they appear.—

I am &c.—.

* Thomson: *Winter*, line 488.

714

PATRICK HERON OF HERON

Born about 1736, the scion of a Lincolnshire family with ancient Galloway connexions, he moved to south-west Scotland where, in partnership with the Hon. Archibald Douglas, he founded the Ayr Bank of Douglas, Heron and Company in 1769. This bank expanded too rapidly and with little practical banking expertise. Within four years it had failed spectacularly, bankrupting its investors and precipitating widespread depression in southern Scotland. Twenty years later, however, Heron bounced back. By that time he had recovered his fortune by marrying the daughter of the Earl of Dundonald and purchased the estate of Kirroughtree in the west of the Stewartry. In 1794 Burns, in company with John Syme and David McCulloch of Ardwall, visited Heron; and the following year Heron sought Burns's help during his election campaign as Whig candidate for the Stewartry. Burns was somewhat apprehensive about nailing his political colours to the mast, hence the self-justificatory tone of the following letter, enclosing the *Ballads on Mr Heron's Election* (C.W. pp. 543-9) which helped defeat the Tory candidate, Thomas Gordon of Balmaghie.

The second letter does not bear a superscription, but it has been conjectured that Heron was the intended recipient. It is not known what ballads Burns referred to, but they were probably authored by someone else and circulated with his name. In May 1796 Parliament was dissolved and Heron contested the Stewartry again, being subsequently returned as Member, a position which he held till 1802. In the election of that year he was again successful, but on 10th May 1803 he was unseated and his name erased from the rolls by order of the House. He died soon afterwards, at Grantham, on his way home to Galloway.

I (660)

[Dumfries, March 1795]

Sir,

I inclose you some copies of a couple of political ballads; one of which, I believe, you have never seen. Would to Heaven I could make you master of as many votes in the Stewartry. But—

"Who does the utmost that he can,
"Does well, acts nobly, angels could no more." *

In order to bring my humble efforts to bear with more effect on the foe, I have privately printed a good many copies of both ballads, and have sent them among friends all about the country.

To pillory on Parnassus the rank reprobation of character, the utter dereliction of all principle, in a profligate junto which has not only outraged virtue, but violated common decency; which, spurning even hypocrisy as paltry iniquity below their daring;—to unmask their flagitiousness to the broadest day—to deliver such over to their merited fate, is surely not merely innocent, but laudable; is not only propriety, but virtue.—You have already, as your auxiliary, the sober detestation of mankind on the heads of your opponents; and I swear by the lyre of Thalia to muster on your side all the votaries of honest laughter, and fair, candid ridicule!

I am extremely obliged to you for your kind mention of my interests in a letter which Mr. Syme shewed me. At present, my situation in life must be in a great measure stationary, at least for two or three years. The statement is this—I am on the supervisors' list, and as we come on there by precedency, in two or three years I shall be at the head of that list, and be appointed, *of course. Then*, a FRIEND might be of service to me in getting me into a place of the kingdom which I would like. A supervisor's income varies from about a hundred and twenty, to two hundred a year; but the business is an incessant drudgery, and would be nearly a compleat bar to every species of literary pursuit. The moment I am appointed supervisor, in the common routine, I may be nominated on the

715

collector's list; and this is always a business purely of political
patronage. A collectorship varies much, from better than two
hundred a year to near a thousand. They also come forward by
precedency on the list; and have besides a handsome income, a life
of compleat leisure. A life of literary leisure with a decent
competence, is the summit of my wishes. It would be the prudish
affectation of silly pride in me to say that I do not need, or would
not be indebted to a political friend; at the same time, Sir, I by no
means lay my affairs before you thus, to hook my dependant
situation on your benevolence. If, in my progress of life, an opening
should occur where the good offices of a gentleman of your public
character and political consequence might bring me forward, I shall
petition your goodness with the same frankness as I now do myself
the honor to subscribe myself, &c.

* Young: *Night Thoughts*, Night II, lines 91-2, misquoted.

II (662A)

Dumfries, 24th April 1795

Sir,

The inclosed ballads having fallen into my hands, I send them to you
as a flagrant instance of the Poetica Licentia.—The Poet, whoever he
is, seems to have some little wit with a great deal of illnature; & I
pray that he may fall among hands who will reward him as he
deserves! If his interests come in your way, I am confident that your
zeal will not be wanting in placing this Byblow of Thalia in his
proper point of view.—

I am, Sir,
Ever your obliged & obedient humble servant
Robt Burns

RICHARD ALEXANDER OSWALD

Born in 1771, the son of Mrs Mary Oswald of Auchencruive whose funeral
cortege so incommoded Burns that he was inspired to pen his savage *Ode*
(C.W. p. 342). In 1793 Oswald married Lucy Johnston of Hilton-on-Merse,
who died of tuberculosis in 1797. Ten years later Richard married Lady Lilias
Montgomerie, daughter of the twelfth Earl of Eglinton and widow of Robert
Dundas Macqueen of Braxfield. Oswald was MP for Ayrshire for some time,
and died in 1841. The following letter does not bear his name, but Chambers
(who first published it in 1851) identified Oswald as the recipient. Although
Oswald was mentioned in the second *Heron Election Ballad* (C.W. p. 545) it is
not known what lines were enclosed.

(662)

Dumfries, 23rd April 1795.

Sir—

You see the danger of patronising the rhyming tribe: you flatter the
poet's vanity—a most potent ingredient in the composition of a son
of rhyme—by a little notice; and he, in return persecutes your good-
nature with his acquaintance. In these days of volunteering, I have
come forward with my services, as poet-laureate to a highly
respectable political party, of which you are a distinguished member.
The enclosed are, I hope, only a beginning to the songs of triumph
which you will earn in that contest.—

I have the honour to be, sir,
your obliged and devoted humble servant,
R. Burns

JOHN EDGAR

An accountant employed by the Board of Excise and Salt Duties in Edinburgh until 1816, he was the recipient of the following letter, written by Burns in his official capacity and protesting against the likelihood of incurring censure for being late in sending in a return, and pleading inexperience for the delay.

(663)

Dumfries, 25th April 1795

Sir,

I understand that I am to incur censure by the Wine-Account of this District not being sent in.—Allow me to state the following circumstances to you, which, if they do not apologise for, will at least extenuate my part of the offence.—

The General Letter was put into my hands sometime about the beginning of this month, as I was then in charge of the District, Mr Findlater being indisposed.—I immediately, as far as in my power, made a survey of the Wine-Stocks; & where I could not personally survey, I wrote the officer of the Division. In a few days more, & previous to Collection-week, Mr Findlater resumed charge; & as in the course of Collection he would have both the Officers by him, & the Old Books among his hands, it very naturally occurred to me the Wine-account business would rest with him.—At the close of that week, I got a note from the Collector that the Account making up was thrown on my hands.—I immediately set about it; but one Officer's books, James Graham of Sanquhar, not being at hand I wrote him to send me them by first post. Mr Graham has not thought proper to pay the least attention to my request, & today I have sent an express for his Stock-book.—

This, Sir, is a plain state of Facts; & if I must still be thought censurable, I hope it will be considered, that this Officiating Job being my first, I cannot be supposed to be completely master of all the etiquette of the business.—

If my supposed neglect is to be laid before the Honorable BOARD, I beg you will have the goodness to accompany the complaint with this letter.—

I am, Sir, your very humble servant
Robt Burns

LADY MARY DOUGLAS-HAMILTON

Born in 1773, the daughter of Dunbar Douglas-Hamilton, fourth Earl of Selkirk, Lord Lieutenant of the Stewartry, and sister of Basil William, Lord Daer (1763-94) who had been the first member of the aristocracy whom Burns ever met socially, an event which inspired the verses *On Meeting with Lord Daer* (C.W. p. 254). St Mary's Isle referred to in this letter was an estate near Kirkcudbright which the earls of Selkirk had purchased from the Heron family in 1704. Burns was entertained there during his visit to Kirkcudbright in June 1793. Lady Mary never married and died some five years later.

(664)

Dumfries, 2nd May 1795

My Lady,

the original music of the beautiful old song you mention is in existence, but I have not yet been able to procure it.—The moment I can find it, I will do myself the honor to transmit it to St Mary's Isle.—

The Orpheus Caledonius is useful to me at present, in some Musical researches; & as your Ladyship is so very good as permit me, I will keep it a little longer.—

The fifth Volume of the Sc. M. Museum is in hands, but not published.—We are in doubts that we have not so many Scotish airs, as make out the number.—I have advised the Editor to finish what is wanting in his hundred songs, (the number for each volume,) by adding some Irish airs, which either have no verses at all, or verses of no merit.—To these I propose making Scotish songs; & in fact, have already composed four or five.—I have written for, Captain Okean, Humors of glen, & a delightful Air, called, The Irish cronoch; & one or two of less celebrity.—If there are any airs of this description, which are favorites in Saint Mary's Isle, the Poet will think himself highly honored by their commands.—I send your Ladyship one of my late compositions in this way—a small but sincere mark of that profound respect with which I have the honor to be,

My Lady,
Your Ladyship's very humble servant
Robt Burns

Scotish Song—Tune, My lodging is on the cold ground—

Behold, my Love, how green the groves,
The primrose banks how fair;

[C.W. p. 531]

719

COLONEL ARENT SCHUYLER DE PEYSTER

Born in 1736, of Dutch-Huguenot descent, in New York, the elder son of Pierre de Peyster and Catherine Schuyler. His boyhood was spent partly in Holland and partly in Britain and in 1755 he obtained a commission in the 50th Foot which had been raised in Massachusetts in 1748. He later transferred to the 51st Regiment and then the 8th (King's Liverpool) serving no fewer than 47 years with the latter. He campaigned in Germany during the Seven Years War (1756-63), but then served in Canada (1768-85) latterly as Military Adminstrator in the Great Lakes area, with the rank of colonel. From 1787 till his retirement in 1794, he served in England and Ireland. He had married Jane Blair, John McMurdo's sister-in-law and daughter of Provost David Blair of Dumfries, so in April 1794 he purchased Mavis Grove on the Nith, three miles from the town. When the Dumfries Volunteers were formed in March 1795 De Peyster was appointed major-commandant. In that capacity he headed Burns's funeral the following year. In response to an enquiry about his health, in January 1795, Burns wrote his verse-epistle 'My honor'd Colonel, deep I feel' (C.W. p. 564). When it was proposed to raise funds for the Volunteers by a public subscription the following letter was drafted and signed by 25 of the members. The manuscript of this document is a transcript in the *Record for the Meetings and Proceedings of Royal Dumfries Volunteers* (1795-1802), now preserved in the Ewart Library, and though itself undated appears with the minutes of 19th May 1795. While Burns is not actually named as the author it has the unmistakeable hallmarks of his style.

Colonel De Peyster was something of a poet himself, and in 1813 published a collection of verse under the title *Miscellanies by an Officer*. He had a vigorous active life right up to the end, and died in 1822 as the result of an accident, at the age of 86.

(666)

Copy of the Letter received by the Major Commandant and referred to in the preceeding Minutes

Monday Evening
[18th May 1795]

Sir

From what we have learned of the proceedings of our Committee to day, we cannot help expressing our disapprobation of the mendicant business of asking a public contribution for defraying the expenses of our Association.— That our Secretary should have waited on those Gentlemen and others of that rank of life, who from the first, offered pecuniary assistance, meets our idea as highly proper but that the Royal Dumfries Volunteers should go a begging, with the burnt out Cottager and Ship-wrecked Sailor, is a measure of which we must disapprove.—

Please then, Sir, to call a meeting as soon as possible, and be so very good also as to put a stop to the degrading business, until the voice of the Corps be heard.

We have the honour to be
Your very humble Servant

Robt Primrose	Kinloch Winlaw
Sam Clark Junr	Thomas Gordon
Will Hyslop Junr	Robt Burns
James Grieve	James Gray
Robt Grainger	Will Hyslop
Wm Hamilton Junr	John McVitie
Robt Clugston	McCornock Junr
John Lawson Junr	John McMorine
William Johnston	George Grieve
	James Scott
	Jno Brand
	Riddle McNaught
	William Richardson
	Thomas Halliday
	John Weems
	Alexr Douglas

WILLIAM LORIMER, SENIOR

Born about 1750, he married Agnes Carson of Morton, Dumfriesshire in 1772 and settled at Craigieburn, near Moffat. His daughter Jean, the 'Chloris' of Burns's songs, was born in 1775. Subsequently the Lorimer family moved to Kemmishall, two miles from Ellisland, where they made Burns's acquaintance. In May 1791 Burns wrote to John Somerville in Edinburgh (see page 567) introducing Lorimer 'as a gentleman worth your knowing'. Within a few weeks, however, he was informed by Findlater that Lorimer was engaging in 'the dark manoeuvres of a smuggler'. Burns promised to be extra-vigilant thereafter (see page 540). Eventually Lorimer went bankrupt, lost his farm and moved into Dumfries. Burns was evidently not the cause of these reversals in fortune for, as the following letter shows, he and the Lorimers were on the best of terms in the last year of his life when recurring illness made him less sociable than heretofore. Douglas (1877) identified the guests at this dinner party as John Syme, Dr Maxwell, and Dr Mundell. One of the two Midlothian farmers was probably Robert Cleghorn. Mrs Hyslop of the Globe Inn, the poet's favourite howff, was aunt of Anna Park whose daughter, Elizabeth, was fathered by Burns in 1791.

(678)

[August 1795]

My dear Sir,—

I called for you yester-night, both at your own house, and at your favorite lady's—Mrs Hyslop of the Globe—but could not find you. I want you to dine with me to-day. I have two honest Midlothian Farmers with me, who have travelled threescore miles to renew old friendship with the poet; and I promise you a pleasant party, a plateful of hotch-potch and a bottle of good sound port.

Mrs Burns desired me yesternight to beg the favor of Jeany to come and partake with her, and she was so obliging as to promise that she would. Jeany and you are all the people, besides my Edinburgh friends, whom I wish to see; and if you can come I shall take it very kind.

Yours,
Robt Burns

(Dinner at three.)

JAMES ARMOUR

The poet's father-in-law, a prosperous master-mason and building contractor who is believed to have been responsible for the construction of Dumfries House (Cumnock), Skeldon House (Dalrymple) and numerous bridges in Ayrshire. His wife, Mary Smith, was the daughter of another mason in Mauchline. He is regarded as a rather dour, pharisaical individual whose original dislike of Burns was probably motivated more by the poet's radicalism and poor prospects, than on purely moral grounds. In March 1786, when apprised of his daughter's pregnancy, he fainted and his wife had to 'run for a cordial' to revive him. When he had recovered his composure Armour tried to get Burns's marriage annulled by mutilating the document which the poet had given Jean; and not content with that, instigated legal proceedings against him. Armour modified his attitude after Burns had achieved fame. Indeed, Burns was quite disgusted by Armour's 'new servility' when he visited Mauchline in the early summer of 1787. When Armour discovered that his daughter had become pregnant a second time his anger knew no bounds. Jean was summarily banished in disgrace, and it was not till late in the following February that Burns managed to arrange accommodation for her. Armour only became reconciled to Burns in August 1788, when the marriage between Burns and Jean was formally recognised by Mauchline Kirk Session. It is ironic that two of Burns's very last letters should be written to his old adversary. Mrs Armour was staying in Fife at the time, but hastened to Dumfries to help her daughter. It is interesting to note Burns signing the first letter 'Your most affectionate son'.

I (701)

10th July [1796]

For Heaven's sake & as you value the welfare of your daughter, & my wife, do, my dearest Sir, write to Fife to Mrs Armour to come if possible.–My wife thinks she can yet reckon upon a fortnight.–The Medical people order me, *as I value my existence,* to fly to seabathing & country quarters, so it is ten thousand chances to one that I shall not be within a dozen miles of her when her hour comes.–What a situation for her, poor girl, without a single friend by her on such a serious moment.–

I have now been a week at salt water, & though I think I have got some good by it, yet I have some secret fears that this business will be dangerous if not fatal.–

Your most affectionate son–
RBurns

II (710)

Dumfries, 18th July 1796

My dear Sir,

Do, for heaven's sake, send Mrs. Armour here immediately. My wife is hourly expecting to be put to bed. Good God! what a situation for her to be in, poor girl, without a friend! I returned from sea-bathing quarters to-day, and my medical friends would almost persuade me that I am better, but I think and feel that my strength is so gone that the disorder will prove fatal to me.

Your son-in-law,
R.B.

MISS GORDON

The following two letters were written by Burns on behalf of a farmer named Johnston who lived at Catlins 'near Dumfries', according to an endorsement dated 22nd March 1836. The only farm of that name, however, is about three miles north-east of Lockerbie. Chambers, who first published these letters in 1851, stated that the farmer was of Rockhall five miles east of Dumfries but did not give his name. Authority for the Catlins attribution was John Gibson of Whitehaven who possessed these letters when Chambers saw them in 1850. They are undated, and could have been written at any time during the poet's Dumfries period (1791-6).

I (713)

Madam,

what excuse to make for the liberty I am going to assume in this letter, I am utterly at a loss.—If the most unfeigned respect for your accomplished worth, if the most ardent attachment, if sincerity & truth—if these on my part, will in any degree weigh with you, my apology [*word missing*] is these & these alone.--Little as I have had the pleasure of your acquaintance it has been enough to convince me what enviable happiness must be his, whom you shall honor with your particular regard, & more than enough to inform me how unworthy I am to offer myself a candidate for that partiality. In this kind of trembling hope Madam, I intend very soon doing myself the honor of waiting on you; persuaded that however little Miss Gordon may be disposed to attend to the suit of a lover as unworthy of her as I am, she is still too good to despise an honest man, whose only fault, as to her, is loving her too much for his own peace.—

> I have the honor to be Madam,
> your most devoted humble servant
> Robt Burns

II (714)

Dear Madam—

The passion of love has need to be productive of much delight; as where it takes thorough possession of the man, it almost unfits him for anything else. The lover who is certain of an equal return of affection, is surely the happiest of men; but he who is a prey to the horrors of anxiety and dreaded disappointment, is a being whose situation is by no means enviable. Of this, my present experience gives me sufficient proof. To me, amusement seems impertinent, and business intrusion, while you alone engross every faculty of my mind. May I request you to drop me a line, to inform me when I may wait on you? For pity's sake, do; and let me have it soon. In the meantime, allow me, in all the artless sincerity of truth, to assure you, that I truly am,

> my dearest madam,
> your ardent lover, and devoted humble servant

UNIDENTIFIED CORRESPONDENTS

The following seven letters do not bear a superscription, and their recipients cannot be identified by the nature of the contents. Ferguson tentatively suggested Thomas Sloan as the addressee of the fourth letter (429), possibly on account of the reference to Robert Riddell. The publisher of the newspaper (691) is not known, nor the details of the 'poetic bagatelle' which was enclosed on that occasion. The lady to whom the undated letter (715) was addressed may not even have been an acquaintance of Burns at all, as it bears an endorsement of 1859 stating that it was written by Burns on behalf of someone else - a service which he occasionally performed for his friends. This letter was first collated by Professor Ross Roy, from the manuscript now in the Bachelors' Club, Tarbolton.

(180A)

[Enclosing *On the death of the late Lord President Dundas.*]

[C.W. p.300]

Edinburgh 16th January, 1788

I inclose you some verses I made on the loss, I am afraid irreparable loss, our Country sustains in the death of the late Lord President. Little new can be said, at this time of day, in Elegy.

Robt Burns

(207A)

[Edinburgh? December 1786-March 1788?]

Excuse me this short epistle- I was up yesternight untill four in the morning with Mr Nicol.- Expect a longer epistle on wedensday.- God bless you.-

Robt Burns

(275A)

Mauchline, 29th September 1788.

I send you the book, dear sir, along with this letter, by our Mauchline Carrier. I am just arrived from Nithsdale, jaded and fatigued to death; so I shall only say, the book is to me as a right hand, or a right eye, so I know you will take proper care of it and return it soon. Drop me a line, by post or return of Carrier, if the book comes to hand.

I am most truly, my dear sir,
Yours
Robt Burns

(429)

Ellisland, Friday morn:
[31st December 1790]

Dear Sir,

Can you come tomorrow & spend your New year day with us? I intend writing Captain Riddel soon, & would be glad you would furnish me with the specimen we spoke of. A Dieu je vous commende.

Robt Burns

Unidentified Correspondents

(454)

[Ellisland, 1791?]

Dear Sir,

I am exceedingly to blame in not writing you long ago; but the truth is, that I am the most indolent of all human beings; and when I matriculate in the Herald's office, I intend that my supporters shall be two sloths, my crest a slow-worm, and the motto, "Deil tak the foremost!" So much by way of apology for not thanking you sooner for your kind execution of my commission.

I would have sent you the poem: but somehow or other it found its way into the public papers, where you must have seen it. . . .

I am ever, dear Sir, yours sincereiy,
Robert Burns

(691)

Dumfries 25th February 1796

Sir

I have by accident seen two or three numbers of your Newspaper, & am so pleased with their honest independence & literary merit, that I wish to be included in the list of your Subscribers.—

Please let me have the very first paper you publish after receipt of this.—My address is Mr Burns, Dumfries.—Punctual payment you may depend on.—

On the other leaf you have a poetic bagatelle which, if worth a corner, is at your service.

I am, Sir, your very humble servant
Robt Burns

(715)

[Dumfries? late 1791-6]

Madam,

Will you forgive me this epistle?—In fact, whether you forgive me or not, I must on with it.—I am much mistaken of your heart, if you are capable of despising a poor fellow, whatever rank or position in life he may hold, whose only fault, to you is loving you too much for his peace.—That fault to you, Madam, has been very much mine, for some time past.—I have often wished to tell you so, but could never muster courage to do it; but now the murder is out, & if you should use me like a dog for this my plain declaration in the simplicity of my mood, I must insist, [but with? . . .] can nor wish to help it.—In Plain-dealing, Madam, for plain-dealing only I profess; whatever I am or have; full of imperfections as is the first, & little as may be the last; I beg leave to offer to share them with you in the honest, beaten path of Love & Honor.—

This address, you will say, is blunt; & so is, Madam, your most devoted humble servant

A FLYTING

The following is not a letter as such, but a literary exercise in the traditional Scottish form of a flyting. Who but the Scots would raise the employment of abusive language to the level of a fine art? The text was contributed to the *Gentleman's Magazine* (August 1832) by V.H., who said that it had been sent by Burns to William Cruikshank whose grand-daughter had married Dr Andrew Henderson of Berwick-upon-Tweed, in whose possession the manuscript then was. Both Ferguson and Ross Roy tentatively ascribe a date of 1791 to this document, though adding in a footnote that 1787 or 1788 seem more probable.

(455)

[1791?]

Literary Scolding—Hints—

Thou Eunuch of language—Thou Englishman who never was south the Tweed—Thou servile echo of fashionable barbarisms—Thou Quack, vending the nostrums of Empirical elocution—Thou Marriage-maker between vowels and consonants on the Gretna-green of Caprice—Thou Cobler, botching the flimsy socks of bombast Oratory—Thou Blacksmith, hammering the rivets of Absurdity—Thou Butcher, embruing thy hands in the bowels of Orthography—Thou Arch-heretic in Pronunciation—thou Pitch-pipe of affected Emphasis—Thou Carpenter, mortoising the aukward joints of jarring sentences—Thou squeaking dissonance of cadence—Thou Pimp of Gender—Thou Lyon-Herald to silly Etymology—Thou Antipode of Grammar—Thou executioner of Construction—Thou brood of the speech-distracting builders of the tower of Babel—Thou lingual confusion worse confounded—Thou scape-gallows from the land of Syntax—Thou scavenger of mood and tense—Thou murderous Accoucheur of Infant-learning—Thou Ignisfatuus, misleading the steps of benighted Ignorance—Thou Pickleherring in the puppet-show of Nonsense—Thou faithful recorder of barbarous idiom—Thou Persecutor of Syllabication—Thou baleful meteor, foretelling and facilitating the rapid approach of Nox and Erebus—

APPENDIX I
CURRIE'S LIST OF LETTERS TO BURNS

The following list was compiled by, or on behalf of, Dr. James Currie in the course of preparing his 1800 edition of *The Works of Robert Burns.* It is an inventory of some, if not all, of the letters addressed to Burns which were in his possession when he died. Each letter was numbered, with brief details of the date and place of despatch and the name of the sender. These details were accompanied by short summaries of the contents, the whole amounting to some 56 folio sheets. Regrettably this important manuscript was badly damaged by damp and the precis of contents in particular has suffered as a result. The manuscript eventually came into the hands of the Trustees of the Birthplace Museum, at Alloway, by whose kind permission the List was published in full in the 1933 *Burns Chronicle* (pp. 20-75). Apart from immense general interest, this List is invaluable for the light it sheds on correspondents to whom no letters from Burns are known to exist. It must be assumed, however, that the letters which Burns received from them were either in reply to letters from him, or were letters that the poet subsequently answered; so that this fact alone should alert us to the possible existence of many other letters of Burns hitherto unrecorded.

ALPHABETICAL LIST OF CORRESPONDENTS' NAMES

References are to letter numbers in Currie's List

____te [Thomas White?] : 91
Ainslie (Robert) 116
Anderson (Dr. James) 164
Armour (James) 273

Baillie (Robert) 275
Baird (Revd. George H.) 176
Ballantyne (John) 9
Benson (Anna Dorothea) 235, 294
Blacklock (Revd. Thomas) 26, 83, 113(2), 163
Blair (David) 79
Blair (Dr. Hugh) 16
Brown (John) 239
Brown (Richard) 45, 46, 47, 70, 72, 120, 129
Bruntins (Miss) 228
Buchan (Earl of) 187, 195, 196, 247, 248, 257, 270
Burgess (Revd. John) 89
Burns (Gilbert) 84, 87, 92, 103, 106, 112, 134, 138, 144, 150, 153, 172, 245, 285
Burns (William) 88, 149

Campbell (Cha.) 65
Candlish (James) 33
Canongate-Kirk-funds (Managers of) 12
Carfrae (Revd. Patrick) 77

Chalmers (Margaret) 32, 204(2), 278, 283; as Mrs. Lewis Hay: 207, 290
Clark (Samuel) *jun.* 99
Clarke (Stephen) 223
Cleghorn (Robert) 50, 58, 85, 166, 177, 271
Corbet (William) 175
Coutts (Alexander) 184
Craik (Helen) 286, 289, 297, 298
Craik (William) 203
Creech (William) 36, 37, 39, 42, 43, 80(1), 188, 190, 213, 214, 222, 232, 279
Cruickshank [Cruikshank] (William) 62, 75, 124, 155
Cummyng (James) 29
Cunningham (Alexander) 59, 60, 76, 95, 127, 136, 139, 147, 152, 154, 159, 167(2), 171, 179, 182, 183(1), 192, 211, 212, 216, 240, 243, 262, 268, 269, 274
Cunningham (Lady Elizabeth) 135, 167(1), 198, 209
Cunningham (Sir William) 137

Dalziel (Alexander) 5, 8, 13, 158, 169, 186, 209
Davies (Deborah Duff) 197
Dick (J.) 41
Don (Lady Harriet) 201

Douglas (Lady Mary) 267
Dunbar (William) 15, 48, 54, 90, 148, 160
Dunlop (Anthony) 49
Dunlop (Mrs. Frances A.) 220, 244, 276(2)
Elliot (Cha.) 40

Fall (Mrs.) 44
Fergusson (Tho.) 10, 14
Fontenelle (Louisa) 272
Fowler (John) 82

Geddes (Bishop John) 81
Graham (Revd. John) 244
Graham (Robert of Fintry) 68, 102, 140,
    161, 206, 217, 227, 246, 250, 276(1)
Graham (Robert) *jun.* 162
Graham (Mrs. Robert) 156, 205
Grant (D.) 117: Letter to D. G.
Gregory (Prof. James) 97
Grose (Capt. Francis) 174
Guion (F. J.) 233
Hamilton (Gavin) 1
Hamilton (Mrs.) 111
Hay (Mrs. Lewis)
    See Chalmers (Margaret)
Hill (Peter) 61, 69, 80(2), 100, 107, 109,
    128, 146, 181, 191, 210, 215, 258, 264,
    266
Hooper (Sam) 259
Hoy (James) 28
Hutchison (John) 2, 71

Johnson (Caroline Isabella) 288
Johnson (James) 67, 73, 119, 121, 141, 236
Johnston (Capt. William) 224
Joy (Henry) 226

Kennedy (James) 118, 126
Kennedy (John) 122, 168
Kennedy (Margaret) 4

Lawrie (Revd. George) 1

Little (Revd. James) 189
Little (Janet) 115, 292
Lockhart (George) 123

Mabane (Isabella) 281, 284
McAdam (John) 6
McIndoe (Robert) 63, 64
Mackenzie (Henry) 280, 282
Macleod (Isabella) 287
Macleod (John) 255, 260, 263

McMurdo (Jane) 242
Macnab (W. G.) 208
Marshall (Jean) 241
Masterton (Allan) 125, 132(2)
Maxwell (Provost Robert) 131
Meikle (William) 101
Miller (Patrick) 3, 193, 237
Miller (Patrick) *jun.* 253, 265
Mitchell (And.) 22
Mitchell (Ja.) 113(1)
Moore (Dr. John) 11, 18, 21, 98, 183(2),
    254, 261
Muir (Robert) 7
Mullar (Luke) 249
Murdoch (John) 27
Murray (James) 170

Nicol (William) 66, 133, 145, 151, 231
Niven (Alexander) 53
Niven (William) 35

Oswald (Mrs.) 299, 300

Parker (William) 56

Queensberry (Duke of) 202

Ramsay (David) 74
Ramsay (John) 24, 25, 26
Reid (William) 225
Renwick (John) 130
Riddell (Mrs. Maria) 234
Riddell (Capt. Robert) 86, 173
Riddell (Robert Andrew) 256
Robertson (Major William) 296
Rose (Mrs. Elizabeth) 31
Ross (Sawney) 291

Scott (Mrs. Elizabeth) 34, 38
Sillar (David) 114
Skinner (Revd. John) 30, 51
Sloan (Thomas) 142
Smellie (William) 238, 251
Smith (John) 57
Sommerville (John) 55
Staig (Jessy) 295
Stewart (Bell) 52
Stewart (Mrs. General) 17
Stewart (T.) 178
Stewart (William) 110, 230
Stokes (W.) 293
Stuart (Peter) 93, 94, 105
Sutherland (George S.) 78, 143, 165
Syme (John) 301

728

Telford (Thomas) 219
Tennant (William) 23
Thompson (Samuel) 185, 252
Thomson (George) 218
Touch (Dr.) 157
Tytler (Alexander Fraser) 180, 204(1), 221.
    277

Walker (Josiah) 20
White (Thomas?) 229
Whitefoord (Sir John) 96, 199
Williams (Helen Maria) 19, 108
Williamson (John B.) 302
Wilson (Alexander) 132(1), 194
Wyat (Robert) 104

Young (Revd. Walter) 25

No. Date   *From whom*
      1786
1   St. Margaret's Hill
      6 September   Revd. George Lawrie to Gavin Hamilton

Inclosing an extract of one from Dr. . . . poems & regrets his inability to clothe
hi . . . time before read him three of the poems — . . . edition being all sold off,
the Doctor advise . . . extensive circulation. — Q. Is this the letter . . .

2   Jamaica
      10 July
      (Received 23 September)   John Hutchison

Has recd. one from Burns dated D . . . Will be glad to return the kindness . . .
B. in the planting line, tho' he must . . . good advice. — Thanks for account h . . .

3   Dalswinton
      4 October [1787]   P. Miller Esqr., Senr.

Ask Burns to come & look at . . . it if a better offer has occurred . . .

4   Mauchline
      15 October   Miss M. Kennedy

A card of thanks for a song

5   Frome
      1 November   Mr. Alexander Dalziel

Rejoices that he has given up his . . . Has laid a copy of his poems before . . .
& his wishes to befriend their author — & . . . unpublished manuscripts —
Dalziel . . .

6   Berbeth
      7 November   Jo. McAdam of Craigengillan

Requesting three copies of the new edi . . .

7   17 December   Robert Muir, Kilmarnock

Dalziel's conduct had at first see . . . given the bard — Description of . . . his
success in Edinr. Introduc . . . & commissions 60 copies of the . . . forward it.

8   Irvine
      22 December   Alex. Dalziel

Capt. Hamilton of Bourtreehill . . . is perfectly right—) & that the Cale . . . tion
papers — Advises him to get h . . .

9   Ayr
      30 December   John Ballantyne

Wants subscription bills — Gratifie . . . for the consequences of a sudden
chang . . . opinion of the excise scheme that . . . Asks for proofsheets of his new
poem . . .

1787

10 Wr. Callie
   22 January   Tho. Fergusson

Answer of a letter to Janet Ramsay spouse to . . . ter in the wicked city —
2dly hearing that she ha . . . to Burns for advising her home — 4th The Girl . . .
will be a dutiful child in time to come — 5th July . . . letter is indorsed
"Poor Bell Stewart!"

11 Clifford Street
   23 January   Dr. Moore

Complains of Mrs. Dunlop for shewing B . . . from the irritability ascribed to
poets by Ho . . . Admires his Patriotism & Humanity & Indepe . . . Scotland —
Congratulates the bard in the pa˙. . . inclosed to a Mr. Morthland, Advocate,
a So . . . Daisy." Presents Burns with his "View . . .

12 22 February   Managers of the Canongate-Kirk-funds

Edict granting liberty to Burns to erect . . .

13 Irvine
   8 March   Alex. Dalziel

Has dispersed some subscription-bills . . . with reluctance — More information
. . . cairn — a truly good man — Mentions . . . tich referring to it from Butler's
tomb — . . . 18d. for a copy of his works! — Ask . . . Understands Burns is in
great req ˙. . .

14 Wester Callie
   17 March   Tho. Fergusson

Bell Stewart has been cordially . . . will write herself soon —

15 St. David's Street
   20 March   Will. Dunbar, W.S.

Approves of an alteration B. has made in . . . requests to meet him at a mason
lodge . . .

16 Argyle Street
   4 May   Dr. Blair

Thanks B. for his portrait — Is ha . . . Ossian's poems into notice & con . . .
that Burns has stood his charge . . . his future conduct — Is happy . . .

17 22 May   Mrs. Stewart of Stair

A card which had inclosed a po . . .

18 Clifford Street
   23 May   Dr. Moore

Burns thought it incumbent . . . — money each had subscribed . . . Observations
on the new edition — . . . script pieces which his friends had p . . . farm & hopes
he will not forsake . . .

731

19 London
    20 June   Miss H. M. Williams

Writes (for Dr. Moore) to thank Burn . . . is Scotch & the dialect is familiar
to her — . . . of them —

20 Athole House
    30 September   Mr. Josiah Walker

Describes the impression Burns . . . mention of a stratagem devised by the . . .
— Miss Cathcart's generosity & sensibility on . . . Bids Burns seize the pencil &
paint th . . . When he visits Octertyre, Mr. & Mrs. Graham of Bal . . . possession
— The Dutchess wishes to see the Letter to . . .

21 Clifford Street
    30 September   Dr. Moore

Acknowledges receiving his letter of 2d . . . to the name of Poet —

22 London
    6 October   And. Mitchell

Solicits liberty to publish Burn's . . . "dainty Rob" in Scotch verse —

23 Glenconner
    14 October   Will. Tennant

A Preacher of the Gospel solicit . . . him a kirk —

24 Ochtertyre
    22 October   John Ramsay of Ochtertyre

Neither the words of "Down the burn . . . Incloses inscription & a letter to . . .
& [which] Mr. R. recommends as the sub . . . ting the plot — & the study
requisite . . . ing to a farm — Advises him to . . . him to keep clear of satire
— reflec . . . Her poem is a specimen of . . .

25 Ochtertyre   Mr. Ramsay to
    22 October   Rev^d. Walter Young at Erskine

Inclosed in the above — Introd . . . or songs — Begs Mr. Y. to shew Burns . . .
words, hopes to see one sung on the . . .

26 Ochtertyre
    27 October   John Ramsay to Dr. Blacklock

Thanks the Dr. for introducing B . . . as a boarder — Col. Geo. Craw . . .
"The Bush aboon Traquair" . . . Stewart of Castle-milk — . . .

27 London
    28 October   John Murdoch

Burns's poems often quoted . . . great city would furnish matt . . . time in the
literary world & asks . . . his childn. in the state into [which] th . . . the welfare
of all the family of Burns . . .

28　Gordon Castle
　　31 October　　　　　　　　　James Hoy

Sends "Cauld kail" to Johnston's C . . . lished — The Dutchess of Gordon
ascribe . . . author, wished it had been written in Scotc . . . on Gordon Castle
& the family —

29　Lyon Office　　　　　　　　James Cummyng,
　　14 November　　　　　　　　Keeper of the Lyon records

Certificate of the arms of *Burn*

30　Linshart
　　14 November　　　　　　　　John Skinner

A classical education does not create . . . & unassisted, it has a prior claim to
adm . . . getting the black gown he ceased to exercis . . . favorite tunes — Can
be of little assistance . . . from his own pen, one to the tune of "Dun . . . the
other to the stanza of "Tune your fiddl . . . writer in Edinr. — Mentions a song
by . . . Has heard of another by a plowman to the . . . Advises B. not to sheathe
his own weap . . . than dozens from clergymen like hi . . .

31　Kilravock-Castle
　　30 November　　　　　　　　Mrs. Rose

Incloses some highland songs . . . seems to have escaped the confus . . . ship will
maintain the ground . . .

32　Harvieston
　　1 December　　　　　　　　　Miss Chalmers

Incloses an answer to an inq . . . has complimented her in a song . . . may not
publish it — Hopes his aff . . . to Mauchline — inquires if he has got . . . of
hers — & if he has read "Las Incas" wh . . .

33　Glasgow
　　4 December　　　　　　　　　James Candlish

Incloses "Pompey's Ghost" which . . . attempt to give the world a com . . . those
of antiquity & gives the p . . .

34　Waughope
　　27 December　　　　　　　　Mrs. Scott

Had written him a letter in . . . mountains had elevated his imagi . . . Once began
a parody on "The rock . . . pickle ink — wishes B. wd. carry . . . impartial
opinion of her poetry —

　　1788
35　Maybole
　　3 January　　　　　　　　　　Will. Niven

Compts. of the season — Sorry to hear he . . . matches they had had at Kirkoswald
school — . . . their oratory — Congratulates him on his success . . . make himself
known to the great of this kingd .. . the height of his ambition — independancy
— by the tim . . .

36   Edinburgh
     14 January   Creech

Apologises for not calling to see him in his c . . . in half an hour after —

37   Edinburgh
     19 January   Do.

Must leave town on Monday if not inc . . .

38   Waughope
     23 January   Mrs. Scott

Thanks Burns for "owning her relation to th . . . a beautiful ballad long known
& admired — In . . . professed receptacle of the rhyming tribe — Lady . . . Gilbert's
kindness to her by introducing him to . . . no one else —

39   Edinburgh
     23 January   Creech

Important affairs have retarded the se . . . go about his business & the acct. will
be se . . .

40   Dalkeith
     31 January

                                   Cha. Elliot

Incloses "Ca' the ewes to the knows" . . . lads o' Gala water"

41   Dalkeith
     31 January   J. Dick

An attempt to address the bard . . .

42   Friday afternoon   Creech

Promises on his honor to bring . . .

43   Edinburgh
     13 February   Do.

A manly, & seemingly candid . . . ten him —

44   Dunbar
     13 February   Mrs. Fall

The perplexity of her husband's affairs h . . . -tunate Shepherdess" — which,
however, Mrs. Sin . . .

45   Greenock
     13 February   Richd. Brown

Has anxiously expected to see him . . . Promises to accompany him to Ayrshire
. . . that has detained him in Edinr.

46   Greenock
     28 February   Do.

Will forward Burns' book across . . . Asks how he felt at meeting Jean . . .

47   Greenock
     16 March   Do.

Is detained by unforeseen accidents . . . burn, a passionate admirer of B . . . excise-commission having been signed . . . plan —

48   St. David's Street
     17 March   Will Dunbar

Thanks him for his visit. Presents him . . . Hamilton when B. has got to his farm . . .

49   London
     6 April   Anthy. Dunlop

Regrets that he is prevented from culti . . . cessity he is under of leaving the island . . . mends "Zadig" & "Candid" — Hopes to hear . . . Coila to which she is very partial — This to . . .

50   Saughton Mills
     27 April   Rob. Cleghorn

Thanks for sending a song to his favorite "C . . . after the fatal battle of Culloden — Offers to ass . . .

51   Linshart
     28 April   Rev^d. John Skinner

Thanks for a present — expresses esteem — In . . . Buchan plowman beginning "Some sings of . . . Song" beginning "O why should old age so mu . . . tive of his own sentiments — He had dabbled in . . . green" & "Batrachomyomachia."

52   2 April   Bell Stewart

"Cannot stay with her mother"?—

53   Sundrum
     20 May   Alexr. Niven

Burns had promised to write his epitaph . . . book — Hears B. has undergone a wonderfu . . . good letter"—

54   Edinburgh
     27 May   Will. Dunbar

Is afflicted with excessive sensibility

55   Edinburgh
     30 May   John Sommerville

Fears Creech is incapable of disinter . . . Congratulates him on his marriage . . .

56   Kilmarnock
     18 June   Will. Parker

Would write in poetry if he could — . . . had sent him from Edinburgh — . . .

57   Glasgow
     9 July   John Smith

Bookseller in Glasgow's Account —

58   Saughton Mills
      21 July   Robt. Cleghorn

Thanks for the "Chevalier's Lament" & . . . to write something in the memory of the . . . to night — Sir James Foulis a great . . . the sooner the better

59   James' Square,
      Edinburgh
      7 May   A. Cunningham

Passed a day lately with Cleghorn witho . . . more than two present — The society in . . . & judgement — asks B. to give him a hear . . . on the war at the Society" & is not a hopel . . . sonnet

60   James' Square,
      Edinburgh
      21 July   A. Cunningham

Asks if Burns had recd. the above letter . . . poem he had asked him to transcribe . . . ever she was there again — C. respects . . . B.'s new productions that he may shew the . . . above — is more distractedly enamoured . . . mends Syme to his acquaintance — C. ha . . .

61   Edinburgh
      24 July   Peter Hill

A Friend sends him Cowper's Poems vol. 2d. — The . . . -ther that he has got — Sends 3 of Smollet's works — thi . . . enquires if it is his — & asks for a compleat . . .

62   Edinburgh
      26 July   W. Cruickshank

Thanks him for a present — congratu . . . B.'s poems [which] he cannot compare to Gr . . . to the best in antiquity — Mentions a pe . . . prosecution for calling the rector a foo

63   Glasgow
      7 August   Robert McIndoe

With 15 yds. Black Lutstring for *her Lady* . . .

64   Glasgow
      13 August   Robert McIndoe

Has recd. the price of the above Lutst . . . William, a cheel & a lass —

65   Hilsea Barracks
      13 August   Cha: Campbell

Indolence has been the cause of . . . varied & he is pleased with the . . . revisit Scotland before his departure for . . . among the English — Begs some poe

66   Edinburgh
      18 August   Will. Nicol

Thanks for a cheese — Had heard Fintry . . . £100 a year — Approves of his marriage . . . up the name of the lady who said he . . .

67 Edinburgh
28 August   James Johnson

Acknowledgements of favors received . . . lication — He incloses the notes of the . . .

68 George's Street
14 September   Graham of Fintry

Had received the verses address . . . charge of improper conduct preferred ag . . . case Burns will get his present pla . . . rent was — observations on farming, in . . . This is the answer to that of Burns . . .

69 Edinburgh
16 September   Peter Hill

Had recd. B.'s original & diverting . . . of the Courant offers to send the Paper gr . . .

70 Port Glasgow
28 September   Richd. Brown

Just arrived with his vessel — Inquires . . .

71 Jamaica, St. Ann's
15 October   John Hutchison

Thanks for the 2d Editn. of his poems . . . & procured him the friendship of the . . . Clergy. Hackneyed arguments for the conti . . . of [which] Burns will see his own poems —

72 Port Glasgow
15 November   Richd. Brown

The "Ode to Spring" had been pro . . . is anxious to see Burns & is passionately atta . . . ling Castle" with the answer by "Maxwell poet in P . . .

73 Edinburgh
19 November   James Johnson

Had recd. two good additions to his Collection . . . to chuse tunes to [which] he may adapt word . . . B. a list in his last

74 Edinburgh
24 November   David Ramsay

Has recd. a volume of poems [which] he will . . . depend on secrecy when he trusts him w . . . a jeu d'esprit on the revolution —

75 Edinburgh
13 December   W. Cruickshank

Had recd. a piece of B.'s manufacture . . . situation — He had made too free with . . . is made a magistrate — is a patron . . . is still pleaing wt. Nicol. Burns m . . .

737

1789

76 Edinburgh
    5 January   A. Cunningham

In the dumps — His betroth'd . . .

77 Morham
    2 January   The Rev^d. Pat. Carfrae

Character of Mylne the Poet — . . . 8vo vol. Transmits verses he wrote . . . some periodical work — The anti . . .

78 Dumfries
    5 January   Geo. S. Sutherland

The actor — thanks him for the lines he . . . "the blue-eyed lassie," but Scotch words . . . The pedantry of the Scotch had exclude . . . enthusiastic love of Shakespeare & proposes . . . Garrick is his model, but he disdains . . .

79 Birmingham
    4 February   Dav. Blair

Acknowledges a letter from B . . . to Birmingham soon

80 Edinburgh
(1) 6 February   Mr. Creech

Will be happy to see him — If B . . . price, Creech will do the rest — Inclo . . .

80 Edinburgh
(2) 9 February   P. Hill

Acknowledges an excellent letter — Is . . . general subject of conversation in London — Ther . . . poems — Urges him to it.

81 Blackfriar's Wynd,
    Edinburgh
    12 February   Bp. Geddes

Acknowledges receipt of B.'s poems & poe . . . is married — hopes to see him & his Jean in the . . . was then in Ayrshire — This letter shews mu . . .

82 Ballybay, Ireland
    15 February   John Fowler

A country-man of B. — Hears he is comp . . . & offers his services in procuring Subscription . . .

84 Mossgiel
    3 March   Gilbert Burns

On farming business — intends writing . . .

85 Edinburgh
    11 March   Rob. Cleghorn

Has sent 2 Bolls of seed Tares, & gives directio . . . book for Burns to fill for him — Mr. Dunbar . . .

86　Friars Carse
　　16 March　　　　　　　　　Capt. Riddell

Sends books for the new library — Hopes . . . illiterate & superstitious neighbours — As soon . . . paper —

87　Mossgiel
　　18 March　　　　　　　　　Gilbert Burns

The road to Sanquhar impassible — business . . . Mentions "MacGill's commemoration . . . pistle from the Pope to W. — . . . to publish —

88　Sunday
　　22 March　　　　　　　　　Wm. Burns

Sends for his hat & fine shirt — . . .

89　Kirkmichael
　　25 March　　　　　　　　　Reverend Dr. Burgess

Sends a list of 56 songs inserted in the . . .

90　Edinburgh
　　26 March　　　　　　　　　W. Dunbar

Inclosing verses on the King's *suppose* . . . Ld. Hailes's selection of Scottish poems . . . his engagements to assist Johnson —

91　Dumfries
　　30 March　　　　　　　　　—te [Thomas White?]

Inclosing a paper he had written . . . admission into the Journal to which it . . . exert himself in behalf of the bard, tho' he . . .

92　Mossgiel
　　7 April　　　　　　　　　　Gilbert Burns

Farming — Wants his mother home — . . .

93　London
　　16 April　　　　　　　　　P. Stuart, Editor of the Morning Star

Thanks him for the honour of corresp . . . peared in the paper — Will send Burns . . .

94　London
　　17 April　　　　　　　　　Do.

Apologising for an alteration he had made . . .

95　26 April　　　　　　　　　A. Cunningham

Miss Hutson at Melville Mill the . . . no danger of being again intrapped — Inquires . . . into Stuart's Star — Has seen B.'s letters in the . . . the Gazetteer — & intreats B. to have nothing . . . Cumm.'s conduct agt. the aspersions of Mrs. Dew . . .

96　Edinburgh
　　29 May　　　　　　　　　　Sir John Whiteford

Returning a verdict in favor of "The Fête . . . be tried by a Jury

97 Edinburgh
    2 June   J. Gregory

Thanks Burns for sending his "Wounded . . . a Mrs. Hunter as being correct & highly p . . . he reveres "the iron justice of Dr. Gregory" . . .

98 Clifford Street
    10 June   Dr. Moore

Advises Burns to correct, polish, select, & . . . & offers his services in promoting the su . . . B.'s impartial opinion of it — N.B. There . . .

99 Dumfries
    24 June   Sam. Clark, Junr.

Inclosing "Riddell's Acct. of the . . . decanter, & presenting another in . . .

100 Edinburgh
    1 July   Peter Hill

Has recd. Miss Carmichael's Poems . . . the girl — Sends a copy of "Shakes . . . B.'s picture is framed & ready to se . . .

101 Dumbarton
    13 July   William Meikle

Letter from a poor man im . . .

102 Edinburgh
    19 July   Graham of Fintry

In consequence of B.'s "Wounded hare" . . . Asks B. to concert a plan for his promotion wh . . . he has read . . . will forward a new . . . be able . . . Mr. Smith himself . . .

103 Mossgiel
    26 July   Gilbert Burns

Sends a cheese & books — Observation . . .

104 Carlisle
    1 August   Robert Wyat

Sends Burns a copy of his "The . . . nal as a monument of the friend . . . the utility of memoirs of great me . . . busy preparing to take holy orders . . .

105 London
    5 August   P. Stuart

Informs B. that he has resigned . . . with the instance B. has given of his . . . intimate Friend of Stuart's — Character . . .

106 Mossgiel
    6 August   Gilbert Burns

Private affairs — Congratulates him . . . go into the excise, but not to abando . . . management of the latter.

107 Edinburgh
    7 April   Peter Hill

Cleghorn has a MS. of B.'s which he ... Morng. Star — A certain magistrate ...
books & a nonsensical pamplet [which] ... MSS. — This letter was misdated ...

108 London
    7 August   Miss Williams

Approves of B.'s criticism of her poem except in ... mired, not only by her, but
by everybody.

109 Edinburgh
    8 August   Peter Hill

Condoles with him on his hypochondr ... has not finished his picture —
Smellie's ... Poems out of print.

110 Closeburn-Castle
    4 August   Will. Stewart

Incloses buttons from Collr. M ...

111 Shaws
    13 August   Mrs. Hamilton

Incloses a letter from Dr. Moore — ... & another to Mrs. Dunlop — He thought
Bu ... waits for his opinion of Zeluco that he ...

112 Mossgiel
    18 August   Gilbert Burns

Has seen B.'s ballad — & is please ... so harshly, as he had shewn him favor
... on the Douglas, Heron & co. bank. M ...

113 Carlisle
(1)   21 August   Mr. Ja. Mitchell

With Bed-Furniture — Had recd. ...

113 Edinburgh
(2)   24 August   Dr. Blacklock

In poetry — Inquires into his ... & spirits

114 Irvine
    29 August   David Sillar

Is going to print 1000 copies of his own ... posing — Sends the letter by a Mr.
R ... marine character —

115 Loudon-House
    12 July   Jenny Little

The rhyming Scotch Milkmaid, has sp ... Mrs. Henri, daughter to Mrs. Dunlop
— Transcri ...

116 Lethim
    19 September   Rob. Ainslie, W.S.

Writes from a farm-house on a . . . B. had sent for her — The cares of . . . before him — Anecdote of a cobler . . . woman —

117 Ayr
    23 September   *To* Mr. D. Grant

An extract from the English review . . . quests to have a sight of the book —

118 Glenlee Mill
    24 September   James Kennedy

Had been almost sent *"to the stygian* . . . cure him the school of Dunscore — but . . . dyke, that he may raise money to prov . . . if safely delivered.

119 Edinburgh
    25 September   James Johnson

Will expunge, as desired, the song of "Ces . . . land hills I hied" — Requests words for a fre . . . Asks for a preface & index & begs B. to return . . .

120 Port-Glasgow
    5 October   Richd. Brown

Has arrived from his 2d voyage to the . . . vision, as he hears government have augment . . . & wishes he could fall in with B. in his way — Pr . . . delivery of a boy.

121 Edinburgh
    16 October   James Johnson

Had sent B. 20 proofs more of his third . . .

122 Dumfries-house
    7 October   John Kennedy

Requesting a copy of Burns's song about . . . ly at Dumfries-house

123 Glasgow
    12 October   Geo. Lockhart

Invective against the persecutors of D . . . subject — Advises Burns to improve . . .

124 Edinburgh
    12 October   Cruickshank

Congratulates him on his excise appo . . . A brother of C.'s is also in the excise . . . to temptations too powerful for him to resist . . . duty. C.'s cousin Cormack has suffered for . . . at war with Adam — Proposes this cor . . .

125 Edinburgh
    17 October   Allan Masterton

Sore eyes have been epidemical in Edin . . . got it from them by dint of sympathy . . . applied to for the names of the auth . . . the occasion — & hopes to hear soon if . . .

126 Glenlee-Mill,
near New Galloway
19 October   Ja. Kennedy

Makes farther enquiries relative to Duns . . . building is of more service than learn
. . . asks for his Greek Grammar —

127 James's Square
26 October   Alexander Cunningham

A song of B.'s has been admired by C.'s . . . have been singularly tried in love-
affair . . . ject of a poem — But advises B. not to . . . Promises to send an
excellent . . .

128 Edinburgh
28 October   Peter Hill

Promises to send books commissi . . .

129 Port Glasgow
29 October   Richd. Brown

Has had no answer to his last — Is go . . . had the prospect of meeting B. there . . .

130 Kirkurd
30 October   John Renwick

School-master at Kirkurd near B . . . *weese* or door-cheekbield, at a count . . .
ther poem on the same subject, for . . .

131 Lochmaben
5 November   Provost Maxwell

Tries to thank Burns in metre for . . .

132 Edinburgh
(1)   8 November   Alex. Wilson

A youth — A stranger — expresses in . . .

132 Edinburgh
(2)   16 November   Allan Masterton

Thanks Burns for introducing him in a song . . .

133 Edinburgh
27 November   Wm. Nicol

Wishes to examine the farm of Lagg . . . Little Masterton the writing master, . . .
of a pupil of his, heiress to £800 a year —

134 Mossgiel
29 November   Gilbert Burns

Sympathizes with his brother on his *alarming* pain . . . Is too much in the dumps
to think of ma . . . sinking soul as himself to encumber himself . . . may give
to Miss M. or Miss B. — Had given . . . son of *singit Sawney* bids fair to be a
clever p . . . Holy Willy —

135 Coates
   9 December   Lady B. Cunningham

Incloses a poem which she think p . . . Her brother has heard that B. intends publi . . .

136 Edinburgh
   9 December   A. Cunningham

Sends "Johnston's thoughts on Farming . . . the poem on "Mary" — Incloses a poem in . . . promise of writing a parody of the lines . . .

137 Auchenskieth
   13 December   Sir W. Cunningham

Thanks B. for his poem on the British . . . a hearty welcome at his house — Has some . . . arrival — Offers his services to Gilbert . . . be happy to serve the bard —

138 Mossgiel
   13 December   Gilbert Burns

His prospects are gloomy & depress him . . . Mrs. Alexander — Inquires about his . . .

139 Edinburgh
   17 December   A. Cunningham

Some account of the "Je ne scai . . .

140 Edinburgh
   17 December   Robt. Graham of Fintry

Answer to a letter of Burns (Folio 91) inclo . . . Among others that "on Dr. Macgill" — "on Capt . . . & a song or elegy, which last Mr. & Mrs. . . . He will send others —

141 Edinburgh
   22 December   James Johnson

Wishes B. to return some proofs he . . . to his work he must look to Burns who . . .

142 Tuesday Eve.   T. Sloan

Burns had entrusted Sloan with some . . . that secret was already publicly known, writes . . .

143 Sunday   G. Sutherland

the player — Multiplicity of business preven . . . they will "have their *hurl* together" — Mrs. S . . . may perfect himself in it —

144 Mossgiel
   Sunday Eve.   Gilbert Burns

Private farming business — will inclose a . . . thering B.'s old books at this time —

1790
145 Edinburgh
2 January   Will. Nicol

On receiving B.'s letter, he purchased . . . enjoys so many blessings & has such
. . . he can for his (N.'s) old mare — a duel in . . .

146 Edinburgh
13 January   Peter Hill

Is anxious to hear from Burns —

147 Edinburgh
28 January   A. Cunningham

Is anxious to hear from Burns . . . fries Journal — C. is B.'s champion whe . . .

148 Edinburgh
4 February   Will. Dunbar

The projected trip to Ellisland is deferred . . . & misses a pretty little song B. &
he ha . . . for the 4th vol. — D. appproves of B.'s adoption . . . customs —

149 London
21 March   Wm. Burns

Has been in London nearly three weeks . . . workmen, & there is little encourag . . .
he hopes with industry & temperance to be enabled to . . . shirts & an Ayrshire-
cheese — He will have . . . Scotch acquaintances — Has heard . . . London in
his next —

150 Mossgiel
2 April   Gilbt. Burns

Returns "the rural economy of Gloster . . . cheese-making — Observations on
cows . . . excellent dairy . . .

151 Edinburgh
11 May   W. Nicol

Begs Burns not to distress him . . . N. bought her imposed upon him . . . is called
limestone on the . . . such as he hopes they are . . .

152 Edinburgh
25 May   A. Cunningham

Miss Burnet is in the . . . of Burns's late productions . . . of Miss M. A. Johnston
has cured . . . Has shewn the correspondence on . . . Heiress &c. who admired
B.'s letter so much . . .

153 Mossgiel
31 May   Gilbt. Burns

Rural economy — friendly —

154 Edinburgh:
James' Square
7 June   A. Cunningham

inclosing a letter from Dr. . . .

155 Edinburgh
    5 July   W. Cruickshank

Had received an enlarged edition of . . . Begs leave to publish it in the Courant
. . . who lives in the same place with C.'s brothe . . . is appointed school-master
of Mid-Calder . . .

156 5 July   Mrs. Graham of Fintry
                                       "The lovely Matron"

Thanks for a poem & the handsome . . . loss whether to admire his poetry or
his p . . . last winter — The whole of this letter e . . .

157 Edinburgh
    13 July   Dr. Touch

Requesting a copy of "Holy Willy"

158 Finlayston
    21 July   Alex. Dalziel

Requesting the particulars of Miss . . . cretly attached — Ld. Glencairn is go . . .
Fears he will be unsuccessful — W . . . of independence, but of late every . . .

159 James' Square
    Edinburgh
    22 July   A. Cunningham

Criticism on "Q. Mary's Lam . . . & country burials —

160 Edinburgh
    Tea-time, 5th dish,
    2 August   Will. Dunbar

Begs permission to get the . . . Compts. to Capt. Riddell . . .

161 Excise Office
    17 August   Graham of Fintry

Mr. Grose had recommended . . . to Dundee where Gr. wd. . . . Had intended
visiting B. & Close . . .

162 Edinburgh   Robert Graham,
    30 August   Junr., of Fintry

"Sir — My father desires me to send . . . *Theory of Moral Sentiments*, wh . . .

163 Edinburgh
    1 September   Dr. Blacklock

in rhyme — Solicits B. . . . Burns commence Supervisor . . .

164 Cotfield, near Edinburgh
    2 September   Dr. Anderson

Incloses his prospectus — requests . . . work when it shall be published . . .

165 Greenock
    6 September   George Stephens Sutherland, the Actor

Has quarrelled with one of his com . . . mence manager — Has been play . . .
to admire B. — Will postpone his vi . . . is ripe, & wishes to have the piece . . .
wants butter from Mrs. B.

166 Saughton-Mills
    Sunday, 5 September   Robt. Cleghorn

For the elegy on Capt. Mat. Henderson . . . will have exhausted his stock of
praise . . . he may judge from symptoms of decay . . . Tennant, the bearer of
a letter from B. — When . . . not a little vain — Incloses Dr. Anderson's about
his farm —

167 Coates
(1)   10 October   Lady Betty Cunningham

B.'s elegy on her Brother Earl Glenca . . . to be published, but begs B. to
consu . . .tion for her brother's memory, approach . . . pearing in the place
B. mentions — E . . . alteration, in the last line but one, of . . .

167 Edinburgh
(2)   14 October   A. Cunningham

Thanks B. for the "ode on Sen . . . happiness in high life with that in . . . poem
on Thomson — C. incloses a pol . . . a song on each season of the year . . .

168 Cumnock
    20 October   John Kennedy

Lady Dumfries had subscribed . . . had never seen them . . . gram — Burns is
suspected as the a . . . the real author — F . . .

169 Finlayston
    25 October   Alexr. Dalziel

Particular account of You . . . to his embarkation for Lisbon . . . Maxwell is
prejudiced agt. Miss G . . .

170 Birmingham   James Murray,
    9 November   Prest. of the Caledonian Society

A poetical address — Accou . . . their rules into Scotch . . .

171 Edinburgh
    26 November   A. Cunningham

Extracts part of a letter from . . . tone —

172 Mossgiel
    Sunday morn.   Gilbt. Burns

Private business — Conversation with . . . der's farm — Will wait on Sir W . . .
with him — Is sorry to hear B . . . tended going to London — from which . . .

173 Friars Carse
    Sunday   Capt. Riddel

Invitation to dinner in verse

1791
174 London
    3 January   Capt. Grose

Thanks for a proof-sheet — Will be . . . his Scotch work this spring, all but the w . . . appear again in the house of Mrs. Riddell, Jun. . . . good qualities — His son will sail in a few da . . .

175 Stirling
    17 January   W. Corbet

Burns may soon expect to hear of his prom . . . character of him

176 London
    8 February   Geo. Baird

Proposed to publish a new edition of . . . begs Burns to revise the MSS. & ad . . . for Bruce's Tombstone — See the ans . . .

177 Saughton Mills
    1 March   Rob. Cleghorn

Acknowledges receiving a poem — Keeps . . . ples — Any B. may intrust him with . . . Is in terms for 24 acres of parks at £3 . . .

178 Dumfries
    5 March   T. Stewart

Asks B. for Miss Craik's "Helen," wh . . . to see him — See No. 298

179 Edinburgh
    8 March   A. Cunningham

Has recd. "Holy Willy" for Dr. . . . death of Ld. Glencairn — Begs for the . . . B. to come to town to see Mrs. Esten . . . on the passions" insuperable . . .

180 Edinburgh
    12 March   Al. Frazer Tytler

Eulogy of "Tam o' Shan . . .

181 Edinburgh
    16 March   P. Hill

Acknowledges three guineas . . . the letter . . .

182 Edinburgh
    18 March   A. Cunningham

"Mrs. Esten performs Rosalind on Mon . . .

183 Edinburgh
(1)   2 March   A. Cunningham

Acknowledges the "Elegy on . . . cher's song & to assist him incloses . . . history of the Royal company a . . . Raeburn the painter wishes to . . . B. in Edinr.

183 London
(2)   23 March   Dr. Moore

See folio 51

184 Whitehaven
   21 April   A. Coutts

A poetical address

185 Temple, Patrick,
   near Belfast
   2 May   Sam Thompson

A great admirer of Burns — . . . edition of Scotch poets — Was unhappy . . .
triffles for the Miscellany but waits . . .

186 Finlayston
   16 June   Alex. Dalziel

Ld. Glencairn is not to be buried . . . D. likes B.'s idea of going into mourning . . .
Earl — & of his Lady — His Lop. wants to . . . Mrs. Burns had discovered the
late Earl . . .

187 Dryburgh-Abbey
   17 June   Lord Buchan

Invites Burns to make one at the . . . Hopes B. will catch inspiration by the
b . . . ode for the occasion —

188 Edinburgh
   4 July   W. Creech

Had informed B. that he meant to pu . . . or additions, but had had no
answer — . . . (See the letter to Hill, for . . .

189 Colvend
   8 July   Reverend James Little

Will be glad to see Burns any ti . . . company will be a great treat after . . .

190 Edinburgh
   27 July   W. Creech

Has shewn Profr. D. Stewart a letter . . . Profr. again requests B. to send h . . .
them in the new edition —

191 Edinburgh
   7 August   P. Hill

Incloses a Sonnet written by . . . He is a great admirer & good frie . . . son had
sent the bard a pres . . . script to remind B. that he . . .

192 Allan's-Close,
   Edinburgh
   10 August   A. Cunningham

Presents a book — Sends so . . . has been in London & has heard . . .

193 Dalswinton
   15 August   P. Miller, Esqr.

Has no objection to Burns continuing . . . a cow, provided the liberty of doing
so does . . .

194 Paisley
    7 September   Alex. Wilson

This letter contains another written . . . hurt — Wilson apologizes & asserts . . . an enthusiastic admirer of B. & enclo . . . of *the bard* himself, — requesting strictures . . .

195 Dryburgh-Abbey
    5 September   Earl of Buchan

Has recd. B.'s "Address to Thomson" . . .

196 Dryburgh-Abbey
    16 September   Earl of Buchan

Suggesting Harvest-home as a subje . . . have an opportunity of *perpetuating the* . . . cution of it

197 Drungans-Lodge
    10 October   Miss Deborah Duff Davies

Is vain of the "poem addressed to her" — . . . notwithstanding the Jacobite sentiments it . . .

198 Coates
    10 October   Lady Betty Cunningham

The "Elegy on her brother, E. Glencairn . . . but begs Burns to consult her sister with reg . . . pearing in the place B. mentions. Expresses . . . Professes much esteem for Burns — Suggests . . . Glencairn" would read "*thee*, Glencairn." A very frien . . .

199 Cloncaird,
    near Maybole
    16 October   Sr. John Whiteford

Thanks B. for the "Lament on E. Glenca . . .

200 Finlayston
    17 October   Alex. Dalziel

Was affected by the "Lament on . . . verses will go to him. — Was happy to hea . . . at Glasgow or Greenock —

201 Newton Don
    30 October   Lady Harriet Don

Admires the Elegy on her Brother — Her elder . . . Advises to publish it in the Edinr. Maga . . .

202 Piccadilly
    3 November   Duke of Queensberry

Polite thanks for "the Whistle" — see f . . .

203 Arbigland
    22 November   Wm. Craik, Esqr.

Incloses a letter for Mr. Alison in Edinr. [which] B . . . must come often to Arbigland

204 Edinburgh
(1)   27 November   Al. Frazer Tytler

Acknowledges having recd. "The Whistle" . . .

204 Harvieston
(2)   17 December   Margt. Chalmers

Laments B.'s misfortune & . . . Rejoices to hear B. is reading . . . superior used
every day to pray that . . . prayer for B. who wants but little to . . . for it —
Lady Mckenzie is better, & wishe . . . to him." "As to happiness . . .

205 1792
     Edinburgh
     2 January [1793]   Mrs. Graham of Fintry

Nothing gave Mr. G. more pain th . . . him more satisfaction th . . .

206 Excise Office
     3 January [1793]   Mrs. Graham of Fintry

Had heard that B. had made . . . not in justice ask any man to prefer a . . . whose
principles are in danger of being sapped . . .passive. Has done every thing in
his . . . motion — Sends publications of the times & . . . This & the preceding
are . . . No. 227 where mention is made of the . . .

207 Edinburgh
     10 January   Mrs. Hay

Sends the words & music of "Some . . . Hamilton & his wife who are both ill . . .

208 Edinburgh
     15 January   H. G. Macnab

Is about to publish "on the Coal Tax . . . miseries it produces in Engld. as well
a . . .

209 Coates
     23 January   Lady Betty Cunningham

Is mortified at having been from ho . . . to send his new poems — Hears of one
. . . those sent —

210 Edinburgh
     16 February   Peter Hill

Has disposed of B.'s money as desired . . . Hill means a present to him . . .

211 Edinburgh
     4 March   A. Cunningham

Clark, school-master, is honor . . . "an unfortunate attachment," by a yo . . .
a happy evening with Miss M. (an acquain . . . departure for Jamaica —

212 Edinburgh
     11 April   A. Cunningham

Is about to marry Miss Moir — In . . . of Rl. Scsh. Archers —

213 Edinburgh
   13 April   Wm. Creech

Has begun a new edition of the . . . will perhaps read the proofs . . .

214 Edinburgh
   17 April   Wm. Creech

In answer to one of Burns . . . reasonable — Name his books, he . . . be sent —
Profr. Stewart is . . . country idle — C. wd. have . . .

215 Edinburgh
   21 May   Peter Hill

Congratulates B. on . . . him to send MSS. Poems . . . & wishes Burns to send
her all . . . Riddell has published a b . . .

216 Edinburgh
   2 June   A. Cunningham

Introducing Robt. Welsh of . . . B. a vol. of songs

217 Edinburgh
   27 July   R. Graham, Esqr., of Fintry

Burns is put on the examine [*deleted*] . . . Athole's death prevented his ack . . .

218 Trustees' Office,
   Edinburgh
   12 September   Geo. Thomson

Belongs to a society for the impro . . . chaste collection of songs set by . . . as
deserve better than have falle . . . apology for troubling Burns —
   The inclosed is from A1 . . . favor — Envies Mr. Clarke (the organist . . .
McMurdo's) the pleasure he enjoys in . . . stanzas in Burns's praise —

219 Shrewsbury Castle   Thos. Telford, Architect

Inclosing a beautiful poem address . . .

220 Morham,
   near Haddington
   16 October   F. A. D[unlop]

Melancholy letter from a mother la . . . the fancied interest of a child who w . . .

221 Edinburgh
   21 October   Fraser Tytler

The illness of his wife & the death of . . . MSS. — The 2d. Epistle to Fintry
bett . . . enlarged edition of "Nidside" alone is to . . . if it is meant as a parody
of the English . . . the proofs — The terms of B.'s bargain to . . . ask an
unreasonable number of copies f . . . that may arise —

222 Edinburgh
   13 November   Wm. Creech

Thanks B. for a stanza — Wants . . . balance — the books you want sha . . .
"Darwin's Bot! Garden & Loves of the . . .

223 Edinburgh
    15 November   Stepn. Clarke

Arrived jaded with his journey . . . the influenza — Hopes to hear . . . is better —

224 Edinburgh
    22 November   W. Johnston

Thanks B. for his attention . . . "Chairman of the Friends of the . . . neglect to pay his compts. to . . .

225 London
    26 September   William Reid, a Mason

Informs B. of his election . . .

226 Belfast
    8 December   Henry Joy, Printer of a . . .

Was the first in Ireland to . . .

    1793
227 Edinburgh
    10 January   Robert Graham Esqr., of Fintry

Sends a few stores & some late . . . true — Dr. Hardy's "Patriot" cont . . . bestowed *in his last on Capt.* . . . patriot till refused a sinecure . . . lent Ministerialist till he was . . . whose brother Sir John places the . . . licitors of Excise for receiving bribes . . .

228 Belfast
    20 January   Miss Bruntins

Send[s] two pound of Dublin Snu . . .

229 Dumfries
    22 January   Mr. White

Returns "The sad Shepherd" which . . . The notes in B.'s hand-writing are . . brew & scotch

230 Hillside
    5 February   Wm. Stewart

Cannot save the poor wretch . . . bear the correction she deserves — Advises B. to apply to Dumfries . . .

231 Edinburgh
    10 February   Wm. Nicol

Alludes to the reports circulated with . . . in a fit of devotion & wishes she & her chi . . . to shift for themselves, as reprobates — Mr. . . . blesses him —

232 Edinburgh
    2 March   Wm. Creech

Sends 20 copies of the new edition of . . . impressions arrive they shall be fo . . .

233 Langholm
     5 March   F. J. Guion, the Actor

The pain of his fracture was encreas . . . Will not be able to remit the fare of
the . . . Wishes to know what is due to Robertson . . .

234 Woodley-Park
     11 March   Mrs. Riddell

Thanks for his present of the new . . .

235 York
     27 March   Miss A. Dorothea Benson

B.'s letter to her so exactly & so . . . to copy it & send it back, mutatis . . .
Expresses much esteem & friends . . . a pilgrimage to York Cathedral — . . .
knowledging the Capt.'s hospitality . . . him with her (Miss B.'s) eyes . . .

236 Edinburgh
     11 April   James Johnson

Gratitude to Burns who has . . . trouble — Has sent him the . . . he ought to
have his copy gratis . . . list of tunes made out by Clarke . . .

237 Dalswinton
     15 April   Peter [Patrick] Miller, Esqr.

Thanks for the 3d Edition of the . . . but wd. have him carefully revi . . .

238 Edinburgh
     16 April   Wm. Smellie

Is about to print a poem wri . . . to add a few Scotch lines by . . .

239 Edinburgh
     30 April   John Brown

Incloses a copy of the P. of . . . on genealogy & wishes to know . . . make it
worth his while to . . . but is convinced of B.'s public sp . . .

240 Edinburgh
     12 May   A. Cunningham

Differed from B. in Politics . . . asks leave to Send Hardy's "Patriot" & "The . . .
Is glad B. knows his friend G . . . Gray" — The name of Burns al . . . & to see
his affable wife —

241 Edinburgh
     27 May   Jean Marishall

Petitioning for a prologue to . . . prologue wd. not answer, & besides . . . so soon
after the Dr.'s death —

242 Drumlanrig
     16 August   Jane McMurdo

Acknowledges the honor he has to do . . . fit by the advice contained in B.'s . . .

243 Edinburgh
    30 October   A. Cunningham

Urbani had advertised that Burns . . . tion he was publishing — C. wishes . . .
is a disgrace to the music he p . . . correct & elegant —

244 Manse of Kirkinner   The Reverend John Graham
    5 November   to Mrs. Dunlop of Dunlop

Laments the loss of a friend — . . . memorials of a justly honored friend . . .
Mrs. D. for her present of a book — Is g . . . & of Little's poems —

245 Mossgiel
    1 December   Gilbert Burns

Bell, their sister, is this day . . . John Begg — Only knew of it . . . the world
poor, but the ma . . . in matchmaking — *His wife* . . .

246 Edinburgh
    12 December   Robert Graham, Esqr., of Fintry

Feels unfeigned pleasure . . . has been unable to lift . . . thank B. for the edition
of . . . thing better than mere thanks . . .

247 Dryburgh-Abbey
    18 January   Earl of Buchan

Tho' descended from Baliol, his Lop . . . having escaped the contagion of his
count . . . ment — Bids B. cultivate indepen . . .

248 Dryburgh-Abbey
    3 February   Earl of Buchan

Plans a poem for Burns "on . . . Ramsay's American Revolution, . . . his Lop.
& Fox's encomium on . . .

249 Auchleand, near Wigton   Luke Mullar,
    February   An Irishman

Poetical Address to the Bard . . .

250 Edinburgh
    2 March   Graham of F.

Mr. Finlater has no authority to say he . . . in Edinr. & hopes he will be able
to . . . by her present —

251 Edinburgh
    4 March   Wm. Smellie

Sends a quarto volume as a specimen . . . own account, & wishes B. to write a
po . . .

252 Carngrasiny,
    near Belfast
    March   Saml. Thomson [?Thompson]

State of Ireland — Overthrow of the rag . . . Sends a pound of blackguard —
will be . . . *off* — it *fell off* spontaneously — T.'s sticks by him . . . him his
paper — the Northern Star — Tha . . .

253 London
   26 March   P. Miller, Esqr., Junior

Perry, proprietor of the Morning Chronicle, offe . . .

254 London
   1 April   Dr. Moore

B. had recommended Mundell, surgeon, to . . . The Dr. has quoted some fine
lines of Burns . . . rejoice with him in the honorable mention . . .

255 Stevenson,
   near Haddington
   16 May   J. McLeod of Colbecks

Is happy in having met with B. in D . . . not now for Woodley-park — Carse
f . . . of it —

256 London
   2 July   Robt. Andw. Riddell

— Polite present of his drawings . . .

257 Banks of Tweed
   6 July   Earl of Buchan

Again recommends "the K . . . on the 22d Septr. the anniversary . . . Lop's hall
of anct. virtue — & will . . . tuned his reed — none shall be . . . sung
"Bannockburn" in his Lop.'s . . . strive against a scoundrel na . . .

258 Edinburgh
   5 August   Peter Hill

Wd. like to see B.'s ms. lett . . . no means endanger the char^r he . . . he was
with altered their route . . .

259 London
   22 August   Sam Hooper

Knows B. well — not personally . . . genial soul with B. & often to . . . "the
Caricature" a juvenile . . .

260 Stevenson
   8 September   John Macleod of Colbecks

Thanks B. for procuring . . . purchase Friars Carse . . . join in inviting Burns
to see . . .

261 —   Dr. Moore

Agrees with B. in thinking . . . tique on the "Sonnet on the . . . vise them —
& to make . . . a description of manners & customs . . . and one from modern
times, as of . . . a good subject for a poem —

1795
262 Edinburgh
22 January A. Cunningham

J. Syme is to him a brother — The . . . lize his name — T.'s work will be a
co . . . dotes B. means to give will mu . . . now but sit'' was composed by one
Halket . . . & to whom he afterwards paid his addresses — . . .

263 Stevenson
22 January John Macleod of Colbecks

Has got a Son & Heir — to be christened . . . in the East Indies & has left his
widow, . . . She is Mr. M^{cl}.'s darling Sister — She will . . . him a bottle of Claret,
a haggis, & his own so . . .

264 Edinburgh
27 January Peter Hill

Has sent B. a barrel of oysters & his . . . nors of Herriot's hospital want B.
to . . . music

265 London
9 February P. Miller, Esq., Junr.

Sends a specimen of Dr. Geddes's p . . . been in the list of Stewards for
celebra . . . so doing. Hopes his conduct will . . . rying the vessel of the state to . . .

266 Edinburgh
9 February Peter Hill

Incloses a poem which had been . . . in a verse of it

267 St. Mary's Isle
18 April Lady Mary Douglas

Requests the original music . . . got the words of it from Burns . . . the *Orpheus
Caledonius* returned . . .

268 Edinburgh
4 July A. Cunningham

Requests to have "Lord Gregory . . . a literary party & sung some of B.'s
songs . . . writer in the world. Wd. he . . .

269 Edinburgh
24 July A. Cunningham

Wishes to hear from B. C.'s wife . . . house if he will come to Reekie . . . by
edition of Burns. Disapproves . . . of a sprig of poetry "From the . . .

270 kirkhill
29 August Earl of Buchan

Two eggs of a Surry Nightingale . . . taken to their wings. Ld. B . . . 7 or 14
Augt. — Fears B.'s late . . . niversary

271 Saughton-Mills
　　9 October　　　　　　　　Rob. Cleghorn

Presents B. with "Gavin Dou . . . — "Tytler on Scotch Breweries" — & . . .
which he sings over his whiskey — . . . Dined with a party where they sung
wi . . . -quests leave to send "a' that & a' that" . . . -ted democrate here was,
immed . . . Service of the United States — Toast . . . of "the Soldiers return"
from Burns . . . sent her

272 Dumfries
　　December?　　　　　　　　Miss Fontenelle

the Actress — Thanking Burns for the . . . See folios 60 & 70. This letter is ve . . .

273 Mauchline
　　13 December　　　　　　　James Armour

B.'s father-in-law, is sorry to hear . . . Sorry to hear of Robert's misfortune . . .
Sends stockings for William —

　　1796
274 Edinburgh
　　16 February　　　　　　　A. Cunningham

Begs a copy of "O let me in . . . of the Plants" — C. wishes to sing the . . .

275 Irvine
　　1 March　　　　　　　　　Robert Baillie

Harry Erskine has been dismissed . . . T. on the occasion — Baillie req . . . not
to enter much into politics . . . has encreased his expenses £100 . . . folly of
continental alliances — . . . Burns at least to correct them . . . of Cummertrees
neglects . . .

276 Excise Office
(1)　11 July　　　　　　　　Graham of Fintry

Is truly sorry to hear of B.'s . . . pay while off duty? (See folio 76) because . . .
-closes a triffle which he hopes . . . Graham has been . . . his interest at heart . . .

276
(2)　14 November [1786]　　　Mrs. Dunlop

Commissions 12 Copies of B . . .

277 Edinburgh
　　George's Square
　　10 March　　　　　　　　Fraser Tytler

Translation of a passage . . . grove

278 Harvieston
　　17 December [1787]　　　Margt. Chalmers

Laments B.'s misfortune . . . -mily might have nursed . . . When she was au
couvent . . . he read the lessons, that God . . . She offers up the same prayer
for . . . The songs B. addressed to her are . . . wishes to see B. at Harvieston
on . . . "As to happiness awaiting her — it awai . . .

279 Edinburgh
    Friday [1787-88]   Wm. Creech

Puts off his engagement. with B. ti . . . is ready & can be settled in 5 min . . .

280 Edinburgh:
    Brown-Square
    13 February [1787]   Henry Mackenzie

by business, indisposition, &c., has b . . . lameness has prevented his enquiring af . . . Mc. will conduct him to them tomor . . .

281 Edinburgh:
    North St. David Street
    Monday [December, 1787]   Isabella Mabane

Values a box for what B. has done . . . her house —

282 Brown Square
    Friday [May, 1787?]   Henry Mackenzie

Thanks for an engraving and a letter . . . Wishes B. a pleasant Journey & suc . . . to Mr. Brydone or McK. wd. have w . . . I think in Roxburgh-sh. or Berwick-sh.

283 Wednesday Eveng.
    [before 9 December, 1788]   Margt. Chalmers

Burns had apprehended neglect fr . . . Soliciting a post or settlement — Th . . . those who have nothing to bestow — . . . Charlotte's husband has a good heart, b . . . *fate* — Miss C. admires B.'s hau . . . be more fortunate than hith . . .

284 Thursday Morng.
    [before 12 September, 1791] Isabella Mabane

Thanks for a poem — Happ . . .

285 Mauchline
    Wednesday   Gilbert Burns

Wants a bull — has finished . . . the 2d. Is much obliged to the . . .

286 Carlisle
    26 March [1792?]   Miss Helen Craik

Sends a poem which she . . . -ture painter for the Author — . . . view of the society at Carlisle . . . by Q. Mary during her confinement . . .

287 Auchinbowie, by Stirling   Isabella MacLeod: Sister to
    18 August [1787]   McLeod of Colbecks?
                              See No. 263

Acknowledges Burns' verses on . . . was her darling — reflections . . . -tions Mr. Monro, br^r. to Dr. . . .

288 Longtown   Carn^e. Isab^a. Johnson of
    12 August [1787]   King Street, Norwich

Thanks him for his company . . . him once or twice a year —

289 Arbigland
  14 August [1790]   Helen Craik

Thanks B. for some poems . . . may expect him as she would . . . J.'s lives of
the Poets — See Folio 99 . . .

290 Parliament Square
  Friday Evening
    after 9 December, [1788]   Mrs. Hay

Invites him to her house —

291 Kirkcudbright
  21 February, 1789   Sawney Ross, School-master

A letter in Scotch verse — Wishes . . . ports circulated about him

292 Dunlop House
  14 November [1789?]   Jenny Little

Acknowledges B.'s kindness. Inclos . . . hearing from Burns

293 Dublin College
  11 November [1793]   W. Stokes

Sends Preston's poems just published — . . . It is founded on fact. Will send more
. . . pleasantest hours of his life in B.'s company

294 After January, [1791]   Anna Benson

Incloses a pamphlet & Poems tr . . . B.'s poems — the "Lament for E. Glenc
. . . The poems are more read & spoken . . . had thoughts of writing his life &
so ste . . . his bust —

295 Dumfries
  Wednesday   Jessy Staig

Returns the songs B. had lent . . .

296 Dumfries
  Wednesday
  [December 1793?]   Major Robertson

Thanks B. for the manner . . . does honor to its Author —

297 Arbigland
  Sunday, 15 December [1790?] Miss H. Craik

returns poems & thanks B . . . at finding B. had left Arbig . . .

298 Arbigland
  10 January 1791? [1792]   Helen Craik

Requests permission for Miss . . . poems — Sends a copy of her . . . Dated
5 March 1791

299 Dumfries
  Tuesday   Mrs. Oswald

regrets not having lately . . . — Adieu!

300 Dumfries
     Wednesday   Mrs. Oswald

Thanks B. for his polite ca . . . production of B.'s pen excites . . .

301 Dumfries
     Wedy. Eveg.   J. Syme

Asks B.'s songs with P . . . to the inn where they . . .

302 Edinburgh   John B. Williamson

the Actor — Has got . . . B. sent him — its brevity . . . minster School — He
had . . . "The modest water saw its . . . be remembered — She improves . . .
gaged in a tedious Law —

     14 November   Mrs. Dunlop

see of this fo. 87

APPENDIX II
THE FORGERIES OF BURNS MANUSCRIPTS BY 'ANTIQUE' SMITH

A century ago, a 27 year-old solicitor's clerk was given the task one day of clearing out bundles of old papers which had been earmarked for destruction. Poring over the musty documents before disposing of them the young clerk chanced upon the manuscript of a poem written in the unmistakable handwriting of Robert Burns. Imagine his excitement at this great find!

The clerk was Alexander Howland Smith, and he was in the employment of T. H. Ferrier, Writer to the Signet. Smith took his precious find to James Stillie, an octogenarian who maintained The Old Book Establishment at 19 George Street, Edinburgh. Stillie had been an antiquarian bookseller for over half a century. As a youth, he had served his apprenticeship with John Ballantyne & Company, Booksellers and Auctioneers of 6 Hanover Street. Sir Walter Scott was a partner in this company and one of Stillie's most prized possessions was the original manuscript pertaining to Scott's partnership. Sir Walter often sent in scrap-books to be bound and the young Stillie's antiquarian interests were kindled by perusing these volumes of miscellanea. He was inspired to begin his own collection of literary odds and ends and eventually he turned professional.

Stillie became at one period in his life a sales representative for the *Edinburgh Weekly Journal* and his work took him to Haddington, where he became intimate with Gilbert Burns. He also paid an extended visit to Ayrshire each year and knew John Wilson, the publisher of the Kilmarnock Edition. He became an avid collector of Burnsiana and later reminisced: 'In early life I used to meet a few young literary friends, and at one of our meetings a Burns Letter was offered for sale. It was addressed to Robert Ainslie, Esq., W.S., upon perusal, it was found to be so offensive to the memory of Burns, that we joined and bought it for £4, and put it into the fire. This Ainslie was one of Burns' worst enemies, and an odious character.'

Although he was at such pains to protect the reputation of his hero, Stillie was, towards the end of his long career, to play a dubious part in one of the greatest literary hoaxes of all time. Exactly what was Stillie's role in the *cause célèbre* has never been made clear, but there can be no doubt whatsoever that he was heavily implicated. When he purchased the genuine Burns manuscript from young Smith in 1887, Stillie probably remarked that he could use any amount of Burns material. Smith certainly needed no encouragement. His official duties as scrivener, or letter-copier for the legal firm, developed in him an extraordinary talent for calligraphy. Furthermore, the muniment room of his employer was a goldmine of old paper, vellum and parchment. Smith assiduously culled the scraps of blank paper and parchment from the bundles of legal documents. He took the trouble to study such niceties as inks and watermarks, and then set to with considerable enthusiasm.

Burns was an obvious and easy target for Smith's peculiar skills. The fashion for collecting Burns relics reached manic proportions in the late 1880s. Sufficient genuine examples of the poet's manuscripts were easily available, not only in museum collections but also in facsimile editions, lithographed or engraved for sale to the public, that Smith had little trouble in mastering the poet's angular script. He became so practised in this art that he could write at speed and great length exactly as Burns had done. This very facility, however, was ultimately to prove his undoing.

Alexander Smith was not content to leave it at that. His output was prodigious and astonishing in range. Letters and documents of Mary Queen of Scots, Lord Darnley, the Earl of Bothwell, the entire Dynasty of Stuart kings, Bonnie Prince Charlie, Flora Macdonald, Oliver Cromwell, the Duke of Wellington, Scott, Hogg, Thackeray, Carlyle, Montrose, Nelson, Pitt, Burke and countless other historic celebrities were represented in his repertoire. Did this gentleman desire a letter written by Graham of Claverhouse? it could be obtained in a few days. Did that library wish to possess an original copy of the National Covenant? Very well, it could be delivered. A few days sufficed for any miracle — a poetic trifle, a worm-eaten charter or an archaic palimpsest. You could pay your money and take your pick.

Such was Stillie's unsullied reputation that collectors never questioned the provenance or authenticity of the manuscripts offered to them from this source. Undoubtedly, however, other antiquarian booksellers must have been involved, and it later transpired that one of the accomplices in this monumental deception was an Edinburgh chemist called Mackenzie, residing at Rillbank Crescent. Mackenzie called his collection the Rillbank Crescent Manuscripts and, as such, it was offered for sale at Dowell's auction-rooms in 1891. The sale of this material created an enormous furore at the time, but the suspicions of three of the most prominent collectors were then alerted.

W. Craibe Angus of Glasgow, H.D. Colvill-Scott of Surrey and William Riach, Editor of the *Edinburgh Evening Dispatch*, were the gentlemen primarily responsible for exposing the true nature of the Rillbank Crescent collection. Angus and Colvill-Scott initially challenged the genuineness of some items in the collection, triggering off a controversy in the press, in which the arrogant Mackenzie came off second best. Riach then took up the matter editorially and in a series of articles alleged that Edinburgh had become the 'plague-spot of a corrupt traffic in literary and historical documents'. The national dailies took up the story and in no time at all the press, and especially the London newspapers, were clamouring for a full-blown enquiry. Agitation was fanned by reports flooding in from all parts of the globe, regarding the authenticity of manuscripts which had been purchased over the preceding four or five years from Edinburgh dealers. Many of these doubtful manuscripts were submitted to the Department of Manuscripts at the British Museum for expert examination. The vast majority of them were pronounced worthless forgeries.

The most notable victim of this literary fraud was John S. Kennedy of New York who had assembled a most impressive collection of autographed documents, many of which he had generously donated to a number of libraries, museums and academic institutions in the United States. These were all gratefully and unsuspectingly received, and Kennedy fulsomely hailed in the American press as a great benefactor. Kennedy was first uneasy, then alarmed, by the news emanating from Scotland, and began his own enquiry. He succeeded in retrieving all 202 items which were sent to the British Museum for scrutiny. The verdict was staggering: only one tiny fragment of paper was pronounced to be genuine, and it was the least significant document in the entire collection.

As the press agitation mounted, more and more victims came forward, and what amounted to boards of examiners — literary students and scholars, professors, antiquarians, archivists and dealers of unquestionable integrity — were kept busy in Edinburgh, Glasgow and London. The victims ranged from private individuals to libraries, galleries and museums. Few literary and academic institutions appear to have been immune to the problem. Regarding these enquiries which continued for much of 1891, James Stillie had this to say — in, of all places, a two-page advertisement in the very first issue of the *Burns Chronicle:*

'I have been sadly annoyed with certain self-elected Experts and Pretenders regarding Burns Manuscripts, in the West of Scotland, chiefly in Glasgow, one hitherto respectable firm wrote me a particular account of Forgeries of Burns in Edinburgh, I immediately challenged them for their Authority and required the name but they giving me no Authority I wrote them that the statement was quite untrue, and a malicious Scandal on Edinburgh.'

This cut no ice with John Kennedy who instituted legal proceedings against Stillie. These civil proceedings were later withdrawn on account of Stillie's advanced years — he was then aged 87. Stillie would not leave well alone, however, but continued to huff and puff his innocence. Both he and Mackenzie vigorously defended the authenticity of their wares with a fanatical zeal which only vanished when the army of experts relentlessly demonstrated how many of the poems which they claimed had come fron the hand of Burns had actually appeared in periodicals before Burns was born, and pointed out numerous irregularities of spelling, incoherencies of diction and obvious anachronisms, which made further protest ridiculous.

These private enquiries were soon followed by police action. It became obvious that the spurious material vended by Stillie and Mackenzie came from one source, but who was actually the perpetrator? The press began to circulate rumours concerning a mysterious 'Mr Smith' and it was said that he was an Edinburgh man. The *Daily Telegraph* expressed in forthright terms the indignation then universally felt, demanding:

'Punishment sufficiently severe for the Scotsman who would forge letters and poems by Scott and Burns in order to beguile the inexperienced collector could hardly be either imagined or invented. Hurling him from the top of the Castle Rock at Edinburgh would be far too mild for the offence.'

Inevitably, various people now came forward and implicated Alexander Smith in the fraud. He was found to have not only peddled his wares around the booksellers and art-dealers of the capital, but also visited private collectors, public institutions and even city pawnshops, offering valuable manuscripts singly or in bulk, for sums ranging between five shillings and a couple of pounds. On 5th December 1892 he was arrested and remanded in custody on charges of falsehood, fraud and wilful imposition. He was committed for trial in January 1893 and was eventually found guilty on all counts at the High Court on 27th June 1893.

At his trial Smith stoutly maintained his innocence and glibly spoke of secret drawers filled with ancient parchments and old deed boxes in Ferrier's offices which were alleged to be the source of the copious supply of historical documents and letters. The truth, however, was unearthed in a wooden shed in some allotments down Leith Walk and behind Hope Crescent. Here the police discovered Smith's *atelier* where he forged documents. It was then that the full extent of his talents was unmasked, for he was apparently also adept at painting, and many a Samuel Bough,

Wintour and Orchardson (probably undetected and greatly admired to this day) had come from the versatile palette of 'Antique' Smith.

In retrospect, it is difficult to understand how the collecting fraternity were so easily duped. To be sure, he possessed a rare skill as a calligrapher and, of course, did have access to a seemingly inexhaustible supply of authentic materials of the right age; but in the end he became too greedy and careless. Mention has already been made of his incredible facility in writing exactly as Burns had done. In the end he made the cardinal mistake of using the *same* handwriting in the endorsement of some documents. Such endorsement would have been applied by the recipient of letters before 'docketing' them, or perhaps by some later possessor to annotate the document with its provenance. When letters purporting to have been written by Burns were found to be docketed as having been purchased at the Gibson Craig and Whitefoord Mackenzie sales in the handwriting used by Burns in 1793, the game was up.

It may seem surprising that no one ever questioned Smith's right to be selling such a vast quantity of material from the Ferrier muniment room. On at least one occasion Smith's credentials were, indeed, questioned; but he obligingly produced Ferrier's will in which Smith was named as sole heir. The will, of course, was yet another of Smith's forgeries!

Even this source of supply must eventually have dried up. Smith then took to buying old theological works, for which there was virtually no market. An outlay of a few pence gave him the blank end-leaves which he disbound and used to fabricate letters. Letters were written direct on to such leaves using a quill pen. The ink was of the right composition, but it was artificially faded either by simple dilution with water, or adulterated with sepia or some acid or solution of iron. The document was then 'distressed' in the time-honoured manner of literary forgers. It could be steeped in a weak solution of tea and stained here and there with some tobacco juice. To dirty it Smith would crease the paper and then rub it on a dusty slate which had first been dampened. Paper would be rubbed on stone and the edges scraped to simulate the appearance of the deckle-edge found on handmade paper.

Haste in manufacturing documents latterly gave the game away. Smith had become so cocksure that he did not always take the trouble to remove the perforated edge of sheets ripped from old books, and these telltale signs of the bookbinder betrayed their true origins. Of course, it is not impossible that Burns could have ripped pages from old books himself as a source of notepaper. Stillie himself, in his *Chronicle* advertisement, stated:

'When inspecting Burns' Manuscripts, I first examined the Paper, as Burns chiefly wrote on Excise Paper, and I had the opinion of Cowan & Co., the Eminent and Oldest Paper Makers in Scotland, that the Paper was made only for Government, previous to 1787, and I found that Burns adopted only one signature chiefly . . .' Stillie went on to claim that he had acquired the collection of manuscripts which had belonged to John Maitland, Surveyor of Excise and Port Collector at Dumfries and Stranraer. Maitland is not a name that figures in the Burns canon at all, but according to Stillie, Burns presented Maitland on 17th January 1794 with a handsome bound volume, *A Plain Account of the Nature and End of the Sacrament of the Lord's Supper* (1735), with an inscription 'As a Token of Esteem and Regard, Robt. Burns'. This book was accompanied by 'a loveable letter' — 'for the many favours you have granted me'. Doubtless the book was one of those worthless old theological treatises that Smith acquired for coppers, normally to disbind for its blank end-leaves, but on this occasion he went further and embellished it with a suitable inscription to transform it into a bibliophilic rarity. Sanctimonious old hypocrite that he was, Stillie concluded his advertisement: 'After a long and happy life (87) amongst old Books and Manuscripts which I sincerely trust has been a life of Purity and Honour to Ayrshire' (*sic*). In the advertisement itself Stillie was offering such gems as a letter from Burns to Maitland introducing 'my friend Captain Grose . . . treat him as you have already, Robt Burns' for which fifteen guineas was asked.

Pages ripped from old books are often worm-eaten, the holes made by *Anobium punctatum* burrowing vertically through many pages. Smith welcomed such worm-eaten leaves, as the holes tended to lend antiquity to his productions; but here again he often slipped up by taking care to avoid the holes with his writing. One would have expected a fair proportion of the handwriting to be pitted by worm holes, but the obliging worms invariably dodged the ink! To lend an air of authenticity, Smith would add docketing and occasionally he would 'gild the lily' by pasting on the bookplate of some famous collector of a bygone age, whose library had previously been sold. These bookplates came from some of the inconsequential volumes that Smith picked up for next to nothing. In some cases Smith was even able to add cuttings from sale catalogues pertaining to the dispersal of these old libraries, in such a way as to imply the provenance of his spurious manuscripts.

In bringing in a verdict of guilty, the jury recommended the prisoner to mercy, on the ground that his had been an unusual crime, and because of the easy facility of disposing of the spurious documents afforded him. The Lord Justice Clerk, in pronouncing sentence, said: 'Alexander Howland Smith, the crime of which you have been convicted is a serious one, particularly in the view that you evidently were following the course of concocting documents in order practically to make a livelihood by selling them. I am giving all the effect I can to the recommendation of the jury in abstaining from pronouncing a sentence of penal servitude, and sentencing you to imprisonment for twelve calendar months.'

After serving his sentence 'Antique' Smith used the antiquarian expertise he had acquired and set himself up as a dealer on his own account, buying and selling antiques, curios, books and autographed manuscripts. One cannot help speculating whether he ever learned his lesson and stuck to the straight and narrow path. There is no doubt that he shielded those who had marketed his productions and refused to give them away at his trial. In the murky half-world of the antiquarian book trade in Edinburgh at the turn of the century 'Antique' Smith probably had his uses. It may have been no coincidence that Smith plied his trade in the early years of this century from 26 George Street — very close to Stillie's old establishment.

In the years following the trial, rumours persisted that Smith could not have perpetrated so many forgeries single-handed and that there had been a conspiracy afoot. Smith remained unrepentant to the end and maintained that he, and he alone, had been the perpetrator of 'all the fac-similes'. A letter from Smith, dated 20th November 1905, was reproduced in the *Burns Chronicle* of 1921. The recipient of the letter was James Cameron, a bookseller in St David Street Edinburgh — 'a fine specimen of the old school of bibliophiles' commented Duncan McNaught, the *Chronicle* Editor, though whether in an ironic mood cannot now be ascertained.

Even to this day spurious letters and poetic manuscripts of Burns continue to surface. As recently as 1986 a letter purporting to be from Burns to the engraver Beugo was sold at an auction in Glasgow. Although this had been pronounced spurious by experts it was nonetheless sold without comment to some unsuspecting collector. Truly, the evil that men do lives on, compounded by ignorant and unscrupulous persons to the present time.

LIST OF SUBSCRIBERS

Aberdeen Burns Club
Aberdeen City Library, Rosemount Viaduct, Aberdeen
William Adair, 36 Woodlands Ave, Gartcosh, Glasgow
James Adam, 39A Titchfield Rd, Troon
Hector A W Adams, Neriliander, 7 Island View, Ardrossan
James K D Adams, 27 Whinmoor Way, Leeds
James Adamson, 1031 Parkwood Way S.E., Calgary, Canada
James Adamson, Rossieden, Tweeddale Cres, Gifford
Mrs Caroline S Addison, Torreagles, Clola, Mintlaw
William Adie, 75 Derran Drive, Cardenden
Robert Aitken, 2 Quarrybrae Gardens, Uddingston
Hugh Alexander, 98 Hunters Avenue, Ayr
Sam G B Alexander, Marchbank, Fenwick
Alexandria Burns Club
Thomas Allan, 37 Croftfoot Road, Glasgow
Allanton Jolly Beggars Burns Club
H V Allen, Hame, Kingswood Road, Gunnislake
Alloway Burns Club (2 copies)
Wilfrid J Allsop, 18 James Grove, Kirkcaldy
George Anderson, 49c Upper Bourtree Drive, Burnside
William A Anderson, 3 Jubilee Place, Stewarton
John Andrew, 134 Bank St, Irvine
Mrs Mary Andrews, 16 Fernhill Rd, Annaclone, Banbridge
Ms Pamela E Apkarian-Russell, P O Box 499, Winchester, NH, USA
Leslie G Archibald, 912 Ingersoll St, Winnipeg, Canada
Robert Armstrong, 44 Tollerton Drive, Irvine
Mrs Marion Morrison Ash, Charter Avenue, St John's, Nfld, Canada
Walter Ashenhurst, Hillrigg, 74 Towers Road, Airdrie
David W L Auld, The Dales, Springs, Stair, Mauchline
Mrs Mary Auld, 27 Baidland Ave, Dalry, Ayrshire
Ayr Burns Club, Tam O Shanter Museum, High St, Ayr (3 copies)
Ayrshire Association of Burns Clubs (5 copies)
David A Baillie, 15 Blair Street, Galston
Alex Baird, 19 Frew Terrace, Irvine
Dr Thomas Baird, 43 St Paul's Road, Coventry
William B Baird, 52 Alexander Terrace, Mauchline
Mrs Agnes Barbour, 16 Bruce St, Dumfries
Sandy Barbour, 1 Templars Crescent, Kinghorn
Thomas R Barker, 12411 51A Avenue, Edmonton, Canada

Dr Tom H Barlow, Lochindaal, Dumbuck Cres, Dumbarton
David W J Barr, Harkieston, Maybole
Thomas H Bartlett, 17 Ewart Drive, Dumfries
Miss Linda Bates, 17 Carseloch Road, Ayr
Andrew Baxter, 18 Abbotsford Road, Lochore
Andrew Baxter, 14 Erskine Place, Kilmarnock
Robert Bayne, 12 Cadham Villas, Glenrothes
William D Beaton, 79 Meadowlands Dr, Ottawa, Canada
John Beattie, 59 Newmains Road, Renfrew
Frank Beaumont, 34 Easdale Drive, Glasgow
David M Begg, House C, Gold Chalet, Clearwater Bay, Hong Kong
Dr James A Begg, 19A Ewenfield Road, Ayr
Mrs Shirley Bell, Skyline Hotel, Irish St, Dumfries
Thomas Bell, Braeside, 49 Drum Brae Sth, Edinburgh
William M Bell, 114 Meadow Road, Coventry
Ian Alastair Bennett, 9 Lowca Lane, Seaton, Workington
Mrs Phyllis M Bennett, 61 Braehead, Girdle Toll, Irvine
George R Beveridge, 11 Dashwood Sq, Newton Stewart
Robert & Jean Beveridge, 37 Ochil View, Kinross
Thomas & Pamela Beveridge, 21A Dogwood Acres, Chapel Hill, USA
Herbert G Bews, 15 Glenlochay Road, Perth
James Bicker, 14 Ardmory Road, Rothesay
John Biggart, 33 Mains Road, Beith
Miss Irene Birch, Alick's House, Kirkby
Birnbeck Burns Club No 951, Weston-super-Mare
Miss Susanne C Black, 897 Cumbernauld Rd, Glasgow
William G Black, 5 Kidsneuk, Irvine
William T K Black, 29 Whalley Rd, Read, Burnley
Robert Blakley, Hillview, 14 Abbey Gardens, Coupar Angus
Andrew L T Blance, 4 White Wisp Gardens, Dollar
Blane Valley Burns Club, Blanefield
Alexander C Bogue, 41 Arrowsmith Ave, Glasgow
Edward R Bonnar, 29 Gagiebank, Wellbank, Dundee
Alan R Booth & Sondra D Stigen, Annapolis, USA
Miss Madge Borland, Mallaig Rd, Port Glasgow
Mrs Cecilia Bottomley, LRAM, 23 Kingswood Gardens, Leeds
Elizabeth Boulton, Broomfield Terrace, Marsh, Huddersfield
Mrs Sarah Bowie, 48 Lowana St, Villawood, Australia
William Bowie, 48 Lowana St, Villawood, Australia
Charles Bowman, JP, 13 Ancrum Gardens, Dundee
Dr John J Boyd, 12023 Aspen Dr W, Edmonton, Canada
Andrew Boyle, 14 Arran Gardens, Troon
Robert M Boyle, 13 Lapwing Close, Blyth
William Boyle, 40 Hillcrest Drive, Stevenston

Leslie M Braby, 35 St John's Road, London
Joseph S Brady, 11 Woodside St, Bedlington
James Brew, 15 Friendly Drive, Islington, Canada
George W Brodie, Marconi Place, St John's, Newfoundland, Canada
John L Broom, 21A Franklin Rd, Stromness
Jack A Brown, Piersland House Hotel, Craigend Rd, Troon
James & Catherine Brown, 31 Magnolia Close, Driffield
John L Brown, 5 Overton Crescent, Falkirk
Malcolm Brown, Ardath, Kirkfield Place, Arrochar
Norman R Brown, 9 Northfield Avenue, Ayr
Robert Brown, 190 Lutterworth Road, Nuneaton
Cllr Robert Brown, SNP, KLDC, Steward Irvine Burns Club
David Brownlie, Taransay, Rhu Road Higher, Helensburgh
Richard F Bruce, 24 Greenock Avenue, Cathcart, Glasgow
Miss Jean G Bryan, 9 Rozelle Terrace, Ayr
Hugh Bryson, 8D Headland Road, Hong Kong
Mrs Mary Bryson, 53 Braehead, Girdle Toll, Irvine
William Bryson, 21 Beechwood Rd, Tarbolton
Mrs Freda Buddie, 49 Jerviston Road, Motherwell
John H Bull, 49 Annahill Ave, Kilmarnock
C Douglas Burgess, 1 Wolfe Ave, Newton Mearns
Robert Burnett, 223 Kirkintilloch Rd, Bishopbriggs
Dr Robin R Burnett, 79 Bank Street, Irvine
Burns House Museum, Mauchline
Alexander Burns, JP, 88 Livingstone Terrace, Irvine
James Burns, 43 Douglas St, Motherwell
James Burns, 43 Eglinton St, Beith
Robert M Burns, Alloway, 19 Durham Close, Cheltenham
Thomas & Elspeth Burns, 548 Lake St, St Catharines, Canada
E Burstow, Latimer, Hermitage, Newbury
Renton Byars, 19 Bathhurst Drive, Alloway, Ayr
Thomas Byrne, 91 Ashcroft Drive, Glasgow
John Cairney, 44 St Vincent Cres, Glasgow
Graeme T Cairns, 69 Boydfield Avenue, Prestwick
J J Caldwell, Director, Irvine Burns Club, Irvine
Miss Leigh Caldwell, 65A Albert Street, Stromness, Orkney
Caledonian Society of Sheffield
Calgary Burns Club
Mrs Patricia Callander, Blaiket Mains, Crocketford Rd, Dumfries
Robert A Callander, Milnfaulds, Boghead Rd, Dumbarton
Alistair C Cameron, 5E Cedar Place, Barrhead
William Cameron, 72 Springhill Ave, Crosshouse
Dr Allan J M Campbell, 2 Dunlin Crescent, Houston
Dr Archibald J Campbell, 221 Glasgow Road, Paisley

Douglas G Campbell, 8 Overtoun Drive, Rutherglen, Glasgow
Mrs Helen Campbell, Bridge Street, Kirkcudbright
James Campbell, 23 Burnside Place, Irvine
James B Campbell, 6 School Lane, Upper Poppleton, York
Joe Campbell, 30 Racecourse Road, Ayr
Joe Campbell, Shandon House, 80 Station Rd, Thornton
Lionel Campbell, BA, MEd, 2 Maple Leaf Court, Cottingham
Cllr Robert Campbell, 28 Thornwood Avenue, Ayr
Robert McK Campbell, 21 Garden St, Tarbolton
Mrs Rose Campbell, 28 Hawkhill Rd, Kincardine
James M Cannell, 77 Marchburn Ave, Prestwick
Capt Alistair T Cant, 11 Denbigh Gdns, Southampton
Robert F Carey, 18 Aldergreen St, Irvine
Maj O Frank & Lilian Carroll, Raven Hills Court, Colorado Springs, USA
Evans J Casso, 108 North Gatehouse Dr, Metairie, USA
James L Chalmers, JP, 39 Cardowan Dr, Stepps, Glasgow
Thomas Chalmers, 4 Harbour Street, Peterhead
Tom Chalmers, Burntisland
Mrs Dorothy M Chase, Grand River, Richmond, NS, Canada
William Cheyne, 16 Mackerel Hall, Royston
Mrs Jean A Chisolm, 1 Catmoor Rd, Scone
John Chisolm, Ravenstone, Auchinleck Rd, Cumnock
Edward Clark, 14826 Delbarton Dr, Houston USA
Gordon A Clark, Cladach, Ainslie Road, Girvan
James Clark, 10 Trench Knowe, Edinburgh
James Howie Clark, Latimer Gardens, Glasgow
James J Clark, Lornewood, Islesteps, Dumfries
Mrs Sally M Clark, Nia-Roo, Nethergribton, Dumfries
James M Clarke, 13 Ralston Road, Dundee
John M Clayton, 33 Blackford Cres, Prestwick
William Cleary, 49 Strathern Road, Dundee
Robert B Cleland, 20 Oakfield Tower, Motherwell
Donald E Clerk, South West Fullarton, Meigle, Perth
Douglas Clifford, 17 Glebe Rd, Hinckley
Ian C Climie, 9 The Beeches, Brookfield, Johnstone
Mrs Elizabeth M Clinton, 560 Balmore Rd, Glasgow
John B Clow, 111 Ainsdale Rd, Leicester
Coalsnaughton Burns Club
Eric G R Cochrane, 14 Boghead Road, Dumbarton
Mrs Sylvia E Colclough, 18 Monkwood Place, Alloway
Dr A Collinson, 112 Westgate, Southwell
Ian Colquhoun, 29 Maxton Terrace, Glasgow
David A Conn, MA, Laloki, Papua New Guinea
James Bell Conn, 5 Avon Place, Kilmarnock

Allan E Connor, Jefton Crescent, Mississauga, Canada
Mrs Bunty Connor, 41 Indian Road, London, Canada
Dr Jim Connor, President Burns Federation (2 copies)
Jim T H Connor, 22/1220 Royal York Rd, London, Canada
John W Conway, 39 Watters Cres, Lochgelly
Daniel Cook, Mardan, 10 Barnton Drive, Dumfries (2 copies)
Michael D Cook, 5 Ewart Drive, Dumfries
Alexander M Cooper, 47 Raemoir Avenue, Banchory
Edward R Copper, Kirkintilloch, Glasgow
James Corbett, 11 Towerhill Ave, Kilmaurs
George Couper, Greenock Burns Club
William Cowan, Norwood, 75 Bank Street, Irvine
William R Cowan, 2473 Malcolm Dr, Palm Harbor, USA
Robert Crabbe, 129 Portland St, Troon
George Craig, 180 Glentanar Rd, Glasgow (2 copies)
Mrs Constance M Craine, 150 Bradford St, Bolton
Peter Crammond, Tillybirnie, Teesdale Rd, Barnard Castle
Hugh W J Crawford, 24 Minto St, Edinburgh
Miss Isabel C Crawford, Rose Mount, Bank Avenue, Cumnock
Mr & Mrs Alan J Crawley, 11 Garfield Lane, St Catharines, Canada
Mr & Mrs Alex W Crawley, 5 Castlemere Ct, St Catharines, Canada
Oliver S Creelman, 47 Bute Crescent, Dykehead, Shotts
Mrs Joan E Creighton, 36 Windmill Heights, Enniskillen
D R H Crichton, Hillview Avenue, Dumfries
John Crilley, 34 Farmeloan Road, Rutherglen
John K Crockett, Kinlet, 35 Drumellan Rd, Alloway
Mrs Jean M Crombie, 80 Standalane, Annan
T Crosbie, Flat 17, 9 Mansfield Rd, Hong Kong
Alex Cross, 203-211 Laxdal Rd, Winnipeg, Canada
Miss Kathleen Crossan, 3 Clochrie Court, Locharbriggs, Dumfries
Mrs Elma G Cruickshank, 3 Clochrie Crt, Locharbriggs, Dumfries
Cumbernauld & District Burns Club No 581
Mrs Elizabeth Cumming, 11 Sandyridge, Nether Poppleton, York
Leonard D Cumming, 3 Royal Terrace, Craigmore, Bute
Cumnock & Doon Valley District Library
Mrs Catherine R Cunningham, 10 Willow Park, Ayr
Ewen Cunningham, 53A Main St, Prestwick
George M Cunningham, 2463 Stonecroft Dr, Horseheads, NY, USA
Graham Cunningham, 11 Linnburn Terrace, Ardrossan
James M Cunningham, 23 Carlyle Drive, Kitchener, Canada
Robert Cunningham, BSc, MSc, 3 Merrick Place, Symington
William M Cunningham, 27 Fern Drive, Barrhead
Frank J Curran, 12 Barnton Drive, Dumfries
Charles C M Currie, Drumadoon, Blackwaterfoot, Arran

Iain H M Currie, Tighnacrioch, Penpont, Dumfries
Dr James Currie, Calgary, Canada
Rev James Currie, The Manse, Dunlop
John M Currie, Ashbank, Graham Terrace, Stewarton
Thomas H Currie, 11 Deveron Road, Troon
William Angus Currie, 70 Bryant Road, Kettering
Mrs Janet M Cutting, 56 Dean Road West, Hinckley
Cutty Sark Scots Whisky
George Darroch, 7 Caddlehill St, Greenock
Elizabeth C Davidson, 22 Wellington Cres, Kirkton, Dumfries
Jimmy Davie, Hon President Burns Federation (3 copies)
Robert Davie, 3 Tontine Path, Rutherglen
Eric Davies, 6 Cottage Farm Rd, Coventry
John Davis, 28 Springhall Rd, Garrowhill, Glasgow
Cath & George Dawes, 5 Laurieston Court, Dundonald
Miss Elaine A M Dawes, 5 Laurieston Court, Dundonald
Ian Day, USA
Ian & Maureen Day, 4295 Adell Avenue, New Berlin, USA
George Dean, London
John Dempster, 11 Wellpark Ave, Kilmarnock (2 copies)
Mrs M Dempster, 16 Hoylake Square, Ashgrove, Kilwinning
Ian G Dick, 3/2 Springfield, Edinburgh
John K Dickie, Flat 3, South Main St, Wigtown
Mrs Ina G Diggle, 18 Gorses Mount, Bolton
Robert Dinwiddie & Co, 34 Great King St, Dumfries (12 copies)
Hugh S Docherty, 11 Kirkshotts Terrace, Cardenden
Norman R Dodds, 3 Eglinton Drive, Troon
Fraser W Doig, Pak Sha Wan, Sai Kung, Hong Kong
Robert Donaldson, Oamaru, Abbotseat Rd, Kelso
Mr & Mrs Robert W Donaldson, Oakleigh Forest, Severna Park, MD, USA
Alan C Donnet, 79 Bisney Road, Hong Kong
Hugh Douglas, 146 Broadway, Peterborough
Robert B Douglas, 31 Hollywood, Greenock Rd, Largs
Ian A Dow, 8 Orchard Brae Ave, Edinburgh
Robin B Dow, Box 478, Bragg Creek, Canada
Dr Arthur L Down, 13319 Myrtlea, Houston, Texas, USA
Joseph J Downes, Stewarton
William Duffy, 98 Leander Crescent, Renfrew
Dumbarton Burns Club
Dumfries & Galloway College of Technology donated by Howff Club
Dumfries & Galloway Regional Council (6 copies)
Dumfries & Galloway Regional Council Library Service
Dumfries Academy donated by Burns Howff Club
Dumfries Burns Club

Dumfries Burns Howff Club
Dumfries High School donated by Burns Howff Club
Dumfries Ladies Burns Club No 1
William W Dunbar, 22 Braehead, Alloa
George & Eliz Duncan, 2 Paterson Crescent, Irvine
William Duncan, 50 Kilbagie St, Kincardine
Dundee Burns Club
Mrs Elza E W Dunlop, Dinarth, 16 Half Edge Lane, Eccles
Professor Charles W Dunn, 25 Longfellow Rd, Cambridge, MA, USA
Ian M Duthie, 7 South Headlands Cres, Newtonhill
John Duthie, 9 Balmoor Terrace, Peterhead
David Dyer, 4 Seafield Court, Aberdeen
George Eastcroft, 5 Kirkburn Drive, Strathblane, Glasgow
Mrs Muriel M Easton, 55 Rosehill Drive, Aberdeen
Hugh Edgar, 5 Southpark Avenue, Prestwick
Mrs Rose Edgar, Dalmalinn, Terregles, Dumfries
Roy Edmundson, 93 Broomfield Rd, Glasgow
Mr & Mrs Arthur N Elliot, 5 Academy Place, Langholm
Alison Mae Elliott, 1 Garden Place, Troon
John Urquhart Elliott, 1 Garden Place, Troon
Lynne Frances Elliott, 1 Garden Place, Troon
Ellisland Trust, Municipal Chambers, Dumfries
Scott A Erdmann, 1836 Old Hardin Rd, Billings, USA
Mr & Mrs Joseph Erdos, 31 Wakefield Crescent, London, Canada
William J Esplin, Ardvorlich, Lochearn Cres, Airdrie
Stanley G Evans, 16 Laburnum Lea, Hamilton
Humphrey N Evry, 24 Bilsland Road, Glenrothes
James Ewan, 39 Kirkburn Drive, Cardenden
Ewart Public Library, Dumfries
J W M Fairbairn, Priors Wood, Church Road, Holywood
Robert Fairbairn, 10 Woodhall Close, Stanningley
Kenneth J Falconer, 28 Crosswood Crescent, Balerno
Dr Ralph Fallows, St Andrews, 51 Main St, Dundonald
George Farquharson, Geomar, Thorniecroft Drive, Cumbernauld
William M Farrell, 7 Craigvale Court, Dumfries
Mrs Henrietta B Ferguson, 5 Ferguson Avenue, Brechin
James & Carol Ferguson, 157 Ladyton Estate, Bonhill
James G Ferguson, 20 Dalmorglen Park, Stirling
Mr & Mrs J M Ferguson, 89 Woodhill Crescent, Irvine
John & Roma Ferguson, 55 Bellesleyhill Avenue, Ayr
Robert W Ferguson, Dunblane
Thomas Ferguson, 10 Knowehead Rd, Kilmarnock
Steven Ferns, 4 Flagholme, Cotgrave
Rinaldo G Ferrari, Maranella, Inverugie St, Peterhead

G G Ferrier, 4 St Margaret's Park, Whitehills, Forfar
Mrs Mattie M Ferris, 123 Pozieres Road, Brisbane, Australia
James M Fisher, 76 Dunlop Terrace, Ayr
Neil Fisher, 40 Strathayr Place, Ayr
Raymond FitzGerald, 38 Rowallan Drive, Kilmarnock
John N Fleming, 33 Milne Avenue, Auchinleck
Peter Fleming, Oxton Lawn Cottage, Oxton
Dr Tom Fleming, OBE, Tomfarclas, Ballindalloch
William R Fleming, 26 Ochil Court, Irvine
James Flockhart, Shalimar, Gunsgreen Crescent, Eyemouth
Robert W Ford, 7 Ledi Road, Glasgow
Richard Fowler, 26 Cathkin Place, Kilwinning
George E Frame, 27 Eckford St, Glasgow
William Francis, 9 Redmire Crescent, Allanton, Shotts
Douglas Fraser, 3 Hunt Street, Corby
Mrs Elisabeth M Fraser, 24 Marlborough St, Edinburgh
Cllr Hugh D G Fraser, 181 Braid Road, Edinburgh
John Fraser, 4 Ramsay Crescent, Aberdeen
Joseph & Elizabeth Freeman, 270/79 Buffalo Rd, E Aurora, USA
James Frew, Tynron, 249 Cumbernauld Rd, Muirhead
Mr & Mrs Thomas Frew, 3 Cockersand Avenue, Hutton, Preston
Elizabeth Frontczak, Kirklees Highland Association
Flora B Fulton, 515/55 Oakmount Rd, Toronto, Canada
William J & Elinor L Gallagher, Meadowlawn Rd, Cheektowaga, USA
Stuart I Galley, Sa Goba, Wickham Way, East Brent
John Gaskin, 15 Goodman Drive, London, Canada
Mrs Anne Gaw, 7 Highfield Place, Girdle Toll, Irvine
Lena S Gaw, Camasunary, 2 Kidsneuk, Irvine
Samuel K Gaw, President 1979-80
David S Gibb, 29 Beechgrove, Ayr
Gordon M Gibson, 82 Bonnyton Road, Kilmarnock
James Gibson, Craigowan Cottage, Symington
John McC Gibson, 24 Blairderry Rd, London
Mrs May D Gibson, MA, 60 Glasgow Rd, Kilmarnock
Mrs Nan Gibson, 205 Yoakum Parkway, Alexandria, USA
Peter Gibson, 205 Yoakum Parkway, Alexandria, USA
Robert S Gibson, 47 Napsbury Lane, St Albans
John & Cath Gillon, 7 Steele Walk, Balloch
Paul & Jennifer Gillon, Hawfield House, Cupar Rd, Kennoway
Vince & Helen Gillon, 33 Jasper Cres, Brampton, Canada
Ian A Gilmour, Corbiere, 57 Round Riding Rd, Dumbarton
Paul S Gionfriddo, 1281 Atwater St, San Diego, USA
Ian Givens, 66 Morris Cres, Hurlford
Glasgow Masonic Burns Club No 263

Glasgow University Library, Hillhead St, Glasgow
James Glass, 31 Glenconner Rd, Ayr
The Globe Inn, 56 High St, Dumfries
Dr James Goldie, The Minack, 7 Graham Cres, Cardross
John & Jessie Goodall, 1 Officials Terrace, Lanchester
Robert J D Goodall, 71 Kingswood Road, Bishopton
Donald S Goodbrand, 8 Birch Polygon, Manchester
David L Goodloe, 208 Gayland St, Midway, KY, USA
Charles B Gordon, 30 Back St, Tarbolton
Mrs Wilma Gordon, 48 Allison Ave, Erskine
Malise J Graham, 8719 Lee Boulevard, Leawood, KS, USA
Charles B Grant, Field House, Wickenby
Gordon Grant, 1 Newmills Court, Balerno
Mrs Johan Ina Grant, 2 Gilchrist Square, Dornoch
Keith W Grant, 20 Kerrfield, Romsey Rd, Winchester
William J Gray, 51 Eastpark Drive, Kilmaurs
William M Gray, An Eilein, Station Road, Mauchline
Greenock Burns Club
Dr Gordon C Greig, 67 Fairfield Rd, Elizabeth, Australia
Rev James Greig, The Manse of Irvine, Golffields, Irvine
Mrs Elaine K Griffiths, 9 Dalry Road, Kilwinning
Robert H Haddow, Glenrossie, Geirston Rd, Kilbirnie
Marshall T Hahn, Jnr, USA
Richard J Hainey, 10 Melville Road, Coventry
Mrs Elizabeth Haining, 74 Laghall Ct, Kingholm Quay, Dumfries
William A. Hair, 18 Brodick Avenue, Kilwinning
Mrs Catherine MacK Hall, 15 Studland Road, Byfleet, Weybridge
Alan K T Halyburton, Benview, Invercargill, East Kilbride
Alex R Hamilton, P O Box 12343, G.P.O., Hong Kong
Mrs Elizabeth M Hamilton, 20 Merryton Tower, Motherwell
Mrs Lily M Hamilton, Gartmore, Annan Rd, Dumfries
James B Hannah, 24 Kilmaurs Rd, Knockentiber
Sam Hannah, 55 Ayr Road, Kilmarnock
William Harcus, 4 Miller Avenue, Abbey Village, Chorley
Mrs Jeanne C Hare, 17 Wentworth Close, Hinckley
John M Harkins, The Kennels, Yaxham Rd, Dereham
T E Harkness, 114 Deyes Lane, Maghull
W S Harland, Greenbank, The Shore, Bolton-le-Sands
Alastair N Harman, 8 Pine Rd, Kilmarnock
Robert Harper, 87 Dundonald Rd, Kilmarnock
Alexander M Harrison, Ar-Tigh, 95 Carlogie Rd, Carnoustie
Mrs Edyth E Harrison, 28 Nant-Y-Felin, Pentraeth
Mrs Ruth Harrison, 75 Bradley Rd, Huddersfield
Miss Tarn J Harrison, Rosewain, Drymen

Miss Margaret Harvie, Speybank, 52 Dalry Road, Kilwinning
Kenneth M Haughan, 30 Cumnock Rd, Mauchline
Colin W Hay, 18 Dunvegan Place, Irvine
John M Hay, Mosscoyle, 7 Newark Crescent, Ayr
Mrs Margaret Hay, 18 Dunvegan Place, Irvine
Walter Hay, 42B Fenwickland Ave, Ayr
Mrs Catherine Hayball, 42 Humberston Ave, Grimsby
Mrs Doris M Heaney, 53 Vale Road, Mitcham
Diana & Peter Hemphill, Knoweside, Failford
James L Hempstead, Inchyra, 10 Chapelton Gardens, Dumbarton
Miss Betty Henderson, 53 Auchendoon Cres, Ayr
John Henderson, 42 Scott Crescent, Alloa
James & Catherine Henry, 16 South Dean Road, Kilmarnock
Mrs Elizabeth S D Herbertson, 45 James Cres, Irvine
Dr D T Herriot, 6 Battery Place, Rothesay
Jimmie R Herron, 217 St Andrews Cres, Rosetown, Canada
W Campbell Heselwood, 4 Whiteley Wood Rd, Sheffield
Thomas P Highet, 37 Devonshire Rd, Sheffield
Mrs Frances A D Highway, 36 Eaves Green, Meriden
Mrs Grizelle M Hill, 76 Summerfield Drive, Annapolis, USA
Ian D Hill, The Cedars, Main St, Urquhart
Mr & Mrs Fred Hinton, 189 Evan St, South Penrith, Australia
Joseph Hobkirk, 47 Craiglockhart Terrace, Edinburgh
Hugh C Hodge, 43 Merksworth Ave, Dalry
Thomas F Hodge, Wurrbak, 42 Elmroyd Ave, Potters Bar
Mrs David Hood, Strathairlie, Craigneil Dr, Prestwick
Thomas Hopton, 15 Parliament Place, Kinglassie
Mrs Margaret Fay Howard, 60A Chorley Rd, Westhoughton, Bolton
Mrs Mabel Evelyn Hughes, 5 Ashley Piece, Ramsbury, Marlborough
John Hume, 5307 Aspen St, Bellaire, Texas, USA
David P Hunter, 123 Overslade Cres, Coventry
Ellen Hunter, Glenartney, 102 Bank St, Irvine
Hugh Hunter, 20 Orchard St, Renfrew
Harry Hutchison, 50 Archers Court Road, Dover
James Hutton, Ailsa, Barloan Cres, Dumbarton
Peter Hutton, 13 Well Rd, Glenrothes
Mrs H M Hyslop, 4 Seaforth Avenue, Annan
Robert Hyslop, 26 Smallwood Terr, Cheektowaga, USA
Iain M Inglis, 19 Gullane Place, Kilwinning
Mr & Mrs John M M Inglis, 16 Berry Drive, Irvine (5 copies)
Mrs Mary B Ingram, 10 Mortain Road, Rotherham
Irvine Burns Club
Alex J Irving, 74 Moyness Park Drive, Blairgowrie
James Irving, Screel, 45 Gillbrae Crescent, Dumfries

W Jack, Ford Cottage, Ford Drive, Mirfield
Alexander M Jackson, Lismore, 3 Downfield Gdns, Bothwell
James J Jeffrey, 59 Bracadale Rd, Baillieston, Glasgow
Graham W D Jenkins, 37 Campsie View, Muirhead
Richard W Jenner, P O Box 13, Civic Centre, Kilmarnock
Brian A Johnston, 52 Hill Street, Dysart
Wilson D Johnston, 337 Columbia Ave, Kerrobert, Canada
Brian Johnstone, Picton St, Niagara-on-the-Lake, Canada
Miss Elizabeth M M Johnstone, 15 Ardwall Road, Dumfries
James Johnstone, 2 Horsburgh Gardens, Pilmuir, Balerno
Jim & Vena Johnstone, Picton St, Niagara-on-the-Lake, Canada
John Johnstone, 20 Montague St, Dumfries
Lawrence Johnstone, 22 John Wilson Drive, Kilsyth
Thomas Johnstone, 7 Hermitage Cres, Dumfries
Derek J Jones, 23 Aynho Close, Coventry
Mrs Isa Jones, 41 Lockhart Place, Wishaw
William Jones, Sheriff Clerk, Dumfries
William Jones, Mossgiel, 7 Kenilworth Ave, Helensburgh
Miss Millicent G Jordan, 56 Oakfield Avenue, Markfield
Douglas Junner, 8 Fereneze Ave, Barrhead
James Junner, 36 Kirktonfield Road, Neilston
William Junner, 8 Thorn Lea Close, Bolton
J M Keegan, 48 Ainslie Road, Cumbernauld
James Kelly, 4C William St, Johnstone
John Kelly, 17 Henley Mill Lane, Coventry
Lewis Kelly, 20 Royal Avenue, Stranraer
Mrs Mary C Kelly, 117 Blairbeth Rd, Glasgow
Rankin Kelly, 38 Kylemore Lane, Greenock
Robert Pitt Kelly, Arros House, Prospecthill Rd, Glasgow
Charles B Kelman, 1 Clerkhill Place, Peterhead
Charles B Kelman, Jr, 6 Grangepark Rd, Peterhead
Charles B Kelman, III, 6 Grangepark Rd, Peterhead
Jan & John Kelso, Burns House Museum, Castle St, Mauchline
Dr Martin Kelvin, 5 Southern Cres, Stockport
Charles Kennedy, 101 Dundonald Park, Cardenden
T Eric Kenwright, Roucanlee, Torthorwald, Dumfries
Mrs Kerr, 13Burgage Court, Southwell
George Kerr, 23 Coronation Drive, Crawford
James W Kerr, Taits Lane, Dundee
Mrs Vivian Kerr, 21 Glencaple Ave, Dumfries
William Kerr, Mountain Meadows Dr, Sussex, USA
Thomas Kettles, Ardmore, Walker St, Kincardine on Forth
Kilmarnock and Loudoun District Libraries (11 copies)
John Kyle Kilpatrick, Minard, 21 Inglewood Cres, East Kilbride

Joseph S King, 14 Hyslop St, Kirkconnel
Thomas Kirby, Friars' Carse, Auldgirth, Dumfries
Mrs Elizabeth Kirkland, 15 Parkhead Drive, Dumfries
John Kirkwood, 202-50 Ridout St S, London, Canada
Mrs Sheila Kurczynski, Picton St, Niagara-on-the-Lake, Canada
Mrs Jean Kvarfordt, 7A Husebybakken, Oslo, Norway 3
Kyle & Carrick District Council
Mrs Dorothy M Laing, Thornlie, 8 Johnston Place, Denny
Marshall G Laing, Lan Tao, 3 Richmond Avenue, Dumfries
Callum Lamont, Glendale, Abernethy
Raymond Lamont-Brown, 3 Crawford House, North St, St Andrews
Lanarkshire Association of Burns Clubs
Mrs Elizabeth Lapsley, 2 Goukscroft Pk, Ayr
Samuel Hannah Lapsley, 4 Woodland-Park, Rainworth, Mansfield
Larkhall Burns Club
Alex Lauchlan, 471 Rooney Cres, Edmonton, Canada
John Lauder, 3 Georgetown Crescent, Dumfries
Miss Vida L Lauder, 5 Whyte Avenue, Irvine
Albert Lawrie, 39 Bankfield St, Bolton
James Lees, Glencoe, 2 Breck Ave, Paisley
John R Lees, 12 Barrhill Rd, Cumnock
Andrew Leitch, 1 Doncaster Close, Coventry
George Leitch, Dockers Club, The Docks, Sharpness
Mrs Alice Lennon, 63 Fergushill Rd, Kilwinning
Mr & Mrs Hugh Lennon, 206 Plank St, Warsaw, USA
Henry Lennox, 50 Yarrow Cres, Wishaw
Mrs Fiona Lindop, 174 Cambridge Road, Hitchin
Charles McC K Lindsay, 72 Lothian Road, Stewarton
David Lindsay, 15 Ninians Terrace, Kilwinning
Mrs Katharine M E Liston, Rock Cottage, Gartocharn, Alexandria
Mrs Bessie T Little, 26 Bristol St, Hamilton, Canada
John Little, 26 Bristol St, Hamilton, Canada
Thomas Little, 10 Avocado Lane, Rochester, USA
Hugh Livingston, 90 Kirk St, Peterhead
David Livingstone, 63 Broadway, Peterborough
Dr Gordon Livingstone
James Livingstone, Ashbank, Gorebridge
Stewart J Livingstone, 63 Broadway, Peterborough
William B Livingstone, 11 Linburn Road, Dunfermline
Bill Llewellyn, 288 High St, Kirkcaldy
Desmond Lock, 8 Anchor Blds, Seedhill, Paisley
Mrs Rosemary Lockerbie, 14 Loganbarns Rd, Dumfries
William Lockhart, Greystones, Kilwinning Rd, Irvine
Mrs Enez Logan, 6 Hugh Watt Place, Kilmaurs

Miss Ida S Logan, 29 Polnessan St, Patna
William G Logan, Golden Meadows Cres, Nanaimo, Canada
London (Ont) Burns Club
Mrs Annette G M Lonsdale, 59 Ringmore Way, Plymouth
Miss Jean Loudon, 9 Ailsa St, Prestwick
Dane Love, 80 Holland Cres, Cumnock
Dr John C Lovie, 7 Milgarholm Ave, Irvine
Luath Press Ltd, Barr, Girvan
Alex W Lumsden, 12 Cloverhill, Ayr
Adam Fraser Lyle, Flat 7/2, 22 Viewpoint Place, Glasgow
William Dougall Lyle, 1 Midton Avenue, Prestwick
Andrew Lynn, 11 Crocus Grove, Irvine
Thomas Mabon, 2E Richardland Place, Kilmarnock
Alan J McAdam, 3 Tinto Square, Renfrew
Mrs Elizabeth McAdam, 1 Callendar Place, Ayr
Mrs Anne McAndrew, 18 Jubilee Grove, Glenrothes
Archie McArthur, 33 Inchmead Drive, Kelso
Helen & Frank McAvoy, 6 Shalloch Park, Ayr
Robert McBride, Hayfield, Darvel
Rev George McCabe, TD, 17 Etive Drive, Airdrie
James H McCall, Via Mil Cumbres, Solana Beach, USA
I R A MacCallum, 601 Prince's Building, Hong Kong
Robert McCallum, 34 Oswald Rd, Ayr
William McCallum, 2 Redwood Crescent, Bishopton
James McCambley, 38 Kirkland Road, Dumfries
Arthur McClune, 39 Thomson Crescent, Port Seton
David McConnell, 6 Coila Avenue, Prestwick
Derek H. McCorquindale, R R 2, Calgary, Canada
Edward McCue, 5 Deanburn Park, Linlithgow
Alexander F McDonald, Twin Trails Dr, San Diego, USA (5 copies)
Mrs Anne Macdonald, 13 Laverockbank Grove, Edinburgh
David McDonald, 8B Morison House, Burns Rd, Cumbernauld
Rev Ian U & Mrs Macdonald, The Manse, Tarbolton
Mrs Margaret M McDonald, Arnish, 8 Morven Crescent, Peterhead
James A McDougall, 2 Woodside Close, Ferndown
Murray J MacDougall, 58 Hillbury Ave, Kenton
Alex M McDowall, 5 Fairways Close, Coventry
James McDowall, 124 Crawfordland Rd, Kilmarnock
Sydney T McEwan, 17 Mactaggart Rd, Cumbernauld
Miss Charlotte M T McFadden, Braeside, Moffat Road, Dumfries
John A C McFadden, Braeside, Moffat Road, Dumfries
John A V McFadden, Braeside, Moffat Road, Dumfries
Miss Rachel L W McFadden, Braeside, Moffat Road, Dumfries
Alistair P McFadyen, Stonecroft, Bridge of Allan

William C B McFadzean, 98 Howbury Street, Bedford
Norman M Macfarlane, 10 Marchmont Gdns, Bishopbriggs, Glasgow
David K McFayden, 8 Park Crescent, Torrance, Glasgow
I McGeachie, 16 Woodlea, Kincardine
John A McGee, Real Colegio de Escoceses, Valladolid
Hugh McGhee, 28 Kilnholm St, Newmilns, Ayrshire
James McGinn, 72 Forth Street, Glasgow
Rev J Walter McGinty, The Manse, Alloway
Robert McGlasson, 10 Ravenswood Dr, Doncaster
Iain McGovern, 62 Cloglands, Forth
Archie MacGregor, 9 Doral Villas, Clearwater, USA (2 copies)
Dr Donald F Macgregor, Goroka Base Hospital, Papua New Guinea
Edward B Macgregor, 35 Loch Laxford, East Kilbride
Ronald McGuigan, 14/5 Murrayburn Grove, Edinburgh
Miss Liz McHattie, 2 Balmoral Avenue, Dumfries
Thomas D McIlwraith, 8 Silverknowes Bank, Edinburgh
George MacInnes, 100 Camnethan St, Stonehouse
Hugh MacInnes, Dalriada, 4 Ferryfield Rd, Connel, Oban
Dr Ronald McInroy, West Royd, Allerton Rd, Bradford (2 copies)
Keith W Macintosh, 106A Sinclair Street, Helensburgh
William Craig Macintosh, 7 High Oaks, Crawley
George McIntyre, Lexington, Kentucky, USA
Dr Stephen G MacIsaac, 1650 Cedar Ave, Montreal, Canada
Alastair A Mackay, Amersham
Alastair L Mackay, 8 Blaven Head, Irvine
Miss Christine C Mackay, 79 Fotheringay Rd, Glasgow
Donald C McKay, 7 Castle Croft, Dalmellington
Hew A Mackay, Kintraw, Barbreck, Lochgilphead
Ian M Mackay, FRICS, 38 The Paddock, Perceton, Irvine
James A Mackay, Newall Terrace, Dumfries
John McKay, 15 Milncroft Place, Glasgow
Joyce M Mackay, Newall Terrace, Dumfries
Malcolm C M McKay, Lyn Vaar, Cardross Road, Dumbarton
Malcolm J Mackay, OBE, 20 Lochy Road, Inverlochy
Mrs M S Mackay, St John St, Creetown
Andrew J McKee, 27 Balfron Road, Paisley
Thomas R McKee, Dunlukin, Cairnhill Rd, Airdrie
Mrs Martha McKellar, 125 Hillfoot Road, Ayr
John D McKendrick, 62 High Park Ave, Toronto Canada
Miss Ardil MacKenzie, Woodend, 134 Culduthel Rd, Inverness
Miss Ismay McKenzie, Stewarton
Mrs Margaret J C Mackenzie, 2 Brookfield Court, Ramsey
Lord Mackenzie-Stuart, Court of Justice, Luxembourg
H George McKerrow, Whiterne, Albert Rd, Dumfries

Alistair Mackie, Fairyknowe, 108 Clyde St, Carluke
Robert McKinnon, 26 St Blane's Drive, Bankhead, Glasgow
Alexander G Mackintosh, 3708 Howden Drive, Nanaimo, Canada
Bryan T McKirgan, 4 Balmoral Drive, Cambuslang, Glasgow
Lachlan McLachlan, 91 Bellfield Rd, Coalburn
Samuel McLarty, 38 Corserine Tce, Dalmellington
Gordon M Mackley, Sydney, Australia
James H McLatchie, 37 Wester Broom Place, Edinburgh
R G McLaughlan, 5 Longridge Rd, Whitburn
Mrs Duncan Maclay, 5 Middleton Bldgs, London
Capt Allan J Maclean, Duart, 59 Buffies Brae, Dunfermline
John C MacLean, 88 Boxwood Ave, Cranston, USA
Donald D McLeay, 6 Crosslet Ave, Dumbarton
Mrs Isobel MacLennan, 9 Birnie Terrace, Inverness
Frank Macleod, OBE, Tokeh, 6 Anson Way, Buckie
William K McLeod, 93 Bridgeburn Dr, Chryston, Glasgow
Ronald W McLucas, 86 Mary St, Toowoomba, Australia
Mrs Jean B Macmillan, 15c Bonnyton Rd, Kilmarnock
P G MacMillan, 25 Fairfield Drive, Clitheroe
Russell G McNab, 54 Montgomery St, Grangemouth
Dr Raymond N McNamee, 77 Bonhill Rd, Dumbarton
James McNaughton, London
John W McNay, 68 Makbrar Road, Dumfries
Charles & Catherine Macphee, 9 Creeth St, Bendigo, Australia
John McPhee, 6 Meadow St, Coventry
Alexander Macpherson, 15 Burnton Road, Dalrymple
Kenneth S MacPherson, II, 908 Sunset St, Pasadena, USA
Thomas McQueen, 72 North St, Coventry
George Macrae, 4023 Westbenden Drive, Murrysville, USA
George L McRobb, 26 Miller Ave, Ashburton, New Zealand
Alex McWilliam, 45 Avondale Ave, East Kilbride
Malcolm Main, Legana, 10 Glenfield Gdns, Cowdenbeath
Peter Fox Mallan, 23 Tinto Rd, Newlands, Glasgow
D B Malloy, Caol Ila, 20 Stanely Drive, Paisley
David F Manclark, 97 Glenvarloch St, Edinburgh
James H A Manderson, 46 Bathurst Drive, Ayr
James Marsh, 1 Rosepark West, Belfast
Albert E R Marshall, 372 Kedleston Rd, Allestree, Derby
Charles M Marshall, 177 Farne Drive, Glasgow
Ivor Marshall, 17 Millar Crescent, Edinburgh
T K Marshall, 46 Beech Avenue, Nairn
William R Marshall, 14 Tregunter Path, Hong Kong
Daniel A Martinez, Atlanta, USA
Robert W Marwick, Ardvohr, 9 Dunbeath Ave, Coatbridge

Gilbert Masiye, 4178 Nangwenya Road, Lusaka, Zambia
Mrs Agnes Lapraik Masterton, 20 Old Road, Elderslie
Derek L G Masterton, Deanfield, Bank Street, Irvine
Mr & Mrs David Matheson, 60 Spynie Street, Bishopmill, Elgin
Mrs Euphemia M Matheson, 2 Milburn Road, Alexandria
Andrew Mathieson, Ettrick Bank, 33 Ayr Rd, Prestwick
Mauchline Burns Club
Maxwelltown High School, donated by Burns Howff Club
Thomas C Meiklejohn, C/o 37 Titchfield Rd, Troon
Angus A Meldrum, Lochgreen, Gryffe Rd, Kilmacolm
Jas Meldrum, 36 MacLean Place, Gorebridge
Dr Patrick Menneteau, Univ. of Haute-Alsace, Mulhouse, France
Colin H Menzies, 49 Kilwinning Rd, Irvine
William H Miles, 27 Crichton Avenue, Pathhead
Andrew Miller, 3 Gladstone Terrace, Lerwick, Shetland
Mrs Ellen J Miller, 7 Dunbeath Ave, Newton Mearns
R Miller, 27 Kellywood Crescent, Kincardine
Cllr James Mills, Leader Labour Group, KLDC
Albert P Milne, 23 Ellon Road, Aberdeen
Ina & Tom Milne, Hespeler Rd, Cambridge, Canada
James N Milne, 57 Glencaple Ave, Dumfries
Kenneth M Milne, 22 Lomond Drive, Dumbarton
Mr & Mrs Peter Milne, 2 Woodside, West Kilbride
Robert W Milton, 11 A Auldlea Road, Beith
Mitchell Library, Glasgow
Glenne Mitchell, Bowbridge Lane, Prestbury, Cheltenham
James Mitchell, 62A Rosetta Rd, Peebles (2 copies)
Peter R Mitchell, 25 Maybury Avenue, Cheshunt
Mrs Margaret E Moffat, 9 Cornal Court, Beattock, Moffat
James S Mollison, 25 Lanchester Rd, Coventry
Jim Mollison, Ulithi, Kerr Place, Irvine
Margaret & Bill Molloy, Westgate Park Dr, St Catharines, Canada
Stewart Monro, 30 Hilary Crescent, Ayr
Andrew Montgomery, 9 Cumbernauld Rd, Mollinsburn
Dr James Montgomery, 229 Bank Street, Irvine
James M Montgomery, 5263 Glenridge Dr, Atlanta, USA
Percy Montgomery, 89 Kelvin Drive, Moodiesburn, Chryston
Mrs Mona J Moore, Marchmont, 11 Bellevue Rd, Ayr
Robert L Morris, 175 Saxmundham Rd, Aldeburgh
Mrs Christina J Morrison, 95 Main St, Callander
Finlay Morrison, 9 Regis Court, Edinburgh
James H Morrison, 10 Milne Avenue, Auchinleck
John Morrison, 85 Broom Crescent, Ochiltree
William & Jessie Morrison, 12 Brook Lane, Ainthrope, Danby

Mr & Mrs James Morrow, 7a Ranald Gdns, Rutherglen
A Lawrie Morton, Highfield, 67 Gartmore Rd, Paisley
George R Moyes, 12 Fair Acres, Bolton
Peter M Moyes, 2 Pennine Close, Wakefield
Dr John R Muir, 60 Hillpark Avenue, Edinburgh
Robert S Muir, 6 Taylors Road, Larbert
Thomas Muir, 16 May Terrace, Glasgow
Peter J Mulholland, 12 Cramond Ave, Renfrew
Dr Cameron Munro, 11 Summer Place, Aberdeen
James Murdoch, 84 George St, Stranraer
Adrian Murphy, 24 Lamington Rd, Glasgow
David R Murray, Woodcot, Strachen Crescent, Dollar
Donald L Murray, Glasgow
Mrs Janette Dunlop Murray, Conheath, Glencaple, Dumfries
Jim Murray, Heritage Blvd, North Vancouver, Canada
John Murray, 23 Craigie Road, Hurlford
John S Murray, 56 Frederick Road, Rainham
Leonard G Murray, 34 Buchanan Drive, Bearsden, Glasgow
William Burns Murray, Sherbule, 2 John Knox St, Galston
Cyril M Mutch, 50 Craigie Park, Aberdeen
Thomas B Myles, 7B Wallace House, Cumbernauld
Allan J Nadeau, USA
James Naismith, 4515 63rd Street, San Diego, USA
Stevenson Naismith, 77 North Orchard St, Motherwell
Nanaimo Burns Club 1041, Canada
National Library of Scotland, George IV Bridge, Edinburgh
Raoul P Neil, 15 Barnehurst St, Brisbane, Australia
David M Nelson, Netherlea, 2 McNab Street, Dollar
J Moir Nelson, Croit Mhor, 44 Ledrish Ave, Balloch
John Nelson, Campleslacks House, Closeburn, Dumfries
John Nelson, 46 Round Riding Rd, Dumbarton
John Paterson Newlands, 54 Garrowhill Drive, Baillieston
Newton Burns Club, Ayr
Robert Newton, 169 East 35th Street, Hamilton, Canada
Mrs Agnes M Nicol, 108 Allan Tower, Motherwell
Archibald Nicol, Seaview, Largiebeg, Whiting Bay, Arran
James Nicol, Craigewan, 8 Langside Drive, Comrie
John M Nicol, 17 Polmaise Crescent, Fallin, Stirling
Nithsdale District Council, Dumfries (2 copies)
Alexander R Niven, Perceton Paddock, Irvine
William A Niven, Sawmill Cottage, Ballochmyle, Mauchline
John Nobbs, 66 Lomond Rd, Coatbridge
William A Nolan, West Park, West Road, Irvine
Mrs Barbara L D K Noonan, 56 Kirkland Gds, Ballingry

Donald Norval, 51 Swanston Avenue, Scorguie, Inverness
David S Ogilvie, Lingerwood, 2 Nelson St, Dumfries
Mr & Mrs D W Ogilvie, Lingerwood, 2 Nelson St, Dumfries
Arnold O'Hara, 6 Hillfoot Cres, Ayr
James O'Lone, 9 Windsor Rd, East Fremantle, Australia
William H Olson, 8162 North Seneca Rd, Fox Point, USA
Albert Oswald, Schiehallion, 40 Derwent Way, Newark
Mrs Sarah Paling, Claremont, 7 Newall Terrace, Dumfries
I Park, 26 Ramsay Lane, Kincardine
James Parnham, North Lane Gardens, Roundhay, Leeds
Clifford F Parr, 22 Moy Terrace, Inverness
Eric Parr, Craggan Mhor, Wormit, Fife
Miss Eilidh-Dawn Paterson, Craiglea, Craig Rd, Dingwall
Frank Paterson, Alligin, Main St, Askhambryan
James Paterson, 49 Ford Crescent, Thornton
James Paterson, 133 Wellhall Road, Hamilton
Major John C Paterson, 35 Shorncliffe Rd, Folkestone
Mrs Ruth Paterson, 84 Stirling Dr, Bishopbriggs, Glasgow
Donald N M Paton, 75 Needless Road, Perth
Gordon Paton, 3 Dean Range, Simonstone
Harry A Paton, 6 Heys Street, Barrhead, Glasgow
Rev Dr Johnstone G Patrick, 8 North Street, Braunton
John Peacock, Sunnyfield, Sunnyhill, Hawick (2 copies)
Thomas G Pendleton, Longview Drive, Waukesna, USA
Tom A Peoples, MBE, JP, Riverside, Ballyclare (2 copies)
Mr & Mrs George Sim Peterkin, 24 Pansport Road, Elgin
Miss Marion Alice Peterkin, 22 Newburgh St, Bridge of Don, Aberdeen
Mrs Elizabeth Petrie, Ashley Cottage, 23 Slug Rd, Stonehaven
John & Margaret Phillips, 69 Morningside Dr, Grand Island, USA
Miss Kimberly M Phillips, 69 Morningside Dr, Grand Island, USA
Neil Thomas Phillips, 69 Morningside Dr, Grand Island, USA
James R Picken, 69 Monach Gardens, Dreghorn
Robert J Pine, Springside, Pier Road, Tarbert
William R Platt, 18 Silverknowes Drive, Edinburgh
Miss Ellen Pollock, 6 Kirkhill Cres, Neilston
John Pollock, 178 Landemer Drive, Rutherglen
John R Pollock, Shian, 9 Sunnyside Ave, Bathgate
John Poolman, 19 Princess Cres, Freuchie
John C Porteous, 18 Norman Cres, Irvine (4 copies)
Mrs Dorothy Ruth Prakke-Sclater, Flat 3, 18 Rutland Rd, Harrogate
Grace B Preston, 1150 Onyx Lane, New Port Richey, USA
Prestwick Burns Club (2 copies)
James McI Price, 4 Cullen, Northbarr, Erskine
Steven J Pritchard, 8 Mossview, Georgetown, Dumfries

John Prott, 8 Hannahston Ave, Drongan
Dr David W Purdie, The University, Leeds
Roy Ramage, 15 Glenwinnel Rd, Alva
John W Raper, 12 Castlehill Dr, Newton Mearns, Glasgow
Robert W Rapp, 2043 Brannon Drive SW, Austell, USA
Maurice L J Rattigan, 11 Saxon Road, Coventry
Luciano Rebecchi, 1 Old Inverkip Rd, Greenock
Robert Redmond, 23 Wyburn Place, Ayr
Mrs Jenny Reid, 134 Caledonia Road, Ayr
William J Rennie, Adenaich, High St, New Pitsligo
Robert A Reoch, 2317 Robinhood Place, Orange, USA
Mr & Mrs Richardson, Nundah, Brisbane, Australia
Andrew Richmond, 12 Innisbrook Cres, Thornhill, Canada
Mrs Mary J L Riddell, Lochlea, 37 Muirs, Kinross
Mrs Mary S Riddell, 8 Meadow View, Cumbernauld
Thomas S Riddock, 39 Newbiggin Cres, Tullibody
Andrew Duncan Rigg, 28 Main Street, Dundonald
Daniel M Ritchie, 24 Hendry Cres, Kirkcaldy
Robert Burns Club of San Diego, USA
Robert Burns Society of Annapolis Ltd
Ian F Roberts, 28 Broad St, Peterhead
Hugh P Robertson, Oakdene, 81 Bonhill Rd, Dumbarton
James D Robertson, 26 King St, New Elgin
John J Robertson, 6 Cessnock Place, Galston
Peter C Robertson, 21 Reid St, Elgin
Thomas F Robertson, Lintknowe, West Main St, Darvel
Brian Robinson, 5 Maple Close, Newcastle-upon-Tyne
William Robinson, 8 Woodland Ave, Corby
Miss Diane Robson, 191 Waverley Crescent, Bonnyrigg
Robert Rodger, 5 Joanne Court, Sefton, Australia
Mathew & Mary Roger, 71 Santin Dr, Cheektowaga, USA
Derek D Rogerson, 49 Gillbrae Crescent, Dumfries
Chris J Rollie, 21 Burnock St, Ochiltree
William R B Ronald, Koo-Man-Goo-Nong, Pakenham, Australia
Dilys & Joseph Roney, 70 Calder Tower, East Kilbride
John D Ross, 7 Centennial Court, Fredericton, Canada
Munro H Ross, Flat 25, Chelmsford Mews, Wigan
Tom Routledge, 43 Dipton Grove, Cramlington
Prof G Ross Roy, University of South Carolina, USA
Royal Scots College, Valladolid, Spain
James Ruddie, 9 Hillhouse Place, Stewarton
Andrew Russell, 20 Keltyhill Road, Kelty
Andrew John Russell, 2 Tolmount Cres, Montrose
St Joseph's College, Dumfries, donated by Burns Howff Club

Werner O Salge, 3070 O'Hagan Drive, Mississauga, Canada
Mrs Maria Saunders, 47 Charlotte St, Carlisle
Rev Melville & Christine Schofield, Laigh Kirk Manse, Kilmarnock
Mrs Jennifer C Schoon, 37 Radlett Park Road, Radlett
Robert A Schumacher, USA
Donald F Scott, 2 Keir St, Cowdenbeath
Harold F Scott, Ivy Bank, Station Rd, Lochgelly
James Scott, 8 Noblehill Pl, Dumfries
James Jarvis Scott, 34 Dawson Road, Broughty Ferry
Rev Dr John Miller Scott, 19 Ruthven Place, St Andrews
Robert Scott, Strathern, Caledonian Rd, Stevenston
Roy Scott, Garrion, 27 Forestview, Cumbernauld
William Scott, Oakfield, Ayr Road, Larkhall
John W Scoular, 731 Dunboyne Cres, London, Canada
Graham L Settles, 8 Gearholm Road, Ayr
Thos Shanks, Melville Park, Calderwood, East Kilbride
Miss Carol M Sharp, 268 Canongate, Edinburgh
Duncan McN C Sharp, 14A Randolph Crescent, Edinburgh
Sir George Sharp, OBE, DL, JP, 56 Station Road, Thornton
Dr N C Craig Sharp, 14A Randolph Crescent, Edinburgh (2 copies)
Robert G C Sharp, 1 Blanefield Terrace, Blanefield
Robert K Sharp, Mo Dhachaidh, Strone, Argyll
George A Shepherd, 183 Claremont St, Alloa
G W Shepherd, The Old Rectory, Market Overton, Oakham
Mrs Isabella A Shepherd, 238 Duddingston Drive, Kirkcaldy
Robert Shepherd, 238 Duddingston Drive, Kirkcaldy
Robert T Shepherd, 66 Keirs Brae, Cardenden
Fiona & Paul Shutler, Chesham
David D Sibbald, 6 Brentham Crescent, Stirling
Maj Earle B B McD Simpson, Woodend House, Dalcross, Inverness
Frederick Sinden, Hon Vice President Sunderland Burns Club
Robert Skinner, 10 Glebe Gardens, Bonhill, Alexandria
David S Skipper, 8198 Wenonga Ct, Tallahassee, USA
Thomas Slaven, 11 St Davids Close, Chepstow
Hugh David Sloan, 34 Gilbert Circle, Dumfries
Mrs Marjorie J I P Sloan, 47 Homebriar House, Barns Park, Ayr
Stanislaus C Sloan, 130 Invergarry Dr, Glasgow
Ian Small, 15 Atholl Street, Dundee
John L Smart, 29 Valley Rd, Clevedon
Alex G M Smith, 6 Coronation St, Wishaw
Andrew Smith, 85 Montrose Rd, Foxbar, Paisley
David Smith, Cargenbridge Ave, Dumfries
James Smith, 22 Glencairn Street, Cumnock

John Smith, 3 Muircot Place, Coalsnaughton
Mrs Mary J Smith, 49 McNeish Drive, Annan
Mr & Mrs T J J Smith, 24 Totley Lane, Bradway, Sheffield
William R Smith, 17 Miller St, Millport
Mark Roy Solomon, 34 Waun-y-Groes Rd, Rhiwbina, Cardiff
Kenneth D K Somerville, 8 Hoi Ping Road, Causeway Bay, Hong Kong
Robert G Somerville, 12 Lowther Bank, Irvine
John Fleming Sorbie, 16 Chapelton Gardens, Dumbarton
H H Souter, Plymouth, Devon
John C Speirs, 48 Tweed Street, Ayr
J M Spittal, Les Bourgs, St Andrew, Guernsey
William M Sprowl, Eastlands Farm, Rothesay, Bute
Alan R Stalker, Struan, The Loan, Gattonside, Melrose
John Stark, 58 Hinkar Way, Eyemouth
Kenny Stark, 52 Westermains Avenue, Kirkintilloch
Carl H C Stephens, Sarsgrove, Churchill, Oxon
George Stevenson, Tanzieknowe, Bentinck Drive, Troon
Robert C Stevenson, 15 Gray Crescent, Irvine
T B Stevenson, 1501 Hutchinson House, Hong Kong
Alexander J Stewart, 10 Hallcraig Place, Carluke
Allister McL Stewart, Ardvorlich, Terang, Australia
Bryan G Stewart, 15 Epping Grove, Perth, Australia
Dr Gordon Stewart, Dundonald Burns Club
Henry S Stewart, 118 Caledonia Rd, Ayr
Jock Stewart, 35 Stanley St, Croydon Park, Australia
T L Stewart, 60 Colinhill Rd, Strathaven
Dr George S Stirling, Phyllis Park, Murraythwaite, Dalton
Allan Stoddart, 35 Morton Avenue, Ayr
Rev Samuel Stokes, 33 North Road, Carrickfergus, Antrim
Strathclyde "Bonnie Jean" Burns Club
Charles F Street, 9 Bensley Ave, Irvine
R Strickland, 2 Ladypark Farm, Ladypark, Gateshead
Charles W M Stuart, 352 Main St, Alexandria
Jack Stuart, 9 St Mathias Court, St Mathias St, Leeds
Sandy Stuart, 51 Raeden Crescent, Aberdeen
James Sturgeon, 6 Birch Road, Ayr
Stanley J Sullivan, 10 Oxgangs Ave, Edinburgh
William Summers, 14 Links Terrace, Peterhead
Rev Alex S Sutherland, The Manse, 16 Kerrix Rd, Symington
Mrs Betsy Sutherland, Spragatup, Haroldswick, Unst, Shetland
Ian G Sutherland, Travilla, 13 Blackhouse Tce, Peterhead
William A Sutherland, 36 Glencaple Ave, Dumfries
William J Sutherland, Coillebhar, Main St, Urquhart
Mrs Mary Ross Sutton, 205 Linwood Ave, Goldsboro, USA

John Sweeney, 22 Mansewood Road, Glasgow
Miss Nancie J Symons, Edina, 15 Cross Lane, Bebington
Donald F Tait, 40 Carabob Court, Scarborough, Canada
Tam O'Shanter Club, Hertford Place, Coventry
Mrs Heather I Taylor, 23 Heathmoor Drive, York
Rev John Taylor, 62 Woodlands Grove, Kilmarnock
Harold Thomas, 24 Cessnock Place, Holmston, Ayr
David M Thomson, 41 Gilloch Cres, Dumfries
George Thomson, Craigenroan, Dalbeattie Rd, Dumfries
Ian R Thomson, 105 Main St, Dreghorn
Matthew Thomson, 73 Marchburn Ave, Prestwick
Mrs Peggy Thomson, 52A Dundonald Road, Kilmarnock
Stewart Thomson, 23 Salisbury Ave, Northshields
T Alex Thomson, MC, Crabtree Cottage, Henton, Chinnor
William D Thomson, 32 Tarfside Gdns, Glasgow
William M Thomson, 39 Adamton Road North, Prestwick
Mrs Jean E F Thow, The Wicket, Carleton Gardens, Prestwick
Mrs M Thow, 50 Midton Road, Prestwick
David Tindall, 1 Briar Grove, Ayr
George Hay Tinning, 235 Ayr Road, Newton Mearns, Glasgow
Mrs Rose Cunningham Trigg, Country Club Drive, Colorado Springs, USA
David McInnes Turnbull, 68 Dunalastair Dr, Stepps
Dick & Rita Turner, 50 West Crescent, Troon
Mrs Emma Turner, Sakura, 11 Silvertonhill Ave, Hamilton
Donald R Urquhart, Glebe House, 39 Glebe St, Dumfries
Robert J Utterson, Oak Cottage, Kirknewton
J L Scott Veitch, 4 Cramond Regis, Edinburgh
Arthur George Wake, 3 Smiddy Row, North Berwick
James S Wales, 14 Whyte Avenue, Irvine
Brian E Walker, 35 Longmeanygate, Leyland
Charles T Walker, 8 Caldecott Rd, Kowloon, Hong Kong
Mrs Gillian I G Walker, 6 Dalmailing Ave, Dreghorn
James A Walker, 97 Hilton Rd, Bishopbriggs, Glasgow
John Smith Walker, 44 Newfields, Berwick-upon-Tweed
Robert Walker, Park Terrace Guest House, Irvine
William Walker, 19 Gleneagles Court, Whitley Bay
Dr Alastair Bruce Wallace, Cheltenham
Stuart M Wallace, Juliston, Eastwoodmains Rd, Clarkston
Charles Ward, 38 Lower Ford St, Coventry
Alexander H Watson, 102 Crowhill Rd, Bishopbriggs
Miss Angela Watson, 102 Crowhill Rd, Bishopbriggs
David Watson, 17 North Street, Falkirk
George W Watson, Hamifield, Kilwinning Rd, Irvine
James H Watson, Meadow Cottage, 23 Quarry Rd, Irvine

James U Watson, 102 Crowhill Rd, Bishopbriggs
Miss Lorna Watson, 102 Crowhill Rd, Bishopbriggs
Tom H H Watson, Eaglesham
George R Watt, Cherry Valley, Ontario, Canada
A Norman Watters, 17 Townsend Cres, Kirkcaldy
David A K Watters, Department of Surgery, Lusaka, Zambia
Robert A Wayman, Holmcroft, West Kilbride Rd, Dalry
Miss W R Webster, 23 Glenshee Drive, Blairgowrie
Mrs Hazel M Weierter, 5 William St, Kirkcaldy
Alexander N Weir, 30 Corslet Road, Currie
John Weir, North Logan, Catrine, Mauchline
John A Weir, Spencer Drive, Lawrence, Kansas, USA
Peter J Westwood, 28 Stranka Avenue, Paisley
Mrs A C White, Dungannon, Little Wynd, Edzell
Dr Ian R White, BSc, PhD, FBCS, FRAS, Daymer Gdns, Pinner
William A Whiteford, Ryeland St, Strathhaven
Ian A Whitehead, 9 Rowanbank Rd, Dumfries
John T Whitelock, 363 Glamorgan Cres SW, Calgary, Canada
Archie Whyte, 63 Oakfield Tower, Motherwell
Mrs Janet D Whyte, Holmbrae House, Strathblane Rd, Milngavie
Miss Megan H Whyte, 32 Colthill Road, Aberdeen
Ms Nan Whyte, 7 Bank St, Irvine
James B Wighton, 83 Glenalla Crescent, Ayr
J R Wignall, 67 Aylestone Lane, Wigston, Leicester
Paul L Wilbert, 311 Winwood, Pittsburg, Kansas, USA
Dr Lindsay Wilkie, OStJ, St Mary's St, Willunga, Australia
Mrs Dorothy M J Williams, 40 Hillbury Ave, Kenton
Mrs Janet Williamson, 202 Grangemoor, Runcorn, Cheshire
Rockwell B Williamson, 12 Miller Avenue, Fairlie
William Williamson, 30 Ivanhoe Road, Paisley
Alex W Wilson, 9 Lodge Avenue, Elstree
Mr & Mrs G R Wilson, Crinan, 15A Burgh Rd, Prestwick
James Wilson, 6 Oswald Place, Ayr
James G Wilson, 373 Hampton Heath Rd, Burlington, Canada
John Wilson, 47 Reid Street, Hamilton
Mrs Marion Wilson, Tighnamor, Gloucester Ave, Dumfries
Dr Robert B Wilson, Mile Ash, Edinburgh Road, Dumfries
Susan & David Wilson, 18 Waverley Gdns, Shawlands, Glasgow
W Stewart Wilson, Ibiscus, Rosehill Crescent, Banchory
Andrew S Winton, 12 Ventor Terrace, Edinburgh
Dr Ian H Y Wood, Kincraig, Kilwinning Rd, Irvine
Herbert H Wright, 7212 Masonville Dr, Annandale, VA, USA
John Wyness, 203-2181 Avenue Rd, Toronto, Canada
Mr & Mrs Brian J Wynne, 52 Smith Drive, Elgin

James Wyper, 2 Watson Terrace, Irvine
James Yates, Eildon, Airlie House, Larbert
David S Young, 42 Route de Remich, Roedt, Luxembourg
Mrs Elizabeth Young, 76 Silcoates Lane, Wakefield
Francis B Young, 65 Glenconner Road, Ayr
Hugh Young, 432 Manora Rise NE, Calgary, Canada
Iain D Young, 52 Mowbray, Calderwood, East Kilbride
Robert Young, 10816 Maplecrest Rd, Calgary, Canada
William J Young, 74 Beechwood Drive, Glasgow
William B Yule, 1 Balwearie Crescent, Kirkcaldy

CHRONOLOGICAL LIST OF LETTERS

Roman numerals denote the number in the sequence of each recipient's letters.
Numbers in brackets are those in the Clarendon Press edition (1985).

1780   Page
(1)   I   William Niven, 29th July.   37
(2)   II   William Niven, 3rd November.   38

1781
(3)   III   William Niven, 12th June.   39
(4)   William Burnes, 27th December.   41
(5)   I   Alison Begbie?, 'What you may think of this letter . . .'.   43
(6)   II   Alison Begbie?, 'I verily believe . . .'.   44
(7)   III   Alison Begbie?, 'I do not remember . . .'.   44
(8)   IV   Alison Begbie?, 'I have often thought . . .'.   46
(9)   V   Alison Begbie?, 'I ought, in good manners . . .'.   47

1782
(10)   I   Thomas Orr, 7th September.   49
(11)   II   Thomas Orr, 17th November.   49
(12)   I   Sir John Whitefoord, [November].   51

1783
(13)   I   John Murdoch, 15th January.   54
(14)   I   James Burness, 21st June.   57
(15)   I   Gavin Hamilton, 18th October.   65

1784
(16)   II   James Burness, 17th February.   59
(17)   III   James Burness, 3rd August.   59
(18)   I   John Tennant, Jr., 13th September.   72
(19)   III   Thomas Orr, 11th November.   50

1785
(20)   Margaret Kennedy, [early October].   75

1786
(21)   I   John Richmond, 17th February.   76
(22)   I   John Kennedy, 3rd March.   83
(23)   I   Robert Muir, 20th March.   86
(24)   I   Robert Aiken, 3rd April.   91
(25)   II   Gavin Hamilton, [15th April].   65
(26)   I   John Ballantine, [April].   97
(27)   ____ McWhinnie, 17th April.   106
(28)   II   John Kennedy, 20th April.   83
(29)   John Arnot, [April].   107
(30)   III   John Kennedy, 16th May.   84
(31)   I   David Brice, 12th June.   111

			Page
(32)	IV	James Burness, 5th July.	60
(33)	II	John Richmond, 9th July.	77
(34)	II	David Brice, 17th July.	112
(35)		Deed of Assignment, 22nd July.	115
(36)	III	John Richmond, 30th July.	77
(37)	II	James Smith, [1st August?].	117
(38)	IV	John Kennedy, [10th?] August.	84
(39)	I	John Logan, 10th August.	123
(40)	III	James Smith, [14th August].	118
(41)		Thomas Campbell, [19th August].	124
(42)	IV	William Niven, 30th August.	40
(43)	IV	John Richmond, 1st September.	78
(44)	II	Dr John Mackenzie, [3rd September].	32
(45)	V	John Richmond, 3rd September.	79
(46)	II	Robert Muir, [8th September].	86
(47)	I	Mrs Stewart of Stair, [September].	125
(48)	V	John Kennedy, 26th September.	84
(49)	VI	John Richmond, [27th September].	79
(51)	II	John Ballantine, [27th September].	97
(51 B)	II	Robert Aiken, [about 27th September].	92
(51 C)	III	John Ballantine, [late September or early October].	98
(53)	III	Robert Aiken, [8th October?].	92
(53 A)	III	Dr John Mackenzie, 25th October.	113
(54)	I	Archibald Lawrie, 13th November.	127
(55)	I	Mrs [Frances] Dunlop, 15th November.	131
(56)		Wilhelmina Alexander, 18th November.	216
(57)	III	Robert Muir, 18th November.	87
(58)	I	William Chalmers, 20th November.	218
(59)	IV	John Ballantine, 20th November.	98
(60)	I	George Reid, 29th November.	220
(61)	II	Sir John Whitefoord, 1st December.	52
(61 A)	IV	Dr John Mackenzie, [6th December].	114
(62)	III	Gavin Hamilton, 7th December.	66
(63)	V	John Ballantine, 13th December.	99
(64)	IV	Robert Muir, 15th December.	87
(65)	IV	Robert Aiken, 16th December.	94
(66)		The Rev. William Greenfield, December.	221
(67)	V	Robert Muir, 20th December.	88
(67 A)	I	John Tennant, 20th December.	222
(68)	II	William Chalmers, 27th December.	218
(69)		Lord Monboddo, [30th December].	223
(70)	I	Henry Erskine, [December].	224

1787

(71)		James Sibbald, [January].	225
(72)	IV	Gavin Hamilton, 7th January.	67
(73)	V	Dr John Mackenzie, 11th January.	114
(75)	I	James, Earl of Glencairn, 13th January.	226

(76)	I	Margaret Chalmers?, [January?].	229
(77)	VI	John Ballantine, 14th January.	100
(78)	II	Mrs Dunlop, 15th January.	132
(78 A)	I	Patrick Miller, [15th January].	239
(79)	I	Dr John Moore, January.	245
(80)		The Rev. George Lawrie, 5th February.	262
(81)		The Bailies of the Canongate, 6th February.	264
(82)	I	The Earl of Buchan, 7th February.	265
(83)	II	Archibald Lawrie, [February?].	127
(84)		James Dalrymple, February.	268
(85)	II	Dr John Moore, 15th February.	246
(86)	VII	John Ballantine, 24th February.	101
(86 A)		The Earl of Eglinton [and others], [February].	270
(88)	V	Gavin Hamilton, 8th March.	67
(89)	I	James Candlish, 21st March.	271
(90)	III	Mrs Dunlop, 22nd March.	134
(91)	I	Robert Cleghorn.	273
(92)	III	Archibald Lawrie, 'I cannot be with you . . .'.	128
(93)	I	Lady Henrietta Don, 26th March.	279
(94)	IV	Mrs Dunlop, 15th April.	135
(95)	VIII	John Ballantine, 18th April.	102
(96)	II	George Reid, 19th April.	220
(96 A)		Miss Farquhar, about 20th April.	280
(97)	III	Dr John Moore, 23rd April.	246
(98)	V	Mrs Dunlop, 30th April.	136
(99)	I	William Dunbar, [30th April].	281
(101)		Rev. Dr Hugh Blair, [4th May].	287
(101 A)		Henry Mackenzie, [4th May].	288
(102)	I	William Tytler, 4th May.	290
(103)	II	James, Earl of Glencairn, 4th May.	227
(104)	I	James Johnson, 4th May.	291
(105)		Dr M. Fyffe, 5th May.	303
(106)	I	William Creech, 13th May.	304
(107)		Alexander Pattison, 17th May.	307
(108)	I	Peter Hill, 17th May.	308
(109)	II	Peter Hill, 24th May.	308
(109 A)	I	William Scott, 24th May.	325
(110)	I	Robert Ainslie, 29th May.	326
(112)	I	William Nicol, 1st June.	342
(113)	III	James Smith, 11th June.	118
(114)	II	William Nicol, 18th June.	343
(115)	II	William Creech, 24th June.	304
(116)	II	Robert Ainslie, 25th June.	327
(117)	IV	James Smith, 30th June.	119
(118)		Will ___, 2nd July.	351
(119)	VII	John Richmond, 7th July.	80
(120)	V	Robert Aiken, [14th July].	95
(121)	III	Peter Hill, 19th July.	308

Page

(122)	III	Robert Ainslie, 23rd July.	327
(122 A)	IV	Robert Ainslie, 29th July.	328
(123)	III	William Nicol, 29th July.	345
(124)	VI	Mrs Dunlop, 30th July.	137
(125)	IV	Dr John Moore, 2nd August.	247
(126)	II	William Tytler, [August].	290
(127)	IV	Archibald Lawrie, 14th August.	128
(128)	II	William Scott.	328
(129)		St James's Lodge, Tarbolton, 23rd August.	352
(130)	V	Robert Ainslie, 23rd August.	329
(131)	VI	Robert Muir, 26th August.	88
(132)	VI	Gavin Hamilton, 28th August.	68
(133)		William Inglis, [4th September].	353
(134)	V	James Burness, 4th September.	61
(135)	I	Josiah Walker, 5th September.	354
(136)	VI	James Burness, [13th September].	61
(137)	I	Gilbert Burns, 17th September.	357
(138)	VII	James Burness, 19th September.	62
(139)	II	Patrick Miller, 28th September.	240
(140)	II	Josiah Walker, 29th September.	355
(141)	IV	William Nicol, [8th October].	345
(142)	I	William Cruikshank, [8th October].	359
(144)	III	Patrick Miller, 20th October.	241
(145)	I	James Hoy, 20th October.	361
(145 A)	II	Margaret Chalmers, [21st October].	230
(146)	VIII	John Richmond, 25th October.	81
(147)	I	The Rev. John Skinner, [25th October].	363
(147 A)	II	James Johnson, [October or November].	291
(149)	II	James Hoy, 6th November.	362
(150)	III	Margaret Chalmers, 6th November.	231
(150 A)		Robert P____n, 14th November.	365
(151)	III	James Johnson, [November].	292
(152)	IV	Margaret Chalmers, 21st November.	232
(152 A)	VII	Mrs Dunlop, 24th November.	137
(153)	VI	Robert Ainslie, 25th November.	330
(153 A)	II	James Candlish, [late November].	271
(153 B)		Thomas Whyter, [end of November?].	366
(154)		Miss Isobel or Isabella Mabane, [1st December?].	367
(155)	V	Margaret Chalmers, 1st December.	232
(156)	I	John Beugo, [December?].	368
(157)	VII	Gavin Hamilton, [December].	70
(158)	I	Mrs [Agnes] McLehose, [6th December], 'I had set . . .'.	371
(159)	II	Mrs McLehose, [8th December], 'I can say with truth . . .'.	372
(159 A)		William Hamilton, [12th December].	413
(160)	VI	Margaret Chalmers, 12th December.	233
(161)	III	Mrs McLehose, [12th December], 'I stretch a point . . .'.	372
(162)	VII	Margaret Chalmers, 19th December.	233
(163)	IV	Mrs McLehose, [20th December], 'Your last, my dear Madam . . .'.	373

			Page
(164)		Charles Hay, [24th December].	414
(164 A)		_____ Thomson, [10th-24th December].	415
(165)		James Stewart, [26th December].	416
(166)	V	Mrs McLehose, [28th December], 'I beg your pardon . . .'.	374
(167)		Francis Howden, [December].	417
(168)	I	Richard Brown, 30th December.	418

1788

(169)	VI	Mrs McLehose, [3rd January], 'Your verses . . .'.	375
(170)	VII	Mrs McLehose, [4th January], 'You are right . . .'.	376
(171)	VIII	Mrs McLehose, [5th January], 'Some days, some nights . . .'.	378
(172)	I	Robert Graham, [January].	424
(173)	IX	John Ballantine?, 'I have been wandering . . .'.	102
(174)	IX	Mrs McLehose, [8th January], 'I am delighted . . .'.	378
(175)	X	Mrs McLehose, [10th January], 'I am certain I saw . . .'.	380
(176)	XI	Mrs McLehose, [12th January], 'Your thoughts on religion . . .'.	381
(177)	XII	Mrs McLehose, [12th January], 'You talk of weeping . . .'.	382
(178)	XIII	Mrs McLehose, [14th January], 'Why have I not heard . . .'.	382
(179)	XIV	Mrs McLehose, [15th January], 'That you have faults . . .'.	383
(180)	XV	Mrs McLehose, [16th January], 'Clarinda, your letter . . .'.	384
(180 A)		An Unidentified Correspondent, 16 January.	724
(181)	XVI	Mrs McLehose, [19th January], 'There is no time . . .'.	384
(182)	XVII	Mrs McLehose, [20th January], 'The impertinence of fools . . .'.	386
(183)	XVIII	Mrs McLehose, [21st January], 'I am discontented . . .'.	388
(184)	VIII	Mrs Dunlop, 21st January .	139
(185)	VIII	Margaret Chalmers, [22nd January].	234
(185 A)	III	William Creech, [24th January].	305
(186)	XIX	Mrs McLehose, [24th January], 'I have been tasking . . .'.	388
(187)	XX	Mrs McLehose, [25th January], 'Clarinda, my life . . .'.	389
(188)	XXI	Mrs McLehose, [26th January], 'I was on the way . . .'.	390
(189)	IX	Mrs McLehose, [27th January], 'I have almost given up . . .'.	390
(190)	XXIII	Mrs McLehose, [29th January], 'I cannot go out today . . .'.	391
(191)	XXIV	Mrs McLehose, [1st February], 'Your fears for Mary . . .'.	392
(192)	III	James, Earl of Glencairn, 1st February.	227
(194)	XXV	Mrs McLehose, [3rd February], 'I have just been before . . .'.	392
(195)	XXVI	Mrs McLehose, [7th February], 'I cannot be easy . . .'.	394
(196)	IX	John Richmond, 7th February.	81
(197)	II	John Tennant, 7th February.	222
(198)	IX	Mrs Dunlop, 12th February.	139
(199)	XXVII	Mrs McLehose, [13th February], 'I make a numerous . . .'.	394
(199 A)	II	William Dunbar, [13th February].	281
(200)	XXVIII	Mrs McLehose, [13th February], 'After a wretched day . . .'.	395
(201)	XXIX	Mrs McLehose, [14th February], 'I am distressed . . .'.	396
(202)	XXX	Mrs McLehose, [14th February], 'I just now received . . .'.	396
(203)	II	The Rev. John Skinner, 14th February.	364
(204)	XXXI	Mrs McLehose, [15th February], 'When matters, my Love . . .'.	397

			Page
(205)	II	Richard Brown, 15th February.	419
(206)		Mrs Elizabeth Rose, 17th February.	441
(207)	IX	Margaret Chalmers, [17th February].	235
(207 A)		An Unidentified Correspondent, [December 1786-March 1788?].	724
(207 B)		Anthony Dunlop, [October 1787-February 1788].	443
(208)	XXXII	Mrs McLehose, [18th February], 'The attraction of love . . .'.	398
(209)	XXXIII	Mrs McLehose, [22nd February], 'I wrote you . . .'.	398
(210)	XXXIV	Mrs McLehose, [23rd February], 'I have just now . . .'.	399
(211)	III	Richard Brown, 24th February.	419
(212)	X	Mrs Dunlop, 29th February.	140
(213)	XXXV	Mrs McLehose, 2nd March, 'I hope, and am certain . . .'.	400
(214)	II	William Cruikshank, 3rd March.	359
(214 A)	IV	Patrick Miller, 3rd March.	241
(215)	VII	Robert Ainslie, 3rd March.	330
(217)	XXXVI	Mrs McLehose, [6th March], 'I own myself guilty . . .'.	401
(218)	XXXVII	Mrs McLehose, [7th March], 'Clarinda, I have been . . .'.	402
(219)	XI	Mrs Dunlop, 7th March.	141
(220)	IV	Richard Brown, 7th March.	420
(221)	VII	Robert Muir, 7th March.	89
(222)	VIII	Gavin Hamilton, [7th March].	70
(222 A)	V	William Nicol?, 8th March.	345
(222 B)	XXXVIII	Mrs McLehose, [12th March], 'Clarinda, will that . . .'.	403
(223)	X	Margaret Chalmers, 14th March.	235
(224)	XXXIX	Mrs McLehose, [14th March], 'I am just now come in . . .'.	404
(224 A)	V	Patrick Miller, [16th March].	242
(225)	XL	Mrs McLehose, [17th March], 'I will meet you . . .'.	404
(225 A)	XLI	Mrs McLehose, 17th March, 'Fair Empress of the Poet's soul . . .'.	405
(226)	XLII	Mrs McLehose, [18th March], 'I am just hurrying . . .'.	405
(228)	V	Richard Brown, 20th March.	421
(228 A)	I	William Stewart, 21st March.	444
(228 B)	II	Robert Graham, 25th March.	425
(229)	XII	Mrs Dunlop, 26th March.	142
(230)	II	Robert Cleghorn, 31st March.	273
(231)	IV	William Creech, 31st March.	305
(233)	XIII	Mrs Dunlop, 31st March.	143
(234)		Alexander Blair, 3rd April.	447
(235)	XI	Margaret Chalmers, 7th April.	235
(236)	III	William Dunbar, 7th April.	282
(237)	V	James Smith, 28th April.	121
(238)	XIV	Mrs Dunlop, 28th April.	143
(239)	I	Dugald Stewart, 3rd May.	448
(240)		Samuel Brown, 4th May.	451
(241)	XV	Mrs Dunlop, 4th May.	145
(242)	IV	James Johnson, 25th May.	292
(243)	VIII	Robert Ainslie, 26th May.	331
(244)	XVI	Mrs Dunlop, 27th May.	

(245)		Andrew Dunlop, 31st May.	452
(246)	IX	Robert Ainslie, [early June].	331
(247)	XVII	Mrs Dunlop, 13th June.	147
(248)	X	Robert Ainslie, 14th June.	332
(248 A)		Hugh Parker, [11th-30th June?].	33
(249)	XI	Robert Ainslie, [June?].	332
(250)	XII	Robert Ainslie, 23rd June.	334
(251)	VI	James Smith, 26th June.	122
(252)	XIII	Robert Ainslie, 30th June.	334
(253)	II	William Stewart, [9th July?].	444
(254)	XVIII	Mrs Dunlop, [17th July].	148
(255)	IV	Peter Hill, 18th July.	309
(256)		George Lockhart, 18th July.	453
(256 A)	I	John Smith, 18th July.	454
(257)	I	Alexander Cunningham, 27th July.	455
(258)	V	James Johnson, [28th July?].	293
(259)	X	John Ballantine, [August?].	103
(260)	XIX	Mrs Dunlop, 2nd August.	150
(261)		Miss Rachel Dunlop, 2nd August.	475
(262)		Robert McIndoe, 5th August.	476
(264)	XX	Mrs Dunlop, 16th August.	152
(265)	XXI	Mrs Dunlop, 21st August.	154
(266)	XIV	Robert Ainslie, 23rd August.	335
(267)	VI	James Johnson, 2nd September.	293
(267 A)	XXII	Mrs Dunlop, 5th September.	155
(268)	II	John Beugo, 9th September.	368
(269)	III	Robert Graham, 10th September.	425
(270)	I	Jean Armour Burns, 12th September.	477
(271)	I	Robert Riddell, [16th September].	480
(272)	XII	Margaret Chalmers, 16th September.	236
(273)	IV	Robert Graham, 23rd September.	427
(274)	IV	William Dunbar, 25th September.	283
(275)	XXIII	Mrs Dunlop, 27th September.	156
(275 A)		An Unidentified Correspondent, 29th September.	724
(276)	V	Peter Hill, 1st October.	310
(277)	I	Dr James Mundell, 'As my symptoms . . .'.	485
(278)	II	Jean Armour Burns, 14th October.	478
(279)	XV	Robert Ainslie, 18th October.	336
(280)	XXIV	Mrs Dunlop, 23rd October.	157
(281)	XXV	Mrs Dunlop, 29th October.	158
(282)		Miss Agnes Dunlop, [November?].	486
(283)		The *Edinburgh Evening Courant*, 8th November.	487
(284)		Bruce Campbell, 13th November.	489
(285)	XXVI	Mrs Dunlop, 13th November.	159
(286)	V	Archibald Lawrie, 15th November.	129
(287)	I	Dr Thomas Blacklock, 15th November.	490
(288)	VII	James Johnson, 15th November.	294
(289)	I	John McMurdo, 26th November.	492

Page

(290)	XXVII	Mrs Dunlop, 7th December.	160
(291)	II	John Tennant, Jr., 22nd December.	73
(292)	III	William Cruikshank, [December 1788-January 1789].	360

1789

(293)	XXVIII	Mrs. Dunlop, 1st January.	163
(294)	V	Dr John Moore, 4th January.	256
(295)	XVI	Robert Ainslie, 6th January.	336
(296)	II	John McMurdo, 9th January.	492
(296 A)	II	John Smith, 17th January.	454
(297)	II	Dugald Stewart, 20th January.	448
(298)	I	Lady Elizabeth Cunningham, 22nd January.	496
(299)	II	Henry Erskine?, 22nd January.	224
(300)		Peter Morison, 22nd January.	501
(301)	I	David Blair, 23rd January.	502
(302)	III	Robert Cleghorn, 23rd January.	274
(303)	VIII	James Johnson, 23rd January.	294
(304)	I	Alexander Dalziel?, 'I sit down to write . . .'.	505
(305)	XXIX	Mrs Dunlop, [January], 'No ill-weather . . .'.	165
(306)	III	William Stewart, 'In honest Bacon's ingleneuk . . .'.	445
(307)	II	Alexander Cunningham, 24th January.	456
(308)		Bishop John Geddes, 3rd February.	507
(309)	V	William Dunbar, 'In vain do we talk . . .'.	284
(310)	XXX	Mrs Dunlop, 5th February.	165
(311)		William Pitt [*Address of the Scottish Distillers*].	509
(312)		Mrs Edward Wigham, 7th February.	512
(313)	I	Thomas Boyd, [8th February], 'I see at last . . .'.	513
(314)	VIII	James Burness, 9th February.	62
(315)	III	Jean Armour Burns, [20th February].	478
(316)	XXXI	Mrs Dunlop, 21st February.	167
(317)	II	Thomas Boyd, [1st March].	513
(318)	I	William Burns, 2nd March.	514
(319)	XXXII	Mrs Dunlop, 4th March.	168
(320)	XLIII	Mrs McLehose, 9th March.	405
(321)	II	William Burns, [10th March].	514
(322)	VI	Dr John Moore, 23rd March.	258
(323)	III	William Burns, 25th March.	515
(324)	XXXIII	Mrs Dunlop, 25th March.	169
(325)	VI	Peter Hill, 2nd April.	312
(326)	XXXIV	Mrs Dunlop, 3rd April.	171
(326 A)	I	[Peter Stuart, April? 1789?].	520
(327)		The Editor of the *Gazetteer*, 10th April.	525
(328)	II	The Editor of *Stuart's Star*, 13th April.	521
(329)	IV	William Burns, 15th April.	515
(330)	XXXV	Mrs Dunlop, 21st April.	171
(331)	IX	James Johnson, 24th April.	294
(331 A)	III	The Editor of the *Morning Star*, 25th April.	522
(332)	I	James Hamilton, 27th April.	526

(333)		The Rev. Patrick Carfrae, 27th April.	527
(334)		Mrs Jane Blair McMurdo [2nd May].	529
(335)	XXXVI	Mrs Dunlop, 4th May.	172
(336)	III	Alexander Cunningham, 4th May.	457
(337)	V	William Burns, 5th May.	516
(338)	IV	The Editor of the *Morning Star*, 7th May.	522
(339)	V	Peter Stuart, 7th May.	522
(340)	II	Robert Riddell, 'I wish from my inmost soul . . .'.	481
(341)	V	Robert Graham, 13th May.	428
(342)	II	Lady Elizabeth Cunningham, 15th May.	497
(343)	VI	Peter Stuart, 18th May.	523
(343 A)		The Editor of the *Belfast News-Letter*, 18th May.	530
(344)	VI	Richard Brown, 21st May.	421
(345)	II	James Hamilton, 26th May.	526
(346)		John McAuley, 4th June.	531
(347)	XVII	Robert Ainslie, 8th June.	337
(348)	X	James Johnson, 19th June.	295
(349)	VI	Patrick Miller, 21st June.	243
(350)	XXXVII	Mrs Dunlop, 21st June.	173
(351)	XXXVIII	Mrs Dunlop, 7th July.	175
(352)	XXXIX	Mrs Dunlop, 17th July.	176
(353)	VI	Robert Graham, 31st July.	429
(353 A)	VII	Peter Stuart, [June-July].	
(353 B)		Helen Maria Williams, [late July or early August].	532
(354)	VI	Robert Aiken, 'Whether in the way of my trade . . .'.	
(355)	III	David Sillar, 5th August.	536
(356)	II	John Logan, 7th August.	123
(357)	VI	William Burns, 14th August.	516
(359)	XL	Mrs Dunlop, 19th August.	177
(360)	II	David Blair, 27th August.	503
(361)	VIII	Peter Stuart, [late August or early September].	523
(362)	XLI	Mrs Dunlop, 6th September.	178
(363)	XLII	Mrs Dunlop, 2nd October.	179
(364)		Alexander Fergusson, [October?].	538
(364 A)	I	Alexander Findlater, [October?].	535
(365)	III	Robert Riddell, 16th October.	483
(365 A)	IV	Robert Riddell? [16th October?].	3
(365 B)	II	Dr Thomas Blacklock, 21st October.	3
(366)		Robert Moore, 26th October.	54
(366 A)	II	Alexander Findlater, 28th October.	536
(367)	XVIII	Robert Ainslie, 1st November.	338
(368)		Mrs Patrick Miller, 2nd November.	244
(369)	VII	Richard Brown, 4th November.	422
(370)	I	David Newall, 7th November.	54
(371)	XLIII	Mrs Dunlop, 8th November.	180
(372)	VII	William Burns, 10th November.	517
(373)	VII	Robert Graham, 9th December.	43
(374)	XLIV	Mrs Dunlop, 13th December.	18

(375)	VI	William Nicol, [13th December?].	346
(376)	III	David Blair, [December].	503
(377)	I	Lady Winifred Maxwell Constable, 16th December.	546
(378)		Robert Maxwell, 20th December.	548
(379)	III	Lady Elizabeth Cunningham, 23rd December.	498
(380)	I	George Sutherland, [31st December].	549
(380 A)	III	Alexander Findlater, [1789?].	540

1790

(381)	II	Gilbert Burns, [11th January].	358
(382)	VI	William Dunbar, 14th January.	284
(383)	II	Dr James Mundell, 'The bearer, Janet Nievison . . .'.	485
(384)	IV	David Sillar, 22nd January.	536
(385)	XLV	Mrs Dunlop, 25th January.	183
(385 A)		An Unidentified Correspondent, [Summer 1789-January 1790].	34
(387)	VII	Peter Hill, 2nd February.	314
(388)	XLIV	Mrs McLehose, [February?], 'I have indeed been ill . . .'.	406
(389)	XLV	Mrs McLehose, 5th February , 'I could not answer . . .'.	407
(390)	VII	William Nicol, 9th February.	346
(391)	VIII	William Burns, 10th February.	518
(392)	IV	Alexander Cunningham, 13th February.	458
(393)	IV	Alexander Findlater, 'Mrs. B ____, like a true good wife . . .'.	540
(394)	I	David Staig, [1st March].	551
(394 A)	II	George S. Sutherland, [1st March?], 'I was much disappointed . . .'.	549
(395)	VIII	Peter Hill, 2nd March.	315
(396)	XLVI	Mrs Dunlop, [March].	184
(397)	XLVII	Mrs Dunlop, 10th April.	185
(398)	II	David Newall, 'Inclosed is a state . . .'.	545
(398 A)	VIII	William Nicol, 28th May.	348
(399)	XLVIII	Mrs Dunlop, 6th June.	187
(400)	IX	William Burns, 7th June.	518
(401)	I	Francis Grose, 'Among the many Witch Stories . . .'.	557
(402)	I	Mrs Robert Graham, 10th June.	555
(402 A)	VIII	Robert Graham, 10th June.	433
(403)	XLIX	Mrs Dunlop, 9th July.	188
(404)	VII	Dr John Moore, 14th July.	259
(405)	II	John Murdoch, 16th July.	55
(406)	X	William Burns, 16th July.	519
(407)	IV	Robert Cleghorn, 23rd July.	274
(408)	II	Francis Grose, [July].	559
(409)	III	Dugald Stewart, [July].	449
(410)	IV	Dugald Stewart, 30th July.	449
(411)	L	Mrs Dunlop, 30th July.	190
(411 A)	III	John McMurdo, 2nd August.	493
(411 B)	V	Alexander Cunningham, 8th August.	459
(412)	LI	Mrs Dunlop, 8th August.	191

Page

(413)	I	Helen Craik, 9th August.	561
(414)	V	Alexander Findlater, 'Sending a letter . . .'.	540
(416)	V	Robert Cleghorn, 29th August.	275
(417)	I	John Mitchell, 'I shall not fail . . .'.	563
(418)		Answers to the Petition of Thomas Johnston, [September].	564
(419)	IX	Robert Graham, 4th September.	433
(420)		John Wilson, 11th September.	566
(421)	I	John Somerville, 11th September.	567
(422)	II	Alexander Dalziel, 5th October.	505
(423)	LII	Mrs Dunlop, 6th October.	191
(424)		Alexander Crombie & Co., 8th October.	568
(425)		Crauford Tait, 15th October.	569
(426)		Dr James Anderson, 1st November.	571
(427)	LIII	Mrs Dunlop, [November].	192
(427 A)	III	Francis Grose, December.	559
(428)	LIV	Mrs Dunlop, 6th December.	192
(429)		An Unidentified Correspondent, [31st December].	724

1791

(430)	IX	Peter Hill, 17th January.	316
(431)	VII	William Dunbar, 17th January.	286
(432)		John Gillespie, 'The inclosed song . . .'.	572
(433)	VI	Alexander Cunningham, 23rd January.	460
(434)	III	John Tennant, Jr., [2nd February].	74
(435)	LV	Mrs Dunlop, 7th February.	193
(436)		The Rev. Archibald Alison, 14th February.	573
(437)	VIII	Dr John Moore, 28th February.	260
(438)		The Rev. George H. Baird, 28th February.	574
(439)	III	Alexander Dalziel, 10th March.	506
(440)	X	Peter Hill, [March].	317
(441)	VII	Alexander Cunningham, 11th March.	461
(442)	XI	John Ballantine, [March?].	103
(443)	LVI	Mrs Dunlop, 11th April.	194
(444)	I	Thomas Sloan, [April].	576
(445)	I	Alexander Fraser Tytler, [April].	578
(446)		Charles Sharpe, 22nd April.	580
(447)	I	James Gracie, [April?], 'I have sent your letter anent Crombie's bill . . .'.	582
(448)	II	Lady Winifred Maxwell Constable, 25th April.	540
(449)		Preface to the Glenriddell MS. of Poems, 27th April.	482
(450)		Alexander Coutts, 28th April.	583
(451)	II	John Somerville, 11th May.	567
(452)	XI	James Johnson, 'I received . . . the Proofs . . .'.	29
(454)		An Unidentified Correspondent, 'I am exceedingly to blame . . .'.	725
(455)		Literary Scolding.	726
(456)	VIII	Alexander Cunningham, 11th June.	462
(457)	II	John Mitchell, [16th June].	563

			Page
458)	III	Thomas Boyd, 16th June.	513
459)		The Lord Provost of Edinburgh [James Stirling], [June].	584
460 A)	IX	William Nicol, [21st June 1791?].	349
460)	VI	Alexander Findlater, [June], 'I am both much surprised . . .'.	540
461)	V	David Sillar, [early summer].	537
462)	XLVI	Mrs McLehose, [July?], 'I have recd. both your last letters . . .'.	407
462 A)		The Rev. Thomas Smith, 4th July.	585
463)	IX	Alexander Cunningham, [summer or early autumn], 'It gave me the highest . . .'.	464
465)	II	The Earl of Buchan, 29th August.	266
466)	II	Thomas Sloan, 1st September.	576
467)	IV	Lady Elizabeth Cunningham, [late September].	499
468)	XII	John Ballantine, [September].	104
469)		Sir John Sinclair, [August or September].	586
470)		Letter written for James Clarke, to Mr Williamson, [September].	588
471)		The Duke of Queensberry, 24th September.	589
472)	V	Robert Riddell, [27th September].	482
472 A)	I	Miss Deborah Duff Davies, [early October?].	590
473)	VI	Robert Cleghorn, [October?].	275
473 A)	VI	Robert Riddell, [September-October].	483
473 B)	VII	Robert Riddell, [September-October].	483
474)		Col. William Fullarton, 3rd October.	593
475)	XI	Peter Hill, [October?].	319
475 A)	III	Sir John Whitefoord, [early October].	34
476)	X	Robert Graham, 6th October.	435
477)	II	Mrs Stewart of Stair, Prefatory Note to the Afton Lodge MS, [October].	126
478)		The Rev. Joseph Kirkpatrick, [22nd? October].	594
479)	II	Lady Hariot [Henrietta] Don, 23rd October.	279
480)	XIII	John Ballantine, 25th October.	105
481)	LVII	Mrs Dunlop, 26th October.	195
481 A)	VIII	Robert Riddell, [June 1788-October 1791].	33
481 B)	IX	Robert Riddell, [June 1788-October 1791].	33
482)	XIX	Robert Ainslie, [November?], 'Can you minister . . .'.	339
483)	XLVII	Mrs McLehose, 23rd November, 'It is extremely . . .'.	407
484)	XLVIII	Mrs McLehose, 11th December, 'Such, My dearest Nancy . . .'.	408
485)	XLIX	Mrs McLehose, 15th December, 'I have some merit . . .'.	409
485 A)	LVIII	Mrs. Dunlop 17th December.	195
486)	L	Mrs McLehose, 27th December, 'I have yours . . .'.	409

1792

487)		Prefatory Note to Abridgement of the First Commonplace Book.	483
488)	VII	Robert Cleghorn, 'My best compliments . . .'.	276
489)	I	James Clarke, 10th January.	595
490)	II	Helen Craik, 12th January.	562
491)	LIX	Mrs Dunlop, 14th January.	196

(492)		William Smellie, [22nd January].	597
(493)	LX	Mrs Dunlop, 3rd February.	197
(494)	I	William Corbet, [February?], 'I have in my time . . .'.	598
(495)	XII	Peter Hill, 5th February.	320
(496)	X	Alexander Cunningham, 5th February.	464
(497)	I	Maria Riddell, [February].	601
(498)		The Rev. William Moodie, [early February].	613
(499)	II	James Clarke, 17th February.	595
(499 A)	IV	John McMurdo, [February?].	493
(500)		John Leven, [March?].	614
(502)	V	William Creech, 16th April.	305
(502 A)	XI	Alexander Cunningham, [April or May].	465
(503)	XII	James Johnson, [May], 'This will be presented . . .'.	296
(504)		Stephen Clarke, 16th July.	615
(505)	LXI	Mrs Dunlop, 22nd August.	198
(506)	XII	Alexander Cunningham, 10th September.	465
(507)	I	George Thomson, 16th September.	617
(508)	II	William Corbet, [September], 'When I was honoured . . .'.	598
(509)	II	Maria Riddell, 'Fate seems determined . . .'.	601
(510)	LXII	Mrs Dunlop, 24th September.	200
(511)	II	George Thomson, 26th October.	618
(512)	LXIII	Mrs Dunlop, 'I had been from home . . .'.	201
(513)	XIII	James Johnson [October], 'I would have returned . . .'.	296
(514)	III	George Thomson, 8th November.	620
(515)	I	William Johnston, 13th November.	681
(517)	III	Maria Riddell, [November], 'I return you my most sincere . . .'.	601
(518)	IV	George Thomson, 14th November.	621
(519)	I	Louisa Fontenelle, [22nd? November], 'In such a bad world . . .'.	682
(520)	II	Louisa Fontenelle?, [November], 'I am thinking to send . . .'.	682
(520 A)	II	William Johnston, 27th November.	681
(521)	III	John Mitchell, 30th November.	564
(522)	V	George Thomson, 1st December.	621
(523)	VI	George Thomson, 4th December.	622
(524)	LXIV	Mrs Dunlop, 6th December.	201
(525)		Mary Peacock, 6th December.	684
(526)	II	Alexander Fraser Tytler, 6th December.	571
(527)	VIII	Robert Cleghorn, 12th December.	276
(528)	XI	Robert Graham, 31st December.	433
(529)	LXV	Mrs Dunlop, 31st December.	202
(—)	VI	William Creech, [late 1792].	306

1793

(530)	XII	Robert Graham, 5th January.	436
(531)	II	Mrs Robert Graham, 5th January.	55
(532)	VII	George Thomson, [7th January].	622
(533)	XIII	Robert Graham, 7th January.	434
(533 A)	IV	Maria Riddell? [8th January?].	60

Page

533 B)	II	David Staig, [10th January].	551
534)	III	David Staig, [January?].	552
535)	VIII	George Thomson, 26th January.	622
536)	XIII	Alexander Cunningham, 20th February.	467
537)	IX	William Nicol, [20th February].	349
538)	VII	William Creech, 28th February.	306
539)	III	Thomas Sloan, 18th March.	577
540)	IX	George Thomson, 20th March.	623
541)		Miss A. D. Benson, 21st March.	685
542)		The Provost and Bailies of Dumfries [March].	553
542 A)	V	John McMurdo, [March?].	494
544)	LI	Mrs McLehose, [March?], 'I suppose, my dear Madam . . .'.	410
545)	VII	Patrick Miller, [mid-March].	243
546)		John, Earl of Glencairn, [mid-March].	686
546 A)	VIII	Patrick Miller, [mid-March].	243
547)	III	Mrs Robert Graham, [mid-March].	556
547 A)		Elizabeth Burns, [mid-March].	35
547 B)		Mrs John Gillespie, [mid-March].	35
548)	X	Robert Riddell, [mid-March].	489
549)	VI	John McMurdo, [mid-March].	494
550)	V	Lady Elizabeth Cunningham, [mid-March].	500
550A)	V	Maria Riddell, [mid-March].	602
551)	IV	David Blair, [mid-March].	503
552)		Thomas White, [mid-March].	687
552 A)	X	George Thomson, 27th March.	624
553)	XIII	Peter Hill, [April].	320
554)	XI	George Thomson, [April].	624
554 A)	VI	Maria Riddell, [April].	602
554 B)		Jessie Staig, [spring].	688
556 A)	II	Deborah Duff Davies, 6th April.	591
557)	XII	George Thomson, 7th April.	626
558)		John Francis Erskine, [13th April].	689
559)	XIII	George Thomson, 26th April.	628
561)	XX	Robert Ainslie, 26th April.	340
561 A)	VII	Alexander Findlater, [early May].	541
562)		Miss Lesley Baillie, [May].	692
563)	LXVI	Mrs Dunlop, [June].	205
564)	III	Deborah Duff Davies, [June?], 'Happy is the man . . .'.	592
565)	XIV	Peter Hill, 13th June.	320
566)	XIV	George Thomson, [25th June?].	629
567)	XV	George Thomson, 30th June.	630
568)	XVI	George Thomson, [2nd July?], 'I have just finished . . .'.	631
569)	XVII	George Thomson, [July], 'I assure you, my dear Sir . . .'.	631
570)	VII	Robert Aiken, 16th July.	96
571)	VII	John McMurdo, [July?].	494
572)		Miss Jean McMurdo, [July].	693
574)	XVIII	George Thomson, [August], 'I hold the pen . . .'.	633

CHRONOLOGICAL LIST OF LETTERS

Page

(574 A)	XIX	Deed of Assignment of Copyright to George Thomson, 2nd August.	63
(575)	XX	George Thomson, 13th August.	63
(576)	XXI	George Thomson, [mid-August], 'That crinkum crankum tune . . .'.	63
(577)	XXII	George Thomson, 19th August.	63
(578)	XXIII	George Thomson, [about 25th August], 'You may readily trust . . .'.	63
(579)	LXVII	Mrs Dunlop, 25th August, 'I have got a Frank for you . . .'.	20
(580)	XXIV	George Thomson, [28th August], 'That tune, Cauld kail . . .'.	63
(581)	XXV	George Thomson, 28th August, 'I have written you . . .'.	63
(582)	XXVI	George Thomson, [about 30th August], 'You know that my pretensions . . .'.	63
(583)	XXVII	George Thomson, [September], 'I dare say, my dear Sir . . .'.	63
(584)	XXVIII	George Thomson, [8th September], 'I am happy, my dear Sir . . .'.	64
(585)		Miss Janet Miller, 9th September.	24
(586)	XXIX	George Thomson, [early September], 'I have received your list . . .'.	64
(587)	XXX	George Thomson, [15th September], 'Who shall decide . . .'.	64
(588)	XXXI	George Thomson, [September], 'I have been turning over . . .'.	64
(590)	VII	Maria Riddell, [October], 'I am extremely sorry . . .'.	60
(591)	XIV	James Johnson, [October].	29
(592)	IX	Robert Cleghorn, 25th October.	27
(593)	XXXII	George Thomson, 29th October.	65
(593 A)	XIV	Alexander Cunningham, [November], 'Urbani has told . . .'.	46
(594)	VIII	Maria Riddell, [November?], 'I meant to have called . . .'.	60
(595)	IX	Maria Riddell, [November?], 'On the conditions and capitulations . . .'.	60
(595 A)	X	Maria Riddell, [November].	60
(598)		Edward Whigham.	51
(599)	III	Louisa Fontenelle, [about 1st December], 'Inclosed is the "Address". . .'.	68
(599 A)	XI	Maria Riddell, [late November or December], 'I have at last . . .'.	60
(600)	I	William Robertson, [3rd December], 'Heated as I was . . .'.	6
(600 A)	XII	Maria Riddell, [December?], 'I will wait on you . . .'.	60
(601)	VIII	To Alexander Findlater, 'Will you give and receive . . .'.	5
(602)	XXXIII	George Thomson, [December], 'Tell me, my dear Sir . . .'.	65
(603)	LXVIII	Mrs Dunlop, 'I mentioned to you . . .'.	20
(603 A)	XIII	Maria Riddell, [December].	60
(605)	LXIX	Mrs Dunlop, 15th December.	20
(606)	IV	William Stewart, 'Smellie's Philosophy . . .'.	4
(607)	VIII	John McMurdo, [December?], 'I just finished the inclosed . . .'.	4
(608)		Mrs Robert Riddell.	6

1794

(609)	XIV	Maria Riddell, [January], 'I have this very moment . . .'.	6

Page

(610)	XIV	Robert Graham, [7th January].	438
(610 A)	XV	Maria Riddell, [early January].	607
(611)	XVI	Maria Riddell, 12th January, 'I return your . . .'.	607
(612)	III	The Earl of Buchan, 12th January.	267
(613)	I	Patrick Miller, Jr., [January].	699
(614)	XV	Peter Hill, [February], 'I am half angry with you . . .'.	321
(615)	IX	Alexander Findlater, [February], 'Inclosed are the two schemes . . .'.	541
(615 A)	XV	Robert Graham, [February], 'The language of supplication . . .'	440
(616)	XV	James Johnson, [5th February].	297
(617)	II	William Robertson, [February or March], 'Mr Burns presents . . .'.	695
(618)	I	Samuel Clark, 'I recollect something . . .'.	702
(619)	XV	Alexander Cunningham, 25th February.	469
(620)	XVI	Alexander Cunningham, 3rd March.	471
(620 A)	LXX	Mrs Dunlop, [13th March].	209
(620 B)	II	Patrick Miller, Jr., [mid-March].	699
(620 C)	I	Captain John Hamilton, 24th March.	703
(620 D)		Lady Elizabeth Heron, 3rd April.	705
(621)	I	John Clark, [21st April].	706
(623)	XVI	Peter Hill, [May], 'Allow me to introduce . . .'.	321
(624)		Miss Eleanor or Sophy Riddell?, [May].	707
(624 A)	I	John Syme, [May].	708
(625)	XXXIV	George Thomson, [May], 'I return you the plates . . .'.	652
(626)		John McLeod, 18th June.	710
(627)		David McCulloch, 21st June.	712
(628)	LXXI	Mrs Dunlop, 25th June.	210
(629)	LII	Mrs McLehose, [25th June?], 'Before you ask me why . . .'.	411
(630)	XVI	James Johnson, 29th June.	297
(631)	II	Samuel Clark, 'I was, I know, drunk . . .'.	702
(632)	XXXV	George Thomson, [July], 'Is there no news yet . . .'.	653
(633)	II	Captain John Hamilton, [July].	703
(635)	XXXVI	George Thomson, 30th August.	654
(635 A)		Dr William Maxwell, [early September].	33
(636)	XXXVII	George Thomson, [September], 'Little do the Trustees . . .'.	654
(637)	XXXVIII	George Thomson, [September], 'Do you know, my dear Sir . . .'.	655
(638)	LXXII	Mrs Dunlop, [September].	210
(639)	X	Alexander Findlater?, [September], 'This is the second letter . . .'.	541
(640)		Robert Andrew Riddell, 22nd September.	713
(643)	XVII	Peter Hill, [October], 'By a carrier of yesterday . . .'.	322
(644)	XXXIX	George Thomson, 19th October.	658
(645)	LXXIII	Mrs Dunlop, 29th October.	212
(646)	XL	George Thomson, [November], 'Many thanks to you, my dear Sir . . .'.	662
(647)	XLI	George Thomson, 19th November.	665
(648)	XLII	George Thomson, 9th December.	668

(649)   LXXIV   Mrs Dunlop, 20th December.   212

1795

(650)   XVII   Maria Riddell, [January?], 'Mr. Burns's compliments . . .'.   608

(651)   XLIII   George Thomson, [January], 'I fear that my songs . . .'.   669

(652)   V   William Stewart, 15th January.   445

(652 A)   An Unidentified Correspondent, 15th January.

(653)   III   Captain John Hamilton, 29th January.   704

(654)   The Editors of the *Morning Chronicle*, [January].   714

(655)   IV   Captain John Hamilton, [31st January].   704

(656)   XLIV   George Thomson, [6th February].   670

(657)   XLV   George Thomson, 7th February.   671

(658)   XVIII   Maria Riddell, [March?], 'I cannot express my gratitude . . .'.   608

(659)   III   Patrick Miller, Jr., 8th March.   700

(660)   Patrick Heron of Heron, [March].   715

(661)   XLVI   George Thomson, [April].   672

(662)   Richard A. Oswald?, 23rd April.   71

(662 A)   An Unidentified Correspondent — Patrick Heron?, 24th April.   716

(663)   John Edgar, 25th April.   718

(664)   Lady Mary Douglas, 2nd May.   719

(665)   XLVII   George Thomson, [3rd May].   673

(666)   Col. A. S. de Peyster, [18th May].   720

(667)   XVII   James Johnson, 'Now to the subject of your songs . . .'.   298

(668)   XIX   Maria Riddell, [spring], 'Par accident . . .'.   609

(669)   II   John Syme, [May?].   708

(670)   XLVIII   George Thomson, [May], 'Ten thousand thanks . . .'.   673

(671)   XVIII   Peter Hill?, 30th May.   323

(672)   XLIX   George Thomson, [June], 'How do you like it . . .'.   674

(673)   L   George Thomson, [3rd July].   674

(673 A)   XX   Maria Riddell, [summer], 'I think there is little doubt . . .'.   609

(674)   XXI   Maria Riddell, [June or July], 'The health you wished me . . .'.   610

(676)   LI   George Thomson, 3rd August.   675

(677)   XVII   Alexander Cunningham, [3rd August].   477

(678)   William Lorimer, [August].   72

(680)   X   Robert Cleghorn, [21st August].   277

(682)   V   David Blair, 25th August.   504

(683)   LXXV   Mrs Dunlop, 'I am afraid, dear Madam . . .'.   214

(684)   XVIII   James Johnson, [August or September], 'Without any apology . . .'.   299

(690)   XIX   James Johnson, [23rd September].   30

(685)   XXII   Maria Riddell, [October or November], 'A severe domestic misfortune . . .'.   61

(685 A)   XXIII   Maria Riddell, [November?], 'I have been a grievous sinner . . .'.   61

(685 B)   III   John Syme, 17th December.   3

(685 C)   IV   John Mitchell, 31st December.   3

(685 D)   XXIV   Maria Riddell, [December 1795 or January 1796], 'I have perused . . .'.   61

1796

(686)	XIX	Peter Hill, 29th January.	324
(687)	XI	Robert Cleghorn, [January].	278
(688)	LXXVI	Mrs Dunlop, 31st January.	214
(689)	LII	George Thomson, [February].	676
(691)		The Publishers of a Newspaper, 25th February.	725
(692)	XX	James Johnson, [March?].	301
(693)	LIII	George Thomson, [April].	677
(694)	LIV	George Thomson, [May], 'I once mentioned to you . . .'.	678
(695)	LV	George Thomson, [about 18th May], 'Inclosed is a certi-ficate . . .'.	679
(696)	XXI	James Johnson, [1st June?].	302
(697)	XXV	Maria Riddell, [1st June?].	611
(698)	III	James Clarke, 26th June.	596
(698 A)		Jessie Lewars, 26th June.	32
(699)	LVI	George Thomson, 4th July.	679
(700)	XVIII	Alexander Cunningham, 7th July.	473
(701)	I	James Armour, 10th July.	722
(702)	LXXVII	Mrs Dunlop, 10th July.	215
(703)	III	Gilbert Burns, 10th July.	358
(704)	XIX	Alexander Cunningham, 12th July.	474
(705)	IX	James Burness, 12th July.	63
(706)	LVII	George Thomson, 12th July.	679
(707)	II	James Gracie, [13th July].	582
(708)	IV	Jean Armour Burns, [14th July].	479
(709)	II	John Clark, [16th July].	706
(710)	II	James Armour, 18th July.	722
(711)		Simon McKenzie, [1796?].	32
(712)	X	William Nicol, [1787-96].	350
(713)	I	Miss ____ Gordon, [1791-6].	723
(714)	II	Miss ____ Gordon, [1791-6].	723
(715)		An Unidentified Correspondent [1791-6].	725

INDEX

INDEX

The titles of poems and songs by Burns have been entered under the heading Poems and Songs. In those cases where Burns himself did not give a title, the works are indexed according to the first line. Other titles of poems, songs and separate works are given under the names of their authors where known, and cross-referenced. The titles of airs to which songs were set are listed under Airs, the entries being given within quotation marks. For books of the Bible, see under Bible. For plays by Shakespeare, see under Shakespeare. All other works are listed individually and cross-referenced to their authors. Names which appear in Currie's List of Letters to Burns are not included in this Index, as they will be found separately indexed in that Appendix.

Aaron 310, 331
Aberdeen 60, 223, 330, 357, 363, 507, 571
Aberdeen Almanac 66
The Aberdeen Prognostication 435, 593
Aberdeenshire 363, 563, 627
Absalom (Biblical figure) 188
Achilles 184
Achitophel (Biblical figure) 108, 330
Act and Testimony — see Adam Gib
Adair, Anne McKittrick 281
Adair, Charlotte Hamilton 69, 127, 230, 231, 233, 234
Adair, Dr James McKittrick 127, 130, 413
Adam (Biblical figure) 108
Adam, Dr Alexander 335, 342, 360
Adamhill 66
Adams, Jean:
 There's nae luck about the house 420, 645, 660, 664
Addison, Joseph 186, 214
 The Campaign 266, 441
 Cato 16, 117, 270, 391, 426
 How are thy Servants Blest, O Lord 249, 391, 396
 Letter from Italy 699
 The Spectator 16, 251, 314, 391, 392, 396, 587
 The Vision of Mirza 15, 164
Address to Loch Lomond — see James Cririe
Admetus 659
Adonis 627
The Adventurer 318, 587
Advocates' Library 193
Aeneid — see Virgil
Afton Lodge MS 125
Afton River 166
Agnew, Eleanora 130
Agnew, Lieutenant 209
Ah, Chloris, could I now but sit 618
Ah Dear Marcella 641
Ahasuerus 331
Aiken, Andrew Hunter 37, 91, 99, 103
 Letters to 32
Aiken, Grace 91
Aiken, Robert 21, 65-6, 76, 94, 97, 99, 101, 103, 219, 477
 Letters to 91-6

INDEX

Aikin, John 669
   Essays on Song-Writing 449-50
Ailsa Craig 451
Ainslie, Douglas 328
Ainslie, James 335
Ainslie, Miss Rachel 326, 328
Ainslie, Robert 18, 19, 96, 103, 360, 371, 390, 400, 403, 406, 411, 514, 762
   Letters to 327-41
Ainslie, Robert, senior 103
Ainslie, Mrs Robert, senior 103
Aird, James: *Selection of Scotch . . . Airs* 294
Airs
   'Allan Water' 206, 636
   'All the Nights o the Year, the Chapman Drinks nae Water' 512
   'Andrew and his Cutty-Gun' 659
   'Auld Lang Syne' 628, 646, 667
   'The Auld Man's Mare's Dead' 301
   'Auld Rob Morris' 619, 621
   'Auld Sir Symon' 548, 644
   'The Auld Yowe Jumpt o'er the Tether' 512
   'Ay Waukin O' 672
   'Balinamona and Ora' 677
   'Ballendalloch's Reel' 461
   'The Banks of Ayr' 624
   'Banks of Banna' 649
   'The Banks of Cree' 652, 653, 705
   'Banks of Dee' 628, 643
   'The Banks of Doon' 664
   'The Banks of Spey' 376
   'Black Joke' 329
   'The Bob o Dumblane' 300
   'The Bonie Brucket Lassie' 643, 660
   'Bonie Dundee' 624, 625, 641, 642
   'Bonie Jean' 642
   'The Braes o Ballochmyle' 296
   'The Caledonian Hunt's Delight' 294, 295, 296, 664, 666, 675
   'Camdelmore' 461
   'The Campbells are Comin'' 656
   'Captain Okean' 274, 644, 677, 719
   'Cauld Kail in Aberdeen' 162, 361, 625, 634, 635, 637, 660, 662, 678, 679
   'Caun der Delish' — see 'Oran Gaoil'
   'Chevy Chase' 347
   'The Collier's bonie Dochter (Lassie)' 620, 648, 664
   'Cooleen' 644
   'The Cordwainer's March' 299
   'Corn Riggs are Bonie' 625
   'Cowdenknowes' 248, 641
   'Craigieburn-Wood' 296, 297, 572, 642, 666, 672
   'Cumnock Psalms' 657
   'Dainty Davie' 637, 638, 644, 663
   'De'il Tak the Wars' 649, 661, 662, 673
   'Despairing beside a Clear Stream' 642
   'Down the Burn Davie' 627, 641
   'Druimionn dubh' 642

'Dumbarton Drums' 364
'Duncan Gray' 660
'Ewe Bughts Marion' 301, 619
'Fair Eliza' 660
'Fair Helen' 642
'Fee him Father' 644, 649
'The Flowers of Edinburgh' 653, 705
'For a' that and a' that' 669
'Fy, let us a' to the Bridal' 649
'Gaffer Gray' 279
'Galla Water' 619
'Gill Morice' 642, 646
'Ginglan Geordie' — see 'The Highland Laddie'
'Ginglan Johnie' — see 'The Highland Laddie'
'Go From my Window Love, Do' 300
'Gramachree' 635, 667
'Green Grow the Rashes' 162
'The Grey Cock' 647
'Ha a Chaillich air mo Dheith' 232
'Had I the Wyte she bade me' 301
'Hazel Green' 301
'A Health to Betty' 300
'The Hemp-dresser' 614
'Here awa' 292
'Here's a Health to them that's Awa' 301, 474
'Hey Tutti Taitie' 638
'The Highland Laddie' 299, 643
'Hughie Graham' 627, 632, 642
'Humors of Glen' 644, 672, 677, 719
'I hae laid a Herrin in Sawt' 649
'The Irish Cronoch' 719
'I wish my love was in a Mire' 628
'Jackie Hume's Lament' 299, 626
'John Anderson my Jo' 627, 647, 650, 673
'Johnnie Cope' 672
'Jo Janet' — see 'My Jo Janet'
'Katherine Ogie' 620, 629, 641
'Killiecrankie' 294
'Laddie Lie Near Me' 643, 672, 673, 678
'The Lammy' 672
'Langolee' 628, 643
'The Last Time I Came o'er the Moor' 637, 640, 653
'The Lazy Mist' 491
'The Lee-rig' 629
'Leiger m' Choss' — see Liggeram Cosh'
'Let me in this ae Night' 632, 634, 674
'Lewis Gordon' 208, 641
'Liggeram Cosh' 464, 630, 631, 650, 659-60, 675
'Lochaber' 622
'Loch Eireachd Side' 672
'The Lochmaben Harper' 299
'Logan Water' 206, 626, 629, 642
'Logie o Buchan' 667
'The Lothian Lassie' 674

'Love Never More shall give me Pain'   661
'Lumps o Puddins'   300, 664, 666
'McGregor of Roro's Lament'   649
'Madam Cossy'   614
'Maggie Lauder'   645
'Marquis of Huntly'   364
'The Merry Beggars'   162
'The Mill Mill O'   294, 618, 625, 627, 630
'Minnie's ay Glowrin o'er Me'   278
'Morag'   441, 659
'The Moudiewort'   660
The Muckin o Geordie's Byre'   637, 645, 648
'Muirland Willie'   648, 667
'My Dearie, and thou Die'   662
'My Jocky Blythe'   301
'My Jo Janet'   652
'My Lodging is on the cold Ground'   603, 625, 642, 661, 662, 719
'My Love, Annie's very Bonie'   636
'My Nanie O'   618
'My Wife's a Wanton wee Thing'   620
'Nansy's to the Green-Wood Gane'   647, 653, 664
'Nine Nights awa, Welcome Hame my Dearie'   512
'O bonie Lass will ye lie in a Barrack'   643
'O'er the Hills and Far Away'   649, 654
'Oonagh's Waterfall, or the Lock that Scattered Oonagh's Piss'   655, 677
'Oran an Aoig' (The Song of Death)   196
'Oran Gaoil'   635, 640, 667
'Peg a Ramsey'   278-9
'Peggy I must Love Thee'   642
'The Pier of Leith'   294
'The Poor Thresher'   296
'Push about the Brisk Bowl'   176
'The Quaker's Wife' (see also 'Liggeram Cosh')   614
'Rigs of Barley'   627
'Robin Adair'   634, 635
'Rory Dall's Port'   409
'Roslin Castle'   659
'Rothiemurche's Rant'   656, 663, 665, 666, 679-80
'Roy's Wife of Aldivaloch'   642, 649, 666, 667
'Saw ye may Father'   245, 645, 660, 662
'Saw ye nae my Peggy' (or 'Saw ye my Maggie')   644, 649
'Scotch Queen'   293
'Shepherds I have lost my Love'   628
'She rose and loot me in'   625
'The Song of Death' — see 'Oran an Aoig'
'The Sow's Tail to Geordie'   623, 656, 664, 665
'Strathallan's Lament'   659
'The Sutor's Dochter'   471, 700
'Take your auld Cloak about ye'   648
'There'll never be Peace till Jamie comes Hame'   462, 642, 668
'There's my Thumb, I'll ne'er Beguile You'   667
'There's nae Luck about the House'   649
'There was a Lass and She was Fair'   642
'This is no my ain House'   649, 675, 676

'The Tither Morn'   664, 669
'Todlin Hame'   278, 645, 648, 649, 666, 668
'Three Guid Fellows Ayont Yon Glen'   457
'Tranent Muir'   645, 646
'Up and warn a' Willie'   669
'Waes my Heart that we should Sunder'   643
'We'll Gang nae Mair to yon Town'   671, 672
'Whar'll Bonie Annie Lie'   672
'When I was a young Thing'   301
'When she Cam Ben she Bobbit'   645, 667
'Whistle, and I'll Come to ye, my Lad'   647, 667
'The White Cockade'   644
'Will ye Lend me your Loom Lass'   632
'Willy was a Wanton Wag'   648, 693
'Woo'd an Married and a''   674
'The Yellow-haired Laddie'   627
Ajax   95
Akenside, Mark: *Pleasures of the Imagination*   257
Alexander, Claud   216, 447
Alexander, Wilhelmina   68, 125-6, 370
   Letter to   216-17
Alexander the Great   621
Alfonso X of Spain   168
Alfred, A Masque — see James Thomson
Alfred the Great   174
Alison, Rev Archibald: Letter to   573
   Essays on the Nature and Principles of Taste   573
Allan – – –   278, 279
Allan, David   472, 619, 635, 673
   Illustrations   652, 667-8
      Jenny said to Jocky   678
      Turnimspyke   678
      Woo'd and Married and a'   678
Allen, John   274
Allen – –, see David Allan
Alloway   54, 222, 536
Alloway Kirk   557, 559
   Tales concerning Tam o Shanter   557
Alnwick   365
Alva   359
Amelia — see Henry Fielding
American Congress   488
American Revolution   58, 480, 485, 487, 488, 598, 695
Anacharsis Travels   600, 608
Ancient and Modern Scottish Songs — see David Herd
Anderson, Mr (Dumfries shoemaker)   516
Anderson, Dr James: Letter to   571
Anderson, John: *A Collection of New Highland Strathspey Reels*   296
Andrew and his Cutty-Gun   659, 666
Angola, histoire indienne — see Rochette de la Morlière
Angus, W. Craibe   763
Annan   22, 179, 198, 342, 432, 490, 552
Annandale   189, 514, 557

INDEX

Annotation, Burns's practice of   208
Answer to Hamilton — see Allan Ramsay
Antiburgher   398
Antigua   466, 600
Antiquities of Scotland — see Francis Grose
Arabian Nights Entertainments   318
Arbela, battle of   109
Arbigland   296, 561, 685
Archers, Royal Company of   653
Ardwell   278
Armour, James   63, 66, 78, 91, 107, 149, 477
  Letters to   722
Armour, Mrs James   77, 78, 722
Armour, Jean — see Jean Armour Burns
Armstrong, John   315
Arnot, James   107
Arnot, John   477
  Letter to   107-110
Arrochar   328
Athole (Atholl) family   354
Athole House   574
Athole, Jane Cathcart, Duchess of   354
Athole, John, 4th Duke of   354, 357, 453
Auchtertyre — see Ochtertyre
Augustus (Roman emperor)   185
The Auld Man's Mare's dead   301
Auld, Walter (Dumfries)   296, 314, 516, 536
Auld, Rev William (Mauchline)   65, 70, 77, 112, 122, 477
Autobiographical letter to Dr Moore   41, 115, 137, 246, 248-57, 490
Ayr   19, 54, 65, 90, 91, 97, 98, 104, 106, 137, 160, 216, 218, 249, 358, 425, 558, 708
Ayr races   212
Ayrshire   37, 51, 58, 63, 67, 69, 70, 96, 103, 124, 131, 159, 177, 190, 199, 201, 209, 215, 232, 237, 259, 271, 274, 330, 333, 337, 368, 379, 410, 418, 419, 422, 426, 444, 448, 455, 478, 517, 559, 577, 593, 627, 684, 717, 722

Bab at the Bowster   119
Babington, Rev Dr William   209
Babylon   513
The Bachelor's Garland   433
Bacon, Mrs Catherine   444
Badenoch   357
Bailies of the Canongate: Letter to   265, 524
Bailies of Dumfries: Letter to   553-4
Baillie, Mr   198-9
Baillie, Lesley   198, 467, 592, 620
  Letter to   692
Baillie, the Misses   198, 453
Baillie, Robert   692
Baird, Rev George Husband: Letter to   574-5
Balaam   611
Balak   611
Balfour   363
Ballantine, John   18, 21, 90, 91, 92, 94, 219, 240, 576
  Letters to   97-105

Ballochmyle   51, 66, 216
Balmerino, Arthur Elphinstone, 6th Lord   298, 504
Bank of Scotland   240, 517, 551
Bankes Rev Thomas: *The Christian's New and Compleat Family Bible*   310
Bankton, Lord   152
Bannockburn   89
Bannockburn, battle of   109, 208, 268, 638-9
Barbara Allan   646
Barber, William T   56
Barbeth   218
Barbour, John: *Life of Bruce*   193
Barclay, Anthony   295
The Bard — see Thomas Gray
Barquharrie   73, 220, 269
The Battle of Sheriff-Muir   646
Bawdry   218, 274, 315, 339, 643
Bawdy poetry   276, 277, 444-5, 548, 701
   Burns's collection   494
Beattie, Dr James   247, 305, 361, 363, 622
   The Minstrel   364
   To Mr Alexander Ross   141
The Bee   280, 296, 485, 571
Beethoven, Ludwig van   20, 615, 616
Begbie, Alison (Elison)   18, 49, 51
   Letters to   43-8
The Beggar's Opera — see John Gay
The Belfast New Almanac   433
Belfast Newsletter   530
Belisaire — see Jean-François Marmontel
Bell (ship)   78
Bell, Henry Glassford   307
Bell, Sandy   154
Ben Lomond   119, 311
Benson, Anna Dorothea: Letter to   685
Benson, James   685
Berrywell   326, 327
Berwickshire   280, 305, 327, 359
Beugo, John   102, 288, 314, 652, 767
   Letters to   368-9
Beveridge, William (Bishop of St Asaph's): *Private Thoughts*   316
Bible   234
   Acts   16, 376
   Colossians   272
   1 Corinthians   200, 270
   2 Corinthians   344
   Deutoronomy   321
   Daniel   510
   Ecclesiastes   200, 248, 255
   Esther   310
   Exodus   304, 453
   Genesis   16, 171, 182, 200, 378, 455
   Hebrews   16, 146, 404
   Isaiah   363, 465, 467, 513, 522, 523
   James   163, 427, 444

Jeremiah 108, 459, 653, 707
Job 16, 102, 110, 178, 251, 260, 269, 362, 363, 373, 398, 401
John 16, 379, 653
Joshua 16, 234, 404
Lamentations 333
Luke 16, 101, 157, 161, 179, 185, 362, 385
Mark 362
Matthew 78, 150, 161, 252, 254, 355, 361, 362, 445, 580, 583
Metrical Psalms 152, 205, 237, 238, 274, 329, 368, 498, 531, 538
Numbers 16, 287, 321, 390, 563, 611
1 Peter 460
2 Peter 255
Philippians 459
Proverbs 16, 66-7, 151, 231, 266, 392, 490, 526
Psalms 16, 356, 403, 677
Revelation 41, 197, 219, 260, 317, 602, 621
Romans 140, 261, 442, 551, 601, 611, 619, 683
1 Samuel 16, 108, 127, 161, 221, 399, 460
2 Samuel 177, 189, 310, 387, 396
Song of Solomon 16, 327, 344, 392, 403
Bickerstaffe, Isaac:
    Love in a Village 385
    The Spoilt Child 682
Bield Inn, Tweedsmuir 472
The bird that charm's his Summer Day 670
Birthplace Museum, Alloway 125
Bishop, Colonel Sir Henry 30
Bishop marks 30, 302, 345, 474, 478, 497, 518, 628, 634, 640, 668, 675
Bixby, W. K. 507
Black, Mrs Elizabeth 58
Black Bull Inn, Glasgow 419
Blacklock, Rev Dr Thomas 32, 128, 157, 159, 230, 231, 258, 263, 292, 294, 334, 361, 363, 571
    Letter to 490-1
Blacklock, Mrs Thomas 490
Blair, Alexander: Letter to 447
Blair, David (Birmingham) 35
    Letters to 502-4
Blair, David (Dumfries) 505
Blair of Athole (Blair Atholl) 354, 357
Blair, Rev Dr Hugh 87, 99, 114, 221, 305
    Letter to 288
    Sermons 318, 587
Blair, Robert: *The Grave* 90, 100, 134, 182, 200, 436, 459
Blairquhan 51
Blan, Thomas 703
Blind Harry — see William Hamiton of Gilbertfield
    Metrical History of Sir William Wallace 193
Boanerges 70
Board of Trustees 616, 654
The Bob o Dumblane 300
Boileau-Despreux, Nicolas: *L'Art poetique* 144, 585
Bolingbroke, Henry St John, Viscount 15, 335, 381
The Bonnie Brucket Lassie 632

Bordeaux 558
Border Tour 327
Borrowstouness 89
Boston, Rev Thomas: *Human Nature in its Fourfold Estate* 260, 318
Boswell, James 489
Bothwell Bridge 66
Bourn, Rev Samuel: *A Series of Discourses on . . . Natural Religion* 191
The Bower of Bliss 444
Bowie, John 671
Boyd, Thomas 22, 537, 549
  Letters to 513
Boyle, Andrew 501
Boyle, Robert: *The Voyages and Adventures of Captain Robert Boyle* 251, 318
Braes of Bellenden 622
Brand, John 720
Brand, William 357
Brandenburg 653
Brandy 198
Breadalbane, Earl of 83
Breadalbane's Fencibles 635
Breckenridge, Jean (Mrs Gilbert Burns) 357
Brice, David 477
  Letters to 111-12
Bridgend (Maxwelltown) 22, 439, 552-3, 708
Briton A — see Burns's pseudonyms
Brodie of Brodie, James 358
Brodie, Miss Sophia 442
Broun — see Brown
Brow on Solway 473, 477, 479, 582, 600, 706, 708
Brown, George 434
Brown, Gilbert (poet's grandfather) 451
Brown, Rev John: *Essay on Satire* 272
Brown, Captain Richard 254, 398
  Letters to 418-23
Brown, Mrs Richard 418, 420, 421, 423
Brown, Samuel (poet's uncle): Letter to 451
Brown, Tom: *Celia's Roundlet of Brandy* 647
Brownhill 444
Brownrigg, John 419
Bruar, falls of 354, 355, 453
Bruce, Andrew 62, 88, 89, 219
Bruce, John 659
Bruce (jeweller) 409
Bruce, King Robert 89, 638-9
Bruce, Michael 574, 659
Brunswick, Karl Wilhelm Ferdinand, Duke of 437
Bryan, James 77
Bryce — see Brice
Brydges, Sir Samuel 12
Buccleuch, Henry Scott, 3rd Duke of 189, 589
Buchan, David Stewart Erskine, 11th Earl of 104, 282, 607, 686
  Letters to 266-8
Buchan, Mrs Elspat 59-60
Buchanan, George (character in *Zeluco*) — see John Moore

Buff and blue — see Whigs
Bundle and Go 80
Bunyan, John 66
Burgoyne, General Sir John 109
Burke, Edmund 211, 657
Burn, Robert (architect) 265, 309, 321
Burnes — see also Burness or Burns
Burnes, Fanny (cousin of the poet) 63
Burnes, James (uncle of the poet) 57
Burnes, John (cousin of the poet) 63
Burnes, Robert (uncle of the poet) 63
Burnes, William (father of the poet) 54, 58, 59, 113, 181, 222, 251, 357, 514
    Letter to 19, 41-2
Burnes, William (cousin of the poet) 63
Burness, Isabel (Mrs Willam Brand, aunt of the poet) 357
Burness, James (cousin of the poet) 19, 357
    Letters to 57-64
Burness, Mrs James 58, 62, 63
Burness, Jean (aunt of the poet) 357
Burness, William (father of the poet) — see William Burnes
Burnett, Miss Elizabeth of Monboddo 69, 193, 194, 219, 223, 458, 460
Burns — see also Burnes, Burness
Burns, Mrs Agnes Brown (poet's mother) 41, 175, 357, 358, 426, 517
Burns, Sir Alexander 57
Burns, Annabella (sister of the poet) 515, 516
Burns Chronicle 617, 708, 713, 727
Burns, Elizabeth (Paton, daughter of the poet) 115, 118
  Book inscribed to 35
Burns, Elizabeth Riddell (daughter of the poet) 215, 611
Burns, Francis Wallace (son of the poet) 167-8, 170, 177, 178, 180, 184, 185, 194, 198, 200, 347, 485, 517, 518
Burns, Gilbert (brother of the poet) 19, 54, 64, 65, 70, 97, 103, 115, 130, 175, 218, 233-4, 263, 425, 426, 474, 478, 514, 516, 517, 549, 563, 617, 762
    Letters to 357-8
Burns, Isabella (poet's sister) 43
Burns, James Glencairn (son of the poet) 211, 212
Burns, Jean Armour 11, 19, 57, 62, 63, 66, 76, 77, 78, 79, 81, 82, 86, 87, 107, 111, 112, 117, 148-9, 194, 211, 278, 292, 331, 333, 348, 368, 399, 406, 420, 421, 423, 455, 475, 485, 503, 526, 531, 540, 572, 577, 594, 600, 631, 659, 671, 673, 706, 708, 713, 721
    Letters to 477-9
  Recognised as wife 113, 122, 148, 237-8, 258, 293, 371, 418, 477, 490, 507
Burns, Margaret 315
Burns, Nanny — see Annabella Burns
Burns, Robert (son of the poet) 57, 87, 200, 222, 347, 378, 399, 401, 455
Burns, William (brother of the poet) 19, 54, 56, 190, 398
    Letters to 514-19
Burns, William Nicol (son of the poet) 546, 567, 673
Burnside, Rev William 344
Bushby, Thomas 549
Butterworth, Edmund 497
Byron, Lord George 274

C– –, Miss 72
'Ça Ira' 202, 307, 436

Caird, John   57, 59, 357
Caldwell, Charlie   471
Caledonian Hunt   66, 99, 114, 212, 226, 685
The Caledonian Pocket Companion — see James Oswald
Caligula   95
Cameron (papermaker)   309, 322, 325
Cameron, May (or Peggy)   327, 332, 370, 477
The Campaign — see Joseph Addison
Campbell, Mr – – – (Edinburgh innkeeper)   22, 295, 465
Campbell, Archibald   263
Campbell, Bruce   123
  Letter to   489
Campbell, David   358
Campbell, Sir Ilay   224, 569
Campbell, Mary (Highland Mary)   86, 182, 477
Campbell, Maxwell (Skerrington)   67
Campbell, Mrs Maxwell   67-8, 91, 456
Campbell, Thomas (poet)   230
Campbell, Thomas (Pencloe): Letter to   124
Campbell, Mrs William (Fairfield)   91
Candlish, James   14, 319
  Letter to   272-3
Canongate (Edinburgh)   265, 359
Canongate Kilwinning Lodge   224, 269
Canton   107
Cardonnel — see Lawson, Adam de Cardonnel
Carfrae, Rev Patrick   169
  Letter to   527-8
The Carl he cam o'er the Craft   300
Carlisle   342, 514
Carlyle, Thomas   685
Carnegie, Thomas   61
Carnell House   43
Carrick   177, 218, 233, 558
Carse   73
Cassilis, Earl of   75
Castle Douglas   210, 371, 411
Cathcart, Captain   78
Cathcart, David (advocate)   96
Cathcart, Miss (Blair Atholl)   354, 355
Cato — see Joseph Addison
Cato (pseudonym of Robert Riddell)   437, 681
Catrine   447, 448, 501, 559
Caudron Linn   68
Cauvin, Louis   349, 368
Cawdor   357
Centlivre, Susan (née Carroll):
  The wonder, a Woman Keeps a Secret   682
Cervantes, Miguel: *Don Quixote*   318, 587
  Dulcinea   139
  Rosinante   120, 121
Chalmers, James   230
Chalmers, – – (Margaret's sister)   237
Chalmers, Mrs Euphemia (Harviestoun)   69, 570

INDEX

Chalmers, Margaret (Mrs Lewis Hay)   18, 20, 69, 127, 370, 381, 413, 570
   Letters to   230-9
Chalmers, Peggy — see Margaret Chalmers
Chalmers, William (Ayr)   218, 503
   Letter to   218
Chambers, Robert   12, 367, 617, 717, 723
Charles Edward Stuart, Prince   416
Charles V, Holy Roman Emperor   463
Charles XII of Sweden   109
Charteris, Francis   100
Chesterfield, Philip 4th Earl of   186
Chloris — see Jean Lorimer
Christ's Kirk on the Grene — see James I
Chrysal — see Charles Johnstone
Churchill, Charles   246
   The Rosciad   444
Cibber, Colley   316
Cincinnatus   428
Clackmannanshire   413
Clarinda — see Agnes McLehose
   First use of name   16, 374
Clark, John (Locherwoods): Letters to   706
Clark, Samuel junior   720
   Letters to   702
Clarke, Mr – – of Liverpool   103
Clarke, James (Moffat)   462-3, 465, 584, 588, 613
   Letters to   595-6
Clarke, John   710
Clarke, Stephen   293, 294, 295, 296, 297, 298, 302, 321, 361, 492, 494, 601, 604, 628, 631, 633, 637, 645, 653, 656, 658, 660, 664, 665, 667, 670, 674, 676, 677, 693
   Letter to   615
   On composition of Scottish airs   615
   Six Sonatas for the Harpsichord   610, 611, 615, 654
Claverhouse   424
Cleghorn, Miss – – (Edinburgh)   276, 279
Cleghorn, Robert   314, 322, 444, 455, 457, 459, 678
   Letters to   274-9
Cleghorn, Mrs Robert   274, 275, 276, 279
Clint, Henry   494
Clochnahill   41, 57
Closeburn   444
Clow, Jenny   370, 408, 477
Clugston, Robert   720
Clunie (or Clunzie), Rev John   655
Clyde River   78, 184, 343
Coates House   496
Cochrane, Commissioner of Excise   136
Cockburn, Alison Rutherford (Mrs Patrick Cockburn)   632-3
Cockburn, Lord   224, 414, 616
   Memorial of his Times   342
Coila   142, 473, 475, 637
   Rachel Dunlop's portrait of   141
Coles, Elisha: *On God's Sovereignty*   318
Collection of Strathspeys — see Angus Cumming

Collessie 288
Collins, Anthony 247, 386
Collins, William 267
Colman, George (the younger): *Inkle and Yarico* 212, 323
Colman, George (the elder) 316
Colossus of Rhodes 257
Colvill-Scott, H. D. 763
Come Fill me a Bumper 668
Commonplace Book (first) 221, 266, 483-4
Commonplace Book (second) 288, 305
Commons, House of 211, 657
The Complete Works of Robert Burns 7, 17, 30
Confessions of Faith 318
Confucius 548
Congreve, William 316
Connaught 254, 418
Connel, James (carrier) 76, 77, 78, 79, 80, 118, 122, 129, 295
Constable, Lady Winifred Maxwell: Letters to 546-7
Contented with little 674
Cooke, C 310
Copyright 617, 627
Corbet, William 21, 184-5, 191, 197, 203, 434, 439, 440, 539, 690, 702
     Letters to 598-9
Corbet, Mrs William 598, 599
Cork-rumps 269
Corneille, Pierre 316
Cornwallis, Charles Earl of 209
Corri, Domenico 301, 616, 635
Corsan, Dr – – (Kilmarnock) 88
Corstorphine 274
Court of Session 75, 240, 370
Coutts, Alexander: Letter to 583
Coutts and Co., London 608
Cowan, James 103, 308, 309
Coverley, Sir Roger de 318-9
Cowper, William 284, 310
     The Task 208
Craig, Andrew 370
Craig, William 370
Craigie 61
Craigieburnwood 628
Craik, Mr – – (Helen's father) 562
Craik, Helen (Arbigland) 685
     Letters to 561-2
Craik, Captain William 296, 562, 685
Crawford, Mr – – 421
Crawford, Robert 641, 648
Creech, William 20, 35, 61, 87, 94, 99, 100, 139, 170, 228, 232, 235, 241, 258, 259, 293, 308, 320, 329, 345, 360, 370, 403, 421, 479
     Letters to 305-7
Creech, Rev William 305
Crieff 206, 357
Crighton family 179
Cririe, Rev James: *Address to Loch Lomond* 311
Criticism of novels, by Burns 186-7

Crochallan Fencibles 19, 274, 282, 319, 414, 457, 597
  see also *The Merry Muses*
Crombie, Alexander 22, 513, 537, 568, 582
Crombie, Messrs (Dumfries): Letter to 568
Cromek, Robert Hartley 11, 12, 117, 230, 234, 714
Crosbie, – – 277
Cruikshank, Janet (or Jeany) 262, 359, 360
Cruikshank, William 81, 273, 335, 343, 345, 362, 364, 366, 726
  Letters to 359-60
Cruikshank, Mrs William 343, 345, 360
Culloden 269
Cumberland, Duke of 363
Cumming, Angus: *Collection of Strathspeys* 461
Cumnock 83, 332, 400
Cumnock Psalms 657
Cunningham, Mrs (Lainshaw) 91
Cunningham, Agnes Moir (Mrs Alexander Cunningham) 455, 456
Cunningham, Alexander 18, 19, 22, 276, 285, 319, 322, 619, 622, 635, 674, 708
  Letters to 455-74
Cunningham, Allan 230, 360, 539, 590, 685
Cunningham, Ann 443
Cunningham district 177, 218
Cunningham, Lady Elizabeth (Betty) 35, 99, 280
  Letters to 496-500
Cunningham, Sir William 482, 627
Currie, Dr James 11, 12, 19, 130, 357, 480, 539, 600, 617, 650, 697, 707, 727
Currie, John 73
Customs service 609
Cyclops 252

Daer, Basil William, Lord 432, 448, 719
Dale, David 447
Dalgarnock 676
Daljarrock 65
Dalkeith 305
Dalquhatswood 107
Dalrymple, Charles 269
Dalrymple of Orangefield, James 66, 94, 99, 220, 224, 226, 505
  Letter to 269-70
Dalrymple, Rev Dr 54
Dalrymple, Sir John: *Memoirs of Great Britain and Ireland* 322
Dalrymple, William (of Cranstoun) 650
Dalswinton 100, 189, 240, 241, 242, 568
Dalzell, Prof. Andrew 449
Dalziel, Alexander 88, 226
  Letters to 505-6
Dancing 251-2
Darien Scheme 288
Darius III 109
Dasswinton — see Dalswinton
Dasti, Charles Theodore 624
David (Biblical figure) 127, 161, 162, 188, 221
Davies, Deborah Duff 324
  Letters to 590-2

Dean, Jamie 379
Dean of Dunglass 327
Debt
  Gilbert's to Robert 64, 70, 103, 115, 170, 227-8
  Burns's 63-4, 444, 445, 679, 703-4
Dee River 628
Deed of Assignment 115-16, 357, 617, 633-4
De Lolme, Jean Louis: *The British Constitution* 35
Deluded Swain, the Pleasure — see Poems and Songs
De Peyster, Colonel Arent Schuyster: Letter to 720
The Deserted Village — see Oliver Goldsmith
Despairing beside a clear Stream 642
Devon 68
Dewar, Professor 17
Dickens, Charles 616
Dickson, Mr – – (Exciseman) 425
Dickson, Adam — see Jethro Tull
Dinning 357
Diogenes 644
Dirom, Major Alexander 209, 674
Distillers 509-11
Doddridge, Rev Philip: *Free Thoughts on . . . the Dissenting Interest* 318
Dods, Captain 702
Don, Elizabeth and Mary 280
Don, Lady Henrietta 14, 305, 464
  Letters to 280
Don MS 14, 280
Donne, John 69
  The Second Anniversary 69
Donocht-head 659
Don Quixote — see Cervantes
Doon River 558
Doonholm 41
Douglas — see John Home
Douglas, Alexander 720
Douglas Cause 260
Douglas, Charles 118
Douglas, Gawin 279
Douglas, Heron Bank 51, 58, 708, 715
Douglas, house of 327, 466
Douglas Dr Patrick 118
Douglas, William Scott 367, 400
Douglas-Hamilton, Dunbar, 4th Earl of Selkirk 719
Douglas-Hamilton, Lady Mary: Letter to 719
Dow, Daniel 232
Dow, John 118
Down the Burn Davie 627, 641
Drama, Burns's plans for 426, 499
Draper, Eliza — see Laurence Sterne
Drumlanrig 492, 529, 589, 601, 615
Drummond, John 206
Drunkenness 22-3, 339, 359, 465, 480, 516, 538, 671, 685, 697, 702
Dryden, John 144, 145, 316
  Prologue to the Tempest 340

Dumbarton   80, 119, 328, 531
Dumbretton   342
Dumfries, Earl of   113
Dumfries   21, 35, 60, 62, 73, 74, 96, 100, 150, 165, 176, 179, 185, 199, 206, 212, 215, 222, 224, 231, 232, 234, 242, 307, 328, 344, 346, 371, 399, 424, 432, 433, 439, 477, 478, 480, 485, 486, 513, 516, 543, 551, 552, 563, 585, 598, 626, 634, 665, 671, 681, 687, 702, 703-4, 714, 721, 723
Dumfries House, Cumnock   83
Dumfries Volunteers   22, 485, 544, 582, 703, 720
Dumfriesshire   399, 400
Dun, David   40
Dunaskin   218
Dunbar   343, 527
Dunbar, Colonel William   276, 292, 319, 322
   Letters to   282-7
Duncan, William   81, 569
Dundas, Henry   520, 525
Dundas, Robert junior   461
Dundas, Robert, Lord Arniston (Lord President)   461
Dundee   63, 81, 355
Dundonald   354, 593
Dunkeld   357, 574
Dunlop, Miss Agnes Eleanor: Letter to   486
Dunlop, Major Andrew: Letter to   452
Dunlop, Anthony   161, 182, 183, 187
   Letter to   443
Dunlop, Miss Frances   140
Dunlop, Mrs Frances Anna Wallace   14, 17, 19, 21, 23, 35, 86, 246, 247, 357, 443, 452, 474, 475, 486, 517, 522, 527, 598
   Letters to   130-215
   Poem by   146, 169
Dunlop House   137, 138, 143, 147, 169, 175, 201, 399, 486
Dunlop James   182, 209
Dunlop, Captain John   130, 137, 171, 177, 190, 206, 209, 214-15
Dunlop, Miss Keith   140, 159, 161, 214
Dunlop, Miss Rachel   159
   Letter to   475
Dunlop, Miss Susan — see Mrs James Henri
Dunlop, Wallace (John Alexander Agnew)   209
Dunnottar   41
Dunscore   347, 586-7, 594
Dunse (Duns)   103, 326, 327, 330, 359
D'Urfey, Thomas: *Wit and Mirth, or Pills to Purge Melancholy*   663
Durie, George   419
Duty and Office of a Messenger — see Robert Thomson

East Indian air   661
Ecclefechan   342, 671
Edgar, John: Letter to   718
Edinburgh   12, 13, 19, 30, 58, 61, 62, 66, 69, 76, 81, 83, 86, 96, 99, 113, 122, 127, 130, 142, 168, 218, 219, 220, 229, 248, 256, 259, 270, 275, 282, 304, 305, 326, 330, 338, 348, 363, 368, 372, 399, 400, 421, 422, 443, 448, 459, 472, 490, 496, 513, 559, 566, 570, 573, 584, 595, 597, 613, 614, 615, 616, 630, 692, 708, 721, 762, 764

827

Edinburgh Evening Courant 160, 309, 314, 319, 509
   Letter to 487-8
Edinburgh Gazetteer 437, 681
Edinburgh Herald 229
Edinburgh Literary Journal 307
Edinburgh Magazine 229, 597
Edinburgh Review 11
Ednam-hill 104
Edward and Eleonora — see James Thomson
Edward II 109
Eglinton, Archibald Montgomerie, 11th Earl of 114, 132
   Letter to 271
Eglinton Woods 418
Egypt 345
Election Ballads (Heron) 499
Elegy in a Country Churchyard — see Thomas Gray
Elibanks and Elibraes 340
Elihu (Biblical figure) 260
Elisha (Biblical figure) 331
Elizabeth I of England 261
Elliot, Mr – – 159, 227
Ellisland 14, 32, 62, 73, 95, 97, 124, 126, 147, 222, 236, 240, 259, 310, 331, 422, 434, 485,
   490, 513, 539, 544, 563, 572, 594, 699
Eloisa 402
Eloisa to Abelard — see Alexander Pope
Elphinstone, James 140, 382
Encyclopaedia Britannica 159, 597
England 327, 392, 593
Epitaph of John Hildebroad 191
Epithalamion of the Dauphin and Mary Stuart — see George Buchanan
Erebean 138
Erskine, Mr – – (Excise officer) 541
Erskine, Captain Andrew 113, 224, 616, 624, 627, 628, 650, 676
Erskine, Henry 14, 66, 114, 266
   Letters to 224-5
Erskine, John Francis, later 27th Earl of Mar: Letter to 689-91
Erskine, John Thomas, later 28th Earl of Mar 240
Essays, Burns's desire to write 700
Essays on Men, Manners and Things — see William Shenstone
Essays on Song-writing — see John Aikin
Essays on the Principles of Taste — see Archibald Allison
Ettles Hotel, Inverness 353
Ettrick district 292
Euclid's *Elements* 573
Eugene, Prince 442
Ewe bughts, Marion 301, 619
Ewie wi the Crooked Horn — see John Skinner
Excise 63, 93, 104, 144, 170, 177, 179, 181, 184, 197, 203, 204, 213, 227, 236, 238, 240,
   258, 262, 275, 285, 313, 315, 332, 336, 338, 360, 399, 404-5, 406, 422, 424-40, 465,
   473, 496, 498, 503, 507, 517, 518, 539-42, 543, 553-4, 563-5, 572, 598-9, 601, 606,
   608, 609-10, 614, 669, 699, 715, 718
Eyemouth 327

INDEX

Faa, Johnie — see Pseudonyms of Burns
Fabricius 428
Fairly shote of her 301
Falconer, William: *The Shipwreck* 183
Falkirk 68, 89
Familiar Epistle to Robie Burns — see John Skinner
Fanny Fair 294
Farming 358, 368, 421, 426, 427, 428, 429, 444, 447, 496, 523
Farquhar, Miss – – of Edinburgh: Letter to 281
Farquhar, James 281
The Fated Marriage — see Thomas Southerne
Fawkes, Guy 487
Fee him, Father 644, 649
Ferdinand Count Fathom — see Tobias Smollett
Ferguson, Professor John De Lancey 7, 8, 12, 14, 16, 17, 22, 43, 76, 81, 221, 230, 307, 327, 401, 447, 576, 617, 707, 724, 726
Fergusson, Alexander (Craigdarroch) 320, 464, 563, 595
    Letter to 538
Fergusson, Mrs Alexander 156
Fergusson, Robert 16, 76, 309, 362, 505, 520, 524
    Influence of 16
    Job, Chapter II, Paraphrased 677
    Memorial to 265, 520, 524
Ferrier, Mr – – (Paisley) 585
Ferrier, Jane 32
Fielding, Henry 260, 262
    Amelia 380
    Joseph Andrews 318, 587
Fife 288, 722
Findlater, Alexander 21, 32, 322-3, 439, 440, 445, 553, 563, 571, 598, 718, 721
    Letters to 539-42
Findlater, James Ogilvy, 7th Earl of 525
Findlay, James 425
Fingal — see James Macpherson
Fingland 230
Finlaystone 226, 496, 506
The First Epistle of the First Book of Horace Imitated — see Alexander Pope
First Epistle to Mr Pope — see Edward Young
Fisher, Edward: *Marrow of Modern Divinity* 318
Flanders 653
The Flowers of the Forest 632, 642
Flyting 726
Fontaine, Jean de la: *Contes* 433
Fontenelle, Miss Louisa 202, 208, 437, 681
    Letters to 682-3
Foote, Samuel 316
Forbes, Hunter & Co 230
Fordyce, Mrs – – of Edinburgh 284, 285
For o'er lang biding here 300
Forres 357
Forsyth, Mr – – (bookseller) 102
Fort George 357
Forth River 89

Fortunate Shepherdess — see Alexander Ross
Fotheringham, Frederick 66
Fourfold State — see Thomas Boston
Fox, Charles James 173, 226, 589
Foxites 179, 482
France 390, 392, 543, 590, 652, 695, 703, 712
  Burns's opinion of 437, 488
Franking privilege 161, 187, 206, 210, 213, 260, 278, 354, 358, 437, 457, 481-2, 483, 506, 593, 654, 675
Franklin, Benjamin 490, 548
Fraser, Simon 288
Fraser, Thomas 630, 638
Frederick the Great, King of Prussia 655
French, John 512
French Revolution 54, 130, 509, 593, 653, 712
Friars' Carse 239, 275, 480, 481, 538, 557, 595, 600, 697, 710
Friends of the People 509
Fullarton, Colonel William 483
  Letter to 593
Fyars (Foyers), falls of 354
Fye let us a' to the Bridal 649
Fyffe, Dr M: Letter to 304
Fy gie me my Coggie, Sirs 649

G− −, Miss 505, 698
Gaelic parson — see Rev Joseph Macgregor
Galashiels 617
Gallovidia 653
Galloway 274, 278, 390, 438, 701, 708, 715
Galloway, John Stewart, 7th Earl of 125
Galston 89, 489
Gardenstone, Francis Garden, Lord 62
Garrick, David 316
Garthland — see William McDowall
Gateslack 676
Gatehouse 712
Gath 108, 205
Gaw, Molly 367
Gaw, Willie 100
Gay, John: *The Beggar's Opera* 300, 682
The Gazetteer 521
  Letter to 525
Geddes, Jenny (Burns's mare) 80, 120, 121, 147, 330
Geddes, Jenny (religious agitator) 121
Geddes, Right Rev John: Letter to 507-8
General Assembly of the Church of Scotland 144, 221, 574
General Post Office 30
Gentle Shepherd — see Allan Ramsay
Geographical Grammar — see William Guthrie
George III 171-2, 437, 589
George, Prince of Wales 417, 520, 523, 589
George Inn, Dumfries 22, 505
Georgics — see Virgil
Georgium Sidus (Uranus) 452, 633

INDEX

Gib, Rev Adam: *The Present Truth, a Display of the Secession Testimony* 316, 318
Gibraltar 200
Gilderoy 617
Gillespie, John: Letter to 572
Gillespie, Mrs John: Letter to 35
Gill Morice 645
Girvan 619
Gladstone, Hugh 707
Glauber's salts 368
The Glancing o her Apron 301
Glasgow 58, 59, 61, 89, 90, 112, 122, 137, 216, 246, 272, 283, 305, 332, 354, 359, 398,
  419, 420, 454, 476, 526, 566, 670, 764, 767
Glen Afton 124
Glenbuck 219
Glencairn, Lady Elizabeth — see Elizabeth Cunningham
Glencairn, Elizabeth McGuire, Dowager Countess of 87, 99, 222, 496
Glencairn, James Cunningham, 14th Earl of 35, 51, 66, 94, 99, 114, 128, 134, 224, 258,
  262, 269, 280, 305, 435, 464, 496, 497, 499, 500, 574, 686
  Letter to 226-8
Glencairn, John Cunningham, 15th Earl of: Letter to 686
Glencairn, William Cunningham, 13th Earl of 280, 496
Glenconner — see John Tennant
Glendinning, – – (Parton) 505
Glendinning, Mrs – – (Parton) 505
Glenlee 240
Glenriddell MS 14-15, 107, 209, 216, 323, 349, 410, 480, 481, 482, 509, 561, 569, 584,
  588, 589, 689-91, 707
Glens 712
Globe Tavern, Dumfries 105, 302, 354, 677
Glorious Revolution — see Revolution of 1688
Gloucester, Vale of 571
Glover, John 454, 526
God, Burns's concept of 174
God Save the King 202
Goethe, Wolfgang: *Werther* 561, 600, 606
Goldie (Goudie), John: Letter to 32
Goldie, Colonel Thomas 600, 710
Goldsmith, Oliver: *The Deserted Village* 185, 383
  The Traveller 147, 400
Goliath (Biblical figure) 205, 221, 322
Gomorrah 109
Good Night and Joy be wi you a' 382, 626
Gordon, Miss – – (Dumfries): Letters to 723
Gordon, Mr – – 243
Gordon, Alexander, 4th Duke of 358, 361, 362
Gordon Castle 358, 361
Gordon, house of 361, 466
Gordon, Lord George 269, 431
Gordon, Jane, Duchess of 87, 99, 114, 130, 358, 361, 457, 521, 525
Gordon, John (Kenmure) 635, 677
Gordon, Robie 538
Gordon, Thomas (Afton and Stair) 125
Gordon, Thomas (Dumfries) 715, 720
Goudie — see Goldie

INDEX

Gow, Nathaniel 667
Gow, Niel 232, 298
Gracie, James 301, 537
 Letters to 582
Graham, Miss Anne (of Fintry) 440, 654
Graham, James (Excise officer) 718
Graham, James, Marquis of 94
Graham, John (son of Graham of Fintry) 430
Graham, Sir John 89
Graham, Margaret Elizabeth Mylne (Mrs Robert Graham) 354, 428, 432, 435, 436
 Letters to 555-6
Graham, Robert (of Fintry) 14, 18, 21, 35, 63, 156, 170-1, 184, 204, 225, 258, 354, 448,
 478, 496, 498, 548, 555, 563, 654, 689
 Letters to 424-40
Graham, Robert Cunningham (of Gartmore) 316
Graham, Mrs Thomas 354
Grain, prices of 57
Grainger, Robert 720
Grand Lodge of Scotland 100
Grant Castle 289
Grant, Mrs − − (Carron) 477
Grant, Sir James 357
The Grave — see Robert Blair
Gray, Miss Hanna 453
Gray, Forbes 414
Gray, James 278, 684, 720
Gray, Symon 32
Gray, Thomas 140, 246
 The Bard 16, 394, 407
 Elegy in a Country Churchyard 83, 143, 520
Greenfield, Rev William 99, 114
 Letter to 221
Green Grow the Rashes 162
Greenland 367
Greenock 78, 84, 123, 184, 256, 419, 434, 505
Gregory (by Peter Pindar) 623
Gregory, Prof James 87, 374
Gregory, Dr John 449, 573
Grenada 421
The Grey Goose and its Gled 656-7
Gribbel Collection 351
Grierson of Dalgoner 76
Grieve, George 720
Grieve, James 720
Groningen 223
Grose, Captain Francis 176-7, 245, 431, 434, 448, 449, 450, 540, 578, 697
 Antiquities of England and Wales 176
 Antiquities of Scotland 176, 261, 559, 578
 Letters to 557-60
Groves, Dr David 572
Gude night & joy be wi' you a' 301
Guion, F J 552, 602
Guthrie, William:
 A New Geographical, Historical and Commercial Grammar 251, 314, 318
Guthrie, Rev William: *Trial of a Saving Interest* 459

INDEX

Haddington 144, 157, 452, 527, 563, 762
Had I the Wyte she Bade me 301
Hall, Sir James 327
Halliday, James 544, 545
Halliday, Thomas 720
Hamilton, Miss – – (Dumfries) 685
Hamilton, Alexander (Grange) 199
Hamilton, Charlotte — see Charlotte Adair
Hamilton, Douglas, 8th Duke of 260-1
Hamilton, Gavin 32, 75, 76, 83, 87, 91, 95, 118, 123, 230, 400
    Letters to 65-71
Hamilton, Grace (of Harviestoun) 69
Hamilton, Helen Kennedy (Mrs Gavin) 65, 69, 70, 75, 83, 570
Hamilton, house of 246, 466
Hamilton, Jacobina (Beenie) 69
Hamilton, James (Glasgow grocer) 526
    Letters to 526
Hamilton, James junior (of Bangour) 334, 336
Hamilton, Captain John (Dumfries) 296
    Letters to 703-4
Hamilton, John (Sundrum) 69
Hamilton, Mary 183
Hamilton, Mrs Rachel 107
Hamilton, Wilhelmina (Willie) 69
Hamilton, William (Edinburgh) 570
    Letter to 413
Hamilton, William (of Gilbertfield):
    The Life and Heroic Actions of Sir William Wallace 131, 193, 641
Hamilton, William (of Harviestoun) 69
Hamilton, William junior (Dumfries) 69, 720
Handel, George Frederick: *The Messiah* 531
Hannibal 131, 171, 249
Harviestoun 65, 68, 230, 231, 359, 413, 569
Haugh Miln 66
Hay, Charles (Lord Newton): Letter to 414
Hay, Lewis 230
Hay, Mrs Lewis — see Margaret Chalmers
Haydn, Josef 615, 616
A Health to Betty 300
Heard ye e'er of Sir John Malcolm 540
Hector 95
Hell, Letter from 23, 697-8
Hellespont 373
Henderson, Andrew (Berwick) 726
Henderson, Matthew 275, 434, 449
Henri, Mrs James (Susan Dunlop) 157, 175, 185, 188, 189, 190, 192, 195, 200
Henriques, Benjamin 419
Henry of Ercildoune:
    Metrical History of Sir William Wallace — see Blind Harry
Henry the Minstrel — see William Hamilton
Herald, Edinburgh 248, 725
Heraldic seal of Burns 248-9, 471-2, 652, 653, 667-8, 679
Herd, David: *The Ancient and Modern Scots Songs* 119-20, 300, 542, 629-30, 640
Hereafter, Burns's belief in 86, 90, 93, 181-2, 188-9, 387

Here's a Health to them that's Awa 301, 474
Heron, – – (Edinburgh) 405
Heron, Major Basil 299
Heron, Lady Elizabeth 652, 664, 715
  Letter to 705
Heron, Patrick 125, 299, 705
  Letters to 715-6
Heron, Robert 299, 539, 617
Herrick, Robert 648
Hervey, James: *Meditations* 317, 384, 393
Highland and Agricultural Society 289
Highland Mary — see Mary Campbell
Highlands 241, 289, 354
Hildebroad, John 191
Hill, Elizabeth Lindsay (Mrs Peter Hill) 309, 316, 321, 323
Hill, Peter 18, 21, 29, 167, 265, 272, 297, 308, 348, 455, 480, 482, 681
  Letters to 309-25
History of Scottish Music — see William Tytler
History of Sir William Wallace see Henry of Ercildoune and William Hamilton of
  Gilbertfield
History of the Late Rebellion — see Peter Rae
History of the Reformation — see John Knox
The Hive 383
Hog, James (of Edinburgh) 332
Holland 437, 720
Home, John 616
  Douglas 149, 193, 486, 616, 653
Homer 145, 184, 640
  The Iliad 178
  The Odyssey 252
Hood, Thomas 327
Hopetoun, James Hope, 3rd Earl of 189, 464, 588, 595
Horace, Book I, Ode XI to WD — see Allan Ramsay's *Tea-Table Miscellany*
How are thy Servants Blest — see Joseph Addison
Howard, John: *The State of the Prisons in England and Wales* 210
Howden, Francis: Letter to 417
Howie, John: *Scots Worthies* 318
Hoy, James: Letters to 361-2
Huber, Marie 222, 312
Hudson, Mr – – 62
Hughoc — see Hugh Parker
Human Nature in its Fourfold Estate — see Thomas Boston
Hume, David 291, 490
  History of England 587
Humphrey Clinker — see Tobias Smollett
Hunter & Co Bank 107
Hurdis Rev James: *The Village Curate* 315
A Hymn on the Seasons — see James Thomson
Hypochondria 23, 235, 358, 469
Hyslop, Margaret (Mrs William) 677, 721
Hyslop, Edward (writer, Dumfries) 74, 541
Hyslop, William (Dumfries innkeeper) 301-2, 571, 720
Hyslop, William junior 720

I− −, Miss   697
Iceland   369
I Chappit at the Study   301
The Idler   318, 587
I had a Horse   645
Iliad — see Homer
Illegitimate children   72
Ill health   427, 435, 473, 505, 610, 611, 677, 678, 679, 722
In April when Primroses   625
Incas, Les — see Jean-François Marmontel
Inchbald, Mrs Elizabeth Simpson   499
An Index to Excise Laws — see Jellinger Symons
Inglis, Bailie William: Letter to   353
Inkle and Yarico — see George Colman the younger
Innes, Cosmo   441
Inveraray   80
Inverness   57, 61, 68, 81, 88, 234, 330, 353, 357, 635
Ireland   635
Irish music — see Music
Irvin, Miss − −   230
Irvine   19, 41, 59, 113, 253-4, 418, 443, 536
Isle   513, 515, 544
Isle of Man   443, 664
Israel   390, 392, 404, 453, 611
I wish I were where Helen lies   627, 632

Jacob   331, 390, 611
Jacobites   416, 487, 504, 543, 546, 590
Jacobite rebellions   41
Jacobite songs   622, 632, 649
Jaffray, Rev Andrew   548
Jamaica   78, 84, 110, 111, 118, 119, 125, 154, 218, 352, 370, 371, 419, 477
James I of Scotland: *Christ's Kirk on the Grene*   189
James IV   300
James VII   487
James the Less   219
James the Apostle   219
Jardine family of Annandale   189
Jeany, where hast Thou Been   299-300
Jeffrey, Francis   11
Jeffry, Mr − − — see Jaffray, Rev Andrew
Jenny's Bawbee   301
Jerusalem   237, 392
Jesus Christ   159, 174, 182, 379
Job (Biblical figure)   333, 580, 590
Jock's Lodge   343, 345
Jocky and Jenny   645
John the Apostle   219
John o Badenyon — see John Skinner
John Ochiltree   301
Johnson, James   18, 20, 361, 362, 468, 615, 617, 626, 627, 645, 666
  Letters to   292-303
  The Scots Musical Museum   153, 157, 166, 234, 238, 245, 285, 291, 337, 361, 363, 376, 409, 441, 457, 468, 478, 480, 615, 616, 624, 626, 630, 636, 637, 644, 653, 656, 661, 664, 719
    Burns's authorship   157
    Identification of contributors   157, 159

INDEX

Johnson, Samuel 135, 236, 314, 490
  Lives of the Poets 561
Johnston Miss – – (of Edinburgh) 490
Johnston, Mr – – (Catlins) 723
Johnston family 189, 359
Johnston, Thomas (Mirecleugh): Letter to 564-5
Johnston, William (Dumfries) 595, 720
Johnston, Captain William (Edinburgh) 437
  Letters to 681
Johnstone, Charles: *Chrysal* 587
Johnstone, Sir James (Westerhall) 179, 189, 240, 432
Johnstone, John (Alva) 359
Joktan (Biblical figure) 171
Jones's Directory 421
Jonson, Ben 316
Joseph Andrews — see Henry Fielding
Journal, Burns's of the Highland Tour 441
Journal During a Residence in France — see John Moore
Jove 411
Judas Iscariot 261-2, 393, 470
Justice, James: *British Gardener's Directory* 251

Kabul 57
Keith family 249
Kellie, Earl of 224
Kellock, Mrs – – (Thornhill) 565
Kelso 326, 616
Kemble, Mrs Elizabeth 212, 323, 324
Kemp, Rev John 397, 399
Kempis, Thomas à 66
Kennedy, Miss – – 707
Kennedy, Mr – – 56
Kennedy, Helen 65
Kennedy, James (Dumbarton) 531
Kennedy, Miss Jane (Mauchline) 236-7
Kennedy, John (factor to Lord Dumfries): Letters to 83-5
Kennedy, John S 763-4
Kennedy, Mrs John 85
Kennedy, Miss Margaret (Daljarrock) 67, 68, 69, 70, 83
  Letter to 75
Kennedy, Robert (Daljarrock) 75
Kent (county) 571
Kent — see Shakespeare, *King Lear*
Ker, Gilbert 326
Ker, William (Secretary of the Post Office) 161
Kerr, Robert 597
Kerr, William (Broomlands, Kelso) 493
Ketch, Jack 522
Kilbarchan 403
Kildrummie 442
Kilmarnock 60, 76, 84, 86, 89, 123, 163, 169, 226, 269, 308, 332, 339, 419, 431, 454, 482, 489, 563, 566
Kilmarnock Edition — see *Poems, Chiefly in the Scottish Dialect* (1786)
Kilmaurs 157, 231

INDEX

Kilpatrick, J.: *The Highlander* 492
Kilpatrick, Nelly 250-1
Kilravock 289, 441
Kilwinning Abbey 560
Kincaid & Bell 305
Kincardineshire 223
King's Arms, Dumfries 494
Kirkbean 347, 561
Kirkcudbright 125, 179, 432, 490, 708
Kirkgunzeon 347
Kirkmahoe 347
Kirkmichael 263
Kirkoswald 18, 37, 49, 451
Kirkpatrick, Rev Joseph 173, 347, 487
  Letter to 594
Kirroughtree 299, 712, 715
Kist Yestreen 542
Knockshinnoch 123
Knox, John: *History of the Reformation* 316
Kozeluch 670
Kyle district 177, 218, 310

La Fontaine, Jean de: *Les Contes* 578
Laggan farm 346, 348, 349
Lamie, James 117
Lang, Rev William 220
Lansdowne, William Petty, 1st Marquis of 714
Lapraik, John 32
L'Art poetique — see Nicolas Boileau-Despreaux
The Lass of Patie's Mill — see Allan Ramsay
The last Time I came o'er the Moor 603, 625
Launcelot Greaves — see Tobias Smollett
Laura — see Gavin Turnbull
Laurie, Sir Robert 481
Lawrie, Rev Archibald 263, 281
  Letters to 128-9
Lawrie, Christina 128, 263
Lawrie, Rev George 127, 490
  Letter to 263-4
Lawrie, Mary Campbell (Mrs George) 263
Lawson, Adam de Cardonnel 540
Lawson, Rev Archibald 191, 347
Lawson, John 103
Lawson, John junior 720
Lawson, William 614
Lawther Hills — see Lowther Hills
Lay thy Loof in mine, Lassie 299
Leadbetter, Charles: *The Royal Gauger* 430-1
Leadhills 408
Leah (Biblical figure) 328
Leglen Wood 131
Leith 67, 77, 609
L'Enclos, Ninon de 392
Leonidas 174

Let me in this ae Night   632, 634, 674
Letter from Italy — see Joseph Addison
Letters — see Rev John Newton
Letters on the Religion Essential to Man — see Marie Huber
Let us all be Unhappy Together   611
Leven, Earl of   288
Leven, John: Letter to   614
Lewars, Jessy   32, 303, 479, 572
Lewars, John (Supervisor of Excise)   130, 322, 571
Lewars, John junior (Excise officer)   572, 678
Liberty, Burns on   638-9
Life of Bruce — see John Barbour
Lindsay, Bishop   121
Lindsay, Maurice   248, 304, 354, 455, 578
Linlithgow   89, 117
Literary Magnet   365
Literary scolding   726
Little Haymarket Theatre   682
Little, Janet   178, 184, 193, 197
Littleton, Mr – – (poet)   247
Liverpool   103
Lives of the Poets — see Samuel Johnson
Lizars (Edinburgh)   368
Lochaber   622
Loch Erroch Side   119
Lochlea   18, 38, 39, 41, 44-9, 57, 536
Loch Lomond   80, 119
Loch Long   80
Lochmaben   179, 189, 432, 548
The Lochmaben Harper   299
Locke, John   386
    Essay on Human Understanding   251, 386
Lockhart, George   539, 712
    Letter to   453
Logan, Hugh   269
Logan, John (poet)   647
Logan, John (Laight)   21, 157, 478
    Letters to   123-4
Logan, Martha Macadam (Mrs John)   157
Logan, Miss Susan   137
Logan Water   206
Logan, Captain William   32
Logie o Buchan   585
London   54, 107, 190, 206, 212, 308, 392, 518, 557, 600, 626, 713
London Star — see Peter Stuart
Lone Vale   626
Longtown   514, 515
Lord Gregory   623, 642
Lords, House of   226, 271
Lorimer, Agnes Carson (Mrs William)   540, 721
Lorimer, Jean   324, 406, 473, 540, 572, 658, 662, 665, 671, 677, 721
Lorimer, William   540, 567, 571
    Letter to   721
Loretto   131

The Lothian Lassie 674
Lothians 67, 305
Loudoun Castle 190
Loudoun, John Earl of 65, 107, 627
Loudoun parish 127, 263
Louis XVI of France 130, 214
The Lounger 100, 114, 185, 186, 314, 316, 587
Lovat, Lord 288
Love in a Village — see Isaac Bickerstaffe
Love never more shall give me Pain 661
Love of Fame — see Edward Young
Low down in the Broom 641
Lowe, Rev John: *Mary's Dream* 455
Lowrie — see Lawrie
Lowther Hills 676
Loyal Natives 485
Loyalty: Burns's questioned 436, 539, 598, 681, 689-91
Lucky Nansie 644
Lugar 619
Lumps o Puddins 628
Lunardi, Vincenzo 644

Mabane Isabella (or Isobel): Letter to 367
McAdam, Miss (of Craigengillan) 114, 130
McAdam, John 32, 218
MacAdam, Martha (of Laight) 123
McAuley, John: Letter to 531
McCandlish — see Candlish
McCartney, Mr – – (Edinburgh) 304
McCauslin, Miss – – (Kilmarnock) 89
McCornock, Hugh junior 720
McCulloch, Andrew 476
McCulloch, David junior 715
   Letter to 712
McCulloch, David senior 278, 712
McDonald, Patrick: *A Collection of Highland Vocal Airs* 196, 625
McDoual, Captain Andrew 75
McDowall, Elizabeth 368
McDowall, William 610
McFarlane, John 438
McGibbon, William 292
McGill, Rev. William 95, 124, 138, 176, 431, 499
   A Practical Essay on the Death of Jesus Christ 431
Macgregor, Rev Joseph Robertson 635
McGuire, Miss Macrae 269
McGuirk, Carol 12-13
Machlin, Machline — see Mauchline
McIlhose, see McLehose
McIndoe, Robert: Letter to 476
Mack, Mrs – – see Agnes McLehose
Mackay, Francis 408
McKay, Georgina 159, 161, 162
Mackenna, Dr Robert 11-12

Mackenzie, Lady Cochrane   69, 231, 237, 570
Mackenzie, Henry   99, 114, 142, 186, 253, 305, 306, 441, 497
   Letter to   289-90
      Man of Feeling   16, 55, 208, 253, 263, 289, 307, 314, 316, 497, 587
      Man of the World   16, 55, 314, 316, 587
Mackenzie, Mrs Henry   289
Mackenzie, Dr. John   32, 52, 69, 352
   Letters to   113-14
Mackenzie, Rev John (Portpatrick)   176
Mackenzie, Simon   32
Mackinlay, Rev. John   76, 269-70, 448
Mackinlay, Rev William   226
McKnight, Samuel   679
McKune, – – (innkeeper, Gatehouse of Fleet)   712
McLeerie, Duncan — see pseudonyms of Burns
McLehose, Mrs Agnes Craig   11, 16, 18, 35, 230, 308, 327, 335, 336, 600, 661, 662, 684
   Letters to   370-412
      To a Blackbird   388, 661
McLehose, James (husband of Agnes)   370, 371, 395
McLeod, Isabella   32, 241
McLeod, John: Letter to   710-11
McMath, Rev. John   33
McMorine, John   720
McMurdo, Mrs Jane Blair   493, 693, 720
   Letter to   529
McMurdo, Miss Jean   495, 631, 634, 637
   Letter to   693-4
McMurdo, John   35, 155, 444, 464, 595, 601, 615, 631, 633, 693, 720
   Letters to   492-5
McMurdo, Miss Phillis   637, 693
MacNaghten, Angus   697
McNaught, Dr Duncan   767
McNaught, Riddle   720
McNish, Robert   482
Macao   107
Macpherson, James   55
   Fingal   16, 405
Macpherson's Farewell   646
McVitie, John   720
McWhinnie, David: Letter to   106
Maitland, Lord James   114
Malaga   162
Man of Feeling — see Henry Mackenzie
Man of the World — see Henry Mackenzie
Manchester   480, 483, 595
Manson, James   352
Marie Antionette, Queen   130, 214
Marlborough, John Churchill, Duke of   442
Marmontel, Jean-François:
   Belisaire   140
   Les Incas, ou la destruction de l'empire du Perou   232
Marquess, Hugh   571
Marriage: Burns's opinion of   72, 108-9, 466-7
Marrow of Modern Divinity — see Edward Fisher

Marshall, Rev. Walter: *On Sanctification* 459
Marshall, William: *The Rural Economy of Yorkshire* 428, 433
Martial 140, 382
Mary – – (Bonie Mary) 277
Mary and Jean (ship) 418
Mary Queen of Scots 187, 291, 546, 547
Masson, Arthur: *A Collection of English Prose and Verse* 15, 16, 249
Masterton, Allan 315, 316, 359, 482, 659
Mauchline 15, 19, 20, 30, 52, 60, 65, 76, 78, 80, 86, 111, 117, 118, 145, 149, 230, 231, 239,
    283, 305, 309, 310, 332, 356, 369, 400, 401, 418, 447, 455, 475, 477, 501, 504, 526, 722
Mauchline Races 477
Maule, Ramsay 212
Maunderson, Mr – – (Dumfries) 74
Maxwell, Colonel – – 67, 209
Maxwell, David (Cardoness) 205, 324
Maxwell, Frederick (Terregles) 505, 571
Maxwell, George (Carruchan) 546, 562
Maxwell, James 433
Maxwell, John (Terraughty) 33
Maxwell, Provost Robert (Lochmaben) 432
    Letter to 548
Maxwell, Dr William (Dumfries) 33, 211, 278, 485, 502, 504, 543, 657, 708
Maybole 40
Meal Riots 215
Medes and Persians 310
Meditations — see James Hervey
Menteath, Rev James Stuart 710
Mentieth, Captain (of Closeburn) 314
Mercury 387
Merry, J 124
The Merry Muses of Caledonia 444-5
Metrical Psalms — see Bible
Mickle, William Julius: *There's nae luck about the house* 645, 660
Miers, John 334, 394, 417
Miller, Eliza or Bettsey 80
Miller, Helen (Mauchline) 113
Miller, James (Edinburgh) 422, 664
Miller, Miss Janet (of Dalswinton) 240, 245
Miller, Patrick (of Dalswinton) 35, 89, 99, 100, 152, 170, 229, 231, 236, 320, 331, 359,
    399, 444, 480, 544, 546, 568, 615, 633, 688, 699
    Letters to 240-5
Miller, Captain Patrick junior 179, 189, 206, 210, 213, 240, 432
    Letters to 699-701
Miller, Mrs Patrick 152, 240
    Letter to 245
Miller, Peter — see Patrick Miller
Miller, Sir Thomas 240
Miller, William 154-5, 240, 688
Mills, James — see James Mylne
Milton, John 141, 380
    Paradise Lost 16, 108, 119, 136, 138, 219, 226, 269, 378, 379, 433, 612
The Minstrel — see James Beattie

INDEX

The Mirror 186, 314, 316, 587
Mitchell, John 21, 33, 428, 429, 431, 434, 435, 438, 354, 614
  Letters to 563-5
Mitchelson, Samuel 329
Moffat 462, 465, 584, 595, 721
Moffat Grammar School 584, 588, 595, 613
Moir, Agnes — see Mrs Alexander Cunningham
Moliere, Jean Baptiste 316
Momus 579
Monboddo, James Burnett, Lord 219
  Letter to 223
Monkland Friendly Society 21, 309, 314, 315, 316, 480, 586-7
Montague, Lady Mary Wortley 392
Montgomerie, Captain James 67-8, 456
Montgomerie, Colonel Hugh 271
Montrose 57, 357
Moodie, Rev William: Letter to 613
Moore, Rev Charles 246
Moore, Dr John 15, 17, 20, 41, 43, 132, 134, 137, 175, 195, 378, 532, 575
  Letters to 246-62
  Journal During a Residence in France 214
  View of Society and Manners in France, Switzerland and Germany 132, 134, 213-14,
    246, 656
  Zeluco 177, 179, 208, 214, 246, 260, 262, 575
    George Buchanan (character) 261
    Duncan Targe (character) 261
Moore, Robert 21
  Letter to 543
More, Hannah 91
Moreham Mains 157, 160, 185
Morham 527
Morison, Peter: Letter to 501
Morison, R. (Perth) 193
Morlière, Rochette de la: *Angola, histoire indienne* 433
The Morning Chronicle 699
  Letter to 714
Morning Star — see Peter Stuart
Morris, Captain: *The Plenipotentiary* 444-5
Moses 234, 548, 590
Mossgiel 40, 50, 59, 65, 70, 76, 80, 97, 106, 113, 115, 127, 309, 357, 371, 419, 477
Mount Oliphant 41, 54, 222
Muir, Robert 181-2
  Letters to 86-90
Muir, Mrs William 96
Muirkirklands 66
Mundell, Dr James 279, 553, 571, 606
  Letters to 485
Munny Begum 250
Murdoch, John 13, 72, 357, 518, 519, 713
  Letters to 54-6
Murdoch, Mrs John 55, 56
Murphy, Arthur 141
  The Way to Keep Him 602

Murray, Miss Euphemia 659
Murray, Sir William 242, 354, 428
Music — see also letters to James Johnson and George Thomson
  Difficulty in ascertaining origins of 665, 667
  English songs, Burns's dislike of 299, 617, 660
  Irish 294, 608, 628, 635, 644, 649, 664, 667, 677
  Sacred (burlesqued) 657
Mylne, James 167-8, 527
  To Mr Burns, on his Poems 167, 527
Mylnefield 424
My Patie is a Lover gay 627

Nairn 282, 357
Nairn, Tibbie 334
Nancy (brig) 78
Nantz (brandy) 198
Nasmyth, Alexander 369, 652
Nathaniel (Biblical figure) 113
Nelson, Mr — see Rev Edward Nielson
Nettle, Tim — see Pseudonyms of Burns
Nevin, Margaret 451
Newall, David 22, 478
  Letters to 544-5
Newbattle 305
Newcastle 327, 516, 518, 614, 659
New Cumnock 124, 157, 166, 259
Newhaven 281
New Jerusalem Tavern 316-7
Newmills (Newmilns) 89, 107, 127, 263
Newton, Sir Isaac 398, 514
Newton, Rev John: *Letters* 318
New York 357
Niagara Falls 110
Nicol, Edward 'Neddy' 348, 349
Nicol, William 17, 61, 88-9, 330, 335-6, 354, 359, 360, 361, 502, 673, 724
  Letters to 342-50
Nicol, Mrs William 348, 349
Nielson, Rev Edward (Kirkbean) 259, 315, 347
Nievison, Janet 485
Night Thoughts — see Edward Young
The Nightingale — see Gavin Turnbull
Nimmo, Miss Erskine 231, 236, 372, 377, 381, 387, 390, 391, 402, 403, 570
Nith, River 62, 154, 166, 225, 236, 239, 242, 428, 451, 508, 513, 551, 553, 637, 676, 700, 708, 720
Nithsdale 149, 150, 156, 158, 167, 189, 275, 310, 345, 357, 431, 448, 453, 455, 475, 478, 485, 490, 496, 512, 514, 519, 546, 557, 586, 724
Niven, Mr – – (carrier, Dumfries) 314
Niven, Bailie Robert 40
Niven, Mrs Robert 40
Niven, William 18, 49
  Letters to 37-40
Northumberland 327

The Observer 318, 587
Ochil Hills 359

Ochiltree   72, 220, 222, 499
Ochtertyre   241, 345, 356, 359
O Condescend Dear Charming Maid — see Gavin Turnbull
Ode, to Mrs A R — see Allan Ramsay's *Tea-Table Miscellany*
Odyssey — see Homer
Og, King of Bashan (Biblical figure)   205
O gin my Love were yon red Rose   630
O' Keefe, John   499, 682
Old Major — see Andrew Dunlop
Old Place, Galston   43
Old Rome Foord   77
One Day I heard Mary Say   627
On God's Sovereignty — see Elisha Coles
On Sanctification — see Rev Walter Marshall
The Oracle   520, 524
The Orphan — see Thomas Otway
Orpheus Caledonius — see William Thomson
Orr, John   342
Orr, Thomas: Letters to   49-50
Osburn, Henry   323
Ossian   16, 55, 127, 358, 405
   — see also James Macpherson
Oswald, James: *The Caledonian Pocket Companion*   162, 293, 296, 299, 632, 643
Oswald, Lucy Johnston (Mrs Richard Oswald)   708, 717
Oswald, Mrs Mary Ramsay   165, 259, 512, 522, 523, 701, 717
Oswald, Richard Alexander (Auchencruive)   66, 708
   Letter to   717
O this is nae my ain Body   675
Otway, Sylvester   523
Otway, Thomas   316
   The Orphan   79
   Venice Preserved   118

Paisley   79, 137, 198, 308, 398, 419, 433, 459, 477, 585
Paisley Union Bank   104, 206
Pamela — see Samuel Richardson
Paris   246, 533
Park, Anna   477
Parker, Hugh   33, 89
Parker, William   87, 88, 89
Parliamentary reform   315, 436, 509, 591, 689
Paterson, G   111
Paterson, James   651
Paterson, Robert   72
Paterson, Mrs Robert   72
Patie's Mill   627
Patmos   219
Paton, Elizabeth   115, 118, 370
Pattison, Alexander   309, 398
   Letter to   308
Pau   230
Peacock, Miss Mary   410
   Letter to   684

INDEX

Pearson, Andrew 439
A Peasant — see Pseudonyms of Burns
Peebles, Rev William 113
Pegasus 259, 558, 674
Pen, William 571
Penitence 572
Percy, Right Rev. Thomas: *Reliques of Ancient English Poetry* 261
Peregrine Pickle — see Tobias Smollett
Perry, James 699, 700
Perth 305, 354
Perth Courier 354
Peterkin, Alexander 539
Pharaoh (Biblical figure) 109
Pharsalia, battle of 109
Philistines 322
Philippi 445
The Philosophy of Natural History — see William Smellie
Pilgarlick 639
Pindar, Peter — see John Wolcot
Pinkerton, John: *Scottish Tragic Ballads* 627, 632, 641
Piper, Thomas 37, 40
Pitt, William 214, 520, 533
   Letter to 509-11
Pleasures of the Imagination — see Mark Akenside
The Plenipotentiary — see Captain Morris
Pleyel, Ignaz Josef 245, 440, 495, 608, 615, 616, 629, 652-3, 670, 693
P– – – –n, Robert (Alnwick): Letter to 365
Poems:
   Burns's reluctance of commissioned 631
   Composition of 630, 643
   Plans for publication 679
Poems, Chiefly in the Scottish Dialect (1786) 65, 77, 79, 86, 91, 106, 111, 115, 226, 229,
   255-6, 352, 418, 448, 477, 490, 505, 520
   Proposals for 65-6, 83, 88, 91
Poems, Chiefly in the Scottish Dialect (1787) 97, 99, 132, 220, 326, 363, 453, 507, 531, 567
   Distribution 57, 62, 102, 281, 454
   Profit from 62
Poems, Chiefly in the Scottish Dialect (1793) 578
   Inscribed copies 240, 244, 484, 500, 503, 556, 602, 686, 687, 691
Poems and Songs of Burns:
   Act Sederunt 277
   Address to the Deil 76
   Address to Edinburgh 218
   Address Spoken by Miss Fontenelle 683
   Address to the Haggis 501
   Address to the Shade of Thomson 104, 266, 267
   Address to the Woodlark 672
   Adown winding Nith 637
   Ae Fond Kiss 12, 371, 409
   Afton Water 166
   Allan Water 206, 636
   Anna, thy Charms my Bosom fire 139
   Auld Lang Syne 161, 162-3, 628, 646
   The Auld Man's Winter Thought 661

Auld Rob Morris   622, 623
The Author's Earnest Crynd Prayer   271
Banks of Cree   652
The Banks of Devon   234
The Banks of Doon   645, 664
Behold, My Love, How Green the Groves   719
Behold the hour   409, 640
The Blue-eyed lassie   158
Blythe hae I been   592, 631, 644, 692
Bonie Dundee   624, 625, 641, 642
Bonie Jean   693
Bonie Peggy Alison   43
The Bonie Wee Thing   591
Braw Lads o Galla Water   622, 624
The Braw Wooer   676
The Brigs of Ayr   92, 97
Caledonian Hunt   294, 295, 296, 664, 666, 675
The Calf   86, 113
Can you Leave me thus, my Katy   609, 667
Castle Gordon   361
Ca' the Yowes to the Knowes   323, 655
Clarinda, Mistress of my Soul   139, 161, 402
Come cowe me, Minnie   278
Come let me take Thee   637
Come rede me, dame   505
Contented wi Little and Cantie wi Mair   666, 674
The Cotter's Saturday Night   41, 76, 83, 91, 130, 616, 652
The Court of Equity   76
Craigieburn-wood   572, 658, 665, 670
Dainty Davie   637, 638
The Day Returns   239, 480
Death and Dr Hornbook   97, 566
The Death and Dying Words of Poor Mailie   253, 269
Dedication to Gavin Hamilton   108
The Deil's awa wi' the Exciseman   307, 614
Delia, an Ode   523, 530
Deluded Swain   648
Down the Burn, Davie   636
The Dumfries Volunteers   214, 302
Duncan Gray   622, 660
The Election — A New Song   433
Election Ballad for Westerha'   240
Elegy for Sir James Hunter Blair   32, 95, 139
Elegy on Capt Matthew Henderson   190, 261, 275, 434, 493
Elegy on the late Miss Burnet   194, 460
Epigrams on Lord Galloway   324
Epistle to a Young Friend   32, 37, 91
Epistle to Davie, a Brother Poet   33
Epistle to John Goldie   32
Epistle to John Lapraik   32
Epistle to John Rankine   33, 84
Epistle to Captain William Logan   32
Epistle to the Revd John McMath   33
Epistle to Hugh Parker   33

INDEX

Epistle to Mr Tytler 291, 416, 546
Epitaph for J H Writer 162
Epitaph, Here lies Robert Fergusson, Poet 520
Epitaph on John Bushby 324
Epitaph on R Muir 182
Extempore in the Court of Session 224
Extempore — On being shewn a beautiful Country Seat 324
Extempore — On some Commemorations of Thomson 437
Extempore, Pinned to Mrs Riddell's Carriage 324, 412, 600, 700
Extempore Verses on Dining with Lord Daer 113, 719
Fairest Maid on Devon Banks 680
Fair Jenny 245
The Farewell. To the Brethren of St James's Lodge, Tarbolton 301, 352
Farewell, thou Stream 208, 603, 605, 629, 653, 664
The Fête Champêtre 103, 489
The Five Carlins 180, 431, 503, 544, 699
For a' that and a' that 669, 676
Forlorn, my Love, no Comfort Near 674, 675
Friday first's the day appointed 113
From thee Eliza, I must go 618
Galla Water 619
Gloomy December 299, 409, 684
The Gloomy Night 624
Go Fetch to me a Pint of Wine 163, 643
Green Grow the Rashes 79, 97, 625
Gude Ale Comes, and Gude Ale Goes 299
Had I a Cave 635
Here awa, there awa 292, 624
Here is the Glen, and here the Bower 652-3, 664, 705
Here's a Health to ane I Lo'e Dear 474, 678
The Heron Ballads 75, 715, 716, 717
Hey for a Lass wi a Tocher 677
The Highland Lassie 644
Highland Mary 620, 623, 629
The Holy Fair 113, 255
Holy Willie's Prayer 228, 255, 443
How Cruel are the Parents 673
How Lang and Dreary is the Night 660
Hughie Graham 627, 632, 642
The Humble Petition of Bruar Water 354
Husband, Husband, cease your Strife 652
I'll tell you a tale of a Wife 548
I see a Form, I see a Face 676
I wish I were where Helen lies 632
In summer when the hay was mawn 660
It was the Charming Month of May 662
J−s−s Ch−−−, O Cardoness 205, 324
John Anderson my Jo 627, 643
John Barleycorn 253
The Jolly Beggars 67, 644
Ken ye ought o Capt Grose 540
Ken ye what Meg o the Mill has gotten 229, 649-50
Killiecrankie 541
The Kirk's Alarm 123-4, 176, 431

INDEX

The Lament 293
Lament for James, Earl of Glencairn 51, 280, 496, 499
Lament of Mary Queen of Scots 187, 261, 408, 546, 555
The Lass o Ballochmyle 68, 125-6, 216
The Lass of Cessnock banks 18, 43
Lassie wi the Lintwhite Locks 656, 663, 666
Last May a Braw Wooer 674
The Last Time I came o'er the Moor 627, 628, 629
The Lea-Rig 618
Let me in this ae Night 632, 634, 670, 672
Let not Woman e'er Complain 660
Lines, sent to Sir John Whitefoord 579
Lines written in Friars' Carse Hermitage 151, 162, 163, 239, 275, 285, 480, 502
Logan Braes 629, 634, 649
Long, Long the Night 609
Lord Gregory 473, 623
Love and Liberty — see *The Jolly Beggars*
Lovely Davies 590
Lovely Polly Stewart 444
The Lover's Morning Salute to his Mistress 661
McPherson's Farewell 659
Man was Made to Mourn 698
Mark Yonder Pomp of Costly Fashion 673
Mary Morison 623
The Mauchline Wedding 155
Monody on Maria 209, 412, 600
A Mother's Lament 156, 491
Mr Gavin Hamilton, Mauchline 65
My Chloris mark how green the Grass 213, 324, 609, 662
My Girl She's Airy 329
My Highland Lassie 644
My Lady's Gown 299
My Nanie O 618, 621
My Nanie's Awa 668
My Peggy's Face 293
My Wife's a winsome wee Thing 620, 621
Nae Gentle Dames — see *The Highland Lassie*
A New Psalm for the Chapel of Kilmarnock 173
New Year's Day 164
Nithsdale's Welcome Hame 546
Now Spring has Clad the Grove in Green 472
O Bonie was yon Rosy Brier 472, 611
Occasional Address, Spoken by Miss Fontenelle 208, 437
Ochel-Hills — see *Where Braving Angry Winter's Storms*
Ode, for General Washington's Birthday 131, 210
Ode, Sacred to the Memory of Mrs Oswald 165, 259, 512, 522, 701
Ode to the departed Regency-bill 171, 499, 509
Ode to Spring 669
O, for Ane and Twenty Tam 660
Of A' the Airts the Wind can Blaw 477
O Lassie art thou sleeping yet — see *Let me in this ae Night*
O, Logan, sweetly dost thou glide 206
O my Luve's Like a Red Red Rose 468, 632
On being asked why God had made Miss Davies so little 205, 324

INDEX

On Capt Lascelles 324
On Capt William Roddick 324, 604, 700
On Cessnock Banks a Lassie Dwells 18, 43
On Chloris being Ill 672
On hearing a Thrush Sing 468
On James Morrine 324
On Maxwell of Cardoness 205, 324
On meeting with Lord Daer 113, 719
On reading . . . the Death of John Macleod 151
On Seeing a Wounded Hare 171, 457
On Seeing Mrs Kemble in Yarico 212, 323, 324
On some Commemorations of Thomson 681
On the Death of the late Lord President Dundas 374, 414, 724
On the Late Captain Grose's Peregrinations 240, 431, 557
On the Seas and far away 654
On Walter Riddell 211, 323, 600
On William Graham 324
Open the Door to me Oh 624
O Philly, Happy be that Day 656
O Poortith Cauld 622, 627, 635
Orananaoig or, the Song of Death 196
The Ordination 76, 226
O saw ye Bonie Lesley 199, 467, 620, 621, 692
O saw ye my Dear 667
O that I had ne'er been Married 207
O this is no my ain Lassie 676
O wat ye wha's in yon Town 585, 671, 672, 708
O were I on Parnassus Hill 637
O were my Love yon Lilack fair 630
O Whistle and I'll come to ye, my Lad 636, 675
Passion's Cry 166, 456
Peggy Alison 18
Phillis the Fair 634
Philly and Willy 665-6
Praise Woman Still 607
Poet's Progress — see *To Robert Graham*
A Poet's Welcome to his Love-begotten Daughter 256, 351
The Posie 659
The Primrose 648
Prologue for Mrs Sutherland's benefit night 185, 358, 519, 549, 551, 577, 683
Rattlin, roarin Willie 282, 628
Raving winds around her blowing 153, 649
Revision for Clarinda 661
Rights of Woman 202, 555, 681, 682
Rigs of Barley 627
Robert Bruce's March to Bannockburn 208, 268, 605, 638-9, 640, 653, 695, 699
Robin shure in hairst 337
The Rosebud 262, 359
Saw ye my Phely [Phillis] 659
Scotch Drink 76, 86
Scots wha hae — see *Robert Bruce's March*
Second Epistle to Davie 33
Second Epistle to John Lapraik 32, 118
Sensibility how charming 407, 409
She says She loves Me Best of A' 655, 677

849

INDEX

Sketch. Inscribed to the Rt Hon Charles J Fox 173
Sleep'st Thou 663
The Small Birds Rejoice 274
The Soger's Return — see *When wild War's deadly blast*
The Song of Death 196
Sonnet to Robert Graham 178
Sonnet, on the Death of Robert Riddell 706
Stanzas on Naething 65
Sweet Afton 166
Tam Glen 295
Tam o Shanter 105, 192, 408, 462, 557, 559, 573, 574, 578, 711
   deletions 578
   genesis of 559
Tam Samson's Elegy 87
That there is Falsehood in his Looks 209
Their Groves o Sweet Myrtle 609, 672
There'll never be Peace till Jamie comes Hame 462, 632, 634
There's naught but Care on ev'ry Han' 627
There was a Lass and she was fair 495, 626, 631, 693
There was twa Wives 277
Thine am I, my Chloris Fair 406, 542, 603, 650, 660, 675
Thou has left me ever 644
Thou Lingering Star 181, 432
To Alexander Cunningham 455
To Alexander Findlater 539
To a Mountain-Daisy 83
To a Mouse 646
To Dr Blacklock 32
To Dr John Mackenzie 32, 352
To Dr Maxwell, on Miss Jessy Staig's Recovery 33, 211, 688
To James Smith 33
To James Tennant 33
To John Syme (No more of your Guests) 33
To John Syme (O had the Malt thy Strength of Mind) 708
To Miss Ferrier 32
To Miss Isabella Macleod 32
To Mr Elphinstone 140, 382
To Mr Gavin Hamilton 32
To Mr John Taylor 33
To Mr McMurdo 492, 529
To Mr Mitchell 33
To Mr S McKenzie 32
To Peter Stuart 33
To Renton of Lamerton 33
To Robert Graham 155, 158, 164, 429, 435
To Robert Graham of Fintry Esqr with a Request for an Excise Division 151, 225, 258, 284, 320, 425, 433, 496
To Symon Gray 32
To Terraughty 33
To the beautiful Miss Eliza J– – –n 324
To the Honorable Mr R Maule of Panmure 212
To William Simson 33
Twa Dogs 76, 250
'Twas na her Bonie Blue E'e was my Ruin 673

Up and warn a' Willie 669
Verses intended to be Written Below a Noble Earl's Picture 226
The Vision 593
Wandering Willie 624
When Guilford Good . . . 97, 224
When Princes and Prelates — see *Why shouldna poor Folk Mowe?*
When she cam ben she bobbed 658, 659
When wild War's deadly Blast 669
Where are the Joys 645, 647
Where Braving Angry Winter's Storms 234
The Whistle 480, 481, 483, 538, 589
Whistle o'er the Lave o't 295, 659
Why shouldna poor Folk Mowe? 437, 653, 656
Wi braw new Branks 218
William Smellie: a Sketch 157
Willie brew'd a peck of maut 472
Will ye go to the Indies 619
Wilt thou be my Dearie 471, 585, 653, 695, 700
A Winter Night 98
Ye Banks and Braes o Bonie Doon 104
Ye Gallants Bright 627
The Young Highland Rover 659
Young Jessy 624, 688
Young Jockey was the Blythest Lad 664
Young Peggy 68, 75
Poetic plans 578, 662
Poetry: Burns's estimate of his 618-19
Politics 548
  Burns's opinions of 432, 435-6, 468, 499
Poltava, battle of 109
Pompey 109
Pompey's Ghost 273
Poor Robin's Almanac 66
The Poor Soldier 672
The Poor Thresher 296
Pope, Alexander 15, 16, 145
  Chorus of Youths and Virgins 70
  Eloisa to Abelard 16, 46, 386, 407, 662
  Epistle I 362
  Essay on Man 16, 41-2, 55, 248, 256, 392
  The First Epistle of the First Book of Horace Imitated 160, 443
  January and May 55, 249, 418
  Moral Epistles 238
  Moral Essays 646-7
  Prologue to the Satires 16, 381, 382
  The Rape of the Lock 607
  Satires 50
  The Temple of Fame 681
  To Mrs M B 404
Port Antonio 118
Port Glasgow 184-5, 418, 422, 433
Portland, 3rd Duke of 94
Portpatrick 572, 580

INDEX

Portraits of Burns:
  by John Beugo 102, 288, 314
  by John Miers 334, 417
  by Alexander Nasmyth 652, 673
  by Alexander Reid 609, 674
Postage 15, 119, 161, 202, 260, 412, 503, 515
Postmarks (see Bishop marks) 30-1
A Practical Discovery of God's Sovereignty — see Elisha Coles
Practical Essay on the Death of Jesus Christ — see William McGill
Predestination 144
Prentice, Archibald 220
Presbyterianism 97
Presbytery Relief 59
Prestwick Airport 269
The Present Truth — see Adam Gib
Price, Rev Dr Richard: *Dissertations on Providence, Prayer, Death and Miracles* 318
Priestley, Joseph 548
Primrose, Robert 720
Professorship of agriculture at Edinburgh University: Burns proposed for 130, 171, 175
Prologue to the Satires — see Alexander Pope
Prologue to the Tempest — see John Dryden
Prostitution 489, 518
Proverbs — see Scottish proverbs and sayings
Provost of Dumfries: Letter to 553-4
Provost of Edinburgh: Letter to 584
Prussia 653
Psalmody 657
Pseudonyms used by Burns:
  A Briton 160, 487
  Duncan McLeerie 173, 536
  John Barleycorn 511
  Johnie Faa 580-1
  A Peasant 587
  Spunkie 340
  Sylvander — see letters to Agnes McLehose
  Tim Nettle 522
Publication — see *Poems, Chiefly in the Scottish Dialect*
Public Library, Dumfries: Letter to 35
Pulteney, William Johnstone 175
Purdon, John 453

Quarterly Review 221
Queensberry, William Douglas, 4th Duke of 179, 240, 259, 262, 320, 432, 458, 492, 693, 699
  Letter to 589
Quotations, Burns on 16

Rachel (Biblical figure) 328
Racine, Jean 316
Rae, Peter: *History of the Late Rebellion* (1715) 316
Raeburn, Sir Henry 368
Raleigh, Sir Walter 206
  Wrong not, Sweet Mistress of my Heart 672
The Rambler 185

Ramsay, Allan 16, 251, 362, 472, 621, 625, 626, 627, 637, 640
  Answer to Hamilton of Gilbertfield's Second Epistle 91, 418
  The Gentle Shepherd 626
  The Lass of Patie's Mill 625
  The Tea-Table Miscellany 300, 373, 542, 647, 648, 662, 668-9
Ramsay, David (Editor of the *Evening Courant*) 309, 314, 319, 323, 325
Ramsay, John (Ochtertyre) 345, 359
Randolph, Lady Agnes 282
Randolph, Lady — see John Home
Rankine, John: Letter to 33
Rankine & Sons (Newcastle upon Tyne) 614
The Rape of the Lock — see Alexander Pope
Rape of the Sabine Women 22-3, 480, 600, 697-8, 712
Rebellion of 1715 41, 488, 546
Rebellion of 1745 269, 363, 488, 504
Red Sea 109
Reform party 315, 436
The Rehearsal — see George Villiers
Reid, Agnes Tennant 220
Reid, Alexander 609, 674
Reid, George 222, 269
  Letters to 220
Reid, J B 385
Reid, Jenny 220
Religion 174, 208, 213, 376, 378-9, 381, 393, 404, 466, 548
Remuneration for songs 631
Reni, Guido 354
Renton John 33, 580
Republicanism 436
Revolution of 1688 435, 436, 487, 594
Riach, William 763
Richardson, Archibald 301, 553
Richardson, Gabriel 485, 553
Richardson, Samuel 260, 262
  Pamela 254
Richardson, William 720
Richmond, Charles Lenox, 3rd Duke of 533
Richmond, John 117, 326
  Letters to 76-82
Riddell, Miss Eleanor (Elinor) or Sophy: Letter to 707
Riddell, Elizabeth Kennedy (Mrs Robert) 480, 483, 707
  Letter to 697-8
Riddell, Maria Banks Woodley (Mrs Walter) 18, 35, 412, 485, 597, 615, 633, 697, 707
  Letters to 600-12
  To thee, Loved Nith 508
  Voyages to the Madeira and Leeward and Caribee Islands 597, 600, 601
Riddell, Captain Robert (of Glenriddell) 14, 21, 33, 35, 173, 176, 296, 314, 316, 321, 437,
    464, 549, 557, 563, 575, 577, 586, 590, 595-6, 601, 633, 676, 681, 689, 695, 697, 706,
    710, 724
  Letters to 480-4
  New Music for the Piano Forte or Harpsichord 296-7, 298, 480
Riddell, Robert A (London): Letter to 713
Riddell, Walter 211, 480, 600, 633, 635, 676, 697, 710
Rillbank Crescent MSS 763

INDEX

Ritson, Joseph   664, 665
  Scottish Song   301, 659, 661, 664, 670
  A Select Collection of English Songs   661, 662, 665, 672
Robertson, William   291, 455, 463
  History of Scotland   587
Robertson, Major William (Lude): Letters to   695-6
Robinson, Julia   49
The Rock and the Wee Pickle Tow   299-300
Roddick, Captain William   603
Roderick Random — see Tobias Smollet
Rodger, Hugh   13, 18, 37, 49, 451
Ronald, Miss Jean (?)   72
Ronald, John (Mauchline)   122, 358, 476, 526
Ronald, William (of Bennals)   518
Ronald, William (Mauchline)   220, 517-8
Rosa, Salvator   12
The Rosciad — see Charles Churchill
Roscoe, William: *Poetical Works*   214
Rose, Miss – –   441, 442
Rose, Mrs Elizabeth   289
  Letter to   441-2
Rose, Dr Hugh   441
Rosebery, Archibald Philip Primrose, 5th Earl of   569
Ross, Alexander   362, 363
  The Fortunate Shepherdess   368
  Woo'd and Married an a'   678
Rowe, Nicholas: *Colin's Complaint*   610
Roxburghshire   292, 305, 632
Roy, Professor George Ross   7-8, 9, 17, 31, 43, 266, 304, 307, 360, 401, 415, 454, 714,
  724, 726
Royal Bank, Glasgow   206, 308
Royal College of Surgeons   304
Royal Company of Archers — see Archers
Royal Museum of Scotland   502
Royal Society   289
Roy's Wife of Aldivaloch   642, 649, 666, 667
Ruddick — see William Roddick
Russell, Rev John   269
Rutherford, Julie   334
St Andrews   263, 480
St David's Lodge   51, 352
St Giles Cathedral   288
St James's (Kilwinning Lodge, Tarbolton)   51, 113, 566
  Letter to   352
St Lucia   117, 695
St Mary's Isle   719
St Michael's, Dumfries   486
St Peter   269
Salmon, Thomas: *A New Geographical and Historical Grammar*   251
Salt Office   130
Salt permits   334
Samson (Biblical figure)   329
Samson, Charles   87,˙88, 89
Samson, John   220, 269

Samson, Thomas — see *Tam Samson's Elegy*
Sanquhar 157, 179, 189, 259, 432, 512, 718
Sappho 184, 402
Saratoga, battle of 109
Sarmatia 653
Satan 378, 531
Saughton Mills 274
Saul (Biblical figure) 127, 221, 399, 525
Savannah la Mar 118
Savoy 437
Saw ye my Father 245, 645, 660, 662
Saw ye na my Peggy 644
Schetky, Johann Georg Christoff 139, 389, 391
Scot, Mrs – – (Dumfries) 609
Scottish Song — see Joseph Ritson
Scots Magazine 176, 206
The Scots Musical Museum — James Johnson
Scots Worthies — see John Howie
Scott, Mrs Elizabeth 33
Scott, James and William 326, 720
Scott, Jean 671
Scott, Sir Walter 221, 266, 371, 444, 712, 762
Scott, William 309-10
  Letters to 326
Scottish proverbs and sayings 103, 121, 153, 217, 233, 330, 334, 355, 379, 390, 399, 403, 417, 515, 617, 625, 644
Scottish Tragic Ballads — see John Pinkerton
Scriptural Doctrines of Original Sin — see John Taylor
Sea-bathing 473
Seals, Burns's 471-2, 679
Sedition Trial 639
Sedley, Sir Charles: *The Mulberry Garden* 542
A Select Collection of Original Scotish Airs — see George Thomson
A Selection of Scotch Airs — see James Aird
Selkirk 305, 343
Selkirk, Dunbar Douglas, 4th Earl of 468
A Series of Discourses on Natural Religion — see Samuel Brown
Seringapatam 209
Shakespeare, William:
  As You Like It 138
  Hamlet 16, 109, 151, 215, 258, 379, 408, 460, 465, 612
  1 Henry IV 277
  2 Henry IV 103
  Henry V 277
  Henry VIII 109, 168, 344
  Julius Caesar 16, 249, 408, 445, 457
    Brutus 113
  King John 143
  King Lear 140, 424, 444, 664
  Macbeth 16, 339, 391, 470, 605
    Duncan 357
    Macbeth 357
  Much Ado About Nothing 282
  Othello 16, 56, 136, 229, 235, 380, 420-1

Pericles 361
Romeo and Juliet 458, 522
The Tempest — see John Dryden
Troilus and Cressida 596
Twelfth Night 278-9
Sharpe, Charles 677
 Letter to 580-1
Shaw, Mr – – 609
Shaw, David 102
Shawood 66
Shenstone, William 55, 246, 253, 394
 Elegy VII 132, 221
 Elegy IX 420
 Elegy XX 152
 Essays on Men, Manners, and Things 233, 238
Sheridan, Richard Brindsley 316, 664
 La Duenna 663, 664
She Rose an' loot me in 625
Sherriff, – – – (of Duns) 327
The Shipwreck — see William Falconer
Shoe manufacture 57
Sibbald, James 99, 240
 Letter to 229
Sillar, David (Irvine) 33
 Letters to 536-7
Sillar, Mrs David 536, 537
Sime, David 606
Simpson William (Ochiltree) 33
Sinclair, George: *Satan's Invisible World Discovered* 284
Sinclair, Sir John 594
 Letter to 586-7
 Statistical Account of Scotland 527, 586, 627
Sinclairs of Scalloway 363
Sirius 387
Skinner, Rev John 231, 362
 Letters to 363-4
 Ewie wi the Crooked Horn 363
 Familiar Epistle to Robie Burns 231, 363, 364
 John o Badenyon 363
 Tullochgorum 119, 362, 363, 364, 627
The Slave-Trade — see Helen Maria Williams
Sloan, Thomas 22, 35, 481, 483, 571, 724
 Letters to 576-7
Small, James: *A Treatise on Ploughs and Wheel Carriages* 326
Smallpox 212, 518, 601
Smeaton, Rev D 231
Smellie, William 94, 315, 322, 600
 Letter to 597
 The Philosophy of Natural History 322, 445, 597
Smith, Captain – – 78, 118
Smith, Adam: *Wealth of Nations* 428, 433
Smith, Dr Adam 136, 430
Smith, Alexander Howland 'Antique' 447, 762-7
Smith, Charlotte 177, 260

Smith, Rev George (Galston) 343
Smith, James (Mauchline) 19, 21, 33, 76, 78, 79, 82, 272, 332
   Letters to 117-22
Smith, Jean 117, 272
Smith, John (Glasgow bookseller) 305, 454
Smith, John junior (Glasgow bookseller): Letters to 454
Smith, Leonard 426
Smith, Rev Thomas: Letter to 585
Smollett, Tobias 260, 460
   Ferdinand Count Fathom 254, 310
   Humphrey Clinker 310
   Launcelot Greaves 310
   Peregrine Pickle 310
   Roderick Random 310, 318
Smuggling 58, 439, 451, 540, 721
Snyder, Franklin B 19
Society 17, 19, 212, 370
Society of Antiquarians (Antiquaries), Edinburgh 193, 268, 291
Socrates 113
Sodom 378
Sodomy 335, 618
Solemn League and Covenant 431, 472
Solomon (Biblical figure) 248, 392
Solway Firth 62
Somerville, John 305, 319, 721
   Letters to 567
Songs by Burns — see Poems and Songs
Song Complaining of Absence — see Allan Ramsay's *Tea-Table Miscellany*
Sorn 76, 559
Southerne, Thomas: *The Fatal Marriage* 16, 381
Spencer, Edmund 140, 282
Spey River 357
Spring — see James Thomson
Sprott, William 520
Spunkie — see Pseudonyms of Burns
Stackhouse, Thomas: *A New History of the Holy Bible* 251
Staig, David 21-2, 211
   Letters to 551-4
Staig, Jessy 211
   Letter to 688
Stair 125
Star (newspaper) — see Peter Stuart
Statistical Account of Scotland — see Sir John Sinclair
Sterne, Laurence 55, 135, 214, 253
   Letters of Yorick to Eliza 658
   Tristram Shandy 162, 253
      Uncle Toby 626
Stewart, Alexander (Stair) 125
Stewart, Anne 324, 390, 455, 457
Stewart, Catherine Gordon (Stair): Letters to 125-6
Stewart, Dugald 87, 99, 100, 113, 114, 138, 305, 306-7, 447, 559
   Letters to 448-50
Stewart (or Steuart), James: Letter to 416

Stewart, Dr Matthew 448
Stewart, William 571, 710
  Letters to 444-6
Stewarton 137, 452, 475
Stewartry 125, 715
Stillie, James 762, 763, 764, 765-6
Stirling 58, 68, 86, 88, 206, 246, 359, 390
Stirling, James (Lord Provost of Edinburgh): Letter to 584
Stodart, Mr and Mrs James 220
Stoddart, Mr − − 601
Stonehaven (Stonhive) 57, 61, 357
Straiton 218
Strasbourg 121-2, 608
Strathcarron 424
Strathspey district 357
Stuart dynasty 291, 487
Stuart, Peter 21, 33, 525
  Letters to 520-4
Stuart's Star and Evening Advertiser 173, 457, 520, 523
  Letter to 521
Surgeoner, Jenny 76, 79
Sutherland, George S 185, 347, 358, 551, 624, 682
  Letters to 549-50
Sutherland, Mrs George 549
Swift, Jonathan 15, 214, 335, 381, 514
Switzerland 608
Sylvander — see Pseudonyms of Burns
Syme, John 33, 278, 541, 617, 653, 677, 705, 712, 715
  Letters to 708-9
Symington, William 240
Symons, Jelinger: *An Index to the Excise Laws* 316, 430-1

Tait, Mr − − 359
Tait, Crauford 413
  Letter to 569-70
Tait, Miss Elizabeth (Harviestoun) 570
Tait, John (Harviestoun) 413, 569, 570
Talk not of Love — see Agnes McLehose
Tarbolton 19, 96, 352, 425, 536, 566, 724
Targe, Duncan — see John Moore
The Task — see William Cowper
Tasso 144
Taylor, John 33
  Scriptural Doctrines of Original Sin 251
Taymouth 357
Tay River 357
The Tea-Table Miscellany — see Allan Ramsay
Tennant, Agnes 220
Tennant, Charles 72
Tennant, James 33, 222
Tennant, John (Glenconner) 72, 89, 220, 242, 276
  Letters to 222
Tennant, John junior (Auchenbay)
  Letters to 72-4

INDEX

Tennant, Mrs John junior   72
Terregles   546, 594
Thalia   715-6
Thames   254
Theatre Royal, Dumfries   127-8, 208, 436, 513, 600, 682-3, 695
Theatre Royal, Edinburgh   549, 682
Theatrical company, Dumfries   202, 212, 347, 604, 624
There's nae luck about the House — see Jean Adams and William Mickle
There was a Lass and she was Fair   615
Thomas the Rhymer   119
Thomson, Mr − −: Letter to   415
Thomson, Archibald   571
Thomson, George   16, 18, 19-20, 278, 292, 302, 342, 406, 468, 472, 474, 603, 608, 615,
     699, 705, 712
   Letters to   616-80
   A Select Collection of Original Scotish Airs   206, 541, 616
Thomson, Mrs George   656
Thomson, James   55, 104, 132, 253, 266, 284, 394
   Alfred, A Masque   188, 202, 337, 378, 515, 517, 576, 595
   Autumn   55, 131, 311, 384, 534
   Edward and Eleanora   147, 201, 207
   A Hymn on the Seasons   398, 470
   The Seasons   246, 385
   Spring   169, 388
   Winter   481, 534, 550, 683, 714
Thomson, James (Exciseman, Dumfries)   572
Thomson, Robert: *A Treatise on the Duty and Office of a Messenger*   321
Thomson, Peggy   50
Thomson, William: *Orpheus Caledonius*   719
Thornhill Meeting House   565
Thou art gane awa   642
Tibbie Fowler   628
Tinnock, Nanse   117
The Tither Morn   664, 669
Titus (Roman emperor)   219
To a Blackbird — see Agnes McLehose
Todlin Hame   278-9
To Fanny fair could I impart   618
To Mr Alexander Ross — see James Beattie
To Mrs MB — see Alexander Pope
Toothache   325, 675
Tory Party   432
Townfield   61
Tranent Muir   645
The Traveller — see Oliver Goldsmith
Treasury Warrant   434
Treatise on Agriculture see Jethro Tull
A Treatise on Ploughs — see James Small
Trial of a Saving Interest — see William Guthrie
Tristram Shandy — see Laurence Sterne
Tudor dynasty   487
Tull, Jethro and Dickson, Adam: *Treatise on Agriculture*   251
Tullibardine, Marquis of   354
Tullochgorum — see John Skinner

Turnbull, Gavin   526, 651
  Laura   651
  The Nightingale   651
  O Condescend, dear charming maid   651
Turnimspyke   678
Tweedside   248, 267, 617
Tyne River   327
Tytler, Alexander Fraser   306-7, 361
  Letters to   578-9
Tytler, James 'Balloon'   159, 632-3, 644, 646
Tytler, William   578, 622
  Letters to   291
  History of Scottish Music   646

Uncle Toby — see Laurence Sterne
Unidentified correspondents   34, 724-5
Uranus — see Georgium Sidus
Urbani, Pietro   299, 468, 605, 636, 639, 645

Vaccination   212
Vair, Mr – –   349
Valladolid   507
Vatican   144
Venice Preserved — see Thomas Otway
Venus   387, 417
Versailles   392
Vespasian (Roman emperor)   219
View of Society and Manners in France, Switzerland and Germany — John Moore
The Village Curate — see Rev James Hurdis
Villiers, George, 2nd Duke of Buckingham: *The Rehearsal*   272
Virgil   144, 145
  The Aenid   145
  Georgics   145
The Vision of Mirza — see Joseph Addison
Voltaire, François Marie   130, 316, 687
Voyages to the Madeira and Leeward and Caribee Islands — see Maria Riddell

Wabster's Grace   233
Walker, Rev Josiah   575, 617, 625
  Letters to   354-6
Walker, Thomas   33
Wallace, – – (Dumfries lawyer)   298
Wallace, Lady Antonia   142, 197
Wallace, Lady Eglintoune Maxwell   130
Wallace, Sir Thomas   130
Wallace, William (editor)   12, 131, 361, 707
Wallace, Sir William   89, 130, 131, 171, 210, 250, 443, 640
Wanlockhead   189, 576
Washington, General George   210
Waterloo, battle of   131
Waters, Robie   340
Watson, Rev Thomas: *Body of Divinity*   316
Watts, John: *Musical Miscellany*   650
Wauchope, John   271
The Way to Keep Him — see Arthur Murphy
Wealth of Nations — see Adam Smith

Webster, Dr – – (Edinburgh) 364
Weems, John 720
Welsh, Jane 685
Westminster divines 94, 109
Wharton, Thomas 434
When I was a young Thing 301
Whigham, Edward 259
  Letter to 512
Whigham, Mrs Edward: Letter to 512
Whigkirk 398
Whigs 179, 320, 432
Whisky 73, 167, 504, 509-11
White, Mr and Mrs – – (Jamaica) 118
White, Thomas 35
  Letter to 687
Whitefoord, John junior 114
Whitefoord, Sir John 34, 87, 99, 113, 114, 579
  Letters to 51-3
Whiter, Thomas: Letter to 366
Whithorn 343
Whyte, Rev Hugh 59
Whyter, Thomas — see Thomas Whiter
Wight, (?Andrew, of Ormiston) 278, 279
Wigtownshire 75, 572
Will, – –: Letter to 351
Williams, Miss Helen Maria 136, 247, 248, 258, 261
  Letter to 532-5
  Slave-Trade 532
    Burns's criticism of 533-5
Williamson, Alexander: Letter to 588
Williamson, David (Dumfries) 616, 679
Williamson, John Brown 682
Willie's rare and Willie's fair 301
Wilson, Alexander (Glasgow) 263
Wilson, Alexander (Paisley) 198
Wilson, John (Kilmarnock) 21, 88, 92, 127, 489, 536, 762
Wilson, John (Tarbolton) 536, 567
  Letter to 566
Wilson, Mrs John 566
Winlaw, Kinloch 720
Winter — see James Thomson
Wit and Mirth or Pills to Purge Melancholy — see Thomas D'Urfey
Witherspoon — see David Herd
Wolcot, John (Peter Pindar pseud.) 213, 623, 636, 660, 668, 676
Women, Burns's opinion of 662
The Wonder, A Woman Keeps a Secret — see Susan Centlivre
Wood, Alexander 360, 461
Woo'd and married an a' — see Alexander Ross
Woodley Park, Dumfries 590, 606, 697, 710
Wordsworth, William 424
The World Unmasked — see Maria Huber
Wotherspoon, John — see David Herd
Wright, Mrs Colonel 367

Wyat, – – 575
Wycherley, William 316

Xerxes 373

Yarico — see George Colman, the younger
Yarrow 248
The Yellow-haired Laddie 624-5
York dynasty 487
Young, Mrs – – (Dumfries) 546
Young, Edward:
  First Epistle to Mr Pope 16, 380
  Love of Fame 459
  Night Thoughts 16, 142, 149, 153, 158, 215, 233, 337, 384, 385, 397, 516, 517, 576,
    595, 715
Young Philander Woo'd Me Lang 294

Zebedee (Biblical figure) 219
Zeluco — see John Moore
Zimri (Biblical figure) 330
Zion 127